Crafting and Executing Strategy

The Quest for Competitive Advantage

CONCEPTS AND CASES

16th Edition

Arthur A. Thompson, Jr.
The University of Alabama

A. J. Strickland III
The University of Alabama

John E. Gamble
University of

 McGraw-Hill Irwin

Boston   Burr Ridge, IL   Dubuque, IA   New York
San Francisco   St. Louis   Bangkok   Bogotá   Caracas   Kuala Lumpur
Lisbon   London   Madrid   Mexico City   Milan   Montreal   New Delhi
Santiago   Seoul   Singapore   Sydney   Taipei   Toronto

D1344824

 **McGraw-Hill Irwin**

CRAFTING AND EXECUTING STRATEGY: THE QUEST FOR COMPETITIVE ADVANTAGE: CONCEPTS AND CASES

Published by McGraw-Hill/Irwin, a business unit of The McGraw-Hill Companies, Inc., 1221 Avenue of the Americas, New York, NY, 10020. Copyright © 2008, 2007, 2005, 2003, 2001, 1999, 1998, 1996, 1995, 1993, 1992, 1990, 1987, 1984, 1981, 1978 by The McGraw-Hill Companies, Inc. All rights reserved. No part of this publication may be reproduced or distributed in any form or by any means, or stored in a database or retrieval system, without the prior written consent of The McGraw-Hill Companies, Inc., including, but not limited to, in any network or other electronic storage or transmission, or broadcast for distance learning.

Some ancillaries, including electronic and print components, may not be available to customers outside the United States.

This book is printed on acid-free paper.

1 2 3 4 5 6 7 8 9 0 DOW/DOW 0 9 8 7

ISBN 978-0-07-128590-2
MHID 0-07-128590-3

Photo Credits: Chapter 1, p.2, © Cary Henrie/CORBIS; Chapter 2, p.18, ©Rob Colvin/CORBIS; Chapter 3, p.48, ©John S. Dykes/CORBIS; Chapter 4, p.94, ©Leon Zernitsky/CORBIS; Chapter 5, p.132, DigitalVision/Getty Images/MGH-DIL; Chapter 6, p.160, ©Eric Westbrook/CORBIS; Chapter 7, p.194, DigitalVision/Getty Images/MGH-DIL; Chapter 8, p.230, DigitalVision/Getty Images/MGH-DIL; Chapter 9, p.266, ©Rob Colvin/CORBIS; Chapter 10, p.316, DigitalVision-Getty Images/MGH-DIL; Chapter 11, p.358, ©Rob Colvin/CORBIS; Chapter 12, p.388, ©Rob Day/CORBIS; Chapter 13, p.414, ©Paul Anderson/CORBIS.

To our families and especially our wives:
Hasseline, Kitty, and Debra

Arthur A. Thompson, Jr., earned his B.S. and Ph.D. degrees in economics from The University of Tennessee, spent three years on the economics faculty at Virginia Tech, and served on the faculty of The University of Alabama's College of Commerce and Business Administration for 24 years. In 1974 and again in 1982, Dr. Thompson spent semester-long sabbaticals as a visiting scholar at the Harvard Business School.

His areas of specialization are business strategy, competition and market analysis, and the economics of business enterprises. In addition to publishing over 30 articles in some 25 different professional and trade publications, he has authored or co-authored five textbooks and six computer-based simulation exercises that are used in colleges and universities worldwide.

Dr. Thompson spends much of his off-campus time giving presentations, putting on management development programs, working with companies, and helping operate a business simulation enterprise in which he is a major partner.

Dr. Thompson and his wife of 47 years have two daughters, two grandchildren, and a Yorkshire terrier.

Dr. A. J. (Lonnie) Strickland, a native of North Georgia, attended the University of Georgia, where he received a bachelor of science degree in math and physics in 1965. Afterward he entered the Georgia Institute of Technology, where he received a master of science in industrial management. He earned a Ph.D. in business administration from Georgia State University in 1969. He currently holds the title of Professor of Strategic Management in the Graduate School of Business at The University of Alabama.

Dr. Strickland's experience in consulting and executive development is in the strategic management area, with a concentration in industry and competitive analysis. He has developed strategic planning systems for such firms as The Southern Company, BellSouth, South Central Bell, American Telephone and Telegraph, Gulf States Paper, Carraway Methodist Medical Center, Delco Remy, Mark IV Industries, Amoco Oil Company, USA Group, General Motors, and Kimberly Clark Corporation (Medical Products). He is a very popular speaker on the subject of implementing strategic change and serves on several corporate boards.

John E. Gamble is currently Associate Dean and Professor of Management in the Mitchell College of Business at the University of South Alabama. His teaching specialty at USA is strategic management and he also conducts a course in strategic management in Germany, which is sponsored by the University of Applied Sciences in Worms.

Dr. Gamble's research interests center on strategic issues in entrepreneurial, health care, and manufacturing settings. His work has been published in various scholarly journals and he is the author or co-author of more than 30 case studies published in an assortment of strategic management and strategic marketing texts. He has done consulting on industry and market analysis for clients in a diverse mix of industries.

Professor Gamble received his Ph.D. in management from The University of Alabama in 1995. Dr. Gamble also has a Bachelor of Science degree and a Master of Arts degree from The University of Alabama.

This 16th edition, coming on the heels of the 15th edition published in mid-2006, features 31 of the latest and best cases in strategic management and the very same 13-chapter presentation that appeared in the 15th edition. The purpose of this 16th edition is to satisfy the market's legitimate and understandable yearning for newly-researched cases involving high-interest companies and headline strategic issues. Both professors and students have long preferred that assigned cases be as up-to-the-minute as possible. Class discussions are prone to take on added sparkle and liveliness when a case is hot off the press and poses issues that company managers are still wrestling with or that involve situations where the jury remains out on the wisdom of prior actions taken by management. Sometimes, fast changing industry and company circumstances cause an otherwise good case in an older edition to lose its appeal (because outcomes are known or the issues are rendered moot by subsequent events). Moreover, with so many business schools offering the strategic management course every term, the case collection in any one edition "wears out" after a few terms.

We made a commitment that extends as far back as our 8th edition to endeavor to keep you well-supplied with a highly appealing stream of brand new cases eminently suitable for courses in strategic management. This edition follows in the footsteps of that longstanding tradition. Only 3 of the 31 cases in this 16th edition are carryovers from the 15th edition, and all three—the classic two-page Robin Hood case, the equally classic three-page Dilemma at Devil's Den case, and the provocative Smithfield Foods case—are truly timeless and teach so exceptionally well that including them here made perfect sense. The remaining 28 cases are newly written and provide altogether fresh and engaging choices for making cutting-edge case assignments.

THE 16TH EDITION: WHAT TO EXPECT

As compared to the 14th edition, the two hallmarks of the 15th and 16th editions are a fresh, refined presentation in every chapter and a powerhouse collection of well-researched, well-written cases loaded with intriguing decision issues and important teaching points. A bigger portion of each 15th/16th edition chapter has been revised and rewritten than in any previous edition. Coverage was trimmed in some areas, expanded in others. Every paragraph on every page of the 14th edition was revisited, producing a host of both major and minor changes in exposition in the 15th/16th edition chapters. Pains were taken to improve and enliven the explanations of core concepts and analytical tools. The latest research findings from the literature and best practices of companies were incorporated to keep in step with both theory and current application. Scores of new examples were added to complement the new and updated Illustration Capsules. The number of the chapter-end exercises was increased and their caliber markedly improved. The result is a 13-chapter treatment with more punch, greater clarity, and quicker comprehension. But none of the changes have altered the fundamental character that has driven the text's success over the years. The chapter content continues to be solidly mainstream and balanced, mirroring *both* the best academic thinking and the best strategic thinking of practitioners.

Complementing the text presentation is a truly appealing lineup of 31 diverse, timely, and thoughtfully crafted cases. Many involve high-profile companies and all are framed around issues and circumstances tightly linked to the content of the 13 chapters, thus pushing students to apply the concepts and analytical tools they have read about. We are confident you will be impressed with how well these cases will teach and the amount of student interest they will spark. And there's an array of support materials in the Instructor Resources package to equip you with enormous course design flexibility and a powerful kit of teaching/learning tools. We've done our very best to ensure that the 16th edition package will work especially well for you in the classroom, help you economize on the time needed to be well prepared for each class, and cause students to conclude that your course is one of the very best they have ever taken—from the standpoint of both enjoyment and learning a lot.

A TEXT WITH ON-TARGET CONTENT

In our view, for a senior/MBA-level strategy text to qualify as having on-target content, it must:

- Explain core concepts in language that students can grasp and provide examples of their relevance and use by actual companies.
- Take care to thoroughly describe the tools of strategic analysis, how they are used, and where they fit into the managerial process of crafting and executing strategy.
- Be up-to-date and comprehensive, with solid coverage of the landmark changes in competitive markets and company strategies being driven by globalization and Internet technology.
- Focus squarely on what every student needs to know about crafting, implementing, and executing business strategies in today's market environments.
- Contain freshly researched, value-adding cases that feature interesting products and companies, illustrate the important kinds of strategic challenges managers face, link closely to the chapter content, contain valuable teaching points, and ignite lively class discussions.

We believe this 16th edition measures up on all five of these criteria. Chapter discussions cut straight to the chase about what students really need to know. Our explanations of core concepts and analytical tools are covered in enough depth to make them understandable and usable—the rationale being that a shallow explanation carries little punch and has almost no instructional value. All the chapters are flush with convincing examples to which students can easily relate. There's a straightforward, integrated flow from one chapter to the next. All the latest research findings pertinent to a first course in strategy have been woven into the chapters. We have deliberately adopted a pragmatic, down-to-earth writing style, not only to better communicate to an audience of students (who, for the most part, will soon be practicing managers) but also to convince readers that the subject matter deals directly with what managers and companies do in the real world.

And, thanks to the talented efforts of dedicated case researchers in strategic management across the world, this edition contains a set of high-interest cases with unusual ability to work magic in the classroom. Great cases make it far easier for you to drive home valuable lessons in the whys and hows of successful crafting and executing strategy.

ORGANIZATION, CONTENT, AND FEATURES OF THE TEXT CHAPTERS

Although the chapter organization in the 15th/16th editions parallels that of the 14th edition, we worked diligently to make quantum improvements in overall content appeal, ease of student comprehension, and the care with which core concepts and analytical tools are described and explained. As a consequence, we think you'll be amply convinced that *no other leading text does a better job of setting forth the principles of strategic management and linking these principles to both sound theory and best practices.* You'll find up-to-date coverage of the continuing march of industries and companies to wider globalization, the growing scope and strategic importance of collaborative alliances, the spread of high-velocity change to more industries and company environments, how online technology is driving fundamental changes in both strategy and internal operations in companies across the world, the keys to successful diversification, pertinent corporate governance issues, and how Six Sigma, best practices, benchmarking, proper workforce compensation, and a strategy-supportive corporate culture act to promote operating excellence and effective strategy execution. Furthermore, the refreshing facelift given to every chapter as concerns sharper definitions, more thorough explanations, and a greater number of current examples has made the chapters' presentations easier for students to read and understand. Effective communication of core concepts and analytical tools in the chapters reduces the need for detailed lectures on your part and frees time for more in-class debate and discussion, coverage of late-breaking stories in the business press, and other means of driving home the principles of strategy.

No other leading strategy text comes close to matching our treatment of the resource-based theory of the firm. The relevance and role of company resources and competitive strengths is prominently and comprehensively integrated into our coverage of crafting both single-business and multi-business strategies. Chapters 3 through 9 make it crystal clear that a company's strategy *must* be matched *both* to its external market circumstances and to its internal resources and competitive capabilities. Moreover, Chapters 11, 12, and 13 on various aspects of executing strategy have a strong resource-based perspective that also makes it crystal clear how and why the tasks of assembling intellectual capital and building core competencies and competitive capabilities are absolutely critical to successful strategy execution and operating excellence.

No other leading strategy text comes close to matching our coverage of business ethics, values, and social responsibility. We have embellished the highly important chapter on "Strategy, Ethics, and Social Responsibility" with new discussions and material so that it can better fulfill the important functions of (1) alerting students to the role and importance of incorporating business ethics and social responsibility into decision-making and (2) addressing the accreditation requirements of the AACSB that business ethics be visibly and thoroughly embedded in the core curriculum. Moreover, there are substantive discussions of the roles of values and ethics in Chapters 1, 2,

11, and 13, thus providing you with a very meaty and comprehensive treatment of business ethics and socially responsible behavior as it applies to crafting and executing company strategies.

The following rundown summarizes the noteworthy chapter features and topical emphasis in this edition:

- Chapter 1 continues to focus on the central questions of "What is strategy?", and "Why is it important?" It defines what is meant by the term *strategy*, identifies the different elements of a company's strategy, and explains why management efforts to craft a company's strategy entail a quest for competitive advantage. Following Henry Mintzberg's pioneering research, we stress how and why a company's strategy is partly planned and partly reactive and why a company's strategy tends to evolve over time. There's an enhanced discussion of what is meant by the term *business model* and how it relates to the concept of strategy. The thrust of this first chapter is to convince students that good strategy + good strategy execution = good management. The chapter is a perfect accompaniment for your opening day lecture on what the course is all about and why it matters.

- Chapter 2 delves into the managerial process of actually crafting and executing a strategy—it makes a great assignment for the second day of class and is a perfect follow-on to your first day's lecture. The focal point of the chapter is the five-step managerial process of crafting and executing strategy: (1) forming a strategic vision of where the company is headed and why, (2) setting objectives and performance targets that measure the company's progress, (3) crafting a strategy to achieve these targets and move the company toward its market destination, (4) implementing and executing the strategy, and (5) monitoring progress and making corrective adjustments as needed. Students are introduced to such core concepts as strategic visions, mission statements, strategic versus financial objectives, and strategic intent. There's a section underscoring that *all managers are on a company's strategy-making, strategy-executing team* and that a company's strategic plan is a collection of strategies devised by different managers at different levels in the organizational hierarchy. The chapter winds up with a substantially-expanded section on corporate governance.

- Chapter 3 sets forth the now-familiar analytical tools and concepts of industry and competitive analysis and demonstrates the importance of tailoring strategy to fit the circumstances of a company's industry and competitive environment. The standout feature of this chapter is a presentation of Michael E. Porter's "five forces model of competition" that we think is the clearest, most straightforward discussion of any text in the field. Globalization and Internet technology are treated as potent driving forces capable of reshaping industry competition—their roles as change agents have become factors that most companies in most industries must reckon with in forging winning strategies.

- Chapter 4 establishes the equal importance of doing solid company situation analysis as a basis for matching strategy to organizational resources, competencies, and competitive capabilities. The roles of core competences and organizational resources and capabilities in creating customer value and helping build competitive advantage are *center stage* in the discussions of company resource strengths and weaknesses. SWOT analysis is cast as a simple, easy-to-use way to assess a company's resources and overall situation. There is much clearer coverage of value chain analysis, benchmarking, and competitive strength assessments—standard tools for appraising a company's relative cost position and market standing vis-à-vis rivals. *An important addition to this chapter is a table showing how key financial and operating ratios are calculated and how to interpret them;* students will find this table handy in doing the number-crunching needed to evaluate whether a company's strategy is delivering good financial performance.

- Chapter 5 deals with a company's quest for competitive advantage and is framed around the five generic competitive strategies—low-cost leadership, differentiation, best-cost provider, focused differentiation, and focused low-cost.

- Chapter 6 extends the coverage of the previous chapter and deals with what *other strategic actions* a company can take to complement its choice of a basic competitive strategy. The chapter features sections on what use to make of strategic alliances and collaborative partnerships; merger and acquisition strategies; vertical integration strategies; outsourcing strategies; offensive and defensive strategies; and the different types of Web site strategies that companies can employ to position themselves in the marketplace. The discussion of offensive strategies has been totally overhauled and features a new section on blue ocean strategy. The concluding section of this chapter provides a much enhanced treatment of first-mover advantages and disadvantages.

- Chapter 7 explores the full range of strategy options for competing in foreign markets: export strategies; licensing; franchising; multicountry strategies; global strategies; and collaborative strategies involving heavy reliance on strategic alliances and joint ventures. The spotlight is trained on two strategic issues unique to competing multinationally: (1) whether to customize the company's offerings in each different country market to match the tastes and preferences of local buyers or whether to offer a mostly standardized product worldwide and (2) whether to employ essentially the same basic competitive strategy in the markets of all countries where it operates or whether to modify the company's competitive approach country-by-country as may be needed to fit the specific market conditions and competitive circumstances it encounters. There's also coverage of the concepts of profit sanctuaries and cross-market subsidization; the ways to achieve competitive advantage by operating multinationally; the special issues of competing in the markets of emerging countries; and the strategies that local companies in emerging countries can use to defend against global giants.

- The role of Chapter 8 is to hammer home the points made in Chapters 3 and 4 that winning strategies have to be matched both to industry and competitive conditions and to company resources and capabilities. The first portion of the chapter covers the broad strategy options for companies competing in six representative industry and competitive situations: (1) emerging industries, (2) rapid growth industries, (3) mature, slow-growth industries, (4) stagnant or declining industries, (5) turbulent, high velocity industries, and (6) fragmented industries. The second portion of the chapters looks at matching strategy to the resources and capabilities of four representative types of companies: (1) companies pursuing rapid growth, (2) companies in industry-leading positions, (3) companies in runner-up positions, and (4) companies in competitively weak positions or plagued by crisis conditions. The detail with which these ten concrete examples are covered in Chapter 8 should enable you to convince students why it is management's job to craft a strategy that is tightly matched to a company's internal and external circumstances.

- Our rather meaty treatment of diversification strategies for multibusiness enterprises in Chapter 9 begins by laying out the various paths for becoming diversified, explains how a company can use diversification to create or compound competitive advantage for its business units, and examines the strategic options an already-diversified company has to improve its overall performance. In the middle part of the chapter, the analytical spotlight is on the techniques and procedures for assessing the strategic attractiveness of a diversified company's business portfolio—the relative attractiveness of the various businesses the company has diversified into, a multi-industry company's competitive strength in each of its lines of business, and the *strategic fits* and *resource fits* among a diversified company's different businesses. The chapter concludes with a brief survey of a company's four main post-diversification strategy alternatives: (1) broadening the diversification base, (2) divesting some businesses and retrenching to a narrower diversification base, (3) restructuring the makeup of the company's business lineup, and (4) multinational diversification.

- Chapter 10 reflects the very latest in the literature on (1) whether and why a company has a *duty* to operate according to ethical standards and (2) whether and why a company has a *duty* or *obligation* to contribute to the betterment of society independent of the needs and preferences of the customers it serves. Is there a credible business case for operating ethically and/or operating in a socially responsible manner? The opening section of the chapter addresses whether ethical standards are universal (as maintained by the school of ethical universalism) or dependent on local norms and situational circumstances (as maintained by the school of ethical relativism) or a combination of both (as maintained by integrative social contracts theory). Following this is a section on the three categories of managerial morality (moral, immoral, and amoral), a section on the drivers of unethical strategies and shady business behavior, a section on the approaches to managing a company's ethical conduct, a section on linking a company's strategy to its ethical principles and core values, a section on the concept of a "social responsibility strategy," and sections that explore the business case for ethical and socially responsible behavior. The chapter will give students some serious ideas to chew on and, hopefully, make them far more ethically-conscious. It has been written as a "stand-alone" chapter that can be assigned in the early, middle, or late part of the course.

- The three-chapter module on executing strategy (Chapters 11–13) is anchored around a pragmatic, compelling conceptual framework: (1) building the resource strengths and organizational capabilities needed to execute the strategy in competent fashion; (2) allocating ample resources to strategy-critical activities; (3) ensuring that policies and procedures facilitate rather than impede strategy execution; (4) instituting best practices and pushing for continuous improvement in how value chain activities are performed; (5) installing information and operating systems that enable company personnel to better carry out their strategic roles proficiently; (6) tying rewards and incentives directly to the achievement of performance targets and good strategy execution; (7) shaping the work environment and corporate culture to fit the strategy; and (8) exerting the internal leadership needed to drive execution forward.

- We have reworked and refreshed the content all three chapters. You will see thoroughly overhauled discussions of staffing the organization, building capabilities, corporate culture, strategic leadership, and the roles of best practices and Six Sigma in facilitating the drive for operating excellence.

- As with the 14th edition, the recurring theme of these three chapters is that implementing and executing strategy entails figuring out the specific actions, behaviors, and conditions that are needed for a smooth strategy-supportive operation and then following through to get things done and deliver results— the goal here is to ensure that students understand the strategy-implementing/ strategy-executing phase is a make-things-happen and make-them-happen-right kind of managerial exercise.

We have done our best to ensure that the 13 chapters hit the bull's-eye in covering the essentials of a senior/MBA course in strategy and convey the best thinking of academics and practitioners. There are new and updated "strategy in action" capsules in each chapter that tie core concepts to real-world management practice and that complement the dramatically expanded number of examples in each chapter. We've provided a host of interesting chapter-end exercises that you can use as a basis for class discussion or written assignments or team presentations. We are confident you'll find this 13-chapter presentation superior to our prior editions as concerns coverage, readability, and convincing examples. The ultimate test of the text, of course, is the positive pedagogical impact it has in the classroom. If this edition sets a more effective stage for your lectures and does a better job of helping you persuade students that the discipline of strategy merits their rapt attention, then it will have fulfilled its purpose.

THE CASE COLLECTION

The 31-case lineup in this edition is flush with interesting companies and valuable lessons for students in the art and science of crafting and executing strategy. There's a good blend of cases from a length perspective—close to a fourth are under 15 pages, yet offer plenty for students to chew on; about a fourth are medium-length cases; and the remainder are detail-rich cases that call for more sweeping analysis.

At least 25 of the 31 cases involve companies, products, or people that students will have heard of, know about from personal experience, or can easily identify with. There are two "dot-com" company cases and two cases involving companies with big online operations, thus giving students ample opportunity to wrestle with e-commerce strategy issues. The lineup includes at least 8 cases that will provide students with insight into the special demands of competing in industry environments where technological developments are an everyday event, product life cycles are short, and competitive maneuvering among rivals comes fast and furious. Over 20 of the cases involve situations where company resources and competitive capabilities play as large a role in the strategy-making, strategy-executing scheme of things as industry and competitive conditions do. Scattered throughout the lineup are 13 cases concerning non-U.S. companies, globally competitive industries, and/or cross-cultural situations. These cases, in conjunction with the globalized content of the text chapters, provide abundant material for linking the study of strategic management tightly to the ongoing globalization of the world economy. You'll also find 5 cases dealing with the strategic problems of family-owned or relatively small entrepreneurial businesses and 22 cases involving public companies about which students can do further research on the

Internet. Ten of the cases have accompanying videotape segments that can be shown either at the beginning of the class or during the case discussion to provide additional information and further engage students in the issues at hand.

We believe you will find the collection of 31 cases quite appealing, eminently teachable, and very suitable for drilling students in the use of the concepts and analytical treatments in Chapters 1 through 13. With this case lineup, you should have no difficulty whatsoever assigning cases that will capture the interest of students from start to finish.

TWO ACCOMPANYING ONLINE, FULLY-AUTOMATED SIMULATION EXERCISES—*THE BUSINESS STRATEGY GAME AND GLO-BUS*

The Business Strategy Game and GLO-BUS: *Developing Winning Competitive Strategies*—two competition-based strategy simulations that are delivered online and that feature automated processing of decisions and grading of performance—are being marketed by the publisher as companion supplements for use with this and other texts in the field. *The Business Strategy Game* is the world's leading strategy simulation, having been played by over 450,000 students at more than 500 universities worldwide. *GLO-BUS,* a somewhat streamlined online strategy simulation that we introduced in 2004, has been played by over 20,000 students at more than 125 universities across the world. Both simulations involve competing in a global market environment because globalization of the marketplace is an ever-widening reality and global strategy issues are a standard part of the strategic management course. Plus, of course, accreditation standards for business school programs routinely require that the core curriculum include international business topics and the managerial challenges of operating in a globally competitive marketplace.

The Compelling Case for Incorporating a Simulation

We think there are powerful, convincing reasons for using a simulation as a cornerstone, if not a centerpiece, of strategy courses for seniors and MBA students:

- Assigning students to run a company that competes head-to-head against companies run by other class members *gives students immediate opportunity to experiment with various strategy options and to gain proficiency in applying the core concepts and analytical tools that they have been reading about in the chapters.* The whole teaching/learning enterprise is facilitated when what the chapters have to say about the managerial tasks of crafting and executing strategy matches up with the strategy-making challenges that students confront in the simulation.

- Most *students desperately need the experience of actively managing a close-to-real-life company where they can practice and hone their business and decision-making skills.* The always new and slightly different market and competitive conditions that flow from each round of decision making turns the simulation into a "live, semester-long case" that puts class members squarely in the middle of the action and under the gun of competition to display their command of the subject matter and exercise good managerial judgment. Having class members run a company and repeatedly make a set of wide-ranging decisions forces them into the role of a practicing manager charged with reading the signs of industry change, reacting to the moves of competitors, evaluating strengths and weaknesses in the company's competitive position, and deciding what to do to improve a company's financial performance in light of all the surrounding circumstances. All this is *highly valuable practice* and *such skills-building is the essence of senior and MBA courses in business strategy.*

- *A competition-based strategy simulation adds an enormous amount of student interest and excitement.* Being an active manager in running a company in which they have a stake makes students' task of learning about crafting and executing winning strategies more enjoyable. Their company becomes "real" and takes on a life of its own as the simulation unfolds—and it doesn't take long for students to establish a healthy rivalry with other class members that are running rival companies. Because the competition in the simulation typically gets very personal, most students become immersed in what's going on in their industry—as compared to the more impersonal engagement that occurs when they are assigned a case to analyze.

- *Using both case analysis and a simulation to reinforce and drive home the lessons of the text chapters is far more pedagogically powerful and lasting than just the use of case analysis alone.* What a simulation does that the case analysis part of the course cannot is give students immediate and unmistakable feedback on the caliber of their managerial decisions and actions. In contrast, in analyzing cases and making action recommendations for the company being studied, there is little way to provide students with credible feedback on the caliber of their action recommendations/decisions beyond that of subjecting their views to the scrutiny of the whole class and at the end of the case discussion telling the class what's happened at the company since the case was written. The potent and highly effective "learn-by-doing" pedagogy of a simulation helps explain the fast-growing use of strategy simulations in undergraduate and MBA courses in strategy.

- Students are *more motivated* to buckle down and figure out what strategic moves will make their simulation company perform better than they are to wrestle with the strategic issues posed in an assigned case (which entails reading the case thoroughly, diagnosing the company's situation, and proposing well-reasoned action recommendations). In a strategy simulation, students have to take the analysis of market conditions, the strategies and actions of competitors, and the condition of their company *seriously*—they are held fully accountable for their decisions and their company's performance. It is to students' advantage to avoid faulty analysis and flawed strategies—*nothing gets students' attention quicker than the adverse grade consequences of a decline in their company's performance or the loss of an industry position.* And no other type of assignment does a better job of spurring students to fully exercise their strategic wits and analytical prowess—*company co-managers have a strong grade incentive to spend quality time debating and deciding how best to boost the performance of their company.*

- A first-rate simulation produces a "WOW! Not only is this fun but I am learning a lot!" reaction from students. *The element of competition ingrained in strategy simulations stirs students' competitive juices and emotionally engages them in the subject matter.* Most students will thoroughly enjoy the *learn-by-doing* character of a simulation, recognize the practical value of having to make all kinds of decisions and run a whole company, and gain confidence from working with all the financial and operating statistics—all of which tends to (a) make the strategy course *a livelier, richer learning experience* and (b) result in higher instructor evaluations at the end of the course.

- Strategy simulations like *The Business Strategy Game* or *GLO-BUS* that have exceptionally close ties between the industry and company circumstances in the simulation and the topics covered in the text chapters, *provide instructors with a host of first-rate examples of how the material in the text applies both to the experience that students are having in running their companies and to real-world management.* Since *students can easily relate to these examples,* they are much more apt to say "aha, now I see how this applies and why I need to know about it and use it." The host of examples the simulation experience provides to create this "aha effect" thus adds real value. (There is information posted in the Instructor Centers for both *The Business Strategy Game* and *GLO-BUS* showing specific links between the pages of this text and the simulation.)

- Because a simulation involves making decisions relating to production operations, worker compensation and training, sales and marketing, distribution, customer service, and finance and requires analysis of company financial statements and market data, *the simulation helps students synthesize the knowledge gained in a variety of different business courses. The cross-functional, integrative nature of a strategy simulation helps make courses in strategy much more of a true capstone experience.*

In sum, *a three-pronged text-case-simulation course model has significantly more teaching/learning power than the traditional text-case model.* Indeed, a very convincing argument can be made that a competition-based strategy simulation is *the single most powerful vehicle that instructors can use to effectively teach the discipline of business and competitive strategy and to build student proficiencies in crafting and executing a winning strategy.* Mounting instructor recognition of the teaching/learning effectiveness of a good strategy simulation, along with the amazingly minimal start-up and administrative time requirements of an online simulation, accounts for why strategy simulations have earned a prominent place in so many of today's strategy courses.

And, happily, there's another positive side benefit to using a simulation—*it lightens the grading burden for instructors.* Since a simulation can entail 20 or more hours of student time over the course of a term (depending on the number of decisions and the extent of accompanying assignments), most adopters compensate by trimming the total number of assigned cases or substituting the simulation for one (or two) written cases and/or an hour exam. This results in less time spent grading because both *The Business Strategy Game* and *GLO-BUS* have built-in grading features that require no instructor effort (beyond setting the grading weights).

A Birds-Eye View of **The Business Strategy Game**

The setting for *The Business Strategy Game (BSG)* is the global athletic footwear industry. The athletic footwear business is particularly suitable for a strategy simulation because the product is used worldwide, there's competition among companies from several continents, production is concentrated in low-cost locations, and the real-world marketplace is populated with companies employing a variety of competitive approaches and business strategies. In the simulation, global market demand for footwear grows at the rate of 7–9% annually for the first five years and 5–7% annually for the second five years. However, market growth rates vary by geographic region—North America, Latin America, Europe-Africa, and Asia-Pacific.

Companies begin the competition producing branded and private-label footwear in two plants, one in North America and one in Asia. They have the option to establish production facilities in Latin America and Europe-Africa, either by constructing new plants or buying previously-constructed plants that have been sold by competing companies. Company co-managers exercise control over production costs based on the styling and quality they opt to manufacture, plant location (wages and incentive compensation vary from region to region), the use of best practices and Six Sigma programs to reduce the production of defective footwear and to boost worker productivity, and compensation practices.

All newly-produced footwear is shipped in bulk containers to one of four geographic distribution centers. All sales in a geographic region are made from footwear inventories in that region's distribution center. Costs at the four regional distribution centers are a function of inventory storage costs, packing and shipping fees, import tariffs paid on incoming pairs shipped from foreign plants, and exchange rate impacts. At the start of the simulation, import tariffs average $4 per pair in Europe-Africa, $6 per pair in Latin America, and $8 in the Asia-Pacific region. However, the Free Trade Treaty of the Americas allows tariff-free movement of footwear between North America and Latin America. Instructors have the option to alter tariffs as the game progresses.

Companies market their brand of athletic footwear to footwear retailers worldwide and to individuals buying online at the company's Web site. Each company's sales and market share in the branded footwear segments hinge on its competitiveness on 11 factors: attractive pricing, footwear styling and quality, product line breadth, advertising, the use of mail-in rebates, the appeal of celebrities endorsing a company's brand, success in convincing footwear retailers dealers to carry its brand, the number of weeks it takes to fill retailer orders, the effectiveness of a company's online sales effort at its Web site, and customer loyalty. Sales of private-label footwear hinge solely on being the low-price bidder.

All told, company co-managers make 47 types of decisions each period that cut across production operations (up to 10 decisions each plant, with a maximum of 4 plants), plant capacity additions/sales/upgrades (up to 6 decisions per plant), worker compensation and training (3 decisions per plant), shipping (up to 8 decisions each plant), pricing and marketing (up to 10 decisions in 4 geographic regions), bids to sign celebrities (2 decision entries per bid), and financing of company operations (up to 8 decisions).

Each time company co-managers make a decision entry, an assortment of on-screen calculations instantly shows the projected effects on unit sales, revenues, market shares, unit costs, profit, earnings per share, return on equity (ROE), and other operating statistics. The on-screen calculations help team members evaluate the relative merits of one decision entry versus another and put together a promising strategy.

Companies can employ any of the five generic competitive strategy options in selling branded footwear—low-cost leadership, differentiation, best-cost provider, focused low-cost, and focused differentiation. They can pursue essentially the same strategy worldwide or craft slightly or very different strategies for the Europe-Africa, Asia-Pacific, Latin America, and North America markets. They can strive for competitive advantage based on more advertising or a wider selection of models or more appealing styling/quality, or bigger rebates, and so on.

Any well-conceived, well-executed competitive approach is capable of succeeding, provided it is not overpowered by the strategies of competitors or defeated by the presence of too many copycat strategies that dilute its effectiveness. The challenge for each company's management team is to craft and execute a competitive strategy that produces good performance on five measures: earnings per share, return on equity investment, stock price appreciation, credit rating, and brand image.

All activity for *The Business Strategy Game* takes place at www.bsg-online.com.

A Birds-Eye View of GLO-BUS.

The industry setting for *GLO-BUS* is the digital camera industry. Global market demand grows at the rate of 8–10% annually for the first five years and 4–6% annually for the second five years. Retail sales of digital cameras are seasonal, with about 20 percent of consumer demand coming in each of the first three quarters of each calendar year and 40 percent coming during the big fourth-quarter retailing season.

Companies produce entry-level and upscale, multi-featured cameras of varying designs and quality in a Taiwan assembly facility and ship assembled cameras directly to retailers in North America, Asia-Pacific, Europe-Africa, and Latin America. All cameras are assembled as retail orders come in and shipped immediately upon completion of the assembly process—companies maintain no finished goods inventories and all parts and components are delivered on a just-in-time basis (which eliminates the need to track inventories and simplifies the accounting for plant operations and costs). Company co-managers exercise control over production costs based on the designs and components they specify for their cameras, work force compensation and training, the length of warranties offered (which affects warranty costs), the amount spent for technical support provided to buyers of the company's cameras, and their management of the assembly process.

Competition in each of the two product market segments (entry-level and multi-featured digital cameras) is based on 10 factors: price, camera performance and quality, number of quarterly sales promotions, length of promotions in weeks, the size of the promotional discounts offered, advertising, the number of camera models, size of retail dealer network, warranty period, and the amount/caliber of technical support provided to camera buyers. Low-cost leadership, differentiation strategies, best-cost provider strategies, and focus strategies are all viable competitive options. Rival companies can strive to be the clear market leader in either entry-level cameras or upscale multi-featured cameras or both. They can focus on one or two geographic regions or strive for geographic balance. They can pursue essentially the same strategy worldwide or craft slightly or very different strategies for the Europe-Africa, Asia-Pacific, Latin America, and North America markets. Just as with *The Business Strategy Game,* most any well-conceived, well-executed competitive approach is capable of succeeding, *provided it is not overpowered by the strategies of competitors or defeated by the presence of too many copycat strategies that dilute its effectiveness.*

Company co-managers make 44 types of decisions each period, ranging from R&D, camera components, and camera performance (10 decisions) to production operations and worker compensation (15 decisions) to pricing and marketing (15 decisions) to the financing of company operations (4 decisions). Each time participants make a decision entry, an assortment of on-screen calculations instantly shows the projected effects on unit sales, revenues, market shares, unit costs, profit, earnings per share, ROE, and other operating statistics. These on-screen calculations help team members evaluate the relative merits of one decision entry versus another and stitch the separate decisions into a cohesive and promising strategy. Company performance is judged on five criteria: earnings per share, return on equity investment, stock price, credit rating, and brand image.

All activity for *GLO-BUS* occurs at www.glo-bus.com.

Administration and Operating Features of the Two Simulations

The online delivery and user-friendly designs of both *BSG* and *GLO-BUS* make them incredibly easy to administer, even for first-time users. And the menus and controls are so similar that you can readily switch between the two simulations or use one in your undergraduate class and the other in a graduate class. If you have not yet used either of the two simulations, you may find the following of particular interest:

- Time requirements for instructors are minimal. Setting up the simulation for your course is done online and takes about 10–15 minutes. Once setup is completed, no other administrative actions are required beyond that of moving participants to a different team (should the need arise) and monitoring the progress of the simulation (to whatever extent desired).

- There's no software for students or administrators to download and no disks to fool with. All work must be done online and the speed for participants using dial-up modems is quite satisfactory. The servers dedicated to hosting the two simulations have appropriate backup capability and are maintained by a prominent Web-hosting service that guarantees 99.99 percentage reliability on a 24/7/365 basis—as long as students or instructors are connected to the Internet, the servers are virtually guaranteed to be operational.

- Participant's Guides are delivered at the Web site—students can read it on their monitors or print out a copy, as they prefer.

- There are extensive built-in "Help" screens explaining (a) each decision entry, (b) the information on each page of the Industry Reports, and (c) the numbers presented in the Company Reports. *The Help screens allow company co-managers to figure things out for themselves, thereby curbing the need for students to always run to the instructor with questions about "how things work."*

- The results of each decision are processed automatically and are typically available to all participants *15 minutes* after the decision deadline specified by the instructor/game administrator.

- Participants and instructors are notified via e-mail when the results are ready.

- Decision schedules are instructor-determined. Decisions can be made once per week, twice per week, or even twice daily, depending on how instructors want to conduct the exercise. One popular decision schedule involves 1 or 2 practice decisions, 6–10 regular decisions, and weekly decisions across the whole term. A second popular schedule is 1 or 2 practice decisions, 6–8 regular decisions, and bi-weekly decisions, all made during last 4 to 6 weeks of the course (when it can be assumed that students have pretty much digested the contents of Chapters 1–6, gotten somewhat comfortable with what is involved in crafting strategy for a single-business company situation, and have prepared several assigned cases). A third popular schedule is to use the simulation as a "final exam" for the course, with daily decisions (Monday through Friday) for the last two weeks of the term.

- Instructors have the flexibility to prescribe 0, 1, or 2 practice decisions and from 3 to 10 regular decisions.

- Company teams can be composed of 1 to 5 players each and the number of companies in a single industry can range from 4 to 12. If your class size is too large for a single industry, then it is a simple matter to create two or more industries for a single class section.

- Following each decision, participants are provided with a complete set of reports—a six-page Industry Report, a one-page Competitive Intelligence report for each geographic region that includes strategic group maps and bulleted lists of competitive strengths and weaknesses, and a set of Company Reports (income statement, balance sheet, cash flow statement, and assorted production, marketing, and cost statistics).

- Two "open-book" multiple choice tests of 20 questions (optional, but strongly recommended) are included as part of each of the two simulations. The quizzes are taken online and automatically graded, with scores reported instantaneously to participants and automatically recorded in the instructor's electronic grade book. Students are automatically provided with three sample questions for each test.

- Both simulations contain a three-year strategic plan option that you can assign. Scores on the plan are automatically recorded in the instructor's online grade book.

- At the end of the simulation, you can have students complete online peer evaluations (again, the scores are automatically recorded in your online grade book).

- Both simulations have a Company Presentation feature that enables students to easily prepare PowerPoint slides for use in describing their strategy and summarizing their company's performance in a presentation either to the class, the instructor, or an "outside" board of directors.

- *A Learning Assurance Report provides you with hard data concerning how well your students performed vis-à-vis students playing the simulation worldwide over the past 12 months.* The report is based on Eight measures of student proficiency, business know-how, and decision-making skill and can also be used in evaluating the extent to which your school's academic curriculum produces the desired degree of student learning insofar as accreditation standards are concerned.

For more details on either simulation, please consult the Instructor's Manual or visit the simulation Web sites (www.bsg-online.com and www.glo-bus.com). Once you register (there's no obligation), you'll be able to access the Instructor's Guide and a set of PowerPoint Presentation slides that you can skim to preview the two simulations in some depth. If you call the senior author of this text at (205) 348-8923, the simulation authors will be glad to provide you with a personal tour of either or both Web sites (while you are on your PC) and walk you through the many features that are built into the simulations. We think you'll be quite impressed with the capabilities that have been programmed into *The Business Strategy Game* and *GLO-BUS,* the simplicity with which both simulations can be administered, and their exceptionally tight connection to the text chapters, core concepts, and standard analytical tools.

Adopters of the text who also want to incorporate use of one of the two simulation supplements can either have students register at the simulation Web site via a credit card or you can instruct your bookstores to order the "book-simulation package"—the publisher has a special ISBN number for new texts that contain a special card shrink-wrapped with each text. Printed on the enclosed card is a pre-paid access code that student can use to register for either simulation and gain full access to the student portion of the Web site. However, bookstore markups on the book-simulation package often result in a higher student cost for the simulation than will registering via credit card at the Web site.

STUDENT SUPPORT MATERIALS FOR THE 16TH EDITION

Key Points Summaries

At the end of each chapter is a synopsis of the core concepts, analytical tools and other key points discussed in the chapter. These chapter-end synopses, along with the margin notes scattered throughout each chapter, help students focus on basic strategy principles, digest the messages of each chapter, and prepare for tests.

Chapter-End Exercises

Each chapter contains a much-embellished set of exercises that you can use as the basis for class discussion, oral presentation assignments, and/or short written reports. A few of the exercises (and many of the Illustration Capsules) qualify as "mini-cases"; these can be used to round out the rest of a 75-minute class period should your lecture on a chapter only last for 50 minutes.

Online Learning Center (OLC)

Students gain access to the publisher's OLC for the 16th edition by visiting www.mhhe .com/thompson. The student section of this site contains a number of helpful aids:

- **Concept-TUTOR:** 20-question self-grading chapter quizzes that students can take to measure their grasp of the material presented in each of the 13 chapters.
- A **"Guide to Case Analysis"** containing sections on what a case is, why cases are a standard part of courses in strategy, preparing a case for class discussion, doing a written case analysis, doing an oral presentation, and using financial ratio analysis to assess a company's financial condition. We suggest having students read this Guide prior to the first class discussion of a case.
- A select number of **PowerPoint** *slides* for each chapter.

Purchasing access to our premium learning resources right on the OLC Web site provides student with the following value added resources:

- **Pre- and Post-Tests.** Students can access the online pre-test prior to reading the chapter, answer the questions, study the chapter, and then take the post-test to see what they have learned.
- **Downloadable Content.** Quizzes, pre- and post-tests, narrated slides, and videos are available for iPod download to help students prepare for exams.
- **Case-TUTOR.** One of the most important and useful student aids at the 16th edition Web site is a set of downloadable files called Case-TUTOR that consists of (1) files containing assignment questions for all 31 cases in the text and (2) files containing analytically-structured exercises for 11 of the cases—these 11 "case preparation exercises" coach students in doing the strategic thinking needed to arrive at solid answers to the assignment questions for that case. Conscientious completion of the case preparation exercises helps students gain

quicker command of the concepts and analytical techniques and points them toward doing good strategic analysis. The 11 cases with an accompanying case preparation exercise are indicated by the Case-TUTOR logo in the case listing section of the Table of Contents (the Case-TUTOR logo also appears on the first page of cases for which there is an exercise).

All the directions that students need to use the Case-TUTOR files appear on the opening screens, and the menus are self-evident and intuitive. The Case-TUTOR courseware can be used only on Windows-based PCs loaded with Microsoft Excel (either the Office 2000, Office XP, Office 2003, or Office 2007 versions).

To purchase Case-TUTOR (or any other premium resources) students can visit www.mhhe.com/thompson, click on the Student Edition link, then click on the Case-TUTOR link, and then make a purchase via an eCommerce transaction.

INSTRUCTOR SUPPORT MATERIALS FOR THE 16TH EDITION

Instructor's Manual

Prepared by the textbook authors, the accompanying IM contains a section on suggestions for organizing and structuring your course, sample syllabi and course outlines, a set of lecture notes on each chapter, a copy of the test bank, and comprehensive case teaching notes for each of the cases.

Test Bank

There is a test bank prepared by the co-authors containing over 1,000 multiple choice questions and short-answer/essay questions. It has now been tagged with Bloom's Taxonomy and AACSB criteria.

AACSB Statement McGraw-Hill Companies is a pround corporate member of AACSB International. Recognizing the importance and value of AACSB accreditation, the authors of Thompson 16e have sought to recognize the curricula guidelines detailed in AACSB standards for business accreditation by connecting selected questions in Thompson 16e or its test bank the general knowledge and skill guidelines found in the AACSB standards. It is important to note that the statements contained in Thompson 16e are provided only as a guide for the users of this text.

The statements contained in Thompson 16e are provided only as a guide for the users of this text. The AACSB leaves content coverage and assessment clearly within the realm and control of individual schools, the mission of the school, and the faculty. The AACSB does also charge schools with the obligation of doing assessment against their own content and learning goals. While Thompson 16e and its teaching package make no claim of any specific AACSB qualification or evaluation, we have, within Thompson 16e labeled selected questions according to the six general knowledge and skills areas. The labels or tags within Thompson 16e are as indicated. There are of course, many more within the test bank, the text, and the teaching package which might be used as as 'standard' for your course. However, the labeled questions are suggested for your consideration.

EZ Test, a computerized version of the test bank, can be found on the Instructor's Resource CD-ROM. This flexible and easy-to-use electronic testing program allows instructors to create multiple versions of tests from book-specific items with a wide range of question types, including adding their own. And any test can be exported for use with course management systems.

NEW: McGraw-Hill EZ Test Online is accessible to busy instructors virtually anywhere—in their office, at home or while traveling—and eliminates the need for software installation. It gives instructors access to hundreds of textbook question banks and millions of questions when creating tests. Instructors can view question banks associated with their textbook or easily create their own questions. Multiple versions of tests can be saved for future delivery as a paper test or online. When created and delivered with EZ Test Online individual tests are immediately scored, saving instructors valuable time and providing prompt test feedback to students. To register please visit: http://www.eztestonline.com/

PowerPoint Slides

To facilitate delivery preparation of your lectures and to serve as chapter outlines, you'll have access to approximately 500 colorful and professional-looking slides displaying core concepts, analytical procedures, key points, and all the figures in the text chapters. The slides, prepared in close collaboration with the text authors, are the creation of Professor Jana Kuzmicki of Troy State University.

Instructor's Resource CD-ROM

All of our instructor supplements are available in this one-stop multimedia resource, which includes the complete Instructor's Manual, Computerized Test Bank (EZ Test), accompanying PowerPoint slides, and the Digital Image Library with all the figures from the text.

Accompanying Case Videos

Ten of the cases (Shearwater Adventures, Costo Wholesale, The Battle in Radio Broadcasting, Competition in Bottled Water in 2006, Blue Nile—World's Largest Online, Diamond Retailer, Panera Bread, Wild Oats Market, Zune: Microsoft's Emtry into the Digital Music Player Market, Competition in Video Game Consoles, and New Balance Athletic Shoe have accompanying videotape segments that can be shown in conjunction with the case discussions. Suggestions for using each video are contained in the teaching note for that case.

Online Learning Center (OLC)

The instructor section of www.mhhe.com/thompson also includes the Instructor's Manual, PowerPoint sides, Group and Video Course Manual as well as additional resources.

Enhanced Cartridge for Blackboard and WebCT*

The Enhanced Cartridge is the perfect tool for instructors teaching a hybrid course or a course completely online requiring substantial online content. Resources such as Case Tutor, the iPod content, pre- and post-tests, interactive skills exercises, and self-assessments help students to learn and apply concepts and allow you to monitor their progress.

---

*Please ask your McGraw-Hill rep about availability of McGraw-Hill's Enhanced Cartridge materials for other course management platforms.

The Business Strategy Game and GLO-BUS Online Simulations

Using one of the two companion simulations is a powerful and constructive way of emotionally connecting students to the subject matter of the course. We know of no more effective and interesting way to stimulate the competitive energy of students and prepare them for the rigors of real-world business decision making than to have them match strategic wits with classmates in running a company in head-to-head competition for global market leadership. Equally important is the extent to which use of a fully automated simulation economizes on course preparation time and grading.

Additional Resources

McGraw-Hill/Primis Custom Publishing   You can readily customize this text. McGraw-Hill/Primis Online's digital database offers you the flexibility to create custom material from a diverse online collection of textbooks, readings, and cases from all of our recent editions (as well as other case sources). To facilitate your putting together a custom casebook in less than fifteen minutes, we have recommended case lineups with 6, 8, 10 and 12 quality cases. Select the number of cases you want to assign for your course, customize if you like, and request a review copy and ISBN for your bookstore. (For more information, please visit www.primisonline.com/thompson, or call 800-228-0634.) Your McGraw-Hill rep can also provide you with other resources that may be of interest, including a Group and Video Resource Manual, Manager's Hot Seat, and eBook format options.

We've done our level best in this 16th edition to provide you with a full-featured teaching/learning package that raises the bar for what a text package in the discipline of strategy ought to deliver and that provides all the resources and materials you'll need to design and deliver a top-flight, pedagogically effective course in strategic management.

ACKNOWLEDGEMENTS

We heartily acknowledge the contributions of the case researchers whose case-writing efforts appear herein and the companies whose cooperation made the cases possible. To each one goes a very special thank-you. We cannot overstate the importance of timely, carefully researched cases in contributing to a substantive study of strategic management issues and practices. From a research standpoint, strategy-related cases are invaluable in exposing the generic kinds of strategic issues which companies face, in forming hypotheses about strategic behavior, and in drawing experienced-based generalizations about the practice of strategic management. From an instructional standpoint, strategy cases give students essential practice in diagnosing and evaluating the strategic situations of companies and organizations, in applying the concepts and tools of strategic analysis, in weighing strategic options and crafting strategies, and in tackling the challenges of successful strategy execution. Without a continuing stream of fresh, well-researched, and well-conceived cases, the discipline of strategic management would lose its close ties to the very institutions whose strategic actions and behavior it is aimed at explaining. There's no question, therefore, that first-class case research constitutes a valuable scholarly contribution to the theory and practice of strategic management.

In addition, a great number of colleagues and students at various universities, business acquaintances, and people at McGraw-Hill provided inspiration, encouragement, and counsel during the course of this project. Like all text authors in the strategy field, we are intellectually indebted to the many academics whose research and writing have blazed new trails and advanced the discipline of strategic management. The following reviewers provided seasoned advice and splendid suggestions for improving the chapters in the 15th and 16th edition packages:

- Lynne Patten, Clark Atlanta University
- Nancy E. Landrum, Morehead State University
- Jim Goes, Walden University
- Jon Kalinowski, Minnesota State University–Mankato
- Rodney M. Walter Jr., Western Illinois University
- Judith D. Powell, Virginia Union University

We also express our thanks to Seyda Deligonul, David Flanagan, Esmerelda Garbi, Mohsin Habib, Kim Hester, Jeffrey E. McGee, Diana J, Wong, F. William Brown, Anthony F. Chelte, Gregory G. Dess, Alan B. Eisner, John George, Carle M. Hunt, Theresa Marron-Grodsky, Sarah Marsh, Joshua D. Martin, William L. Moore, Donald Neubaum, George M. Puia, Amit Shah, Lois M. Shelton, Mark Weber, Steve Barndt, J. Michael Geringer, Ming-Fang Li, Richard Stackman, Stephen Tallman, Gerardo R. Ungson, James Boulgarides, Betty Diener, Daniel F. Jennings, David Kuhn, Kathryn Martell, Wilbur Mouton, Bobby Vaught, Tuck Bounds, Lee Burk, Ralph Catalanello, William Crittenden, Vince Luchsinger, Stan Mendenhall, John Moore, Will Mulvaney, Sandra Richard, Ralph Roberts, Thomas Turk, Gordon VonStroh, Fred Zimmerman, S. A. Billion, Charles Byles, Gerald L. Geisler, Rose Knotts, Joseph Rosenstein, James B. Thurman, Ivan Able, W. Harvey Hegarty, Roger Evered, Charles B. Saunders, Rhae M. Swisher, Claude I. Shell, R. Thomas Lenz, Michael C. White, Dennis Callahan, R. Duane Ireland, William E. Burr II, C. W. Millard, Richard Mann, Kurt Christensen, Neil W. Jacobs, Louis W. Fry, D. Robley Wood, George J. Gore, and William R. Soukup. These reviewers provided valuable guidance in steering our efforts to improve earlier editions.

As always, we value your recommendations and thoughts about the book. Your comments regarding coverage and contents will be taken to heart, and we always are grateful for the time you take to call our attention to printing errors, deficiencies, and other shortcomings. Please e-mail us at athompso@cba.ua.edu, astrickl@cba.ua.edu, or jgamble@usouthal.edu; fax us at (205) 348-6695; or write us at P. O. Box 870225, Department of Management and Marketing, The University of Alabama, Tuscaloosa, Alabama 35487-0225.

Arthur A. Thompson

A. J. Strickland

John E. Gamble

Guided Tour

Chapter Structure and Organization

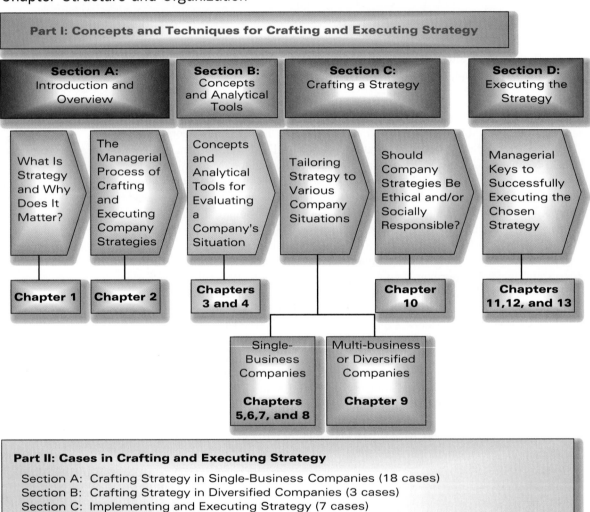

Part I: Concepts and Techniques for Crafting and Executing Strategy

Section A: Introduction and Overview		Section B: Concepts and Analytical Tools	Section C: Crafting a Strategy		Section D: Executing the Strategy
What Is Strategy and Why Does It Matter?	The Managerial Process of Crafting and Executing Company Strategies	Concepts and Analytical Tools for Evaluating a Company's Situation	Tailoring Strategy to Various Company Situations	Should Company Strategies Be Ethical and/or Socially Responsible?	Managerial Keys to Successfully Executing the Chosen Strategy
Chapter 1	**Chapter 2**	**Chapters 3 and 4**		**Chapter 10**	**Chapters 11,12, and 13**

Single-Business Companies
Chapters 5,6,7, and 8

Multi-business or Diversified Companies
Chapter 9

Part II: Cases in Crafting and Executing Strategy

Section A: Crafting Strategy in Single-Business Companies (18 cases)
Section B: Crafting Strategy in Diversified Companies (3 cases)
Section C: Implementing and Executing Strategy (7 cases)
Section D: Strategy, Ethics, and Social Responsibility (3 cases)

chapter one

What Is Strategy and Why Is It Important?

Strategy means making clear-cut choices about how to compete.
—**Jack Welch**
Former CEO, General Electric

A strategy is a commitment to undertake one set of actions rather than another.
—**Sharon Oster**
Professor, Yale University

The process of developing superior strategies is part planning, part trial and error, until you hit upon something that works.
—**Costas Markides**
Professor, London Business School

Without a strategy the organization is like a ship without a rudder.
—**Joel Ross and Michael Kami**
Authors and Consultants

Managers face three central questions in evaluating their company's business prospects: What's the company's present situation? Where does the company need to go from here? How should it get there? Arriving at a probing answer to the question "What's the company's present situation?" prompts managers to evaluate industry conditions and competitive pressures, the company's current performance and market standing, its resource strengths and capabilities, and its competitive weaknesses. The question "Where does the company need to go from here?" pushes managers to make choices about the direction the company should be headed—what new or different customer groups and customer needs it should endeavor to satisfy, what market positions it should be staking out, what changes in its business makeup are needed. The question "How should it get there?" challenges managers to craft and execute a strategy capable of moving the company in the intended direction, growing its business, and improving its financial and market performance.

In this opening chapter, we define the concept of strategy and describe its many facets. We shall indicate the kinds of actions that determine what a company's strategy is, why strategies are partly proactive and partly reactive, and why company strategies tend to evolve over time. We will look at what sets a winning strategy apart from ho-hum or flawed strategies and why the caliber of a company's strategy determines whether it will enjoy a competitive advantage or be burdened by competitive disadvantage. By the end of this chapter, you will have a pretty clear idea of why the tasks of crafting and executing strategy are core management functions and why excellent execution of an excellent strategy is the most reliable recipe for turning a company into a standout performer.

WHAT DO WE MEAN BY *STRATEGY*?

A company's **strategy** is management's action plan for running the business and conducting operations. The crafting of a strategy represents a managerial *commitment to pursue a particular set of actions* in growing the business, attracting and pleasing customers, competing successfully, conducting operations, and improving the company's financial and market performance. Thus a company's strategy is all about *how—how* management intends to grow the business, *how* it will build a loyal clientele and outcompete rivals, *how* each functional piece of the business (research and development,

Each chapter begins with a series of pertinent **quotes** and an introductory preview of its contents.

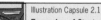

Chapter 2   The Managerial Process of Crafting and Executing Strategy   23

Illustration Capsule 2.1
Examples of Strategic Visions—How Well Do They Measure Up?

Using the information in Tables 2.2 and 2.3, critique the following strategic visions and rank them from 1 (best) to 7 (in need of substantial improvement).

RED HAT
To extend our position as the most trusted Linux and open source provider to the enterprise. We intend to grow the market for Linux through a complete range of enterprise Red Hat Linux software, a powerful Internet management platform, and associated support and services.

WELLS FARGO
We want to satisfy all of our customers' financial needs, help them succeed financially, be the premier provider of financial services in every one of our markets, and be known as one of America's great companies.

HILTON HOTELS CORPORATION
Our vision is to be the first choice of the world's travelers. Hilton intends to build on the rich heritage and strength of our brands by:
- Consistently delighting our customers
- Investing in our team members
- Delivering innovative products and services
- Continuously improving performance
- Increasing shareholder value

- Creating a culture of pride
- Strengthening the loyalty of our constituents

THE DENTAL PRODUCTS DIVISION OF 3M CORPORATION
Become THE supplier of choice to the global dental professional markets, providing world-class quality and innovative products.
[*Note:* All employees of the division wear badges bearing these words, and whenever a new product or business procedure is being considered, management asks "Is this representative of THE leading dental company?"]

CATERPILLAR
Be the global leader in customer value.

eBAY
Provide a global trading platform where practically anyone can trade practically anything.

H. J. HEINZ COMPANY
Be the world's premier food company, offering nutritious, superior tasting foods to people everywhere. Being the premier food company does not mean being the biggest but it does mean being the best in terms of consumer value, customer service, employee talent, and consistent and predictable growth.

Sources: Company documents and Web sites.

In-depth examples—**Illustration Capsules**—appear in boxes throughout each chapter to illustrate important chapter topics, connect the text presentation to real world companies, and convincingly demonstrate "strategy in action." Some can be used as "mini-cases" for purposes of class discussion.

Margin notes define core concepts and call attention to important ideas and principles.

Strategy and the Quest for Competitive Advantage

The heart and soul of any strategy are the actions and moves in the marketplace that managers are taking to improve the company's financial performance, strengthen its long-term competitive position, and gain a competitive edge over rivals. A creative, distinctive strategy that sets a company apart from rivals and yields a competitive advantage is a company's most reliable ticket for earning above-average profits. Competing in the marketplace with a competitive advantage tends to be more profitable than competing with no advantage. And a company is almost certain to earn significantly higher profits when it enjoys a competitive advantage as opposed to when it is hamstrung by competitive disadvantage. Furthermore, if a company's competitive edge holds promise for being durable and sustainable (as opposed to just temporary), then so much the better for both the strategy and the company's future profitability. It's nice when a company's strategy produces at least a temporary competitive edge, but a **sustainable competitive advantage** is plainly much better. What makes a competitive advantage sustainable as opposed to temporary are actions and elements in the strategy that cause an attractive number of buyers to have a *lasting preference* for a company's products or services as compared to the offerings of competitors. Competitive advantage is the key to above-average profitability and financial performance because strong buyer preferences for the company's product offering translate into higher sales volumes (Wal-Mart) and/or the ability to command a higher price (Häagen-Dazs), thus driving up earnings, return on investment, and other measures of financial performance.

Core Concept
A company achieves *sustainable competitive advantage* when an attractive number of buyers prefers its products or services over the offerings of competitors and when the basis for this preference is durable.

Four of the most frequently used and dependable strategic approaches to setting a company apart from rivals, building strong customer loyalty, and winning a sustainable competitive advantage are:

Figures scattered throughout the chapters provide conceptual and analytical frameworks.

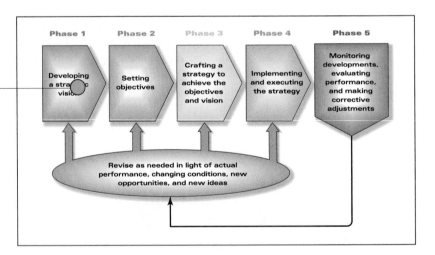

As you tackle the following pages, ponder the following observation by the essayist and poet Ralph Waldo Emerson: "Commerce is a game of skill which many people
play, but which few play well." If the content of this book helps you become a more
savvy player and equips you to succeed in business, then your journey through these
pages will indeed be time well spent.

Key Points

The tasks of crafting and executing company strategies are the heart and soul of managing a business enterprise and winning in the marketplace. A company's strategy is
the game plan management is using to stake out a market position, conduct its operations, attract and please customers, compete successfully, and achieve organizational
objectives. The central thrust of a company's strategy is undertaking moves to build and
strengthen the company's long-term competitive position and financial performance
and, ideally, gain a competitive advantage over rivals that then becomes a company's
ticket to above-average profitability. A company's strategy typically evolves and reforms over time, emerging from a blend of (1) proactive and purposeful actions on the
part of company managers and (2) as-needed reactions to unanticipated developments
and fresh market conditions.

Key Points sections
at the end of each
chapter provide a handy
summary of essential
ideas and things to
remember.

the company's product offerings and competitive approaches will generate a revenue
stream and have an associated cost structure that produces attractive earnings and return
on investment—in effect, a company's business model sets forth the economic logic
for making money in a particular business, given the company's current strategy.

A winning strategy fits the circumstances of a company's external situation and its
internal resource strengths and competitive capabilities, builds competitive advantage,
and boosts company performance.

Crafting and executing strategy are core management functions. Whether a company wins or loses in the marketplace is directly attributable to the caliber of a company's strategy and the proficiency with which the strategy is executed.

Exercises

1.   Go to Red Hat's Web site (www.redhat.com) and check whether the company's
     recent financial reports indicate that its business model is working. Is the company
     sufficiently profitable to validate its business model and strategy? Is its revenue
     stream from selling training, consulting, and engineering services growing or
     declining as a percentage of total revenues? Does your review of the company's
     recent financial performance suggest that its business model and strategy are
     changing? Read the company's latest statement about its business model and
     about why it is pursuing the subscription approach (as compared to Microsoft's
     approach of selling copies of its operating software directly to PC manufacturers
     and individuals).

Value-added **exercises**
at the end of each
chapter provide a basis
for class discussion, oral
presentations, and
written assignments.
Several chapters have
exercises that qualify as
"mini-cases."

FOR STUDENTS: An Assortment of Support Materials

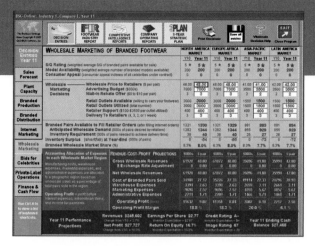

www.mhhe.com/thompson

The student portion of the Web site features a "Guide to Case Analysis," with special sections on what a case is, why cases are a standard part of courses in strategy, preparing a case for class discussion, doing a written case analysis, doing an oral presentation, and using financial ratio analysis to assess a company's financial condition. In addition, there are 20-question, self-scoring chapter tests and a select number of PowerPoint slides for each chapter.

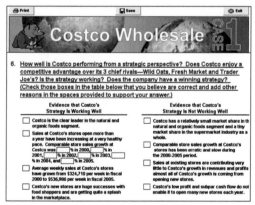

Case-Tutor: A set of downloadable files containing assignment questions for each of the 31 cases in the text, plus analytically structured exercises for 11 of the cases that coach students in doing the strategic thinking needed to arrive at solid answers to the assignment questions for that case. Conscientious completion of the 11 case exercises aids quicker command of the concepts and analytical techniques and facilitates good strategic analysis and thorough preparation of assigned cases.

***The Business Strategy Game* or *GLO-BUS* Simulation Exercises** Either one of these text supplements involves teams of students managing companies in a head-to-head contest for global market leadership. Company co-managers have to make decisions relating to product quality, production, work force compensation and training, pricing and marketing, and financing of company operations. The challenge is to craft and execute a strategy that is powerful enough to deliver good financial performance despite the competitive efforts of rival companies. Each company competes in North America, Latin America, Europe-Africa, and Asia-Pacific.

Section B: Core Concepts and Analytical Tools

3. Evaluating a Company's External Environment   48

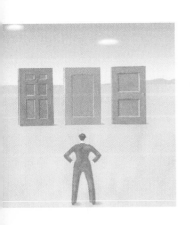

Illustration Capsules

6. Supplementing the Chosen Competitive Strategy: *Other Important Strategy Choices*   160

10. Strategy, Ethics, and Social Responsibility   316

13. Corporate Culture and Leadership: Keys to Good Strategy Execution   414

Part Two   Cases

part one 1

Concepts and Techniques for Crafting and Executing Strategy

What Is Strategy and Why Is It Important?

Strategy means making clear-cut choices about how to compete.

—Jack Welch
Former CEO, General Electric

A strategy is a commitment to undertake one set of actions rather than another.

—Sharon Oster
Professor, Yale University

The process of developing superior strategies is part planning, part trial and error, until you hit upon something that works.

—Costas Markides
Professor, London Business School

Without a strategy the organization is like a ship without a rudder.

—Joel Ross and Michael Kami
Authors and Consultants

anagers face three central questions in evaluating their company's business prospects: What's the company's present situation? Where does the company need to go from here? How should it get there? Arriving at a probing answer to the question "What's the company's present situation?" prompts managers to evaluate industry conditions and competitive pressures, the company's current performance and market standing, its resource strengths and capabilities, and its competitive weaknesses. The question "Where does the company need to go from here?" pushes managers to make choices about the direction the company should be headed—what new or different customer groups and customer needs it should endeavor to satisfy, what market positions it should be staking out, what changes in its business makeup are needed. The question "How should it get there?" challenges managers to craft and execute a strategy capable of moving the company in the intended direction, growing its business, and improving its financial and market performance.

In this opening chapter, we define the concept of strategy and describe its many facets. We shall indicate the kinds of actions that determine what a company's strategy is, why strategies are partly proactive and partly reactive, and why company strategies tend to evolve over time. We will look at what sets a winning strategy apart from ho-hum or flawed strategies and why the caliber of a company's strategy determines whether it will enjoy a competitive advantage or be burdened by competitive disadvantage. By the end of this chapter, you will have a pretty clear idea of why the tasks of crafting and executing strategy are core management functions and why excellent execution of an excellent strategy is the most reliable recipe for turning a company into a standout performer.

WHAT DO WE MEAN BY *STRATEGY*?

A company's **strategy** is management's action plan for running the business and conducting operations. The crafting of a strategy represents a managerial *commitment to pursue a particular set of actions* in growing the business, attracting and pleasing customers, competing successfully, conducting operations, and improving the company's financial and market performance. Thus a company's strategy is all about *how—how* management intends to grow the business, *how* it will build a loyal clientele and outcompete rivals, *how* each functional piece of the business (research and development,

Core Concept

A company's *strategy* consists of the competitive moves and business approaches that managers are employing to grow the business, attract and please customers, compete successfully, conduct operations, and achieve the targeted levels of organizational performance.

supply chain activities, production, sales and marketing, distribution, finance, and human resources) will be operated, *how* performance will be boosted. In choosing a strategy, management is in effect saying, "Among all the many different business approaches and ways of competing we could have chosen, we have decided to employ this particular combination of competitive and operating approaches in moving the company in the intended direction, strengthening its market position and competitiveness, and boosting performance." The strategic choices a company makes are seldom easy decisions, and some of them may turn out to be wrong—but that is not an excuse for not deciding on a concrete course of action.[1]

In most industries companies have considerable freedom in choosing the hows of strategy.[2] Thus, some rivals strive to improve their performance and market standing by achieving lower costs than rivals, while others pursue product superiority or personalized customer service or the development of competencies and capabilities that rivals cannot match. Some target the high end of the market, while others go after the middle or low end; some opt for wide product lines, while others concentrate their energies on a narrow product lineup. Some competitors position themselves in only one part of the industry's chain of production/distribution activities (preferring to be just in manufacturing or wholesale distribution or retailing), while others are partially or fully integrated, with operations ranging from components production to manufacturing and assembly to wholesale distribution or retailing. Some competitors deliberately confine their operations to local or regional markets; others opt to compete nationally, internationally (several countries), or globally (all or most of the major country markets worldwide). Some companies decide to operate in only one industry, while others diversify broadly or narrowly, into related or unrelated industries, via acquisitions, joint ventures, strategic alliances, or internal start-ups.

At companies intent on gaining sales and market share at the expense of competitors, managers typically opt for offensive strategies, frequently launching fresh initiatives of one kind or another to make the company's product offering more distinctive and appealing to buyers. Companies already in a strong industry position are more prone to strategies that emphasize gradual gains in the marketplace, fortifying the company's market position, and defending against the latest maneuvering of rivals and other developments that threaten the company's well-being. Risk-averse companies often prefer conservative strategies, preferring to follow the successful moves of pioneering companies whose managers are more entrepreneurial and willing to take the risks of being first to make a bold and perhaps pivotal move that reshapes the contest among market rivals.

There is no shortage of opportunity to fashion a strategy that both tightly fits a company's own particular situation and is discernibly different from the strategies of rivals. In fact, a company's managers normally attempt to make strategic choices about the key building blocks of its strategy that differ from the choices made by competitors—not 100 percent different but at least different in several important respects. A strategy stands a better chance of succeeding when it is predicated on actions, business approaches, and competitive moves aimed at (1) appealing to buyers in ways that set a company apart from rivals and (2) carving out its own market position. Simply copying what successful companies in the industry are doing and trying to mimic their market position rarely works. Rather, there needs to be some distinctive "aha" element to the strategy that draws in customers and produces a competitive edge. Carbon-copy strategies among companies in the same industry are the exception rather than the rule.

For a concrete example of the actions and approaches that comprise strategy, see Illustration Capsule 1.1, which describes Comcast's strategy to revolutionize the cable TV business.

Illustration Capsule 1.1

Comcast's Strategy to Revolutionize the Cable Industry

In 2004–2005 cable TV giant Comcast put the finishing touches on a bold strategy to change the way people watched television and to grow its business by introducing Internet phone service. With revenues of $18 billion and almost 22 million of the 74 million U.S. cable subscribers, Comcast became the industry leader in the U.S. market in 2002 when it acquired AT&T Broadband, along with its 13 million cable subscribers, for about $50 billion. Comcast's strategy had the following elements:

- *Continue to roll out high-speed Internet or broadband service to customers via cable modems.* With more than 8 million customers that generated revenues approaching $5 billion annually, Comcast was already America's number one provider of broadband service. It had recently upgraded its broadband service to allow download speeds of up to six megabits per second— considerably faster than the DSL-type broadband service available over telephone lines.

- *Continue to promote a relatively new video-on-demand service that allowed digital subscribers to watch TV programs whenever they wanted to watch them.* The service allowed customers to use their remotes to choose from a menu of thousands of programs, stored on Comcast's servers as they were first broadcast, and included network shows, news, sports, and movies. Viewers with a Comcast DVR set-top box had the ability to pause, stop, restart, and save programs, without having to remember to record them when they were broadcast. Comcast had signed up more than 10 million of its cable customers for digital service, and it was introducing enhanced digital and high-definition television (HDTV) service in additional geographic markets at a brisk pace.

- *Promote a video-on-demand service whereby digital customers with a set-top box could order and watch pay-per-view movies using a menu on their remote.* Comcast's technology enabled viewers to call up the programs they wanted with a few clicks of the remote. In 2005, Comcast had almost 4000 program choices and customers were viewing about 120 million videos per month.

- *Partner with Sony, MGM, and others to expand Comcast's library of movie offerings.* In 2004, Comcast agreed to develop new cable channels using MGM and Sony libraries, which had a combined 7,500 movies and 42,000 TV shows—it took about 300 movies to feed a 24-hour channel for a month.

- *Use Voice over Internet Protocol (VoIP) technology to offer subscribers Internet-based phone service at a fraction of the cost charged by other providers.* VoIP is an appealing low-cost technology widely seen as the most significant new communication technology since the invention of the telephone. Comcast was on track to make its Comcast Digital Voice (CDV) service available to 41 million homes by year-end 2006. CDV had many snazzy features, including call forwarding, caller ID, and conferencing, thus putting Comcast in position to go after the customers of traditional telephone companies.

- *Use its video-on-demand and CDV offerings to combat mounting competition from direct-to-home satellite TV providers.* Satellite TV providers such as EchoStar and DIRECTV had been using the attraction of lower monthly fees to steal customers away from cable TV providers. Comcast believed that the appeal of video-on-demand and low-cost CDV service would overcome its higher price. And satellite TV providers lacked the technological capability to provide either two-way communications connection to homes (necessary to offer video-on-demand) or reliable high-speed Internet access.

- *Employ a sales force (currently numbering about 3,200 people) to sell advertising to businesses that were shifting some of their advertising dollars from sponsoring network programs to sponsoring cable programs.* Ad sales generated revenues of about $1.6 billion, and Comcast had cable operations in 21 of the 25 largest markets in the United States.

- *Significantly improve Comcast's customer service.* Most cable subscribers were dissatisfied with the caliber of customer service offered by their local cable companies. Comcast management believed that service would be a big issue given the need to support video-on-demand, cable modems, HDTV, phone service, and the array of customer inquiries and problems such services entailed. In 2004, Comcast employed about 12,500 people to answer an expected volume of 200 million phone calls. Newly hired customer service personnel were given five weeks of classroom training, followed by three weeks of taking calls while a supervisor listened in—it cost Comcast about $7 to handle each call. The company's goal was to answer 90 percent of calls within 30 seconds.

Sources: Information posted at www.comcast.com (accessed August 6, 2005); Marc Gunter, "Comcast Wants to Change the World, But Can It Learn to Answer the Phone?" *Fortune,* October 16, 2004, pp. 140–56; and Stephanie N. Mehta, "The Future Is on the Line," *Fortune,* July 26, 2004, pp. 121–30.

Strategy and the Quest for Competitive Advantage

The heart and soul of any strategy are the actions and moves in the marketplace that managers are taking to improve the company's financial performance, strengthen its long-term competitive position, and gain a competitive edge over rivals. A creative, distinctive strategy that sets a company apart from rivals and yields a competitive advantage is a company's most reliable ticket for earning above-average profits. Competing in the marketplace with a competitive advantage tends to be more profitable than competing with no advantage. And a company is almost certain to earn significantly higher profits when it enjoys a competitive advantage as opposed to when it is hamstrung by competitive disadvantage. Furthermore, if a company's competitive edge holds promise for being durable and sustainable (as opposed to just temporary), then so much the better for both the strategy and the company's future profitability. It's nice when a company's strategy produces at least a temporary competitive edge, but a **sustainable competitive advantage** is plainly much better. What makes a competitive advantage sustainable as opposed to temporary are actions and elements in the strategy that cause an attractive number of buyers to have a *lasting preference* for a company's products or services as compared to the offerings of competitors. Competitive advantage is the key to above-average profitability and financial performance because strong buyer preferences for the company's product offering translate into higher sales volumes (Wal-Mart) and/or the ability to command a higher price (Häagen-Dazs), thus driving up earnings, return on investment, and other measures of financial performance.

Core Concept
A company achieves *sustainable competitive advantage* when an attractive number of buyers prefers its products or services over the offerings of competitors and when the basis for this preference is durable.

Four of the most frequently used and dependable strategic approaches to setting a company apart from rivals, building strong customer loyalty, and winning a sustainable competitive advantage are:

1. *Striving to be the industry's low-cost provider, thereby aiming for a cost-based competitive advantage over rivals.* Wal-Mart and Southwest Airlines have earned strong market positions because of the low-cost advantages they have achieved over their rivals and their consequent ability to underprice competitors. Achieving lower costs than rivals can produce a durable competitive edge when rivals find it hard to match the low-cost leader's approach to driving costs out of the business. Despite years of trying, discounters like Kmart and Target have struck out trying to match Wal-Mart's frugal operating practices, super-efficient distribution systems, and its finely honed supply chain approaches that allow it to obtain merchandise from manufacturers at super-low prices.

2. *Outcompeting rivals based on such differentiating features as higher quality, wider product selection, added performance, value-added services, more attractive styling, technological superiority, or unusually good value for the money.* Successful adopters of differentiation strategies include Johnson & Johnson in baby products (product reliability), Harley-Davidson (bad-boy image and king-of-the-road styling), Chanel and Rolex (top-of-the-line prestige), Mercedes-Benz and BMW (engineering design and performance), L. L. Bean (good value), and Amazon.com (wide selection and convenience). Differentiation strategies can be powerful so long as a company is sufficiently innovative to thwart clever rivals in finding ways to copy or closely imitate the features of a successful differentiator's product offering.

3. *Focusing on a narrow market niche and winning a competitive edge by doing a better job than rivals of serving the special needs and tastes of buyers comprising*

the niche. Prominent companies that enjoy competitive success in a specialized market niche include eBay in online auctions, Jiffy Lube International in quick oil changes, McAfee in virus protection software, Starbucks in premium coffees and coffee drinks, Whole Foods Market in natural and organic foods, CNBC and The Weather Channel in cable TV.

4. *Developing expertise and resource strengths that give the company competitive capabilities that rivals can't easily imitate or trump with capabilities of their own*. FedEx has superior capabilities in next-day delivery of small packages. Walt Disney has hard-to-beat capabilities in theme park management and family entertainment. Over the years, Toyota has developed a sophisticated production system that allows it to produce reliable, largely defect-free vehicles at low cost. IBM has wide-ranging expertise in helping corporate customers develop and install cutting-edge information systems. Ritz-Carlton and Four Seasons have uniquely strong capabilities in providing their hotel guests with an array of personalized services. Very often, winning a durable competitive edge over rivals hinges more on building competitively valuable expertise and capabilities than it does on having a distinctive product. Clever rivals can nearly always copy the attributes of a popular or innovative product, but for rivals to match experience, know-how, and specialized competitive capabilities that a company has developed and perfected over a long period of time is substantially harder to duplicate and takes much longer.

The tight connection between competitive advantage and profitability means that the quest for sustainable competitive advantage always ranks center stage in crafting a strategy. The key to successful strategy making is to come up with one or more differentiating strategy elements that act as a magnet to draw customers and yield a lasting competitive edge. Indeed, what separates a powerful strategy from a run-of-the-mill or ineffective one is management's ability to forge a series of moves, both in the marketplace and internally, that sets the company apart from its rivals, tilts the playing field in the company's favor by giving buyers reason to prefer its products or services, and produces a sustainable competitive advantage over rivals. The bigger and more sustainable the competitive advantage, the better the company's prospects for winning in the marketplace and earning superior long-term profits relative to its rivals. Without a strategy that leads to competitive advantage, a company risks being outcompeted by stronger rivals and/or locked in to mediocre financial performance. Hence, company managers deserve no gold stars for coming up with a ho-hum strategy that results in ho-hum financial performance and a ho-hum industry standing.

Identifying a Company's Strategy

The best indicators of a company's strategy are its actions in the marketplace and the statements of senior managers about the company's current business approaches, future plans, and efforts to strengthen its competitiveness and performance. Figure 1.1 shows what to look for in identifying the key elements of a company's strategy.

Once it is clear what to look for, the task of identifying a company's strategy is mainly one of researching information about the company's actions in the marketplace and business approaches. In the case of publicly owned enterprises, the strategy is often openly discussed by senior executives in the company's annual report and 10-K report, in press releases and company news (posted on the company's Web site), and in the information provided to investors at the company's Web site. To maintain the confidence of investors and Wall Street, most public companies have to be fairly open about their strategies. Company executives typically lay out key elements of their strategies in

Figure 1.1   **Identifying a Company's Strategy—What to Look for**

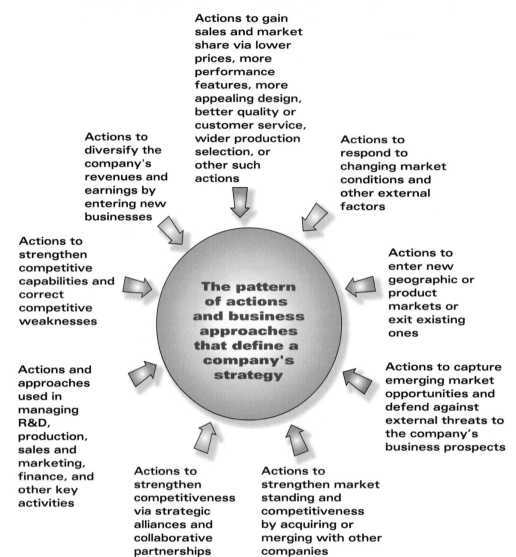

presentations to securities analysts (the accompanying PowerPoint slides are sometimes posted in the investor relations section of the company's Web site), and stories in the business media about the company often include aspects of the company's strategy. Hence, except for some about-to-be-launched moves and changes that remain under wraps and in the planning stage, there's usually nothing secret or undiscoverable about a company's present strategy.

Why a Company's Strategy Evolves over Time

Irrespective of where the strategy comes from—be it the product of top executives or the collaborative product of numerous company personnel—it is unlikely that the strategy, as originally conceived, will prove entirely suitable over time. Every company must be willing and ready to modify its strategy in response to changing market conditions, advancing technology, the fresh moves of competitors, shifting buyer needs and preferences, emerging market opportunities, new ideas for improving the strategy, and mounting evidence that the strategy is not working well. Thus, *a company's strategy is always a work in progress.*

Most of the time a company's strategy evolves incrementally from management's ongoing efforts to fine-tune this or that piece of the strategy and to adjust certain strategy elements in response to unfolding events. But, on occasion, major strategy shifts are called for, such as when a strategy is clearly failing and the company faces a financial crisis, when market conditions or buyer preferences change significantly, or when important technological breakthroughs occur. In some industries, conditions change at a fairly slow pace, making it feasible for the major components of a good strategy to remain in place for long periods. But in industries where industry and competitive conditions change frequently and in sometimes dramatic ways, the life cycle of a given strategy is short. Industry environments characterized by *high-velocity change* require companies to rapidly adapt their strategies.[3] For example, companies in industries with rapid-fire advances in technology—like medical equipment, electronics, and wireless devices—often find it essential to adjust one or more key elements of their strategies several times a year, sometimes even finding it necessary to reinvent their approach to providing value to their customers. Companies in online retailing and the travel and resort industries find it necessary to adapt their strategies to accommodate sudden bursts of new spending or sharp drop-offs in demand, often updating their market prospects and financial projections every few months.

> **Core Concept**
> Changing circumstances and ongoing management efforts to improve the strategy cause a company's strategy to evolve over time—a condition that makes the task of crafting a strategy a work in progress, not a one-time event.

> A company's strategy is shaped partly by management analysis and choice and partly by the necessity of adapting and learning by doing.

But regardless of whether a company's strategy changes gradually or swiftly, the important point is that a company's present strategy is always temporary and on trial, pending new ideas for improvement from management, changing industry and competitive conditions, and any other new developments that management believes warrant strategy adjustments. Thus, a company's strategy at any given point is fluid, representing the temporary outcome of an ongoing process that, on the one hand, involves reasoned and creative management efforts to craft an effective strategy and, on the other hand, involves ongoing responses to market change and constant experimentation and tinkering. Adapting to new conditions and constantly learning what is working well enough to continue and what needs to be improved is consequently a normal part of the strategy-making process and results in an evolving strategy.

A Company's Strategy Is Partly Proactive and Partly Reactive

The evolving nature of a company's strategy means that the typical company strategy is a blend of (1) proactive actions to improve the company's financial performance and secure a competitive edge and (2) as-needed reactions to unanticipated developments and fresh market conditions (see Figure 1.2).[4] The biggest portion of a company's current strategy flows from previously initiated actions and business approaches that are working well enough to merit continuation and newly launched initiatives aimed at boosting financial performance and edging out rivals. Typically, managers proactively modify this or that aspect of their strategy as new learning emerges about which pieces of the strategy are working well and which aren't, and as they hit upon new ideas for strategy improvement. This part of management's action plan for running the company is deliberate and proactive, standing as the current product of management's latest and best strategy ideas.

Figure 1.2   **A Company's Strategy Is a Blend of Proactive Initiatives and Reactive Adjustments**

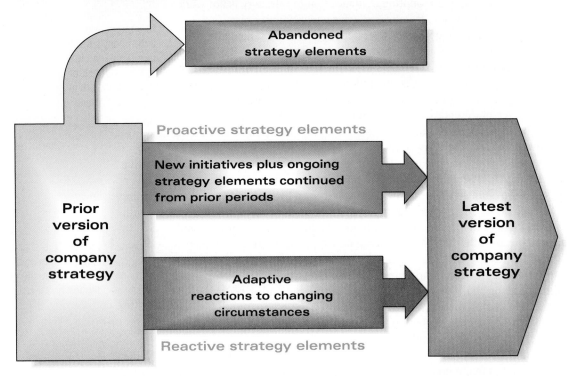

But managers must always be willing to supplement or modify all the proactive strategy elements with as-needed reactions to unanticipated developments. Inevitably, there will be occasions when market and competitive conditions take an unexpected turn that calls for some kind of strategic reaction or adjustment. Hence, a portion of a company's strategy is always developed on the fly, coming as a response to fresh strategic maneuvers on the part of rival firms, unexpected shifts in customer requirements and expectations, fast-changing technological developments, newly appearing market opportunities, a changing political or economic climate, or other unanticipated happenings in the surrounding environment. These adaptive strategy adjustments form the reactive strategy elements.

As shown in Figure 1.2, a company's strategy evolves from one version to the next as managers abandon obsolete or ineffective strategy elements, settle upon a set of *proactive/intended strategy elements*, and then adapt the strategy as new circumstances unfold, thus giving rise to *reactive/adaptive strategy elements*. A company's strategy thus tends to be a *combination* of proactive and reactive elements. In the process, some strategy elements end up being abandoned because they have become obsolete or ineffective.

STRATEGY AND ETHICS: PASSING THE TEST OF MORAL SCRUTINY

In choosing from among strategic alternatives, company managers are well advised to embrace actions that are aboveboard and can pass the test of moral scrutiny. Just keeping a company's strategic actions within the bounds of what is legal does not mean the strategy is ethical. Ethical and moral standards are not governed by what is legal. Rather, they involve issues of both right versus wrong and *duty*—what one *should* do. A strategy is ethical only if (1) it does not entail actions and behaviors that cross the line from "should do" to "should not do" (because such actions are unsavory, unconscionable, or injurious to other people or unnecessarily harmful to the environment) and (2) it allows management to fulfill its ethical duties to all stakeholders— owners/shareholders, employees, customers, suppliers, the communities in which it operates, and society at large.

> **Core Concept**
> A strategy cannot be considered ethical just because it involves actions that are legal. To meet the standard of being ethical, a strategy must entail actions that can pass moral scrutiny and that are aboveboard in the sense of not being shady, unconscionable, injurious to others, or unnecessarily harmful to the environment.

Admittedly, it is not always easy to categorize a given strategic behavior as definitely ethical or definitely unethical. Many strategic actions fall in a gray zone in between, and whether they are deemed ethical or unethical hinges on how clearly the boundaries are defined. For example, is it ethical for advertisers of alcoholic products to place ads in media having an audience of as much as 50 percent underage viewers? (In 2003, growing concerns about underage drinking prompted some beer and distilled spirits companies to agree to place ads in media with an audience at least 70 percent adult, up from a standard of 50 percent adult.) Is it ethical for an apparel retailer attempting to keep prices attractively low to source clothing from foreign manufacturers who pay substandard wages, use child labor, or subject workers to unsafe working conditions? Many people would say no, but some might argue that a company is not unethical simply because it does not police the business practices of its suppliers. Is it ethical for the makers of athletic uniforms, shoes, and other sports equipment to pay coaches large sums of money to induce them to use the manufacturer's products in their sport? (The compensation contracts of many college coaches include substantial payments from sportswear and sports equipment manufacturers, and the teams subsequently end up wearing the uniforms and using the products of those manufacturers.) Is it ethical for manufacturers of life-saving drugs to charge higher prices in some countries than they charge in others? (This is a fairly common practice that has recently come under scrutiny because it raises the costs of health care for consumers who are charged higher prices.) Is it ethical for a company to turn a blind eye to the damage its operations do to the environment even though its operations are in compliance with current environmental regulations—especially if it has the know-how and the means to alleviate some of the environmental impacts by making relatively inexpensive changes in its operating practices?

Senior executives with strong ethical convictions are generally proactive in linking strategic action and ethics: They forbid the pursuit of ethically questionable business opportunities and insist that all aspects of company strategy reflect high ethical standards.[5] They make it clear that all company personnel are expected to act with integrity, and they put organizational checks and balances into place to monitor behavior, enforce ethical codes of conduct, and provide guidance to employees regarding any gray areas. Their commitment to conducting the company's business in an ethical manner is genuine, not hypocritical.

Instances of corporate malfeasance, ethical lapses, and fraudulent accounting practices at Enron, WorldCom, Tyco, Adelphia, HealthSouth, and other companies leave no room to doubt the damage to a company's reputation and business that can result from ethical misconduct, corporate misdeeds, and even criminal behavior on the part of company personnel. Aside from just the embarrassment and black marks that accompany headline exposure of a company's unethical practices, the hard fact is that many customers and many suppliers are wary of doing business with a company that engages in sleazy practices or that turns a blind eye to illegal or unethical behavior on the part of employees. They are turned off by unethical strategies or behavior and, rather than become victims or get burned themselves, wary customers will quickly take their business elsewhere and wary suppliers will tread carefully. Moreover, employees with character and integrity do not want to work for a company whose strategies are shady or whose executives lack character and integrity. There's little lasting benefit to unethical strategies and behavior, and the downside risks can be substantial. Besides, such actions are plain wrong.

THE RELATIONSHIP BETWEEN A COMPANY'S STRATEGY AND ITS BUSINESS MODEL

Core Concept
A company's **business model** explains the rationale for why its business approach and strategy will be a moneymaker. Absent the ability to deliver good profitability, the strategy is not viable and the survival of the business is in doubt.

Closely related to the concept of strategy is the concept of a company's **business model.** While the word *model* conjures up images of ivory-tower ideas that may be loosely connected to the real world, such images do not apply here. A company's business model is management's story line for how the strategy will be a moneymaker. The story line sets forth the key components of the enterprise's business approach, indicates how revenues will be generated, and makes a case for why the strategy can deliver value to customers in a profitable manner.[6] A company's business model thus explains why its business approach and strategy will generate ample revenues to cover costs and capture a profit.

The nitty-gritty issue surrounding a company's business model is whether the chosen strategy makes good business sense. Why is there convincing reason to believe that the strategy is capable of producing a profit? How will the business generate its revenues? Will those revenues be sufficient to cover operating costs? Will customers see enough value in what the business does for them to pay a profitable price? The concept of a company's business model is, consequently, more narrowly focused than the concept of a company's business strategy. A company's strategy *relates broadly to its competitive initiatives and action plan for running the business* (but it may or may not lead to profitability). However, a company's business model zeros in on *how and why the business will generate revenues sufficient to cover costs and produce attractive profits and return on investment.* Absent the ability to deliver good profits, the strategy is not viable, the business model is flawed, and the business itself is in jeopardy of failing.

Companies that have been in business for a while and are making acceptable profits have a proven business model—because there is hard evidence that their strategies are capable of profitability. Companies that are in a start-up mode or that are losing money have questionable business models; their strategies have yet to produce good bottom-line results, putting their story line about how they intend to make money and their viability as business enterprises in doubt.

Magazines and newspapers employ a business model based on generating sufficient subscriptions and advertising to cover the costs of delivering their products to readers. Cable TV companies, cell-phone providers, record clubs, satellite radio companies, and Internet service providers also employ a subscription-based business model. The business model of network TV and radio broadcasters entails providing free programming to audiences but charging advertising fees based on audience size. McDonald's invented the business model for fast food—economical quick-service meals at clean, convenient locations. Wal-Mart has perfected the business model for big-box discount retailing—a model also used by Home Depot, Costco, and Target. Gillette's business model in razor blades involves selling a "master product"—the razor—at an attractively low price and then making money on repeat purchases— the razor blades. Printer manufacturers like Hewlett-Packard, Lexmark, and Epson pursue much the same business model as Gillette—selling printers at a low (virtually break-even) price and making large profit margins on the repeat purchases of printer supplies, especially ink cartridges. Companies like Dell and Avon employ a direct sales business model that helps keep prices low by cutting out the costs of reaching consumers through distributors and retail dealers. Illustration Capsule 1.2 discusses the contrasting business models of Microsoft and Red Hat.

WHAT MAKES A STRATEGY A WINNER?

Three questions can be used to test the merits of one strategy versus another and distinguish a winning strategy from a so-so or flawed strategy:

1. *How well does the strategy fit the company's situation?* To qualify as a winner, a strategy has to be well matched to industry and competitive conditions, a company's best market opportunities, and other aspects of the enterprise's external environment. At the same time, it has to be tailored to the company's resource strengths and weaknesses, competencies, and competitive capabilities. Unless a strategy exhibits tight fit with both the external and internal aspects of a company's overall situation, it is likely to produce less than the best possible business results.

> **Core Concept**
> A winning strategy must fit the enterprise's external and internal situation, build sustainable competitive advantage, and improve company performance.

2. *Is the strategy helping the company achieve a sustainable competitive advantage?* Winning strategies enable a company to achieve a competitive advantage that is durable. The bigger and more durable the competitive edge that a strategy helps build, the more powerful and appealing it is.

3. *Is the strategy resulting in better company performance?* A good strategy boosts company performance. Two kinds of performance improvements tell the most about the caliber of a company's strategy: (*a*) gains in profitability and financial strength, and (*b*) gains in the company's competitive strength and market standing.

Once a company commits to a particular strategy and enough time elapses to assess how well it fits the situation and whether it is actually delivering competitive advantage and better performance, then one can determine what grade to assign that strategy. Strategies that come up short on one or more of the above questions are plainly less appealing than strategies that pass all three test questions with flying colors.

Managers can also use the same questions to pick and choose among alternative strategic actions. A company evaluating which of several strategic options to employ can evaluate how well each option measures up against each of the three questions. The strategic option with the highest prospective passing scores on all three questions can be regarded as the best or most attractive strategic alternative.

Other criteria for judging the merits of a particular strategy include internal consistency and unity among all the pieces of strategy, the degree of risk the strategy poses as compared to alternative strategies, and the degree to which it is flexible and adaptable to changing circumstances. These criteria are relevant and merit consideration, but they seldom override the importance of the three test questions posed above.

Illustration Capsule 1.2

Microsoft and Red Hat: Two Contrasting Business Models

The strategies of rival companies are often predicated on strikingly different business models. Consider, for example, the business models for Microsoft and Red Hat in operating system software for personal computers (PCs).

Microsoft's business model for making money from its Windows operating system products is based on the following revenue-cost-profit economics:

- Employ a cadre of highly skilled programmers to develop proprietary code; keep the source code hidden so as to keep the inner workings of the software proprietary.

- Sell the resulting operating system and software package to PC makers and to PC users at relatively attractive prices (around $75 to PC makers and about $100 at retail to PC users); strive to maintain a 90 percent or more market share of the 150 million PCs sold annually worldwide.

- Strive for big-volume sales. Most of Microsoft's costs arise on the front end in developing the software and are thus fixed; the variable costs of producing and packaging the CDs provided to users are only a couple of dollars per copy—once the break-even volume is reached, Microsoft's revenues from additional sales are almost pure profit.

- Provide a modest level of technical support to users at no cost.

- Keep rejuvenating revenues by periodically introducing next-generation software versions with features that will induce PC users to upgrade the operating system on previously purchased PCs to the new version.

Red Hat, a company formed to market its own version of the Linux open-source operating system, employs a business model based on sharply different revenue-cost-profit economics:

- Rely on the collaborative efforts of volunteer programmers from all over the world who contribute bits and pieces of code to improve and polish the Linux system. The global community of thousands of programmers who work on Linux in their spare time do what they do because they love it, because they are fervent believers that all software should be free (as in free speech), and in some cases because they are anti-Microsoft and want to have a part in undoing what they see as a Microsoft monopoly.

- Collect and test enhancements and new applications submitted by the open-source community of volunteer programmers. Linux's originator, Linus Torvalds, and a team of 300-plus Red Hat engineers and software developers evaluate which incoming submissions merit inclusion in new releases of Linux—the evaluation and integration of new submissions are Red Hat's only upfront product development costs.

- Market the upgraded and tested family of Red Hat products to large enterprises and charge them a subscription fee that includes 24/7 support within one hour in seven languages. Provide subscribers with updated versions of Linux every 12–18 months to maintain the subscriber base.

- Make the source code open and available to all users, allowing them to create customized versions of Linux.

- Capitalize on the specialized expertise required to use Linux in multiserver, multiprocessor applications by providing fees-based training, consulting, software customization, and client-directed engineering to Linux users. Red Hat offers Linux certification training programs at all skill levels at more than 60 global locations—Red Hat certification in the use of Linux is considered the best in the world.

Microsoft's business model—sell proprietary code software and give service away free—is a proven moneymaker that generates billions in profits annually. In contrast, the jury is still out on Red Hat's business model of selling subscriptions to open-source software to large corporations and deriving substantial revenues from the sales of technical support (included in the subscription cost), training, consulting, software customization, and engineering to generate revenues sufficient to cover costs and yield a profit. Red Hat posted losses of $140 million on revenues of $79 million in fiscal year 2002 and losses of $6.6 million on revenues of $91 million in fiscal year 2003, but it earned $14 million on revenues of $126 million in fiscal 2004. The profits came from a shift in Red Hat's business model that involved putting considerably more emphasis on getting large corporations to purchase subscriptions to the latest Linux updates. In 2005, about 75 percent of Red Hat's revenues came from large enterprise subscriptions, compared to about 53 percent in 2003.

Source: Company documents and information posted on www.microsoft.com and www.redhat.com. (accessed August 10, 2005).

WHY ARE CRAFTING AND EXECUTING STRATEGY IMPORTANT?

Crafting and executing strategy are top-priority managerial tasks for two very big reasons. First, there is a compelling need for managers to *proactively shape*, or *craft*, how the company's business will be conducted. A clear and reasoned strategy is management's prescription for doing business, its road map to competitive advantage, its game plan for pleasing customers and improving financial performance. Winning in the marketplace requires a well-conceived, opportunistic strategy, usually one characterized by strategic offensives to outinnovate and outmaneuver rivals and secure sustainable competitive advantage, then using this market edge to achieve superior financial performance. A powerful strategy that delivers a home run in the marketplace can propel a firm from a trailing position into a leading one, clearing the way for its products/services to become the industry standard. High-achieving enterprises are nearly always the product of astute, creative, proactive strategy making that sets a company apart from its rivals. Companies don't get to the top of the industry rankings or stay there with imitative strategies or with strategies built around timid actions to try to do better. And only a handful of companies can boast of strategies that hit home runs in the marketplace due to lucky breaks or the good fortune of having stumbled into the right market at the right time with the right product. There can be little argument that a company's strategy matters—and matters a lot.

Second, a *strategy-focused enterprise* is more likely to be a strong bottom-line performer than a company whose management views strategy as secondary and puts its priorities elsewhere. There's no escaping the fact that the quality of managerial strategy making and strategy execution has a highly positive impact on revenue growth, earnings, and return on investment. A company that lacks clear-cut direction, has vague or undemanding performance targets, has a muddled or flawed strategy, or can't seem to execute its strategy competently is a company whose financial performance is probably suffering, whose business is at long-term risk, and whose management is sorely lacking. In contrast, when crafting and executing a winning strategy drive management's whole approach to operating the enterprise, the odds are much greater that the initiatives and activities of different divisions, departments, managers, and work groups will be unified into a *coordinated, cohesive effort*. Mobilizing the full complement of company resources in a total team effort behind good execution of the chosen strategy and achievement of the targeted performance allows a company to operate at full power. The chief executive officer of one successful company put it well when he said:

> In the main, our competitors are acquainted with the same fundamental concepts and techniques and approaches that we follow, and they are as free to pursue them as we are. More often than not, the difference between their level of success and ours lies in the relative thoroughness and self-discipline with which we and they develop and execute our strategies for the future.

Good Strategy + Good Strategy Execution = Good Management

Crafting and executing strategy are core management functions. Among all the things managers do, nothing affects a company's ultimate success or failure more fundamentally than how well its management team charts the company's direction, develops

Core Concept

Excellent execution of an excellent strategy is the best test of managerial excellence—and the most reliable recipe for turning companies into standout performers.

competitively effective strategic moves and business approaches, and pursues what needs to be done internally to produce good day-in, day-out strategy execution and operating excellence. Indeed, *good strategy and good strategy execution are the most trustworthy signs of good management.* Managers don't deserve a gold star for designing a potentially brilliant strategy but failing to put the organizational means in place to carry it out in high-caliber fashion—weak implementation and execution undermine the strategy's potential and pave the way for shortfalls in customer satisfaction and company performance. Competent execution of a mediocre strategy scarcely merits enthusiastic applause for management's efforts either. The rationale for using the twin standards of good strategy making and good strategy execution to determine whether a company is well managed is therefore compelling: *The better conceived a company's strategy and the more competently it is executed, the more likely that the company will be a standout performer in the marketplace.*

Throughout the text chapters to come and the accompanying case collection, the spotlight is trained on the foremost question in running a business enterprise: What must managers do, and do well, to make a company a winner in the marketplace? The answer that emerges, and that becomes the message of this book, is that doing a good job of managing inherently requires good strategic thinking and good management of the strategy-making, strategy-executing process.

The mission of this book is to provide a solid overview of what every business student and aspiring manager needs to know about crafting and executing strategy. This requires exploring what good strategic thinking entails; presenting the core concepts and tools of strategic analysis; describing the ins and outs of crafting and executing strategy; and, through the cases, helping you build your skills both in diagnosing how well the strategy-making, strategy-executing task is being performed in actual companies and in prescribing actions for how the companies in question can improve their approaches to crafting and executing their strategies. At the very least, we hope to convince you that capabilities in crafting and executing strategy are basic to managing successfully and merit a place in a manager's tool kit.

As you tackle the following pages, ponder the following observation by the essayist and poet Ralph Waldo Emerson: "Commerce is a game of skill which many people play, but which few play well." If the content of this book helps you become a more savvy player and equips you to succeed in business, then your journey through these pages will indeed be time well spent.

Key Points

The tasks of crafting and executing company strategies are the heart and soul of managing a business enterprise and winning in the marketplace. A company's strategy is the game plan management is using to stake out a market position, conduct its operations, attract and please customers, compete successfully, and achieve organizational objectives. The central thrust of a company's strategy is undertaking moves to build and strengthen the company's long-term competitive position and financial performance and, ideally, gain a competitive advantage over rivals that then becomes a company's ticket to above-average profitability. A company's strategy typically evolves and reforms over time, emerging from a blend of (1) proactive and purposeful actions on the part of company managers and (2) as-needed reactions to unanticipated developments and fresh market conditions.

Closely related to the concept of strategy is the concept of a company's business model. A company's business model is management's story line for how and why the company's product offerings and competitive approaches will generate a revenue stream and have an associated cost structure that produces attractive earnings and return on investment—in effect, a company's business model sets forth the economic logic for making money in a particular business, given the company's current strategy.

A winning strategy fits the circumstances of a company's external situation and its internal resource strengths and competitive capabilities, builds competitive advantage, and boosts company performance.

Crafting and executing strategy are core management functions. Whether a company wins or loses in the marketplace is directly attributable to the caliber of a company's strategy and the proficiency with which the strategy is executed.

Exercises

1. Go to Red Hat's Web site (www.redhat.com) and check whether the company's recent financial reports indicate that its business model is working. Is the company sufficiently profitable to validate its business model and strategy? Is its revenue stream from selling training, consulting, and engineering services growing or declining as a percentage of total revenues? Does your review of the company's recent financial performance suggest that its business model and strategy are changing? Read the company's latest statement about its business model and about why it is pursuing the subscription approach (as compared to Microsoft's approach of selling copies of its operating software directly to PC manufacturers and individuals).

2. From your perspective as a cable or satellite service consumer, does Comcast's strategy as described in Illustration Capsule 1.1 seem to be well matched to industry and competitive conditions? Does the strategy seem to be keyed to maintaining a cost advantage, offering differentiating features, serving the unique needs of a niche, or developing resource strengths and competitive capabilities rivals can't imitate or trump (or a mixture of these)? Do you think Comcast's strategy has evolved in recent years? Why or why not? What is there about Comcast's strategy that can lead to sustainable competitive advantage?

3. In 2003, Levi Strauss & Company announced it would close its two remaining U.S. apparel plants to finalize its transition from a clothing manufacturer to a marketing, sales, and design company. Beginning in 2004, all Levi's apparel would be produced by contract manufacturers located in low-wage countries. As recently as 1990, Levi Strauss had produced 90 percent of its apparel in company-owned plants in the United States employing over 20,000 production workers. With every plant closing, Levi Strauss & Company provided severance and job retraining packages to affected workers and cash payments to small communities where its plants were located. However, the economies of many small communities had yet to recover and some employees had found it difficult to match their previous levels of compensation and benefits.

    Review Levi Strauss & Company's discussion of its Global Sourcing and Operating Guidelines at www.levistrauss.com/responsibility/conduct. Does the company's strategy fulfill the company's ethical duties to all stakeholders—owners/shareholders, employees, customers, suppliers, the communities in which it operates, and society at large? Does Levi Strauss's strategy to outsource all of its manufacturing operations to low-wage countries pass the moral scrutiny test given that 20,000 workers lost their jobs?

The Managerial Process of Crafting and Executing Strategy

Unless we change our direction we are likely to end up where we are headed.

—Ancient Chinese proverb

If we can know where we are and something about how we got there, we might see where we are trending—and if the outcomes which lie naturally in our course are unacceptable, to make timely change.

—Abraham Lincoln

If you don't know where you are going, any road will take you there.

—The Koran

Management's job is not to see the company as it is . . . but as it can become.

—John W. Teets
Former CEO

rafting and executing strategy are the heart and soul of managing a business enterprise. But exactly what is involved in developing a strategy and executing it proficiently? What are the various components of the strategy-making, strategy-executing process? And to what extent are company personnel—aside from top executives—involved in the process? In this chapter we present an overview of the managerial ins and outs of crafting and executing company strategies. Special attention will be given to management's direction-setting responsibilities—charting a strategic course, setting performance targets, and choosing a strategy capable of producing the desired outcomes. We will also examine which kinds of strategic decisions are made at which levels of management and the roles and responsibilities of the company's board of directors in the strategy-making, strategy-executing process.

WHAT DOES THE STRATEGY-MAKING, STRATEGY-EXECUTING PROCESS ENTAIL?

The managerial process of crafting and executing a company's strategy consists of five interrelated and integrated phases:

1. *Developing a strategic vision* of where the company needs to head and what its future product/market/customer technology focus should be.
2. *Setting objectives* and using them as yardsticks for measuring the company's performance and progress.
3. *Crafting a strategy to achieve the objectives* and move the company along the strategic course that management has charted.
4. *Implementing and executing the chosen strategy efficiently and effectively.*
5. *Evaluating performance and initiating corrective adjustments* in the company's long-term direction, objectives, strategy, or execution in light of actual experience, changing conditions, new ideas, and new opportunities.

Figure 2.1 displays this five-phase process. Let's examine each phase in enough detail to set the stage for the forthcoming chapters and give you a bird's-eye view of what this book is about.

Figure 2.1 **The Strategy-Making, Strategy-Executing Process**

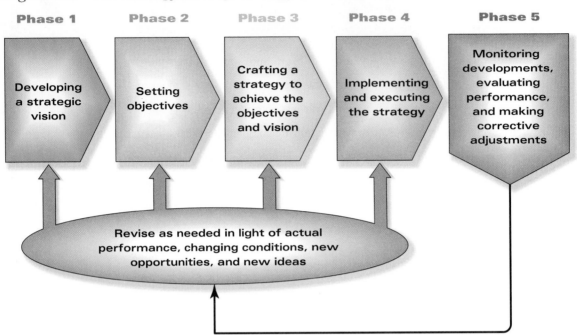

DEVELOPING A STRATEGIC VISION: PHASE 1 OF THE STRATEGY-MAKING, STRATEGY-EXECUTING PROCESS

Very early in the strategy-making process, a company's senior managers must wrestle with the issue of what path the company should take and what changes in the company's product/market/customer/technology focus would improve its market position and future prospects. Deciding to commit the company to one path versus another pushes managers to draw some carefully reasoned conclusions about how to modify the company's business makeup and what market position it should stake out. A number of direction-shaping factors need to be considered in deciding where to head and why such a direction makes good business sense—see Table 2.1.

Top management's views and conclusions about the company's direction and future product/market/customer/technology focus constitute a **strategic vision** for the company. A strategic vision delineates management's aspirations for the business, providing a panoramic view of "where we are going" and a convincing rationale for why this makes good business sense for the company. A strategic vision thus points an organization in a particular direction, charts a strategic path, and molds organizational identity. A clearly articulated strategic vision communicates management's aspirations to stakeholders and helps steer the energies of company personnel in a common direction. For instance, Henry Ford's vision of a car in every garage had power because it captured the imagination of others, aided internal efforts to mobilize the Ford Motor Company's resources, and served as a reference point for gauging the merits of the company's strategic actions.

Core Concept
A *strategic vision* describes the route a company intends to take in developing and strengthening its business. It lays out the company's strategic course in preparing for the future.

Table 2.1   **Factors to Consider in Deciding to Commit the Company to One Path versus Another**

External Considerations	Internal Considerations
• Is the outlook for the company promising if it simply maintains its product/market/customer/technology focus? Does sticking with the company's current strategic course present attractive growth opportunities? • Are changes under way in the market and competitive landscape acting to enhance or weaken the company's prospects? • What, if any, new customer groups and/or geographic markets should the company get in position to serve? • Which emerging market opportunities should the company pursue? Which ones should not be pursued? • Should the company plan to abandon any of the markets, market segments, or customer groups it is currently serving?	• What are the company's ambitions? What industry standing should the company have? • Will the company's present business generate sufficient growth and profitability in the years ahead to please shareholders? • What organizational strengths ought to be leveraged in terms of adding new products or services and getting into new businesses? • Is the company stretching its resources too thin by trying to compete in too many markets or segments, some of which are unprofitable? • Is the company's technological focus too broad or too narrow? Are any changes needed?

Well-conceived visions are *distinctive* and *specific* to a particular organization; they avoid generic feel-good statements like "We will become a global leader and the first choice of customers in every market we choose to serve"—which could apply to any of hundreds of organizations.[1] And they are not the product of a committee charged with coming up with an innocuous but well-meaning one-sentence vision that wins consensus approval from various stakeholders. Nicely worded vision statements with no specifics about the company's product/market/customer/technology focus fall well short of what it takes for a vision to measure up. A strategic vision proclaiming management's quest "to be the market leader" or "to be the first choice of customers" or "to be the most innovative" or "to be recognized as the best company in the industry" offers scant guidance about a company's direction and what changes and challenges lie on the road ahead.

For a strategic vision to function as a valuable managerial tool, it must (1) provide understanding of what management wants its business to look like and (2) provide managers with a reference point in making strategic decisions and preparing the company for the future. It must say something definitive about how the company's leaders intend to position the company beyond where it is today. A good vision always needs to be a bit beyond a company's reach, but progress toward the vision is what unifies the efforts of company personnel. Table 2.2 lists some characteristics of an effectively worded strategic vision.

A sampling of strategic visions currently in use shows a range from strong and clear to overly general and generic. A surprising number of the visions found on company Web sites and in annual reports are vague and unrevealing, saying very little about the company's future product/market/customer/technology focus. Some are nice-sounding but say little. Others read like something written by a committee to win the support of different stakeholders. And some are so short on specifics as to apply to most any company in any industry. Many read like a public relations statement—high-sounding words that someone came up with because it is fashionable for companies to have an official vision statement.[2] Table 2.3 provides a list of the most

Table 2.2   **Characteristics of an Effectively Worded Strategic Vision**

Graphic	Paints a picture of the kind of company that management is trying to create and the market position(s) the company is striving to stake out.
Directional	Is forward-looking; describes the strategic course that management has charted and the kinds of product/market/customer/technology changes that will help the company prepare for the future.
Focused	Is specific enough to provide managers with guidance in making decisions and allocating resources.
Flexible	Is not a once-and-for-all-time statement—the directional course that management has charted may have to be adjusted as product/market/customer/technology circumstances change.
Feasible	Is within the realm of what the company can reasonably expect to achieve in due time.
Desirable	Indicates why the chosen path makes good business sense and is in the long-term interests of stakeholders (especially shareowners, employees, and customers).
Easy to communicate	Is explainable in 5–10 minutes and, ideally, can be reduced to a simple, memorable slogan (like Henry Ford's famous vision of "a car in every garage").

Source: Based partly on John P. Kotter, *Leading Change* (Boston: Harvard Business School Press, 1996), p. 72.

common shortcomings in strategic vision statements. The one- or two-sentence vision statements most companies make available to the public, of course, provide only a glimpse of what company executives are really thinking and the strategic course they have charted—company personnel nearly always have a much better understanding of where the company is headed and why that is revealed in the official vision. But the real purpose of a strategic vision is to serve as a management tool for giving the organization a sense of direction. Like any tool, it can be used properly or improperly, either clearly conveying a company's strategic course or not.

Table 2.3   **Common Shortcomings in Company Vision Statements**

Vague or incomplete	Is short on specifics about where the company is headed or what the company is doing to prepare for the future.
Not forward-looking	Does not indicate whether or how management intends to alter the company's current product/market/customer/technology focus.
Too broad	Is so umbrella-like and all-inclusive that the company could head in most any direction, pursue most any opportunity, or enter most any business.
Bland or uninspiring	Lacks the power to motivate company personnel or inspire shareholder confidence about the company's direction or future prospects.
Not distinctive	Provides no unique company identity; could apply to companies in any of several industries (or at least several rivals operating in the same industry or market arena).
Too reliant on superlatives	Does not say anything specific about the company's strategic course beyond the pursuit of such lofty accolades as *best, most successful, recognized leader, global or worldwide leader,* or *first choice of customers.*

Sources: Based on information in Hugh Davidson, *The Committed Enterprise: How to Make Vision and Values Work* (Oxford: Butterworth Heinemann, 2002), Chapter 2, and Michel Robert, *Strategy Pure and Simple II* (New York: McGraw-Hill, 1992), Chapters 2, 3, and 6.

Illustration Capsule 2.1

Examples of Strategic Visions—How Well Do They Measure Up?

Using the information in Tables 2.2 and 2.3, critique the following strategic visions and rank them from 1 (best) to 7 (in need of substantial improvement).

RED HAT

To extend our position as the most trusted Linux and open source provider to the enterprise. We intend to grow the market for Linux through a complete range of enterprise Red Hat Linux software, a powerful Internet management platform, and associated support and services.

WELLS FARGO

We want to satisfy all of our customers' financial needs, help them succeed financially, be the premier provider of financial services in every one of our markets, and be known as one of America's great companies.

HILTON HOTELS CORPORATION

Our vision is to be the first choice of the world's travelers. Hilton intends to build on the rich heritage and strength of our brands by:

- Consistently delighting our customers
- Investing in our team members
- Delivering innovative products and services
- Continuously improving performance
- Increasing shareholder value

- Creating a culture of pride
- Strengthening the loyalty of our constituents

THE DENTAL PRODUCTS DIVISION OF 3M CORPORATION

Become THE supplier of choice to the global dental professional markets, providing world-class quality and innovative products.

[*Note:* All employees of the division wear badges bearing these words, and whenever a new product or business procedure is being considered, management asks "Is this representative of THE leading dental company?"]

CATERPILLAR

Be the global leader in customer value.

eBAY

Provide a global trading platform where practically anyone can trade practically anything.

H. J. HEINZ COMPANY

Be the world's premier food company, offering nutritious, superior tasting foods to people everywhere. Being the premier food company does not mean being the biggest but it does mean being the best in terms of consumer value, customer service, employee talent, and consistent and predictable growth.

Sources: Company documents and Web sites.

Illustration Capsule 2.1 provides examples of strategic visions of several prominent companies. See if you can tell which ones are mostly meaningless or nice-sounding and which ones are managerially useful in communicating "where we are headed and the kind of company we are trying to become".

A Strategic Vision Covers Different Ground than the Typical Mission Statement

The defining characteristic of a well-conceived *strategic vision* is what it says about the company's *future strategic course*—"the direction we are headed and what our future product/market/customer/technology focus will be."

In contrast, the *mission statements* that one finds in company annual reports or posted on company Web sites typically provide a brief overview of the company's *present* business purpose and raison d'être, and sometimes its geographic coverage or standing as a market leader. They may or may not single out the company's present products/services, the buyer needs it is seeking to satisfy, the customer groups it serves, or its technological and business capabilities. But rarely do company mission statements say anything about where the company is headed, the anticipated changes in its business, or its aspirations; hence, they lack the essential forward-looking quality of a strategic vision in specifying a company's direction and *future* product/market/customer/technology focus.

Consider, for example, the mission statement of Trader Joe's (a specialty grocery chain):

> The mission of Trader Joe's is to give our customers the best food and beverage values that they can find anywhere and to provide them with the information required for informed buying decisions. We provide these with a dedication to the highest quality of customer satisfaction delivered with a sense of warmth, friendliness, fun, individual pride, and company spirit.

Note that Trader Joe's mission statement does a good job of conveying "who we are, what we do, and why we are here," but provides no sense of "where we are headed." (Some companies use the term *business purpose* instead of *mission statement* in describing themselves; in practice, there seems to be no meaningful difference between the terms *mission statement* and *business purpose*—which one is used is a matter of preference.)

The distinction between a strategic vision and a mission statement is fairly clear-cut: A strategic vision portrays a company's *future* business scope ("where we are going"), whereas a company's mission typically describes its *present* business and purpose ("who we are, what we do, and why we are here").

There is value in distinguishing between the forward-looking concept of a strategic vision and the here-and-now theme of the typical mission statement. Thus, to mirror actual practice, we will use the term *mission statement* to refer to an enterprise's description of its *present* business and its purpose for existence. Ideally, a company mission statement is sufficiently descriptive to *identify the company's products/services and specify the buyer needs it seeks to satisfy, the customer groups or markets it is endeavoring to serve, and its approach to pleasing customers.* Not many company mission statements fully reveal *all* of these facets (and a few companies have worded their mission statements so obscurely as to mask what they are about), but most company mission statements do a decent job of indicating "who we are, what we do, and why we are here."

An example of a well-formed mission statement with ample specifics is that of the U.S. government's Occupational Safety and Health Administration (OSHA): "to assure the safety and health of America's workers by setting and enforcing standards; providing training, outreach, and education; establishing partnerships; and encouraging continual improvement in workplace safety and health." Google's mission statement, while short, still captures the essence of the company: "to organize the world's information and make it universally accessible and useful." Likewise, Blockbuster has a brief mission statement that cuts right to the chase: "To help people transform ordinary nights into BLOCKBUSTER nights by being their complete source for movies and games."

An example of a not-so-revealing mission statement is that of the present-day Ford Motor Company: "We are a global family with a proud heritage passionately committed to providing personal mobility for people around the world. We anticipate consumer need and deliver outstanding products and services that improve people's lives." A person who has never heard of Ford would not know from reading the company's mission statement that it is a global producer of motor vehicles. Similarly, Microsoft's mission statement—"to help people and businesses throughout the world realize their full potential"—says nothing about its products or business makeup and could apply to many companies in many different industries. Coca-Cola, which markets nearly 400 beverage brands in over 200 countries, also has an overly general mission statement: "to benefit and refresh everyone it touches." A mission statement that provides scant indication of "who we are and what we do" has no substantive value.

Occasionally, companies couch their mission statements in terms of making a profit. This is misguided. Profit is more correctly an *objective* and a *result* of what a company does. Moreover, earning a profit is the obvious intent of every commercial enterprise. Such companies as BMW, McDonald's, Shell Oil, Procter & Gamble, Nintendo, and Nokia are each striving to earn a profit for shareholders; but plainly the fundamentals of their businesses are substantially different when it comes to "who we are and what we do." It is management's answer to "Make a profit doing what and for whom?" that reveals a company's true substance and business purpose. *A well-conceived mission statement distinguishes a company's business makeup from that of other profit-seeking enterprises in language specific enough to give the company its own identity.*

Communicating the Strategic Vision

Effectively communicating the strategic vision down the line to lower-level managers and employees is as important as choosing a strategically sound long-term direction. Not only do people have a need to believe that senior management knows where it's trying to take the company and understand what changes lie ahead both externally and internally, but unless and until frontline employees understand why the strategic course that management has charted is reasonable and beneficial, they are unlikely to rally behind managerial efforts to get the organization moving in the intended direction.

Winning the support of organization members for the vision nearly always means putting "where we are going and why" in writing, distributing the written vision organizationwide, and having executives personally explain the vision and its rationale to as many people as feasible. Ideally, executives should present their vision for the company in a manner that reaches out and grabs people. An engaging and convincing strategic vision has enormous motivational value—for the same reason that a stonemason is more inspired by "building a great cathedral for the ages" than by "laying stones to create floors and walls." When managers articulate a vivid and compelling case for where the company is headed, organization members begin to say, "This is interesting and has a lot of merit. I want to be involved and do my part to helping make it happen." The more that a vision evokes positive support and excitement, the greater its impact in terms of arousing a committed organizational effort and getting company personnel to move in a common direction.[3] Thus executive ability to paint a convincing and inspiring picture of a company's journey and destination is an important element of effective strategic leadership.

> **Core Concept**
> An effectively communicated vision is a valuable management tool for enlisting the commitment of company personnel to actions that get the company moving in the intended direction.

Expressing the Essence of the Vision in a Slogan   The task of effectively conveying the vision to company personnel is assisted when management can capture the vision of where to head in a catchy or easily remembered slogan. A number of organizations have summed up their vision in a brief phrase:

- Levi Strauss & Company: "We will clothe the world by marketing the most appealing and widely worn casual clothing in the world."
- Nike: "To bring innovation and inspiration to every athlete in the world."

- Mayo Clinic: "The best care to every patient every day."
- Scotland Yard: "To make London the safest major city in the world."
- Greenpeace: "To halt environmental abuse and promote environmental solutions."
- Charles Schwab: "To provide customers with the most useful and ethical financial services in the world."

Strategic visions become real only when the vision statement is imprinted in the minds of organization members and then translated into hard objectives and strategies.

Creating a short slogan to illuminate an organization's direction and purpose and then using it repeatedly as a reminder of "where we are headed and why" helps rally organization members to hurdle whatever obstacles lie in the company's path and maintain their focus.

Breaking Down Resistance to a New Strategic Vision   It is particularly important for executives to provide a compelling rationale for a dramatically *new* strategic vision and company direction. When company personnel don't understand or accept the need for redirecting organizational efforts, they are prone to resist change. Hence, reiterating the basis for the new direction, addressing employee concerns head-on, calming fears, lifting spirits, and providing updates and progress reports as events unfold all become part of the task of mobilizing support for the vision and winning commitment to needed actions.

Just stating the case for a new direction once is not enough. Executives must repeat the reasons for the new direction often and convincingly at company gatherings and in company publications, and they must reinforce their pronouncements with updates about how the latest information confirms the choice of direction and the validity of the vision. Unless and until more and more people are persuaded of the merits of management's new vision and the vision gains wide acceptance, it will be a struggle to move the organization down the newly chosen path.

Recognizing Strategic Inflection Points   Sometimes there's an order-of-magnitude change in a company's environment that dramatically alters its prospects and mandates radical revision of its strategic course. Intel's former chairman Andrew Grove has called such occasions *strategic inflection points*—Illustration Capsule 2.2 relates Intel's two encounters with strategic inflection points and the resulting alterations in its strategic vision. As the Intel example forcefully demonstrates, when a company reaches a strategic inflection point, management has some tough decisions to make about the company's course. Often it is a question of what to do to sustain company success, not just how to avoid possible disaster. Responding quickly to unfolding changes in the marketplace lessens a company's chances of becoming trapped in a stagnant or declining business or letting attractive new growth opportunities slip away.

Understanding the Payoffs of a Clear Vision Statement   In sum, a well-conceived, forcefully communicated strategic vision pays off in several respects: (1) it crystallizes senior executives' own views about the firm's long-term direction; (2) it reduces the risk of rudderless decision making; (3) it is a tool for winning the support of organizational members for internal changes that will help make the vision a reality; (4) it provides a beacon for lower-level managers in forming departmental missions, setting departmental objectives, and crafting functional and departmental strategies that are in sync with the company's overall strategy; and (5) it helps an organization prepare for the future. When management is able to demonstrate significant progress in achieving these five benefits, the first step in organizational direction setting has been successfully completed.

Illustration Capsule 2.2
Intel's Two Strategic Inflection Points

Intel Corporation has encountered two strategic inflection points within the past 20 years. The first came in the mid-1980s, when memory chips were Intel's principal business and Japanese manufacturers, intent on dominating the memory chip business, began cutting their prices 10 percent below the prices charged by Intel and other U.S. memory chip manufacturers. Each time U.S. companies matched the Japanese price cuts, the Japanese manufacturers responded with another 10 percent price cut. Intel's management explored a number of strategic options to cope with the aggressive pricing of its Japanese rivals—building a giant memory chip factory to overcome the cost advantage of Japanese producers, investing in research and development (R&D) to come up with a more advanced memory chip, and retreating to niche markets for memory chips that were not of interest to the Japanese.

At the time, Gordon Moore, Intel's chairman and cofounder, and Andrew Grove, Intel's chief executive officer (CEO), jointly concluded that none of these options offered much promise and that the best long-term solution was to abandon the memory chip business even though it accounted for 70 percent of Intel's revenue. Grove, with the concurrence of both Moore and the board of directors, then proceeded to commit Intel's full energies to the business of developing ever more powerful microprocessors for personal computers. Intel had invented microprocessors in the early 1970s but had recently been concentrating on memory chips because of strong competition and excess capacity in the market for microprocessors.

Grove's bold decision to withdraw from memory chips, absorb a $173 million write-off in 1986, and go all out in microprocessors produced a new strategic vision for Intel—becoming the preeminent supplier of microprocessors to the personal computing industry, making the personal computer (PC) the central appliance in the workplace and the home, and being the undisputed leader in driving PC technology forward. Grove's new vision for Intel and the strategic course he charted in 1985 produced spectacular results. Since 1996, over 80 percent of the world's PCs have been made with Intel microprocessors and Intel has become the world's most profitable chip maker.

Intel encountered a second inflection point in 1998, opting to refocus on becoming the preeminent building-block supplier to the Internet economy and spurring efforts to make the Internet more useful. Starting in early 1998 and responding to the mushrooming importance of the Internet, Intel's senior management launched major new initiatives to direct attention and resources to expanding the capabilities of both the PC platform and the Internet. It was this strategic inflection point that led to Intel's latest strategic vision of playing a major role in getting a billion computers connected to the Internet worldwide, installing millions of servers, and building an Internet infrastructure that would support trillions of dollars of e-commerce and serve as a worldwide communication medium.

Source: Andrew S. Grove, *Only the Paranoid Survive* (New York: Doubleday-Currency, 1996), company documents and press releases, and information posted at www.intel.com.

Linking the Vision/Mission with Company Values

Many companies have developed a statement of values to guide the company's pursuit of its vision/mission, strategy, and ways of operating. By **values** (or *core values,* as they are often called), we mean the beliefs, traits, and ways of doing things that management has determined should guide the pursuit of its vision and strategy, the conduct of company's operations, and the behavior of company personnel.

Values, good and bad, exist in every organization. They relate to such things as fair treatment, integrity, ethical behavior, innovation, teamwork, top-notch quality, superior customer service, social responsibility, and community citizenship. Most companies have built their statements of values around four to eight traits that company personnel are expected to display and that are supposed to be mirrored in how the company conducts its business.

Core Concept

A company's **values** are the beliefs, traits, and behavioral norms that company personnel are expected to display in conducting the company's business and pursuing its strategic vision and strategy.

At Kodak, the core values are respect for the dignity of the individual, uncompromising integrity, unquestioned trust, constant credibility, continual improvement and personal renewal, and open celebration of individual and team achievements. Home Depot embraces eight values (entrepreneurial spirit, excellent customer service, giving back to the community, respect for all people, doing the right thing, taking care of people, building strong relationships, and creating shareholder value) in its quest to be the world's leading home improvement retailer by operating warehouse stores filled with a wide assortment of products at the lowest prices with trained associates giving absolutely the best customer service in the industry. Toyota preaches respect for and development of its employees, teamwork, getting quality right the first time, learning, continuous improvement, and embracing change in its pursuit of low-cost, top-notch manufacturing excellence in motor vehicles.[4] DuPont stresses four values—safety, ethics, respect for people, and environmental stewardship; the first three have been in place since the company was founded 200 years ago by the DuPont family. Heinz uses the acronym PREMIER to identify seven values that "define to the world and to ourselves who we are and what we stand for":

- *P*assion . . . to be passionate about winning and about our brands, products and people, thereby delivering superior value to our shareholders.
- *R*isk Tolerance . . . to create a culture where entrepreneurship and prudent risk taking are encouraged and rewarded.
- *E*xcellence . . . to be the best in quality and in everything we do.
- *M*otivation . . . to celebrate success, recognizing and rewarding the achievements of individuals and teams.
- *I*nnovation . . . to innovate in everything, from products to processes.
- *E*mpowerment . . . to empower our talented people to take the initiative and to do what's right.
- *R*espect . . . to act with integrity and respect towards all.

Do companies practice what they preach when it comes to their professed values? Sometimes no, sometimes yes—it runs the gamut. At one extreme are companies with window-dressing values; the values statement is merely a collection of nice words and phrases that may be given lip service by top executives but have little discernible impact on either how company personnel behave or how the company operates. Such companies have values statements because such statements are in vogue and are seen as making the company look good. At the other extreme are companies whose executives take the stated values very seriously—the values are widely adopted by company personnel, are ingrained in the corporate culture, and are mirrored in how company personnel conduct themselves and the company's business on a daily basis. Top executives at companies on this end of the values-statement gamut genuinely believe in the importance of grounding company operations on sound values and ways of doing business. In their view, holding company personnel accountable for displaying the stated values is a way of infusing the company with the desired character, identity, and behavioral norms—the values become the company's equivalent of DNA.

At companies where the stated values are real rather than cosmetic, managers connect values to the pursuit of the strategic vision and mission in one of two ways. In companies with long-standing values that are deeply entrenched in the corporate culture, senior managers are careful to craft a vision, mission, and strategy that match established values, and they reiterate how the values-based behavioral norms contribute to the company's business success. If the company changes to a different vision or strategy, executives take care to explain how and why the core values continue to be relevant. Few companies with sincere commitment to established core values ever undertake strategic moves that conflict with ingrained values.

In new companies or companies with weak or incomplete sets of values, top management considers what values, behaviors, and business conduct should characterize the company and that will help drive the vision and strategy forward. Then values and behaviors that complement and support vision are drafted and circulated among managers and employees for discussion and possible modification. A final values statement that incorporates the desired behaviors and traits and that connects to the vision/mission is then officially adopted. Some companies combine their vision and values into a single statement or document, circulate it to all organization members, and in many instances post the vision/mission and values statement on the company's Web site. Illustration Capsule 2.3 describes the connection between Yahoo's mission and its core values.

Of course, a wide gap sometimes opens between a company's stated values and its actual business practices. Enron, for example, touted four corporate values—respect, integrity, communication, and excellence—but some top officials engaged in dishonest and fraudulent maneuvers that were concealed by "creative" accounting; the lack of integrity on the part of Enron executives and their deliberate failure to accurately communicate with shareholders and regulators in the company's financial filings led directly to the company's dramatic bankruptcy and implosion over a six-week period, along with criminal indictments, fines, or jail terms for over a dozen Enron executives. Once one of the world's most distinguished public accounting firms, Arthur Andersen was renowned for its commitment to the highest standards of audit integrity, but its high-profile audit failures and ethical lapses at Enron, WorldCom, and other companies led to Andersen's demise—in 2002, it was indicted for destroying Enron-related documents to thwart investigators.

SETTING OBJECTIVES: PHASE 2 OF THE STRATEGY-MAKING, STRATEGY-EXECUTING PROCESS

The managerial purpose of setting **objectives** is to convert the strategic vision into specific performance targets—results and outcomes the company's management wants to achieve. Objectives represent a managerial commitment to achieving particular results and outcomes. Well-stated objectives are *quantifiable,* or *measurable,* and contain a *deadline for achievement.* As Bill Hewlett, cofounder of Hewlett-Packard, shrewdly observed, "You cannot manage what you cannot measure. . . . And what gets measured gets done."[5] Concrete, measurable objectives are managerially valuable because they serve as yardsticks for tracking a company's performance and progress—a company that consistently meets or beats its performance targets is generally a better overall performer than a company that frequently falls short of achieving its objectives. Indeed, the experiences of countless companies and managers teach that precisely spelling out *how much* of *what kind* of performance *by when* and then pressing forward with actions and incentives calculated to help achieve the targeted outcomes greatly improve a company's actual performance. Such an approach definitely beats setting vague targets like "maximize profits," "reduce costs," "become more efficient," or "increase sales," which specify neither how much nor when. Similarly, exhorting

> **Core Concept**
> ***Objectives*** are an organization's performance targets—the results and outcomes management wants to achieve. They function as yardsticks for measuring how well the organization is doing.

Illustration Capsule 2.3

The Connection between Yahoo's Mission and Core Values

Our mission is to be the most essential global Internet service for consumers and businesses. How we pursue that mission is influenced by a set of core values—the standards that guide interactions with fellow Yahoos, the principles that direct how we service our customers, the ideals that drive what we do and how we do it. Many of our values were put into practice by two guys in a trailer some time ago; others reflect ambitions as our company grows. All of them are what we strive to achieve every day.

EXCELLENCE

We are committed to winning with integrity. We know leadership is hard won and should never be taken for granted. We aspire to flawless execution and don't take shortcuts on quality. We seek the best talent and promote its development. We are flexible and learn from our mistakes.

INNOVATION

We thrive on creativity and ingenuity. We seek the innovations and ideas that can change the world. We anticipate market trends and move quickly to embrace them. We are not afraid to take informed, responsible risks.

CUSTOMER FIXATION

We respect our customers above all else and never forget that they come to us by choice. We share a personal responsibility to maintain our customers' loyalty and trust. We listen and respond to our customers and seek to exceed their expectations.

TEAMWORK

We treat one another with respect and communicate openly. We foster collaboration while maintaining individual accountability. We encourage the best ideas to surface from anywhere within the organization. We appreciate the value of multiple perspectives and diverse expertise.

COMMUNITY

We share an infectious sense of mission to make an impact on society and empower consumers in ways never before possible. We are committed to serving both the Internet community and our own communities.

FUN

We believe humor is essential to success. We applaud irreverence and don't take ourselves too seriously. We celebrate achievement. We yodel.

WHAT YAHOO DOESN'T VALUE

At the end of its values statement, Yahoo made a point of singling out 54 things that it did not value, including bureaucracy, losing, good enough, arrogance, the status quo, following, formality, quick fixes, passing the buck, micromanaging, Monday morning quarterbacks, 20/20 hindsight, missing the boat, playing catch-up, punching the clock, and "shoulda coulda woulda."

Source: http://docs.yahoo.com/info/values (accessed August 20, 2005).

company personnel to try hard or do the best they can, and then living with whatever results they deliver, is clearly inadequate.

The Imperative of Setting Stretch Objectives   Ideally, managers ought to use the objective-setting exercise as a tool for *stretching an organization to perform at its full potential and deliver the best possible results.* Challenging company personnel to go all out and deliver "stretch" gains in performance pushes an enterprise to be more inventive, to exhibit more urgency in improving both its financial performance and its business position, and to be more intentional and focused in its actions. Stretch objectives spur exceptional performance and help companies guard against contentment with modest gains in organizational performance. As Mitchell Leibovitz, former CEO of the auto parts and service retailer Pep Boys, once said, "If you want to have ho-hum results, have ho-hum objectives." *There's no better way to avoid ho-hum results than by setting stretch objectives and*

> Setting stretch objectives is an effective tool for avoiding ho-hum results.

using compensation incentives to motivate organization members to achieve the stretch performance targets.

What Kinds of Objectives to Set: The Need for a Balanced Scorecard

Two very distinct types of performance yardsticks are required: those relating to *financial performance* and those relating to *strategic performance*—outcomes that indicate a company is strengthening its marketing standing, competitive vitality, and future business prospects. Examples of commonly used **financial objectives** and **strategic objectives** include the following:

> **Core Concept**
> *Financial objectives* relate to the financial performance targets management has established for the organization to achieve. *Strategic objectives* relate to target outcomes that indicate a company is strengthening its market standing, competitive vitality, and future business prospects.

Financial Objectives	Strategic Objectives
• An *x* percent increase in annual revenues	• Winning an *x* percent market share
• Annual increases in after-tax profits of *x* percent	• Achieving lower overall costs than rivals
• Annual increases in earnings per share of *x* percent	• Overtaking key competitors on product performance or quality or customer service
• Annual dividend increases	• Deriving *x* percent of revenues from the sale of new products introduced within the past five years
• Larger profit margins	
• An *x* percent return on capital employed (ROCE) or return on equity (ROE)	• Achieving technological leadership
• Increased shareholder value—in the form of an upward trending stock price and annual dividend increases	• Having better product selection than rivals
	• Strengthening the company's brand-name appeal
• Strong bond and credit ratings	• Having stronger national or global sales and distribution capabilities than rivals
• Sufficient internal cash flows to fund new capital investment	• Consistently getting new or improved products to market ahead of rivals
• Stable earnings during periods of recession	

Achieving acceptable financial results is a must. Without adequate profitability and financial strength, a company's pursuit of its strategic vision, as well as its long-term health and ultimate survival, is jeopardized. Furthermore, subpar earnings and a weak balance sheet not only alarm shareholders and creditors but also put the jobs of senior executives at risk. However, good financial performance, by itself, is not enough. Of equal or greater importance is a company's strategic performance—outcomes that indicate whether a company's market position and competitiveness are deteriorating, holding steady, or improving.

The Case for a Balanced Scorecard: Improved Strategic Performance Fosters Better Financial Performance A company's financial performance measures are really *lagging indicators* that reflect the results of past decisions and organizational activities.[6] But a company's past or current financial performance is not a reliable indicator of its future prospects—poor financial performers often turn things around and do better, while good financial performers can fall on hard times. The best and most reliable *leading indicators* of a company's future financial performance and business prospects are strategic outcomes that indicate whether the

> **Core Concept**
> A company that pursues and achieves strategic outcomes that boost its competitiveness and strength in the marketplace is in much better position to improve its future financial performance.

company's competitiveness and market position are stronger or weaker. For instance, if a company has set aggressive strategic objectives and is achieving them—such that its competitive strength and market position are on the rise, then there's reason to expect that its *future* financial performance will be better than its current or past performance. If a company is losing ground to competitors and its market position is slipping— outcomes that reflect weak strategic performance (and, very likely, failure to achieve its strategic objectives), then its ability to maintain its present profitability is highly suspect. Hence, the degree to which a company's managers set, pursue, and achieve stretch strategic objectives tends to be a reliable leading indicator of whether its future financial performance will improve or stall.

Consequently, a *balanced scorecard* for measuring company performance—one that tracks the achievement of both financial objectives and strategic objectives—is optimal.[7] Just tracking a company's financial performance overlooks the fact that what ultimately enables a company to deliver better financial results from its operations is the achievement of strategic objectives that improve its competitiveness and market strength. Indeed, *the surest path to boosting company profitability quarter after quarter and year after year is to relentlessly pursue strategic outcomes that strengthen the company's market position and produce a growing competitive advantage over rivals.*

Roughly 36 percent of global companies and over 100 nonprofit and governmental organizations used the balanced scorecard approach in 2001.[8] A more recent survey of 708 companies on five continents found that 62 percent were using a balanced scorecard to track performance.[9] Organizations that have adopted the balanced scorecard approach to setting objectives and measuring performance include Exxon Mobil, CIGNA, United Parcel Service, Sears, Nova Scotia Power, BMW, AT&T Canada, Chemical Bank, DaimlerChrysler, DuPont, Motorola, Siemens, Wells Fargo, Wendy's, Saatchi & Saatchi, Duke Children's Hospital, U.S. Department of the Army, Tennessee Valley Authority, the United Kingdom's Ministry of Defense, the University of California at San Diego, and the City of Charlotte, North Carolina.[10]

Illustration Capsule 2.4 shows selected objectives of five prominent companies— all employ a combination of strategic and financial objectives.

Both Short-Term and Long-Term Objectives Are Needed   As a rule, a company's set of financial and strategic objectives ought to include both near-term and longer-term performance targets. Having quarterly and annual objectives focuses attention on delivering immediate performance improvements. Targets to be achieved within three to five years prompt considerations of what to do *now* to put the company in position to perform better later. A company that has an objective of doubling its sales within five years can't wait until the third or fourth year to begin growing its sales and customer base. By spelling out annual (or perhaps quarterly) performance targets, management indicates the *speed* at which longer range targets are to be approached. Long-term objectives take on particular importance because it is generally in the best interest of shareholders for companies to be managed for optimal long-term performance. When trade-offs have to be made between achieving long-run objectives and achieving short-run objectives, long-run objectives should take precedence (unless the achievement of one or more short-run performance targets have unique importance). Shareholders are seldom well-served by repeated management actions that sacrifice better long-term performance in order to make quarterly or annual targets.

Strategic Intent: Relentless Pursuit of an Ambitious Strategic Objective

Very ambitious companies often establish a long-term strategic objective that clearly

Illustration Capsule 2.4

Examples of Company Objectives

NISSAN

Increase sales to 4.2 million cars and trucks by 2008 (up from 3 million in 2003); cut purchasing costs 20% and halve the number of suppliers; have zero net debt; maintain a return on invested capital of 20%; maintain a 10% or better operating margin.

McDONALD'S

Place more emphasis on delivering an exceptional customer experience; add approximately 350 net new McDonald's restaurants; reduce general and administrative spending as a percent of total revenues; achieve systemwide sales and revenue growth of 3% to 5%, annual operating income growth of 6% to 7%, and annual returns on incremental invested capital in the high teens.

H. J. HEINZ COMPANY

Achieve 4–6% sales growth, 7–10% growth in operating income, EPS in the range of $2.35 to $2.45, and operating free cash flow of $900 million to $1 billion in fiscal 2006; pay dividends equal to 45–50 percent of earnings; increase the focus on the company's 15 power brands and give top resource priority to those brands with number one and two market positions; continue to introduce new and improved food products; add to the Heinz portfolio of brands by acquiring companies with brands that complement existing brands; increase sales in Russia, Indonesia, China and India by 50 percent in fiscal year 2006 to roughly 6 percent of total sales; and by the end of fiscal 2008, derive approximately 50 percent of sales and profits from North America, 30 percent from Europe, and 20 percent from all other markets.

SEAGATE TECHNOLOGY

Solidify the company's No. 1 position in the overall market for hard-disk drives; get more Seagate drives into popular consumer electronics products; take share away from Western Digital in providing disk drives for Microsoft's Xbox; maintain leadership in core markets and achieve leadership in emerging markets; grow revenues by 10 percent per year; maintain gross margins of 24–26 percent; hold internal operating expenses to 13–13.5 percent of revenue.

3M CORPORATION

To achieve long term sales growth of 5–8% organic plus 2–4% from acquisitions; annual growth in earnings per share of 10% or better, on average; a return on stockholders' equity of 20%–25%; a return on capital employed of 27% or better; double the number of qualified new 3M product ideas and triple the value of products that win in the marketplace; and build the best sales and marketing organization in the world.

Sources: Information posted on company Web sites (accessed August 21, 2005); and "Nissan's Smryna Plant Produces 7 Millionth Vehicle," *Automotive Intelligence News,* August 2, 2005, p. 5.

signals **strategic intent** to be a winner in the marketplace, often against long odds.[11] A company's strategic intent can entail unseating the existing industry leader, becoming the dominant market share leader, delivering the best customer service of any company in the industry (or the world), or turning a new technology into products capable of changing the way people work and live. Nike's strategic intent during the 1960s was to overtake Adidas; this intent connected nicely with Nike's core purpose "to experience the emotion of competition, winning, and crushing competitors." Canon's strategic intent in copying equipment was to "beat Xerox." For some years, Toyota has been driving to overtake General Motors as the world's largest motor vehicle producer—and it surpassed Ford Motor Company in total vehicles sold in 2003, to move into second place. Toyota has expressed its strategic intent in the form of a global market share objective of 15 percent by 2010, up from 5 percent in 1980 and 10 percent in 2003. Starbucks' strategic intent is to make the Starbucks brand the world's most recognized and respected brand.

Core Concept

A company exhibits *strategic intent* when it relentlessly pursues an ambitious strategic objective, concentrating the full force of its resources and competitive actions on achieving that objective.

Ambitious companies that establish exceptionally bold strategic objectives and have an unshakable commitment to achieving them almost invariably begin with strategic intents that are out of proportion to their immediate capabilities and market grasp. But they pursue their strategic target relentlessly, sometimes even obsessively. They rally the organization around efforts to make the strategic intent a reality. They go all out to marshal the resources and capabilities to close in on their strategic target (which is often global market leadership) as rapidly as they can. They craft potent offensive strategies calculated to throw rivals off-balance, put them on the defensive, and force them into an ongoing game of catch-up. They deliberately try to alter the market contest and tilt the rules for competing in their favor. As a consequence, capably managed up-and-coming enterprises with strategic intents exceeding their present reach and resources are a force to be reckoned with, often proving to be more formidable competitors over time than larger, cash-rich rivals that have modest strategic objectives and market ambitions.

The Need for Objectives at All Organizational Levels   Objective setting should not stop with top management's establishing of companywide performance targets. Company objectives need to be broken down into performance targets for each of the organization's separate businesses, product lines, functional departments, and individual work units. Company performance can't reach full potential unless each organizational unit sets and pursues performance targets that contribute directly to the desired companywide outcomes and results. Objective setting is thus a top-down process that must extend to the lowest organizational levels. And it means that each organizational unit must take care to set performance targets that support—rather than conflict with or negate—the achievement of companywide strategic and financial objectives.

The ideal situation is a team effort in which each organizational unit strives to produce results in its area of responsibility that contribute to the achievement of the company's performance targets and strategic vision. Such consistency signals that organizational units know their strategic role and are on board in helping the company move down the chosen strategic path and produce the desired results.

Objective Setting Needs to Be Top-Down Rather than Bottom-Up   To appreciate why a company's objective-setting process needs to be more top-down than bottom-up, consider the following example. Suppose the senior executives of a diversified corporation establish a corporate profit objective of $500 million for next year. Suppose further that, after discussion between corporate management and the general managers of the firm's five different businesses, each business is given a stretch profit objective of $100 million by year-end (i.e., if the five business divisions contribute $100 million each in profit, the corporation can reach its $500 million profit objective). A concrete result has thus been agreed on and translated into measurable action commitments at two levels in the managerial hierarchy. Next, suppose the general manager of business unit A, after some analysis and discussion with functional area managers, concludes that reaching the $100 million profit objective will require selling 1 million units at an average price of $500 and producing them at an average cost of $400 (a $100 profit margin times 1 million units equals $100 million profit). Consequently, the general manager and the manufacturing manager settle on a production objective of 1 million units at a unit cost of $400; and the general manager and the marketing manager agree on a sales objective of 1 million units and a target selling price of $500. In turn, the marketing manager, after consultation with regional sales personnel, breaks the sales objective of 1 million units into unit sales targets for each sales territory, each item in the product line, and each salesperson. It is logical for organizationwide objectives and strategy to be established first so they can guide objective setting and strategy making at lower levels.

A top-down process of setting companywide performance targets first and then insisting that the financial and strategic performance targets established for business units, divisions, functional departments, and operating units be directly connected to the achievement of company objectives has two powerful advantages: One, it helps produce *cohesion* among the objectives and strategies of different parts of the organization. Two, it helps *unify internal efforts* to move the company along the chosen strategic path. If top management, desirous of involving many organization members, allows objective setting to start at the bottom levels of an organization without the benefit of companywide performance targets as a guide, then lower-level organizational units have no basis for connecting their performance targets to the company's. Bottom-up objective setting, with little or no guidance from above, nearly always signals an absence of strategic leadership on the part of senior executives.

CRAFTING A STRATEGY: PHASE 3 OF THE STRATEGY-MAKING, STRATEGY-EXECUTING PROCESS

The task of crafting a strategy entails answering a series of hows: *how* to grow the business, *how* to please customers, *how* to outcompete rivals, *how* to respond to changing market conditions, *how* to manage each functional piece of the business and develop needed competencies and capabilities, *how* to achieve strategic and financial objectives. It also means exercising astute entrepreneurship in choosing among the various strategic alternatives—proactively searching for opportunities to do new things or to do existing things in new or better ways.[12] The faster a company's business environment is changing, the more critical the need for its managers to be good entrepreneurs in diagnosing the direction and force of the changes under way and in responding with timely adjustments in strategy. Strategy makers have to pay attention to early warnings of future change and be willing to experiment with dare-to-be-different ways to alter their market position in preparing for new market conditions. When obstacles unexpectedly appear in a company's path, it is up to management to adapt rapidly and innovatively. *Masterful strategies come partly (maybe mostly) by doing things differently from competitors where it counts—outinnovating them, being more efficient, being more imaginative, adapting faster—rather than running with the herd.* Good strategy making is therefore inseparable from good business entrepreneurship. One cannot exist without the other.

Who Participates in Crafting a Company's Strategy?

A company's senior executives obviously have important strategy-making roles. The chief executive officer (CEO) wears the mantles of chief direction setter, chief objective setter, chief strategy maker, and chief strategy implementer for the total enterprise. Ultimate responsibility for *leading* the strategy-making, strategy-executing process rests with the CEO. In some enterprises the CEO functions as strategic visionary and chief architect of strategy, personally deciding what the key elements of the company's strategy will be, although others may well assist with data gathering and analysis, and the CEO may seek the advice of other senior managers and key employees in fashioning an overall strategy and deciding on important strategic moves. A CEO-centered approach to strategy development is characteristic of small owner-managed companies and sometimes large corporations that have been founded by the present CEO or that have CEOs with strong strategic leadership skills. Meg Whitman at eBay, Andrea Jung at Avon, Jeffrey Immelt at General Electric, and Howard Schultz at Starbucks are prominent examples of corporate CEOs who have wielded a heavy hand in shaping their company's strategy.

In most companies, however, strategy is the product of more than just the CEO's handiwork. Typically, other senior executives—business unit heads, the chief financial officer, and vice presidents for production, marketing, human resources, and other functional departments—have influential strategy-making roles and help fashion the chief strategy components. Normally, a company's chief financial officer (CFO) is in charge of devising and implementing an appropriate financial strategy; the production vice president takes the lead in developing the company's production strategy; the marketing vice president orchestrates sales and marketing strategy; a brand manager is in charge of the strategy for a particular brand in the company's product lineup; and so on.

But even here it is a mistake to view strategy making as a *top* management function, the exclusive province of owner-entrepreneurs, CEOs, and other senior executives. The more that a company's operations cut across different products, industries, and geographical areas, the more that headquarters executives have little option but to delegate considerable strategy-making authority to down-the-line managers in charge of particular subsidiaries, divisions, product lines, geographic sales offices, distribution centers, and plants. On-the-scene managers with authority over specific operating units are in the best position to evaluate the local situation in which the strategic choices must be made and can be expected to have detailed familiarity with local market and competitive conditions, customer requirements and expectations, and all the other aspects surrounding the strategic issues and choices in their arena of authority. This gives them an edge over headquarters executives in keeping the local aspects of the company's strategy responsive to local market and competitive conditions.

Take a company like Toshiba, a $43 billion corporation with 300 subsidiaries, thousands of products, and operations extending across the world. While top-level Toshiba executives may well be personally involved in shaping Toshiba's *overall* strategy and fashioning *important* strategic moves, it doesn't follow that a few senior executives at Toshiba headquarters have either the expertise or a sufficiently detailed understanding of all the relevant factors to wisely craft all the strategic initiatives taken for 300 subsidiaries and thousands of products. They simply cannot know enough about the situation in every Toshiba organizational unit to decide upon every strategy detail and direct every strategic move made in Toshiba's worldwide organization. Rather, it takes involvement on the part of Toshiba's whole management team—top executives, subsidiary heads, division heads, and key managers in such geographic units as sales offices, distribution centers, and plants—to craft the thousands of strategic initiatives that end up comprising the whole of Toshiba's strategy. The same can be said for a company like General Electric, which employs 300,000 people in businesses ranging from jet engines to plastics, power generation equipment to appliances, medical equipment to TV broadcasting, and locomotives to financial services (among many others) and that sells to customers in over 100 countries.

While managers farther down in the managerial hierarchy obviously have a narrower, more specific strategy-making role than managers closer to the top, the important understanding here is that in most of today's companies *every company manager typically has a strategy-making role—ranging from minor to major—for the area he or she heads.* Hence, any notion that an organization's strategists are at the top of the management hierarchy and that midlevel and frontline personnel merely carry out the strategic directives of senior managers needs to be cast aside. In companies with wide-ranging operations, it is far more accurate to view strategy making as a *collaborative or team effort* involving managers (and sometimes key employees) down through the whole organizational hierarchy.

> **Core Concept**
> In most companies, crafting and executing strategy is a team effort in which every manager has a role for the area he or she heads. It is flawed thinking to view crafting and executing strategy as something only high-level managers do.

In fact, the necessity of delegating some strategy-making authority to down-the-line managers has resulted in it being fairly common for key pieces of a company's strategy to originate in a company's middle and lower ranks.[13] Electronic Data Systems conducted a yearlong strategy review involving 2,500 of its 55,000 employees and coordinated by a core of 150 managers and staffers from all over the world.[14] J. M. Smucker, best-known for its jams and jellies, formed a team of 140 employees (7 percent of its 2,000-person workforce) who spent 25 percent of their time over a six-month period looking for ways to rejuvenate the company's growth. Involving teams of people to dissect complex situations and come up with strategic solutions is an often-used component of the strategy-making process because many strategic issues are complex or cut across multiple areas of expertise and operating units, thus calling for the contributions of many disciplinary experts and the collaboration of managers from different parts of the organization. A valuable strength of collaborative strategy-making is that the team of people charged with crafting the strategy can easily include the very people who will also be charged with implementing and executing it. Giving people an influential stake in crafting the strategy they must later help implement and execute not only builds motivation and commitment but also means those people can be held accountable for putting the strategy into place and making it work—the excuse of "It wasn't my idea to do this" won't fly.

The Strategy-Making Role of Corporate Intrapreneurs   In some companies, top management makes a regular practice of encouraging individuals and teams to develop and champion proposals for new product lines and new business ventures. The idea is to unleash the talents and energies of promising "corporate intrapreneurs," letting them try out untested business ideas and giving them the room to pursue new strategic initiatives. Executives judge which proposals merit support, give the chosen intrapreneurs the organizational and budgetary support they need, and let them proceed freely. Thus, important pieces of company strategy can originate with those intrapreneurial individuals and teams who succeed in championing a proposal through the approval stage and then end up being charged with the lead role in launching new products, overseeing the company's entry into new geographic markets, or heading up new business ventures. W. L. Gore and Associates, a privately owned company famous for its Gore-Tex waterproofing film, is an avid and highly successful practitioner of the corporate intrapreneur approach to strategy making. Gore expects all employees to initiate improvements and to display innovativeness. Each employee's intrapreneurial contributions are prime considerations in determining raises, stock option bonuses, and promotions. Gore's commitment to intrapreneurship has produced a stream of product innovations and new strategic initiatives that have kept the company vibrant and growing for nearly two decades.

A Company's Strategy-Making Hierarchy

It thus follows that *a company's overall strategy is a collection of strategic initiatives and actions* devised by managers and key employees up and down the whole organizational hierarchy. The larger and more diverse the operations of an enterprise, the more points of strategic initiative it has and the more managers and employees at more levels of management that have a relevant strategy-making role. Figure 2.2 shows who is generally responsible for devising what pieces of a company's overall strategy.

In diversified, multibusiness companies where the strategies of several different businesses have to be managed, the strategy-making task involves four distinct types or levels of strategy, each of which involves different facets of the company's overall strategy:

1. *Corporate strategy* consists of the kinds of initiatives the company uses to establish business positions in different industries, the approaches corporate executives pursue to boost the combined performance of the set of businesses the company has diversified into, and the means of capturing cross-business synergies and turning them into competitive advantage. Senior corporate executives normally have lead responsibility for devising corporate strategy and for choosing from among whatever recommended actions bubble up from the organization below. Key business-unit heads may also be influential, especially in strategic decisions affecting the businesses they head. Major strategic decisions are usually reviewed and approved by the company's board of directors. We will look deeper into the strategy-making process at diversified companies when we get to Chapter 9.

2. *Business strategy* concerns the actions and the approaches crafted to produce successful performance in one specific line of business. The key focus is crafting responses to changing market circumstances and initiating actions to strengthen market position, build competitive advantage, and develop strong competitive capabilities. Orchestrating the development of business-level strategy is the responsibility of the manager in charge of the business. The business head has at least two other strategy-related roles: (*a*) seeing that lower-level strategies are well conceived, consistent, and adequately matched to the overall business strategy, and (*b*) getting major business-level strategic moves approved by corporate-level officers (and sometimes the board of directors) and keeping them informed of emerging strategic issues. In diversified companies, business-unit heads may have the additional obligation of making sure business-level objectives and strategy conform to corporate-level objectives and strategy themes.

3. *Functional-area strategies* concern the actions, approaches, and practices to be employed in managing particular functions or business processes or key activities within a business. A company's marketing strategy, for example, represents the managerial game plan for running the sales and marketing part of the business. A company's product development strategy represents the managerial game plan for keeping the company's product lineup fresh and in tune with what buyers are looking for. Functional strategies add specifics to the hows of business-level strategy. Plus, they aim at establishing or strengthening a business unit's competencies and capabilities in performing strategy-critical activities so as to enhance the business's market position and standing with customers. The primary role of a functional strategy is to *support* the company's overall business strategy and competitive approach.

   Lead responsibility for functional strategies within a business is normally delegated to the heads of the respective functions, with the general manager of

Figure 2.2   **A Company's Strategy-Making Hierarchy**

Orchestrated by the CEO and other senior executives.

Corporate Strategy

The companywide game plan for managing a set of businesses

In the case of a single-business company, these two levels of the strategy-making hierarchy merge into one level—*business strategy*—that is orchestrated by the company's CEO and other top executives.

Two-Way Influence

Orchestrated by the general managers of each of the company's different lines of business, often with advice and input from the heads of functional area activities within each business and other key people.

Business Strategy
(one for each business the company has diversified into)

• How to strengthen market position and build competitive advantage
• Actions to build competitive capabilities

Two-Way Influence

Crafted by the heads of major functional activities within a particular business—often in collaboration with other key people.

Functional-area strategies within each business

• Add relevant detail to the hows of overall business strategy
• Provide a game plan for managing a particular activity in ways that support the overall business strategy

Two-Way Influence

Crafted by brand managers; the operating managers of plants, distribution centers, and geographic units; and the managers of strategically important activities like advertising and Web site operations—often key employees are involved.

Operating strategies within each business

• Add detail and completeness to business and functional strategy
• Provide a game plan for managing specific lower-echelon activities with strategic significance

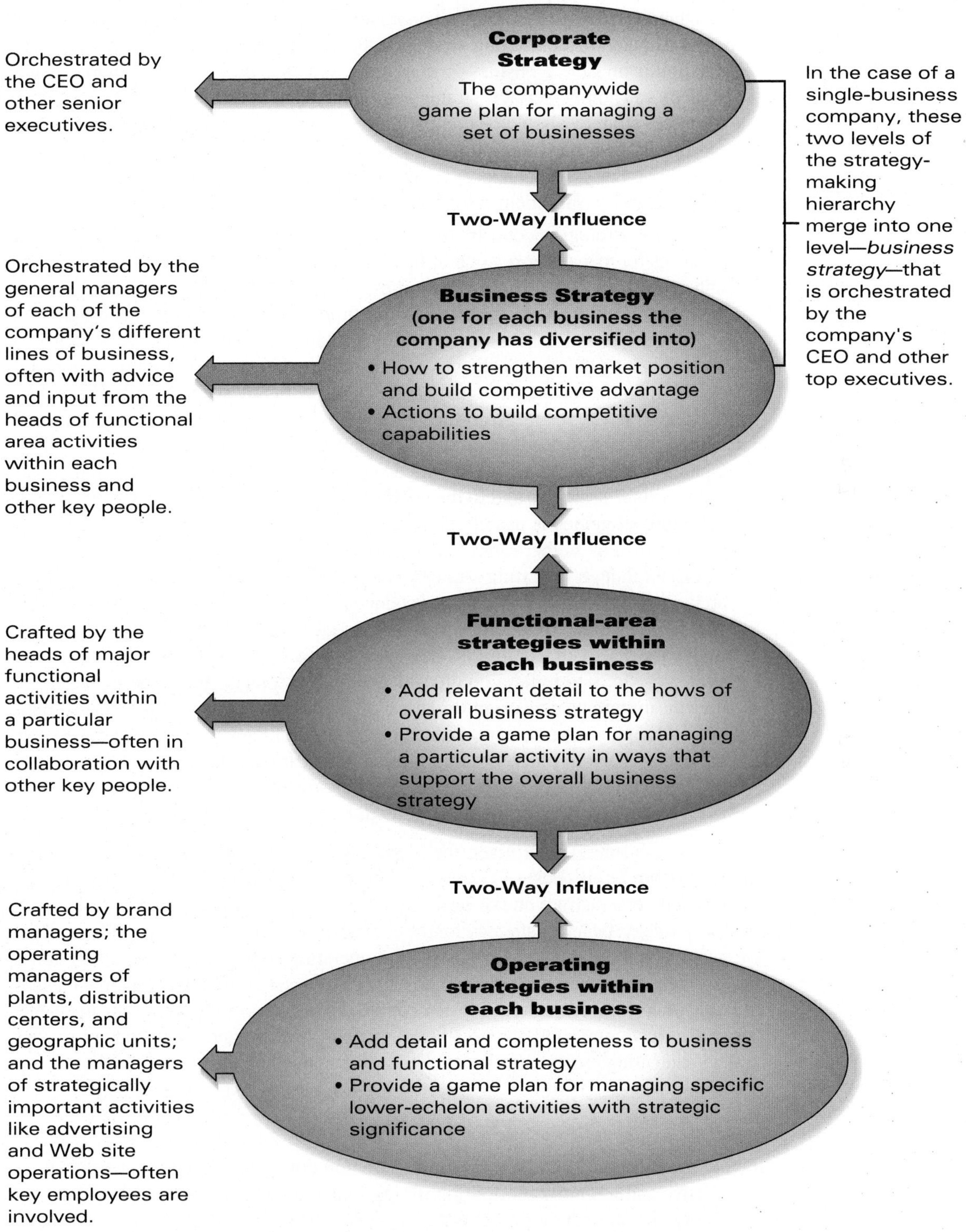

the business having final approval and perhaps even exerting a strong influence over the content of particular pieces of the strategies. To some extent, functional managers have to collaborate and coordinate their strategy-making efforts to avoid uncoordinated or conflicting strategies. For the overall business strategy to have maximum impact, a business's marketing strategy, production strategy, finance strategy, customer service strategy, product development strategy, and human resources strategy should be compatible and mutually reinforcing rather than each serving its own narrower purposes. If inconsistent functional-area strategies are sent up the line for final approval, the business head is responsible for spotting the conflicts and getting them resolved.

4. *Operating strategies* concern the relatively narrow strategic initiatives and approaches for managing key operating units (plants, distribution centers, geographic units) and specific operating activities with strategic significance (advertising campaigns, the management of specific brands, supply chain–related activities, and Web site sales and operations). A plant manager needs a strategy for accomplishing the plant's objectives, carrying out the plant's part of the company's overall manufacturing game plan, and dealing with any strategy-related problems that exist at the plant. A company's advertising manager needs a strategy for getting maximum audience exposure and sales impact from the ad budget. Operating strategies, while of limited scope, add further detail and completeness to functional strategies and to the overall business strategy. Lead responsibility for operating strategies is usually delegated to frontline managers, subject to review and approval by higher-ranking managers.

   Even though operating strategy is at the bottom of the strategy-making hierarchy, its importance should not be downplayed. A major plant that fails in its strategy to achieve production volume, unit cost, and quality targets can undercut the achievement of company sales and profit objectives and wreak havoc with strategic efforts to build a quality image with customers. Frontline managers are thus an important part of an organization's strategy-making team because many operating units have strategy-critical performance targets and need to have strategic action plans in place to achieve them. One cannot reliably judge the strategic importance of a given action simply by the strategy level or location within the managerial hierarchy where it is initiated.

In single-business enterprises, the corporate and business levels of strategy making merge into one level—business strategy—because the strategy for the whole company involves only one distinct line of business. Thus, a single-business enterprise has three levels of strategy: business strategy for the company as a whole, functional-area strategies for each main area within the business, and operating strategies undertaken by lower-echelon managers to flesh out strategically significant aspects for the company's business and functional-area strategies. Proprietorships, partnerships, and owner-managed enterprises may have only one or two strategy-making levels since their strategy-making, strategy-executing process can be handled by just a few key people.

Uniting the Strategy-Making Effort

Ideally, the pieces of a company's strategy up and down the strategy hierarchy should be cohesive and mutually reinforcing, fitting together like a jigsaw puzzle. To achieve such unity, the strategizing process requires leadership from the top. It is the responsibility of top executives to provide strategy-making direction and clearly articulate key strategic themes that paint the white lines for lower-level strategy-making efforts. *Mid-level and frontline managers cannot craft unified strategic moves without first understanding the company's long-term direction and knowing the major components of the overall and business strategies that their strategy-making efforts are supposed to support and enhance.* Thus, as a general rule, strategy making must start at the top of the organization and then proceed downward through the hierarchy from the corporate level to the business level and then from the business level to the associated functional and operating levels. Strategy cohesion requires that business-level strategies complement and be compatible with the overall corporate strategy. Likewise, functional and operating strategies have to complement and support the overall business-level strategy of which they are a part. When the strategizing process is mostly top-down, with lower-level strategy-making efforts taking their cues from the higher-level strategy elements they are supposed to complement and support, there's less potential for strategy conflict between different levels. An absence of strong strategic leadership from the top sets the stage for some degree of strategic disunity. The strategic disarray that occurs in an organization when there is weak leadership and too few strategy guidelines coming from top executives is akin to what would happen to a football team's offensive performance if the quarterback decided not to call a play for the team but instead let each player do whatever he/thought would work best at his respective position. In business, as in sports, all the strategy makers in a company are on the same team and the many different pieces of the overall strategy crafted at various organizational levels need to be in sync. *Anything less than a unified collection of strategies weakens the overall strategy and is likely to impair company performance.*

> **Core Concept**
> A company's strategy is at full power only when its many pieces are united.

There are two things that top-level executives can do to drive consistent strategic action down through the organizational hierarchy. One is to effectively communicate the company's vision, objectives, and major strategy components to down-the-line managers and key personnel. The greater the numbers of company personnel who know, understand, and buy into the company's long-term direction and overall strategy, the smaller the risk that organization units will go off in conflicting strategic directions when strategy making is pushed down to frontline levels and many people are given a strategy-making role. The second is to exercise due diligence in reviewing lower-level strategies for consistency and support of higher level strategies. Any strategy conflicts must be addressed and resolved, either by modifying the lower-level strategies with conflicting elements or by adapting the higher-level strategy to accommodate what may be more appealing strategy ideas and initiatives bubbling from below. Thus, the process of synchronizing the strategy initiatives up and down the organizational hierarchy does not necessarily mean that lower-level strategies must be changed whenever conflicts and inconsistencies are spotted. When more attractive strategies ideas originate at lower organizational levels, it makes sense to adapt higher-level strategies to accommodate them.

A Strategic Vision + Objectives + Strategy = A Strategic Plan

Developing a strategic vision and mission, setting objectives, and crafting a strategy are basic direction-setting tasks. They map out where a company is headed, the targeted strategic and financial outcomes, and the competitive moves and internal action approaches to be used in achieving the desired business results. Together, they constitute a **strategic plan** for coping with industry and competitive conditions, the expected actions of the industry's key players, and the challenges and issues that stand as obstacles to the company's success.[15]

> **Core Concept**
> A **strategic plan** lays out the company's future direction, performance targets, and strategy.

In companies that do regular strategy reviews and develop explicit strategic plans, the strategic plan usually ends up as a written document that is circulated to most managers and perhaps selected employees. Near-term performance targets are the part of the strategic plan most often spelled out explicitly and communicated to managers and employees. A number of companies summarize key elements of their strategic plans in the company's annual report to shareholders, in postings on their Web site, or in statements provided to the business media. Other companies, perhaps for reasons of competitive sensitivity, make only vague, general statements about their strategic plans. In small, privately owned companies, it is rare for strategic plans to exist in written form. Small companies' strategic plans tend to reside in the thinking and directives of owners/ executives, with aspects of the plan being revealed in meetings and conversations with company personnel, and the understandings and commitments among managers and key employees about where to head, what to accomplish, and how to proceed.

IMPLEMENTING AND EXECUTING THE STRATEGY: PHASE 4 OF THE STRATEGY-MAKING, STRATEGY-EXECUTING PROCESS

Managing the implementation and execution of strategy is an operations-oriented, make-things-happen activity aimed at performing core business activities in a strategy-supportive manner. It is easily the most demanding and time-consuming part of the strategy management process. Converting strategic plans into actions and results tests a manager's ability to direct organizational change, motivate people, build and strengthen company competencies and competitive capabilities, create and nurture a strategy-supportive work climate, and meet or beat performance targets. Initiatives to put the strategy in place and execute it proficiently have to be launched and managed on many organizational fronts.

Management's action agenda for implementing and executing the chosen strategy emerges from assessing what the company will have to do differently or better, given its particular operating practices and organizational circumstances, to execute the strategy competently and achieve the targeted financial and strategic performance. Each company manager has to think through the answer to "What has to be done in my area to execute my piece of the strategic plan, and what actions should I take to get the process under way?" How much internal change is needed depends on how much of the strategy is new, how far internal practices and competencies deviate from what the strategy requires, and how well the present work climate/culture supports good strategy execution. Depending on the amount of internal change involved, full implementation and proficient execution of company strategy (or important new pieces thereof) can take several months to several years.

In most situations, managing the strategy execution process includes the following principal aspects:

- Staffing the organization with the needed skills and expertise, consciously building and strengthening strategy-supportive competencies and competitive capabilities, and organizing the work effort.
- Allocating ample resources to those activities critical to strategic success.
- Ensuring that policies and procedures facilitate rather than impede effective execution.

- Using best practices to perform core business activities and pushing for continuous improvement. Organizational units have to periodically reassess how things are being done and diligently pursue useful changes and improvements.
- Installing information and operating systems that enable company personnel to better carry out their strategic roles day in and day out.
- Motivating people to pursue the target objectives energetically and, if need be, modifying their duties and job behavior to better fit the requirements of successful strategy execution.
- Tying rewards and incentives directly to the achievement of performance objectives and good strategy execution.
- Creating a company culture and work climate conducive to successful strategy execution.
- Exerting the internal leadership needed to drive implementation forward and keep improving on how the strategy is being executed. When stumbling blocks or weaknesses are encountered, management has to see that they are addressed and rectified in timely and effective fashion.

Good strategy execution requires diligent pursuit of operating excellence. It is a job for a company's whole management team. And success hinges on the skills and cooperation of operating managers who can push needed changes in their organization units and consistently deliver good results. Strategy implementation can be considered successful if things go smoothly enough that the company meets or beats its strategic and financial performance targets and shows good progress in achieving management's strategic vision.

EVALUATING PERFORMANCE AND INITIATING CORRECTIVE ADJUSTMENTS: PHASE 5 OF THE STRATEGY-MAKING, STRATEGY-EXECUTING PROCESS

The fifth phase of the strategy management process—monitoring new external developments, evaluating the company's progress, and making corrective adjustments—is the trigger point for deciding whether to continue or change the company's vision, objectives, strategy, or strategy execution methods. So long as the company's direction and strategy seem well matched to industry and competitive conditions, and performance targets are being met, company executives may well decide to stay the course. Simply fine-tuning the strategic plan and continuing with efforts to improve strategy execution are sufficient.

> **Core Concept**
> A company's vision, objectives, strategy, and approach to strategy execution are never final; managing strategy is an ongoing process, not an every-now-and-then task.

But whenever a company encounters disruptive changes in its environment, questions need to be raised about the appropriateness of its direction and strategy. If a company experiences a downturn in its market position or persistent shortfalls in performance, then company managers are obligated to ferret out the causes—do they relate to poor strategy, poor strategy execution, or both?—and take timely corrective action. A company's direction, objectives, and strategy have to be revisited anytime external or internal conditions warrant. It is to be expected that a company will modify its strategic vision, direction, objectives, and strategy over time.

Likewise, it is not unusual for a company to find that one or more aspects of its strategy implementation and execution are not going as well as intended. Proficient strategy execution is always the product of much organizational learning. It is achieved unevenly—coming quickly in some areas and proving nettlesome in others. It is both normal and desirable to periodically assess strategy execution to determine which aspects are working well and which need improving. Successful strategy execution entails vigilantly searching for ways to improve and then making corrective adjustments whenever and wherever it is useful to do so.

CORPORATE GOVERNANCE: THE ROLE OF THE BOARD OF DIRECTORS IN THE STRATEGY-MAKING, STRATEGY-EXECUTING PROCESS

Although senior managers have *lead responsibility* for crafting and executing a company's strategy, it is the duty of the board of directors to exercise *strong oversight* and see that the five tasks of strategic management are done in a manner that benefits shareholders (in the case of investor-owned enterprises) or stakeholders (in the case of not-for-profit organizations). In watching over management's strategy-making, strategy-executing actions and making sure that executive actions are not only proper but also aligned with the interests of stakeholders, a company's board of directors has four important obligations to fulfill:

1. *Be inquiring critics and oversee the company's direction, strategy, and business approaches.* Board members must ask probing questions and draw on their business acumen to make independent judgments about whether strategy proposals have been adequately analyzed and whether proposed strategic actions appear to have greater promise than alternatives. If executive management is bringing well-supported and reasoned strategy proposals to the board, there's little reason for board members to aggressively challenge or pick apart everything put before them. Asking incisive questions is usually sufficient to test whether the case for management's proposals is compelling. However, when the company's strategy is failing or is plagued with faulty execution, and certainly when there is a precipitous collapse in profitability, board members have a duty to express their concerns about the validity of the strategy and/or operating methods, initiate debate about the company's strategic path, hold one-on-one discussions with key executives and other board members, and perhaps directly intervene as a group to alter the company's executive leadership and, ultimately, its strategy and business approaches.

2. *Evaluate the caliber of senior executives' strategy-making and strategy-executing skills.* The board is always responsible for determining whether the current CEO is doing a good job of strategic leadership (as a basis for awarding salary increases and bonuses and deciding on retention or removal). Boards must also exercise due diligence in evaluating the strategic leadership skills of other senior executives in line to succeed the CEO. When the incumbent CEO steps down or leaves for a position elsewhere, the board must elect a successor, either going with an insider or deciding that a better-qualified outsider is needed to perhaps radically change the company's strategic course.

3. *Institute a compensation plan for top executives that rewards them for actions and results that serve stakeholder interests, and most especially those of shareholders.* A basic principle of corporate governance is that the owners of a corporation delegate operating authority and managerial control to top management in return for compensation. In their role as an *agent* of shareholders, top executives have a

clear and unequivocal duty to make decisions and operate the company in accord with shareholder interests (but this does not mean disregarding the interests of other stakeholders, particularly those of employees, with whom they also have an agency relationship). Most boards of directors have a compensation committee, composed entirely of outside directors, to develop a salary and incentive compensation plan that makes it in the self-interest of executives to operate the business in a manner that benefits the owners; the compensation committee's recommendations are presented to the full board for approval. But in addition to creating compensation plans intended to align executive actions with owner interests, the board of directors must put a halt to self-serving executive perks and privileges that simply line the financial pockets of executives. Numerous media reports have recounted instances in which boards of directors have gone along with opportunistic executive efforts to secure excessive, if not downright obscene, compensation of one kind or another (multimillion-dollar interest-free loans, personal use of corporate aircraft, lucrative severance and retirement packages, outsized stock incentive awards, and so on).

4.   *Oversee the company's financial accounting and financial reporting practices.* While top managers, particularly the company's CEO and CFO, are primarily responsible for seeing that the company's financial statements fairly and accurately report the results of the company's operations, it is well established that board members have a fiduciary duty to protect shareholders by exercising oversight of the company's financial practices, ensuring that generally accepted accounting principles (GAAP) are properly used in preparing the company's financial statements, and determining whether proper financial controls are in place to prevent fraud and misuse of funds. Virtually all boards of directors monitor the financial reporting activities by appointing an audit committee, always composed entirely of outside directors. The members of the audit committee have lead responsibility for overseeing the company's financial officers and consulting with both internal and external auditors to ensure accurate financial reporting and adequate financial controls.

   The number of prominent companies penalized because of the actions of scurrilous or out-of-control CEOs and CFOs, the growing propensity of disgruntled stockholders to file lawsuits alleging director negligence, and the escalating costs of liability insurance for directors all underscore the responsibility that a board of directors has for overseeing a company's strategy-making, strategy-executing process and ensuring that management actions are proper and responsible. Moreover, holders of large blocks of shares (mutual funds and pension funds), regulatory authorities, and the financial press consistently urge that board members, especially outside directors, be active and diligent in their oversight of company strategy and maintain a tight rein on executive actions.

Every corporation should have a strong, independent board of directors that (1) is well informed about the company's performance, (2) guides and judges the CEO and other top executives, (3) has the courage to curb inappropriate or unduly risky management actions, (4) certifies to shareholders that the CEO is doing what the board expects, (5) provides insight and advice to management, and (6) is intensely involved in debating the pros and cons of key decisions and actions.[14] Boards of directors that lack the backbone to challenge a strong-willed or imperial CEO or that rubber-stamp most anything the CEO recommends without probing inquiry and debate (perhaps because the board is stacked with the CEO's cronies) abdicate their duty to represent and protect shareholder interests. The whole fabric of effective corporate governance is undermined when boards of directors shirk their responsibility to maintain ultimate control over the company's strategic direction, the major elements of its strategy, the business approaches management is using to implement and execute the strategy, executive compensation, and the financial reporting process. Thus, even though lead responsibility for crafting and executing strategy falls to top executives, boards of directors have a very important oversight role in the strategy-making, strategy-executing process.

Key Points

The managerial process of crafting and executing a company's strategy consists of five interrelated and integrated phases:

1. *Developing a strategic vision* of where the company needs to head and what its future product/market/customer/technology focus should be. This managerial step provides long-term direction, infuses the organization with a sense of purposeful action, and communicates management's aspirations to stakeholders.

2. *Setting objectives* to spell out for the company *how much* of *what kind* of performance is expected, and *by when.* The objectives need to require a significant amount of organizational stretch. A balanced scorecard approach for measuring company performance entails setting both *financial objectives* and *strategic objectives.*

3. *Crafting a strategy to achieve the objectives* and move the company along the strategic course that management has charted. Crafting strategy is concerned principally with forming responses to changes under way in the external environment, devising competitive moves and market approaches aimed at producing sustainable competitive advantage, building competitively valuable competencies and capabilities, and uniting the strategic actions initiated in various parts of the company. The more that a company's operations cut across different products, industries, and geographical areas, the more that strategy making becomes a *team effort* involving managers and company personnel at many organizational levels. The total strategy that emerges in such companies is really a collection of strategic actions and business approaches initiated partly by senior company executives, partly by the heads of major business divisions, partly by functional-area managers, and partly by frontline operating managers. The larger and more diverse the operations of an enterprise, the more points of strategic initiative it has and the more managers and employees at more levels of management that have a relevant strategy-making role. A single business enterprise has three levels of strategy—business strategy for the company as a whole, functional-area strategies for each main area within the business, and operating strategies undertaken by lower-echelon managers to flesh out strategically significant aspects for the company's business and functional-area strategies. In diversified, multibusiness companies, the strategy-making task involves four distinct types or levels of strategy: corporate strategy for the company as a whole, business strategy (one for each business the company has diversified into), functional-area strategies within each business, and operating strategies. Typically, the strategy-making task is more top-down than bottom-up, with higher-level strategies serving as the guide for developing lower-level strategies.

4. *Implementing and executing the chosen strategy efficiently and effectively.* Managing the implementation and execution of strategy is an operations-oriented, make-things-happen activity aimed at shaping the performance of core business activities in a strategy-supportive manner. Management's handling of the strategy implementation process can be considered successful if things go smoothly

enough that the company meets or beats its strategic and financial performance targets and shows good progress in achieving management's strategic vision.

5. *Evaluating performance and initiating corrective adjustments* in vision, long-term direction, objectives, strategy, or execution in light of actual experience, changing conditions, new ideas, and new opportunities. This phase of the strategy management process is the trigger point for deciding whether to continue or change the company's vision, objectives, strategy, and/or strategy execution methods.

A company's strategic vision, objectives, and strategy constitute a *strategic plan* for coping with industry and competitive conditions, outcompeting rivals, and addressing the challenges and issues that stand as obstacles to the company's success.

Boards of directors have a duty to shareholders to play a vigilant role in overseeing management's handling of a company's strategy-making, strategy-executing process. A company's board is obligated to (1) critically appraise and ultimately approve strategic action plans; (2) evaluate the strategic leadership skills of the CEO and others in line to succeed the incumbent CEO; (3) institute a compensation plan for top executives that rewards them for actions and results that serve stakeholder interests, most especially those of shareholders; and (4) ensure that the company issues accurate financial reports and has adequate financial controls.

Exercises

1. Go to the Investors section of Heinz's Web site (www.heinz.com) and read the letter to the shareholders in the company's fiscal 2003 annual report. Is the vision for Heinz articulated by Chairman and CEO William R. Johnson sufficiently clear and well defined? Why or why not? Are the company's objectives well stated and appropriate? What about the strategy that Johnson outlines for the company? If you were a shareholder, would you be satisfied with what Johnson has told you about the company's direction, performance targets, and strategy?

2. Consider the following mission statement of the American Association of Retired People (AARP):

AARP Mission Statement

- AARP is a nonprofit, nonpartisan membership organization for people age 50 and over.
- AARP is dedicated to enhancing quality of life for all as we age. We lead positive social change and deliver value to members through information, advocacy and service.
- AARP also provides a wide range of unique benefits, special products, and services for our members. These benefits include AARP Web site at www.aarp.org, "AARP The Magazine," the monthly "AARP Bulletin," and a Spanish-language newspaper, "Segunda Juventud."
- Active in every state, the District of Columbia, Puerto Rico, and the U.S. Virgin Islands, AARP celebrates the attitude that age is just a number and life is what you make it.

Is AARP's mission statement well-crafted? Does it do an adequate job of indicating "who we are, what we do, and why we are here"? Why or why not?

3. How would you rewrite/restate the strategic vision for Caterpillar in Illustration Capsule 2.1 so as to better exemplify the characteristics of effective vision statements presented in Tables 2.2 and 2.3? Visit www.caterpillar.com to get more information about Caterpillar and figure out how a more appropriate strategic vision might be worded.

chapter three

Evaluating a Company's External Environment

Analysis is the critical starting point of strategic thinking.

—Kenichi Ohmae
Consultant and Author

Things are always different—the art is figuring out which differences matter.

—Laszlo Birinyi
Investments Manager

Competitive battles should be seen not as one-shot skirmishes but as a dynamic multiround game of moves and countermoves.

—Anil K. Gupta
Professor

anagers are not prepared to act wisely in steering a company in a different direction or altering its strategy until they have a deep understanding of the pertinent factors surrounding the company's situation. As indicated in the opening paragraph of Chapter 1, one of the three central questions that managers must address in evaluating their company's business prospects is "What's the company's present situation?" Two facets of a company's situation are especially pertinent: (1) the industry and competitive environment in which the company operates and the forces acting to reshape this environment, and (2) the company's own market position and competitiveness—its resources and capabilities, its strengths and weaknesses vis-à-vis rivals, and its windows of opportunity.

Insightful diagnosis of a company's external and internal environment is a prerequisite for managers to succeed in crafting a strategy that is an excellent fit with the company's situation, is capable of building competitive advantage, and holds good prospect for boosting company performance—the three criteria of a winning strategy. As depicted in Figure 3.1, the task of crafting a strategy thus should always begin with an appraisal of the company's external and internal situation (as a basis for developing strategic vision of where the company needs to head), then move toward an evaluation of the most promising alternative strategies and business models, and culminate in choosing a specific strategy.

This chapter presents the concepts and analytical tools for zeroing in on those aspects of a single-business company's external environment that should be considered in making strategic choices. Attention centers on the competitive arena in which a company operates, the drivers of market change, and what rival companies are doing. In Chapter 4 we explore the methods of evaluating a company's internal circumstances and competitiveness.

THE STRATEGICALLY RELEVANT COMPONENTS OF A COMPANY'S EXTERNAL ENVIRONMENT

All companies operate in a "macroenvironment" shaped by influences emanating from the economy at large; population demographics; societal values and lifestyles; governmental legislation and regulation; technological factors; and, closer to home, the

Figure 3.1   **From Thinking Strategically about the Company's Situation to Choosing a Strategy**

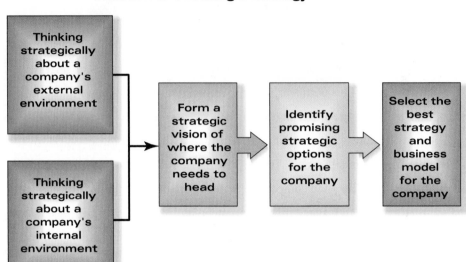

industry and competitive arena in which the company operates (see Figure 3.2). Strictly speaking, a company's macroenvironment includes *all relevant factors and influences* outside the company's boundaries; by relevant, we mean important enough to have a bearing on the decisions the company ultimately makes about its direction, objectives, strategy, and business model. Strategically relevant influences coming from the outer ring of the macroenvironment can sometimes have a high impact on a company's business situation and have a very significant impact on the company's direction and strategy. The strategic opportunities of cigarette producers to grow their business are greatly reduced by antismoking ordinances and the growing cultural stigma attached to smoking. Motor vehicle companies must adapt their strategies (especially as concerns the fuel mileage of their vehicles) to customer concerns about gasoline prices. The demographics of an aging population and longer life expectancies are having a dramatic impact on the business prospects and strategies of health care and prescription drug companies. Companies in most all industries have to craft strategies that are responsive to environmental regulations, growing use of the Internet and broadband technology, and energy prices. Companies in the food-processing, restaurant, sports, and fitness industries have to pay special attention to changes in lifestyles, eating habits, leisure-time preferences, and attitudes toward nutrition and exercise in fashioning their strategies.

Happenings in the outer ring of the macroenvironment may occur rapidly or slowly, with or without advance warning. The impact of outer-ring factors on a company's choice of strategy can range from big to small. But even if the factors in the outer ring of the macroenvironment change slowly or have such a comparatively low impact on a company's situation that only the edges of a company's direction and strategy are affected, there are enough strategically relevant outer-ring trends and events to justify a watchful eye. As company managers scan the external environment, they must be alert for potentially important outer-ring developments, assess their impact and influence, and adapt the company's direction and strategy as needed.

Figure 3.2 **The Components of a Company's Macroenvironment**

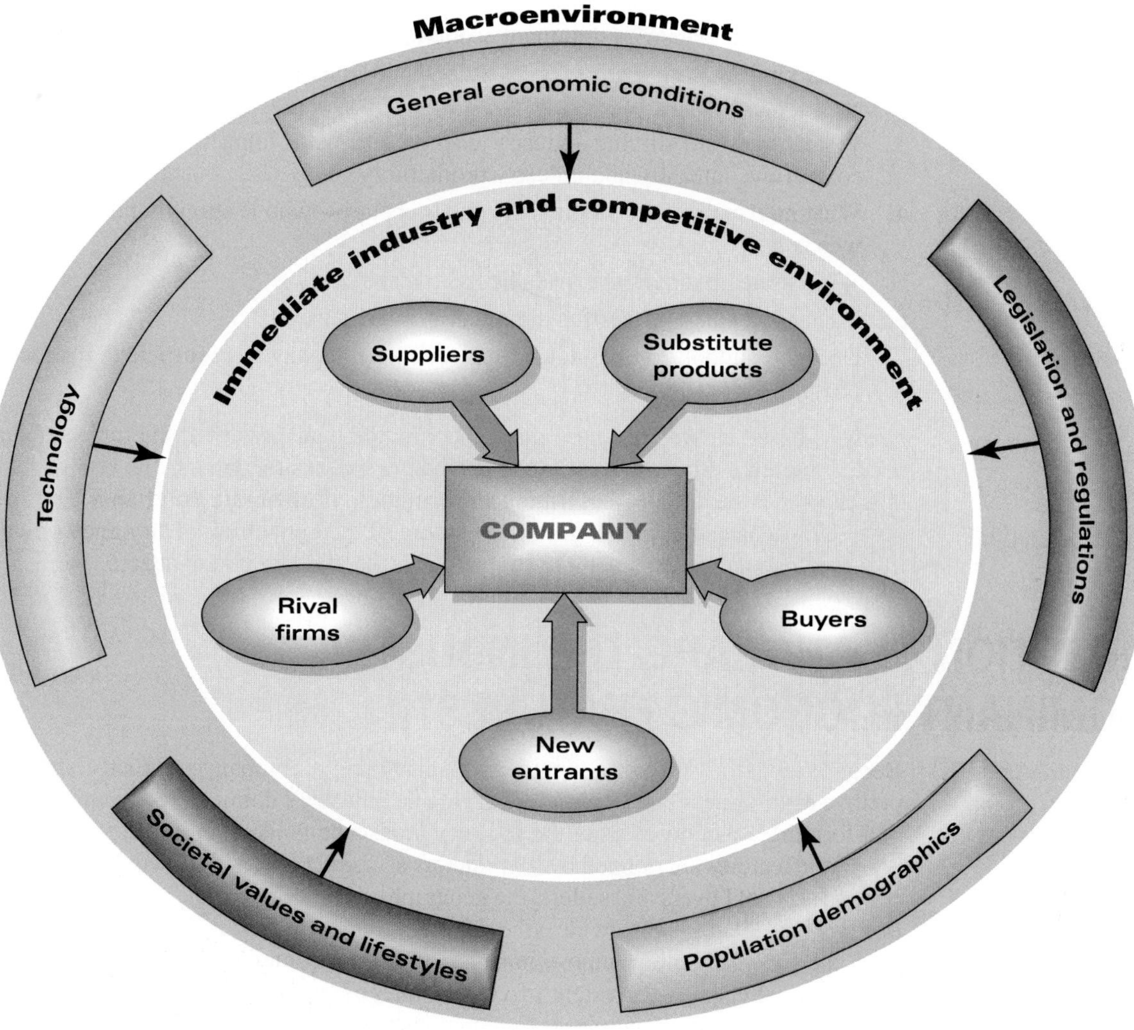

However, the factors and forces in a company's macroenvironment having the *biggest* strategy-shaping impact typically pertain to the company's immediate industry and competitive environment—competitive pressures, the actions of rival firms, buyer behavior, supplier-related considerations, and so on. Consequently, it is on a company's industry and competitive environment that we concentrate our attention in this chapter.

THINKING STRATEGICALLY ABOUT A COMPANY'S INDUSTRY AND COMPETITIVE ENVIRONMENT

To gain a deep understanding of a company's industry and competitive environment, managers do not need to gather all the information they can find and spend lots of time digesting it. Rather, the task is much more focused. Thinking strategically about a company's industry and competitive environment entails using some well-defined concepts and analytical tools to get clear answers to seven questions:

1. What are the industry's dominant economic features?
2. What kinds of competitive forces are industry members facing and how strong is each force?
3. What forces are driving industry change and what impacts will they have on competitive intensity and industry profitability?
4. What market positions do industry rivals occupy—who is strongly positioned and who is not?
5. What strategic moves are rivals likely to make next?
6. What are the key factors for future competitive success?
7. Does the outlook for the industry present the company with sufficiently attractive prospects for profitability?

Analysis-based answers to these questions provide managers with the understanding needed to craft a strategy that fits the company's external situation. The remainder of this chapter is devoted to describing the methods of obtaining solid answers to the seven questions and explaining how the nature of a company's industry and competitive environment weighs upon the strategic choices of company managers.

QUESTION 1: WHAT ARE THE INDUSTRY'S DOMINANT ECONOMIC FEATURES?

Because industries differ so significantly, analyzing a company's industry and competitive environment begins with identifying an industry's dominant economic features and forming a picture of what the industry landscape is like. An industry's dominant economic features are defined by such factors as market size and growth rate, the number and sizes of buyers and sellers, the geographic boundaries of the market (which can extend from local to worldwide), the degree to which sellers' products are differentiated, the pace of product innovation, market supply/demand conditions, the pace of technological change, the extent of vertical integration, and the extent to which costs are affected by scale economies (i.e., situations in which large-volume operations result in lower unit costs) and learning/experience curve effects (i.e., situations in which costs decline as a company gains knowledge and experience). Table 3.1 provides a convenient summary of what economic features to look at and the corresponding questions to consider in profiling an industry's landscape.

Getting a handle on an industry's distinguishing economic features not only sets the stage for the analysis to come but also promotes understanding of the kinds of strategic moves that industry members are likely to employ. For example, in industries characterized by one product advance after another, companies must invest in research and development (R&D) and develop strong product innovation capabilities—a strategy of continuous product innovation becomes a condition of survival in such industries as video games, mobile phones, and pharmaceuticals. An industry that has recently passed through the rapid-growth stage and is looking at single-digit percentage increases in buyer demand is likely to be experiencing a competitive shake-out and much stronger strategic emphasis on cost reduction and improved customer service.

In industries like semiconductors, strong *learning/experience curve effects* in manufacturing cause unit costs to decline about 20 percent each time *cumulative* production

Table 3.1 **What to Consider in Identifying an Industry's Dominant Economic Features**

Economic Feature	Questions to Answer
Market size and growth rate	• How big is the industry and how fast is it growing? • What does the industry's position in the life cycle (early development, rapid growth and takeoff, early maturity and slowing growth, saturation and stagnation, decline) reveal about the industry's growth prospects?
Number of rivals	• Is the industry fragmented into many small companies or concentrated and dominated by a few large companies? • Is the industry going through a period of consolidation to a smaller number of competitors?
Scope of competitive rivalry	• Is the geographic area over which most companies compete local, regional, national, multinational, or global? • Is having a presence in the foreign country markets becoming more important to a company's long-term competitive success?
Number of buyers	• Is market demand fragmented among many buyers? • Do some buyers have bargaining power because they purchase in large volume?
Degree of product differentiation	• Are the products of rivals becoming more differentiated or less differentiated? • Are increasingly look-alike products of rivals causing heightened price competition?
Product innovation	• Is the industry characterized by rapid product innovation and short product life cycles? • How important is R&D and product innovation? • Are there opportunities to overtake key rivals by being first-to-market with next-generation products?
Supply/demand conditions	• Is a surplus of capacity pushing prices and profit margins down? • Is the industry overcrowded with too many competitors? • Are short supplies creating a sellers' market?
Pace of technological change	• What role does advancing technology play in this industry? • Are ongoing upgrades of facilities/equipment essential because of rapidly advancing production process technologies? • Do most industry members have or need strong technological capabilities?
Vertical integration	• Do most competitors operate in only one stage of the industry (parts and components production, manufacturing and assembly, distribution, retailing) or do some competitors operate in multiple stages? • Is there any cost or competitive advantage or disadvantage associated with being fully or partially integrated?
Economies of scale	• Is the industry characterized by economies of scale in purchasing, manufacturing, advertising, shipping, or other activities? • Do companies with large-scale operations have an important cost advantage over small-scale firms?
Learning/experience curve effects	• Are certain industry activities characterized by strong learning/experience curve effects ("learning by doing") such that unit costs decline as a company's experience in performing the activity builds? • Do any companies have significant cost advantages because of their learning/experience in performing particular activities?

volume doubles. With a 20 percent experience curve effect, if the first 1 million chips cost $100 each, the unit cost would be $80 (80 percent of $100) by a production volume of 2 million, the unit cost would be $64 (80 percent of $80) by a production volume of 4 million, and so on.[1] The bigger the learning/experience curve effect, the bigger the cost advantage of the company with the largest *cumulative* production volume.

Thus, when an industry is characterized by important learning/experience curve effects (or by economies of scale), industry members are strongly motivated to adopt volume-increasing strategies to capture the resulting cost-saving economies and maintain their competitiveness. Unless small-scale firms succeed in pursuing strategic options that allow them to grow sales sufficiently to remain cost-competitive with larger-volume rivals, they are unlikely to survive. The bigger the learning/experience curve effects and/or scale economies in an industry, the more imperative it becomes for competing sellers to pursue strategies to win additional sales and market share—the company with the biggest sales volume gains sustainable competitive advantage as the low-cost producer.

QUESTION 2: WHAT KINDS OF COMPETITIVE FORCES ARE INDUSTRY MEMBERS FACING?

The character, mix, and subtleties of the competitive forces operating in a company's industry are never the same from one industry to another. Far and away the most powerful and widely used tool for systematically diagnosing the principal competitive pressures in a market and assessing the strength and importance of each is the *five-forces model of competition*.[2] This model, depicted in Figure 3.3, holds that the state of competition in an industry is a composite of competitive pressures operating in five areas of the overall market:

1. Competitive pressures associated with the market maneuvering and jockeying for buyer patronage that goes on among *rival sellers* in the industry.
2. Competitive pressures associated with the threat of *new entrants* into the market.
3. Competitive pressures coming from the attempts of companies in other industries to win buyers over to their own *substitute products*.
4. Competitive pressures stemming from *supplier* bargaining power and supplier–seller collaboration.
5. Competitive pressures stemming from *buyer* bargaining power and seller–buyer collaboration.

The way one uses the five-forces model to determine the nature and strength of competitive pressures in a given industry is to build the picture of competition in three steps:

- *Step 1:* Identify the specific competitive pressures associated with each of the five forces.
- *Step 2:* Evaluate how strong the pressures comprising each of the five forces are (fierce, strong, moderate to normal, or weak).
- *Step 3:* Determine whether the collective strength of the five competitive forces is conducive to earning attractive profits.

Figure 3.3   **The Five-Forces Model of Competition: A Key Analytical Tool**

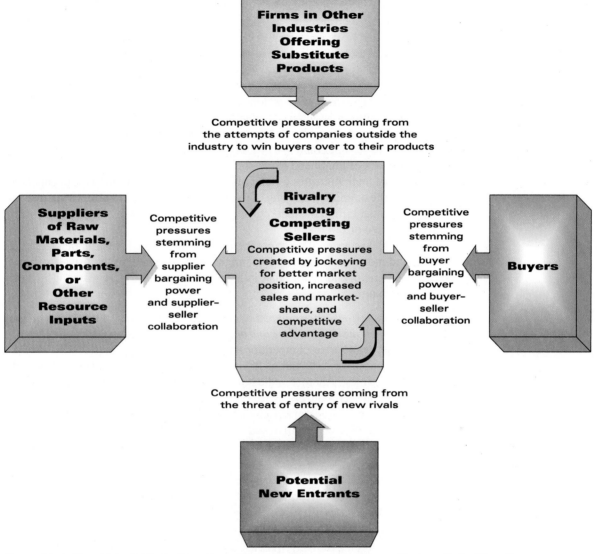

Source: Adapted from Michael E. Porter, "How Competitive Forces Shape Strategy," *Harvard Business Review* 57, no. 2 (March–April 1979), pp. 137–45.

Competitive Pressures Associated with the Jockeying among Rival Sellers

The strongest of the five competitive forces is nearly always the market maneuvering and jockeying for buyer patronage that goes on among rival sellers of a product or service. In effect, *a market is a competitive battlefield* where there's no end to the jockeying for buyer patronage. Rival sellers are prone to employ whatever weapons they

Core Concept
Competitive jockeying among industry rivals is ever changing, as rivals initiate fresh offensive and defensive moves and emphasize first one mix of competitive weapons and then another in efforts to improve their market positions.

have in their business arsenal to improve their market positions, strengthen their market position with buyers, and earn good profits. The challenge is to craft a competitive strategy that, at the very least, allows a company to hold its own against rivals and that, ideally, *produces a competitive edge over rivals.* But competitive contests are ongoing and dynamic. When one firm makes a strategic move that produces good results, its rivals typically respond with offensive or defensive countermoves, shifting their strategic emphasis from one combination of product attributes, marketing tactics, and capabilities to another. This pattern of action and reaction, move and countermove, adjust and readjust produces a continually evolving competitive landscape in which the market battle ebbs and flows, sometimes takes unpredictable twists and turns, and produces winners and losers. But the winners—the current market leaders— have no guarantees of continued leadership; their market success is no more durable than the power of their strategies to fend off the strategies of ambitious challengers. In every industry, the ongoing jockeying of rivals leads to one or another companies gaining or losing momentum in the marketplace according to whether their latest strategic maneuvers succeed or fail.

Figure 3.4 shows a sampling of competitive weapons that firms can deploy in battling rivals and indicates the factors that influence the intensity of their rivalry. A brief discussion of some of the factors that influence the tempo of rivalry among industry competitors is in order:[3]

- *Rivalry intensifies when competing sellers are active in launching fresh actions to boost their market standing and business performance.* One indicator of active rivalry is lively price competition, a condition that puts pressure on industry members to drive costs out of the business and threatens the survival of high-cost companies. Another indicator of active rivalry is rapid introduction of next-generation products—when one or more rivals frequently introduce new or improved products, competitors that lack good product innovation capabilities feel considerable competitive heat to get their own new and improved products into the marketplace quickly. Other indicators of active rivalry among industry members include:
  - Whether industry members are racing to differentiate their products from rivals by offering better performance features or higher quality or improved customer service or a wider product selection.
  - How frequently rivals resort to such marketing tactics as special sales promotions, heavy advertising, rebates, or low-interest-rate financing to drum up additional sales.
  - How actively industry members are pursuing efforts to build stronger dealer networks or establish positions in foreign markets or otherwise expand their distribution capabilities and market presence.
  - How hard companies are striving to gain a market edge over rivals by developing valuable expertise and capabilities that rivals are hard pressed to match.

  Normally, competitive jockeying among rival sellers is active and fairly intense because competing companies are highly motivated to launch whatever fresh actions and creative market maneuvers they can think of to try to strengthen their market positions and business performance.

- *Rivalry intensifies as the number of competitors increases and as competitors become more equal in size and capability.* Rivalry is not as vigorous in micro-processors for PCs, where Advanced Micro Devices (AMD) is one of the few

Figure 3.4 **Weapons for Competing and Factors Affecting the Strength of Rivalry**

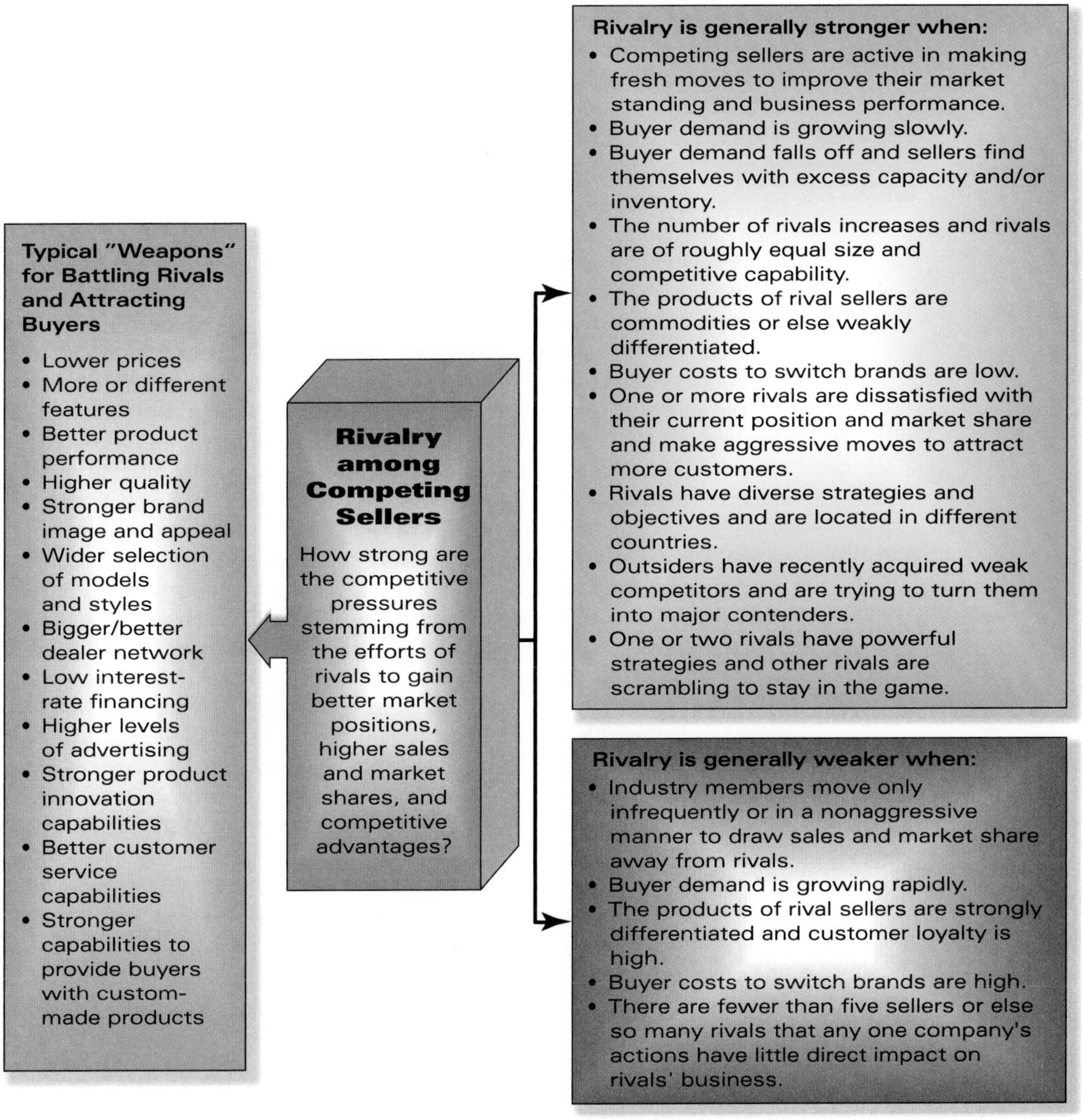

Rivalry is generally stronger when:
- Competing sellers are active in making fresh moves to improve their market standing and business performance.
- Buyer demand is growing slowly.
- Buyer demand falls off and sellers find themselves with excess capacity and/or inventory.
- The number of rivals increases and rivals are of roughly equal size and competitive capability.
- The products of rival sellers are commodities or else weakly differentiated.
- Buyer costs to switch brands are low.
- One or more rivals are dissatisfied with their current position and market share and make aggressive moves to attract more customers.
- Rivals have diverse strategies and objectives and are located in different countries.
- Outsiders have recently acquired weak competitors and are trying to turn them into major contenders.
- One or two rivals have powerful strategies and other rivals are scrambling to stay in the game.

Typical "Weapons" for Battling Rivals and Attracting Buyers
- Lower prices
- More or different features
- Better product performance
- Higher quality
- Stronger brand image and appeal
- Wider selection of models and styles
- Bigger/better dealer network
- Low interest-rate financing
- Higher levels of advertising
- Stronger product innovation capabilities
- Better customer service capabilities
- Stronger capabilities to provide buyers with custom-made products

Rivalry among Competing Sellers

How strong are the competitive pressures stemming from the efforts of rivals to gain better market positions, higher sales and market shares, and competitive advantages?

Rivalry is generally weaker when:
- Industry members move only infrequently or in a nonaggressive manner to draw sales and market share away from rivals.
- Buyer demand is growing rapidly.
- The products of rival sellers are strongly differentiated and customer loyalty is high.
- Buyer costs to switch brands are high.
- There are fewer than five sellers or else so many rivals that any one company's actions have little direct impact on rivals' business.

challengers to Intel, as it is in fast-food restaurants, where numerous sellers are actively jockeying for buyer patronage. Up to a point, the greater the number of competitors, the greater the probability of fresh, creative strategic initiatives. In addition, when rivals are nearly equal in size and capability, they can usually compete on a fairly even footing, making it harder for one or two firms to win commanding market shares and confront weaker market challenges from rivals.

- *Rivalry is usually stronger in slow-growing markets and weaker in fast-growing markets.* Rapidly expanding buyer demand produces enough new business for all industry members to grow. Indeed, in a fast-growing market, a company may find itself stretched just to keep abreast of incoming orders, let alone devote resources to stealing customers away from rivals. But in markets where growth is sluggish or where buyer demand drops off unexpectedly, expansion-minded firms and firms with excess capacity often are quick to cut prices and initiate other sales-increasing tactics, thereby igniting a battle for market share that can result in a shake-out of weak, inefficient firms.

- *Rivalry is usually weaker in industries comprised of so many rivals that the impact of any one company's actions is spread thin across all industry members; likewise, it is often weak when there are fewer than five competitors.* A progressively larger number of competitors can actually begin to weaken head-to-head rivalry once an industry becomes populated with so many rivals that the impact of successful moves by any one company is spread thin across many industry members. To the extent that a company's strategic moves ripple out to have little discernible impact on the businesses of its many rivals, then industry members soon learn that it is not imperative to respond every time one or another rival does something to enhance its market position—an outcome that weakens the intensity of head-to-head battles for market share. Rivalry also *tends* to be weak if an industry consists of just two or three or four sellers. In a market with few rivals, each competitor soon learns that aggressive moves to grow its sales and market share can have immediate adverse impact on rivals' businesses, almost certainly provoking vigorous retaliation and risking an all-out battle for market share that is likely to lower the profits of all concerned. Companies that have a few strong rivals thus come to understand the merits of *restrained* efforts to wrest sales and market share from competitors as opposed to undertaking hard-hitting offensives that escalate into a profit-eroding arms-race or price war. However, some caution must be exercised in concluding that rivalry is weak just because there are only a few competitors. Thus, although occasional warfare can break out (the fierceness of the current battle between Red Hat and Microsoft and the decades-long war between Coca-Cola and Pepsi are prime examples), competition among the few normally produces a live-and-let-live approach to competing because rivals see the merits of restrained efforts to wrest sales and market share from competitors as opposed to undertaking hard-hitting offensives that escalate into a profit-eroding arms race or price war.

- *Rivalry increases when buyer demand falls off and sellers find themselves with excess capacity and/or inventory.* Excess supply conditions create a "buyers' market," putting added competitive pressure on industry rivals to scramble for profitable sales levels (often by price discounting).

- *Rivalry increases as it becomes less costly for buyers to switch brands.* The less expensive it is for buyers to switch their purchases from the seller of one brand to the seller of another brand, the easier it is for sellers to steal customers away from rivals. But the higher the costs buyers incur to switch brands, the less prone they are to brand switching. Even if consumers view one or more rival brands as more attractive, they may not be inclined to switch because of the added time and inconvenience or the psychological costs of abandoning a familiar brand. Distributors and retailers may not switch to the brands of rival manufacturers because they are hesitant to sever long-standing supplier relationships, incur any technical support costs or retraining expenses in making the switchover, go to the trouble of testing the quality and reliability of the rival brand, or devote resources to marketing the new brand (especially if the brand is lesser known).

Apple Computer, for example, has been unable to convince PC users to switch from Windows-based PCs because of the time burdens and inconvenience associated with learning Apple's operating system and because so many Windows-based applications will not run on a MacIntosh due to operating system incompatibility. Consequently, unless buyers are dissatisfied with the brand they are presently purchasing, high switching costs can significantly weaken the rivalry among competing sellers.

- *Rivalry increases as the products of rival sellers become more standardized and diminishes as the products of industry rivals become more strongly differentiated.* When the offerings of rivals are identical or weakly differentiated, buyers have less reason to be brand-loyal—a condition that makes it easier for rivals to convince buyers to switch to their offering. And since the brands of different sellers have comparable attributes, buyers can shop the market for the best deal and switch brands at will. In contrast, strongly differentiated product offerings among rivals breed high brand loyalty on the part of buyers—because many buyers view the attributes of certain brands as better suited to their needs. Strong brand attachments make it tougher for sellers to draw customers away from rivals. Unless meaningful numbers of buyers are open to considering new or different product attributes being offered by rivals, the high degrees of brand loyalty that accompany strong product differentiation work against fierce rivalry among competing sellers. *The degree of product differentiation also affects switching costs.* When the offerings of rivals are identical or weakly differentiated, it is usually easy and inexpensive for buyers to switch their purchases from one seller to another. Strongly differentiated products raise the probability that buyers will find it costly to switch brands.

- *Rivalry is more intense when industry conditions tempt competitors to use price cuts or other competitive weapons to boost unit volume.* When a product is perishable, seasonal, or costly to hold in inventory, competitive pressures build quickly any time one or more firms decide to cut prices and dump supplies on the market. Likewise, whenever fixed costs account for a large fraction of total cost, such that unit costs tend to be lowest at or near full capacity, then firms come under significant pressure to cut prices or otherwise try to boost sales whenever they are operating below full capacity. Unused capacity imposes a significant cost-increasing penalty because there are fewer units over which to spread fixed costs. The pressure of high fixed costs can push rival firms into price concessions, special discounts, rebates, low-interest-rate financing, and other volume-boosting tactics.

- *Rivalry increases when one or more competitors become dissatisfied with their market position and launch moves to bolster their standing at the expense of rivals.* Firms that are losing ground or in financial trouble often pursue aggressive (or perhaps desperate) turnaround strategies that can involve price discounts, more advertising, acquisition of or merger with other rivals, or new product introductions—such strategies can turn competitive pressures up a notch.

- *Rivalry becomes more volatile and unpredictable as the diversity of competitors increases in terms of visions, strategic intents, objectives, strategies, resources, and countries of origin.* A diverse group of sellers often contains one or more mavericks willing to try novel or high-risk or rule-breaking market approaches, thus generating a livelier and less predictable competitive environment. Globally competitive markets often contain rivals with different views about where the industry is headed and a willingness to employ perhaps radically different competitive approaches. Attempts by cross-border rivals to gain stronger footholds in each other's domestic markets usually boost the intensity of rivalry, especially when the aggressors have lower costs or products with more attractive features.

- *Rivalry increases when strong companies outside the industry acquire weak firms in the industry and launch aggressive, well-funded moves to transform their newly acquired competitors into major market contenders.* A concerted effort to turn a weak rival into a market leader nearly always entails launching well-financed strategic initiatives to dramatically improve the competitor's product offering, excite buyer interest, and win a much bigger market share—actions that, if successful, put added pressure on rivals to counter with fresh strategic moves of their own.

- *A powerful, successful competitive strategy employed by one company greatly intensifies the competitive pressures on its rivals to develop effective strategic responses or be relegated to also-ran status.*

Rivalry can be characterized as *cutthroat* or *brutal* when competitors engage in protracted price wars or habitually employ other aggressive tactics that are mutually destructive to profitability. Rivalry can be considered *fierce* to *strong* when the battle for market share is so vigorous that the profit margins of most industry members are squeezed to bare-bones levels. Rivalry can be characterized as *moderate* or *normal* when the maneuvering among industry members, while lively and healthy, still allows most industry members to earn acceptable profits. Rivalry is *weak* when most companies in the industry are relatively well satisfied with their sales growth and market shares, rarely undertake offensives to steal customers away from one another, and have comparatively attractive earnings and returns on investment.

Competitive Pressures Associated with the Threat of New Entrants

Several factors determine whether the threat of new companies entering the marketplace poses significant competitive pressure (see Figure 3.5). One factor relates to the size of the pool of likely entry candidates and the resources at their command. As a rule, the bigger the pool of entry candidates, the stronger the threat of potential entry. This is especially true when some of the likely entry candidates have ample resources and the potential to become formidable contenders for market leadership. Frequently, the strongest competitive pressures associated with potential entry come not from outsiders, but from current industry participants looking for growth opportunities. *Existing industry members are often strong candidates for entering market segments or geographic areas where they currently do not have a market presence.* Companies already well established in certain product categories or geographic areas often possess the resources, competencies, and competitive capabilities to hurdle the barriers of entering a different market segment or new geographic area.

A second factor concerns whether the likely entry candidates face high or low entry barriers. High barriers reduce the competitive threat of potential entry, while low barriers make entry more likely, especially if the industry is growing and offers attractive profit opportunities. The most widely encountered barriers that entry candidates must hurdle include:[4]

- *The presence of sizable economies of scale in production or other areas of operation*—When incumbent companies enjoy cost advantages associated with

Figure 3.5   **Factors Affecting the Threat of Entry**

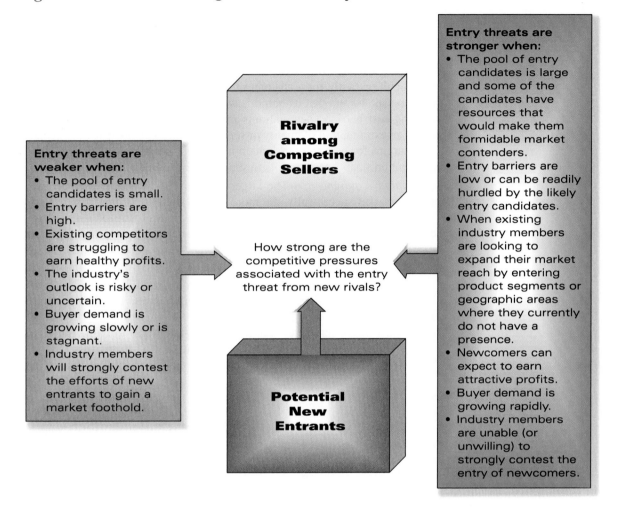

Entry threats are weaker when:
- The pool of entry candidates is small.
- Entry barriers are high.
- Existing competitors are struggling to earn healthy profits.
- The industry's outlook is risky or uncertain.
- Buyer demand is growing slowly or is stagnant.
- Industry members will strongly contest the efforts of new entrants to gain a market foothold.

Rivalry among Competing Sellers

How strong are the competitive pressures associated with the entry threat from new rivals?

Potential New Entrants

Entry threats are stronger when:
- The pool of entry candidates is large and some of the candidates have resources that would make them formidable market contenders.
- Entry barriers are low or can be readily hurdled by the likely entry candidates.
- When existing industry members are looking to expand their market reach by entering product segments or geographic areas where they currently do not have a presence.
- Newcomers can expect to earn attractive profits.
- Buyer demand is growing rapidly.
- Industry members are unable (or unwilling) to strongly contest the entry of newcomers.

large-scale operation, outsiders must either enter on a large scale (a costly and perhaps risky move) or accept a cost disadvantage and consequently lower profitability. Trying to overcome the disadvantages of small size by entering on a large scale at the outset can result in long-term overcapacity problems for the new entrant (until sales volume builds up), and it can so threaten the market shares of existing firms that they launch strong defensive maneuvers (price cuts, increased advertising and sales promotion, and similar blocking actions) to maintain their positions and make things hard on a newcomer.

- *Cost and resource disadvantages not related to scale of operation*—Aside from enjoying economies of scale, there are other reasons why existing firms may have low unit costs that are hard to replicate by newcomers. Industry incumbents can have cost advantages that stem from learning/experience curve effects, the possession of key patents or proprietary technology, partnerships with the best and cheapest suppliers of raw materials and components, favorable locations, and low fixed costs (because they have older facilities that have been mostly depreciated).

- *Strong brand preferences and high degrees of customer loyalty*—The stronger the attachment of buyers to established brands, the harder it is for a newcomer to break into the marketplace. In such cases, a new entrant must have the financial resources to spend enough on advertising and sales promotion to overcome customer loyalties and build its own clientele. Establishing brand recognition and building customer loyalty can be a slow and costly process. In addition, if it is difficult or costly for a customer to switch to a new brand, a new entrant must persuade buyers that its brand is worth the switching costs. To overcome switching-cost barriers, new entrants may have to offer buyers a discounted price or an extra margin of quality or service. All this can mean lower expected profit margins for new entrants, which increases the risk to start-up companies dependent on sizable early profits to support their new investments.

- *High capital requirements*—The larger the total dollar investment needed to enter the market successfully, the more limited the pool of potential entrants. The most obvious capital requirements for new entrants relate to manufacturing facilities and equipment, introductory advertising and sales promotion campaigns, working capital to finance inventories and customer credit, and sufficient cash to cover start-up costs.

- *The difficulties of building a network of distributors or retailers and securing adequate space on retailers' shelves*—A potential entrant can face numerous distribution channel challenges. Wholesale distributors may be reluctant to take on a product that lacks buyer recognition. Retailers have to be recruited and convinced to give a new brand ample display space and an adequate trial period. When existing sellers have strong, well-functioning distributor or retailer networks, a newcomer has an uphill struggle in squeezing its way in. Potential entrants sometimes have to "buy" their way into wholesale or retail channels by cutting their prices to provide dealers and distributors with higher markups and profit margins or by giving them big advertising and promotional allowances. As a consequence, a potential entrant's own profits may be squeezed unless and until its product gains enough consumer acceptance that distributors and retailers are anxious to carry it.

- *Restrictive regulatory policies*—Government agencies can limit or even bar entry by requiring licenses and permits. Regulated industries like cable TV, telecommunications, electric and gas utilities, radio and television broadcasting, liquor retailing, and railroads entail government-controlled entry. In international markets, host governments commonly limit foreign entry and must approve all foreign investment applications. Stringent government-mandated safety regulations and environmental pollution standards are entry barriers because they raise entry costs.

- *Tariffs and international trade restrictions*—National governments commonly use tariffs and trade restrictions (antidumping rules, local content requirements, quotas, etc.) to raise entry barriers for foreign firms and protect domestic producers from outside competition.

- *The ability and inclination of industry incumbents to launch vigorous initiatives to block a newcomer's successful entry*—Even if a potential entrant has or can acquire the needed competencies and resources to attempt entry, it must still worry about the reaction of existing firms.[5] Sometimes, there's little that incumbents can do to throw obstacles in an entrant's path—for instance, existing restaurants have little in their arsenal to discourage a new restaurant from opening or to dissuade people from trying the new restaurant. But there are times when incumbents do all they can to make it difficult for a new entrant, using price cuts, increased advertising, product improvements, and whatever else they can think of to prevent the entrant from building a clientele. Cable TV companies vigorously fight the entry of satellite TV companies; Sony and Nintendo have mounted strong defenses to thwart Microsoft's entry in video games with its Xbox; existing hotels try to combat the opening of new hotels with loyalty programs, renovations of their own, the addition of new services, and so on. A potential entrant can have second thoughts when financially strong incumbent firms send clear signals that they will give newcomers a hard time.

Whether an industry's entry barriers ought to be considered high or low depends on the resources and competencies possessed by the pool of potential entrants. Companies with sizable financial resources, proven competitive capabilities, and a respected brand name may be able to hurdle an industry's entry barriers rather easily. Small start-up enterprises may find the same entry barriers insurmountable. Thus, how hard it will be for potential entrants to compete on a level playing field is always relative to the financial resources and competitive capabilities of likely entrants. For example, when Honda opted to enter the U.S. lawn-mower market in competition against Toro, Snapper, Craftsman, John Deere, and others, it was easily able to hurdle entry barriers that would have been formidable to other newcomers because it had long-standing expertise in gasoline engines and because its well-known reputation for quality and durability gave it instant credibility with shoppers looking to buy a new lawn mower. Honda had to spend relatively little on advertising to attract buyers and gain a market foothold, distributors and dealers were quite willing to handle the Honda lawn-mower line, and Honda had ample capital to build a U.S. assembly plant.

In evaluating whether the threat of additional entry is strong or weak, company managers must look at (1) how formidable the entry barriers are for each type of potential entrant—start-up enterprises, specific candidate companies in other industries, and current industry participants looking to expand their market reach—and (2) how attractive the growth and profit prospects are for new entrants. Rapidly growing market demand and high potential profits act as magnets, motivating potential entrants to commit the resources needed to hurdle entry barriers.[6] When profits are sufficiently attractive, entry barriers are unlikely to be an effective entry deterrent. At most, they limit the pool of candidate entrants to enterprises with the requisite competencies and resources and with the creativity to fashion a strategy for competing with incumbent firms.

Hence, *the best test of whether potential entry is a strong or weak competitive force in the marketplace is to ask if the industry's growth and profit prospects are strongly attractive to potential entry candidates*. When the answer is no, potential entry is a weak competitive force. When the answer is yes and there are entry candidates with sufficient expertise and resources, then potential entry adds significantly to competitive pressures in the marketplace. The stronger the threat of entry, the more that incumbent firms are driven to seek ways to fortify their positions against newcomers, pursuing strategic moves not only to protect their market shares but also to make entry more costly or difficult.

One additional point: *The threat of entry changes as the industry's prospects grow brighter or dimmer and as entry barriers rise or fall*. For example, in the pharmaceutical industry the expiration of a key patent on a widely prescribed drug virtually guarantees that one or more drug makers will enter with generic offerings of their own. Growing use of the Internet for shopping is making it much easier for Web-based retailers to enter into competition

> High entry barriers and weak entry threats today do not always translate into high entry barriers and weak entry threats tomorrow.

against such well-known retail chains as Sears, Circuit City, and Barnes and Noble. In international markets, entry barriers for foreign-based firms fall as tariffs are lowered, as host governments open up their domestic markets to outsiders, as domestic wholesalers and dealers seek out lower-cost foreign-made goods, and as domestic buyers become more willing to purchase foreign brands.

Competitive Pressures from the Sellers of Substitute Products

Companies in one industry come under competitive pressure from the actions of companies in a closely adjoining industry whenever buyers view the products of the two industries as good substitutes. For instance, the producers of sugar experience competitive pressures from the sales and marketing efforts of the makers of artificial sweeteners. Similarly, the producers of eyeglasses and contact lenses are currently facing mounting competitive pressures from growing consumer interest in corrective laser surgery. Newspapers are feeling the competitive force of the general public turning to cable news channels for late-breaking news and using Internet sources to get information about sports results, stock quotes, and job opportunities. The makers of videotapes and VCRs have watched demand evaporate as more and more consumers have been attracted to substitute use of DVDs and DVD recorders/players. Traditional providers of telephone service like BellSouth, AT&T, Verizon, and Qwest are feeling enormous competitive pressure from cell phone providers, as more and more consumers find cell phones preferable to landline phones.

Just how strong the competitive pressures are from the sellers of substitute products depends on three factors:

1. *Whether substitutes are readily available and attractively priced.* The presence of readily available and attractively priced substitutes creates competitive pressure by placing a ceiling on the prices industry members can charge without giving customers an incentive to switch to substitutes and risking sales erosion.[7] This price ceiling, at the same time, puts a lid on the profits that industry members can earn unless they find ways to cut costs. When substitutes are cheaper than an industry's product, industry members come under heavy competitive pressure to reduce their prices and find ways to absorb the price cuts with cost reductions.

2. *Whether buyers view the substitutes as being comparable or better in terms of quality, performance, and other relevant attributes.* The availability of substitutes inevitably invites customers to compare performance, features, ease of use, and other attributes as well as price. For example, ski boat manufacturers are experiencing strong competition from personal water-ski craft because water sports enthusiasts see personal water skis as fun to ride and less expensive. The users of paper cartons constantly weigh the performance trade-offs with plastic containers and metal cans. Camera users consider the convenience and performance trade-offs when deciding whether to substitute a digital camera for a film-based camera. Competition from good-performing substitutes unleashes competitive pressures on industry participants to incorporate new performance features and attributes that makes their product offerings more competitive.

3. *Whether the costs that buyers incur in switching to the substitutes are high or low.* High switching costs deter switching to substitutes, while low switching costs make it easier for the sellers of attractive substitutes to lure buyers to their offering.[8] Typical switching costs include the time and inconvenience that may be involved, the costs of additional equipment, the time and cost in testing the quality

Figure 3.6   **Factors Affecting Competition from Substitute Products**

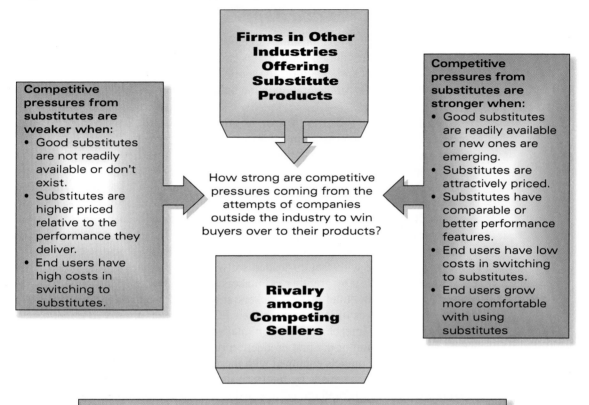

Firms in Other Industries Offering Substitute Products

Competitive pressures from substitutes are weaker when:
• Good substitutes are not readily available or don't exist.
• Substitutes are higher priced relative to the performance they deliver.
• End users have high costs in switching to substitutes.

How strong are competitive pressures coming from the attempts of companies outside the industry to win buyers over to their products?

Competitive pressures from substitutes are stronger when:
• Good substitutes are readily available or new ones are emerging.
• Substitutes are attractively priced.
• Substitutes have comparable or better performance features.
• End users have low costs in switching to substitutes.
• End users grow more comfortable with using substitutes

Rivalry among Competing Sellers

Signs That Competition from Substitutes Is Strong
• Sales of substitutes are growing faster than sales of the industry being analyzed (an indication that the sellers of substitutes are drawing customers away from the industry in question).
• Producers of substitutes are moving to add new capacity.
• Profits of the producers of substitutes are on the rise.

and reliability of the substitute, the psychological costs of severing old supplier relationships and establishing new ones, payments for technical help in making the changeover, and employee retraining costs. High switching costs can materially weaken the competitive pressures that industry members experience from substitutes unless the sellers of substitutes are successful in offsetting the high switching costs with enticing price discounts or additional performance enhancements.

Figure 3.6 summarizes the conditions that determine whether the competitive pressures from substitute products are strong, moderate, or weak.

As a rule, the lower the price of substitutes, the higher their quality and performance, and the lower the user's switching costs, the more intense the competitive pressures posed by substitute products. Other market indicators of the competitive strength of substitute products include (1) whether the sales of substitutes are growing faster than the sales of the industry being analyzed (a sign that the sellers of substitutes may be drawing customers away from the industry in question), (2) whether the producers of substitutes are moving to add new capacity, and (3) whether the profits of the producers of substitutes are on the rise.

Competitive Pressures Stemming from Supplier Bargaining Power and Supplier–Seller Collaboration

Whether supplier–seller relationships represent a weak or strong competitive force depends on (1) whether the major suppliers can exercise sufficient bargaining power to influence the terms and conditions of supply in their favor, and (2) the nature and extent of supplier–seller collaboration in the industry.

How Supplier Bargaining Power Can Create Competitive Pressures

Whenever the major suppliers to an industry have considerable leverage in determining the terms and conditions of the item they are supplying, then they are in a position to exert competitive pressure on one or more rival sellers. For instance, Microsoft and Intel, both of which supply personal computer (PC) makers with products that most PC users consider essential, are known for using their dominant market status not only to charge PC makers premium prices but also to leverage PC makers in other ways. Microsoft pressures PC makers to load only Microsoft products on the PCs they ship and to position the icons for Microsoft software prominently on the screens of new computers that come with factory-loaded software. Intel pushes greater use of Intel microprocessors in PCs by granting PC makers sizable advertising allowances on PC models equipped with "Intel Inside" stickers; it also tends to give PC makers that use the biggest percentages of Intel chips in their PC models top priority in filling orders for newly introduced Intel chips. Being on Intel's list of preferred customers helps a PC maker get an allocation of the first production runs of Intel's latest and greatest chips and thus get new PC models equipped with these chips to market ahead of rivals who are heavier users of chips made by Intel's rivals. The ability of Microsoft and Intel to pressure PC makers for preferential treatment of one kind or another in turn affects competition among rival PC makers.

Several other instances of supplier bargaining power are worth citing. Small-scale retailers must often contend with the power of manufacturers whose products enjoy prestigious and well-respected brand names; when a manufacturer knows that a retailer needs to stock the manufacturer's product because consumers expect to find the product on the shelves of retail stores where they shop, the manufacturer usually has some degree of pricing power and can also push hard for favorable shelf displays. Motor vehicle manufacturers typically exert considerable power over the terms and conditions with which they supply new vehicles to their independent automobile dealerships. The operators of franchised units of such chains as McDonald's, Dunkin' Donuts, Pizza Hut, Sylvan Learning Centers, and Hampton Inns must frequently agree not only to source some of their supplies from the franchisor at prices and terms favorable to that franchisor but also to operate their facilities in a manner largely dictated by the franchisor.

Strong supplier bargaining power is a competitive factor in industries where unions have been able to organize the workforces of some industry members but not others; those industry members that must negotiate wages, fringe benefits, and working conditions with powerful unions (which control the supply of labor) often find themselves with higher labor costs than their competitors with nonunion labor forces. The bigger the gap between union and nonunion labor costs in an industry, the more that unionized industry members must scramble to find ways to relieve the competitive pressure associated with their disadvantage on labor costs. High labor costs are proving a huge competitive liability to unionized supermarket chains like Kroger and Safeway in trying to combat the market share gains being made by Wal-Mart in supermarket retailing—Wal-Mart has a nonunion workforce, and the prices for supermarket items at its Supercenters tend to run 5 to 20 percent lower than those at unionized supermarket chains.

The factors that determine whether any of the suppliers to an industry are in a position to exert substantial bargaining power or leverage are fairly clear-cut:[9]

- *Whether the item being supplied is a commodity that is readily available from many suppliers at the going market price.* Suppliers have little or no bargaining power or leverage whenever industry members have the ability to source their requirements at competitive prices from any of several alternative and eager suppliers, perhaps dividing their purchases among two or more suppliers to promote lively competition for orders. The suppliers of commodity items have market power only when supplies become quite tight and industry members are so eager to secure what they need that they agree to terms more favorable to suppliers.

- *Whether a few large suppliers are the primary sources of a particular item.* The leading suppliers may well have pricing leverage unless they are plagued with excess capacity and are scrambling to secure additional orders for their products. Major suppliers with good reputations and strong demand for the items they supply are harder to wring concessions from than struggling suppliers striving to broaden their customer base or more fully utilize their production capacity.

- *Whether it is difficult or costly for industry members to switch their purchases from one supplier to another or to switch to attractive substitute inputs.* High switching costs signal strong bargaining power on the part of suppliers, whereas low switching costs and ready availability of good substitute inputs signal weak bargaining power. Soft-drink bottlers, for example, can counter the bargaining power of aluminum can suppliers by shifting or threatening to shift to greater use of plastic containers and introducing more attractive plastic container designs.

- *Whether certain needed inputs are in short supply.* Suppliers of items in short supply have some degree of pricing power, whereas a surge in the availability of particular items greatly weakens supplier pricing power and bargaining leverage.

- *Whether certain suppliers provide a differentiated input that enhances the performance or quality of the industry's product.* The more valuable that a particular input is in terms of enhancing the performance or quality of the products of industry members or of improving the efficiency of their production processes, the more bargaining leverage its suppliers are likely to possess.

- *Whether certain suppliers provide equipment or services that deliver valuable cost-saving efficiencies to industry members in operating their production processes.* Suppliers who provide cost-saving equipment or other valuable or necessary production-related services are likely to possess bargaining leverage. Industry members that do not source from such suppliers may find themselves at a cost disadvantage and thus under competitive pressure to do so (on terms that are favorable to the suppliers).

- *Whether suppliers provide an item that accounts for a sizable fraction of the costs of the industry's product.* The bigger the cost of a particular part or component, the more opportunity for the pattern of competition in the marketplace to be affected by the actions of suppliers to raise or lower their prices.

- *Whether industry members are major customers of suppliers.* As a rule, suppliers have less bargaining leverage when their sales to members of this one industry constitute a big percentage of their total sales. In such cases, the well-being of suppliers is closely tied to the well-being of their major customers.

Suppliers then have a big incentive to protect and enhance their customers' competitiveness via reasonable prices, exceptional quality, and ongoing advances in the technology of the items supplied.

- *Whether it makes good economic sense for industry members to integrate backward and self-manufacture items they have been buying from suppliers.* The make-or-buy issue generally boils down to whether suppliers who specialize in the production of a particular part or component and make them in volume for many different customers have the expertise and scale economies to supply as good or better component at a lower cost than industry members could achieve via self-manufacture. Frequently, it is difficult for industry members to self-manufacture parts and components more economically than they can obtain them from suppliers who specialize in making such items. For instance, most producers of outdoor power equipment (lawn mowers, rotary tillers, leaf blowers, etc.) find it cheaper to source the small engines they need from outside manufacturers who specialize in small-engine manufacture rather than make their own engines because the quantity of engines they need is too small to justify the investment in manufacturing facilities, master the production process, and capture scale economies. Specialists in small-engine manufacture, by supplying many kinds of engines to the whole power equipment industry, can obtain a big enough sales volume to fully realize scale economies, become proficient in all the manufacturing techniques, and keep costs low. As a rule, suppliers are safe from the threat of self-manufacture by their customers *until* the volume of parts a customer needs becomes large enough for the customer to justify backward integration into self-manufacture of the component. Suppliers also gain bargaining power when they have the resources and profit incentive to integrate forward into the business of the customers they are supplying and thus become a strong rival.

Figure 3.7 summarizes the conditions that tend to make supplier bargaining power strong or weak.

How Seller–Supplier Partnerships Can Create Competitive Pressures

In more and more industries, sellers are forging strategic partnerships with select suppliers in efforts to (1) reduce inventory and logistics costs (e.g., through just-in-time deliveries), (2) speed the availability of next-generation components, (3) enhance the quality of the parts and components being supplied and reduce defect rates, and (4) squeeze out important cost savings for both themselves and their suppliers. Numerous Internet technology applications are now available that permit real-time data sharing, eliminate paperwork, and produce cost savings all along the supply chain. The many benefits of effective seller–supplier collaboration can translate into competitive advantage for industry members that do the best job of managing supply chain relationships.

Dell Computer has used strategic partnering with key suppliers as a major element in its strategy to be the world's lowest-cost supplier of branded PCs, servers, and workstations. Because Dell has managed its supply chain relationships in ways that contribute to a low-cost, high-quality competitive edge in components supply, it has put enormous pressure on its PC rivals to try to imitate its supply chain management practices. Effective partnerships with suppliers on the part of one or more industry members can thus become a major source of competitive pressure for rival firms.

The more opportunities that exist for win–win efforts between a company and its suppliers, the less their relationship is characterized by who has the upper hand in

Figure 3.7   **Factors Affecting the Bargaining Power of Suppliers**

Supplier bargaining power is stronger when:
- Industry members incurs high costs in switching their purchases to alternative suppliers.
- Needed inputs are in short supply (which gives suppliers more leverage in setting prices).
- A supplier has a differentiated input that enhances the quality or performance of sellers' products or is a valuable or critical part of sellers' production process.
- There are only a few suppliers of a particular input.
- Some suppliers threaten to integrate forward into the business of industry members and perhaps become a powerful rival.

Supplier bargaining power is weaker when:
- The item being supplied is a commodity that is readily available from many suppliers at the going market price.
- Seller switching costs to alternative suppliers are low.
- Good substitute inputs exist or new ones emerge.
- There is a surge in the availability of supplies (thus greatly weakening supplier pricing power).
- Industry members account for a big fraction of suppliers' total sales and continued high volume purchases are important to the well-being of suppliers.
- Industry members are a threat to integrate backward into the business of suppliers and to self-manufacture their own requirements.
- Seller collaboration or partnering with selected suppliers provides attractive win–win opportunities.

bargaining with the other. Collaborative partnerships between a company and a supplier tend to last so long as the relationship is producing valuable benefits for both parties. Only if a supply partner is falling behind alternative suppliers is a company likely to switch suppliers and incur the costs and trouble of building close working ties with a different supplier.

Competitive Pressures Stemming from Buyer Bargaining Power and Seller–Buyer Collaboration

Whether seller–buyer relationships represent a weak or strong competitive force depends on (1) whether some or many buyers have sufficient bargaining leverage to obtain price concessions and other favorable terms and conditions of sale, and (2) the extent and competitive importance of seller–buyer strategic partnerships in the industry.

How Buyer Bargaining Power Can Create Competitive Pressures   As with suppliers, the leverage that certain types of buyers have in negotiating favorable terms can range from weak to strong. Individual consumers, for example, rarely have much bargaining power in negotiating price concessions or other favorable terms with sellers; the primary exceptions involve situations in which price haggling is customary, such as the purchase of new and used motor vehicles, homes, and certain big-ticket items like luxury watches, jewelry, and pleasure boats. For most consumer goods and services, individual buyers have no bargaining leverage—their option is to pay the seller's posted price or take their business elsewhere.

In contrast, large retail chains like Wal-Mart, Best Buy, Staples, and Home Depot typically have considerable negotiating leverage in purchasing products from manufacturers because of manufacturers' need for broad retail exposure and the most appealing shelf locations. Retailers may stock two or three competing brands of a product but rarely all competing brands, so competition among rival manufacturers for visibility on the shelves of popular multistore retailers gives such retailers significant bargaining strength. Major supermarket chains like Kroger, Safeway, and Royal Ahold, which provide access to millions of grocery shoppers, have sufficient bargaining power to demand promotional allowances and lump-sum payments (called slotting fees) from food products manufacturers in return for stocking certain brands or putting them in the best shelf locations. Motor vehicle manufacturers have strong bargaining power in negotiating to buy original equipment tires from Goodyear, Michelin, Bridgestone/Firestone, Continental, and Pirelli not only because they buy in large quantities but also because tire makers believe they gain an advantage in supplying replacement tires to vehicle owners if their tire brand is original equipment on the vehicle. "Prestige" buyers have a degree of clout in negotiating with sellers because a seller's reputation is enhanced by having prestige buyers on its customer list.

Even if buyers do not purchase in large quantities or offer a seller important market exposure or prestige, they gain a degree of bargaining leverage in the following circumstances:[10]

- *If buyers' costs of switching to competing brands or substitutes are relatively low*—Buyers who can readily switch brands or source from several sellers have more negotiating leverage than buyers who have high switching costs. When the products of rival sellers are virtually identical, it is relatively easy for buyers to switch from seller to seller at little or no cost and anxious sellers may be willing to make concessions to win or retain a buyer's business.

- *If the number of buyers is small or if a customer is particularly important to a seller*—The smaller the number of buyers, the less easy it is for sellers to find alternative buyers when a customer is lost to a competitor. The prospect of losing a customer not easily replaced often makes a seller more willing to grant concessions of one kind or another.

- *If buyer demand is weak and sellers are scrambling to secure additional sales of their products*—Weak or declining demand creates a "buyers' market"; conversely, strong or rapidly growing demand creates a "sellers' market" and shifts bargaining power to sellers.

- *If buyers are well informed about sellers' products, prices, and costs*—The more information buyers have, the better bargaining position they are in. The mushrooming availability of product information on the Internet is giving added bargaining power to individuals. Buyers can easily use the Internet to compare prices and features of vacation packages, shop for the best interest rates on mortgages and loans, and find the best prices on big-ticket items such as digital cameras. Bargain-hunting individuals can shop around for the best deal on the Internet and use that information to negotiate a better deal from local retailers; this method is becoming commonplace in buying new and used motor vehicles. Further, the Internet has created opportunities for manufacturers, wholesalers, retailers, and sometimes individuals to join online buying groups to pool their purchasing power and approach vendors for better terms than could be gotten individually. A multinational manufacturer's geographically scattered purchasing groups can use Internet technology to pool their orders with parts and components suppliers and bargain for volume discounts. Purchasing agents at some companies are banding together at third-party Web sites to pool corporate purchases to get better deals or special treatment.

- *If buyers pose a credible threat of integrating backward into the business of sellers*—Companies like Anheuser-Busch, Coors, and Heinz have integrated backward into metal can manufacturing to gain bargaining power in obtaining the balance of their can requirements from otherwise powerful metal can manufacturers. Retailers gain bargaining power by stocking and promoting their own private-label brands alongside manufacturers' name brands. Wal-Mart, for example, has elected to compete against Procter & Gamble (P&G), its biggest supplier, with its own brand of laundry detergent, called Sam's American Choice, which is priced 25 to 30 percent lower than P&G's Tide.

- *If buyers have discretion in whether and when they purchase the product*—Many consumers, if they are unhappy with the present deals offered on major appliances or hot tubs or home entertainment centers, may be in a position to delay purchase until prices and financing terms improve. If business customers are not happy with the prices or security features of bill-payment software systems, they can either delay purchase until next-generation products become available or attempt to develop their own software in-house. If college students believe that the prices of new textbooks are too high, they can purchase used copies.

Figure 3.8 highlights the factors causing buyer bargaining power to be strong or weak.

A final point to keep in mind is that *not all buyers of an industry's product have equal degrees of bargaining power with sellers*, and some may be less sensitive than others to price, quality, or service differences. For example, independent tire retailers have less bargaining power in purchasing tires than do Honda, Ford, and DaimlerChrysler (which buy in much larger quantities), and they are also less sensitive to quality. Motor vehicle manufacturers are very particular about tire quality and tire performance because of the effects on vehicle performance, and they drive a hard bargain with tire manufacturers on both price and quality. Apparel manufacturers confront significant bargaining power when selling to big retailers like JCPenney, Macy's, or L. L. Bean but they can command much better prices selling to small owner-managed apparel boutiques.

How Seller–Buyer Partnerships Can Create Competitive Pressures   Partnerships between sellers and buyers are an increasingly important element of the competitive picture in *business-to-business relationships* (as opposed to business-to-consumer relationships). Many sellers that provide items to business customers have found it in their mutual interest to collaborate closely on such matters as just-in-time deliveries, order processing, electronic invoice payments, and data sharing. Wal-Mart, for example, provides the manufacturers with which it does business (like Procter & Gamble) with daily sales at each of its stores so that the manufacturers can maintain sufficient inventories at Wal-Mart's distribution centers to keep the shelves at each Wal-Mart store amply stocked. Dell has partnered with its largest PC customers to create

Figure 3.8 **Factors Affecting the Bargaining Power of Buyers**

Buyer bargaining power is stronger when:
- Buyer switching costs to competing brands or substitute products are low.
- Buyers are large and can demand concessions when purchasing large quantities.
- Large-volume purchases by buyers are important to sellers.
- Buyer demand is weak or declining.
- There are only a few buyers—so that each one's business is important to sellers.
- Identity of buyer adds prestige to the seller's list of customers.
- Quantity and quality of information available to buyers improves.
- Buyers have the ability to postpone purchases until later if they do not like the present deals being offered by sellers.
- Some buyers are a threat to integrate backward into the business of sellers and become an important competitor.

Buyer bargaining power is weaker when:
- Buyers purchase the item infrequently or in small quantities.
- Buyer switching costs to competing brands are high.
- There is a surge in buyer demand that creates a "sellers' market."
- A seller's brand reputation is important to a buyer.
- A particular seller's product delivers quality or performance that is very important to buyer and that is not matched in other brands.
- Buyer collaboration or partnering with selected sellers provides attractive win–win opportunities.

online systems for over 50,000 corporate customers, providing their employees with information on approved product configurations, global pricing, paperless purchase orders, real-time order tracking, invoicing, purchasing history, and other efficiency tools. Dell loads a customer's software at the factory and installs asset tags so that customer setup time is minimal; it also helps customers upgrade their PC systems to next-generation hardware and software. Dell's partnerships with its corporate customers have put significant competitive pressure on other PC makers.

Is the Collective Strength of the Five Competitive Forces Conducive to Good Profitability?

Scrutinizing each of the five competitive forces one by one provides a powerful diagnosis of what competition is like in a given market. Once the strategist has gained an understanding of the specific competitive pressures comprising each force and determined whether these pressures constitute a strong, moderate, or weak competitive force, the next step is to evaluate the collective strength of the five forces and determine whether the state of competition is conducive to good profitability. Is the collective impact of the five competitive forces stronger than "normal"? Are some of the competitive forces sufficiently strong to undermine industry profitability? Can companies in this industry reasonably expect to earn decent profits in light of the prevailing competitive forces?

Is the Industry Competitively Attractive or Unattractive?   *As a rule, the stronger the collective impact of the five competitive forces, the lower the combined profitability of industry participants.* The most extreme case of a competitively unattractive industry is when all five forces are producing strong competitive pressures: Rivalry among sellers is vigorous, low entry barriers allow new rivals to gain a market foothold, competition from substitutes is intense, and both suppliers and customers are able to exercise considerable bargaining leverage. Fierce to strong competitive pressures coming from all five directions nearly always drive industry profitability to unacceptably low levels, frequently producing losses for many industry members and forcing some out of business. But an industry can be competitively unattractive even when not all five competitive forces are strong. Intense competitive pressures from just two or three of the five forces may suffice to destroy the conditions for good profitability and prompt some companies to exit the business. The manufacture of disk drives, for example, is brutally competitive; IBM recently announced the sale of its disk drive business to Hitachi, taking a loss of over $2 billion on its exit from the business. Especially intense competitive conditions seem to be the norm in tire manufacturing and apparel, two industries where profit margins have historically been thin.

> The stronger the forces of competition, the harder it becomes for industry members to earn attractive profits.

In contrast, when the collective impact of the five competitive forces is moderate to weak, an industry is competitively attractive in the sense that industry members can reasonably expect to earn good profits and a nice return on investment. The ideal competitive environment for earning superior profits is one in which both suppliers and customers are in weak bargaining positions, there are no good substitutes, high barriers block further entry, and rivalry among present sellers generates only moderate competitive pressures. Weak competition is the best of all possible worlds for also-ran companies because even they can usually eke out a decent profit—if a company can't make a decent profit when competition is weak, then its business outlook is indeed grim.

In most industries, the collective strength of the five competitive forces is somewhere near the middle of the two extremes of very intense and very weak, typically ranging from slightly stronger than normal to slightly weaker than normal and typically allowing well-managed companies with sound strategies to earn attractive profits.

Matching Company Strategy to Competitive Conditions   Working through the five-forces model step by step not only aids strategy makers in assessing whether the intensity of competition allows good profitability but also promotes sound strategic thinking about how to better match company strategy to the specific competitive character of the marketplace. Effectively matching a company's strategy to prevailing competitive conditions has two aspects:

> A company's strategy is increasingly effective the more it provides some insulation from competitive pressures and shifts the competitive battle in the company's favor.

1. Pursuing avenues that shield the firm from as many of the different competitive pressures as possible.
2. Initiating actions calculated to produce sustainable competitive advantage, thereby shifting competition in the company's favor, putting added competitive pressure on rivals, and perhaps even defining the business model for the industry.

But making headway on these two fronts first requires identifying competitive pressures, gauging the relative strength of each of the five competitive forces, and gaining a deep enough understanding of the state of competition in the industry to know which strategy buttons to push.

QUESTION 3: WHAT FACTORS ARE DRIVING INDUSTRY CHANGE AND WHAT IMPACTS WILL THEY HAVE?

An industry's present conditions don't necessarily reveal much about the strategically relevant ways in which the industry environment is changing. All industries are characterized by trends and new developments that gradually or speedily produce changes important enough to require a strategic response from participating firms. A popular hypothesis states that industries go through a life cycle of takeoff, rapid growth, early maturity and slowing growth, market saturation, and stagnation or decline. This hypothesis helps explain industry change—but it is far from complete.[11] There are more causes of industry change than an industry's normal progression through the life cycle—these need to be identified and their impacts understood.

The Concept of Driving Forces

Core Concept
Industry conditions change because important forces are *driving* industry participants (competitors, customers, or suppliers) to alter their actions; the ***driving forces*** in an industry are the *major underlying causes* of changing industry and competitive conditions—they have the biggest influence on how the industry landscape will be altered. Some driving forces originate in the outer ring of macroenvironment and some originate from the inner ring.

While it is important to track where an industry is in the life cycle, there's more analytical value in identifying the other factors that may be even stronger drivers of industry and competitive change. The point to be made here is that industry and competitive conditions change because forces are enticing or pressuring certain industry participants (competitors, customers, suppliers) to alter their actions in important ways.[12] The most powerful of the change agents are called **driving forces** because they have the biggest influences in reshaping the industry landscape and altering competitive conditions. Some driving forces originate in the outer ring of the company's macroenvironment (see Figure 3.2), but most originate in the company's more immediate industry and competitive environment.

Driving-forces analysis has three steps: (1) identifying what the driving forces are; (2) assessing whether the drivers of change are, on the whole, acting to make the industry more or less attractive; and (3) determining what strategy changes are needed to prepare for the impacts of the driving forces. All three steps merit further discussion.

Identifying an Industry's Driving Forces

Many developments can affect an industry powerfully enough to qualify as driving forces. Some drivers of change are unique and specific to a particular industry situation, but most drivers of industry and competitive change fall into one of the following categories:[13]

- *Emerging new Internet capabilities and applications*—Since the late 1990s, the Internet has woven its way into everyday business operations and the social fabric of life all across the world. Mushrooming Internet use, growing acceptance of Internet shopping, the emergence of high-speed Internet service and Voice over Internet Protocol (VoIP) technology, and an ever-growing series of Internet applications and capabilities have been major drivers of change in industry after industry. Companies are increasingly using online technology (1) to collaborate closely with suppliers and streamline their supply chains and (2) to revamp internal operations and squeeze out cost savings. Manufacturers can use their Web sites to access customers directly rather than distribute exclusively through traditional wholesale and retail channels. Businesses of all types can use Web stores to extend their geographic reach and vie for sales in areas where they formerly did not have a presence. The ability of companies to reach consumers via the Internet increases the number of rivals a company faces and often escalates rivalry by pitting pure online sellers against combination brick-and-click sellers against pure brick-and-mortar sellers. The Internet gives buyers unprecedented ability to research the product offerings of competitors and shop the market for the best value. Mounting ability of consumers to download music from the Internet via either file sharing or online music retailers has profoundly and re-shaped the music industry and the business of traditional brick-and-mortar music retailers. Widespread use of e-mail has forever eroded the business of providing fax services and the first-class mail delivery revenues of government postal services worldwide. Videoconferencing via the Internet can erode the demand for business travel. Online course offerings at universities have the potential to revolutionize higher education. The Internet of the future will feature faster speeds, dazzling applications, and over a billion connected gadgets performing an array of functions, thus driving further industry and competitive changes. But Internet-related impacts vary from industry to industry. The challenges here are to assess precisely how emerging Internet developments are altering a particular industry's landscape and to factor these impacts into the strategy-making equation.

- *Increasing globalization*—Competition begins to shift from primarily a regional or national focus to an international or global focus when industry members begin seeking out customers in foreign markets or when production activities begin to migrate to countries where costs are lowest. Globalization of competition really starts to take hold when one or more ambitious companies precipitate a race for worldwide market leadership by launching initiatives to expand into more and more country markets. Globalization can also be precipitated by the blossoming of consumer demand in more and more countries and by the actions of government officials in many countries to reduce trade barriers or open up once-closed markets to foreign competitors, as is occurring in many parts of Europe, Latin America, and Asia. Significant differences in labor costs among countries give manufacturers a strong incentive to locate plants for labor-intensive products in low-wage countries and use these plants to supply market demand across the world. Wages in China, India, Singapore, Mexico, and Brazil, for example, are about one-fourth those in the United States, Germany, and Japan. The forces of globalization are sometimes such a strong driver that companies find it highly advantageous, if not necessary, to spread their operating reach into more and more country markets. Globalization is very much a driver of industry change in such industries as credit cards, cell phones, digital cameras, golf and ski equipment, motor vehicles, steel, petroleum, personal computers, video games, public accounting, and textbook publishing.

- *Changes in an industry's long-term growth rate*—Shifts in industry growth up or down are a driving force for industry change, affecting the balance between industry supply and buyer demand, entry and exit, and the character and strength of competition. An upsurge in buyer demand triggers a race among established firms and newcomers to capture the new sales opportunities; ambitious companies with trailing market shares may see the upturn in demand as a golden opportunity to launch offensive strategies to broaden their customer base and move up several notches in the industry standings. A slowdown in the rate at which demand is growing nearly always portends mounting rivalry and increased efforts by some firms to maintain their high rates of growth by taking sales and market share away from rivals. If industry sales suddenly turn flat or begin to shrink after years of rising at double-digit levels, competition is certain to intensify as industry members scramble for the available business and as mergers and acquisitions result in industry consolidation to a smaller number of competitively stronger participants. Stagnating sales usually prompt both competitively weak and growth-oriented companies to sell their business operations to those industry members who elect to stick it out; as demand for the industry's product continues to shrink, the remaining industry members may be forced to close inefficient plants and retrench to a smaller production base—all of which results in a much-changed competitive landscape.

- *Changes in who buys the product and how they use it*—Shifts in buyer demographics and new ways of using the product can alter the state of competition by opening the way to market an industry's product through a different mix of dealers and retail outlets; prompting producers to broaden or narrow their product lines; bringing different sales and promotion approaches into play; and forcing adjustments in customer service offerings (credit, technical assistance, maintenance, and repair). The mushrooming popularity of downloading music from the Internet, storing music files on PC hard drives, and burning custom discs has forced recording companies to reexamine their distribution strategies and raised questions about the future of traditional retail music stores; at the same time, it has stimulated sales of disc burners and blank discs. Longer life expectancies and growing percentages of relatively well-to-do retirees are driving changes in such industries as health care, prescription drugs, recreational living, and vacation travel. The growing percentage of households with PCs and Internet access is opening opportunities for banks to expand their electronic bill-payment services and for retailers to move more of their customer services online.

- *Product innovation*—Competition in an industry is always affected by rivals racing to be first to introduce one new product or product enhancement after another. An ongoing stream of product innovations tends to alter the pattern of competition in an industry by attracting more first-time buyers, rejuvenating industry growth, and/or creating wider or narrower product differentiation among rival sellers. Successful new product introductions strengthen the market positions of the innovating companies, usually at the expense of companies that stick with their old products or are slow to follow with their own versions of the new product. Product innovation has been a key driving force in such industries as digital cameras, golf clubs, video games, toys, and prescription drugs.

- *Technological change and manufacturing process innovation*—Advances in technology can dramatically alter an industry's landscape, making it possible to produce new and better products at lower cost and opening up whole new industry frontiers. For instance, Voice over Internet Protocol (VoIP) technology has spawned low-cost, Internet-based phone networks that are stealing large numbers of customers away from traditional telephone companies worldwide (whose higher cost technology depends on hardwired connections via overhead and underground telephone lines). Flat-screen technology for PC monitors is killing the demand for conventional cathode ray tube (CRT) monitors. Liquid crystal display (LCD), plasma screen technology, and high-definition technology are precipitating a revolution in the television industry and driving use of cathode ray technology (CRT) into the background. MP3 technology is transforming how people listen to music. Digital technology is driving huge changes in the camera and film industries. Satellite radio technology is allowing satellite radio companies with their largely commercial-free programming to draw millions of listeners away from traditional radio stations whose revenue streams from commercials are dependent on audience size. Technological developments can also produce competitively significant changes in capital requirements, minimum efficient plant sizes, distribution channels and logistics, and learning/experience curve effects. In the steel industry, ongoing advances in electric arc minimill technology (which involve recycling scrap steel to make new products) have allowed steelmakers with state-of-the-art minimills to gradually expand into the production of more and more steel products, steadily taking sales and market share from higher-cost integrated producers (which make steel from scratch using iron ore, coke, and traditional blast furnace technology). Nucor Corporation, the leader of the minimill technology revolution in the United States, began operations in 1970 and has ridden the wave of technological advances in minimill technology to become the biggest U.S. steel producer (as of 2004) and ranks among the lowest-cost producers in the world. In a space of 30 years, advances in minimill technology have changed the face of the steel industry worldwide.

- *Marketing innovation*—When firms are successful in introducing new ways to *market* their products, they can spark a burst of buyer interest, widen industry demand, increase product differentiation, and lower unit costs—any or all of which can alter the competitive positions of rival firms and force strategy revisions. Online marketing is shaking up competition in electronics (where there are dozens of online electronics retailers, often with deep-discount prices) and office supplies (where Office Depot, Staples, and Office Max are using their Web sites to market office supplies to corporations, small businesses, schools and universities, and government agencies). Increasing numbers of music artists are marketing their recordings at their own Web sites rather than entering into contracts with recording studios that distribute through online and brick-and-mortar music retailers.

- *Entry or exit of major firms*—The entry of one or more foreign companies into a geographic market once dominated by domestic firms nearly always shakes up competitive conditions. Likewise, when an established domestic firm from another industry attempts entry either by acquisition or by launching its own start-up venture, it usually applies its skills and resources in some innovative fashion that pushes competition in new directions. Entry by a major firm thus often produces a new ball game, not only with new key players but also with new rules for competing. Similarly, exit of a major firm changes the competitive structure by reducing the number of market leaders (perhaps increasing the dominance of the leaders who remain) and causing a rush to capture the exiting firm's customers.

- *Diffusion of technical know-how across more companies and more countries*—As knowledge about how to perform a particular activity or execute a particular manufacturing technology spreads, the competitive advantage held by firms originally possessing this know-how erodes. Knowledge diffusion can occur through scientific journals, trade publications, on-site plant tours, word of mouth among suppliers and customers, employee migration, and Internet sources. It can also occur when those possessing technological knowledge license others to use that knowledge for a royalty fee or team up with a company interested in turning the technology into a new business venture. Quite often, technological know-how can be acquired by simply buying a company that has the wanted skills, patents, or manufacturing capabilities. In recent years, *rapid technology transfer across national boundaries has been a prime factor in causing industries to become more globally competitive.* As companies worldwide gain access to valuable technical know-how, they upgrade their manufacturing capabilities in a long-term effort to compete head-on with established companies. Cross-border technology transfer has made the once domestic industries of automobiles, tires, consumer electronics, telecommunications, computers, and others increasingly global.

- *Changes in cost and efficiency*—Widening or shrinking differences in the costs among key competitors tend to dramatically alter the state of competition. The low cost of fax and e-mail transmission has put mounting competitive pressure on the relatively inefficient and high-cost operations of the U.S. Postal Service—sending a one-page fax is cheaper and far quicker than sending a first-class letter; sending e-mail is faster and cheaper still. In the steel industry, the lower costs of companies using electric-arc furnaces to recycle scrap steel into new steel products has forced traditional manufacturers that produce steel from iron ore using blast furnace technology to overhaul their plants and to withdraw totally from making those steel products where they could no longer be cost competitive. Shrinking cost differences in producing multifeatured mobile phones is turning the mobile phone market into a commodity business and causing more buyers to base their purchase decisions on price.

- *Growing buyer preferences for differentiated products instead of a commodity product (or for a more standardized product instead of strongly differentiated products)*—When buyer tastes and preferences start to diverge, sellers can win a loyal following with product offerings that stand apart from those of rival sellers. In recent years, beer drinkers have grown less loyal to a single brand and have begun to drink a variety of domestic and foreign beers; as a consequence, beer manufacturers have introduced a host of new brands and malt beverages with different tastes and flavors. Buyer preferences for motor vehicles are becoming increasingly diverse, with few models generating sales of more than 250,000 units annually. When a shift from standardized to differentiated products occurs, the driver of change is the contest among rivals to cleverly outdifferentiate one another.

    However, buyers sometimes decide that a standardized, budget-priced product suits their requirements as well as or better than a premium-priced product with lots of snappy features and personalized services. Online brokers, for example, have used the lure of cheap commissions to attract many investors willing to place their own buy–sell orders via the Internet; growing acceptance of online trading has put significant competitive pressures on full-service brokers whose business model has always revolved around convincing clients of the value of asking for personalized advice from professional brokers and paying their high commission fees to make trades. Pronounced shifts toward greater product standardization usually spawn lively price competition and force rival sellers to drive down their costs to maintain profitability. The lesson here is that competition is driven partly by whether the market forces in motion are acting to increase or decrease product differentiation.

- *Reductions in uncertainty and business risk*—An emerging industry is typically characterized by much uncertainty over potential market size, how much time and money will be needed to surmount technological problems, and what distribution channels and buyer segments to emphasize. Emerging industries tend to attract only risk-taking entrepreneurial companies. Over time, however, if the business model of industry pioneers proves profitable and market demand for the product appears durable, more conservative firms are usually enticed to enter the market. Often, these later entrants are large, financially strong firms looking to invest in attractive growth industries.

   Lower business risks and less industry uncertainty also affect competition in international markets. In the early stages of a company's entry into foreign markets, conservatism prevails and firms limit their downside exposure by using less risky strategies like exporting, licensing, joint marketing agreements, or joint ventures with local companies to accomplish entry. Then, as experience accumulates and perceived risk levels decline, companies move more boldly and more independently, making acquisitions, constructing their own plants, putting in their own sales and marketing capabilities to build strong competitive positions in each country market, and beginning to link the strategies in each country to create a more globalized strategy.

- *Regulatory influences and government policy changes*—Government regulatory actions can often force significant changes in industry practices and strategic approaches. Deregulation has proved to be a potent pro-competitive force in the airline, banking, natural gas, telecommunications, and electric utility industries. Government efforts to reform Medicare and health insurance have become potent driving forces in the health care industry. In international markets, host governments can drive competitive changes by opening their domestic markets to foreign participation or closing them to protect domestic companies. Note that this driving force is spawned by forces in a company's macroenvironment.

- *Changing societal concerns, attitudes, and lifestyles*—Emerging social issues and changing attitudes and lifestyles can be powerful instigators of industry change. Growing antismoking sentiment has emerged as a major driver of change in the tobacco industry; concerns about terrorism are having a big impact on the travel industry. Consumer concerns about salt, sugar, chemical additives, saturated fat, cholesterol, carbohydrates, and nutritional value have forced food producers to revamp food-processing techniques, redirect R&D efforts into the use of healthier ingredients, and compete in developing nutritious, good-tasting products. Safety concerns have driven product design changes in the automobile, toy, and outdoor power equipment industries, to mention a few. Increased interest in physical fitness has spawned new industries in exercise equipment, biking, outdoor apparel, sports gyms and recreation centers, vitamin and nutrition supplements, and medically supervised diet programs. Social concerns about air and water pollution have forced industries to incorporate expenditures for controlling pollution into their cost structures. Shifting societal concerns, attitudes, and lifestyles alter the pattern of competition, usually favoring those

Table 3.2   **The Most Common Driving Forces**

1. Emerging new Internet capabilities and applications
2. Increasing globalization
3. Changes in an industry's long-term growth rate
4. Changes in who buys the product and how they use it
5. Product innovation
6. Technological change and manufacturing process innovation
7. Marketing innovation
8. Entry or exit of major firms
9. Diffusion of technical know-how across more companies and more countries
10. Changes in cost and efficiency
11. Growing buyer preferences for differentiated products instead of a commodity product (or for a more standardized product instead of strongly differentiated products)
12. Reductions in uncertainty and business risk
13. Regulatory influences and government policy changes
14. Changing societal concerns, attitudes, and lifestyles

players that respond quickly and creatively with products targeted to the new trends and conditions. As with the preceding driving force, this driving force springs from factors at work in a company's macroenvironment.

Table 3.2 lists these 14 most common driving forces.

That there are so many different potential driving forces explains why it is too simplistic to view industry change only in terms of moving through the different stages in an industry's life cycle and why a full understanding of all types of change drivers is a fundamental part of industry analysis. However, while many forces of change may be at work in a given industry, no more than three or four are likely to be true driving forces powerful enough to qualify as the *major determinants* of why and how the industry is changing. Thus company strategists must resist the temptation to label every change they see as a driving force; the analytical task is to evaluate the forces of industry and competitive change carefully enough to separate major factors from minor ones.

Assessing the Impact of the Driving Forces

An important part of driving-forces analysis is to determine whether the collective impact of the driving forces will be to increase or decrease market demand, make competition more or less intense, and lead to higher or lower industry profitability.

Just identifying the driving forces is not sufficient, however. The second, and more important, step in driving-forces analysis is to determine whether the prevailing driving forces are, on the whole, acting to make the industry environment more or less attractive. Answers to three questions are needed here:

1. Are the driving forces collectively acting to cause demand for the industry's product to increase or decrease?
2. Are the driving forces acting to make competition more or less intense?
3. Will the combined impacts of the driving forces lead to higher or lower industry profitability?

Getting a handle on the collective impact of the driving forces usually requires looking at the likely effects of each force separately, since the driving forces may not all be pushing change in the same direction. For example, two driving forces may be acting to spur demand for the industry's product while one driving force may be working to curtail demand. Whether the net effect on industry demand is up or down hinges on which driving forces are the more powerful. The analyst's objective here is to get a good grip on what external factors are shaping industry change and what difference these factors will make.

Developing a Strategy That Takes the Impacts of the Driving Forces into Account

The third step of driving-forces analysis—where the real payoff for strategy making comes—is for managers to draw some conclusions about what strategy adjustments will be needed to deal with the impacts of the driving forces. The real value of doing driving-forces analysis is to gain better understanding of what strategy adjustments will be needed to cope with the drivers of industry change and the impacts they are likely to have on market demand, competitive intensity, and industry profitability. In short, the strategy-making challenge that flows from driving-forces analysis is what to do to prepare for the industry and competitive changes being wrought by the driving forces. Indeed, without understanding the forces driving industry change and the impacts these forces will have on the character of the industry environment and on the company's business over the next one to three years, managers are ill-prepared to craft a strategy tightly matched to emerging conditions. Similarly, if managers are uncertain about the implications of one or more driving forces, or if their views are incomplete or off base, it's difficult for them to craft a strategy that is responsive to the driving forces and their consequences for the industry. So driving-forces analysis is not something to take lightly; it has practical value and is basic to the task of thinking strategically about where the industry is headed and how to prepare for the changes ahead.

> Driving-forces analysis, when done properly, pushes company managers to think about what's around the corner and what the company needs to be doing to get ready for it.

> The real payoff of driving-forces analysis is to help managers understand what strategy changes are needed to prepare for the impacts of the driving forces.

QUESTION 4: WHAT MARKET POSITIONS DO RIVALS OCCUPY—WHO IS STRONGLY POSITIONED AND WHO IS NOT?

Since competing companies commonly sell in different price/quality ranges, emphasize different distribution channels, incorporate product features that appeal to different types of buyers, have different geographic coverage, and so on, it stands to reason that some companies enjoy stronger or more attractive market positions than other companies. Understanding which companies are strongly positioned and which are weakly positioned is an integral part of analyzing an industry's competitive structure. The best technique for revealing the market positions of industry competitors is **strategic group mapping.**[14] This analytical tool is useful for comparing the market positions of each firm separately or for grouping them into like positions when an industry has so many competitors that it is not practical to examine each one in depth.

> **Core Concept**
> ***Strategic group mapping*** is a technique for displaying the different market or competitive positions that rival firms occupy in the industry.

Using Strategic Group Maps to Assess the Market Positions of Key Competitors

A **strategic group** consists of those industry members with similar competitive approaches and positions in the market.[15] Companies in the same strategic group can resemble one another in any of several ways: They may have comparable product-line breadth, sell in the same price/quality range, emphasize the same distribution channels, use essentially the same product attributes to appeal to similar types of buyers, depend on identical technological approaches, or offer buyers similar services and technical assistance.[16] An industry contains only one strategic group when all sellers pursue essentially identical strategies and have comparable market positions. At the other extreme, an industry may contain as many strategic groups as there are competitors when each rival pursues a distinctively different competitive approach and occupies a substantially different market position.

Core Concept
A **strategic group** is a cluster of industry rivals that have similar competitive approaches and market positions.

The procedure for constructing a *strategic group map* is straightforward:

- Identify the competitive characteristics that differentiate firms in the industry. Typical variables are price/quality range (high, medium, low); geographic coverage (local, regional, national, global); degree of vertical integration (none, partial, full); product-line breadth (wide, narrow); use of distribution channels (one, some, all); and degree of service offered (no-frills, limited, full).
- Plot the firms on a two-variable map using pairs of these differentiating characteristics.
- Assign firms that fall in about the same strategy space to the same strategic group.
- Draw circles around each strategic group, making the circles proportional to the size of the group's share of total industry sales revenues.

This produces a two-dimensional diagram like the one for the retailing industry in Illustration Capsule 3.1.

Several guidelines need to be observed in mapping the positions of strategic groups in the industry's overall strategy space.[17] First, the two variables selected as axes for the map should *not* be highly correlated; if they are, the circles on the map will fall along a diagonal and strategy makers will learn nothing more about the relative positions of competitors than they would by considering just one of the variables. For instance, if companies with broad product lines use multiple distribution channels while companies with narrow lines use a single distribution channel, then looking at broad versus narrow product lines reveals just as much about who is positioned where as looking at single versus multiple distribution channels; that is, one of the variables is redundant. Second, the variables chosen as axes for the map should expose big differences in how rivals position themselves to compete in the marketplace. This, of course, means analysts must identify the characteristics that differentiate rival firms and use these differences as variables for the axes and as the basis for deciding which firm belongs in which strategic group. Third, the variables used as axes don't have to be either quantitative or continuous; rather, they can be discrete variables or defined in terms of distinct classes and combinations. Fourth, drawing the sizes of the circles on the map proportional to the combined sales of the firms in each strategic group allows the map to reflect the relative sizes of each strategic group. Fifth, if more than two good competitive variables can be used as axes for the map, several maps can be drawn to give different exposures to the competitive positioning relationships present

Illustration Capsule 3.1

Comparative Market Positions of Selected Retail Chains: A Strategic Group Map Application

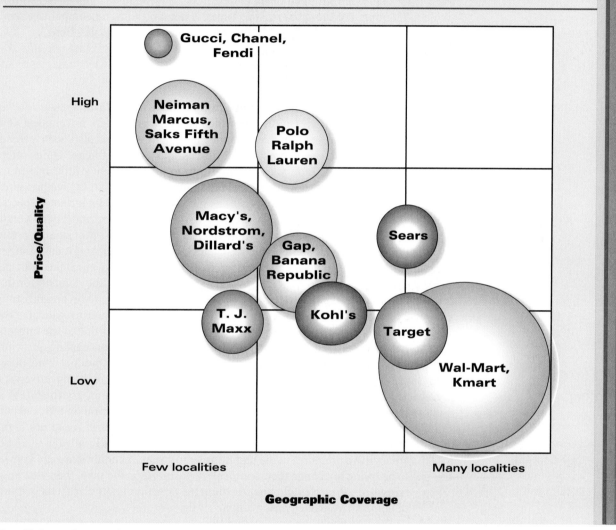

Note: Circles are drawn roughly proportional to the sizes of the chains, based on revenues.

in the industry's structure. Because there is not necessarily one best map for portraying how competing firms are positioned in the market, it is advisable to experiment with different pairs of competitive variables.

What Can Be Learned from Strategic Group Maps?

Strategic group maps are revealing in several respects. The most important has to do with which rivals are similarly positioned and are thus close rivals and which are distant rivals. Generally speaking, *the closer strategic groups are to each other on the*

Strategic group maps reveal which companies are close competitors and which are distant competitors.

map, the stronger the cross-group competitive rivalry tends to be. Although firms in the same strategic group are the closest rivals, the next closest rivals are in the immediately adjacent groups.[18] Often, firms in strategic groups that are far apart on the map hardly compete at all. For instance, Wal-Mart's clientele, merchandise selection, and pricing points are much too different to justify calling them close competitors of Neiman Marcus or Saks Fifth Avenue in retailing. For the same reason, Timex is not a meaningful competitive rival of Rolex, and Subaru is not a close competitor of Lincoln or Mercedes-Benz.

The second thing to be gleaned from strategic group mapping is that *not all positions on the map are equally attractive.* Two reasons account for why some positions can be more attractive than others:

1. *Prevailing competitive pressures and industry driving forces favor some strategic groups and hurt others.*[19] Discerning which strategic groups are advantaged and disadvantaged requires scrutinizing the map in light of what has also been learned from the prior analysis of competitive forces and driving forces. Quite often the strength of competition varies from group to group—there's little reason to believe that all firms in an industry feel the same degrees of competitive pressure, since their strategies and market positions may well differ in important respects. For instance, the competitive battle among Wal-Mart, Target, and Sears/Kmart (Kmart acquired Sears in 2005) is more intense (with consequently smaller profit margins) than the rivalry among Gucci, Chanel, Fendi, and other high-end fashion retailers. Likewise, industry driving forces may be acting to grow the demand for the products of firms in some strategic groups and shrink the demand for the products of firms in other strategic groups—as is the case in the radio broadcasting industry where satellite radio firms like XM and Sirius stand to gain market ground at the expense of commercial-based radio broadcasters due to the impacts of such driving forces as technological advances in satellite broadcasting, growing buyer preferences for more diverse radio programming, and product innovation in satellite radio devices. Firms in strategic groups that are being adversely impacted by intense competitive pressures or driving forces may try to shift to a more favorably situated group. But shifting to a different position on the map can prove difficult when entry barriers for the target strategic group are high. Moreover, attempts to enter a new strategic group nearly always increase competitive pressures in the target strategic group. If certain firms are known to be trying to change their competitive positions on the map, then attaching arrows to the circles showing the targeted direction helps clarify the picture of competitive maneuvering among rivals.

Core Concept
Not all positions on a strategic group map are equally attractive.

2. *The profit potential of different strategic groups varies due to the strengths and weaknesses in each group's market position.* The profit prospects of firms in different strategic groups can vary from good to ho-hum to poor because of differing growth rates for the principal buyer segments served by each group, differing degrees of competitive rivalry within strategic groups, differing degrees of exposure to competition from substitute products outside the industry, and differing degrees of supplier or customer bargaining power from group to group.

Thus, part of strategic group map analysis always entails drawing conclusions about where on the map is the "best" place to be and why. Which companies/strategic groups are destined to prosper because of their positions? Which companies/strategic groups seem destined to struggle because of their positions? What accounts for why some parts of the map are better than others?

QUESTION 5: WHAT STRATEGIC MOVES ARE RIVALS LIKELY TO MAKE NEXT?

Unless a company pays attention to what competitors are doing and knows their strengths and weaknesses, it ends up flying blind into competitive battle. As in sports, scouting the opposition is essential. *Competitive intelligence* about rivals' strategies, their latest actions and announcements, their resource strengths and weaknesses, the efforts being made to improve their situation, and the thinking and leadership styles of their executives is valuable for predicting or anticipating the strategic moves competitors are likely to make next in the marketplace. Having good information to predict the strategic direction and likely moves of key competitors allows a company to prepare defensive countermoves, to craft its own strategic moves with some confidence about what market maneuvers to expect from rivals, and to exploit any openings that arise from competitors' missteps or strategy flaws.

> Good scouting reports on rivals provide a valuable assist in anticipating what moves rivals are likely to make next and outmaneuvering them in the marketplace.

Identifying Competitors' Strategies and Resource Strengths and Weaknesses

Keeping close tabs on a competitor's strategy entails monitoring what the rival is doing in the marketplace, what its management is saying in company press releases, information posted on the company's Web site (especially press releases and the presentations management has recently made to securities analysts), and such public documents as annual reports and 10-K filings, articles in the business media, and the reports of securities analysts. (Figure 1.1 in Chapter 1 indicates what to look for in identifying a company's strategy.) Company personnel may be able to pick up useful information from a rival's exhibits at trade shows and from conversations with a rival's customers, suppliers, and former employees.[20] Many companies have a competitive intelligence unit that sifts through the available information to construct up-to-date strategic profiles of rivals—their current strategies, resource strengths and competitive capabilities, competitive shortcomings, press releases, and recent executive pronouncements. Such profiles are typically updated regularly and made available to managers and other key personnel.

Those who gather competitive intelligence on rivals, however, can sometimes cross the fine line between honest inquiry and unethical or even illegal behavior. For example, calling rivals to get information about prices, the dates of new product introductions, or wage and salary levels is legal, but misrepresenting one's company affiliation during such calls is unethical. Pumping rivals' representatives at trade shows is ethical only if one wears a name tag with accurate company affiliation indicated. Avon Products at one point secured information about its biggest rival, Mary Kay Cosmetics (MKC), by having its personnel search through the garbage bins outside MKC's headquarters.[21] When MKC officials learned of the action and sued, Avon claimed it did nothing illegal, since a 1988 Supreme Court case had ruled that trash left on public property (in this case, a sidewalk) was anyone's for the taking. Avon even produced a videotape of its removal of the trash at the MKC site. Avon won the lawsuit—but Avon's action, while legal, scarcely qualifies as ethical.

In sizing up competitors, it makes sense for company strategists to make three assessments:

1. Which competitor has the best strategy? Which competitors appear to have flawed or weak strategies?

2. Which competitors are poised to gain market share, and which ones seem destined to lose ground?

3. Which competitors are likely to rank among the industry leaders five years from now? Do one or more up-and-coming competitors have powerful strategies and sufficient resource capabilities to overtake the current industry leader?

The industry's *current* major players are generally easy to identify, but some of the leaders may be plagued with weaknesses that are causing them to lose ground; other notable rivals may lack the resources and capabilities to remain strong contenders given the superior strategies and capabilities of up-and-coming companies. In evaluating which competitors are favorably or unfavorably positioned to gain market ground, company strategists need to focus on why there is potential for some rivals to do better or worse than other rivals. Usually, a competitor's prospects are a function of whether it is in a strategic group that is being favored or hurt by competitive pressures and driving forces, whether its strategy has resulted in competitive advantage or disadvantage, and whether its resources and capabilities are well suited for competing on the road ahead.

> Today's market leaders don't automatically become tomorrow's.

Predicting Competitors' Next Moves

Predicting the next strategic moves of competitors is the hardest yet most useful part of competitor analysis. Good clues about what actions a specific company is likely to undertake can often be gleaned from how well it is faring in the marketplace, the problems or weaknesses it needs to address, and how much pressure it is under to improve its financial performance. Content rivals are likely to continue their present strategy with only minor fine-tuning. Ailing rivals can be performing so poorly that fresh strategic moves are virtually certain. Ambitious rivals looking to move up in the industry ranks are strong candidates for launching new strategic offensives to pursue emerging market opportunities and exploit the vulnerabilities of weaker rivals.

Since the moves a competitor is likely to make are generally predicated on the views their executives have about the industry's future and their beliefs about their firm's situation, it makes sense to closely scrutinize the public pronouncements of rival company executives about where the industry is headed and what it will take to be successful, what they are saying about their firm's situation, information from the grapevine about what they are doing, and their past actions and leadership styles. Other considerations in trying to predict what strategic moves rivals are likely to make next include the following:

- Which rivals badly need to increase their unit sales and market share? What strategic options are they most likely to pursue: lowering prices, adding new models and styles, expanding their dealer networks, entering additional geographic markets, boosting advertising to build better brand-name awareness, acquiring a weaker competitor, or placing more emphasis on direct sales via their Web site?
- Which rivals have a strong incentive, along with the resources, to make major strategic changes, perhaps moving to a different position on the strategic group map? Which rivals are probably locked in to pursuing the same basic strategy with only minor adjustments?
- Which rivals are good candidates to be acquired? Which rivals may be looking to make an acquisition and are financially able to do so?

- Which rivals are likely to enter new geographic markets?
- Which rivals are strong candidates to expand their product offerings and enter new product segments where they do not currently have a presence?

To succeed in predicting a competitor's next moves, company strategists need to have a good feel for each rival's situation, how its managers think, and what the rival's best strategic options are. Doing the necessary detective work can be tedious and time-consuming, but scouting competitors well enough to anticipate their next moves allows managers to prepare effective countermoves (perhaps even beat a rival to the punch) and to take rivals' probable actions into account in crafting their own best course of action.

> Managers who fail to study competitors closely risk being caught napping when rivals make fresh and perhaps bold strategic moves.

QUESTION 6: WHAT ARE THE KEY FACTORS FOR FUTURE COMPETITIVE SUCCESS?

An industry's **key success factors (KSFs)** are those competitive factors that most affect industry members' ability to prosper in the marketplace—the particular strategy elements, product attributes, resources, competencies, competitive capabilities, and market achievements that spell the difference between being a strong competitor and a weak competitor—and sometimes between profit and loss. KSFs by their very nature are so important to future competitive success that *all firms* in the industry must pay close attention to them or risk becoming an industry also-ran. To indicate the significance of KSFs another way, how well a company's product offering, resources, and capabilities measure up against an industry's KSFs determines just how financially and competitively successful that company will be. Identifying KSFs, in light of the prevailing and anticipated industry and competitive conditions, is therefore always a top-priority analytical and strategy-making consideration. Company strategists need to understand the industry landscape well enough to separate the factors most important to competitive success from those that are less important.

> **Core Concept**
> **Key success factors** are the product attributes, competencies, competitive capabilities, and market achievements with the greatest impact on future competitive success in the marketplace.

In the beer industry, the KSFs are full utilization of brewing capacity (to keep manufacturing costs low), a strong network of wholesale distributors (to get the company's brand stocked and favorably displayed in retail outlets where beer is sold), and clever advertising (to induce beer drinkers to buy the company's brand and thereby pull beer sales through the established wholesale/retail channels). In apparel manufacturing, the KSFs are appealing designs and color combinations (to create buyer interest) and low-cost manufacturing efficiency (to permit attractive retail pricing and ample profit margins). In tin and aluminum cans, because the cost of shipping empty cans is substantial, one of the keys is having can-manufacturing facilities located close to end-use customers. Key success factors thus vary from industry to industry, and even from time to time within the same industry, as driving forces and competitive conditions change. Table 3.3 lists the most common types of industry key success factors.

An industry's key success factors can usually be deduced from what was learned from the previously described analysis of the industry and competitive environment. Which factors are most important to future competitive success flow directly from the industry's dominant characteristics, what competition is like, the impacts of the driving forces, the comparative market positions of industry members, and the likely

Table 3.3 **Common Types of Industry Key Success Factors**

Technology-related KSFs	• Expertise in a particular technology or in scientific research (important in pharmaceuticals, Internet applications, mobile communications, and most high-tech industries) • Proven ability to improve production processes (important in industries where advancing technology opens the way for higher manufacturing efficiency and lower production costs)
Manufacturing-related KSFs	• Ability to achieve scale economies and/or capture learning/experience curve effects (important to achieving low production costs) • Quality control know-how (important in industries where customers insist on product reliability) • High utilization of fixed assets (important in capital-intensive, high-fixed-cost industries) • Access to attractive supplies of skilled labor • High labor productivity (important for items with high labor content) • Low-cost product design and engineering (reduces manufacturing costs) • Ability to manufacture or assemble products that are customized to buyer specifications
Distribution-related KSFs	• A strong network of wholesale distributors/dealers • Strong direct sales capabilities via the Internet and/or having company-owned retail outlets • Ability to secure favorable display space on retailer shelves
Marketing-related KSFs	• Breadth of product line and product selection • A well-known and well-respected brand name • Fast, accurate technical assistance • Courteous, personalized customer service • Accurate filling of buyer orders (few back orders or mistakes) • Customer guarantees and warranties (important in mail-order and online retailing, big-ticket purchases, new product introductions) • Clever advertising
Skills and capability-related KSFs	• A talented workforce (important in professional services like accounting and investment banking) • National or global distribution capabilities • Product innovation capabilities (important in industries where rivals are racing to be first-to-market with new product attributes or performance features) • Design expertise (important in fashion and apparel industries) • Short delivery time capability • Supply chain management capabilities • Strong e-commerce capabilities—a user-friendly Web site and/or skills in using Internet technology applications to streamline internal operations
Other types of KSFs	• Overall low costs (not just in manufacturing) so as to be able to meet customer expectations of low price • Convenient locations (important in many retailing businesses) • Ability to provide fast, convenient after-the-sale repairs and service • A strong balance sheet and access to financial capital (important in newly emerging industries with high degrees of business risk and in capital-intensive industries) • Patent protection

next moves of key rivals. In addition, the answers to three questions help identify an industry's key success factors:

1. On what basis do buyers of the industry's product choose between the competing brands of sellers? That is, what product attributes are crucial?
2. Given the nature of competitive rivalry and the competitive forces prevailing in the marketplace, what resources and competitive capabilities does a company need to have to be competitively successful?
3. What shortcomings are almost certain to put a company at a significant competitive disadvantage?

Only rarely are there more than five or six key factors for future competitive success. And even among these, two or three usually outrank the others in importance. Managers should therefore bear in mind the purpose of identifying key success factors— to determine which factors are most important to future competitive success— and resist the temptation to label a factor that has only minor importance a KSF. To compile a list of every factor that matters even a little bit defeats the purpose of concentrating management attention on the factors truly critical to long-term competitive success.

Correctly diagnosing an industry's KSFs raises a company's chances of crafting a sound strategy. The goal of company strategists should be to design a strategy aimed at stacking up well on all of the industry's future KSFs and trying to be *distinctively better* than rivals on one (or possibly two) of the KSFs. Indeed, companies that stand out or excel on a particular KSF are likely to enjoy a stronger market position—*being distinctively better than rivals on one or two key success factors tends to translate into competitive advantage.* Hence, using the industry's KSFs as *cornerstones* for the company's strategy and trying to gain sustainable competitive advantage by excelling at one particular KSF is a fruitful competitive strategy approach.[22]

> **Core Concept**
> A sound strategy incorporates the intent to stack up well on all of the industry's key success factors and to excel on one or two KSFs.

QUESTION 7: DOES THE OUTLOOK FOR THE INDUSTRY PRESENT THE COMPANY WITH AN ATTRACTIVE OPPORTUNITY?

The final step in evaluating the industry and competitive environment is to use the preceding analysis to decide whether the outlook for the industry presents the company with a sufficiently attractive business opportunity. The important factors on which to base such a conclusion include:

- The industry's growth potential.
- Whether powerful competitive forces are squeezing industry profitability to subpar levels and whether competition appears destined to grow stronger or weaker.
- Whether industry profitability will be favorably or unfavorably affected by the prevailing driving forces.
- The degrees of risk and uncertainty in the industry's future.
- Whether the industry as a whole confronts severe problems—regulatory or environmental issues, stagnating buyer demand, industry overcapacity, mounting competition, and so on.

- The company's competitive position in the industry vis-à-vis rivals. (Being a well-entrenched leader or strongly positioned contender in a lackluster industry may present adequate opportunity for good profitability; however, having to fight a steep uphill battle against much stronger rivals may hold little promise of eventual market success or good return on shareholder investment, even though the industry environment is attractive.)

- The company's potential to capitalize on the vulnerabilities of weaker rivals, perhaps converting a relatively unattractive *industry* situation into a potentially rewarding *company* opportunity.

- Whether the company has sufficient competitive strength to defend against or counteract the factors that make the industry unattractive.

- Whether continued participation in this industry adds importantly to the firm's ability to be successful in other industries in which it may have business interests.

Core Concept

The degree to which an industry is attractive or unattractive is not the same for all industry participants and all potential entrants; the attractiveness of the opportunities an industry presents depends heavily on whether a company has the resource strengths and competitive capabilities to capture them.

As a general proposition, *if an industry's overall profit prospects are above average, the industry environment is basically attractive; if industry profit prospects are below average, conditions are unattractive.* However, it is a mistake to think of a particular industry as being equally attractive or unattractive to all industry participants and all potential entrants. Attractiveness is relative, not absolute, and conclusions one way or the other have to be drawn from the perspective of a particular company. Industries attractive to insiders may be unattractive to outsiders. Companies on the outside may look at an industry's environment and conclude that it is an unattractive business for them to get into, given the prevailing entry barriers, the difficulty of challenging current market leaders with their particular resources and competencies, and the opportunities they have elsewhere. Industry environments unattractive to weak competitors may be attractive to strong competitors. A favorably positioned company may survey a business environment and see a host of opportunities that weak competitors cannot capture.

When a company decides an industry is fundamentally attractive and presents good opportunities, a strong case can be made that it should invest aggressively to capture the opportunities it sees and to improve its long-term competitive position in the business. When a strong competitor concludes an industry is relatively unattractive and lacking in opportunity, it may elect to simply protect its present position, investing cautiously if at all and looking for opportunities in other industries. A competitively weak company in an unattractive industry may see its best option as finding a buyer, perhaps a rival, to acquire its business.

Key Points

Thinking strategically about a company's external situation involves probing for answers to the following seven questions:

1. *What are the industry's dominant economic features?* Industries differ significantly on such factors as market size and growth rate, the number and relative sizes of both buyers and sellers, the geographic scope of competitive rivalry, the degree of product differentiation, the speed of product innovation, demand–supply conditions, the extent of vertical integration, and the extent of scale economies and learning-curve effects. In addition to setting the stage for the analysis to come,

identifying an industry's economic features also promotes understanding of the kinds of strategic moves that industry members are likely to employ.

2. *What kinds of competitive forces are industry members facing, and how strong is each force?* The strength of competition is a composite of five forces: (1) competitive pressures stemming from the competitive jockeying and market maneuvering among industry rivals, (2) competitive pressures associated with the market inroads being made by the sellers of substitutes, (3) competitive pressures associated with the threat of new entrants into the market, (4) competitive pressures stemming from supplier bargaining power and supplier–seller collaboration, and (5) competitive pressures stemming from buyer bargaining power and seller–buyer collaboration. The nature and strength of the competitive pressures associated with these five forces have to be examined force by force to identify the specific competitive pressures they each comprise and to decide whether these pressures constitute a strong or weak competitive force. The next step in competition analysis is to evaluate the collective strength of the five forces and determine whether the state of competition is conducive to good profitability. Working through the five-forces model step by step not only aids strategy makers in assessing whether the intensity of competition allows good profitability but also promotes sound strategic thinking about how to better match company strategy to the specific competitive character of the marketplace. Effectively matching a company's strategy to the particular competitive pressures and competitive conditions that exist has two aspects: (1) pursuing avenues that shield the firm from as many of the prevailing competitive pressures as possible, and (2) initiating actions calculated to produce sustainable competitive advantage, thereby shifting competition in the company's favor, putting added competitive pressure on rivals, and perhaps even defining the business model for the industry.

3. *What factors are driving industry change and what impact will they have on competitive intensity and industry profitability?* Industry and competitive conditions change because forces are in motion that create incentives or pressures for change. The first phase is to identify the forces that are driving change in the industry; the most common driving forces include the Internet and Internet technology applications, globalization of competition in the industry, changes in the long-term industry growth rate, changes in buyer composition, product innovation, entry or exit of major firms, changes in cost and efficiency, changing buyer preferences for standardized versus differentiated products or services, regulatory influences and government policy changes, changing societal and lifestyle factors, and reductions in uncertainty and business risk. The second phase of driving-forces analysis is to determine whether the driving forces, taken together, are acting to make the industry environment more or less attractive. Are the driving forces causing demand for the industry's product to increase or decrease? Are the driving forces acting to make competition more or less intense? Will the driving forces lead to higher or lower industry profitability?

4. *What market positions do industry rivals occupy—who is strongly positioned and who is not?* Strategic group mapping is a valuable tool for understanding the similarities, differences, strengths, and weaknesses inherent in the market positions of rival companies. Rivals in the same or nearby strategic groups are close competitors, whereas companies in distant strategic groups usually pose little or no immediate threat. The lesson of strategic group mapping is that some positions on the map are more favorable than others. The profit potential of different strategic groups varies due to strengths and weaknesses in each group's market

position. Often, industry driving forces and competitive pressures favor some strategic groups and hurt others.

5. *What strategic moves are rivals likely to make next?* This analytical step involves identifying competitors' strategies, deciding which rivals are likely to be strong contenders and which are likely to be weak, evaluating rivals' competitive options, and predicting their next moves. Scouting competitors well enough to anticipate their actions can help a company prepare effective countermoves (perhaps even beating a rival to the punch) and allows managers to take rivals' probable actions into account in designing their own company's best course of action. Managers who fail to study competitors risk being caught unprepared by the strategic moves of rivals.

6. *What are the key factors for future competitive success?* An industry's key success factors (KSFs) are the particular strategy elements, product attributes, competitive capabilities, and business outcomes that spell the difference between being a strong competitor and a weak competitor—and sometimes between profit and loss. KSFs by their very nature are so important to competitive success that *all firms* in the industry must pay close attention to them or risk becoming an industry also-ran. Correctly diagnosing an industry's KSFs raises a company's chances of crafting a sound strategy. The goal of company strategists should be to design a strategy aimed at stacking up well on all of the industry KSFs and trying to be *distinctively better* than rivals on one (or possibly two) of the KSFs. Indeed, using the industry's KSFs as *cornerstones* for the company's strategy and trying to gain sustainable competitive advantage by excelling at one particular KSF is a fruitful competitive strategy approach.

7. *Does the outlook for the industry present the company with sufficiently attractive prospects for profitability?* If an industry's overall profit prospects are above average, the industry environment is basically attractive; if industry profit prospects are below average, conditions are unattractive. Conclusions regarding industry attractive are a major driver of company strategy. When a company decides an industry is fundamentally attractive and presents good opportunities, a strong case can be made that it should invest aggressively to capture the opportunities it sees and to improve its long-term competitive position in the business. When a strong competitor concludes an industry is relatively unattractive and lacking in opportunity, it may elect to simply protect its present position, investing cautiously if at all and looking for opportunities in other industries. A competitively weak company in an unattractive industry may see its best option as finding a buyer, perhaps a rival, to acquire its business. On occasion, an industry that is unattractive overall is still very attractive to a favorably situated company with the skills and resources to take business away from weaker rivals.

A competently conducted industry and competitive analysis generally tells a clear, easily understood story about the company's external environment. Different analysts can have varying judgments about competitive intensity, the impacts of driving forces, how industry conditions will evolve, how good the outlook is for industry profitability, and the degree to which the industry environment offers the company an attractive business opportunity. However, while no method can guarantee that all analysts will come to identical conclusions about the state of industry and competitive conditions and an industry's future outlook, this doesn't justify shortcutting hardnosed strategic analysis and relying instead on opinion and casual observation. Managers become better strategists when they know what questions to pose and what tools to use. This is why this chapter has concentrated on suggesting the right questions to ask, explaining concepts and analytical approaches, and indicating the kinds of things to look for. There's no substitute for doing cutting edge strategic thinking about a company's external situation—anything less weakens managers' ability to craft strategies that are well matched to industry and competitive conditions.

Exercises

1. As the owner of a fast-food enterprise seeking a loan from a bank to finance the construction and operation of three new store locations, you have been asked to provide the loan officer with a brief analysis of the competitive environment in fast food. Draw a five-forces diagram for the fast-food industry, and briefly discuss the nature and strength of each of the five competitive forces in fast food. Do whatever Internet research is required to expand your understanding of competition in the fast-food industry and do a competent five-forces analysis.

2. Based on the strategic group map in Illustration Capsule 3.1: Who are Polo Ralph Lauren's closest competitors? Between which two strategic groups is competition the strongest? Why do you think no retailers are positioned in the upper right-hand corner of the map? Which company/strategic group faces the weakest competition from the members of other strategic groups?

3. With regard to the ice cream industry, which of the following factors might qualify as possible driving forces capable of causing fundamental change in the industry's structure and competitive environment?

    a. Increasing sales of frozen yogurt and frozen sorbets.

    b. The potential for additional makers of ice cream to enter the market.

    c. Growing consumer interest in low-calorie/low-fat/low-carb/sugar-free dessert alternatives.

    d. A slowdown in consumer purchases of ice cream products.

    e. Rising prices for milk, sugar, and other ice cream ingredients.

    f. A decision by Häagen-Dazs to increase its prices by 10 percent.

    g. A decision by Ben & Jerry's to add five new flavors to its product line.

Evaluating a Company's Resources and Competitive Position

Before executives can chart a new strategy, they must reach common understanding of the company's current position.

**—W. Chan Kim and
Rene Mauborgne**

The real question isn't how well you're doing today against your own history, but how you're doing against your competitors.

—Donald Kress

Organizations succeed in a competitive marketplace over the long run because they can do certain things their customers value better than can their competitors.

**—Robert Hayes, Gary Pisano,
and David Upton**

Only firms who are able to continually build new strategic assets faster and cheaper than their competitors will earn superior returns over the long term.

**—C. C. Markides and
P. J. Williamson**

In Chapter 3 we described how to use the tools of industry and competitive analysis to assess a company's external environment and lay the groundwork for matching a company's strategy to its external situation. In this chapter we discuss the techniques of evaluating a company's resource capabilities, relative cost position, and competitive strength vis-á-vis its rivals. The analytical spotlight will be trained on five questions:

1. How well is the company's present strategy working?

2. What are the company's resource strengths and weaknesses, and its external opportunities and threats?

3. Are the company's prices and costs competitive?

4. Is the company competitively stronger or weaker than key rivals?

5. What strategic issues and problems merit front-burner managerial attention?

We will describe four analytical tools that should be used to probe for answers to these questions—SWOT analysis, value chain analysis, benchmarking, and competitive strength assessment. All four are valuable techniques for revealing a company's competitiveness and for helping company managers match their strategy to the company's own particular circumstances.

QUESTION 1: HOW WELL IS THE COMPANY'S PRESENT STRATEGY WORKING?

In evaluating how well a company's present strategy is working, a manager has to start with what the strategy is. Figure 4.1 shows the key components of a single-business company's strategy. The first thing to pin down is the company's competitive approach. Is the company striving to be a low-cost leader *or* stressing ways to differentiate its product offering from rivals? Is it concentrating its efforts on serving a broad spectrum of customers *or* a narrow market niche? Another strategy-defining consideration is the firm's competitive scope within the industry—what its geographic market coverage is and whether it operates in just a single stage of the industry's production/distribution chain or is vertically integrated across several stages. Another good indication of the company's strategy is whether the company has made moves recently to improve its competitive position and performance—for instance, by cutting prices, improving design, stepping up advertising, entering a new geographic market (domestic or foreign),

Figure 4.1   **Identifying the Components of a Single-Business Company's Strategy**

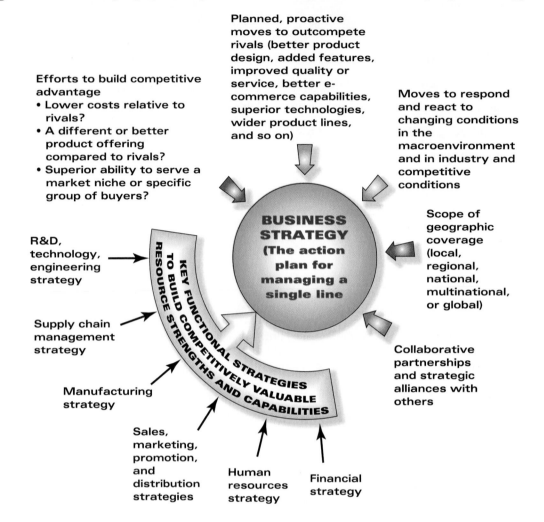

or merging with a competitor. The company's functional strategies in R&D, production, marketing, finance, human resources, information technology, and so on further characterize company strategy.

While there's merit in evaluating the strategy from a *qualitative* standpoint (its completeness, internal consistency, rationale, and relevance), the best *quantitative* evidence of how well a company's strategy is working comes from its results. The two best empirical indicators are (1) whether the company is achieving its stated financial and strategic objectives, and (2) whether the company is an above-average industry performer. Persistent shortfalls in meeting company performance targets and weak performance relative to rivals are reliable warning signs that the company suffers from poor strategy making, less-than-competent strategy execution, or both. Other indicators of how well a company's strategy is working include:

- Whether the firm's sales are growing faster, slower, or about the same pace as the market as a whole, thus resulting in a rising, eroding, or stable market share.

- Whether the company is acquiring new customers at an attractive rate as well as retaining existing customers.
- Whether the firm's profit margins are increasing or decreasing and how well its margins compare to rival firms' margins.
- Trends in the firm's net profits and return on investment and how these compare to the same trends for other companies in the industry.
- Whether the company's overall financial strength and credit rating are improving or on the decline.
- Whether the company can demonstrate continuous improvement in such internal performance measures as days of inventory, employee productivity, unit cost, defect rate, scrap rate, misfilled orders, delivery times, warranty costs, and so on.
- How shareholders view the company based on trends in the company's stock price and shareholder value (relative to the stock price trends at other companies in the industry).
- The firm's image and reputation with its customers.
- How well the company stacks up against rivals on technology, product innovation, customer service, product quality, delivery time, price, getting newly developed products to market quickly, and other relevant factors on which buyers base their choice of brands.

The stronger a company's current overall performance, the less likely the need for radical changes in strategy. The weaker a company's financial performance and market standing, the more its current strategy must be questioned. Weak performance is almost always a sign of weak strategy, weak execution, or both.

> The stronger a company's financial performance and market position, the more likely it has a well-conceived, well-executed strategy.

Table 4.1 provides a compilation of the financial ratios most commonly used to evaluate a company's financial performance and balance sheet strength.

QUESTION 2: WHAT ARE THE COMPANY'S RESOURCE STRENGTHS AND WEAKNESSES AND ITS EXTERNAL OPPORTUNITIES AND THREATS?

Appraising a company's resource strengths and weaknesses and its external opportunities and threats, commonly known as **SWOT analysis,** provides a good overview of whether the company's overall situation is fundamentally healthy or unhealthy. Just as important, a first-rate SWOT analysis provides the basis for crafting a strategy that capitalizes on the company's resources, aims squarely at capturing the company's best opportunities, and defends against the threats to its well-being.

> **Core Concept**
> *SWOT analysis* is a simple but powerful tool for sizing up a company's resource capabilities and deficiencies, its market opportunities, and the external threats to its future well-being.

Identifying Company Resource Strengths and Competitive Capabilities

A *resource strength* is something a company is good at doing or an attribute that enhances its competitiveness in the marketplace. Resource strengths can take any of several forms:

Table 4.1   **Key Financial Ratios: How to Calculate Them and What They Mean**

Ratio	How Calculated	What It Shows
Profitability ratios		
1. Gross profit margin	$\dfrac{\text{Sales} - \text{Cost of goods sold}}{\text{Sales}}$	Shows the percentage of revenues available to cover operating expenses and yield a profit. Higher is better, and the trend should be upward.
2. Operating profit margin (or return on sales)	$\dfrac{\text{Sales} - \text{Operating expenses}}{\text{Sales}}$ or $\dfrac{\text{Operating income}}{\text{Sales}}$	Shows the profitability of current operations without regard to interest charges and income taxes. Higher is better, and the trend should be upward.
3. Net profit margin (or net return on sales)	$\dfrac{\text{Profits after taxes}}{\text{Sales}}$	Shows after-tax profits per dollar of sales. Higher is better, and the trend should be upward.
4. Return on total assets	$\dfrac{\text{Profits after taxes} + \text{Interest}}{\text{Total assets}}$	A measure of the return on total investment in the enterprise. Interest is added to after-tax profits to form the numerator since total assets are financed by creditors as well as by stockholders. Higher is better, and the trend should be upward.
5. Return on stockholders' equity	$\dfrac{\text{Profits after taxes}}{\text{Total stockholders' equity}}$	Shows the return stockholders are earning on their investment in the enterprise. A return in the 12–15 percent range is "average," and the trend should be upward.
6. Earnings per share	$\dfrac{\text{Profits after taxes}}{\text{Number of shares of common stock outstanding}}$	Shows the earnings for each share of common stock outstanding. The trend should be upward, and the bigger the annual percentage gains, the better.
Liquidity ratios		
1. Current ratio	$\dfrac{\text{Current assets}}{\text{Current liabilities}}$	Shows a firm's ability to pay current liabilities using assets that can be converted to cash in the near term. Ratio should definitely be higher than 1.0; ratios of 2 or higher are better still.
2. Quick ratio (or acid-test ratio)	$\dfrac{\text{Current assets} - \text{Inventory}}{\text{Current liabilities}}$	Shows a firm's ability to pay current liabilities without relying on the sale of its inventories.
3. Working capital	Current assets – Current liabilities	Bigger amounts are better because the company has more internal funds available to (1) pay its current liabilities on a timely basis and (2) finance inventory expansion, additional accounts receivable, and a larger base of operations without resorting to borrowing or raising more equity capital.
Leverage ratios		
1. Debt-to-assets ratio	$\dfrac{\text{Total debt}}{\text{Total assets}}$	Measures the extent to which borrowed funds have been used to finance the firm's operations. Low fractions or ratios are better—high fractions indicate overuse of debt and greater risk of bankruptcy.

(Continued)

Table 4.1   **Continued**

Ratio	How Calculated	What It Shows
2. Debt-to-equity ratio	$$\frac{\text{Total debt}}{\text{Total stockholders' equity}}$$	Should usually be less than 1.0. High ratios (especially above 1.0) signal excessive debt, lower creditworthiness, and weaker balance sheet strength.
3. Long-term debt-to-equity ratio	$$\frac{\text{Long-term debt}}{\text{Total stockholders' equity}}$$	Shows the balance between debt and equity in the firm's *long-term* capital structure. Low ratios indicate greater capacity to borrow additional funds if needed.
4. Times-interest-earned (or coverage) ratio	$$\frac{\text{Operating income}}{\text{Interest expenses}}$$	Measures the ability to pay annual interest charges. Lenders usually insist on a minimum ratio of 2.0, but ratios above 3.0 signal better creditworthiness.
Activity ratios		
1. Days of inventory	$$\frac{\text{Inventory}}{\text{Cost of goods sold} \div 365}$$	Measures inventory management efficiency. Fewer days of inventory are usually better.
2. Inventory turnover	$$\frac{\text{Cost of goods sold}}{\text{Inventory}}$$	Measures the number of inventory turns per year. Higher is better.
3. Average collection period	$$\frac{\text{Accounts receivable}}{\text{Total sales} \div 365}$$ or $$\frac{\text{Accounts receivable}}{\text{Average daily sales}}$$	Indicates the average length of time the firm must wait after making a sale to receive cash payment. A shorter collection time is better.
Other important measures of financial performance		
1. Dividend yield on common stock	$$\frac{\text{Annual dividends per share}}{\text{Current market price per share}}$$	A measure of the return that shareholders receive in the form of dividends. A "typical" dividend yield is 2–3%. The dividend yield for fast-growth companies is often below 1% (may be even 0); the dividend yield for slow-growth companies can run 4–5%.
2. Price/earnings ratio	$$\frac{\text{Current market price per share}}{\text{Earnings per share}}$$	P/E ratios above 20 indicate strong investor confidence in a firm's outlook and earnings growth; firms whose future earnings are at risk or likely to grow slowly typically have ratios below 12.
3. Dividend payout ratio	$$\frac{\text{Annual dividends per share}}{\text{Earnings per share}}$$	Indicates the percentage of after-tax profits paid out as dividends.
4. Internal cash flow	After tax profits + Depreciation	A quick and rough estimate of the cash a company's business is generating after payment of operating expenses, interest, and taxes. Such amounts can be used for dividend payments or funding capital expenditures.

- *A skill, specialized expertise, or competitively important capability*—skills in low-cost operations, technological expertise, expertise in defect-free manufacture, proven capabilities in developing and introducing innovative products, cutting-edge supply chain management capabilities, expertise in getting new products to market quickly, strong e-commerce expertise, expertise in providing consistently good customer service, excellent mass merchandising skills, or unique advertising and promotional talents.

- *Valuable physical assets*—state-of-the-art plants and equipment, attractive real estate locations, worldwide distribution facilities, or ownership of valuable natural resource deposits.

- *Valuable human assets and intellectual capital*—an experienced and capable workforce, talented employees in key areas, cutting-edge knowledge in technology or other important areas of the business, collective learning embedded in the organization and built up over time, or proven managerial know-how.[1]

- *Valuable organizational assets*—proven quality control systems, proprietary technology, key patents, state-of-the-art systems for doing business via the Internet, ownership of important natural resources, a cadre of highly trained customer service representatives, a strong network of distributors or retail dealers, sizable amounts of cash and marketable securities, a strong balance sheet and credit rating (thus giving the company access to additional financial capital), or a comprehensive list of customers' e-mail addresses.

- *Valuable intangible assets*—a powerful or well-known brand name, a reputation for technological leadership, or strong buyer loyalty and goodwill.

- *An achievement or attribute that puts the company in a position of market advantage*—low overall costs relative to competitors, market share leadership, a superior product, a wider product line than rivals, wide geographic coverage, or award-winning customer service.

- *Competitively valuable alliances or cooperative ventures*—fruitful partnerships with suppliers that reduce costs and/or enhance product quality and performance; alliances or joint ventures that provide access to valuable technologies, specialized know-how, or geographic markets.

> **Core Concept**
> A company's resource strengths represent *competitive assets* and are big determinants of its competitiveness and ability to succeed in the marketplace.

A company's resource strengths represent its endowment of *competitive assets.* The caliber of a firm's resource strengths is a big determinant of its competitiveness—whether it has the wherewithal to be a strong competitor in the marketplace or whether its capabilities and competitive strengths are modest, thus relegating it to a trailing position in the industry.[2] Plainly, a company's resource strengths may or may not enable it to improve its competitive position and financial performance.

Assessing a Company's Competencies and Capabilities—What Activities Does It Perform Well?   One of the most important aspects of appraising a company's resource strengths has to do with its competence level in performing key pieces of its business—such as supply chain management, research and development (R&D), production, distribution, sales and marketing, and customer service. Which activities does it perform especially well? And are there any activities it performs better than rivals? A company's proficiency in conducting different facets of its operations can range from merely a competence in performing an activity to a core competence to a distinctive competence:

1. A **competence** is something an organization is good at doing. It is nearly always the product of experience, representing an accumulation of learning and the buildup

of proficiency in performing an internal activity. Usually a company competence originates with deliberate efforts to develop the organizational ability to do something, however imperfectly or inefficiently. Such efforts involve selecting people with the requisite knowledge and skills, upgrading or expanding individual abilities as needed, and then molding the efforts and work products of individuals into a cooperative group effort to create organizational ability. Then, as experience builds, such that the company gains proficiency in performing the activity consistently well and at an acceptable cost, the ability evolves into a true competence and company capability. Some competencies relate to fairly specific skills and expertise (like just-in-time inventory control or low-cost manufacturing efficiency or picking locations for new stores or designing an unusually appealing and user-friendly Web site); they spring from proficiency in a single discipline or function and may be performed in a single department or organizational unit. Other competencies, however, are inherently multidisciplinary and cross-functional—they are the result of effective collaboration among people with different expertise working in different organizational units. A competence in continuous product innovation, for example, comes from teaming the efforts of people and groups with expertise in market research, new product R&D, design and engineering, cost-effective manufacturing, and market testing.

> **Core Concept**
> A **competence** is an activity that a company has learned to perform well.

2. A **core competence** is a proficiently performed internal activity that is *central* to a company's strategy and competitiveness. A core competence is a more valuable resource strength than a competence because of the well-performed activity's core role in the company's strategy and the contribution it makes to the company's success in the marketplace. A core competence can relate to any of several aspects of a company's business: expertise in integrating multiple technologies to create families of new products, know-how in creating and operating systems for cost-efficient supply chain management, the capability to speed new or next-generation products to market, good after-sale service capabilities, skills in manufacturing a high-quality product at a low cost, or the capability to fill customer orders accurately and swiftly. A company may have more than one core competence in its resource portfolio, but rare is the company that can legitimately claim more than two or three core competencies. Most often, *a core competence is knowledge-based, residing in people and in a company's intellectual capital and not in its assets on the balance sheet.* Moreover, a core competence is more likely to be grounded in cross-department combinations of knowledge and expertise rather than being the product of a single department or work group. 3M Corporation has a core competence in product innovation—its record of introducing new products goes back several decades and new product introduction is central to 3M's strategy of growing its business. Ben & Jerry's Homemade, a subsidiary of Unilever, has a core competence in creating unusual flavors of ice cream and marketing them with catchy names like Chunky Monkey, Wavy Gravy, Chubby Hubby, The Gobfather, Dublin Mudslide, and Marsha Marsha Marshmallow.

> **Core Concept**
> A **core competence** is a *competitively important* activity that a company performs better than other internal activities.

3. A **distinctive competence** is a competitively valuable activity that a company *performs better than its rivals.* A distinctive competence thus signifies even greater proficiency than a core competence. But what is especially important about a distinctive competence is that the company enjoys *competitive superiority*

> **Core Concept**
> A ***distinctive competence*** is a competitively important activity that a company performs better than its rivals—it thus represents *a competitively superior resource strength.*

in performing that activity—a distinctive competence represents a level of proficiency that rivals do not have. Because a distinctive competence represents uniquely strong capability relative to rival companies, it qualifies as a *competitively superior resource strength* with competitive advantage potential. This is particularly true when the distinctive competence enables a company to deliver standout value to customers (in the form of lower costs and prices or better product performance or superior service). Toyota has worked diligently over several decades to establish a distinctive competence in low-cost, high-quality manufacturing of motor vehicles; its "lean production" system is far superior to that of any other automaker's, and the company is pushing the boundaries of its production advantage with a new type of assembly line—called the Global Body line—that costs 50 percent less to install and can be changed to accommodate a new model for 70 percent less than its previous production system.[3] Starbucks' distinctive competence in innovative coffee drinks and store ambience has propelled it to the forefront among coffee retailers.

The conceptual differences between a competence, a core competence, and a distinctive competence draw attention to the fact that a company's resource strengths and competitive capabilities are not all equal.[4] Some competencies and competitive capabilities merely enable market survival because most rivals have them—indeed, not having a competence or capability that rivals have can result in competitive disadvantage. If an apparel company does not have the competence to produce its apparel items cost-efficiently, it is unlikely to survive given the intensely price-competitive nature of the apparel industry. Every Web retailer requires a basic competence in designing an appealing and user-friendly Web site.

Core competencies are *competitively* more important resource strengths than competencies because they add power to the company's strategy and have a bigger positive impact on its market position and profitability. Distinctive competencies are even more competitively important. A distinctive competence is a competitively potent resource strength for three reasons: (1) it gives a company competitively valuable capability that is unmatched by rivals, (2) it has potential for being the cornerstone of the company's strategy, and (3) it can produce a competitive edge in the marketplace since it represents a level of proficiency that is superior to rivals. It is always easier for a company to build competitive advantage when it has a distinctive competence in performing an activity important to market success, when rival companies do not have offsetting competencies, and when it is costly and time-consuming for rivals to imitate the competence. A distinctive competence is thus potentially the mainspring of a company's success—unless it is trumped by more powerful resources possessed by rivals.

> **Core Concept**
> A distinctive competence is a competitively potent resource strength for three reasons: (1) it gives a company competitively valuable capability that is unmatched by rivals, (2) it can underpin and add real punch to a company's strategy, and (3) it is a basis for sustainable competitive advantage.

What Is the Competitive Power of a Resource Strength?

It is not enough to simply compile a list of a company's resource strengths and competitive capabilities. What is most telling about a company's resource strengths, individually and collectively, is how powerful they are in the marketplace. The competitive power of a resource strength is measured by how many of the following four tests it can pass:[5]

1. *Is the resource strength hard to copy?* The more difficult and more expensive it is to imitate a company's resource strength, the greater its potential competitive

value. Resources tend to be difficult to copy when they are unique (a fantastic real estate location, patent protection), when they must be built over time in ways that are difficult to imitate (a brand name, mastery of a technology), and when they carry big capital requirements (a cost-effective plant to manufacture cutting-edge microprocessors). Wal-Mart's competitors have failed miserably in their attempts over the past two decades to match Wal-Mart's super-efficient state-of-the-art distribution capabilities. Hard-to-copy strengths and capabilities are valuable competitive assets, adding to a company's market strength and contributing to sustained profitability.

2. *Is the resource strength durable—does it have staying power?* The longer the competitive value of a resource lasts, the greater its value. Some resources lose their clout in the marketplace quickly because of the rapid speeds at which technologies or industry conditions are moving. The value of Eastman Kodak's resources in film and film processing is rapidly being undercut by the growing popularity of digital cameras. The investments that commercial banks have made in branch offices is a rapidly depreciating asset because of growing use of direct deposits, debit cards, automated teller machines, and telephone and Internet banking options.

3. *Is the resource really competitively superior?* Companies have to guard against pridefully believing that their core competencies are distinctive competencies or that their brand name is more powerful than the brand names of rivals. Who can really say whether Coca-Cola's consumer marketing prowess is better than Pepsi-Cola's or whether the Mercedes-Benz brand name is more powerful than that of BMW or Lexus? Although many retailers claim to be quite proficient in product selection and in-store merchandising, a number run into trouble in the marketplace because they encounter rivals whose competencies in product selection and in-store merchandising are better than theirs. Apple's operating system for its MacIntosh PCs is by most accounts a world beater (compared to Windows XP), but Apple has failed miserably in converting its resource strength in operating system design into competitive success in the global PC market—it is an also-ran with a paltry 2–3 percent market share worldwide.

4. *Can the resource strength be trumped by the different resource strengths and competitive capabilities of rivals?* Many commercial airlines have invested heavily in developing the resources and capabilities to offer passengers safe, reliable flights at convenient times, along with an array of in-flight amenities. However, Southwest Airlines and JetBlue in the United States and Ryanair and easyJet in Europe have been quite successful deploying their resources in ways that enable them to provide commercial air services at radically lower fares. Amazon.com's strengths in online retailing of books have put a big dent in the business prospects of brick-and-mortar bookstores. Whole Foods Market has a resource lineup that enables it to merchandise a dazzling array of natural and organic food products in a supermarket setting, thus putting strong competitive pressure on Kroger, Safeway, Albertson's, and other prominent supermarket chains. The prestigious brand names of Cadillac and Lincoln have faded because Mercedes, BMW, Audi, and Lexus have used their resources to design, produce, and market more appealing luxury vehicles.

The vast majority of companies are not well endowed with standout resource strengths, much less with one or more competitively superior resources (or distinctive competencies) capable of passing all four tests with high marks. Most firms have a mixed bag of resources—one or two quite valuable, some good, many satisfactory to mediocre.

Companies in the top tier of their industry may have as many as two core competencies in their resource strength lineup. But only a few companies, usually the strongest industry leaders or up-and-coming challengers, have a resource strength that truly qualifies as a distinctive competence. Even so, a company can still marshal the resource strengths to be competitively successful without having a competitively superior resource or distinctive competence. A company can achieve considerable competitive vitality, maybe even competitive advantage, from a collection of good-to-adequate resource strengths that collectively give it competitive power in the marketplace. A number of fast-food chains—for example, Wendy's, Taco Bell, and Subway—have achieved a respectable market position competing against McDonald's with satisfactory sets of resource strengths and no apparent distinctive competence. The same can be said for Lowe's, which competes against industry leader Home Depot, and such regional banks as Compass, State Street, Keybank, PNC, BB&T, and AmSouth, which increasingly find themselves in competition with the top five U.S. banks—JPMorgan Chase, Bank of America, Citibank, Wachovia, and Wells Fargo.

> **Core Concept**
> A company's ability to succeed in the marketplace hinges to a considerable extent on the competitive power of its resources—the set of competencies, capabilities, and competitive assets at its command.

Identifying Company Resource Weaknesses and Competitive Deficiencies

A *resource weakness,* or *competitive deficiency,* is something a company lacks or does poorly (in comparison to others) or a condition that puts it at a disadvantage in the marketplace. A company's resource weaknesses can relate to (1) inferior or unproven skills, expertise, or intellectual capital in competitively important areas of the business; (2) deficiencies in competitively important physical, organizational, or intangible assets; or (3) missing or competitively inferior capabilities in key areas. *Internal weaknesses are thus shortcomings in a company's complement of resources and represent competitive liabilities.* Nearly all companies have competitive liabilities of one kind or another. Whether a company's resource weaknesses make it competitively vulnerable depends on how much they matter in the marketplace and whether they are offset by the company's resource strengths.

> **Core Concept**
> A company's resource strengths represent competitive assets; its resource weaknesses represent competitive liabilities.

Table 4.2 lists the kinds of factors to consider in compiling a company's resource strengths and weaknesses. Sizing up a company's complement of resource capabilities and deficiencies is akin to constructing a *strategic balance sheet,* where resource strengths represent *competitive assets* and resource weaknesses represent *competitive liabilities.* Obviously, the ideal condition is for the company's competitive assets to outweigh its competitive liabilities by an ample margin—a 50–50 balance is definitely not the desired condition!

Identifying a Company's Market Opportunities

Market opportunity is a big factor in shaping a company's strategy. Indeed, managers can't properly tailor strategy to the company's situation without first identifying its market opportunities and appraising the growth and profit potential each one holds. Depending on the prevailing circumstances, a company's opportunities can be plentiful or scarce, fleeting or lasting, and can range from wildly attractive (an absolute "must" to pursue) to marginally interesting (because the growth and profit potential are questionable) to unsuitable (because there's not a good match with the company's

Table 4.2   **What to Look for in Identifying a Company's Strengths, Weaknesses, Opportunities, and Threats**

Potential Resource Strengths and Competitive Capabilities	Potential Resource Weaknesses and Competitive Deficiencies
• A powerful strategy • Core competencies in _____ • A distinctive competence in _____ • A product that is strongly differentiated from those of rivals • Competencies and capabilities that are well matched to industry key success factors • A strong financial condition; ample financial resources to grow the business • Strong brand-name image/company reputation • An attractive customer base • Economy of scale and/or learning/experience curve advantages over rivals • Proprietary technology/superior technological skills/important patents • Superior intellectual capital relative to key rivals • Cost advantages over rivals • Strong advertising and promotion • Product innovation capabilities • Proven capabilities in improving production processes • Good supply chain management capabilities • Good customer service capabilities • Better product quality relative to rivals • Wide geographic coverage and/or strong global distribution capability • Alliances/joint ventures with other firms that provide access to valuable technology, competencies, and/or attractive geographic markets	• No clear strategic direction • Resources that are not well matched to industry key success factors • No well-developed or proven core competencies • A weak balance sheet; burdened with too much debt • Higher overall unit costs relative to key competitors • Weak or unproven product innovation capabilities • A product/service with ho-hum attributes or features inferior to those of rivals • Too narrow a product line relative to rivals • Weak brand image or reputation • Weaker dealer network than key rivals and/or lack of adequate global distribution capability • Behind on product quality, R&D, and/or technological know-how • In the wrong strategic group • Losing market share because . . . • Lack of management depth • Inferior intellectual capital relative to leading rivals • Subpar profitability because . . . • Plagued with internal operating problems or obsolete facilities • Behind rivals in e-commerce capabilities • Short on financial resources to grow the business and pursue promising initiatives • Too much underutilized plant capacity
Potential Market Opportunities	**Potential External Threats to a Company's Future Prospects**
• Openings to win market share from rivals • Sharply rising buyer demand for the industry's product • Serving additional customer groups or market segments • Expanding into new geographic markets • Expanding the company's product line to meet a broader range of customer needs • Using existing company skills or technological know-how to enter new product lines or new businesses • Online sales • Integrating forward or backward • Falling trade barriers in attractive foreign markets • Acquiring rival firms or companies with attractive technological expertise or capabilities • Entering into alliances or joint ventures to expand the firm's market coverage or boost its competitive capability • Openings to exploit emerging new technologies	• Increasing intensity of competition among industry rivals—may squeeze profit margins • Slowdowns in market growth • Likely entry of potent new competitors • Loss of sales to substitute products • Growing bargaining power of customers or suppliers • A shift in buyer needs and tastes away from the industry's product • Adverse demographic changes that threaten to curtail demand for the industry's product • Vulnerability to unfavorable industry driving forces • Restrictive trade policies on the part of foreign governments • Costly new regulatory requirements

resource strengths and capabilities). A checklist of potential market opportunities is included in Table 4.2.

While stunningly big or "golden" opportunities appear fairly frequently in volatile, fast-changing markets (typically due to important technological developments or rapidly shifting consumer preferences), they are nonetheless hard to see before most all companies in the industry identify them. The more volatile and thus unpredictable market conditions are, the more limited a company's ability to do market reconnaissance and spot important opportunities much ahead of rivals—there are simply too many variables in play for managers to peer into the fog of the future, identify one or more upcoming opportunities, and get a jump on rivals in pursuing it.[6] In mature markets, unusually attractive market opportunities emerge sporadically, often after long periods of relative calm—but future market conditions may be less foggy, thus facilitating good market reconnaissance and making emerging opportunities easier for industry members to detect. But in both volatile and stable markets, the rise of a golden opportunity is almost never under the control of a single company or manufactured by company executives—rather, it springs from the simultaneous alignment of several external factors. For instance, in China the recent upsurge in demand for motor vehicles was spawned by a convergence of many factors—increased disposable income, rising middle-class aspirations, a major road-building program by the government, the demise of employer-provided housing, and easy credit.[7] But golden opportunities are nearly always seized rapidly—and the companies that seize them are usually those that have been actively waiting, staying alert with diligent market reconnaissance, and preparing themselves to capitalize on shifting market conditions by patiently assembling an arsenal of competitively valuable resources—talented personnel, technical know-how, strategic partnerships, and a war chest of cash to finance aggressive action when the time comes.[8]

> A company is well advised to pass on a particular market opportunity unless it has or can acquire the resources to capture it.

In evaluating a company's market opportunities and ranking their attractiveness, managers have to guard against viewing every *industry* opportunity as a *company* opportunity. Not every company is equipped with the resources to successfully pursue each opportunity that exists in its industry. Some companies are more capable of going after particular opportunities than others, and a few companies may be hopelessly outclassed. *The market opportunities most relevant to a company are those that match up well with the company's financial and organizational resource capabilities, offer the best growth and profitability, and present the most potential for competitive advantage.*

Identifying the External Threats to a Company's Future Profitability

Often, certain factors in a company's external environment pose *threats* to its profitability and competitive well-being. Threats can stem from the emergence of cheaper or better technologies, rivals' introduction of new or improved products, the entry of lower-cost foreign competitors into a company's market stronghold, new regulations that are more burdensome to a company than to its competitors, vulnerability to a rise in interest rates, the potential of a hostile takeover, unfavorable demographic shifts, adverse changes in foreign exchange rates, political upheaval in a foreign country where the company has facilities, and the like. A list of potential threats to a company's future profitability and market position is shown in Table 4.2.

External threats may pose no more than a moderate degree of adversity (all companies confront some threatening elements in the course of doing business), or they may be so imposing as to make a company's situation and outlook quite tenuous. On rare occasions, market shocks can give birth to a *sudden-death* threat that throws a company into an immediate crisis and battle to survive. Many of the world's major airlines have been plunged into unprecedented financial crisis by the perfect storm of the September 11, 2001, terrorist attacks, rising prices for jet fuel, mounting competition from low-fare carriers, shifting traveler preferences for low fares as opposed to lots of in-flight amenities, and out-of-control labor costs. It is management's job to identify the threats to the company's future prospects and to evaluate what strategic actions can be taken to neutralize or lessen their impact.

What Do the SWOT Listings Reveal?

SWOT analysis involves more than making four lists. The two most important parts of SWOT analysis are *drawing conclusions* from the SWOT listings about the company's overall situation, and *translating these conclusions into strategic actions* to better match the company's strategy to its resource strengths and market opportunities, to correct the important weaknesses, and to defend against external threats. Figure 4.2 shows the three steps of SWOT analysis.

Just what story the SWOT listings tell about the company's overall situation is often revealed in the answers to the following sets of questions:

> Simply making lists of a company's strengths, weaknesses, opportunities, and threats is not enough; the payoff from SWOT analysis comes from the conclusions about a company's situation and the implications for strategy improvement that flow from the four lists.

- Does the company have an attractive set of resource strengths? Does it have any strong core competencies or a distinctive competence? Are the company's strengths and capabilities well matched to the industry key success factors? Do they add adequate power to the company's strategy, or are more or different strengths needed? Will the company's current strengths and capabilities matter in the future?

- How serious are the company's weaknesses and competitive deficiencies? Are they mostly inconsequential and readily correctable, or could one or more prove fatal if not remedied soon? Are some of the company's weaknesses in areas that relate to the industry's key success factors? Are there any weaknesses that if uncorrected, would keep the company from pursuing an otherwise attractive opportunity? Does the company have important resource gaps that need to be filled for it to move up in the industry rankings and/or boost its profitability?

- Do the company's resource strengths and competitive capabilities (its competitive assets) outweigh its resource weaknesses and competitive deficiencies (its competitive liabilities) by an attractive margin?

- Does the company have attractive market opportunities that are well suited to its resource strengths and competitive capabilities? Does the company lack the resources and capabilities to pursue any of the most attractive opportunities?

- Are the threats alarming, or are they something the company appears able to deal with and defend against?

Figure 4.2 **The Three Steps of SWOT Analysis: Identify, Draw Conclusions, Translate into Strategic Action**

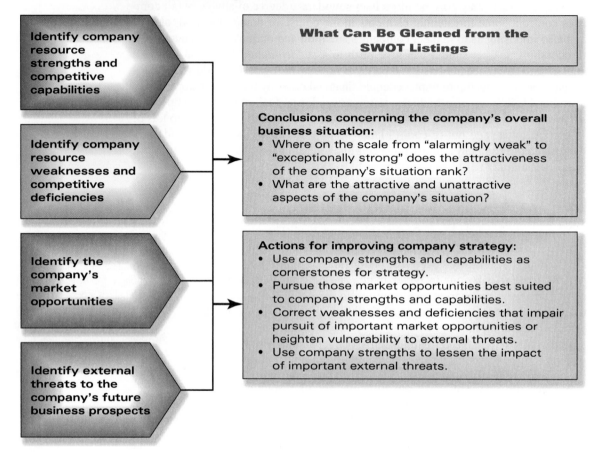

- All things considered, how strong is the company's overall situation? Where on a scale of 1 to 10 (1 being alarmingly weak and 10 exceptionally strong) should the firm's position and overall situation be ranked? What aspects of the company's situation are particularly attractive? What aspects are of the most concern?

The final piece of SWOT analysis is to translate the diagnosis of the company's situation into actions for improving the company's strategy and business prospects. The following questions point to implications the SWOT listings have for strategic action:

- Which competitive capabilities need to be strengthened immediately, so as to add greater power to the company's strategy and boost sales and profitability? Do new types of competitive capabilities need to be put in place to help the company better respond to emerging industry and competitive conditions? Which resources and capabilities need to be given greater emphasis, and which merit less emphasis? Should the company emphasize leveraging its existing resource strengths and capabilities, or does it need to create new resource strengths and capabilities?
- What actions should be taken to reduce the company's competitive liabilities? Which weaknesses or competitive deficiencies are in urgent need of correction?

- Which market opportunities should be top priority in future strategic initiatives (because they are good fits with the company's resource strengths and competitive capabilities, present attractive growth and profit prospects, and/or offer the best potential for securing competitive advantage)? Which opportunities should be ignored, at least for the time being (because they offer less growth potential or are not suited to the company's resources and capabilities)?
- What should the company be doing to guard against the threats to its well-being?

A company's resource strengths should generally form the cornerstones of strategy because they represent the company's best chance for market success.[9] As a rule, strategies that place heavy demands on areas where the company is weakest or has unproven ability are suspect and should be avoided. If a company doesn't have the resources and competitive capabilities around which to craft an attractive strategy, managers need to take decisive remedial action either to upgrade existing organizational resources and capabilities and add others as needed or to acquire them through partnerships or strategic alliances with firms possessing the needed expertise. Plainly, managers have to look toward correcting competitive weaknesses that make the company vulnerable, hold down profitability, or disqualify it from pursuing an attractive opportunity.

At the same time, sound strategy making requires sifting through the available market opportunities and aiming strategy at capturing those that are most attractive and suited to the company's circumstances. Rarely does a company have the resource depth to pursue all available market opportunities simultaneously without spreading itself too thin. How much attention to devote to defending against external threats to the company's market position and future performance hinges on how vulnerable the company is, whether there are attractive defensive moves that can be taken to lessen their impact, and whether the costs of undertaking such moves represent the best use of company resources.

QUESTION 3: ARE THE COMPANY'S PRICES AND COSTS COMPETITIVE?

Company managers are often stunned when a competitor cuts its price to "unbelievably low" levels or when a new market entrant comes on strong with a very low price. The competitor may not, however, be "dumping" (an economic term for selling at prices that are below cost), buying its way into the market with a super-low price, or waging a desperate move to gain sales—it may simply have substantially lower costs. One of the most telling signs of whether a company's business position is strong or precarious is whether its prices and costs are competitive with industry rivals. For a company to compete successfully, its costs must be *in line* with those of close rivals.

> The higher a company's costs are above those of close rivals, the more competitively vulnerable it becomes.

Price–cost comparisons are especially critical in a commodity-product industry where the value provided to buyers is the same from seller to seller, price competition is typically the ruling market force, and low-cost companies have the upper hand. But even in industries where products are differentiated and competition centers on the different attributes of competing brands as much as on price, rival companies have to keep their costs in line and make sure that any added costs they incur, and any price premiums they charge, create ample value that buyers are willing to pay extra for.

While some cost disparity is justified so long as the products or services of closely competing companies are sufficiently differentiated, a high-cost firm's market position becomes increasingly vulnerable the more its costs exceed those of close rivals.

Two analytical tools are particularly useful in determining whether a company's prices and costs are competitive: value chain analysis and benchmarking.

The Concept of a Company Value Chain

Core Concept
A company's *value chain* identifies the primary activities that create customer value and the related support activities.

Every company's business consists of a collection of activities undertaken in the course of designing, producing, marketing, delivering, and supporting its product or service. All of the various activities that a company performs internally combine to form a **value chain**—so called because the underlying intent of a company's activities is to do things that ultimately *create value for buyers*. A company's value chain also includes an allowance for profit because a markup over the cost of performing the firm's value-creating activities is customarily part of the price (or total cost) borne by buyers—unless an enterprise succeeds in creating and delivering sufficient value to buyers to produce an attractive profit, it can't survive for long.

As shown in Figure 4.3, a company's value chain consists of two broad categories of activities: the *primary activities* that are foremost in creating value for customers and the requisite *support activities* that facilitate and enhance the performance of the primary activities.[10] For example, the primary value-creating activities for a maker of bakery goods include supply chain management, recipe development and testing, mixing and baking, packaging, sales and marketing, and distribution; related support activities include quality control, human resource management, and administration. A wholesaler's primary activities and costs deal with merchandise selection and purchasing, inbound shipping and warehousing from suppliers, and outbound distribution to retail customers. The primary activities for a department store retailer include merchandise selection and buying, store layout and product display, advertising, and customer service; its support activities include site selection, hiring and training, and store maintenance, plus the usual assortment of administrative activities. A hotel chain's primary activities and costs are in site selection and construction, reservations, operation of its hotel properties (check-in and check-out, maintenance and housekeeping, dining and room service, and conventions and meetings), and managing its lineup of hotel locations; principal support activities include accounting, hiring and training hotel staff, advertising, building a brand and reputation, and general administration. Supply chain management is a crucial activity for Nissan and Amazon.com but is not a value chain component at Google or a TV and radio broadcasting company. Sales and marketing are dominant activities at Procter & Gamble and Sony but have minor roles at oil drilling companies and natural gas pipeline companies. Delivery to buyers is a crucial activity at Domino's Pizza but comparatively insignificant at Starbucks. Thus, what constitutes a primary or secondary activity varies according to the specific nature of a company's business, meaning that you should view the listing of the primary and support activities in Figure 4.3 as illustrative rather than definitive.

A Company's Primary and Support Activities Identify the Major Components of Its Cost Structure   Segregating a company's operations into different types of primary and support activities is the first step in understanding its cost structure. Each activity in the value chain gives rise to costs and ties up assets.

Figure 4.3   **A Representative Company Value Chain**

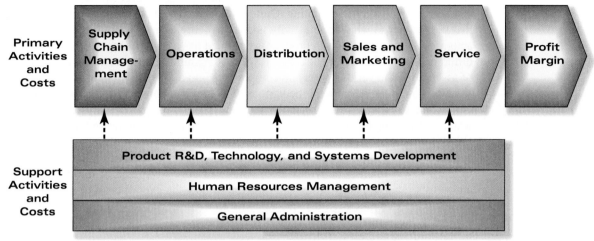

PRIMARY ACTIVITIES

- **Supply chain management**—activities, costs, and assets associated with purchasing fuel, energy, raw materials, parts and components, merchandise, and consumable items from vendors; receiving, storing, and disseminating inputs from suppliers; inspection; and inventory management.

- **Operations**—activities, costs, and assets associated with converting inputs into final product from (production, assembly, packaging, equipment maintenance, facilities, operations, quality assurance, environmental protection).

- **Distribution**—activities, costs, and assets dealing with physically distributing the product to buyers (finished goods warehousing, order processing, order picking and packing, shipping, delivery vehicle operations, establishing and maintaining a network of dealers and distributors).

- **Sales and marketing**—activities, costs, and assets related to sales force efforts, advertising and promotion, market research and planning, and dealer/distributor support.

- **Service**—activities, costs, and assets associated with providing assistance to buyers, such as installation, spare parts delivery, maintenance and repair, technical assistance, buyer inquiries, and complaints.

SUPPORT ACTIVITIES

- **Product R&D, technology, and systems development**—activities, costs, and assets relating to product R&D, process R&D, process design improvement, equipment design, computer software development, telecommunications systems, computer-assisted design and engineering, database capabilities, and development of computerized support systems.

- **Human resources management**—activities, costs, and assets associated with the recruitment, hiring, training, development, and compensation of all types of personnel; labor relations activities; and development of knowledge-based skills and core competencies.

- **General administration**—activities, costs, and assets relating to general management, accounting and finance, legal and regulatory affairs, safety and security, management information systems, forming strategic alliances and collaborating with strategic partners, and other overhead functions.

Source: Based on the discussion in Michael E. Porter, *Competitive Advantage* (New York: Free Press, 1985), pp. 37–43.

Assigning the company's operating costs and assets to each individual activity in the chain provides cost estimates and capital requirements—a process that accountants call activity-based cost accounting. Quite often, there are links between activities such that the manner in which one activity is done can affect the costs of performing other activities. For instance, how a product is designed has a huge impact on the number of different parts and components, their respective manufacturing costs, and the expense of assembling the various parts and components into a finished product.

The combined costs of all the various activities in a company's value chain define the company's internal cost structure. Further, the cost of each activity contributes to whether the company's overall cost position relative to rivals is favorable or unfavorable. The tasks of value chain analysis and benchmarking are to develop the data for comparing a company's costs activity-by-activity against the costs of key rivals and to learn which internal activities are a source of cost advantage or disadvantage. A company's relative cost position is a function of how the overall costs of the activities it performs in conducting business compare to the overall costs of the activities performed by rivals.

Why the Value Chains of Rival Companies Often Differ

A company's value chain and the manner in which it performs each activity reflect the evolution of its own particular business and internal operations, its strategy, the approaches it is using to execute its strategy, and the underlying economics of the activities themselves.[11] Because these factors differ from company to company, the value chains of rival companies sometimes differ substantially—a condition that complicates the task of assessing rivals' relative cost positions. For instance, music retailers like Blockbuster and Musicland, which purchase CDs from recording studios and wholesale distributors and sell them in their own retail store locations, have value chains and cost structures different from those of rival online music stores like Apple's iTunes and Musicmatch, which sell downloadable music files directly to music shoppers. Competing companies may differ in their degrees of vertical integration. The operations component of the value chain for a manufacturer that *makes* all of its own parts and assembles them into a finished product differs from the operations component of a rival producer that *buys* the needed parts from outside suppliers and performs assembly operations only. Likewise, there is legitimate reason to expect value chain and cost differences between a company that is pursuing a low-cost/low-price strategy and a rival that is positioned on the high end of the market. The costs of certain activities along the low-cost company's value chain should indeed be relatively low, whereas the high-end firm may understandably be spending relatively more to perform those activities that create the added quality and extra features of its products.

Moreover, cost and price differences among rival companies can have their origins in activities performed by suppliers or by distribution channel allies involved in getting the product to end users. Suppliers or wholesale/retail dealers may have excessively high cost structures or profit margins that jeopardize a company's cost-competitiveness even though its costs for internally performed activities are competitive. For example, when determining Michelin's cost-competitiveness vis-à-vis Goodyear and Bridgestone in supplying replacement tires to vehicle owners, we have to look at more than whether Michelin's tire manufacturing costs are above or below Goodyear's and Bridgestone's. Let's say that a motor vehicle owner looking for a new set of tires has to pay $400 for a set of Michelin tires and only $350 for a set of Goodyear or Bridgestone tires. Michelin's $50 price disadvantage can stem not only from higher manufacturing costs (reflecting, perhaps, the added costs of Michelin's strategic efforts to build a better-quality tire with more performance features) but also from (1) differences in what the three tire makers pay their suppliers for materials and tire-making components, and (2) differences in the operating efficiencies, costs, and markups of Michelin's wholesale–retail dealer outlets versus those of Goodyear and Bridgestone.

The Value Chain System for an Entire Industry

As the tire industry example makes clear, a company's value chain is embedded in a larger system of activities that includes the value chains of its suppliers and the value chains of whatever distribution channel allies it uses in getting its product or service to end users.[12] Suppliers' value chains are relevant because suppliers perform activities and incur costs in creating and delivering the purchased inputs used in a company's own value-creating activities. The costs, performance features, and quality of these inputs influence a company's own costs and product differentiation capabilities. Anything a company can do to help its suppliers' drive down the costs of their value chain activities or improve the quality and performance of the items being supplied can enhance its own competitiveness—a powerful reason for working collaboratively with suppliers in managing supply chain activities.[13]

The value chains of forward channel partners and/or the customers to whom a company sells are relevant because (1) the costs and margins of a company's distributors and retail dealers are part of the price the ultimate consumer pays, and (2) the activities that distribution allies perform affect customer satisfaction. For these reasons, companies normally work closely with their forward channel allies (who are their direct customers) to perform value chain activities in mutually beneficial ways. For instance, motor vehicle manufacturers work closely with their local automobile dealers to keep the retail prices of their vehicles competitive with rivals' models and to ensure that owners are satisfied with dealers' repair and maintenance services. Some aluminum can producers have constructed plants next to beer breweries and deliver cans on overhead conveyors directly to the breweries' can-filling lines; this has resulted in significant savings in production scheduling, shipping, and inventory costs for both container producers and breweries.[14] Many automotive parts suppliers have built plants near the auto assembly plants they supply to facilitate just-in-time deliveries, reduce warehousing and shipping costs, and promote close collaboration on parts design and production scheduling. Irrigation equipment companies, suppliers of grape-harvesting and winemaking equipment, and firms making barrels, wine bottles, caps, corks, and labels all have facilities in the California wine country to be close to the nearly 700 winemakers they supply.[15] The lesson here is that a company's value chain activities are often closely linked to the value chains of their suppliers and the forward allies or customers to whom they sell.

As a consequence, *accurately assessing a company's competitiveness from the perspective of the consumers who ultimately use its products or services thus requires that company managers understand an industry's entire value chain system for delivering a product or service to customers, not just the company's own value chain.* A typical industry value chain that incorporates the value chains of suppliers and forward channel allies (if any) is shown in Figure 4.4. However, industry value chains

> A company's cost-competitiveness depends not only on the costs of internally performed activities (its own value chain) but also on costs in the value chains of its suppliers and forward channel allies.

Figure 4.4 **Representative Value Chain for an Entire Industry**

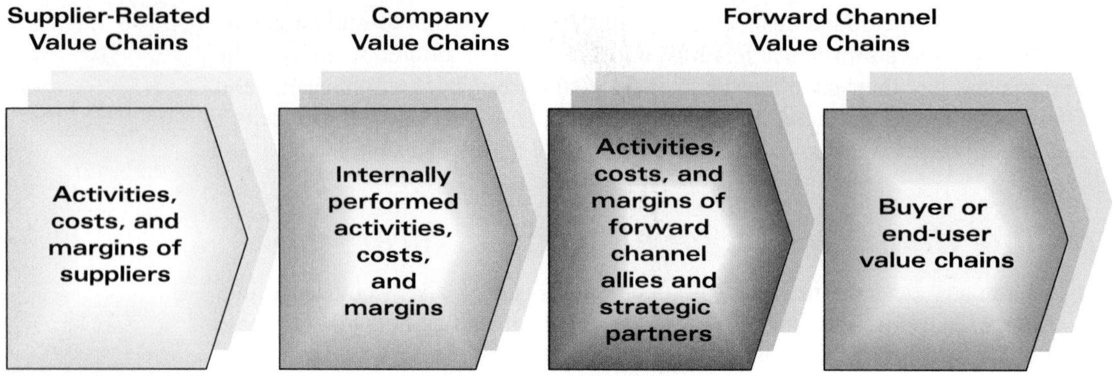

Supplier-Related Value Chains	Company Value Chains	Forward Channel Value Chains	
Activities, costs, and margins of suppliers	Internally performed activities, costs, and margins	Activities, costs, and margins of forward channel allies and strategic partners	Buyer or end-user value chains

Source: Based in part on the single-industry value chain displayed in Michael E. Porter, *Competitive Advantage* (New York: Free Press, 1985), p. 35.

vary significantly by industry. The primary value chain activities in the pulp and paper industry (timber farming, logging, pulp mills, and papermaking) differ from the primary value chain activities in the home appliance industry (parts and components manufacture, assembly, wholesale distribution, retail sales). The value chain for the soft-drink industry (processing of basic ingredients and syrup manufacture, bottling and can filling, wholesale distribution, advertising, and retail merchandising) differs from that for the computer software industry (programming, disk loading, marketing, distribution). Producers of bathroom and kitchen faucets depend heavily on the activities of wholesale distributors and building supply retailers in winning sales to homebuilders and do-it-yourselfers, but producers of papermaking machines internalize their distribution activities by selling directly to the operators of paper plants. Illustration Capsule 4.1 shows representative costs for various activities performed by the producers and marketers of music CDs.

Activity-Based Costing: A Tool for Assessing a Company's Cost Competitiveness

Once the company has identified its major value chain activities, the next step in evaluating its cost competitiveness involves determining the costs of performing specific value chain activities, using what accountants call activity-based costing.[16] Traditional accounting identifies costs according to broad categories of expenses—wages and salaries, employee benefits, supplies, maintenance, utilities, travel, depreciation, R&D, interest, general administration, and so on. But activity-based cost accounting involves establishing expense categories for specific value chain activities and assigning costs to the activity responsible for creating the cost. An illustrative example is shown in Table 4.3 on page 116. Perhaps 25 percent of the companies that have explored the feasibility of activity-based costing have adopted this accounting approach.

Illustration Capsule 4.1

Estimated Value Chain Costs for Recording and Distributing Music CDs through Traditional Music Retailers

The following table presents the representative costs and markups associated with producing and distributing a music CD retailing for $15 in music stores (as opposed to Internet sources).

Value Chain Activities and Costs in Producing and Distributing a CD		
1. Record company direct production costs:		$2.40
Artists and repertoire	$0.75	
Pressing of CD and packaging	1.65	
2. Royalties		0.99
3. Record company marketing expenses		1.50
4. Record company overhead		1.50
5. Total record company costs		6.39
6. Record company's operating profit		1.86
7. Record company's selling price to distributor/wholesaler		8.25
8. Average wholesale distributor markup to cover distribution activities and profit margins		1.50
9. Average wholesale price charged to retailer		9.75
10. Average retail markup over wholesale cost		5.25
11. Average price to consumer at retail		$15.00

Source: Developed from information in "Fight the Power," a case study prepared by Adrian Aleyne, Babson College, 1999.

The degree to which a company's costs should be disaggregated into specific activities depends on how valuable it is to develop cross-company cost comparisons for narrowly defined activities as opposed to broadly defined activities. Generally speaking, cost estimates are needed at least for each broad category of primary and secondary activities, but finer classifications may be needed if a company discovers that it has a cost disadvantage vis-à-vis rivals and wants to pin down the exact source or activity causing the cost disadvantage. It can also be necessary to develop cost estimates for activities performed in the competitively relevant portions of suppliers' and customers' value chains—which requires going to outside sources for reliable cost information.

Once a company has developed good cost estimates for each of the major activities in its value chain, and perhaps has cost estimates for subactivities within each primary/ secondary value chain activity, then it is ready to see how its costs for these activities compare with the costs of rival firms. This is where benchmarking comes in.

Table 4.3   **The Difference between Traditional Cost Accounting and Activity-Based Cost Accounting: A Supply Chain Activity Example**

Traditional Cost Accounting Categories for Supply Chain Activities		Cost of Performing Specific Supply Chain Activities Using Activity-Based Cost Accounting	
Wages and salaries	$450,000	Evaluate supplier capabilities	$150,000
Employee benefits	95,000	Process purchase orders	92,000
Supplies	21,500	Collaborate with suppliers on just-in-time deliveries	180,000
Travel	12,250	Share data with suppliers	69,000
Depreciation	19,000	Check quality of items purchased	94,000
Other fixed charges (office space, utilities)	112,000	Check incoming deliveries against purchase orders	50,000
Miscellaneous operating expenses	40,250	Resolve disputes	15,000
	$750,000	Conduct internal administration	100,000
			$750,000

Source: Developed from information in Terence P. Par, "A New Tool for Managing Costs," *Fortune,* June 14, 1993, pp. 124–29.

Benchmarking: A Tool for Assessing Whether a Company's Value Chain Costs Are in Line

Core Concept
Benchmarking is a potent tool for learning which companies are best at performing particular activities and then using their techniques (or "best practices") to improve the cost and effectiveness of a company's own internal activities.

Many companies today are **benchmarking** their costs of performing a given activity against competitors' costs (and/or against the costs of a noncompetitor that efficiently and effectively performs much the same activity in another industry). *Benchmarking is a tool that allows a company to determine whether its performance of a particular function or activity represents the "best practice" when both cost and effectiveness are taken into account.*

Benchmarking entails comparing how different companies perform various value chain activities—how materials are purchased, how suppliers are paid, how inventories are managed, how products are assembled, how fast the company can get new products to market, how the quality control function is performed, how customer orders are filled and shipped, how employees are trained, how payrolls are processed, and how maintenance is performed—and then making cross-company comparisons of the costs of these activities.[17] The objectives of benchmarking are to identify the best practices in performing an activity, to learn how other companies have actually achieved lower costs or better results in performing benchmarked activities, and to take action to improve a company's competitiveness whenever benchmarking reveals that its costs and results of performing an activity are not on a par with what other companies (either competitors or noncompetitors) have achieved.

Xerox became one of the first companies to use benchmarking when, in 1979, Japanese manufacturers began selling midsize copiers in the United States for $9,600 each—less than Xerox's production costs.[18] Xerox management suspected its Japanese competitors were dumping, but it sent a team of line managers to Japan, including the head of manufacturing, to study competitors' business processes and costs. With the aid of Xerox's joint venture partner in Japan, Fuji-Xerox, which knew the competitors well, the team found that Xerox's costs were excessive due to gross inefficiencies in the company's manufacturing processes and business practices. The findings triggered a major internal effort at Xerox to become cost-competitive and prompted Xerox to begin benchmarking 67 of its key work processes against companies identified as employing the best practices. Xerox quickly decided not to restrict its benchmarking efforts to its office equipment rivals but to extend them to any company regarded as world class in performing *any activity* relevant to Xerox's business. Other companies quickly picked up on Xerox's approach. Toyota managers got their idea for just-in-time inventory deliveries by studying how U.S. supermarkets replenished their shelves. Southwest Airlines reduced the turnaround time of its aircraft at each scheduled stop by studying pit crews on the auto racing circuit. Over 80 percent of Fortune 500 companies reportedly use benchmarking for comparing themselves against rivals on cost and other competitively important measures.

The tough part of benchmarking is not whether to do it, but rather how to gain access to information about other companies' practices and costs. Sometimes benchmarking can be accomplished by collecting information from published reports, trade groups, and industry research firms and by talking to knowledgeable industry analysts, customers, and suppliers. Sometimes field trips to the facilities of competing or noncompeting companies can be arranged to observe how things are done, ask questions, compare practices and processes, and perhaps exchange data on productivity, staffing levels, time requirements, and other cost components—but the problem here is that such companies, even if they agree to host facilities tours and answer questions, are unlikely to share competitively sensitive cost information. Furthermore, comparing one company's costs to another's costs may not involve comparing apples to apples if the two companies employ different cost accounting principles to calculate the costs of particular activities.

> Benchmarking the costs of company activities against rivals provides hard evidence of whether a company is cost-competitive.

However, a third and fairly reliable source of benchmarking information has emerged. The explosive interest of companies in benchmarking costs and identifying best practices has prompted consulting organizations (e.g., Accenture, A. T. Kearney, Benchnet—The Benchmarking Exchange, Towers Perrin, and Best Practices) and several councils and associations (e.g., the American Productivity and Quality Center, the Qualserve Benchmarking Clearinghouse, and the Strategic Planning Institute's Council on Benchmarking) to gather benchmarking data, distribute information about best practices, and provide comparative cost data without identifying the names of particular companies. Having an independent group gather the information and report it in a manner that disguises the names of individual companies avoid having the disclosure of competitively sensitive data and lessens the potential for unethical behavior on the part of company personnel in gathering their own data about competitors. Illustration Capsule 4.2 presents a widely recommended code of conduct for engaging in benchmarking that is intended to help companies avoid any improprieties in gathering and using benchmarking data.

Strategic Options for Remedying a Cost Disadvantage

Value chain analysis and benchmarking can reveal a great deal about a firm's cost competitiveness. Examining the costs of a company's own value chain activities and comparing them to rivals' indicates who has how much of a cost advantage or

Illustration Capsule 4.2

Benchmarking and Ethical Conduct

Because discussions between benchmarking partners can involve competitively sensitive data, conceivably raising questions about possible restraint of trade or improper business conduct, many benchmarking organizations urge all individuals and organizations involved in benchmarking to abide by a code of conduct grounded in ethical business behavior. Among the most widely used codes of conduct is the one developed by the American Productivity and Quality Center and advocated by the Qualserve Benchmarking Clearinghouse; it is based on the following principles and guidelines:

- Avoid discussions or actions that could lead to or imply an interest in restraint of trade, market and/or customer allocation schemes, price fixing, dealing arrangements, bid rigging, or bribery. Don't discuss costs with competitors if costs are an element of pricing.

- Refrain from the acquisition of trade secrets from another by any means that could be interpreted as improper including the breach or inducement of a breach of any duty to maintain secrecy. Do not disclose or use any trade secret that may have been obtained through improper means or that was disclosed by another in violation of duty to maintain its secrecy or limit its use.

- Be willing to provide the same type and level of information that you request from your benchmarking partner to your benchmarking partner.

- Communicate fully and early in the relationship to clarify expectations, avoid misunderstanding, and establish mutual interest in the benchmarking exchange.

- Be honest and complete.

- Treat benchmarking interchange as confidential to the individuals and companies involved. Information must not be communicated outside the partnering organizations without the prior consent of the benchmarking partner who shared the information.

- Use information obtained through benchmarking only for purposes stated to the benchmarking partner.

- The use or communication of a benchmarking partner's name with the data obtained or practices observed requires the prior permission of that partner.

- Respect the corporate culture of partner companies and work within mutually agreed-on procedures.

- Use benchmarking contacts designated by the partner company, if that is the company's preferred procedure.

- Obtain mutual agreement with the designated benchmarking contact on any hand-off of communication or responsibility to other parties.

- Make the most of your benchmarking partner's time by being fully prepared for each exchange.

- Help your benchmarking partners prepare by providing them with a questionnaire and agenda prior to benchmarking visits.

- Follow through with each commitment made to your benchmarking partner in a timely manner.

- Understand how your benchmarking partner would like to have the information he or she provides handled and used, and handle and use it in that manner.

Note: Identification of firms, organizations, and contacts visited is prohibited without advance approval from the organization.

Sources: The American Productivity and Quality Center, www.apqc.org, and the Qualserve Benchmarking Clearinghouse, www.awwa.org (accessed September 14, 2005).

disadvantage and which cost components are responsible. Such information is vital in strategic actions to eliminate a cost disadvantage or create a cost advantage. One of the fundamental insights of value chain analysis and benchmarking is that *a company's competitiveness on cost depends on how efficiently it manages its value chain activities relative to how well competitors manage theirs.*[19] There are three main areas in a company's overall value chain where important differences in the costs of competing firms can occur: a company's own activity segments, suppliers' part of the industry value chain, and the forward channel portion of the industry chain.

Remedying an Internal Cost Disadvantage   When a company's cost disadvantage stems from performing internal value chain activities at a higher cost than key rivals, then managers can pursue any of several strategic approaches to restore cost parity:[20]

1. Implement the use of best practices throughout the company, particularly for high-cost activities.

2. Try to eliminate some cost-producing activities altogether by revamping the value chain. Examples include cutting out low-value-added activities or bypassing the value chains and associated costs of distribution allies and marketing directly to end users. Dell has used this approach in PCs, and airlines have begun bypassing travel agents by getting passengers to purchase their tickets directly at airline Web sites.

3. Relocate high-cost activities (such as manufacturing) to geographic areas—such as China, Latin America, or Eastern Europe—where they can be performed more cheaply.

4. See if certain internally performed activities can be outsourced from vendors or performed by contractors more cheaply than they can be done in-house.

5. Invest in productivity-enhancing, cost-saving technological improvements (robotics, flexible manufacturing techniques, state-of-the-art electronic networking).

6. Find ways to detour around the activities or items where costs are high—computer chip makers regularly design around the patents held by others to avoid paying royalties; automakers have substituted lower-cost plastic and rubber for metal at many exterior body locations.

7. Redesign the product and/or some of its components to facilitate speedier and more economical manufacture or assembly.

8. Try to make up the internal cost disadvantage by reducing costs in the supplier or forward channel portions of the industry value chain—usually a last resort.

Remedying a Supplier-Related Cost Disadvantage   Supplier-related cost disadvantages can be attacked by pressuring suppliers for lower prices, switching to lower-priced substitute inputs, and collaborating closely with suppliers to identify mutual cost-saving opportunities.[21] For example, just-in-time deliveries from suppliers can lower a company's inventory and internal logistics costs and may also allow its suppliers to economize on their warehousing, shipping, and production scheduling costs—a win–win outcome for both. In a few instances, companies may find that it is cheaper to integrate backward into the business of high-cost suppliers and make the item in-house instead of buying it from outsiders. If a company strikes out in wringing savings out of its high-cost supply chain activities, then it must resort to finding cost savings either in-house or in the forward channel portion of the industry value chain to offset its supplier-related cost disadvantage.

Remedying a Cost Disadvantage Associated with Activities Performed by Forward Channel Allies   There are three main ways to combat a cost disadvantage in the forward portion of the industry value chain:

1. Pressure dealer-distributors and other forward channel allies to reduce their costs and markups so as to make the final price to buyers more competitive with the prices of rivals.

2. Work closely with forward channel allies to identify win–win opportunities to reduce costs. For example, a chocolate manufacturer learned that by shipping its bulk chocolate in liquid form in tank cars instead of 10-pound molded bars, it could not only save its candy bar manufacturing customers the costs associated with unpacking and melting but also eliminate its own costs of molding bars and packing them.

3. Change to a more economical distribution strategy, including switching to cheaper distribution channels (perhaps direct sales via the Internet) or perhaps integrating forward into company-owned retail outlets.

If these efforts fail, the company can either try to live with the cost disadvantage or pursue cost-cutting earlier in the value chain system.

Translating Proficient Performance of Value Chain Activities into Competitive Advantage

Performing value chain activities in ways that give a company the capabilities to either outmatch the competencies and capabilities of rivals or else beat them on costs are two good ways to secure competitive advantage.

A company that does a *first-rate job* of managing its value chain activities *relative to competitors* stands a good chance of achieving sustainable competitive advantage. As shown in Figure 4.5, outmanaging rivals in performing value chain activities can be accomplished in either or both of two ways: (1) by astutely developing core competencies and maybe a distinctive competence that rivals don't have or can't quite match and that are instrumental in helping it deliver attractive value to customers, and/or (2) by simply doing an overall better job than rivals of lowering its combined costs of performing all the various value chain activities, such that it ends up with a low-cost advantage over rivals.

The first of these two approaches begins with management efforts to build more organizational expertise in performing certain competitively important value chain activities, deliberately striving to develop competencies and capabilities that add power to its strategy and competitiveness. If management begins to make selected competencies and capabilities cornerstones of its strategy and continues to invest resources in building greater and greater proficiency in performing them, then over time one (or maybe several) of the targeted competencies/capabilities may rise to the level of a core competence. Later, following additional organizational learning and investments in gaining still greater proficiency, a core competence could evolve into a distinctive competence, giving the company superiority over rivals in performing an important value chain activity. Such superiority, if it gives the company significant competitive clout in the marketplace, can produce an attractive competitive edge over rivals and, more important, prove difficult for rivals to match or offset with competencies and capabilities of their own making. As a general rule, it is substantially harder for rivals to achieve best-in-industry proficiency in performing a key value chain activity than it is for them to clone the features and attributes of a hot-selling product or service.[22] This is especially true when a company with a distinctive competence avoids becoming complacent and works diligently to maintain its industry-leading expertise and capability. GlaxoSmithKline, one of the world's most competitively capable pharmaceutical companies, has built its business position around expert performance of a few competitively crucial activities: extensive R&D to achieve first discovery of new drugs, a carefully constructed approach to patenting, skill in gaining rapid and thorough clinical clearance through regulatory bodies, and unusually strong distribution and sales-force

Figure 4.5   **Translating Company Performance of Value Chain Activities into Competitive Advantage**

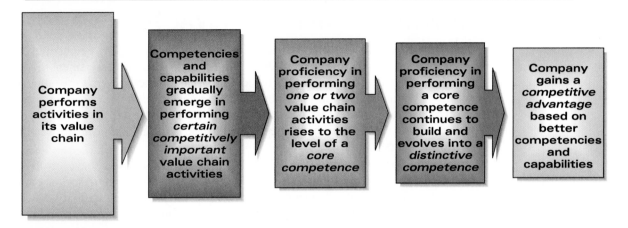

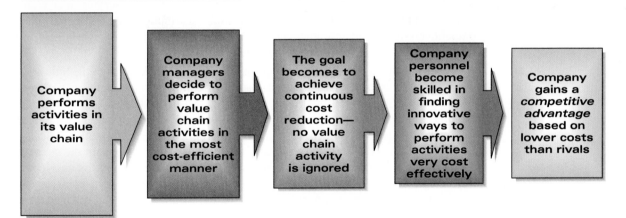

capabilities.[23] FedEx's astute management of its value chain has produced unmatched competencies and capabilities in overnight package delivery.

The second approach to building competitive advantage entails determined management efforts to be cost-efficient in performing value chain activities. Such efforts have to be ongoing and persistent, and they have to involve each and every value chain activity. The goal must be continuous cost reduction, not a one-time or on-again/off-again effort. Companies whose managers are truly committed to low-cost performance of value chain activities and succeed in engaging company personnel to discover innovative ways to drive costs out of the business have a real chance of gaining a durable low-cost edge over rivals. It is not as easy as it seems to imitate a company's low-cost practices. Companies like Wal-Mart, Dell, Nucor Steel, Southwest Airlines,

Toyota, and French discount retailer Carrefour have been highly successful in managing their value chains in a low-cost manner.

QUESTION 4: IS THE COMPANY COMPETITIVELY STRONGER OR WEAKER THAN KEY RIVALS?

Using value chain analysis and benchmarking to determine a company's competitiveness on price is necessary but not sufficient. A more comprehensive assessment needs to be made of the company's overall competitive strength. The answers to two questions are of particular interest: First, how does the company rank relative to competitors on each of the important factors that determine market success? Second, all things considered, does the company have a net competitive advantage or disadvantage versus major competitors?

An easy-to-use method for answering the two questions posed above involves developing quantitative strength ratings for the company and its key competitors on each industry key success factor and each competitively pivotal resource capability. Much of the information needed for doing a competitive strength assessment comes from previous analyses. Industry and competitive analysis reveals the key success factors and competitive capabilities that separate industry winners from losers. Benchmarking data and scouting key competitors provide a basis for judging the competitive strength of rivals on such factors as cost, key product attributes, customer service, image and reputation, financial strength, technological skills, distribution capability, and other competitively important resources and capabilities. SWOT analysis reveals how the company in question stacks up on these same strength measures.

Step 1 in doing a competitive strength assessment is to make a list of the industry's key success factors and most telling measures of competitive strength or weakness (6 to 10 measures usually suffice). Step 2 is to rate the firm and its rivals on each factor. Numerical rating scales (e.g., from 1 to 10) are best to use, although ratings of stronger (+), weaker (−), and about equal (=) may be appropriate when information is scanty and assigning numerical scores conveys false precision. Step 3 is to sum the strength ratings on each factor to get an overall measure of competitive strength for each company being rated. Step 4 is to use the overall strength ratings to draw conclusions about the size and extent of the company's net competitive advantage or disadvantage and to take specific note of areas of strength and weakness.

Table 4.5 provides two examples of competitive strength assessment, using the hypothetical ABC Company against four rivals. The first example employs an *unweighted rating system*. With unweighted ratings, each key success factor/competitive strength measure is assumed to be equally important (a rather dubious assumption). Whichever company has the highest strength rating on a given measure has an implied competitive edge on that factor; the size of its edge is mirrored in the margin of difference between its rating and the ratings assigned to rivals—a rating of 9 for one company versus ratings of 5, 4, and 3, respectively, for three other companies indicates a bigger advantage than a rating of 9 versus ratings of 8, 7, and 6. Summing a company's ratings on all the measures produces an overall strength rating. The higher a company's overall strength rating, the stronger its overall competitiveness versus rivals. The bigger the difference between a company's overall rating and the scores of *lower-rated* rivals, the greater its implied *net competitive advantage.* Conversely, the bigger the difference between a company's overall rating and the scores of *higher-rated* rivals, the greater its implied

Table 4.5 **Illustrations of Unweighted and Weighted Competitive Strength Assessments**

A. An Unweighted Competitive Strength Assessment

	Strength Rating (Scale: 1 = Very weak; 10 = Very strong)				
Key Success Factor/Strength Measure	ABC Co.	Rival 1	Rival 2	Rival 3	Rival 4
Quality/product performance	8	5	10	1	6
Reputation/image	8	7	10	1	6
Manufacturing capability	2	10	4	5	1
Technological skills	10	1	7	3	8
Dealer network/distribution capability	9	4	10	5	1
New product innovation capability	9	4	10	5	1
Financial resources	5	10	7	3	1
Relative cost position	5	10	3	1	4
Customer service capabilities	5	7	10	1	4
Unweighted overall strength rating	**61**	**58**	**71**	**25**	**32**

B. A Weighted Competitive Strength Assessment
(Rating Scale: 1 = Very weak; 10 = Very strong)

Key Success Factor/Strength Measure	Importance Weight	ABC Co.		Rival 1		Rival 2		Rival 3		Rival 4	
		Strength Rating	Score	Strength Rating	Score	Strength Rating	Score	Strength Rating	Score	Strength Rating	Score
Quality/product performance	0.10	8	0.80	5	0.50	10	1.00	1	0.10	6	0.60
Reputation/image	0.10	8	0.80	7	0.70	10	1.00	1	0.10	6	0.60
Manufacturing capability	0.10	2	0.20	10	1.00	4	0.40	5	0.50	1	0.10
Technological skills	0.05	10	0.50	1	0.05	7	0.35	3	0.15	8	0.40
Dealer network/distribution capability	0.05	9	0.45	4	0.20	10	0.50	5	0.25	1	0.05
New product innovation capability	0.05	9	0.45	4	0.20	10	0.50	5	0.25	1	0.05
Financial resources	0.10	5	0.50	10	1.00	7	0.70	3	0.30	1	0.10
Relative cost position	0.30	5	1.50	10	3.00	3	0.95	1	0.30	4	1.20
Customer service capabilities	0.15	5	0.75	7	1.05	10	1.50	1	0.15	4	0.60
Sum of importance weights	1.00										
Weighted overall strength rating		61	**5.95**	58	**7.70**	71	**6.85**	25	**2.10**	32	**3.70**

123

net competitive disadvantage. Thus, ABC's total score of 61 (see the top half of Table 4.5) signals a much greater net competitive advantage over Rival 4 (with a score of 32) than over Rival 1 (with a score of 58) but indicates a moderate net competitive disadvantage against Rival 2 (with an overall score of 71).

However, a better method is a *weighted rating system* (shown in the bottom half of Table 4.5) because the different measures of competitive strength are unlikely to be equally important. In an industry where the products/services of rivals are virtually identical, for instance, having low unit costs relative to rivals is nearly always the most important determinant of competitive strength. In an industry with strong product differentiation, the most significant measures of competitive strength may be brand awareness, amount of advertising, product attractiveness, and distribution capability. In a weighted rating system each measure of competitive strength is assigned a weight based on its perceived importance in shaping competitive success. A weight could be as high as 0.75 (maybe even higher) in situations where one particular competitive variable is overwhelmingly decisive, or a weight could be as low as 0.20 when two or three strength measures are more important than the rest. Lesser competitive strength indicators can carry weights of 0.05 or 0.10. No matter whether the differences between the importance weights are big or little, *the sum of the weights must equal 1.0.*

> A weighted competitive strength analysis is conceptually stronger than an unweighted analysis because of the inherent weakness in assuming that all the strength measures are equally important.

Weighted strength ratings are calculated by rating each competitor on each strength measure (using the 1 to 10 rating scale) and multiplying the assigned rating by the assigned weight (a rating of 4 times a weight of 0.20 gives a weighted rating, or score, of 0.80). Again, the company with the highest rating on a given measure has an implied competitive edge on that measure, with the size of its edge reflected in the difference between its rating and rivals' ratings. The weight attached to the measure indicates how important the edge is. Summing a company's weighted strength ratings for all the measures yields an overall strength rating. Comparisons of the weighted overall strength scores indicate which competitors are in the strongest and weakest competitive positions and who has how big a net competitive advantage over whom.

Note in Table 4.5 that the unweighted and weighted rating schemes produce different orderings of the companies. In the weighted system, ABC Company drops from second to third in strength, and Rival 1 jumps from third to first because of its high strength ratings on the two most important factors. Weighting the importance of the strength measures can thus make a significant difference in the outcome of the assessment.

Interpreting the Competitive Strength Assessments

> High competitive strength ratings signal a strong competitive position and possession of competitive advantage; low ratings signal a weak position and competitive disadvantage.

Competitive strength assessments provide useful conclusions about a company's competitive situation. The ratings show how a company compares against rivals, factor by factor or capability by capability, thus revealing where it is strongest and weakest, and against whom. Moreover, the overall competitive strength scores indicate how all the different factors add up—whether the company is at a net competitive advantage or disadvantage against each rival. The firm with the largest overall competitive strength rating enjoys the strongest competitive position, with the size of its net competitive advantage reflected by how much its score exceeds the scores of rivals.

In addition, the strength ratings provide guidelines for designing wise offensive and defensive strategies. For example, consider the ratings and weighted scores in the bottom half of Table 4.5. If ABC Company wants to go on the offensive to win additional sales and market share, such an offensive probably needs to be aimed directly at winning customers away from Rivals 3 and 4 (which have lower overall strength scores) rather than Rivals 1 and 2 (which have higher overall strength scores). Moreover, while ABC has high ratings for quality/product performance (an 8 rating), reputation/image (an 8 rating), technological skills (a 10 rating), dealer network/distribution capability (a 9 rating), and new product innovation capability (a 9 rating), these strength measures have low importance weights—meaning that ABC has strengths in areas that don't translate into much competitive clout in the marketplace. Even so, it outclasses Rival 3 in all five areas, plus it enjoys lower costs than Rival 3: On relative cost position ABC has a 5 rating versus a 1 rating for Rival 3—and relative cost position carries the highest importance weight of all the strength measures. ABC also has greater competitive strength than Rival 3 as concerns customer service capabilities (which carries the second-highest importance weight). Hence, because ABC's strengths are in the very areas where Rival 3 is weak, ABC is in good position to attack Rival 3—it may well be able to persuade a number of Rival 3's customers to switch their purchases over to ABC's product.

But in mounting an offensive to win customers away from Rival 3, ABC should note that Rival 1 has an excellent relative cost position—its rating of 10, combined with the importance weight of 0.30 for relative cost, means that Rival 1 has meaningfully lower costs in an industry where low costs are competitively important. Rival 1 is thus strongly positioned to retaliate against ABC with lower prices if ABC's strategy offensive ends up drawing customers away from Rival 1. Moreover, Rival 1's very strong relative cost position vis-à-vis all the other companies arms it with the ability to use its lower-cost advantage to underprice all of its rivals and gain sales and market share at their expense. If ABC wants to defend against its vulnerability to potential price cutting by Rival 1, then it needs to aim a portion of its strategy at lowering its costs.

> A company's competitive strength scores pinpoint its strengths and weaknesses against rivals and point directly to the kinds of offensive/defensive actions it can use to exploit its competitive strengths and reduce its competitive vulnerabilities.

The point here is that a competitively astute company should use the strength assessment in deciding what strategic moves to make—which strengths to exploit in winning business away from rivals and which competitive weaknesses to try to correct. When a company has important competitive strengths in areas where one or more rivals are weak, it makes sense to consider offensive moves to exploit rivals' competitive weaknesses. When a company has important competitive weaknesses in areas where one or more rivals are strong, it makes sense to consider defensive moves to curtail its vulnerability.

QUESTION 5: WHAT STRATEGIC ISSUES AND PROBLEMS MERIT FRONT-BURNER MANAGERIAL ATTENTION?

The final and most important analytical step is to zero in on exactly what strategic issues that company managers need to address—and resolve—for the company to be more financially and competitively successful in the years ahead. This step involves drawing on the results of both industry and competitive analysis and the evaluations of the company's own competitiveness. The task here is to get a clear fix on exactly what strategic and competitive challenges confront the company, which of the company's competitive shortcomings need fixing, what obstacles stand in the way of improving the company's competitive position in the marketplace, and what specific problems

Zeroing in on the strategic issues a company faces and compiling a "worry list" of problems and roadblocks creates a strategic agenda of problems that merit prompt managerial attention.

Actually deciding upon a strategy and what specific actions to take is what comes *after* developing the list of strategic issues and problems that merit front-burner management attention.

A good strategy must contain ways to deal with all the strategic issues and obstacles that stand in the way of the company's financial and competitive success in the years ahead.

merit front-burner attention by company managers. *Pinpointing the precise things that management needs to worry about sets the agenda for deciding what actions to take next to improve the company's performance and business outlook.*

The "worry list" of issues and problems that have to be wrestled with can include such things as *how* to stave off market challenges from new foreign competitors, *how* to combat the price discounting of rivals, *how* to reduce the company's high costs and pave the way for price reductions, *how* to sustain the company's present rate of growth in light of slowing buyer demand, *whether* to expand the company's product line, *whether* to correct the company's competitive deficiencies by acquiring a rival company with the missing strengths, *whether* to expand into foreign markets rapidly or cautiously, *whether* to reposition the company and move to a different strategic group, *what to do* about growing buyer interest in substitute products, and *what to do* to combat the aging demographics of the company's customer base. The worry list thus always centers on such concerns as "how to . . .," "what to do about . . .," and "whether to . . ."—the purpose of the worry list is to identify the specific issues/problems that management needs to address, not to figure out what specific actions to take. Deciding what to do—which strategic actions to take and which strategic moves to make—comes later (when it is time to craft the strategy and choose from among the various strategic alternatives).

If the items on the worry list are relatively minor—which suggests the company's strategy is mostly on track and reasonably well matched to the company's overall situation—then company managers seldom need to go much beyond fine-tuning of the present strategy. If, however, the issues and problems confronting the company are serious and indicate the present strategy is not well suited for the road ahead, the task of crafting a better strategy has got to go to the top of management's action agenda.

Key Points

There are five key questions to consider in analyzing a company's own particular competitive circumstances and its competitive position vis-à-vis key rivals:

1. *How well is the present strategy working?* This involves evaluating the strategy from a qualitative standpoint (completeness, internal consistency, rationale, and suitability to the situation) and also from a quantitative standpoint (the strategic and financial results the strategy is producing). The stronger a company's current overall performance, the less likely the need for radical strategy changes. The weaker a company's performance and/or the faster the changes in its external situation (which can be gleaned from industry and competitive analysis), the more its current strategy must be questioned.

2. *What are the company's resource strengths and weaknesses, and its external opportunities and threats?* A SWOT analysis provides an overview of a firm's situation and is an essential component of crafting a strategy tightly matched to the company's situation. The two most important parts of SWOT analysis are (*a*) drawing conclusions about what story the compilation of strengths, weaknesses, opportunities, and threats tells about the company's overall situation, and

(*b*) acting on those conclusions to better match the company's strategy, to its resource strengths and market opportunities, to correct the important weaknesses, and to defend against external threats. A company's resource strengths, competencies, and competitive capabilities are strategically relevant because they are the most logical and appealing building blocks for strategy; resource weaknesses are important because they may represent vulnerabilities that need correction. External opportunities and threats come into play because a good strategy necessarily aims at capturing a company's most attractive opportunities and at defending against threats to its well-being.

3. *Are the company's prices and costs competitive?* One telling sign of whether a company's situation is strong or precarious is whether its prices and costs are competitive with those of industry rivals. Value chain analysis and benchmarking are essential tools in determining whether the company is performing particular functions and activities cost-effectively, learning whether its costs are in line with competitors, and deciding which internal activities and business processes need to be scrutinized for improvement. Value chain analysis teaches that how competently a company manages its value chain activities relative to rivals is a key to building a competitive advantage based on either better competencies and competitive capabilities or lower costs than rivals.

4. *Is the company competitively stronger or weaker than key rivals?* The key appraisals here involve how the company matches up against key rivals on industry key success factors and other chief determinants of competitive success and whether and why the company has a competitive advantage or disadvantage. Quantitative competitive strength assessments, using the method presented in Table 4.5, indicate where a company is competitively strong and weak, and provide insight into the company's ability to defend or enhance its market position. As a rule a company's competitive strategy should be built around its competitive strengths and should aim at shoring up areas where it is competitively vulnerable. When a company has important competitive strengths in areas where one or more rivals are weak, it makes sense to consider offensive moves to exploit rivals' competitive weaknesses. When a company has important competitive weaknesses in areas where one or more rivals are strong, it makes sense to consider defensive moves to curtail its vulnerability.

5. *What strategic issues and problems merit front-burner managerial attention?* This analytical step zeros in on the strategic issues and problems that stand in the way of the company's success. It involves using the results of both industry and competitive analysis and company situation analysis to identify a "worry list" of issues to be resolved for the company to be financially and competitively successful in the years ahead. The worry list always centers on such concerns as "how to . . .," "what to do about . . .," and "whether to . . ."—the purpose of the worry list is to identify the specific issues/problems that management needs to address. Actually deciding upon a strategy and what specific actions to take is what comes after the list of strategic issues and problems that merit front-burner management attention is developed.

Good company situation analysis, like good industry and competitive analysis, is a valuable precondition for good strategy making. A competently done evaluation of a company's resource capabilities and competitive strengths exposes strong and weak points in the present strategy and how attractive or unattractive the company's competitive position is and why. Managers need such understanding to craft a strategy that is well suited to the company's competitive circumstances.

Exercises

1. Review the information in Illustration Capsule 4.1 concerning the costs of the different value chain activities associated with recording and distributing music CDs through traditional brick-and-mortar retail outlets. Then answer the following questions:

   a. Does the growing popularity of downloading music from the Internet give rise to a new music industry value chain that differs considerably from the traditional value chain? Explain why or why not.

   b. What costs are cut out of the traditional value chain or bypassed when *online music retailers* (Apple, Sony, Microsoft, Musicmatch, Napster, Cdigix, and others) sell songs directly to online buyers? (Note: In 2005, online music stores were selling download-only titles for $0.79 to $0.99 per song and $9.99 for most albums.)

   c. What costs would be cut out of the traditional value chain or bypassed in the event that *recording studios* sell downloadable files of artists' recordings directly to online buyers?

   d. What happens to the traditional value chain if more and more music lovers use peer-to-peer file-sharing software to download music from the Internet to play music on their PCs or MP3 players or make their own CDs? (Note: It was estimated that, in 2004, about 1 billion songs were available for online trading and file sharing via such programs as Kazaa, Grokster, Shareaza, BitTorrent, and eDonkey, despite the fact that some 4,000 people had been sued by the Recording Industry Association of America for pirating copyrighted music via peer-to-peer file sharing.)

2. Using the information in Table 4.1 and the following financial statement information for Avon Products, calculate the following ratios for Avon for both 2003 and 2004:

   a. Gross profit margin.

   b. Operating profit margin.

   c. Net profit margin.

   d. Return on total assets.

   e. Return on stockholders' equity.

   f. Debt-to-equity ratio.

   g. Times-interest-earned.

   h. Days of inventory.

   i. Inventory turnover ratio.

   j. Average collection period.

   Based on these ratios, did Avon's financial performance improve, weaken, or remain about the same from 2003 to 2004?

Avon Products Inc., Consolidated Statements of Income
(in millions, except per share data)

| | Years Ended December 31 | |
	2004	2003
Net sales	$7,656.2	$6,773.7
Other revenue	91.6	71.4
Total revenue	7,747.8	6,845.1
Costs, expenses and other:		
Cost of sales	2,911.7	2,611.8
Marketing, distribution and administrative expenses	3,610.3	3,194.4
Special charges, net	(3.2)	(3.9)
Operating profit	1,229.0	1,042.8
Interest expense	33.8	33.3
Interest income	(20.6)	(12.6)
Other expense (income), net	28.3	28.6
Total other expenses	41.5	49.3
Income before taxes and minority interest	1,187.5	993.5
Income taxes	330.6	318.9
Income before minority interest	856.9	674.6
Minority interest	(10.8)	(9.8)
Net income	$ 846.1	$ 664.8
Earnings per share:		
Basic	$ 1.79	$ 1.41
Diluted	$ 1.77	$ 1.39
Weighted-average shares outstanding (in millions):		
Basic	472.35	471.08
Diluted	477.96	483.13

Avon Products Inc. Consolidated Balance Sheets (in millions)

	December 31	
	2004	2003
Current assets		
Cash, including cash equivalents of $401.2 and $373.8	$ 769.6	$ 694.0
Accounts receivable (less allowances of $101.0 and $81.1)	599.1	553.2
Inventories	740.5	653.4
Prepaid expenses and other	397.2	325.5
Total current assets	$2,506.4	$2,226.1
Property, plant and equipment, at cost:		
Land	$ 61.7	$ 58.6
Buildings and improvements	886.8	765.9
Equipment	1,006.7	904.4
	1,955.2	1,728.9
Less accumulated depreciation	(940.4)	(873.3)
	1,014.8	855.6
Other assets	626.9	499.9
Total assets	$4,148.1	$3,581.6
Liabilities and shareholders' equity		
Current liabilities		
Debt maturing within one year	$ 51.7	$ 244.1
Accounts payable	490.1	400.1
Accrued compensation	164.5	149.5
Other accrued liabilities	360.1	332.6
Sales and taxes other than income	154.4	139.5
Income taxes	304.7	341.2
Total current liabilities	$1,525.5	$1,607.0
Long-term debt	$ 866.3	$ 877.7
Employee benefit plans	620.6	502.1
Deferred income taxes	12.1	50.6
Other liabilities (including minority interest of $42.5 and $46.0)	173.4	172.9
Total liabilities	$3,197.9	$3,210.3

(*Continued*)

	December 31	
	2004	2003
Shareholders' equity		
Common stock, par value $.25—authorized 1,500 shares; issued 728.61 and 722.25 shares	182.2	90.3
Additional paid-in capital	1,356.8	1,188.4
Retained earnings	2,693.5	2,202.4
Accumulated other comprehensive loss	(679.5)	(729.4)
Treasury stock, at cost—257.08 and 251.66 shares	(2,602.8)	(2,380.4)
Total shareholders' equity	950.2	371.3
Total liabilities and shareholders' equity	$4,148.1	$3,581.6

Source: Avon Products Inc., 2004 10-K

The Five Generic Competitive Strategies

Which One to Employ?

Competitive strategy is about being different. It means deliberately choosing to perform activities differently or to perform different activities than rivals to deliver a unique mix of value.

—Michael E. Porter

Strategy . . . is about first analyzing and then experimenting, trying, learning, and experimenting some more.

—Ian C. McMillan and Rita Gunther McGrath

Winners in business play rough and don't apologize for it. The nicest part of playing hardball is watching your competitors squirm.

—George Stalk Jr. and Rob Lachenauer

The essence of strategy lies in creating tomorrow's competitive advantages faster than competitors mimic the ones you possess today.

—Gary Hamel and C. K. Prahalad

This chapter describes the *five basic competitive strategy options*—which of the five to employ is a company's first and foremost choice in crafting an overall strategy and beginning its quest for competitive advantage. A company's **competitive strategy** deals exclusively with the specifics of management's game plan for competing successfully—its specific efforts to please customers, its offensive and defensive moves to counter the maneuvers of rivals, its responses to whatever market conditions prevail at the moment, its initiatives to strengthen its market position, and its approach to securing a competitive advantage vis-à-vis rivals. Companies the world over are imaginative in conceiving competitive strategies to win customer favor. At most companies the aim, quite simply, is to do a significantly better job than rivals of providing what buyers are looking for and thereby secure an upper hand in the marketplace.

A company achieves competitive advantage whenever it has some type of edge over rivals in attracting buyers and coping with competitive forces. There are many routes to competitive advantage, but they all involve giving buyers what they perceive as superior value compared to the offerings of rival sellers. Superior value can mean a good product at a lower price; a superior product that is worth paying more for; or a best-value offering that represents an attractive combination of price, features, quality, service, and other appealing attributes. Delivering superior value—whatever form it takes—nearly always requires performing value chain activities differently than rivals and building competencies and resource capabilities that are not readily matched.

> **Core Concept**
> A *competitive strategy* concerns the specifics of management's game plan for competing successfully and securing a competitive advantage over rivals.

> **Core Concept**
> The objective of competitive strategy is to knock the socks off rival companies by doing a better job of satisfying buyer needs and preferences.

THE FIVE GENERIC COMPETITIVE STRATEGIES

There are countless variations in the competitive strategies that companies employ, mainly because each company's strategic approach entails custom-designed actions to fit its own circumstances and industry environment. The custom-tailored nature of each company's strategy makes the chances remote that any two companies—even companies in the same industry—will employ strategies that are exactly alike in every detail. Managers at different companies always have a slightly different spin on future market conditions and how to best align their company's strategy with these conditions; moreover, they have different notions of how they intend to outmaneuver rivals and what strategic options make the most sense for their particular company. However, when one strips away the details to get at the real substance, the biggest and most important differences among competitive strategies boil down to (1) whether a company's market target is broad or narrow, and (2) whether the company is pursuing a competitive advantage linked to low costs or product differentiation. Five distinct competitive strategy approaches stand out:[1]

1. *A low-cost provider strategy*—striving to achieve lower overall costs than rivals and appealing to a broad spectrum of customers, usually by underpricing rivals.

2. *A broad differentiation strategy*—seeking to differentiate the company's product offering from rivals' in ways that will appeal to a broad spectrum of buyers.

3. *A best-cost provider strategy*—giving customers more value for their money by incorporating good-to-excellent product attributes at a lower cost than rivals; the target is to have the lowest (best) costs and prices compared to rivals offering products with comparable attributes.

Figure 5.1   **The Five Generic Competitive Strategies: Each Stakes Out a Different Market Position**

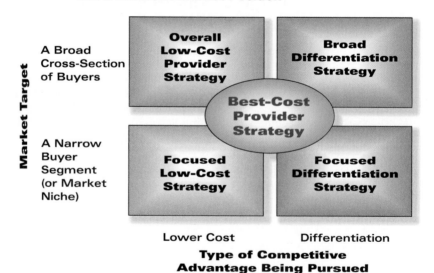

Source: This is an author-expanded version of a three-strategy classification discussed in Michael E. Porter, *Competitive Strategy: Techniques for Analyzing Industries and Competitors* (New York: Free Press, 1980), pp. 35–40.

4. *A focused (or market niche) strategy based on low costs*—concentrating on a narrow buyer segment and outcompeting rivals by having lower costs than rivals and thus being able to serve niche members at a lower price.

5. *A focused (or market niche) strategy based on differentiation*—concentrating on a narrow buyer segment and outcompeting rivals by offering niche members customized attributes that meet their tastes and requirements better than rivals' products.

Each of these five generic competitive approaches stakes out a different market position, as shown in Figure 5.1. Each involves distinctively different approaches to competing and operating the business. The remainder of this chapter explores the ins and outs of the five generic competitive strategies and how they differ.

LOW-COST PROVIDER STRATEGIES

Striving to be the industry's overall low-cost provider is a powerful competitive approach in markets with many price-sensitive buyers. A company achieves low-cost leadership when it becomes the industry's lowest-cost provider rather than just being one of perhaps several competitors with comparatively low costs. A low-cost provider's strategic target is meaningfully lower costs than rivals—but not necessarily the absolutely lowest possible cost. In striving for a cost advantage over rivals, managers must take care to include features and services that buyers consider essential—*a product offering that is too frills-free sabotages the attractiveness of the company's product and can turn buyers off even if it is priced lower than competing products.* For maximum effectiveness, companies employing a low-cost provider strategy need to achieve their cost advantage in ways difficult for rivals to copy or match. If rivals find it relatively easy or inexpensive to imitate the leader's low-cost methods, then the leader's advantage will be too short-lived to yield a valuable edge in the marketplace.

> **Core Concept**
> A low-cost leader's basis for competitive advantage is lower overall costs than competitors. Successful low-cost leaders are exceptionally good at finding ways to drive costs out of their businesses.

A company has two options for translating a low-cost advantage over rivals into attractive profit performance. Option 1 is to use the lower-cost edge to underprice competitors and attract price-sensitive buyers in great enough numbers to increase total profits. The trick to profitably underpricing rivals is either to keep the size of the price cut smaller than the size of the firm's cost advantage (thus reaping the benefits of both a bigger profit margin per unit sold and the added profits on incremental sales) or to generate enough added volume to increase total profits despite thinner profit margins (larger volume can make up for smaller margins provided the underpricing of rivals brings in enough extra sales). Option 2 is to maintain the present price, be content with the present market share, and use the lower-cost edge to earn a higher profit margin on each unit sold, thereby raising the firm's total profits and overall return on investment.

Illustration Capsule 5.1 describes Nucor Corporation's strategy for gaining low-cost leadership in manufacturing a variety of steel products.

The Two Major Avenues for Achieving a Cost Advantage

To achieve a low-cost edge over rivals, a firm's cumulative costs across its overall value chain must be lower than competitors' cumulative costs—and the means of achieving

Illustration Capsule 5.1

Nucor Corporation's Low-Cost Provider Strategy

Nucor Corporation is the world's leading minimill producer of such steel products as carbon and alloy steel bars, beams, sheet, and plate; steel joists and joist girders; steel deck; cold finished steel; steel fasteners; metal building systems; and light gauge steel framing. In 2004, it had close to $10 billion in sales, 9,000 employees, and annual production capacity of nearly 22 million tons, making it the largest steel producer in the United States and one of the 10 largest in the world. The company has pursued a strategy that has made it among the world's lowest-cost producers of steel and has allowed the company to consistently outperform its rivals in terms of financial and market performance.

Nucor's low-cost strategy aims to give it a cost and pricing advantage in the commodity-like steel industry and leaves no part of the company's value chain neglected. The key elements of the strategy include the following:

- Using electric arc furnaces where scrap steel and directly reduced iron ore are melted and then sent to a continuous caster and rolling mill to be shaped into steel products, thereby eliminating an assortment of production processes from the value chain used by traditional integrated steel mills. Nucor's minimill value chain makes the use of coal, coke, and iron ore unnecessary; cuts investment in facilities and equipment (eliminating coke ovens, blast furnaces, basic oxygen furnaces, and ingot casters); and requires fewer employees than integrated mills.

- Striving hard for continuous improvement in the efficiency of its plants and frequently investing in state-of-the-art equipment to reduce unit costs. Nucor is known for its technological leadership and its aggressive pursuit of production process innovation.

- Carefully selecting plant sites to minimize inbound and outbound shipping costs and to take advantage of low rates for electricity (electric arc furnaces are heavy users of electricity). Nucor tends to avoid locating new plants in geographic areas where labor unions are a strong influence.

- Hiring a nonunion workforce that uses team-based incentive compensation systems (often opposed by unions). Operating and maintenance employees and supervisors are paid weekly bonuses based on the productivity of their work group. The size of the bonus is based on the capabilities of the equipment employed and ranges from 80 percent to 150 percent of an employee's base pay; no bonus is paid if the equipment is not operating. Nucor's compensation program has boosted the company's labor productivity to levels nearly double the industry average while rewarding productive employees with annual compensation packages that exceed what their union counterparts earn by as much as 20 percent. Nucor has been able to attract and retain highly talented, productive, and dedicated employees. In addition, the company's healthy culture and results-oriented self-managed work teams allow the company to employ fewer supervisors than what would be needed with an hourly union workforce.

- Heavily emphasizing consistent product quality and has rigorous quality systems.

- Minimizing general and administrative expenses by maintaining a lean staff at corporate headquarters (fewer than 125 employees) and allowing only four levels of management between the CEO and production workers. Headquarters offices are modestly furnished and located in an inexpensive building. The company minimizes reports, paperwork, and meetings to keep managers focused on value-adding activities. Nucor is noted not only for its streamlined organizational structure but also for its frugality in travel and entertainment expenses—the company's top managers set the example by flying coach class, avoiding pricey hotels, and refraining from taking customers out for expensive dinners.

In 2001–2003, when many U.S. producers of steel products were in dire economic straits because of weak demand for steel and deep price discounting by foreign rivals, Nucor began acquiring state-of-the-art steelmaking facilities from bankrupt or nearly bankrupt rivals at bargain-basement prices, often at 20 to 25 percent of what it cost to construct the facilities. This has given Nucor much lower depreciation costs than rivals having comparable plants.

Nucor management's outstanding execution of its low-cost strategy and its commitment to drive down costs throughout its value chain has allowed it to compete aggressively on price, earn higher profit margins than rivals, and grow its business at a considerably faster rate than its integrated steel mill rivals.

Source: Company annual reports, news releases, and Web site.

the cost advantage must be durable. There are two ways to accomplish this:[2]

1. Do a better job than rivals of performing value chain activities more cost-effectively.

2. Revamp the firm's overall value chain to eliminate or bypass some cost-producing activities.

Let's look at each of the two approaches to securing a cost advantage.

Cost-Efficient Management of Value Chain Activities   For a company to do a more cost-efficient job of managing its value chain than rivals, managers must launch a concerted, ongoing effort to ferret out cost-saving opportunities in every part of the value chain. No activity can escape cost-saving scrutiny, and all company personnel must be expected to use their talents and ingenuity to come up with innovative and effective ways to keep costs down. All avenues for performing value chain activities at a lower cost than rivals have to be explored. Attempts to outmanage rivals on cost commonly involve such actions as:

1. *Striving to capture all available economies of scale.* Economies of scale stem from an ability to lower unit costs by increasing the scale of operation—there are many occasions when a large plant is more economical to operate than a small or medium-size plant or when a large distribution warehouse is more cost efficient than a small warehouse. Often, manufacturing economies can be achieved by using common parts and components in different models and/or by cutting back on the number of models offered (especially slow-selling ones) and then scheduling longer production runs for fewer models. In global industries, making separate products for each country market instead of selling a mostly standard product worldwide tends to boost unit costs because of lost time in model changeover, shorter production runs, and inability to reach the most economic scale of production for each country model.

2. *Taking full advantage of learning/experience curve effects.* The cost of performing an activity can decline over time as the learning and experience of company personnel builds. Learning/experience curve economies can stem from debugging and mastering newly introduced technologies, using the experiences and suggestions of workers to install more efficient plant layouts and assembly procedures, and the added speed and effectiveness that accrues from repeatedly picking sites for and building new plants, retail outlets, or distribution centers. Aggressively managed low-cost providers pay diligent attention to capturing the benefits of learning and experience and to keeping these benefits proprietary to whatever extent possible.

3. *Trying to operate facilities at full capacity.* Whether a company is able to operate at or near full capacity has a big impact on units costs when its value chain contains activities associated with substantial fixed costs. Higher rates of capacity utilization allow depreciation and other fixed costs to be spread over a larger unit volume, thereby lowering fixed costs per unit. The more capital-intensive the business, or the higher the percentage of fixed costs as a percentage of total costs, the more important that full-capacity operation becomes because there's such a stiff unit-cost penalty for underutilizing existing capacity. In such cases, finding ways to operate close to full capacity year-round can be an important source of cost advantage.

4. *Pursuing efforts to boost sales volumes and thus spread such costs as R&D, advertising, and selling and administrative costs out over more units.* The more units

a company sells, the more it lowers its unit costs for R&D, sales and marketing, and administrative overhead.

5. *Improving supply chain efficiency.* Many companies pursue cost reduction by partnering with suppliers to streamline the ordering and purchasing process via online systems, reduce inventory carrying costs via just-in-time inventory practices, economize on shipping and materials handling, and ferret out other cost-saving opportunities. A company with a core competence (or better still a distinctive competence) in cost-efficient supply chain management can sometimes achieve a sizable cost advantage over less adept rivals.

6. *Substituting the use of low-cost for high-cost raw materials or component parts.* If the costs of raw materials and parts are too high, a company can either substitute the use of lower-cost items or maybe even design the high-cost components out of the product altogether.

7. *Using online systems and sophisticated software to achieve operating efficiencies.* Data sharing, starting with customer orders and going all the way back to components production, coupled with the use of enterprise resource planning (ERP) and manufacturing execution system (MES) software, can make custom manufacturing just as cheap as mass production—and sometimes cheaper. Online systems and software can also greatly reduce production times and labor costs. Lexmark used ERP and MES software to cut its production time for inkjet printers from four hours to 24 minutes. Southwest Airlines uses proprietary software to schedule flights and assign flight crews cost-effectively.

8. *Adopting labor-saving operating methods.* Examples of ways for a company to economize on labor costs include the following: installing labor-saving technology, shifting production from geographic areas where labor costs are high to geographic areas where labor costs are low, avoiding the use of union labor where possible (because of work rules that can stifle productivity and because of union demands for above-market pay scales and costly fringe benefits), and using incentive compensation systems that promote high labor productivity.

9. *Using the company's bargaining power vis-à-vis suppliers to gain concessions.* Many large enterprises (e.g., Wal-Mart, Home Depot, the world's major motor vehicle producers) have used their bargaining clout in purchasing large volumes to wrangle good prices on their purchases from suppliers. Having greater buying power than rivals can be an important source of cost advantage.

10. *Being alert to the cost advantages of outsourcing and vertical integration.* Outsourcing the performance of certain value chain activities can be more economical than performing them in-house if outside specialists, by virtue of their expertise and volume, can perform the activities at lower cost. Indeed, outsourcing has in recent years become a widely used cost-reduction approach. However, there can be times when integrating the activities of either suppliers or distribution channel allies can allow an enterprise to detour suppliers or buyers who have an adverse impact on costs because of their considerable bargaining power.

In addition to the above means of achieving lower costs than rivals, managers can also achieve important cost savings by deliberately opting for an inherently economical strategy keyed to a frills-free product offering. For instance, a company can bolster its attempts to open up a durable cost advantage over rivals by:

- Having lower specifications for purchased materials, parts, and components than rivals do. Thus, a maker of personal computers (PCs) can use the cheapest hard drives, microprocessors, monitors, DVD drives, and other components it can find so as to end up with lower production costs than rival PC makers.

- Distributing the company's product only through low-cost distribution channels and avoiding high-cost distribution channels.
- Choosing to use the most economical method for delivering customer orders (even if it results in longer delivery times).

These strategy-related means of keeping costs low don't really involve "outmanaging" rivals, but they can nonetheless contribute materially to becoming the industry's low-cost leader.

Revamping the Value Chain to Curb or Eliminate Unnecessary Activities

Dramatic cost advantages can emerge from finding innovative ways to cut back on or entirely bypass certain cost-producing value chain activities. There are six primary ways companies can achieve a cost advantage by reconfiguring their value chains:

1. *Cutting out distributors and dealers by selling directly to customers.* Selling directly and bypassing the activities and costs of distributors or dealers can involve (1) having the company's own direct sales force (which adds the costs of maintaining and supporting a sales force but may well be cheaper than accessing customers through distributors or dealers) and/or (2) conducting sales operations at the company's Web site (Web site operations may be substantially cheaper than distributor or dealer channels). Costs in the wholesale/retail portions of the value chain frequently represent 35–50 percent of the price final consumers pay. There are several prominent examples in which companies have instituted a sell-direct approach to cutting costs out of the value chain. Software developers allow customers to download new programs directly from the Internet, eliminating the costs of producing and packaging CDs and cutting out the host of activities, costs, and markups associated with shipping and distributing software through wholesale and retail channels. By cutting all these costs and activities out of the value chain, software developers have the pricing room to boost their profit margins and still sell their products below levels that retailers would have to charge. The major airlines now sell most of their tickets directly to passengers via their Web sites, ticket counter agents, and telephone reservation systems, allowing them to save hundreds of millions of dollars in commissions once paid to travel agents.

2. *Replacing certain value chain activities with faster and cheaper online technology.* In recent years the Internet and Internet technology applications have become powerful and pervasive tools for conducting business and reengineering company and industry value chains. For instance, Internet technology has revolutionized supply chain management, turning many time-consuming and labor-intensive activities into paperless transactions performed instantaneously. Company procurement personnel can—with only a few mouse clicks—check materials inventories against incoming customer orders, check suppliers' stocks, check the latest prices for parts and components at auction and e-sourcing Web sites, and check FedEx delivery schedules. Various e-procurement software packages streamline the purchasing process by eliminating paper documents such as requests for quotations, purchase orders, order acceptances, and shipping notices. There's software that permits the relevant details of incoming customer orders to be instantly shared with the suppliers of needed parts and components. All this facilitates

just-in-time deliveries of parts and components and matching the production of parts and components to assembly plant requirements and production schedules, cutting out unnecessary activities and producing savings for both suppliers and manufacturers. Retailers can install online systems that relay data from cash register sales at the check-out counter back to manufacturers and their suppliers. Manufacturers can use online systems to collaborate closely with parts and components suppliers in designing new products and shortening the time it takes to get them into production. Online systems allow warranty claims and product performance problems involving supplier components to be instantly relayed to the relevant suppliers so that corrections can be expedited. Online systems have the further effect of breaking down corporate bureaucracies and reducing over-head costs. The whole back-office data management process (order processing, invoicing, customer accounting, and other kinds of transaction costs) can be handled fast, accurately, and with less paperwork and fewer personnel.

3. *Streamlining operations by eliminating low-value-added or unnecessary work steps and activities.* Examples include using computer-assisted design techniques, standardizing parts and components across models and styles, having suppliers collaborate to combine parts and components into modules so that products can be assembled in fewer steps, and shifting to an easy-to-manufacture product design. At Wal-Mart, some items supplied by manufacturers are delivered directly to retail stores rather than being routed through Wal-Mart's distribution centers and delivered by Wal-Mart trucks; in other instances, Wal-Mart unloads incoming shipments from manufacturers' trucks arriving at its distribution centers directly onto outgoing Wal-Mart trucks headed to particular stores without ever moving the goods into the distribution center. Many supermarket chains have greatly reduced in-store meat butchering and cutting activities by shifting to meats that are cut and packaged at the meat-packing plant and then delivered to their stores in ready-to-sell form.

4. *Relocating facilities so as to curb the need for shipping and handling activities.* Having suppliers locate facilities adjacent to the company's plant or locating the company's plants or warehouses near customers can help curb or eliminate shipping and handling costs.

5. *Offering a frills-free product.* Deliberately restricting a company's product offering to the essentials can help the company cut costs associated with snazzy attributes and a full lineup of options and extras. Activities and costs can also be eliminated by incorporating fewer performance and quality features into the product and by offering buyers fewer services. Stripping extras like first-class sections, meals, and reserved seating is a favorite technique of budget airlines like Southwest, Ryanair (Europe), easyJet (Europe), and Gol (Brazil).

6. *Offering a limited product line as opposed to a full product line.* Pruning slow-selling items from the product lineup and being content to meet the needs of most buyers rather than all buyers can eliminate activities and costs associated with numerous product versions and wide selection.

Illustration Capsule 5.2 describes how Wal-Mart has managed its value chain in the retail grocery portion of its business to achieve a dramatic cost advantage over rival supermarket chains and become the world's biggest grocery retailer.

Examples of Companies That Revamped Their Value Chains to Reduce Costs   Iowa Beef Packers (IBP), now a subsidiary of Tyson Foods, pioneered the

Ilustration Capsule 5.2

How Wal-Mart Managed Its Value Chain to Achieve a Huge Low-Cost Advantage over Rival Supermarket Chains

Wal-Mart has achieved a very substantial cost and pricing advantage over rival supermarket chains both by revamping portions of the grocery retailing value chain and by out-managing its rivals in efficiently performing various value chain activities. Its cost advantage stems from a series of initiatives and practices:

- Instituting extensive information sharing with vendors via online systems that relay sales at its checkout counters directly to suppliers of the items, thereby providing suppliers with real-time information on customer demand and preferences (creating an estimated 6 percent cost advantage). It is standard practice at Wal-Mart to collaborate extensively with vendors on all aspects of the purchasing and store delivery process to squeeze out mutually beneficial cost savings. Procter & Gamble, Wal-Mart's biggest supplier, went so far as to integrate its enterprise resource planning (ERP) system with Wal-Mart's.

- Pursuing global procurement of some items and centralizing most purchasing activities so as to leverage the company's buying power (creating an estimated 2.5 percent cost advantage).

- Investing in state-of-the-art automation at its distribution centers, efficiently operating a truck fleet that makes daily deliveries to Wal-Mart's stores, and putting assorted other cost-saving practices into place at its headquarters, distribution centers, and stores (resulting in an estimated 4 percent cost advantage).

- Striving to optimize the product mix and achieve greater sales turnover (resulting in about a 2 percent cost advantage).

- Installing security systems and store operating procedures that lower shrinkage rates (producing a cost advantage of about 0.5 percent).

- Negotiating preferred real estate rental and leasing rates with real estate developers and owners of its store sites (yielding a cost advantage of 2 percent).

- Managing and compensating its workforce in a manner that produces lower labor costs (yielding an estimated 5 percent cost advantage)

Altogether, these value chain initiatives give Wal-Mart an approximately 22 percent cost advantage over Kroger, Safeway, and other leading supermarket chains. With such a sizable cost advantage, Wal-Mart has been able to underprice its rivals and become the world's leading supermarket retailer in little more than a decade.

Source: Developed by the authors from information at www.wal-mart.com (accessed September 15, 2004) and in Marco Iansiti and Roy Levien, "Strategy as Ecology," *Harvard Business Review* 82, no. 3 (March 2004), p. 70.

development of a cheaper value chain system in the beef-packing industry.[3] The traditional cost chain involved raising cattle on scattered farms and ranches; shipping them live to labor-intensive, unionized slaughtering plants; and then transporting whole sides of beef to grocery retailers whose butcher departments cut them into smaller pieces and packaged them for sale to grocery shoppers. IBP revamped the traditional chain with a radically different strategy: It built large automated plants employing nonunion workers near cattle supplies. Near the plants it arranged to set up large feed lots (or holding pens) where cattle were fed grain for a short time to fatten them up prior to slaughter. The meat was butchered at the processing plant into small, high-yield cuts. Some of the trimmed and boned cuts were vacuum-sealed in plastic casings for further butchering in supermarket meat departments, but others were trimmed and/or boned, put in plastic-sealed ready-to-sell trays, boxed, and shipped to retailers. IBP's strategy was to increase the volume of prepackaged, "case-ready" cuts that retail grocers could unpack from boxes and place directly into the meat case. In addition, IBP provided meat retailers with individually wrapped quick-frozen steaks, as well as precooked roasts, beef tip, and meatloaf selections that could be prepared in a matter of minutes. Iowa Beef's inbound cattle transportation expenses, traditionally a major cost item, were cut significantly by avoiding the weight losses that occurred when live animals were shipped long distances just prior to slaughter. Sizable major outbound shipping cost savings were achieved by not having to ship whole sides of beef, which had a high waste factor. Meat retailers had to do far less butchering to stock their meat cases. IBP value chain revamping was so successful that the company became the largest U.S. meatpacker.

Southwest Airlines has reconfigured the traditional value chain of commercial airlines to lower costs and thereby offer dramatically lower fares to passengers. Its mastery of fast turnarounds at the gates (about 25 minutes versus 45 minutes for rivals) allows its planes to fly more hours per day. This translates into being able to schedule more flights per day with fewer aircraft, allowing Southwest to generate more revenue per plane on average than rivals. Southwest does not offer in-flight meals, assigned seating, baggage transfer to connecting airlines, or first-class seating and service, thereby eliminating all the cost-producing activities associated with these features. The company's fast, user-friendly online reservation system facilitates e-ticketing and reduces staffing requirements at telephone reservation centers and airport counters. Its use of automated check-in equipment reduces staffing requirements for terminal check-in.

Dell has created the best, most cost-efficient value chain in the global personal computer industry. Whereas Dell's major rivals (Hewlett-Packard, Lenovo, Sony, and Toshiba) produce their models in volume and sell them through independent resellers and retailers, Dell has elected to market directly to PC users, building its PCs to customer specifications as orders come in and shipping them to customers within a few days of receiving the order. Dell's value chain approach has proved cost-effective in coping with the PC industry's blink-of-an-eye product life cycle. The build-to-order strategy enables the company to avoid misjudging buyer demand for its various models and being saddled with quickly obsolete excess components and finished-goods inventories—all parts and components are obtained on a just-in-time basis from vendors, many of which deliver their items to Dell assembly plants several times a day in volumes matched to the Dell's daily assembly schedule. Also, Dell's sell-direct strategy slices reseller/retailer costs and margins out of the value chain (although some of these savings are offset by the cost of Dell's direct marketing and customer support activities—functions that would otherwise be performed by resellers and retailers). Partnerships with suppliers that facilitate just-in-time deliveries of components and minimize Dell's inventory costs, coupled with Dell's extensive use of e-commerce technologies further reduce Dell's costs. Dell's value chain approach is widely considered to have made it the global low-cost leader in the PC industry.

The Keys to Success in Achieving Low-Cost Leadership

To succeed with a low-cost-provider strategy, company managers have to scrutinize each cost-creating activity and determine what factors cause costs to be high or low. Then they have to use this knowledge to keep the unit costs of each activity low, exhaustively pursuing cost efficiencies throughout the value chain. They have to be proactive in restructuring the value chain to eliminate nonessential work steps and low-value activities. Normally, low-cost producers work diligently to create cost-conscious corporate cultures that feature broad employee participation in continuous cost improvement efforts and limited perks and frills for executives. They strive to operate with exceptionally small corporate staffs to keep administrative costs to a minimum.

Many successful low-cost leaders also use benchmarking to keep close tabs on how their costs compare with rivals and firms performing comparable activities in other industries.

> Success in achieving a low-cost edge over rivals comes from outmanaging rivals in figuring out how to perform value chain activities most cost effectively and eliminating or curbing non essential value chain activities

But while low-cost providers are champions of frugality, they are usually aggressive in investing in resources and capabilities that promise to drive costs out of the business. Wal-Mart, one of the foremost practitioners of low-cost leadership, employs state-of-the-art technology throughout its operations—its distribution facilities are an automated showcase, it uses online systems to order goods from suppliers and manage inventories, it equips its stores with cutting-edge sales-tracking and check-out systems, and it sends daily point-of-sale data to 4,000 vendors. Wal-Mart's information and communications systems and capabilities are more sophisticated than those of virtually any other retail chain in the world.

Other companies noted for their successful use of low-cost provider strategies include Lincoln Electric in arc welding equipment, Briggs & Stratton in small gasoline engines, Bic in ballpoint pens, Black & Decker in power tools, Stride Rite in footwear, Beaird-Poulan in chain saws, and General Electric and Whirlpool in major home appliances.

When a Low-Cost Provider Strategy Works Best

A competitive strategy predicated on low-cost leadership is particularly powerful when:

1. *Price competition among rival sellers is especially vigorous*—Low-cost providers are in the best position to compete offensively on the basis of price, to use the appeal of lower price to grab sales (and market share) from rivals, to win the business of price-sensitive buyers, to remain profitable in the face of strong price competition, and to survive price wars.

2. *The products of rival sellers are essentially identical and supplies are readily available from any of several eager sellers*—Commodity-like products and/or ample supplies set the stage for lively price competition; in such markets, it is less efficient, higher-cost companies whose profits get squeezed the most.

3. *There are few ways to achieve product differentiation that have value to buyers*—When the differences between brands do not matter much to buyers, buyers are nearly always very sensitive to price differences and shop the market for the best price.

4. *Most buyers use the product in the same ways*—With common user requirements, a standardized product can satisfy the needs of buyers, in which case low selling price, not features or quality, becomes the dominant factor in causing buyers to choose one seller's product over another's.

5. *Buyers incur low costs in switching their purchases from one seller to another*—Low switching costs give buyers the flexibility to shift purchases to lower-priced sellers having equally good products or to attractively priced substitute products. A low-cost leader is well positioned to use low price to induce its customers not to switch to rival brands or substitutes.

6. *Buyers are large and have significant power to bargain down prices*—Low-cost providers have partial profit-margin protection in bargaining with high-volume buyers, since powerful buyers are rarely able to bargain price down past the survival level of the next most cost-efficient seller.

7. *Industry newcomers use introductory low prices to attract buyers and build a customer base*—The low-cost leader can use price cuts of its own to make it harder

A low-cost provider is in the best position to win the business of price-sensitive buyers, set the floor on market price, and still earn a profit.

for a new rival to win customers; the pricing power of the low-cost provider acts as a barrier for new entrants.

As a rule, the more price-sensitive buyers are, the more appealing a low-cost strategy becomes. A low-cost company's ability to set the industry's price floor and still earn a profit erects protective barriers around its market position.

The Pitfalls of a Low-Cost Provider Strategy

Perhaps the biggest pitfall of a low-cost provider strategy is getting carried away with overly aggressive price cutting and ending up with lower, rather than higher, profitability. A low-cost/low-price advantage results in superior profitability only if (1) prices are cut by less than the size of the cost advantage or (2) the added gains in unit sales are large enough to bring in a bigger total profit despite lower margins per unit sold. A company with a 5 percent cost advantage cannot cut prices 20 percent, end up with a volume gain of only 10 percent, and still expect to earn higher profits!

A second big pitfall is not emphasizing avenues of cost advantage that can be kept proprietary or that relegate rivals to playing catch-up. The value of a cost advantage depends on its sustainability. Sustainability, in turn, hinges on whether the company achieves its cost advantage in ways difficult for rivals to copy or match.

A low-cost provider's product offering must always contain enough attributes to be attractive to prospective buyers—low price, by itself, is not always appealing to buyers.

A third pitfall is becoming too fixated on cost reduction. Low cost cannot be pursued so zealously that a firm's offering ends up being too features-poor to generate buyer appeal. Furthermore, a company driving hard to push its costs down has to guard against misreading or ignoring increased buyer interest in added features or service, declining buyer sensitivity to price, or new developments that start to alter how buyers use the product. A low-cost zealot risks losing market ground if buyers start opting for more upscale or features-rich products.

Even if these mistakes are avoided, a low-cost competitive approach still carries risk. Cost-saving technological breakthroughs or the emergence of still-lower-cost value chain models can nullify a low-cost leader's hard-won position. The current leader may have difficulty in shifting quickly to the new technologies or value chain approaches because heavy investments lock it in (at least temporarily) to its present value chain approach.

BROAD DIFFERENTIATION STRATEGIES

Core Concept
The essence of a broad differentiation strategy is to be unique in ways that are valuable to a wide range of customers.

Differentiation strategies are attractive whenever buyers' needs and preferences are too diverse to be fully satisfied by a standardized product or by sellers with identical capabilities. A company attempting to succeed through differentiation must study buyers' needs and behavior carefully to learn what buyers consider important, what they think has value, and what they are willing to pay for. Then the company has to incorporate buyer-desired attributes into its product or service offering that will clearly set it apart from rivals. Competitive advantage results once a sufficient number of buyers become strongly attached to the differentiated attributes.

Successful differentiation allows a firm to:

- Command a premium price for its product, and/or
- Increase unit sales (because additional buyers are won over by the differentiating features), and/or

- Gain buyer loyalty to its brand (because some buyers are strongly attracted to the differentiating features and bond with the company and its products).

Differentiation enhances profitability whenever the extra price the product commands outweighs the added costs of achieving the differentiation. Company differentiation strategies fail when buyers don't value the brand's uniqueness and when a company's approach to differentiation is easily copied or matched by its rivals.

Types of Differentiation Themes

Companies can pursue differentiation from many angles: a unique taste (Dr Pepper, Listerine); multiple features (Microsoft Windows, Microsoft Office); wide selection and one-stop shopping (Home Depot, Amazon.com); superior service (FedEx); spare parts availability (Caterpillar); engineering design and performance (Mercedes, BMW); prestige and distinctiveness (Rolex); product reliability (Johnson & Johnson in baby products); quality manufacture (Karastan in carpets, Michelin in tires, Toyota and Honda in automobiles); technological leadership (3M Corporation in bonding and coating products); a full range of services (Charles Schwab in stock brokerage); a complete line of products (Campbell's soups); and top-of-the-line image and reputation (Ralph Lauren and Starbucks).

The most appealing approaches to differentiation are those that are hard or expensive for rivals to duplicate. Indeed, resourceful competitors can, in time, clone almost any product or feature or attribute. If Coca-Cola introduces a vanilla-flavored soft drink, so can Pepsi; if Ford offers a 50,000-mile bumper-to-bumper warranty on its new vehicles, so can Volkswagen and Nissan. If Nokia introduces cell phones with cameras and Internet capability, so can Motorola and Samsung. As a rule, differentiation yields a longer-lasting and more profitable competitive edge when it is based on product innovation, technical superiority, product quality and reliability, comprehensive customer service, and unique competitive capabilities. Such differentiating attributes tend to be tough for rivals to copy or offset profitably, and buyers widely perceive them as having value.

> Easy-to-copy differentiating features cannot produce sustainable competitive advantage; differentiation based on competencies and capabilities tend to be more sustainable.

Where along the Value Chain to Create the Differentiating Attributes

Differentiation is not something hatched in marketing and advertising departments, nor is it limited to the catchalls of quality and service. Differentiation opportunities can exist in activities all along an industry's value chain; possibilities include the following:

- *Supply chain activities* that ultimately spill over to affect the performance or quality of the company's end product. Starbucks gets high ratings on its coffees partly because it has very strict specifications on the coffee beans purchased from suppliers.

- *Product R&D activities* that aim at improved product designs and performance features, expanded end uses and applications, more frequent first-on-the-market victories, wider product variety and selection, added user safety, greater recycling capability, or enhanced environmental protection.

- *Production R&D and technology-related activities* that permit custom-order manufacture at an efficient cost; make production methods safer for the environment; or improve product quality, reliability, and appearance. Many manufacturers have developed flexible manufacturing systems that allow different models and product versions to be made on the same assembly line. Being able to provide buyers with made-to-order products can be a potent differentiating capability.

- *Manufacturing activities* that reduce product defects, prevent premature product failure, extend product life, allow better warranty coverages, improve economy of use, result in more end-user convenience, or enhance product appearance. The quality edge enjoyed by Japanese automakers stems partly from their distinctive competence in performing assembly-line activities.

- *Distribution and shipping activities* that allow for fewer warehouse and on-the-shelf stockouts, quicker delivery to customers, more accurate order filling, and/or lower shipping costs.

- *Marketing, sales, and customer service activities* that result in superior technical assistance to buyers, faster maintenance and repair services, more and better product information provided to customers, more and better training materials for end users, better credit terms, quicker order processing, or greater customer convenience.

Managers need keen understanding of the sources of differentiation and the activities that drive uniqueness to evaluate various differentiation approaches and design durable ways to set their product offering apart from those of rival brands.

The Four Best Routes to Competitive Advantage via a Broad Differentiation Strategy

While it is easy enough to grasp that a successful differentiation strategy must entail creating buyer value in ways unmatched by rivals, the big issue in crafting a differentiation strategy is which of four basic routes to take in delivering unique buyer value via a broad differentiation strategy. Usually, building a sustainable competitive advantage via differentiation involves pursuing one of four basic routes to delivering superior value to buyers.

One route is to *incorporate product attributes and user features that lower the buyer's overall costs of using the company's product.* Making a company's product more economical for a buyer to use can be done by reducing the buyer's raw materials waste (providing cut-to-size components), reducing a buyer's inventory requirements (providing just-in-time deliveries), increasing maintenance intervals and product reliability so as to lower a buyer's repair and maintenance costs, using online systems to reduce a buyer's procurement and order processing costs, and providing free technical support. Rising costs for gasoline have dramatically spurred the efforts of motor vehicle manufacturers worldwide to introduce models with better fuel economy and reduce operating costs for motor vehicle owners.

A second route is to *incorporate features that raise product performance.*[4] This can be accomplished with attributes that provide buyers greater reliability, ease of use, convenience, or durability. Other performance-enhancing options include making the company's product or service cleaner, safer, quieter, or more maintenance-free than rival brands. Cell phone manufacturrs are in a race to introduce next-generation phones with trendsetting features and options.

A third route to a differentiation-based competitive advantage is to *incorporate features that enhance buyer satisfaction in noneconomic or intangible ways.* Goodyear's Aquatread tire design appeals to safety-conscious motorists wary of slick roads. Rolls Royce, Ralph Lauren, Gucci, Tiffany, Cartier, and Rolex have differentiation-based competitive advantages linked to buyer desires for status, image, prestige, upscale fashion, superior craftsmanship, and the finer things in life. L. L. Bean makes its mail-order customers feel secure in their purchases by providing an unconditional guarantee with no time limit: "All of our products are guaranteed to give 100 percent satisfaction in every way. Return anything purchased from us at any time if it proves otherwise. We will replace it, refund your purchase price, or credit your credit card, as you wish."

> **Core Concept**
> A differentiator's basis for competitive advantage is either a product/service offering whose attributes differ significantly from the offerings of rivals or a set of capabilities for delivering customer value that rivals don't have.

The fourth route is to *deliver value to customers by differentiating on the basis of competencies and competitive capabilities that rivals don't have or can't afford to match.*[5] The importance of cultivating competencies and capabilities that add power to a company's resource strengths and competitiveness comes into play here. Core and/or distinctive competencies not only enhance a company's ability to compete successfully in the marketplace but can also be unique in delivering value to buyers. There are numerous examples of companies that have differentiated themselves on the basis of capabilities. Because Fox News and CNN have the capability to devote more air time to breaking news stories and get reporters on the scene very quickly compared to the major networks, many viewers turn to the cable networks when a major news event occurs. Microsoft has stronger capabilities to design, create, distribute, and advertise an array of software products for PC applications than any of its rivals. Avon and Mary Kay Cosmetics have differentiated themselves from other cosmetics and personal care companies by assembling a sales force numbering in the hundreds of thousands that gives them direct sales capability—their sales associates can demonstrate products to interested buyers, take their orders on the spot, and deliver the items to buyers' homes. Japanese automakers have the capability to satisfy changing consumer preferences for one vehicle style versus another because they can bring new models to market faster than American and European automakers.

The Importance of Perceived Value and Signaling Value

Buyers seldom pay for value they don't perceive, no matter how real the unique extras may be.[6] Thus, the price premium commanded by a differentiation strategy reflects *the value actually delivered* to the buyer and *the value perceived* by the buyer (even if not actually delivered). Actual and perceived value can differ whenever buyers have trouble assessing what their experience with the product will be. Incomplete knowledge on the part of buyers often causes them to judge value based on such signals as price (where price connotes quality), attractive packaging, extensive ad campaigns (i.e., how well-known the product is), ad content and image, the quality of brochures and sales presentations, the seller's facilities, the seller's list of customers, the firm's market share, the length of time the firm has been in business, and the professionalism, appearance, and personality of the seller's employees. Such signals of value may be as important as actual value (1) when the nature of differentiation is subjective or hard to quantify, (2) when buyers are making a first-time purchase, (3) when repurchase is infrequent, and (4) when buyers are unsophisticated.

When a Differentiation Strategy Works Best

Differentiation strategies tend to work best in market circumstances where:

- *Buyer needs and uses of the product are diverse*—Diverse buyer preferences present competitors with a bigger window of opportunity to do things differently and set themselves apart with product attributes that appeal to particular buyers. For instance, the diversity of consumer preferences for menu selection, ambience, pricing, and customer service gives restaurants exceptionally wide latitude in creating a differentiated product offering. Other companies having many ways to strongly differentiate themselves from rivals include the publishers of magazines, the makers of motor vehicles, and the manufacturers of cabinetry and countertops.

- *There are many ways to differentiate the product or service and many buyers perceive these differences as having value*—There is plenty of room for retail apparel competitors to stock different styles and quality of apparel merchandise but very little room for the makers of paper clips, copier paper, or sugar to set their products apart. Likewise, the sellers of different brands of gasoline or orange juice have little differentiation opportunity compared to the sellers of high-definition TVs, patio furniture, or breakfast cereal. Unless different buyers have distinguishably different preferences for certain features and product attributes, profitable differentiation opportunities are very restricted.

- *Few rival firms are following a similar differentiation approach*—The best differentiation approaches involve trying to appeal to buyers on the basis of attributes that rivals are not emphasizing. A differentiator encounters less head-to-head rivalry when it goes its own separate way in creating uniqueness and does not try to outdifferentiate rivals on the very same attributes—when many rivals are all claiming "Ours tastes better than theirs" or "Ours gets your clothes cleaner than theirs," the most likely result is weak brand differentiation and "strategy overcrowding"—a situation in which competitors end up chasing the same buyers with very similar product offerings.

- *Technological change is fast-paced and competition revolves around rapidly evolving product features*—Rapid product innovation and frequent introductions of next-version products not only provide space for companies to pursue separate differentiating paths but also heighten buyer interest. In video game hardware and video games, golf equipment, PCs, cell phones, and MP3 players, competitors are locked into an ongoing battle to set themselves apart by introducing the best next-generation products—companies that fail to come up with new and improved products and distinctive performance features quickly lose out in the marketplace. In network TV broadcasting in the United States, NBC, ABC, CBS, Fox, and several others are always scrambling to develop a lineup of TV shows that will win higher audience ratings and pave the way for charging higher advertising rates and boosting ad revenues.

The Pitfalls of a Differentiation Strategy

Differentiation strategies can fail for any of several reasons. *A differentiation strategy is always doomed when competitors are able to quickly copy most or all of the appealing product attributes a company comes up with.* Rapid imitation means that no rival achieves differentiation, since whenever one firm introduces some aspect of uniqueness that strikes the fancy of buyers, fast-following copycats quickly reestablish similarity. This is why a firm must search out sources of uniqueness that are time-consuming or burdensome for rivals to match if it hopes to use differentiation to win a competitive edge over rivals.

> **Core Concept**
> Any differentiating feature that works well is a magnet for imitators.

A second pitfall is that the company's differentiation strategy produces a ho-hum market reception because buyers see little value in the unique attributes of a company's product. Thus, even if a company sets the attributes of its brand apart from the brands of rivals, its strategy can fail because of trying to differentiate on the basis of something that does not deliver adequate value to buyers (such as lowering a buyer's cost to use the product or enhancing a buyer's well-being). Anytime many potential buyers look at a company's differentiated product offering and conclude "So what?" the company's differentiation strategy is in deep trouble—buyers will likely decide the product is not worth the extra price, and sales will be disappointingly low.

The third big pitfall of a differentiation strategy is overspending on efforts to differentiate the company's product offering, thus eroding profitability. Company efforts to achieve differentiation nearly always raise costs. The trick to profitable differentiation is either to keep the costs of achieving differentiation below the price premium the differentiating attributes can command in the marketplace (thus increasing the profit margin per unit sold) or to offset thinner profit margins per unit by selling enough additional units to increase total profits. If a company goes overboard in pursuing costly differentiation efforts and then unexpectedly discovers that buyers are unwilling to pay a sufficient price premium to cover the added costs of differentiation, it ends up saddled with unacceptably thin profit margins or even losses. The need to contain differentiation costs is why many companies add little touches of differentiation that add to buyer satisfaction but are inexpensive to institute. Upscale restaurants often provide valet parking. Ski resorts provide skiers with complimentary coffee or hot apple cider at the base of the lifts in the morning and late afternoon. FedEx, UPS, and many catalog and online retailers have installed software capabilities that allow customers to track packages in transit. Some hotels and motels provide free continental breakfasts, exercise facilities, and in-room coffeemaking amenities. Publishers are using their Web sites to deliver supplementary educational materials to the buyers of their textbooks. Laundry detergent and soap manufacturers add pleasing scents to their products.

Other common pitfalls and mistakes in crafting a differentiation strategy include:[7]

- *Overdifferentiating so that product quality or service levels exceed buyers' needs.* Even if buyers like the differentiating extras, they may not find them sufficiently valuable for their purposes to pay extra to get them. Many shoppers shy away from buying top-of-the-line items because they have no particular interest in all the bells and whistles; for them, a less deluxe model or style makes better economic sense.

- *Trying to charge too high a price premium.* Even if buyers view certain extras or deluxe features as nice to have, they may still conclude that the added cost is excessive relative to the value they deliver. A differentiator must guard against turning off would-be buyers with what is perceived as price gouging. Normally, the bigger the price premium for the differentiating extras, the harder it is to keep buyers from switching to the lower-priced offerings of competitors.

- *Being timid and not striving to open up meaningful gaps in quality or service or performance features vis-à-vis the products of rivals.* Tiny differences between rivals' product offerings may not be visible or important to buyers. If a company wants to generate the fiercely loyal customer following needed to earn superior profits and open up a differentiation-based competitive advantage over rivals, then its strategy must result in strong rather than weak product differentiation. In markets where differentiators do no better than achieve weak product differentiation (because the attributes of rival brands are fairly similar in the minds of many buyers), customer loyalty to any one brand is weak, the costs of buyers to switch to rival brands are fairly low, and no one company has enough of a market edge that it can get by with charging a price premium over rival brands.

A low-cost provider strategy can defeat a differentiation strategy when buyers are satisfied with a basic product and don't think extra attributes are worth a higher price.

BEST-COST PROVIDER STRATEGIES

Core Concept
The competitive advantage of a best-cost provider is lower costs than rivals in incorporating upscale attributes, putting the company in a position to underprice rivals whose products have similar upscale attributes.

Best-cost provider strategies aim at giving customers *more value for the money*. The objective is to deliver superior value to buyers by satisfying their expectations on key quality/features/performance/service attributes and beating their expectations on price (given what rivals are charging for much the same attributes). *A company achieves best-cost status from an ability to incorporate attractive or upscale attributes at a lower cost than rivals.* The attractive attributes can take the form of appealing features, good-to-excellent product performance or quality, or attractive customer service. When a company has the resource strengths and competitive capabilities to incorporate these upscale attributes into its product offering *at a lower cost than rivals,* it enjoys best-cost status—it is the low-cost provider *of an upscale product.*

Being a best-cost provider is different from being a low-cost provider because the additional upscale features entail additional costs (that a low-cost provider can avoid by offering buyers a basic product with few frills). As Figure 5.1 indicates, best-cost provider strategies stake out a middle ground between pursuing a low-cost advantage and a differentiation advantage and between appealing to the broad market as a whole and a narrow market niche. From a competitive positioning standpoint, best-cost strategies are thus a *hybrid,* balancing a strategic emphasis on low cost against a strategic emphasis on differentiation (upscale features delivered at a price that constitutes superior value).

The competitive advantage of a best-cost provider is its capability to include upscale attributes at a lower cost than rivals whose products have comparable attributes. A best-cost provider can use its low-cost advantage to underprice rivals whose products have similar upscale attributes—it is usually not difficult to entice customers away from rivals charging a higher price for an item with highly comparable features, quality, performance, and/or customer service attributes. To achieve competitive advantage with a best-cost provider strategy, it is critical that a company have the resources and capabilities to incorporate upscale attributes at a lower cost than rivals. In other words, it must be able to (1) incorporate attractive features at a lower cost than rivals whose products have similar features, (2) manufacture a good-to-excellent quality product at a lower cost than rivals with good-to-excellent product quality, (3) develop a product that delivers good-to-excellent performance at a lower cost than rivals whose products also entail good-to-excellent performance, or (4) provide attractive customer service at a lower cost than rivals who provide comparably attractive customer service.

What makes a best-cost provider strategy so appealing is being able to incorporate upscale attributes at a lower cost than rivals and then using the company's low-cost advantage to underprice rivals whose products have similar upscale attributes.

The target market for a best-cost provider is value-conscious buyers—buyers that are looking for appealing extras at an appealingly low price. Value-hunting buyers (as distinct from buyers looking only for bargain-basement prices) often constitute a very sizable part of the overall market. Normally, value-conscious buyers are willing to pay a fair price for extra features, but they shy away from paying top dollar for items having all the bells and whistles. It is the desire to cater to *value-conscious buyers* as opposed to *budget-conscious buyers* that sets a best-cost provider apart from a low-cost provider—the two strategies aim at distinguishably different market targets.

When a Best-Cost Provider Strategy Works Best

A best-cost provider strategy works best in markets where buyer diversity makes product differentiation the norm and where many buyers are also sensitive to price and value. This is because a best-cost provider can position itself near the middle of the market with either a medium-quality product at a below-average price or a high-quality product at an average or slightly higher price. Often, substantial numbers of buyers prefer midrange products rather than the cheap, basic products of low-cost producers or the expensive products of top-of-the-line differentiators. But unless a company has the resources, know-how, and capabilities to incorporate upscale product or service attributes at a lower cost than rivals, adopting a best-cost strategy is ill advised—a winning strategy must always be matched to a company's resource strengths and capabilities.

Illustration Capsule 5.3 describes how Toyota has applied the principles of a best-cost provider strategy in producing and marketing its Lexus brand.

The Big Risk of a Best-Cost Provider Strategy

A company's biggest vulnerability in employing a best-cost provider strategy is getting squeezed between the strategies of firms using low-cost and high-end differentiation strategies. Low-cost providers may be able to siphon customers away with the appeal of a lower price (despite their less appealing product attributes). High-end differentiators may be able to steal customers away with the appeal of better product attributes (even though their products carry a higher price tag). Thus, to be successful, a best-cost provider must offer buyers *significantly* better product attributes in order to justify a price above what low-cost leaders are charging. Likewise, it has to achieve *significantly* lower costs in providing upscale features so that it can outcompete high-end differentiators on the basis of a *significantly* lower price.

FOCUSED (OR MARKET NICHE) STRATEGIES

What sets focused strategies apart from low-cost leadership or broad differentiation strategies is concentrated attention on a narrow piece of the total market. The target segment, or niche, can be defined by geographic uniqueness, by specialized requirements in using the product, or by special product attributes that appeal only to niche members. Community Coffee, the largest family-owned specialty coffee retailer in the United States, is a company that focused on a geographic market niche; despite having a national market share of only 1.1 percent, Community has won a 50 percent share of the coffee business in supermarkets in southern Louisiana in competition

Illustration Capsule 5.3

Toyota's Best-Cost Producer Strategy for Its Lexus Line

Toyota Motor Company is widely regarded as a low-cost producer among the world's motor vehicle manufacturers. Despite its emphasis on product quality, Toyota has achieved low-cost leadership because it has developed considerable skills in efficient supply chain management and low-cost assembly capabilities, and because its models are positioned in the low-to-medium end of the price spectrum, where high production volumes are conducive to low unit costs. But when Toyota decided to introduce its new Lexus models to compete in the luxury-car market, it employed a classic best-cost provider strategy. Toyota took the following four steps in crafting and implementing its Lexus strategy:

- Designing an array of high-performance characteristics and upscale features into the Lexus models so as to make them comparable in performance and luxury to other high-end models and attractive to Mercedes, BMW, Audi, Jaguar, Cadillac, and Lincoln buyers.

- Transferring its capabilities in making high-quality Toyota models at low cost to making premium-quality Lexus models at costs below other luxury-car makers. Toyota's supply chain capabilities and low-cost assembly know-how allowed it to incorporate high-tech performance features and upscale quality into Lexus models at substantially less cost than comparable Mercedes and BMW models.

- Using its relatively lower manufacturing costs to underprice comparable Mercedes and BMW models. Toyota believed that with its cost advantage it could price attractively equipped Lexus cars low enough to draw price-conscious buyers away from Mercedes and BMW and perhaps induce dissatisfied Lincoln and Cadillac owners to switch to a Lexus. Lexus's pricing advantage over Mercedes and BMW was sometimes quite significant. For example, in 2006 the Lexus RX 330, a midsized SUV, carried a sticker price in the $36,000–$45,000 range (depending on how it was equipped), whereas variously equipped Mercedes M-class SUVs had price tags in the $50,000–$65,000 range and a BMW X5 SUV could range anywhere from $42,000 to $70,000, depending on the optional equipment chosen.

- Establishing a new network of Lexus dealers, separate from Toyota dealers, dedicated to providing a level of personalized, attentive customer service unmatched in the industry.

Lexus models have consistently ranked first in the widely watched J. D. Power & Associates quality survey, and the prices of Lexus models are typically several thousand dollars below those of comparable Mercedes and BMW models—clear signals that Toyota has succeeded in becoming a best-cost producer with its Lexus brand.

---

against Starbucks, Folger's, Maxwell House, and asserted specialty coffee retailers. Community Coffee's geographic version of a focus strategy has allowed it to capture sales in excess of $100 million annually by catering to the tastes of coffee drinkers across an 11-state region. Examples of firms that concentrate on a well-defined market niche keyed to a particular product or buyer segment include Animal Planet and the History Channel (in cable TV); Google (in Internet search engines); Porsche (in sports cars); Cannondale (in top-of-the-line mountain bikes); Domino's Pizza (in pizza delivery); Enterprise Rent-a-Car (a specialist in providing rental cars to repair garage customers); Bandag (a specialist in truck tire recapping that promotes its recaps aggressively at over 1,000 truck stops), CGA Inc. (a specialist in providing insurance to cover the cost of lucrative hole-in-one prizes at golf tournaments); Match.com (the world's largest online dating service); and Avid Technology (the world leader in digital technology products to create 3D animation and to edit films, videos, TV broadcasts, video games, and audio recordings). Microbreweries, local bakeries, bed-and-breakfast inns, and local owner-managed retail boutiques are all good examples of enterprises that have scaled their operations to serve narrow or local customer segments.

A Focused Low-Cost Strategy

A focused strategy based on low cost aims at securing a competitive advantage by serving buyers in the target market niche at a lower cost and lower price than rival competitors. This strategy has considerable attraction when a firm can lower costs significantly by limiting its customer base to a well-defined buyer segment. The avenues to achieving a cost advantage over rivals also serving the target market niche are the same as for low-cost leadership—outmanage rivals in keeping the costs of value chain activities contained to a bare minimum and search for innovative ways to reconfigure the firm's value chain and bypass or reduce certain value chain activities. The only real difference between a low-cost provider strategy and a focused low-cost strategy is the size of the buyer group that a company is trying to appeal to—the former involves a product offering that appeals broadly to most all buyer groups and market segments whereas the latter at just meeting the needs of buyers in a narrow market segment.

Focused low-cost strategies are fairly common. Producers of private-label goods are able to achieve low costs in product development, marketing, distribution, and advertising by concentrating on making generic items imitative of name-brand merchandise and selling directly to retail chains wanting a basic house brand to sell to price-sensitive shoppers. Several small printer-supply manufacturers have begun making low-cost clones of the premium-priced replacement ink and toner cartridges sold by Hewlett-Packard, Lexmark, Canon, and Epson; the clone manufacturers dissect the cartridges of the name-brand companies and then reengineer a similar version that won't violate patents. The components for remanufactured replacement cartridges are aquired from various outside sources, and the clones are then marketed at prices as much as 50 percent below the name-brand cartridges. Cartridge remanufacturers have been lured to focus on this market because replacement cartridges constitute a multibillion-dollar business with considerable profit potential given their low costs and the premium pricing of the name-brand companies. Illustration Capsule 5.4 describes how Motel 6 has kept its costs low in catering to budget-conscious travelers.

A Focused Differentiation Strategy

A focused strategy keyed to differentiation aims at securing a competitive advantage with a product offering carefully designed to appeal to the unique preferences and needs of a narrow, well-defined group of buyers (as opposed to a broad differentiation strategy aimed at many buyer groups and market segments). Successful use of a focused differentiation strategy depends on the existence of a buyer segment that is looking for special product attributes or seller capabilities and on a firm's ability to stand apart from rivals competing in the same target market niche.

Companies like Godiva Chocolates, Chanel, Gucci, Rolls-Royce, Häagen-Dazs, and W. L. Gore (the maker of Gore-Tex) employ successful differentiation-based focused strategies targeted at upscale buyers wanting products and services with world-class attributes. Indeed, most markets contain a buyer segment willing to pay a big price premium for the very finest items available, thus opening the strategic window for some competitors to pursue differentiation-based focused strategies aimed at the very top of the market pyramid. Another successful focused differentiator is Trader Joe's, a 150-store East and West Coast "fashion food retailer" that is a combination gourmet deli and grocery warehouse.[8] Customers shop Trader Joe's as much for entertainment as for conventional grocery items—the store stocks out-of-the-ordinary culinary treats like raspberry salsa, salmon burgers, and jasmine fried rice,

Illustration Capsule 5.4
Motel 6's Focused Low-Cost Strategy

Motel 6 caters to price-conscious travelers who want a clean, no-frills place to spend the night. To be a low-cost provider of overnight lodging, Motel 6 (1) selects relatively inexpensive sites on which to construct its units (usually near interstate exits and high-traffic locations but far enough away to avoid paying prime site prices); (2) builds only basic facilities (no restaurant or bar and only rarely a swimming pool); (3) relies on standard architectural designs that incorporate inexpensive materials and low-cost construction techniques; and (4) provides simple room furnishings and decorations. These approaches lower both investment costs and operating costs. Without restaurants,

bars, and all kinds of guest services, a Motel 6 unit can be operated with just front-desk personnel, room cleanup crews, and skeleton building-and-grounds maintenance.

To promote the Motel 6 concept with travelers who have simple overnight requirements, the chain uses unique, recognizable radio ads done by nationally syndicated radio personality Tom Bodett; the ads describe Motel 6's clean rooms, no-frills facilities, friendly atmosphere, and dependably low rates (usually under $40 a night).

Motel 6's basis for competitive advantage is lower costs than competitors in providing basic, economical overnight accommodations to price-constrained travelers.

---

as well as the standard goods normally found in supermarkets. What sets Trader Joe's apart is not just its unique combination of food novelties and competitively priced grocery items but also its capability to turn an otherwise mundane grocery excursion into a whimsical treasure hunt that is just plain fun.

Illustration Capsule 5.5 describes Progressive Insurance's focused differentiation strategy.

When a Focused Low-Cost or Focused Differentiation Strategy Is Attractive

A focused strategy aimed at securing a competitive edge based on either low cost or differentiation becomes increasingly attractive as more of the following conditions are met:

- The target market niche is big enough to be profitable and offers good growth potential.
- Industry leaders do not see that having a presence in the niche is crucial to their own success—in which case focusers can often escape battling head-to-head against some of the industry's biggest and strongest competitors.
- It is costly or difficult for multisegment competitors to put capabilities in place to meet the specialized needs of buyers comprising the target market niche and at the same time satisfy the expectations of their mainstream customers.
- The industry has many different niches and segments, thereby allowing a focuser to pick a competitively attractive niche suited to its resource strengths and capabilities. Also, with more niches, there is more room for focusers to avoid each other in competing for the same customers.

Illustration Capsule 5.5
Progressive Insurance's Focused Differentiation Strategy in Auto Insurance

Progressive Insurance has fashioned a strategy in auto insurance focused on people with a record of traffic violations who drive high-performance cars, drivers with accident histories, motorcyclists, teenagers, and other so-called high-risk categories of drivers that most auto insurance companies steer away from. Progressive discovered that some of these high-risk drivers are affluent and pressed for time, making them less sensitive to paying premium rates for their car insurance. Management learned that it could charge such drivers high enough premiums to cover the added risks, plus it differentiated Progressive from other insurers by expediting the process of obtaining insurance and decreasing the annoyance that such drivers faced in obtaining insurance coverage. Progressive pioneered the low-cost direct sales model of allowing customers to purchase insurance online and over the phone.

Progressive also studied the market segments for insurance carefully enough to discover that some motorcycle owners were not especially risky (middle-aged suburbanites who sometimes commuted to work or used their motorcycles mainly for recreational trips with their friends). Progressive's strategy allowed it to become a leader in the market for luxury-car insurance for customers who appreciated Progressive's streamlined approach to doing business.

In further differentiating and promoting Progressive policies, management created teams of roving claims adjusters who would arrive at accident scenes to assess claims and issue checks for repairs on the spot. Progressive introduced 24-hour claims reporting, now an industry standard. In addition, it developed a sophisticated pricing system so that it could quickly and accurately assess each customer's risk and weed out unprofitable customers.

By being creative and excelling at the nuts and bolts of its business, Progressive has won a 7 percent share of the $150 billion market for auto insurance and has the highest underwriting margins in the auto-insurance industry.

Sources: www.progressiveinsurance.com; Ian C. McMillan, Alexander van Putten, and Rita Gunther McGrath, "Global Gamesmanship," *Harvard Business Review* 81, no. 5 (May 2003), p. 68; and *Fortune,* May 16, 2005, p. 34.

- Few, if any, other rivals are attempting to specialize in the same target segment—a condition that reduces the risk of segment overcrowding.
- The focuser has a reservoir of customer goodwill and loyalty (accumulated from having catered to the specialized needs and preferences of niche members over many years) that it can draw on to help stave off ambitious challengers looking to horn in on its business.

The advantages of focusing a company's entire competitive effort on a single market niche are considerable, especially for smaller and medium-sized companies that may lack the breadth and depth of resources to tackle going after a broad customer base with a "something for everyone" lineup of models, styles, and product selection. eBay has made a huge name for itself and very attractive profits for shareholders by focusing its attention on online auctions—at one time a very small niche in the overall auction business that eBay's focus strategy turned into the dominant piece of the global auction industry. Google has capitalized on its specialized expertise in Internet search engines to become one of the most spectacular growth companies of the past 10 years. Two hippie entrepreneurs, Ben Cohen and Jerry Greenfield, built Ben & Jerry's Homemade into an impressive business by focusing their energies and resources solely on the superpremium segment of the ice cream market.

The Risks of a Focused Low-Cost or Focused Differentiation Strategy

Focusing carries several risks. One is the chance that competitors will find effective ways to match the focused firm's capabilities in serving the target niche—perhaps by coming up with products or brands specifically designed to appeal to buyers in the target niche or by developing expertise and capabilities that offset the focuser's strengths. In the lodging business, large chains like Marriott and Hilton have launched multibrand strategies that allow them to compete effectively in several lodging segments simultaneously. Marriott has flagship hotels with a full complement of services and amenities that allow it to attract travelers and vacationers going to major resorts, it has J. W. Marriot hotels usually located in downtown metropolitan areas that cater to business travelers; the Courtyard by Marriott brand is for business travelers looking for moderately priced lodging; Marriott Residence Inns are designed as a home away from home for travelers staying five or more nights; and the 530 Fairfield Inn locations cater to travelers looking for quality lodging at an affordable price. Similarly, Hilton has a lineup of brands (Conrad Hotels, Doubletree Hotels, Embassy Suite Hotels, Hampton Inns, Hilton Hotels, Hilton Garden Inns, and Homewood Suites) that enable it to operate in multiple segments and compete head-to-head against lodging chains that operate only in a single segment. Multibrand strategies are attractive to large companies like Marriott and Hilton precisely because they enable a company to enter a market niche and siphon business away from companies that employ a focus strategy.

A second risk of employing a focus strategy is the potential for the preferences and needs of niche members to shift over time toward the product attributes desired by the majority of buyers. An erosion of the differences across buyer segments lowers entry barriers into a focuser's market niche and provides an open invitation for rivals in adjacent segments to begin competing for the focuser's customers. A third risk is that the segment may become so attractive it is soon inundated with competitors, intensifying rivalry and splintering segment profits.

THE CONTRASTING FEATURES OF THE FIVE GENERIC COMPETITIVE STRATEGIES: A SUMMARY

Deciding which generic competitive strategy should serve as the framework for hanging the rest of the company's strategy is not a trivial matter. Each of the five generic competitive strategies positions the company differently in its market and competitive environment. Each establishes a central theme for how the company will endeavor to outcompete rivals. Each creates some boundaries or guidelines for maneuvering as market circumstances unfold and as ideas for improving the strategy are debated. Each points to different ways of experimenting and tinkering with the basic strategy—for example, employing a low-cost leadership strategy means experimenting with ways that costs can be cut and value chain activities can be streamlined, whereas a broad differentiation strategy means exploring ways to add new differentiating features or to perform value chain activities differently if the result is to add value for customers in ways they are willing to pay for. Each entails differences in terms of product line, production emphasis, marketing emphasis, and means of sustaining the strategy—as shown in Table 5.1.

Table 5.1 **Distinguishing Features of the Five Generic Competitive Strategies**

	Low-Cost Provider	Broad Differentiation	Best-Cost Provider	Focused Low-Cost Provider	Focused Differentiation
Strategic target	• A broad cross-section of the market	• A broad cross-section of the market	• Value-conscious buyers	• A narrow market niche where buyer needs and preferences are distinctively different	• A narrow market niche where buyer needs and preferences are distinctively different
Basis of competitive advantage	• Lower overall costs than competitors	• Ability to offer buyers something attractively different from competitors	• Ability to give customers more value for the money	• Lower overall cost than rivals in serving niche members	• Attributes that appeal specifically to niche members
Product line	• A good basic product with few frills (acceptable quality and limited selection)	• Many product variations, wide selection; emphasis on differentiating features	• Items with appealing attributes; assorted upscale features	• Features and attributes tailored to the tastes and requirements of niche members	• Features and attributes tailored to the tastes and requirements of niche members
Production emphasis	• A continuous search for cost reduction without sacrificing acceptable quality and essential features	• Build in whatever differentiating features buyers are willing to pay for; strive for product superiority	• Build in upscale features and appealing attributes at lower cost than rivals	• A continuous search for cost reduction while incorporating features and attributes matched to niche member preferences	• Custom-made products that match the tastes and requirements of niche members
Marketing emphasis	• Try to make a virtue out of product features that lead to low cost	• Tout differentiating features • Charge a premium price to cover the extra costs of differentiating features	• Tout delivery of best value • Either deliver comparable features at a lower price than rivals or else match rivals on prices and provide better features	• Communicate attractive features of a budget-priced product offering that fits niche buyers' expectations	• Communicate how product offering does the best job of meeting niche buyers' expectations
Keys to sustaining the strategy	• Economical prices/ good value • Strive to manage costs down, year after year, in every area of the business	• Stress constant innovation to stay ahead of imitative competitors • Concentrate on a few key differentiating features	• Unique expertise in simultaneously managing costs down while incorporating upscale features and attributes	• Stay committed to serving the niche at lowest overall cost; don't blur the firm's image by entering other market segments or adding other products to widen market appeal	• Stay committed to serving the niche better than rivals; don't blur the firm's image by entering other market segments or adding other products to widen market appeal

Thus, a choice of which generic strategy to employ spills over to affect several aspects of how the business will be operated and the manner in which value chain activities must be managed. Deciding which generic strategy to employ is perhaps the most important strategic commitment a company makes—it tends to drive the rest of the strategic actions a company decides to undertake.

One of the big dangers in crafting a competitive strategy is that managers, torn between the pros and cons of the various generic strategies, will opt for *stuck-in-the-middle strategies* that represent compromises between lower costs and greater differentiation and between broad and narrow market appeal. Compromise or middle-ground strategies rarely produce sustainable competitive advantage or a distinctive competitive position—a well-executed, best-cost producer strategy is the only compromise between low cost and differentiation that succeeds. Usually, companies with compromise strategies end up with a middle-of-the-pack industry ranking—they have average costs, some but not a lot of product differentiation relative to rivals, an average image and reputation, and little prospect of industry leadership. Having a competitive edge over rivals is the single most dependable contributor to above-average company profitability. Hence, only if a company makes a strong and unwavering commitment to one of the five generic competitive strategies does it stand much chance of achieving sustainable competitive advantage that such strategies can deliver if properly executed.

Key Points

Early in the process of crafting a strategy company managers have to decide which of the five basic competitive strategies to employ—overall low-cost, broad differentiation, best-cost, focused low-cost, or focused differentiation.

In employing a low-cost provider strategy and trying to achieve a low-cost advantage over rivals, a company must do a better job than rivals of cost-effectively managing value chain activities and/or find innovative ways to eliminate or bypass cost-producing activities. Low-cost provider strategies work particularly well when the products of rival sellers are virtually identical or very weakly differentiated and supplies are readily available from eager sellers, when there are not many ways to differentiate that have value to buyers, when many buyers are price sensitive and shop the market for the lowest price, and when buyer switching costs are low.

Broad differentiation strategies seek to produce a competitive edge by incorporating attributes and features that set a company's product/service offering apart from rivals in ways that buyers consider valuable and worth paying for. Successful differentiation allows a firm to (1) command a premium price for its product, (2) increase unit sales (because additional buyers are won over by the differentiating features), and/or (3) gain buyer loyalty to its brand (because some buyers are strongly attracted to the differentiating features and bond with the company and its products). Differentiation strategies work best in markets with diverse buyer preferences where there are big windows of opportunity to strongly differentiate a company's product offering from those of rival brands, in situations where few other rivals are pursuing a similar differentiation approach, and in circumstances where companies are racing to bring out the most appealing next-generation product. A differentiation strategy is doomed when competitors are able to quickly copy most or all of the appealing product attributes a company comes up with, when a company's differentiation efforts meet with a ho-hum or "so what" market reception, or when a company erodes profitability by overspending on efforts to differentiate its product offering.

Best-cost provider strategies combine a strategic emphasis on low cost with a strategic emphasis on more than minimal quality, service, features, or performance. The aim is to create competitive advantage by giving buyers more value for the money— an approach that entails matching close rivals on key quality/service/features/ performance attributes and beating them on the costs of incorporating such attributes into the product or service. A best-cost provider strategy works best in markets where buyer diversity makes product differentiation the norm and where many buyers are also sensitive to price and value.

A focus strategy delivers competitive advantage either by achieving lower costs than rivals in serving buyers comprising the target market niche or by developing specialized ability to offer niche buyers an appealingly differentiated offering than meets their needs better than rival brands. A focused strategy based on either low cost or differentiation becomes increasingly attractive when the target market niche is big enough to be profitable and offers good growth potential, when it is costly or difficult for multi-segment competitors to put capabilities in place to meet the specialized needs of the target market niche and at the same time satisfy the expectations of their mainstream customers, when there are one or more niches that present a good match with a focuser's resource strengths and capabilities, and when few other rivals are attempting to specialize in the same target segment.

Deciding which generic strategy to employ is perhaps the most important strategic commitment a company makes—it tends to drive the rest of the strategic actions a company decides to undertake and it sets the whole tone for the pursuit of a competitive advantage over rivals.

Exercises

1. Go to www.google.com and do a search for "low-cost producer." See if you can identify five companies that are pursuing a low-cost strategy in their respective industries.

2. Using the advanced search function at www.google.com, enter "best-cost producer" in the exact-phrase box and see if you can locate three companies that indicate they are employing a best-cost producer strategy.

3. Go to BMW's Web site (www.bmw.com) click on the link for BMW Group. The site you find provides an overview of the company's key functional areas, including R&D and production activities. Explore each of the links on the Research & Development page—People & Networks, Innovation & Technology, and Mobility & Traffic—to better understand the company's approach. Also review the statements under Production focusing on vehicle production and sustainable production. How do these activities contribute to BMW's differentiation strategy and the unique position in the auto industry that BMW has achieved?

4. Which of the five generic competitive strategies do you think the following companies are employing (do whatever research at the various company Web sites might be needed to arrive at and support your answer):

   a. The Saturn division of General Motors
   b. Abercrombie & Fitch
   c. Amazon.com
   d. Home Depot
   e. Mary Kay Cosmetics
   f. *USA Today*

Supplementing the Chosen Competitive Strategy

Other Important Strategy Choices

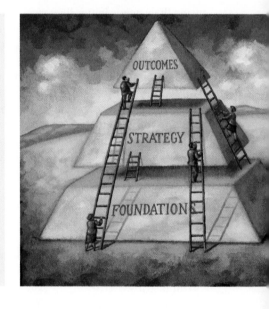

Don't form an alliance to correct a weakness and don't ally with a partner that is trying to correct a weakness of its own. The only result from a marriage of weaknesses is the creation of even more weaknesses.

—**Michel Robert**

Strategies for taking the hill won't necessarily hold it.

—**Amar Bhide**

The sure path to oblivion is to stay where you are.

—**Bernard Fauber**

Successful business strategy is about actively shaping the game you play, not just playing the game you find.

—**Adam M. Brandenburger and Barry J. Nalebuff**

O nce a company has settled on which of the five generic strategies to employ, attention turns to what other *strategic actions* it can take to complement its choice of a basic competitive strategy. Several decisions have to be made:

- What use to make of strategic alliances and collaborative partnerships.
- Whether to bolster the company's market position via merger or acquisitions.
- Whether to integrate backward or forward into more stages of the industry value chain.
- Whether to outsource certain value chain activities or perform them in-house.
- Whether and when to employ offensive and defensive moves.
- Which of several ways to use the Internet as a distribution channel in positioning the company in the marketplace.

This chapter contains sections discussing the pros and cons of each of the above complementary strategic options. The next-to-last section in the chapter discusses the need for strategic choices in each functional area of a company's business (R&D, production, sales and marketing, finance, and so on) to support its basic competitive approach and complementary strategic moves. The chapter concludes with a brief look at the competitive importance of timing strategic moves—when it is advantageous to be a first-mover and when it is better to be a fast-follower or late-mover.

Figure 6.1 shows the menu of strategic options a company has in crafting a strategy and the order in which the choices should generally be made. The portion of Figure 6.1 below the five generic competitive strategy options illustrates the structure of this chapter and the topics that will be covered.

Figure 6.1 **A Company's Menu of Strategy Options**

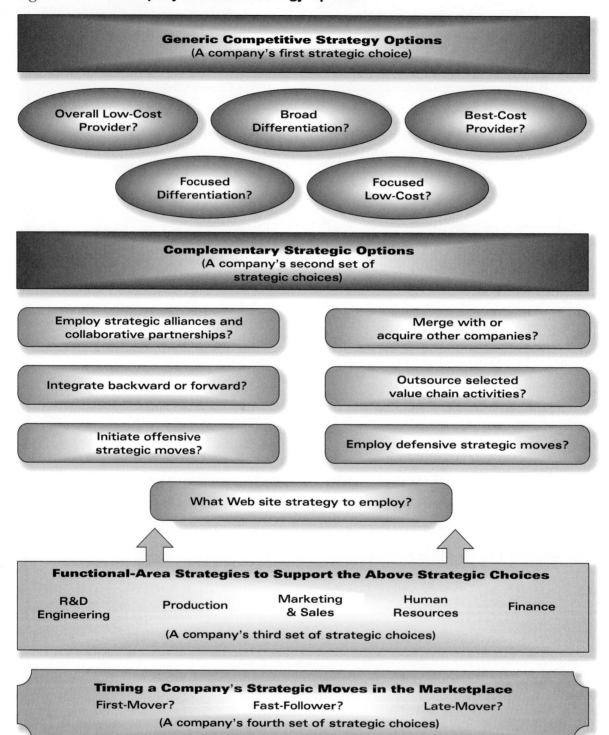

COLLABORATIVE STRATEGIES: ALLIANCES AND PARTNERSHIPS

Companies in all types of industries and in all parts of the world have elected to form strategic alliances and partnerships to complement their own strategic initiatives and strengthen their competitiveness in domestic and international markets. This is an about-face from times past, when the vast majority of companies were content to go it alone, confident that they already had or could independently develop whatever resources and know-how were needed to be successful in their markets. But globalization of the world economy; revolutionary advances in technology across a broad front; and untapped opportunities in Asia, Latin America, and Europe—whose national markets are opening up, deregulating, and/or undergoing privatization—have made strategic partnerships of one kind or another integral to competing on a broad geographic scale.

Many companies now find themselves thrust into two very demanding competitive races: (1) *the global race to build a market presence in many different national markets* and join the ranks of companies recognized as global market leaders, and (2) *the race to seize opportunities on the frontiers of advancing technology* and build the resource strengths and business capabilities to compete successfully in the industries and product markets of the future.[1] Even the largest and most financially sound companies have concluded that simultaneously running the races for global market leadership and for a stake in the industries of the future requires more diverse and expansive skills, resources, technological expertise, and competitive capabilities than they can assemble and manage alone. Such companies, along with others that are missing the resources and competitive capabilities needed to pursue promising opportunities, have determined that the fastest way to fill the gap is often to form alliances with enterprises having the desired strengths. Consequently, these companies form strategic alliances or collaborative partnerships in which two or more companies jointly work to achieve mutually beneficial strategic outcomes. Thus, a **strategic alliance** is a formal agreement between two or more separate companies in which there is strategically relevant collaboration of some sort, joint contribution of resources, shared risk, shared control, and mutual dependence. Often, alliances involve joint marketing, joint sales or distribution, joint production, design collaboration, joint research, or projects to jointly develop new technologies or products. The relationship between the partners may be contractual or merely collaborative; the arrangement commonly stops short of formal ownership ties between the partners (although there are a few strategic alliances where one or more allies have minority ownership in certain of the other alliance members). Five factors make an alliance strategic, as opposed to just a convenient business arrangement:[2]

> **Core Concept**
> ***Strategic alliances*** are collaborative arrangements where two or more companies join forces to achieve mutually beneficial strategic outcomes.

1. It is critical to the company's achievement of an important objective.
2. It helps build, sustain, or enhance a core competence or competitive advantage.
3. It helps block a competitive threat.
4. It helps open up important new market opportunities.
5. It mitigates a significant risk to a company's business.

Strategic cooperation is a much-favored, indeed necessary, approach in industries where new technological developments are occurring at a furious pace along many different paths and where advances in one technology spill over to affect others (often blurring industry boundaries). Whenever industries are experiencing high-velocity technological advances in many areas simultaneously, firms find it virtually essential to have cooperative relationships with other enterprises to stay on the leading edge of technology and product performance even in their own area of specialization.

Companies in many different industries all across the world have made strategic alliances a core part of their overall strategy; U.S. companies alone announced nearly 68,000 alliances from 1996 through 2003.[3] In the personal computer (PC) industry, alliances are pervasive because the different components of PCs and the software to run them are supplied by so many different companies—one set of companies provides the microprocessors, another group makes the motherboards, another the monitors, another the disk drives, another the memory chips, and so on. Moreover, their facilities are scattered across the United States, Japan, Taiwan, Singapore, Malaysia, and parts of Europe. Strategic alliances among companies in the various parts of the PC industry facilitate the close cross-company collaboration required on next-generation product development, logistics, production, and the timing of new product releases.

> Company use of alliances is quite widespread.

Toyota has forged long-term strategic partnerships with many of its suppliers of automotive parts and components, both to achieve lower costs and to improve the quality and reliability of its vehicles. Microsoft collaborates very closely with independent software developers to ensure that their programs will run on the next-generation versions of Windows. Genentech, a leader in biotechnology and human genetics, has a partnering strategy to increase its access to novel biotherapeutics products and technologies and has formed alliances with over 30 companies to strengthen its research and development (R&D) pipeline. During the 1998–2004 period, Samsung Electronics, a South Korean corporation with $54 billion in sales, entered into over 50 major strategic alliances involving such companies as Sony, Yahoo, Hewlett-Packard, Nokia, Motorola, Intel, Microsoft, Dell, Mitsubishi, Disney, IBM, Maytag, and Rockwell Automation; the alliances involved joint investments, technology transfer arrangements, joint R&D projects, and agreements to supply parts and components—all of which facilitated Samsung's strategic efforts to transform itself into a global enterprise and establish itself as a leader in the worldwide electronics industry.

Studies indicate that large corporations are commonly involved in 30 to 50 alliances and that some have hundreds of alliances. One recent study estimated that about 35 percent of corporate revenues in 2003 came from activities involving strategic alliances, up from 15 percent in 1995.[4] Another study reported that the typical large corporation relied on alliances for 15 to 20 percent of its revenues, assets, or income.[5] Companies that have formed a host of alliances have a need to manage their alliances like a portfolio—terminating those that no longer serve a useful purpose or that have produced meager results, forming promising new alliances, and restructuring certain existing alliances to correct performance problems and/or redirect the collaborative effort.[6]

Why and How Strategic Alliances Are Advantageous

The most common reasons why companies enter into strategic alliances are to expedite the development of promising new technologies or products, to overcome deficits in their own technical and manufacturing expertise, to bring together the personnel and expertise needed to create desirable new skill sets and capabilities, to improve supply chain efficiency, to gain economies of scale in production and/or marketing, and to acquire or improve market access through joint marketing agreements.[7] In bringing together firms with different skills and knowledge bases, alliances open up learning opportunities that help partner firms better leverage their own resource strengths.[8] In industries where technology is advancing rapidly, alliances are all about fast cycles of learning, staying abreast of the latest developments, and gaining quick access to the latest round of technological know-how and capability.

> The best alliances are highly selective, focusing on particular value chain activities and on obtaining a particular competitive benefit. They tend to enable a firm to build on its strengths and to learn.

There are several other instances in which companies find strategic alliances particularly valuable. A company that is racing for *global market leadership* needs alliances to:

- Get into critical country markets quickly and accelerate the process of building a potent global market presence.
- *Gain inside knowledge about unfamiliar markets and cultures* through alliances with local partners. For example, U.S., European, and Japanese companies wanting to build market footholds in the fast-growing Chinese market have pursued partnership arrangements with Chinese companies to help in getting products through the tedious and typically corrupt customs process, to help guide them through the maze of government regulations, to supply knowledge of local markets, to provide guidance on adapting their products to better match the buying preferences of Chinese consumers, to set up local manufacturing capabilities, and to assist in distribution, marketing, and promotional activities. The Chinese government has long required foreign companies operating in China to have a state-owned Chinese company as a minority or maybe even 50 percent partner—only recently has it backed off this requirement for foreign companies operating in selected parts of the Chinese economy.
- *Access valuable skills and competencies* that are concentrated in particular geographic locations (such as software design competencies in the United States, fashion design skills in Italy, and efficient manufacturing skills in Japan and China).

A company that is racing to *stake out a strong position in an industry of the future* needs alliances to:

- *Establish a stronger beachhead* for participating in the target industry.
- *Master new technologies and build new expertise and competencies* faster than would be possible through internal efforts.
- *Open up broader opportunities* in the target industry by melding the firm's own capabilities with the expertise and resources of partners.

Allies can learn much from one another in performing joint research, sharing technological know-how, and collaborating on complementary new technologies and products—sometimes enough to enable them to pursue other new opportunities on their own.[9] Manufacturers frequently pursue alliances with parts and components suppliers to gain the efficiencies of better supply chain management and to speed new products to market. By joining forces in components production and/or final assembly, companies may be able to realize cost savings not achievable with their own small volumes—German automakers Volkswagen, Audi, and Porsche formed a strategic alliance to spur mutual development of a gasoline-electric hybrid engine and transmission system that they could each then incorporate into their motor vehicle models; BMW, General

> The competitive attraction of alliances is in allowing companies to bundle competencies and resources that are more valuable in a joint effort than when kept separate.

Motors, and DaimlerChrysler formed a similar partnership. Both alliances were aimed at closing the gap on Toyota, generally said to be the world leader in fuel-efficient hybrid engines. Information systems consultant Accenture has developed strategic alliances with such leading technology providers as SAP, Oracle, Siebel, Microsoft, BEA, and Hewlett-Packard to give it greater capabilities in designing and integrating information systems for its corporate clients. Johnson & Johnson and Merck entered into an alliance to market Pepcid AC; Merck developed the stomach distress remedy, and Johnson & Johnson functioned as marketer—the alliance made Pepcid products the best-selling remedies for acid indigestion and heartburn. United Airlines, American Airlines, Continental, Delta, and Northwest created an alliance to form Orbitz, an Internet travel site to compete head-to-head against Expedia and Travelocity, thereby strengthening their access to travelers and vacationers shopping online for airfares, rental cars, lodging, cruises, and vacation packages.

Capturing the Benefits of Strategic Alliances

The extent to which companies benefit from entering into alliances and collaborative partnerships seems to be a function of six factors:[10]

1. *Picking a good partner*—A good partner not only has the desired expertise and capabilities but also shares the company's vision about the purpose of the alliance. Experience indicates that it is generally wise to avoid a partnership in which there is strong potential of direct competition because of overlapping product lines or other conflicting interests—agreements to jointly market each other's products hold much potential for conflict unless the products are complements rather than substitutes and unless there is good chemistry among key personnel. Experience also indicates that alliances between strong and weak companies rarely work because the alliance is unlikely to provide the strong partner with useful resources or skills and because there's a greater chance of the alliance producing mediocre results.

2. *Being sensitive to cultural differences*—Unless the outsider exhibits respect for the local culture and local business practices, productive working relationships are unlikely to emerge.

3. *Recognizing that the alliance must benefit both sides*—Information must be shared as well as gained, and the relationship must remain forthright and trustful. Many alliances fail because one or both partners grow unhappy with what they are learning. Also, if either partner plays games with information or tries to take advantage of the other, the resulting friction can quickly erode the value of further collaboration.

4. *Ensuring that both parties live up to their commitments*—Both parties have to deliver on their commitments for the alliance to produce the intended benefits. The division of work has to be perceived as fairly apportioned, and the caliber of the benefits received on both sides has to be perceived as adequate.

5. *Structuring the decision-making process so that actions can be taken swiftly when needed*—In many instances, the fast pace of technological and competitive changes dictates an equally fast decision-making process. If the parties get bogged down in discussion or in gaining internal approval from higher-ups, the alliance can turn into an anchor of delay and inaction.

6. *Managing the learning process and then adjusting the alliance agreement over time to fit new circumstances*—One of the keys to long-lasting success is adapting the nature and structure of the alliance to be responsive to shifting market conditions, emerging technologies, and changing customer requirements. Wise allies are quick

to recognize the merit of an evolving collaborative arrangement, where adjustments are made to accommodate changing market conditions and to overcome whatever problems arise in establishing an effective working relationship. Most alliances encounter troubles of some kind within a couple of years—those that are flexible enough to evolve are better able to recover.

Most alliances that aim at technology sharing or providing market access turn out to be temporary, fulfilling their purpose after a few years because the benefits of mutual learning have occurred and because the businesses of both partners have developed to the point where they are ready to go their own ways. In such cases, it is important for each partner to learn thoroughly and rapidly about the other partner's technology, business practices, and organizational capabilities and then promptly transfer valuable ideas and practices into its own operations. Although long-term alliances sometimes prove mutually beneficial, most partners don't hesitate to terminate the alliance and go it alone when the payoffs run out.

Alliances are more likely to be long-lasting when (1) they involve collaboration with suppliers or distribution allies and each party's contribution involves activities in different portions of the industry value chain, or (2) both parties conclude that continued collaboration is in their mutual interest, perhaps because new opportunities for learning are emerging or perhaps because further collaboration will allow each partner to extend its market reach beyond what it could accomplish on its own.

Why Many Alliances Are Unstable or Break Apart

The stability of an alliance depends on how well the partners work together, their success in responding and adapting to changing internal and external conditions, and their willingness to renegotiate the bargain if circumstances so warrant. A successful alliance requires real in-the-trenches collaboration, not merely an arm's-length exchange of ideas. Unless partners place a high value on the skills, resources, and contributions each brings to the alliance and the cooperative arrangement results in valuable win–win outcomes, it is doomed. A surprisingly large number of alliances never live up to expectations. A 1999 study by Accenture, a global business consulting organization, revealed that 61 percent of alliances were either outright failures or "limping along." In 2004, McKinsey & Company estimated that the overall success rate of alliances was around 50 percent, based on whether the alliance achieved the stated objectives.[11] Many alliances are dissolved after a few years. The high "divorce rate" among strategic allies has several causes—diverging objectives and priorities, an inability to work well together (an alliance between Disney and Pixar came apart because of clashes between high-level executives—in 2005, after one of the feuding executives retired, Disney acquired Pixar), changing conditions that render the purpose of the alliance obsolete, the emergence of more attractive technological paths, and marketplace rivalry between one or more allies.[12] Experience indicates that *alliances stand a reasonable chance of helping a company reduce competitive disadvantage, but very rarely have they proved a strategic option for gaining a durable competitive edge over rivals.*

The Strategic Dangers of Relying Heavily on Alliances and Collaborative Partnerships

The Achilles heel of alliances and collaborative partnerships is dependence on another company for *essential* expertise and capabilities. To be a market leader (and perhaps even a serious market contender), a company must ultimately develop its own capabilities in areas where internal strategic control is pivotal to protecting its competitiveness and building competitive advantage. Moreover, some alliances hold only limited potential because the partner guards its most valuable skills and expertise; in such instances, acquiring or merging with a company possessing the desired know-how and resources is a better solution.

MERGER AND ACQUISITION STRATEGIES

Mergers and acquisitions are much-used strategic options—for example, U.S. companies alone made 90,000 acquisitions from 1996 through 2003.[13] Mergers and acquisitions are especially suited for situations in which alliances and partnerships do not go far enough in providing a company with access to needed resources and capabilities.[14] Ownership ties are more permanent than partnership ties, allowing the operations of the merger/acquisition participants to be tightly integrated and creating more in-house control and autonomy. A *merger* is a pooling of equals, with the newly created company often taking on a new name. An *acquisition* is a combination in which one company, the acquirer, purchases and absorbs the operations of another, the acquired. The difference between a merger and an acquisition relates more to the details of ownership, management control, and financial arrangements than to strategy and competitive advantage. The resources, competencies, and competitive capabilities of the newly created enterprise end up much the same whether the combination is the result of acquisition or merger.

> Combining the operations of two companies, via merger or acquisition, is an attractive strategic option for achieving operating economies, strengthening the resulting company's competences and competitiveness, and opening up avenues of new market opportunity.

Many mergers and acquisitions are driven by strategies to achieve any of five strategic objectives:[15]

1. *To create a more cost-efficient operation out of the combined companies*—When a company acquires another company in the same industry, there's usually enough overlap in operations that certain inefficient plants can be closed or distribution activities partly combined and downsized (when nearby centers serve some of the same geographic areas), or sales-force and marketing activities combined and downsized (when each company has salespeople calling on the same customer). The combined companies may also be able to reduce supply chain costs because of buying in greater volume from common suppliers and from closer collaboration with supply chain partners. Likewise, it is usually feasible to squeeze out cost savings in administrative activities, again by combining and downsizing such administrative activities as finance and accounting, information technology, and human resources. The merger that formed DaimlerChrysler was motivated in large part by the fact that the motor vehicle industry had far more production capacity worldwide than was needed; top executives at both Daimler-Benz and Chrysler believed that the efficiency of the two companies could be significantly improved by shutting some plants and laying off workers; realigning which models were produced at which plants; and squeezing out efficiencies by combining supply chain activities, product design, and administration. Quite a number of acquisitions are undertaken with the objective of transforming two or more otherwise high-cost companies into one lean competitor with average or below-average costs.

2. *To expand a company's geographic coverage*—One of the best and quickest ways to expand a company's geographic coverage is to acquire rivals with operations in the desired locations. And if there is some geographic overlap, then a side benefit is being able to reduce costs by eliminating duplicate facilities in those geographic areas where undesirable overlap exists. Banks like Wells Fargo, Bank

of America, Wachovia, and Suntrust have pursued geographic expansion by making a series of acquisitions over the years, enabling them to establish a market presence in an ever-growing number of states and localities. Many companies use acquisitions to expand internationally; for example, food products companies like Nestlé, Kraft, Unilever, and Procter & Gamble—all racing for global market leadership—have made acquisitions an integral part of their strategies to widen their geographic reach.

3. *To extend the company's business into new product categories*—Many times a company has gaps in its product line that need to be filled. Acquisition can be a quicker and more potent way to broaden a company's product line than going through the exercise of introducing a company's own new product to fill the gap. PepsiCo acquired Quaker Oats chiefly to bring Gatorade into the Pepsi family of beverages. While Coca-Cola has expanded its beverage lineup by introducing its own new products (like Powerade and Dasani), it has also expanded its lineup by acquiring Fanta (carbonated fruit beverages), Minute Maid (juices and juice drinks), Odwalla (juices), and Hi-C (ready-to-drink fruit beverages).

4. *To gain quick access to new technologies or other resources and competitive capabilities*—Making acquisitions to bolster a company's technological know-how or to fill resource holes is a favorite of companies racing to establish a position in an industry or product category about to be born. Making acquisitions aimed at filling meaningful gaps in technological expertise allows a company to bypass a time-consuming and perhaps expensive R&D effort (which might not succeed). Cisco Systems purchased over 75 technology companies to give it more technological reach and product breadth, thereby buttressing its standing as the world's biggest supplier of systems for building the infrastructure of the Internet. Intel has made over 300 acquisitions in the past five or so years to broaden its technological base, obtain the resource capabilities to produce and market a variety of Internet-related and electronics-related products, and make it less dependent on supplying microprocessors for PCs.

5. *To try to invent a new industry and lead the convergence of industries whose boundaries are being blurred by changing technologies and new market opportunities*—Such acquisitions are the result of a company's management betting that two or more distinct industries are converging into one and deciding to establish a strong position in the consolidating markets by bringing together the resources and products of several different companies. Examples include the merger of AOL and media giant Time Warner—a move predicated on the belief that entertainment content would ultimately converge into a single industry (much of which would be distributed over the Internet)—and News Corporation's purchase of satellite TV companies to complement its media holdings in TV broadcasting (the Fox network and TV stations in various countries); cable TV (Fox News, Fox Sports, and FX); filmed entertainment (Twentieth Century Fox and Fox Studios); and newspaper, magazine, and book publishing.

Numerous companies have employed an acquisition strategy to catapult themselves from the ranks of the unknown into positions of market leadership. During the 1990s, North Carolina National Bank (NCNB) pursued a series of acquisitions to transform itself into a major regional bank in the Southeast. But NCNB's strategic vision was to become a bank with offices across most of the United States, so the company changed its name to NationsBank. In 1998, NationsBank acquired Bank of America for $66 billion and adopted its name. In 2004, Bank of America acquired Fleet Boston Financial for $48 billion. Then in mid-2005, Bank of America spent $35 billion to acquire MBNA,

Illustration Capsule 6.1

Clear Channel Communications: Using Mergers and Acquisitions to Become a Global Market Leader

Going into 2006, Clear Channel Communications was the world's fourth largest media company, behind Disney, Time Warner, and Viacom/CBS. The company, founded in 1972 by Lowry Mays and Billy Joe McCombs, got its start by acquiring an unprofitable country-music radio station in San Antonio, Texas. Over the next 10 years, Mays learned the radio business and slowly bought other radio stations in a variety of states. Going public in 1984 helped the company raise the equity capital needed to continue acquiring radio stations in additional geographic markets.

In the late 1980s, when the Federal Communications Commission loosened the rules regarding the ability of one company to own both radio and TV stations, Clear Channel broadened its strategy and began acquiring small, struggling TV stations. By 1998, Clear Channel had used acquisitions to build a leading position in radio and television stations. Domestically, it owned, programmed, or sold airtime for 69 AM radio stations, 135 FM stations, and 18 TV stations in 48 local markets in 24 states. Clear Channel's big move was to begin expanding internationally, chiefly by acquiring interests in radio station properties in a variety of countries.

In 1997, Clear Channel used acquisitions to establish a major position in outdoor advertising. Its first acquisition was Phoenix-based Eller Media Company, an outdoor advertising company with over 100,000 billboard facings. This was quickly followed by additional acquisitions of outdoor advertising companies, the most important of which were ABC Outdoor in Milwaukee, Wisconsin; Paxton Communications (with operations in Tampa and Orlando, Florida); Universal Outdoor; the More Group, with outdoor operations and 90,000 displays in 24 countries; and the Ackerley Group.

Then in October 1999, Clear Channel made a major move by acquiring AM-FM Inc. and changed its name to Clear Channel Communications; the AM-FM acquisition gave Clear Channel operations in 32 countries, including 830 radio stations, 19 TV stations, and more than 425,000 outdoor displays.

Additional acquisitions were completed during the 2000–2003 period. The emphasis was on buying radio, TV, and outdoor advertising properties with operations in many of the same local markets, which made it feasible to (1) cut costs by sharing facilities and staffs, (2) improve programming, and (3) sell advertising to customers in packages for all three media simultaneously. Packaging ads for two or three media not only helped Clear Channel's advertising clients distribute their messages more effectively but also allowed the company to combine its sales activities and have a common sales force for all three media, achieving significant cost savings and boosting profit margins. But in 2000 Clear Channel broadened its media strategy by acquiring SFX Entertainment, one of the world's largest promoters, producers, and presenters of live entertainment events.

At year-end 2005, Clear Channel owned radio and television stations, outdoor displays, and entertainment venues in 66 countries around the world. It operated approximately 1,200 radio and 40 television stations in the United States and had equity interests in over 240 radio stations internationally. It also operated a U.S. radio network of syndicated talk shows with about 180 million weekly listeners. In addition, the company owned or operated over 820,000 outdoor advertising displays, including billboards, street furniture, and transit panels around the world. In late 2005, the company spun off its Clear Channel Entertainment division (which was a leading promoter, producer, and marketer of about 32,000 live entertainment events annually and also owned leading athlete management and sports marketing companies) as a separate entity via an initial public offering of stock.

Sources: Information posted at www.clearchannel.com (accessed September 2005), and *BusinessWeek,* October 19, 1999, p. 56.

a leading credit card company. Going into 2006, Bank of America had a network of 5,900 branch banks in 29 states and the District of Columbia, and was managing $140 billion in credit card balances. It was the largest U.S. bank in terms of deposits, the second largest in terms of assets, and the fifth most profitable company in the world (with 2005 profits of about $17 billion).

Illustration Capsule 6.1 describes how Clear Channel Worldwide has used acquisitions to build a leading global position in outdoor advertising and radio and TV broadcasting.

All too frequently, mergers and acquisitions do not produce the hoped-for outcomes.[16] Cost savings may prove smaller than expected. Gains in competitive capabilities may take substantially longer to realize or, worse, may never materialize at all. Efforts to mesh the corporate cultures can stall due to formidable resistance from organization members. Managers and employees at the acquired company may argue forcefully for continuing to do certain things the way they were done prior to the acquisition. Key employees at the acquired company can quickly become disenchanted and leave; morale can drop to disturbingly low levels because personnel who remain disagree with newly instituted changes. Differences in management styles and operating procedures can prove hard to resolve. The managers appointed to oversee the integration of a newly acquired company can make mistakes in deciding what activities to leave alone and what activities to meld into their own operations and systems.

A number of previously applauded mergers/acquisitions have yet to live up to expectations—the merger of America Online (AOL) and Time Warner, the merger of Daimler-Benz and Chrysler, Hewlett-Packard's acquisition of Compaq Computer, Ford's acquisition of Jaguar, and Kmart's acquisition of Sears are prime examples. The AOL-Time Warner merger has proved to be mostly a disaster, partly because AOL's once-rapid growth has evaporated, partly because of a huge clash of corporate cultures, and partly because most of the expected benefits from industry convergence have yet to materialize. Ford paid a handsome price to acquire Jaguar but has yet to make the Jaguar brand a major factor in the luxury-car segment in competition against Mercedes, BMW, and Lexus. Novell acquired WordPerfect for $1.7 billion in stock in 1994, but the combination never generated enough punch to compete against Microsoft Word and Microsoft Office—Novell sold WordPerfect to Corel for $124 million in cash and stock less than two years later. In 2001 electronics retailer Best Buy paid $685 million to acquire Musicland, a struggling 1,300-store music retailer that included stores operating under the names Musicland, Sam Goody, Suncoast, Media Play, and On Cue. But Musicland's sales, already declining, dropped even further. In June 2003, Best Buy "sold" Musicland to a Florida investment firm—no cash changed hands and the "buyer" received shares of stock in Best Buy in return for assuming Musicland's liabilities.

VERTICAL INTEGRATION STRATEGIES: OPERATING ACROSS MORE STAGES OF THE INDUSTRY VALUE CHAIN

Vertical integration extends a firm's competitive and operating scope within the same industry. It involves expanding the firm's range of activities backward into sources of supply and/or forward toward end users. Thus, if a manufacturer invests in facilities to produce certain component parts that it formerly purchased from outside suppliers, it remains in essentially the same industry as before. The only change is that it has operations in two stages of the industry value chain. Similarly, if a paint manufacturer, Sherwin-Williams for example, elects to integrate forward by opening 100 retail stores to market its paint products directly to consumers, it remains in the paint business even though its competitive scope extends from manufacturing to retailing.

Vertical integration strategies can aim at *full integration* (participating in all stages of the industry value chain) or *partial integration* (building positions in selected stages of the industry's total value chain). A firm can pursue vertical integration by starting its own operations in other stages in the industry's activity chain or by acquiring a company already performing the activities it wants to bring in-house.

The Advantages of a Vertical Integration Strategy

The two best reasons for investing company resources in vertical integration are to strengthen the firm's competitive position and/or boost its profitability.[17] Vertical integration has no real payoff profitwise or strategywise unless it produces sufficient cost savings or profit increases to justify the extra investment, adds materially to a company's technological and competitive strengths, or helps differentiate the company's product offering.

Integrating Backward to Achieve Greater Competitiveness   It is harder than one might think to generate cost savings or boost profitability by integrating backward into activities such as manufacturing parts and components (which could otherwise be purchased from suppliers with specialized expertise in making these parts and components). For backward integration to be a viable and profitable strategy, a company must be able to (1) achieve the same scale economies as outside suppliers and (2) match or beat suppliers' production efficiency with no drop-off in quality. Neither outcome is a slam-dunk. To begin with, a company's in-house requirements are often too small to reach the optimum size for low-cost operation—for instance, if it takes a minimum production volume of 1 million units to achieve mass-production economies and a company's in-house requirements are just 250,000 units, then the company falls way short of being able to capture the scale economies of outside suppliers (which may readily find buyers for 1 million or more units). Furthermore, matching the production efficiency of suppliers is fraught with problems when suppliers have considerable production experience of their own, when the technology they employ has elements that are hard to master, or when substantial R&D expertise is required to develop next-version parts and components or keep pace with advancing technology in parts/components production.

But that being said, there are still occasions when a company can improve its cost position and competitiveness by performing a broad range of value chain activities in-house. The best potential for being able to reduce costs via a backward integration strategy exists in situations where suppliers have outsized profit margins, where the item being supplied is a major cost component, and where the requisite technological skills are easily mastered or can be gained by acquiring a supplier with the desired technological know-how. Furthermore, when a company has proprietary know-how that it is beneficial to keep away from rivals, then in-house performance of value chain activities related to this know-how is beneficial even if such activities could be performed by outsiders. For example, Krispy Kreme Doughnuts has successfully employed a backward vertical integration strategy that involves internally producing both the doughnut-making equipment and ready-mixed doughnut ingredients that company-owned and franchised retail stores used in making Krispy Kreme doughnuts—the company earned substantial profits from producing these items internally rather than having them supplied by outsiders. Furthermore, Krispy Kreme's vertical integration strategy made good competitive sense because both its doughnut-making equipment and its doughnut recipe were proprietary; keeping its equipment manufacturing know-how and its secret recipe out of the hands of outside suppliers helped Krispy Kreme protect its doughnut offering from would-be imitators.

Backward vertical integration can produce a differentiation-based competitive advantage when a company, by performing activities internally rather than using outside suppliers, ends up with a better-quality product/service offering, improves the caliber of its customer service, or in other ways enhances the performance of its final product. On occasion, integrating into more stages along the industry value chain can add to a company's differentiation capabilities by allowing the company to build or strengthen its core competencies, better master key skills or strategy-critical technologies, or add features that deliver greater customer value. Other potential advantages of backward integration include sparing a company the uncertainty of being dependent on suppliers for crucial components or support services and lessening a company's vulnerability to powerful suppliers inclined to raise prices at every opportunity.

Integrating Forward to Enhance Competitiveness   The strategic impetus for forward integration is to gain better access to end users and better market visibility. In many industries, independent sales agents, wholesalers, and retailers handle competing brands of the same product; having no allegiance to any one company's brand, they tend to push whatever sells and earns them the biggest profits. An independent insurance agency, for example, represents a number of different insurance companies—in trying to find the best match between a customer's insurance requirements and the policies of alternative insurance companies, there's plenty of opportunity for independent agents to end up promoting certain insurance companies' policies ahead of others'. An insurance company may therefore conclude that it is better off setting up its own local sales offices with its own local agents to exclusively promote its policies. Likewise, a manufacturer can be frustrated in its attempts to win higher sales and market share or get rid of unwanted inventory or maintain steady, near-capacity production if it must distribute its products through distributors and/or retailers who are only halfheartedly committed to promoting and marketing its brand as opposed to those of rivals. In such cases, it can be advantageous for a manufacturer to integrate forward into wholesaling or retailing via company-owned distributorships or a chain of retail stores. For instance, both Goodyear and Bridgestone opted to integrate forward into tire retailing rather than to use independent distributors and retailers that stocked multiple brands because the independent distributors/retailers stressed selling the tire brands on which they earned the highest profit margins. A number of housewares and apparel manufacturers have integrated forward into retailing so as to move seconds, overstocked items, and slow-selling merchandise through their own branded retail outlet stores located in discount malls. Some producers have opted to integrate forward into retailing by selling directly to customers at the company's Web site. Bypassing regular wholesale/retail channels in favor of direct sales and Internet retailing can have appeal if it lowers distribution costs, produces a relative cost advantage over certain rivals, and results in lower selling prices to end users.

The Disadvantages of a Vertical Integration Strategy

Vertical integration has some substantial drawbacks, however.[18] As it boosts a firm's capital investment in the industry, it increases business risk (what if industry growth and profitability go sour?) and increases the company's vested interests in sticking with its vertically integrated value chain (what if some aspects of its technology and production facilities become obsolete before they are worn out or fully depreciated?). Vertically integrated companies that have invested heavily in a particular technology or in parts/components manufacture are often slow to embrace technological advances or more efficient production methods compared to partially integrated or nonintegrated firms. This is because less integrated firms can pressure suppliers to provide only the latest and best parts and components (even going so far as to shift their purchases from one supplier to another if need be), whereas a vertically integrated firm that is saddled with older technology or facilities that make items it no longer needs is looking at the high costs of premature abandonment. Second, integrating forward or backward locks a firm into relying on its own in-house activities and sources of supply (which later may prove more costly than outsourcing) and potentially results in less flexibility in accommodating shifting buyer preferences or a product design that doesn't include parts and components that it makes in-house. *In today's world of close working relationships with suppliers and efficient supply chain management systems, very few businesses can make a case for integrating backward into the business of suppliers to ensure a reliable supply of materials and components or to reduce production costs.* The best materials and components suppliers stay abreast of advancing technology and are adept in boosting their efficiency and keeping their costs and prices as low as possible. A company that pursues a vertical integration strategy and tries to produce many parts and components in-house is likely to find itself hard-pressed to keep up with technological advances and cutting-edge production practices for each part and component used in making its product.

Third, vertical integration poses all kinds of capacity-matching problems. In motor vehicle manufacturing, for example, the most efficient scale of operation for making axles is different from the most economic volume for radiators, and different yet again for both engines and transmissions. Building the capacity to produce just the right number of axles, radiators, engines, and transmissions in-house—and doing so at the lowest unit cost for each—is much easier said than done. If internal capacity for making transmissions is deficient, the difference has to be bought externally. Where internal capacity for radiators proves excessive, customers need to be found for the surplus. And if by-products are generated—as occurs in the processing of many chemical products—they require arrangements for disposal. Consequently, integrating across several production stages in ways that achieve the lowest feasible costs is not as easy as it might seem.

Fourth, integration forward or backward often calls for radical changes in skills and business capabilities. Parts and components manufacturing, assembly operations, wholesale distribution and retailing, and direct sales via the Internet are different businesses with different key success factors. Managers of a manufacturing company should consider carefully whether it makes good business sense to invest time and money in developing the expertise and merchandising skills to integrate forward into wholesaling and retailing. Many manufacturers learn the hard way that company-owned wholesale/retail networks present many headaches, fit poorly with what they do best, and don't always add the kind of value to their core business they thought they would. Selling to customers via the Internet poses still another set of problems—it is usually easier to use the Internet to sell to business customers than to consumers.

Finally, integrating backward into parts and components manufacture can impair a company's operating flexibility when it comes to changing out the use of certain parts and components. It is one thing to design out a component made by a supplier and another to design out a component being made in-house (which can mean laying off employees and writing off the associated investment in equipment and facilities). Companies that alter designs and models frequently in response to shifting buyer preferences often find that outsourcing the needed parts and components is cheaper and less complicated than producing them in-house. Most of the world's automakers, despite their expertise in automotive technology and manufacturing, have concluded that purchasing many of their key parts and components from manufacturing specialists results in higher quality, lower costs, and greater design flexibility than does the vertical integration option.

Weighing the Pros and Cons of Vertical Integration   All in all, therefore, a strategy of vertical integration can have both important strengths and weaknesses. The tip of the scales depends on (1) whether vertical integration can enhance the performance of strategy-critical activities in ways that lower cost, build expertise, protect proprietary know-how, or increase differentiation; (2) the impact of vertical integration on investment costs, flexibility and response times, and the administrative costs of coordinating operations across more value chain activities; and (3) whether vertical integration substantially enhances a company's competitiveness and profitability. *Vertical integration strategies have merit according to which capabilities and value-chain activities truly need to be performed in-house and which can be performed better or cheaper by outsiders.* Absent solid benefits, integrating forward or backward is not likely to be an attractive strategy option.

OUTSOURCING STRATEGIES: NARROWING THE BOUNDARIES OF THE BUSINESS

Outsourcing involves a conscious decision to abandon or forgo attempts to perform certain value chain activities internally and instead to farm them out to outside specialists and strategic allies. The two big drivers for outsourcing are that (1) outsiders can often perform certain activities better or cheaper and (2) outsourcing allows a firm to focus its entire energies on those activities at the center of its expertise (its core competencies) and that are the most critical to its competitive and financial success.

> **Core Concept**
> *Outsourcing* involves farming out certain value chain activities to outside vendors.

The current interest of many companies in making outsourcing a key component of their overall strategy and their approach to supply chain management represents a big departure from the way that companies used to deal with their suppliers and vendors. In years past, it was common for companies to maintain arm's-length relationships with suppliers and outside vendors, insisting on items being made to precise specifications and negotiating long and hard over price.[19] Although a company might place orders with the same supplier repeatedly, there was no expectation that this would be the case; price usually determined which supplier was awarded an order, and companies used the threat of switching suppliers to get the lowest possible prices. To enhance their bargaining power and, to make the threat of switching credible, it was standard practice for companies to source key parts and components from several suppliers as opposed to dealing with only a single supplier. But today most companies are abandoning such approaches in favor of forging alliances and strategic partnerships with a small number of highly capable suppliers. Collaborative relationships are replacing contractual, purely price-oriented relationships because companies have discovered that many of the advantages of performing value chain activities in-house can be captured and many of the disadvantages avoided by forging close, long-term cooperative partnerships with able suppliers and vendors and tapping into the expertise and capabilities that they have painstakingly developed.

When Outsourcing Strategies Are Advantageous

Outsourcing pieces of the value chain to narrow the boundaries of a firm's business makes strategic sense whenever:

- *An activity can be performed better or more cheaply by outside specialists.* Many PC makers, for example, have shifted from assembling units in-house to using contract assemblers because of the sizable scale economies associated with purchasing PC components in large volumes and assembling PCs. German shoemaker Birkenstock, by outsourcing the distribution of shoes made in its two plants in Germany to UPS, cut the time for delivering orders to U.S. footwear retailers from seven weeks to three weeks.[20]

- *The activity is not crucial to the firm's ability to achieve sustainable competitive advantage and won't hollow out its core competencies, capabilities, or technical know-how.* Outsourcing of maintenance services, data processing and data storage, fringe benefit management, Web site operations, and similar administrative support activities to specialists has become commonplace. American Express, for instance, recently entered into a seven-year, $4 billion deal whereby IBM's Services division would host American Express's Web site, network servers, data storage, and help desk; American Express indicated that it would save several hundred million dollars by paying only for the services it needed when it needed them (as opposed to funding its own full-time staff). A number of companies have begun outsourcing their call center operations to foreign-based contractors who have access to lower-cost labor supplies and can employ lower-paid call center personnel to respond to customer inquiries or requests for technical support.

> **Core Concept**
> A company should generally *not* perform any value chain activity internally that can be performed more efficiently or effectively by outsiders—the chief exception is when a particular activity is strategically crucial and internal control over that activity is deemed essential.

- *It reduces the company's risk exposure to changing technology and/or changing buyer preferences.* When a company outsources certain parts, components, and services, its suppliers must bear the burden of incorporating state-of-the-art technologies and/or undertaking redesigns and upgrades to accommodate a company's plans to introduce next-generation products. If what a supplier provides falls out of favor with buyers or is designed out of next-generation products, it is the supplier's business that suffers rather than a company's own internal operations.

- *It improves a company's ability to innovate.* Collaborative partnerships with world-class suppliers who have cutting-edge intellectual capital and are early adopters of the latest technology give a company access to ever better parts and components—such supplier-driven innovations, when incorporated into a company's own product offering, fuel a company's ability to introduce its own new and improved products.

- *It streamlines company operations in ways that improve organizational flexibility and cuts the time it takes to get new products into the marketplace.* Outsourcing gives a company the flexibility to switch suppliers in the event that its present supplier falls behind competing suppliers. To the extent that its suppliers can speedily get next-generation parts and components into production, then a company can get its own next-generation product offerings into the marketplace quicker. Moreover, seeking out new suppliers with the needed capabilities already in place is frequently quicker, easier, less risky, and cheaper than hurriedly retooling internal operations to replace obsolete capabilities or try to install and master new technologies.

- *It allows a company to assemble diverse kinds of expertise speedily and efficiently.* A company can nearly always gain quicker access to first-rate capabilities and expertise by partnering with suppliers who already have them in place than it can by trying to build them from scratch with its own company personnel.

- *It allows a company to concentrate on its core business, leverage its key resources, and do even better what it already does best.* A company is better able to build and develop its own competitively valuable competencies and capabilities when it concentrates its full resources and energies on performing those activities internally that it can perform better than outsiders and/or that it needs to have under its direct control. Cisco Systems, for example, devotes its energy to designing new generations of switches, routers, and other Internet-related equipment, opting to outsource the more mundane activities of producing and assembling its routers and switching equipment to contract manufacturers that together operate 37 factories, all closely monitored and overseen by Cisco personnel via online systems. Cisco's contract suppliers work so closely with Cisco that they can ship Cisco products to Cisco customers without a Cisco employee ever touching the gear. This system of alliances saves $500 million to $800 million annually.[21]

Dell Computer's partnerships with the suppliers of PC components have allowed it to operate with only three days of inventory (just a couple of hours of inventory in the case of some components), to realize substantial savings in inventory costs, and to get PCs equipped with next-generation components into the marketplace in less than a week after the newly upgraded components start shipping. Hewlett-Packard, IBM, Silicon Graphics (now SGI), and others have sold plants to suppliers and then contracted to purchase the output. Starbucks has found purchasing coffee beans from independent growers far more advantageous than trying to integrate backward into the coffee-growing business.

The Big Risk of an Outsourcing Strategy

The biggest danger of outsourcing is that a company will farm out too many or the wrong types of activities and thereby hollow out its own capabilities.[22] In such cases, a company loses touch with the very activities and expertise that over the long run determine its success. But most companies are alert to this danger and take actions to protect against being held hostage by outside suppliers. Cisco Systems guards against loss of control and protects its manufacturing expertise by designing the production methods that its contract manufacturers must use. Cisco keeps the source code for its designs proprietary, thereby controlling the initiation of all improvements and safeguarding its innovations from imitation. Further, Cisco uses the Internet to monitor the factory operations of contract manufacturers around the clock and can therefore know immediately when problems arise and whether to get involved.

OFFENSIVE STRATEGIES: IMPROVING MARKET POSITION AND BUILDING COMPETITIVE ADVANTAGE

Most every company must at times go on the offensive to improve its market position and try to build a competitive advantage or widen an existing one. Companies like Dell, Wal-Mart, and Toyota play hardball, aggressively pursuing competitive advantage and trying to reap the benefits a competitive edge offers—a leading market share, excellent profit margins and rapid growth (as compared to rivals), and all the intangibles of being known as a company on the move and one that plays to win.[23] The best offensives tend to incorporate several behaviors and principles: (1) focusing relentlessly on building competitive advantage and then striving to convert competitive advantage into decisive advantage, (2) employing the element of surprise as opposed to doing what rivals expect and are prepared for, (3) applying resources where rivals are least able to defend themselves, and (4) being impatient with the status quo and displaying a strong bias for swift, decisive actions to boost a company's competitive position vis-à-vis rivals.[24]

Offensive strategies are also important when a company has no choice but to try to whittle away at a strong rival's competitive advantage and when it is possible to gain profitable market share at the expense of rivals despite whatever resource strengths and capabilities they have. How long it takes for an offensive to yield good results varies with the competitive circumstances.[25] It can be short if buyers respond immediately (as can occur with a dramatic price cut, an imaginative ad campaign, or an especially appealing new product). Securing a competitive edge can take much longer if winning consumer acceptance of an innovative product will take some time or if the firm may need several years to debug a new technology or put new production capacity in place or develop and perfect new competitive capabilities. Ideally, an offensive move will improve a company's market standing or result in a competitive edge fairly quickly; the longer it takes, the more likely it is that rivals will spot the move, see its potential, and begin a counterresponse.

> **Core Concept**
>
> It takes successful offensive strategies to build competitive advantage—good defensive strategies can help protect competitive advantage but rarely are the basis for creating it.

The principal offensive strategy options include the following:

1. *Offering an equally good or better product at a lower price.* This is the classic offensive for improving a company's market position vis-à-vis rivals. Advanced Micro Devices (AMD), wanting to grow its sales of microprocessors for PCs, has on several occasions elected to attack Intel head-on, offering a faster alternative to Intel's Pentium chips at a lower price. Believing that the company's survival depends on eliminating the performance gap between AMD chips and Intel chips, AMD management has been willing to risk that a head-on offensive might prompt Intel to counter with lower prices of its own and accelerated development of next-generation chips. Lower prices can produce market share gains if competitors don't respond with price cuts of their own and if the challenger convinces buyers that its product is just as good or better. However, such a strategy increases total profits only if the gains in additional unit sales are enough to offset the impact of lower prices and thinner margins per unit sold. Price-cutting offensives generally work best when a company *first achieves a cost advantage and then hits competitors with a lower price.*[26]

2. *Leapfrogging competitors by being the first adopter of next-generation technologies or being first to market with next-generation products.* In 2004–2005, Microsoft waged an offensive to get its next-generation Xbox to market four to six months ahead of Sony's PlayStation 3, anticipating that such a lead time would allow help it convince video gamers to switch to the Xbox rather than wait for the new PlayStation to hit the market in 2006.

3. *Pursuing continuous product innovation to draw sales and market share away from less innovative rivals.* Aggressive and sustained efforts to trump the products of rivals by introducing new or improved products with features calculated to win customers away from rivals can put rivals under tremendous competitive pressure, especially when their new product development capabilities are weak or suspect. But such offensives work only if a company has potent product innovation skills of its own and can keep its pipeline full of ideas that are consistently well received in the marketplace.

4. *Adopting and improving on the good ideas of other companies (rivals or otherwise).*[27] The idea of warehouse-type hardware and home improvement centers did not

originate with Home Depot founders Arthur Blank and Bernie Marcus; they got the big-box concept from their former employer Handy Dan Home Improvement. But they were quick to improve on Handy Dan's business model and strategy and take Home Depot to the next plateau in terms of product line breadth and customer service. Casket maker Hillenbrand greatly improved its market position by adapting Toyota's production methods to casket making. Ryanair has succeeded as a low-cost airline in Europe by imitating many of Southwest Airlines' operating practices and applying them in a different geographic market. Companies that like to play hardball are willing to take any good idea (not nailed down by a patent or other legal protection), make it their own, and then aggressively apply it to create competitive advantage for themselves.[28]

5. *Deliberately attacking those market segments where a key rival makes big profits.*[29] Dell Computer's recent entry into printers and printer cartridges—the market arena where number-two PC maker Hewlett-Packard (HP) enjoys hefty profit margins and makes the majority of its profits—while mainly motivated by Dell's desire to broaden its product line and save its customers money (because of Dell's lower prices), nonetheless represented a hardball offensive calculated to weaken HP's market position in printers. To the extent that Dell might be able to use lower prices to woo away some of HP's printer customers, the move would erode HP's "profit sanctuary," distract HP's attention away from PCs, and reduce the financial resources HP has available for battling Dell in the global market for PCs.

6. *Attacking the competitive weaknesses of rivals.* Offensives aimed at rivals' weaknesses present many options. One is to go after the customers of those rivals whose products lag on quality, features, or product performance. If a company has especially good customer service capabilities, it can make special sales pitches to the customers of those rivals who provide subpar customer service. Aggressors with a recognized brand name and strong marketing skills can launch efforts to win customers away from rivals with weak brand recognition. There is considerable appeal in emphasizing sales to buyers in geographic regions where a rival has a weak market share or is exerting less competitive effort. Likewise, it may be attractive to pay special attention to buyer segments that a rival is neglecting or is weakly equipped to serve.

7. *Maneuvering around competitors and concentrating on capturing unoccupied or less contested market territory.* Examples include launching initiatives to build strong positions in geographic areas where close rivals have little or no market presence and trying to create new market segments by introducing products with different attributes and performance features to better meet the needs of selected buyers.

8. *Using hit-and-run or guerrilla warfare tactics to grab sales and market share from complacent or distracted rivals.* Options for "guerrilla offensives" include occasional lowballing on price (to win a big order or steal a key account from a rival); surprising key rivals with sporadic but intense bursts of promotional activity (offering a 20 percent discount for one week to draw customers away from rival brands); or undertaking special campaigns to attract buyers away from rivals plagued with a strike or problems in meeting buyer demand.[30] Guerrilla offensives are particularly well suited to small challengers who have neither the resources nor the market visibility to mount a full-fledged attack on industry leaders.

9. *Launching a preemptive strike to secure an advantageous position that rivals are prevented or discouraged from duplicating.*[31] What makes a move preemptive

is its one-of-a-kind nature—whoever strikes first stands to acquire competitive assets that rivals can't readily match. Examples of preemptive moves include (1) securing the best distributors in a particular geographic region or country; (2) moving to obtain the most favorable site along a heavily traveled thoroughfare, at a new interchange or intersection, in a new shopping mall, in a natural beauty spot, close to cheap transportation or raw material supplies or market outlets, and so on; (3) tying up the most reliable, high-quality suppliers via exclusive partnership, long-term contracts, or even acquisition; and (4) moving swiftly to acquire the assets of distressed rivals at bargain prices. To be successful, a preemptive move doesn't have to totally block rivals from following or copying; it merely needs to give a firm a prime position that is not easily circumvented.

Blue Ocean Strategy: A Special Kind of Offensive

A "blue ocean strategy" seeks to gain a dramatic and durable competitive advantage *by abandoning efforts to beat out competitors in existing markets and, instead, inventing a new industry or distinctive market segment (a wide-open blue ocean of possibility) that renders existing competitors largely irrelevant and allows a company to create and capture altogether new demand.*[32] This strategy views the business universe as consisting of two distinct types of market space. One is where industry boundaries are defined and accepted, the competitive rules of the game are well understood by all industry members, and companies try to outperform rivals by capturing a bigger share of existing demand; in such markets, lively competition constrains a company's prospects for rapid growth and superior profitability since rivals move quickly to either imitate or counter the successes of competitors. In the second type of market space, the industry does not really exist yet, is untainted by competition, and offers wide-open opportunity for profitable and rapid growth if a company can come up with a product offering and strategy that allows it to create new demand rather than fight over existing demand. A terrific example of such a blue ocean market space is the online auction industry that eBay created and now dominates.

Another company that has employed a blue ocean strategy is Cirque du Soleil, which increased its revenues by 22 times during the 1993–2003 period in the circus business, an industry that had been in long-term decline for 20 years. How did Cirque du Soleil pull this off against legendary industry leader Ringling Bros. and Barnum & Bailey? By reinventing the circus, creating a distinctively different market space for its performances (Las Vegas nightclubs and theater-type settings), and pulling in a whole new group of customers—adults and corporate clients—who were noncustomers of traditional circuses and were willing to pay several times more than the price of a conventional circus ticket to have an "entertainment experience" featuring sophisticated clowns and star-quality acrobatic acts in a comfortable big-tent atmosphere. Cirque studiously avoided the use of animals because of costs and because of concerns over their treatment by traditional circus organizations. Cirque's market research led management to conclude that the lasting allure of the traditional circus came down to just three factors: the clowns, classic acrobatic acts, and a tentlike stage. As of 2005, Cirque du Soleil was presenting nine different shows, each with its own theme and story line; was performing before audiences of about 7 million people annually; and had performed 250 engagements in 100 cities before 50 million spectators since its formation in 1984.

Other examples of companies that have achieved competitive advantages by creating blue ocean market spaces include AMC via its pioneering of megaplex movie theaters, The Weather Channel in cable TV, Home Depot in big-box retailing of hardware and building supplies, and FedEx in overnight package delivery. Companies that create blue ocean market spaces can usually sustain their initially won competitive advantage without encountering major competitive challenge for 10 to 15 years because of high barriers to imitation and the strong brand-name awareness that a blue ocean strategy can produce.

Choosing Which Rivals to Attack

Offense-minded firms need to analyze which of their rivals to challenge as well as how to mount that challenge. The following are the best targets for offensive attacks:[33]

- *Market leaders that are vulnerable*—Offensive attacks make good sense when a company that leads in terms of size and market share is not a true leader in terms of serving the market well. Signs of leader vulnerability include unhappy buyers, an inferior product line, a weak competitive strategy with regard to low-cost leadership or differentiation, strong emotional commitment to an aging technology the leader has pioneered, outdated plants and equipment, a preoccupation with diversification into other industries, and mediocre or declining profitability. Offensives to erode the positions of market leaders have real promise when the challenger is able to revamp its value chain or innovate to gain a fresh cost-based or differentiation-based competitive advantage.[34] To be judged successful, attacks on leaders don't have to result in making the aggressor the new leader; a challenger may "win" by simply becoming a stronger runner-up. Caution is well advised in challenging strong market leaders— there's a significant risk of squandering valuable resources in a futile effort or precipitating a fierce and profitless industrywide battle for market share.

- *Runner-up firms with weaknesses in areas where the challenger is strong*— Runner-up firms are an especially attractive target when a challenger's resource strengths and competitive capabilities are well suited to exploiting their weaknesses.

- *Struggling enterprises that are on the verge of going under*—Challenging a hard-pressed rival in ways that further sap its financial strength and competitive position can weaken its resolve and hasten its exit from the market.

- *Small local and regional firms with limited capabilities*—Because small firms typically have limited expertise and resources, a challenger with broader capabilities is well positioned to raid their biggest and best customers— particularly those who are growing rapidly, have increasingly sophisticated requirements, and may already be thinking about switching to a supplier with more full-service capability.

Choosing the Basis for Competitive Attack

As a rule, challenging rivals on competitive grounds where they are strong is an uphill struggle.[35] Offensive initiatives that exploit competitor weaknesses stand a better chance of succeeding than do those that challenge competitor strengths, especially if the weaknesses represent important vulnerabilities and weak rivals can be caught by surprise with no ready defense.[36]

> **Core Concept**
> The best offensives use a company's resource strengths to attack rivals in those competitive areas where they are weak.

Strategic offensives should, as a general rule, be grounded in a company's competitive assets and strong points—its core competencies, competitive capabilities, and such resource strengths as a better-known brand name, a cost advantage in manufacturing or distribution, greater technological capability, or a superior product. If the attacker's resource strengths give it a competitive advantage over the targeted rivals, so much the better. Ignoring the need to tie a strategic offensive to a company's competitive strengths is like going to war with a popgun—the prospects for success are dim. For instance, it is foolish for a company with relatively high costs to employ a price-cutting offensive—price-cutting offensives are best left to financially strong companies whose costs are relatively low in comparison to those of the companies being attacked. Likewise, it is ill advised to pursue a product innovation offensive without having proven expertise in R&D, new product development, and speeding new or improved products to market.

DEFENSIVE STRATEGIES: PROTECTING MARKET POSITION AND COMPETITIVE ADVANTAGE

It is just as important to discern when to fortify a company's present market position with defensive actions as it is to seize the initiative and launch strategic offensives.

In a competitive market, all firms are subject to offensive challenges from rivals. The purposes of defensive strategies are to lower the risk of being attacked, weaken the impact of any attack that occurs, and influence challengers to aim their efforts at other rivals. While defensive strategies usually don't enhance a firm's competitive advantage, they can definitely help fortify its competitive position, protect its most valuable resources and capabilities from imitation, and defend whatever competitive advantage it might have. Defensive strategies can take either of two forms: actions to block challengers and signaling the likelihood of strong retaliation.

Blocking the Avenues Open to Challengers

There are many ways to throw obstacles in the path of would-be challengers.

The most frequently employed approach to defending a company's present position involves actions that restrict a challenger's options for initiating competitive attack. There are any number of obstacles that can be put in the path of would-be challengers.[37] A defender can participate in alternative technologies as a hedge against rivals attacking with a new or better technology. A defender can introduce new features, add new models, or broaden its product line to close off gaps and vacant niches to opportunity-seeking challengers. It can thwart the efforts of rivals to attack with a lower price by maintaining economy-priced options of its own. It can try to discourage buyers from trying competitors' brands by lengthening warranties, offering free training and support services, developing the capability to deliver spare parts to users faster than rivals can, providing coupons and sample giveaways to buyers most prone to experiment, and making early announcements about impending new products or price changes to induce potential buyers to postpone switching. It can challenge the quality or safety of rivals' products. Finally, a defender can grant volume discounts or better financing terms to dealers and distributors to discourage them from experimenting with other suppliers, or it can convince them to handle its product line *exclusively* and force competitors to use other distribution outlets.

Signaling Challengers that Retaliation Is Likely

The goal of signaling challengers that strong retaliation is likely in the event of an attack is either to dissuade challengers from attacking at all or to divert them to less threatening options. Either goal can be achieved by letting challengers know the battle will cost more than it is worth. Would-be challengers can be signaled by:[38]

- Publicly announcing management's commitment to maintain the firm's present market share.
- Publicly committing the company to a policy of matching competitors' terms or prices.
- Maintaining a war chest of cash and marketable securities.
- Making an occasional strong counterresponse to the moves of weak competitors to enhance the firm's image as a tough defender.

WEB SITE STRATEGIES

One of the biggest strategic issues facing company executives across the world is just what role the company's Web site should play in a company's competitive strategy. In particular, to what degree should a company use the Internet as a distribution channel for accessing buyers? Should a company use its Web site *only as a means of disseminating product information* (with traditional distribution channel partners making all sales to end users), as a *secondary or minor channel* for selling directly to buyers of its product, as *one of several important distribution channels* for accessing customers, as *the primary distribution channel* for accessing customers, or as *the exclusive channel* for transacting sales with customers?[39] Let's look at each of these strategic options in turn.

> Companies today must wrestle with the strategic issue of how to use their Web sites in positioning themselves in the marketplace—whether to use their Web sites just to disseminate product information or whether to operate an e-store to sell direct to online shoppers.

Product Information–Only Web Strategies: Avoiding Channel Conflict

Operating a Web site that contains extensive product information but that relies on click-throughs to the Web sites of distribution channel partners for sales transactions (or that informs site users where nearby retail stores are located) is an attractive market positioning option for manufacturers and/or wholesalers that have invested heavily in building and cultivating retail dealer networks and that face nettlesome channel conflict issues if they try to sell online in direct competition with their dealers. A manufacturer or wholesaler that aggressively pursues online sales to end users is signaling both a weak strategic commitment to its dealers and a willingness to cannibalize dealers' sales and growth potential.

To the extent that strong partnerships with wholesale and/or retail dealers are critical to accessing end users, selling directly to end users via the company's Web site is a very tricky road to negotiate. A manufacturer's efforts to use its Web site to sell around its dealers is certain to anger its wholesale distributors and retail dealers, which may respond by putting more effort into marketing the brands of rival manufacturers that don't sell online. In sum, the manufacturer may stand to lose more sales by offending its dealers than it gains from its own online sales effort. Moreover, dealers may be in better position to employ a brick-and-click strategy than a manufacturer is because dealers have a local presence to complement their online sales approach (which consumers may find appealing). Consequently, in industries where the strong support and goodwill of dealer networks is essential, manufacturers may conclude that their Web site should be designed to partner with dealers rather than compete with them—just as the auto manufacturers are doing with their franchised dealers.

Web Site e-Stores as a Minor Distribution Channel

A second strategic option is to use online sales as a relatively minor distribution channel for achieving incremental sales, gaining online sales experience, and doing marketing research. If channel conflict poses a big obstacle to online sales, or if only a small fraction of buyers can be attracted to make online purchases, then companies are well advised to pursue online sales with the strategic intent of gaining experience, learning more about buyer tastes and preferences, testing reaction to new products, creating added market buzz about their products, and boosting overall sales volume a few percentage points. Sony and Nike, for example, sell most all of their products at their Web sites without provoking resistance from their retail dealers since most buyers of their products prefer to do their buying at retail stores rather than online. They use their Web site not so much to make sales as to glean valuable marketing research data from tracking the browsing patterns of Web site visitors. The behavior and actions of Web surfers are a veritable gold mine of information for companies seeking to keep their finger on the market pulse and respond more precisely to buyer preferences and interests.

Despite the channel conflict that exists when a manufacturer sells directly to end users at its Web site in head-to-head competition with its distribution channel allies, manufacturers might still opt to pursue online sales at their Web sites and try to establish online sales as an important distribution channel because (1) their profit margins from online sales are bigger than they earned from selling to their wholesale/retail customers; (2) encouraging buyers to visit the company's Web site helps educate them to the ease and convenience of purchasing online and, over time, prompts more and more buyers to purchase online (where company profit margins are greater)—which makes incurring channel conflict in the short term and competing against traditional distribution allies potentially worthwhile—and (3) selling directly to end users allows a manufacturer to make greater use of build-to-order manufacturing and assembly, which, if met with growing buyer acceptance of and satisfaction, would increase the rate at which sales migrate from distribution allies to the company's Web site—such migration could lead to streamlining the company's value chain and boosting its profit margins.

Brick-and-Click Strategies

Brick-and-click strategies have two big strategic appeals for wholesale and retail enterprises: They are an economic means of expanding a company's geographic reach, and they give both existing and potential customers another choice of how to communicate with the company, shop for product information, make purchases, or resolve customer service problems. Software developers, for example, have come to rely on the Internet as a highly effective distribution channel to complement sales through brick-and-mortar wholesalers and retailers. Selling online directly to end users has the advantage of eliminating the costs of producing and packaging CDs, as well as cutting out the costs and margins of software wholesalers and retailers (often 35 to 50 percent of the retail price). However, software developers are still strongly motivated to continue to distribute their products through wholesalers and retailers (to maintain broad access to existing and potential users who, for whatever reason, may be reluctant to buy online). Chain retailers like Wal-Mart and Circuit City operate online stores for their products primarily as a convenience to customers who want to buy online rather than making a shopping trip to nearby stores.

Many brick-and-mortar companies can enter online retailing at relatively low cost—all they need is a Web store and systems for filling and delivering individual customer orders. Brick-and-mortar distributors and retailers (as well as manufacturers with company-owned retail stores) can employ brick-and-click strategies by using their current distribution centers and/or retail stores for picking orders from on-hand inventories and making deliveries. Blockbuster, the world's largest chain of video and DVD rental stores, uses the inventories at its stores to fill orders for its online subscribers, who pay a monthly fee for unlimited DVDs delivered by mail carrier; using local stores to fill orders typically allows delivery in 24 hours versus 48 hours for shipments made from a regional shipping center. Walgreen's, a leading drugstore chain, allows customers to order a prescription online and then pick it up at the drive-through window or inside counter of a local store. In banking, a brick-and-click strategy allows customers to use local branches and ATMs for depositing checks and getting cash while using online systems to pay bills, check account balances, and transfer funds. Many industrial distributors are finding it efficient for customers to place their orders over the Web rather than phoning them in or waiting for salespeople to call in person. Illustration Capsule 6.2 describes how office supply chains like Office Depot, Staples, and OfficeMax have successfully migrated from a traditional brick-and-mortar distribution strategy to a combination brick-and-click distribution strategy.

Strategies for Online Enterprises

A company that elects to use the Internet as its exclusive channel for accessing buyers is essentially an online enterprise from the perspective of the customer. The Internet becomes the vehicle for transacting sales and delivering customer services; except for advertising, the Internet is the sole point of all buyer–seller contact. Many so-called pure dot-com enterprises have chosen this strategic approach—prominent examples include eBay, Yahoo, Amazon.com, Buy.com, Overstock.com, and Priceline.com. For a company to succeed in using the Internet as its exclusive distribution channel, its product or service must be one for which buying online holds strong appeal.

A company that decides to use online sales as its exclusive method for sales transactions must address several strategic issues:

- *How it will deliver unique value to buyers*—Online businesses must usually attract buyers on the basis of low price, convenience, superior product information, build-to-order options, or attentive online service.

- *Whether it will pursue competitive advantage based on lower costs, differentiation, or better value for the money*—For an online-only sales strategy to succeed in head-to-head competition with brick-and-mortar and brick-and-click rivals, an online seller's value chain approach must hold potential for a low-cost advantage, competitively valuable differentiating attributes, or a best-cost provider advantage. If an online firm's strategy is to attract customers by selling at cut-rate prices, then it must possess cost advantages in those activities it performs, and it must outsource the remaining activities to low-cost specialists. If an online seller is going to differentiate itself on the basis of a superior buying experience and top-notch customer service, then it needs to concentrate on having an easy-to-navigate Web site, an array of functions and conveniences for customers, Web reps who can answer questions online, and logistical capabilities to deliver products quickly and accommodate returned merchandise. If it is going to deliver more value for the money, then it must manage value chain activities so as to deliver upscale products and services at lower costs than rivals.

Illustration Capsule 6.2

Brick-and-Click Strategies in the Office Supplies Industry

Office Depot was in the first wave of retailers to adopt a combination brick-and-click strategy. Management quickly saw the merits of allowing business customers to use the Internet to place orders instead of having to make a call, generate a purchase order, and pay an invoice—while still getting same-day or next-day delivery from one of Office Depot's local stores.

Office Depot already had an existing network of retail stores, delivery centers and warehouses, delivery trucks, account managers, sales offices, and regional call centers that handled large business customers. In addition, it had a solid brand name and enough purchasing power with its suppliers to counter discount-minded online rivals trying to attract buyers of office supplies on the basis of super-low prices. Office Depot's incremental investment to enter the e-commerce arena was minimal since all it needed to add was a Web site where customers could see pictures and descriptions of the 14,000 items it carried, their prices, and in-stock availability. Marketing costs to make customers aware of its Web store option ran less than $10 million.

Office Depot's online prices were the same as its store prices, the strategy being to promote Web sales on the basis of service, convenience, and lower customer costs for order processing and inventories. Customers reported that doing business with Office Depot online cut their transaction costs by up to 80 percent; plus, Office Depot's same-day or next-day delivery capability allowed them to reduce office supply inventories.

The company set up customized Web pages for 37,000 corporate and educational customers that allowed the customer's employees varying degrees of freedom to buy supplies. A clerk might be able to order only copying paper, toner cartridges, computer disks, and paper clips up to a preset dollar limit per order, while a vice president might have carte blanche to order any item Office Depot sold.

Web site sales cost Office Depot less than $1 per $100 of goods ordered, compared with about $2 for phone and fax orders. And since Web sales eliminate the need to key in transactions, order-entry errors were virtually eliminated and product returns cut by 50 percent. Billing is handled electronically.

In 2005, over 50 percent of Office Depot's major customers were ordering most of their supplies online. Online sales accounted for almost $3 billion in 2004 (about 24 percent of Office Depot's total revenues), up from $982 million in 2000 and making Office Depot the third-largest online retailer. Its online operations were profitable from the start.

Office Depot's successful brick-and-click strategy prompted its two biggest rivals—Staples and OfficeMax—to adopt brick-and-click strategies too. In 2005, all three companies were enjoying increasing success with selling online to business customers and using local stores to fill orders and make deliveries.

Sources: Information posted at www.officedepot.com (accessed September 28, 2005); "Office Depot's e-Diva," *BusinessWeek Online* (www.businessweek.com)**,** August 6, 2001; Laura Lorek, "Office Depot Site Picks Up Speed," *Interactive Week* (www.zdnet.com/intweek), June 25, 2001; "Why Office Depot Loves the Net," *BusinessWeek,* September 27, 1999, pp. EB 66, EB 68; and *Fortune,* November 8, 1999, p. 17.

- *Whether it will have a broad or a narrow product offering*—A one-stop shopping strategy like that employed by Amazon.com (which offers over 30 million items for sale at its Web sites in the United States, Britain, France, Germany, Denmark, and Japan) has the appealing economics of helping spread fixed operating costs over a wide number of items and a large customer base. Other e-tailers, such as E-Loan and Hotel.com, have adopted classic focus strategies and cater to a sharply defined target audience shopping for a particular product or product category.

- *Whether to perform order fulfillment activities internally or to outsource them*—Building central warehouses, stocking them with adequate inventories, and developing systems to pick, pack, and ship individual orders all require substantial start-up capital but may result in lower overall unit costs than would paying the fees of order fulfillment specialists who make a business of providing warehouse space, stocking inventories, and shipping orders for e-tailers. However, outsourcing order fulfillment activities is likely to be more economical unless an e-tailer has high unit volume and the capital to invest in its own order fulfillment capabilities. Buy.com, an online superstore consisting of some 30,000 items, obtains products from name-brand manufacturers and uses outsiders to stock and ship those products; thus, its focus is not on manufacturing or order fulfillment but rather on selling.

- *How it will draw traffic to its Web site and then convert page views into revenues*—Web sites have to be cleverly marketed. Unless Web surfers hear about the site, like what they see on their first visit, and are intrigued enough to return again and again, the site is unlikely to generate adequate revenues. Marketing campaigns that result only in heavy site traffic and lots of page views are seldom sufficient; the best test of effective marketing and the appeal of an online company's product offering is the ratio at which page views are converted into revenues (the "look-to-buy" ratio). For example, in 2001 Yahoo's site traffic averaged 1.2 *billion* page views daily but generated only about $2 million in daily revenues; in contrast, the traffic at brokerage firm Charles Schwab's Web site averaged only 40 *million* page views per day but resulted in an average of $5 million daily in online commission revenues.

CHOOSING APPROPRIATE FUNCTIONAL-AREA STRATEGIES

A company's strategy is not complete until company managers have made strategic choices about how the various functional parts of the business—R&D, production, human resources, sales and marketing, finance, and so on—will be managed in support of its basic competitive strategy approach and the other important competitive moves being taken. Normally, functional-area strategy choices rank third on the menu of choosing among the various strategy options, as shown in Figure 6.1 (see p. 162). But whether commitments to particular functional strategies are made before or after the choices of complementary strategic options shown in Figure 6.1 is beside the point—what's really important is what the functional strategies are and how they mesh to enhance the success of the company's higher-level strategic thrusts.

In many respects, the nature of functional strategies is dictated by the choice of competitive strategy. For example, a manufacturer employing a low-cost provider strategy needs an R&D and product design strategy that emphasizes cheap-to-incorporate features and facilitates economical assembly and a production strategy that stresses capture of scale economies and actions to achieve low-cost manufacture (such as high labor productivity, efficient supply chain management, and automated production processes), and a low-budget marketing strategy. A business pursuing a high-end differentiation strategy needs a production strategy geared to top-notch quality and a marketing strategy aimed at touting differentiating features and using advertising and a trusted brand name to "pull" sales through the chosen distribution channels. A company using a focused differentiation strategy needs a marketing strategy that stresses growing the niche. For example, the Missouri-based franchise Panera Bread has been growing its business by getting more people hooked on fresh-baked specialty breads and patronizing its bakery-cafés, keeping buyer interest in Panera's all-natural specialty breads at a high level, and protecting its specialty bread niche against invasion by outsiders.

Beyond very general prescriptions, it is difficult to say just what the content of the different functional-area strategies should be without first knowing what higher-level strategic choices a company has made, the industry environment in which it operates, the resource strengths that can be leveraged, and so on. Suffice it to say here that company personnel—both managers and employees charged with strategy-making responsibility down through the organizational hierarchy—must be clear about which higher-level strategies top management has chosen and then must tailor the company's functional-area strategies accordingly.

FIRST-MOVER ADVANTAGES AND DISADVANTAGES

Core Concept

Because of first-mover advantages and disadvantages, competitive advantage can spring from *when* a move is made as well as from *what* move is made.

When to make a strategic move is often as crucial as *what* move to make. Timing is especially important when *first-mover advantages* or *disadvantages* exist.[40] Being first to initiate a strategic move can have a high payoff when (1) pioneering helps build a firm's image and reputation with buyers; (2) early commitments to new technologies, new-style components, new or emerging distribution channels, and so on can produce an absolute cost advantage over rivals; (3) first-time customers remain strongly loyal to pioneering firms in making repeat purchases; and (4) moving first constitutes a preemptive strike, making imitation extra hard or unlikely. The bigger the first-mover advantages, the more attractive making the first move becomes.[41] In e-commerce, companies like America Online, Amazon.com, Yahoo, eBay, and Priceline.com that were first with a new technology, network solution, or business model enjoyed lasting first-mover advantages in gaining the visibility and reputation needed to remain market leaders. However, other first-movers such as Xerox in fax machines, eToys (an online toy retailer), Webvan and Peapod (in online groceries), and scores of other dot-com companies never converted their first-mover status into any sort of competitive advantage. Sometimes markets are slow to accept the innovative product offering of a first-mover; sometimes, a fast-follower with greater resources and marketing muscle can easily overtake the first-mover (as Microsoft was able to do when it introduced Internet Explorer against Netscape, the pioneer of Internet browsers with the lion's share of the market); and sometimes furious technological change or product innovation makes a first-mover vulnerable to quickly appearing next-generation technology or products. Hence, just being a first-mover by itself is seldom enough to win a sustainable competitive advantage.[42]

To sustain any advantage that may initially accrue to a pioneer, a first-mover needs to be a fast learner and continue to move aggressively to capitalize on any initial pioneering advantage. It helps immensely if the first-mover has deep financial pockets, important competencies and competitive capabilities, and astute managers. If a first-mover's skills, know-how, and actions are easily copied or even surpassed, then fast-followers and even late-movers can catch or overtake the first-mover in a relatively short period. What makes being a first-mover strategically important is not being the first company to do something but rather being the first competitor to put together the precise combination of features, customer value, and sound revenue/cost/profit economics that gives it an edge over rivals in the battle for market leadership.[43] If the marketplace quickly takes to a first-mover's innovative product offering, a first-mover must have large-scale production, marketing, and distribution capabilities if it is to stave off fast-followers who possess these resources capabilities. If technology is advancing at torrid pace, a first-mover cannot hope to sustain its lead without having strong capabilities in R&D, design, and new product development, along with the financial strength to fund these activities.

The Potential for Late-Mover Advantages or First-Mover Disadvantages

There are instances when there are actually *advantages* to being an adept follower rather than a first-mover. Late-mover advantages (or *first-mover disadvantages*) arise in four instances:

- When pioneering leadership is more costly than imitating followership and only negligible learning/experience curve benefits accrue to the leader—a condition that allows a follower to end up with lower costs than the first-mover.

- When the products of an innovator are somewhat primitive and do not live up to buyer expectations, thus allowing a clever follower to win disenchanted buyers away from the leader with better-performing products.

- When the demand side of the marketplace is skeptical about the benefits of a new technology or product being pioneered by a first-mover.

- When rapid market evolution (due to fast-paced changes in either technology or buyer needs and expectations) gives fast-followers and maybe even cautious late-movers the opening to leapfrog a first-mover's products with more attractive next-version products.

To Be a First-Mover or Not

In weighing the pros and cons of being a first-mover versus a fast-follower versus a slow-mover, it matters whether the race to market leadership in a particular industry is a marathon or a sprint. In marathons, a slow-mover is not unduly penalized—first-mover advantages can be fleeting, and there is ample time for fast-followers and sometimes even late-movers to play catch-up.[44] Thus, the speed at which the pioneering innovation is likely to catch on matters considerably as companies struggle with whether to pursue a particular emerging market opportunity aggressively (as a first-mover or fast-follower) or cautiously (as a late-mover). For instance, it took 18 months for 10 million users to sign up for Hotmail, 5.5 years for worldwide mobile phone use to grow from 10 million to 100 million worldwide, 7 years for videocassette recorders to find their way into 1 million U.S. homes, and close to 10 years for the number of at-home broadband subscribers to grow to 100 million worldwide. The lesson here is that there is a market-penetration curve for every emerging opportunity; typically, the curve has an inflection point at which all the pieces of the business model fall into place, buyer demand explodes, and the market takes off. The inflection point can come early on a fast-rising curve (like use of e-mail) or further up on a slow-rising curve (like the use of broadband). Any company that seeks competitive advantage by being a first-mover thus needs to ask some hard questions:

- Does market takeoff depend on the development of complementary products or services that currently are not available?

- Is new infrastructure required before buyer demand can surge?

- Will buyers need to learn new skills or adopt new behaviors? Will buyers encounter high switching costs?

- Are there influential competitors in a position to delay or derail the efforts of a first-mover?

Illustration Capsule 6.3

The Battle in Consumer Broadband:
First-Movers versus Late-Movers

In 1988 an engineer at the Bell companies' research labs figured out how to rush signals along ordinary copper wire at high speed using digital technology, thus creating the digital subscriber line (DSL). But the regional Bells, which dominated the local telephone market in the United States, showed little interest over the next 10 years, believing it was more lucrative to rent T-1 lines to businesses that needed fast data transmission capability and rent second phone lines to households wanting an Internet connection that didn't disrupt their regular telephone service. Furthermore, telephone executives were skeptical about DSL technology—there were a host of technical snarls to overcome, and early users encountered annoying glitches. Many executives doubted that it made good sense to invest billions of dollars in the infrastructure needed to roll out DSL to residential and small business customers, given the success they were having with T-1 and second-line rentals. As a consequence, the Bells didn't seriously begin to market DSL until the late 1990s, two years after the cable TV companies began their push to market cable broadband.

Cable companies were more than happy to be the first-movers in marketing broadband service via their copper cable wires, chiefly because their business was threatened by satellite TV technology and they saw broadband as an innovative service they could provide that the satellite companies could not. (Delivering broadband service via satellite has yet to become a factor in the marketplace, winning only a 1 percent share in 2003.) Cable companies were able to deploy broadband on their copper wire economically because during the 1980s and early 1990s most cable operators had spent about $60 billion to upgrade their systems with fiber-optic technology in order to handle two-way traffic rather than just one-way TV signals and thereby make good on their promises to local governments to develop "interactive" cable systems if they were awarded franchises. Although the early interactive services were duds, technicians discovered in the mid-1990s that the two-way systems enabled high-speed Internet hookups.

With Internet excitement surging in the late 1990s, cable executives saw high-speed Internet service as a no-brainer and began rolling it out to customers in 1998, securing about 362,000 customers by year-end versus only about 41,000 for DSL. Part of the early success of cable broadband was due to a cost advantage in modems—cable executives, seeing the potential of cable broadband several years earlier, had asked CableLabs to standardize the technology for cable modems, a move that lowered costs and made cable modems marketable in consumer electronics stores. DSL modems were substantially more complicated, and it took longer to drive the costs down from several hundred dollars each to under $100—in 2004, both cable and phone companies paid about $50 for modems, but cable modems got there much sooner.

As cable broadband began to attract more and more attention in the 1998–2002 period, the regional Bells continued to move slowly on DSL. The technical problems lingered, and early users were disgruntled by a host of annoying and sometimes horrendous installation difficulties and service glitches. Not only did providing users with convenient and reliable service prove to be a formidable challenge, but some regulatory issues stood in the way as well. Even in 2003 phone company executives found it hard to justify multibillion-dollar investments to install the necessary equipment and support systems to offer, market, manage, and maintain DSL service on the vast scale of a regional Bell company. SBC Communications figured it would cost at least $6 billion to roll out DSL to its customers. Verizon estimated that it would take 3.5 to 4 million customers to make DSL economics work, a number it would probably not reach until the end of 2005.

In 2003–2004, high-speed consumer access to the Internet was a surging business with a bright outlook—the number of U.S. Internet users upgrading to high-speed service increased by close to 500,000 monthly. In 2005, cable broadband was the preferred choice—70 percent of U.S. broadband users had opted for cable modems supplied by cable TV companies, with cable modem subscribers outnumbering DSL subscribers 30 million to 10.6 million. Its late start made it questionable whether DSL would be able to catch cable broadband in the U.S. marketplace, although DSL providers added 1.4 million subscribers in the first three months of 2005 compared to 1.2 million new subscribers for cable. In the rest of the world, however, DSL was the broadband connection of choice—there were an estimated 200 million broadband subscribers worldwide at the end of 2005.

Source: Developed from information in Shawn Young and Peter Grant, "How Phone Firms Lost to Cable in Consumer Broadband Market," *The Wall Street Journal,* March 13, 2003, pp. A1, A6, and Cnet's www.news.com site (accessed September 22, 2005).

When the answers to any of these questions are yes, then a company must be careful not to pour too many resources into getting ahead of the market opportunity—the race is likely going to be more of a 10-year marathon than a 2-year sprint. Being first out of the starting block is competitively important only when pioneering early introduction of a technology or product delivers clear and substantial benefits to early adopters and buyers, thus winning their immediate support, perhaps giving the pioneer a reputational head-start advantage, and forcing competitors to quickly follow the pioneer's lead. In the remaining instances where the race is more of a marathon, the companies that end up capturing and dominating new-to-the-world markets are almost never the pioneers that gave birth to those markets—there is time for a company to marshal the needed resources and to ponder its best time and method of entry.[45] Furthermore, being a late-mover into industries of the future has the advantages of being less risky and skirting the costs of pioneering.

But while a company is right to be cautious about quickly entering virgin territory, where all kinds of risks abound, rarely does a company have much to gain from consistently being a late-mover whose main concern is avoiding the mistakes of first-movers. Companies that are habitual late-movers regardless of the circumstances, while often able to survive, can find themselves scrambling to keep pace with more progressive and innovative rivals and fighting to retain their customers. For a habitual late-mover to catch up, it must count on first-movers to be slow learners and complacent in letting their lead dwindle. It also has to hope that buyers will be slow to gravitate to the products of first-movers, again giving it time to catch up. And it has to have competencies and capabilities that are sufficiently strong to allow it to close the gap fairly quickly once it makes its move. Counting on all first-movers to stumble or otherwise be easily overtaken is usually a bad bet that puts a late-mover's competitive position at risk.

Illustration Capsule 6.3 describes the challenges that late-moving telephone companies have in winning the battle to supply at-home high-speed Internet access and overcoming the first-mover advantages of cable companies.

Key Points

Once a company has selected which of the five basic competitive strategies to employ in its quest for competitive advantage, then it must decide whether to supplement its choice of a basic competitive strategy approach, as shown in Figure 6.1 (p. 162).

Many companies are using strategic alliances and collaborative partnerships to help them in the race to build a global market presence or be a leader in the industries of the future. Strategic alliances are an attractive, flexible, and often cost-effective means by which companies can gain access to missing technology, expertise, and business capabilities.

Mergers and acquisitions are another attractive strategic option for strengthening a firm's competitiveness. When the operations of two companies are combined via merger or acquisition, the new company's competitiveness can be enhanced in any of several ways—lower costs; stronger technological skills; more or better competitive capabilities; a more attractive lineup of products and services; wider geographic coverage; and/or greater financial resources with which to invest in R&D, add capacity, or expand into new areas.

Vertically integrating forward or backward makes strategic sense only if it strengthens a company's position via either cost reduction or creation of a differentiation-based advantage. Otherwise, the drawbacks of vertical integration (increased investment, greater business risk, increased vulnerability to technological changes, and less flexibility in making product changes) are likely to outweigh any advantages.

Outsourcing pieces of the value chain formerly performed in-house can enhance a company's competitiveness whenever an activity (1) can be performed better or more cheaply by outside specialists; (2) is not crucial to the firm's ability to achieve sustainable competitive advantage and won't hollow out its core competencies, capabilities, or technical know-how; (3) reduces the company's risk exposure to changing technology or changing buyer preferences; (4) streamlines company operations in ways that improve organizational flexibility, cut cycle time, speed decision making, and reduce coordination costs; or (5) allows a company to concentrate on its core business and do what it does best.

One of the most pertinent strategic issues that companies face is how to use the Internet in positioning the company in the marketplace—whether to use the Internet as *only a means of disseminating product information* (with traditional distribution channel partners making all sales to end users), as *a secondary or minor channel*, as *one of several important distribution channels*, as *the company's primary distribution channel,* or as *the company's exclusive channel for accessing customers.*

Companies have a number of offensive strategy options for improving their market positions and trying to secure a competitive advantage: offering an equal or better product at a lower price, leapfrogging competitors by being first to adopt next-generation technologies or the first to introduce next-generation products, pursuing sustained product innovation, attacking competitors weaknesses, going after less contested or unoccupied market territory, using hit-and-run tactics to steal sales away from unsuspecting rivals, and launching preemptive strikes. A blue ocean strategy seeks to gain a dramatic and durable competitive advantage by abandoning efforts to beat out competitors in existing markets and, instead, inventing a new industry or distinctive market segment that renders existing competitors largely irrelevant and allows a company to create and capture altogether new demand.

Defensive strategies to protect a company's position usually take the form of making moves that put obstacles in the path of would-be challengers and fortify the company's present position while undertaking actions to dissuade rivals from even trying to attack (by signaling that the resulting battle will be more costly to the challenger than it is worth).

Once all the higher-level strategic choices have been made, company managers can turn to the task of crafting functional and operating-level strategies to flesh out the details of the company's overall business and competitive strategy.

The timing of strategic moves also has relevance in the quest for competitive advantage. Company managers are obligated to carefully consider the advantages or disadvantages that attach to being a first-mover versus a fast-follower versus a late-mover.

Exercises

1. Go to Google or another Internet search engine and do a search on "strategic alliances." Identify at least two companies in different industries that are making a significant use of strategic alliances as a core part of their strategies. In addition, identify who their alliances are with and describe the purpose of the alliances.

2. Go to Google or another Internet search engine and do a search on "acquisition strategy." Identify at least two companies in different industries that are using

acquisitions to strengthen their market positions. Identify some of the companies that have been acquired, and research the purpose behind the acquisitions.

3. Go to www.goodyear.com/investor and read Goodyear's most recent annual report. To what extent is the company vertically integrated? What segments of the industry value chain has the company chosen to perform? Based on the company's discussion of business unit performance, does it appear the company is becoming more vertically integrated or choosing to narrow its range of internally performed activities?

4. Illustration Capsule 6.3 describes how cable companies used fiber-optic networks to gain a first-mover advantage over telephone companies in providing high-speed Internet access to home subscribers. Telephone companies are attempting to catch up with cable companies in the broadband access market with the widespread rollout of DSL to telephone customers. In addition, phone companies are pursuing fiber-to-the-premises (FTTP) and outdoor wireless networks (outdoor WLAN) technologies to supplement or replace DSL. Conduct Web searches on FTTP and outdoor WLAN, and discuss how use of these technologies by telephone companies might offset the first-mover advantage currently held by cable companies in the high-speed Internet market.

5. Go to the Web sites of various companies (such as those appearing on the Fortune 500) and identify two companies using each of the following Web site strategies and explain why the approach is well matched to the company's business model:

   a. Product information only.

   b. E-store as a minor distribution strategy.

   c. Brick-and-click.

   d. Online enterprise.

Competing in Foreign Markets

You have no choice but to operate in a world shaped by globalization and the information revolution. There are two options: Adapt or die.

—Andrew S. Grove

Former Chairman, Intel Corporation

You do not choose to become global. The market chooses for you; it forces your hand.

—Alain Gomez

CEO, Thomson SA

[I]ndustries actually vary a great deal in the pressures they put on a company to sell internationally.

—Niraj Dawar and Tony Frost

Professors, Richard Ivey School of Business

A ny company that aspires to industry leadership in the 21st century must think in terms of global, not domestic, market leadership. The world economy is globalizing at an accelerating pace as countries previously closed to foreign companies open up their markets, as the Internet shrinks the importance of geographic distance, and as ambitious, growth-minded companies race to build stronger competitive positions in the markets of more and more countries. Companies in industries that are already globally competitive or in the process of becoming so are under the gun to come up with a strategy for competing successfully in foreign markets.

This chapter focuses on strategy options for expanding beyond domestic boundaries and competing in the markets of either a few or a great many countries. The spotlight will be on four strategic issues unique to competing multinationally:

1. Whether to customize the company's offerings in each different country market to match the tastes and preferences of local buyers or to offer a mostly standardized product worldwide.

2. Whether to employ essentially the same basic competitive strategy in all countries or modify the strategy country by country.

3. Where to locate the company's production facilities, distribution centers, and customer service operations so as to realize the greatest location advantages.

4. How to efficiently transfer the company's resource strengths and capabilities from one country to another in an effort to secure competitive advantage.

In the process of exploring these issues, we will introduce a number of core concepts—multicountry competition, global competition, profit sanctuaries, and cross-market subsidization. The chapter includes sections on cross-country differences in cultural, demographic, and market conditions; strategy options for entering and competing in foreign markets; the growing role of alliances with foreign partners; the importance of locating operations in the most advantageous countries; and the special circumstances of competing in such emerging markets as China, India, Brazil, Russia, and Eastern Europe.

WHY COMPANIES EXPAND INTO FOREIGN MARKETS

A company may opt to expand outside its domestic market for any of four major reasons:

1. *To gain access to new customers*—Expanding into foreign markets offers potential for increased revenues, profits, and long-term growth and becomes an especially attractive option when a company's home markets are mature. Firms like Cisco Systems, Dell, Sony, Nokia, Avon, and Toyota, which are racing for global leadership in their respective industries, are moving rapidly and aggressively to extend their market reach into all corners of the world.

2. *To achieve lower costs and enhance the firm's competitiveness*—Many companies are driven to sell in more than one country because domestic sales volume is not large enough to fully capture manufacturing economies of scale or learning/experience curve effects and thereby substantially improve the firm's cost-competitiveness. The relatively small size of country markets in Europe explains why companies like Michelin, BMW, and Nestlé long ago began selling their products all across Europe and then moved into markets in North America and Latin America.

3. *To capitalize on its core competencies*—A company may be able to leverage its competencies and capabilities into a position of competitive advantage in foreign markets as well as just domestic markets. Nokia's competencies and capabilities in mobile phones have propelled it to global market leadership in the wireless telecommunications business. Wal-Mart is capitalizing on its considerable expertise in discount retailing to expand into China, Latin America, and parts of Europe—Wal-Mart executives believe the company has tremendous growth opportunities in China.

4. *To spread its business risk across a wider market base*—A company spreads business risk by operating in a number of different foreign countries rather than depending entirely on operations in its domestic market. Thus, if the economies of certain Asian countries turn down for a period of time, a company with operations across much of the world may be sustained by buoyant sales in Latin America or Europe.

In a few cases, companies in industries based on natural resources (e.g., oil and gas, minerals, rubber, and lumber) often find it necessary to operate in the international arena because attractive raw material supplies are located in foreign countries.

The Difference Between Competing Internationally and Competing Globally

Typically, a company will start to compete internationally by entering just one or maybe a select few foreign markets. Competing on a truly global scale comes later, after the company has established operations on several continents and is racing against rivals for global market leadership. Thus, there is a meaningful distinction between the competitive scope of a company that operates in a few foreign countries (with perhaps modest ambitions to enter several more country markets) and a company that markets its products in 50 to 100 countries and is expanding its operations into additional country markets annually. The former is most accurately termed an *international competitor,* whereas the latter qualifies as a *global competitor.* In the discussion that follows, we'll continue to make a distinction between strategies for competing internationally and strategies for competing globally.

CROSS-COUNTRY DIFFERENCES IN CULTURAL, DEMOGRAPHIC, AND MARKET CONDITIONS

Regardless of a company's motivation for expanding outside its domestic markets, the strategies it uses to compete in foreign markets must be situation-driven. Cultural, demographic, and market conditions vary significantly among the countries of the world.[1] Cultures and lifestyles are the most obvious areas in which countries differ; market demographics and income levels are close behind. Consumers in Spain do not have the same tastes, preferences, and buying habits as consumers in Norway; buyers differ yet again in Greece, Chile, New Zealand, and Taiwan. Less than 20 percent of the populations of Brazil, India, and China have annual purchasing power equivalent to $25,000. Middle-class consumers represent a much smaller portion of the population in these and other emerging countries than in North America, Japan, and much of Western Europe—China's middle class numbers about 125 million out of a population of 1.3 billion.[2]

Sometimes product designs suitable in one country are inappropriate in another—for example, in the United States electrical devices run on 110-volt systems, but in some European countries the standard is a 240-volt system, necessitating the use of different electrical designs and components. In France consumers prefer top-loading washing machines, while in most other European countries consumers prefer front-loading machines. Northern Europeans want large refrigerators because they tend to shop once a week in supermarkets; southern Europeans can get by on small refrigerators because they shop daily. In parts of Asia refrigerators are a status symbol and may be placed in the living room, leading to preferences for stylish designs and colors—in India bright blue and red are popular colors. In other Asian countries household space is constrained and many refrigerators are only four feet high so that the top can be used for storage. In Hong Kong the preference is for compact European-style appliances, but in Taiwan large American-style appliances are more popular. In Italy, most people use automatic washing machines but prefer to hang the clothes out to dry on a clothesline—there is a strongly entrenched tradition and cultural belief that sun-dried clothes are fresher, which virtually shuts down any opportunities for appliance makers to market clothes dryers in Italy. In China, many parents are reluctant to purchase personal computers (PCs) even when they can afford them because of concerns that their children will be distracted from their schoolwork by surfing the Web, playing PC-based video games, and downloading and listening to pop music.

Similarly, market growth varies from country to country. In emerging markets like India, China, Brazil, and Malaysia, market growth potential is far higher than in the more mature economies of Britain, Denmark, Canada, and Japan. In automobiles, for example, the potential for market growth is explosive in China, where 2005 sales of new vehicles amounted to less than 5 million in a country with 1.3 billion people. In India there are efficient, well-developed national channels for distributing trucks, scooters, farm equipment, groceries, personal care items, and other packaged products to the country's 3 million retailers, whereas in China distribution is primarily local and there is no national network for distributing most products. The marketplace is intensely competitive in some countries and only moderately contested in others. Industry driving forces may be one thing in Spain, quite another in Canada, and different yet again in Turkey or Argentina or South Korea.

One of the biggest concerns of companies competing in foreign markets is whether to customize their offerings in each different country market to match the tastes and preferences of local buyers or whether to offer a mostly standardized product worldwide. While making products that are closely matched to local tastes makes them more appealing to local buyers, customizing a company's products country by country may have the effect of raising production and distribution costs due to the greater variety of designs and components, shorter production runs, and the complications of added inventory handling and distribution logistics. Greater standardization of a global company's product offering, however, can lead to scale economies and experience/learning curve effects, thus contributing to the achievement of a low-cost advantage. *The tension between the market pressures to localize a company's product offerings country by country and the competitive pressures to lower costs is one of the big strategic issues that participants in foreign markets have to resolve.*

Aside from the basic cultural and market differences among countries, a company also has to pay special attention to location advantages that stem from country-to-country variations in manufacturing and distribution costs, the risks of adverse shifts in exchange rates, and the economic and political demands of host governments.

Gaining Competitive Advantage Based on Where Activities Are Located

Differences in wage rates, worker productivity, inflation rates, energy costs, tax rates, government regulations, and the like create sizable variations in manufacturing costs from country to country. Plants in some countries have major manufacturing cost advantages because of lower input costs (especially labor), relaxed government regulations, the proximity of suppliers, or unique natural resources. In such cases, the low-cost countries become principal production sites, with most of the output being exported to markets in other parts of the world. Companies that build production facilities in low-cost countries (or that source their products from contract manufacturers in these countries) have a competitive advantage over rivals with plants in countries where costs are higher. The competitive role of low manufacturing costs is most evident in low-wage countries like China, India, Pakistan, Cambodia, Vietnam, Mexico, Brazil, Guatemala, the Philippines, and several countries in Africa that have become production havens for manufactured goods with high labor content (especially textiles and apparel). Labor costs in China averaged about $0.70 an hour in 2004–2005 versus about $1.50 in Russia, $4.60 in Hungary, $4.90 in Portugal, $16.50 in Canada, $21.00 in the United States, $23.00 in Norway, and $25.00 in Germany.[3] China is fast becoming the manufacturing capital of the world—virtually all of the world's major manufacturing companies now have facilities in China, and China attracted more foreign direct investment in 2002 and 2003 than any other country in the world. Likewise, concerns about short delivery times and low shipping costs make some countries better locations than others for establishing distribution centers.

The quality of a country's business environment also offers locational advantages—the governments of some countries are anxious to attract foreign investments and go all out to create a business climate that outsiders will view as favorable. A good example is Ireland, which has one of the world's most pro-business environments. Ireland offers companies very low corporate tax rates, has a government that is responsive to the needs of industry, and aggressively recruits high-tech manufacturing facilities and multinational companies. Such policies were a significant force in making Ireland the most dynamic, fastest-growing nation in Europe during the 1990s. Ireland's policies were a major factor in Intel's decision to choose Leixlip, County Kildare, as the site for a $2.5 billion chip manufacturing plant that employs over 4,000 people. Another locational advantage is the clustering of suppliers of components and capital equipment; infrastructure suppliers (universities, vocational training providers, research enterprises); trade associations; and makers of complementary products in a geographic area—such clustering can be an important source of cost savings in addition to facilitating close collaboration with key suppliers.

The Risks of Adverse Exchange Rate Shifts

The volatility of exchange rates greatly complicates the issue of geographic cost advantages. Currency exchange rates often move up or down 20 to 40 percent annually. Changes of this magnitude can either totally wipe out a country's low-cost advantage or transform a former high-cost location into a competitive-cost location. For instance, in the mid-1980s, when the dollar was strong relative to the Japanese yen (meaning that $1 would purchase, say, 125 yen as opposed to only 100 yen), Japanese heavy-equipment maker Komatsu was able to undercut U.S.-based Caterpillar's prices by as much as 25 percent, causing Caterpillar to lose sales and market share. But starting in 1985, when exchange rates began to shift and the dollar grew steadily weaker against the yen (meaning that $1 was worth fewer and fewer yen, and that a Komatsu product made in Japan at a cost of 20 million yen translated into costs of many more dollars than before), Komatsu had to raise its prices to U.S. buyers six times over two years. With its competitiveness against Komatsu restored because of the weaker dollar and Komatsu's higher prices, Caterpillar regained sales and market share. *The lesson of fluctuating exchange rates is that companies that export goods to foreign countries always gain in competitiveness when the currency of the country in which the goods are manufactured is weak. Exporters are disadvantaged when the currency of the country where goods are being manufactured grows stronger.* Sizable long-term shifts in exchange rates thus shuffle the global cards of which rivals have the upper hand in the marketplace and which countries represent the low-cost manufacturing location.

> **Core Concept**
> Companies with manufacturing facilities in a particular country are more cost-competitive in exporting goods to world markets when the local currency is weak (or declines in value relative to other currencies); their competitiveness erodes when the local currency grows stronger relative to the currencies of the countries to which the locally made goods are being exported.

As a further illustration of the risks associated with fluctuating exchange rates, consider the case of a U.S. company that has located manufacturing facilities in Brazil (where the currency is reals—pronounced *ray-alls*) and that exports most of the Brazilian-made goods to markets in the European Union (where the currency is euros). To keep the numbers simple, assume that the exchange rate is 4 Brazilian reals for 1 euro and that the product being made in Brazil has a manufacturing cost of 4 Brazilian reals (or 1 euro). Now suppose that for some reason the exchange rate shifts from 4 reals per euro to 5 reals per euro (meaning that the real has declined in value and that the euro is stronger). Making the product in Brazil is now more cost-competitive because a Brazilian good costing 4 reals to produce has fallen to only 0.8 euros at the new exchange rate. If, in contrast, the value of the Brazilian real grows stronger in relation to the euro—resulting in an exchange rate of 3 reals to 1 euro—the same good costing 4 reals to produce now has a cost of 1.33 euros. Clearly, the attraction of manufacturing a good in Brazil and selling it in Europe is far greater when the euro is strong (an exchange rate of 1 euro for 5 Brazilian reals) than when the euro is weak and exchanges for only 3 Brazilian reals.

Insofar as U.S.-based manufacturers are concerned, declines in the value of the U.S. dollar against foreign currencies act to reduce or eliminate whatever cost advantage foreign manufacturers might have over U.S. manufacturers and can even prompt foreign companies to establish production plants in the United States. Likewise, a weak euro enhances the cost competitiveness of companies manufacturing goods in Europe for export to foreign markets; a strong euro versus other currencies weakens the cost competitiveness of European plants that manufacture goods for export.

In 2002, when the Brazilian real declined in value by about 25 percent against the dollar, the euro, and several other currencies, the ability of companies with manufacturing plants in Brazil to compete in world markets was greatly enhanced—of course, in the future years this windfall gain in cost advantage might well be eroded by sustained rises in the value of the Brazilian real against these same currencies. Herein lies the risk: *Currency exchange rates are rather unpredictable, swinging first one way and then another way, so the competitiveness of any company's facilities in any country is partly dependent on whether exchange rate changes over time have a favorable or unfavorable cost impact.* Companies producing goods in one country for export abroad always improve their cost competitiveness when the country's currency grows weaker relative to currencies of the countries where the goods are being exported to, and they find their cost competitiveness eroded when the local currency grows stronger. In contrast, domestic companies that are under pressure from lower-cost imported goods become more cost competitive when their currency grows weaker in relation to the currencies of the countries where the imported goods are made—in other words, a U.S. manufacturer views a weaker U.S. dollar as a *favorable exchange rate shift* because such shifts help make its costs more competitive versus those of foreign rivals.

Core Concept

Fluctuating exchange rates pose significant risks to a company's competitiveness in foreign markets. Exporters win when the currency of the country where goods are being manufactured grows weaker, and they lose when the currency grows stronger. Domestic companies under pressure from lower-cost imports are benefited when their government's currency grows weaker in relation to the countries where the imported goods are being made.

Host Governments' Policies

National governments enact all kinds of measures affecting business conditions and the operation of foreign companies in their markets. Host governments may set local content requirements on goods made inside their borders by foreign-based companies, have rules and policies that protect local companies from foreign competition, put restrictions on exports to ensure adequate local supplies, regulate the prices of imported and locally produced goods, enact deliberately burdensome procedures and requirements for imported goods to pass customs inspection, and impose tariffs or quotas on the imports of certain goods—until 2002, when it joined the World Trade Organization, China imposed a 100 percent tariff on motor vehicle imports. The European Union imposes quotas on textile and apparel imports from China, as a measure to protect European producers in southern Europe. India imposed excise taxes on newly purchased motor vehicles in 2005 ranging from 24 to 40 percent—a policy that has significantly dampened the demand for new vehicles in India (though down from as much as 50 percent in prior years). Governments may or may not have burdensome tax structures, stringent environmental regulations, or strictly enforced worker safety standards. Sometimes outsiders face a web of regulations regarding technical standards, product certification, prior approval of capital spending projects, withdrawal of funds from the country, and required minority (sometimes majority) ownership of foreign company operations by local companies or investors. A few governments may be hostile to or suspicious of foreign companies operating within their borders. Some governments provide subsidies and low-interest loans to domestic companies to help them compete against foreign-based companies. Other governments, anxious to obtain new plants and jobs, offer foreign companies a helping hand in the form of subsidies, privileged market access, and technical assistance. All of these possibilities explain why the managers of companies opting to compete in foreign markets have to take a close look at a country's politics and policies toward business in general, and foreign companies in particular, in deciding which country markets to participate in and which ones to avoid.

THE CONCEPTS OF MULTICOUNTRY COMPETITION AND GLOBAL COMPETITION

There are important differences in the patterns of international competition from industry to industry.[4] At one extreme is **multicountry competition,** in which there's so much cross-country variation in market conditions and in the companies contending for leadership that the market contest among rivals in one country is not closely connected to the market contests in other countries. The standout features of multicountry competition are that (1) buyers in different countries are attracted to different product attributes, (2) sellers vary from country to country, and (3) industry conditions and competitive forces in each national market differ in important respects. Take the banking industry in Italy, Brazil, and Japan as an example—the requirements and expectations of banking customers vary among the three countries, the lead banking competitors in Italy differ from those in Brazil or in Japan, and the competitive battle going on among the leading banks in Italy is unrelated to the rivalry taking place in Brazil or Japan. Thus, with multicountry competition, rival firms battle for national championships, and winning in one country does not necessarily signal the ability to fare well in other countries. In multicountry competition, the power of a company's strategy and resource capabilities in one country may not enhance its competitiveness to the same degree in other countries where it operates. Moreover, any competitive advantage a company secures in one country is largely confined to that country; the spillover effects to other countries are minimal to nonexistent. Industries characterized by multicountry competition include radio and TV broadcasting, consumer banking, life insurance, apparel, metals fabrication, many types of food products (coffee, cereals, breads, canned goods, frozen foods), and retailing.

> **Core Concept**
> ***Multicountry competition*** exists when competition in one national market is not closely connected to competition in another national market—there is no global or world market, just a collection of self-contained country markets.

At the other extreme is **global competition,** in which prices and competitive conditions across country markets are strongly linked and the term *global market* has true meaning. In a globally competitive industry, much the same group of rival companies competes in many different countries, but especially so in countries where sales volumes are large and where having a competitive presence is strategically important to building a strong global position in the industry. Thus, a company's competitive position in one country both affects and is affected by its position in other countries. In global competition, a firm's overall competitive advantage grows out of its entire worldwide operations; the competitive advantage it creates at its home base is supplemented by advantages growing out of its operations in other countries (having plants in low-wage countries, being able to transfer expertise from country to country, having the capability to serve customers who also have multinational operations, and brand-name recognition in many parts of the world). Rival firms in globally competitive industries vie for worldwide leadership. Global competition exists in motor vehicles, television sets, tires, mobile phones, personal computers, copiers, watches, digital cameras, bicycles, and commercial aircraft.

> **Core Concept**
> ***Global competition*** exists when competitive conditions across national markets are linked strongly enough to form a true international market and when leading competitors compete head to head in many different countries.

An industry can have segments that are globally competitive and segments in which competition is country by country.[5] In the hotel/motel industry, for example, the low- and medium-priced segments are characterized by multicountry competition—competitors serve travelers mainly within the same country. In the business and luxury segments, however, competition is more globalized. Companies like Nikki, Marriott, Sheraton, and Hilton have hotels at many international locations, use worldwide reservation systems, and establish common quality and service standards to gain marketing advantages in serving businesspeople and other travelers who make frequent international trips. In lubricants, the marine engine segment is globally competitive—ships move from port to port and require the same oil everywhere they stop. Brand reputations in marine lubricants have a global scope, and successful marine engine lubricant producers (ExxonMobil, BP Amoco, and Shell) operate globally. In automotive motor oil, however, multicountry competition dominates—countries have different weather conditions and driving patterns, production of motor oil is subject to limited scale economies, shipping costs are high, and retail distribution channels differ markedly from country to country. Thus, domestic firms—like Quaker State and Pennzoil in the United States and Castrol in Great Britain—can be leaders in their home markets without competing globally.

It is also important to recognize that an industry can be in transition from multicountry competition to global competition. In a number of today's industries—beer and major home appliances are prime examples—leading domestic competitors have begun expanding into more and more foreign markets, often acquiring local companies or brands and integrating them into their operations. As some industry members start to build global brands and a global presence, other industry members find themselves pressured to follow the same strategic path—especially if establishing multinational operations results in important scale economies and a powerhouse brand name. As the industry consolidates to fewer players, such that many of the same companies find themselves in head-to-head competition in more and more country markets, global competition begins to replace multicountry competition.

At the same time, consumer tastes in a number of important product categories are converging across the world. Less diversity of tastes and preferences opens the way for companies to create global brands and sell essentially the same products in most all countries of the world. Even in industries where consumer tastes remain fairly diverse, companies are learning to use "custom mass production" to economically create different versions of a product and thereby satisfy the tastes of people in different countries.

In addition to taking the obvious cultural and political differences between countries into account, a company has to shape its strategic approach to competing in foreign markets according to whether its industry is characterized by multicountry competition, global competition, or a transition from one to the other.

STRATEGY OPTIONS FOR ENTERING AND COMPETING IN FOREIGN MARKETS

There are a host of generic strategic options for a company that decides to expand outside its domestic market and compete internationally or globally:

1. *Maintain a national (one-country) production base and export goods to foreign markets,* using either company-owned or foreign-controlled forward distribution channels.

2. *License foreign firms to use the company's technology or to produce and distribute the company's products.*

3. *Employ a franchising strategy.*

4. *Follow a multicountry strategy,* varying the company's strategic approach (perhaps a little, perhaps a lot) from country to country in accordance with local conditions and differing buyer tastes and preferences.

5. *Follow a global strategy,* using essentially the same competitive strategy approach in all country markets where the company has a presence.

6. *Use strategic alliances or joint ventures with foreign companies as the primary vehicle for entering foreign markets* and perhaps also using them as an ongoing strategic arrangement aimed at maintaining or strengthening its competitiveness.

The following sections discuss the first five options in more detail; the sixth option is discussed in a separate section later in the chapter.

Export Strategies

Using domestic plants as a production base for exporting goods to foreign markets is an excellent initial strategy for pursuing international sales. It is a conservative way to test the international waters. The amount of capital needed to begin exporting is often quite minimal; existing production capacity may well be sufficient to make goods for export. With an export strategy, a manufacturer can limit its involvement in foreign markets by contracting with foreign wholesalers experienced in importing to handle the entire distribution and marketing function in their countries or regions of the world. If it is more advantageous to maintain control over these functions, however, a manufacturer can establish its own distribution and sales organizations in some or all of the target foreign markets. Either way, a home-based production and export strategy helps the firm minimize its direct investments in foreign countries. Such strategies are commonly favored by Chinese, Korean, and Italian companies—products are designed and manufactured at home and then distributed through local channels in the importing countries; the primary functions performed abroad relate chiefly to establishing a network of distributors and perhaps conducting sales promotion and brand awareness activities.

Whether an export strategy can be pursued successfully over the long run hinges on the relative cost competitiveness of the home-country production base. In some industries, firms gain additional scale economies and experience/learning curve benefits from centralizing production in one or several giant plants whose output capability exceeds demand in any one country market; obviously, a company must export to capture such economies. However, an export strategy is vulnerable when (1) manufacturing costs in the home country are substantially higher than in foreign countries where rivals have plants, (2) the costs of shipping the product to distant foreign markets are relatively high, or (3) adverse shifts occur in currency exchange rates. Unless an exporter can both keep its production and shipping costs competitive with rivals and successfully hedge against unfavorable changes in currency exchange rates, its success will be limited.

Licensing Strategies

Licensing makes sense when a firm with valuable technical know-how or a unique patented product has neither the internal organizational capability nor the resources to enter foreign markets. Licensing also has the advantage of avoiding the risks of committing resources to country markets that are unfamiliar, politically volatile, economically unstable, or otherwise risky. By licensing the technology or the production rights to foreign-based firms, the firm does not have to bear the costs and risks of entering foreign markets on its own, yet it is able to generate income from royalties. The big disadvantage of licensing is the risk of providing valuable technological know-how to foreign companies and thereby losing some degree of control over its use; monitoring licensees and safeguarding the company's proprietary know-how can prove quite difficult in some circumstances. But if the royalty potential is considerable and the companies to whom the licenses are being granted are both trustworthy and reputable, then licensing can be a very attractive option. Many software and pharmaceutical companies use licensing strategies.

Franchising Strategies

While licensing works well for manufacturers and owners of proprietary technology, franchising is often better suited to the global expansion efforts of service and retailing enterprises. McDonald's, Yum! Brands (the parent of Pizza Hut, KFC, and Taco Bell), The UPS Store, Jani-King International (the world's largest commercial cleaning franchisor), Roto-Rooter, 7-Eleven, and Hilton Hotels have all used franchising to build a presence in foreign markets. Franchising has much the same advantages as licensing. The franchisee bears most of the costs and risks of establishing foreign locations; a franchisor has to expend only the resources to recruit, train, support, and monitor franchisees. The big problem a franchisor faces is maintaining quality control; foreign franchisees do not always exhibit strong commitment to consistency and standardization, especially when the local culture does not stress the same kinds of quality concerns. Another problem that can arise is whether to allow foreign franchisees to make modifications in the franchisor's product offering so as to better satisfy the tastes and expectations of local buyers. Should McDonald's allow its franchised units in Japan to modify Big Macs slightly to suit Japanese tastes? Should the franchised KFC units in China be permitted to substitute spices that appeal to Chinese consumers? Or should the same menu offerings be rigorously and unvaryingly required of all franchisees worldwide?

Localized Multicountry Strategies or a Global Strategy?

The issue of whether to vary the company's competitive approach to fit specific market conditions and buyer preferences in each host country or whether to employ essentially the same strategy in all countries is perhaps the foremost strategic issue that companies must address when they operate in two or more foreign markets. Figure 7.1 shows a company's options for resolving this issue.

Core Concept

A *localized* or *multicountry* strategy is one where a company varies its product offering and competitive approach from country to country in an effort to be responsive to differing buyer preferences and market conditions.

Think-Local, Act-Local Approaches to Strategy Making   The bigger the differences in buyer tastes, cultural traditions, and market conditions in different countries, the stronger the case for a think-local, act-local approach to strategy making, in which a company tailors its product offerings and perhaps its basic competitive strategy to fit buyer tastes and market conditions in each country where it opts to compete. The strength of employing a set of *localized* or *multicountry strategies* is that the company's actions and business approaches are deliberately crafted to accommodate the

Figure 7.1 **A Company's Strategic Options for Dealing with Cross-Country Variations in Buyer Preferences and Market Conditions**

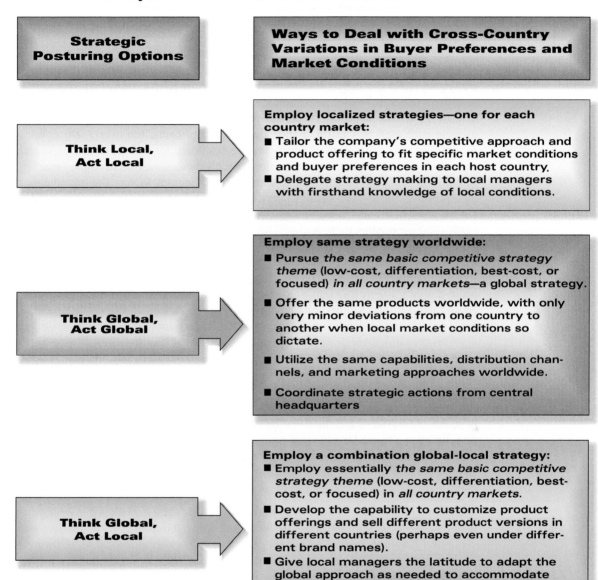

differing tastes and expectations of buyers in each country and to stake out the most attractive market positions vis-à-vis local competitors. A think-local, act-local approach means giving local managers considerable strategy-making latitude. It means having plants produce different product versions for different local markets, and adapting marketing and distribution to fit local customs and cultures. The bigger the country-to-country variations, the more that a company's overall strategy is a collection of its localized country strategies rather than a common or global strategy.

A think-local, act-local approach to strategy making is essential when there are significant country-to-country differences in customer preferences and buying habits, when there are significant cross-country differences in distribution channels and marketing methods, when host governments enact regulations requiring that products sold locally meet strict manufacturing specifications or performance standards, and when the trade restrictions of host governments are so diverse and complicated that they preclude a uniform, coordinated worldwide market approach. With localized strategies, a company often has different product versions for different countries and sometimes sells them under different brand names. Sony markets a different Walkman in Norway than in Sweden to better meet the somewhat different preferences and habits of the users in each market. Castrol, a specialist in oil lubricants, has over 3,000 different formulas of lubricants, many of which have been tailored for different climates, vehicle types and uses, and equipment applications that characterize different country markets. In the food products industry, it is common for companies to vary the ingredients in their products and sell the localized versions under local brand names in order to cater to country-specific tastes and eating preferences. Motor vehicle manufacturers routinely produce smaller, more fuel-efficient vehicles for markets in Europe where roads are often narrower and gasoline prices two or three times higher than they produce for the North American market; the models they manufacture for the Asian market are different yet again. DaimlerChrysler, for example, equips all of the Jeep Grand Cherokees and many of its Mercedes cars sold in Europe with fuel-efficient diesel engines. The Buicks that General Motors sells in China are small compacts, whereas those sold in the United States are large family sedans and SUVs.

However, think-local, act-local strategies have two big drawbacks: They hinder transfer of a company's competencies and resources across country boundaries (since the strategies in different host countries can be grounded in varying competencies and capabilities), and they do not promote building a single, unified competitive advantage—especially one based on low cost. Companies employing highly localized or multicountry strategies face big hurdles in achieving low-cost leadership *unless* they find ways to customize their products and *still* be in position to capture scale economies and experience/learning curve effects. Companies like Dell Computer and Toyota, because they have mass customization production capabilities, can cost effectively adapt their product offerings to local buyer tastes.

Think-Global, Act-Global Approaches to Strategy Making   While multicountry or localized strategies are best suited for industries where multicountry competition dominates and a fairly high degree of local responsiveness is competitively imperative, global strategies are best suited for globally competitive industries. A *global strategy* is one in which the company's approach is predominantly the same in all countries—it sells the same products under the same brand names everywhere, uses much the same distribution channels in all countries, and competes on the basis of the same capabilities and marketing approaches worldwide. Although the company's strategy or product offering may be adapted in very minor ways to accommodate specific situations in a few host countries, the company's fundamental competitive approach (low-cost, differentiation, best-cost, or focused) remains very much intact worldwide, and local managers stick close to the global strategy. A think-global, act-global strategic theme prompts company managers to integrate and coordinate the company's strategic moves worldwide and to expand into most if not all nations where there is significant buyer demand. It puts considerable strategic

Core Concept

A *global strategy* is one where a company employs the same basic competitive approach in all countries where it operates, sells much the same products everywhere, strives to build global brands, and coordinates its actions worldwide.

emphasis on building a *global* brand name and aggressively pursuing opportunities to transfer ideas, new products, and capabilities from one country to another.[6] Indeed, with a think global, act global approach to strategy making, a company's operations in each country can be viewed as experiments that result in learning and in capabilities that may merit transfer to other country markets.

Whenever country-to-country differences are small enough to be accommodated within the framework of a global strategy, a global strategy is preferable to localized strategies because a company can more readily unify its operations and focus on establishing a brand image and reputation that is uniform from country to country. Moreover, with a global strategy a company is better able to focus its full resources on building the resource strengths and capabilities to secure a sustainable low-cost or differentiation-based competitive advantage over both domestic rivals and global rivals racing for world market leadership. Figure 7.2 summarizes the basic differences between a localized or multicountry strategy and a global strategy.

Think-Global, Act-Local Approaches to Strategy Making Often, a company can accommodate cross-country variations in buyer tastes, local customs, and market conditions with a think-global, act-local approach to developing strategy. This middle-ground approach entails using the same basic competitive theme (low-cost, differentiation, best-cost, or focused) in each country but allowing local managers the latitude to (1) incorporate whatever country-specific variations in product attributes are needed to best satisfy local buyers and (2) make whatever adjustments in production, distribution, and marketing are needed to be responsive to local market conditions and compete successfully against local rivals. Slightly different product versions sold under the same brand name may suffice to satisfy local tastes, and it may be feasible to accommodate these versions rather economically in the course of designing and manufacturing the company's product offerings. The build-to-order component of Dell's strategy in PCs for example, makes it simple for Dell to be responsive to how buyers in different parts of the world want their PCs equipped. However, Dell has not wavered in its strategy to sell directly to customers rather than through local retailers, even though the majority of buyers in countries such as China are concerned about ordering online and prefer to personally inspect PCs at stores before making a purchase.

As a rule, most companies that operate multinationally endeavor to employ as global a strategy as customer needs and market conditions permit. Philips Electronics, the Netherlands-based electronics and consumer products company, operated successfully with localized strategies for many years but has recently begun moving more toward a unified strategy within the European Union and within North America.[7] Whirlpool has been globalizing its low-cost leadership strategy in home appliances for over 15 years, striving to standardize parts and components and move toward worldwide designs for as many of its appliance products as possible. But it has found it necessary to continue producing significantly different versions of refrigerators, washing machines, and cooking appliances for consumers in different regions of the world because the needs and tastes of local buyers for appliances of different sizes and designs have not converged sufficiently to permit standardization of Whirlpool's product offerings worldwide. General Motors began an initiative in 2004 to insist that its worldwide units share basic parts and work together to design vehicles that can be sold, with modest variations, anywhere around the world; by reducing the types of radios used in its cars and trucks from 270 to 50, it expected to save 40 percent in radio costs.

Illustration Capsule 7.1 on page 209 describes how two companies localize their strategies for competing in country markets across the world.

Figure 7.2 **How a Localized or Multicountry Strategy Differs from a Global Strategy**

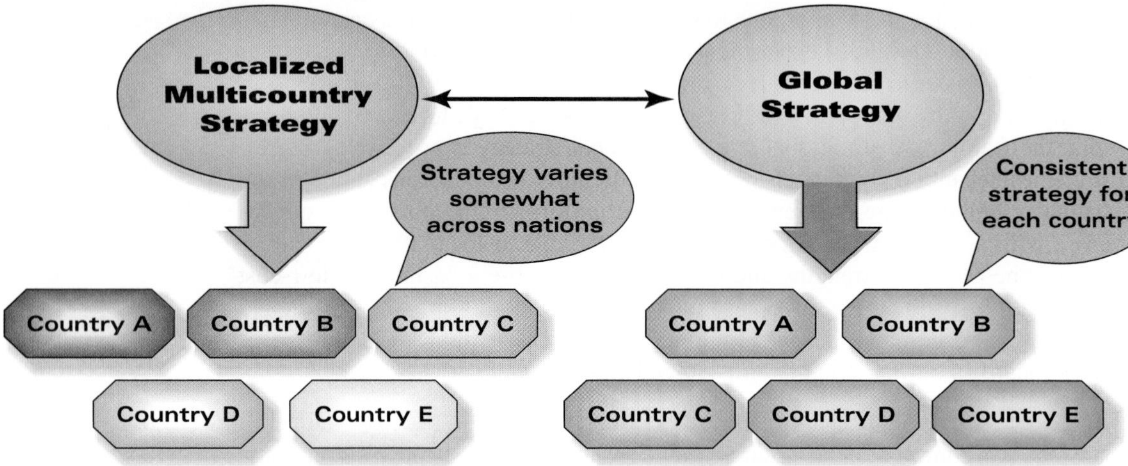

Localized Multicountry Strategy

Strategy varies somewhat across nations

Country A   Country B   Country C

Country D   Country E

- Customize the company's competitive approach as needed to fit market and business circumstances in each host country—strong responsiveness to local conditions.
- Sell different product versions in different countries under different brand names—adapt product attributes to fit buyer tastes and preferences country by country.
- Scatter plants across many host countries, each producing product versions for local markets.
- Preferably use local suppliers (some local sources may be required by host government).
- Adapt marketing and distribution to local customs and culture of each country.
- Transfer competencies and capabilities from country to country where feasible.
- Give country managers fairly wide strategy-making latitude and autonomy over local operations.

Global Strategy

Consistent strategy for each country

Country A   Country B

Country C   Country D   Country E

- Pursue same basic competitive strategy worldwide (low-cost, differentiation, best-cost, focused low-cost, focused differentiation), with minimal responsiveness to local conditions.
- Sell same products under same brand name worldwide; focus efforts on building global brands as opposed to strengthening local/regional brands sold in local/regional markets.
- Locate plants on basis of maximum locational advantage, usually in countries where production costs are lowest but plants may be scattered if shipping costs are high or other locational advantages dominate.
- Use best suppliers from anywhere in world.
- Coordinate marketing and distribution worldwide; make minor adaptation to local countries where needed.
- Compete on basis of same technologies, competencies, and capabilities worldwide; stress rapid transfer of new ideas, products, and capabilities to other countries.
- Coordinate major strategic decisions worldwide; expect local managers to stick close to global strategy.

Illustration Capsule 7.1

Multicountry Strategies at Electronic Arts and Coca-Cola

ELECTRONIC ARTS' MULTICOUNTRY STRATEGY IN VIDEO GAMES

Electronic Arts (EA), the world's largest independent developer and marketer of video games, designs games that are suited to the differing tastes of game players in different countries and also designs games in multiple languages. EA has two major design studios—one in Vancouver, British Columbia, and one in Los Angeles—and smaller design studios in San Francisco, Orlando, London, and Tokyo. This dispersion of design studios helps EA to design games that are specific to different cultures—for example, the London studio took the lead in designing the popular FIFA Soccer game to suit European tastes and to replicate the stadiums, signage, and team rosters; the U.S. studio took the lead in designing games involving NFL football, NBA basketball, and NASCAR racing. No other game software company had EA's ability to localize games

or to launch games on multiple platforms in multiple countries in multiple languages. EA's game Harry Potter and the Chamber of Secrets was released simultaneously in 75 countries, in 31 languages, and on seven platforms.

COCA-COLA'S MULTICOUNTRY STRATEGY IN BEVERAGES

Coca-Cola strives to meet the demands of local tastes and cultures, offering 300 brands in some 200 countries. Its network of bottlers and distributors is distinctly local, and the company's products and brands are formulated to cater to local tastes. The ways in which Coca-Cola's local operating units bring products to market, the packaging that is used, and the company's advertising messages are all intended to match the local culture and fit in with local business practices. Many of the ingredients and supplies for Coca-Cola's products are sourced locally.

Sources: Information posted at www.ea.com and www.cocacola.com (accessed September 2004).

THE QUEST FOR COMPETITIVE ADVANTAGE IN FOREIGN MARKETS

There are three important ways in which a firm can gain competitive advantage (or offset domestic disadvantages) by expanding outside its domestic market:[8] One, it can use location to lower costs or achieve greater product differentiation. Two, it can transfer competitively valuable competencies and capabilities from its domestic markets to foreign markets. And three, it can use cross-border coordination in ways that a domestic-only competitor cannot.

Using Location to Build Competitive Advantage

To use location to build competitive advantage, a company must consider two issues: (1) whether to concentrate each activity it performs in a few select countries or to disperse performance of the activity to many nations, and (2) in which countries to locate particular activities.[9]

> Companies that compete multinationally can pursue competitive advantage in world markets by locating their value chain activities in whatever nations prove most advantageous.

When to Concentrate Activities in a Few Locations   Companies tend to concentrate their activities in a limited number of locations in the following circumstances:

- *When the costs of manufacturing or other activities are significantly lower in some geographic locations than in others*—For example, much of the world's athletic footwear is manufactured in Asia (China and Korea) because of low labor costs; much of the production of motherboards for PCs is located in Taiwan because of both low costs and the high-caliber technical skills of the Taiwanese labor force.

- *When there are significant scale economies*—The presence of significant economies of scale in components production or final assembly means that a company can gain major cost savings from operating a few superefficient plants as opposed to a host of small plants scattered across the world. Important marketing and distribution economies associated with multinational operations can also yield low-cost leadership. In situations where some competitors are intent on global dominance, being the worldwide low-cost provider is a powerful competitive advantage. Achieving low-cost provider status often requires a company to have the largest worldwide manufacturing share, with production centralized in one or a few world-scale plants in low-cost locations. Some companies even use such plants to manufacture units sold under the brand names of rivals. Manufacturing share (as distinct from brand share or market share) is significant because it provides more certain access to production-related scale economies. Japanese makers of VCRs, microwave ovens, TVs, and DVD players have used their large manufacturing share to establish a low-cost advantage.[10]

- *When there is a steep learning curve associated with performing an activity in a single location*—In some industries experience/learning curve effects in parts manufacture or assembly are so great that a company establishes one or two large plants from which it serves the world market. The key to riding down the learning curve is to concentrate production in a few locations to increase the accumulated volume at a plant (and thus the experience of the plant's workforce) as rapidly as possible.

- *When certain locations have superior resources, allow better coordination of related activities, or offer other valuable advantages*—A research unit or a sophisticated production facility may be situated in a particular nation because of its pool of technically trained personnel. Samsung became a leader in memory chip technology by establishing a major R&D facility in Silicon Valley and transferring the know-how it gained back to headquarters and its plants in South Korea. Where just-in-time inventory practices yield big cost savings and/or where an assembly firm has long-term partnering arrangements with its key suppliers, parts manufacturing plants may be clustered around final assembly plants. An assembly plant may be located in a country in return for the host government's allowing freer import of components from large-scale, centralized parts plants located elsewhere. A customer service center or sales office may be opened in a particular country to help cultivate strong relationships with pivotal customers located nearby.

When to Disperse Activities Across Many Locations   There are several instances when dispersing activities is more advantageous than concentrating them. Buyer-related activities—such as distribution to dealers, sales and advertising, and after-sale service—usually must take place close to buyers. This means physically locating the capability to perform such activities in every country market where a global firm has major customers (unless buyers in several adjoining countries can be served quickly from a nearby central location). For example, firms that make mining and oil-drilling equipment maintain operations in many international locations to support customers' needs for speedy equipment repair and technical assistance. The four biggest public accounting firms have numerous international offices to service the foreign operations of their multinational corporate clients. A global competitor that effectively disperses its buyer-related activities can gain a service-based competitive edge in world markets over rivals whose buyer-related activities are more concentrated—this is one reason the Big Four public accounting firms (PricewaterhouseCoopers, KPMG, Deloitte & Touche, and Ernst & Young) have been so successful relative to regional and national firms. Dispersing activities to many locations is also competitively advantageous when high transportation costs, diseconomies of large size, and trade barriers make it too expensive to operate from a central location. Many companies distribute their products from multiple locations to shorten delivery times to customers. In addition, it is strategically advantageous to disperse activities to hedge against the risks of fluctuating exchange rates; supply interruptions (due to strikes, mechanical failures, and transportation delays); and adverse political developments. Such risks are greater when activities are concentrated in a single location.

The classic reason for locating an activity in a particular country is low cost.[11] Even though multinational and global firms have strong reason to disperse buyer-related activities to many international locations, such activities as materials procurement, parts manufacture, finished goods assembly, technology research, and new product development can frequently be decoupled from buyer locations and performed wherever advantage lies. Components can be made in Mexico; technology research done in Frankfurt; new products developed and tested in Phoenix; and assembly plants located in Spain, Brazil, Taiwan, or South Carolina. Capital can be raised in whatever country it is available on the best terms.

Using Cross-Border Transfers of Competencies and Capabilities to Build Competitive Advantage

One of the best ways for a company with valuable competencies and resource strengths to secure competitive advantage is to use its considerable resource strengths to enter additional country markets. A company whose resource strengths prove particularly potent in competing successfully in newly entered country markets not only grows sales and profits but also may find that its competitiveness is sufficiently enhanced to produce competitive advantage over one or more rivals and contend for global market leadership. Transferring competencies, capabilities, and resource strengths from country to country contributes to the development of broader or deeper competencies and capabilities—ideally helping a company achieve dominating depth in some competitively valuable area. Dominating depth in a competitively valuable capability, resource, or value chain activity is a strong basis for sustainable competitive advantage over other multinational or global competitors, and especially so over domestic-only competitors. A one-country customer base is often too small to support the resource buildup needed to achieve such depth; this is particularly true when the market is just emerging and sophisticated resources have not been required.

Whirlpool, the leading global manufacturer of home appliances, with plants in 14 countries and sales in 170 countries, has used the Internet to create a global information technology platform that allows the company to transfer key product innovations and production processes across regions and brands quickly and effectively. Wal-Mart is slowly but forcefully expanding its operations with a strategy that involves transferring its considerable domestic expertise in distribution and discount retailing to store operations recently established in China, Japan, Latin America, and Europe. Its status as the largest, most resource-deep, and most sophisticated user of distribution/ retailing know-how has served it well in building its foreign sales and profitability. But Wal-Mart is not racing madly to position itself in many foreign markets; rather, it is establishing a strong presence in select country markets and learning how to be successful in these before tackling entry into other countries well-suited to its business model.

However, cross-border resource transfers are not a guaranteed recipe for success. Philips Electronics sells more color TVs and DVD recorders in Europe than any other company does; its biggest technological breakthrough was the compact disc, which it invented in 1982. Philips has worldwide sales of about 38 billion euros, but as of 2005 Philips had lost money for 17 consecutive years in its U.S. consumer electronics business. In the United States, the company's color TVs and DVD recorders (sold under the Magnavox and Philips brands) are slow sellers. Philips notoriously lags in introducing new products into the U.S. market and has been struggling to develop an able sales force that can make inroads with U.S. electronics retailers and change its image as a low-end brand.

Using Cross-Border Coordination to Build Competitive Advantage

Coordinating company activities across different countries contributes to sustainable competitive advantage in several different ways.[12] Multinational and global competitors can choose where and how to challenge rivals. They may decide to retaliate against an aggressive rival in the country market where the rival has its biggest sales volume or its best profit margins in order to reduce the rival's financial resources for competing in other country markets. They may also decide to wage a price-cutting offensive against weak rivals in their home markets, capturing greater market share and subsidizing any short-term losses with profits earned in other country markets.

If a firm learns how to assemble its product more efficiently at, say, its Brazilian plant, the accumulated expertise can be quickly communicated via the Internet to assembly plants in other world locations. Knowledge gained in marketing a company's product in Great Britain can readily be exchanged with company personnel in New Zealand or Australia. A global or multinational manufacturer can shift production from a plant in one country to a plant in another to take advantage of exchange rate fluctuations, to enhance its leverage with host-country governments, and to respond to changing wage rates, components shortages, energy costs, or changes in tariffs and quotas. Production schedules can be coordinated worldwide; shipments can be diverted from one distribution center to another if sales rise unexpectedly in one place and fall in another.

Using online systems, companies can readily gather ideas for new and improved products from customers and company personnel all over the world, permitting informed decisions about what can be standardized and what should be customized. Likewise, online systems enable multinational companies to involve their best design and engineering personnel (wherever they are located) in collectively coming up with next-generation products—it is easy for company personnel in one location to use the Internet to collaborate closely with personnel in other locations in performing all sorts of strategically relevant activities. Efficiencies can also be achieved by shifting workloads from where they are unusually heavy to locations where personnel are underutilized. Whirlpool's efforts to link its product R&D and manufacturing operations in North America, Latin America, Europe, and Asia allowed it to accelerate the discovery of innovative appliance features, coordinate the introduction of these features in the appliance products marketed in different countries, and create a cost-efficient worldwide supply chain. Whirlpool's conscious efforts to integrate and coordinate its various operations around the world have helped it become a low-cost producer and also speed product innovations to market, thereby giving Whirlpool an edge over rivals in designing and rapidly introducing innovative and attractively priced appliances worldwide.

Furthermore, a multinational company that consistently incorporates the same differentiating attributes in its products worldwide has enhanced potential to build a global brand name with significant power in the marketplace. The reputation for quality that Honda established worldwide first in motorcycles and then in automobiles gave it competitive advantage in positioning Honda lawn mowers at the upper end of the U.S. outdoor power equipment market—the Honda name gave the company immediate credibility with U.S. buyers of power equipment and enabled it to become an instant market contender without all the fanfare and cost of a multimillion-dollar ad campaign to build brand awareness.

PROFIT SANCTUARIES, CROSS-MARKET SUBSIDIZATION, AND GLOBAL STRATEGIC OFFENSIVES

Profit sanctuaries are country markets (or geographic regions) in which a company derives substantial profits because of its strong or protected market position. McDonald's serves about 50 million customers daily at nearly 32,000 locations in 119 countries on five continents; not surprisingly, its biggest profit sanctuary is the United States, which generated 61.2 percent of 2004 profits, despite accounting for just 34.2 percent of 2004 revenues. Nike, which markets its products in 160 countries, has two big profit sanctuaries: the United States (where it earned 41.5 percent of its operating profits in 2005) and Europe, the Middle East, and Africa (where it earned 34.8 percent of 2005 operating profits). Discount retailer Carrefour, which has stores across much of Europe plus stores in Asia and the Americas, also has two principal profit sanctuaries; its biggest is in France (which in 2004 accounted for 49.2 percent of revenues and 60.8 percent of earnings before interest and taxes), and its second biggest is Europe outside of France (which in 2004 accounted for 37.3 percent of revenues and 33.1 percent of earnings before interest and taxes). Japan is the chief profit sanctuary for most Japanese companies because trade barriers erected by the Japanese government effectively block foreign companies from competing for a large share of Japanese sales. Protected from the threat of foreign competition in their home market, Japanese companies can safely charge somewhat higher prices to their Japanese customers and thus earn attractively large profits on sales made in Japan. In most cases, a company's biggest and most strategically crucial profit sanctuary is its home market, but international and global companies may also enjoy profit sanctuary status in other nations where they have a strong competitive position, big sales volume, and attractive profit margins. Companies that compete globally are likely to have more profit sanctuaries than companies that compete in just a few country markets; a domestic-only competitor, of course, can have only one profit sanctuary (see Figure 7.3).

> **Core Concept**
> Companies with large, protected **profit sanctuaries** have competitive advantage over companies that don't have a protected sanctuary. Companies with multiple profit sanctuaries have a competitive advantage over companies with a single sanctuary.

Figure 7.3   **Profit Sanctuary Potential of Domestic-Only, International, and Global Competitors**

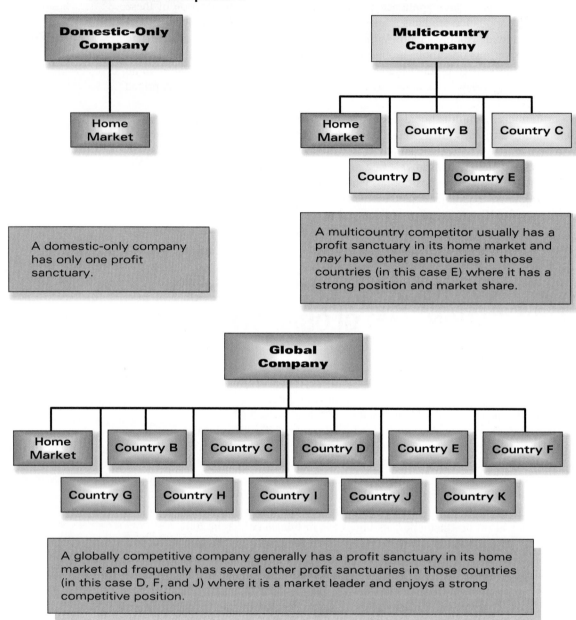

Using Cross-Market Subsidization to Wage a Strategic Offensive

Profit sanctuaries are valuable competitive assets, providing the financial strength to support strategic offensives in selected country markets and fuel a company's race for global market leadership. The added financial capability afforded by multiple profit sanctuaries gives a global or multicountry competitor the financial strength to wage a market offensive against a domestic competitor whose only profit sanctuary is its home market. Consider the case of a purely domestic company in competition with a company that has multiple profit sanctuaries and that is racing for global market leadership. The global company has the flexibility of lowballing its prices in the domestic company's home market and grabbing market share at the domestic company's expense, subsidizing razor-thin margins or even losses with the healthy profits earned in its profit sanctuaries—a practice called **cross-market subsidization.** The global company can adjust the depth of its price cutting to move in and capture market share quickly, or it can shave prices slightly to make gradual market inroads (perhaps over a decade or more) so as not to threaten domestic firms precipitously or trigger protectionist government actions. If the domestic company retaliates with matching price cuts, it exposes its entire revenue and profit base to erosion; its profits can be squeezed substantially and its competitive strength sapped, even if it is the domestic market leader.

> **Core Concept**
> ***Cross-market subsidization*—** supporting competitive offensives in one market with resources and profits diverted from operations in other markets—is a powerful competitive weapon.

Offensive Strategies Suitable for Competing in Foreign Markets

Companies that compete in multiple foreign markets can, of course, fashion an offensive strategy based on any of the approaches discussed in Chapter 6 (pages 160–193)—these types of offensive strategies are universally applicable and are just as suitable for competing in foreign markets as for domestic markets. But there are three additional types of offensive strategies that are suited to companies competing in foreign markets:[13]

- *Attack a foreign rival's profit sanctuaries.* Launching an offensive in a country market where a rival earns its biggest profits can put the rival on the defensive, forcing it to perhaps spend more on marketing/advertising, trim its prices, boost product innovation efforts, or otherwise undertake actions that raise its costs and erode its profits. If a company's offensive succeeds in eroding a rival's profits in its chief profit sanctuary, the rival's financial resources may be sufficiently weakened to enable the attacker to gain the upper hand and build market momentum. While attacking a rival's profit sanctuary violates the principle of attacking competitor weaknesses instead of competitor strengths, it can nonetheless prove valuable when there is special merit in pursuing actions that cut into a foreign rival's profit margins and force it to defend a market that is important to its competitive well-being. This is especially true when the attacker has important resource strengths and profit sanctuaries of its own that it can draw on to support its offensive.

- *Employ cross-market subsidization to win customers and sales away from select rivals in select country markets.* This can be a particularly attractive offensive strategy for companies that compete in multiple country markets with multiple products (several brands of cigarettes or different brands of food products). Competing in multiple country markets gives a company the luxury of drawing upon the resources, profits, and cash flows derived from particular country markets (especially its profit sanctuaries) to support offensives aimed at winning customers away from select rivals in those country markets that it wants either to enter or to boost its sales and market share. Alternatively, a company whose product lineup consists of different items can shift resources from a product category where it is competitively strong and resource deep (say soft drinks) to add firepower to an offensive in those countries with bright growth prospects in another product category (say bottled water or fruit juices).

- *Dump goods at cut-rate prices in the markets of foreign rivals.* A company is said to be dumping when it sells its goods in foreign markets at prices that are (1) well below the prices at which it normally sells in its home market or (2) well below its full costs per unit. Companies that engage in dumping usually keep their selling prices high enough to cover variable costs per unit, thereby limiting their losses on each unit to some percentage of fixed costs per unit. Dumping can be an appealing offensive strategy in either of two instances. One is when dumping drives down the price so far in the targeted country that domestic firms are quickly put in dire financial straits and end up declaring bankruptcy or being driven out of business—for dumping to pay off in this instance, however, the dumping company needs to have deep enough financial pockets to cover any losses from selling at below-market prices, and the targeted domestic companies need to be financially weak. The second instance in which dumping becomes an attractive strategy is when a company with unused production capacity discovers that it is cheaper to keep producing (as long as the selling prices cover average variable costs per unit) than it is to incur the costs associated with idle plant capacity. By keeping its plants operating at or near capacity, a dumping company not only may be able to cover variable costs and earn a contribution to fixed costs but also may be able to use its below-market prices to draw price-sensitive customers away from foreign rivals, then attentively court these new customers and retain their business when prices later begin a gradual rise back to normal market levels. Thus, dumping may prove useful as a way of entering the market of a particular foreign country and establishing a customer base.

> **Core Concept**
> Three strategy offensives that are particularly suitable for competing in foreign markets involve (1) attacking a foreign rival's profit sanctuaries, (2) employing cross-market subsidization, and (3) dumping.

However, dumping strategies run a high risk of host government retaliation on behalf of the adversely affected domestic companies. Indeed, as the trade among nations has mushroomed over the past 10 years, most governments have joined the World Trade Organization (WTO), which promotes fair trade practices among nations and actively polices dumping. The WTO allows member governments to take actions against dumping wherever there is material injury to domestic competitors. In 2002, for example, the U.S. government imposed tariffs of up to 30 percent on selected steel products that Asian and European steel manufacturers were said to be selling at ultra-low prices in the U.S. market. Canada recently investigated charges that companies in Austria, Belgium, France, Germany, Poland and China were dumping supplies of laminate flooring in Canada to the detriment of Canadian producers and concluded that companies in France and China were indeed selling such flooring in Canada at unreasonably low prices.[14] Most all governments can be expected to retaliate against dumping by imposing special tariffs on goods being imported from the countries of the guilty companies. Companies deemed guilty of dumping frequently come under pressure from their government to cease and desist, especially if the tariffs adversely affect innocent companies based in the same country or if the advent of special tariffs raises the specter of a trade war.

A company desirous of employing some type of offensive strategy in foreign markets is well advised to observe the principles for employing offensive strategies in general. For instance, it usually wise to attack foreign rivals on grounds that pit the challenger's competitive strengths against the defender's weaknesses and vulnerabilities. As a rule, trying to steal customers away from foreign rivals with strategies aimed at besting rivals where they are strongest stand a lower chance of succeeding than strategies that attack their competitive weaknesses, especially when the challenger has resource strengths that enable it to exploit rivals' weaknesses and when its attack involves an element of surprise.[15] It nearly always makes good strategic sense to use the challenger's core competencies and best competitive capabilities to spearhead the offensive. Furthermore, strategic offensives in foreign markets should, as a general rule, be predicated on exploiting the challenger's core competencies and best competitive capabilities. The ideal condition for a strategic offensive is when the attacker's resource strengths give it a competitive advantage over the targeted foreign rivals. The only two exceptions to these offensive strategy principles come when a competitively strong company with deep financial pockets sees considerable benefit in attacking a foreign rival's profit sanctuary and/or has the ability to employ cross-market subsidization—both of these offensive strategies can involve attacking a foreign rival's strengths (but they also are grounded in important strengths of the challenger and don't fall into the trap of challenging a competitively strong rival with a strategic offensive based on unproven expertise or inferior technology or a relatively unknown brand name or other resource weaknesses).

STRATEGIC ALLIANCES AND JOINT VENTURES WITH FOREIGN PARTNERS

Strategic alliances, joint ventures, and other cooperative agreements with foreign companies are a favorite and potentially fruitful means for entering a foreign market or strengthening a firm's competitiveness in world markets.[16] Historically, export-minded firms in industrialized nations sought alliances with firms in less-developed countries to import and market their products locally—such arrangements were often necessary to win approval for entry from the host country's government. Both Japanese and American companies are actively forming alliances with European companies to strengthen their ability to compete in the 25-nation European Union (and the five countries that are seeking to become EU members) and to capitalize on the opening up of Eastern European markets. Many U.S. and European companies are allying with Asian companies in their efforts to enter markets in China, India, Malaysia, Thailand, and other Asian countries. Companies in Europe, Latin America, and Asia are using alliances and joint ventures as a means of strengthening their mutual ability to compete across a wider geographical area—for instance, all the countries in the European Union or whole continents or most all country markets where there is sizable demand for the industry's product. Many foreign companies, of course, are particularly interested in strategic partnerships that will strengthen their ability to gain a foothold in the U.S. market.

> Cross-border alliances have proved to be popular and viable vehicles for companies to edge their way into the markets of foreign countries.

However, cooperative arrangements between domestic and foreign companies have strategic appeal for reasons besides gaining better access to attractive country markets.[17] A second big appeal of cross-border alliances is to capture economies of scale in production and/or marketing—cost reduction can be the difference that allows a company to be cost-competitive. By joining forces in producing components, assembling models, and marketing their products, companies can realize cost savings not achievable with their own small volumes. A third motivation for entering into a cross-border alliance is to fill gaps in technical expertise and/or knowledge of local markets (buying habits and product preferences of consumers, local customs, and so on). Allies learn much from one another in performing joint research, sharing technological know-how, studying one another's manufacturing methods, and understanding how to tailor sales and marketing approaches to fit local cultures and traditions. Indeed, one of the win–win benefits of an alliance is to learn from the skills, technological know-how, and capabilities of alliance partners and implant the knowledge and know-how of these partners in personnel throughout the company.

A fourth motivation for cross-border alliances is to share distribution facilities and dealer networks, thus mutually strengthening their access to buyers. A fifth benefit is that cross-border allies can direct their competitive energies more toward mutual rivals and less toward one another; teaming up may help them close the gap on leading companies. A sixth driver of cross-border alliances comes into play when companies desirous of entering a new foreign market conclude that alliances with local companies are an effective way to tap into a partner's local market knowledge and help it establish working relationships with key officials in the host-country government.[18] And, finally, alliances can be a particularly useful way for companies across the world to gain agreement on important technical standards—they have been used to arrive at standards for DVD players, assorted PC devices, Internet-related technologies, high-definition televisions, and mobile phones.

> Cross-border alliances enable a growth-minded company to widen its geographic coverage and strengthen its competitiveness in foreign markets while, at the same time, offering flexibility and allowing a company to retain some degree of autonomy and operating control.

What makes cross-border alliances an attractive strategic means of gaining the above types of benefits (as compared to acquiring or merging with foreign-based companies to gain much the same benefits) is that entering into alliances and strategic partnerships to gain market access and/ or expertise of one kind or another allows a company to preserve its independence (which is not the case with a merger), retain veto power over how the alliance operates, and avoid using perhaps scarce financial resources to fund acquisitions. Furthermore, an alliance offers the flexibility to readily disengage once its purpose has been served or if the benefits prove elusive, whereas an acquisition is more permanent sort of arrangement (although the acquired company can, of course, be divested).[19]

Illustration Capsule 7.2 provides six examples of cross-border strategic alliances.

The Risks of Strategic Alliances with Foreign Partners

Alliances and joint ventures with foreign partners have their pitfalls, however. Cross-border allies typically have to overcome language and cultural barriers and figure out how to deal with diverse (or perhaps conflicting) operating practices. The communication, trust-building, and coordination costs are high in terms of management time.[20] It is not unusual for there to be little personal chemistry among some of the key people on whom success or failure of the alliance depends—the rapport such personnel need to work well together may never emerge. And even if allies are able to develop productive personal relationships, they can still have trouble reaching mutually agreeable ways to deal with key issues or resolve differences. There is a natural tendency for allies to struggle to collaborate effectively in competitively sensitive areas, thus spawning suspicions on both sides about forthright exchanges of information and expertise. Occasionally, the egos of corporate executives can clash—an alliance between Northwest Airlines and KLM Royal Dutch Airlines resulted in a bitter feud among both companies' top officials (who, according to some reports, refused to speak to each other).[21] In addition, there is the thorny problem of getting alliance partners to sort through issues and reach decisions fast enough to stay abreast of rapid advances in technology or fast-changing market conditions.

Illustration Capsule 7.2
Six Examples of Cross-Border Strategic Alliances

1. Two auto firms, Renault of France and Nissan of Japan, formed a broad-ranging global partnership in 1999 and then strengthened and expanded the alliance in 2002. The initial objective was to gain sales for new Nissan vehicles introduced in the European market, but the alliance now extends to full cooperation in all major areas, including the use of common platforms, joint development and use of engines and transmissions, fuel cell research, purchasing and use of common suppliers, and exchange of best practices. When the alliance was formed in 1999, Renault acquired a 36.8 percent ownership stake in Nissan; this was extended to 44.4 percent in 2002 when the alliance was expanded. Also, in 2002, the partners formed a jointly and equally owned strategic management company, named Renault-Nissan, to coordinate cooperative efforts.

2. Intel, the world's largest chip maker, has formed strategic alliances with leading software application providers and computer hardware providers to bring more innovativeness and expertise to the architecture underlying Intel's family of microprocessors and semiconductors. Intel's partners in the effort to enhance Intel's next-generation products include SAP, Oracle, SAS, BEA, IBM, Hewlett-Packard, Dell, Microsoft, Cisco Systems, and Alcatel. One of the alliances between Intel and Cisco involves a collaborative effort in Hong Kong to build next-generation infrastructure for Electronic Product Code/Radio Frequency Identification (EPC/RFID) solutions used to link manufacturers and logistics companies in the Hong Kong region with retailers worldwide. Intel and France-based Alcatel (a leading provider of fixed and mobile broadband access products, marketed in 130 countries) formed an alliance in 2004 to advance the definition, standardization, development, integration, and marketing of WiMAX broadband services solutions. WiMAX was seen as a cost-effective wireless or mobile broadband solution for deployment in both emerging markets and developed countries when, for either economic or technical reasons, it was not feasible to provide urban or rural customers with hardwired DSL broadband access.

3. Verio, a subsidiary of Japan-based NTT Communications and one of the leading global providers of Web hosting services and IP data transport, operates with the philosophy that in today's highly competitive and challenging technology market, companies must gain and share skills, information, and technology with technology leaders across the world. Believing that no company can be all things to all customers in the Web hosting industry, Verio executives have developed an alliance-oriented business model that combines the company's core competencies with the skills and products of best-of-breed technology partners. Verio's strategic partners include Accenture, Cisco Systems, Microsoft, Sun Microsystems,

Oracle, Arsenal Digital Solutions (a provider of worry-free tape backup, data restore, and data storage services), Internet Security Systems (a provider of firewall and intrusion detection systems), and Mercantec (a developer of storefront and shopping cart software). Verio management believes that its portfolio of strategic alliances allows it to use innovative, best-of-class technologies in providing its customers with fast, efficient, accurate data transport and a complete set of Web hosting services. An independent panel of 12 judges recently selected Verio as the winner of the Best Technology Foresight Award for its efforts in pioneering new technologies.

4. Toyota and First Automotive Works, China's biggest automaker, entered into an alliance in 2002 to make luxury sedans, sport-utility vehicles (SUVs), and minivehicles for the Chinese market. The intent was to make as many as 400,000 vehicles annually by 2010, an amount equal to the number that Volkswagen, the company with the largest share of the Chinese market, was making as of 2002. The alliance envisioned a joint investment of about $1.2 billion. At the time of the announced alliance, Toyota was lagging behind Honda, General Motors, and Volkswagen in setting up production facilities in China. Capturing a bigger share of the Chinese market was seen as crucial to Toyota's success in achieving its strategic objective of having a 15 percent share of the world's automotive market by 2010.

5. Airbus Industrie was formed by an alliance of aerospace companies from Britain, Spain, Germany, and France that included British Aerospace, Daimler-Benz Aerospace, and Aerospatiale. The objective of the alliance was to create a European aircraft company capable of competing with U.S.-based Boeing Corporation. The alliance has proved highly successful, infusing Airbus with the know-how and resources to compete head-to-head with Boeing for world leadership in large commercial aircraft (over 100 passengers).

6. General Motors, DaimlerChrysler, and BMW have entered into an alliance to develop a hybrid gasoline-electric engine that is simpler and less expensive to produce than the hybrid engine technology being pioneered by Toyota. Toyota, the acknowledged world leader in hybrid engines, is endeavoring to establish its design as the industry standard by signing up other automakers to use it. But the technology favored by the General Motors/DaimlerChrysler/BMW alliance is said to be less costly to produce and easier to configure for large trucks and SUVs than Toyota's (although it is also less fuel efficient). Europe's largest automaker, Volkswagen, has allied with Porsche to pursue the development of hybrid engines. Ford Motor and Honda, so far, have elected to go it alone in developing hybrid engine technology.

Sources: Company Web sites and press releases; Yves L. Doz and Gary Hamel, *Alliance Advantage: The Art of Creating Value through Partnering* (Boston, MA: Harvard Business School Press, 1998); and Norihiko Shirouzu and Jathon Sapsford, "As Hybrid Cars Gain Traction, Industry Battles over Designs," *The Wall Street Journal,* October 19, 2005, pp. A1, A9B.

It requires many meetings of many people working in good faith over time to iron out what is to be shared, what is to remain proprietary, and how the cooperative arrangements will work. Often, once the bloom is off the rose, partners discover they have conflicting objectives and strategies, deep differences of opinion about how to proceed, or important differences in corporate values and ethical standards. Tensions build up, working relationships cool, and the hoped-for benefits never materialize.[22]

Even if the alliance becomes a win–win proposition for both parties, there is the danger of becoming overly dependent on foreign partners for essential expertise and competitive capabilities. If a company is aiming for global market leadership and needs to develop capabilities of its own, then at some juncture cross-border merger or acquisition may have to be substituted for cross-border alliances and joint ventures. One of the lessons about cross-border alliances is that they are more effective in helping a company establish a beachhead of new opportunity in world markets than they are in enabling a company to achieve and sustain global market leadership. Global market leaders, while benefiting from alliances, usually must guard against becoming overly dependent on the assistance they get from alliance partners—otherwise, they are not masters of their own destiny.

> Strategic alliances are more effective in helping establish a beachhead of new opportunity in world markets than in achieving and sustaining global leadership.

When a Cross-Border Alliance May Be Unnecessary

Experienced multinational companies that market in 50 to 100 or more countries across the world find less need for entering into cross-border alliances than do companies in the early stages of globalizing their operations.[23] Multinational companies make it a point to develop senior managers who understand how "the system" works in different countries; these companies can also avail themselves of local managerial talent and know-how by simply hiring experienced local managers and thereby detouring the hazards of collaborative alliances with local companies. If a multinational enterprise with considerable experience in entering the markets of different countries wants to detour the hazards and hassles of allying with local businesses, it can simply assemble a capable management team consisting of both senior managers with considerable international experience and local managers. The responsibilities of its own in-house managers with international business savvy are (1) to transfer technology, business practices, and the corporate culture into the company's operations in the new country market, and (2) to serve as conduits for the flow of information between the corporate office and local operations. The responsibilities of local managers are (1) to contribute needed understanding of the local market conditions, local buying habits, and local ways of doing business, and (2) in many cases, to head up local operations.

Hence, one cannot automatically presume that a company needs the wisdom and resources of a local partner to guide it through the process of successfully entering the markets of foreign countries. Indeed, experienced multinationals often discover that local partners do not always have adequate local market knowledge—much of the so-called experience of local partners can predate the emergence of current market trends and conditions, and sometimes their operating practices can be archaic.[24]

STRATEGIES THAT FIT THE MARKETS OF EMERGING COUNTRIES

Companies racing for global leadership have to consider competing in emerging markets like China, India, Brazil, Indonesia, and Mexico—countries where the business risks are considerable but where the opportunities for growth are huge, especially as their

Illustration Capsule 7.3

Coca-Cola's Strategy for Growing Its Sales in China and India

In 2004, Coca-Cola developed a strategy to dramatically boost its market penetration in such emerging countries as China and India, where annual growth had recently dropped from about 30 percent in 1994–1998 to 10–12 percent in 2001–2003. Prior to 2003, Coca-Cola had focused its marketing efforts in China and India on making its drinks attractive to status-seeking young people in urbanized areas (cities with populations of 500,000 or more), but as annual sales growth steadily declined in these areas during the 1998–2003 period, Coca-Cola's management decided that the company needed a new, bolder strategy aimed at more rural areas of these countries. It began promoting the sales of 6.5-ounce returnable glass bottles of Coke in smaller cities and outlying towns with populations in the 50,000 to 250,000 range. Returnable bottles (which could be reused about 20 times) were much cheaper than plastic bottles or aluminum cans, and the savings in packaging costs were enough to slash the price of single-serve bottles to one yuan in China and about five rupees in India,

the equivalent in both cases of about 12 cents. Initial results were promising. Despite the fact that annual disposable incomes in these rural areas were often less than $1,000, the one-yuan and five-rupee prices proved attractive. Sales of the small bottles of Coke for one local Coca-Cola distributor in Anning, China, soon accounted for two-thirds of the distributor's total sales; a local distributor in India boosted sales from 9,000 cases in 2002 to 27,000 cases in 2003 and was expecting sales of 45,000 cases in 2004. Coca-Cola management expected that greater emphasis on rural sales would boost its growth rate in Asia to close to 20 percent and help boost worldwide volume growth to the 3–5 percent range as opposed to the paltry 1 percent rate experienced in 2003.

However, Pepsi, which had a market share of about 27 percent in China versus Coca-Cola's 55 percent, was skeptical of Coca-Cola's rural strategy and continued with its all-urban strategy of marketing to consumers in China's 165 cities with populations greater than 1 million people.

Sources: Based on information in Gabriel Kahn and Eric Bellman, "Coke's Big Gamble in Asia: Digging Deeper in China, India," *The Wall Street Journal,* August 11, 2004, pp. A1, A4, plus information at www.cocacola.com (accessed September 20, 2004 and October 6, 2005).

economies develop and living standards climb toward levels in the industrialized world.[25] With the world now comprising more than 6 billion people—fully one-third of whom are in India and China, and hundreds of millions more in other less-developed countries of Asia and in Latin America—a company that aspires to world market leadership (or to sustained rapid growth) cannot ignore the market opportunities or the base of technical and managerial talent such countries offer. For example, in 2003 China's population of 1.3 billion people consumed nearly 33 percent of the world's annual cotton production, 51 percent of the world's pork, 35 percent of all the cigarettes, 31 percent of worldwide coal production, 27 percent of the world's steel production, 19 percent of the aluminum, 23 percent of the TVs, 20 percent of the cell phones, and 18 percent of the washing machines.[26] China is the world's largest consumer of copper, aluminum, and cement and the second largest importer of oil; it is the world's biggest market for mobile phones and the second biggest for PCs, and it is on track to become the second largest market for motor vehicles by 2010.

Illustration Capsule 7.3 describes Coca-Cola's strategy to boost its sales and market share in China.

Tailoring products to fit conditions in an emerging-country market, however, often involves more than making minor product changes and becoming more familiar with local cultures.[27] Ford's attempt to sell a Ford Escort in India at a price of $21,000—a luxury-car price, given that India's best-selling Maruti-Suzuki model sold at the time for $10,000 or less, and that fewer than 10 percent of Indian households have annual purchasing power greater than $20,000—met with a less-than-enthusiastic market response. McDonald's has had to offer vegetable burgers in parts of Asia and to rethink its prices, which are often high by local standards and affordable only by the well-to-do. Kellogg has struggled to introduce its cereals successfully because consumers in many less-developed countries do not eat cereal for breakfast—changing habits is difficult and expensive. In several emerging countries, Coca-Cola has found that advertising its world image does not strike a chord with the local populace in a number of emerging-country markets. Single-serving packages of detergents, shampoos, pickles, cough syrup, and cooking oils are very popular in India because they allow buyers to conserve cash by purchasing only what they need immediately. Thus, many companies find that trying to employ a strategy akin to that used in the markets of developed countries is hazardous.[28] Experimenting with some, perhaps many, local twists is usually necessary to find a strategy combination that works.

Strategy Options

Several strategy options for tailoring a company's strategy to fit the sometimes unusual or challenging circumstances presented in emerging-country markets:

- *Prepare to compete on the basis of low price.* Consumers in emerging markets are often highly focused on price, which can give low-cost local competitors the edge unless a company can find ways to attract buyers with bargain prices as well as better products.[29] For example, when Unilever entered the market for laundry detergents in India, it realized that 80 percent of the population could not afford the brands it was selling to affluent consumers there (or the brands it was selling in wealthier countries). To compete against a low-priced detergent made by a local company, Unilever came up with a low-cost formula that was not harsh to the skin, constructed new low-cost production facilities, packaged the detergent (named Wheel) in single-use amounts so that it could be sold very cheaply, distributed the product to local merchants by handcarts, and crafted an economical marketing campaign that included painted signs on buildings and demonstrations near stores—the new brand quickly captured $100 million in sales and was the number one detergent brand in India in 2004 based on dollar sales. Unilever later replicated the strategy with low-priced packets of shampoos and deodorants in India and in South America with a detergent brand named Ala.

- *Be prepared to modify aspects of the company's business model to accommodate local circumstances (but not so much that the company loses the advantage of global scale and global branding).*[30] For instance when Dell entered China, it discovered that individuals and businesses were not accustomed to placing orders through the Internet (in North America, over 50 percent of Dell's sales in 2002–2005 were online). To adapt, Dell modified its direct sales model to rely more heavily on phone and fax orders and decided to be patient in getting Chinese customers to place Internet orders. Further, because numerous Chinese government departments and state-owned enterprises insisted that hardware vendors make their bids through distributors and systems integrators (as opposed to dealing directly with Dell salespeople as did large enterprises in other countries), Dell opted to use third parties in marketing its products to this buyer segment (although it did sell through its own sales force where it could). But Dell was careful not to abandon those parts of its business model that gave it a competitive edge over rivals. When McDonald's moved into Russia in the 1990s, it was forced to alter its practice of obtaining needed supplies from outside vendors because capable local suppliers were not available; to supply its Russian outlets and stay true to its core principle of serving consistent quality fast food, McDonald's set up its own vertically integrated supply chain (cattle were imported from Holland, russet potatoes were imported from the United States); worked with a select number of Russian bakers for its bread; brought in agricultural specialists from Canada and Europe to improve the management practices of Russian farmers; built its own 100,000-square-foot McComplex to produce hamburgers, French fries, ketchup, mustard, and Big Mac sauce; and set up a trucking fleet to move supplies to restaurants.

- *Try to change the local market to better match the way the company does business elsewhere.*[31] A multinational company often has enough market clout to drive major changes in the way a local country market operates. When Hong Kong–based STAR launched its first satellite TV channel in 1991, it profoundly impacted the TV marketplace in India: The Indian government lost its monopoly on TV broadcasts, several other satellite TV channels aimed at Indian audiences quickly emerged, and the excitement of additional channels triggered a boom in TV manufacturing in India. When Japan's Suzuki entered India in 1981, it triggered a quality revolution among Indian auto parts manufacturers. Local parts and components suppliers teamed up with Suzuki's vendors in Japan and worked with Japanese experts to produce higher-quality products. Over the next two decades, Indian companies became very proficient in making top-notch parts and components for vehicles, won more prizes for quality than companies in any country other than Japan, and broke into the global market as suppliers to many automakers in Asia and other parts of the world.

- *Stay away from those emerging markets where it is impractical or uneconomic to modify the company's business model to accommodate local circumstances.*[32] Home Depot has avoided entry into most Latin American countries because its value proposition of good quality, low prices, and attentive customer service relies on (1) good highways and logistical systems to minimize store inventory costs, (2) employee stock ownership to help motivate store personnel to provide good customer service, and (3) high labor costs for housing construction and home repairs to encourage homeowners to engage in do-it-yourself projects. Relying on these factors in the U.S. market has worked spectacularly for Home Depot, but the company has found that it cannot count on these factors in much of Latin America. Thus, to enter the market in Mexico, Home Depot switched to an acquisition strategy; it has acquired two building supply retailers in Mexico with a total of 40-plus stores. But it has not tried to operate them in the style of its U.S. big-box stores, and it doesn't have retail operations in any other developing nations (although it is exploring entry into China).

Company experiences in entering developing markets like China, India, Russia, and Brazil indicate that profitability seldom comes quickly or easily. Building a market for the company's products can often turn into a long-term process that involves reeducation of consumers, sizable investments in advertising and promotion to alter tastes and buying habits, and upgrades of the local infrastructure (the supplier base, transportation systems, distribution channels, labor markets, and capital markets). In such cases, a company must be patient, work within the system to improve the infrastructure, and lay the foundation for generating sizable revenues and profits once conditions are ripe for market takeoff.

> Profitability in emerging markets rarely comes quickly or easily—new entrants have to adapt their business models and strategies to local conditions and be patient in earning a profit.

Figure 7.4   **Strategy Options for Local Companies in Competing Against Global Companies**

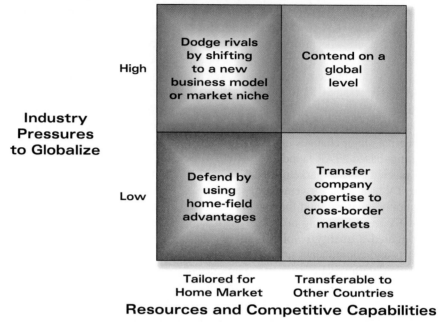

Source: Adapted from Niroj Dawar and Tony Frost, "Competing with Giants: Survival Strategies for Local Companies in Emerging Markets," *Harvard Business Review* 77, no. 1 (January–February 1999), p. 122.

Defending Against Global Giants: Strategies for Local Companies in Emerging Markets

If opportunity-seeking, resource-rich multinational companies are looking to enter emerging markets, what strategy options can local companies use to survive? As it turns out, the prospects for local companies facing global giants are by no means grim. They can employ any of four generic strategic approaches depending on (1) whether their competitive assets are suitable only for the home market or can be transferred abroad, and (2) whether industry pressures to move toward global competition are strong or weak, as shown in Figure 7.4.

Using Home-Field Advantages   When the pressures for competing globally are low and a local firm has competitive strengths well suited to the local market, a good strategy option is to concentrate on the advantages enjoyed in the home market, cater to customers who prefer a local touch, and accept the loss of customers attracted to global brands.[33] A local company may be able to astutely exploit its local orientation— its familiarity with local preferences, its expertise in traditional products, its long-standing customer relationships. In many cases, a local company enjoys a significant cost advantage over global rivals (perhaps because of simpler product design or lower operating and overhead costs), allowing it to compete on the basis of price. Its global competitors often aim their products at upper- and middle-income urban buyers, who tend to be more fashion-conscious, more willing to experiment with new products, and more attracted to global brands.

Another competitive approach is to cater to the local market in ways that pose difficulties for global rivals. A small Middle Eastern cell phone manufacturer competes successfully against industry giants Nokia, Samsung, and Motorola by selling a model designed especially for Muslims—it is loaded with the Koran, alerts people at prayer times, and is equipped with a compass that points them toward Mecca. Several Chinese PC makers have been able to retain customers in competition against global leader Dell because Chinese PC buyers strongly prefer to personally inspect PCs before making a purchase; local PC makers with their extensive retailer networks that allow prospective buyers to check out their offerings in nearby stores have a competitive edge in winning the business of first-time PC buyers vis-à-vis Dell with its build-to-order, sell-direct business strategy (where customers are encouraged to place their orders online or via phone or fax). Bajaj Auto, India's largest producer of scooters, has defended its turf against Honda (which entered the Indian market with local joint venture partner Hero Group to sell scooters, motorcycles, and other vehicles on the basis of its superior technology, quality, and the appeal) by focusing on buyers who wanted low-cost, durable scooters and easy access to maintenance in the countryside. Bajaj designed a rugged, cheap-to-build scooter for India's rough roads, increased its investments in R&D to improve reliability and quality, and created an extensive network of distributors and roadside-mechanic stalls, a strategic approach that allowed it to remain the market leader with a 70–75 percent market share through 2004 despite growing unit sales of Hero Honda motorcycles and scooters.

Transferring the Company's Expertise to Cross-Border Markets   When a company has resource strengths and capabilities suitable for competing in other country markets, launching initiatives to transfer its expertise to cross-border markets becomes a viable strategic option.[34] Televisa, Mexico's largest media company, used its expertise in Spanish culture and linguistics to become the world's most prolific producer of Spanish-language soap operas. Jollibee Foods, a family-owned company with 56 percent of the fast-food business in the Philippines, combated McDonald's entry first by upgrading service and delivery standards and then by using its expertise in seasoning hamburgers with garlic and soy sauce and making noodle and rice meals with fish to open outlets catering to Asian residents in Hong Kong, the Middle East, and California.

Shifting to a New Business Model or Market Niche   When industry pressures to globalize are high, any of the following three options makes the most sense: (1) shift the business to a piece of the industry value chain where the firm's expertise and resources provide competitive advantage, (2) enter into a joint venture with a globally competitive partner, or (3) sell out to (be acquired by) a global entrant into the home market who concludes the company would be a good entry vehicle.[35] When Microsoft entered China, local software developers shifted from cloning Windows products to developing Windows application software customized to the Chinese market. When the Russian PC market opened to IBM, Compaq, and Hewlett-Packard, local Russian PC maker Vist focused on assembling low-cost models, marketing them through exclusive distribution agreements with selected local retailers, and opening company-owned full-service centers in dozens of Russian cities. Vist focused on providing low-cost PCs, giving lengthy warranties, and catering to buyers who felt the need for local service and support. Vist's strategy allowed it to remain the market leader, with a 20 percent share.

An India-based electronics company has been able to carve out a market niche for itself by developing an all-in-one business machine designed especially for India's 1.2 million small shopkeepers that tolerates heat, dust, and power outages and that sells for a modest $180 for the smallest of its three models.[36]

Contending on a Global Level   If a local company in an emerging market has transferable resources and capabilities, it can sometimes launch successful initiatives to meet the pressures for globalization head-on and start to compete on a global level itself.[37] Lenovo, China's biggest PC maker, recently purchased IBM's PC business, moved its headquarters to New York City, put the Lenovo brand on IBM's PCs, and launched initiative to become a global PC maker alongside leaders Dell and Hewlett-Packard. When General Motors (GM) decided to outsource the production of radiator caps for all of its North American vehicles, Sundaram Fasteners of India pursued the opportunity; it purchased one of GM's radiator cap production lines, moved it to India, and became GM's sole supplier of radiator caps in North America—at 5 million units a year. As a participant in GM's supplier network, Sundaram learned about emerging technical standards, built its capabilities, and became one of the first Indian companies to achieve QS 9000 certification, a quality standard that GM now requires for all suppliers. Sundaram's acquired expertise in quality standards enabled it then to pursue opportunities to supply automotive parts in Japan and Europe. Chinese communications equipment maker Huawei has captured a 16 percent share in the global market for Internet routers because its prices are up to 50 percent lower than those of industry leaders like Cisco Systems; Huawei's success in low-priced Internet networking gear has allowed it to expand aggressively outside China, into such country markets as Russia and Brazil, and achieve the number two worldwide market share in broadband networking gear.[38] In 2005 Chinese automakers were laying plans to begin exporting fuel-efficient small cars to the United States and begin the long-term process of competing internationally against the world's leading automakers.

Key Points

Most issues in competitive strategy that apply to domestic companies apply also to companies that compete internationally. But there are four strategic issues unique to competing across national boundaries:

1. Whether to customize the company's offerings in each different country market to match the tastes and preferences of local buyers or offer a mostly standardized product worldwide.

2. Whether to employ essentially the same basic competitive strategy in all countries or modify the strategy country by country to fit the specific market conditions and competitive circumstances it encounters.

3. Where to locate the company's production facilities, distribution centers, and customer service operations so as to realize the greatest locational advantages.

4. Whether and how to efficiently transfer the company's resource strengths and capabilities from one country to another in an effort to secure competitive advantage.

Multicountry competition refers to situations where competition in one national market is largely independent of competition in another national market—there is no "international market," just a collection of self-contained country (or maybe regional) markets. Global competition exists when competitive conditions across national markets are linked strongly enough to form a true world market and when leading competitors compete head-to-head in many different countries.

In posturing to compete in foreign markets, a company has three basic options: (1) a think-local, act-local approach to crafting a strategy, (2) a think-global, act-global approach to crafting a strategy, and (3) a combination think-global, act-local approach. A think-local, act-local, or multicountry, strategy is appropriate for industries where multicountry competition dominates; a localized approach to strategy making calls for a company to vary its product offering and competitive approach from country to country in order to accommodate differing buyer preferences and market conditions. A think-global, act-global approach (or global strategy) works best in markets that are globally competitive or beginning to globalize; global strategies involve employing the same basic competitive approach (low-cost, differentiation, best-cost, focused) in all country markets and marketing essentially the same products under the same brand names in all countries where the company operates. A think-global, act-local approach can be used when it is feasible for a company to employ essentially the same basic competitive strategy in all markets but still customize its product offering and some aspect of its operations to fit local market circumstances.

Other strategy options for competing in world markets include maintaining a national (one-country) production base and exporting goods to foreign markets, licensing foreign firms to use the company's technology or produce and distribute the company's products, employing a franchising strategy, and using strategic alliances or other collaborative partnerships to enter a foreign market or strengthen a firm's competitiveness in world markets.

Strategic alliances with foreign partners have appeal from several angles: gaining wider access to attractive country markets, allowing capture of economies of scale in production and/or marketing, filling gaps in technical expertise and/or knowledge of local markets, saving on costs by sharing distribution facilities and dealer networks, helping gain agreement on important technical standards, and helping combat the impact of alliances that rivals have formed. Cross-border strategic alliances are fast reshaping competition in world markets, pitting one group of allied global companies against other groups of allied global companies.

There are three ways in which a firm can gain competitive advantage (or offset domestic disadvantages) in global markets. One way involves locating various value chain activities among nations in a manner that lowers costs or achieves greater product differentiation. A second way involves efficient and effective transfer of competitively valuable competencies and capabilities from its domestic markets to foreign markets. A third way draws on a multinational or global competitor's ability to deepen or broaden its resource strengths and capabilities and to coordinate its dispersed activities in ways that a domestic-only competitor cannot.

Profit sanctuaries are country markets in which a company derives substantial profits because of its strong or protected market position. They are valuable competitive assets. A company with multiple profit sanctuaries has the financial strength to support competitive offensives in one market with resources and profits diverted from its operations in other markets—a practice called *cross-market subsidization*. The ability of companies with multiple profit sanctuaries to employ cross-subsidization gives them a powerful offensive weapon and a competitive advantage over companies with a single sanctuary.

Companies racing for global leadership have to consider competing in emerging markets like China, India, Brazil, Indonesia, and Mexico—countries where the business risks are considerable but the opportunities for growth are huge. To succeed in these markets, companies often have to (1) compete on the basis of low price, (2) be prepared to modify aspects of the company's business model to accommodate local circumstances (but not so much that the company loses the advantage of global scale and global branding), and/or (3) try to change the local market to better match the way the company does business elsewhere. Profitability is unlikely to come quickly or easily in emerging markets, typically because of the investments needed to alter buying habits and tastes and/or the need for infrastructure upgrades. And there may be times when a company should simply stay away from certain emerging markets until conditions for entry are better suited to its business model and strategy.

Local companies in emerging country markets can seek to compete against multinational companies by (1) defending on the basis of home-field advantages, (2) transferring their expertise to cross-border markets, (3) dodging large rivals by shifting to a new business model or market niche, or (4) launching initiatives to compete on a global level themselves.

Exercises

1. Go to Caterpillar's Web site (www.caterpillar.com) and search for information about the company's strategy in foreign markets. Is Caterpillar pursuing a global strategy or a localized multicountry strategy? Support your answer.

2. Assume you are in charge of developing the strategy for a multinational company selling products in some 50 different countries around the world. One of the issues you face is whether to employ a multicountry strategy or a global strategy.

    a. If your company's product is personal computers, do you think it would make better strategic sense to employ a multicountry strategy or a global strategy? Why?

    b. If your company's product is dry soup mixes and canned soups, would a multicountry strategy seem to be more advisable than a global strategy? Why?

    c. If your company's product is washing machines, would it seem to make more sense to pursue a multicountry strategy or a global strategy? Why?

    d. If your company's product is basic work tools (hammers, screwdrivers, pliers, wrenches, saws), would a multicountry strategy or a global strategy seem to have more appeal? Why?

3. The Hero Group is among the 10 largest corporations in India, with 19 business segments and annual revenues of $2.75 billion in fiscal 2004–2005. Many of the corporation's business units have used strategic alliances with foreign partners to compete in new product and geographic markets. Review the company's statements concerning its alliances and international business operations at www.herogroup.com and prepare a two-page report that outlines Hero's successful use of international strategic alliances.

4. Using this chapter's discussion of strategies for local companies competing against global rivals and Figure 7.4, develop a strategic approach for a manufacturer or service company in your community that might be forced to compete with a global firm. How might the local company exploit a home-field advantage? Would it make sense for the local company to attempt to transfer its capabilities or expertise to cross-border markets? Or change its business model or market niche? Or join the fight on a global level? Explain.

Tailoring Strategy to Fit Specific Industry and Company Situations

Strategy is all about combining choices of what to do and what not to do into a system that creates the requisite fit between what the environment needs and what the company does.

—Costas Markides

Competing in the marketplace is like war. You have injuries and casualties, and the best strategy wins.

—John Collins

It is much better to make your own products obsolete than allow a competitor to do it.

—Michael A. Cusamano and Richard W. Selby

In a turbulent age, the only dependable advantage is reinventing your business model before circumstances force you to.

—Gary Hamel and Liisa Välikangas

Prior chapters have emphasized the analysis and options that go into matching a company's choice of strategy to (1) industry and competitive conditions and (2) its own resource strengths and weaknesses, competitive capabilities, opportunities and threats, and market position. But there's more to be revealed about the hows of matching the choices of strategy to a company's circumstances. This chapter looks at the strategy-making task in 10 commonly encountered situations:

1. Companies competing in emerging industries.

2. Companies competing in rapidly growing markets.

3. Companies competing in maturing industries.

4. Companies competing in stagnant or declining industries.

5. Companies competing in turbulent, high-velocity markets.

6. Companies competing in fragmented industries.

7. Companies striving to sustain rapid growth.

8. Companies in industry leadership positions.

9. Companies in runner-up positions.

10. Companies in competitively weak positions or plagued by crisis conditions.

We selected these situations to shed still more light on the factors that managers need to consider in tailoring a company's strategy. When you finish this chapter, you will have a stronger grasp of the factors that managers have to weigh in choosing a strategy and what the pros and cons are for some of the heretofore unexplored strategic options that are open to a company.

STRATEGIES FOR COMPETING IN EMERGING INDUSTRIES

An emerging industry is one in the formative stage. Examples include Voice over Internet Protocol (VoIP) telephone communications, high-definition TV, assisted living for the elderly, online education, organic food products, e-book publishing, and electronic banking. Many companies striving to establish a strong foothold in an emerging industry are start-up enterprises busily engaged in perfecting technology, gearing up operations, and trying to broaden distribution and gain buyer acceptance. Important product design issues or technological problems may still have to be worked out. The business models and strategies of companies in an emerging industry are unproved—they may look promising but may or may not ever result in attractive profitability.

The Unique Characteristics of an Emerging Industry

Competing in emerging industries presents managers with some unique strategy-making challenges:[1]

- Because the market is in its infancy, there's usually much speculation about how it will function, how fast it will grow, and how big it will get. The little historical information available is virtually useless in making sales and profit projections. There's lots of guesswork about how rapidly buyers will be attracted and how much they will be willing to pay. For example, there is much uncertainty about how many users of traditional telephone service will be inclined to switch over to VoIP telephone technology and how rapidly any such switchovers will occur.

- In many cases, much of the technological know-how underlying the products of emerging industries is proprietary and closely guarded, having been developed in-house by pioneering firms. In such cases, patents and unique technical expertise are key factors in securing competitive advantage. In other cases, numerous companies have access to the requisite technology and may be racing to perfect it, often in collaboration with others. In still other instances, there can be competing technological approaches, with much uncertainty over whether multiple technologies will end up competing alongside one another or whether one approach will ultimately win out because of lower costs or better performance—such a battle is currently under way in the emerging market for gasoline-electric hybrid engines (where demand is mushrooming because of greater fuel efficiency without a loss of power and acceleration). Toyota has pioneered one design; an alliance among General Motors, DaimlerChrysler, and BMW is pursuing another design; a Volkswagen-Porsche alliance is looking at a third technological approach; and Ford and Honda have their own slightly different hybrid engine designs.

- Just as there may be uncertainties surrounding an emerging industry's technology, there may also be no consensus regarding which product attributes will prove decisive in winning buyer favor. Rivalry therefore centers on each firm's efforts to get the market to ratify its own strategic approach to technology, product design, marketing, and distribution. Such rivalry can result in wide differences in product quality and performance from brand to brand.

- Since in an emerging industry all buyers are first-time users, the marketing task is to induce initial purchase and to overcome customer concerns about product features, performance reliability, and conflicting claims of rival firms.

- Many potential buyers expect first-generation products to be rapidly improved, so they delay purchase until technology and product design mature and second- or third-generation products appear on the market.

- Entry barriers tend to be relatively low, even for entrepreneurial start-up companies. Large, well-known, opportunity-seeking companies with ample resources and competitive capabilities are likely to enter if the industry has promise for explosive growth or if its emergence threatens their present business. For instance, many traditional local telephone companies, seeing the potent threat of wireless communications technology and VoIP, have opted to enter the mobile communications business and begin offering landline customers a VoIP option.

- Strong experience/learning curve effects may be present, allowing significant price reductions as volume builds and costs fall.
- Sometimes firms have trouble securing ample supplies of raw materials and components (until suppliers gear up to meet the industry's needs).
- Undercapitalized companies, finding themselves short of funds to support needed R&D and get through several lean years until the product catches on, end up merging with competitors or being acquired by financially strong outsiders looking to invest in a growth market.

Strategy Options for Emerging Industries

The lack of established rules of the game in an emerging industry gives industry participants considerable freedom to experiment with a variety of different strategic approaches. Competitive strategies keyed either to low cost or differentiation are usually viable. Focusing makes good sense when resources and capabilities are limited and the industry has too many technological frontiers or too many buyer segments to pursue at once. Broad or focused differentiation strategies keyed to technological or product superiority typically offer the best chance for early competitive advantage.

> **Core Concept**
> Companies in an emerging industry have wide latitude in experimenting with different strategic approaches.

In addition to choosing a competitive strategy, companies in an emerging industry usually have to fashion a strategy containing one or more of the following actions:[2]

1. Push to perfect the technology, improve product quality, and develop additional attractive performance features. Out-innovating the competition is often one of the best avenues to industry leadership.

2. Consider merging with or acquiring another firm to gain added expertise and pool resource strengths.

3. As technological uncertainty clears and a dominant technology emerges, try to capture any first-mover advantages by adopting it quickly. However, while there's merit in trying to be the industry standard-bearer on technology and to pioneer the dominant product design, firms have to beware of betting too heavily on their own preferred technological approach or product design—especially when there are many competing technologies, R&D is costly, and technological developments can quickly move in surprising new directions.

4. Acquire or form alliances with companies that have related or complementary technological expertise as a means of helping outcompete rivals on the basis of technological superiority.

5. Pursue new customer groups, new user applications, and entry into new geographical areas (perhaps using strategic partnerships or joint ventures if financial resources are constrained).

6. Make it easy and cheap for first-time buyers to try the industry's first-generation product.

7. As the product becomes familiar to a wide portion of the market, shift the advertising emphasis from creating product awareness to increasing frequency of use and building brand loyalty.

8. Use price cuts to attract the next layer of price-sensitive buyers into the market.

9. Form strategic alliances with key suppliers whenever effective supply chain management provides important access to specialized skills, technological capabilities, and critical materials or components.

Young companies in emerging industries face four strategic hurdles: (1) raising the capital to finance initial operations until sales and revenues take off, profits appear, and cash flows turn positive; (2) developing a strategy to ride the wave of industry growth (what market segments and competitive advantages to go after?); (3) managing the rapid expansion of facilities and sales in a manner that positions them to contend for industry leadership; and (4) defending against competitors trying to horn in on their success.[3] Up-and-coming companies can help their cause by selecting knowledgeable members for their boards of directors and by hiring entrepreneurial managers with experience in guiding young businesses through the start-up and takeoff stages. *A firm that develops solid resource capabilities, an appealing business model, and a good strategy has a golden opportunity to shape the rules and establish itself as the recognized industry front-runner.*

But strategic efforts to win the early race for growth and market share leadership in an emerging industry have to be balanced against the longer-range need to build a durable competitive edge and a defendable market position.[4] The initial front-runners in a fast-growing emerging industry that shows signs of good profitability will almost certainly have to defend their positions against ambitious challengers striving to overtake the current market leaders. Well-financed outsiders can be counted on to enter with aggressive offensive strategies once industry sales take off, the perceived risk of investing in the industry lessens, and the success of current industry members becomes apparent. Sometimes a rush of new entrants, attracted by the growth and profit potential, overcrowds the market and forces industry consolidation to a smaller number of players. Resource-rich latecomers, aspiring to industry leadership, may become major players by acquiring and merging the operations of weaker competitors and then using their own perhaps considerable brand name recognition to draw customers and build market share. Hence, the strategies of the early leaders must be aimed at competing for the long haul and making a point of developing the resources, capabilities, and market recognition needed to sustain early successes and stave off competition from capable, ambitious newcomers.

STRATEGIES FOR COMPETING IN RAPIDLY GROWING MARKETS

Companies that have the good fortune to be in an industry growing at double-digit rates have a golden opportunity to achieve double-digit revenues and profit growth.

In a fast-growing market, a company needs a strategy predicated on growing faster than the market average, so that it can boost its market share and improve its competitive standing vis-à-vis rivals.

If market demand is expanding 20 percent annually, a company can grow 20 percent annually simply by doing little more than contentedly riding the tide of market growth—it has to simply be aggressive enough to secure enough new customers to realize a 20 percent gain in sales, not a particularly impressive strategic feat. What is more interesting, however, is to craft a strategy that enables sales to grow at 25 or 30 percent when the overall market is growing by 20 percent, such that the company's market share and competitive position improve relative to rivals, on average. Should a company's strategy only deliver sales growth of 12 percent in a market growing at

20 percent, then it is actually losing ground in the marketplace—a condition that signals a weak strategy and an unappealing product offering. The point here is that, in a rapidly growing market, a company must aim its strategy at producing gains in revenue that exceed the market average; otherwise, the best it can hope for is to maintain its market standing (if it is able to boost sales at a rate equal to the market average) and its market standing may indeed erode if its sales rise by less than the market average.

To be able to grow at a pace exceeding the market average, a company generally must have a strategy that incorporates one or more of the following elements:

- *Driving down costs per unit so as to enable price reductions that attract droves of new customers.* Charging a lower price always has strong appeal in markets where customers are price-sensitive, and lower prices can help push up buyers demand by drawing new customers into the marketplace. But since rivals can lower their prices also, a company must really be able to drive its unit costs down *faster than rivals*, such that it can use its low-cost advantage to underprice rivals. The makers of liquid crystal display (LCD) and high-definition TVs are aggressively pursuing cost reduction to bring the prices of their TV sets down under $1,000 and thus make their products more affordable to more consumers.

- *Pursuing rapid product innovation, both to set a company's product offering apart from rivals and to incorporate attributes that appeal to growing numbers of customers.* Differentiation strategies, when keyed to product attributes that draw in large numbers of new customers, help bolster a company's reputation for product superiority and lay the foundation for sales gains in excess of the overall rate of market growth. If the market is one where technology is advancing rapidly and product life cycles are short, then it becomes especially important to be first-to-market with next-generation products. But product innovation strategies require competencies in R&D and new product development and design, plus organizational agility in getting new and improved products to market quickly. At the same time they are pursuing cost reductions, the makers of LCD and high-definition TVs are pursuing all sorts of product improvements to enhance product quality and performance and boost screen sizes, so as to match or beat the picture quality and reliability of conventional TVs (with old-fashioned cathode-ray tubes) and drive up sales at an even faster clip.

- *Gaining access to additional distribution channels and sales outlets.* Pursuing wider distribution access so as to reach more potential buyers is a particularly good strategic approach for realizing above-average sales gains. But usually this requires a company to be a first-mover in positioning itself in new distribution channels and forcing rivals into playing catch-up.

- *Expanding the company's geographic coverage.* Expanding into areas, either domestic or foreign, where the company does not have a market presence can also be an effective way to reach more potential buyers and pave the way for gains in sales that outpace the overall market average.

- *Expanding the product line to add models/styles that appeal to a wider range of buyers.* Offering buyers a wider selection can be an effective way to draw new customers in numbers sufficient to realize above-average sales gains. Makers of MP3 players and cell phones are adding new models to stimulate buyer demand; Starbucks is adding new drinks and other menu selections to build store traffic; and marketers of VoIP technology are rapidly introducing a wider variety of plans to broaden their appeal to customers with different calling habits and needs.

STRATEGIES FOR COMPETING IN MATURING INDUSTRIES

A *maturing industry* is one that is moving from rapid growth to significantly slower growth. An industry is said to be *mature* when nearly all potential buyers are already users of the industry's products and growth in market demand closely parallels that of the population and the economy as a whole. In a mature market, demand consists mainly of replacement sales to existing users, with growth hinging on the industry's abilities to attract the few remaining new buyers and to convince existing buyers to up their usage. Consumer goods industries that are mature typically have a growth rate under 5 percent—roughly equal to the growth of the customer base or economy as a whole.

How Slowing Growth Alters Market Conditions

An industry's transition to maturity does not begin on an easily predicted schedule. Industry maturity can be forestalled by the emergence of new technological advances, product innovations, or other driving forces that keep rejuvenating market demand. Nonetheless, when growth rates do slacken, the onset of market maturity usually produces fundamental changes in the industry's competitive environment:[5]

1. *Slowing growth in buyer demand generates more head-to-head competition for market share.* Firms that want to continue on a rapid-growth track start looking for ways to take customers away from competitors. Outbreaks of price cutting, increased advertising, and other aggressive tactics to gain market share are common.

2. *Buyers become more sophisticated, often driving a harder bargain on repeat purchases.* Since buyers have experience with the product and are familiar with competing brands, they are better able to evaluate different brands and can use their knowledge to negotiate a better deal with sellers.

3. *Competition often produces a greater emphasis on cost and service.* As sellers all begin to offer the product attributes buyers prefer, buyer choices increasingly depend on which seller offers the best combination of price and service.

4. *Firms have a "topping-out" problem in adding new facilities.* Reduced rates of industry growth mean slowdowns in capacity expansion for manufacturers—adding too much plant capacity at a time when growth is slowing can create oversupply conditions that adversely affect manufacturers' profits well into the future. Likewise, retail chains that specialize in the industry's product have to cut back on the number of new stores being opened to keep from saturating localities with too many stores.

5. *Product innovation and new end-use applications are harder to come by.* Producers find it increasingly difficult to create new product features, find further uses for the product, and sustain buyer excitement.

6. *International competition increases.* Growth-minded domestic firms start to seek out sales opportunities in foreign markets. Some companies, looking for ways to cut costs, relocate plants to countries with lower wage rates. Greater product standardization and diffusion of technological know-how reduce entry barriers and make it possible for enterprising foreign companies to become serious market contenders in more countries. Industry leadership passes to companies that succeed in building strong competitive positions in most of the world's major geographic markets and in winning the biggest global market shares.

7. *Industry profitability falls temporarily or permanently.* Slower growth, increased competition, more sophisticated buyers, and occasional periods of overcapacity put pressure on industry profit margins. Weaker, less-efficient firms are usually the hardest hit.

8. *Stiffening competition induces a number of mergers and acquisitions among former competitors, driving industry consolidation to a smaller number of larger players.* Inefficient firms and firms with weak competitive strategies can achieve respectable results in a fast-growing industry with booming sales. But the intensifying competition that accompanies industry maturity exposes competitive weakness and throws second- and third-tier competitors into a survival-of-the-fittest contest.

Strategies that Fit Conditions in Maturing Industries

As the new competitive character of industry maturity begins to hit full force, any of several strategic moves can strengthen a firm's competitive position: pruning the product line, improving value chain efficiency, trimming costs, increasing sales to present customers, acquiring rival firms, expanding internationally, and strengthening capabilities.[6]

Pruning Marginal Products and Models   A wide selection of models, features, and product options sometimes has competitive value during the growth stage, when buyers' needs are still evolving. But such variety can become too costly as price competition stiffens and profit margins are squeezed. Maintaining many product versions works against achieving design, parts inventory, and production economies at the manufacturing levels and can increase inventory stocking costs for distributors and retailers. In addition, the prices of slow-selling versions may not cover their true costs. Pruning marginal products from the line opens the door for cost savings and permits more concentration on items whose margins are highest and/or where a firm has a competitive advantage. General Motors has been cutting slow-selling models and brands from its lineup of offerings—it has eliminated the entire Oldsmobile division and is said to be looking at whether it can eliminate its Saab lineup. Textbook publishers are discontinuing publication of those books that sell only a few thousand copies annually (where profits are marginal at best) and instead focusing their resources on texts that generate sales of at least 5,000 copies per edition.

Improving Value Chain Efficiency   Efforts to reinvent the industry value chain can have a fourfold payoff: lower costs, better product or service quality, greater capability to turn out multiple or customized product versions, and shorter design-to-market cycles. Manufacturers can mechanize high-cost activities, redesign production lines to improve labor efficiency, build flexibility into the assembly process so that customized product versions can be easily produced, and increase use of advanced technology (robotics, computerized controls, and automated assembly). Suppliers of parts and components, manufacturers, and distributors can collaboratively deploy online systems and product coding techniques to streamline activities and achieve cost savings all along the value chain—from supplier-related activities all the way through distribution, retailing, and customer service.

Trimming Costs   Stiffening price competition gives firms extra incentive to drive down unit costs. Company cost-reduction initiatives can cover a broad front. Some of the most frequently pursued options are pushing suppliers for better prices, implementing tighter supply chain management practices, cutting low-value activities out of the value chain, developing more economical product designs, reengineering internal processes using e-commerce technology, and shifting to more economical distribution arrangements.

Increasing Sales to Present Customers   In a mature market, growing by taking customers away from rivals may not be as appealing as expanding sales to existing customers. Strategies to increase purchases by existing customers can involve adding more sales promotions, providing complementary items and ancillary services, and finding more ways for customers to use the product. Convenience stores, for example, have boosted average sales per customer by adding video rentals, automated teller machines, gasoline pumps, and deli counters.

Acquiring Rival Firms at Bargain Prices   Sometimes a firm can acquire the facilities and assets of struggling rivals quite cheaply. Bargain-priced acquisitions can help create a low-cost position if they also present opportunities for greater operating efficiency. In addition, an acquired firm's customer base can provide expanded market coverage and opportunities for greater scale economies. The most desirable acquisitions are those that will significantly enhance the acquiring firm's competitive strength.

Expanding Internationally   As its domestic market matures, a firm may seek to enter foreign markets where attractive growth potential still exists and competitive pressures are not so strong. Many multinational companies are expanding into such emerging markets as China, India, Brazil, Argentina, and the Philippines, where the long-term growth prospects are quite attractive. Strategies to expand internationally also make sense when a domestic firm's skills, reputation, and product are readily transferable to foreign markets. For example, even though the U.S. market for soft drinks is mature, Coca-Cola has remained a growth company by upping its efforts to penetrate emerging markets where soft-drink sales are expanding rapidly.

Building New or More Flexible Capabilities   The stiffening pressures of competition in a maturing or already mature market can often be combated by strengthening the company's resource base and competitive capabilities. This can mean adding new competencies or capabilities, deepening existing competencies to make them harder to imitate, or striving to make core competencies more adaptable to changing customer requirements and expectations. Microsoft has responded to challenges by such competitors as Google and Linux by expanding its competencies in search engine software and revamping its entire approach to programming next-generation operating systems. Chevron has developed a best-practices discovery team and a best-practices resource map to enhance the speed and effectiveness with which it is able to transfer efficiency improvements from one oil refinery to another.

Strategic Pitfalls in Maturing Industries

Perhaps the biggest strategic mistake a company can make as an industry matures is steering a middle course between low cost, differentiation, and focusing—blending efforts to achieve low cost with efforts to incorporate differentiating features and efforts to focus on a limited target market. Such strategic compromises typically leave the firm *stuck in the middle* with a fuzzy strategy, too little commitment to winning a competitive advantage, an average image with buyers, and little chance of springing into the ranks of the industry leaders.

Other strategic pitfalls include being slow to mount a defense against stiffening competitive pressures, concentrating more on protecting short-term profitability than on building or maintaining long-term competitive position, waiting too long to respond to price cutting by rivals, overexpanding in the face of slowing growth, overspending on advertising and sales promotion efforts in a losing effort to combat the growth slow-down, and failing to pursue cost reduction soon enough or aggressively enough.

STRATEGIES FOR COMPETING IN STAGNANT OR DECLINING INDUSTRIES

Many firms operate in industries where demand is growing more slowly than the economy-wide average or is even declining. The demand for an industry's product can decline for any of several reasons: (1) advancing technology gives rise to better-performing substitute products (slim LCD monitors displace bulky CRT monitors; DVD players replace VCRs; wrinkle-free fabrics replace the need for laundry/dry-cleaning services) or lower costs (cheaper synthetics replace expensive leather); (2) the customer group shrinks (baby foods are in less demand when birthrates fall); (3) changing lifestyles and buyer tastes (cigarette smoking and wearing dress hats go out of vogue); (4) the rising costs of complementary products (higher gasoline prices drive down purchases of gas-guzzling vehicles).[7] The most attractive declining industries are those in which sales are eroding only slowly, there are pockets of stable or even growing demand, and some market niches present good profit opportunities. But in some stagnant or declining industries, decaying buyer demand precipitates a desperate competitive battle among industry members for the available business, replete with price discounting, costly sales promotions, growing amounts of idle plant capacity, and fast-eroding profit margins. It matters greatly whether buyer demand falls gradually or sharply and whether competition proves to be fierce or moderate.

Businesses competing in stagnant or declining industries have to make a fundamental strategic choice—whether to remain committed to the industry for the long term despite the industry's dim prospects or whether to pursue an end-game strategy to withdraw gradually or quickly from the market. Deciding to stick with the industry despite eroding market demand can have considerable merit. Stagnant demand by itself is not enough to make an industry unattractive. Market demand may be decaying slowly. Some segments of the market may still present good profit opportunities. Cash flows from operations may still remain strongly positive. Strong competitors may well be able to grow and boost profits by taking market share from weaker competitors.[8] Furthermore, the acquisition or exit of weaker firms creates opportunities for the remaining companies to capture greater market share. On the one hand, striving to become the market leader and be one of the few remaining companies in a declining industry can lead to above-average profitability even though overall market demand is stagnant or eroding. On the other hand, if the market environment of a declining industry is characterized by bitter warfare for customers and lots of overcapacity, such that companies are plagued with heavy operating losses, then an early exit makes much more strategic sense.

If a company decides to stick with a declining industry—because top management is encouraged by the remaining opportunities or sees merit in striving for market share

> It is erroneous to assume that companies in a declining industry are doomed to having declining revenues and profits.

leadership (or even just being one of the few remaining companies in the industry), then its three best strategic alternatives are usually the following:[9]

1. *Pursue a focused strategy aimed at the fastest-growing or slowest-decaying market segments within the industry.* Stagnant or declining markets, like other markets, are composed of numerous segments or niches. Frequently, one or more of these segments is growing rapidly (or at least decaying much more slowly), despite stagnation in the industry as a whole. An astute competitor who zeros in on fast-growing segments and does a first-rate job of meeting the needs of buyers comprising these segments can often escape stagnating sales and profits and even gain decided competitive advantage. For instance, both Ben & Jerry's and Häagen-Dazs have achieved success by focusing on the growing luxury or superpremium segment of the otherwise stagnant market for ice cream; revenue growth and profit margins are substantially higher for high-end ice creams sold in supermarkets and in scoop shops than is the case in other segments of the ice cream market. Companies that focus on the one or two most attractive market segments in a declining business may well decide to ignore the other segments altogether—withdrawing from them entirely or at least gradually or rapidly disinvesting in them. But the key is to *move aggressively* to establish a strong position in the most attractive parts of the stagnant or declining industry.

2. *Stress differentiation based on quality improvement and product innovation.* Either enhanced quality or innovation can rejuvenate demand by creating important new growth segments or inducing buyers to trade up. Successful product innovation opens up an avenue for competing that bypasses meeting or beating rivals' prices. Differentiation based on successful innovation has the additional advantage of being difficult and expensive for rival firms to imitate. New Covent Garden Soup has met with success by introducing packaged fresh soups for sale in major supermarkets, where the typical soup offerings are canned or dry mixes. Procter & Gamble has rejuvenated sales of its toothbrushes with its new line of Crest battery-powered spin toothbrushes, and it has revitalized interest in tooth care products with a series of product innovations related to teeth whitening. Bread makers are fighting declining sales of white breads that use bleached flour by introducing all kinds of whole-grain breads (which have far more nutritional value).

3. *Strive to drive costs down and become the industry's low-cost leader.* Companies in stagnant industries can improve profit margins and return on investment by pursuing innovative cost reduction year after year. Potential cost-saving actions include (*a*) cutting marginally beneficial activities out of the value chain; (*b*) outsourcing functions and activities that can be performed more cheaply by outsiders; (*c*) redesigning internal business processes to exploit cost-reducing e-commerce technologies; (*d*) consolidating underutilized production facilities; (*e*) adding more distribution channels to ensure the unit volume needed for low-cost production; (*f*) closing low-volume, high-cost retail outlets; and (*g*) pruning marginal products from the firm's offerings. Japan-based Asahi Glass (a low-cost producer of flat glass), PotashCorp and IMC Global (two low-cost leaders in potash production), Alcan Aluminum, Nucor Steel, and Safety Components International (a low-cost producer of air bags for motor vehicles) have all been successful in driving costs down in competitively tough and largely stagnant industry environments.

These three strategic themes are not mutually exclusive.[10] Introducing innovative versions of a product can create a fast-growing market segment. Similarly, relentless pursuit of greater operating efficiencies permits price reductions that create price-conscious growth segments. Note that all three themes are spinoffs of the five generic competitive strategies, adjusted to fit the circumstances of a tough industry environment.

End-Game Strategies for Declining Industries

An *end-game strategy* can take either of two paths: (1) a *slow-exit strategy* that involves a gradual phasing down of operations coupled with an objective of getting the most cash flow from the business even if it means sacrificing market position or profitability and (2) a *fast-exit* or *sell-out-quickly strategy* to disengage from the industry during the early stages of the decline and recover as much of the company's investment as possible for deployment elsewhere.[11]

A Slow-Exit Strategy   With a slow-exit strategy, *the key objective is to generate the greatest possible harvest of cash from the business for as long as possible.* Management either eliminates or severely curtails new investment in the business. Capital expenditures for new equipment are put on hold or given low financial priority (unless replacement needs are unusually urgent); instead, efforts are made to stretch the life of existing equipment and make do with present facilities as long as possible. Old plants with high costs may be retired from service. The operating budget is chopped to a rock-bottom level. Promotional expenses may be cut gradually, quality reduced in not-so-visible ways, nonessential customer services curtailed, and maintenance of facilities held to a bare minimum. The resulting increases in cash flow (and perhaps even bottom-line profitability and return on investment) compensate for whatever declines in sales might be experienced. Withering buyer demand is tolerable if sizable amounts of cash can be reaped in the interim. If and when cash flows dwindle to meager levels as sales volumes decay, the business can be sold or, if no buyer can be found, closed down.

A Fast-Exit Strategy   The challenge of a sell-out-quickly strategy is to find a buyer willing to pay an agreeable price for the company's business assets. Buyers may be scarce since there's a tendency for investors to shy away from purchasing a stagnant or dying business. And even if willing buyers appear, they will be in a strong bargaining position once it's clear that the industry's prospects are permanently waning. How much prospective buyers will pay is usually a function of how rapidly they expect the industry to decline, whether they see opportunities to rejuvenate demand (at least temporarily), whether they believe that costs can be cut enough to still produce attractive profit margins or cash flows, whether there are pockets of stable demand where buyers are not especially price sensitive, and whether they believe that fading market demand will weaken competition (which could enhance profitability) or trigger strong competition for the remaining business (which could put pressure on profit margins). Thus, the expectations of prospective buyers will tend to drive the price they are willing to pay for the business assets of a company wanting to sell out quickly.

STRATEGIES FOR COMPETING IN TURBULENT, HIGH-VELOCITY MARKETS

Many companies operate in industries characterized by rapid technological change, short product life cycles, the entry of important new rivals, lots of competitive maneuvering by rivals, and fast-evolving customer requirements and expectations—all occurring in a manner that creates swirling market conditions. Since news of this or that important competitive development arrives daily, it is an imposing task just to monitor and assess developing events. High-velocity change is plainly the prevailing condition in computer/server hardware and software, video games, networking, wireless tele-communications, medical equipment, biotechnology, prescription drugs, and online retailing.

Ways to Cope with Rapid Change

The central strategy-making challenge in a turbulent market environment is managing change.[12] As illustrated in Figure 8.1, a company can assume any of three strategic postures in dealing with high-velocity change:[13]

- *It can react to change.* The company can respond to a rival's new product with a better product. It can counter an unexpected shift in buyer tastes and buyer demand by redesigning or repackaging its product, or shifting its advertising emphasis to different product attributes. Reacting is a defensive strategy and is therefore unlikely to create fresh opportunity, but it is nonetheless a necessary component in a company's arsenal of options.
- *It can anticipate change.* The company can make plans for dealing with the expected changes and follow its plans as changes occur (fine-tuning them as may be needed). Anticipation entails looking ahead to analyze what is likely to occur and then preparing and positioning for that future. It entails studying buyer behavior, buyer needs, and buyer expectations to get insight into how the market will evolve, then lining up the necessary production and distribution capabilities ahead of time. Like reacting to change, anticipating change is still fundamentally defensive in that forces outside the enterprise are in the driver's seat. Anticipation, however, can open up new opportunities and thus is a better way to manage change than just pure reaction.
- *It can lead change.* Leading change entails initiating the market and competitive forces that others must respond to—it is an offensive strategy aimed at putting a company in the driver's seat. Leading change means being first to market with an important new product or service. It means being the technological leader, rushing next-generation products to market ahead of rivals, and having products whose features and attributes shape customer preferences and expectations. It means proactively seeking to shape the rules of the game.

A sound way to deal with turbulent market conditions is to try to lead change with proactive strategic moves while at the same time trying to anticipate and prepare for upcoming changes and being quick to react to unexpected developments.

As a practical matter, a company's approach to managing change should, ideally, incorporate all three postures (though not in the same proportion). The best-performing companies in high-velocity markets consistently seek to lead change with proactive strategies that often entail the flexibility to pursue any of several strategic options, depending on how the market actually evolves. Even so, an environment of relentless change makes it incumbent on any company to anticipate and prepare for the future and to react quickly to unpredictable or uncontrollable new developments.

Strategy Options for Fast-Changing Markets

Competitive success in fast-changing markets tends to hinge on a company's ability to improvise, experiment, adapt, reinvent, and regenerate as market and competitive conditions shift rapidly and sometimes unpredictably.[14] It has to constantly reshape its

Figure 8.1 **Meeting the Challenge of High-Velocity Change**

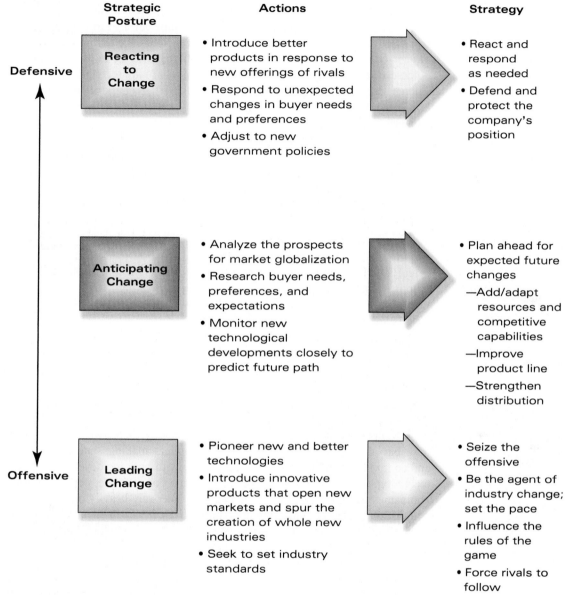

Source: Adapted from Shona L. Brown and Kathleen M. Eisenhardt, *Competing on the Edge: Strategy as Structured Chaos* (Boston, MA: Harvard Business School Press, 1998) p. 5.

strategy and its basis for competitive advantage. While the process of altering offensive and defensive moves every few months or weeks to keep the overall strategy closely matched to changing conditions is inefficient, the alternative—a fast-obsolescing strategy—is worse. The following five strategic moves seem to offer the best payoffs:

1. *Invest aggressively in R&D to stay on the leading edge of technological know-how.* Translating technological advances into innovative new products (and remaining close on the heels of whatever advances and features are pioneered by rivals) is a necessity in industries where technology is the primary driver of change. But it is often desirable to focus the R&D effort on a few critical areas, not only to avoid stretching the company's resources too thin but also to deepen the firm's expertise, master the technology, fully capture experience/learning curve effects, and become the dominant leader in a particular technology or product category.[15] When a fast-evolving market environment entails many technological areas and product categories, competitors have little choice but to employ some type of focus strategy and concentrate on being the leader in a particular product/technology category.

2. *Keep the company's products and services fresh and exciting enough to stand out in the midst of all the change that is taking place.* One of the risks of rapid change is that products and even companies can get lost in the shuffle. The marketing challenge here is to keep the firm's products and services in the limelight and, further, to keep them innovative and well matched to the changes that are occurring in the marketplace.

3. *Develop quick-response capability.* Because no company can predict all of the changes that will occur, it is crucial to have the organizational capability to be able to react quickly, improvising if necessary. This means shifting resources internally, adapting existing competencies and capabilities, creating new competencies and capabilities, and not falling far behind rivals. Companies that are habitual late-movers are destined to be industry also-rans.

4. *Rely on strategic partnerships with outside suppliers and with companies making tie-in products.* In many high-velocity industries, technology is branching off to create so many new technological paths and product categories that no company has the resources and competencies to pursue them all. Specialization (to promote the necessary technical depth) and focus (to preserve organizational agility and leverage the firm's expertise) are desirable strategies. Companies build their competitive position not just by strengthening their own internal resource base but also by partnering with those suppliers making state-of-the-art parts and components and by collaborating closely with both the developers of related technologies and the makers of tie-in products. For example, personal computer companies like Gateway, Dell, Compaq, and Acer rely heavily on the developers and manufacturers of chips, monitors, hard drives, DVD players, and software for innovative advances in PCs. None of the PC makers have done much in the way of integrating backward into parts and components because they have learned that the most effective way to provide PC users with a state-of-the-art product is to outsource the latest, most advanced components from technologically sophisticated suppliers who make it their business to stay on the cutting edge of their specialization and who can achieve economies of scale by mass-producing components for many PC assemblers. An outsourcing strategy also allows a company the flexibility to replace suppliers that fall behind on technology or product features or that cease to be competitive on price. The managerial challenge here is to strike a good balance between building a rich internal resource base that, on the one hand, keeps the firm from being at the mercy of its suppliers and allies and, on the other hand, maintains organizational agility by relying on the resources and expertise of capable (and perhaps best-in-world) outsiders.

5. *Initiate fresh actions every few months, not just when a competitive response is needed.* In some sense, change is partly triggered by the passage of time rather

than solely by the occurrence of events. A company can be proactive by making time-paced moves—introducing a new or improved product every four months, rather than when the market tapers off or a rival introduces a next-generation model.[16] Similarly, a company can expand into a new geographic market every six months rather than waiting for a new market opportunity to present itself; it can also refresh existing brands every two years rather than waiting until their popularity wanes. The keys to successfully using time pacing as a strategic weapon are choosing intervals that make sense internally and externally, establishing an internal organizational rhythm for change, and choreographing the transitions. 3M Corporation has long pursued an objective of having 25 percent of its revenues come from products less than four years old, a force that established the rhythm of change and created a relentless push for new products. Recently, the firm's CEO upped the tempo of change at 3M by increasing the goal from 25 to 30 percent.

Cutting-edge know-how and first-to-market capabilities are very valuable competitive assets in fast-evolving markets. Moreover, action-packed competition demands that a company have quick reaction times and flexible, adaptable resources—organizational agility is a huge competitive asset. Even so, companies will make mistakes and take some actions that do not work out well. When a company's strategy doesn't seem to be working well, it has to quickly regroup—probing, experimenting, improvising, and trying again and again until it finds something that strikes the right chord with buyers and that puts it in sync with market and competitive realities.

STRATEGIES FOR COMPETING IN FRAGMENTED INDUSTRIES

A number of industries are populated by hundreds, even thousands, of small and medium-sized companies, many privately held and none with a substantial share of total industry sales.[17] The standout competitive feature of a fragmented industry is the absence of market leaders with king-sized market shares or widespread buyer recognition. Examples of fragmented industries include book publishing, landscaping and plant nurseries, real estate development, convenience stores, banking, health and medical care, mail order catalog sales, computer software development, custom printing, kitchen cabinets, trucking, auto repair, restaurants and fast food, public accounting, apparel manufacture and apparel retailing, paperboard boxes, hotels and motels, and furniture.

Reasons for Supply-Side Fragmentation

Any of several reasons can account for why the supply side of an industry comprises hundreds or even thousands of companies:

- *The product or service is delivered at neighborhood locations so as to be conveniently accessible to local residents.* Retail and service businesses, for example, are inherently local—gas stations and car washes, pharmacies, dry-cleaning services, nursing homes, auto repair firms, furniture stores, flower shops, and lawn care enterprises. Whenever it takes thousands of locations to adequately serve the market, the way is opened for many enterprises to be engaged in providing products/services to local residents and businesses (and such enterprises can operate at just one location or at multiple locations).

- *Buyer preferences and requirements are so diverse that very large numbers of firms can easily coexist trying to accommodate differing buyer tastes, expectations, and pocketbooks.* This is true in the market for apparel, where there are thousands of apparel manufacturers making garments of various styles and price ranges. There's a host of different hotels and restaurants in places like New York City, London, Buenos Aires, Mexico City, and Tokyo. The software development industry is highly fragmented because there are so many types of software applications and because the needs and expectations of software users are so highly diverse—hence, there's ample market space for a software company to concentrate its attention on serving a particular market niche.

- *Low entry barriers allow small firms to enter quickly and cheaply.* Such tends to be the case in many areas of retailing, residential real estate, insurance sales, beauty shops, and the restaurant business.

- *An absence of scale economies permits small companies to compete on an equal cost footing with larger firms.* The markets for business forms, interior design, kitchen cabinets, and picture framing are fragmented because buyers require relatively small quantities of customized products; since demand for any particular product version is small, sales volumes are not adequate to support producing, distributing, or marketing on a scale that yields cost advantages to a large-scale firm. A locally owned pharmacy can be cost competitive with the pharmacy operations of large drugstore chains like Walgreen's or Rite Aid or CVS. Small trucking companies can be cost-competitive with companies that have huge truck fleets. A local pizzeria is not cost-disadvantaged in competing against such chains as Pizza Hut, Domino's, and Papa John's.

- *The scope of the geographic market for the industry's product or service is transitioning from national to global.* A broadening of geographic scope puts companies in more and more countries in the same competitive market arena (as in the apparel industry, where increasing numbers of garment makers across the world are shifting their production operations to low-wage countries and then shipping their goods to retailers in several countries).

- *The technologies embodied in the industry's value chain are exploding into so many new areas and along so many different paths that specialization is essential just to keep abreast in any one area of expertise.* Technology branching accounts for why the manufacture of electronic parts and components is fragmented and why there's fragmentation in prescription drug research.

- *The industry is young and crowded with aspiring contenders.* In most young industries, no firm has yet developed the resource base, competitive capabilities, and market recognition to command a significant market share (as in online e-tailing).

Competitive Conditions in a Fragmented Industry

Competitive rivalry in fragmented industries can vary from moderately strong to fierce. Low barriers tend to make entry of new competitors an ongoing threat. Competition from substitutes may or may not be a major factor. The relatively small size of companies in fragmented industries puts them in a relatively weak position to bargain with powerful suppliers and buyers, although sometimes they can become members of a cooperative formed for the purpose of using their combined leverage to negotiate better sales and purchase terms. In such an environment, the best a firm can expect is to cultivate a loyal customer base and grow a bit faster than the industry average.

Some fragmented industries consolidate over time as growth slows and the market matures. The stiffer competition that accompanies slower growth produces a shake-out of weak, inefficient firms and a greater concentration of larger, more visible sellers. Others remain atomistic because it is inherent in their businesses. And still others remain stuck in a fragmented state because existing firms lack the resources or ingenuity to employ a strategy powerful enough to drive industry consolidation.

Strategy Options for Competing in a Fragmented Industry

In fragmented industries, firms generally have the strategic freedom to pursue broad or narrow market targets and low-cost or differentiation-based competitive advantages. Many different strategic approaches can exist side by side (unless the industry's product is highly standardized or a commodity—like concrete blocks, sand and gravel, or paperboard boxes). Fragmented industry environments are usually ideal for focusing on a well-defined market niche—a particular geographic area or buyer group or product type. In an industry that is fragmented due to highly diverse buyer tastes or requirements, focusing usually offers more competitive advantage potential than trying to come up with a product offering that has broad market appeal.

Some of the most suitable strategy options for competing in a fragmented industry include:

- *Constructing and operating "formula" facilities*—This strategic approach is frequently employed in restaurant and retailing businesses operating at multiple locations. It involves constructing standardized outlets in favorable locations at minimum cost and then operating them cost-effectively. This is a favorite approach for locally owned fast-food enterprises and convenience stores that have multiple locations serving a geographically limited market area. Major fast-food chains like Yum! Brands—the parent of Pizza Hut, Taco Bell, KFC, Long John Silver's, and A&W restaurants—and big convenience store retailers like 7-Eleven have, of course, perfected the formula facilities strategy.

- *Becoming a low-cost operator*—When price competition is intense and profit margins are under constant pressure, companies can stress no-frills operations featuring low overhead, high-productivity/low-cost labor, lean capital budgets, and dedicated pursuit of total operating efficiency. Successful low-cost producers in a fragmented industry can play the price-discounting game and still earn profits above the industry average. Many e-tailers compete on the basis of bargain prices; so do budget motel chains like Econo Lodge, Super 8, and Days Inn.

- *Specializing by product type*—When a fragmented industry's products include a range of styles or services, a strategy to focus on one product or service category can be effective. Some firms in the furniture industry specialize in only one furniture type such as brass beds, rattan and wicker, lawn and garden, or Early American. In auto repair, companies specialize in transmission repair, body work, or speedy oil changes.

- *Specializing by customer type*—A firm can stake out a market niche in a fragmented industry by catering to those customers who are interested in low prices,

Illustration Capsule 8.1
Exertris's Focus Strategy in the Fragmented Exercise Equipment Industry

The exercise equipment industry is largely fragmented from a global perspective—there are hundreds of companies across the world making exercise and fitness products of one kind or another. The window of opportunity for employing a focus strategy is big. In 2001, three fitness enthusiasts in Great Britain came up with a novel way to make exercise more interesting. Their idea was to create an exercise bike equipped with a video game console, a flat-screen display, and an on-board PC that allowed users to play a video game while doing their workout.

After creating a prototype and forming a company called Exertris, the three fitness entrepreneurs approached a product design company for help in turning the prototype into a marketable product. The design company quickly determined that the task was not trivial and required significant additional product development. But the company was enthusiastic about the product and put up the capital to fund the venture as a minority partner. The partners set a goal of having six prototypes ready in time for a major leisure products trade show scheduled to be held in the United Kingdom in several months. The design company assumed responsibility for engineering the product, finding a contract manufacturer, and managing the supply chain; certain other specialty tasks were outsourced. The three cofounders concentrated on developing gaming software where the exerciser's pedaling performance had direct consequences for particular elements of the game; for example, the exerciser had to pedal harder to power a spaceship's weapon systems or move cards around in a game of Solitaire.

The Exertris bike won the "best new product" award at the trade show. It featured four games (Gems, Orbit, Solitaire, and Space Tripper), and new games and features could be added as they were released. Exercisers could play solo or competitively against other people, with the option of handicapping for multiplayer games. The recommended workout included an automatic warm-up and cool-down period. The bike had an armrest, a monitor, and a seat that optimized posture. The LCD display used the latest 3D graphics, and the on-board PC (positioned under the mounting step) used Microsoft Windows XP Embedded and was compatible with Polar heart rate monitors. Earphones were optional, and the game pad and menu control were sweat-proof and easy to clean.

Production by contract manufacturers started soon after the show. In the ensuing months, the Exertris bike was well received by gyms and fitness enthusiasts (for whom the addictive nature of video games broke the monotony and made exercise time fly by). The first interactive fitness arcade featuring 25 linked Exertris Interactive Bikes opened in Great Britain in April 2003. In 2005, the Exertris exercise bike was being marketed online in Great Britain at Amazon's Web site (www.amazon-leisure.co.uk) at a price of £675 (or about $1,150); it could also be purchased at Broadcast Vision Entertainment's online store. Exertris's strategy of focusing on this one niche product in exercise equipment was, however, producing unexpectedly weak results—sales were much slower than initially expected.

Sources: Information posted at www.betterproductdesign.com (accessed October 14, 2005), www.embedded-resources.com (accessed October 14, 2005), and www.broadcastvision.com (accessed December 31, 2005).

unique product attributes, customized features, carefree service, or other extras. A number of restaurants cater to take-out customers; others specialize in fine dining, and still others cater to the sports bar crowd. Bed-and-breakfast inns cater to a particular type of traveler/vacationer (and also focus on a very limited geographic area).

- *Focusing on a limited geographic area*—Even though a firm in a fragmented industry can't win a big share of total industrywide sales, it can still try to dominate a local or regional geographic area. Concentrating company efforts on a limited territory can produce greater operating efficiency, speed delivery and customer services, promote strong brand awareness, and permit saturation advertising, while avoiding the diseconomies of stretching operations out over a much wider area. Several locally owned banks, drugstores, and sporting goods retailers successfully operate multiple locations within a limited geographic area. Numerous local restaurant operators have pursued operating economies by opening anywhere from 4 to 10 restaurants (each with each its own distinctive theme and menu) scattered across a single metropolitan area like Atlanta or Denver or Houston.

Illustration Capsule 8.1 describes how a new start-up company in Great Britain has employed a product niche type of focus strategy in the fragmented exercise equipment industry.

STRATEGIES FOR SUSTAINING RAPID COMPANY GROWTH

Companies that strive to grow their revenues and earnings at double-digit rates year after year (or at rates exceeding the overall market average so that they are growing faster than rivals and gaining market share) generally have to craft *a portfolio of strategic initiatives* covering three horizons:[18]

- *Horizon 1: "Short-jump" strategic initiatives to fortify and extend the company's position in existing businesses*—Short-jump initiatives typically include adding new items to the company's present product line, expanding into new geographic areas where the company does not yet have a market presence, and launching offensives to take market share away from rivals. The objective is to capitalize fully on whatever growth potential exists in the company's present business arenas.

- *Horizon 2: "Medium-jump" strategic initiatives to leverage existing resources and capabilities by entering new businesses with promising growth potential*— Growth companies have to be alert for opportunities to jump into new businesses where there is promise of rapid growth and where their experience, intellectual capital, and technological know-how will prove valuable in gaining rapid market penetration. While Horizon 2 initiatives may take a back seat to Horizon 1 initiatives as long as there is plenty of untapped growth in the company's present businesses, they move to the front as the onset of market maturity dims the company's growth prospects in its present business(es).

- *Horizon 3: "Long-jump" strategic initiatives to plant the seeds for ventures in businesses that do not yet exist*—Long-jump initiatives can entail pumping funds into long-range R&D projects, setting up an internal venture capital fund to invest in promising start-up companies attempting to create the industries of the future, or acquiring a number of small start-up companies experimenting with technologies and product ideas that complement the company's present businesses. Intel, for example, set up a multibillion-dollar venture fund to invest in over 100 different projects and start-up companies, the intent being to plant seeds for Intel's future, broadening its base as a global leader in supplying building blocks for PCs and the worldwide Internet economy. Royal Dutch/ Shell, with over $140 billion in revenues and over 100,000 employees, spent over $20 million on rule-breaking, game-changing ideas put forth by free-thinking employees; the objective was to inject a new spirit of entrepreneurship into the company and sow the seeds of faster growth.[19]

Figure 8.2 **The Three Strategy Horizons for Sustaining Rapid Growth**

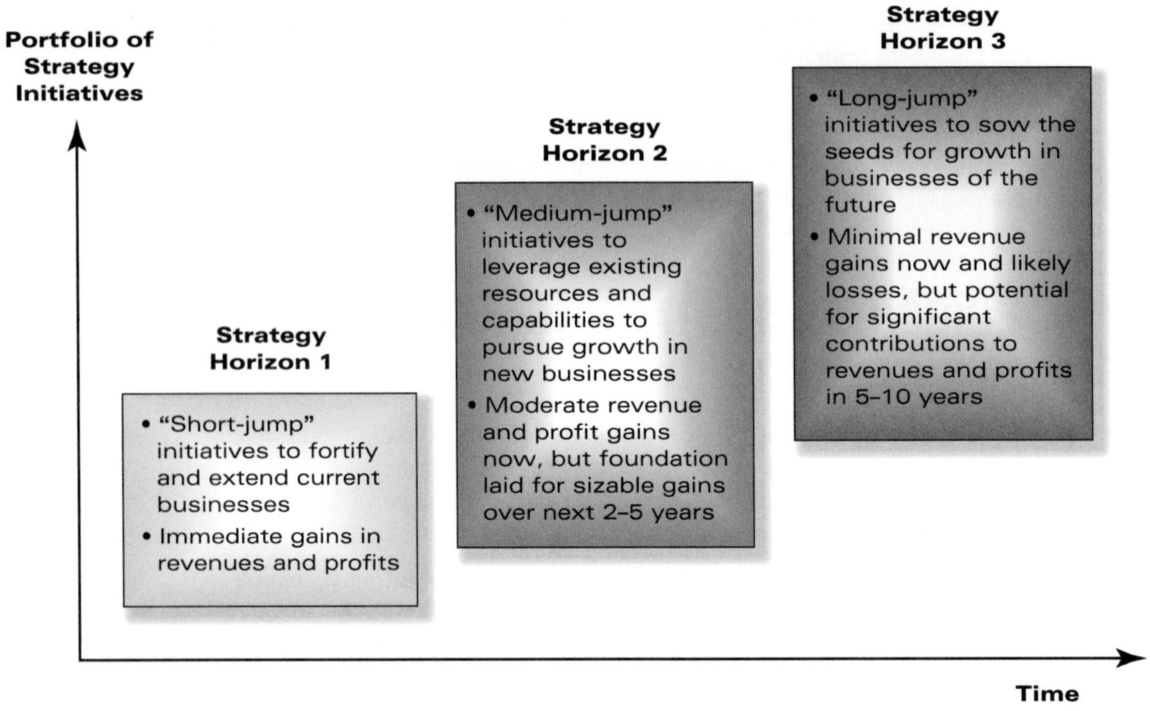

Portfolio of Strategy Initiatives

Strategy Horizon 1
- "Short-jump" initiatives to fortify and extend current businesses
- Immediate gains in revenues and profits

Strategy Horizon 2
- "Medium-jump" initiatives to leverage existing resources and capabilities to pursue growth in new businesses
- Moderate revenue and profit gains now, but foundation laid for sizable gains over next 2–5 years

Strategy Horizon 3
- "Long-jump" initiatives to sow the seeds for growth in businesses of the future
- Minimal revenue gains now and likely losses, but potential for significant contributions to revenues and profits in 5–10 years

Time

Source: Adapted from Eric D. Beinhocker, "Robust Adaptive Strategies," *Sloan Management Review* 40. No. 3 (Spring 1999), p. 101.

The three strategy horizons are illustrated in Figure 8.2. Managing such a portfolio of strategic initiatives to sustain rapid growth is not easy, however. The tendency of most companies is to focus on Horizon 1 strategies and devote only sporadic and uneven attention to Horizon 2 and 3 strategies. But a recent McKinsey & Company study of 30 of the world's leading growth companies revealed a relatively balanced portfolio of strategic initiatives covering all three horizons. The lesson of successful growth companies is that keeping a company's record of rapid growth intact over the long term entails crafting a diverse population of strategies, ranging from short-jump incremental strategies to grow present businesses to long-jump initiatives with a 5- to 10-year growth payoff horizon.[20] Having a mixture of short-jump, medium-jump, and long-jump initiatives not only increases the odds of hitting a few home runs but also provides some protection against unexpected adversity in present or newly entered businesses.

The Risks of Pursuing Multiple Strategy Horizons

There are, of course, risks to pursuing a diverse strategy portfolio aimed at sustained growth. A company cannot, of course, place bets on every opportunity that appears on its radar screen, lest it stretch its resources too thin. And medium-jump and long-jump initiatives can cause a company to stray far from its core competencies and end up trying to compete in businesses for which it is ill-suited. Moreover, it can be difficult to achieve competitive advantage in medium- and long-jump product families and businesses that prove not to mesh well with a company's present businesses and resource strengths. The payoffs of long-jump initiatives often prove elusive; not all of the seeds a company sows will bear fruit, and only a few may evolve into truly significant contributors to the company's revenue and profit growth. The losses from those long-jump ventures that do not take root may significantly erode the gains from those that do, resulting in disappointingly modest gains in overall profits.

STRATEGIES FOR INDUSTRY LEADERS

The competitive positions of industry leaders normally range from "stronger than average" to "powerful." Leaders typically are well known, and strongly entrenched leaders have proven strategies (keyed either to low-cost leadership or to differentiation). Some of the best-known industry leaders are Anheuser-Busch (beer), Starbucks (coffee drinks), Microsoft (computer software), Callaway (golf clubs), McDonald's (fast food), Procter & Gamble (laundry detergents and soaps), Campbell's (canned soups), Gerber (baby food), Hewlett-Packard (printers), Sony (video game consoles), Black & Decker (power tools), Intel (semiconductors and chip sets), Wal-Mart and Carrefour (discount retailing), Amazon.com (online shopping), eBay (online auctions), Apple (MP3 players), and Ocean Spray (cranberries).

The main strategic concern for a leader revolves around how to defend and strengthen its leadership position, perhaps becoming the dominant leader as opposed to just a leader. However, the pursuit of industry leadership and large market share is primarily important because of the competitive advantage and profitability that accrue to being the industry's biggest company. Three contrasting strategic postures are open to industry leaders:[21]

1. *Stay-on-the-offensive strategy*—The central goal of a stay-on-the-offensive strategy is to be a first-mover and a proactive market leader.[22] It rests on the principle that playing hardball, moving early and frequently, and forcing rivals into a catch-up mode is the surest path to industry prominence and potential market dominance—as the saying goes, the best defense is a good offense. Furthermore, *an offensive-minded industry leader relentlessly concentrates on achieving a competitive advantage over rivals and then widening this advantage over time to achieve extreme competitive advantage.*[23] Being the industry standard setter thus requires being impatient with the status quo, seizing the initiative, and pioneering continuous improvement and innovation—this can mean being first-to-market with technological improvements, new or better products, more attractive performance features, quality enhancements, or customer service improvements. It can mean aggressively seeking out ways to cut operating costs, ways to establish competitive capabilities that rivals cannot match, or ways to make it easier and less costly for potential customers to switch their purchases from runner-up firms to the leader's own products. It can mean aggressively attacking the profit sanctuaries of important rivals, perhaps with bursts of advertising or price-cutting or approaching its customers with special deals.[24]

> The governing principle underlying an industry leader's use of a stay-on-the-offensive strategy is to be an action-oriented first-mover, impatient with the status quo.

A low-cost leader must set the pace for cost reduction, and a differentiator must constantly initiate new ways to keep its product set apart from the brands of imitative rivals in order to be the standard against which rivals' products are judged. The array of options for a potent stay-on-the-offensive strategy can also include initiatives to expand overall industry demand—spurring the creation of new families of products, making the product more suitable for consumers in emerging-country markets, discovering new uses for the product, attracting new users of the product, and promoting more frequent use.

Illustration Capsule 8.2
ESPN's Strategy to Dominate Sports Entertainment

Via a series of offensive initiatives over the past 10 years, ESPN has parlayed its cable TV sports programming franchise into a dominating and pervasive general store of sports entertainment. The thrust of ESPN's strategy has been to stay on the offensive by (1) continually enhancing its program offerings and (2) extending the ESPN brand into a host of cutting-edge sports businesses. Examples of ESPN's enhanced product offering include the ESPY Awards for top achievements in sports, the X Games (an annual extreme sports competition for both winter and summer sports), the addition of *Monday Night Football* (starting in 2006), making new movies to show on ESPN, and producing its own shows (such as *ESPN Hollywood, Cold Pizza,* and *Bound for Glory*). The appeal of ESPN's programming was so powerful that ESPN was able to charge cable operators an estimated $2.80 per subscriber per month—nearly twice as much as the next most popular cable channel (CNN, for instance, was only able to command a monthly fee of roughly $0.40 per subscriber).

But the most important element of ESPN's strategic offensive had been to start up a series of new ESPN-branded businesses—all of which were brainstormed by ESPN's entrepreneurially talented management team. The company's brand extension offensive has produced nine TV channels (the most prominent of which are ESPN, ESPN2, ESPN Classic, ESPNews, and ESPN Desportes); the ESPN radio network, with 700 affiliate stations; ESPN. com (which in 2005 attracted some 16 million unique visitors monthly to view its bazaar of wide-ranging sports stories and information); *ESPN: The Magazine* (with a fast-growing base of 1.8 million subscribers that could in time overtake the barely growing 3.3 million subscriber

base of longtime leader *Sports Illustrated*); ESPN Motion (an online video service); ESPN360 (which offers sports information and video-clip programming tailored for broadband providers—it had 5 million subscribers in 2005 and was available from 14 broadband providers); Mobile ESPN (an ESPN-branded cell phone service provided in partnership with Sprint Nextel); ESPN Zones (nine sports-themed restaurants in various cities); ESPN branded video games (video game developer Electronic Arts has 15-year licensing rights to use the ESPN name for a series of sports-related games), and a business unit that distributes ESPN sports programming in 11 languages in over 180 countries.

In 2005, the empire of ESPN consisted of some 50 different businesses that generated annual revenues in excess of $5 billion and hefty annual operating profits of about $2 billion—about 40 percent of its revenues came from advertising and 60 percent from subscriptions and distribution fees. ESPN, a division of Disney, was one of Disney's most profitable and fastest-growing operations (Disney was also the parent of ABC Broadcasting).

So far, ESPN's stay-a-step-ahead strategy had left lesser rivals in the dust. But Comcast, the largest U.S. cable operator, with 22 million subscribers, was maneuvering to create its own cable TV sports channel; Comcast already owned the Philadelphia 76ers, the Philadelphia Flyers, and a collection of regional sports networks in cities from Philadelphia to Chicago to Los Angeles. And Rupert Murdoch's expansion-minded News Corporation, a worldwide media conglomerate whose many businesses included Fox Broadcasting and DIRECTV, was said to be looking at melding its 15 regional U.S. sports channels into a national sports channel.

Source: Developed from information in Tom Lowry, "ESPN the Zone," *BusinessWeek,* October 17, 2005, pp. 66–78.

A stay-on-the-offensive strategy cannot be considered successful unless it results in growing sales and revenues faster than the industry as a whole and wresting market share from rivals—a leader whose sales growth is only 5 percent in a market growing at 8 percent is losing ground to some of its competitors. Only if an industry's leader's market share is already so dominant that it presents a threat of antitrust action (a market share under 60 percent is usually safe) should an industry leader deliberately back away from aggressively pursuing market share gains.

Illustration Capsule 8.2 describes ESPN's stay-on-the-offensive strategy to dominate the sports entertainment business.

2. *Fortify-and-defend strategy*—The essence of "fortify and defend" is to make it harder for challengers to gain ground and for new firms to enter. The goals of a strong defense are to hold on to the present market share, strengthen current market position, and protect whatever competitive advantage the firm has. Specific defensive actions can include:

- Attempting to raise the competitive ante for challengers and new entrants via increased spending for advertising, higher levels of customer service, and bigger R&D outlays.
- Introducing more product versions or brands to match the product attributes that challenger brands have or to fill vacant niches that competitors could slip into.
- Adding personalized services and other extras that boost customer loyalty and make it harder or more costly for customers to switch to rival products.
- Keeping prices reasonable and quality attractive.
- Building new capacity ahead of market demand to discourage smaller competitors from adding capacity of their own.
- Investing enough to remain cost-competitive and technologically progressive.
- Patenting the feasible alternative technologies.
- Signing exclusive contracts with the best suppliers and dealer/distributors.

A fortify-and-defend strategy best suits firms that have already achieved industry dominance and don't wish to risk antitrust action. It is also well suited to situations where a firm wishes to milk its present position for profits and cash flow because the industry's prospects for growth are low or because further gains in market share do not appear profitable enough to go after. But a fortify-and-defend strategy always entails trying to grow as fast as the market as a whole (to stave off market-share slippage) and requires reinvesting enough capital in the business to protect the leader's ability to compete.

3. *Muscle-flexing strategy*—Here a dominant leader plays competitive hardball (presumably in an ethical and competitively legal manner) when smaller rivals rock the boat with price cuts or mount new market offensives that directly threaten its position. Specific responses can include quickly matching and perhaps exceeding challengers' price cuts, using large promotional campaigns to counter challengers' moves to gain market share, and offering better deals to their major customers. Dominant leaders may also court distributors assiduously to dissuade them from carrying rivals' products, provide salespersons with documented information about the weaknesses of competing products, or try to fill any vacant positions in their own firms by making attractive offers to the better executives of rivals that get out of line.

The leader may also use various arm-twisting tactics to pressure present customers not to use the products of rivals. This can range from simply forcefully communicating its displeasure should customers opt to use the products of rivals to pushing them to agree to exclusive arrangements in return for better prices to charging them a higher price if they use any competitors' products. As a final resort, a leader may grant certain customers special discounts or preferred treatment if they do not use any products of rivals.

The obvious risks of a muscle-flexing strategy are running afoul of laws prohibiting monopoly practices and unfair competition and using bullying tactics that arouse adverse public opinion. Microsoft paid Real Networks $460 million in 2005 to resolve all of Real Network's antitrust complaints and settle a long-standing feud over Microsoft's repeated bullying of PC makers to include Windows Media Player instead of Real's media player as standard installed software on their PCs. In 2005 AMD filed an antitrust suit against Intel, claiming that Intel unfairly and monopolistically coerced 38 named companies on three continents in efforts to get them to use Intel chips instead of AMD chips in the computer products they manufactured or marketed. Consequently, a company that throws its weight around to protect and enhance its market dominance has got to be judicious, lest it cross the line from allowable muscle-flexing to unethical or illegal competitive bullying.

STRATEGIES FOR RUNNER-UP FIRMS

Runner-up, or second-tier, firms have smaller market shares than first-tier industry leaders. Some runner-up firms are often advancing market challengers, employing offensive strategies to gain market share and build a stronger market position. Other runner-up competitors are focusers, seeking to improve their lot by concentrating their attention on serving a limited portion of the market. There are, of course, always a number of firms in any industry that are destined to be perennial runners-up, either because they are content to follow the trendsetting moves of the market leaders or because they lack the resources and competitive strengths to do much better in the marketplace than they are already doing. But it is erroneous to view runner-up firms as inherently less profitable or unable to hold their own against the biggest firms. Many small and medium-sized firms earn healthy profits and enjoy good reputations with customers.

Obstacles for Firms with Small Market Shares

There are times when runner-up companies face significant hurdles in contending for market leadership. In industries where big size is definitely a key success factor, firms with small market shares have four obstacles to overcome: (1) less access to economies of scale in manufacturing, distribution, or marketing and sales promotion; (2) difficulty in gaining customer recognition (since the products and brands of the market leaders are much better known); (3) less money to spend on mass-media advertising; and (4) limited funds for capital expansion or making acquisitions.[25] Some runner-up companies may be able to surmount these obstacles. Others may not. When significant scale economies give large-volume competitors a dominating cost advantage, small-share firms have only two viable strategic options: initiate offensive moves aimed at building sufficient sales volume to approach the scale economies and lower unit costs enjoyed by larger rivals or withdraw from the business (gradually or quickly) because of the inability to achieve low enough costs to compete effectively against the market leaders.

Offensive Strategies to Build Market Share

A runner-up company desirous of closing in on the market leaders has to make some waves in the marketplace if it wants to make big market share gains—this means coming up with distinctive strategy elements that set it apart from rivals and draw buyer attention. If a challenger has a 5 percent market share and needs a 15 to 20 percent share to contend for leadership and earn attractive profits, it requires a more creative approach to competing than just "Try harder" or "Follow in the footsteps of current industry leaders." Rarely can a runner-up significantly improve its competitive position by imitating the strategies of leading firms. A cardinal rule in offensive strategy is to avoid attacking a leader head-on with an imitative strategy, regardless of the resources and staying power an underdog may have.[26] What an aspiring challenger really needs is a strategy aimed at building a competitive advantage of its own (and certainly a strategy capable of quickly eliminating any important competitive disadvantages).

The best "mover-and-shaker" offensives for a second-tier challenger aiming to join the first-tier ranks usually involve one of the following five approaches:

1. Making a series of acquisitions of smaller rivals to greatly expand the company's market reach and market presence. *Growth via acquisition* is perhaps the most frequently used strategy employed by ambitious runner-up companies to form an enterprise that has greater competitive strength and a larger share of the overall market. For an enterprise to succeed with this strategic approach, senior management must be skilled in quickly assimilating the operations of the acquired companies, eliminating duplication and overlap, generating efficiencies and cost savings, and structuring the combined resources in ways that create substantially stronger competitive capabilities. Many banks and public accounting firms owe their growth during the past decade to acquisition of smaller regional and local banks. Likewise, a number of book publishers have grown by acquiring small publishers, and public accounting firms have grown by acquiring lesser-sized accounting firms with attractive client lists.

2. Finding innovative ways to dramatically drive down costs and then using the attraction of lower prices to win customers from higher-cost, higher-priced rivals. This is a necessary offensive move when a runner-up company has higher costs than larger-scale enterprises (either because the latter possess scale economies or have benefited from experience/learning curve effects). A challenger firm can pursue aggressive cost reduction by eliminating marginal activities from its value chain, streamlining supply chain relationships, improving internal operating efficiency, using various e-commerce techniques, and merging with or acquiring rival firms to achieve the size needed to capture greater scale economies.

3. Crafting an attractive differentiation strategy based on premium quality, technological superiority, outstanding customer service, rapid product innovation, or convenient online shopping options.

4. Pioneering a leapfrog technological breakthrough—an attractive option if an important technological breakthrough is within a challenger's reach and rivals are not close behind.

5. Being first-to-market with new or better products and building a reputation for product leadership. A strategy of product innovation has appeal if the runner-up company possesses the necessary resources—cutting-edge R&D capability and organizational agility in speeding new products to market.

Other possible, but likely less effective, offensive strategy options include (1) outmaneuvering slow-to-change market leaders in adapting to evolving market conditions and customer expectations and (2) forging productive strategic alliances with key distributors, dealers, or marketers of complementary products.

Without a potent offensive strategy to capture added market share, runner-up companies have to patiently nibble away at the lead of market leaders and build sales at a moderate pace over time.

Other Strategic Approaches for Runner-Up Companies

There are five other strategies that runner-up companies can employ.[27] While none of the five is likely to move a company from second-tier to first-tier status, all are capable of producing attractive profits and returns for shareholders.

Vacant-Niche Strategy   A version of a focused strategy, the vacant-niche strategy involves concentrating on specific customer groups or end-use applications that market leaders have bypassed or neglected. An ideal vacant niche is of sufficient size and scope to be profitable, has some growth potential, is well suited to a firm's own capabilities, and for one reason or another is hard for leading firms to serve. Two examples where vacant-niche strategies have worked successfully are (1) regional commuter airlines serving cities with too few passengers to fill the large jets flown by major airlines and (2) health-food producers (like Health Valley, Hain, and Tree of Life) that cater to local health-food stores—a market segment that until recently has been given little attention by such leading companies as Kraft, Nestlé, and Unilever.

Specialist Strategy   A specialist firm trains its competitive effort on one technology, product or product family, end use, or market segment (often one in which buyers have special needs). The aim is to train the company's resource strengths and capabilities on building competitive advantage through leadership in a specific area. Smaller companies that successfully use this focused strategy include Formby's (a specialist in stains and finishes for wood furniture, especially refinishing); Blue Diamond (a California-based grower and marketer of almonds); Cuddledown (a specialty producer and retailer of down and synthetic comforters, featherbeds, and other bedding products); and American Tobacco (a leader in chewing tobacco and snuff). Many companies in high-tech industries concentrate their energies on being the clear leader in a particular technological niche; their competitive advantage is superior technological depth, technical expertise that is highly valued by customers, and the capability to consistently beat out rivals in pioneering technological advances.

Superior Product Strategy   The approach here is to use a differentiation-based focused strategy keyed to superior product quality or unique attributes. Sales and marketing efforts are aimed directly at quality-conscious and performance-oriented buyers. Fine craftsmanship, prestige quality, frequent product innovations, and/or close contact with customers to solicit their input in developing a better product usually undergird the superior product approach. Some examples include Samuel Adams in beer, Tiffany in diamonds and jewelry, Chicago Cutlery in premium-quality kitchen knives, Baccarat in fine crystal, Cannondale in mountain bikes, Bally in shoes, and Patagonia in apparel for outdoor recreation enthusiasts.

Distinctive-Image Strategy   Some runner-up companies build their strategies around ways to make themselves stand out from competitors. A variety of distinctive-image strategies can be used: building a reputation for charging the lowest prices (Dollar General), providing high-end quality at a good price (Orvis, Lands' End, and L. L. Bean), going all out to give superior customer service (Four Seasons hotels), incorporating unique product attributes (Omega-3 enriched eggs), making a product with disctinctive styling (General Motors' Hummer), or devising unusually creative advertising (AFLAC's duck ads on TV). Other examples include Dr Pepper's strategy in calling attention to its distinctive taste, Apple Computer's making it easier and more interesting for people to use its Macintosh PCs, and Mary Kay Cosmetics' distinctive use of the color pink.

Content Follower Strategy   Content followers deliberately refrain from initiating trendsetting strategic moves and from aggressive attempts to steal customers away from the leaders. Followers prefer approaches that will not provoke competitive retaliation, often opting for focus and differentiation strategies that keep them out of the leaders' paths. They react and respond rather than initiate and challenge. They prefer defense to offense. And they rarely get out of line with the leaders on price. They are content to simply maintain their market position, albeit sometimes struggling to do so. Followers have no urgent strategic questions to confront beyond "What strategic changes are the leaders initiating and what do we need to do to follow along and maintain our present position?" The marketers of private-label products tend to be followers, imitating many of the newly introduced features of name brand products and content to sell to price-conscious buyers at prices modestly below those of well-known brands.

STRATEGIES FOR WEAK AND CRISIS-RIDDEN BUSINESSES

A firm in an also-ran or declining competitive position has four basic strategic options. If it can come up with the financial resources, it can launch a turnaround strategy keyed either to "low-cost" or "new" differentiation themes, pouring enough money and talent into the effort to move up a notch or two in the industry rankings and become a respectable market contender within five years or so. It can employ a fortify-and-defend strategy, using variations of its present strategy and fighting hard to keep sales, market share, profitability, and competitive position at current levels. It can opt for a fast-exit strategy and get out of the business, either by selling out to another firm or by closing down operations if a buyer cannot be found. Or it can employ an end-game or slow-exit strategy, keeping reinvestment to a bare-bones minimum and taking actions to maximize short-term cash flows in preparation for orderly market withdrawal.

Turnaround Strategies for Businesses in Crisis

Turnaround strategies are needed when a business worth rescuing goes into crisis. The objective is to arrest and reverse the sources of competitive and financial weakness as quickly as possible. Management's first task in formulating a suitable turnaround strategy is to diagnose what lies at the root of poor performance. Is it an unexpected downturn in sales brought on by a weak economy? An ill-chosen competitive strategy? Poor execution of an otherwise viable strategy? High operating costs? Important resource deficiencies? An overload of debt? The next task is to decide whether the business can be saved or whether the situation is hopeless. Understanding what is wrong with the business and how serious its strategic problems are is essential because different diagnoses lead to different turnaround strategies.

Some of the most common causes of business trouble are taking on too much debt, overestimating the potential for sales growth, ignoring the profit-depressing effects of an overly aggressive effort to "buy" market share with deep price cuts, being burdened with heavy fixed costs because weak sales don't permit near-full capacity utilization, betting on R&D efforts but failing to come up with effective innovations, betting on technological long shots, being too optimistic about the ability to penetrate new markets, making frequent changes in strategy (because the previous strategy didn't work out), and being overpowered by more successful rivals. Curing these kinds of problems and achieving a successful business turnaround can involve any of the following actions:

- Selling off assets to raise cash to save the remaining part of the business.
- Revising the existing strategy.
- Launching efforts to boost revenues.

- Pursuing cost reduction.
- Using a combination of these efforts.

Selling Off Assets   Asset-reduction strategies are essential when cash flow is a critical consideration and when the most practical ways to generate cash are (1) through sale of some of the firm's assets (plant and equipment, land, patents, inventories, or profitable subsidiaries) and (2) through retrenchment (pruning of marginal products from the product line, closing or selling older plants, reducing the workforce, withdrawing from outlying markets, cutting back customer service). Sometimes crisis-ridden companies sell off assets not so much to unload losing operations as to raise funds to save and strengthen the remaining business activities. In such cases, the choice is usually to dispose of noncore business assets to support strategy renewal in the firm's core businesses.

Strategy Revision   When weak performance is caused by bad strategy, the task of strategy overhaul can proceed along any of several paths: (1) shifting to a new competitive approach to rebuild the firm's market position; (2) overhauling internal operations and functional-area strategies to better support the same overall business strategy; (3) merging with another firm in the industry and forging a new strategy keyed to the newly merged firm's strengths; and (4) retrenching into a reduced core of products and customers more closely matched to the firm's strengths. The most appealing path depends on prevailing industry conditions, the firm's particular strengths and weaknesses, its competitive capabilities vis-à-vis rival firms, and the severity of the crisis. A situation analysis of the industry, the major competitors, and the firm's own competitive position is a prerequisite for action. As a rule, successful strategy revision must be tied to the ailing firm's strengths and near-term competitive capabilities and directed at its best market opportunities.

Boosting Revenues   Revenue-increasing turnaround efforts aim at generating increased sales volume. The chief revenue-building options include price cuts, increased advertising, a bigger sales force, added customer services, and quickly achieved product improvements. Attempts to increase revenues and sales volumes are necessary (1) when there is little or no room in the operating budget to cut expenses and still break even, and (2) when the key to restoring profitability is increased use of existing capacity. If buyers are not especially price-sensitive (because many are strongly attached to various differentiating features in the company's product offering), the quickest way to boost short-term revenues may be to raise prices rather than opt for volume-building price cuts. A price increase in the 2–4 percent range may well be feasible if the company's prices are already below those of key rivals.

Cutting Costs   Cost-reducing turnaround strategies work best when an ailing firm's value chain and cost structure are flexible enough to permit radical surgery, when operating inefficiencies are identifiable and readily correctable, when the firm's costs are obviously bloated, and when the firm is relatively close to its break-even point. Accompanying a general belt-tightening can be an increased emphasis on paring administrative overheads, elimination of nonessential and low-value-added activities in the firm's value chain, modernization of existing plant and equipment to gain greater productivity, delay of nonessential capital expenditures, and debt restructuring to reduce interest costs and stretch out repayments.

Illustration Capsule 8.3
Sony's Turnaround Strategy—Will It Work?

Electronics was once Sony's star business, but Sony's electronics business was a huge money-loser in 2003–2004, pushing the company's stock price down about 65 percent. Once the clear leader in top-quality TVs, in 2005 Sony lagged miserably behind Samsung, Panasonic, and Sharp in popular flat-panel LCD and plasma TVs, where sales were growing fastest. Apple Computer's iPod players had stolen the limelight in the handheld music market, where Sony's Walkman had long ruled.

In the fall of 2005, Sony management announced a turnaround strategy. Howard Stringer, a dual American and British citizen who was named Sony's CEO in early 2005 and was the first foreigner ever to head Sony, unveiled a plan centered on cutting 10,000 jobs (about 6 percent of Sony's workforce), closing 11 of Sony's 65 manufacturing plants, and shrinking or eliminating 15 unprofitable

electronics operations by March 2008 (the unprofitable operations were not identified). These initiatives were projected to reduce costs by $1.8 billion. In addition to the cost cuts, Sony said it would focus on growing its sales of "champion products" like the next-generation Sony PlayStation 3 video game console, a newly introduced line of Bravia LCD TVs, and Walkman MP3 music players.

Analysts were not impressed by the turnaround plan. Standard & Poor's cut its credit rating for Sony, citing doubts about the company's turnaround strategy and forecasting "substantially" lower profitability and cash flow in fiscal 2005. Moody's put Sony on its watch list for a credit rating downgrade. Other analysts said Stringer's strategy lacked vision and creativity because it was in the same mold as most corporate streamlining efforts.

Sources: Company press releases; Yuri Kageyama, "Sony Announcing Turnaround Strategy," www.yahoo.com (accessed October 20, 2005); *Mainichi Daily News*, October 14, 2005 (accessed on Google News, October 20, 2005); and "Sony to Cut 10,000 Jobs," www.cnn.com (accessed October 20, 2005).

Combination Efforts   Combination turnaround strategies are usually essential in grim situations that require fast action on a broad front. Likewise, combination actions frequently come into play when new managers are brought in and given a free hand to make whatever changes they see fit. The tougher the problems, the more likely it is that the solutions will involve multiple strategic initiatives—see the story of turnaround efforts at Sony in Illustration Capsule 8.3.

The Chances of a Successful Turnaround Are Not High   Turnaround efforts tend to be high-risk undertakings; some return a company to good profitability, but most don't. A landmark study of 64 companies found no successful turnarounds among the most troubled companies in eight basic industries.[28] Many of the troubled businesses waited too long to begin a turnaround. Others found themselves short of both the cash and entrepreneurial talent needed to compete in a slow-growth industry characterized by a fierce battle for market share. Better-positioned rivals simply proved too strong to defeat in a long, head-to-head contest. Even when successful, turnaround may involve numerous attempts and management changes before long-term competitive viability and profitability are finally restored. A recent study found that troubled companies that did nothing and elected to wait out hard times had only a 10 percent chance of recovery.[29] This same study also found that, of the companies studied, the chances of recovery were boosted 190 percent if the turnaround strategy involved buying assets that strengthened the company's business in its core markets; companies that both bought assets or companies in their core markets while selling off noncore assets increased their chances of recovery by 250 percent.

Harvest Strategies for Weak Businesses

When a struggling company's chances of pulling off a successful turnaround are poor, the wisest option may be to forget about trying to restore the company's competitiveness and profitability and, instead employ a *harvesting strategy* that aims at generating the largest possible cash flows from the company's operations for as long as possible. A losing effort to transform a competitively weak company into a viable market contender has little appeal when there are opportunities to generate potentially sizable amounts of cash by running the business in a manner calculated to either maintain the status quo or even let the business slowly deteriorate over a long period.

As is the case with a slow-exit strategy, a harvesting strategy entails trimming operating expenses to the bone and spending the minimum amount on capital projects to keep the business going. Internal cash flow becomes the key measure of how well the company is performing, and top priority is given to cash-generating actions. Thus,

> The overriding objective of a harvesting strategy is to maximize short-term cash flows from operations.

advertising and promotional costs are kept at minimal levels; personnel who leave for jobs elsewhere or retire may not be replaced; and maintenance is performed with an eye toward stretching the life of existing facilities and equipment. Even though a harvesting strategy is likely to lead to a gradual decline in the company's business over time, the ability to harvest sizable amounts of cash in the interim makes such an outcome tolerable.

The Conditions That Make a Harvesting Strategy Attractive   A strategy of harvesting the cash flows from a weak business is a reasonable option in the following circumstances:[30]

1. *When industry demand is stagnant or declining and there's little hope that either market conditions will improve*—The growing popularity of digital cameras has forever doomed market demand for camera film.

2. *When rejuvenating the business would be too costly or at best marginally profitable*—A struggling provider of dial-up Internet access is likely to realize more benefit from harvesting than from a losing effort to grow its business in the face of the unstoppable shift to high-speed broadband service.

3. *When trying to maintain or grow the company's present sales is becoming increasingly costly*—A money-losing producer of pipe tobacco and cigars is unlikely to make market headway in gaining sales and market share against the top-tier producers (which have more resources to compete for the business that is still available).

4. *When reduced levels of competitive effort will not trigger an immediate or rapid falloff in sales*—the makers of corded telephones will not likely experience much of a decline in sales if they spend all of their R&D and marketing budgets on wireless phone systems.

5. *When the enterprise can redeploy the freed resources in higher-opportunity areas*—The makers of food products with "bad-for-you" ingredients (saturated fats, high transfats, and sugar) are better off devoting their resources to the development, production, and sale of "good-for-you" products (those with no transfats, more fiber, and good types of carbohydrates).

6. *When the business is not a crucial or core component of a diversified company's overall lineup of businesses*—Harvesting a sideline business and perhaps

hastening its decay is strategically preferable to harvesting a mainline or core business (where even a gradual decline may not be a very attractive outcome).

The more of these six conditions that are present, the more ideal the business is for harvesting.

Liquidation: The Strategy of Last Resort

Sometimes a business in crisis is too far gone to be salvaged and presents insufficient harvesting potential to be interesting. Closing down a crisis-ridden business and liquidating its assets is sometimes the best and wisest strategy. But it is also the most unpleasant and painful strategic alternative due to the hardships of job eliminations and the economic effects of business closings on local communities. Nonetheless, in hopeless situations, an early liquidation effort usually serves owner-stockholder interests better than an inevitable bankruptcy. Prolonging the pursuit of a lost cause further erodes an organization's resources and leaves less to salvage, not to mention the added stress and potential career impairment for all the people involved. The problem, of course, is differentiating between when a turnaround is achievable and when it isn't. It is easy for owners or managers to let their emotions and pride overcome sound judgment when a business gets in such deep trouble that a successful turnaround is remote.

10 COMMANDMENTS FOR CRAFTING SUCCESSFUL BUSINESS STRATEGIES

Company experiences over the years prove again and again that disastrous strategies can be avoided by adhering to good strategy-making principles. We've distilled the lessons learned from the strategic mistakes companies most often make into 10 commandments that serve as useful guides for developing sound strategies:

1. *Place top priority on crafting and executing strategic moves that enhance the company's competitive position for the long term.* The glory of meeting one quarter's or one year's financial performance targets quickly fades, but an everstronger competitive position pays off year after year. Shareholders are never well served by managers who let short-term financial performance considerations rule out strategic initiatives that will meaningfully bolster the company's longer-term competitive position and competitive strength. The best way to ensure a company's long-term profitability is with a strategy that strengthens the company's long-term competitiveness and market position.

2. *Be prompt in adapting to changing market conditions, unmet customer needs, buyer wishes for something better, emerging technological alternatives, and new initiatives of competitors.* Responding late or with too little often puts a company in the precarious position of having to play catch-up. While pursuit of a consistent strategy has its virtues, adapting strategy to changing circumstances is normal and necessary. Moreover, long-term strategic commitments to achieve top quality or lowest cost should be interpreted relative to competitors' products as well as customers' needs and expectations; the company should avoid singlemindedly striving to make the absolute highest-quality or lowest-cost product no matter what.

3. *Invest in creating a sustainable competitive advantage.* Having a competitive edge over rivals is the single most dependable contributor to above-average profitability.

As a general rule, a company must play aggressive offense to build competitive advantage and aggressive defense to protect it.

4. *Avoid strategies capable of succeeding only in the most optimistic circumstances.* Expect competitors to employ countermeasures and expect times of unfavorable market conditions. A good strategy works reasonably well and produces tolerable results even in the worst of times.

5. *Consider that attacking competitive weakness is usually more profitable and less risky than attacking competitive strength.* Attacking capable, resourceful rivals is likely to fail unless the attacker has deep financial pockets and a solid basis for competitive advantage despite the strengths of the competitor being attacked.

6. *Strive to open up very meaningful gaps in quality or service or performance features when pursuing a differentiation strategy.* Tiny differences between rivals' product offerings may not be visible or important to buyers.

7. *Be wary of cutting prices without an established cost advantage.* Price cuts run the risk that rivals will retaliate with matching or deeper price cuts of their own. The best chance for remaining profitable if the price-cutting contest turns into a price war is to have lower costs than rivals.

8. *Don't underestimate the reactions and the commitment of rival firms.* Rivals are most dangerous when they are pushed into a corner and their well-being is threatened.

9. *Avoid stuck-in-the-middle strategies that represent compromises between lower costs and greater differentiation and between broad and narrow market appeal.* Compromise strategies rarely produce sustainable competitive advantage or a distinctive competitive position—a well-executed best-cost producer strategy is the only exception in which a compromise between low cost and differentiation succeeds. Companies with compromise strategies most usually end up with average costs, an average product, an average reputation, and *no distinctive image in the marketplace.* Lacking any strategy element that causes them to stand out in the minds of buyers, companies with compromise strategies are destined for a middle-of-the-pack industry ranking, with little prospect of ever becoming an industry leader.

10. *Be judicious in employing aggressive moves to wrest market share away from rivals that often provoke retaliation in the form of escalating marketing and sales promotion, a furious race to be first-to-market with next-version products or a price war—to the detriment of everyone's profits.* Aggressive moves to capture a bigger market share invite cutthroat competition, especially when many industry members, plagued with high inventories and excess production capacity, are also scrambling for additional sales.

Key Points

The lessons of this chapter are that (1) some strategic options are better suited to certain specific industry and competitive environments than others and (2) some strategic options are better suited to certain specific company situations than others. Crafting a strategy tightly matched to a company's situation thus involves being alert to which strategy alternatives are likely to work well and which alternatives are unlikely to work well. Specifically:

1. What basic type of industry environment (emerging, rapid-growth, mature/slow-growth, stagnant/declining, high-velocity/turbulent, fragmented) does the company operate in? What strategic options and strategic postures are usually best suited to this generic type of environment?
2. What position does the firm have in the industry (leader, runner-up, or weak/distressed)? Given this position, which strategic options merit strong consideration and which options should definitely be ruled out?

In addition, creating a tight strategy-situation fit entails considering all the external and internal situational factors discussed in Chapters 3 and 4 and then revising the list of strategy options accordingly to take account of competitive conditions, industry driving forces, the expected moves of rivals, and the company's own competitive strengths and weaknesses. Listing the pros and cons of the candidate strategies is nearly always a helpful step. In weeding out the least attractive strategic alternatives and weighing the pros and cons of the most attractive ones, the answers to four questions often help point to the best course of action:

1. What kind of competitive edge can the company realistically achieve, given its resource strengths, competencies, and competitive capabilities? Is the company in a position to lead industry change and set the rules by which rivals must compete?
2. Which strategy alternative best addresses all the issues and problems the firm confronts.
3. Are any rivals particularly vulnerable and, if so, what sort of an offensive will it take to capitalize on these vulnerabilities? Will rivals counterattack? What can be done to blunt their efforts?
4. Are any defensive actions needed to protect against rivals' likely moves or other external threats to the company's future profitability?

In picking and choosing among the menu of strategic options, there are four pitfalls to avoid:

1. Designing an overly ambitious strategic plan—one that overtaxes the company's resources and capabilities.
2. Selecting a strategy that represents a radical departure from or abandonment of the cornerstones of the company's prior success—a radical strategy change need not be rejected automatically, but it should be pursued only after careful risk assessment.
3. Choosing a strategy that goes against the grain of the organization's culture.
4. Being unwilling to commit wholeheartedly to one of the five competitive strategies—picking and choosing features of the different strategies usually produces so many compromises between low cost, best cost, differentiation, and focusing that the company fails to achieve any kind of advantage and ends up stuck in the middle.

Table 8.1 provides a generic format for outlining a strategic action plan for a single-business enterprise. It contains all of the pieces of a comprehensive strategic action plan that we discussed at various places in these first eight chapters.

Table 8.1   **Sample Format for a Strategic Action Plan**

1. Strategic Vision and Mission	**5.** Supporting Functional Strategies
	• Production
2. Strategic Objectives	
• Short-term	• Marketing/sales
• Long-term	• Finance
3. Financial Objectives	• Personnel/human resources
• Short-term	
	• Other
• Long-term	
	6. Recommended Actions to Improve Company Performance
4. Overall Business Strategy	• Immediate
	• Longer-range

Exercises

1. Listed below are 10 industries. Classify each one as (*a*) emerging, (*b*) rapid-growth, (*c*) mature/slow-growth, (*d*) stagnant/declining, (*e*) high-velocity/turbulent, and (*f*) fragmented. Do research on the Internet, if needed, to locate information on industry conditions and reach a conclusion on what classification to assign each of the following:

   a. Exercise and fitness industry.

   b. Dry-cleaning industry.

   c. Poultry industry.

   d. Camera film and film-developing industry.

   e. Wine, beer, and liquor retailing.

   f. Watch industry.

   g. Cell-phone industry.

   h. Recorded music industry (DVDs, CDs, tapes).

   i. Computer software industry.

   j. Newspaper industry.

2. Toyota overtook Ford Motor Company in 2003 to become the world's second-largest maker of motor vehicles, behind General Motors. Toyota is widely regarded as having aspirations to overtake General Motors as the global leader in motor vehicles within the next 10 years. Do research on the Internet or in the library to determine what strategy General Motors is pursuing to maintain its status as the industry leader. Then research Toyota's strategy to overtake General Motors.

3. Review the discussion in Illustration Capsule 8.1 concerning the focused differentiation strategy that Exertris has employed in the exercise equipment industry. Then answer the following:

    a. What reasons can you give for why sales of the Exertris exercise bike have not taken off?

    b. What strategic actions would you recommend to the cofounders of Exertris to spark substantially greater sales of its innovative exercise bike and overcome the apparent market apathy for its video-game-equipped exercise bike? Should the company consider making any changes in its product offering? What distribution channels should it emphasize? What advertising and promotional approaches should be considered? How can it get gym owners to purchase or at least try its bikes?

    c. Should the company just give up on its product innovation (because the bike is not ever likely to get good reception in the marketplace)? Or should the cofounders try to sell their fledgling business to another exercise equipment company with a more extensive product line and wider geographic coverage?

4. Review the information in Illustration Capsule 8.3 concerning the turnaround strategy Sony launched in the fall of 2005. Go to the company's Web site and check out other Internet sources to see how Sony's strategy to revitalize its electronics business is coming along. Does your research indicate that Sony's turnaround strategy is a success or a failure, or is it still too early to tell? Explain.

5. Yahoo competes in an industry characterized by high-velocity change. Read the company's press releases at http://yhoo.client.shareholder.com/releases.cfm and answer the following questions:

    a. Does it appear that the company has dealt with change in the industry by reacting to change, anticipating change, or leading change? Explain.

    b. What are its key strategies for competing in fast-changing markets? Describe them.

chapter nine

Diversification

Strategies for Managing a Group of Businesses

To acquire or not to acquire: that is the question.

—Robert J. Terry

Fit between a parent and its businesses is a two-edged sword: a good fit can create value; a bad one can destroy it.

—Andrew Campbell, Michael Goold, and Marcus Alexander

Achieving superior performance through diversification is largely based on relatedness.

—Philippe Very

Make winners out of every business in your company. Don't carry losers.

—Jack Welch
Former CEO, General Electric

We measure each of our businesses against strict criteria: growth, margin, and return-on-capital hurdle rate, and does it have the ability to become number one or two in its industry? We are quite pragmatic. If a business does not contribute to our overall vision, it has to go.

—Richard Wambold
CEO, Pactiv

In this chapter, we move up one level in the strategy-making hierarchy, from strategy making in a single-business enterprise to strategy making in a diversified enterprise. Because a diversified company is a collection of individual businesses, the strategy-making task is more complicated. In a one-business company, managers have to come up with a plan for competing successfully in only a single industry environment—the result is what we labeled in Chapter 2 as *business strategy* (or *business-level strategy*). But in a diversified company, the strategy-making challenge involves assessing multiple industry environments and developing a *set* of business strategies, one for each industry arena in which the diversified company operates. And top executives at a diversified company must still go one step further and devise a company-wide or *corporate strategy* for improving the attractiveness and performance of the company's overall business lineup and for making a rational whole out of its diversified collection of individual businesses.

In most diversified companies, corporate-level executives delegate considerable strategy-making authority to the heads of each business, usually giving them the latitude to craft a business strategy suited to their particular industry and competitive circumstances and holding them accountable for producing good results. But the task of crafting a diversified company's overall or corporate strategy falls squarely in the lap of top-level executives and involves four distinct facets:

1. *Picking new industries to enter and deciding on the means of entry*—The first concerns in diversifying are what new industries to get into and whether to enter by starting a new business from the ground up, acquiring a company already in the target industry, or forming a joint venture or strategic alliance with another company. A company can diversify narrowly into a few industries or broadly into many industries. The choice of whether to enter an industry via a start-up operation; a joint venture; or the acquisition of an established leader, an up-and-coming company, or a troubled company with turnaround potential shapes what position the company will initially stake out for itself.

2. *Initiating actions to boost the combined performance of the businesses the firm has entered*—As positions are created in the chosen industries, corporate strategists typically zero in on ways to strengthen the long-term competitive positions and profits of the businesses the firm has invested in. Corporate parents can help their business subsidiaries by providing financial resources, by supplying missing skills or technological know-how or managerial expertise to better perform key value chain activities, and by providing new avenues for cost reduction. They can also acquire another company in the same industry and merge the two operations into a stronger business, or acquire new businesses that strongly complement existing businesses. Typically, a company will pursue rapid-growth strategies in its most promising businesses, initiate turnaround efforts in weak-performing businesses with potential, and divest businesses that are no longer attractive or that don't fit into management's long-range plans.

3. *Pursuing opportunities to leverage cross-business value chain relationships and strategic fits into competitive advantage*—A company that diversifies into businesses with competitively important value chain matchups (pertaining to technology, supply chain logistics, production, overlapping distribution channels, or common customers) gains competitive advantage potential not open to a company that diversifies into businesses whose value chains are totally unrelated. Capturing this competitive advantage potential requires that corporate strategists spend considerable time trying to capitalize on such cross-business opportunities as transferring skills or technology from one business to another, reducing costs via sharing use of common facilities and resources, and using the company's well-known brand names and distribution muscle to grow the sales of newly acquired products.

4. *Establishing investment priorities and steering corporate resources into the most attractive business units*—A diversified company's different businesses are usually not equally attractive from the standpoint of investing additional funds. It is incumbent on corporate management to (*a*) decide on the priorities for investing capital in the company's different businesses, (*b*) channel resources into areas where earnings potentials are higher and away from areas where they are lower, and (*c*) divest business units that are chronically poor performers or are in an increasingly unattractive industry. Divesting poor performers and businesses in unattractive industries frees up unproductive investments either for redeployment to promising business units or for financing attractive new acquisitions.

The demanding and time-consuming nature of these four tasks explains why corporate executives generally refrain from becoming immersed in the details of crafting and implementing business-level strategies, preferring instead to delegate lead responsibility for business strategy to the heads of each business unit.

In the first portion of this chapter we describe the various means a company can use to become diversified and explore the pros and cons of related versus unrelated diversification strategies. The second part of the chapter looks at how to evaluate the attractiveness of a diversified company's business lineup, decide whether it has a good diversification strategy, and identify ways to improve its future performance. In the chapter's concluding section, we survey the strategic options open to already-diversified companies.

WHEN TO DIVERSIFY

So long as a company has its hands full trying to capitalize on profitable growth opportunities in its present industry, there is no urgency to pursue diversification. The big risk of a single-business company, of course, is having all of the firm's eggs in one industry basket. If demand for the industry's product is eroded by the appearance of alternative technologies, substitute products, or fast-shifting buyer preferences, or if the industry becomes competitively unattractive and unprofitable, then a company's prospects can quickly dim. Consider, for example, what digital cameras have done to erode the revenues of companies dependent on making camera film and doing film processing, what CD and DVD technology have done to business outlook for producers of cassette tapes and 3.5-inch disks, and what cell-phone companies with their no-long-distance-charge plans and marketers of Voice over Internet Protocol (VoIP) are doing to the revenues of such once-dominant long-distance providers as AT&T, British Telecommunications, and NTT in Japan.

Thus, diversifying into new industries always merits strong consideration whenever a single-business company encounters diminishing market opportunities and stagnating sales in its principal business—most landline-based telecommunications companies across the world are quickly diversifying their product offerings to include wireless and VoIP services. But there are four other instances in which a company becomes a prime candidate for diversifying:[1]

1.   When it spots opportunities for expanding into industries whose technologies and products complement its present business.

2.   When it can leverage existing competencies and capabilities by expanding into businesses where these same resource strengths are key success factors and valuable competitive assets.

3.   When diversifying into closely related businesses opens new avenues for reducing costs.

4.   When it has a powerful and well-known brand name that can be transferred to the products of other businesses and thereby used as a lever for driving up the sales and profits of such businesses.

The decision to diversify presents wide-open possibilities. A company can diversify into closely related businesses or into totally unrelated businesses. It can diversify its present revenue and earning base to a small extent (such that new businesses account for less than 15 percent of companywide revenues and profits) or to a major extent (such that new businesses produce 30 or more percent of revenues and profits). It can move into one or two large new businesses or a greater number of small ones. It can achieve multibusiness/multi-industry status by acquiring an existing company already in a business/industry it wants to enter, starting up a new business subsidiary from scratch, or forming a joint venture with one or more companies to enter new businesses.

BUILDING SHAREHOLDER VALUE: THE ULTIMATE JUSTIFICATION FOR DIVERSIFYING

Diversification must do more for a company than simply spread its business risk across various industries. In principle, diversification cannot be considered a success unless it results in *added shareholder value*—value that shareholders cannot capture on their own by purchasing stock in companies in different industries or investing in mutual funds so as to spread their investments across several industries.

For there to be reasonable expectations that a company's diversification efforts can produce added value, a move to diversify into a new business must pass three tests:[2]

1. *The industry attractiveness test*—The industry to be entered must be attractive enough to yield consistently good returns on investment. Whether an industry is attractive depends chiefly on the presence of industry and competitive conditions that are conducive to earning as good or better profits and return on investment than the company is earning in its present business(es). It is hard to justify diversifying into an industry where profit expectations are *lower* than in the company's present businesses.

2. *The cost-of-entry test*—The cost to enter the target industry must not be so high as to erode the potential for good profitability. A catch-22 can prevail here, however. The more attractive an industry's prospects are for growth and good long-term profitability, the more expensive it can be to get into. Entry barriers for start-up companies are likely to be high in attractive industries; were barriers low, a rush of new entrants would soon erode the potential for high profitability. And buying a well-positioned company in an appealing industry often entails a high acquisition cost that makes passing the cost-of-entry test less likely. For instance, suppose that the price to purchase a company is $3 million and that the company is earning after-tax profits of $200,000 on an equity investment of $1 million (a 20 percent annual return). Simple arithmetic requires that the profits be tripled if the purchaser (paying $3 million) is to earn the same 20 percent return. Building the acquired firm's earnings from $200,000 to $600,000 annually could take several years—and require additional investment on which the purchaser would also have to earn a 20 percent return. Since the owners of a successful and growing company usually demand a price that reflects their business's profit prospects, it's easy for such an acquisition to fail the cost-of-entry test.

3. *The better-off test*—Diversifying into a new business must offer potential for the company's existing businesses and the new business to perform better together under a single corporate umbrella than they would perform operating as independent, stand-alone businesses. For example, let's say that company A diversifies by purchasing company B in another industry. If A and B's consolidated profits in the years to come prove no greater than what each could have earned on its own, then A's diversification won't provide its shareholders with added value. Company A's shareholders could have achieved the same $1 + 1 = 2$ result by merely purchasing stock in company B. Shareholder value is not created by diversification unless it produces a $1 + 1 = 3$ effect where sister businesses *perform better together* as part of the same firm than they could have performed as independent companies.

> **Core Concept**
> Creating added value for shareholders via diversification requires building a multibusiness company where the whole is greater than the sum of its parts.

Diversification moves that satisfy all three tests have the greatest potential to grow shareholder value over the long term. Diversification moves that can pass only one or two tests are suspect.

STRATEGIES FOR ENTERING NEW BUSINESSES

The means of entering new businesses can take any of three forms: acquisition, internal start-up, or joint ventures with other companies.

Acquisition of an Existing Business

Acquisition is the most popular means of diversifying into another industry. Not only is it quicker than trying to launch a brand-new operation, but it also offers an effective way to hurdle such entry barriers as acquiring technological know-how, establishing supplier relationships, becoming big enough to match rivals' efficiency and unit costs, having to spend large sums on introductory advertising and promotions, and securing adequate distribution. Buying an ongoing operation allows the acquirer to move directly to the task of building a strong market position in the target industry, rather than getting bogged down in going the internal start-up route and trying to develop the knowledge, resources, scale of operation, and market reputation necessary to become an effective competitor within a few years.

The big dilemma an acquisition-minded firm faces is whether to pay a premium price for a successful company or to buy a struggling company at a bargain price.[3] If the buying firm has little knowledge of the industry but ample capital, it is often better off purchasing a capable, strongly positioned firm—unless the price of such an acquisition flunks the cost-of-entry test. However, when the acquirer sees promising ways to transform a weak firm into a strong one and has the resources, the know-how, and the patience to do it, a struggling company can be the better long-term investment.

Internal Start-Up

Achieving diversification through *internal start-up* involves building a new business subsidiary from scratch. This entry option takes longer than the acquisition option and poses some hurdles. A newly formed business unit not only has to overcome entry barriers but also has to invest in new production capacity, develop sources of supply, hire and train employees, build channels of distribution, grow a customer base, and so on. Generally, forming a start-up subsidiary to enter a new business has appeal only when (1) the parent company already has in-house most or all of the skills and resources it needs to piece together a new business and compete effectively; (2) there is ample time to launch the business; (3) internal entry has lower costs than entry via acquisition; (4) the targeted industry is populated with many relatively small firms such that the new start-up does not have to compete head-to-head against larger, more powerful rivals; (5) adding new production capacity will not adversely impact the supply–demand balance in the industry; and (6) incumbent firms are likely to be slow or ineffective in responding to a new entrant's efforts to crack the market.[4]

> The biggest drawbacks to entering an industry by forming an internal start-up are the costs of overcoming entry barriers and the extra time it takes to build a strong and profitable competitive position.

Joint Ventures

Joint ventures entail forming a new corporate entity owned by two or more companies, where the purpose of the joint venture is to pursue a mutually attractive opportunity. The terms and conditions of a joint venture concern joint operation of a mutually owned business, which tends to make the arrangement more definitive and perhaps more durable than a strategic alliance—in a strategic alliance, the arrangement between the partners is one of limited collaboration for a limited purpose and a partner can choose to simply walk away or reduce its commitment at any time.

A joint venture to enter a new business can be useful in at least three types of situations.[5] First, a joint venture is a good vehicle for pursuing an opportunity that is too complex, uneconomical, or risky for one company to pursue alone. Second, joint ventures make sense when the opportunities in a new industry require a broader range of competencies and know-how than a company can marshal. Many of the opportunities in satellite-based telecommunications, biotechnology, and network-based systems that blend hardware, software, and services call for the coordinated development of complementary innovations and tackling an intricate web of financial, technical, political, and regulatory factors simultaneously. In such cases, pooling the resources and competencies of two or more companies is a wiser and less risky way to proceed.

Third, companies sometimes use joint ventures to diversify into a new industry when the diversification move entails having operations in a foreign country—several governments require foreign companies operating within their borders to have a local partner that has minority, if not majority, ownership in the local operations. Aside from fulfilling host government ownership requirements, companies usually seek out a local partner with expertise and other resources that will aid the success of the newly established local operation.

However, as discussed in Chapters 6 and 7, partnering with another company—in either a joint venture or a collaborative alliance—has significant drawbacks due to the potential for conflicting objectives, disagreements over how to best operate the venture, culture clashes, and so on. Joint ventures are generally the least durable of the entry options, usually lasting only until the partners decide to go their own ways.

CHOOSING THE DIVERSIFICATION PATH: RELATED VERSUS UNRELATED BUSINESSES

Core Concept
Related businesses possess competitively valuable cross-business value chain matchups; *unrelated businesses* have dissimilar value chains, containing no competitively useful cross-business relationships.

Once a company decides to diversify, its first big strategy decision is whether to diversify into related businesses, unrelated businesses, or some mix of both (see Figure 9.1). *Businesses are said to be related when their value chains possess competitively valuable cross-business relationships that present opportunities for the businesses to perform better under the same corporate umbrella than they could by operating as stand-alone entities.* The big appeal of related diversification is to build shareholder value by leveraging these cross-business relationships into competitive advantage, thus allowing the company as a whole to perform better than just the sum of its individual businesses. *Businesses are said to be unrelated when the activities comprising their respective value chains are so dissimilar that no competitively valuable cross-business relationships are present.*

The next two sections of this chapter explore the ins and outs of related and unrelated diversification.

THE CASE FOR DIVERSIFYING INTO RELATED BUSINESSES

A related diversification strategy involves building the company around businesses whose value chains possess competitively valuable strategic fits, as shown in Figure 9.2. **Strategic fit** exists whenever one or more activities comprising the value chains of different businesses are sufficiently similar as to present opportunities for:[6]

- Transferring competitively valuable expertise, technological know-how, or other capabilities from one business to another.

Figure 9.1   **Strategy Alternatives for a Company Looking to Diversify**

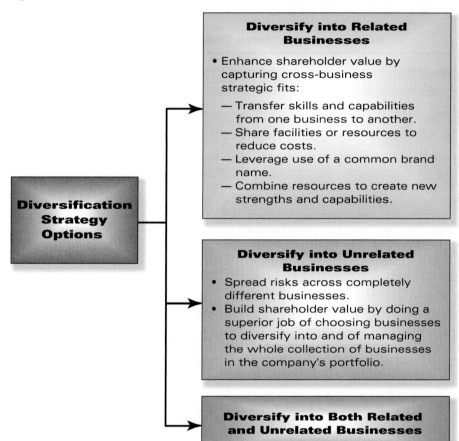

- Combining the related value chain activities of separate businesses into a single operation to achieve lower costs. For instance, it is often feasible to manufacture the products of different businesses in a single plant or use the same warehouses for shipping and distribution or have a single sales force for the products of different businesses (because they are marketed to the same types of customers).
- Exploiting common use of a well-known and potent brand name. For example, Honda's name in motorcycles and automobiles gave it instant credibility and recognition in entering the lawn-mower business, allowing it to achieve a significant market share without spending large sums on advertising to establish a brand identity for its lawn mowers. Canon's reputation in photographic equipment was a competitive asset that facilitated the company's diversification into copying equipment. Sony's name in consumer electronics made it easier and cheaper for Sony to enter the market for video games with its PlayStation console and lineup of PlayStation video games.
- Cross-business collaboration to create competitively valuable resource strengths and capabilities.

> **Core Concept**
> **Strategic fit** exists when the value chains of different businesses present opportunities for cross-business resource transfer, lower costs through combining the performance of related value chain activities, cross-business use of a potent brand name, and cross-business collaboration to build new or stronger competitive capabilities.

Figure 9.2 **Related Businesses Possess Related Value Chain Activities and Competitively Valuable Strategic Fits**

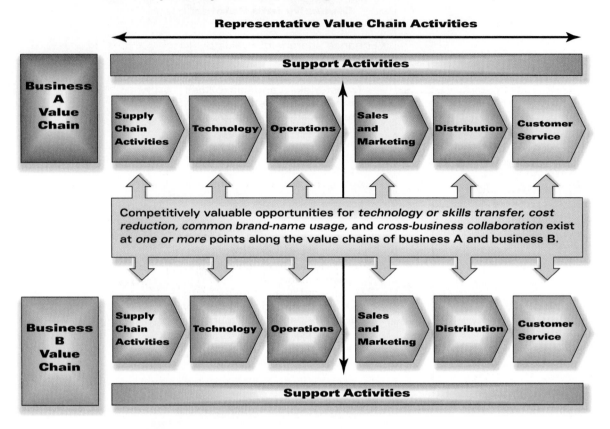

Related diversification thus has strategic appeal from several angles. It allows a firm to reap the competitive advantage benefits of skills transfer, lower costs, a powerful brand name, and/or stronger competitive capabilities and still spread investor risks over a broad business base. Furthermore, the relatedness among the different businesses provides sharper focus for managing diversification and a useful degree of strategic unity across the company's various business activities.

Identifying Cross-Business Strategic Fits along the Value Chain

Cross-business strategic fits can exist anywhere along the value chain—in R&D and technology activities, in supply chain activities and relationships with suppliers, in manufacturing, in sales and marketing, in distribution activities, or in administrative support activities.[7]

Strategic Fits in R&D and Technology Activities   Diversifying into businesses where there is potential for sharing common technology, exploiting the full range of business opportunities associated with a particular technology and its derivatives, or transferring technological know-how from one business to another has considerable appeal. Businesses with technology-sharing benefits can perform better together than apart because of potential cost savings in R&D and potentially shorter times in getting new products to market; also, technological advances in one business can lead to increased sales for both. Technological innovations have been the driver behind the efforts of cable TV companies to diversify into high-speed Internet access (via the use of cable modems) and, further, to explore providing local and long-distance telephone service to residential and commercial customers in either a single wire or using VoIP technology.

Strategic Fits in Supply Chain Activities   Businesses that have supply chain strategic fits can perform better together because of the potential for skills transfer in procuring materials, greater bargaining power in negotiating with common suppliers, the benefits of added collaboration with common supply chain partners, and/or added leverage with shippers in securing volume discounts on incoming parts and components. Dell Computer's strategic partnerships with leading suppliers of microprocessors, motherboards, disk drives, memory chips, flat-panel displays, wireless capabilities, long-life batteries, and other PC-related components have been an important element of the company's strategy to diversify into servers, data storage devices, MP3 players, and LCD TVs—products that include many components common to PCs and that can be sourced from the same strategic partners that provide Dell with PC components.

Manufacturing-Related Strategic Fits   Cross-business strategic fits in manufacturing-related activities can represent an important source of competitive advantage in situations where a diversifier's expertise in quality manufacture and cost-efficient production methods can be transferred to another business. When Emerson Electric diversified into the chain-saw business, it transferred its expertise in low-cost manufacture to its newly acquired Beaird-Poulan business division; the transfer drove Beaird-Poulan's new strategy—to be the low-cost provider of chain-saw products—and fundamentally changed the way Beaird-Poulan chain saws were designed and manufactured. Another benefit of production-related value chain matchups is the ability to consolidate production into a smaller number of plants and significantly reduce overall production costs. When snowmobile maker Bombardier diversified into motorcycles, it was able to set up motorcycle assembly lines in the same manufacturing facility where it was assembling snowmobiles. When Smuckers acquired Procter & Gamble's Jif peanut butter business, it was able to combine the manufacture of its own Smucker's peanut butter products with those of Jif; in addition, it gained greater leverage with vendors in purchasing its peanut supplies.

Distribution-Related Strategic Fits   Businesses with closely related distribution activities can perform better together than apart because of potential cost savings in sharing the same distribution facilities or using many of the same wholesale distributors and retail dealers to access customers. When Sunbeam acquired Mr. Coffee, it was able to consolidate its own distribution centers for small household appliances with those of Mr. Coffee, thereby generating considerable cost savings. Likewise, since Sunbeam products were sold to many of the same retailers as Mr. Coffee products (Wal-Mart, Kmart, Target, department stores, home centers, hardware chains, supermarket chains, and drugstore chains), Sunbeam was able to convince many of the retailers carrying Sunbeam appliances to also take on the Mr. Coffee line and vice versa.

Strategic Fits in Sales and Marketing Activities   Various cost-saving opportunities spring from diversifying into businesses with closely related sales and marketing activities. The same distribution centers can be used for warehousing and shipping the products of different businesses. When the products are sold directly to the same customers, sales costs can often be reduced by using a single sales force and avoiding having two different salespeople call on the same customer. The products of related businesses can be promoted at the same Web site, and included in the same media ads and sales brochures. After-sale service and repair organizations for the products of closely related businesses can often be consolidated into a single operation. There may be opportunities to reduce costs by consolidating order processing and billing and using common promotional tie-ins (cents-off couponing, free samples and trial offers, seasonal specials, and the like). When global power-tool maker Black & Decker acquired General Electric's domestic small household appliance business, it was able to use its own global sales force and distribution facilities to sell and distribute the newly acquired GE line of toasters, irons, mixers, and coffeemakers because the types of customers that carried its power tools (discounters like Wal-Mart and Target, home centers, and hardware stores) also stocked small appliances. The economies Black & Decker achieved for both product lines were substantial.

A second category of benefits arises when different businesses use similar sales and marketing approaches; in such cases, there may be competitively valuable opportunities to transfer selling, merchandising, advertising, and product differentiation skills from one business to another. Procter & Gamble's product lineup includes Folgers coffee, Tide laundry detergent, Crest toothpaste, Ivory soap, Charmin toilet tissue, Gillette razors and blades, Duracell batteries, Oral-B toothbrushes, and Head & Shoulders shampoo. All of these have different competitors and different supply chain and production requirements, but they all move through the same wholesale distribution systems, are sold in common retail settings to the same shoppers, are advertised and promoted in much the same ways, and require the same marketing and merchandising skills.

Strategic Fits in Managerial and Administrative Support Activities
Often, different businesses require comparable types managerial know-how, thereby allowing know-how in one line of business to be transferred to another. At General Electric (GE), managers who were involved in GE's expansion into Russia were able to expedite entry because of information gained from GE managers involved in expansions into other emerging markets. The lessons GE managers learned in China were passed along to GE managers in Russia, allowing them to anticipate that the Russian government would demand that GE build production capacity in the country rather than enter the market through exporting or licensing. In addition, GE's managers in Russia were better able to develop realistic performance expectations and make tough upfront decisions since experience in China and elsewhere warned them (1) that there would likely be increased short-term costs during the early years of start-up and (2) that if GE committed to the Russian market for the long term and aided the country's economic development it could eventually expect to be given the freedom to pursue profitable penetration of the Russian market.[8]

Likewise, different businesses can often use the same administrative and customer service infrastructure. For instance, an electric utility that diversifies into natural gas, water, appliance sales and repair services, and home security services can use the same customer data network, the same customer call centers and local offices, the same

Illustration Capsule 9.1

Related Diversification at L'Oréal, Johnson & Johnson, PepsiCo, and Darden Restaurants

See if you can identify the value chain relationships that make the businesses of the following companies related in competitively relevant ways. In particular, you should consider whether there are cross-business opportunities for (1) transferring skills/technology, (2) combining related value chain activities to achieve lower costs, (3) leveraging use of a well-respected brand name, and/or (4) establishing cross-business collaboration to create new resource strengths and capabilities.

L'ORÉAL

- Maybelline, Lancôme, Helena Rubenstein, Kiehl's, Garner, and Shu Uemura cosmetics.
- L'Oréal and Soft Sheen/Carson hair care products.
- Redken, Matrix, L'Oréal Professional, and Kerastase Paris professional hair care and skin care products.
- Ralph Lauren and Giorgio Armani fragrances.
- Biotherm skin care products.
- La Roche–Posay and Vichy Laboratories dermocosmetics.

JOHNSON & JOHNSON

- Baby products (powder, shampoo, oil, lotion).
- Band-Aids and other first-aid products.
- Women's health and personal care products (Stayfree, Carefree, Sure & Natural).
- Neutrogena and Aveeno skin care products.

- Nonprescription drugs (Tylenol, Motrin, Pepcid AC, Mylanta, Monistat).
- Prescription drugs.
- Prosthetic and other medical devices.
- Surgical and hospital products.
- Accuvue contact lenses.

PEPSICO

- Soft drinks (Pepsi, Diet Pepsi, Pepsi One, Mountain Dew, Mug, Slice).
- Fruit juices (Tropicana and Dole).
- Sports drinks (Gatorade).
- Other beverages (Aquafina bottled water, SoBe, Lipton ready-to-drink tea, Frappucino—in partnership with Starbucks, international sales of 7UP).
- Snack foods (Fritos, Lay's, Ruffles, Doritos, Tostitos, Santitas, Smart Food, Rold Gold pretzels, Chee-tos, Grandma's cookies, Sun Chips, Cracker Jack, Frito-Lay dips and salsas).
- Cereals, rice, and breakfast products (Quaker oatmeal, Cap'n Crunch, Life, Rice-A-Roni, Quaker rice cakes, Aunt Jemima mixes and syrups, Quaker grits).

DARDEN RESTAURANTS

- Olive Garden restaurant chain (Italian-themed).
- Red Lobster restaurant chain (seafood-themed).
- Bahama Breeze restaurant chain (Caribbean-themed).

Source: Company Web sites, annual reports, and 10-K reports.

---

billing and customer accounting systems, and the same customer service infrastructure to support all of its products and services.

Illustration Capsule 9.1 lists the businesses of five companies that have pursued a strategy of related diversification.

Strategic Fit, Economies of Scope, and Competitive Advantage

What makes related diversification an attractive strategy is the opportunity to convert cross-business strategic fits into a competitive advantage over business rivals whose operations do not offer comparable strategic-fit benefits. The greater the relatedness among a diversified company's sister businesses, the bigger a company's window for converting strategic fits into competitive advantage via (1) skills transfer, (2) combining related value chain activities to achieve lower costs, (3) leveraging use of a well-respected brand name, and/or (4) cross-business collaboration to create new resource strengths and capabilities.

Economies of Scope: A Path to Competitive Advantage   One of the most important competitive advantages that a related diversification strategy can produce is lower costs than competitors. Related businesses often present opportunities to eliminate or reduce the costs of performing certain value chain activities; such cost savings are termed **economies of scope**—a concept distinct from *economies of scale*. Economies of *scale* are cost savings that accrue directly from a larger-sized operation; for example, unit costs may be lower in a large plant than in a small plant, lower in a large distribution center than in a small one, and lower for large-volume purchases of components than for small-volume purchases. Economies of *scope,* however, stem directly from cost-saving strategic fits along the value chains of related businesses. Such economies are open only to a multibusiness enterprise and are the result of a related diversification strategy that allows sister businesses to share technology, perform R&D together, use common manufacturing or distribution facilities, share a common sales force or distributor/dealer network, use the same established brand name, and/or share the same administrative infrastructure. *The greater the cross-business economies associated with cost-saving strategic fits, the greater the potential for a related diversification strategy to yield a competitive advantage based on lower costs than rivals.*

> **Core Concept**
> *Economies of scope* are cost reductions that flow from operating in multiple businesses; such economies stem directly from strategic fit efficiencies along the value chains of related businesses.

From Competitive Advantage to Added Profitability and Gains in Shareholder Value   The competitive advantage potential that flows from economies of scope and the capture of other strategic-fit benefits is what enables a company pursuing related diversification to achieve $1 + 1 = 3$ financial performance and the hoped-for gains in shareholder value. The strategic and business logic is compelling: Capturing strategic fits along the value chains of its related businesses gives a diversified company a clear path to achieving competitive advantage over undiversified competitors and competitors whose own diversification efforts don't offer equivalent strategic-fit benefits.[9] Such competitive advantage potential provides a company with a dependable basis for earning profits and a return on investment that exceed what the company's businesses could earn as stand-alone enterprises. Converting the competitive advantage potential into greater profitability is what fuels $1 + 1 = 3$ gains in shareholder value—the necessary outcome for satisfying the better-off test and proving the business merit of a company's diversification effort.

> **Core Concept**
> Diversifying into related businesses where competitively valuable strategic fit benefits can be captured puts sister businesses in position to perform better financially as part of the same company than they could have performed as independent enterprises, thus providing a clear avenue for boosting shareholder value.

There are three things to bear in mind here. One, capturing cross-business strategic fits via a strategy of related diversification builds shareholder value in ways that shareholders cannot undertake by simply owning a portfolio of stocks of companies in different industries. Two, the capture of cross-business strategic-fit benefits is possible only via a strategy of related diversification. Three, the benefits of cross-business strategic fits are not automatically realized when a company diversifies into related businesses; *the benefits materialize only after management has successfully pursued internal actions to capture them.*

Figure 9.3   **Unrelated Businesses Have Unrelated Value Chains and No Strategic Fits**

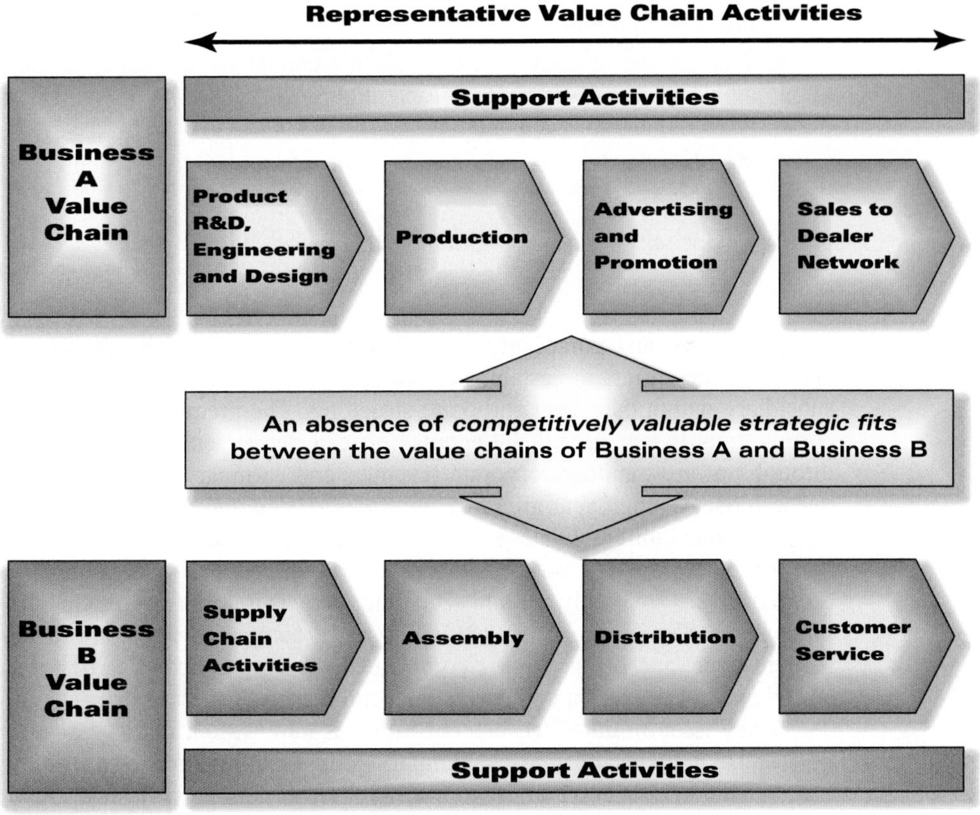

Representative Value Chain Activities

Support Activities

| Business A Value Chain | Product R&D, Engineering and Design | Production | Advertising and Promotion | Sales to Dealer Network |

An absence of *competitively valuable strategic fits* between the value chains of Business A and Business B

| Business B Value Chain | Supply Chain Activities | Assembly | Distribution | Customer Service |

Support Activities

THE CASE FOR DIVERSIFYING INTO UNRELATED BUSINESSES

An unrelated diversification strategy discounts the merits of pursuing cross-business strategic fits and, instead, focuses squarely on entering and operating businesses in industries that allow the company as a whole to grow its revenues and earnings. Companies that pursue a strategy of unrelated diversification generally exhibit a willingness to diversify into *any industry* where senior managers see *opportunity* to realize consistently good financial results—*the basic premise of unrelated diversification is that any company or business that can be acquired on good financial terms and that has satisfactory growth and earnings potential represents a good acquisition and a good business opportunity.* With a strategy of unrelated diversification, the emphasis is on satisfying the attractiveness and cost-of-entry tests and each business's prospects for good financial performance. As indicated in Figure 9.3, there's no deliberate effort to satisfy the better-off test in the sense of diversifying only into businesses having strategic fits with the firm's other businesses.

Thus, with an unrelated diversification strategy, company managers spend much time and effort screening acquisition candidates and evaluating the pros and cons or keeping or divesting existing businesses, using such criteria as:

- Whether the business can meet corporate targets for profitability and return on investment.

- Whether the business is in an industry with attractive growth potential.
- Whether the business is big enough to contribute *significantly* to the parent firm's bottom line.
- Whether the business has burdensome capital requirements (associated with replacing out-of-date plants and equipment, growing the business, and/or providing working capital).
- Whether the business is plagued with chronic union difficulties and labor problems.
- Whether there is industry vulnerability to recession, inflation, high interest rates, tough government regulations concerning product safety or the environment, and other potentially negative factors.

Companies that pursue unrelated diversification nearly always enter new businesses by acquiring an established company rather than by forming a start-up subsidiary within their own corporate structures. The premise of acquisition-minded corporations is that growth by acquisition can deliver enhanced shareholder value through upward-trending corporate revenues and earnings and a stock price that *on average* rises enough year after year to amply reward and please shareholders. Three types of acquisition candidates are usually of particular interest: (1) businesses that have bright growth prospects but are short on investment capital—cash-poor, opportunity-rich businesses are highly coveted acquisition targets for cash-rich companies scouting for good market opportunities; (2) undervalued companies that can be acquired at a bargain price; and (3) struggling companies whose operations can be turned around with the aid of the parent company's financial resources and managerial know-how.

A key issue in unrelated diversification is how wide a net to cast in building a portfolio of unrelated businesses. In other words, should a company pursuing unrelated diversification seek to have few or many unrelated businesses? How much business diversity can corporate executives successfully manage? A reasonable way to resolve the issue of how much diversification comes from answering two questions: "What is the least diversification it will take to achieve acceptable growth and profitability?" and "What is the most diversification that can be managed, given the complexity it adds?"[10] The optimal amount of diversification usually lies between these two extremes.

Illustration Capsule 9.2 lists the businesses of three companies that have pursued unrelated diversification. Such companies are frequently labeled *conglomerates* because their business interests range broadly across diverse industries.

The Merits of an Unrelated Diversification Strategy

A strategy of unrelated diversification has appeal from several angles:

1. Business risk is scattered over a set of truly *diverse* industries. In comparison to related diversification, unrelated diversification more closely approximates *pure* diversification of financial and business risk because the company's investments are spread over businesses whose technologies and value chain activities bear no close relationship and whose markets are largely disconnected.[11]
2. The company's financial resources can be employed to maximum advantage by (*a*) investing in *whatever industries* offer the best profit prospects (as opposed to considering only opportunities in industries with related value chain activities) and (*b*) diverting cash flows from company businesses with lower growth and profit prospects to acquiring and expanding businesses with higher growth and profit potentials.

Illustration Capsule 9.2

Unrelated Diversification at General Electric, United Technologies, American Standard, and Lancaster Colony

The defining characteristic of unrelated diversification is few competitively valuable cross-business relationships. Peruse the business group listings for General Electric, United Technologies, American Standard, and Lancaster Colony and see if you can confirm why these four companies have unrelated diversification strategies.

GENERAL ELECTRIC

- Advanced materials (engineering thermoplastics, silicon-based products and technology platforms, and fused quartz and ceramics)—revenues of $8.3 billion in 2004.
- Commercial and consumer finance (loans, operating leases, financing programs and financial services provided to corporations, retailers, and consumers in 38 countries)—revenues of $39.2 billion in 2004.
- Major appliances, lighting, and integrated industrial equipment, systems and services—revenues of $13.8 billion in 2004.
- Commercial insurance and reinsurance products and services for insurance companies, Fortune 1000 companies, self-insurers, health care providers and other groups—revenues of $23.1 billion in 2004.
- Jet engines for military and civil aircraft, freight and passenger locomotives, motorized systems for mining trucks and drills, and gas turbines for marine and industrial applications—revenues of $15.6 billion in 2004.
- Electric power generation equipment, power transformers, high-voltage breakers, distribution transformers and breakers, capacitors, relays, regulators, substation equipment, metering products—revenues of $17.3 billion in 2004.
- Medical imaging and information technologies, medical diagnostics, patient monitoring systems, disease research, drug discovery and biopharmaceuticals—revenues of $13.5 billion in 2004.
- NBC Universal—owns and operates the NBC television network, a Spanish-language network (Telemundo), several news and entertainment networks (CNBC, MSNBC, Bravo, Sci-Fi Channel, USA Network), Universal Studios, various television production operations, a group of television stations, and theme parks—revenues of $12.9 billion in 2004.
- Chemical treatment programs for water and industrial process systems; precision sensors; security and safety systems for intrusion and fire detection, access and

building control, video surveillance, explosives and drug detection; and real estate services—revenues of $3.4 billion in 2004.
- Equipment services, including Penske truck leasing; operating leases, loans, sales, and asset management services for owners of computer networks, trucks, trailers, railcars, construction equipment, and shipping containers—revenues of $8.5 billion in 2004.

UNITED TECHNOLOGIES

- Pratt & Whitney aircraft engines—2005 revenues of $9.3 billion.
- Carrier heating and air-conditioning equipment—2005 revenues of $12.5 billion.
- Otis elevators and escalators—2005 revenues of $9.6 billion.
- Sikorsky helicopters and Hamilton Sunstrand aerospace systems—2005 revenues of $7.2 billion.
- Chubb fire detection and security systems—2005 revenues of $4.3 billion.

AMERICAN STANDARD

- Trane and American Standard furnaces, heat pumps, and air conditioners—2005 revenues of $6.0 billion.
- American Standard, Ideal Standard, Standard, and Porcher lavatories, toilets, bath tubs, faucets, whirlpool baths, and shower basins—2005 revenues of $2.4 billion.
- Commercial and utility vehicle braking and control systems—2005 revenues of $1.8 billion.

LANCASTER COLONY

- Specialty food products: Cardini, Marzetti, Girard's, and Pheiffer salad dressings; Chatham Village croutons; New York Brand, Sister Schubert, and Mamma Bella frozen breads and rolls; Reames and Aunt Vi's frozen noodles and pastas; Inn Maid and Amish dry egg noodles; and Romanoff caviar—fiscal 2005 revenues of $674 million.
- Candles and glassware: Candle-lite candles; Indiana Glass and Fostoria drinkware and tabletop items; Colony giftware; and Brody floral containers—fiscal 2005 revenues of $234 million.
- Automotive products: Rubber Queen automotive floor mats; Dee Zee aluminum accessories and running boards for light trucks; Protecta truck bed mats; and assorted other truck accessories—fiscal 2005 revenues of $224 million.

Source: Company Web sites, annual reports, and 10-K reports.

3. To the extent that corporate managers are exceptionally astute at spotting bargain-priced companies with big upside profit potential, shareholder wealth can be enhanced by buying distressed businesses at a low price, turning their operations around fairly quickly with infusions of cash and managerial know-how supplied by the parent company, and then riding the crest of the profit increases generated by the newly acquired businesses.

4. Company profitability may prove somewhat more stable over the course of economic upswings and downswings because market conditions in all industries don't move upward or downward simultaneously—in a broadly diversified company, there's a chance that market downtrends in some of the company's businesses will be partially offset by cyclical upswings in its other businesses, thus producing somewhat less earnings volatility. (In actual practice, however, there's no convincing evidence that the consolidated profits of firms with unrelated diversification strategies are more stable or less subject to reversal in periods of recession and economic stress than the profits of firms with related diversification strategies.)

Unrelated diversification certainly merits consideration when a firm is trapped in or overly dependent on an endangered or unattractive industry, especially when it has no competitively valuable resources or capabilities it can transfer to an adjacent industry. A case can also be made for unrelated diversification when a company has a strong preference for spreading business risks widely and not restricting itself to investing in a family of closely related businesses.

Building Shareholder Value via Unrelated Diversification   Given the absence of cross-business strategic fits with which to capture added competitive advantage, the task of building shareholder value via unrelated diversification ultimately hinges on the business acumen of corporate executives. To succeed in using a strategy of unrelated diversification to produce companywide financial results above and beyond what the businesses could generate operating as stand-alone entities, corporate executives must:

- Do a superior job of diversifying into new businesses that can produce consistently good earnings and returns on investment (thereby satisfying the attractiveness test).
- Do an excellent job of negotiating favorable acquisition prices (thereby satisfying the cost-of-entry test).
- Do such a good job overseeing the firm's business subsidiaries and contributing to how they are managed—by providing expert problem-solving skills, creative strategy suggestions, and high caliber decision-making guidance to the heads of the various business subsidiaries—that the subsidiaries perform at a higher level than they would otherwise be able to do through the efforts of the business-unit heads alone (a possible way to satisfy the better-off test).
- Be shrewd in identifying when to shift resources out of businesses with dim profit prospects and into businesses with above-average prospects for growth and profitability.
- Be good at discerning when a business needs to be sold (because it is on the verge of confronting adverse industry and competitive conditions and probable declines in long-term profitability) and also finding buyers who will pay a price higher than the company's net investment in the business (so that the sale of divested businesses will result in capital gains for shareholders rather than capital losses).

To the extent that corporate executives are able to craft and execute a strategy of unrelated diversification that produces enough of the above outcomes to result in a stream of dividends and capital gains for stockholders greater than a $1 + 1 = 2$ outcome, a case can be made that shareholder value has truly been enhanced.

The Drawbacks of Unrelated Diversification

Unrelated diversification strategies have two important negatives that undercut the pluses: demanding managerial requirements and limited competitive advantage potential.

> **Core Concept**
> The two biggest drawbacks to unrelated diversification are the difficulties of competently managing many different businesses and being without the added source of competitive advantage that cross-business strategic fit provides.

Demanding Managerial Requirements   Successfully managing a set of fundamentally different businesses operating in fundamentally different industry and competitive environments is an exceptionally challenging proposition for corporate-level managers. It is difficult because key executives at the corporate level, while perhaps having personally worked in one or two of the company's businesses, rarely have the time and expertise to be sufficiently familiar with all the circumstances surrounding each of the company's businesses to be in a position to give high-caliber guidance to business-level managers. Indeed, the greater the number of businesses a company is in and the more diverse they are, the harder it is for corporate managers to (1) stay abreast of what's happening in each industry and each subsidiary and thus judge whether a particular business has bright prospects or is headed for trouble, (2) know enough about the issues and problems facing each subsidiary to pick business-unit heads having the requisite combination of managerial skills and know-how, (3) be able to tell the difference between those strategic proposals of business-unit managers that are prudent and those that are risky or unlikely to succeed, and (4) know what to do if a business unit stumbles and its results suddenly head downhill.[12]

In a company like General Electric (see Illustration Capsule 9.2) or Tyco International (which acquired over 1,000 companies during the 1990–2001 period), corporate executives are constantly scrambling to stay on top of fresh industry developments and the strategic progress and plans of each subsidiary, often depending on briefings by business-level managers for many of the details. As a rule, the more unrelated businesses that a company has diversified into, the more corporate executives are dependent on briefings from business unit heads and "managing by the numbers"—that is, keeping a close track on the financial and operating results of each subsidiary and assuming that the heads of the various subsidiaries have most everything under control so long as the latest key financial and operating measures look good. Managing by the numbers works if the heads of the various business units are quite capable and consistently meet their numbers. But the problem comes when things start to go awry in a business despite the best effort of business-unit managers and corporate management has to get deeply involved in turning around a business it does not know all that much about—as the former chairman of a Fortune 500 company advised, "Never acquire a business you don't know how to run." Because every business tends to encounter rough sledding, a good way to gauge the merits of acquiring a company in an unrelated industry is to ask, "If the business got into trouble, is corporate management likely to know how to bail it out?" When the answer is no (or even a qualified yes or maybe), growth via acquisition into unrelated businesses is a chancy strategy.[13] Just one or two unforeseen declines or big strategic mistakes (misjudging the importance of certain competitive forces or the impact of driving forces or key success factors, encountering unexpected problems in a newly acquired business, or being too optimistic about turning around a struggling subsidiary) can cause a precipitous drop in corporate earnings and crash the parent company's stock price.

Relying solely on the expertise of corporate executives to wisely manage a set of unrelated businesses is a much weaker foundation for enhancing shareholder value than is a strategy of related diversification where corporate performance can be boosted by competitively valuable cross-business strategic fits.

Hence, competently overseeing a set of widely diverse businesses can turn out to be much harder than it sounds. In practice, comparatively few companies have proved up to the task. There are far more companies whose corporate executives have failed at delivering consistently good financial results with an unrelated diversification strategy than there are companies with corporate executives who have been successful.[14] It is simply very difficult for corporate executives to achieve $1 + 1 = 3$ gains in shareholder value based on their expertise in (*a*) picking which industries to diversify into and which companies in these industries to acquire, (*b*) shifting resources from low-performing businesses into high-performing businesses, and (*c*) giving high-caliber decision-making guidance to the general managers of their business subsidiaries. The odds are that the result of unrelated diversification will be $1 + 1 = 2$ or less.

Limited Competitive Advantage Potential   The second big negative is that *unrelated diversification offers no potential for competitive advantage beyond what each individual business can generate on its own.* Unlike a related diversification strategy, there are no cross-business strategic fits to draw on for reducing costs, beneficially transferring skills and technology, leveraging use of a powerful brand name, or collaborating to build mutually beneficial competitive capabilities and thereby *adding to any competitive advantage possessed by individual businesses.* Yes, a cash-rich corporate parent pursuing unrelated diversification can provide its subsidiaries with much-needed capital and maybe even the managerial know-how to help resolve problems in particular business units, but otherwise it has little to offer in the way of enhancing the competitive strength of its individual business units. *Without the competitive advantage potential of strategic fits, consolidated performance of an unrelated group of businesses stands to be little or no better than the sum of what the individual business units could achieve if they were independent.*

COMBINATION RELATED–UNRELATED DIVERSIFICATION STRATEGIES

There's nothing to preclude a company from diversifying into both related and unrelated businesses. Indeed, in actual practice the business makeup of diversified companies varies considerably. Some diversified companies are really *dominant-business enterprises*—one major "core" business accounts for 50 to 80 percent of total revenues and a collection of small related or unrelated businesses accounts for the remainder. Some diversified companies are *narrowly diversified* around a few (two to five) related or unrelated businesses. Others are *broadly diversified* around a wide-ranging collection of related businesses, unrelated businesses, or a mixture of both. And a number of multibusiness enterprises have diversified into unrelated areas but have a collection of related businesses within each area—thus giving them a business portfolio consisting of *several unrelated groups of related businesses.* There's ample room for companies to customize their diversification strategies to incorporate elements of both related and unrelated diversification, as may suit their own risk preferences and strategic vision.

Figure 9.4   **Identifying a Diversified Company's Strategy**

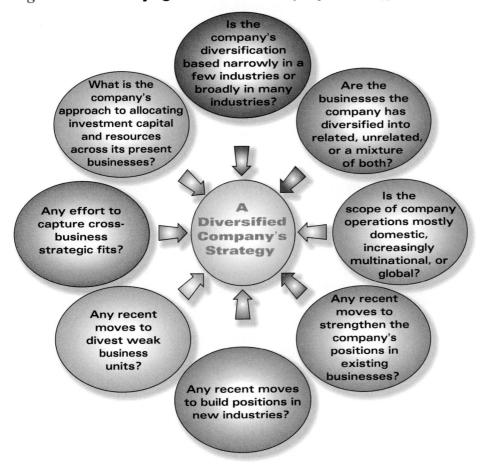

Figure 9.4 indicates what to look for in identifying the main elements of a company's diversification strategy. Having a clear fix on the company's current corporate strategy sets the stage for evaluating how good the strategy is and proposing strategic moves to boost the company's performance.

EVALUATING THE STRATEGY OF A DIVERSIFIED COMPANY

Strategic analysis of diversified companies builds on the concepts and methods used for single-business companies. But there are some additional aspects to consider and a couple of new analytical tools to master. The procedure for evaluating the pluses and minuses of a diversified company's strategy and deciding what actions to take to improve the company's performance involves six steps:

1. Assessing the attractiveness of the industries the company has diversified into, both individually and as a group.
2. Assessing the competitive strength of the company's business units and determining how many are strong contenders in their respective industries.

3. Checking the competitive advantage potential of cross-business strategic fits among the company's various business units.

4. Checking whether the firm's resources fit the requirements of its present business lineup.

5. Ranking the performance prospects of the businesses from best to worst and determining what the corporate parent's priority should be in allocating resources to its various businesses.

6. Crafting new strategic moves to improve overall corporate performance.

The core concepts and analytical techniques underlying each of these steps merit further discussion.

Step 1: Evaluating Industry Attractiveness

A principal consideration in evaluating a diversified company's business makeup and the caliber of its strategy is the attractiveness of the industries in which it has business operations. Answers to several questions are required:

1. *Does each industry the company has diversified into represent a good business for the company to be in?* Ideally, each industry in which the firm operates will pass the attractiveness test.

2. *Which of the company's industries are most attractive and which are least attractive?* Comparing the attractiveness of the industries and ranking them from most to least attractive is a prerequisite to wise allocation of corporate resources across the various businesses.

3. *How appealing is the whole group of industries in which the company has invested?* The answer to this question points to whether the group of industries holds promise for attractive growth and profitability. A company whose revenues and profits come chiefly from businesses in relatively unattractive industries probably needs to look at divesting businesses in unattractive industries and entering industries that qualify as highly attractive.

The more attractive the industries (both individually and as a group) a diversified company is in, the better its prospects for good long-term performance.

Calculating Industry Attractiveness Scores for Each Industry into Which the Company Has Diversified   A simple and reliable analytical tool involves calculating quantitative industry attractiveness scores, which can then be used to gauge each industry's attractiveness, rank the industries from most to least attractive, and make judgments about the attractiveness of all the industries as a group.

The following measures are typically used to gauge an industry's attractiveness:

- *Market size and projected growth rate*—Big industries are more attractive than small industries, and fast-growing industries tend to be more attractive than slow-growing industries, other things being equal.

- *The intensity of competition*—Industries where competitive pressures are relatively weak are more attractive than industries where competitive pressures are strong.

- *Emerging opportunities and threats*—Industries with promising opportunities and minimal threats on the near horizon are more attractive than industries with modest opportunities and imposing threats.

- *The presence of cross-industry strategic fits*—The more the industry's value chain and resource requirements match up well with the value chain activities of other industries in which the company has operations, the more attractive the industry is to a firm pursuing related diversification. However, cross-industry strategic fits may be of no consequence to a company committed to a strategy of unrelated diversification.

- *Resource requirements*—Industries having resource requirements within the company's reach are more attractive than industries where capital and other resource requirements could strain corporate financial resources and organizational capabilities.

- *Seasonal and cyclical factors*—Industries where buyer demand is relatively steady year-round and not unduly vulnerable to economic ups and downs tend to be more attractive than industries where there are wide swings in buyer demand within or across years. However, seasonality may be a plus for a company that is in several seasonal industries, if the seasonal highs in one industry correspond to the lows in another industry, thus helping even out monthly sales levels. Likewise, cyclical market demand in one industry can be attractive if its up-cycle runs counter to the market down-cycles in another industry where the company operates, thus helping reduce revenue and earnings volatility.

- *Social, political, regulatory, and environmental factors*—Industries with significant problems in such areas as consumer health, safety, or environmental pollution or that are subject to intense regulation are less attractive than industries where such problems are not burning issues.

- *Industry profitability*—Industries with healthy profit margins and high rates of return on investment are generally more attractive than industries where profits have historically been low or unstable.

- *Industry uncertainty and business risk*—Industries with less uncertainty on the horizon and lower overall business risk are more attractive than industries whose prospects for one reason or another are quite uncertain, especially when the industry has formidable resource requirements.

After settling on a set of attractiveness measures that suit a diversified company's circumstances, each attractiveness measure is assigned a weight reflecting its relative importance in determining an industry's attractiveness—it is weak methodology to assume that the various attractiveness measures are equally important. The intensity of competition in an industry should nearly always carry a high weight (say, 0.20 to 0.30). Strategic-fit considerations should be assigned a high weight in the case of companies with related diversification strategies; but, for companies with an unrelated diversification strategy, strategic fits with other industries may be given a low weight or even dropped from the list of attractiveness measures altogether. Seasonal and cyclical factors generally are assigned a low weight (or maybe even eliminated from the analysis) unless a company has diversified into industries strongly characterized by seasonal demand and/or heavy vulnerability to cyclical upswings and downswings. The importance weights must add up to 1.0.

Next, each industry is rated on each of the chosen industry attractiveness measures, using a rating scale of 1 to 10 (where a *high* rating signifies *high* attractiveness and a *low* rating signifies *low* attractiveness). *Keep in mind here that the more intensely competitive an industry is, the lower the attractiveness rating for that industry.* Likewise, the higher the capital and resource requirements associated with being in a particular industry, the lower the attractiveness rating. And an industry that is subject

Table 9.1   **Calculating Weighted Industry Attractiveness Scores**

Industry Attractiveness Measure	Importance Weight	Industry A Rating/ Score	Industry B Rating/ Score	Industry C Rating/ Score	Industry D Rating/ Score
Market size and projected growth rate	0.10	8/0.80	5/0.50	7/0.70	3/0.30
Intensity of competition	0.25	8/2.00	7/1.75	3/0.75	2/0.50
Emerging opportunities and threats	0.10	2/0.20	9/0.90	4/0.40	5/0.50
Cross-industry strategic fits	0.20	8/1.60	4/0.80	8/1.60	2/0.40
Resource requirements	0.10	9/0.90	7/0.70	10/1.00	5/0.50
Seasonal and cyclical influences	0.05	9/0.45	8/0.40	10/0.50	5/0.25
Societal, political, regulatory, and environmental factors	0.05	10/1.00	7/0.70	7/0.70	3/0.30
Industry profitability	0.10	5/0.50	10/1.00	3/0.30	3/0.30
Industry uncertainty and business risk	0.05	5/0.25	7/0.35	10/0.50	1/0.05
Sum of the assigned weights	1.00				
Overall industry attractiveness scores		**7.70**	**7.10**	**5.45**	**3.10**

Rating scale: 1 = Very unattractive to company; 10 = Very attractive to company.

to stringent pollution control regulations or that causes societal problems (like cigarettes or alcoholic beverages) should usually be given a low attractiveness rating. Weighted attractiveness scores are then calculated by multiplying the industry's rating on each measure by the corresponding weight. For example, a rating of 8 times a weight of 0.25 gives a weighted attractiveness score of 2.00. The sum of the weighted scores for all the attractiveness measures provides an overall industry attractiveness score. This procedure is illustrated in Table 9.1.

Interpreting the Industry Attractiveness Scores   Industries with a score much below 5.0 probably do not pass the attractiveness test. If a company's industry attractiveness scores are all above 5.0, it is probably fair to conclude that the group of industries the company operates in is attractive as a whole. But the group of industries takes on a decidedly lower degree of attractiveness as the number of industries with scores below 5.0 increases, especially if industries with low scores account for a sizable fraction of the company's revenues.

For a diversified company to be a strong performer, a substantial portion of its revenues and profits must come from business units with relatively high attractiveness scores. It is particularly important that a diversified company's principal businesses be in industries with a good outlook for growth and above-average profitability. Having a big fraction of the company's revenues and profits come from industries with slow growth, low profitability, or intense competition tends to drag overall company performance down. Business units in the least attractive industries are potential candidates for divestiture, unless they are positioned strongly enough to overcome the unattractive aspects of their industry environments or they are a strategically important component of the company's business makeup.

The Difficulties of Calculating Industry Attractiveness Scores   There are two hurdles to calculating industry attractiveness scores. One is deciding on appropriate weights for the industry attractiveness measures. Not only may different analysts have different views about which weights are appropriate for the different attractiveness measures but also different weightings may be appropriate for different companies—based on their strategies, performance targets, and financial circumstances. For instance, placing a low weight on industry resource requirements may be justifiable for a cash-rich company, whereas a high weight may be more appropriate for a financially strapped company. The second hurdle is gaining sufficient command of the industry to assign accurate and objective ratings. Generally, a company can come up with the statistical data needed to compare its industries on such factors as market size, growth rate, seasonal and cyclical influences, and industry profitability. Cross-industry fits and resource requirements are also fairly easy to judge. But the attractiveness measure where judgment weighs most heavily is that of intensity of competition. It is not always easy to conclude whether competition in one industry is stronger or weaker than in another industry because of the different types of competitive influences that prevail and the differences in their relative importance. In the event that the available information is too skimpy to confidently assign a rating value to an industry on a particular attractiveness measure, then it is usually best to use a score of 5, which avoids biasing the overall attractiveness score either up or down.

But despite the hurdles, calculating industry attractiveness scores is a systematic and reasonably reliable method for ranking a diversified company's industries from most to least attractive—numbers like those shown for the four industries in Table 9.1 help pin down the basis for judging which industries are more attractive and to what degree.

Step 2: Evaluating Business-Unit Competitive Strength

The second step in evaluating a diversified company is to appraise how strongly positioned each of its business units are in their respective industry. Doing an appraisal of each business unit's strength and competitive position in its industry not only reveals its chances for industry success but also provides a basis for ranking the units from competitively strongest to competitively weakest and sizing up the competitive strength of all the business units as a group.

Calculating Competitive Strength Scores for Each Business Unit   Quantitative measures of each business unit's competitive strength can be calculated using a procedure similar to that for measuring industry attractiveness. The following factors are using in quantifying the competitive strengths of a diversified company's business subsidiaries:

- *Relative market share*—A business unit's *relative market share* is defined as the ratio of its market share to the market share held by the largest rival firm in the industry, with market share measured in unit volume, not dollars. For instance, if business A has a market-leading share of 40 percent and its largest rival has 30 percent, A's relative market share is 1.33. (Note that only business units that are market share leaders in their respective industries can have relative market shares greater than 1.0.) If business B has a 15 percent market share and B's largest rival has 30 percent, B's relative market share is 0.5. *The further below 1.0 a business unit's relative market share is, the weaker its competitive strength and market position vis-à-vis rivals.* A 10 percent market share, for example, does not signal much competitive strength if the leader's share is 50 percent

> Using relative market share to measure competitive strength is analytically superior to using straight-percentage market share.

(a 0.20 relative market share), but a 10 percent share is actually quite strong if the leader's share is only 12 percent (a 0.83 relative market share)—this is why a company's relative market share is a better measure of competitive strength than a company's market share based on either dollars or unit volume.

- *Costs relative to competitors' costs*—Business units that have low costs relative to key competitors' costs tend to be more strongly positioned in their industries than business units struggling to maintain cost parity with major rivals. Assuming that the prices charged by industry rivals are about the same, there's reason to expect that business units with higher relative market shares have lower unit costs than competitors with lower relative market shares because their greater unit sales volumes offer the possibility of economies from larger-scale operations and the benefits of any experience/learning curve effects. Another indicator of low cost can be a business unit's supply chain management capabilities. The only time when a business unit's competitive strength may not be undermined by having higher costs than rivals is when it has incurred the higher costs to strongly differentiate its product offering and its customers are willing to pay premium prices for the differentiating features.

- *Ability to match or beat rivals on key product attributes*—A company's competitiveness depends in part on being able to satisfy buyer expectations with regard to features, product performance, reliability, service, and other important attributes.

- *Ability to benefit from strategic fits with sister businesses*—Strategic fits with other businesses within the company enhance a business unit's competitive strength and may provide a competitive edge.

- *Ability to exercise bargaining leverage with key suppliers or customers*—Having bargaining leverage signals competitive strength and can be a source of competitive advantage.

- *Caliber of alliances and collaborative partnerships with suppliers and/or buyers*—Well-functioning alliances and partnerships may signal a potential competitive advantage vis-à-vis rivals and thus add to a business's competitive strength. Alliances with key suppliers are often the basis for competitive strength in supply chain management.

- *Brand image and reputation*—A strong brand name is a valuable competitive asset in most industries.

- *Competitively valuable capabilities*—Business units recognized for their technological leadership, product innovation, or marketing prowess are usually strong competitors in their industry. Skills in supply chain management can generate valuable cost or product differentiation advantages. So can unique production capabilities. Sometimes a company's business units gain competitive strength because of their knowledge of customers and markets and/or their proven managerial capabilities. *An important thing to look for here is how well a business unit's competitive assets match industry key success factors.* The more a business unit's resource strengths and competitive capabilities match the industry's key success factors, the stronger its competitive position tends to be.

- *Profitability relative to competitors*—Business units that consistently earn above-average returns on investment and have bigger profit margins than their rivals usually have stronger competitive positions. Moreover, above-average profitability signals competitive advantage, while below-average profitability usually denotes competitive disadvantage.

Table 9.2   **Calculating Weighted Competitive Strength Scores for a Diversified Company's Business Units**

Competitive Strength Measure	Importance Weight	Business A in Industry A Rating/ Score	Business B in Industry B Rating/ Score	Business C in Industry C Rating/ Score	Business D in Industry D Rating/ Score
Relative market share	0.15	10/1.50	1/0.15	6/0.90	2/0.30
Costs relative to competitors' costs	0.20	7/1.40	2/0.40	5/1.00	3/0.60
Ability to match or beat rivals on key product attributes	0.05	9/0.45	4/0.20	8/0.40	4/0.20
Ability to benefit from strategic fits with sister businesses	0.20	8/1.60	4/0.80	8/0.80	2/0.60
Bargaining leverage with suppliers/ buyers; caliber of alliances	0.05	9/0.90	3/0.30	6/0.30	2/0.10
Brand image and reputation	0.10	9/0.90	2/0.20	7/0.70	5/0.50
Competitively valuable capabilities	0.15	7/1.05	2/0.20	5/0.75	3/0.45
Profitability relative to competitors	0.10	5/0.50	1/0.10	4/0.40	4/0.40
Sum of the assigned weights	1.00				
Overall industry attractiveness scores		**8.30**	**2.35**	**5.25**	**3.15**

Rating scale: 1 = Very weak; 10 = Very strong.

After settling on a set of competitive strength measures that are well matched to the circumstances of the various business units, weights indicating each measure's importance need to be assigned. A case can be made for using different weights for different business units whenever the importance of the strength measures differs significantly from business to business, but otherwise it is simpler just to go with a single set of weights and avoid the added complication of multiple weights. As before, the importance weights must add up to 1.0. Each business unit is then rated on each of the chosen strength measures, using a rating scale of 1 to 10 (where a *high* rating signifies competitive *strength* and a *low* rating signifies competitive *weakness*). In the event that the available information is too skimpy to confidently assign a rating value to a business unit on a particular strength measure, then it is usually best to use a score of 5, which avoids biasing the overall score either up or down. Weighted strength ratings are calculated by multiplying the business unit's rating on each strength measure by the assigned weight. For example, a strength score of 6 times a weight of 0.15 gives a weighted strength rating of 0.90. The sum of weighted ratings across all the strength measures provides a quantitative measure of a business unit's overall market strength and competitive standing. Table 9.2 provides sample calculations of competitive strength ratings for four businesses.

Interpreting the Competitive Strength Scores   Business units with competitive strength ratings above 6.7 (on a scale of 1 to 10) are strong market contenders in their industries. Businesses with ratings in the 3.3 to 6.7 range have moderate competitive strength vis-à-vis rivals. Businesses with ratings below 3.3 are in competitively weak market positions. If a diversified company's business units all have competitive strength scores above 5.0, it is fair to conclude that its business units are all fairly strong market contenders in their respective industries. But as the number of business units with scores below 5.0 increases, there's reason to question whether the company can perform well with so many businesses in relatively weak competitive positions. This concern takes on even more importance when business units with low scores account for a sizable fraction of the company's revenues.

Using a Nine-Cell Matrix to Simultaneously Portray Industry Attractiveness and Competitive Strength   The industry attractiveness and competitive strength scores can be used to portray the strategic positions of each business in a diversified company. Industry attractiveness is plotted on the vertical axis, and competitive strength on the horizontal axis. A nine-cell grid emerges from dividing the vertical axis into three regions (high, medium, and low attractiveness) and the horizontal axis into three regions (strong, average, and weak competitive strength). As shown in Figure 9.5, high attractiveness is associated with scores of 6.7 or greater on a rating scale of 1 to 10, medium attractiveness to scores of 3.3 to 6.7, and low attractiveness to scores below 3.3. Likewise, high competitive strength is defined as a score greater than 6.7, average strength as scores of 3.3 to 6.7, and low strength as scores below 3.3. *Each business unit is plotted on the nine-cell matrix according to its overall attractiveness score and strength score, and then shown as a bubble.* The size of each bubble is scaled to what percentage of revenues the business generates relative to total corporate revenues. The bubbles in Figure 9.5 were located on the grid using the four industry attractiveness scores from Table 9.1 and the strength scores for the four business units in Table 9.2.

The locations of the business units on the attractiveness–strength matrix provide valuable guidance in deploying corporate resources to the various business units. In general, *a diversified company's prospects for good overall performance are enhanced by concentrating corporate resources and strategic attention on those business units having the greatest competitive strength and positioned in highly attractive industries*—specifically, businesses in the three cells in the upper left portion of the attractiveness–strength matrix, where industry attractiveness and competitive strength/ market position are both favorable. The general strategic prescription for businesses falling in these three cells (for instance, business A in Figure 9.5) is "grow and build," with businesses in the high–strong cell standing first in line for resource allocations by the corporate parent.

Next in priority come businesses positioned in the three diagonal cells stretching from the lower left to the upper right (businesses B and C in Figure 9.5). Such businesses usually merit medium or intermediate priority in the parent's resource allocation ranking. However, some businesses in the medium-priority diagonal cells may have brighter or dimmer prospects than others. For example, a small business in the upper right cell of the matrix (like business B), despite being in a highly attractive industry, may occupy too weak a competitive position in its industry to justify the investment and resources needed to turn it into a strong market contender and shift its position leftward in the matrix over time. If, however, a business in the upper right cell has attractive opportunities for rapid growth and a good potential for winning a much stronger market position over time, it may merit a high claim on the corporate parent's resource allocation ranking and be given the capital it needs to pursue a grow-and-build strategy–the strategic objective here would be to move the business leftward in the attractiveness–strength matrix over time.

Businesses in the three cells in the lower right corner of the matrix (like business D in Figure 9.5) typically are weak performers and have the lowest claim on corporate resources. Most such businesses are good candidates for being divested (sold to other companies) or else managed in a manner calculated to squeeze out the maximum cash flows from operations—the cash flows from low-performing/low-potential businesses

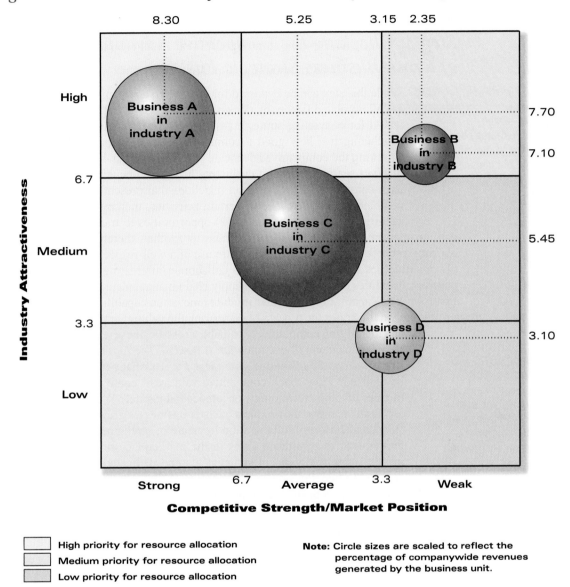

Figure 9.5   **A Nine-Cell Industry Attractiveness–Competitive Strength Matrix**

can then be diverted to financing expansion of business units with greater market opportunities. In exceptional cases where a business located in the three lower right cells
is nonetheless fairly profitable (which it might be if it is in the low–average cell) or has
the potential for good earnings and return on investment, the business merits retention
and the allocation of sufficient resources to achieve better performance.

The nine-cell attractiveness–strength matrix provides clear, strong logic for why
a diversified company needs to consider both industry attractiveness and business
strength in allocating resources and investment capital to its different businesses. A
good case can be made for concentrating resources in those businesses that enjoy
higher degrees of attractiveness and competitive strength, being very selective in
making investments in businesses with intermediate positions on the grid, and

withdrawing resources from businesses that are lower in attractiveness and strength unless they offer exceptional profit or cash flow potential.

Step 3: Checking the Competitive Advantage Potential of Cross-Business Strategic Fits

Core Concept
A company's related diversification strategy derives its power in large part from the presence of competitively valuable strategic fits among its businesses.

While this step can be bypassed for diversified companies whose businesses are all unrelated (since, by design, no strategic fits are present), a high potential for converting strategic fits into competitive advantage is central to concluding just how good a company's related diversification strategy is. Checking the competitive advantage potential of cross-business strategic fits involves searching for and evaluating how much benefit a diversified company can gain from value chain matchups that present (1) opportunities to combine the performance of certain activities, thereby reducing costs and capturing economies of scope; (2) opportunities to transfer skills, technology, or intellectual capital from one business to another, thereby leveraging use of existing resources; (3) opportunities to share use of a well-respected brand name; and (4) opportunities for sister businesses to collaborate in creating valuable new competitive capabilities (such as enhanced supply chain management capabilities, quicker first-to-market capabilities, or greater product innovation capabilities).

Figure 9.6 illustrates the process of comparing the value chains of sister businesses and identifying competitively valuable cross-business strategic fits. *But more than just strategic fit identification is needed. The real test is what competitive value can be generated from these fits.* To what extent can cost savings be realized? How much competitive value will come from cross-business transfer of skills, technology, or intellectual capital? Will transferring a potent brand name to the products of sister businesses grow sales significantly? Will cross-business collaboration to create or strengthen competitive capabilities lead to significant gains in the marketplace or in financial performance? Absent significant strategic fits and dedicated company efforts to capture the benefits, one has to be skeptical about the potential for a diversified company's businesses to perform better together than apart.

Core Concept
The greater the value of cross-business strategic fits in enhancing a company's performance in the marketplace or on the bottom line, the more competitively powerful is its strategy of related diversification.

Step 4: Checking for Resource Fit

Core Concept
Sister businesses possess *resource fit* when they add to a company's overall resource strengths and when a company has adequate resources to support their requirements.

The businesses in a diversified company's lineup need to exhibit good **resource fit.** Resource fit exists when (1) businesses add to a company's overall resource strengths and (2) a company has adequate resources to support its entire group of businesses without spreading itself too thin. One important dimension of resource fit concerns whether a diversified company can generate the internal cash flows sufficient to fund the capital requirements of its businesses, pay its dividends, meet its debt obligations, and otherwise remain financially healthy.

Financial Resource Fits: Cash Cows versus Cash Hogs   Different businesses have different cash flow and investment characteristics. For example, business units in rapidly growing industries are often **cash hogs**—so labeled because the cash flows they are able to generate from internal operations aren't big enough to fund their expansion. To keep pace with rising buyer demand, rapid-growth businesses frequently need sizable annual capital investments—for new facilities and equipment, for

Figure 9.6   **Identifying the Competitive Advantage Potential of Cross-Business Strategic Fits**

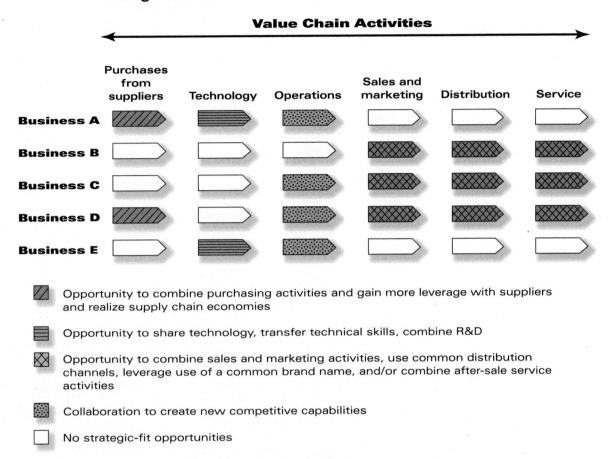

Value Chain Activities

	Purchases from suppliers	Technology	Operations	Sales and marketing	Distribution	Service
Business A	▨	▤	▒	□	□	□
Business B	□	□	□	▩	▩	▩
Business C	□	□	▒	▩	▩	▩
Business D	▨	□	▒	▩	▩	▩
Business E	□	▤	▒	□	□	□

▨ Opportunity to combine purchasing activities and gain more leverage with suppliers and realize supply chain economies

▤ Opportunity to share technology, transfer technical skills, combine R&D

▩ Opportunity to combine sales and marketing activities, use common distribution channels, leverage use of a common brand name, and/or combine after-sale service activities

▒ Collaboration to create new competitive capabilities

□ No strategic-fit opportunities

new product development or technology improvements, and for additional working capital to support inventory expansion and a larger base of operations. A business in a fast-growing industry becomes an even bigger cash hog when it has a relatively low market share and is pursuing a strategy to become an industry leader. Because a cash hog's financial resources must be provided by the corporate parent, corporate managers have to decide whether it makes good financial and strategic sense to keep pouring new money into a business that continually needs cash infusions.

In contrast, business units with leading market positions in mature industries may, however, be **cash cows**—businesses that generate substantial cash surpluses over what is needed to adequately fund their operations. Market leaders in slow-growth industries often generate sizable positive cash flows *over and above what is needed for growth and reinvestment* because their industry-leading positions tend to give them the sales volumes and reputation to earn attractive profits and because the slow-growth nature of their industry often entails relatively modest annual investment requirements. Cash cows, though not always attractive from a growth standpoint, are valuable businesses from a financial resource perspective. The surplus cash flows they generate can be used to pay corporate dividends, finance acquisitions, and provide

> **Core Concept**
> A *cash hog* generates cash flows that are too small to fully fund its operations and growth; a cash hog requires cash infusions to provide additional working capital and finance new capital investment.

funds for investing in the company's promising cash hogs. It makes good financial and strategic sense for diversified companies to keep cash cows in healthy condition, fortifying and defending their market position so as to preserve their cash-generating capability over the long term and thereby have an ongoing source of financial resources to deploy elsewhere. The cigarette business is one of the world's biggest cash cows. General Electric, whose business lineup is shown in Illustration Capsule 9.2, considers that its advanced materials, equipment services, and appliance and lighting businesses are cash cows.

Viewing a diversified group of businesses as a collection of cash flows and cash requirements (present and future) is a major step forward in understanding what the financial ramifications of diversification are and why having businesses with good financial resource fit is so important. For instance, *a diversified company's businesses exhibit good financial resource fit when the excess cash generated by its cash cows is sufficient to fund the investment requirements of promising cash hogs.* Ideally, investing in promising cash hog businesses over time results in growing the hogs into self-supporting *star businesses* that have strong or market-leading competitive positions in attractive, high-growth markets and high levels of profitability. Star businesses are often the cash cows of the future—when the markets of star businesses begin to mature and their growth slows, their competitive strength should produce self-generated cash flows more than sufficient to cover their investment needs. The "success sequence" is thus cash hog to young star (but perhaps still a cash hog) to self-supporting star to cash cow.

If, however, a cash hog has questionable promise (either because of low industry attractiveness or a weak competitive position), then it becomes a logical candidate for divestiture. Pursuing an aggressive invest-and-expand strategy for a cash hog with an uncertain future seldom makes sense because it requires the corporate parent to keep pumping more capital into the business with only a dim hope of eventually turning the cash hog into a future star and realizing a good return on its investments. Such financially draining businesses fail the resource fit test because they strain the corporate parent's ability to adequately fund its other businesses. Divesting a cash hog is usually the best alternative unless (1) it has valuable strategic fits with other business units or (2) the capital infusions needed from the corporate parent are modest relative to the funds available and there's a decent chance of growing the business into a solid bottom-line contributor yielding a good return on invested capital.

Other Tests of Resource Fit   Aside from cash flow considerations, there are four other factors to consider in determining whether the businesses comprising a diversified company's portfolio exhibit good resource fit:

- *Does the business adequately contribute to achieving companywide performance targets?* A business has good financial fit when it contributes to the achievement of corporate performance objectives (growth in earnings per share, above-average return on investment, recognition as an industry leader, etc.) and when it materially enhances shareholder value via helping drive increases in the company's stock price. A business exhibits poor financial fit if it soaks up a disproportionate share of the company's financial resources, makes subpar or inconsistent bottom-line contributions, is unduly risky and failure would jeopardize the entire enterprise, or remains too small to make a material earnings contribution even though it performs well.

- *Does the company have adequate financial strength to fund its different businesses and maintain a healthy credit rating?* A diversified company's strategy fails the resource fit test when its financial resources are stretched across so many businesses that its credit rating is impaired. Severe financial strain sometimes occurs when a company borrows so heavily to finance new acquisitions that it has to trim way back on capital expenditures for existing businesses and use the big majority of its financial resources to meet interest obligations and to pay down debt. Time Warner, Royal Ahold, and AT&T, for example, have found themselves so financially overextended that they have had to sell off some of their business units to raise the money to pay down burdensome debt obligations and continue to fund essential capital expenditures for the remaining businesses.

- *Does the company have or can it develop the specific resource strengths and competitive capabilities needed to be successful in each of its businesses?*[15] Sometimes the resource strengths a company has accumulated in its core or mainstay business prove to be a poor match with the key success factors and competitive capabilities needed to succeed in one or more businesses it has diversified into. For instance, BTR, a multibusiness company in Great Britain, discovered that the company's resources and managerial skills were quite well suited for parenting industrial manufacturing businesses but not for parenting its distribution businesses (National Tyre Services and Texas-based Summers Group); as a consequence, BTR decided to divest its distribution businesses and focus exclusively on diversifying around small industrial manufacturing.[16] One company with businesses in restaurants and retailing decided that its resource capabilities in site selection, controlling operating costs, management selection and training, and supply chain logistics would enable it to succeed in the hotel business and in property management; but what management missed was that these businesses had some significantly different key success factors—namely, skills in controlling property development costs, maintaining low overheads, product branding (hotels), and ability to recruit a sufficient volume of business to maintain high levels of facility use.[17] Thus, a mismatch between the company's resource strengths and the key success factors in a particular business can be serious enough to warrant divesting an existing business or not acquiring a new business. In contrast, when a company's resources and capabilities are a good match with the key success factors of industries it is not presently in, it makes sense to take a hard look at acquiring companies in these industries and expanding the company's business lineup.

- *Are recently acquired businesses acting to strengthen a company's resource base and competitive capabilities or are they causing its competitive and managerial resources to be stretched too thin?* A diversified company has to guard against overtaxing its resource strengths, a condition that can arise when (1) it goes on an acquisition spree and management is called on to assimilate and oversee many new businesses very quickly or (2) when it lacks sufficient resource depth to do a creditable job of transferring skills and competences from one of its businesses to another (especially, a large acquisition or several lesser ones). The broader the diversification, the greater the concern about whether the company has sufficient managerial depth to cope with the diverse range of operating problems its wide business lineup presents. And the more a company's diversification strategy is tied to transferring its existing know-how or technologies to new businesses, the more it has to develop a big enough and deep enough resource pool to supply these businesses with sufficient capability to create competitive advantage.[18] Otherwise its strengths end up being thinly spread across many businesses and the opportunity for competitive advantage slips through the cracks.

A Cautionary Note About Transferring Resources from One Business to Another   Just because a company has hit a home run in one business doesn't mean it can easily enter a new business with similar resource requirements and hit a second home run.[19] Noted British retailer Marks & Spencer, despite possessing a range of impressive resource capabilities (ability to choose excellent store locations, having a supply chain that gives it both low costs and high merchandise quality, loyal employees, an excellent reputation with consumers, and strong management expertise) that have made it one of Britain's premier retailers for 100 years, has failed repeatedly in its efforts to diversify into department store retailing in the United States. Even though Philip Morris (now named Altria) had built powerful consumer marketing capabilities in its cigarette and beer businesses, it floundered in soft drinks and ended up divesting its acquisition of 7UP after several frustrating years of competing against strongly entrenched and resource-capable rivals like Coca-Cola and PepsiCo. Then in 2002 it decided to divest its Miller Brewing business—despite its long-standing marketing successes in cigarettes and in its Kraft Foods subsidiary—because it was unable to grow Miller's market share in head-to-head competition against the considerable marketing prowess of Anheuser-Busch.

Step 5: Ranking the Performance Prospects of Business Units and Assigning a Priority for Resource Allocation

Once a diversified company's strategy has been evaluated from the perspective of industry attractiveness, competitive strength, strategic fit, and resource fit, the next step is to rank the performance prospects of the businesses from best to worst and determine which businesses merit top priority for resource support and new capital investments by the corporate parent.

The most important considerations in judging business-unit performance are sales growth, profit growth, contribution to company earnings, and return on capital invested in the business. Sometimes cash flow is a big consideration. Information on each business's past performance can be gleaned from a company's financial records. While past performance is not necessarily a good predictor of future performance, it does signal whether a business already has good-to-excellent performance or has problems to overcome.

Furthermore, the industry attractiveness/business strength evaluations provide a solid basis for judging a business's prospects. Normally, strong business units in attractive industries have significantly better prospects than weak businesses in unattractive industries. And, normally, the revenue and earnings outlook for businesses in fast-growing industries is better than for businesses in slow-growing industries—one important exception is when a business in a slow-growing industry has the competitive strength to draw sales and market share away from its rivals and thus achieve much faster growth than the industry as whole. As a rule, the prior analyses, taken together, signal which business units are likely to be strong performers on the road ahead and which are likely to be laggards. And it is a short step from ranking the prospects of business units to drawing conclusions about whether the company as a whole is capable of strong, mediocre, or weak performance in upcoming years.

Figure 9.7 **The Chief Strategic and Financial Options for Allocating a Diversified Company's Financial Resources**

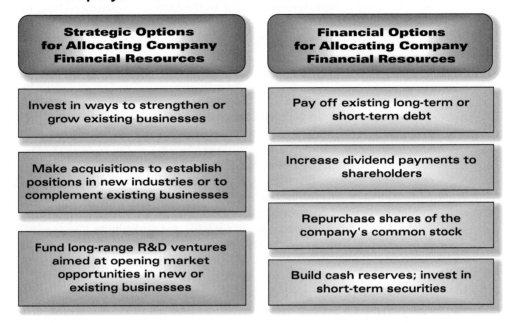

The rankings of future performance generally determine what priority the corporate parent should give to each business in terms of resource allocation. The task here is to decide which business units should have top priority for corporate resource support and new capital investment and which should carry the lowest priority. *Business subsidiaries with the brightest profit and growth prospects and solid strategic and resource fits generally should head the list for corporate resource support.* More specifically, corporate executives need to consider whether and how corporate resources can be used to enhance the competitiveness of particular business units. And they must be diligent in steering resources out of low-opportunity areas and into high-opportunity areas. Divesting marginal businesses is one of the best ways of freeing unproductive assets for redeployment. Surplus funds from cash cows also add to the corporate treasury.

Figure 9.7 shows the chief strategic and financial options for allocating a diversified company's financial resources. Ideally, a company will have enough funds to do what is needed, both strategically and financially. If not, strategic uses of corporate resources should usually take precedence unless there is a compelling reason to strengthen the firm's balance sheet or divert financial resources to pacify shareholders.

Step 6: Crafting New Strategic Moves to Improve Overall Corporate Performance

The diagnosis and conclusions flowing from the five preceding analytical steps set the agenda for crafting strategic moves to improve a diversified company's overall performance. The strategic options boil down to five broad categories of actions:

1. Sticking closely with the existing business lineup and pursuing the opportunities these businesses present.

2. Broadening the company's business scope by making new acquisitions in new industries.

3. Divesting certain businesses and retrenching to a narrower base of business operations.

4. Restructuring the company's business lineup and putting a whole new face on the company's business makeup.

5. Pursuing multinational diversification and striving to globalize the operations of several of the company's business units.

The option of sticking with the current business lineup makes sense when the company's present businesses offer attractive growth opportunities and can be counted on to generate good earnings and cash flows. As long as the company's set of existing businesses puts it in good position for the future and these businesses have good strategic and/or resource fits, then rocking the boat with major changes in the company's business mix is usually unnecessary. Corporate executives can concentrate their attention on getting the best performance from each of its businesses, steering corporate resources into those areas of greatest potential and profitability. The specifics of "what to do" to wring better performance from the present business lineup have to be dictated by each business's circumstances and the preceding analysis of the corporate parent's diversification strategy.

However, in the event that corporate executives are not entirely satisfied with the opportunities they see in the company's present set of businesses and conclude that changes in the company's direction and business makeup are in order, they can opt for any of the four other strategic alternatives listed above. These options are discussed in the following section.

AFTER A COMPANY DIVERSIFIES: THE FOUR MAIN STRATEGY ALTERNATIVES

Diversifying is by no means the final chapter in the evolution of a company's strategy. Once a company has diversified into a collection of related or unrelated businesses and concludes that some overhaul is needed in the company's present lineup and diversification strategy, there are four main strategic paths it can pursue (see Figure 9.8). To more fully understand the strategic issues corporate managers face in the ongoing process of managing a diversified group of businesses, we need to take a brief look at the central thrust of each of the four postdiversification strategy alternatives.

Strategies to Broaden a Diversified Company's Business Base

Diversified companies sometimes find it desirable to build positions in new industries, whether related or unrelated. There are several motivating factors. One is sluggish growth that makes the potential revenue and profit boost of a newly acquired business look attractive. A second is vulnerability to seasonal or recessionary influences or to threats from emerging new technologies. A third is the potential for transferring resources and capabilities to other related or complementary businesses. A fourth is rapidly changing conditions in one or more of a company's core businesses brought on by technological, legislative, or new product innovations that alter buyer requirements and preferences. For instance, the passage of legislation in the United States allowing

Figure 9.8   **A Company's Four Main Strategic Alternatives After It Diversifies**

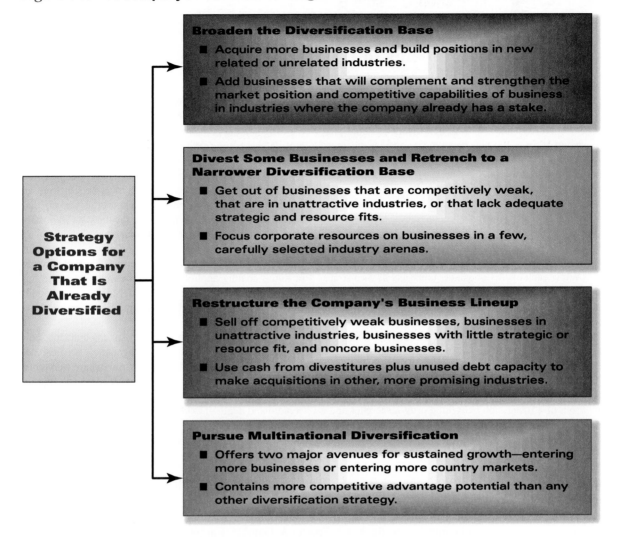

Strategy Options for a Company That Is Already Diversified

Broaden the Diversification Base
- Acquire more businesses and build positions in new related or unrelated industries.
- Add businesses that will complement and strengthen the market position and competitive capabilities of business in industries where the company already has a stake.

Divest Some Businesses and Retrench to a Narrower Diversification Base
- Get out of businesses that are competitively weak, that are in unattractive industries, or that lack adequate strategic and resource fits.
- Focus corporate resources on businesses in a few, carefully selected industry arenas.

Restructure the Company's Business Lineup
- Sell off competitively weak businesses, businesses in unattractive industries, businesses with little strategic or resource fit, and noncore businesses.
- Use cash from divestitures plus unused debt capacity to make acquisitions in other, more promising industries.

Pursue Multinational Diversification
- Offers two major avenues for sustained growth—entering more businesses or entering more country markets.
- Contains more competitive advantage potential than any other diversification strategy.

banks, insurance companies, and stock brokerages to enter each other's businesses spurred a raft of acquisitions and mergers to create full-service financial enterprises capable of meeting the multiple financial needs of customers. Citigroup, already the largest U.S. bank, with a global banking franchise, acquired Salomon Smith Barney to position itself in the investment banking and brokerage business and acquired insurance giant Travelers Group to enable it to offer customers insurance products.

A fifth, and often very important, motivating factor for adding new businesses is to complement and strengthen the market position and competitive capabilities of one or more of its present businesses. Procter & Gamble's recent acquisition of Gillette strengthened and extended P&G's reach into personal care and household products—Gillette's businesses included Oral-B toothbrushes, Gillette razors and razor blades, Duracell batteries, Braun shavers and small appliances (coffeemakers, mixers, hair dryers, and electric toothbrushes), and toiletries (Right Guard, Foamy, Soft & Dry, White Rain, and Dry Idea). Unilever, a leading maker of food and personal care products, expanded its business lineup by acquiring SlimFast, Ben & Jerry's Homemade,

Illustration Capsule 9.3

Managing Diversification at Johnson & Johnson: The Benefits of Cross-Business Strategic Fits

Johnson & Johnson (J&J), once a consumer products company known for its Band-Aid line and its baby care products, has evolved into a $42 billion diversified enterprise consisting of some 200-plus operating companies organized into three divisions: drugs, medical devices and diagnostics, and consumer products. Over the past decade J&J has acquired 56 businesses at a cost of about $30 billion; about 10 to 15 percent of J&J's annual growth in revenues has come from acquisitions. Much of the company's recent growth has been in the pharmaceutical division, which in 2004 accounted for 47 percent of J&J's revenues and 57 percent of its operating profits.

While each of J&J's business units sets its own strategies and operates with its own finance and human resource departments, corporate management strongly encourages cross-business cooperation and collaboration, believing that many of the advances in 21st century medicine will come from applying advances in one discipline to another. J&J had 9,300 scientists working in 40 research labs in 2003, and the frequency of cross-disciplinary collaboration was increasing. One of J&J's new drug-coated stents grew out of a discussion between a drug researcher and a researcher in the company's stent business. (When stents are inserted to prop open arteries following angioplasty, the drug coating helps prevent infection.) A gene technology database compiled by the company's gene research lab was shared with personnel from the diagnostics division, who developed a test that the drug R&D people could use to predict which patients would most benefit from an experimental cancer therapy. J&J experts in various diseases have been meeting quarterly for the past five years to share information, and top management is setting up cross-disciplinary groups to focus on new treatments for particular diseases. J&J's new liquid Band-Aid product (a liquid coating applied to hard-to-cover places like fingers and knuckles) is based on a material used in a wound-closing product sold by the company's hospital products company.

J&J's corporate management maintains that close collaboration among people in its diagnostics, medical devices, and pharmaceuticals businesses—where numerous cross-business strategic fits exist—gives J&J an edge on competitors, most of whom cannot match the company's breadth and depth of expertise.

Sources: Amy Barrett, "Staying on Top," *BusinessWeek,* May 5, 2003, pp. 60–68, and www.jnj.com (accessed October 19, 2005).

and Bestfoods (whose brands included Knorr's soups, Hellman's mayonnaise, Skippy peanut butter, and Mazola cooking oils). Unilever saw these businesses as giving it more clout in competing against such other diversified food and household products companies as Nestlé, Kraft, Procter & Gamble, Campbell Soup, and General Mills.

Usually, expansion into new businesses is undertaken by acquiring companies already in the target industry. Some companies depend on new acquisitions to drive a major portion of their growth in revenues and earnings, and thus are always on the acquisition trail. Cisco Systems built itself into a worldwide leader in networking systems for the Internet by making 95 technology-based acquisitions during 1993–2005 to extend its market reach from routing and switching into Internet Protocol (IP) telephony, home networking, wireless local-area networking (LAN), storage networking, network security, broadband, and optical and broadband systems. Tyco International, now recovering from charges of looting on the part of several top executives, transformed itself from an obscure company in the early 1990s into a $40 billion global manufacturing enterprise with operations in over 100 countries as of 2005 by making over 1,000 acquisitions; the company's far-flung diversification includes businesses in electronics, electrical components, fire and security systems, health care products, valves, undersea telecommunications systems, plastics, and adhesives. Tyco made over 700 acquisitions of small companies in the 1999–2001 period alone. As a group, Tyco's businesses were cash cows, generating a combined free cash flow in 2005 of around $4.4 billion.

Illustration Capsule 9.3 describes how Johnson & Johnson has used acquisitions to diversify far beyond its well-known Band-Aid and baby care businesses and become a major player in pharmaceuticals, medical devices, and medical diagnostics.

Divestiture Strategies Aimed at Retrenching to a Narrower Diversification Base

A number of diversified firms have had difficulty managing a diverse group of businesses and have elected to get out of some of them. Retrenching to a narrower diversification base is usually undertaken when top management concludes that its diversification strategy has ranged too far afield and that the company can improve long-term performance by concentrating on building stronger positions in a smaller number of core businesses and industries. Hewlett-Packard spun off its testing and measurement businesses into a stand-alone company called Agilent Technologies so that it could better concentrate on its PC, workstation, server, printer and peripherals, and electronics businesses. PepsiCo divested its cash-hog group of restaurant businesses, consisting of KFC, Pizza Hut, Taco Bell, and California Pizza Kitchens, to provide more resources for strengthening its soft-drink business (which was losing market share to Coca-Cola) and growing its more profitable Frito-Lay snack foods business. Kmart divested OfficeMax, Sports Authority, and Borders Bookstores in order to refocus management attention and all of the company's resources on restoring luster to its distressed discount retailing business, which was (and still is) being totally outclassed in the marketplace by Wal-Mart and Target. In 2003–2004, Tyco International began a program to divest itself of some 50 businesses, including its entire undersea fiber-optics telecommunications network and an assortment of businesses in its fire and security division; the initiative also involved consolidating 219 manufacturing, sales, distribution, and other facilities and reducing its workforce of some 260,000 people by 7,200. Lucent Technology's retrenchment strategy is described in Illustration Capsule 9.4.

> Focusing corporate resources on a few core and mostly related businesses avoids the mistake of diversifying so broadly that resources and management attention are stretched too thin.

But there are other important reasons for divesting one or more of a company's present businesses. Sometimes divesting a business has to be considered because market conditions in a once-attractive industry have badly deteriorated. A business can become a prime candidate for divestiture because it lacks adequate strategic or resource fit, because it is a cash hog with questionable long-term potential, or because it is weakly positioned in its industry with little prospect the corporate parent can realize a decent return on its investment in the business. Sometimes a company acquires businesses that, down the road, just do not work out as expected even though management has tried all it can think of to make them profitable—mistakes cannot be completely avoided because it is hard to foresee how getting into a new line of business will actually work out. Subpar performance by some business units is bound to occur, thereby raising questions of whether to divest them or keep them and attempt a turnaround. Other business units, despite adequate financial performance, may not mesh as well with the rest of the firm as was originally thought.

Illustration Capsule 9.4
Lucent Technology's Retrenchment Strategy

At the height of the telecommunications boom in 1999–2000, Lucent Technology was a company with $38.3 billion in revenues and 157,000 employees; it was the biggest maker of telecommunications equipment in the United States and a recognized leader worldwide. The company's strategy was to build positions in a number of blossoming technologies and industry arenas and achieve 20 percent annual revenue growth in each of 11 different business groups. But when customers' orders for new equipment began to evaporate in 2000–2001, Lucent's profits vanished and the once-growing company found itself battling to overcome bloated costs, deep price discounting, and customer defaults on the $7.5 billion in loans Lucent had made to finance their purchases. As it became clear that equipment sales and prices would never return to former levels, Lucent executives concluded that the company had overextended itself trying to do too many things and needed to pare its lineup of businesses.

Alongside efforts to curtail lavish spending at the company's fabled Bell Labs research unit, make deep workforce cutbacks, streamline order-taking and billing systems, shore up the balance sheet, and conserve cash by ending dividend payments, management launched a series of retrenchment initiatives:

- Of the 40 businesses Lucent acquired since 1996, 27 were sold, closed, or spun off.

- Lucent ceased all manufacturing operations, opting to outsource everything.

- It stopped making gear for wireless phone networks based on global system for mobile communication (GSM) technology (the dominant technology used in Europe and much of the world) in order to focus more fully on wireless gear using code division multiple access (CDMA) technology (a technology prevalent in the United States and some developing nations). As of 2004 Lucent had an estimated 45 percent share in the CDMA market and the CDMA gear division was the company's chief revenue and profit producer.

- The wireline and wireless business units were combined to form a single, unified organization called Network Solutions.

- All the remaining businesses were grouped into a unit called Lucent Worldwide Services that was engaged in designing, implementing, integrating, and managing sophisticated voice and data networks for service providers in 45 countries.

- The role of Bell Labs was narrowed to supporting the efforts of both the Network Solutions group and the Worldwide Services group.

Lucent's strategic moves to retrench stemmed a string of 13 straight money-losing quarters. In fiscal 2004 Lucent reported profits of $2 billion from continuing operations (equal to EPS of $0.47 but still far below the levels of $0.93 in 2000 and $1.12 in 1999). In May 2004, Lucent announced its first acquisition in four years, buying a maker of Internet transmission technology for $300 million to help it become a leader in Internet telephony technology. Going into 2006, Lucent was a company with sales of about $9 billion (versus $38 billion in 1999) and a workforce of about 30,000 (versus 157,000 in 1999). The company's stock price, which reached a high of $62 in 1999 before crashing to below $1 in 2002, languished in the $3–$4 range for most of 2004–2005, indicating continuing investor skepticism about Lucent's prospects despite its having retreated to businesses where it was strongest.

Sources: Shawn Young, "Less May Be More," *The Wall Street Journal,* October 23, 2004, p. R10, and www.lucent.com (accessed October 19, 2005).

On occasion, a diversification move that seems sensible from a strategic-fit standpoint turns out to be a poor *cultural fit.*[20] Several pharmaceutical companies had just this experience. When they diversified into cosmetics and perfume, they discovered their personnel had little respect for the "frivolous" nature of such products compared to the far nobler task of developing miracle drugs to cure the ill. The absence of shared values and cultural compatibility between the medical research and chemical-compounding expertise of the pharmaceutical companies and the fashion/marketing orientation of the cosmetics business was the undoing of what otherwise was diversification into businesses with technology-sharing potential, product-development fit, and some overlap in distribution channels.

There's evidence indicating that pruning businesses and narrowing a firm's diversification base improves corporate performance.[21] Corporate parents often end up selling off businesses too late and at too low a price, sacrificing shareholder value.[22] A useful guide to determine whether or when to divest a business subsidiary is to ask, "If we were not in this business today, would we want to get into it now?"[23] When the answer is no or probably not, divestiture should be considered. Another signal that a business should become a divestiture candidate is whether it is worth more to another company than to the present parent; in such cases, shareholders would be well served if the company sells the business and collects a premium price from the buyer for whom the business is a valuable fit.[24]

> Diversified companies need to divest low-performing businesses or businesses that don't fit in order to concentrate on expanding existing businesses and entering new ones where opportunities are more promising.

The Two Options for Divesting a Business: Selling It or Spinning It Off as an Independent Company

Selling a business outright to another company is far and away the most frequently used option for divesting a business. But sometimes a business selected for divestiture has ample resource strengths to compete successfully on its own. In such cases, a corporate parent may elect to spin the unwanted business off as a financially and managerially independent company, either by selling shares to the investing public via an initial public offering or by distributing shares in the new company to existing shareholders of the corporate parent. When a corporate parent decides to spin off one of its businesses as a separate company, it must decide whether or not to retain partial ownership. Retaining partial ownership makes sense when the business to be divested has a hot product or technological capabilities that give it good profit prospects. When 3Com elected to divest its PalmPilot business, which investors then saw as having very promising profit potential, it elected to retain a substantial ownership interest so as to provide 3Com shareholders a way of participating in whatever future market success that PalmPilot (now Palm Inc.) might have on its own. In 2001, when Philip Morris (now Altria) became concerned that its popular Kraft Foods subsidiary was suffering because of its affiliation with Philip Morris's cigarette business (antismoking groups were leading a national boycott of Kraft macaroni and cheese, and a Harris poll revealed that about 16 percent of people familiar with Philip Morris had boycotted its products), Philip Morris executives opted to spin Kraft Foods off as an independent public company but retained a controlling ownership interest. R. J. Reynolds Tobacco was also spun off from Nabisco Foods in 1999 in an effort to distance the tobacco operations part of the company from the food operations part. (Nabisco was then acquired by Philip Morris in 2000 and integrated into Kraft Foods.) In 2005, Cendant announced it would split its diversified businesses into four separate publicly traded companies—one for vehicle rental services (which consisted of Avis and Budget car rental companies); one for real estate and mortgage services (which included Century 21, Coldwell Banker, ERA, Sotheby's International Realty, and NRT—a residential real estate brokerage company); one for hospitality and lodging (consisting of such hotels and motel chains as Wyndam, Ramada, Days Inn, Howard Johnson, Travelodge, AmeriHost Inn, and Knights Inn, plus an assortment of time-share resort properties); and one for travel (consisting of various travel agencies, online ticket and vacation travel sites like Orbitz and Cheap Tickets, and vacation rental operations handling some 55,000 villas and condos). Cendant said the reason for the split-up was that shareholders would realize more value from operating the businesses independently—a clear sign that

Cendant's diversification strategy had failed to deliver added shareholder value and that the parts were worth more than the whole.

Selling a business outright requires finding a buyer. This can prove hard or easy, depending on the business. As a rule, a company selling a troubled business should not ask, "How can we pawn this business off on someone, and what is the most we can get for it?"[25] Instead, it is wiser to ask, "For what sort of company would this business be a good fit, and under what conditions would it be viewed as a good deal?" Enterprises for which the business is a good fit are likely to pay the highest price. Of course, if a buyer willing to pay an acceptable price cannot be found, then a company must decide whether to keep the business until a buyer appears; spin it off as a separate company; or, in the case of a crisis-ridden business that is losing substantial sums, simply close it down and liquidate the remaining assets. Liquidation is obviously a last resort.

Strategies to Restructure a Company's Business Lineup

Core Concept
Restructuring involves divesting some businesses and acquiring others so as to put a whole new face on the company's business lineup.

Restructuring strategies involve divesting some businesses and acquiring others so as to put a whole new face on the company's business lineup. Performing radical surgery on a company's group of businesses is an appealing strategy alternative when its financial performance is being squeezed or eroded by:

- Too many businesses in slow-growth, declining, low-margin, or otherwise unattractive industries (a condition indicated by the number and size of businesses with industry attractiveness ratings below 5 and located on the bottom half of the attractiveness–strength matrix—see Figure 9.5).
- Too many competitively weak businesses (a condition indicated by the number and size of businesses with competitive strength ratings below 5 and located on the right half of the attractiveness–strength matrix).
- Ongoing declines in the market shares of one or more major business units that are falling prey to more market-savvy competitors.
- An excessive debt burden with interest costs that eat deeply into profitability.
- Ill-chosen acquisitions that haven't lived up to expectations.

Restructuring can also be mandated by the emergence of new technologies that threaten the survival of one or more of a diversified company's important businesses or by the appointment of a new CEO who decides to redirect the company. On occasion, restructuring can be prompted by special circumstances—as when a firm has a unique opportunity to make an acquisition so big and important that it has to sell several existing business units to finance the new acquisition, or when a company needs to sell off some businesses in order to raise the cash for entering a potentially big industry with wave-of-the-future technologies or products.

Candidates for divestiture in a corporate restructuring effort typically include not only weak or up-and-down performers or those in unattractive industries but also business units that lack strategic fit with the businesses to be retained, businesses that are cash hogs or that lack other types of resource fit, and businesses incompatible with the company's revised diversification strategy (even though they may be profitable or in an attractive industry). As businesses are divested, corporate restructuring generally involves aligning the remaining business units into groups with the best strategic fits and then redeploying the cash flows from the divested business to either pay down debt or make new acquisitions to strengthen the parent company's business position in the industries it has chosen to emphasize.[26]

Over the past decade, corporate restructuring has become a popular strategy at many diversified companies, especially those that had diversified broadly into many different industries and lines of business. For instance, one struggling diversified company over a two-year period divested four business units, closed down the operations of four others, and added 25 new lines of business to its portfolio (16 through acquisition and 9 through internal start-up). PerkinElmer used a series of divestitures and new acquisitions to transform itself from a supplier of low-margin services sold to the government agencies into an innovative high-tech company with operations in over 125 countries and businesses in four industry groups—life sciences (drug research and clinical screening), optoelectronics, medical instruments, and fluid control and containment services (for customers in aerospace, power generation, and semiconductors). In 2005, PerkinElmer took a second restructuring step by divesting its entire fluid control and containment business group so that it could concentrate on its higher-growth health sciences and optoelectronics businesses; the company's CEO said, "While fluid services is an excellent business, it does not fit with our long-term strategy."[27] Before beginning a restructuring effort in 1995, British-based Hanson PLC owned companies with more than $20 billion in revenues in industries as diverse as beer, exercise equipment, tools, construction cranes, tobacco, cement, chemicals, coal mining, electricity, hot tubs and whirlpools, cookware, rock and gravel, bricks, and asphalt. By early 1997, Hanson had restructured itself into a $3.8 billion enterprise focused more narrowly on gravel, crushed rock, cement, asphalt, bricks, and construction cranes; the remaining businesses were divided into four groups and divested.

During Jack Welch's first four years as CEO of General Electric (GE), the company divested 117 business units, accounting for about 20 percent of GE's assets; these divestitures, coupled with several important acquisitions, provided GE with 14 major business divisions and led to Welch's challenge to the managers of GE's divisions to become number one or number two in their industry. Ten years after Welch became CEO, GE was a different company, having divested operations worth $9 billion, made new acquisitions totaling $24 billion, and cut its workforce by 100,000 people. Then, during the 1990–2001 period, GE continued to reshuffle its business lineup, acquiring over 600 new companies, including 108 in 1998 and 64 during a 90-day period in 1999. Most of the new acquisitions were in Europe, Asia, and Latin America and were aimed at transforming GE into a truly global enterprise. In 2003, GE's new CEO, Jeffrey Immelt, began a further restructuring of GE's business lineup with three initiatives: (1) spending $10 billion to acquire British-based Amersham and extend GE's Medical Systems business into diagnostic pharmaceuticals and biosciences, thereby creating a $15 billion business designated as GE Healthcare; (2) acquiring the entertainment assets of debt-ridden French media conglomerate Vivendi Universal Entertainment (Universal Studios, five Universal theme parks, USA Network, Sci-Fi Channel, the Trio cable channel, and Spanish-language broadcaster Telemundo) and integrate its operations into GE's NBC division (the owner of NBC, 29 television stations, and cable networks CNBC, MSNBC, and Bravo), thereby creating a broad-based $13 billion media business positioned to compete against Walt Disney, Time Warner, Fox, and Viacom; and (3) beginning a withdrawal from the insurance business by divesting several companies in its insurance division and preparing to spin off its remaining life and mortgage insurance businesses through an initial public offering of stock for a new company called Genworth Financial.

In a study of the performance of the 200 largest U.S. corporations from 1990 to 2000, McKinsey & Company found that those companies that actively managed their business portfolios through acquisitions and divestitures created substantially more shareholder value than those that kept a fixed lineup of businesses.[28]

Multinational Diversification Strategies

The distinguishing characteristics of a multinational diversification strategy are a *diversity of businesses* and a *diversity of national markets*.[29] Such diversity makes multinational diversification a particularly challenging and complex strategy to conceive and execute. Managers have to develop business strategies for each industry (with as many multinational variations as conditions in each country market dictate). Then they have to pursue and manage opportunities for cross-business and cross-country collaboration and strategic coordination in ways calculated to result in competitive advantage and enhanced profitability.

Moreover, the geographic operating scope of individual businesses within a diversified multinational corporation (DMNC) can range from one country only to several countries to many countries to global. Thus, each business unit within a DMNC often competes in a somewhat different combination of geographic markets than the other businesses do—adding another element of strategic complexity, and perhaps an element of opportunity.

Illustration Capsule 9.5 shows the scope of four prominent DMNCs.

The Appeal of Multinational Diversification: More Opportunities for Sustained Growth and Maximum Competitive Advantage Potential

Despite their complexity, multinational diversification strategies have great appeal. They contain *two major avenues* for growing revenues and profits: One is to grow by entering additional businesses, and the other is to grow by extending the operations of existing businesses into additional country markets. Moreover, a strategy of multinational diversification also contains six attractive paths to competitive advantage, *all of which can be pursued simultaneously:*

1. *Full capture of economies of scale and experience/learning curve effects.* In some businesses, the volume of sales needed to realize full economies of scale and/or benefit fully from experience/learning curve effects is rather sizable, often exceeding the volume that can be achieved operating within the boundaries of a single country market, especially a small one. *The ability to drive down unit costs by expanding sales to additional country markets is one reason why a diversified multinational may seek to acquire a business and then rapidly expand its operations into more and more foreign markets.*

2. *Opportunities to capitalize on cross-business economies of scope.* Diversifying into related businesses offering economies of scope can drive the development of a low-cost advantage over less diversified rivals. For example, a DMNC that uses mostly the same distributors and retail dealers worldwide can diversify into new businesses using these same worldwide distribution channels at relatively little incremental expense. The cost savings of piggybacking distribution activities can be substantial. Moreover, with more business selling more products in more countries, a DMNC acquires more bargaining leverage in its purchases from suppliers and more bargaining leverage with retailers in securing attractive display space for its products. Consider, for example, the competitive power that Sony derived

Illustration Capsule 9.5

The Global Scope of Four Prominent Diversified Multinational Corporations

Company	Global Scope	Businesses into Which the Company Has Diversified
Sony	Operations in more than 100 countries and sales offices in more than 200 countries	• Televisions, VCRs, DVD players, Walkman MP3 players, radios, digital cameras and video equipment, Vaio PCs, and Trinitron computer monitors; PlayStation game consoles and video game software; Columbia, Epic, and Sony Classical pre-recorded music; Columbia TriStar motion pictures; syndicated television programs; entertainment complexes, and insurance
Nestlé	Operations in 70 countries and sales offices in more than 200 countries	• Beverages (Nescafé and Taster's Choice coffees, Nestea, Perrier, Arrowhead, & Calistoga mineral and bottled waters); milk products (Carnation, Gloria, Neslac, Coffee Mate, Nestlé ice cream and yogurt); pet foods (Friskies, Alpo, Fancy Feast, Mighty Dog); Contadina, Libby's, and Stouffer's food products and prepared dishes; chocolate and confectionery products (Nestlé Crunch, Smarties, Baby Ruth, Butterfinger, KitKat); and pharmaceuticals (Alcon opthalmic products, Galderma dermatological products)
Siemens	Operations in 160 countries and sales offices in more than 190 countries	• Electrical power generation, transmission, and distribution equipment and products; manufacturing automation systems; industrial motors, machinery, and tools; plant construction and maintenance; corporate communication networks; telephones; PCs, mainframes, computer network products, consulting services; mass transit and light rail systems, rail cars, locomotives, lighting products (bulbs, lamps, theater and television lighting systems); semiconductors; home appliances; vacuum cleaners; and financial, procurement, and logistics services
Samsung	Operations in more than 60 countries and sales offices in more than 200 countries	• Notebook computers, hard disk drives, CD/DVD-ROM drives, monitors, printers, and fax machines; televisions (big-screen TVs, plasma-screen TVs, and LCD-screen TVs); DVD and MP3 players; Cell phones and various other telecommunications products; compressors; home appliances; DRAM chips, flash memory chips, and graphics memory chips; and optical fibers, fiber-optic cables, and fiber-optic connectors

Source: Company annual reports and Web sites.

from these very sorts of economies of scope when it decided to diversify into the video game business with its PlayStation product line. Sony had in place capability to go after video game sales in all country markets where it presently did business in other electronics product categories (TVs, computers, DVD players, VCRs, radios, CD players, and camcorders). And it had the marketing clout and brand-name credibility to persuade retailers to give Sony's PlayStation products prime shelf space and visibility. These strategic-fit benefits helped Sony quickly overtake long-time industry leaders Nintendo and Sega and defend its market leadership against Microsoft's new Xbox.

3. *Opportunities to transfer competitively valuable resources both from one business to another and from one country to another.* A company pursuing related diversification can gain a competitive edge over less diversified rivals by transferring competitively valuable resources from one business to another; a multinational company can gain competitive advantage over rivals with narrower geographic coverage by transferring competitively valuable resources from one country to another. But a strategy of multinational diversification enables simultaneous pursuit of both sources of competitive advantage.

4. *Ability to leverage use of a well-known and competitively powerful brand name.* Diversified multinational companies whose businesses have brand names that are well known and respected across the world possess a valuable strategic asset with competitive advantage potential. For example, Sony's well-established global brand-name recognition gives it an important marketing and advertising advantage over rivals with lesser-known brands. When Sony goes into a new marketplace with the stamp of the Sony brand on its product families, it can command prominent display space with retailers. It can expect to win sales and market share simply on the confidence that buyers place in products carrying the Sony name. While Sony may spend money to make consumers aware of the availability of its new products, it does not have to spend nearly as much on achieving brand recognition and market acceptance as would a lesser-known competitor looking at the marketing and advertising costs of entering the same new product/business/country markets and trying to go head-to-head against Sony. Further, if Sony moves into a new country market for the first time and does well selling Sony PlayStations and video games, it is easier to sell consumers in that country Sony TVs, digital cameras, PCs, MP3 players, and so on—plus, the related advertising costs are likely to be less than they would be without having already established the Sony brand strongly in the minds of buyers.

5. *Ability to capitalize on opportunities for cross-business and cross-country collaboration and strategic coordination.*[30] A multinational diversification strategy allows competitively valuable cross-business and cross-country coordination of certain value chain activities. For instance, by channeling corporate resources directly into a combined R&D/technology effort for all related businesses, as opposed to letting each business unit fund and direct its own R&D effort however it sees fit, a DMNC can merge its expertise and efforts *worldwide* to advance core technologies, expedite cross-business and cross-country product improvements, speed the development of new products that complement existing products, and pursue promising technological avenues to create altogether new businesses—all significant contributors to competitive advantage and better corporate performance.[31] Honda has been very successful in building R&D expertise in gasoline engines and transferring the resulting technological advances to its businesses in automobiles, motorcycles, outboard engines, snow blowers, lawn mowers, garden tillers, and portable power generators. Further, a DMNC can reduce costs through cross-business and cross-country coordination of purchasing and procurement from suppliers, from collaborative introduction and shared use of e-commerce technologies and online sales efforts, and from coordinated product introductions and promotional campaigns. Firms that are less diversified and less global in scope have less such cross-business and cross-country collaborative opportunities.

6. *Opportunities to use cross-business or cross-country subsidization to outcompete rivals.* A financially successful DMNC has potentially valuable organizational resources and multiple profit sanctuaries in both certain country markets and certain businesses that it can draw on to wage a market offensive. In comparison, a one-business domestic company has only one profit sanctuary—its home market. A diversified one-country competitor may have profit sanctuaries in several businesses, but all are in the same country market. A one-business multinational company may have profit sanctuaries in several country markets, but all are in the same business. All three are vulnerable to an offensive in their more limited profit sanctuaries by an aggressive DMNC willing to lowball its prices or spend extravagantly on advertising to win market share at their expense. A DMNC's ability to keep hammering away at competitors with low prices year after year may reflect either a cost advantage growing out of its related diversification strategy or a willingness to accept low profits or even losses in the market being attacked because it has ample earnings from its other profit sanctuaries. For example, Sony's global-scale diversification strategy gives it unique competitive strengths in outcompeting Nintendo and Sega, neither of which are diversified. If need be, Sony can maintain low prices on its PlayStations or fund high-profile promotions for its latest video game products, using earnings from its other business lines to fund its offensive to wrest market share away from Nintendo and Sega in video games. At the same time, Sony can draw on its considerable resources in R&D, its ability to transfer electronics technology from one electronics product family to another, and its expertise in product innovation to introduce better and better video game players, perhaps players that are multifunctional and do more than just play video games. Such competitive actions not only enhance Sony's own brand image but also make it very tough for Nintendo and Sega to match Sony's prices, advertising, and product development efforts and still earn acceptable profits.

The Combined Effects of These Advantages Is Potent A strategy of diversifying into *related* industries and then competing *globally* in each of these industries thus has great potential for being a winner in the marketplace because of the long-term growth opportunities it offers and the multiple corporate-level competitive advantage opportunities it contains. Indeed, *a strategy of multinational diversification contains more competitive advantage potential* (above and beyond what is achievable through a particular business's own competitive strategy) *than any other diversification strategy.*

> **Core Concept**
> A strategy of multinational diversification has more built-in potential for competitive advantage than any other diversification strategy.

The strategic key to maximum competitive advantage is for a DMNC to concentrate its diversification efforts in those industries where there are resource-sharing and resource-transfer opportunities and where there are important economies of scope and brand-name benefits. The more a company's diversification strategy yields these kinds of strategic-fit benefits, the more powerful a competitor it becomes and the better its profit and growth performance is likely to be.

However, it is important to recognize that while, in theory, a DMNC's cross-subsidization capabilities are a potent competitive weapon, cross-subsidization can, in actual practice, be used only sparingly. It is one thing to *occasionally* divert a portion of the profits and cash flows from existing businesses to help fund entry into a new business or country market or wage a competitive offensive against select rivals. It is quite another thing to *regularly* use cross-subsidization tactics and thereby weaken overall company performance. A DMNC is under the same pressures as any other company to demonstrate consistently acceptable profitability across its whole operation.[32] At some juncture, every business and every country market needs to make a profit contribution or become a candidate for abandonment. As a general rule, *cross-subsidization tactics are justified only when there is a good prospect that the short-term impairment to corporate profitability will be offset by stronger competitiveness and better overall profitability over the long term.*

Key Points

The purpose of diversification is to build shareholder value. Diversification builds shareholder value when a diversified group of businesses can perform better under the auspices of a single corporate parent than they would as independent, stand-alone businesses—the goal is not to achieve just a $1 + 1 = 2$ result, but rather to realize important $1 + 1 = 3$ performance benefits. Whether getting into a new business has potential to enhance shareholder value hinges on whether a company's entry into that business can pass the attractiveness test, the cost-of-entry test, and the better-off test.

Entry into new businesses can take any of three forms: acquisition, internal start-up, or joint venture/strategic partnership. Each has its pros and cons, but acquisition is the most frequently used; internal start-up takes the longest to produce home-run results, and joint venture/strategic partnership, though used second most frequently, is the least durable.

There are two fundamental approaches to diversification—into related businesses and into unrelated businesses. The rationale for *related* diversification is *strategic*: Diversify into businesses with strategic fits along their respective value chains, capitalize on strategic-fit relationships to gain competitive advantage, and then use competitive advantage to achieve the desired $1 + 1 = 3$ impact on shareholder value.

The basic premise of unrelated diversification is that any business that has good profit prospects and can be acquired on good financial terms is a good business to diversify into. Unrelated diversification strategies surrender the competitive advantage potential of strategic fit in return for such advantages as (1) spreading business risk over a variety of industries and (2) providing opportunities for financial gain (if candidate acquisitions have undervalued assets, are bargain priced and have good upside potential given the right management, or need the backing of a financially strong parent to capitalize on attractive opportunities). However, the greater the number of businesses a company has diversified into and the more diverse these businesses are, the harder it is for corporate executives to select capable managers to run each business, know when the major strategic proposals of business units are sound, or decide on a wise course of recovery when a business unit stumbles.

Analyzing how good a company's diversification strategy is a six-step process:

1. *Evaluate the long-term attractiveness of the industries into which the firm has diversified.* Industry attractiveness needs to be evaluated from three angles: the attractiveness of each industry on its own, the attractiveness of each industry relative to the others, and the attractiveness of all the industries as a group.

2. *Evaluate the relative competitive strength of each of the company's business units.* Again, quantitative ratings of competitive strength are preferable to subjective

judgments. The purpose of rating the competitive strength of each business is to gain clear understanding of which businesses are strong contenders in their industries, which are weak contenders, and the underlying reasons for their strength or weakness. The conclusions about industry attractiveness can be joined with the conclusions about competitive strength by drawing an industry attractiveness–competitive strength matrix that helps identify the prospects of each business and what priority each business should be given in allocating corporate resources and investment capital.

3. *Check for cross-business strategic fits.* A business is more attractive strategically when it has value chain relationships with sister business units that offer potential to (*a*) realize economies of scope or cost-saving efficiencies; (*b*) transfer technology, skills, know-how, or other resource capabilities from one business to another; (*c*) leverage use of a well-known and trusted brand name; and (*d*) to build new or stronger resource strengths and competitive capabilities via cross-business collaboration. Cross-business strategic fits represent a significant avenue for producing competitive advantage beyond what any one business can achieve on its own.

4. *Check whether the firm's resource strengths fit the resource requirements of its present business lineup.* Resource fit exists when (*a*) businesses add to a company's resource strengths, either financially or strategically; (*b*) a company has the resources to adequately support the resource requirements of its businesses as a group without spreading itself too thin; and (*c*) there are close matches between a company's resources and industry key success factors. One important test of financial resource fit involves determining whether a company has ample cash cows and not too many cash hogs.

5. *Rank the performance prospects of the businesses from best to worst and determine what the corporate parent's priority should be in allocating resources to its various businesses.* The most important considerations in judging business-unit performance are sales growth, profit growth, contribution to company earnings, and the return on capital invested in the business. Sometimes, cash flow generation is a big consideration. Normally, strong business units in attractive industries have significantly better performance prospects than weak businesses or businesses in unattractive industries. Business subsidiaries with the brightest profit and growth prospects and solid strategic and resource fits generally should head the list for corporate resource support.

6. *Crafting new strategic moves to improve overall corporate performance.* This step entails using the results of the preceding analysis as the basis for devising actions to strengthen existing businesses, make new acquisitions, divest weak-performing and unattractive businesses, restructure the company's business lineup, expand the scope of the company's geographic reach multinationally or globally, and otherwise steer corporate resources into the areas of greatest opportunity.

Once a company has diversified, corporate management's task is to manage the collection of businesses for maximum long-term performance. There are four different strategic paths for improving a diversified company's performance: (1) broadening the firm's business base by diversifying into additional businesses, (2) retrenching to a narrower diversification base by divesting some of its present businesses, (3) restructuring the company, and (4) diversifying multinationally.

Exercises

1. Consider the business lineup of General Electric (GE) shown in Illustration Capsule 9.2. What problems do you think the top executives at GE encounter in trying to stay on top of all the businesses the company is in? How might they decide the merits of adding new businesses or divesting poorly performing businesses? What types of advice might they be in a position to give to the general managers of each of GE's business units?

2. The Walt Disney Company is in the following businesses:
   - Theme parks.
   - Disney Cruise Line.
   - Resort properties.
   - Movie, video, and theatrical productions (for both children and adults).
   - Television broadcasting (ABC, Disney Channel, Toon Disney, Classic Sports Network, ESPN and ESPN2, E!, Lifetime, and A&E networks).
   - Radio broadcasting (Disney Radio).
   - Musical recordings and sales of animation art.
   - Anaheim Mighty Ducks NHL franchise.
   - Anaheim Angels major league baseball franchise (25 percent ownership).
   - Books and magazine publishing.
   - Interactive software and Internet sites.
   - The Disney Store retail shops.

   Given the above listing, would you say that Walt Disney's business lineup reflects a strategy of related or unrelated diversification? Explain your answer in terms of the extent to which the value chains of Disney's different businesses seem to have competitively valuable cross-business relationships.

3. Newell Rubbermaid is in the following businesses:
   - Cleaning and organizations businesses: Rubbermaid storage, organization, and cleaning products; Blue Ice ice substitute; Roughneck storage item; Stain Shield and TakeAlongs food storage containers; and Brute commercial-grade storage and cleaning products (25 percent of annual revenues).
   - Home and family businesses: Calphalon cookware and bakeware, Cookware Europe, Graco strollers, Little Tikes children's toys and furniture, and Goody hair accessories (20 percent of annual sales).
   - Home fashions: Levolor and Kirsch window blinds, shades, and hardware in the United States; Swish, Gardinia and Harrison Drape home furnishings in Europe (15 percent of annual revenues).
   - Office products businesses: Sharpie markers, Sanford highlighters, Eberhard Faber and Berol ballpoint pens, Paper Mate pens and pencils, Waterman and Parker fine writing instruments, and Liquid Paper (25 percent of annual revenues).

   Would you say that Newell Rubbermaid's strategy is one of related diversification, unrelated diversification or a mixture of both? Explain.

4. Explore the Web sites of the following companies and determine whether the company is pursuing a strategy of related diversification, unrelated diversification, or a mixture of both:

- Berkshire Hathaway
- News Corporation
- Dow Jones & Company
- Kimberly Clark

Strategy, Ethics, and Social Responsibility

When morality comes up against profit, it is seldom profit that loses.

—Shirley Chisholm
Former Congresswoman

But I'd shut my eyes in the sentry box so I didn't see nothing wrong.

—Rudyard Kipling
Author

Values can't just be words on a page. To be effective, they must shape action.

—Jeffrey R. Immelt
CEO, General Electric

Leaders must be more than individuals of high character. They must "lead" others to behave ethically.

—Linda K. Treviňo and Michael E. Brown
Professors

Integrity violations are no-brainers. In such cases, you don't need to hesitate for a moment before firing someone or fret about it either. Just do it, and make sure the organization knows why, so that the consequences of breaking the rules are not lost on anyone.

—Jack Welch
Former CEO, General Electric

There is one and only one social responsibility of business—to use its resources and engage in activities designed to increase its profits so long as it stays within the rules of the game, which is to say engages in free and open competition, without deception or fraud.

—Milton Friedman
Nobel Prize–winning economist

Corporations are economic entities, to be sure, but they are also social institutions that must justify their existence by their overall contribution to society.

—Henry Mintzberg, Robert Simons, and Kunal Basu
Professors

Clearly, a company has a responsibility to make a profit and grow the business—in capitalistic, or market, economies, management's fiduciary duty to create value for shareholders is not a matter for serious debate. Just as clearly, a company and its personnel also have a duty to obey the law and play by the rules of fair competition. But does a company have a duty to operate according to the ethical norms of the societies in which it operates—should it be held to some standard of ethical conduct? And does it have a duty or obligation to contribute to the betterment of society independent of the needs and preferences of the customers it serves? Should a company display a social conscience and devote a portion of its resources to bettering society?

The focus of this chapter is to examine what link, if any, there should be between a company's efforts to craft and execute a winning strategy and its duties to (1) conduct its activities ethically and (2) demonstrate socially responsible behavior by being a committed corporate citizen and directing corporate resources to the betterment of employees, the communities in which it operates, and society as a whole.

WHAT DO WE MEAN BY *BUSINESS ETHICS*?

Business ethics is the application of ethical principles and standards to business behavior.[1] Business ethics does not really involve a special set of ethical standards applicable only to business situations. Ethical principles in business are not materially different from ethical principles in general. Why? Because business actions have to be judged in the context of society's standards of right and wrong, not by a special set of rules that businesspeople decide to apply to their own conduct. If dishonesty is considered to be unethical and immoral, then dishonest behavior in business—whether it relates to customers, suppliers, employees or shareholders—qualifies as equally unethical and immoral. If being ethical entails not deliberately harming others, then recalling a defective or unsafe product is ethically necessary and failing to undertake such a recall or correct the problem in future shipments of the product is likewise unethical. If society deems bribery to be unethical, then it is unethical for company personnel to make payoffs to government officials to facilitate business transactions or bestow gifts and other favors on prospective customers to win or retain their business.

> **Core Concept**
> **Business ethics** concerns the application of general ethical principles and standards to the actions and decisions of companies and the conduct of company personnel.

WHERE DO ETHICAL STANDARDS COME FROM—ARE THEY UNIVERSAL OR DEPENDENT ON LOCAL NORMS AND SITUATIONAL CIRCUMSTANCES?

Notions of right and wrong, fair and unfair, moral and immoral, ethical and unethical are present in all societies, organizations, and individuals. But there are three schools of thought about the extent to which the ethical standards travel across cultures and whether multinational companies can apply the same set of ethical standards in any and all of the locations where they operate.

The School of Ethical Universalism

According to the school of **ethical universalism,** some concepts of what is right and what is wrong are *universal*; that is, they transcend all cultures, societies, and religions.[2] For instance, being truthful (or not lying, or not being deliberately deceitful) is considered right by the peoples of all nations. Likewise, demonstrating integrity of character, not cheating, and treating people with dignity and respect are concepts that resonate with people of most cultures and religions. In most societies, people believe that companies should not pillage or degrade the environment in the course of conducting their operations. In most societies, people would concur that it is unethical to knowingly expose workers to toxic chemicals and hazardous materials or to sell products known to be unsafe or harmful to the users. *To the extent that there is common moral agreement about right and wrong actions and behaviors across multiple cultures and countries, there exists a set of universal ethical standards to which all societies, all companies, and all individuals can be held accountable.* These universal ethical principles or norms put limits on what actions and behaviors fall inside the boundaries of what is right and which ones fall outside. They set forth the traits and behaviors that are considered virtuous and that a good person is supposed to believe in and to display.

> **Core Concept**
>
> According to the school of *ethical universalism,* the same standards of what's ethical and what's unethical resonate with peoples of most societies regardless of local traditions and cultural norms; hence, common ethical standards can be used to judge the conduct of personnel at companies operating in a variety of country markets and cultural circumstances.

Many ethicists believe that the most important moral standards travel well across countries and cultures and thus are *universal*—universal norms include honesty or trustworthiness, respecting the rights of others, practicing the Golden Rule, avoiding unnecessary harm to workers or to the users of the company's product or service, and respect for the environment.[3] In all such instances where there is cross-cultural agreement as to what actions and behaviors are inside and outside ethical and moral boundaries, adherents of the school of ethical universalism maintain that the conduct of personnel at companies operating in a variety of country markets and cultural circumstances can be judged against the resulting set of common ethical standards.

The strength of ethical universalism is that it draws on the collective views of multiple societies and cultures to put some clear boundaries on what constitutes ethical business behavior and what constitutes unethical business behavior no matter what country market or culture a company or its personnel are operating in. This means that whenever basic moral standards really do not vary significantly according to local cultural beliefs, traditions, religious convictions, or time and circumstance, a multinational company can apply a code of ethics more or less evenly across its worldwide operations.[4] It can avoid the slippery slope that comes from having different ethical standards for different company personnel depending on where in the world they are working.

The School of Ethical Relativism

Apart from select universal basics—honesty, trustworthiness, fairness, a regard for worker safety, and respect for the environment—there are meaningful variations in what societies generally agree to be right and wrong in the conduct of business activities. Divergent religious beliefs, historic traditions, social customs, and prevailing political and economic doctrines (whether a country leans more toward a capitalistic market economy or one heavily dominated by socialistic or communistic principles) frequently produce ethical norms that vary from one country to another. The school of **ethical relativism** holds that when there are cross-country or cross-cultural differences in what is deemed fair or unfair, what constitutes proper regard for human rights, and what is considered ethical or unethical in business situations, it is appropriate for local moral standards to take precedence over what the ethical standards may be elsewhere—for instance, in a company's home market. The thesis is that whatever a culture thinks is right or wrong really is right or wrong for that culture.[5] Hence, the school of ethical relativism contends that there are important occasions when cultural norms and the circumstances of the situation determine whether certain actions or behaviors are right or wrong. Consider the following examples.

> **Core Concept**
> According to the school of *ethical relativism* different societal cultures and customs have divergent values and standards of right and wrong—thus what is ethical or unethical must be judged in the light of local customs and social mores and can vary from one culture or nation to another.

The Use of Underage Labor   In industrialized nations, the use of underage workers is considered taboo; social activists are adamant that child labor is unethical and that companies should neither employ children under the age of 18 as full-time employees nor source any products from foreign suppliers that employ underage workers. Many countries have passed legislation forbidding the use of underage labor or, at a minimum, regulating the employment of people under the age of 18. However, in India, Bangladesh, Botswana, Sri Lanka, Ghana, Somalia, Turkey, and 100-plus other countries, it is customary to view children as potential, even necessary, workers.[6] Many poverty-stricken families cannot subsist without the income earned by young family members, and sending their children to school instead of having them participate in the workforce is not a realistic option. In 2000, the International Labor Organization estimated that 211 million children ages 5 to 14 were working around the world.[7] If such children are not permitted to work—due to pressures imposed by activist groups in industrialized nations—they may be forced to seek work in lower-wage jobs in "hidden" parts of the economy of their countries, beg on the street, or even traffic in drugs or engage in prostitution.[8] So if all businesses succumb to the protests of activist groups and government organizations that, based on their values and beliefs, loudly proclaim that underage labor is unethical, then have either businesses or the protesting groups really done something good on behalf of society in general?

The Payment of Bribes and Kickbacks   A particularly thorny area facing multinational companies is the degree of cross-country variability in paying bribes.[9] In many countries in Eastern Europe, Africa, Latin America, and Asia, it is customary to pay bribes to government officials in order to win a government contract, obtain a license or permit, or facilitate an administrative ruling.[10] Senior managers in China often use their power to obtain kickbacks and offer bribes when they purchase materials or other products for their companies.[11] In some developing nations, it is difficult for any company, foreign or domestic, to move goods through customs without paying off low-level officials.[12] Likewise, in many countries it is normal to make payments to prospective customers in order to win or retain their business. A *Wall Street Journal* article reported that 30 to 60 percent of all business transactions in Eastern Europe involved paying bribes, and the costs of bribe payments averaged 2 to 8 percent of revenues.[13] Three recent annual issues of the *Global Corruption Report*, sponsored by Berlin-based Transparency International, provide credible evidence that corruption among public officials and in business transactions is widespread across the world.[14] Some people stretch to justify the payment of bribes and kickbacks on grounds that bribing government officials to get goods through customs or giving kickbacks to customers to retail their business or win an order is simply a payment for services rendered, in the same way that people tip for service at restaurants.[15] But this argument rests on moral quicksand, even though it is a clever and pragmatic way to rationalize why such facilitating payments should be viewed as a normal and maybe unavoidable cost of doing business in some countries.

Companies that forbid the payment of bribes and kickbacks in their codes of ethical conduct and that are serious about enforcing this prohibition face a particularly vexing problem in those countries where bribery and kickback payments have been entrenched as a local custom for decades and are not considered unethical by the local population.[16] Refusing to pay bribes or kickbacks (so as to comply with the company's code of ethical conduct) is very often tantamount to losing business. Frequently, the sales and profits are lost to more unscrupulous companies, with the result that both ethical companies and ethical individuals are penalized. However, winking at the code of ethical conduct and going along with the payment of bribes or kickbacks not only undercuts enforcement of and adherence to the company's code of ethics but can also risk breaking the law. U.S. companies are prohibited by the Foreign Corrupt Practices Act (FCPA) from paying bribes to government officials, political parties, political candidates, or others in all countries where they do business; the FCPA requires U.S. companies with foreign operations to adopt accounting practices that ensure full disclosure of a company's transactions so that illegal payments can be detected. The 35 member countries of the Organization for Economic Cooperation and Development (OECD) in 1997 adopted a convention to combat bribery in international business transactions; the Anti-Bribery Convention obligated the countries to criminalize the bribery of foreign public officials, including payments made to political parties and party officials. So far, however, there has been only token enforcement of the OECD convention and the payment of bribes in global business transactions remains a common practice in many countries.

Ethical Relativism Equates to Multiple Sets of Ethical Standards   The existence of varying ethical norms such as those cited above explains why the adherents of ethical relativism maintain that there are few absolutes when it comes to business ethics and thus few ethical absolutes for consistently judging a company's conduct in various countries and markets. Indeed, the thesis of ethical relativists is that while there are sometimes general moral prescriptions that apply in most every society and business circumstance there are plenty of situations where ethical norms must be contoured to fit the local customs, traditions, and the notions of fairness shared by the parties involved. They argue that a one-size-fits-all template for judging the ethical appropriateness of business actions and the behaviors of company personnel simply does not exist—in other words, ethical problems in business cannot be fully resolved without appealing to the shared convictions of the parties in question.[17] European and American managers may want to impose standards of business conduct that give heavy weight to such core human rights as personal freedom, individual security, political participation, the ownership of property, and the right to subsistence as well as the obligation to respect the dignity of each human person, adequate health and safety standards for all employees, and respect for the environment; managers in China have a much weaker commitment to these kinds of human rights. Japanese managers may prefer ethical standards that show respect for the collective good of society. Muslim managers may wish to apply ethical standards compatible with the teachings of Mohammed. Individual companies may want to give explicit recognition to the importance of company personnel living up to the company's own espoused values and business principles. Clearly, there is merit in the school of ethical relativism's view that what is deemed right or wrong, fair or unfair, moral or immoral, ethical or unethical in business situations depends partly on the context of each country's local customs, religious traditions, and societal norms. Hence, there is a kernel of truth in the argument that businesses need some room to tailor their ethical standards to fit local situations. A company has to be very cautious about exporting its home-country values and ethics to foreign countries where it operates—"photocopying" ethics is disrespectful of other cultures and neglects the important role of moral free space.

> Under ethical relativism, there can be no one-size-fits-all set of authentic ethical norms against which to gauge the conduct of company personnel.

Pushed to Extremes, Ethical Relativism Breaks Down   While the relativistic rule of "When in Rome, do as the Romans do" appears reasonable, it nonetheless presents a big problem—when the envelope starts to be pushed, as will inevitably be the case, *it is tantamount to rudderless ethical standards.* Consider, for instance, the following example: In 1992, the owners of the SS *United States,* an aging luxury ocean liner constructed with asbestos in the 1940s, had the liner towed to Turkey, where a contractor had agreed to remove the asbestos for $2 million (versus a far higher cost in the United States, where asbestos removal safety standards were much more stringent).[18] When Turkish officials blocked the asbestos removal because of the dangers to workers of contracting cancer, the owners had the liner towed to the Black Sea port of Sevastopol, in the Crimean Republic, where the asbestos removal standards were quite lax and where a contractor had agreed to remove more than 500,000 square feet of carcinogenic asbestos for less than $2 million. There are no moral grounds for arguing that exposing workers to carcinogenic asbestos is ethically correct, irrespective of what a country's law allows or the value the country places on worker safety.

A company that adopts the principle of ethical relativism and holds company personnel to local ethical standards necessarily assumes that what prevails as local morality is an adequate guide to ethical behavior. This can be ethically dangerous—it leads to the conclusion that if a country's culture is accepting of bribery or environmental degradation or exposing workers to dangerous conditions (toxic chemicals or bodily harm), then so much the worse for honest people and protection of the environment and safe working conditions. Such a position is morally unacceptable. Even though bribery of government officials in China is a common practice, when Lucent Technologies found that managers in its Chinese operations had bribed government officials, it fired the entire senior management team.[19]

> Managers in multinational enterprises have to figure out how to navigate the gray zone that arises when operating in two cultures with two sets of ethics.

Moreover, from a global markets perspective, ethical relativism results in a maze of conflicting ethical standards for multinational companies wanting to address the very real issue of what ethical standards to enforce companywide. On the one hand, multinational companies need to educate and motivate their employees worldwide to respect the customs and traditions of other nations, and, on the other hand, they must enforce compliance with the company's own particular code of ethical behavior. It is a slippery slope indeed to resolve such ethical diversity without any kind of higher-order moral compass. Imagine, for example, that a multinational company in the name of ethical relativism takes the position that it is okay for company personnel to pay bribes and kickbacks in countries where such payments are customary but forbids company personnel from making such payments in those countries where bribes and kickbacks are considered unethical or illegal. Or that the company says it is ethically fine to use underage labor in its plants in those countries where underage labor is acceptable and ethically inappropriate to employ underage labor at the remainder of its plants. Having thus adopted conflicting ethical standards for operating in different countries, company managers have little moral basis for enforcing ethical standards companywide—rather, the clear message to employees would be that the company has no ethical standards or principles of its own, preferring to let its practices be governed by the countries in which it operates. This is scarcely strong moral ground to stand on.

Ethics and Integrative Social Contracts Theory

Core Concept
According to *integrated social contracts theory,* universal ethical principles or norms based on the collective views of multiple cultures and societies combine to form a "social contract" that all individuals in all situations have a duty to observe. Within the boundaries of this social contract, local cultures or groups can specify other impermissible actions; however, universal ethical norms always take precedence over local ethical norms.

Social contract theory provides a middle position between the opposing views of universalism (that the same set of ethical standards should apply everywhere) and relativism (that ethical standards vary according to local custom).[20] According to **integrative social contracts theory,** the ethical standards a company should try to uphold are governed both by (1) a limited number of universal ethical principles that are widely recognized as putting legitimate ethical boundaries on actions and behavior in *all* situations and (2) the circumstances of local cultures, traditions, and shared values that further prescribe what constitutes ethically permissible behavior and what does not. However, *universal ethical norms take precedence over local ethical norms.* In other words, universal ethical principles apply in those situations where most all societies—endowed with rationality and moral knowledge—have common moral agreement on what is wrong and thereby put limits on what actions and behaviors fall inside the boundaries of what is right and which ones fall outside. *These mostly uniform agreements about what is morally right and wrong form a "social contract" or contract with society that is binding on all individuals, groups, organizations, and businesses in terms of establishing right and wrong and in drawing the line between ethical and unethical behaviors.* But these universal ethical principles or norms nonetheless still leave some moral free space for the people in a particular country (or local culture or even a company) to make specific interpretations of what other actions may or may not be permissible within the bounds defined by universal ethical principles. Hence, while firms, industries, professional associations, and other business-relevant groups are contractually obligated to society to observe universal ethical norms, they have the discretion to go beyond these universal norms and specify other behaviors that are out of bounds and place further limitations on what is considered ethical. Both the legal and medical professions have standards regarding what kinds of advertising are ethically permissible and what kinds are not. Food products companies are beginning to establish ethical guidelines for judging what is and is not appropriate advertising for food products that are inherently unhealthy and may cause dietary or obesity problems for people who eat them regularly or consume them in large quantities.

The strength of integrated social contracts theory is that it accommodates the best parts of ethical universalism and ethical relativism. It is indisputable that cultural differences impact how business is conducted in various parts of the world and that these cultural differences sometimes give rise to different ethical norms. But it is just as indisputable that some ethical norms are more authentic or universally applicable than others, meaning that, in many instances of cross-country differences, one side may be more "ethically correct" or "more right" than another. In such instances, resolving cross-cultural differences entails applying universal, or first-order, ethical norms and overriding the local, or second-order, ethical norms. A good example is the payment of bribes and kickbacks. Yes, bribes and kickbacks seem to be common in some countries, but does this justify paying them? Just because bribery flourishes in a country does not mean that it is an authentic or legitimate ethical norm. Virtually all of the world's major religions (Buddhism, Christianity, Confucianism, Hinduism, Islam, Judaism, Sikhism, and Taoism) and all moral schools of thought condemn bribery and corruption.[21] Bribery is commonplace in India but interviews with Indian CEOs whose companies constantly engaged in payoffs indicated disgust for the practice and they expressed no illusions about its impropriety.[22] Therefore, a multinational company might reasonably conclude that the right ethical standard is one of refusing to condone bribery and kickbacks on the part of company personnel no matter what the local custom is and no matter what the sales consequences are.

Granting an automatic preference to local country ethical norms presents vexing problems to multinational company managers when the ethical standards followed in a foreign country are lower than those in its home country or are in conflict with the company's code of ethics. Sometimes there can be no compromise on what is ethically permissible and what is not. *This is precisely what integrated social contracts theory maintains—universal or first-order ethical norms should always take precedence over local or second-order norms.* Integrated social contracts theory offers managers in multinational companies clear guidance in resolving cross-country ethical differences: Those parts of the company's code of ethics that involve universal ethical norms must be enforced worldwide, but within these boundaries there is room for ethical diversity and opportunity for host country cultures to exert *some* influence in setting their own moral and ethical standards. Such an approach detours the somewhat scary case of a self-righteous multinational company trying to operate as the standard-bearer of moral truth and imposing its interpretation of its code of ethics worldwide no matter what. And it avoids the equally scary case for a company's ethical conduct to be no higher than local ethical norms in situations where local ethical norms permit practices that are generally considered immoral or when local norms clearly conflict with a company's code of ethical conduct. But even with the guidance provided by integrated social contracts theory, there are many instances where cross-country differences in ethical norms create gray areas in which it is tough to draw a line in the sand between right and wrong decisions, actions, and business practices.

THE THREE CATEGORIES OF MANAGEMENT MORALITY

Three categories of managers stand out with regard to ethical and moral principles in business affairs:[23]

- *The moral manager*—Moral managers are dedicated to high standards of ethical behavior, both in their own actions and in their expectations of how the company's business is to be conducted. They see themselves as stewards of ethical behavior and believe it is important to exercise ethical leadership. Moral managers may well be ambitious and have a powerful urge to succeed, but they pursue success in business within the confines of both the letter and the spirit of what is ethical and legal—they typically regard the law as an ethical minimum and have a habit of operating well above what the law requires.

- *The immoral manager*—Immoral managers have no regard for so-called ethical standards in business and pay no attention to ethical principles in making decisions and conducting the company's business. Their philosophy is that good businesspeople cannot spend time watching out for the interests of others and agonizing over "the right thing to do." In the minds of immoral managers, nice guys come in second and the competitive nature of business requires that you either trample on others or get trampled yourself. They believe what really matters is single-minded pursuit of their own best interests—they are living examples of capitalistic greed, caring only about their own or their organization's gains and successes. Immoral managers may even be willing to short-circuit legal and regulatory requirements if they think they can escape detection. And they are always on the lookout for legal loopholes and creative ways to get around rules and regulations that block or constrain actions they deem in their own or their company's self-interest. Immoral managers are thus the bad guys—they have few scruples, little or no integrity, and are willing to do most anything they believe they can get away with. It doesn't bother them much to be seen by others as wearing the black hats.

- *The amoral manager*—Amoral managers appear in two forms: the intentionally amoral manager and the unintentionally amoral manager. Intentionally amoral managers are of the strong opinion that business and ethics are not to be mixed. They are not troubled by failing to factor ethical considerations into their decisions and actions because it is perfectly legitimate for businesses to do anything they wish so long as they stay within legal and regulatory bounds—in other words, if particular actions and behaviors are legal and comply with existing regulations, then they qualify as permissible and should not be seen as unethical. Intentionally amoral managers view the observance of high ethical standards (doing more than what is required by law) as too Sunday-schoolish for the tough competitive world of business, even though observing some higher ethical considerations may be appropriate in life outside of business. Their concept of right and wrong tends to be lawyer-driven—how much can we get by with and can we go ahead even if it is borderline? Thus intentionally amoral managers hold firmly to the view that anything goes, so long as actions and behaviors are not clearly ruled out by prevailing legal and regulatory requirements.

> **Core Concept**
> Amoral managers believe that businesses ought to be able to do whatever current laws and regulations allow them to do without being shackled by ethical considerations—they think that what is permissible and what is not is governed entirely by prevailing laws and regulations, not by societal concepts of right and wrong.

  Unintentionally amoral managers do not pay much attention to the concept of business ethics either, but for different reasons. They are simply casual about, careless about, or inattentive to the fact that certain kinds of business decisions or company activities are unsavory or may have deleterious effects on others—in short, they go about their jobs as best they can without giving serious thought to the ethical dimension of decisions and business actions. They are ethically unconscious when it comes to business matters, partly or mainly because they have just never stopped to consider whether and to what extent business decisions or company actions sometimes spill over to create adverse impacts on others. Unintentionally amoral managers may even see themselves as people of integrity and as personally ethical. But, like intentionally amoral managers, they are of the firm view that businesses ought to be able to do whatever the current legal and regulatory framework allows them to do without being shackled by ethical considerations.

By some accounts, the population of managers is said to be distributed among all three types in a bell-shaped curve, with immoral managers and moral managers occupying the two tails of the curve, and the amoral managers (especially the intentionally amoral managers) occupying the broad middle ground.[24] Furthermore, within the population of managers, there is experiential evidence to support that while the average manager may be amoral most of the time, he or she may slip into a moral or immoral mode on occasion, based on a variety of impinging factors and circumstances.

Evidence of Managerial Immorality in the Global Business Community

There is considerable evidence that a sizable majority of managers are either amoral or immoral. The *2005 Global Corruption Report,* sponsored by Transparency International, found that corruption among public officials and in business transactions is widespread across the world. Table 10.1 shows some of the countries where corruption is believed to be lowest and highest—even in the countries where business practices are deemed to be least corrupt, there is considerable room for improvement in the extent to which managers observe ethical business practices. Table 10.2 presents data showing the perceived likelihood that companies in the 21 largest exporting countries are paying bribes to win business in the markets of 15 emerging-country markets—Argentina, Brazil, Colombia, Hungary, India, Indonesia, Mexico, Morocco, Nigeria, the Philippines, Poland, Russia, South Africa, South Korea, and Thailand.

Table 10.1 **Corruption Perceptions Index, Selected Countries, 2004**

Country	2004 CPI Score*	High–Low Range	Number of Surveys Used	Country	2004 CPI Score*	High–Low Range	Number of Surveys Used
Finland	9.7	9.2–10.0	9	Taiwan	5.6	4.7–6.0	15
New Zealand	9.6	9.2–9.7	9	Italy	4.8	3.4–5.6	10
Denmark	9.5	8.7–9.8	10	South Africa	4.6	3.4–5.8	11
Sweden	9.2	8.7–9.5	11	South Korea	4.5	2.2–5.8	14
Switzerland	9.1	8.6–9.4	10	Brazil	3.9	3.5–4.8	11
Norway	8.9	8.0–9.5	9	Mexico	3.6	2.6–4.5	11
Australia	8.8	6.7–9.5	15	Thailand	3.6	2.5–4.5	14
Netherlands	8.7	8.3–9.4	10	China	3.4	2.1–5.6	16
United Kingdom	8.6	7.8–9.2	12	Saudi Arabia	3.4	2.0–4.5	5
Canada	8.5	6.5–9.4	12	Turkey	3.2	1.9–5.4	13
Germany	8.2	7.5–9.2	11	India	2.8	2.2–3.7	15
Hong Kong	8.0	3.5–9.4	13	Russia	2.8	2.0–5.0	15
United States	7.5	5.0–8.7	14	Philippines	2.6	1.4–3.7	14
Chile	7.4	6.3–8.7	11	Vietnam	2.6	1.6–3.7	11
France	7.1	5.0–9.0	12	Argentina	2.5	1.7–3.7	11
Spain	7.1	5.6–8.0	11	Venezuela	2.3	2.0–3.0	11
Japan	6.9	3.5–9.0	15	Pakistan	2.1	1.2–3.3	7
Israel	6.4	3.5–8.1	10	Nigeria	1.6	0.9–2.1	9
Uruguay	6.2	5.6–7.3	6	Bangladesh	1.5	0.3–2.4	5

* The CPI scores range between 10 (highly clean) and 0 (highly corrupt); the data were collected between 2002 and 2004 and reflect a composite of 18 data sources from 12 institutions, as indicated in the number of surveys used. The CPI score represents the perceptions of the degree of corruption as seen by businesspeople, academics, and risk analysts. CPI scores were reported for 146 countries.

Source: Transparency International, *2005 Global Corruption Report,* www.globalcorruptionreport.org (accessed October 31, 2005), pp. 235–38.

Table 10.2   **The Degree to Which Companies in Major Exporting Countries Are Perceived to Be Paying Bribes in Doing Business Abroad**

Rank/Country	Bribe-Payer Index (10 = Low; 0 = High)	Rank/Country	Bribe-Payer Index (10 = Low; 0 = High)
1. Australia	8.5	12. France	5.5
2. Sweden	8.4	13. United States	5.3
3. Switzerland	8.4	14. Japan	5.3
4. Austria	8.2	15. Malaysia	4.3
5. Canada	8.1	16. Hong Kong	4.3
6. Netherlands	7.8	17. Italy	4.1
7. Belgium	7.8	18. South Korea	3.9
8. Britain	6.9	19. Taiwan	3.8
9. Singapore	6.3	20. China (excluding Hong Kong)	3.5
10. Germany	6.3	21. Russia	3.2
11. Spain	5.8		

Note: The bribe-payer index is based on a questionnaire developed by Transparency International and a survey of some 835 private-sector leaders in 15 emerging countries accounting for 60 percent of all imports into non-Organization for Economic Cooperation and Development countries—actual polling was conducted by Gallup International.

Source: Transparency International, *2003 Global Corruption Report*, www.globalcorruptionreport.org (accessed November 1, 2005), p. 267.

The *2003 Global Corruption Report* cited data indicating that bribery occurred most often in (1) public works contracts and construction, (2) the arms and defense industry, and (3) the oil and gas industry. On a scale of 1 to 10, where 10 indicates negligible bribery, even the "cleanest" industry sectors—agriculture, light manufacturing, and fisheries—only had "passable" scores of 5.9, indicating that bribes are quite likely a common occurrence in these sectors as well (see Table 10.3).

The corruption, of course, extends beyond just bribes and kickbacks. For example, in 2005, four global chip makers (Samsung and Hynix Semiconductor in South Korea, Infineon Technologies in Germany, and Micron Technology in the United States) pleaded guilty to conspiring to fix the prices of dynamic random access memory (DRAM) chips sold to such companies as Dell, Apple Computer, and Hewlett-Packard—DRAM chips generate annual worldwide sales of around $26 billion and are used in computers, electronics products, and motor vehicles.[25] So far, the probe has resulted in fines of $730 million, jail terms for nine executives, and pending criminal charges for three more employees for their role in the global cartel; the guilty companies face hundreds of millions of dollars more in damage claims from customers and from consumer class-action lawsuits.

A global business community that is apparently so populated with unethical business practices and managerial immorality does not bode well for concluding that many companies ground their strategies on exemplary ethical principles or for the vigor with which company managers try to ingrain ethical behavior into company personnel. And, as many business school professors have noted, there are considerable numbers of amoral business students in our classrooms. So efforts to root out shady and corrupt business practices and implant high ethical principles into the managerial process of crafting and executing strategy is unlikely to produce an ethically strong global business climate anytime in the near future, barring major effort to address and correct the ethical laxness of company managers.

Table 10.3   **Bribery in Different Industries**

Business Sector	Bribery Score (10 = Low; 0 = High)
Agriculture	5.9
Light manufacturing	5.9
Fisheries	5.9
Information technology	5.1
Forestry	5.1
Civilian aerospace	4.9
Banking and finance	4.7
Heavy manufacturing	4.5
Pharmaceuticals/medical care	4.3
Transportation/storage	4.3
Mining	4.0
Power generation/transmission	3.7
Telecommunications	3.7
Real estate/property	3.5
Oil and gas	2.7
Arms and defense	1.9
Public works/construction	1.3

Note: The bribery scores for each industry are based on a questionnaire developed by Transparency International and a survey of some 835 private sector leaders in 15 emerging countries accounting for 60 percent of all imports into non-Organization for Economic Cooperation and Development countries—actual polling was conducted by Gallup International.

Source: Transparency International, *2003 Global Corruption Report,* www.globalcorruption report.org (accessed November 1, 2005), p. 268.

DO COMPANY STRATEGIES NEED TO BE ETHICAL?

Company managers may formulate strategies that are ethical in all respects, or they may decide to employ strategies that, for one reason or another, have unethical or at least gray-area components. While most company managers are usually careful to ensure that a company's strategy is within the bounds of what is legal, the available evidence indicates they are not always so careful to ensure that all elements of their strategies are within the bounds of what is generally deemed ethical. Senior executives with strong ethical convictions are normally proactive in insisting that all aspects of company strategy fall within ethical boundaries. In contrast, senior executives who are either immoral or amoral may use shady strategies and unethical or borderline business practices, especially if they are clever at devising schemes to keep ethically questionable actions hidden from view.

During the past five years, there has been an ongoing series of revelations about managers who have ignored ethical standards, deliberately stepped out of bounds, and been called to account by the media, regulators, and the legal system. Ethical misconduct has occurred at Enron, Tyco International, HealthSouth, Rite Aid, Citicorp, Bristol-Myers Squibb, Adelphia, Royal Dutch/Shell, Parmalat (an Italy-based food products company), Mexican oil giant Pemex, Marsh & McLennan and other insurance brokers, several leading brokerage houses and investment banking firms, and a host of mutual fund companies. The consequences of crafting strategies that cannot pass the test of moral scrutiny are manifested in the sharp drops in the stock prices of the guilty companies that have cost shareholders billions of dollars; the frequently devastating public relations hits that the accused companies have taken, the sizes of the fines that have been levied (often amounting to several hundred million dollars); the growing legion of criminal indictments and convictions of company executives; and the number of executives who have either been dismissed from their jobs, shoved into early retirement, and/or suffered immense public embarrassment. The fallout from all these scandals has resulted in heightened management attention to legal and ethical considerations in crafting strategy. Illustration Capsule 10.1 details the ethically flawed strategy at the world's leading insurance broker, and the consequences to those concerned.

What Are the Drivers of Unethical Strategies and Business Behavior?

The apparent pervasiveness of immoral and amoral businesspeople is one obvious reason why ethical principles are an ineffective moral compass in business dealings and why companies may resort to unethical strategic behavior. But apart from thinking that maintains "The business of business is business, not ethics," three other main drivers of unethical business behavior also stand out:[26]

- Faulty oversight such that overzealous or obsessive pursuit of personal gain, wealth, and other selfish interests is overlooked by or escapes the attention of higher-ups (most usually the board of directors).
- Heavy pressures on company managers to meet or beat performance targets.
- A company culture that puts the profitability and good business performance ahead of ethical behavior.

Overzealous Pursuit of Personal Gain, Wealth, and Selfish Interests
People who are obsessed with wealth accumulation, greed, power, status, and other selfish interests often push ethical principles aside in their quest for self-gain. Driven by their ambitions, they exhibit few qualms in skirting the rules or doing whatever is necessary to achieve their goals. The first and only priority of such corporate bad apples is to look out for their own best interests and if climbing the ladder of success means having few scruples and ignoring the welfare of others, so be it. A general disregard for business ethics can prompt all kinds of unethical strategic maneuvers and behaviors at companies. Top executives, directors, and majority shareholders at cable-TV company Adelphia Communications ripped off the company for amounts totaling well over $1 billion, diverting hundreds of millions of dollars to fund their Buffalo Sabres hockey team, build a private golf course, and buy timber rights—among other things—and driving the company into bankruptcy. Their actions, which represent one of the biggest instances of corporate looting and self-dealing in American business, took place despite the company's public pontifications about the principles it would observe in trying to care for customers, employees, stockholders, and the local communities where it operated. Andrew Fastow, Enron's chief financial officer (CFO), set himself up as the manager of one of Enron's off-the-books partnerships and as the part-owner of another, allegedly earning extra compensation of $30 million for his owner-manager roles in the two partnerships; Enron's board of directors agreed to suspend the company's conflict-of-interest rules designed to protect the company from this very kind of executive self-dealing (but directors and perhaps Fastow's superiors were kept in the dark about how much Fastow was earning on the side).

Marsh & McLennan's Ethically Flawed Strategy

In October 2004, *Wall Street Journal* headlines trumpeted that a cartel among insurance brokers had been busted. Among the ringleaders was worldwide industry leader Marsh & McLennan Companies Inc., with 2003 revenues of $11.5 billion and a U.S. market share of close to 20 percent. The gist of the brokers' plan was to cheat corporate clients by rigging the bids brokers solicited for insurance policies and thereby collecting big fees (called contingent commissions) from major insurance companies for steering business their way. Two family members of Marsh & McLennan CEO Jeffery Greenberg were CEOs of major insurance companies to which Marsh sometimes steered business. Greenberg's father was CEO of insurance giant AIG (which had total revenues of $81 billion and insurance premium revenues of $28 billion in 2003), and Greenberg's younger brother was CEO of ACE Ltd., the 24th biggest property-casualty insurer in the United States, with 2003 revenues of $10.7 billion and insurance premium revenues of more than $5 billion worldwide. Prior to joining ACE, Greenberg's younger brother had been president and chief operating officer of AIG, headed by his father.

Several months prior to the cartel bust, a Marsh subsidiary, Putnam Investments, had paid a $110 million fine for securities fraud and another Marsh subsidiary, Mercer Consulting, was placed under Securities and Exchange Commission (SEC) investigation for engaging in pay-to-play practices that forced investment managers to pay fees in order to secure Mercer's endorsement of their services when making recommendations to Mercer's pension fund clients.

The cartel scheme arose from the practice of large corporations to hire the services of such brokers as Marsh & McLennan, Aon Corporation, A. J. Gallaher & Company, Wells Fargo, or BB&T Insurance Services to manage their risks and take out appropriate property and casualty insurance on their behalf. The broker's job was to solicit bids from several insurers and obtain the best policies at the lowest prices for the client.

Marsh's insurance brokerage strategy was to solicit artificially high bids from some insurance companies so that it could guarantee that the bid of a preferred insurer on a given deal would win the bid. Marsh brokers called underwriters at various insurers, often including AIG and ACE, and asked for "B" quotes—bids that were deliberately high. Insurers asked for B quotes knew that Marsh wanted another insurer to win the business, but they were willing to participate because on other policy solicitations Marsh could end up steering the business to them via Marsh's same strategy. Sometimes Marsh even asked underwriters that were providing B quotes to attend a meeting with Marsh's client and make a presentation regarding their policy to help bolster the credibility of their inflated bid.

Since it was widespread practice among insurers to pay brokers contingent commissions based on the volume or profitability of the business the broker directed to them, Marsh's B-quote solicitation strategy allowed it to steer business to those insurers paying the largest contingent commissions—these contingent commissions were in addition to the fees the broker earned from the corporate client for services rendered in conducting the bidding process for the client. A substantial fraction of the policies that Marsh unlawfully steered were to two Bermuda-based insurance companies that it helped start up and in which it also had ownership interests (some Marsh executives also indirectly owned shares of stock in one of the companies); indeed, these two insurance companies received 30–40 percent of their total business from policies steered to them by Marsh.

At Marsh, steering business to insurers paying the highest contingent commission was a key component of the company's overall strategy. Marsh's contingent commissions generated revenues of close to $1.5 billion over the 2001–2003 period, including $845 million in 2003. Without these commission revenues, Marsh's $1.5 billion in net profits would have been close to 40 percent lower in 2003.

Within days of headlines about the cartel bust, Marsh's stock price had fallen by 48 percent (costing shareholders about $11.5 billion in market value) and the company was looking down the barrel of a criminal indictment. To stave off the criminal indictment (something no insurance company had ever survived), board members forced Jeffrey Greenberg to resign as CEO. Another top executive was suspended. Criminal charges against several Marsh executives for their roles in the bid-rigging scheme were filed several weeks thereafter.

In an attempt to lead industry reform, Greenberg's successor quickly announced a new business model for Marsh that included not accepting any contingent commissions from insurers. Marsh's new strategy and business model involved charging fees only to its corporate clients for soliciting bids, placing their insurance, and otherwise managing clients' risks and crises. This eliminated Marsh's conflict of interest in earning fees from both sides of the transactions it made on behalf of its corporate clients. Marsh also committed to provide up-front disclosure to clients of the fees it would earn on their business (in the past such fees had been murky and incomplete). Even so, there were indications that close to 10 lawsuits, some involving class action, would soon be filed against the company.

Meanwhile, all major commercial property-casualty insurers were scrambling to determine whether their payment of contingent commissions was ethical, since such arrangements clearly gave insurance brokers a financial incentive to place insurance with companies paying the biggest contingent commissions, not those with the best prices or terms. Prosecutors of the cartel had referred to the contingent commissions as kickbacks.

Sources: Monica Langley and Theo Francis, "Insurers Reel from Bust of a 'Cartel,'" *The Wall Street Journal,* October 18, 2004, pp. A1, A14; Monica Langley and Ian McDonald, "Marsh Averts Criminal Case with New CEO," *The Wall Street Journal,* October 26, 2004, pp. A1, A10; Christopher Oster and Theo Francis, "Marsh and Aon Have Holdings in Two Insurers," *The Wall Street Journal,* November 1, 2004, p. C1; and Marcia Vickers, "The Secret World of Marsh Mac," *BusinessWeek,* November 1, 2004, pp. 78–89.

According to a civil complaint filed by the Securities and Exchange Commission, the CEO of Tyco International, a well-known $35.6 billion manufacturing and services company, conspired with the company's CFO to steal more than $170 million, including a company-paid $2 million birthday party for the CEO's wife held on Sardinia, an island off the coast of Italy; a $7 million Park Avenue apartment for his wife; and secret low-interest and interest-free loans to fund private businesses and investments and purchase lavish artwork, yachts, estate jewelry, and vacation homes in New Hampshire, Connecticut, Massachusetts, and Utah. The CEO allegedly lived rent-free in a $31 million Fifth Avenue apartment that Tyco purchased in his name, directed millions of dollars of charitable contributions in his own name using Tyco funds, diverted company funds to finance his personal businesses and investments, and sold millions of dollars of Tyco stock back to Tyco itself through Tyco subsidiaries located in offshore bank-secrecy jurisdictions. Tyco's CEO and CFO were further charged with conspiring to reap more than $430 million from sales of stock, using questionable accounting to hide their actions, and engaging in deceptive accounting practices to distort the company's financial condition from 1995 to 2002. At the trial on the charges filed by the SEC, the prosecutor told the jury in his opening statement, "This case is about lying, cheating and stealing. These people didn't win the jackpot—they stole it." Defense lawyers countered that "every single transaction . . . was set down in detail in Tyco's books and records" and that the authorized and disclosed multimillion-dollar compensation packages were merited by the company's financial performance and stock price gains. The two Tyco executives were convicted and sentenced to jail.

Prudential Securities paid a total of about $2 billion in the 1990s to settle misconduct charges relating to practices that misled investors on the risks and rewards of limited-partnership investments. Providian Financial Corporation, despite an otherwise glowing record of social responsibility and corporate citizenship, paid $150 million in 2001 to settle claims that its strategy included systematic attempts to cheat credit card holders. Ten prominent Wall Street securities firms in 2003 paid $1.4 billion to settle charges that they knowingly issued misleading stock research to investors in an effort to prop up the stock prices of client corporations. A host of mutual-fund firms made under-the-table arrangements to regularly buy and sell stock for their accounts at special after-hours trading prices that disadvantaged long-term investors and had to pay nearly $2.0 billion in fines and restitution when their unethical practices were discovered by authorities during 2002–2003. Salomon Smith Barney, Goldman Sachs, Credit Suisse First Boston, and several other financial firms were assessed close to $2 billion in fines and restitution for the unethical manner in which they contributed to the scandals at Enron and WorldCom and for the shady practice of allocating shares of hot initial public offering stocks to a select list of corporate executives who either steered or were in a position to steer investment banking business their way.

Heavy Pressures on Company Managers to Meet or Beat Earnings Targets   When companies find themselves scrambling to achieve ambitious earnings growth and meet the quarterly and annual performance expectations of Wall Street analysts and investors, managers often feel enormous pressure to do whatever it takes to sustain the company's reputation for delivering good financial performance. Executives at high-performing companies know that investors will see the slightest sign of a slowdown in earnings growth as a red flag and drive down the company's stock price. The company's credit rating could be downgraded if it has used lots of debt to finance its growth. The pressure to watch the scoreboard and never miss a quarter—so as not to upset the expectations of Wall Street analysts and fickle stock market investors—prompts managers to cut costs wherever savings show up immediately, squeeze extra sales out of early deliveries, and engage in other short-term maneuvers to make the numbers. As the pressure builds to keep performance numbers looking good, company personnel start stretching the rules further and further, until the limits of ethical conduct are overlooked.[27] Once ethical boundaries are crossed in efforts to "meet or beat the numbers," the threshold for making more extreme ethical compromises becomes lower.

Several top executives at WorldCom (the remains of which is now part of Verizon Communications), a company built with scores of acquisitions in exchange for WorldCom stock, allegedly concocted a fraudulent $11 billion accounting scheme to hide costs and inflate revenues and profit over several years; the scheme was said to have helped the company keep its stock price propped up high enough to make additional acquisitions, support its nearly $30 billion debt load, and allow executives to cash in on their lucrative stock options. At Qwest Communications, a company created by the merger of a go-go telecom start-up and U.S. West (one of the regional Bell companies), management was charged with scheming to improperly book $2.4 billion in revenues from a variety of sources and deals, thereby inflating the company's profits and making it appear that the company's strategy to create a telecommunications company of the future was on track when, in fact, it was faltering badly behind the scenes. Top-level Qwest executives were dismissed, and in 2004 new management agreed to $250 million in fines for all the misdeeds.

At Bristol-Myers Squibb, the world's fifth-largest drug maker, management apparently engaged in a series of numbers-game maneuvers to meet earnings targets, including such actions as:

- Offering special end-of-quarter discounts to induce distributors and local pharmacies to stock up on certain prescription drugs—a practice known as channel stuffing.
- Issuing last-minute price increase alerts to spur purchases and beef up operating profits.
- Setting up excessive reserves for restructuring charges and then reversing some of the charges as needed to bolster operating profits.
- Making repeated asset sales small enough that the gains could be reported as additions to operating profit rather than being flagged as one-time gains. (Some accountants have long used a rule of thumb that says a transaction that alters quarterly profits by less than 5 percent is "immaterial" and need not be disclosed in the company's financial reports.)

Such numbers games were said to be a common "earnings management" practice at Bristol-Myers and, according to one former executive, "sent a huge message across the organization that you make your numbers at all costs."[28]

Company executives often feel pressured to hit financial performance targets because their compensation depends heavily on the company's performance. During the late 1990s, it became fashionable for boards of directors to grant lavish bonuses, stock option awards, and other compensation benefits to executives for meeting specified performance targets. So outlandishly large were these rewards that executives had strong personal incentives to bend the rules and engage in behaviors the allowed the targets to be met. Much of the accounting hocus-pocus at the root of recent corporate scandals has entailed situations in which executives benefited enormously from misleading accounting or other shady activities that allowed them to hit the numbers and receive incentive awards ranging from $10 million to $100 million. At Bristol-Myers Squibb, for example, the pay-for-performance link spawned strong rules-bending incentives. About 94 percent of one top executive's $18.5 million in total compensation in 2001 came from stock-option grants, a bonus, and long-term incentive payments linked to corporate performance; about 92 percent of a second executive's $12.9 million of compensation was incentive-based.[29]

The fundamental problem with a "make the numbers and move on" syndrome is that a company doesn't really serve its customers or its shareholders by going overboard in pursuing bottom-line profitability. In the final analysis, shareholder interests are best served by doing a really good job of serving customers (observing the rule that customers are king) and by improving the company's competitiveness in the marketplace—these outcomes are the most reliable drivers of higher profits and added shareholder value. Cutting ethical corners or stooping to downright illegal actions in the name of profits first carries exceptionally high risk for shareholders—the steep stock-price decline and tarnished brand image that accompany the discovery of scurrilous behavior leaves shareholders with a company worth much less than before—and the rebuilding task can be arduous, taking both considerable time and resources.

Company Cultures That Put the Bottom Line Ahead of Ethical Behavior

When a company's culture spawns an ethically corrupt or amoral work climate, people have a company-approved license to ignore what's right and engage in most any behavior or employ most any strategy they think they can get away with. Such cultural norms as "No one expects strict adherence to ethical standards," "Everyone else does it," and "It is politic to bend the rules to get the job done" permeate the work environment.[30] At such companies, ethically immoral or amoral people play down observance of ethical strategic actions and business conduct. Moreover, the pressures to conform to cultural norms can prompt otherwise honorable people to make ethical mistakes and succumb to the many opportunities around them to engage in unethical practices.

A perfect example of a company culture gone awry on ethics is Enron.[31] Enron's leaders encouraged company personnel to focus on the current bottom line and to be innovative and aggressive in figuring out what could be done to grow current revenues and earnings. Employees were expected to pursue opportunities to the utmost. Enron executives viewed the company as a laboratory for innovation; the company hired the best and brightest people and pushed them to be creative, look at problems and opportunities in new ways, and exhibit a sense of urgency in making things happen. Employees were encouraged to make a difference and do their part in creating an entrepreneurial environment in which creativity flourished, people could achieve their full potential, and everyone had a stake in the outcome. Enron employees got the message—pushing the limits and meeting one's numbers were viewed as survival skills. Enron's annual "rank and yank" formal evaluation process, in which the 15 to 20 percent lowest-ranking employees were let go or encouraged to seek other employment, made it abundantly clear that hitting earnings targets and being *the* mover and shaker in the marketplace were what counted. The name of the game at Enron became devising clever ways to boost revenues and earnings, even if it sometimes meant operating outside established policies and without the knowledge of superiors. In fact, outside-the-lines behavior was celebrated if it generated profitable new business. Enron's energy contracts and its trading and hedging activities grew increasingly more complex and diverse as employees pursued first this avenue and then another to help keep Enron's financial performance looking good.

As a consequence of Enron's well-publicized successes in creating new products and businesses and leveraging the company's trading and hedging expertise into new market arenas, Enron came to be regarded as exceptionally innovative. It was ranked by its corporate peers as the most innovative U.S. company for three consecutive years in *Fortune* magazine's annual surveys of the most-admired companies. A high-performance/high-rewards climate came to pervade the Enron culture, as the best workers (determined by who produced the best bottom-line results) received impressively large incentives and bonuses (amounting to as much as $1 million for traders and even more for senior executives). On Car Day at Enron, an array of luxury sports cars arrived for presentation to the most successful employees. Understandably, employees wanted to be seen as part of Enron's star team and partake in the benefits that being one of Enron's best and smartest employees entailed. The high monetary rewards, the ambitious and hard-driving people that the company hired and promoted, and the competitive, results-oriented culture combined to give Enron a reputation not only for trampling competitors at every opportunity but also for practicing internal ruthlessness. The company's super-aggressiveness and win-at-all-costs mind-set nurtured a culture that gradually and then more rapidly fostered the erosion of ethical standards, eventually making a mockery of the company's stated values of integrity and respect. When it became evident in the fall of 2001 that Enron was a house of cards propped up by deceitful accounting and a myriad of unsavory practices, the company imploded in a matter of weeks—the biggest bankruptcy of all time cost investors $64 billion in losses (between August 2000, when the stock price was at its five-year high, and November 2001), and Enron employees lost their retirement assets, which were almost totally invested in Enron stock.

More recently, a team investigating an ethical scandal at oil giant Royal Dutch/ Shell Group that resulted in the payment of $150 million in fines found that an ethically flawed culture was a major contributor to why managers made rosy forecasts that they couldn't meet and why top executives engaged in maneuvers to mislead investors by overstating Shell's oil and gas reserves by 25 percent (equal to 4.5 billion barrels of oil). The investigation revealed that top Shell executives knew that a variety of internal practices, together with unrealistic and unsupportable estimates submitted by overzealous, bonus-conscious managers in Shell's exploration and production group, were being used to overstate reserves. An e-mail written by Shell's top executive for exploration and production (who was caught up in the ethical misdeeds and later forced to resign) said, "I am becoming sick and tired about lying about the extent of our reserves issues and the downward revisions that need to be done because of our far too aggressive/optimistic bookings."[32]

Illustration Capsule 10.2 describes Philip Morris USA's new strategy for growing the sales of its leading Marlboro cigarette brand—judge for yourself whether the strategy is ethical or shady in light of the undisputed medical links between smoking and lung cancer.

Approaches to Managing a Company's Ethical Conduct

The stance a company takes in dealing with or managing ethical conduct at any given point can take any of four basic forms:[33]

- The unconcerned, or nonissue, approach.
- The damage control approach.
- The compliance approach.
- The ethical culture approach.

The differences in these four approaches are discussed briefly below and summarized in Table 10.4 on page 335.

Illustration Capsule 10.2

Philip Morris USA's Strategy for Marlboro Cigarettes: Ethical or Unethical?

In late 2005, Philip Morris USA and its corporate parent, Altria Group Inc., wrapped up a year of promotions and parties to celebrate the 50th year of selling Marlboro cigarettes. Marlboro commanded a 40 percent share of the U.S. market for cigarettes and was also one of the world's top cigarette brands. Despite sharp advertising restrictions agreed to by cigarette marketers in 1998 and a big jump in state excise taxes on cigarettes since 2002, Marlboro's sales and market share were climbing, thanks to a new trailblazing marketing strategy.

Marlboro had become a major brand in the 1960s and 1970s via a classic mass-marketing strategy anchored by annual ad budgets in the millions of dollars. The company's TV, magazine, and billboard ads for Marlboros always featured a rugged cowboy wearing a Stetson, riding a horse in a mountainous area, and smoking a Marlboro—closely connecting the brand with the American West gave Marlboro a distinctive and instantly recognized brand image. The Marlboro ad campaign was a gigantic success, making Marlboro one of the world's best-known and valuable brands.

But following the ad restrictions in 1998, Philip Morris had to shift to a different marketing strategy to grow Marlboro's sales. It opted for an approach aimed at generating all kinds of marketing buzz for the Marlboro brand and creating a larger cadre of loyal Marlboro smokers (who often felt persecuted by social pressures and antismoking ordinances). Philip Morris directed company field reps to set up promotions at local bars where smokers could sign up for promotional offers like price discounts on Marlboro purchases, a Marlboro Miles program that awarded points for each pack purchased, and sweepstakes prizes that included cash, trips, and Marlboro apparel; some prizes could be purchased with Marlboro Miles points. It also began to sponsor live concerts and other events to generate additional sign-ups among attendees. A Web site was created to spur Internet chatter among the Marlboro faithful and to encourage still more sign-ups

for special deals and contests (some with prizes up to a $1 million)—an online community quickly sprang up around the brand. Via all the sign-ups and calls to an 800 number, Philip Morris created a database of Marlboro smokers that by 2005 had grown to 26 million names. Using direct mail and e-mail, the company sent the members of its database a steady stream of messages and offers, ranging from birthday coupons for free breakfasts to price discounts to chances to attend local concerts, enjoy a day at nearby horse tracks, or win a trip to the company's ranch in Montana (where winners got gifts, five-course meals, massages, and free drinks and could go snowmobiling, fly fishing, or horseback riding).

Meanwhile, Philip Morris also became considerably more aggressive in retail stores, launching an offensive initiative to give discounts and incentives to retailers who utilized special aisle displays and signage for its cigarette brands. One 22-store retail chain reported that, by agreeing to a deal to give Philip Morris brands about 66 percent of its cigarette shelf space, it ended up paying about $5.50 per carton less for its Marlboro purchases than it paid for cartons of Camels supplied by rival R. J. Reynolds. Some Wal-Mart stores were said to have awarded Philip Morris as much as 80 percent of its cigarette shelf space.

Thus, despite being besieged by the costs of defending lawsuits and paying out billions to governments as compensation for the increased health care costs associated with smoking, Philip Morris and other cigarette makers were making very healthy profits: operating margins of nearly 28 percent in 2005 (up from 26 percent in 2004) and net income of about $11.4 billion on sales of $66.3 billion in the United States and abroad.

However, health care officials were highly critical of Philip Morris's marketing tactics for Marlboro, and the U.S. Department of Justice had filed a lawsuit claiming, among other things, that the company knowingly marketed Marlboros to underage people in its database, a charge denied by the company.

Source: Based largely on information in Nanette Byrnes, "Leader of the Packs," *BusinessWeek,* October 31, 2005, pp. 56, 58.

The Unconcerned, or Nonissue, Approach   The unconcerned approach is prevalent at companies whose executives are immoral and unintentionally amoral. Senior executives at companies using this approach ascribe to the view that notions of right and wrong in matters of business are defined entirely by government via the prevailing laws and regulations. They maintain that trying to enforce ethical standards above and beyond what is legally required is a nonissue because businesses are entitled to conduct their affairs in whatever manner they wish so long as

Table 10.4   **Four Approaches to Managing Business Ethics**

	Unconcerned, or Nonissue Approach	Damage Control Approach	Compliance Approach	Ethical Culture Approach
Underlying beliefs	• The business of business is business, not ethics. • All that matters is whether an action is legal. • Ethics has no place in the conduct of business. • Companies should not be morally accountable for their actions.	• The company needs to make a token gesture in the direction of ethical standards (a code of ethics).	• The company must be committed to ethical standards and monitoring ethics performance. • Unethical behavior must be prevented and punished if discovered. • It is important to have a reputation for high ethical standards.	• Ethics is basic to the culture. • Behaving ethically must be a deeply held corporate value and become a way of life. • Everyone is expected to walk the talk.
Ethics management approaches	• There's no need to make decisions concerning business ethics—if its legal, it is okay. • No intervention regarding the ethical component of decisions is needed.	• The company must act to protect against the dangers of unethical strategies and behavior. • Ignore unethical behavior or allow it to go unpunished unless the situation is extreme and requires action.	• The company must establish a clear, comprehensive code of ethics. • The company must provide ethics training for all personnel. • Have formal ethics compliance procedures, an ethics compliance office, and a chief ethics officer.	• Ethical behavior is ingrained and reinforced as part of the culture. • Much reliance on co-worker peer pressure—"That's not how we do things here." • Everyone is an ethics watchdog—whistle-blowing is required. • Ethics heroes are celebrated; ethics stories are told.
Challenges	• Financial consequences can become unaffordable. • Some stakeholders are alienated.	• Credibility problems with stakeholders can arise. • The company is susceptible to ethical scandal. • The company has a subpar ethical reputation—executives and company personnel don't walk the talk.	• Organizational members come to rely on the existing rules for moral guidance—fosters a mentality of what is not forbidden is allowed. • Rules and guidelines proliferate. • The locus of moral control resides in the code and in the ethics compliance system rather than in an individual's own moral responsibility for ethical behavior.	• New employees must go through strong ethics induction program. • Formal ethics management systems can be underutilized. • Relying on peer pressures and cultural norms to enforce ethical standards can result in eliminating some or many of the compliance trappings and, over time, induce moral laxness.

Source: Adapted from Gedeon J. Rossouw and Leon J. van Vuuren, "Modes of Managing Morality: A Descriptive Model of Strategies for Managing Ethics," *Journal of Business Ethics* 46, no. 4 (September 2003), pp. 392–93.

they comply with the letter of what is legally required. Hence, there is no need to spend valuable management time trying to prescribe and enforce standards of conduct that go above and beyond legal and regulatory requirements. In companies where senior managers are immoral, the prevailing view may well be that under-the-table dealing can be good business if it can be kept hidden or if it can be justified on grounds that others are doing it too. Companies in this mode usually engage in most any business practices they believe they can get away with, and the strategies they employ may well embrace elements that are either borderline from a legal perspective or ethically shady and unsavory.

The Damage Control Approach   Damage control is favored at companies whose managers are intentionally amoral but who are wary of scandal and adverse public relations fallout that could cost them their jobs of tarnish their careers. Companies using this approach, not wanting to risk tarnishing the reputations of key personnel or the company, usually make some concession to window-dressing ethics, going so far as to adopt a code of ethics—so that their executives can point to it as evidence of good-faith efforts to prevent unethical strategy making or unethical conduct on the part of company personnel. But the code of ethics exists mainly as nice words on paper, and company personnel do not operate within a strong ethical context—there's a notable gap between talking ethics and walking ethics. Employees quickly get the message that rule bending is tolerated and may even be rewarded if the company benefits from their actions.

> The main objective of the damage control approach is to protect against adverse publicity and any damaging consequences brought on by headlines in the media, outside investigation, threats of litigation, punitive government action, or angry or vocal stakeholders.

Company executives that practice the damage control approach are prone to look the other way when shady or borderline behavior occurs—adopting a kind of "See no evil, hear no evil, speak no evil" stance (except when exposure of the company's actions put executives under great pressure to redress any wrongs that have been done). They may even condone questionable actions that help the company reach earnings targets or bolster its market standing—such as pressuring customers to stock up on the company's product (channel stuffing), making under-the-table payments to win new business, stonewalling the recall of products claimed to be unsafe, bad-mouthing the products of rivals, or trying to keep prices low by sourcing goods from disreputable suppliers in low-wage countries that run sweatshop operations or use child labor. But they are usually careful to do such things in a manner that lessens the risks of exposure or damaging consequences. This generally includes making token gestures to police compliance with codes of ethics and relying heavily on spin to help extricate the company or themselves from claims that the company's strategy has unethical components or that company personnel have engaged in unethical practices.

The Compliance Approach   Anywhere from light to forceful compliance is favored at companies whose managers (1) lean toward being somewhat amoral but are highly concerned about having ethically upstanding reputations or (2) are moral and see strong compliance methods as the best way to impose and enforce ethical rules and high ethical standards. Companies that adopt a compliance mode usually do some or all of the following to display their commitment to ethical conduct: make the code of ethics a visible and regular part of communications with employees, implement ethics training programs, appoint a chief ethics officer or ethics ombudsperson, have ethics committees to give guidance on ethics matters, institute formal procedures for investigating alleged ethics violations, conduct ethics audits to measure and document compliance, give ethics awards to employees for outstanding efforts to create an ethical climate and improve ethical performance, and/or try to deter violations by setting up ethics hotlines for anonymous callers to use in reporting possible violations.

Emphasis here is usually on securing broad compliance and measuring the degree to which ethical standards are upheld and observed. However, violators are disciplined and sometimes subjected to public reprimand and punishment (including dismissal), thereby sending a clear signal to company personnel that complying with ethical standards needs to be taken seriously. The driving force behind the company's commitment to eradicate unethical behavior normally stems from a desire to avoid the cost and damage associated with unethical conduct or else a quest to gain favor from stakeholders (especially ethically conscious customers, employees, and investors) for having a highly regarded reputation for ethical behavior. One of the weaknesses of the compliance approach is that moral control resides in the company's code of ethics and in the ethics compliance system rather than in (1) the strong peer pressures for ethical behavior that come from ingraining a highly ethical corporate culture and (2) an individual's own moral responsibility for ethical behavior.[34]

The Ethical Culture Approach   At some companies, top executives believe that high ethical principles must be deeply ingrained in the corporate culture and function as guides for "how we do things around here." A company using the ethical culture approach seeks to gain employee buy-in to the company's ethical standards, business principles, and corporate values. The ethical principles embraced in the company's code of ethics and/or in its statement of corporate values are seen as integral to the company's identity and ways of operating—they are at the core of the company's soul and are promoted as part of business as usual. The integrity of the ethical culture approach depends heavily on the ethical integrity of the executives who create and nurture the culture—it is incumbent on them to determine how high the bar is to be set and to exemplify ethical standards in their own decisions and behavior. Further, it is essential that the strategy be ethical in all respects and that ethical behavior be ingrained in the means that company personnel employ to execute the strategy. Such insistence on observing ethical standards is what creates an ethical work climate and a workplace where displaying integrity is the norm.

Many of the trappings used in the compliance approach are also manifest in the ethical culture mode, but one other is added—strong peer pressure from co-workers to observe ethical norms. Thus, responsibility for ethics compliance is widely dispersed throughout all levels of management and the rank-and-file. Stories of former and current moral heroes are kept in circulation, and the deeds of company personnel who display ethical values and are dedicated to walking the talk are celebrated at internal company events. The message that ethics matters—and matters a lot—resounds loudly and clearly throughout the organization and in its strategy and decisions. However, one of the challenges to overcome in the ethical culture approach is relying too heavily on peer pressures and cultural norms to enforce ethics compliance rather than on an individual's own moral responsibility for ethical behavior—absent unrelenting peer pressure or strong internal compliance systems, there is a danger that over time company personnel may become lax about its ethical standards. Compliance procedures need to be an integral part of the ethical culture approach to help send the message that management takes the observance of ethical norms seriously and that behavior that falls outside ethical boundaries will have negative consequences.

Why a Company Can Change Its Ethics Management Approach
Regardless of the approach they have used to managing ethical conduct, a company's executives may sense that they have exhausted a particular mode's potential for managing ethics and that they need to become more forceful in their approach to ethics management. Such changes typically occur when the company's ethical failures have made the headlines and created an embarrassing situation for company officials or when the business climate changes. For example, the recent raft of corporate scandals, coupled with aggressive enforcement of anticorruption legislation such as the Sarbanes-Oxley Act of 2002 (which addresses corporate governance and accounting practices), has prompted numerous executives and boards of directors to clean up their acts in accounting and financial reporting, review their ethical standards, and tighten up ethics compliance procedures. Intentionally amoral managers using the unconcerned approach to ethics management may see less risk in shifting to the damage control approach (or, for appearance's sake, maybe a "light" compliance mode). Senior managers who have employed the damage control mode may be motivated by bad experiences to mend their ways and shift to a compliance mode. In the wake of so many corporate scandals, companies in the compliance mode may move closer to the ethical culture approach.

WHY SHOULD COMPANY STRATEGIES BE ETHICAL?

There are two reasons why a company's strategy should be ethical: (1) because a strategy that is unethical in whole or in part is morally wrong and reflects badly on the character of the company personnel involved and (2) because an ethical strategy is good business and in the self-interest of shareholders.

The Moral Case for an Ethical Strategy

Managers do not dispassionately assess what strategic course to steer. Ethical strategy making generally begins with managers who themselves have strong character (i.e., who are honest, have integrity, are ethical, and truly care about how they conduct the company's business). Managers with high ethical principles and standards are usually advocates of a corporate code of ethics and strong ethics compliance, and they are typically genuinely committed to certain corporate values and business principles. They walk the talk in displaying the company's stated values and living up to its business principles and ethical standards. They understand that there is a big difference between adopting values statements and codes of ethics that serve merely as window dressing and those that truly paint the white lines for a company's actual strategy and business conduct. As a consequence, ethically strong managers consciously opt for strategic actions that can pass moral scrutiny—they display no tolerance for strategies with ethically controversial components.

The Business Case for an Ethical Strategy

There are solid business reasons to adopt ethical strategies even if most company managers are not of strong moral character and personally committed to high ethical standards. Pursuing unethical strategies not only damages a company's reputation but can also have costly, wide-ranging consequences. Some of the costs are readily visible; others are hidden and difficult to track down—as shown in Figure 10.1. The costs of

Figure 10.1   **The Business Costs of Ethical Failures**

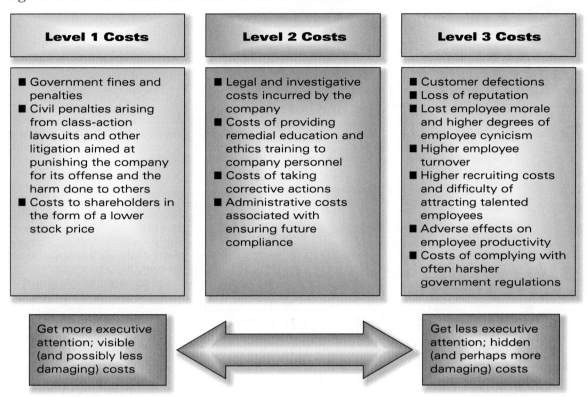

Source: Adapted from Terry Thomas, John R. Schermerhorn, and John W. Dienhart, "Strategic Leadership of Ethical Behavior," *Academy of Management Executive* 18, no. 2 (May 2004), p. 58.

fines and penalties and any declines in the stock price are easy enough to calculate. The administrative cleanup (or Level 2) costs are usually buried in the general costs of doing business and can be difficult to ascribe to any one ethical misdeed. Level 3 costs can be quite difficult to quantify but can sometimes be the most devastating—the aftermath of the Enron debacle left Arthur Andersen's reputation in shreds and led to the once-revered accounting firm's almost immediate demise, and it remains to be seen whether Marsh & McLennan can overcome the problems described in Illustration Capsule 10.1. Merck, once one of the world's most respected pharmaceutical firms, has been struggling against the revelation that senior management deliberately concealed that its Vioxx painkiller, which the company pulled off the market in September 2004, was tied to much greater risk of heart attack and strokes—some 20 million people in the United States had taken Vioxx over the years, and Merck executives had reason to suspect as early as 2000 (and perhaps earlier) that Vioxx had dangerous side effects.[35]

Rehabilitating a company's shattered reputation is time-consuming and costly. Customers shun companies known for their shady behavior. Companies with reputations for unethical conduct have considerable difficulty in recruiting and retaining talented employees. Most hardworking, ethically upstanding people are repulsed by a work environment where unethical behavior is condoned; they don't want to get entrapped in a

> Conducting business in an ethical fashion is in a company's enlightened self-interest.

Illustration Capsule 10.3

A Test of Your Business Ethics

As a gauge of your own ethical and moral standards, take the following quiz and see how you stack up against other members of your class. For the test to be valid, you need to answer the questions candidly, not on the basis of what you think the ethically correct answer is.

1. Do you think that it would be unethical for you to give two Super Bowl tickets to an important customer? Would your answer be different if the customer is likely to place a large order that would qualify you for a large year-end sales bonus?

_____Yes _____No _____Unsure (it depends)

_____Need more information

2. Would it be wrong to accept a case of fine wine from an important customer? Would your answer be different if you have just convinced your superiors to authorize a special price discount on a big order that the customer has just placed?

_____Yes _____No _____Unsure (it depends)

_____Need more information

3. Is it unethical for a high school or college coach to accept a "talent fee" or similar type of payment from a maker of sports apparel or sports equipment when the coach has authority to determine which brand of apparel or equipment to use for his or her team and subsequently chooses the brand of the company making the payment? Is it unethical for the maker of the sports apparel or equipment to make such payments in expectation that the coach will reciprocate by selecting the company's brand? (Would you answer be different if everybody else is doing it?)

_____Yes _____No _____Unsure (it depends)

_____Need more information

4. Is it unethical to accept an invitation from a supplier to spend a holiday weekend skiing at the supplier company's resort home in Colorado? (Would your answer be different if you were presently considering a proposal from that supplier to purchase $1 million worth of components?)

_____Yes _____No _____Unsure (it depends)

_____Need more information

5. Is it unethical for a food products company to incorporate ingredients that have trans fats in its products, given that trans fats are known to be very unhealthy for consumers and that alternative ingredients (which might be somewhat more expensive) can be used in producing the product?

_____Yes _____No _____Unsure (it depends)

_____Need more information

6. Would it be wrong to keep quiet if you, as a junior financial analyst, had just calculated that the projected return on a possible project was 18 percent and your boss (*a*) informed you that no project could be approved without the prospect

of a 25 percent return and (*b*) told you to go back and redo the numbers and "get them right"?

_____Yes _____No _____Unsure (it depends)

_____Need more information

7. Would it be unethical to allow your supervisor to believe that you were chiefly responsible for the success of a new company initiative if it actually resulted from a team effort or major contributions by a co-worker?

_____Yes _____No _____Unsure (it depends)

_____Need more information

8. Would it be unethical for you, as the chief company official in India to (*a*) authorize a $25,000 payment to a local government official to facilitate governmental approval to construct a $200 million petrochemical plant and (*b*) disguise this payment by instructing accounting personnel to classify the payment as part of the cost of obtaining a building permit? (As you can see from Table 10.1, corruption is the norm in India, and bribes and kickbacks are often a "necessary" cost of doing business there.)

_____Yes _____No _____Unsure (it depends)

_____Need more information

9. Is it unethical for a motor vehicle manufacturer to resist recalling some of its vehicles when governmental authorities present it with credible evidence that the vehicles have safety defects?

_____Yes _____No _____Unsure (it depends)

_____Need more information

10. Is it unethical for a credit card company to aggressively try to sign up new accounts when, after an introductory period of interest-free or low-interest charges on unpaid monthly balances, the interest rate on unpaid balances jumps to 1.5 percent or more monthly (even though such high rates of 18 percent or more annually are disclosed in fine print)?

_____Yes _____No _____Unsure (it depends)

_____Need more information

11. Is it unethical to bolster your résumé with exaggerated claims of your credentials and prior job accomplishments in hopes of improving your chances of gaining employment at another company?

_____Yes _____No _____Unsure (it depends)

_____Need more information

12. Is it unethical for a company to spend as little as possible on pollution control when, with some extra effort and expenditures, it could substantially reduce the amount of pollution caused by its operations?

_____Yes _____No _____Unsure (it depends)

_____Need more information

Answers: The answers to questions 1, 2, and 4 probably shift from no/unsure to a definite yes when the second part of the circumstance comes into play. We think a strong case can be made that the answers to the remaining 9 questions are yes, although it can be argued that more information about the circumstances might be needed in responding to questions 5, 7, 9, and 12.

compromising situation, nor do they want their personal reputations tarnished by the actions of an unsavory employer. A 1997 survey revealed that 42 percent of the respondents took into account a company's ethics when deciding whether to accept a job.[36] Creditors are usually unnerved by the unethical actions of a borrower because of the potential business fallout and subsequent risk of default on any loans. To some significant degree, therefore, companies recognize that ethical strategies and ethical conduct are good business. Most companies have strategies that pass the test of being ethical, and most companies are aware that both their reputations and their long-term well-being are tied to conducting their business in a manner that wins the approval of suppliers, employees, investors, and society at large.

As a test your own business ethics and where you stand on the importance of companies having an ethical strategy, take the test on page 340.

LINKING A COMPANY'S STRATEGY TO ITS ETHICAL PRINCIPLES AND CORE VALUES

Many companies have officially adopted a code of ethical conduct and a statement of company values—in the United States, the Sarbanes-Oxley Act, passed in 2002, requires that companies whose stock is publicly traded have a code of ethics or else explain in writing to the Securities and Exchange Commission why they do not. But there's a big difference between having a code of ethics and a values statement that serve merely as a public window dressing and having ethical standards and corporate values that truly paint the white lines for a company's actual strategy and business conduct. If ethical standards and statements of core values are to have more than a cosmetic role, boards of directors and top executives must work diligently to see that they are scrupulously observed in crafting the company's strategy and conducting every facet of the company's business. In other words, living up to the ethical principles and displaying the core values in actions and decisions must become a way of life at the company.

Indeed, the litmus test of whether a company's code of ethics and statement of core values are cosmetic is the extent to which they are embraced in crafting strategy and in operating the business day to day. It is up to senior executives to walk the talk and make a point of considering two sets of questions whenever a new strategic initiative is under review:

- Is what we are proposing to do fully compliant with our code of ethical conduct? Is there anything here that could be considered ethically objectionable?

- Is it apparent that this proposed action is in harmony with our core values? Are any conflicts or concerns evident?

Unless questions of this nature are posed—either in open discussion or by force of habit in the minds of strategy makers, then there's room for strategic initiatives to become disconnected from the company's code of ethics and stated core values. If a company's executives are ethically principled and believe strongly in living up to the company's stated core values, there's a good chance they will pose these types of questions and reject strategic initiatives that don't measure up. There's also a good chance that strategic actions will be scrutinized for their compatibility with ethical standards and core values when the latter are so deeply ingrained in a company's culture and in the

Core Concept
More attention is paid to linking strategy with ethical principles and core values in companies headed by moral executives and in companies where ethical principles and core values are a way of life.

everyday conduct of company personnel that they are automatically taken into account in all that the company does. However, in companies with window-dressing ethics and core values or in companies headed by immoral or amoral managers, any strategy-ethics-values link stems mainly from a desire to avoid the risk of embarrassment, scandal, and possible disciplinary action should strategy makers get called on the carpet and held accountable for approving an unethical strategic initiative.

STRATEGY AND SOCIAL RESPONSIBILITY

The idea that businesses have an obligation to foster social betterment, a much-debated topic in the past 40 years, took root in the 19th century when progressive companies in the aftermath of the industrial revolution began to provide workers with housing and other amenities. The notion that corporate executives should balance the interests of all stakeholders—shareholders, employees, customers, suppliers, the communities in which they operated, and society at large—began to blossom in the 1960s. A group of chief executives of America's 200 largest corporations, calling themselves the Business Roundtable, promoted the concept of corporate social responsibility. In 1981, the Roundtable's "Statement on Corporate Responsibility" said:[37]

> Balancing the shareholder's expectations of maximum return against other priorities is one of the fundamental problems confronting corporate management. The shareholder must receive a good return but the legitimate concerns of other constituencies (customers, employees, communities, suppliers and society at large) also must have the appropriate attention . . . [Leading managers] believe that by giving enlightened consideration to balancing the legitimate claims of all its constituents, a corporation will best serve the interest of its shareholders.

Today, corporate social responsibility is a concept that resonates in Western Europe, the United States, Canada, and such developing nations as Brazil and India.

What Do We Mean by Social Responsibility?

Core Concept

The notion of *social responsibility* as it applies to businesses concerns a company's *duty* to operate in an honorable manner, provide good working conditions for employees, be a good steward of the environment, and actively work to better the quality of life in the local communities where it operates and in society at large.

The essence of socially responsible business behavior is that a company should balance strategic actions to benefit shareholders against the *duty* to be a good corporate citizen. The thesis is that company managers are obligated to display a *social conscience* in operating the business and specifically take into account how management decisions and company actions affect the well-being of employees, local communities, the environment, and society at large. Acting in a socially responsible manner thus encompasses more than just participating in community service projects and donating money to charities and other worthy social causes. Demonstrating social responsibility also entails undertaking actions that earn trust and respect from all stakeholders—operating in an honorable and ethical manner, striving to make the company a great place to work, demonstrating genuine respect for the environment, and trying to make a difference in bettering society. As depicted in Figure 10.2, the menu for demonstrating a social conscience and choosing specific ways to exercise social responsibility includes:

- *Efforts to employ an ethical strategy and observe ethical principles in operating the business*—A sincere commitment to observing ethical principles is

Figure 10.2   **Demonstrating a Social Conscience: The Five Components of Socially Responsible Business Behavior**

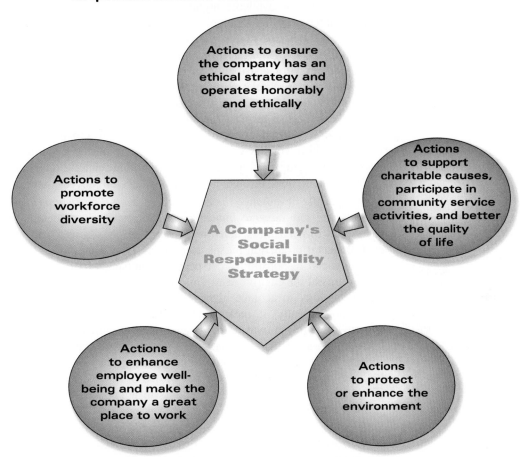

Source: Adapted from material in Ronald Paul Hill, Debra Stephens, and Iain Smith, "Corporate Social Responsibility: An Examination of Individual Firm Behavior," *Business and Society Review* 108, no. 3 (September 2003), p. 348.

necessary here simply because unethical strategies and conduct are incompatible with the concept of good corporate citizenship and socially responsible business behavior.

- *Making charitable contributions, donating money and the time of company personnel to community service endeavors, supporting various worthy organizational causes, and reaching out to make a difference in the lives of the disadvantaged*—Some companies fulfill their corporate citizenship and community outreach obligations by spreading their efforts over a multitude of charitable and community activities; for instance, Microsoft and Johnson & Johnson support a broad variety of community art, social welfare, and environmental programs. Others prefer to focus their energies more narrowly. McDonald's, for example, concentrates on sponsoring the Ronald McDonald House program (which provides a home away from home for the families of seriously ill children receiving treatment at nearby hospitals), preventing child abuse and neglect, and participating in local community service activities; in 2004, there were 240 Ronald McDonald Houses in 25 countries and more than 6,000 bedrooms available nightly. British Telecom gives 1 percent of its profits directly to communities, largely for education—teacher training, in-school workshops, and digital technology. Leading prescription drug maker GlaxoSmithKline and other pharmaceutical companies either donate or heavily discount medicines for distribution in the least-developed nations. Numerous health-related businesses take a leading role in community activities that promote effective health care. Many companies work closely with community officials to minimize the impact of hiring large numbers of new employees (which could put a strain on local schools and utility services) and to provide outplacement services for laid-off workers. Companies frequently reinforce their philanthropic efforts by encouraging employees to support charitable causes and participate in community affairs, often through programs to match employee contributions.

- *Actions to protect or enhance the environment and, in particular, to minimize or eliminate any adverse impact on the environment stemming from the company's own business activities*—Social responsibility as it applies to environmental protection means doing more than what is legally required. From a social responsibility perspective, companies have an obligation to be stewards of the environment. This means using the best available science and technology to achieve higher-than-required environmental standards. Even more ideally, it means putting time and money into improving the environment in ways that extend past a company's own industry boundaries—such as participating in recycling projects, adopting energy conservation practices, and supporting efforts to clean up local water supplies. Retailers such as Home Depot in the United States and B&Q in the United Kingdom have pressured their suppliers to adopt stronger environmental protection practices.[38]

> Business leaders who want their companies to be regarded as exemplary corporate citizens must not only see that their companies operate ethically but they must personally display a social conscience in making decisions that affect employees, the environment, the communities in which they operate, and society at large.

- *Actions to create a work environment that enhances the quality of life for employees and makes the company a great place to work*—Numerous companies go beyond providing the ordinary kinds of compensation and exert extra efforts to enhance the quality of life for their employees, both at work and at home. This can include varied and engaging job assignments, career development programs and mentoring, rapid career advancement, appealing compensation incentives, ongoing training to ensure future employability, added decision-making authority, onsite day care, flexible work schedules for single parents, workplace exercise facilities, special leaves to care for sick family members, work-at-home opportunities, gender pay equity, showcase plants and offices, special safety programs, and the like.

- *Actions to build a workforce that is diverse with respect to gender, race, national origin, and perhaps other aspects that different people bring to the workplace*—Most large companies in the United States have established workforce diversity programs, and some go the extra mile to ensure that their workplaces are attractive to ethnic minorities and inclusive of all groups and perspectives. The pursuit of workforce diversity can be good business—Johnson & Johnson, Pfizer, and Coca-Cola believe that a reputation for workforce diversity makes recruiting employees easier (talented employees from diverse backgrounds often seek out such companies). And at Coca-Cola, where strategic success depends on getting people all over the world to become loyal consumers of the company's beverages, efforts to build a public persona of inclusiveness for people of all races, religions, nationalities, interests, and talents has considerable strategic value. Multinational companies are particularly inclined to make workforce diversity a visible strategic component; they recognize that respecting individual differences and promoting inclusiveness resonate well with people all around the world. At a few companies the diversity initiative extends to suppliers—sourcing items from small businesses owned by women or ethnic minorities.

Crafting a Social Responsibility Strategy: The Starting Point for Demonstrating a Social Conscience

While striving to be socially responsible entails choosing from the menu outlined in the preceding section, there's plenty of room for every company to make its own statement about what charitable contributions to make, what kinds of community service projects to emphasize, what environmental actions to support, how to make the company a good place to work, where and how workforce diversity fits into the picture, and what else it will do to support worthy causes and projects that benefit society. The particular combination of socially responsible endeavors a company elects to pursue defines its **social responsibility strategy.** However, unless a company's social responsibility initiatives become part of the way it operates its business every day, the initiatives are unlikely to catch fire and be fully effective. As an executive at Royal Dutch/Shell put it, corporate social responsibility "is not a cosmetic; it must be rooted in our values. It must make a difference to the way we do business."[39] Thus some companies are integrating social responsibility objectives into their missions and overall performance targets—they see social performance and environmental metrics as an essential component of judging the company's overall future performance. Some 2,500 companies around the world are not only articulating their social responsibility strategies and commitments but they are also issuing annual social responsibility reports (much like an annual report) that set forth their commitments and the progress they are making for all the world to see and evaluate.[40]

> **Core Concept**
> A company's **social responsibility strategy** is defined by the specific combination of socially beneficial activities it opts to support with its contributions of time, money, and other resources.

At Starbucks, the commitment to social responsibility is linked to the company's strategy and operating practices via the tag line "Giving back to our communities is the way we do business"; top management makes the theme come alive via the company's extensive community-building activities, efforts to protect the welfare of coffee growers and their families (in particular, making sure they receive a fair price), a variety of recycling and environmental conservation practices, and the financial support it provides to charities and the disadvantaged through the Starbucks Foundation. At Green Mountain Coffee Roasters, social responsibility includes fair dealing with suppliers and trying to do something about the poverty of small coffee growers; in its dealings with suppliers at small farmer cooperatives in Peru, Mexico, and Sumatra, Green Mountain pays "fair trade" prices for coffee beans (in 2002, the fair trade prices were a minimum of $1.26 per pound for conventional coffee and $1.41 for organically grown versus market prices of 24 to 50 cents per pound). Green Mountain also purchases about 25 percent of its coffee direct from farmers so as to cut out intermediaries and see that farmers realize a higher price for their efforts—coffee is the world's second most heavily traded commodity after oil, requiring the labor of some 20 million people, most of whom live at the poverty level.[41] At Whole Foods Market, a $5 billion supermarket chain specializing in organic and natural foods, the social responsibility emphasis is on supporting organic farming and

> Many companies tailor their strategic efforts to operate in a socially responsible manner to fit their core values and business mission, thereby making their own statement about "how we do business and how we intend to fulfill our duties to all stakeholders and society at large."

sustainable agriculture, recycling, sustainable seafood practices, giving employees paid time off to participate in worthy community service endeavors, and donating 5 percent of after-tax profits in cash or products to charitable causes. At General Mills the social responsibility focus is on service to the community and bettering the employment opportunities for minorities and women. Stonyfield Farm, a producer of yogurt and ice cream products, employs a social responsibility strategy focused on wellness, good nutrition, and earth-friendly actions (10 percent of profits are donated to help protect and restore the earth, and yogurt lids are used as miniature billboards to help educate people about environmental issues); in addition, it is stressing the development of an environmentally friendly supply chain, sourcing from farmers that grow organic products and refrain from using artificial hormones in milk production. Chick-Fil-A, an Atlanta-based fast-food chain with over 1,200 outlets in 38 states, has a charitable foundation; supports 14 foster homes and a summer camp (for some 1,600 campers from 22 states and several foreign countries); funds two scholarship programs (including one for employees that has awarded more than $20 million in scholarships); and maintains a closed-on-Sunday policy to ensure that every Chick-Fil-A employee and restaurant operator has an opportunity to worship, spend time with family and friends, or just plain rest from the workweek.[42] Toys "R" Us supports initiatives addressing the issues of child labor and fair labor practices around the world. Community Pride Food Stores is assisting in revitalizing the inner city of Richmond, Virginia, where the company is based.

It is common for companies engaged in natural resource extraction, electric power production, forestry and paper products, motor vehicles, and chemicals production to place more emphasis on addressing environmental concerns than, say, software and electronics firms or apparel manufacturers. Companies whose business success is heavily dependent on high employee morale or attracting and retaining the best and brightest employees are somewhat more prone to stress the well-being of their employees and foster a positive, high-energy workplace environment that elicits the dedication and enthusiastic commitment of employees, thus putting real meaning behind the claim "Our people are our greatest asset." Ernst & Young, one of the four largest global accounting firms, stresses its "People First" workforce diversity strategy, which focuses on respecting differences, fostering individuality, and promoting inclusiveness so that its 105,000 employees in 140 countries can feel valued, engaged, and empowered in developing creative ways to serve the firm's clients.

Thus, while the strategies and actions of all socially responsible companies have a sameness in the sense of drawing on the five categories of socially responsible behavior shown in Figure 10.2, each company's version of being socially responsible is unique.

The Moral Case for Corporate Social Responsibility

> Every action a company takes can be interpreted as a statement of what it stands for.

The moral case for why businesses should actively promote the betterment of society and act in a manner that benefits all of the company's stakeholders—not just the interests of shareholders—boils down to the fact that it's the right thing to do. Ordinary decency, civic-mindedness, and contributing to the well-being of society should be expected of any business. In today's social and political climate, most business leaders can be expected to acknowledge that socially responsible actions are important and that businesses have a duty to be good corporate citizens. But there is a complementary school of thought that business operates on the basis of an implied social contract with the members of society. According to this contract, society grants a business the right to conduct its business affairs and agrees not to unreasonably restrain its pursuit of a fair profit for the goods or services it sells; in return for this "license to operate," a business is obligated to act as a responsible citizen and do its fair share to promote the general welfare. Such a view clearly puts a moral burden on a company to take corporate citizenship into consideration and to do what's best for shareholders within the confines of discharging its duties to operate honorably, provide good working conditions to employees, be a good environmental steward, and display good corporate citizenship.

The Business Case for Socially Responsible Behavior

Whatever the merits of the moral case for socially responsible business behavior, it has long been recognized that it is in the enlightened self-interest of companies to be good citizens and devote some of their energies and resources to the betterment of employees, the communities in which they operate, and society in general. In short, there are several reasons why the exercise of social responsibility is good business:

- *It generates internal benefits (particularly as concerns employee recruiting, workforce retention, and training costs)*—Companies with deservedly good reputations for contributing time and money to the betterment of society are better able to attract and retain employees compared to companies with tarnished reputations. Some employees just feel better about working for a company committed to improving society.[43] This can contribute to lower turnover and better worker productivity. Other direct and indirect economic benefits include lower costs for staff recruitment and training. For example, Starbucks is said to enjoy much lower rates of employee turnover because of its full benefits package for both full-time and part-time employees, management efforts to make Starbucks a great place to work, and the company's socially responsible practices. When a U.S. manufacturer of recycled paper, taking eco-efficiency to heart, discovered how to increase its fiber recovery rate, it saved the equivalent of 20,000 tons of waste paper—a factor that helped the company become the industry's lowest-cost producer.[44] Various benchmarking and measurement mechanisms have shown that workforce diversity initiatives promote the success of companies that stay behind them. Making a company a great place to work pays dividends in recruiting talented workers, more creativity and energy on the part of workers, higher worker productivity, and greater employee commitment to the company's business mission/vision and success in the marketplace.

- *It reduces the risk of reputation-damaging incidents and can lead to increased buyer patronage*—Firms may well be penalized by employees, consumers, and shareholders for actions that are not considered socially responsible. When a major oil company suffered damage to its reputation on environmental and social grounds, the CEO repeatedly said that the most negative impact the company suffered—and the one that made him fear for the future of the company—was that bright young graduates were no longer attracted to work for the company.[45] Consumer, environmental, and human rights activist groups are quick to criticize businesses whose behavior they consider to be out of line, and they are adept at getting their message into the media and onto the Internet. Pressure groups can generate widespread adverse publicity, promote boycotts, and influence like-minded or sympathetic buyers to avoid an offender's products.

> The higher the public profile of a company or brand, the greater the scrutiny of its activities and the higher the potential for it to become a target for pressure-group action.

Research has shown that product boycott announcements are associated with a decline in a company's stock price.[46] Outspoken criticism of Royal Dutch/Shell by environmental and human rights groups and associated boycotts were said to be major factors in the company's decision to tune in to its social responsibilities. For many years, Nike received stinging criticism for not policing sweatshop conditions in the Asian factories of its contractors, causing Nike CEO Phil Knight to observe that "Nike has become synonymous with slave wages, forced overtime, and arbitrary abuse."[47] In 1997, Nike began an extensive effort to monitor conditions in the 800 overseas factories to which it outsourced its shoes; Knight said, "Good shoes come from good factories, and good factories have good labor relations." Nonetheless, Nike has continually been plagued by complaints from human rights activists that its monitoring procedures are flawed and that it is not doing enough to correct the plight of factory workers. In contrast, to the extent that a company's socially responsible behavior wins applause from consumers and fortifies its reputation, the company may win additional patronage; Ben & Jerry's, Whole Foods Market, Stonyfield Farm, and the Body Shop have definitely expanded their customer bases because of their visible and well-publicized activities as socially conscious companies. More and more companies are recognizing the strategic value of social responsibility strategies that reach out to people of all cultures and demographics—in the United States, women are said to having buying power of $3.7 trillion, retired and disabled people close to $4.1 trillion, Hispanics nearly $600 billion, African Americans some $500 billion, and Asian Americans about $255 billion.[48] So reaching out in ways that appeal to such groups can pay off at the cash register. Some observers and executives are convinced that a strong, visible social responsibility strategy gives a company an edge in differentiating itself from rivals and in appealing to those consumers who prefer to do business with companies that are solid corporate citizens. Yet there is only limited evidence that consumers go out of their way to patronize socially responsible companies if it means paying a higher price or purchasing an inferior product.[49]

- *It is in the best interest of shareholders*—Well-conceived social responsibility strategies work to the advantage of shareholders in several ways. Socially responsible business behavior helps avoid or preempt legal and regulatory actions that could prove costly and otherwise burdensome. Increasing numbers of mutual funds and pension benefit managers are restricting their stock purchases to companies that meet social responsibility criteria. According to one survey, one out of every eight dollars under professional management in the United States involved socially responsible investing.[50] Moreover, the growth in socially responsible investing and identifying socially responsible companies has led to a substantial increase in the number of companies that publish formal reports on their social and environmental activities.[51] The stock prices of companies that rate high on social and environmental performance criteria have been found to perform 35 to 45 percent better than the average of the 2,500 companies comprising the Dow Jones Global Index.[52] A two-year study of leading companies found that improving environmental compliance and developing environmentally friendly products can enhance earnings per share, profitability, and the likelihood of winning contracts.[53] Nearly 100 studies have examined the relationship between corporate citizenship and corporate financial performance over the past 30 years; the majority point to a positive relationship. Of the 80 studies that examined whether a company's social performance is a good predictor of its financial performance, 42 concluded yes, 4 concluded

> There's little hard evidence indicating shareholders are disadvantaged in any meaningful way by a company's actions to be socially responsible.

no, and the remainder reported mixed or inconclusive findings.[54] To the extent that socially responsible behavior is good business, then, a social responsibility strategy that packs some punch and is more than rhetorical flourish turns out to be in the best interest of shareholders.

In sum, companies that take social responsibility seriously can improve their business reputations and operational efficiency while also reducing their risk exposure and encouraging loyalty and innovation. Overall, companies that take special pains to protect the environment (beyond what is required by law), are active in community affairs, and are generous supporters of charitable causes and projects that benefit society are more likely to be seen as good investments and as good companies to work for or do business with. Shareholders are likely to view the business case for social responsibility as a strong one, even though they certainly have a right to be concerned whether the time and money their company spends to carry out its social responsibility strategy outweighs the benefits and reduces the bottom line by an unjustified amount.

Companies are, of course, sometimes rewarded for bad behavior—a company that is able to shift environmental and other social costs associated with its activities onto society as a whole can reap large short-term profits. The major cigarette producers for many years were able to earn greatly inflated profits by shifting the health-related costs of smoking onto others and escaping any responsibility for the harm their products caused to consumers and the general public. Most companies will, of course, try to evade paying for the social harms of their operations for as long as they can. Calling a halt to such actions usually hinges upon (1) the effectiveness of activist social groups in publicizing the adverse consequences of a company's social irresponsibility and marshaling public opinion for something to be done, (2) the enactment of legislation or regulations to correct the inequity, and (3) widespread actions on the part of socially conscious buyers to take their business elsewhere.

The Well-Intentioned Efforts of Do-Good Executives Can Be Controversial

While there is substantial agreement that businesses have obligations to non-owner stakeholders and to society at large, and that these must be factored into a company's overall strategy and into the conduct of its business operations, there is much less agreement about the extent to which "do-good" executives should pursue their personal vision of a better world using company funds. One view holds that any money executives authorize for so-called social responsibility initiatives is effectively theft from a company's shareholders who can, after all, decide for themselves what and how much to give to charity and other causes they deem worthy. A related school of thought says that companies should be wary of taking on an assortment of societal obligations because doing so diverts valuable resources and weakens a company's competitiveness. Many academics and businesspeople believe that businesses best satisfy their social responsibilities through conventional business activities, primarily producing needed goods and services at prices that people can afford. They further argue that spending shareholders' or customers' money for social causes not only muddies decision making by diluting the focus on the company's business mission but also thrusts business executives into the role of social engineers—a role more appropriately performed by charitable and nonprofit organizations and duly elected government officials. Do we really want corporate executives deciding how to best balance the different interests of stakeholders and functioning as social engineers? Are they competent to make such judgments?

Take the case of Coca-Cola and Pepsi bottlers. Local bottlers of both brands have signed contracts with public school districts that provide millions of dollars of support for local schools in exchange for vending-machine distribution rights in the schools.[55] While such contracts would seem to be a win–win proposition, protests from parents concerned about children's sugar-laden diets and commercialism in the schools make such contracts questionable. Opponents of these contracts claim that it is the role of government to provide adequate school funding and that the learning environment in local schools should be free of commercialism and the self-serving efforts of businesses to hide behind providing support for education.

In September 1997, the Business Roundtable changed its stance from one of support for social responsibility and balanced consideration of stakeholder interests to one of skepticism with regard to such actions:

> The notion that the board must somehow balance the interests of stockholders against the interests of other stakeholders fundamentally misconstrues the role of directors. It is, moreover, an unworkable notion because it would leave the board with no criteria for resolving conflicts between the interest of stockholders and of other stakeholders or among different groups of stakeholders.[56]

The new Business Roundtable view implied that the paramount duty of management and of boards of directors is to the corporation's stockholders. Customers may be "king," and employees may be the corporation's "greatest asset" (at least in the rhetoric), but the interests of shareholders rule.[57]

However, there are real problems with disconnecting business behavior from the well-being of non-owner stakeholders and the well-being of society at large.[58] Isolating business from the rest of society when the two are inextricably intertwined is unrealistic. Many business decisions spill over to impact non-owner stakeholders and society. Furthermore, the notion that businesses must be managed solely to serve the interests of shareholders is something of a stretch. Clearly, a business's first priority must be to deliver value to customers. Unless a company does a creditable job of satisfying buyer needs and expectations of reliable and attractively priced goods and services, it cannot survive. While shareholders provide capital and are certainly entitled to a return on their investment, fewer and fewer shareholders are truly committed to the companies whose stock they own. Shareholders can dispose of their holdings in a moment's whim or at the first sign of a downturn in the stock price. Mutual funds buy and sell shares daily, adding and dropping companies whenever they see fit. Day traders buy and sell within hours. Such buying and selling of shares is nothing more than a financial transaction and results in no capital being provided to the company to fund operations except when it entails the purchase of newly issued shares of stock. So why should shareholders—a group distant from the company's operations and adding little to its operations except when new shares of stock are purchased—lay such a large claim on how a company should be managed? Are most shareholders really interested in or knowledgeable about the companies they own? Or do they just own a stock for whatever financial returns it is expected to provide?

While there is legitimate concern about the use of company resources for do-good purposes and the motives and competencies of business executives in functioning as social engineers, it is tough to argue that businesses have no obligations to nonowner stakeholders or to society at large. If one looks at the category of activities that fall under the umbrella of socially responsible behavior (Figure 10.2), there's really very little for shareholders or others concerned about the do-good attempts of executives to object to in principle. Certainly, it is legitimate for companies to minimize or eliminate any adverse impacts of their operations on the environment. It is hard to argue against efforts to make the company a great place to work or to promote workforce diversity. And with regard to charitable contributions, community service projects, and the like, it would be hard to find a company where spending on such activities is so out of control that shareholders might rightfully complain or that the company's competitiveness is being eroded. What is likely to prove most objectionable in the social responsibility arena are the specific activities a company elects to engage in and/or the manner in which a company carries out its attempts to behave in a socially responsible manner.

How Much Attention to Social Responsibility Is Enough?

What is an appropriate balance between the imperative to create value for shareholders and the obligation to proactively contribute to the larger social good? What fraction of a company's resources ought to be aimed at addressing social concerns and bettering the well-being of society and the environment? A few companies have a policy of setting aside a specified percentage of their profits (typically 5 percent or maybe 10 percent) to fund their social responsibility strategy; they view such percentages as a fair amount to return to the community as a kind of thank-you or a tithe to the betterment of society. Other companies shy away from a specified percentage of profits or revenues because it entails upping the commitment in good times and cutting back on social responsibility initiatives in hard times (even cutting out social responsibility initiatives entirely if profits temporarily turn into losses). If social responsibility is an ongoing commitment rooted in the corporate culture and enlists broad participation on the part of company personnel, then a sizable portion of the funding for the company's social responsibility strategy has to be viewed as simply a regular and ongoing cost of doing business.

But judging how far a particular company should go in pursuing particular social causes is a tough issue. Consider, for example, Nike's commitment to monitoring the workplace conditions of its contract suppliers.[59] The scale of this monitoring task is significant: in 2005, Nike had over 800 contract suppliers employing over 600,000 people in 50 countries. How frequently should sites be monitored? How should it respond to the use of underage labor? If only children above a set age are to be employed by suppliers, should suppliers still be required to provide schooling opportunities? At last count, Nike had some 80 people engaged in site monitoring. Should Nike's monitoring budget be $2 million, $5 million, $10 million, or whatever it takes?

Consider another example: If pharmaceutical manufacturers donate or discount their drugs for distribution to low-income people in less-developed nations, what safeguards should they put in place to see that the drugs reach the intended recipients and are not diverted by corrupt local officials for reexport to markets in other countries? Should drug manufacturers also assist in drug distribution and administration in these less-developed countries? How much should a drug company invest in R&D to develop medicines for tropical diseases commonly occurring in less-developed countries when it is unlikely to recover its costs in the foreseeable future?

And how much should a company allocate to charitable contributions? Is it falling short of its responsibilities if its donations are less than 1 percent of profits? Is a company going too far if it allocates 5 percent or even 10 percent of its profits to worthy of one kind or another? The point here is that there is no simple or widely accepted standard for judging when a company has or has not gone far enough in fulfilling its citizenship responsibilities.

Linking Social Performance Targets to Executive Compensation

Perhaps the most surefire way to enlist a genuine commitment to corporate social responsibility initiatives is to link the achievement of social performance targets to executive compensation. If a company's board of directors is serious about corporate citizenship, then it will incorporate measures of the company's social and environmental performance into its evaluation of top executives, especially the CEO. And if the CEO uses compensation incentives to further enlist the support of down-the-line company personnel in effectively crafting and executing a social responsibility strategy, the company will over time build a culture rooted in socially responsible and ethical behavior. According to one survey, 80 percent of surveyed CEOs believe that environmental and social performance metrics are a valid part of measuring a company's overall performance. At Verizon Communications, 10 percent of the annual bonus of the company's top 2,500 managers is tied directly to the achievement of social responsibility targets; for the rest of the staff, there are corporate recognition awards in the form of cash for employees who have made big contributions towards social causes. The corporate social responsibility reports being issued annually by 2,500 companies across the world that detail social responsibility initiatives and the results achieved are a good basis for compensating executives and judging the effectiveness of their commitment to social responsibility.

Key Points

Ethics involves concepts of right and wrong, fair and unfair, moral and immoral. Beliefs about what is ethical serve as a moral compass in guiding the actions and behaviors of individuals and organizations. Ethical principles in business are not materially different from ethical principles in general.

There are three schools of thought about ethical standards:

1. According to the *school of ethical universalism*, the same standards of what's ethical and what's unethical resonate with peoples of most societies regardless of local traditions and cultural norms; hence, common ethical standards can be used to judge the conduct of personnel at companies operating in a variety of country markets and cultural circumstances.

2. According to the *school of ethical relativism* different societal cultures and customs have divergent values and standards of right and wrong—thus, what is ethical or unethical must be judged in the light of local customs and social mores and can vary from one culture or nation to another.

3. According to *integrated social contracts theory*, universal ethical principles or norms based on the collective views of multiple cultures and societies combine to form a "social contract" that all individuals in all situations have a duty to observe. Within the boundaries of this social contract, local cultures can specify other impermissible actions; however, universal ethical norms always take precedence over local ethical norms.

Three categories of managers stand out as concerns their prevailing beliefs in and commitments to ethical and moral principles in business affairs: the moral manager; the immoral manager, and the amoral manager. By some accounts, the population of managers is said to be distributed among all three types in a bell-shaped curve, with immoral managers and moral managers occupying the two tails of the curve, and the amoral managers, especially the intentionally amoral managers, occupying the broad middle ground.

The apparently large numbers of immoral and amoral businesspeople are one obvious reason why some companies resort to unethical strategic behavior. Three other main drivers of unethical business behavior also stand out:

1. Overzealous or obsessive pursuit of personal gain, wealth, and other selfish interests.
2. Heavy pressures on company managers to meet or beat earnings targets.
3. A company culture that puts the profitability and good business performance ahead of ethical behavior.

The stance a company takes in dealing with or managing ethical conduct at any given time can take any of four basic forms:

1. The unconcerned, or nonissue, approach.
2. The damage control approach.
3. The compliance approach.
4. The ethical culture approach.

There are two reasons why a company's strategy should be ethical: (1) because a strategy that is unethical in whole or in part is morally wrong and reflects badly on the character of the company personnel involved, and (2) because an ethical strategy is good business and in the self-interest of shareholders.

The term *corporate social responsibility* concerns a company's *duty* to operate in an honorable manner, provide good working conditions for employees, be a good steward of the environment, and actively work to better the quality of life in the local communities where it operates and in society at large. The menu of actions and behavior for demonstrating social responsibility includes:

1. Employing an ethical strategy and observing ethical principles in operating the business.
2. Making charitable contributions, donating money and the time of company personnel to community service endeavors, supporting various worthy organizational causes, and making a difference in the lives of the disadvantaged. Corporate commitments are further reinforced by encouraging employees to support charitable and community activities.
3. Protecting or enhancing the environment and, in particular, striving to minimize or eliminate any adverse impact on the environment stemming from the company's own business activities.
4. Creating a work environment that makes the company a great place to work.
5. Employing a workforce that is diverse with respect to gender, race, national origin, and perhaps other aspects that different people bring to the workplace.

There is ample room for every company to tailor its social responsibility strategy to fit its core values and business mission, thereby making their own statement about "how we do business and how we intend to fulfill our duties to all stakeholders and society at large."

The moral case for social responsibility boils down to a simple concept: It's the right thing to do. The business case for social responsibility holds that it is in the enlightened self-interest of companies to be good citizens and devote some of their energies and resources to the betterment of such stakeholders as employees, the communities in which it operates, and society in general.

Exercises

1. Given the description of Marsh & McLennan's strategy presented in Illustration Capsule 10.1, would it be fair to characterize the payment of contingent commissions by property-casualty insurers as nothing more than thinly disguised kickbacks? Why or why not? If you or why not? If you were the manager of a company that hired Marsh & McLennan to provide risk management services, would you see that Marsh had a conflict of interest in steering your company's insurance policies to insurers in which it has an ownership interest? Given Marsh's unethical and illegal foray into rigging the bids on insurance policies for its corporate clients, what sort of fines and penalties would you impose on the company for its misdeeds (assuming you were asked to recommend appropriate penalties by the prosecuting authorities). In arriving at a figure, bear in mind that Prudential Securities paid a total of about $2 billion in the 1990s to settle civil regulatory charges and private lawsuits alleging that it misled investors on the risks and rewards of limited-partnership investments. Ten Wall Street securities firms in 2003 paid $1.4 billion to settle civil charges for issuing misleading stock research to investors. Prominent mutual-fund firms were assessed nearly $2 billion in fines and restitution for engaging in after-hours stock trading at prearranged prices that were contrary to the interests of long-term shareholders. And several well-known financial institutions, including Citigroup, Merrill Lynch, Goldmans Sachs, and Credit Suisse First Boston agreed to pay several billion dollars in fines and restitution for their role in scandals at Enron and WorldCom and for improperly allocating initial public offerings of stock. Using Internet research tools, determine what Marsh & McLennan ended up paying in fines and restitution for its unethical and illegal strategic behavior and assess the extent to which the conduct of company personnel damaged shareholders.

2. Consider the following portrayal of strategies employed by major recording studios:[60]

> Some recording artists and the Recording Artists' Coalition claim that the world's five major music recording studios—Universal, Sony, Time Warner, EMI/Virgin, and Bertelsmann—deliberately employ strategies calculated to take advantage of musicians who record for them. One practice to which they strenuously object is that the major-label record companies frequently require artists to sign contracts committing them to do six to eight albums, an obligation that some artists say can entail an indefinite term of indentured servitude. Further, it is claimed that audits routinely detect unpaid royalties to musicians under contract; according to one music industry attorney, record companies misreport and underpay artist royalties by 10 to 40 percent and are "intentionally fraudulent." One music writer was recently quoted as saying the process was "an entrenched system whose prowess and conniving makes Enron look like amateur hour." Royalty calculations are based on complex formulas that are paid only after artists pay for recording costs and other expenses and after any advances are covered by royalty earnings.
>
> A *Baffler* magazine article outlined a hypothetical but typical record deal in which a promising young band is given a $250,000 royalty advance on a new album. The album subsequently sells 250,000 copies, earning $710,000 for the

record company; but the band, after repaying the record company for $264,000 in expenses ranging from recording fees and video budgets to catering, wardrobe, and bus tour costs for promotional events related to the album, ends up $14,000 in the hole, owes the record company money, and is thus paid no royalties on any of the $710,000 in revenues the recording company receives from the sale of the band's music. It is also standard practice in the music industry for recording studios to sidestep payola laws by hiring independent promoters to lobby and compensate radio stations for playing certain records. Record companies are often entitled to damages for undelivered albums if an artist leaves a recording studio for another label after seven years. Record companies also retain the copyrights in perpetuity on all music recorded under contract, a practice that artists claim is unfair. The Dixie Chicks, after a year-long feud with Sony over contract terms, ended up refusing to do another album; Sony sued for breach of contract, prompting a countersuit by the Dixie Chicks charging "systematic thievery" to cheat them out of royalties. The suits were settled out of court. One artist said, "The record companies are like cartels."

Recording studios defend their strategic practices by pointing out that fewer than 5 percent of the signed artists ever deliver a hit and that they lose money on albums that sell poorly. According to one study, only 1 of 244 contracts signed during 1994–1996 was negotiated without the artists being represented by legal counsel, and virtually all contracts renegotiated after a hit album added terms more favorable to the artist.

a. If you were a recording artist, would you be happy with some of the strategic practices of the recording studios? Would you feel comfortable signing a recording contract with studios engaging in any of the practices?

b. Which, if any, of the practices of the recording studios do you view as unethical?

3. Recently, it came to light that three of the world's four biggest public accounting firms may have overbilled clients for travel-related expenses. Pricewaterhouse Coopers, KPMG, and Ernst & Young were sued for systematically charging their clients full price for airline tickets, hotel rooms and car-rental expenses, even though they received volume discounts and rebates of up to 40 percent under their contracts with various travel companies. Large accounting firms, law firms, and medical practices have in recent years used their size and purchasing volumes to negotiate sizable discounts and rebates on up-front travel costs; some of these contracts apparently required that the discounts not be disclosed to other parties, which seemingly included clients.

However, it has long been the custom for accounting and law firms to bill their clients for actual out-of-pocket expenses. The three accounting firms, so the lawsuit alleges, billed clients for the so-called full prices of the airline tickets, hotel rooms, and car-rental expenses rather than for the out-of-pocket discounted amounts. They pocketed the differences to the tune of several million dollars annually in additional profits. Several clients, upon learning of the full-price billing practices, claimed fraud and sued.

Do you consider the accounting firms' billing practice to be unethical? Why or why not?

4. Suppose you found yourself in the following situation: In preparing a bid for a multimillion-dollar contract in a foreign country, you are introduced to a "consultant" who offers to help you in submitting the bid and negotiating with the customer company. You learn in conversing with the consultant that she is well connected in local government and business circles and knows key personnel in the customer company extremely well. The consultant quotes you a six-figure fee.

Later, your local co-workers tell you that the use of such consultants is normal in this country—and that a large fraction of the fee will go directly to people working for the customer company. They further inform you that bidders who reject the help of such consultants have lost contracts to competitors who employed them. What would you do, assuming your company's code of ethics expressly forbids the payments of bribes or kickbacks in any form?

5. Assume that you are the sales manager at a European company that makes sleepwear products for children. Company personnel discover that the chemicals used to flameproof the company's line of children's pajamas might cause cancer if absorbed through the skin. Following this discovery, the pajamas are then banned from sale in the European Union and the United States, but senior executives of your company learn that the children's pajamas in inventory and the remaining flameproof material can be sold to sleepwear distributors in certain East European countries where there are no restrictions against the material's use. Your superiors instruct you to make the necessary arrangements to sell the inventories of banned pajamas and flameproof materials to East European distributors. Would you comply if you felt that your job would be in jeopardy if you didn't?

6. At Salomon Smith Barney (a subsidiary of Citigroup), Credit Suisse First Boston (CSFB), and Goldman Sachs (three of the world's most prominent investment banking companies), part of the strategy for securing the investment banking business of large corporate clients (to handle the sale of new stock issues or new bond issues or advise on mergers and acquisitions) involved (*a*) hyping the stocks of companies that were actual or prospective customers of their investment banking services, and (*b*) allocating hard-to-get shares of hot new initial public offerings (IPOs) to select executives and directors of existing and potential client companies, who then made millions of dollars in profits when the stocks went up once public trading began.[61] Former WorldCom CEO Bernard Ebbers reportedly made more than $11 million in trading profits over a four-year period on shares of IPOs received from Salomon Smith Barney; Salomon served as WorldCom's investment banker on a variety of deals during this period. Jack Grubman, Salomon's top-paid research analyst at the time, enthusiastically touted WorldCom stock and was regarded as the company's biggest cheerleader on Wall Street.

To help draw in business from new or existing corporate clients, CSFB established brokerage accounts for corporate executives who steered their company's investment banking business to CSFB. Apparently, CSFB's strategy for acquiring more business involved promising the CEO and/or CFO of companies about to go public for the first time or needing to issue new long-term bonds that if CSFB was chosen to handle their company's IPO of common stock or a new bond issue, then CSFB would ensure they would be allocated shares at the initial offering price of all subsequent IPOs in which CSFB was a participant. During 1999–2000, it was common for the stock of a hot new IPO to rise 100 to 500 percent above the initial offering price in the first few days or weeks of public trading; the shares allocated to these executives were then sold for a tidy profit over the initial offering price. According to investigative sources, CSFB increased the number of companies whose executives were allowed to participate in its IPO offerings from 26 companies in January 1999 to 160 companies in early 2000; executives received anywhere from 200 to 1,000 shares each of every IPO in which CSFB was a participant in 2000. CSFB's accounts for these executives reportedly generated profits of about $80 million for the participants. Apparently, it was CSFB's practice to curtail access to IPOs for some executives if their companies didn't come through with additional securities business for CSFB or if CSFB concluded that other securities offerings by these companies would be unlikely.

Goldman Sachs also used an IPO-allocation scheme to attract investment banking business, giving shares to executives at 21 companies—among the participants were the CEOs of eBay, Yahoo, and Ford Motor Company. eBay's CEO was a participant in over 100 IPOs managed by Goldman during the 1996–2000 period and was on Goldman's board of directors part of this time; eBay paid Goldman Sachs $8 million in fees for services during the 1996–2001 period.

a. If you were a top executive at Salomon Smith Barney, CSFB, or Goldman Sachs, would you be proud to defend your company's actions?

b. Would you want to step forward and take credit for having been a part of the group who designed or approved of the strategy for gaining new business at any of these three firms?

c. Is it accurate to characterize the allocations of IPO shares to "favored" corporate executives as bribes or kickbacks?

Building an Organization Capable of Good Strategy Execution

The best game plan in the world never blocked or tackled anybody.

—Vince Lombardi
Hall of Fame football coach

Strategies most often fail because they aren't executed well.

—Larry Bossidy and Ram Charan
*CEO Honeywell International;
author and consultant*

A second-rate strategy perfectly executed will beat a first-rate strategy poorly executed every time.

—Richard M. Kovacevich
Chairman and CEO, Wells Fargo

Any strategy, however brilliant, needs to be implemented properly if it is to deliver the desired results.

—Costas Markides
Professor

People are *not* your most important asset. The right people are.

—Jim Collins
Professor and author

Organizing is what you do before you do something, so that when you do it, it is not all mixed up.

—A. A. Milne
Author

Once managers have decided on a strategy, the emphasis turns to converting it into actions and good results. Putting the strategy into place and getting the organization to execute it well call for different sets of managerial skills. Whereas crafting strategy is largely a market-driven activity, implementing and executing strategy is primarily an operations-driven activity revolving around the management of people and business processes. Whereas successful strategy making depends on business vision, solid industry and competitive analysis, and shrewd market positioning, successful strategy execution depends on doing a good job of working with and through others, building and strengthening competitive capabilities, motivating and rewarding people in a strategy-supportive manner, and instilling a discipline of getting things done. Executing strategy is an action-oriented, make-things-happen task that tests a manager's ability to direct organizational change, achieve continuous improvement in operations and business processes, create and nurture a strategy-supportive culture, and consistently meet or beat performance targets.

Experienced managers are emphatic in declaring that it is a whole lot easier to develop a sound strategic plan than it is to execute the plan and achieve the desired outcomes. According to one executive, "It's been rather easy for us to decide where we wanted to go. The hard part is to get the organization to act on the new priorities."[1] *Just because senior managers announce a new strategy doesn't mean that organizational members will agree with it or enthusiastically move forward in implementing it.* Senior executives cannot simply direct immediate subordinates to abandon old ways and take up new ways, and they certainly cannot expect the needed actions and changes to occur in rapid-fire fashion and lead to the desired outcomes. Some managers and employees may be skeptical about the merits of the strategy, seeing it as contrary to the organization's best interests, unlikely to succeed, or threatening to their departments or careers. Moreover, different employees may interpret the new strategy differently or have different ideas about what internal changes are needed to execute it. Long-standing attitudes, vested interests, inertia, and ingrained organizational practices don't melt away when managers decide on a new strategy and begin efforts to implement it—especially when only comparatively few people have been involved in crafting the strategy and when the rationale for strategic change has to be sold to enough organizational members to root out the status quo.

It takes adept managerial leadership to convincingly communicate the new strategy and the reasons for it, overcome pockets of doubt and disagreement, secure the commitment and enthusiasm of concerned parties, identify and build consensus on all the hows of implementation and execution, and move forward to get all the pieces into place. Company personnel have to understand—in their heads and in their hearts— why a new strategic direction is necessary and where the new strategy is taking them.[2] Instituting change is, of course, easier when the problems with the old strategy have become obvious and/or the company has spiraled into a financial crisis.

But the challenge of successfully implementing new strategic initiatives goes well beyond managerial adeptness in overcoming resistance to change. What really makes executing strategy a tougher, more time-consuming management challenge than crafting strategy are the wide array of managerial activities that have to be attended to, the many ways that managers can proceed, and the number of bedeviling issues that must be worked out. It takes first-rate "managerial smarts" to zero in on what exactly needs to be done to put new strategic initiatives in place and, further, how best to get these things done in a timely fashion and in a manner that yields good results. Demanding people-management skills are required. Plus, it takes follow-through and perseverance to get a variety of initiatives launched and moving and to integrate the efforts of many different work groups into a smoothly functioning whole. Depending on how much consensus building and organizational change is involved, the process of implementing strategy changes can take several months to several years. And it takes still longer to achieve *real proficiency* in executing the strategy.

Like crafting strategy, *executing strategy is a job for the whole management team, not just a few senior managers.* While an organization's chief executive officer and the heads of major units (business divisions, functional departments, and key operating units) are ultimately responsible for seeing that strategy is executed successfully, the process typically affects every part of the firm, from the biggest operating unit to the smallest frontline work group. Top-level managers have to rely on the active support and cooperation of middle and lower managers to push strategy changes into functional areas and operating units and to see that the organization actually operates in accordance with the strategy on a daily basis. Middle and lower-level managers not only are responsible for initiating and supervising the execution process in their areas of authority but also are instrumental in getting subordinates to continuously improve on how strategy-critical value chain activities are being performed and in producing the operating results that allow company performance targets to be met—their role on the company's strategy execution team is by no means minimal.

Core Concept

Good strategy execution requires a *team effort*. All managers have strategy-executing responsibility in their areas of authority, and all employees are participants in the strategy execution process.

Strategy execution thus requires every manager to think through the answer to "What does my area have to do to implement its part of the strategic plan, and what should I do to get these things accomplished effectively and efficiently?" The bigger the organization or the more geographically scattered its operating units, the more that successful strategy execution depends on the cooperation and implementing skills of operating managers who can push the needed changes at the lowest organizational levels and, in the process, deliver good results. Only in small organizations can top-level managers get around the need for a team effort on the part of management and personally orchestrate the actions steps required for good strategy execution and operating excellence.

A FRAMEWORK FOR EXECUTING STRATEGY

Implementing and executing strategy entails figuring out all the hows—the specific techniques, actions, and behaviors that are needed for a smooth strategy-supportive operation—and then following through to get things done and deliver results. The idea is to make things happen and make them happen right. The first step in implementing strategic changes is for management to communicate the case for organizational change so clearly and persuasively to organizational members that a determined commitment takes hold throughout the ranks to find ways to put the strategy into place, make it work, and meet performance targets. The ideal condition is for managers to arouse enough enthusiasm for the strategy to turn the implementation process into a companywide crusade. *Management's handling of the strategy implementation process can be considered successful if and when the company achieves the targeted strategic and financial performance and shows good progress in making its strategic vision a reality.*

The specific hows of executing a strategy—the exact items that need to be placed on management's action agenda—always have to be customized to fit the particulars of a company's situation. Making minor changes in an existing strategy differs from implementing radical strategy changes. The hot buttons for successfully executing a low-cost provider strategy are different from those in executing a high-end differentiation strategy. Implementing and executing a new strategy for a struggling company in the midst of a financial crisis is a different job from that of improving strategy execution in a company where the execution is already pretty good. Moreover, some managers are more adept than others at using this or that approach to achieving the desired kinds of organizational changes. Hence, there's no definitive managerial recipe for successful strategy execution that cuts across all company situations and all types of strategies or that works for all types of managers. Rather, the specific hows of implementing and executing a strategy—the to-do list that constitutes management's agenda for action—must always be custom-tailored to fit an individual company's own circumstances and represents management's judgment about how best to proceed.

THE PRINCIPAL MANAGERIAL COMPONENTS OF THE STRATEGY EXECUTION PROCESS

Despite the need to tailor a company's strategy-executing approaches to the particulars of its situation, certain managerial bases have to be covered no matter what the circumstances. Eight managerial tasks crop up repeatedly in company efforts to execute strategy (see Figure 11.1):

1. Building an organization with the competencies, capabilities, and resource strengths to execute strategy successfully.
2. Marshaling sufficient money and people behind the drive for strategy execution.
3. Instituting policies and procedures that facilitate rather than impede strategy execution.
4. Adopting best practices and pushing for continuous improvement in how value chain activities are performed.
5. Installing information and operating systems that enable company personnel to carry out their strategic roles proficiently.

Figure 11.1 **The Eight Components of the Strategy Execution Process**

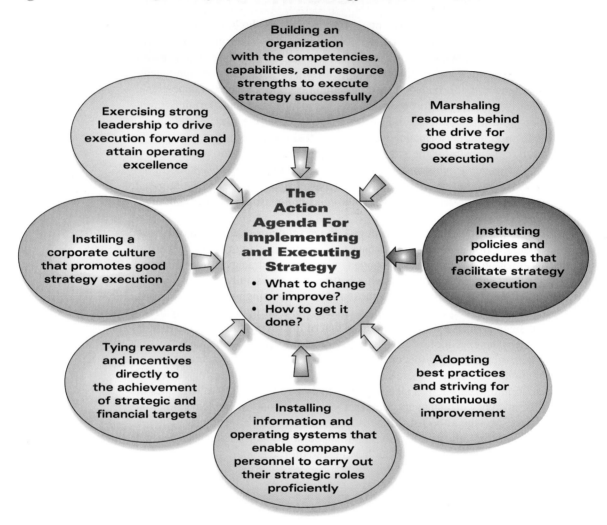

6. Tying rewards directly to the achievement of strategic and financial targets and to good strategy execution.
7. Instilling a corporate culture that promotes good strategy execution.
8. Exercising strong leadership to drive execution forward, keep improving on the details of execution, and achieve operating excellence as rapidly as feasible.

How well managers perform these eight tasks has a decisive impact on whether the outcome is a spectacular success, a colossal failure, or something in between.

In devising an action agenda for implementing and executing strategy, the place for managers to start is with *a probing assessment of what the organization must do differently and better to carry out the strategy successfully.* They should then consider *precisely how to make the necessary internal changes* as rapidly as possible. Successful strategy implementers have a knack for diagnosing what their organizations need to do to execute the chosen strategy well and figuring out how to get things done—they are

When strategies fail, it is often because of poor execution—things that were supposed to get done slip through the cracks.

masters in promoting results-oriented behaviors on the part of company personnel and following through on making the right things happen in a timely fashion.[3]

In big organizations with geographically scattered operating units, the action agenda of senior executives mostly involves communicating the case for change to others, building consensus for how to proceed, installing strong allies in positions where they can push implementation along in key organizational units, urging and empowering subordinates to keep the process moving, establishing measures of progress and deadlines, recognizing and rewarding those who achieve implementation milestones, directing resources to the right places, and personally leading the strategic change process. Thus, the bigger the organization, the more successful strategy execution depends on the cooperation and implementing skills of operating managers who can push needed changes at the lowest organizational levels and deliver results. In small organizations, top managers can deal directly with frontline managers and employees, personally orchestrating the action steps and implementation sequence, observing firsthand how implementation is progressing, and deciding how hard and how fast to push the process along. Regardless of the organization's size and whether implementation involves sweeping or minor changes, the most important leadership traits are a strong, confident sense of what to do and how to do it. Having a strong grip on these two things comes from understanding the circumstances of the organization and the requirements for effective strategy execution. Then it remains for those managers and company personnel in strategy-critical areas to step up to the plate and produce the desired results.

What's Covered in Chapters 11, 12, and 13   In the remainder of this chapter and the next two chapters, we will discuss what is involved in performing the eight key managerial tasks (shown in Figure 11.1) that shape the process of implementing and executing strategy. This chapter explores building an organization with the competencies, capabilities, and resource strengths to execute the strategy successfully. Chapter 12 looks at marshaling resources, instituting strategy-facilitating policies and procedures, adopting best practices, installing operating systems, and tying rewards to the achievement of good results. Chapter 13 deals with creating a strategy-supportive corporate culture and exercising the leadership needed to drive the execution process forward.

BUILDING AN ORGANIZATION CAPABLE OF GOOD STRATEGY EXECUTION

Proficient strategy execution depends heavily on competent personnel, better-than-adequate competitive capabilities, and effective internal organization. Building a capable organization is thus always a top priority in strategy execution. As shown in Figure 11.2, three types of organization-building actions are paramount:

1. *Staffing the organization*—putting together a strong management team, and recruiting and retaining employees with the needed experience, technical skills, and intellectual capital.
2. *Building core competencies and competitive capabilities*—developing proficiencies in performing strategy-critical value chain activities and updating them to match changing market conditions and customer expectations.
3. *Structuring the organization and work effort*—organizing value chain activities and business processes and deciding how much decision-making authority to push down to lower-level managers and frontline employees.

Figure 11.2   **The Three Components of Building an Organization Capable of Proficient Strategy Execution**

Staffing the Organization

■ Putting together a strong management team
■ Recruiting and retaining talented employees

Building Core Competencies and Competitive Capabilities

■ Developing a set of competencies and capabilities suited to the current strategy
■ Updating and revising this set as external conditions and strategy change
■ Training and retraining employees as needed to maintain skills-based competencies

Matching the Organization Structure to Strategy

■ Instituting organizational arrangements that facilitate good strategy execution
■ Deciding how much decision-making authority to push down to lower-level managers and front line employees

A Company with the Competencies and Capabilities Needed for Proficient Strategy Execution

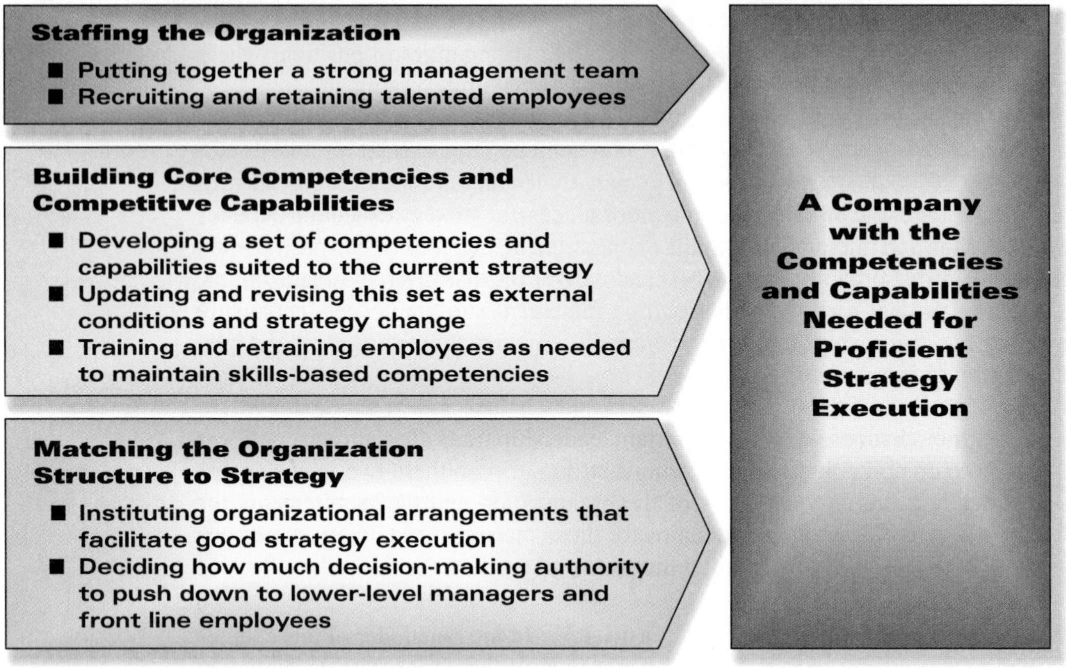

STAFFING THE ORGANIZATION

No company can hope to perform the activities required for successful strategy execution without attracting and retaining talented managers and employees with suitable skills and *intellectual capital.*

Putting Together a Strong Management Team

Assembling a capable management team is a cornerstone of the organization-building task.[4] While different strategies and company circumstances sometimes call for different mixes of backgrounds, experiences, values, beliefs, management styles, and know-how, *the most important consideration is to fill key managerial slots with smart people who are clear thinkers, good at figuring out what needs to be done, and skilled in "making it happen" and delivering good results.*[5] The task of implementing and executing challenging strategic initiatives must be assigned to executives who have the skills and talents to handle them and who can be counted on to turn their decisions and actions into results that meet or beat the established performance targets. It helps enormously when a company's top management team has several people who are particularly good change agents—true believers who champion change, know how to make it happen, and love every second of the process.[6] Without a smart, capable, results-oriented management team, the implementation-execution process ends up being hampered by missed deadlines, misdirected or wasteful efforts, and/or managerial ineptness.[7] Weak executives are serious impediments to getting

Core Concept
Putting together a talented management team with the right mix of experiences, skills, and abilities to get things done is one of the first strategy-implementing steps.

optimal results because they are unable to differentiate between ideas and approaches that have merit and those that are misguided—the caliber of work done under their supervision suffers.[8] In contrast, managers with strong strategy-implementing capabilities have a talent for asking tough, incisive questions. They know enough about the details of the business to be able to challenge and ensure the soundness of the approaches and decisions of the people around them, and they can discern whether the resources people are asking for to put the strategy in place make sense. They are good at getting things done through others, typically by making sure they have the right people under them and that these people are put in the right jobs.[9] They consistently follow through on issues, monitor progress carefully, make adjustments when needed, and not let important details slip through the cracks. In short, they understand how to drive organizational change, and they have the managerial discipline requisite for first-rate strategy execution.

Sometimes a company's existing management team is suitable; at other times it may need to be strengthened or expanded by promoting qualified people from within or by bringing in outsiders whose experiences, talents, and leadership styles better suit the situation. In turnaround and rapid-growth situations, and in instances when a company doesn't have insiders with the requisite know-how, filling key management slots from the outside is a fairly standard organization-building approach. In addition, it is important to ferret out and replace managers who, for whatever reasons, prefer the status quo and who either do not buy into the case for making organizational changes or do not see ways to make things better.[10] For a top management team to be truly effective, it has got to consist of "true believers" who recognize that organizational changes are needed and are ready to get on with the process. Weak executives and die-hard resisters have to be replaced or sidelined (by shifting them to positions of lesser influence where they cannot hamper or derail new strategy execution initiatives).

The overriding aim in building a management team should be to assemble a *critical mass* of talented managers who can function as agents of change and further the cause of first-rate strategy execution—every manager's success is enhanced (or limited) by the quality of their managerial colleagues and the degree to which they freely exchange ideas, debate how to improve approaches that have merit, and join forces to tackle issues and solve problems.[11] When a first-rate manager enjoys the help and support of other first-rate managers, it's possible to create a managerial whole that is greater than the sum of individual efforts—talented managers who work well together as a team can produce organizational results that are dramatically better than what one or two star managers acting individually can achieve. The chief lesson here is that *a company needs to get the right executives on the bus—and the wrong executives off the bus—before trying to drive the bus in the desired direction.*[12]

Illustration Capsule 11.1 describes General Electric's widely acclaimed approach to developing a top-caliber management team.

Recruiting and Retaining Capable Employees

Assembling a capable management team is not enough. Staffing the organization with the right kinds of people must go much deeper than managerial jobs in order for value chain activities to be performed competently. *The quality of an organization's people is always an essential ingredient of successful strategy execution—knowledgeable, engaged employees are a company's best source of creative ideas for the nuts-and-bolts operating improvements that lead to operating excellence.* Companies

Core Concept

In many industries, adding to a company's talent base and building intellectual capital is more important to good strategy execution than additional investments in plants, equipment, and capital projects.

Illustration Capsule 11.1

How General Electric Develops a Talented and Deep Management Team

General Electric (GE) is widely considered to be one of the best-managed companies in the world, partly because of its concerted effort to develop outstanding managers. For starters, GE strives to hire talented people with high potential for executive leadership; it then goes to great lengths to expand the leadership, business, and decision-making capabilities of all its managers. Four key elements undergird GE's efforts to build a talent-rich stable of managers:

- GE makes a practice of transferring managers across divisional, business, or functional lines for sustained periods of time. Such transfers allow managers to develop relationships with colleagues in other parts of the company, help break down insular thinking in business "silos," and promote the sharing of cross-business ideas and best practices. There is an enormous emphasis at GE on transferring ideas and best practices from business to business and making GE a "boundaryless" company.

- In selecting executives for key positions, GE is strongly disposed to candidates who exhibit what are called the four E's—enormous personal *energy,* the ability to motivate and *energize* others, *edge* (a GE code word for instinctive competitiveness and the ability to make tough decisions in a timely fashion, saying yes or no, and not maybe), and *execution* (the ability to carry things through to fruition). Considerable attention is also paid to problem-solving ability, experience in multiple functions or businesses, and experience in driving business growth (as indicated by good market instincts, in-depth knowledge of particular markets, customer touch, and technical understanding).

- All managers are expected to be proficient at what GE calls *workout*—a process in which managers and employees come together to confront issues as soon as they come up, pinpoint the root cause of the issues, and bring about quick resolutions so the business can move forward. Workout is GE's way of training its managers to diagnose what to do and how to do it.

- Each year GE sends about 10,000 newly hired and long-time managers to its Leadership Development Center (generally regarded as one of the best corporate training centers in the world), for a three-week course on the company's Six Sigma quality initiative. Close to 10,000 "master black belt" and "black belt" Six Sigma experts have graduated from the program to drive forward thousands of quality initiatives throughout GE. Six Sigma training is an ironclad requirement for promotion to any professional and managerial position and any stock option award. GE's Leadership Development Center also offers advanced courses for senior managers that may focus on a single management topic for a month. All classes involve managers from different GE businesses and different parts of the world. Some of the most valuable learning comes in between formal class sessions when GE managers from different businesses trade ideas about how to improve processes and better serve the customer. This knowledge sharing not only spreads best practices throughout the organization but also improves each GE manager's knowledge.

All of GE's 85,000 managers and professionals are graded in an annual process that divides them into five tiers: the top 10 percent, the next 15 percent, the middle 50 percent, the next 15 percent, and the bottom 10 percent. Everyone in the top tier gets stock awards, nobody in the fourth tier gets shares of stock, and most of those in the fifth tier become candidates for being weeded out. Business heads are pressured to wean out "C" players. GE's CEO personally reviews the performance of the top 3,000 managers. Senior executive compensation is heavily weighted toward Six Sigma commitment and successful business results.

According to Jack Welch, GE's CEO from 1980 to 2001, "The reality is, we simply cannot afford to field anything but teams of 'A' players."

Sources: General Electric's 1998 and 2003 annual reports; www.ge.com; John A. Byrne, "How Jack Welch Runs GE," *BusinessWeek,* June 8, 1998, p. 90; Miriam Leuchter, "Management Farm Teams," *Journal of Business Strategy,* May 1998, pp. 29–32; and "The House That Jack Built," *The Economist,* September 18, 1999.

like Microsoft, McKinsey & Company, Southwest Airlines, Cisco Systems, Amazon.com, Procter & Gamble, PepsiCo, Nike, Electronic Data Systems, Google, and Intel make a concerted effort to recruit the best and brightest people they can find and then retain them with excellent compensation packages, opportunities for rapid advancement and professional growth, and challenging and interesting assignments. Having a pool of "A players" with strong skill sets and lots of brainpower is essential to their business. Microsoft makes a point of hiring the very brightest and most talented programmers it can find and motivating them with both good monetary incentives and the challenge of working on cutting-edge software design projects. McKinsey & Company, one of the world's premier management consulting companies, recruits only cream-of-the-crop MBAs at the nation's top 10 business schools; such talent is essential to McKinsey's strategy of performing high-level consulting for the world's top corporations. The leading global accounting firms screen candidates not only on the basis of their accounting expertise but also on whether they possess the people skills needed to relate well with clients and colleagues. Southwest Airlines goes to considerable lengths to hire people who can have fun and be fun on the job; it uses special interviewing and screening methods to gauge whether applicants for customer-contact jobs have outgoing personality traits that match its strategy of creating a high-spirited, fun-loving, in-flight atmosphere for passengers; it is so selective that only about 3 percent of the people who apply are offered jobs.

In high-tech companies, the challenge is to staff work groups with gifted, imaginative, and energetic people who can bring life to new ideas quickly and inject into the organization what one Dell Inc. executive calls "hum."[13] The saying "People are our most important asset" may seem hollow, but it fits high-technology companies dead-on. Besides checking closely for functional and technical skills, Dell tests applicants for their tolerance of ambiguity and change, their capacity to work in teams, and their ability to learn on the fly. Companies like Amazon.com, Google, Yahoo, and Cisco Systems have broken new ground in recruiting, hiring, cultivating, developing, and retaining talented employees—most of whom are in their 20s and 30s. Cisco goes after the top 10 percent, raiding other companies and endeavoring to retain key people at the companies it acquires so as to maintain a cadre of star engineers, programmers, managers, salespeople, and support personnel in executing its strategy to remain the world's leading provider of Internet infrastructure products and technology.

In instances where intellectual capital greatly aids good strategy execution, companies have instituted a number of practices aimed at staffing jobs with the best people they can find:

1. Spending considerable effort in screening and evaluating job applicants, selecting only those with suitable skill sets, energy, initiative, judgment, and aptitudes for learning and adaptability to the company's work environment and culture.

2. Putting employees through training programs that continue throughout their careers.

3. Providing promising employees with challenging, interesting, and skill-stretching assignments.

4. Rotating people through jobs that not only have great content but also span functional and geographic boundaries. Providing people with opportunities to gain experience in a variety of international settings is increasingly considered an essential part of career development in multinational or global companies.

5. Encouraging employees to challenge existing ways of doing things, to be creative and innovative in proposing better ways of operating, and to push their ideas for new products or businesses. Progressive companies work hard at creating an environment in which ideas and suggestions bubble up from below and employees are made to feel that their views and suggestions count.

6. Making the work environment stimulating and engaging such that employees will consider the company a great place to work.

7. Striving to retain talented, high-performing employees via promotions, salary increases, performance bonuses, stock options and equity ownership, fringe benefit packages, and other perks.

> The best companies make a point of recruiting and retaining talented employees—the objective is to make the company's entire workforce (managers and rank-and-file employees) a genuine resource strength

8. Coaching average performers to improve their skills and capabilities, while weeding out underperformers and benchwarmers.

It is very difficult for a company to competently execute its strategy and achieve operating excellence without a large band of capable employees who are actively engaged in the process of making ongoing operating improvements.

BUILDING CORE COMPETENCIES AND COMPETITIVE CAPABILITIES

High among the organization-building priorities in the strategy implementing/ executing process is the need to build and strengthen competitively valuable core competencies and organizational capabilities. Whereas managers identify the desired competencies and capabilities in the course of crafting strategy, good strategy execution requires putting the desired competencies and capabilities in place, upgrading them as needed, and then modifying them as market conditions evolve. Sometimes a company already has some semblance of the needed competencies and capabilities, in which case managers can concentrate on strengthening and nurturing them to promote better strategy execution. More usually, however, company managers have to significantly broaden or deepen certain capabilities or even add entirely new competencies in order to put strategic initiatives in place and execute them proficiently.

A number of prominent companies have succeeded in establishing core competencies and capabilities that have been instrumental in making them winners in the marketplace. Intel's core competence is in the design and mass production of complex chips for personal computers, servers, and other electronic products. Procter & Gamble's core competencies reside in its superb marketing/distribution skills and its R&D capabilities in five core technologies—fats, oils, skin chemistry, surfactants, and emulsifiers. Ciba Specialty Chemicals has technology-based competencies that allow it to quickly manufacture products for customers wanting customized products relating to coloration, brightening and whitening, water treatment and paper processing, freshness, and cleaning. General Electric has a core competence in developing professional managers with broad problem-solving skills and proven ability to grow global businesses. Disney has core competencies in theme park operation and family entertainment. Dell Inc. has the capabilities to deliver state-of-the-art products to its customers within days of next-generation components coming available—and to do so at attractively low costs (it has leveraged its collection of competencies and capabilities into being the global low-cost leader in PCs). Toyota's success in motor vehicles is due, in large part, to its legendary "production system," which it has honed and perfected and which gives it the capability to produce high-quality vehicles at relatively low costs.

The Three-Stage Process of Developing and Strengthening Competencies and Capabilities

Building core competencies and competitive capabilities is a time-consuming, managerially challenging exercise. While some organization-building assist can be gotten from discovering how best-in-industry or best-in-world companies perform a particular activity, trying to replicate and then improve on the competencies and capabilities of others is, however, much easier said than done—for the same reasons that one is unlikely to ever become a good golfer just by studying what Tiger Woods does. Putting a new capability in place is more complicated than just forming a new team or department and charging it with becoming highly competent in performing the desired activity, using whatever it can learn from other companies having similar competencies or capabilities. Rather, it takes a series of deliberate and well orchestrated organizational steps to achieve mounting proficiency in performing an activity. The capability-building process has three stages:

> **Core Concept**
> Building competencies and capabilities is a multistage process that occurs over a period of months and years, not something that is accomplished overnight.

> *Stage 1*—First, the organization must develop the *ability* to do something, however imperfectly or inefficiently. This entails selecting people with the requisite skills and experience, upgrading or expanding individual abilities as needed, and then molding the efforts and work products of individuals into a collaborative effort to create organizational ability.

> *Stage 2*—As experience grows and company personnel learn how to perform the activity *consistently well and at an acceptable cost,* the ability evolves into a tried-and-true *competence* or *capability.*

> *Stage 3*—Should company personnel continue to polish and refine their know-how and otherwise sharpen their performance of an activity such that the company eventually becomes *better than rivals* at performing the activity, the core competence rises to the rank of a *distinctive competence* (or the capability becomes a competitively superior capability), thus providing a path to competitive advantage.

Many companies are able to get through stages 1 and 2 in performing a strategy-critical activity, but comparatively few achieve sufficient proficiency in performing strategy-critical activities to qualify for the third stage.

Managing the Process   Four traits concerning core competencies and competitive capabilities are important in successfully managing the organization-building process:[14]

1. *Core competencies and competitive capabilities are bundles of skills and know-how that most often grow out of the combined efforts of cross-functional work groups and departments performing complementary activities at different locations in the firm's value chain.* Rarely does a core competence or capability consist of narrow skills attached to the work efforts of a single department. For instance, a core competence in speeding new products to market involves the collaborative efforts of personnel in research and development (R&D), engineering and design, purchasing, production, marketing, and distribution. Similarly, the capability to provide superior customer service is a team effort among people in customer call centers (where orders are taken and inquiries are answered), shipping and delivery, billing and accounts receivable, and after-sale support. Complex activities (like designing and manufacturing a sports-utility vehicle or creating the capability for secure credit card transactions over the Internet) usually involve a number of component skills, technological disciplines, competencies, and capabilities—some performed in-house and some provided by suppliers/allies. An important part of the organization-building function is to think about which activities of which groups need to be linked and made mutually reinforcing and then to forge the necessary collaboration both internally and with outside resource providers.

2. *Normally, a core competence or capability emerges incrementally out of company efforts either to bolster skills that contributed to earlier successes or to respond to customer problems, new technological and market opportunities, and the*

competitive maneuverings of rivals. Migrating from the one-time ability to do something up the ladder to a core competence or competitively valuable capability is usually an organization-building process that takes months and often years to accomplish—it is definitely not an overnight event.

3. *The key to leveraging a core competence into a distinctive competence (or a capability into a competitively superior capability) is concentrating more effort and more talent than rivals on deepening and strengthening the competence or capability, so as to achieve the dominance needed for competitive advantage.* This does not necessarily mean spending more money on such activities than competitors, but it does mean consciously focusing more talent on them and striving for best-in-industry, if not best-in-world, status. To achieve dominance on lean financial resources, companies like Cray in large computers and Honda in gasoline engines have leveraged the expertise of their talent pool by frequently re-forming high-intensity teams and reusing key people on special projects. The experiences of these and other companies indicate that the usual keys to successfully building core competencies and valuable capabilities are superior employee selection, thorough training and retraining, powerful cultural influences, effective cross-functional collaboration, empowerment, motivating incentives, short deadlines, and good databases—not big operating budgets.

4. *Evolving changes in customers' needs and competitive conditions often require tweaking and adjusting a company's portfolio of competencies and intellectual capital to keep its capabilities freshly honed and on the cutting edge.* This is particularly important in high-tech industries and fast-paced markets where important developments occur weekly. As a consequence, wise company managers work at anticipating changes in customer-market requirements and staying ahead of the curve in proactively building a package of competencies and capabilities that can win out over rivals.

Managerial actions to develop core competencies and competitive capabilities generally take one of two forms: either strengthening the company's base of skills, knowledge, and intellect, or coordinating and networking the efforts of the various work groups and departments. Actions of the first sort can be undertaken at all managerial levels, but actions of the second sort are best orchestrated by senior managers who not only appreciate the strategy-executing significance of strong competencies/capabilities but also have the clout to enforce the necessary networking and cooperation among individuals, groups, departments, and external allies.

One organization-building question is whether to develop the desired competencies and capabilities internally or to outsource them by partnering with key suppliers or forming strategic alliances. The answer depends on what can be safely delegated to outside suppliers or allies versus what internal capabilities are key to the company's long-term success. Either way, though, calls for action. Outsourcing means launching initiatives to identify the most attractive providers and to establish collaborative relationships. Developing the capabilities in-house means marshaling personnel with relevant skills and experience, collaboratively networking the individual skills and related cross-functional activities to form organizational capability, and building the desired levels of proficiency through repetition (practice makes perfect).[15]

Sometimes the tediousness of internal organization building can be shortcut by buying a company that has the requisite capability and integrating its competencies into the firm's value chain. Indeed, a pressing need to acquire certain capabilities quickly is one reason to acquire another company—an acquisition aimed at building greater capability can be every bit as competitively valuable as an acquisition aimed at adding new products or services to the company's business lineup. Capabilities-motivated acquisitions are essential (1) when a market opportunity can slip by faster than a needed capability can be created internally, and (2) when industry conditions, technology, or competitors are moving at such a rapid clip that time is of the essence. But usually there's no good substitute for ongoing internal efforts to build and strengthen the company's competencies and capabilities in performing strategy-critical value chain activities.

Updating and Remodeling Competencies and Capabilities as External Conditions and Company Strategy Change   Even after core competencies and competitive capabilities are in place and functioning, company managers can't relax. Competencies and capabilities that grow stale can impair competitiveness unless they are refreshed, modified, or even phased out and replaced in response to ongoing market changes and shifts in company strategy. Indeed, the buildup of knowledge and experience over time, coupled with the imperatives of keeping capabilities in step with ongoing strategy and market changes, makes it appropriate to view a company as *a bundle of evolving competencies and capabilities.* Management's organization-building challenge is one of deciding when and how to recalibrate existing com petencies and capabilities, and when and how to develop new ones. Although the task is formidable, ideally it produces a dynamic organization with "hum" and momentum as well as a distinctive competence. Toyota, aspiring to overtake General Motors as the global leader in motor vehicles, has been aggressively upgrading its capabilities in fuel-efficient hybrid engine technology and is constantly fine-tuning its famed Toyota Production System to enhance its already proficient capabilities in manufacturing top-quality vehicles at relatively low costs—see Illustration Capsule 11.2. Like-wise, Honda, which has long had a core competence in gasoline engine technology and small engine design, has accelerated its efforts to broaden its expertise and capabilities in hybrid engines so as to stay close behind Toyota. TV broadcasters are upgrading their capabilities in digital broadcasting technology in readiness for the upcoming switchover from analog to digital signal transmission. Microsoft has totally retooled the manner in which its programmers attack the task of writing code for its new operating systems for PCs and servers (the first wave of which was due out in 2006).

The Strategic Role of Employee Training

Training and retraining are important when a company shifts to a strategy requiring different skills, competitive capabilities, managerial approaches, and operating methods. Training is also strategically important in organizational efforts to build skills-based competencies. And it is a key activity in businesses where technical know-how is changing so rapidly that a company loses its ability to compete unless its skilled people have cutting-edge knowledge and expertise. Successful strategy implementers see to it that the training function is both adequately funded and effective. If the chosen strategy calls for new skills, deeper technological capability, or building and using new capabilities, training should be placed near the top of the action agenda.

The strategic importance of training has not gone unnoticed. Over 600 companies have established internal "universities" to lead the training effort, facilitate continuous organizational learning, and help upgrade company competencies and capabilities. Many companies conduct orientation sessions for new employees, fund an assortment

Illustration Capsule 11.2

Toyota's Legendary Production System: A Capability That Translates into Competitive Advantage

The heart of Toyota's strategy in motor vehicles is to outcompete rivals by manufacturing world-class, quality vehicles at lower costs and selling them at competitive price levels. Executing this strategy requires top-notch manufacturing capability and super-efficient management of people, equipment, and materials. Toyota began conscious efforts to improve its manufacturing competence more than 50 years ago. Through tireless trial and error, the company gradually took what started as a loose collection of techniques and practices and integrated them into a full-fledged process that has come to be known as the Toyota Production System (TPS). The TPS drives all plant operations and the company's supply chain management practices. TPS is grounded in the following principles, practices, and techniques:

- *Deliver parts and components just-in-time to the point of vehicle assembly.* The idea here is to cut out all the bits and pieces of transferring materials from place to place and to discontinue all activities on the part of workers that don't add value (particularly activities where nothing ends up being made or assembled).

- *Develop people who can come up with unique ideas for production improvements.*

- *Emphasize continuous improvement.* Workers are expected to use their heads and develop better ways of doing things, rather than mechanically follow instructions. Toyota managers tell workers that the *T* in TPS also stands for "Thinking." The thesis is that a work environment where people have to think generates the wisdom to spot opportunities for making tasks simpler and easier to perform, increasing the speed and efficiency with which activities are performed, and constantly improving product quality.

- *Empower workers to stop the assembly line when there's a problem or a defect is spotted.* Toyota views worker efforts to purge defects and sort out the problem immediately as critical to the whole concept of building quality

into the production process. According to TPS, "If the line doesn't stop, useless defective items will move on to the next stage. If you don't know where the problem occurred, you can't do anything to fix it." The tool for halting the assembly line is the *andon* electric light board, which is visible to everyone on the production floor.

- *Deal with defects only when they occur.* TPS philosophy holds that when things are running smoothly, they should not be subject to control; if attention is directed to fixing problems that are found, quality control along the assembly line can be handled with fewer personnel.

- *Ask yourself "Why?" five times.* While errors need to be fixed whenever they occur, the value of asking "Why?" five times enables identifying the root cause of the error and correcting it so that the error won't recur.

- *Organize all jobs around human motion to create a production/assembly system with no wasted effort.* Work organized in this fashion is called standardized work, and people are trained to observe standardized work procedures (which include supplying parts to each process on the assembly line at the proper time, sequencing the work in an optimal manner, and allowing workers to do their jobs continuously in a set sequence of subprocesses).

- *Find where a part is made cheaply and use that price as a benchmark.*

The TPS uses unique terms (such as *kanban, takt time, jikoda, kaizen, heijunka, monozukuri, poka yoke,* and *muda*) that facilitate precise discussion of specific TPS elements. In 2003, Toyota established a Global Production Center to efficiently train large numbers of shop-floor experts in the latest TPS methods and better operate an increasing number of production sites worldwide. There's widespread agreement that Toyota's ongoing effort to refine and improve on its renowned TPS gives it important manufacturing capabilities that are the envy of other motor vehicle manufacturers.

Sources: Information posted at www.toyotageorgetown.com, and Taiichi Ohno, *Toyota Production System: Beyond Large-Scale Production* (New York: Sheridan, 1988).

of competence-building training programs, and reimburse employees for tuition and other expenses associated with obtaining additional college education, attending professional development courses, and earning professional certification of one kind or another. A number of companies offer online, just-in-time training courses to employees around the clock. Increasingly, employees at all levels are expected to take an active role in their own professional development, assuming responsibility for keeping their skills and expertise up-to-date and in sync with the company's needs.

From Competencies and Capabilities to Competitive Advantage

While strong core competencies and competitive capabilities are a major assist in executing strategy, they are an equally important avenue for securing a competitive edge over rivals in situations where it is relatively easy for rivals to copy smart strategies. Any time rivals can readily duplicate successful strategy features, making it difficult or impossible to outstrategize rivals and beat them in the marketplace with a superior strategy, the chief way to achieve lasting competitive advantage is to outexecute them (beat them by performing certain value chain activities in a superior fashion). *Building core competencies and competitive capabilities that are very difficult or costly for rivals to emulate and that push a company closer to true operating excellence promotes very proficient strategy execution.* Moreover, because cutting-edge core competencies and competitive capabilities represent resource strengths that are often time-consuming and expensive for rivals to match or trump, any competitive edge they produce tends to be sustainable and pave the way for above-average company performance.

> **Core Concept**
> Building competencies and capabilities that are very difficult or costly for rivals to emulate has a huge payoff—improved strategy execution and a potential for competitive advantage.

It is easy to cite instances where companies have gained a competitive edge based on superior competencies and capabilities. Toyota's production capabilities (see Illustration Capsule 11.2) have given it a decided market edge over such rivals as General Motors, Ford, DaimlerChrysler, and Volkswagen. Dell's competitors have spent years and millions of dollars in what so far is a futile effort to match Dell's cost-efficient supply chain management capabilities. FedEx has unmatched capabilities in reliable overnight delivery of documents and small parcels. Various business news media have been unable to match the competence of Dow-Jones in gathering and reporting business news via *The Wall Street Journal.*

EXECUTION-RELATED ASPECTS OF ORGANIZING THE WORK EFFORT

There are few hard-and-fast rules for organizing the work effort to support good strategy execution. Every firm's organization chart is partly a product of its particular situation, reflecting prior organizational patterns, varying internal circumstances, executive judgments about reporting relationships, and the politics of who gets which assignments. Moreover, every strategy is grounded in its own set of key success factors and value chain activities. But some organizational considerations are common to all companies. These are summarized in Figure 11.3 and discussed in turn in the following sections.

Deciding Which Value Chain Activities to Perform Internally and Which to Outsource

The advantages of a company having an outsourcing component in its strategy were discussed in Chapter 6 (pp. 160–193), but there is also a need to consider the role of outsourcing in executing the strategy. Aside from the fact than an outsider, because of

Figure 11.3 **Structuring the Work Effort to Promote Successful Strategy Execution**

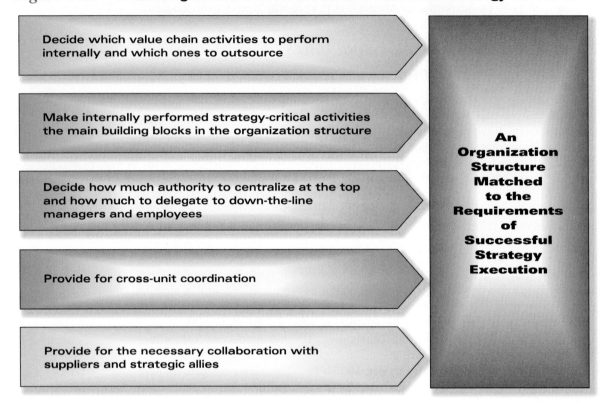

its expertise and specialized know-how, may be able to perform certain value chain activities better or cheaper than a company can perform them internally, outsourcing can also have several organization-related benefits. Managers too often spend inordinate amounts of time, mental energy, and resources haggling with functional support groups and other internal bureaucracies over needed services, leaving less time for them to devote to performing strategy-critical activities in the most proficient manner. One way to reduce such distractions is to outsource the performance of assorted administrative support functions and perhaps even selected core or primary value chain activities to outside vendors, thereby enabling the company to *heighten its strategic focus and concentrate its full energies and resources on even more competently performing those value chain activities that are at the core of its strategy and for which it can create unique value.* For example, E. & J. Gallo Winery outsources 95 percent of its grape production, letting farmers take on the weather and other grape-growing risks while it concentrates its full energies on wine production and sales.[16] A number of personal computer (PC) makers outsource the mundane and highly specialized task of PC assembly, concentrating their energies instead on product design, sales and marketing, and distribution.

When a company uses outsourcing to zero in on ever better performance of those truly strategy-critical activities where its expertise is most needed, then it may be able to realize three very positive benefits:

1. The company improves its chances for outclassing rivals in the performance of strategy-critical activities and turning a core competence into a distinctive competence. At the very least, the heightened focus on performing a select few value chain activities should meaningfully strengthen the company's existing core competences and promote more innovative performance of those activities—either of which could lower costs or materially improve competitive capabilities. Eastman Kodak, Ford, Exxon Mobil, Merrill Lynch, and Chevron have outsourced their data processing activities to computer service firms, believing that outside specialists can perform the needed services at lower costs and equal or better quality. A relatively large number of companies outsource the operation of their Web sites to Web design and hosting enterprises. Many business that get a lot of inquiries from customers or that have to provide 24/7 technical support to users of their products across the world have found that it is considerably less expensive to outsource these functions to specialists (often located in foreign countries where skilled personnel are readily available and worker compensation costs are much lower) than to operate their own call centers.

2. *The streamlining of internal operations that flows from outsourcing often acts to decrease internal bureaucracies, flatten the organization structure, speed internal decision making, and shorten the time it takes to respond to changing market conditions.*[17] In consumer electronics, where advancing technology drives new product innovation, organizing the work effort in a manner that expedites getting next-generation products to market ahead of rivals is a critical competitive capability. Motor vehicle manufacturers have found that they can shorten the cycle time for new models, improve the quality and performance of those models, and lower overall production costs by outsourcing the big majority of their parts and components from independent suppliers and then working closely with their vendors to advance the design and functioning of the items being supplied, to swiftly incorporate new technology, and to better integrate individual parts and components to form engine cooling systems, transmission systems, and electrical systems.

3. *Outsourcing the performance of certain value chain activities to able suppliers can add to a company's arsenal of capabilities and contribute to better strategy execution.* By building, continually improving, and then leveraging its partnerships with able suppliers, a company enhances its overall organizational capabilities and builds resource strengths—strengths that deliver value to customers and consequently pave the way for competitive success. Soft-drink and beer manufacturers all cultivate their relationships with their bottlers and distributors to strengthen access to local markets and build the loyalty, support, and commitment for corporate marketing programs, without which their own sales and growth are weakened. Similarly, fast-food enterprises like McDonald's and Taco Bell find it essential to work hand-in-hand with franchisees on outlet cleanliness, consistency of product quality, in-store ambience, courtesy and friendliness of store personnel, and other aspects of store operations. Unless franchisees continuously deliver sufficient customer satisfaction to attract repeat business, a fast-food chain's sales and competitive standing will suffer quickly. Companies like Boeing, Aerospatiale, Verizon Communications, and Dell have learned that their central R&D groups cannot begin to match the innovative capabilities of a well-managed network of supply chain partners having the ability to advance the technology, lead the development of next-generation parts and components, and supply them at a relatively low price.[18]

As a general rule, companies refrain from outsourcing those value chain activities over which they need direct strategic and operating control in order to build core competencies, achieve competitive advantage, and effectively manage key customer–supplier–distributor relationships. It is the strategically less important activities—like handling customer inquiries and providing technical support, doing the payroll, administering employee benefit programs, providing corporate security, managing stockholder relations, maintaining fleet vehicles, operating the company's Web site, conducting employee training, and managing an assortment of information and data processing functions—where outsourcing is most used.

Even so, a number of companies have found ways to successfully rely on outside vendors to perform strategically significant value chain activities.[19] Broadcom, a global leader in chips for broadband communications systems, outsources the manufacture of its chips to Taiwan Semiconductor, thus freeing company personnel to focus their full energies on R&D, new chip design, and marketing. For years Polaroid Corporation bought its film from Eastman Kodak, its electronics from Texas Instruments, and its cameras from Timex and others, while it concentrated on producing its unique self-developing film packets and designing its next-generation cameras and films. Nike concentrates on design, marketing, and distribution to retailers, while outsourcing virtually all production of its shoes and sporting apparel. Cisco Systems outsources virtually all manufacturing of its routers, switches, and other Internet gear, yet it protects its market position by retaining tight internal control over product design and closely monitors the daily operations of its manufacturing vendors. Large numbers of electronics companies outsource the design, engineering, manufacturing, and shipping of their products to such companies as Flextronics and Solectron, both of which have built huge businesses as providers of such services to companies worldwide. So while performing *core* value chain activities in-house normally makes good sense, there can be times when outsourcing some of them works to good advantage.

The Dangers of Excessive Outsourcing   Critics contend that a company can go overboard on outsourcing and so hollow out its knowledge base and capabilities as to leave itself at the mercy of outside suppliers and short of the resource strengths to be a master of its own destiny.[20] The point is well taken, but most companies appear alert to the danger of taking outsourcing to an extreme or failing to maintain control of the work performed by specialist vendors or offshore suppliers. Many companies refuse to source key components from a single supplier, opting to use two or three suppliers as a way of avoiding single supplier dependence or giving one supplier too much bargaining power. Moreover, they regularly evaluate their suppliers, looking not only at the supplier's overall performance but also at whether they should switch to another supplier or even bring the activity back in-house. To avoid loss of control, companies typically work closely with key suppliers, meeting often and setting up online systems to share data and information, collaborate on work in progress, monitor performance, and otherwise document that suppliers' activities are closely integrated with their own requirements and expectations. Indeed, sophisticated online systems permit companies to work in "real time" with suppliers 10,000 miles away, making rapid response possible whenever concerns or problems arise. Hence *the real debate surrounding outsourcing is not about whether too much outsourcing risks loss of control, but about how to use outsourcing in a manner that produces greater competitiveness.*

Making Strategy-Critical Activities the Main Building Blocks of the Organization Structure

In any business, some activities in the value chain are always more critical to strategic success and competitive advantage than others. For instance, hotel/motel enterprises have to be good at fast check-in/check-out, housekeeping and facilities maintenance, food service, and the creation of a pleasant ambience. For a manufacturer of chocolate bars, buying quality cocoa beans at low prices is vital and reducing production costs by a fraction of a cent per bar can mean a seven-figure improvement in the bottom line. In discount stock brokerage, the strategy-critical activities are fast access to information, accurate order execution, efficient record keeping and transactions processing, and good customer service. In specialty chemicals, the critical activities are R&D, product innovation, getting new products onto the market quickly, effective marketing, and expertise in assisting customers. Where such is the case, it is important for management to build its organization structure around proficient performance of these activities, making them the centerpieces or main building blocks on the organization chart.

The rationale for making strategy-critical activities the main building blocks in structuring a business is compelling: If activities crucial to strategic success are to have the resources, decision-making influence, and organizational impact they need, they have to be centerpieces in the organizational scheme. Plainly, implementing a new or changed strategy is likely to entail new or different key activities, competencies, or capabilities and therefore to require new or different organizational arrangements. If workable organizational adjustments are not forthcoming, the resulting mismatch between strategy and structure can open the door to execution and performance problems.[21] Hence, attempting to carry out a new strategy with an old organization structure is usually unwise.

What Types of Organization Structures Fit Which Strategies?   It is generally agreed that some type of functional structure is the best organizational arrangement when a company is in just one particular business (irrespective of which of the five competitive strategies it opts to pursue). The primary organizational building blocks within a business are usually *traditional functional departments* (R&D, engineering and design, production and operations, sales and marketing, information technology, finance and accounting, and human resources) and *process departments* (where people in a single work unit have responsibility for all the aspects of a certain process like supply chain management, new product development, customer service, quality control, or selling direct to customers via the company's Web site). For instance, a technical instruments manufacturer may be organized around research and development, engineering, supply chain management, assembly, quality control, marketing, technical services, and corporate administration. A hotel may have a functional organization based on front-desk operations, housekeeping, building maintenance, food service, convention services and special events, guest services, personnel and training, and accounting. A discount retailer may organize around such functional units as purchasing, warehousing and distribution, store operations, advertising, merchandising and promotion, customer service, and corporate administrative services.

In enterprises with operations in various countries around the world (or with geographically scattered organizational units within a country), the basic building blocks may also include *geographic organizational units,* each of which has profit/loss responsibility for its assigned geographic area. In vertically integrated firms, the major building blocks are *divisional units performing one or more of the major processing steps along the value chain* (raw materials production, components manufacture, assembly, wholesale distribution, retail store operations); each division in the value chain may operate as a profit center for performance measurement purposes. The typical building blocks of a diversified company are its *individual businesses,* with each business unit usually operating as an independent profit center and with corporate headquarters performing assorted support functions for all of its business units. But a divisional business-unit structure can present problems to a company pursuing related diversification.

Determining the Degree of Authority and Independence to Give Each Unit and Each Employee

In executing the strategy and conducting daily operations, companies must decide how much authority to delegate to the managers of each organization unit—especially the heads of business subsidiaries; functional and process departments; and plants, sales offices, distribution centers, and other operating units—and how much decision-making latitude to give individual employees in performing their jobs. The two extremes are to *centralize decision making* at the top (the CEO and a few close lieutenants) or to *decentralize decision making* by giving managers and employees considerable decision-making latitude in their areas of responsibility. As shown in Table 11.1, the two approaches are based on sharply different underlying principles and beliefs, with each having its pros and cons.

Centralized Decision Making: Pros and Cons   *In a highly centralized organization structure, top executives retain authority for most strategic and operating decisions and keep a tight rein on business-unit heads, department heads, and the*

Table 11.1   **Advantages and Disadvantages of Centralized versus Decentralized Decision Making**

Centralized Organizational Structures	Decentralized Organizational Structures
Basic tenets	**Basic tenets**
• Decisions on most matters of importance should be pushed to managers up the line who have the experience, expertise, and judgment to decide what is the wisest or best course of action.	• Decision-making authority should be put in the hands of the people closest to and most familiar with the situation and these people should be trained to exercise good judgment.
• Frontline supervisors and rank-and-file employees can't be relied on to make the right decisions—because they seldom know what is best for the organization and because they do not have the time or the inclination to properly manage the tasks they are performing (letting them decide "what to do" is thus risky).	• A company that draws on the combined intellectual capital of all its employees can outperform a command-and-control company.
Chief advantage	**Chief advantages**
• Fixes accountability.	• Encourages lower level managers and rank-and-file employees to exercise initiative and act responsibly.
Primary disadvantages	• Promotes greater motivation and involvement in the business on the part of more company personnel.
• Lengthens response times because management bureaucracy must decide on a course of action.	• Spurs new ideas and creative thinking.
• Does not encourage responsibility among lower level managers and rank-and-file employees.	• Allows fast response times.
	• Entails fewer layers of management.
• Discourages lower level managers and rank-and-file employees from exercising any initiative—they are expected to wait to be told what to do.	**Primary disadvantages**
	• Puts the organization at risk if many bad decisions are made at lower levels—top management lacks full control.
	• Impedes cross-business coordination and capture of strategic fits in diversified companies.

managers of key operating units; comparatively little discretionary authority is granted to frontline supervisors and rank-and-file employees. The command-and-control paradigm of centralized structures is based on the underlying assumption that frontline personnel have neither the time nor the inclination to direct and properly control the work they are performing, and that they lack the knowledge and judgment to make wise decisions about how best to do it—hence the need for managerially prescribed policies and procedures, close supervision, and tight control. The thesis underlying authoritarian structures is that strict enforcement of detailed procedures backed by rigorous managerial oversight is the most reliable way to keep the daily execution of strategy on track.

The big advantage of an authoritarian structure is tight control by the manager in charge—it is easy to know who is accountable when things do not go well. But there are some serious disadvantages. Hierarchical command-and-control structures make an organization sluggish in responding to changing conditions because of the time it takes for the review/approval process to run up all the layers of the management bureaucracy. Furthermore, to work well, centralized decision making requires top-level managers to gather and process whatever information is relevant to the decision. When the relevant knowledge resides at lower organizational levels (or is technical, detailed, or hard to express in words), it is difficult and time-consuming to get all the facts and nuances in front of a high-level executive located far from the scene of the action—full understanding of the situation cannot be readily copied from one mind to another. Hence, centralized decision making is often impractical—the larger the company and the more scattered its operations, the more that decision-making authority has to be delegated to managers closer to the scene of the action.

> There are disadvantages to having a small number of top-level managers micromanage the business either by personally making decisions or by requiring lower-level subordinates to gain approval before taking action.

Decentralized Decision Making: Pros and Cons   *In a highly decentralized organization, decision-making authority is pushed down to the lowest organizational level capable of making timely, informed, competent decisions.* The objective is to put adequate decision-making authority in the hands of the people closest to and most familiar with the situation and train them to weigh all the factors and exercise good judgment. Decentralized decision making means that the managers of each organizational unit are delegated lead responsibility for deciding how best to execute strategy (as well as some role in shaping the strategy for the units they head). Decentralization thus requires selecting strong managers to head each organizational unit and holding them accountable for crafting and executing appropriate strategies for their units. Managers who consistently produce unsatisfactory results have to be weeded out.

The case for empowering down-the-line managers and employees to make decisions related to daily operations and executing the strategy is based on the belief that a company that draws on the combined intellectual capital of all its employees can outperform a command-and-control company.[22] Decentralized decision making means, for example, that in a diversified company the various business-unit heads have broad authority to execute the agreed-on business strategy with comparatively little interference from corporate headquarters; moreover, the business-unit heads delegate considerable decision-making latitude to functional and process department heads and the heads of the various operating units (plants, distribution centers, sales offices) in implementing and executing their pieces of the strategy. In turn, work teams may be empowered to manage and improve their assigned value chain activity, and employees with customer contact may be empowered to do what it takes to please customers.

The ultimate goal of decentralized decision making is to put decision-making authority in the hands of those persons or teams closest to and most knowledgeable about the situation.

At Starbucks, for example, employees are encouraged to exercise initiative in promoting customer satisfaction—there's the story of a store employee who, when the computerized cash register system went offline, enthusiastically offered free coffee to waiting customers.[23] *With decentralized decision making, top management maintains control by limiting empowered managers' and employees' discretionary authority and holding people accountable for the decisions they make.*

Decentralized organization structures have much to recommend them. Delegating greater authority to subordinate managers and employees creates a more horizontal organization structure with fewer management layers. Whereas in a centralized vertical structure managers and workers have to go up the ladder of authority for an answer, in a decentralized horizontal structure they develop their own answers and action plans—making decisions in their areas of responsibility and being accountable for results is an integral part of their job. Pushing decision-making authority down to middle and lower-level managers and then further on to work teams and individual employees shortens organizational response times and spurs new ideas, creative thinking, innovation, and greater involvement on the part of subordinate managers and employees. In worker-empowered structures, jobs can be defined more broadly, several tasks can be integrated into a single job, and people can direct their own work. Fewer managers are needed because deciding how to do things becomes part of each person's or team's job. Further, today's online communication systems make it easy and relatively inexpensive for people at all organizational levels to have direct access to data, other employees, managers, suppliers, and customers. They can access information quickly (via the Internet or company intranet), readily check with superiors or co-workers as needed, and take responsible action. Typically, there are genuine gains in morale and productivity when people are provided with the tools and information they need to operate in a self-directed way. Decentralized decision making not only can shorten organizational response times but also can spur new ideas, creative thinking, innovation, and greater involvement on the part of subordinate managers and employees.

The past decade has seen a growing shift from authoritarian, multilayered hierarchical structures to flatter, more decentralized structures that stress employee empowerment. There's strong and growing consensus that authoritarian, hierarchical organization structures are not well suited to implementing and executing strategies in an era when extensive information and instant communication are the norm and when a big fraction of the organization's most valuable assets consists of intellectual capital and resides in the knowledge and capabilities of its employees. Many companies have therefore begun empowering lower-level managers and employees throughout their organizations, giving them greater discretionary authority to make strategic adjustments in their areas of responsibility and to decide what needs to be done to put new strategic initiatives into place and execute them proficiently.

Maintaining Control in a Decentralized Organization Structure

Pushing decision-making authority deep down into the organization structure and empowering employees presents its own organizing challenge: *how to exercise adequate control over the actions of empowered employees so that the business is not put at risk at the same time that the benefits of empowerment are realized.*[24] Maintaining adequate organizational control over empowered employees is generally accomplished by placing limits on the authority that empowered personnel can exercise, holding people accountable for their decisions, instituting compensation incentives that reward people for doing their jobs in a manner that contributes to good company performance, and creating a corporate culture where there's strong peer pressure on individuals to act responsibly.

Capturing Strategic Fits in a Decentralized Structure   Diversified companies striving to capture cross-business strategic fits have to beware of giving business heads full rein to operate independently when cross-business collaboration is essential in order to gain strategic fit benefits. Cross-business strategic fits typically have to be captured either by enforcing close cross-business collaboration or by centralizing performance of functions having strategic fits at the corporate level.[25] For example, if businesses with overlapping process and product technologies have their own independent R&D departments—each pursuing their own priorities, projects, and strategic agendas—it's hard for the corporate parent to prevent duplication of effort, capture either economies of scale or economies of scope, or broaden the company's R&D efforts to embrace new technological paths, product families, end-use applications, and customer groups. Where cross-business R&D fits exist, the best solution is usually to centralize the R&D function and have a coordinated corporate R&D effort that serves both the interests of individual businesses and the company as a whole. Likewise, centralizing the related activities of separate businesses makes sense when there are opportunities to share a common sales force, use common distribution channels, rely on a common field service organization to handle customer requests or provide maintenance and repair services, use common e-commerce systems and approaches, and so on.

The point here is that efforts to decentralize decision making and give organizational units leeway in conducting operations have to be tempered with the need to maintain adequate control and cross-unit coordination—decentralization doesn't mean delegating authority in ways that allow organization units and individuals to do their own thing. There are numerous instances when decision-making authority must be retained at high levels in the organization and ample cross-unit coordination strictly enforced.

Providing for Internal Cross-Unit Coordination

The classic way to coordinate the activities of organizational units is to position them in the hierarchy so that the most closely related ones report to a single person (a functional department head, a process manager, a geographic area head, a senior executive). Managers higher up in the ranks generally have the clout to coordinate, integrate, and arrange for the cooperation of units under their supervision. In such structures, the chief executive officer, chief operating officer, and business-level managers end up as central points of coordination because of their positions of authority over the whole unit. When a firm is pursuing a related diversification strategy, coordinating the related activities of independent business units often requires the centralizing authority of a single corporate-level officer. Also, diversified companies commonly centralize such staff support functions as public relations, finance and accounting, employee benefits, and information technology at the corporate level both to contain the costs of support activities and to facilitate uniform and coordinated performance of such functions within each business unit.

However, close cross-unit collaboration is usually needed to build core competencies and competitive capabilities in strategically important activities—such as speeding new products to market and providing superior customer service—that involve employees scattered across several internal organization units (and perhaps the employees of outside strategic partners or specialty vendors). A big weakness of traditional functionally organized structures is that pieces of strategically relevant activities and capabilities often end up scattered across many departments, with the result that no one group or manager is accountable. Consider, for example, how the following strategy-critical activities cut across different functions:

- *Filling customer orders accurately and promptly*—a process that involves personnel from sales (which wins the order); finance (which may have to check credit terms or approve special financing); production (which must produce the goods and replenish warehouse inventories as needed); warehousing (which has to verify whether the items are in stock, pick the order from the warehouse, and package it for shipping); and shipping (which has to choose a carrier to deliver the goods and release the goods to the carrier).[26]
- *Fast, ongoing introduction of new products*—a cross-functional process involving personnel in R&D, design and engineering, purchasing, manufacturing, and sales and marketing.
- *Improving product quality*—a process that entails the collaboration of personnel in R&D, design and engineering, purchasing, in-house components production, manufacturing, and assembly.
- *Supply chain management*—a collaborative process that cuts across such functional areas as purchasing, inventory management, manufacturing and assembly, and warehousing and shipping.
- *Building the capability to conduct business via the Internet*—a process that involves personnel in information technology, supply chain management, production, sales and marketing, warehousing and shipping, customer service, finance, and accounting.
- *Obtaining feedback from customers and making product modifications to meet their needs*—a process that involves personnel in customer service and after-sale support, R&D, design and engineering, purchasing, manufacturing and assembly, and marketing research.

Handoffs from one department to another lengthen completion time and frequently drive up administrative costs, since coordinating the fragmented pieces can soak up hours of effort on the parts of many people.[27] This is not a fatal flaw of functional organization—organizing around specific functions normally works to good advantage in support activities like finance and accounting, human resource management, and engineering, and in such primary activities as R&D, manufacturing, and marketing. But the tendency for pieces of a strategy-critical activity to be scattered across several functional departments is an important weakness of functional organization and accounts for why a company's competencies and capabilities are typically cross-functional.

Many companies have found that rather than continuing to scatter related pieces of a strategy-critical business process across several functional departments and scrambling to integrate their efforts, it is better to reengineer the work effort and pull the people who performed the pieces in functional departments into a group that works together to perform the whole process, thus creating *process departments* (like customer service or new product development or supply chain management). And sometimes the coordinating mechanisms involve the use of cross-functional task forces, dual reporting relationships, informal organizational networking, voluntary cooperation, incentive compensation tied to measures of group performance, and strong executive-level insistence on teamwork and cross-department cooperation (including removal of recalcitrant managers who stonewall collaborative efforts). At one European-based company, a top executive promptly replaced the managers of several plants who were not fully committed to collaborating closely on eliminating duplication in product development and production efforts among plants in several different countries. Earlier, the executive, noting that negotiations among the managers had stalled on which labs and plants to close, had met with all the managers, asked them to cooperate to find a solution, discussed with them which options were unacceptable, and given them a deadline to find a solution. When the asked-for teamwork wasn't forthcoming, several managers were replaced.

Providing for Collaboration with Outside Suppliers and Strategic Allies

Someone or some group must be authorized to collaborate as needed with each major outside constituency involved in strategy execution. Forming alliances and cooperative relationships presents immediate opportunities and opens the door to future possibilities, but nothing valuable is realized until the relationship grows, develops, and blossoms. Unless top management sees that constructive organizational bridge building with strategic partners occurs and that productive working relationships emerge, the value of alliances is lost and the company's power to execute its strategy is weakened. If close working relationships with suppliers are crucial, then supply chain management must be given formal status on the company's organization chart and a significant position in the pecking order. If distributor/dealer/franchisee relationships are important, someone must be assigned the task of nurturing the relationships with forward channel allies. If working in parallel with providers of complementary products and services contributes to enhanced organizational capability, then cooperative organizational arrangements have to be put in place and managed to good effect.

Building organizational bridges with external allies can be accomplished by appointing "relationship managers" with responsibility for making particular strategic partnerships or alliances generate the intended benefits. Relationship managers have many roles and functions: getting the right people together, promoting good rapport, seeing that plans for specific activities are developed and carried out, helping adjust internal organizational procedures and communication systems, ironing out operating dissimilarities, and nurturing interpersonal cooperation. Multiple cross-organization ties have to be established and kept open to ensure proper communication and coordination.[28] There has to be enough information sharing to make the relationship work and periodic frank discussions of conflicts, trouble spots, and changing situations.[29]

CURRENT ORGANIZATIONAL TRENDS

Many of today's companies are winding up the task of remodeling their traditional hierarchical structures once built around functional specialization and centralized authority. Much of the corporate downsizing movement in the late 1980s and early 1990s was aimed at recasting authoritarian, pyramidal organizational structures into flatter, decentralized structures. The change was driven by growing realization that command-and-control hierarchies were proving a liability in businesses where customer preferences were shifting from standardized products to custom orders and special features, product life cycles were growing shorter, custom mass-production methods were replacing standardized mass-production techniques, customers wanted to be treated as individuals, technological change was ongoing, and market conditions were fluid. Layered management hierarchies with lots of checks and controls that required people to look upward in the organizational structure for answers and approval were failing to deliver responsive customer service and timely adaptations to changing conditions.

The organizational adjustments and downsizing of companies in 2001–2005 brought further refinements and changes to streamline organizational activities and shake out inefficiencies. The goals have been to make companies leaner, flatter, and more responsive to change. Many companies are drawing on five tools of organizational design: (1) managers and workers empowered to act on their own judgments, (2) work process redesign (to achieve greater streamlining and tighter cohesion), (3) self-directed work teams, (4) rapid incorporation of Internet technology applications, and (5) networking with outsiders to improve existing organization capabilities and create new ones. Considerable management attention is being devoted to building a company capable of outcompeting rivals on the basis of superior resource strengths and competitive capabilities—capabilities that are increasingly based on intellectual capital and cross-unit collaboration.

Several other organizational characteristics are emerging:

- Extensive use of Internet technology and e-commerce business practices—real-time data and information systems; greater reliance on online systems for transacting business with suppliers and customers; and Internet-based communication and collaboration with suppliers, customers, and strategic partners.

- Fewer barriers between different vertical ranks, between functions and disciplines, between units in different geographic locations, and between the company and its suppliers, distributors/dealers, strategic allies, and customers—an outcome partly due to pervasive use of online systems.

- Rapid dissemination of information, rapid learning, and rapid response times—also an outcome partly due to pervasive use of online systems.

- Collaborative efforts among people in different functional specialties and geographic locations—essential to create organization competencies and capabilities.

Key Points

Implementing and executing strategy is an operation-driven activity revolving around the management of people and business processes. The managerial emphasis is on converting strategic plans into actions and good results. *Management's handling of the process of implementing and executing the chosen strategy can be considered successful if and when the company achieves the targeted strategic and financial performance and shows good progress in making its strategic vision a reality.* Shortfalls in performance signal weak strategy, weak execution, or both.

The place for managers to start in implementing and executing a new or different strategy is with *a probing assessment of what the organization must do differently and better to carry out the strategy successfully.* They should then consider *precisely how to make the necessary internal changes* as rapidly as possible.

Like crafting strategy, executing strategy is a job for a company's whole management team, not just a few senior managers. Top-level managers have to rely on the active support and cooperation of middle and lower managers to push strategy changes into functional areas and operating units and to see that the organization actually operates in accordance with the strategy on a daily basis.

Eight managerial tasks crop up repeatedly in company efforts to execute strategy:

1. Building an organization with the competencies, capabilities, and resource strengths to execute strategy successfully.

2. Marshaling sufficient money and people behind the drive for strategy execution.

3. Instituting policies and procedures that facilitate rather than impede strategy execution.

4. Adopting best practices and pushing for continuous improvement in how value chain activities are performed.

5. Installing information and operating systems that enable company personnel to carry out their strategic roles proficiently.

6. Tying rewards directly to the achievement of strategic and financial targets and to good strategy execution.

7. Shaping the work environment and corporate culture to fit the strategy.

8. Exercising strong leadership to drive execution forward, keep improving on the details of execution, and achieve operating excellence as rapidly as feasible.

Building an organization capable of good strategy execution entails three types of organization-building actions: (1) *staffing the organization*—assembling a talented, can-do management team, and recruiting and retaining employees with the needed experience, technical skills, and intellectual capital; (2) *building core competencies and competitive capabilities* that will enable good strategy execution and updating them as strategy and external conditions change; and (3) *structuring the organization and work effort*—organizing value chain activities and business processes and deciding how much decision-making authority to push down to lower-level managers and frontline employees.

Building core competencies and competitive capabilities is a time-consuming, managerially challenging exercise that involves three stages: (1) developing the *ability* to do something, however imperfectly or inefficiently, by selecting people with the requisite skills and experience, upgrading or expanding individual abilities as needed, and then molding the efforts and work products of individuals into a collaborative group effort; (2) coordinating group efforts to learn how to perform the activity *consistently well and at an acceptable cost,* thereby transforming the ability into a tried-and-true *competence or capability;* and (3) continuing to polish and refine the organization's know-how and otherwise sharpen performance such that it becomes *better than rivals* at performing the activity, thus raising the core competence (or capability) to the rank of a *distinctive competence* (or competitively superior capability) and opening an avenue to competitive advantage. Many companies manage to get through stages 1 and 2 in performing a strategy-critical activity but comparatively few achieve sufficient proficiency in performing strategy-critical activities to qualify for the third stage.

Strong core competencies and competitive capabilities are an important avenue for securing a competitive edge over rivals in situations where it is relatively easy for rivals to copy smart strategies. Any time rivals can readily duplicate successful strategy features, making it difficult or impossible to *outstrategize* rivals and beat them in the marketplace with a superior strategy, the chief way to achieve lasting competitive advantage is to *outexecute* them (beat them by performing certain value chain activities in superior fashion). *Building core competencies and competitive capabilities that are very difficult or costly for rivals to emulate and that push a company closer to true operating excellence is one of the best and most reliable ways to achieve a durable competitive edge.*

Structuring the organization and organizing the work effort in a strategy-supportive fashion has five aspects: (1) deciding which value chain activities to perform internally and which ones to outsource; (2) making internally performed strategy-critical activities the main building blocks in the organization structure; (3) deciding how much authority to centralize at the top and how much to delegate to down-the-line managers and employees; (4) providing for internal cross-unit coordination and collaboration to build and strengthen internal competencies/capabilities; and (5) providing for the necessary collaboration and coordination with suppliers and strategic allies.

Exercises

1.   As the new owner of a local ice cream store located in a strip mall adjacent to a university campus, you are contemplating how to organize your business—whether to make your ice cream in-house or outsource its production to a nearby ice cream manufacturer whose brand is in most of the local supermarkets, and how much authority to delegate to the two assistant store managers and to employees working the counter and the cash register. You plan to sell 20 flavors of ice cream.

   a.   What are the pros and cons of contracting with the local company to custom-produce your product line?

   b.   Since you do not plan to be in the store during all of the hours it is open, what specific decision-making authority would you delegate to the two assistant store managers?

   c.   To what extent, if any, should store employees—many of whom will be university students working part-time—be empowered to make decisions relating to store operations (opening and closing, keeping the premises clean and attractive, keeping the work area behind the counter stocked with adequate supplies of cups, cones, napkins, and so on)?

   d.   Should you create a policies and procedures manual for the assistant managers and employees, or should you just give oral instructions and have them learn their duties and responsibilities on the job?

   e.   How can you maintain control during the times you are not in the store?

2. Go to Home Depot's corporate home page (www.homedepot.com/corporate) and review the information under the headings About The Home Depot, Investor Relations, and Careers. How does Home Depot go about building core competencies and competitive capabilities? Would any of Home Depot's competencies qualify as a distinctive competence? Please use the chapter's discussion of building core competencies and competitive capabilities as a guide for preparing your answer.

3. Using Google Scholar or your access to EBSCO, InfoTrac, or other online database of journal articles and research in your university's library, do a search for recent writings on self-directed or empowered work teams. According to the articles you found in the various management journals, what are the conditions for the effective use of such teams? Also, how should such teams be organized or structured to better ensure their success?

chapter twelve

Managing Internal Operations

Actions That Promote Good Strategy Execution

Winning companies know how to do their work better.

—Michael Hammer and James Champy

Companies that make best practices a priority are thriving, thirsty, learning organizations. They believe that everyone should always be searching for a better way. Those kinds of companies are filled with energy and curiosity and a spirit of can-do.

—Jack Welch
Former CEO, General Electric

If you want people motivated to do a good job, give them a good job to do.

—Frederick Herzberg

You ought to pay big bonuses for premier performance. . . . Be a top payer, not in the middle or low end of the pack.

—Lawrence Bossidy
CEO, Honeywell International

In Chapter 11 we emphasized the importance of building organization capabilities and structuring the work effort so as to perform strategy-critical activities in a coordinated and highly competent manner. In this chapter we discuss five additional managerial actions that promote the success of a company's strategy execution efforts:

1. Marshaling resources behind the drive for good strategy execution.

2. Instituting policies and procedures that facilitate strategy execution.

3. Adopting best practices and striving for continuous improvement in how value chain activities are performed.

4. Installing information and operating systems that enable company personnel to carry out their strategic roles proficiently.

5. Tying rewards and incentives directly to the achievement of strategic and financial targets and to good strategy execution.

MARSHALING RESOURCES BEHIND THE DRIVE FOR GOOD STRATEGY EXECUTION

Early in the process of implementing and executing a new or different strategy, managers need to determine what resources will be needed and then consider whether the current budgets of organizational units are suitable. Plainly, organizational units must have the budgets and resources for executing their parts of the strategic plan effectively and efficiently. Developing a strategy-driven budget requires top management to determine what funding is needed to execute new strategic initiatives and to strengthen or modify the company's competencies and capabilities. This includes careful screening of requests for more people and more or better facilities and equipment, approving those that hold promise for making a cost-justified contribution to strategy execution, and turning down those that don't. Should internal cash flows prove insufficient to fund the planned strategic initiatives, then management must raise additional funds through borrowing or selling additional shares of stock to willing investors.

A company's ability to marshal the resources needed to support new strategic initiatives and steer them to the appropriate organizational units has a major impact on the strategy execution process. Too little funding (stemming either from constrained financial resources or from sluggish management action to adequately increase the budgets of strategy-critical organizational units) slows progress and impedes the efforts of organizational units to execute their pieces of the strategic plan proficiently. Too much funding wastes organizational resources and reduces financial performance. Both outcomes argue for managers to be deeply involved in reviewing budget proposals and directing the proper kinds and amounts of resources to strategy-critical organization units.

Core Concept

The funding requirements of a new strategy must drive how capital allocations are made and the size of each unit's operating budgets. Underfunding organizational units and activities pivotal to strategic success impedes execution and the drive for operating excellence.

A change in strategy nearly always calls for budget reallocations and resource shifting. Units important in the prior strategy but having a lesser role in the new strategy may need downsizing. Units that now have a bigger and more critical strategic role may need more people, new equipment, additional facilities, and above-average increases in their operating budgets. More resources may have to be devoted to quality control or to adding new product features or to building a better brand image or to cutting costs or to employee retraining. Strategy implementers need to be active and forceful in shifting resources, downsizing some functions and upsizing others, not only to amply fund activities with a critical role in the new strategy but also to avoid inefficiency and achieve profit projections. They have to exercise their power to put enough resources behind new strategic initiatives to make things happen, and they have to make the tough decisions to kill projects and activities that are no longer justified.

Visible actions to reallocate operating funds and move people into new organizational units signal a determined commitment to strategic change and frequently are needed to catalyze the implementation process and give it credibility. Microsoft has made a practice of regularly shifting hundreds of programmers to new high-priority programming initiatives within a matter of weeks or even days. At Harris Corporation, where the strategy was to diffuse research ideas into areas that were commercially viable, top management regularly shifted groups of engineers out of government projects and into new commercial venture divisions. Fast-moving developments in many markets are prompting companies to abandon traditional annual or semiannual budgeting and resource allocation cycles in favor of cycles that match the strategy changes a company makes in response to newly developing events.

The bigger the change in strategy (or the more obstacles that lie in the path of good strategy execution), the bigger the resource shifts that will likely be required. Merely fine-tuning the execution of a company's existing strategy seldom requires big movements of people and money from one area to another. The desired improvements can usually be accomplished through above-average budget increases to organizational units launching new initiatives and below-average increases (or even small cuts) for the remaining organizational units. The chief exception occurs where all the strategy changes or new execution initiatives need to be made without adding to total expenses. Then managers have to work their way through the existing budget line-by-line and activity-by-activity, looking for ways to trim costs in some areas and shift the resources to higher priority activities where new execution initiatives are needed.

INSTITUTING POLICIES AND PROCEDURES THAT FACILITATE GOOD STRATEGY EXECUTION

Core Concept

Well-conceived policies and procedures aid strategy execution; out-of-sync ones are barriers.

A company's policies and procedures can either assist the cause of good strategy execution or be a barrier. Any time a company moves to put new strategy elements in place or improve its strategy execution capabilities, managers are well advised to undertake a careful review of existing policies and procedures, proactively revising or discarding those that are out of sync. A change in strategy or a push for better strategy execution generally requires some changes in work practices and the behavior of company personnel. One way of promoting such changes is by instituting a select set of new policies and procedures deliberately aimed at steering the actions and behavior of company personnel in a direction more conducive to good strategy execution and operating excellence.

Figure 12.1   **How Prescribed Policies and Procedures Facilitate Strategy Execution**

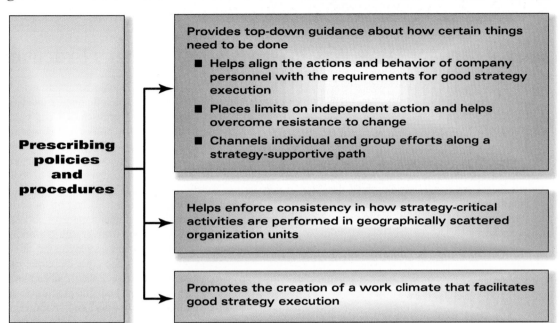

As shown in Figure 12.1, prescribing new policies and operating procedures acts to facilitate strategy execution in three ways:

1. *Instituting new policies and procedures provides top-down guidance regarding how certain things now need to be done.* Asking people to alter established habits and procedures, of course, always upsets the internal order of things. It is normal for pockets of resistance to develop and for people to exhibit some degree of stress and anxiety about how the changes will affect them, especially when the changes may eliminate jobs. But when existing ways of doing things pose a barrier to improving strategy execution, actions and behaviors have to be changed. The managerial role of establishing and enforcing new policies and operating practices is to paint a different set of white lines, place limits on independent behavior, and channel individual and group efforts along a path more conducive to executing the strategy. Policies are a particularly useful way to counteract tendencies for some people to resist change—most people refrain from violating company policy or going against recommended practices and procedures without first gaining clearance or having strong justification.

2. *Policies and procedures help enforce needed consistency in how particular strategy-critical activities are performed in geographically scattered operating units.* Standardization and strict conformity are sometimes desirable components of good strategy execution. Eliminating significant differences in the operating practices of different plants, sales regions, customer service centers, or the individual outlets in a chain operation helps a company deliver consistent product quality and service to customers. Good strategy execution nearly always entails an ability to replicate product quality and the caliber of customer service at every location where the company does business—anything less blurs the company's image and fails to meet customer expectations.

Illustration Capsule 12.1

Granite Construction's Short-Pay Policy: An Innovative Way to Drive Better Strategy Execution

In 1987, the owners of Granite Construction, a 100-plus-year-old supplier of crushed gravel, sand, concrete, and asphalt in Watsonville, California, decided to pursue two strategic targets: total customer satisfaction and a reputation for superior service. To drive the internal efforts to achieve these two objectives and signal both employees and customers that it was deadly serious about these two strategic commitments, top management instituted a short-pay policy that appeared on the bottom of every Granite Construction invoice:

> If you are not satisfied for any reason, don't pay us for it. Simply scratch out the line item, write a brief note about the problem, and return a copy of this invoice along with your check for the balance.

Customers did not have to call and complain and were not expected to return the product. They were given complete discretionary power to decide whether and how much to pay based on their satisfaction level. Management believed that empowering customers not to pay for items or service they found lacking would provide unmistakable feedback and spur company personnel to correct any problems quickly in order to avoid repeated short payments.

The short-pay policy had the desired impact, focusing the attention of company personnel on avoiding short payments by customers and boosting customer satisfaction significantly. Granite has enjoyed compound annual sales gains of 12.2 percent since 2000, while charging a 6 percent price premium for its commodity products in competition against larger rivals.

In addition to its short-pay policy, Granite employs two other policies to help induce company personnel to do their very best to satisfy the company's customers. It has a no-layoff policy (no employees have been laid off in over 80 years), and it sends positive customer comments about employees home for families to read. To make sure its workforce force is properly trained, company employees go through training programs averaging 43 hours per employee annually. And compensation is attractive: Entry-level employees, called job owners, start at $16 an hour and progress to such positions as "accomplished job owner" and "improvement champion" (base pay of $26 an hour); all employees are entitled to 12 company-paid massages annually.

Granite won the prestigious Malcolm Baldrige National Quality Award in 1992, about five years after instituting the short-pay policy. *Fortune* rated Granite as one of the 100 best companies to work for in America in eight of the nine years from 1998 to 2006 (its highest ranking was 16th in 2002, and its lowest was 90th in 2004). The company was on *Fortune*'s "Most Admired Companies" list in 2005 and 2006.

Source: Based on information in Jim Collins, "Turning Goals into Results: The Power of Catalytic Mechanisms," *Harvard Business Review* 77, no. 4 (July–August 1999), pp. 72–73; Robert Levering and Milton Moskowitz, "The 100 Best Companies to Work For," *Fortune,* February 4, 2004, p. 73; Robert Levering and Milton Moskowitz, "The 100 Best Companies to Work For," *Fortune,* January 12, 2005, p. 78; and www.fortune.com (accessed November 11, 2005).

3. *Well-conceived policies and procedures promote the creation of a work climate that facilitates good strategy execution.* Because discarding old policies and procedures in favor of new ones invariably alters the internal work climate, managers can use the policy-changing process as a powerful lever for changing the corporate culture in ways that produce a stronger fit with the new strategy. The trick here, obviously, is to hit upon a new policy that will catch the immediate attention of the whole organization, quickly shift their actions and behavior, and then become embedded in how things are done—as with Granite Construction's short-pay policy discussed in Illustration Capsule 12.1.

In an attempt to steer "crew members" into stronger quality and service behavior patterns, McDonald's policy manual spells out detailed procedures that personnel in each McDonald's unit are expected to observe; for example, "Cooks must turn, never flip, hamburgers," "If they haven't been purchased, Big Macs must be discarded in 10 minutes after being cooked and French fries in 7 minutes," and "Cashiers must make eye contact with and smile at every customer."

Nordstrom's strategic objective is to make sure that each customer has a pleasing shopping experience in its department stores and returns time and again; to get store personnel to dedicate themselves to outstanding customer service, Nordstrom has a policy of promoting only those people whose personnel records contain evidence of "heroic acts" to please customers—especially customers who may have made "unreasonable requests" that require special efforts. To keep its R&D activities responsive to customer needs and expectations, Hewlett-Packard (HP) requires R&D people to make regular visits to customers to learn about their problems and learn their reactions to HP's latest new products.

One of the big policymaking issues concerns what activities need to be rigidly prescribed and what activities ought to allow room for independent action on the part of empowered personnel. Few companies need thick policy manuals to direct the strategy execution process or prescribe exactly how daily operations are to be conducted. Too much policy can erect as many obstacles as wrong policy or be as confusing as no policy. There is wisdom in a middle approach: *Prescribe enough policies to give organization members clear direction in implementing strategy and to place desirable boundaries on their actions; then empower them to act within these boundaries however they think makes sense.* Allowing company personnel to act anywhere between the "white lines" is especially appropriate when individual creativity and initiative are more essential to good strategy execution than standardization and strict conformity. Instituting strategy-facilitating policies can therefore mean more policies, fewer policies, or different policies. It can mean policies that require things to be done a certain way or policies that give employees leeway to do activities the way they think best.

ADOPTING BEST PRACTICES AND STRIVING FOR CONTINUOUS IMPROVEMENT

Company managers can significantly advance the cause of competent strategy execution by pushing organization units and company personnel to identify and adopt the best practices for performing value chain activities and, further, insisting on continuous improvement in how internal operations are conducted. One of the most widely used and effective tools for gauging how well a company is executing pieces of its strategy entails benchmarking the company's performance of particular activities and business processes against best-in-industry and best-in-world performers.[1] It can also be useful to look at best-in-company performers of an activity if a company has a number of different organizational units performing much the same function at different locations. Identifying, analyzing, and understanding how top companies or individuals perform particular value chain activities and business processes provides useful yardsticks for judging the effectiveness and efficiency of internal operations and setting performance standards for organization units to meet or beat.

> **Core Concept**
> Managerial efforts to identify and adopt best practices are a powerful tool for promoting operating excellence and better strategy execution.

How the Process of Identifying and Incorporating Best Practices Works

A **best practice** is a technique for performing an activity or business process that at least one company has demonstrated works particularly well. To qualify as a legitimate best practice, the technique must have a proven record in significantly lowering costs, improving quality or performance, shortening time requirements, enhancing safety, or

Core Concept

A ***best practice*** is any practice that at least one company has proved works particularly well.

delivering some other highly positive operating outcome. Best practices thus identify a path to operating excellence. For a best practice to be valuable and transferable, it must demonstrate success over time, deliver quantifiable and highly positive results, and be repeatable.

Benchmarking is the backbone of the process of identifying, studying, and implementing outstanding practices. A company's benchmarking effort looks outward to find best practices and then proceeds to develop the data for measuring how well a company's own performance of an activity stacks up against the best-practice standard. Informally, benchmarking involves being humble enough to admit that others have come up with world-class ways to perform particular activities yet wise enough to try to learn how to match, and even surpass, them. But, as shown in Figure 12.2, the payoff of benchmarking comes from adapting the top-notch approaches pioneered by other companies in the company's own operation and thereby boosting, perhaps dramatically, the proficiency with which value chain tasks are performed.

However, benchmarking is more complicated than simply identifying which companies are the best performers of an activity and then trying to imitate their approaches—especially if these companies are in other industries. Normally, the outstanding practices of other organizations have to be *adapted* to fit the specific circumstances of a company's own business and operating requirements. Since most companies believe their work is unique, the telling part of any best-practice initiative is how well the company puts its own version of the best practice into place and makes it work.

Indeed, a best practice remains little more than another company's interesting success story unless company personnel buy into the task of translating what can be learned from other companies into real action and results. The agents of change must be frontline employees who are convinced of the need to abandon the old ways of doing things and switch to a best-practice mind-set. *The more that organizational units use best practices in performing their work, the closer a company moves toward performing its value chain activities as effectively and efficiently as possible.* This is what operational excellence is all about.

Legions of companies across the world now engage in benchmarking to improve their strategy execution efforts and, ideally, gain a strategic, operational, and financial advantage over rivals. Scores of trade associations and special interest organizations have undertaken efforts to collect best-practice data relevant to a particular industry or business function and make their databases available online to members—good

Figure 12.2 **From Benchmarking and Best-Practice Implementation to Operating Excellence**

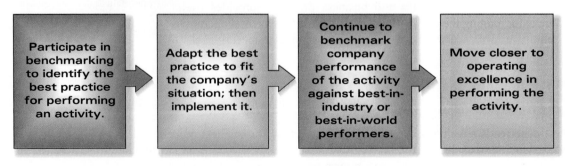

examples include The Benchmarking Exchange's BenchNet (www.benchnet.com), Best Practices LLC (www.best-in-class.com), and the American Productivity and Quality Center (www.apqc.org). Benchmarking and best-practice implementation have clearly emerged as legitimate and valuable managerial tools for promoting operational excellence.

Business Process Reengineering, Six Sigma Quality Programs, and TQM: Tools for Promoting Operating Excellence

In striving for operating excellence, many companies have also come to rely on three other potent management tools: business process reengineering, Six Sigma quality control techniques, and total quality management (TQM) programs. Indeed, these three tools have become globally pervasive techniques for implementing strategies keyed to cost reduction, defect-free manufacture, superior product quality, superior customer service, and total customer satisfaction. The following sections describe how business process reengineering, Six Sigma, and TQM can contribute to operating excellence and better strategy execution.

Business Process Reengineering   Companies scouring for ways to improve their operations have sometimes discovered that the execution of strategy-critical activities is hindered by an organizational arrangement where pieces of the activity are performed in several different functional departments, with no one manager or group being accountable for optimum performance of the entire activity. This can easily occur in such inherently cross-functional activities as customer service (which can involve personnel in order filling, warehousing and shipping, invoicing, accounts receivable, after-sale repair, and technical support), new product development (which can typically involve personnel in R&D, design and engineering, purchasing, manufacturing, and sales and marketing), and supply chain management (which cuts across such areas as purchasing, inventory management, manufacturing and assembly, warehousing, and shipping). Even if personnel in all the different departments and functional areas are inclined to collaborate closely, the activity may not end up being performed optimally or cost-efficiently, such that performance is adversely affected.

To address such shortcomings in strategy execution, many companies during the past decade have opted to *reengineer the work effort* by pulling the pieces of strategy-critical activities out of different departments and unifying their performance in a single department or cross-functional work group. Reorganizing the people who performed the pieces in functional departments into a close-knit group that has charge over the whole process and that can be held accountable for performing the activity in a cheaper, better, and/or more strategy-supportive fashion is called *business process reengineering.*[2]

When done properly, business process reengineering can produce dramatic operating benefits. In the order-processing section of General Electric's circuit breaker division, elapsed time from order receipt to delivery was cut from three weeks to three days by consolidating six production units into one, reducing a variety of former inventory and handling steps, automating the design system to replace a human custom-design process, and cutting the organizational layers between managers and workers from three to one. Productivity rose 20 percent in one year, and unit manufacturing costs dropped 30 percent. Northwest Water, a British utility, used business process reengineering to eliminate 45 work depots that served as home bases to crews who installed and repaired water and sewage lines and equipment. Now crews work directly from their vehicles, receiving assignments and reporting work completion from computer terminals in their trucks. Crew members are no longer employees but rather contractors to Northwest Water. These reengineering efforts not only eliminated the need for the work depots but also allowed Northwest Water to eliminate a big percentage of the bureaucratic personnel and supervisory organization that managed the crews.[3]

Since the early 1990s, reengineering of value chain activities has been undertaken at many companies in many industries all over the world, with excellent results being achieved at some companies.[4] While reengineering has produced only modest results in some instances, usually because of ineptness or lack of wholehearted commitment, reengineering has nonetheless proved itself as a useful tool for streamlining a company's work effort and moving closer to operational excellence.

Total Quality Management Programs

Total quality management (TQM) is a philosophy of managing a set of business practices that emphasizes continuous improvement in all phases of operations, 100 percent accuracy in performing tasks, involvement and empowerment of employees at all levels, team-based work design, benchmarking, and total customer satisfaction.[5] While TQM concentrates on the production of quality goods and fully satisfying customer expectations, it achieves its biggest successes when it is also extended to employee efforts in *all departments*—human resources, billing, R&D, engineering, accounting and records, and information systems—that may lack pressing, customer-driven incentives to improve. It involves reforming the corporate culture and shifting to a total quality/continuous improvement business philosophy that permeates every facet of the organization.[6] TQM aims at instilling enthusiasm and commitment to doing things right from the top to the bottom of the organization. Management's job is to kindle an companywide search for ways to improve, a search that involves all company personnel exercising initiative and using their ingenuity. TQM doctrine preaches that there's no such thing as "good enough" and that everyone has a responsibility to participate in continuous improvement. TQM is thus a race without a finish. Success comes from making little steps forward each day, a process that the Japanese call *kaizen*.

Core Concept
TQM entails creating a total quality culture bent on continuously improving the performance of every task and value chain activity.

TQM takes a fairly long time to show significant results—very little benefit emerges within the first six months. The long-term payoff of TQM, if it comes, depends heavily on management's success in implanting a culture within which TQM philosophies and practices can thrive. TQM is a managerial tool that has attracted numerous users and advocates over several decades, and it can deliver good results when used properly.

Six Sigma Quality Control

Six Sigma quality control consists of a disciplined, statistics-based system aimed at producing not more than 3.4 defects per million iterations for any business process—from manufacturing to customer transactions.[7] The Six Sigma process of define, measure, analyze, improve, and control (DMAIC) is an improvement system for existing processes falling below specification and needing incremental improvement. The Six Sigma process of define, measure, analyze, design, and verify (DMADV) is used to develop *new* processes or products at Six Sigma quality levels. Both Six Sigma processes are executed by personnel who have earned Six Sigma "green belts" and Six Sigma "black belts," and are overseen by personnel who have completed Six Sigma "master black belt" training. According to the Six Sigma Academy, personnel with black belts can save companies approximately $230,000 per project and can complete four to six projects a year.[8]

The statistical thinking underlying Six Sigma is based on the following three principles: All work is a process, all processes have variability, and all processes create data that explains variability.[9] To illustrate how these three principles drive the metrics of DMAIC, consider the case of a janitorial company that wants to improve the caliber of work done by its cleaning crews and thereby boost customer satisfaction. The janitorial company's Six Sigma team can pursue quality enhancement and continuous improvement via the DMAIC process as follows:

- *Define.* Because Six Sigma is aimed at reducing defects, the first step is to define what constitutes a defect. Six Sigma team members might decide that leaving streaks on windows is a defect because it is a source of customer dissatisfaction.

- *Measure.* The next step is to collect data to find out why, how, and how often this defect occurs. This might include a process flow map of the specific ways that cleaning crews go about the task of cleaning a commercial customer's windows. Other metrics may include recording what tools and cleaning products the crews use to clean windows.

- *Analyze.* After the data are gathered and the statistics analyzed, the company's Six Sigma team discovers that the tools and window-cleaning techniques of certain employees are better than those of other employees because their tools and procedures leave no streaked windows—a "best practice" for avoiding window streaking is thus identified and documented.

- *Improve.* The Six Sigma team implements the documented best practice as a standard way of cleaning windows.

- *Control.* The company teaches new and existing employees the best practice technique for window cleaning. Over time, there's significant improvement in customer satisfaction and increased business.

Six Sigma's DMAIC process is a particularly good vehicle for improving performance when there are *wide variations* in how well an activity is performed.[10] For instance, airlines striving to improve the on-time performance of their flights have more to gain from actions to curtail the number of flights that are late by more then 30 minutes than from actions to reduce the number of flights that are late by less than 5 minutes. Likewise, an overnight delivery service might have a 16-hour average delivery time, but if the actual delivery time varies around the 16-hour average from a low of 12 hours to a high of 26 hours such that 10 percent of its packages are delivered more than 6 hours late, then the company has a huge *reliability* problem.

Since the mid-1990s, thousands of companies and nonprofit organizations around the world have begun using Six Sigma programs to promote operating excellence. Such manufacturers as Motorola, Allied Signal, Caterpillar, DuPont, Xerox, Alcan Aluminum, BMW, Volkswagen, Nokia, Owens Corning, and Emerson Electric have employed Six Sigma techniques to good advantage in improving production quality. General Electric (GE), one of the most successful companies implementing Six Sigma training and pursuing Six Sigma perfection, estimated benefits on the order of $10 billion during the first five years of implementation. GE first began Six Sigma in 1995 after Motorola and Allied Signal blazed the Six Sigma trail. One of GE's successes was in its Lighting division, where Six Sigma was used to cut invoice defects and disputes by 98 percent, a particular benefit to Wal-Mart, the division's largest customer. GE Capital Mortgage improved the chances of a caller reaching a "live" GE person from 76 to 99 percent.[11] Illustration Capsule 12.2 describes Whirlpool's use of Six Sigma in its appliance business.

Illustration Capsule 12.2
Whirlpool's Use of Six Sigma to Promote Operating Excellence

Top management at Whirlpool Corporation, the leading global manufacturer and marketer of home appliances in 2005 with 50 manufacturing and technology centers around the globe and sales in some 170 countries, has a vision of Whirlpool appliances in "Every Home, Everywhere." One of management's chief objectives in pursuing this vision is to build unmatched customer loyalty to the Whirlpool brand. Whirlpool's strategy to win the hearts and minds of appliance buyers the world over has been to produce and market appliances with top-notch quality and innovative features that users will find appealing. In addition, Whirlpool's strategy has been to offer a wide selection of models (recognizing that buyer tastes and needs differ) and to strive for low-cost production efficiency, thereby enabling Whirlpool to price its products competitively. Executing this strategy at Whirlpool's operations in North America (where it is the market leader), Latin America (where it is also the market leader), Europe (where it ranks third), and Asia (where it number one in India and has a foothold with huge growth opportunities elsewhere) has involved a strong focus on continuous improvement, lean manufacturing capabilities, and a drive for operating excellence. To marshal the efforts of Whirlpool's 68,000 employees in executing the strategy successfully, management developed a comprehensive Operational Excellence program with Six Sigma as one of the centerpieces.

The Operational Excellence initiative, which began in the 1990s, incorporated Six Sigma techniques to improve the quality of Whirlpool products, while at the same time lowering costs and trimming the time it took to get product innovations into the marketplace. The Six Sigma program helped Whirlpool save $175 million in manufacturing costs in its first three years.

To sustain the productivity gains and cost savings, Whirlpool embedded Six Sigma practices within each of its manufacturing facilities worldwide and instilled a culture based on Six Sigma and lean manufacturing skills and capabilities. Beginning in 2002, each of Whirlpool's operating units began taking the Six Sigma initiative to a higher level by first placing the needs of the customer at the center of every function—R&D, technology, manufacturing, marketing, and administrative support—and then striving to consistently improve quality levels while eliminating all unnecessary costs. The company systematically went through every aspect of its business with the view that company personnel should perform every activity at every level in a manner that delivers value to the customer and that leads to continuous improvement on how things are done.

Whirlpool management believes that the company's Operational Excellence process has been a major contributor in sustaining the company's global leadership in appliances.

Source: Information posted at www.whirlpool.com (accessed September 25, 2003, and November 15, 2005).

Six Sigma is, however, not just a quality-enhancing tool for manufacturers. At one company, product sales personnel typically wined and dined customers to close their deals.[12] But the costs of such entertaining were viewed as excessively high in many instances. A Six Sigma project that examined sales data found that although face time with customers was important, wining, dining, and other types of entertainment were not. The data showed that regular face time helped close sales, but that time could be spent over a cup of coffee instead of golfing at a resort or taking clients to expensive restaurants. In addition, analysis showed that too much face time with customers was counterproductive. A regularly scheduled customer picnic was found to be detrimental to closing sales because it was held at a busy time of year, when customers preferred not to be away from their offices. Changing the manner in which prospective customers were wooed resulted in a 10 percent increase in sales.

A Milwaukee hospital used Six Sigma to map the process as prescriptions originated with a doctor's writeup, were filled by the hospital pharmacy, and then administered by nurses. DMAIC analysis revealed that most mistakes came from misreading the doctor's handwriting.[13] The hospital implemented a program requiring doctors to type the prescription into a computer, which slashed the number of errors dramatically.

A problem tailor-made for Six Sigma occurs in the insurance industry, where it is common for top agents to outsell poor agents by a factor of 10 to 1 or more. If insurance executives offer a trip to Hawaii in a monthly contest to motivate low-performing agents, the typical result is to motivate top agents to be even more productive and make the performance gap even wider. A DMAIC Six Sigma project to reduce the variation in the performance of agents and correct the problem of so many low-performing agents would begin by measuring the performance of all agents, perhaps discovering that the top 20 percent sell 7 times more policies than the bottom 40 percent. Six Sigma analysis would then consider such steps as mapping how top agents spend their day, investigating the factors that distinguish top performers from low performers, learning what techniques training specialists have employed in converting low-performing agents into high performers, and examining how the hiring process could be improved to avoid hiring underperformers in the first place. The next step would be to *test* proposed solutions—better training methods or psychological profiling to identify and weed out candidates likely to be poor performers—to identify and measure which alternative solutions really work, which don't, and why. Only those actions that prove statistically beneficial are then introduced on a wide scale. The DMAIC method thus entails empirical analysis to diagnose the problem (*design, measure, analyze*), test alternative solutions (*improve*) and then *control* the variability in how well the activity is performed by implementing actions shown to truly fix the problem.

A company that systematically applies Six Sigma methods to its value chain, activity by activity, can make major strides in improving the proficiency with which its strategy is executed. As is the case with TQM, obtaining managerial commitment, establishing a quality culture, and fully involving employees are the three most intractable challenges encountered in the implementation of Six Sigma quality programs.[14]

The Difference between Business Process Reengineering and Continuous Improvement Programs Like Six Sigma and TQM

Business process reengineering and continuous improvement efforts like TQM and Six Sigma both aim at improved efficiency and reduced costs, better product quality, and greater customer satisfaction. The essential difference between business process reengineering and continuous improvement programs is that reengineering aims at *quantum gains* on the order of 30 to 50 percent or more whereas total quality programs stress *incremental progress,* striving for inch-by-inch gains again and again in a never-ending stream. The two approaches to improved performance of value chain activities and operating excellence are not mutually exclusive; it makes sense to use them in tandem. Reengineering can be used first to produce a good basic design that yields quick, dramatic improvements in performing a business process. Total quality programs can then be used as a follow-on to reengineering and/or best-practice implementation, delivering gradual improvements. Such a two-pronged approach to implementing operational excellence is like a marathon race in which you run the first four miles as fast as you can, then gradually pick up speed the remainder of the way.

> Business process reengineering aims at one-time quantum improvement; continuous improvement programs like TQM and Six Sigma aim at ongoing incremental improvements.

Capturing the Benefits of Initiatives to Improve Operations

Usually, the biggest beneficiaries of benchmarking and best-practice initiatives, reengineering, TQM, and Six Sigma are companies that view such programs not as ends in themselves but as tools for implementing and executing company strategy more effectively. The skimpiest payoffs occur when company managers seize them as something worth trying—novel ideas that could improve things. In most such instances, they result in strategy-blind efforts to simply manage better. There's an important lesson here. Best practices, TQM, Six Sigma quality, and reengineering all need to be seen and used as part of a bigger-picture effort to execute strategy proficiently. Only strategy can point to which value chain activities matter and what performance targets make the most sense. Absent a strategic framework, managers lack the context in which to fix things that really matter to business-unit performance and competitive success.

Core Concept
The purpose of using benchmarking, best practices, business process reengineering, TQM, Six Sigma, or other operational improvement programs is to improve the performance of strategy-critical activities and enhance strategy execution.

To get the most from initiatives to better execute strategy, managers must have a clear idea of what specific outcomes really matter. Is it a Six Sigma or lower defect rate, high on-time delivery percentages, low overall costs relative to rivals, high percentages of pleased customers and few customer complaints, shorter cycle times, a higher percentage of revenues coming from recently introduced products, or what? Benchmarking best-in-industry and best-in-world performance of most or all value chain activities provides a realistic basis for setting internal performance milestones and longer-range targets.

Then comes the managerial task of building a total quality culture genuinely committed to achieving the performance outcomes that strategic success requires.[15] Managers can take the following action steps to realize full value from TQM or Six Sigma initiatives:[16]

1. Visible, unequivocal, and unyielding commitment to total quality and continuous improvement, including a quality vision and specific, measurable objectives for boosting quality and making continuous improvement.

2. Nudging people toward quality-supportive behaviors by:
   a. Screening job applicants rigorously and hiring only those with attitudes and aptitudes right for quality-based performance.
   b. Providing quality training for most employees.
   c. Using teams and team-building exercises to reinforce and nurture individual effort (the creation of a quality culture is facilitated when teams become more cross-functional, multitask-oriented, and increasingly self-managed).
   d. Recognizing and rewarding individual and team efforts regularly and systematically.
   e. Stressing prevention (doing it right the first time), not inspection (instituting ways to correct mistakes).

3. Empowering employees so that authority for delivering great service or improving products is in the hands of the doers rather than the overseers—*improving quality has to be seen as part of everyone's job.*

4. Using online systems to provide all relevant parties with the latest best practices and actual experiences with them, thereby speeding the diffusion and adoption of best practices throughout the organization and also allowing them to exchange data and opinions about how to upgrade the prevailing best practices.

5. Preaching that performance can, and must, be improved because competitors are not resting on their laurels and customers are always looking for something better.

If the targeted performance measures are appropriate to the strategy and if all organizational members (top executives, middle managers, professional staff, and line employees) buy into a culture of operating excellence, then a company's work climate becomes decidedly more conducive to proficient strategy execution. Benchmarking, best-practice implementation, reengineering, TQM, and Six Sigma initiatives can greatly enhance a company's product design, cycle time, production costs, product quality, service, customer satisfaction, and other operating capabilities—and they can even deliver competitive advantage.[17] Not only do improvements from such initiatives add up over time and strengthen organizational capabilities, but the benefits they produce have hard-to-imitate aspects. While it is relatively easy for rivals to undertake benchmarking, process improvement, and quality training, it is much more difficult and time-consuming for them to instill a deeply ingrained culture of operating excellence (as occurs when such techniques are religiously employed) and top management exhibits lasting commitment to operational excellence throughout the organization.

INSTALLING INFORMATION AND OPERATING SYSTEMS

Company strategies can't be executed well without a number of internal systems for business operations. Southwest, American, Northwest, Delta, and other major airlines cannot hope to provide passenger-pleasing service without a user-friendly online reservation system, an accurate and speedy baggage handling system, and a strict aircraft maintenance program that minimizes equipment failures requiring at-the-gate service and delaying plane departures. FedEx has internal communication systems that allow it to coordinate its over 70,000 vehicles in handling an average of 5.5 million packages a day. Its leading-edge flight operations systems allow a single controller to direct as many as 200 of FedEx's 650 aircraft simultaneously, overriding their flight plans should weather or other special emergencies arise. In addition, FedEx has created a series of e-business tools for customers that allow them to ship and track packages online (either at FedEx's Web site or on their own company intranets or Web sites), create address books, review shipping history, generate custom reports, simplify customer billing, reduce internal warehousing and inventory management costs, purchase goods and services from suppliers, and respond quickly to changing customer demands. All of FedEx's systems support the company's strategy of providing businesses and individuals with a broad array of package delivery services (from premium next-day to economical five-day deliveries) and boosting its competitiveness against United Parcel Service, Airborne Express, and the U.S. Postal Service.

Otis Elevator, the world's largest manufacturer of elevators, has 24-hour communications service centers for customers called OtisLine to coordinate its maintenance efforts for some 1.5 million elevators and escalators it has installed worldwide.[18] Electronic monitors installed on each user's site can detect when an elevator or escalator has any of 325 problems and will automatically place a service call to the nearest service center location. Trained operators take all trouble calls, input critical information on a computer screen, and can dispatch trained mechanics from 325 locations across the world to the local trouble spot when needed. All customers have online access to performance data on each of their Otis elevators. More than 80 percent of mechanics in North America carry Web-enabled phones connected to e*Service that transport needed information quickly and allow mechanics to update data in Otis computers for future reference. The OtisLine system helps keep outage times to less than two and a half hours. All the trouble-call data is relayed to design and manufacturing personnel, allowing them to quickly alter design specifications or manufacturing procedures when needed to correct recurring problems.

Amazon.com ships customer orders from fully computerized, 1,300-by-600-foot warehouses containing about 3 million books, CDs, toys, and houseware items.[19] The warehouses are so technologically sophisticated that they require about as many lines of code to run as Amazon's Web site does. Using complex picking algorithms, computers initiate the order-picking process by sending signals to workers' wireless receivers, telling them which items to pick off the shelves in which order. Computers also generate data on misboxed items, chute backup times, line speed, worker productivity, and shipping weights on orders. Systems are upgraded regularly, and productivity improvements are aggressively pursued. In 2003 Amazon's six warehouses were able to handle three times the volume handled in 1999 at costs averaging 10 percent of revenues (versus 20 percent in 1999); in addition, they turned their inventory over 20 times annually in an industry whose average was 15 turns. Amazon's warehouse efficiency and cost per order filled was so low that one of the fastest-growing and most profitable parts of Amazon's business was using its warehouses to run the e-commerce operations of Toys "R" Us and Target.

Most telephone companies, electric utilities, and TV broadcasting systems have online monitoring systems to spot transmission problems within seconds and increase the reliability of their services. At eBay, there are systems for real-time monitoring of new listings, bidding activity, Web site traffic, and page views. Kaiser Permanente spent $3 billion to digitize the medical records of its 8.2 million members so that it could manage patient care more efficiently.[20] IBM has created a database of 36,000 employee profiles that enable it to better assign the most qualified IBM consultant to the projects it is doing for clients. In businesses such as public accounting and management consulting, where large numbers of professional staff need cutting-edge technical know-how, companies have developed systems that identify when it is time for certain employees to attend training programs to update their skills and know-how. Many companies have cataloged best-practice information on their intranets to promote faster transfer and implementation throughout the organization.[21]

Well-conceived, state-of-the-art operating systems not only enable better strategy execution but also strengthen organizational capabilities—perhaps enough to provide a competitive edge over rivals. For example, a company with a differentiation strategy based on superior quality has added capability if it has systems for training personnel in quality techniques, tracking product quality at each production step, and ensuring that all goods shipped meet quality standards. A company striving to be a low-cost provider is competitively stronger if it has a benchmarking system that identifies opportunities to implement best practices and drive costs out of the business. Fast-growing companies get an important assist from having capabilities in place to recruit and train new employees in large numbers and from investing in infrastructure that gives them the capability to handle rapid growth as it occurs. It is nearly always better to put infrastructure and support systems in place before they are actually needed than to have to scramble to catch up to customer demand.

Core Concept

State-of-the-art support systems can be a basis for competitive advantage if they give a firm capabilities that rivals can't match.

Instituting Adequate Information Systems, Performance Tracking, and Controls

Accurate and timely information about daily operations is essential if managers are to gauge how well the strategy execution process is proceeding. Information systems need to cover five broad areas: (1) customer data, (2) operations data, (3) employee data, (4) supplier/partner/collaborative ally data, and (5) financial performance data. All key strategic performance indicators have to be tracked and reported as often as practical. Monthly profit-and-loss statements and monthly statistical summaries, long the norm, are fast being replaced by daily statistical updates and even up-to-the-minute performance monitoring that online technology makes possible. Many retail companies have automated online systems that generate daily sales reports for each store and maintain up-to-the-minute inventory and sales records on each item. Manufacturing plants typically generate daily production reports and track labor productivity on every shift. Many retailers and manufacturers have online data systems connecting them with their suppliers that monitor the status of inventories, track shipments and deliveries, and measure defect rates.

Real-time information systems permit company managers to stay on top of implementation initiatives and daily operations, and to intervene if things seem to be drifting off course. Tracking key performance indicators, gathering information from operating personnel, quickly identifying and diagnosing problems, and taking corrective actions are all integral pieces of the process of managing strategy implementation and execution and exercising adequate organization control. A number of companies have recently begun creating "electronic scorecards" for senior managers that gather daily or weekly statistics from different databases about inventory, sales, costs, and sales trends; such information enables these managers to easily stay abreast of what's happening and make better decisions on a real-time basis.[22] Telephone companies have elaborate information systems to measure signal quality, connection times, interrupts, wrong connections, billing errors, and other measures of reliability that affect customer service and satisfaction. To track and manage the quality of passenger service, airlines have information systems to monitor gate delays, on-time departures and arrivals, baggage handling times, lost baggage complaints, stockouts on meals and drinks, overbookings, and maintenance delays and failures. Continental Airlines has an online system that alerts the company when planes arrive late and assesses whether connecting flights need to be delayed slightly for late-arriving passengers and carts sent to the gate to shorten the time it will take for passengers to reach their connecting flight. British Petroleum (BP) has outfitted rail cars carrying hazardous materials with sensors and global positioning system (GPS) devices so that it can track the status, location, and other information about these shipments via satellite and relay the data to its corporate intranet. Companies that rely on empowered customer-contact personnel to act promptly and creatively in pleasing customers have installed online information systems that put essential customer data on their computer monitors with a few keystrokes so that they can respond effectively to customer inquiries and deliver personalized customer service.

Statistical information gives managers a feel for the numbers, briefings and meetings provide a feel for the latest developments and emerging issues, and personal contacts add a feel for the people dimension. All are good barometers. Managers have to identify problem areas and deviations from plan before they can take actions to get the organization back on course, by either improving the approaches to strategy execution or fine-tuning the strategy. Jeff Bezos, Amazon's CEO, is an ardent proponent of managing by the numbers—as he puts it, "Math-based decisions always trump opinion and judgment. The trouble with most corporations is that they make judgment-based decisions when data-based decisions could be made."[23]

> **Core Concept**
> Having good information systems and operating data are integral to competent strategy execution and operating excellence.

Exercising Adequate Controls over Empowered Employees

Another important aspect of effectively managing and controlling the strategy execution process is monitoring the performance of empowered workers to see that they are acting within the specified limits.[24] Leaving empowered employees to their own devices in meeting performance standards without appropriate checks and balances can expose an organization to excessive risk.[25] Instances abound of employees' decisions or behavior having gone awry, sometimes costing a company huge sums or producing lawsuits aside from just generating embarrassing publicity.

Managers shouldn't have to devote big chunks of their time to making sure that the decisions and behavior of empowered employees stay between the white lines—this would defeat the major purpose of empowerment and, in effect, lead to the reinstatement of a managerial bureaucracy engaged in constant over-the-shoulder supervision. Yet managers have a clear responsibility to exercise sufficient control over empowered employees to protect the company against out-of-bounds behavior and unwelcome surprises. Scrutinizing daily and weekly operating statistics is one of the important ways in which managers can monitor the results that flow from the actions of empowered subordinates—if the operating results flowing from the actions of empowered employees look good, then it is reasonable to assume that empowerment is working.

But close monitoring of real-time or daily operating performance is only one of the control tools at management's disposal. Another valuable lever of control in companies that rely on empowered employees, especially in those that use self-managed work groups or other such teams, is peer-based control. Most team members feel responsible for the success of the whole team and tend to be relatively intolerant of any team member's behavior that weakens team performance or puts team accomplishments at risk (especially when team performance has a big impact on each team member's compensation). Because peer evaluation is such a powerful control device, companies organized into teams can remove some layers of the management hierarchy and rely on strong peer pressure to keep team members operating between the white lines. This is especially true when a company has the information systems capability to monitor team performance daily or in real time.

TYING REWARDS AND INCENTIVES TO GOOD STRATEGY EXECUTION

It is important for both organization units and individuals to be enthusiastically committed to executing strategy and achieving performance targets. Managers typically use an assortment of motivational techniques and rewards to enlist companywide commitment to executing the strategic plan. A manager has to do more than just talk to everyone about how important new strategic practices and performance targets are to the organization's well-being. No matter how inspiring, talk seldom commands people's best efforts for long. *To get employees' sustained, energetic commitment, management has to be resourceful in designing and using motivational incentives—both monetary and nonmonetary.* The more a manager understands what motivates subordinates and the more he or she relies on motivational incentives as a tool for achieving the targeted strategic and financial results, the greater will be employees' commitment to good day-in, day-out strategy execution and achievement of performance targets.[26]

Core Concept

A properly designed reward structure is management's most powerful tool for mobilizing organizational commitment to successful strategy execution.

Strategy-Facilitating Motivational Practices

Financial incentives generally head the list of motivating tools for trying to gain wholehearted employee commitment to good strategy execution and operating excellence. Monetary rewards generally include some combination of base pay increases, performance bonuses, profit-sharing plans, stock awards, company contributions to employee

401(k) or retirement plans, and piecework incentives (in the case of production workers). But successful companies and managers normally make extensive use of such nonmonetary carrot-and-stick incentives as frequent words of praise (or constructive criticism), special recognition at company gatherings or in the company newsletter, more (or less) job security, stimulating assignments, opportunities to transfer to attractive locations, increased (or decreased) autonomy, and rapid promotion (or the risk of being sidelined in a routine or dead-end job). In addition, companies use a host of other motivational approaches to make their workplaces more appealing and spur stronger employee commitment to the strategy execution process; the following are some of the most important:[27]

> **Core Concept**
> One of management's biggest strategy-executing challenges is to employ motivational techniques that build wholehearted commitment to operating excellence and winning attitudes among employees.

- *Providing attractive perks and fringe benefits*—The various options here include full coverage of health insurance premiums; full tuition reimbursement for work on college degrees; paid vacation time of three or four weeks; on-site child care at major facilities; on-site gym facilities and massage therapists; getaway opportunities at company-owned recreational facilities (beach houses, ranches, resort condos); personal concierge services; subsidized cafeterias and free lunches; casual dress every day; personal travel services; paid sabbaticals; maternity leaves; paid leaves to care for ill family members; telecommuting; compressed workweeks (four 10-hour days instead of five 8-hour days); reduced summer hours; college scholarships for children; on-the-spot bonuses for exceptional performance; and relocation services.

- *Relying on promotion from within whenever possible*—This practice helps bind workers to their employer and employers to their workers; plus, it is an incentive for good performance. Promotion from within also helps ensure that people in positions of responsibility actually know something about the business, technology, and operations they are managing.

- *Making sure that the ideas and suggestions of employees are valued and that those with merit are promptly acted on*—Many companies find that their best ideas for nuts-and-bolts operating improvements come from the suggestions of employees. Moreover, research indicates that the moves of many companies to push decision making down the line and empower employees increases employee motivation and satisfaction, as well as boosting their productivity. The use of self-managed teams has much the same effect.

- *Creating a work atmosphere in which there is genuine sincerity, caring, and mutual respect among workers and between management and employees*—A "family" work environment in which people are on a first-name basis and there is strong camaraderie promotes teamwork and cross-unit collaboration.

- *Stating the strategic vision in inspirational terms that make employees feel they are a part of doing something very worthwhile in a larger social sense*—There's strong motivating power associated with giving people a chance to be part of something exciting and personally satisfying. Jobs with noble purpose tend to turn employees on. At Pfizer, Merck, and most other pharmaceutical companies, it is the notion of helping sick people get well and restoring patients to full life. At Whole Foods Market (a natural foods grocery chain), it is helping customers discover good eating habits and thus improving human health and nutrition.

- *Sharing information with employees about financial performance, strategy, operational measures, market conditions, and competitors' actions*—Broad disclosure and prompt communication send the message that managers trust their workers. Keeping employees in the dark denies them information useful to performing their job, prevents them from being "students of the business," and usually turns them off.

- *Having knockout facilities*—A workplace with appealing features and amenities usually has decidedly positive effects on employee morale and productivity.

- *Being flexible in how the company approaches people management (motivation, compensation, recognition, recruitment) in multinational, multicultural environments*—There is usually some merit in giving local managers in foreign operations to adapt their motivation, compensation, recognition, and recruitment practices to fit local customs, habits, values, and business practices rather than insisting on consistent people-management practices worldwide. But the one area where consistency is essential is conveying the message that the organization values people of all races and cultural backgrounds and that discrimination of any sort will not be tolerated.

For specific examples of the motivational tactics employed by several prominent companies (many of which appear on *Fortune*'s list of "The 100 Best Companies to Work for in America"), see Illustration Capsule 12.3.

Striking the Right Balance between Rewards and Punishment

While most approaches to motivation, compensation, and people management accentuate the positive, companies also embellish positive rewards with the risk of punishment. At General Electric, McKinsey & Company, several global public accounting firms, and other companies that look for and expect top-notch individual performance, there's an "up-or-out" policy—managers and professionals whose performance is not good enough to warrant promotion are first denied bonuses and stock awards and eventually weeded out. A number of companies deliberately give employees heavy workloads and tight deadlines—personnel are pushed hard to achieve "stretch" objectives and expected to put in long hours (nights and weekends if need be). At most companies, senior executives and key personnel in underperforming units are pressured to boost performance to acceptable levels and keep it there or risk being replaced.

As a general rule, it is unwise to take off the pressure for good individual and group performance or play down the stress, anxiety, and adverse consequences of shortfalls in performance. There is no evidence that a no-pressure/no-adverse-consequences work environment leads to superior strategy execution or operating excellence. As the CEO of a major bank put it, "There's a deliberate policy here to create a level of anxiety. Winners usually play like they're one touchdown behind."[28] *High-performing organizations nearly always have a cadre of ambitious people who relish the opportunity to climb the ladder of success, love a challenge, thrive in a performance-oriented environment, and find some competition and pressure useful to satisfy their own drives for personal recognition, accomplishment, and self-satisfaction.*

However, if an organization's motivational approaches and reward structure induce too much stress, internal competitiveness, job insecurity, and unpleasant consequences, the impact on workforce morale and strategy execution can be counterproductive. Evidence shows that managerial initiatives to improve strategy execution should incorporate more positive than negative motivational elements because when cooperation is

Illustration Capsule 12.3

What Companies Do to Motivate and Reward Employees

Companies have come up with an impressive variety of motivational and reward practices to help create a work environment that energizes employees and promotes better strategy execution. Here's a sampling of what companies are doing:

- Google has a sprawling four-building complex known as the Googleplex where the company's roughly 1,000 employees are provided with free food, unlimited ice cream, pool and Ping-Pong tables, and complimentary massages—management built the Googleplex to be "a dream environment." Moreover, the company gives its employees the ability to spend 20 percent of their work time on any outside activity.

- Lincoln Electric, widely known for its piecework pay scheme and incentive bonus plan, rewards individual productivity by paying workers for each nondefective piece produced. Workers have to correct quality problems on their own time—defects in products used by customers can be traced back to the worker who caused them. Lincoln's piecework plan motivates workers to pay attention to both quality and volume produced. In addition, the company sets aside a substantial portion of its profits above a specified base for worker bonuses. To determine bonus size, Lincoln Electric rates each worker on four equally important performance measures: dependability, quality, output, and ideas and cooperation. The higher a worker's merit rating, the higher the incentive bonus earned; the most highly rated workers in good profit years receive bonuses of as much as 110 percent of their piecework compensation.

- At JM Family Enterprises, a Toyota distributor in Florida, employees get a great lease on new Toyotas and are flown to the Bahamas for cruises on the 172-foot company yacht. The company's office facility has such amenities as a heated lap pool, a fitness center, and a free nail salon. Employees get free prescriptions delivered by a "pharmacy concierge" and professionally made take-home dinners.

- Amazon.com hands out Just Do It awards to employees who do something they think will help Amazon *without* getting their boss's permission. The action has to be well thought through but doesn't have to succeed.

- Nordstrom, widely regarded for its superior in-house customer service experience, typically pays its retail salespeople an hourly wage higher than the prevailing rates paid by other department store chains plus a commission on each sale. Spurred by a culture that encourages salespeople to go all out to satisfy customers and to seek out and promote new fashion ideas, Nordstrom salespeople often earn twice the average incomes of sales employees at competing stores. Nordstrom's rules for employees are simple: "Rule #1: Use your good judgment in all situations. There will be no additional rules."

- At W. L. Gore (the maker of Gore-Tex), employees get to choose what project/team they work on and each team member's compensation is based on other team members' rankings of his or her contribution to the enterprise.

- At Ukrop's Super Markets, a family-owned chain, stores stay closed on Sunday; the company pays out 20 percent of pretax profits to employees in the form of quarterly bonuses; and the company picks up the membership tab for employees if they visit their health club 30 times a quarter.

- At biotech leader Amgen, employees get 16 paid holidays, generous vacation time, tuition reimbursements up to $10,000, on-site massages, a discounted car wash, and the convenience of shopping at on-site farmers' markets.

- At Synovus, a financial services and credit card company, the company adds as much as 20 percent annually to each employee's compensation via a "wealth-building" program that includes a 401(k) and profit sharing; plus, it holds an annual bass fishing tournament.

- At specialty chipmaker Xilinx, new hires receive stock option grants; the CEO responds promptly to employee e-mails, and during hard times management takes a 20 percent pay cut instead of laying off employees.

Sources: Fortune's lists of the 100 best companies to work for in America, 2002, 2004, and 2005 (accessed November 14, 2005); Jefferson Graham, "The Search Engine That Could," *USA Today,* August 26, 2003, p. B3; and Fred Vogelstein, "Winning the Amazon Way," *Fortune* (May 26, 2003), p. 73.

positively enlisted and rewarded, rather than strong-armed by orders and threats (implicit or explicit), people tend to respond with more enthusiasm, dedication, creativity, and initiative. Something of a middle ground is generally optimal—not only handing out decidedly positive rewards for meeting or beating performance targets but also imposing sufficiently negative consequences (if only withholding rewards) when actual performance falls short of the target. But the negative consequences of underachievement should never be so severe or demoralizing as to impede a renewed and determined effort to overcome existing obstacles and hit the targets in upcoming periods.

Linking the Reward System to Strategically Relevant Performance Outcomes

The most dependable way to keep people focused on strategy execution and the achievement of performance targets is to *generously* reward and recognize individuals and groups who meet or beat performance targets and deny rewards and recognition to those who don't. *The use of incentives and rewards is the single most powerful tool management has to win strong employee commitment to diligent, competent strategy execution and operating excellence.* Decisions on salary increases, incentive compensation, promotions, key assignments, and the ways and means of awarding praise and recognition are potent attention-getting, commitment-generating devices.

Core Concept
A properly designed reward system aligns the well-being of organization members with their contributions to competent strategy execution and the achievement of performance targets.

Such decisions seldom escape the closest employee scrutiny, saying more about what is expected and who is considered to be doing a good job than about any other factor. Hence, when meeting or beating strategic and financial targets become *the dominating basis* for designing incentives, evaluating individual and group efforts, and handing out rewards, company personnel quickly grasp that it is in their own self-interest to do their best in executing the strategy competently and achieving key performance targets.[29] Indeed, it is usually through the company's system of incentives and rewards that workforce members emotionally ratify their commitment to the company's strategy execution effort.

Ideally, performance targets should be set for every organization unit, every manager, every team or work group, and perhaps every employee—targets that measure whether strategy execution is progressing satisfactorily. If the company's strategy is to be a low-cost provider, the incentive system must reward actions and achievements that result in lower costs. If the company has a differentiation strategy predicated on superior quality and service, the incentive system must reward such outcomes as Six Sigma defect rates, infrequent need for product repair, low numbers of customer complaints, speedy order processing and delivery, and high levels of customer satisfaction. If a company's growth is predicated on a strategy of new product innovation, incentives should be tied to factors such as the percentages of revenues and profits coming from newly introduced products.

Illustration Capsule 12.4 provides two vivid examples of how companies have designed incentives linked directly to outcomes reflecting good strategy execution.

The Importance of Basing Incentives on Achieving Results, Not on Performing Assigned Duties   To create a strategy-supportive system of rewards and incentives, a company must emphasize rewarding people for accomplishing results, not for just dutifully performing assigned tasks. Focusing jobholders' attention and energy on what to *achieve* as opposed to what to *do* makes the work

Illustration Capsule 12.4

Nucor and Bank One: Two Companies that Tie Incentives Directly to Strategy Execution

The strategy at Nucor Corporation, now the biggest steel producer in the United States, is to be *the* low-cost producer of steel products. Because labor costs are a significant fraction of total cost in the steel business, successful implementation of Nucor's low-cost leadership strategy entails achieving lower labor costs per ton of steel than competitors' costs. Nucor management uses an incentive system to promote high worker productivity and drive labor costs per ton below rivals.' Each plant's workforce is organized into production teams (each assigned to perform particular functions), and weekly production targets are established for each team. Base pay scales are set at levels comparable to wages for similar manufacturing jobs in the local areas where Nucor has plants, but workers can earn a 1 percent bonus for each 1 percent that their output exceeds target levels. If a production team exceeds its weekly production target by 10 percent, team members receive a 10 percent bonus in their next paycheck; if a team exceeds its quota by 20 percent, team members earn a 20 percent bonus. Bonuses, paid every two weeks, are based on the prior two weeks' actual production levels measured against the targets.

Nucor's piece-rate incentive plan has produced impressive results. The production teams put forth exceptional effort; it is not uncommon for most teams to beat their weekly production targets anywhere from 20 to 50 percent. When added to their base pay, the bonuses earned by Nucor workers make Nucor's workforce among the highest-paid in the U.S. steel industry. From a management perspective, the incentive system has resulted in Nucor having labor productivity levels 10 to 20 percent above the average of the unionized workforces at several of its largest rivals, which in turn has given Nucor a significant labor cost advantage over most rivals.

At Bank One (recently acquired by JP Morgan Chase), management believed it was strategically important to boost its customer satisfaction ratings in order to enhance its competitiveness vis-à-vis rivals. Targets were set for customer satisfaction and monitoring systems for measuring customer satisfaction at each branch office were put in place. Then, to motivate branch office personnel to be more attentive in trying to please customers and also to signal that top management was truly committed to achieving higher levels of overall customer satisfaction, top management opted to tie pay scales in each branch office to that branch's customer satisfaction rating—the higher the branch's ratings, the higher that branch's pay scales. Management believed its shift from a theme of equal pay for equal work to one of equal pay for equal performance contributed significantly to its customer satisfaction priority.

environment results-oriented. It is flawed management to tie incentives and rewards to satisfactory performance of duties and activities in hopes that the by-products will be the desired business outcomes and company achievements.[30] In any job, performing assigned tasks is not equivalent to achieving intended outcomes. Diligently showing up for work and attending to one's job assignment does not, by itself, guarantee results. As any student knows, the fact that an instructor teaches and students go to class doesn't necessarily mean that the students are learning. The enterprise of education would no doubt take on a different character if teachers were rewarded for the result of student learning rather than for the activity of teaching.

> It is folly to reward one outcome in hopes of getting another outcome.

Incentive compensation for top executives is typically tied to such financial measures as revenue and earnings growth, stock price performance, return on investment, and creditworthiness and perhaps such strategic measures as market share, product quality, or customer satisfaction. However, incentives for department heads, teams, and individual workers may be tied to performance outcomes more closely related to their strategic area of responsibility. In manufacturing, incentive compensation may be tied to unit manufacturing costs, on-time production and shipping, defect rates,

Core Concept
The role of the reward system is to align the well-being of organization members with realizing the company's vision, so that organization members benefit by helping the company execute its strategy competently and fully satisfy customers.

the number and extent of work stoppages due to labor disagreements and equipment breakdowns, and so on. In sales and marketing, there may be incentives for achieving dollar sales or unit volume targets, market share, sales penetration of each target customer group, the fate of newly introduced products, the frequency of customer complaints, the number of new accounts acquired, and customer satisfaction. Which performance measures to base incentive compensation on depends on the situation—the priority placed on various financial and strategic objectives, the requirements for strategic and competitive success, and what specific results are needed in different facets of the business to keep strategy execution on track.

Guidelines for Designing Incentive Compensation Systems   The concepts and company experiences discussed above yield the following prescriptive guidelines for creating an incentive compensation system to help drive successful strategy execution:

1. *Make the performance payoff a major, not minor, piece of the total compensation package.* Payoffs must be at least 10 to 12 percent of base salary to have much impact. Incentives that amount to 20 percent or more of total compensation are big attention-getters, likely to really drive individual or team effort; incentives amounting to less than 5 percent of total compensation have comparatively weak motivational impact. Moreover, the payoff for high-performing individuals and teams must be meaningfully greater than the payoff for average performers, and the payoff for average performers meaningfully bigger than for below-average performers.

2. *Have incentives that extend to all managers and all workers, not just top management.* It is a gross miscalculation to expect that lower-level managers and employees will work their hardest to hit performance targets just so a few senior executives can get lucrative rewards.

3. *Administer the reward system with scrupulous objectivity and fairness.* If performance standards are set unrealistically high or if individual/group performance evaluations are not accurate and well documented, dissatisfaction with the system will overcome any positive benefits.

4. *Tie incentives to performance outcomes directly linked to good strategy execution and financial performance.* Incentives should never be paid just because people are thought to be "doing a good job" or because they "work hard." Performance evaluation based on factors not tightly related to good strategy execution signal that either the strategic plan is incomplete (because important performance targets were left out) or management's real agenda is something other than the stated strategic and financial objectives.

5. *Make sure that the performance targets each individual or team is expected to achieve involve outcomes that the individual or team can personally affect.* The role of incentives is to enhance individual commitment and channel behavior in beneficial directions. This role is not well served when the performance measures by which company personnel are judged are outside their arena of influence.

6. *Keep the time between achieving the target performance outcome and the payment of the reward as short as possible.* Companies like Nucor and Continental Airlines have discovered that weekly or monthly payments for good performance work much better than annual payments. Nucor pays weekly bonuses based on

prior-week production levels; Continental awards employees a monthly bonus for each month that on-time flight performance meets or beats a specified percentage companywide. Annual bonus payouts work best for higher-level managers and for situations where target outcome relates to overall company profitability or stock price performance.

7. *Make liberal use of nonmonetary rewards; don't rely solely on monetary rewards.* When used properly, money is a great motivator, but there are also potent advantages to be gained from praise, special recognition, handing out plum assignments, and so on.

8. *Absolutely avoid skirting the system to find ways to reward effort rather than results.* Whenever actual performance falls short of targeted performance, there's merit in determining whether the causes are attributable to subpar individual/ group performance or to circumstances beyond the control of those responsible. An argument can be made that exceptions should be made in giving rewards to people who've tried hard, gone the extra mile, yet still come up short because of circumstances beyond their control. The problem with making exceptions for unknowable, uncontrollable, or unforeseeable circumstances is that once good excuses start to creep into justifying rewards for subpar results, the door is open for all kinds of reasons why actual performance failed to match targeted performance. A "no excuses" standard is more evenhanded and certainly easier to administer.

Once the incentives are designed, they have to be communicated and explained. Everybody needs to understand how their incentive compensation is calculated and how individual/group performance targets contribute to organizational performance targets. The pressure to achieve the targeted strategic and financial performance and continuously improve on strategy execution should be unrelenting, with few (if any) loopholes for rewarding shortfalls in performance. People at all levels have to be held accountable for carrying out their assigned parts of the strategic plan, and they have to understand their rewards are based on the caliber of results that are achieved. But with the pressure to perform should come meaningful rewards. Without an ample payoff, the system breaks down, and managers are left with the less workable options of barking orders, trying to enforce compliance, and depending on the goodwill of employees.

> **Core Concept**
> The unwavering standard for judging whether individuals, teams, and organizational units have done a good job must be whether they meet or beat performance targets that reflect good strategy execution.

Performance-Based Incentives and Rewards in Multinational Enterprises   In some foreign countries, incentive pay runs counter to local customs and cultural norms. Professor Steven Kerr cites the time he lectured an executive education class on the need for more performance-based pay and a Japanese manager protested, "You shouldn't bribe your children to do their homework, you shouldn't bribe your wife to prepare dinner, and you shouldn't bribe your employees to work for the company."[31] Singling out individuals and commending them for unusually good effort can also be a problem; Japanese culture considers public praise of an individual an affront to the harmony of the group. In some countries, employees have a preference for nonmonetary rewards—more leisure time, important titles, access to vacation villages, and nontaxable perks. Thus, multinational companies have to build some degree of flexibility into the design of incentives and rewards in order to accommodate cross-cultural traditions and preferences.

Key Points

Managers implementing and executing a new or different strategy must identify the resource requirements of each new strategic initiative and then consider whether the current pattern of resource allocation and the budgets of the various subunits are suitable.

Anytime a company alters its strategy, managers should review existing policies and operating procedures, proactively revise or discard those that are out of sync, and formulate new ones to facilitate execution of new strategic initiatives. Prescribing new or freshly revised policies and operating procedures aids the task of strategy execution (1) by providing top-down guidance to operating managers, supervisory personnel, and employees regarding how certain things need to be done and what the boundaries are on independent actions and decisions; (2) by enforcing consistency in how particular strategy-critical activities are performed in geographically scattered operating units; and (3) by promoting the creation of a work climate and corporate culture that promotes good strategy execution.

Competent strategy execution entails visible, unyielding managerial commitment to best practices and continuous improvement. Benchmarking, the discovery and adoption of best practices, reengineering core business processes, and continuous improvement initiatives like total quality management (TQM) or Six Sigma programs, all aim at improved efficiency, lower costs, better product quality, and greater customer satisfaction. *These initiatives are important tools for learning how to execute a strategy more proficiently.*

Company strategies can't be implemented or executed well without a number of support systems to carry on business operations. Well-conceived state-of-the-art support systems not only facilitate better strategy execution but also strengthen organizational capabilities enough to provide a competitive edge over rivals. Real-time information and control systems further aid the cause of good strategy execution.

Strategy-supportive motivational practices and reward systems are powerful management tools for gaining employee commitment. The key to creating a reward system that promotes good strategy execution is to make strategically relevant measures of performance *the dominating basis* for designing incentives, evaluating individual and group efforts, and handing out rewards. Positive motivational practices generally work better than negative ones, but there is a place for both. There's also a place for both monetary and nonmonetary incentives.

For an incentive compensation system to work well (1) the monetary payoff should be a major percentage of the compensation package, (2) the use of incentives should extend to all managers and workers, (3) the system should be administered with care and fairness, (4) the incentives should be linked to performance targets spelled out in the strategic plan, (5) each individual's performance targets should involve outcomes the person can personally affect, (6) rewards should promptly follow the determination of good performance, (7) monetary rewards should be supplemented with liberal use of nonmonetary rewards, and (8) skirting the system to reward nonperformers or subpar results should be scrupulously avoided. Companies with operations in multiple countries often have to build some degree of flexibility into the design of incentives and rewards in order to accommodate cross-cultural traditions and preferences.

Exercises

1. Go to Google or another Internet search engine and, using the advanced search feature, enter "best practices." Browse through the search results to identify at least five organizations that have gathered a set of best practices and are making the best-practice library they have assembled available to members. Explore at least one of the sites to get an idea of the kind of best-practice information that is available.

2. Do an Internet search on "Six Sigma" quality programs. Browse through the search results and (*a*) identify at least three companies that offer Six Sigma training and (*b*) find lists of companies that have implemented Six Sigma programs in their pursuit of operational excellence—you should be able to cite at least 25 companies that are Six Sigma users. Prepare a one-page report to your instructor detailing the experiences and benefits that one company has realized from employing Six Sigma methods in its operations. To learn more about how Six Sigma works, go to www.isixsigma.com and explore the Q&A menu option.

3. Do an Internet search on "total quality management." Browse through the search results and (*a*) identify 10 companies that offer TQM training, (*b*) identify 5 books on TQM programs, and (*c*) find lists of companies that have implemented TQM programs in their pursuit of operational excellence—you should be able to name at least 20 companies that are TQM users.

4. Consult the latest issue of *Fortune* containing the annual "100 Best Companies to Work For" (usually a late-January or early-February issue, or else use a search engine to locate the list online) and identify at least five compensation incentives and work practices that these companies use to enhance employee motivation and reward them for good strategic and financial performance. Choose compensation methods and work practices that are different from those cited in Illustration Capsule 12.3.

5. Review the profiles and applications of the latest Malcolm Baldrige National Quality Award recipients at www.quality.nist.gov. What are the standout features of the companies' approaches to managing operations? What do you find impressive about the companies' policies and procedures, use of best practices, emphasis on continuous improvement, and use of rewards and incentives?

6. Using Google Scholar or your access to online business periodicals in your university's library, search for the term "incentive compensation" and prepare a report of one to two pages to your instructor discussing the successful (or unsuccessful) use of incentive compensation plans by various companies. According to your research, what factors seem to determine whether incentive compensation plans succeed or fail?

Corporate Culture and Leadership

Keys to Good Strategy Execution

The biggest levers you've got to change a company are strategy, structure, and culture. If I could pick two, I'd pick strategy and culture.

—Wayne Leonard
CEO, Entergy

An organization's capacity to execute its strategy depends on its "hard" infrastructure—its organizational structure and systems—and on its "soft" infrastructure—its culture and norms.

—Amar Bhide

Weak leadership can wreck the soundest strategy; forceful execution of even a poor plan can often bring victory.

—Sun Zi

Leadership is accomplishing something through other people that wouldn't have happened if you weren't there. . . . Leadership is being able to mobilize ideas and values that energize other people. . . . Leaders develop a story line that engages other people.

—Noel Tichy

Seeing people in person is a big part of how you drive any change process. You have to show people a positive view of the future and say "we can do it."

—Jeffrey R. Immelt
CEO, General Electric

In the previous two chapters we examined six of the managerial tasks important to good strategy execution and operating excellence—building a capable organization, marshaling the needed resources and steering them to strategy-critical operating units, establishing policies and procedures that facilitate good strategy execution, adopting best practices and pushing for continuous improvement in how value chain activities are performed, creating internal operating systems that enable better execution, and employing motivational practices and compensation incentives that gain wholehearted employee commitment to the strategy execution process. In this chapter we explore the two remaining managerial tasks that shape the outcome of efforts to execute a company's strategy: creating a strategy-supportive corporate culture and exerting the internal leadership needed to drive the implementation of strategic initiatives forward and achieve higher plateaus of operating excellence.

INSTILLING A CORPORATE CULTURE THAT PROMOTES GOOD STRATEGY EXECUTION

Every company has its own unique culture. The character of a company's culture or work climate is a product of the core values and business principles that executives espouse, the standards of what is ethically acceptable and what is not, the work practices and behaviors that define "how we do things around here," the approach to people management and style of operating, the "chemistry" and the "personality" that permeates the work environment, and the stories that get told over and over to illustrate and reinforce the company's values, business practices, and traditions. The meshing together of stated beliefs, business principles, styles of operating, ingrained behaviors and attitudes, and work climate define a company's **corporate culture.** A company's culture is important because it influences the organization's actions and approaches to conducting business—in a very real sense, the culture is the company's "operating system" or organizational DNA.[1]

> **Core Concept**
> **Corporate culture** refers to the character of a company's internal work climate and personality—as shaped by its core values, beliefs, business principles, traditions, ingrained behaviors, work practices, and styles of operating.

The psyche of corporate cultures varies widely. For instance, the bedrock of Wal-Mart's culture is dedication to customer satisfaction, zealous pursuit of low costs and frugal operating practices, a strong work ethic, ritualistic Saturday-morning headquarters meetings to exchange ideas and review problems, and company executives' commitment to visiting stores, listening to customers, and soliciting suggestions from employees. General Electric's culture is founded on a hard-driving, results-oriented atmosphere (where all of the company's business divisions are held to a standard of being number one or two in their industries as well as achieving good business results); extensive cross-business sharing of ideas, best practices, and learning; the reliance on "workout sessions" to identify, debate, and resolve burning issues; a commitment to Six Sigma quality; and globalization of the company. At Occidental Petroleum, the culture is grounded in entrepreneurship on the part of employees; the company's empowered employees are encouraged to be innovative, excel in their fields of specialization, respond quickly to strategic opportunities, and creatively apply state-of-the-art technology in a manner that promotes operating excellence and sets Occidental apart from its competitors. At Nordstrom, the corporate culture is centered on delivering exceptional service to customers; the company's motto is "Respond to unreasonable customer requests"—each out-of-the-ordinary request is seen as an opportunity for a "heroic" act by an employee that can further the company's reputation for a customer-pleasing shopping environment. Nordstrom makes a point of promoting employees noted for their heroic acts and dedication to outstanding service; the company motivates its salespeople with a commission-based compensation system that enables Nordstrom's best salespeople to earn more than double what other department stores pay.

Illustration Capsule 13.1 relates how Google and Alberto-Culver describe their corporate cultures.

Identifying the Key Features of a Company's Corporate Culture

A company's corporate culture is mirrored in the character or "personality" of its work environment—the factors that underlie how the company tries to conduct its business and the behaviors that are held in high esteem. The chief things to look for include the following:

- *The values, business principles, and ethical standards that management preaches and practices.* Actions speak much louder than words here.
- *The company's approach to people management* and the official policies, procedures, and operating practices that paint the white lines for the behavior of company personnel.
- *The spirit and character that pervade the work climate.* Is the workplace vibrant and fun, methodical and all-business, tense and harried, or highly competitive and politicized? Are people excited about their work and emotionally connected to the company's business or are they just there to draw a paycheck? Is there an emphasis on empowered worker creativity or do people have little discretion in how jobs are done?
- *How managers and employees interact and relate to each other.* How much reliance is there on teamwork and open communication? To what extent is there good camaraderie? Are people called by their first names? Do co-workers spend little or lots of time together outside the workplace? What are the dress codes (the accepted styles of attire and whether there are casual days)?
- *The strength of peer pressure to do things in particular ways and conform to expected norms.* What actions and behaviors are approved (and rewarded by management in the form of compensation and promotion) and which ones are frowned on?

Illustration Capsule 13.1

The Corporate Cultures at Google and Alberto-Culver

GOOGLE

Founded in 1998 by Larry Page and Sergey Brin, two Ph.D. students in computer science at Stanford University, Google has beome world-renowned for its search engine technology. Google.com is one of the five most popular sites on the Internet, attracting over 380 million unique visitors monthly from around the world. Google has some unique ways of operating, and its culture is rather quirky. The company describes its culture as follows:

> Though growing rapidly, Google still maintains a small company feel. At the Googleplex headquarters almost everyone eats in the Google café (known as "Charlie's Place"), sitting at whatever table has an opening and enjoying conversations with Googlers from all different departments. Topics range from the trivial to the technical, and whether the discussion is about computer games or encryption or ad serving software, it's not surprising to hear someone say, "That's a product I helped develop before I came to Google."
>
> Google's emphasis on innovation and commitment to cost containment means each employee is a hands-on contributor. There's little in the way of corporate hierarchy and everyone wears several hats. The international webmaster who creates Google's holiday logos spent a week translating the entire site into Korean. The chief operations engineer is also a licensed neurosurgeon. Because everyone realizes they are an equally important part of Google's success, no one hesitates to skate over a corporate officer during roller hockey.
>
> Google's hiring policy is aggressively non-discriminatory and favors ability over experience. The result is a staff that reflects the global audience the search engine serves. Google has offices around the globe and Google engineering centers are recruiting local talent in locations from Zurich to Bangalore. Dozens of languages are spoken by Google staffers, from Turkish to Telugu. When not at work, Googlers pursue interests from cross-country cycling to wine tasting, from flying to Frisbee. As Google expands its development team, it continues to look for those who share an obsessive commitment to creating search perfection and having a great time doing it.

ALBERTO-CULVER

The Alberto-Culver Company, with fiscal 2005 revenues of about $3.5 billion, is the producer and marketer of Alberto VO5, TRESemmé, Consort, and Just for Me hair care products; St. Ives skin care, hair care, and facial care products; and such brands as Molly McButter, Mrs. Dash, Sugar Twin, and Static Guard. Alberto-Culver brands are sold in 120 countries. Its Sally Beauty Company, with over 3,250 stores and 1,250 professional sales consultants, is the largest marketer of professional beauty care products in the world.

At the careers section of its Web site, the company described its culture in the following words:

> Building careers is as important to us as building brands. We believe that passionate people create powerful growth. We believe in a workplace built on values and believe our best people display those same values in their families and their communities. We believe in recognizing and rewarding accomplishment and celebrating our victories.
>
> We believe the best ideas work their way—quickly—up an organization, not down. We believe that we should take advantage of every ounce of your talent on teams and cross-functional activities, not just assign you to a box.
>
> We believe in open communication. We believe that you can improve what you measure, so we survey and spot check all the time. For that same reason, everyone has specific goals so that their expectations are in line with their managers' and the company's.
>
> We believe that victory is a team accomplishment. We believe in personal development. We believe if you talk with us you will catch our enthusiasm and want to be a part of the Alberto-Culver team.

Sources: Information posted at www.google.com and www.alberto.com (accessed November 16, 2005).

- *The company's revered traditions and oft-repeated stories.* Do people talk a lot about "heroic acts" and "how we do things around here"?
- *The manner in which the company deals with external stakeholders (particularly vendors and local communities where it has operations).* Does it treat

suppliers as business partners or does it prefer hardnosed, arm's-length business arrangements? How strong and genuine is its commitment to corporate citizenship?

Some of these sociological forces are readily apparent, and others operate quite subtly.

The values, beliefs, and practices that undergird a company's culture can come from anywhere in the organization hierarchy, most often representing the business philosophy and managerial style of influential executives but also resulting from exemplary actions on the part of company personnel and consensus agreement about "how we ought to do things around here."[2] Typically, key elements of the culture originate with a founder or certain strong leaders who articulated them as a set of business principles, company policies, operating approaches, and ways of dealing with employees, customers, vendors, shareholders, and local communities where the company has operations. Over time, these cultural underpinnings take root, become embedded in how the company conducts its business, come to be accepted by company managers and employees alike, and then persist as new employees are encouraged to adopt and follow the professed values, behaviors, and work practices.

The Role of Stories   Frequently, a significant part of a company's culture is captured in the stories that get told over and over again to illustrate to newcomers the importance of certain values and the depth of commitment that various company personnel have displayed. One of the folktales at FedEx, world renowned for the reliability of its next-day package delivery guarantee, is about a deliveryman who had been given the wrong key to a FedEx drop box. Rather than leave the packages in the drop box until the next day when the right key was available, the deliveryman unbolted the drop box from its base, loaded it into the truck, and took it back to the station. There, the box was pried open and the contents removed and sped on their way to their destination the next day. Nordstrom keeps a scrapbook commemorating the heroic acts of its employees and uses it as a regular reminder of the beyond-the-call-of-duty behaviors that employees are encouraged to display. At Frito-Lay, there are dozens of stories about truck drivers who went to extraordinary lengths in overcoming adverse weather conditions in order to make scheduled deliveries to retail customers and keep store shelves stocked with Frito-Lay products. At Microsoft, there are stories of the long hours programmers put in, the emotional peaks and valleys in encountering and overcoming coding problems, the exhilaration of completing a complex program on schedule, the satisfaction of working on cutting-edge projects, the rewards of being part of a team responsible for a popular new software program, and the tradition of competing aggressively. Such stories serve the valuable purpose of illustrating the kinds of behavior the company encourages and reveres. Moreover, each retelling of a legendary story puts a bit more peer pressure on company personnel to display core values and do their part in keeping the company's traditions alive.

Perpetuating the Culture   Once established, company cultures are perpetuated in six important ways: (1) by screening and selecting new employees that will mesh well with the culture, (2) by systematic indoctrination of new members in the culture's fundamentals, (3) by the efforts of senior group members to reiterate core values in daily conversations and pronouncements, (4) by the telling and retelling of company legends, (5) by regular ceremonies honoring members who display desired cultural behaviors, and (6) by visibly rewarding those who display cultural norms and penalizing those who don't.[3] *The more new employees a company is hiring, the more important it becomes to screen job applicants every bit as much for how well their values, beliefs, and personalities match up with the culture as for their technical skills and experience.*

For example, a company that stresses operating with integrity and fairness has to hire people who themselves have integrity and place a high value on fair play. A company whose culture revolves around creativity, product innovation, and leading change has to screen new hires for their ability to think outside the box, generate new ideas, and thrive in a climate of rapid change and ambiguity. Southwest Airlines—whose two core values, "LUV" and fun, permeate the work environment and whose objective is to ensure that passengers have a positive and enjoyable flying experience—goes to considerable lengths to hire flight attendants and gate personnel who are witty, cheery, and outgoing and who display whistle-while-you-work attitudes. Fast-growing companies risk creating a culture by chance rather than by design if they rush to hire employees mainly for their talents and credentials and neglect to screen out candidates whose values, philosophies, and personalities aren't a good fit with the organizational character, vision, and strategy being articulated by the company's senior executives.

As a rule, companies are attentive to the task of hiring people who will fit in and who will embrace the prevailing culture. And, usually, job seekers lean toward accepting jobs at companies where they feel comfortable with the atmosphere and the people they will be working with. Employees who don't hit it off at a company tend to leave quickly, while employees who thrive and are pleased with the work environment stay on, eventually moving up the ranks to positions of greater responsibility. The longer people stay at an organization, the more they come to embrace and mirror the corporate culture—their values and beliefs tend to be molded by mentors, fellow workers, company training programs, and the reward structure. Normally, employees who have worked at a company for a long time play a major role in indoctrinating new employees into the culture.

Forces That Cause a Company's Culture to Evolve   However, even stable cultures aren't static; just like strategy and organization structure, they evolve. New challenges in the marketplace, revolutionary technologies, and shifting internal conditions—especially eroding business prospects, an internal crisis, or top executive turnover—tend to breed new ways of doing things and, in turn, cultural evolution. An incoming CEO who decides to shake up the existing business and take it in new directions often triggers a cultural shift, perhaps one of major proportions. Likewise, diversification into new businesses, expansion into foreign countries, rapid growth, an influx of new employees, and merger with or acquisition of another company can all precipitate cultural changes of one kind or another.

Company Subcultures: The Problems Posed by New Acquisitions and Multinational Operations   Although it is common to speak about corporate culture in the singular, it is not uncommon for companies to have multiple cultures (or subcultures).[4] Values, beliefs, and practices within a company sometimes vary significantly by department, geographic location, division, or business unit. A company's subcultures can clash, or at least not mesh well, if they embrace conflicting business philosophies or operating approaches, if key executives employ different approaches to people management, or if important differences between a company's culture and those of recently acquired companies have not yet been ironed out. Global and multinational companies tend to be at least partly multicultural because cross-country organization units have different operating histories and work climates, as well as members who have grown up under different social customs and traditions and who have different sets of values and beliefs. The human resources manager of a global pharmaceutical company who took on an assignment in the Far East discovered, to his surprise, that one of his biggest challenges was to persuade his company's managers in China,

Korea, Malaysia, and Taiwan to accept promotions—their cultural values were such that they did not believe in competing with their peers for career rewards or personal gain, nor did they relish breaking ties to their local communities to assume cross-national responsibilities.[5] Many companies that have merged with or acquired foreign companies have to deal with language- and custom-based cultural differences.

Nonetheless, the existence of subcultures does not preclude important areas of commonality and compatibility. For example, General Electric's cultural traits of boundarylessness, workout, and Six Sigma quality can be implanted and practiced successfully in different countries. AES, a global power company with operations in over 25 countries, has found that the four core values of integrity, fairness, fun, and social responsibility underlying its culture are readily embraced by people in most countries. Moreover, AES tries to define and practice its cultural values the same way in all of its locations while still being sensitive to differences that exist among various people groups across the world; top managers at AES express the views that people across the world are more similar than different and that the company's culture is as meaningful in Buenos Aires or Kazakhstan as in Virginia.

In today's globalizing world, multinational companies are learning how to make strategy-critical cultural traits travel across country boundaries and create a workably uniform culture worldwide. Likewise, company managements are quite alert to the importance of cultural compatibility in making acquisitions and the need to address how to merge and integrate the cultures of newly acquired companies—cultural due diligence is often as important as financial due diligence in deciding whether to go forward on an acquisition or merger. On a number of occasions, companies have decided to pass on acquiring particular companies because of culture conflicts that they believed would be hard to resolve.

Strong versus Weak Cultures

Company cultures vary widely in strength and influence. Some are strongly embedded and have a big impact on a company's practices and behavioral norms. Others are weak and have comparatively little influence on company operations.

Strong-Culture Companies   The hallmark of a strong-culture company is the dominating presence of certain deeply rooted values and operating approaches that "regulate" the conduct of a company's business and the climate of its workplace.[6] Strong cultures emerge over a period of years (sometimes decades) and are never an overnight phenomenon. In strong culture companies, senior managers make a point of reiterating these principles and values to organization members and explaining how they relate to its business environment. But, more important, they make a conscious effort to display these principles in their own actions and behavior—they walk the talk, and they *insist that company values and business principles be reflected in the decisions and actions taken by all company personnel.* An unequivocal expectation that company personnel will act and behave in accordance with the adopted values and ways of doing business leads to two important outcomes: (1) Over time, the values come to be widely shared by rank-and-file employees—people who dislike the culture tend to leave—and (2) individuals encounter strong peer pressure from co-workers to observe the culturally approved norms and behaviors. Hence, a strongly implanted corporate culture ends up having a powerful influence on "how we

Core Concept

In a strong-culture company, culturally-approved behaviors and ways of doing things are nurtured while culturally-disapproved behaviors and work practices get squashed.

do things around here" because so many company personnel are accepting of cultural traditions and because this acceptance is reinforced both by management expectations and co-worker peer pressure to conform to cultural norms. Since cultural traditions and norms have such a dominating influence in strong-culture companies, the character of the culture becomes the the company's soul or psyche.

Three factors contribute to the development of strong cultures: (1) a founder or strong leader who establishes values, principles, and practices that are consistent and sensible in light of customer needs, competitive conditions, and strategic requirements; (2) a sincere, long-standing company commitment to operating the business according to these established traditions, thereby creating an internal environment that supports decision making and strategies based on cultural norms; and (3) a genuine concern for the well-being of the organization's three biggest constituencies—customers, employees, and shareholders. Continuity of leadership, small group size, stable group membership, geographic concentration, and considerable organizational success all contribute to the emergence and sustainability of a strong culture.[7]

During the time a strong culture is being implanted, there's nearly always a good strategy–culture fit (which partially accounts for the organization's success). Mismatches between strategy and culture in a strong-culture company tend to occur when a company's business environment undergoes significant change, prompting a drastic strategy revision that clashes with the entrenched culture. A strategy–culture clash can also occur in a strong-culture company whose business has gradually eroded; when a new leader is brought in to revitalize the company's operations, he or she may push the company in a strategic direction that requires substantially different cultural and behavioral norms. In such cases, a major culture-changing effort has to be launched.

In strong-culture companies, values and behavioral norms are so ingrained that they can endure leadership changes at the top—although their strength can erode over time if new CEOs cease to nurture them or move aggressively to institute cultural adjustments. And the cultural norms in a strong-culture company may not change much as strategy evolves and the organization acts to make strategy adjustments, either because the new strategies are compatible with the present culture or because the dominant traits of the culture are somewhat strategy-neutral and compatible with evolving versions of the company's strategy.

> In a strong-culture company, values and behavioral norms are like crabgrass: deeply rooted and hard to weed out.

Weak-Culture Companies   In direct contrast to strong-culture companies, weakculture companies lack values and principles that are consistently preached or widely shared (usually because the company has had a series of CEOs with differing values and differing views about how the company's business ought to be conducted). As a consequence, the company has few widely revered traditions and few culture-induced norms are evident in operating practices. Because top executives at a weak-culture company don't repeatedly espouse any particular business philosophy, exhibit long-standing commitment to particular values, or extol particular operating practices and behavioral norms, individuals encounter little co-worker peer pressure to do things in particular ways. Moreover, a weak company culture breeds no strong employee allegiance to what the company stands for or to operating the business in well-defined ways. While individual employees may well have some bonds of identification with and loyalty toward their department, their colleagues, their union, or their boss, there is neither passion about the company nor emotional commitment to what it is trying to accomplish—a condition that often results in many employees viewing their company as just a place to work and their job as just a way to make a living. Very often, cultural weakness stems from moderately entrenched subcultures that block the emergence of a well-defined companywide work climate.

As a consequence, *weak cultures provide little or no assistance in executing strategy* because there are no traditions, beliefs, values, common bonds, or behavioral norms that management can use as levers to mobilize commitment to executing the chosen strategy. The only plus of a weak culture is that it does not usually pose a strong barrier to strategy execution, but the negative of not providing any support means that culture-building has to be high on management's action agenda. Absent a work climate that channels organizational energy in the direction of good strategy execution, managers are left with the options of either using compensation incentives and other motivational devices to mobilize employee commitment or trying to establish cultural roots that will in time start to nurture the strategy execution process.

Unhealthy Cultures

The distinctive characteristic of an unhealthy corporate culture is the presence of counterproductive cultural traits that adversely impact the work climate and company performance.[8] The following four traits are particularly unhealthy:

1. A highly politicized internal environment in which many issues get resolved and decisions made on the basis of which individuals or groups have the most political clout to carry the day.

2. Hostility to change and a general wariness of people who champion new ways of doing things.

3. An insular "not-invented-here" mind-set that makes company personnel averse to looking outside the company for best practices, new managerial approaches, and innovative ideas.

4. A disregard for high ethical standards and overzealous pursuit of wealth and status on the part of key executives.

Politicized Cultures   What makes a politicized internal environment so unhealthy is that political infighting consumes a great deal of organizational energy, often with the result that what's best for the company takes a backseat to political maneuvering. In companies where internal politics pervades the work climate, empire-building managers jealously guard their decision-making prerogatives. They have their own agendas and operate the work units under their supervision as autonomous "fiefdoms," and the positions they take on issues is usually aimed at protecting or expanding their turf. Collaboration with other organizational units is viewed with suspicion (What are "they" up to? How can "we" protect "our" flanks?), and cross-unit cooperation occurs grudgingly. When an important proposal moves to the front burner, advocates try to ram it through and opponents try to alter it in significant ways or else kill it altogether. The support or opposition of politically influential executives and/or coalitions among departments with vested interests in a particular outcome typically weigh heavily in deciding what actions the company takes. All this maneuvering takes away from efforts to execute strategy with real proficiency and frustrates company personnel who are less political and more inclined to do what is in the company's best interests.

Change-Resistant Cultures   In less-adaptive cultures where skepticism about the importance of new developments and resistance to change are the norm, managers prefer waiting until the fog of uncertainty clears before steering a new course, making fundamental adjustments to their product line, or embracing a major new technology. They believe in moving cautiously and conservatively, preferring to follow others rather than taking decisive action to be in the forefront of change. Change-resistant cultures place a premium on not making mistakes, prompting managers to lean toward safe, don't-rock-the-boat options that will have only a ripple effect on the status quo, protect or advance their own careers, and guard the interests of their immediate work groups.

Change-resistant cultures encourage a number of undesirable or unhealthy behaviors—avoiding risks, not making bold proposals to pursue emerging opportunities, a lax approach to both product innovation and continuous improvement in performing value chain activities, and following rather than leading market change. In change-resistant cultures, word quickly gets around that proposals to do things differently face an uphill battle and that people who champion them may be seen as either something of a nuisance or a troublemaker. Executives who don't value managers or employees with initiative and new ideas put a damper on product innovation, experimentation, and efforts to improve. At the same time, change-resistant companies have little appetite for being first-movers or fast-followers, believing that being in the forefront of change is too risky and that acting too quickly increases vulnerability to costly mistakes. They are more inclined to adopt a wait-and-see posture, carefully analyze several alternative responses, learn from the missteps of early movers, and then move forward cautiously and conservatively with initiatives that are deemed safe. Hostility to change is most often found in companies with multilayered management bureaucracies that have enjoyed considerable market success in years past and that are wedded to the "We have done it this way for years" syndrome.

When such companies encounter business environments with accelerating change, going slow on altering traditional ways of doing things can be become a liability rather than an asset. General Motors, IBM, Sears, and Eastman Kodak are classic examples of companies whose change-resistant bureaucracies were slow to respond to fundamental changes in their markets; clinging to the cultures and traditions that made them successful, they were reluctant to alter operating practices and modify their business approaches. As strategies of gradual change won out over bold innovation and being an early mover, all four lost market share to rivals that quickly moved to institute changes more in tune with evolving market conditions and buyer preferences. These companies are now struggling to recoup lost ground with cultures and behaviors more suited to market success—the kinds of fit that caused them to succeed in the first place.

Insular, Inwardly Focused Cultures   Sometimes a company reigns as an industry leader or enjoys great market success for so long that its personnel start to believe they have all the answers or can develop them on their own. There is a strong tendency to neglect what customers are saying and how their needs and expectations are changing. Such confidence in the correctness of how it does things and in the company's skills and capabilities breeds arrogance—company personnel discount the merits of what outsiders are doing and what can be learned by studying best-in-class performers. Benchmarking and a search for the best practices of outsiders are seen as offering little payoff. Any market share gains on the part of up-and-coming rivals are regarded as temporary setbacks, soon to be reversed by the company's own forthcoming initiatives (which, it is confidently predicted, will be an instant market hit with customers).

Insular thinking, internally driven solutions, and a must-be-invented-here mind-set come to permeate the corporate culture. An inwardly focused corporate culture gives rise to managerial inbreeding and a failure to recruit people who can offer fresh thinking and outside perspectives. The big risk of insular cultural thinking is that the company can underestimate the competencies and accomplishments of rival companies and overestimate its own progress—with a resulting loss of competitive advantage over time.

Unethical and Greed-Driven Cultures   Companies that have little regard for ethical standards or that are run by executives driven by greed and ego gratification are scandals waiting to happen. Enron's collapse in 2001 was largely the product of an ethically dysfunctional corporate culture—while the culture embraced the positives of product innovation, aggressive risk taking, and a driving ambition to lead global change in the energy business, its executives exuded the negatives of arrogance, ego, greed, and an ends-justify-the-means mentality in pursuing stretched revenue and profitability targets.[9] A number of Enron's senior managers were all too willing to wink at unethical behavior, to cross over the line to unethical (and sometimes criminal) behavior themselves, and to deliberately stretch generally accepted accounting principles to make Enron's financial performance look far better than it really was. In the end, Enron came unglued because a few top executives chose unethical and illegal paths to pursue corporate revenue and profitability targets—in a company that publicly preached integrity and other notable corporate values but was lax in making sure that key executives walked the talk. Unethical cultures and executive greed have also produced scandals at WorldCom, Qwest, HealthSouth, Adelphia, Tyco, McWane, Parmalat, Rite Aid, Hollinger International, Refco, and Marsh & McLennan, with executives being indicted and/or convicted of criminal behavior. The U.S. Attorney's office elected not to prosecute the accounting firm KPMG with "systematic" criminal acts to market illegal tax shelters to wealthy clients (which KPMG tried mightily to cover up) because a criminal indictment would have resulted in the immediate collapse of KPMG and cut the number of global public accounting firms from four to just three; instead, criminal charges were filed against the company officials deemed most responsible. In 2005, U.S. prosecutors elected not to press criminal charges against Royal Dutch Petroleum (Shell Oil) for repeatedly and knowingly reporting inflated oil reserves to the U.S. Securities and Exchange Commission and not to indict Tommy Hilfiger USA for multiple tax law violations—but both companies agreed to sign nonprosecution agreements, the terms of which were not made public but which almost certainly involved fines and a long-term company commitment to cease and desist.

High-Performance Cultures

Some companies have high-performance cultures, in which the standout cultural traits are a can-do spirit, pride in doing things right, no-excuses accountability, and a pervasive results-oriented work climate in which people go the extra mile to meet or beat stretch objectives. In high-performance cultures, there is a strong sense of involvement on the part of company personnel and emphasis on individual initiative and creativity. Performance expectations are clearly delineated for the company as a whole, for each organizational unit, and for each individual. Issues and problems are promptly addressed—a strong bias exists for being proactive instead of reactive. There is a razor-sharp focus on what needs to be done. The clear and unyielding expectation is that all company personnel, from senior executives to frontline employees will display high-performance behaviors and a passion for making the company successful. There is respect for the contributions of individuals and groups.

A high-performance culture is a valuable contributor to good strategy execution and operating excellence. High performance, results-oriented cultures are permeated with a spirit of achievement and have a good track record in meeting or beating performance targets.

The challenge in creating a high-performance culture is to inspire high loyalty and dedication on the part of employees, such that they are both energized and preoccupied with putting forth their very best efforts to do things right and be unusually productive. Managers have to reinforce constructive behavior, reward top performers, and purge habits and behaviors that stand in the way of high productivity and good results. They must work at knowing the strengths and weaknesses of their subordinates, so as to better match talent with task and enable people to make meaningful contributions by doing what they do best.[10] They have to stress correcting and learning from mistakes, and they must put an unrelenting emphasis on moving forward and making good progress—in effect, there has to be a disciplined, performance-focused approach to managing the organization.

Adaptive Cultures

The hallmark of adaptive corporate cultures is willingness on the part of organizational members to accept change and take on the challenge of introducing and executing new strategies.[11] Company personnel share a feeling of confidence that the organization can deal with whatever threats and opportunities come down the pike; they are receptive to risk taking, experimentation, and innovation. In direct contrast to change-resistant cultures, adaptive cultures are very supportive of managers and employees at all ranks who propose or help initiate useful change. Internal entrepreneurship on the part of individuals and groups is encouraged and rewarded. Senior executives seek out, support, and promote individuals who exercise initiative, spot opportunities for improvement, and display the skills to implement them. Managers openly evaluate ideas and suggestions, fund initiatives to develop new or better products, and take prudent risks to pursue emerging market opportunities. As in high-performance cultures, the adaptive company exhibits a proactive approach to identifying issues, evaluating the implications and options, and quickly moving ahead with workable solutions. Strategies and traditional operating practices are modified as needed to adjust to or take advantage of changes in the business environment.

> **Core Concept**
> In adaptive cultures, there is a spirit of doing what's necessary to ensure long-term organizational success provided the new behaviors and operating practices that management is calling for are seen as legitimate and consistent with the core values and business principles underpinning the culture.

But why is change so willingly embraced in an adaptive culture? Why are organization members not fearful of how change will affect them? Why does an adaptive culture not become unglued with ongoing changes in strategy, operating practices, and behavioral norms? The answers lie in two distinctive and dominant traits of an adaptive culture: (1) Any changes in operating practices and behaviors must *not* compromise core values and long-standing business principles, and (2) the changes that are instituted must satisfy the legitimate interests of stakeholders—customers, employees, shareowners, suppliers, and the communities in which the company operates.[12] In other words, what sustains an adaptive culture is that organization members perceive the changes that management is trying to institute as legitimate and in keeping with the core values and business principles that form the heart and soul of the culture.

Thus, for an adaptive culture to remain intact over time, top management must orchestrate organizational changes in a manner that (1) demonstrates genuine care for the well-being of all key constituencies and (2) tries to satisfy all their legitimate interests simultaneously. Unless fairness to all constituencies is a decision-making principle and a commitment to doing the right thing is evident to organization members, the changes are not likely to be seen as legitimate and thus be readily accepted and implemented wholeheartedly.[13] Making changes that will please customers and that protect, if not enhance, the company's long-term well-being are generally seen as legitimate and are often seen as the best way of looking out for the interests of employees, stockholders, suppliers, and communities where the company operates. At companies with adaptive cultures, management concern for the well-being of employees is nearly always a big factor in gaining employee support for change—company personnel are usually receptive to change as long as employees understand that changes in their job assignments are part of the process of adapting to new conditions and that their employment security will not be threatened unless the company's business unexpectedly reverses direction. In cases where workforce downsizing becomes necessary, management concern for employees dictates that separation be handled humanely, making employee departure as painless as possible. Management efforts to make the process of adapting to change fair and equitable for customers, employees, stockholders, suppliers, and communities where the company operates, keeping adverse impacts to a minimum insofar as possible, breeds acceptance of and support for change among all organization stakeholders.

> Adaptive cultures are exceptionally well suited to companies with fast-changing strategies and market environments.

Technology companies, software companies, and today's dot-com companies are good illustrations of organizations with adaptive cultures. Such companies thrive on change—driving it, leading it, and capitalizing on it (but sometimes also succumbing to change when they make the wrong move or are swamped by better technologies or the superior business models of rivals). Companies like Google, Intel, Cisco Systems, eBay, Nokia, Amazon. com, and Dell cultivate the capability to act and react rapidly. They are avid practitioners of entrepreneurship and innovation, with a demonstrated willingness to take bold risks to create altogether new products, new businesses, and new industries. To create and nurture a culture that can adapt rapidly to changing to shifting business conditions, they make a point of staffing their organizations with people who are proactive, who rise to the challenge of change, and who have an aptitude for adapting.

In fast-changing business environments, a corporate culture that is receptive to altering organizational practices and behaviors is a virtual necessity. However, adaptive cultures work to the advantage of all companies, not just those in rapid-change environments. Every company operates in a market and business climate that is changing to one degree or another and that, in turn, requires internal operating responses and new behaviors on the part of organization members. *As a company's strategy evolves, an adaptive culture is a definite ally in the strategy-implementing, strategy-executing process as compared to cultures that have to be coaxed and cajoled to change.*

Culture: Ally or Obstacle to Strategy Execution?

A company's present culture and work climate may or may not be compatible with what is needed for effective implementation and execution of the chosen strategy. *When a company's present work climate promotes attitudes and behaviors that are well suited to first-rate strategy execution, its culture functions as a valuable ally in the strategy execution process.* When the culture is in conflict with some aspect of the company's direction, performance targets, or strategy, the culture becomes a stumbling block.[14]

How a Company's Culture Can Promote Better Strategy Execution   A culture grounded in strategy-supportive values, practices, and behavioral norms adds significantly to the power and effectiveness of a company's strategy execution effort.

For example, a culture where frugality and thrift are values widely shared by organizational members nurtures employee actions to identify cost-saving opportunities—the very behavior needed for successful execution of a low-cost leadership strategy. A culture built around such business principles as pleasing customers, fair treatment, operating excellence, and employee empowerment promotes employee behaviors and an esprit de corps that facilitate execution of strategies keyed to high product quality and superior customer service. A culture in which taking initiative, challenging the status quo, exhibiting creativity, embracing change, and collaborating with team members pervade the work climate promotes a company's drive to lead market change—outcomes that are conducive to successful execution of product innovation and technological leadership strategies.[15] Good alignment between in-grained cultural norms and the behaviors needed for good strategy execution makes the culture a valuable ally in the strategy-execution process. In a company where strategy and culture are misaligned, some of the very behaviors needed to execute strategy successfully run contrary to the behaviors and values imbedded in the prevailing culture. Such a clash nearly always produces a roadblock from employees whose actions and behaviors are strongly linked to the present culture. Culture-bred resistance to the actions and behaviors needed for good execution, if strong and widespread, poses a formidable hurdle that has to be cleared for strategy execution to get very far.

> **Core Concept**
> The tighter the culture–strategy fit, the more that the culture steers company personnel into displaying behaviors and adopting operating practices that promote good strategy execution.

A tight culture–strategy matchup furthers a company's strategy execution effort in three ways:[16]

1. *A culture that encourages actions, behaviors, and work practices supportive of good strategy execution not only provides company personnel with clear guidance regarding "how we do things around here" but also produces significant peer pressure from co-workers to conform to culturally acceptable norms.* The stronger the admonishments from top executives about "how we need to do things around here" and the stronger the peer pressure from co-workers, the more the culture influences people to display behaviors and observe operating practices that support good strategy execution.

2. *A deeply embedded culture tightly matched to the strategy aids the cause of competent strategy execution by steering company personnel to culturally approved behaviors and work practices and thus makes it far simpler to root out any operating practice that is a misfit.* This is why it is very much in management's best interests to build and nurture a deeply rooted culture where ingrained behaviors and operating practices marshal organizational energy behind the drive for good strategy execution.

3. *A culture imbedded with values and behaviors that facilitate strategy execution promotes strong employee identification with and commitment to the company's vision, performance targets, and strategy.* When a company's culture is grounded in many of the needed strategy-executing behaviors, employees feel genuinely better about their jobs, the company they work for, and the merits of what the company is trying to accomplish. As a consequence, greater numbers of company personnel exhibit some passion about their work and exert their best efforts to execute the strategy and achieve performance targets. All this helps move the company closer to realizing its strategic vision and, from employees' standpoint, makes the company a more engaging place to work.

These aspects of culture–strategy alignment say something important about the task of managing the strategy executing process: *Closely aligning corporate culture with the requirements for proficient strategy execution merits the full attention of senior*

Core Concept
It is in management's best interest to dedicate considerable effort to embedding a corporate culture that encourages behaviors and work practices conducive to good strategy execution—a tight strategy–culture fit automatically nurtures culturally-approved behaviors and squashes culturally-disapproved behaviors.

executives. The culture-building objective is to create a work climate and style of operating that mobilize the energy and behavior of company personnel squarely behind efforts to execute strategy competently. The more deeply that management can embed strategy-supportive ways of doing things, the more that management can rely on the culture to automatically steer company personnel toward behaviors and work practices that aid good strategy execution and away from ways of doing things that impede it.

Furthermore, culturally astute managers understand that nourishing the right cultural environment not only adds power to their push for proficient strategy execution but also promotes strong employee identification with and commitment to the company's vision, performance targets, and strategy. A culture–strategy fit prompts employees with emotional allegiance to the culture to feel genuinely better about their jobs, the company they work for, and the merits of what the company is trying to accomplish. As a consequence, their morale is higher and their productivity is higher. In addition, greater numbers of company personnel exhibit passion for their work and exert their best efforts to make the strategy succeed and achieve performance targets. All this helps move the company closer to realizing its strategic vision and, from the employees' standpoint, makes the company a more engaging place to work.

The Perils of Strategy–Culture Conflict   Conflicts between behaviors approved by the culture and behaviors needed for good strategy execution pose a real dilemma for company personnel. Should they be loyal to the culture and company traditions (to which they are likely to be emotionally attached) and thus resist or be indifferent to actions and behaviors that will promote better strategy execution—a choice that will certainly weaken the drive for good strategy execution? Or should they go along with the strategy execution effort and engage in actions and behaviors that run counter to the culture—a choice that will likely impair morale and lead to less-than-wholehearted commitment to management's strategy execution efforts? Neither choice leads to desirable outcomes, and the solution is obvious: eliminate the conflict.

When a company's culture is out of sync with the actions and behaviors needed to execute the strategy successfully, the culture has to be changed as rapidly as can be managed—this, of course, presumes that it is one or more aspects of the culture that are out of whack rather than the strategy executions approaches management wishes to institute. While correcting a strategy–culture conflict can occasionally mean revamping a company's approach to executing the strategy to produce good cultural fit, more usually it means altering aspects of the mismatched culture to ingrain new behaviors and work practices that will enable first-rate strategy execution. The more entrenched the mismatched aspects of the culture, the greater the difficulty of implementing and executing new or different strategies until better strategy–culture alignment emerges. A sizable and prolonged strategy–culture conflict weakens and may even defeat managerial efforts to make the strategy work.

Changing a Problem Culture

Once a culture is established, it is difficult to change.

Changing a company culture that impedes proficient strategy execution is among the toughest management tasks because of the heavy anchor of ingrained behaviors and ways of doing things. It is natural for company personnel to cling to familiar practices and to be wary, if not hostile, to new approaches of how things are to be done. Consequently, it takes concerted management action over a period of time to root out certain unwanted behaviors and replace an out-of-sync culture with different behaviors and ways of doing things deemed more conducive to executing the strategy. *The single most visible factor that distinguishes successful culture-change efforts from failed attempts is competent leadership at the top.* Great power is needed to force major cultural change and overcome the springback resistance of entrenched cultures—and great power is possessed only by the most senior executives, especially the CEO. However, while top management must be out front leading the effort, marshaling support for a new culture and, more important, instilling new cultural behaviors are tasks for the whole management team. Middle managers and frontline supervisors play a key role in implementing the new work practices and operating approaches, helping win rank-and-file acceptance of and support for the changes, and instilling the desired behavioral norms.

As shown in Figure 13.1, the first step in fixing a problem culture is for top management to identify those facets of the present culture that are dysfunctional and pose obstacles to executing new strategic initiatives and meeting or beating company performance targets. Second, managers have to clearly define the desired new behaviors and features of the culture they want to create. Third, managers have to convince company personnel why the present culture poses problems and why and how new behaviors and operating approaches will improve company performance—the case for cultural change and the benefits of a reformed culture have to be persuasive. Finally, and most important, all the talk about remodeling the present culture has to be followed swiftly by visible, forceful actions to promote the desired new behaviors and work practices—actions that company personnel will interpret as a determined top management commitment to alter the culture and instill a different work climate and different ways of operating.

Making a Compelling Case for Culture Change   The place for management to begin a major remodeling of the corporate culture is by selling company personnel on

Figure 13.1   **Changing a Problem Culture**

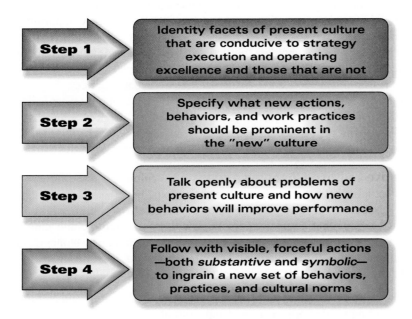

Step 1 — Identify facets of present culture that are conducive to strategy execution and operating excellence and those that are not

Step 2 — Specify what new actions, behaviors, and work practices should be prominent in the "new" culture

Step 3 — Talk openly about problems of present culture and how new behaviors will improve performance

Step 4 — Follow with visible, forceful actions—both *substantive* and *symbolic*—to ingrain a new set of behaviors, practices, and cultural norms the need for new-style behaviors and work practices. This means making a compelling case for why the company's new strategic direction and culture-remodeling efforts are in the organization's best interests and why company personnel should wholeheartedly join the effort to doing things somewhat differently. Skeptics and opinion leaders have to be convinced that all is not well with the status quo. This can be done by:

- Citing reasons why the current strategy has to be modified and why new strategic initiatives that are being undertaken will bolster the company's competitiveness and performance. The case for altering the old strategy usually needs to be predicated on its shortcomings—why sales are growing slowly, why rivals are doing so much better, why too many customers are opting to go with the products of rivals, why costs are too high, why the company's price has to be lowered, and so on. There may be merit in holding events where managers and other key personnel are forced to listen to dissatisfied customers, the complaints of strategic allies, alienated employees, or disenchanted stockholders
- Citing why and how certain behavioral norms and work practices in the current culture pose obstacles to good execution of new strategic initiatives.
- Explaining how certain new behaviors and work practices that are to be introduced and have important roles in the new culture will be more advantageous and produce better results.

It is essential for the CEO and other top executives to personally talk to company personnel all across the company about the reasons for modifying work practices and culture-related behaviors. Senior officers and department heads have to play the lead role in explaining the behaviors, practices, and operating approaches that are to be introduced and why they are beneficial—and the explanations will likely have to be repeated many times. For the culture-change effort to be successful, frontline supervisors and employee opinion leaders must be won over to the cause, which means convincing them of the merits of *practicing* and *enforcing* cultural norms at the lowest levels in the organization. Until a big majority of employees accept the need for a new culture and agree that different work practices and behaviors are called for, there's more work to be done in selling company personnel on the whys and wherefores of culture change. Building widespread organizational support requires taking every opportunity to repeat the messages of why the new work practices, operating approaches, and behaviors are good for company stakeholders (particularly customers, employees, and shareholders). Effective culture-change leaders are good at telling stories to describe the new values and desired behaviors and connect them to everyday practices.

Management's efforts to make a persuasive case for changing what is deemed to be a problem culture must be *quickly followed* by forceful, high-profile actions across several fronts. The actions to implant the new culture must be both substantive and symbolic.

Substantive Culture-Changing Actions   No culture change effort can get very far with just talk about the need for different actions, behaviors, and work practices. Company executives have to give the culture-change effort some teeth by initiating *a series of actions* that company personnel will see as credible and unmistakably indicative of the seriousness of management's commitment to new strategic initiatives and the associated cultural changes. The strongest signs that management is truly committed to instilling a new culture include:

1.   Replacing key executives who are strongly associated with the old culture and are stonewalling needed organizational and cultural changes.

2. Promoting individuals who are known to possess the desired cultural traits, who have stepped forward to advocate the shift to a different culture, and who can serve as role models for the desired cultural behavior.

3. Appointing outsiders with the desired cultural attributes to high-profile positions—bringing in new-breed managers to serve as role models and help drive the culture-change movement sends an unmistakable message that a new era is dawning and acts to reinforce company personnel who have already gotten on board the culture-change effort.

4. Screening all candidates for new positions carefully, hiring only those who appear to fit in with the new culture—this helps build a critical mass of people to help turn the tide in favor of the new culture.

5. Mandating that all company personnel attend culture-training programs to learn more about the new work practices and operating approaches and to better understand the cultured-related actions and behaviors that are expected.

6. Pushing hard to implement new-style work practices and operating procedures.

7. Designing compensation incentives that boost the pay of teams and individuals who display the desired cultural behaviors and hit change resisters in the pocket-book—company personnel are much more inclined to exhibit the desired kinds of actions and behaviors when it is in their financial best interest to do so.

8. Granting generous pay raises to individuals who step out front, lead the adoption of the desired work practices, display the new-style behaviors, and achieve pace-setting results.

9. Revising policies and procedures in ways that will help drive cultural change.

Executives must take care to launch enough companywide culture-change actions at the outset to leave no room for doubt that management is dead serious about changing the present culture and that a cultural transformation is inevitable. To convince doubters and skeptics that they cannot just wait in hopes the culture-change initiative will soon die out, the series of actions initiated by top management must create lots of hallway talk across the whole company, get the change process off to a fast start, and be followed by unrelenting efforts to firmly establish the new work practices and style of operating as standard.

Symbolic Culture-Changing Actions Symbolic managerial actions are necessary to alter a problem culture and tighten the strategy–culture fit. The most important symbolic actions are those that top executives take to *lead by example*. For instance, if the organization's strategy involves a drive to become the industry's low-cost producer, senior managers must display frugality in their own actions and decisions: inexpensive decorations in the executive suite, conservative expense accounts and entertainment allowances, a lean staff in the corporate office, scrutiny of budget requests, few executive perks, and so on. At Wal-Mart, all the executive offices are simply decorated; executives are habitually frugal in their own actions, and they are zealous in their own efforts to control costs and promote greater efficiency. At Nucor, one of the world's low-cost producers of steel products, executives fly coach class and use taxis at airports rather than limousines. If the culture change imperative is to be more responsive to customers' needs and to pleasing customers, the CEO can instill greater customer awareness by requiring all officers and executives to spend a significant portion of each week talking with customers about their needs. Top executives must be alert to the fact that company personnel will be watching their actions and decisions to see if they are walking the talk. Hence, they need to make sure that their current decisions will be construed as consistent with new-culture values and behaviors.[17]

Another category of symbolic actions includes holding ceremonial events to single out and honor people whose actions and performance exemplify what is called for in the new culture. A point is made of holding events to celebrate each culture-change success (and any other outcome that management would like to see happen again). Executives sensitive to their role in promoting strategy–culture fits make a habit of appearing at ceremonial functions to praise individuals and groups that get with the program. They show up at employee training programs to stress strategic priorities, values, ethical principles, and cultural norms. Every group gathering is seen as an opportunity to repeat and ingrain values, praise good deeds, expound on the merits of the new culture, and cite instances of how the new work practices and operating approaches have worked to good advantage.

The use of symbols in culture building is widespread. Many universities give outstanding teacher awards each year to symbolize their commitment to good teaching and their esteem for instructors who display exceptional classroom talents. Numerous businesses have employee-of-the-month awards. The military has a long-standing custom of awarding ribbons and medals for exemplary actions. Mary Kay Cosmetics awards an array of prizes—from ribbons to pink automobiles—to its beauty consultants for reaching various sales plateaus.

How Long Does It Take to Change a Problem Culture?   Planting and growing the seeds of a new culture require a determined effort by the chief executive and other senior managers. Neither charisma nor personal magnetism is essential. But a sustained and persistent effort to reinforce the culture at every opportunity through both word and deed is very definitely required. Changing a problem culture is never a short-term exercise. It takes time for a new culture to emerge and prevail. Overnight transformations simply don't occur. And it takes even longer for a new culture to become deeply embedded The bigger the organization and the greater the cultural shift needed to produce a strategy–culture fit, the longer it takes. In large companies, fixing a problem culture and instilling a new set of attitudes and behaviors can take two to five years. In fact, it is usually tougher to reform an entrenched problematic culture than it is to instill a strategy-supportive culture from scratch in a brand-new organization. Sometimes executives succeed in changing the values and behaviors of small groups of managers and even whole departments or divisions, only to find the changes eroded over time by the actions of the rest of the organization—what is communicated, praised, supported, and penalized by an entrenched majority undermines the new emergent culture and halts its progress. Executives, despite a series of well-intended actions to reform a problem culture, are likely to fail at weeding out embedded cultural traits when widespread employee skepticism about the company's new directions and culture-change effort spawns covert resistance to the cultural behaviors and operating practices advocated by top management. This is why management must take every opportunity to convince employees of the need for culture change and communicate to them how new attitudes, behaviors, and operating practices will benefit the interests of organizational stakeholders.

A company that succeeded in fixing a problem culture is Alberto-Culver—see Illustration Capsule 13.2.

Illustration Capsule 13.2

Changing the Culture in Alberto-Culver's North American Division

In 1993, Carol Bernick—vice chairperson of Alberto-Culver, president of its North American division, and daughter of the company's founders—concluded that her division's existing culture had four problems: Employees dutifully waited for marching orders from their bosses, workers put pleasing their bosses ahead of pleasing customers, some company policies were not family-friendly, and there was too much bureaucracy and paperwork. What was needed, in Bernick's opinion, was a culture in which company employees had a sense of ownership and an urgency to get things done, welcomed innovation, and were willing to take risks.

Alberto-Culver's management undertook a series of actions to introduce and ingrain the desired cultural attributes:

- In 1993, a new position, called growth development leader (GDL), was created to help orchestrate the task of fixing the culture deep in the ranks (there were 70 GDLs in Alberto-Culver's North American division). GDLs came from all ranks of the company's managerial ladder and were handpicked for such qualities as empathy, communication skills, positive attitude, and ability to let their hair down and have fun. GDLs performed their regular jobs in addition to taking on the GDL roles; it was considered an honor to be chosen. Each GDL mentored about 12 people from both a career and a family standpoint. GDLs met with senior executives weekly, bringing forward people's questions and issues and then, afterward, sharing with their groups the topics and solutions that were discussed. GDLs brought a group member as a guest to each meeting. One meeting each year is devoted to identifying "macros and irritations"— attendees are divided into four subgroups and given 15 minutes to identify the company's four biggest challenges (the macros) and the four most annoying aspects of life at the company (the irritations); the whole group votes on which four deserve the company's attention. Those selected are then addressed, and assignments made for follow-up and results.

- Changing the culture was made an issue across the company, starting in 1995 with a two-hour State of the Company presentation to employees covering where the company was and where it wanted to be. The State of the Company address then became an annual event.

- Management created ways to measure the gains in changing the culture. One involved an annual all-employee survey to assess progress against cultural goals and to get 360-degree feedback—the 2000 survey had 180 questions, including 33 relating to the performance of each respondent's GDL. A bonfire celebration was held in the company parking lot to announce that paperwork would be cut by 30 percent.

- A list of 10 cultural imperatives was formalized in 1998—honesty, ownership, trust, customer orientation, commitment, fun, innovation, risk taking, speed and urgency, and teamwork. These imperatives came to be known internally as HOT CC FIRST.

- Numerous celebrations and awards programs were instituted. Most celebrations are scheduled, but some are spontaneous (an impromptu thank-you party for a good fiscal year). Business Builder Awards (initiated in 1997) are given to individuals and teams that make a significant impact on the company's growth and profitability. The best-scoring GDLs on the annual employee surveys are awarded shares of company stock. The company notes all work anniversaries and personal milestones with "Alberto-appropriate" gifts; appreciative company employees sometimes give thank-you gifts to their GDLs. According to Carol Bernick, "If you want something to grow, pour champagne on it. We've made a huge effort—maybe even an over-the-top effort—to celebrate our successes and, indeed, just about everything we'd like to see happen again."

The culture change effort at Alberto-Culver North America was viewed as a major contributor to improved performance. From 1993 (when the effort first began) to 2001, the division's sales increased from just under $350 million to over $600 million and pretax profits rose from $20 million to almost $50 million. Carol Bernick was elevated to chairman of Alberto-Culver's board of directors in 2004.

Source: Based on information in Carol Lavin Bernick, "When Your Culture Needs a Makeover," *Harvard Business Review* 79, no. 6 (June 2001), p. 61 and information posted at the company's Web site, www.alberto.com (accessed November 10, 2005).

Grounding the Culture in Core Values and Ethics

The foundation of a company's corporate culture nearly always resides in its dedication to certain core values and the bar it sets for ethical behavior. The culture-shaping significance of core values and ethical behaviors accounts for why so many companies have developed a formal values statement and a code of ethics—see Table 13.1 for representative core values and the ground usually covered in codes of ethics. Many companies today convey their values and codes of ethics to stakeholders and interested parties in their annual reports and on their Web sites. The trend of making stakeholders aware of a company's commitment to core values and ethical business conduct is attributable to three factors: (1) greater management understanding of the role these statements play in culture building, (2) a renewed focus on ethical standards stemming from the numerous corporate scandals that hit the headlines during 2001–2005, and (3) the sizable fraction of consumers and suppliers who prefer doing business with ethical companies.

> **Core Concept**
> A company's culture is grounded in and shaped by its core values and the bar it sets for ethical behavior.

At Darden Restaurants—the world's largest casual dining company, which employs more than 150,000 people and serves 300 million meals annually at 1,400 Red Lobster, Olive Garden, Bahama Breeze, Smokey Bones Barbeque & Grill, and Seasons 52 restaurants in North America—the core values are operating with integrity and fairness, caring and respect, being of service, teamwork, excellence, always learning and teaching, and welcoming and celebrating workforce diversity. Top executives at

Table 13.1 **Representative Content of Company Values Statements and Codes of Ethics**

Typical Core Values	Areas Covered by Codes of Ethics
• Satisfying and delighting customers	• Expecting all company personnel to display honesty and integrity in their actions and avoid conflicts of interest
• Dedication to superior customer service, top-notch quality, product innovation, and/or technological leadership	• Mandating full compliance with all laws and regulations, specifically:
• A commitment to excellence and results	—Antitrust laws prohibiting anticompetitive practices, conspiracies to fix prices, or attempts to monopolize
• Exhibiting such qualities as integrity, fairness, trustworthiness, pride of workmanship, Golden Rule behavior, respect for co-workers, and ethical behavior	—Foreign Corrupt Practices Act
• Creativity, exercising initiative, and accepting responsibility	—Securities laws and prohibitions against insider trading
• Teamwork and cooperative attitudes	—Environmental and workplace safety regulations
• Fair treatment of suppliers	—Discrimination and sexual harassment regulations
• Making the company a great place to work	—Political contributions and lobbying activities
• A commitment to having fun and creating a fun work environment	• Prohibiting giving or accepting bribes, kickbacks, or gifts
• Being stewards of shareholders' investments and remaining committed to profits and growth	• Engaging in fair selling and marketing practices
• Exercising social responsibility and being a good community citizen	• Not dealing with suppliers that employ child labor or engage in other unsavory practices
• Caring about protecting the environment	• Being above-board in acquiring and using competitively sensitive information about rivals and others
• Having a diverse workforce	• Avoiding use of company assets, resources, and property for personal or other inappropriate purposes
	• Responsibility to protect proprietary information and not divulge trade secrets

Darden believe the company's practice of these values has been instrumental in creating a culture characterized by trust, exciting jobs and career opportunities for employees, and a passion to provide "a terrific dining experience to every guest, every time, in every one of our restaurants."[18]

Of course, sometimes a company's stated core values and codes of ethics are cosmetic, existing mainly to impress outsiders and help create a positive company image. But more usually they have been developed to shape the culture. Many executives want the work climate at their companies to mirror certain values and ethical standards, partly because they are personally committed to these values and ethical standards but mainly because they are convinced that adherence to such values and ethical principles will make the company a much better performer *and* improve its image. As discussed earlier, values-related cultural norms promote better strategy execution and mobilize company personnel behind the drive to achieve stretch objectives and the company's strategic vision. Hence, a corporate culture grounded in well-chosen core values and high ethical standards contributes mightily to a company's long-term strategic success.[19] And, not incidentally, strongly ingrained values and ethical standards reduce the likelihood of lapses in ethical and socially-approved behavior that mar a company's reputation and put its financial performance and market standing at risk.

> A company's values statement and code of ethics communicate expectations of how employees should conduct themselves in the workplace.

The Culture-Building Role of Values and Codes of Ethics   At companies where executives believe in the merits of practicing the values and ethical standards that have been espoused, *the stated core values and ethical principles are the cornerstones of the corporate culture.* As depicted in Figure 13.2, a company's stated core values and ethical principles have two roles in the culture-building process. One, a company that works hard at putting its stated core values and ethical principles into practice fosters a work climate where company personnel share common and strongly held convictions about how the company's business is to be conducted. Second, the stated values and ethical principles provide company personnel with guidance about the manner in which

Figure 13.2   **The Two Culture-Building Roles of a Company's Core Values and Ethical Standards**

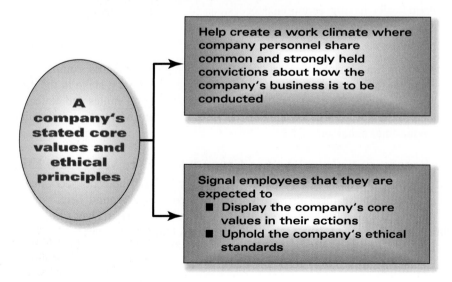

A company's stated core values and ethical principles

Help create a work climate where company personnel share common and strongly held convictions about how the company's business is to be conducted

Signal employees that they are expected to
■ Display the company's core values in their actions
■ Uphold the company's ethical standards

they are to do their jobs—which behaviors and ways of doing things are approved (and expected) and which are out-of-bounds.

Transforming Core Values and Ethical Standards into Cultural Norms

Once values and ethical standards have been formally adopted, they must be institutionalized in the company's policies and practices and embedded in the conduct of company personnel. This can be done in a number of different ways.[20] Tradition-steeped companies with a rich folklore rely heavily on word-of-mouth indoctrination and the power of tradition to instill values and enforce ethical conduct. But most companies employ a variety of techniques to hammer in core values and ethical standards, using some or all of the following:

1. Giving explicit attention to values and ethics in recruiting and hiring to screen out applicants who do not exhibit compatible character traits.

2. Incorporating the statement of values and the code of ethics into orientation programs for new employees and training courses for managers and employees.

3. Having senior executives frequently reiterate the importance and role of company values and ethical principles at company events and internal communications to employees.

4. Using values statements and codes of ethical conduct as benchmarks for judging the appropriateness of company policies and operating practices.

5. Making the display of core values and ethical principles a big factor in evaluating each person's job performance—there's no better way to win the attention and commitment of company personnel than by using the degree to which individuals observe core values and ethical standards as a basis for compensation increases and promotion.

6. Making sure that managers, from the CEO down to frontline supervisors, are diligent in stressing the importance of ethical conduct and observance of core values. Line managers at all levels must give serious and continuous attention to the task of explaining how the values and ethical code apply in their areas.

7. Encouraging everyone to use their influence in helping enforce observance of core values and ethical standards—strong peer pressures to exhibit core values and ethical standards are a deterrent to outside-the-lines behavior.

8. Periodically having ceremonial occasions to recognize individuals and groups who display the values and ethical principles.

9. Instituting ethics enforcement procedures.

To deeply ingrain the stated core values and to high ethical standards, companies must turn them into *strictly enforced cultural norms*. They must put a stake in the ground, making it unequivocally clear that living up to the company's values and ethical standards has to be a way of life at the company and that there will be little toleration of outside-the-lines behavior.

The Benefits of Cultural Norms Grounded in Core Values and Ethical Principles

The more that managers succeed in making the espoused values and ethical principles the main drivers of "how we do things around here," the more that the values and ethical principles function as cultural norms. Over time, a strong culture grounded in the display of core values and ethics may emerge. As shown in Figure 13.3, *cultural norms* rooted in core values and ethical behavior are highly beneficial in three respects.[21] One, the advocated core values and ethical standards accurately

Figure 13.3   **The Benefits of Cultural Norms Strongly Grounded in Core Values and Ethical Principles**

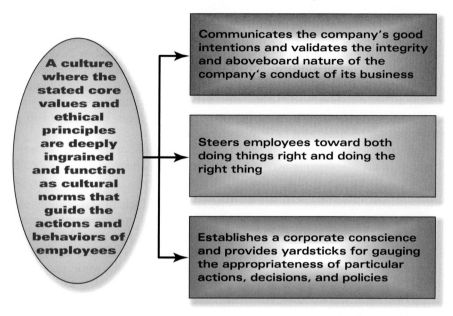

communicate the company's good intentions and validate the integrity and above-board character of its business principles and operating methods. There's nothing cosmetic or fake about the company's values statement and code of ethics—company personnel actually strive to practice what is being preached. Second, the values-based and ethics-based cultural norms steer company personnel toward both doing things right and doing the right thing. Third, they establish a "corporate conscience" and provide yardsticks for gauging the appropriateness of particular actions, decisions, and policies.

Establishing a Strategy–Culture Fit in Multinational and Global Companies

In multinational and global companies, establishing a tight strategy–culture fit is complicated by the diverse societal circumstances surrounding the company's operations in different countries. The nature of the local economies, living conditions, per capita incomes, and lifestyles can give rise to considerable cross-border diversity in a company's workforce and to subcultures within the corporate culture. Leading cross-border culture-change initiatives requires sensitivity to prevailing differences in local circumstances; company managers must discern when local subcultures have to be accommodated and when cross-border differences in the company's corporate culture can be and should be narrowed.[22] Cross-border diversity in a multinational enterprise's corporate culture is more tolerable if the company is pursuing a multicountry strategy and if the company's culture in each country is well aligned with its strategy in that country. But significant cross-country differences in a company's culture are likely to impede execution of a global strategy and have to be addressed.

As discussed earlier in this chapter, *the trick to establishing a workable strategy–culture fit in multinational companies is to ground the culture in strategy-supportive values and operating practices that travel well across country borders* and strike a chord with managers and workers in many different areas of the world, despite varying local customs and traditions. A multinational enterprise with a misfit between its strategy and culture in certain countries where it operates can attack the problem by rewording its values statement so as to express core values in ways that have universal appeal. The alternative is to allow *some leeway* for certain core values to be reinterpreted or de-emphasized or applied somewhat differently from country to country whenever local customs and traditions in a few countries really need to be accommodated. But such accommodation needs to be done in ways that do not impede good strategy execution. Sometimes certain offending operating styles can be modified to good advantage in all locations where the company operates.

Aside from trying to build the corporate culture around a set of core values that have universal appeal, management can seek to minimize the existence of subcultures and promote greater cross-country cultural uniformity by:

- *Instituting culture training in each country.* The goals of this training should be to (1) communicate the meaning of core values in language that resonates with company personnel in that country and (2) explain the case for common operating approaches and work practices. The use of uniform work practices becomes particularly important when the company's work practices are efficient and aid good strategy execution—in such instances, local managers have to find ways to skirt local preferences and win support for "how we do things around here."

- *Creating a cultural climate where the norm is to adopt best practices, use common work procedures, and pursue operating excellence.* Companies may find that a values-based corporate culture is less crucial to good strategy execution that an operations-based, results-oriented culture in which the dominant cultural norm is an all-out effort to do things in the best possible manner, achieve continuous improvement, and meet or beat performance targets. A results-oriented culture keyed to operating excellence and meeting stretch objectives sidesteps many of the problems with trying to get people from different societies and traditions to embrace common values.

- *Giving local managers the flexibility to modify people management approaches or operating styles.* In some situations, adherence to companywide cultural traditions simply doesn't work well. However, local modifications have to be infrequent and done in a manner that doesn't undermine the establishment of a mostly uniform corporate culture.

- *Giving local managers discretionary authority to use somewhat different motivational and compensation incentives to induce local personnel to adopt and practice the desired cultural behaviors.* Personnel in different countries may respond better to some compensation structures and reward systems than to others.

Generally, a high degree of cross-country homogeneity in a multinational company's corporate culture is desirable and has to be pursued, particularly when it comes to ingraining universal core values and companywide enforcement of such ethical standards as the payment of bribes and kickbacks, the use of underage labor, and environmental stewardship. Having too much variation in the culture from country to country not only makes it difficult to use the culture in helping drive the strategy execution process but also works against the establishment of a one-company mind-set and a consistent corporate identity.

LEADING THE STRATEGY EXECUTION PROCESS

The litany of managing the strategy process is simple enough: Craft a sound strategic plan, implement it, execute it to the fullest, adjust it as needed, and win! But the leadership challenges are significant and diverse. Exerting take-charge leadership, being a "spark plug," ramrodding things through, and achieving results thrusts a manager into a variety of leadership roles in managing the strategy execution process: resource acquirer and allocator, capabilities builder, motivator, policymaker, policy enforcer, head cheerleader, crisis solver, decision maker, and taskmaster, to mention a few. There are times when leading the strategy execution process entails being hard-nosed and authoritarian, times when it is best to be a perceptive listener and a compromising decision maker, times when matters are best delegated to people closest to the scene of the action, and times when mentoring or coaching is appropriate. Many occasions call for the manager in charge to assume a highly visible role and put in long hours guiding the process, while others entail only a brief ceremonial performance with the details delegated to subordinates.

For the most part, leading the strategy execution process is a top-down responsibility driven by mandates to get things on the right track and show good results. It must start with a perceptive diagnosis of the requirements for good strategy execution, given the company's circumstances. Then comes diagnosis of the organization's capabilities and preparedness to execute the necessary strategic initiatives and decisions as to which of several ways to proceed to get things done and achieve the targeted results.[23] In general, leading the drive for good strategy execution and operating excellence calls for five actions on the part of the manager-in-charge:

1. Staying on top of what is happening, closely monitoring progress, ferreting out issues, and learning what obstacles lie in the path of good execution.
2. Putting constructive pressure on the organization to achieve good results and operating excellence.
3. Leading the development of stronger core competencies and competitive capabilities.
4. Displaying ethical integrity and leading social responsibility initiatives.
5. Pushing corrective actions to improve strategy execution and achieve the targeted results.

Staying on Top of How Well Things Are Going

To stay on top of how well the strategy execution process is going, a manager needs to develop a broad network of contacts and sources of information, both formal and informal. The regular channels include talking with key subordinates, attending meetings and quizzing the presenters, reading reviews of the latest operating results, talking to customers, watching the competitive reactions of rival firms, exchanging e-mail and holding telephone conversations with people in outlying locations, making on-site visits, and listening to rank-and-file employees. However, some information is more trustworthy than the rest, and the views and perspectives offered by different people can vary widely. Presentations and briefings by subordinates may be colored by wishful thinking or shoddy analysis rather than representing the unvarnished truth. Bad news is sometimes filtered, minimized, or distorted by people pursuing their own agendas, and in some cases not reported at all as subordinates delay conveying failures and problems in hopes that they can turn things around in time. Hence, managers have to decide which information is trustworthy and get an accurate feel for the existing situation. They have to confirm whether things are on track, identify problems, learn what obstacles lie in the path of good strategy execution, ruthlessly assess whether the organization has the talent and attitude needed to drive the required changes, and develop a basis for determining what, if anything, they can personally do to move the process along.[24]

One of the best ways for executives to stay on top of the strategy execution process is by making regular visits to the field and talking with many different people at many different levels—a technique often labeled **managing by walking around (MBWA).** Wal-Mart executives have had a long-standing practice of spending two to three days every week visiting Wal-Mart's stores and talking with store managers and employees. Sam Walton, Wal-Mart's founder, insisted, "The key is to get out into the store and listen to what the associates have to say." Jack Welch, the highly effective CEO of General Electric (GE) from 1980 to 2001, not only spent several days each month personally visiting GE operations and talking with major customers but also arranged his schedule so that he could spend time exchanging information and ideas with GE managers from all over the world who were attending classes at the company's leadership development center near GE's headquarters.

> **Core Concept**
> *Management by walking around (MBWA)* is one of the techniques that effective leaders use to stay informed about how well the strategy execution process is progressing.

Often, customers and suppliers can provide valuable perspectives on how well a company's strategy execution process is going. Joe Tucci, chief operating officer at data-storage leader EMC, when confronted with an unexpected dropoff in EMC's sales in 2001 and not sure whether the downturn represented a temporary slump or a structural market change went straight to the source for hard information: the chief executive officers and chief financial officers to whom chief information officers at customer companies reported and to the consultants who advised them. The information he got was eye-opening—fundamental market shifts were occurring, and the rules of market engagement now called for major strategy changes at EMC followed by quick implementation.

To keep their fingers on the company's pulse, managers at some companies host weekly get-togethers (often on Friday afternoons) to create a regular opportunity for tidbits of information to flow freely between down-the-line employees and executives. Many manufacturing executives make a point of strolling the factory floor to talk with workers and meeting regularly with union officials. Some managers operate out of open cubicles in big spaces so that they can interact easily and frequently with co-workers. Jeff Bezos, Amazon.com's CEO, is noted for his practice of MBWA, firing off a battery of questions when he tours facilities and insisting that Amazon managers spend time in the trenches with their people to avoid abstract thinking and getting disconnected from the reality of what's happening.[25]

Most managers practice MBWA, attaching great importance to spending time with people at various company facilities and gathering information and opinions firsthand from diverse sources about how well various aspects of the strategy execution process are going. They believe facilities visits and face-to-face contacts give them a good feel for what progress is being made, what problems are being encountered, and whether additional resources or different approaches may be needed. Just as important, MBWA provides opportunities to talk informally to many different people at different organizational levels, give encouragement, lift spirits, shift attention from the old to the new priorities, and create some excitement—all of which generate positive energy and help mobilize organizational efforts behind strategy execution.

Putting Constructive Pressure on the Organization to Achieve Good Results and Operating Excellence

Managers have to be out front in mobilizing organizational energy behind the drive for good strategy execution and operating excellence. Part of the leadership requirement here entails nurturing a results-oriented work climate, where performance standards are high and a spirit of achievement is pervasive. The intended outcome is an organization with a good track record in meeting or beating stretch performance targets. A high-performance culture in which there is constructive pressure to achieve good results is a valuable contributor to good strategy execution and operating excellence. If management wants to drive the strategy execution effort by instilling a results-oriented work climate, then senior executives have to take the lead in promoting certain enabling cultural drivers: a strong sense of involvement on the part of company personnel, emphasis on individual initiative and creativity, respect for the contribution of individuals and groups, and pride in doing things right.

Organizational leaders who succeed in creating a results-oriented work climate typically are intensely people-oriented, and they are skilled users of people-management practices that win the emotional commitment of company personnel and inspire them to do their best.[26] They understand that treating employees well generally leads to increased teamwork, higher morale, greater loyalty, and increased employee commitment to making a contribution. All of these foster an esprit de corps that energizes organizational members to contribute to the drive for operating excellence and proficient strategy execution.

Successfully leading the effort to instill a spirit of high achievement into the culture generally entails such leadership actions and managerial practices as:

- *Treating employees with dignity and respect.* This often includes a strong company commitment to training each employee thoroughly, providing attractive career opportunities, emphasizing promotion from within, and providing a high degree of job security. Some companies symbolize the value of individual employees and the importance of their contributions by referring to them as cast members (Disney), crew members (McDonald's), co-workers (Kinko's and CDW Computer Centers), job owners (Granite Construction), partners (Starbucks), or associates (Wal-Mart, Lenscrafters, W. L. Gore, Edward Jones, Publix Supermarkets, and Marriott International). At a number of companies, managers at every level are held responsible for developing the people who report to them.

- *Making champions out of the people who turn in winning performances.* This must be done in ways that promote teamwork and cross-unit collaboration as opposed to spurring an unhealthy footrace among employees to best one another. Would-be champions who advocate radical or different ideas must not be looked on as disruptive or troublesome. The best champions and change agents are persistent, competitive, tenacious, committed, and fanatic about seeing their idea through to success. It is particularly important that people who champion an unsuccessful idea not be punished or sidelined but rather encouraged to try again—encouraging lots of "tries" is important since many ideas won't pan out.

- *Encouraging employees to use initiative and creativity in performing their work.* Operating excellence requires that everybody be expected to contribute ideas, exercise initiative, and pursue continuous improvement. The leadership trick is to keep a sense of urgency alive in the business so that people see change and innovation as necessities. Moreover, people with maverick ideas or out-of-the-ordinary proposals have to be tolerated and given room to operate; anything less tends to squelch creativity and initiative.

- *Setting stretch objectives.* Managers must clearly communicate an expectation that company personnel are to give their best in achieving performance targets.

- *Using the tools of benchmarking, best practices, business process reengineering, TQM, and Six Sigma quality to focus attention on operating excellence.* These are proven approaches to getting better operating results and facilitating better strategy execution.

- *Using the full range of motivational techniques and compensation incentives to inspire company personnel, nurture a results-oriented work climate, and enforce high-performance standards.* Managers cannot mandate innovative improvements by simply exhorting people to "be creative," nor can they make continuous progress toward operating excellence with directives to "try harder." Rather, they have to foster a culture where innovative ideas and experimentation with new ways of doing things can blossom and thrive. Individuals and groups need to be strongly encouraged to brainstorm, let their imaginations fly in all directions, and come up with proposals for improving how things are done. This means giving company personnel enough autonomy to stand out, excel, and contribute. And it means that the rewards for successful champions of new ideas and operating improvements should be large and visible.

- *Celebrating individual, group, and company successes.* Top management should miss no opportunity to express respect for individual employees and their appreciation of extraordinary individual and group effort.[27] Companies like Mary Kay Cosmetics, Tupperware, and McDonald's actively seek out reasons and opportunities to give pins, buttons, badges, and medals for good showings by average performers—the idea being to express appreciation and give a motivational boost to people who stand out in doing ordinary jobs. General Electric and 3M Corporation make a point of ceremoniously honoring individuals who believe so strongly in their ideas that they take it on themselves to hurdle the bureaucracy, maneuver their projects through the system, and turn them into improved services, new products, or even new businesses.

While leadership efforts to instill a results-oriented, high performance culture usually accentuate the positive, there are negative reinforcers too. Managers whose units consistently perform poorly have to be replaced. Low-performing workers and people who reject the results-oriented cultural emphasis have to be weeded out or at least moved to out-of-the-way positions. Average performers have to be candidly counseled that they have limited career potential unless they show more progress in the form of additional effort, better skills, and improved ability to deliver good results.

Leading the Development of Better Competencies and Capabilities

A third avenue to better strategy execution and operating excellence is proactively strengthening core competencies and competitive capabilities to better perform value chain activities and pave the way for better bottom-line results. This often requires top management intervention for two reasons. One, senior managers are more likely to recognize and appreciate the strategy-executing significance of stronger capabilities; this is especially true in multinational companies where it is top executives are in the best position to spot opportunities to leverage existing competencies and competitive capabilities across geographical borders. Two, senior managers usually have to *lead* the strengthening effort because core competencies and competitive capabilities typically reside in the combined efforts of different work groups, departments, and strategic allies and only senior managers have the organizational clout to enforce the necessary networking and collaboration.

Aside from leading efforts to strengthen *existing* competencies and capabilities, effective strategy leaders try to anticipate changes in customer-market requirements and proactively build *new* competencies and capabilities that offer a competitive edge over rivals. Again, senior managers are in the best position to see the need and potential of new capabilities and then to play a lead role in the capability-building, resource-enhancing process. Proactively building new competencies and capabilities ahead of rivals to gain a competitive edge is strategic leadership of the best kind, but strengthening the company's resource base in reaction to newly developed capabilities of pioneering rivals occurs more frequently.

Displaying Ethical Integrity and Leading Social Responsibility Initiatives

For an organization to avoid the pitfalls of scandal and disgrace and consistently display the intent to conduct its business in a principled manner, the CEO and those around the CEO must be openly and unswervingly committed to ethical conduct and socially redeeming business principles and core values. Leading the effort to operate the company's business in an ethically principled fashion has three pieces. First and foremost, the CEO and other senior executives must set an excellent example in their own ethical behavior, demonstrating character and personal integrity in their actions and decisions. The behavior of senior executives sends a clear message to company personnel regarding what the "real" standards of personal conduct are. Moreover, the company's strategy and operating decisions have to be seen as ethical—actions always speak far louder than the words in a company's code of ethics. Second, top management must declare unequivocal support of the company's ethical code and take an uncompromising stand on expecting all company personnel to conduct themselves in an ethical fashion at all times. This means iterating and reiterating to employees that it is their duty to observe the company's ethical codes. Third, top management must be prepared to act as the final arbiter on hard calls; this means removing people from key positions or terminating them when they are guilty of a violation. It also means reprimanding those who have been lax in monitoring and enforcing ethical compliance. Failure to act swiftly and decisively in punishing ethical misconduct is interpreted as a lack of real commitment.

Establishing an Effective Ethics Compliance and Enforcement Process

If a company's executives truly aspire for company personnel to behave ethically, they must personally see to it that strong and effective procedures for enforcing ethical standards and handling potential violations are put in place. Even in an ethically strong company, there can be bad apples—and some of the bad apples may be executives. So it is rarely enough to rely on either the exhortations of senior executives or an ethically principled culture to produce ethics compliance.

Executive action to institute formal ethics compliance and enforcement mechanisms can entail forming an ethics committee to give guidance on ethics matters, appointing an ethics officers to head the compliance effort, establishing an ethics hotline or Web site that employees can use to either anonymously report a possible violation or get confidential advice on a troubling ethics-related situation, and having an annual ethics audit to measure the extent of ethical behavior and identify problem areas. If senior executives are really serious about enforcing ethical behavior, they probably need to do five things:[28]

1. **Have mandatory ethics training programs for employees.** Company personnel have to be educated about what is ethical and what is not and given guidance about the gray areas. Special training programs probably are needed for personnel in such ethically vulnerable areas as procurement, sales, and lobbying. Company personnel assigned to subsidiaries in foreign countries can find themselves trapped in ethical dilemmas if bribery and corruption of public officials are common practices or if suppliers or customers are accustomed to kickbacks of one kind or another.

2. **Openly encourage company personnel to report possible infractions via anonymous calls to a hotline or e-mails sent to a designated address.** Ideally, the company's culture will be sufficiently ethically principled that most company personnel will feel it is their obligation and duty to report possible ethical violations (not so much to get someone in trouble but to prevent further damage and help the company avoid the dire consequences of a debilitating scandal. Furthermore, everyone must be encouraged to raise issues about ethically gray areas and to get confidential advice from the company's ethics specialists.

3. **Conduct an annual audit of each manager's efforts to uphold ethical standards** and require formal reports on the actions taken by managers to remedy deficient conduct.

4. **Require all employees to sign a statement annually certifying that they have complied with the company's code of ethics.**

5. **Make sure that ethical violations carry appropriate punishment, including dismissal if the violation is sufficiently egregious.**

While these actions may seem extreme, they leave little room to doubt the seriousness of executive commitment to ethics compliance. Openly encouraging people to report possible ethical violations heightens awareness of operating within ethical bounds. And while violators have to be disciplined, *the main purpose of the various means of enforcement is to encourage compliance rather than administer punishment.* Most company personnel will think twice about knowingly engaging in unethical conduct when their actions could be reported by watchful co-workers. The same is true when they know their actions will be audited and/or when they have to sign statements certifying compliance with the company's code of ethics.

Top executives in multinational companies face big challenges in enforcing strict ethical standards companywide because what is considered ethical often varies substantially or subtly from country to country. There are shades and variations in what societies generally agree to be right and wrong based on the prevailing circumstances, local customs, and predominant religious convictions. And certainly there are cross-country variations in the *degree* to which certain behaviors are considered unethical.[29] Thus, transnational companies have to make a fundamental decision regarding whether to try to enforce common ethical standards across their operations in all countries or whether to allow some rules to be bent in some cases.

Leading Social Responsibility Initiatives   The exercise of social responsibility, just as with observance of ethical principles, requires top executive leadership. *What separates companies that make a sincere effort to carry their weight in being good corporate citizens from companies that are content to do only what is legally required of them are company leaders who believe strongly that just making a profit is not good enough. Such leaders are committed to a higher standard of performance that includes social and environmental metrics as well as financial and strategic metrics.* Thus, it is up to the CEO and other senior executives to insist that the company go past the rhetoric and cosmetics of corporate citizenship and implement social responsibility initiatives.

> CEOs who are committed to a core value of corporate social responsibility move beyond the rhetorical flourishes and enlist the full support of company personnel behind the execution of social responsibility initiatives.

Among the leadership responsibilities of the CEO and other senior managers, therefore, are to *step out front,* to wave the flag of socially responsible behavior for all to see, to marshal the support of company personnel, and to make social responsibility initiatives an everyday part of how the company conducts its business affairs. Top executives have to use social and environmental metrics in evaluating performance and, ideally, the company's board of directors will elect to tie the company's social and environmental performance to executive compensation—a surefire way to make sure that social responsibility efforts are more than window dressing. To help ensure that it has commitment from senior managers, Verizon Communications ties 10 percent of the annual bonus of the company's top 2,500 managers directly to the achievement of social responsibility targets. One survey found over 60 percent of senior managers believed that a portion of executive compensation should be linked to a company's performance on social and environmental measures. The strength of the commitment from the top—typically a company's CEO and board of directors—ultimately determines whether a company will implement and execute a full-fledged strategy of social responsibility that embraces some customized combination of actions to protect the environment (beyond what is required by law), actively participate in community affairs, be a generous supporter of charitable causes and projects that benefit society, and have a positive impact on workforce diversity and the overall well-being of employees. One of the most reliable signs that company executives are leading an authentic effort to carry out fruitful social responsibility initiatives is whether the company issues an annual report on its social responsibility efforts that cites quantitative and qualitative evidence of the company accomplishments.

Leading the Process of Making Corrective Adjustments

The leadership challenge of making corrective adjustments is twofold: deciding when adjustments are needed and deciding what adjustments to make. Both decisions are a normal and necessary part of managing the strategy execution process, since no scheme for implementing and executing strategy can foresee all the events and problems that will arise. There comes a time at every company when managers have to fine-tune or overhaul the approaches to strategy execution and push for better results. Clearly, when a company's strategy execution effort is not delivering good results and making measurable progress toward operating excellence, it is the leader's responsibility to step forward and push corrective actions.

The *process* of making corrective adjustments varies according to the situation. In a crisis, it is typical for leaders to have key subordinates gather information, identify and evaluate options (crunching whatever numbers may be appropriate), and perhaps prepare a preliminary set of recommended actions for consideration. The organizational leader then usually meets with key subordinates and personally presides over extended discussions of the proposed responses, trying to build a quick consensus among members of the executive inner circle. If no consensus emerges and action is required immediately, the burden falls on the manager in charge to choose the response and urge its support.

When the situation allows managers to proceed more deliberately in deciding when to make changes and what changes to make, most managers seem to prefer a process of incrementally solidifying commitment to a particular course of action.[30] The process that managers go through in deciding on corrective adjustments is essentially the same for both proactive and reactive changes: They sense needs, gather information, broaden and deepen their understanding of the situation, develop options and explore their pros and cons, put forth action proposals, generate partial (comfort-level) solutions, strive for a consensus, and finally formally adopt an agreed-on course of action.[31] Deciding what corrective changes to initiate can take a few hours, a few days, a few weeks, or even a few months if the situation is particularly complicated.

Success in initiating corrective actions usually hinges on thorough analysis of the situation, the exercise of good business judgment in deciding what actions to take, and good implementation of the corrective actions that are initiated. Successful managers are skilled in getting an organization back on track rather quickly; they (and their staffs) are good at discerning what actions to take and in ramrodding them through to a successful conclusion. Managers that struggle to show measurable progress in generating good results and improving the performance of strategy-critical value chain activities are candidates for being replaced.

The challenges of leading a successful strategy execution effort are, without question, substantial.[32] But the job is definitely doable. Because each instance of executing strategy occurs under different organizational circumstances, the managerial agenda for executing strategy always needs to be situation-specific—there's no neat generic procedure to follow. And, as we said at the beginning of Chapter 11, executing strategy is an action-oriented, make-the-right-things-happen task that challenges a manager's ability to lead and direct organizational change, create or reinvent business processes, manage and motivate people, and achieve performance targets. If you now better understand what the challenges are, what approaches are available, which issues need to be considered, and why the action agenda for implementing and executing strategy sweeps across so many aspects of administrative and managerial work, then we will look on our discussion in Chapters 11, 12, and 13 as a success.

A Final Word on Managing the Process of Crafting and Executing Strategy   In practice, it is hard to separate the leadership requirements of executing strategy from the other pieces of the strategy process. As we emphasized in Chapter 1, the job of crafting, implementing, and executing strategy is a five-phase process with much looping and recycling to fine-tune and adjust strategic visions, objectives, strategies, capabilities, implementation approaches, and cultures to fit one another and to fit changing circumstances. The process is continuous, and the conceptually separate acts of crafting and executing strategy blur together in real-world situations. The best tests of good strategic leadership are whether the company has a good strategy and whether the strategy execution effort is delivering the hoped-for results. If these two conditions exist, the chances are excellent that the company has good strategic leadership.

Key Points

The character of a company's culture is a product of the core values and business principles that executives espouse, the standards of what is ethically acceptable and what is not, the work practices and behaviors that define "how we do things around here," its approach to people management and style of operating, the "chemistry" and the "personality" that permeates its work environment, and the stories that get told over and over to illustrate and reinforce the company's values, business practices, and traditions. A company's culture is important because it influences the organization's actions and approaches to conducting business—in a very real sense, the culture is the company's "operating system" or organizational DNA.

The psyche of corporate cultures varies widely. Moreover, company cultures vary widely in strength and influence. Some are strongly embedded and have a big impact on a company's practices and behavioral norms. Others are weak and have comparatively little influence on company operations. There are four types of unhealthy cultures: (1) those that are highly political and characterized by empire building, (2) those that are change resistant, (3) those that are insular and inwardly focused, and (4) those that are ethically unprincipled and are driven by greed. High-performance cultures and adaptive cultures both have positive features that are conducive to good strategy execution.

A culture grounded in values, practices, and behavioral norms that match what is needed for good strategy execution helps energize people throughout the company to do their jobs in a strategy-supportive manner, adding significantly to the power of a company's strategy execution effort and the chances of achieving the targeted results. But when the culture is in conflict with some aspect of the company's direction, performance targets, or strategy, the culture becomes a stumbling block. Thus, an important part of the managing the strategy execution process is establishing and nurturing a good fit between culture and strategy.

A company's present culture and work climate may or may not be compatible with what is needed for effective implementation and execution of the chosen strategy. *When a company's present work climate promotes attitudes and behaviors that are well suited to first-rate strategy execution, its culture functions as a valuable ally in the strategy execution process.* When the culture is in conflict with some aspect of the company's direction, performance targets, or strategy, the culture becomes a stumbling block.

Changing a company's culture, especially a strong one with traits that don't fit a new strategy's requirements, is a tough and often time-consuming challenge. Changing a culture requires competent leadership at the top. It requires symbolic actions and substantive actions that unmistakably indicate serious commitment on the part of top management. The more that culture-driven actions and behaviors fit what's needed for good strategy execution, the less managers have to depend on policies, rules, procedures, and supervision to enforce what people should and should not do.

The taproot of a company's corporate culture nearly always is its dedication to certain core values and the bar it sets for ethical behavior. Of course, sometimes a company's stated core values and codes of ethics are cosmetic, existing mainly to impress outsiders and help create a positive company image. But more usually they have been developed to shape the culture. If management practices what it preaches, a company's core values and ethical standards nurture the corporate culture in three highly positive ways: (1) They communicate the company's good intentions and validate the integrity and above-board character of its business principles and operating methods; (2) they steer company personnel toward both doing the right thing and doing things right; and (3) they establish a corporate conscience that gauges the appropriateness of particular actions, decisions, and policies. Companies that really care about how they conduct their business put a stake in the ground, making it unequivocally clear that company personnel are expected to live up to the company's values and ethical standards—how well individuals display core values and adhere to ethical standards is often part of the job performance evaluations. Peer pressures to conform to cultural norms are quite strong, acting as an important deterrent to outside-the-lines behavior.

Leading the drive for good strategy execution and operating excellence calls for five actions on the part of the manager-in-charge:

1. Staying on top of what is happening, closely monitoring progress, ferreting out issues, and learning what obstacles lie in the path of good execution.

2. Putting constructive pressure on the organization to achieve good results and operating excellence.

3. Leading the development of stronger core competencies and competitive capabilities.

4. Displaying ethical integrity and leading social responsibility initiatives.

5. Pushing corrective actions to improve strategy execution and achieve the targeted results.

Exercises

1. Go to Herman Miller's Web site (www.hermanmiller.com) and read what the company has to say about its corporate culture in its careers sections. Do you think this statement is just public relations, or, based on what else you can learn about the Herman Miller Company from browsing this Web site, is there reason to believe that management has truly built a culture that makes the stated values and principles come alive?

2. Go to the careers section at Qualcomm's Web site (www.qualcomm.com) and see what this company, one of the most prominent companies in mobile communications technology, has to say about life at Qualcomm. Is what's on this Web site just recruiting propaganda, or does it convey the type of work climate that management is actually trying to create? If you were a senior executive at Qualcomm, would you see merit in building and nurturing a culture like what is described in the section "Life at Qualcomm"? Would such a culture represent a tight fit with Qualcomm's high-tech business and strategy? (You can get an overview of the Qualcomm's strategy by exploring the section for investors and some of the recent press releases.) Is your answer consistent with what is presented in the "Awards and Honors" menu selection in the "About Qualcomm" portion of the Web site?

3. Go to the Web site of Johnson & Johnson (www.jnj.com) and read the "J&J Credo," which sets forth the company's responsibilities to customers, employees, the community, and shareholders. Then read the "Our Company" section. Why do you think the credo has resulted in numerous awards and accolades that recognize the company as a good corporate citizen?

4. Do an Internet search or use the resources of your university's library to identify at least five companies that have experienced a failure of strategic leadership on the part of the CEO since 2000. Three candidate companies you might want to research are Adelphia Communications, AIG, and HealthSouth. Then determine which, if any, of the five factors discussed in this chapter's section titled "Leading the Strategy Execution Process" came into play in the CEOs' failure.

5. Dell Inc. has been listed as one of *Fortune*'s most admired companies for several years. Click on the "About Dell" link at www.dell.com. What is your assessment of the company's extensive discussion of accountability, concern for the environment, and community involvement? Does it appear these programs have the support of upper-level management? Is there evidence that this is more than a public relations initiative?

6. Review the material in Illustration Capsule 13.1 on Google's corporate culture; then go to the company's Web site, click on the "About Google" link, then on the "Corporate Info" link and read the "Ten things Google has found to be true" in the "Our Philosophy" section. What relationships do you see between these 10 things and Google's description of its culture? Are the two closely connected? Why or why not? Explain.

part two 2

Cases in Crafting and Executing Strategy

Case 1

Costco Wholesale Corporation: Mission, Business Model, and Strategy

Arthur A. Thompson Jr.
The University of Alabama

Jim Sinegal, cofounder and CEO of Costco Wholesale, was the driving force behind Costco's 23-year march to become the fourth largest retailer in the United States and the seventh largest in the world. He was far from the stereotypical CEO. A grandfatherly 70-year-old, Sinegal dressed casually and unpretentiously, often going to the office or touring Costco stores wearing an open-collared cotton shirt that came from a Costco bargain rack and sporting a standard employee name tag that said, simply, "Jim." His informal dress, mustache, gray hair, and unimposing appearance made it easy for Costco shoppers to mistake him for a store clerk. He answered his own phone, once telling ABC News reporters, "If a customer's calling and they have a gripe, don't you think they kind of enjoy the fact that I picked up the phone and talked to them?"[1]

Sinegal spent much of his time touring Costco stores, using the company plane to fly from location to location and sometimes visiting 8 to 10 stores daily (the record for a single day was 12). Treated like a celebrity when he appeared at a store (the news "Jim's in the store" spread quickly), Sinegal made a point of greeting store employees. He observed, "The employees know that I want to say hello to them, because I like them. We have said from the very beginning: 'We're going to be a company that's on a first-name basis with everyone.'"[2] Employees genuinely seemed to like Sinegal. He talked quietly, in a commonsensical manner that suggested what he was saying was no big deal.[3] He came across as kind yet stern, but

he was prone to display irritation when he disagreed sharply with what people were saying to him.

In touring a Costco store with the local store manager, Sinegal was very much the person-in-charge. He functioned as producer, director, and knowledgeable critic. He cut to the chase quickly, exhibiting intense attention to detail and pricing, wandering through store aisles firing a barrage of questions at store managers about sales volumes and stock levels of particular items, critiquing merchandising displays or the position of certain products in the stores, commenting on any aspect of store operations that caught his eye, and asking managers to do further research and get back to him with more information whenever he found their answers to his questions less than satisfying. It was readily apparent that Sinegal had tremendous merchandising savvy, that he demanded much of store managers and employees, and that his views about discount retailing set the tone for how the company operated. Knowledgeable observers regarded Jim Sinegal's merchandising expertise as being on a par with that of the legendary Sam Walton.

In 2006, Costco's sales totaled almost $59 billion at 496 stores in 37 states, Puerto Rico, Canada, the United Kingdom, Taiwan, Japan, Korea, and Mexico. About 26 million households and 5.2 million businesses had membership cards entitling them to shop at Costco, generating nearly $1.2 billion in membership fees for the company. Annual sales per store averaged about $128 million, nearly double the $67 million figure for Sam's Club, Costco's chief competitor in the membership warehouse retail segment.

COMPANY BACKGROUND

The membership warehouse concept was pioneered by discount merchandising sage Sol Price, who opened the first Price Club in a converted airplane hangar on Morena Boulevard in San Diego in 1976. Price Club lost $750,000 in its first year of operation, but by 1979 it had two stores, 900 employees, 200,000 members, and a $1 million profit. Years earlier, Sol Price had experimented with discount retailing at a San Diego store called Fed-Mart. Jim Sinegal got his start in retailing there at the age of 18, loading mattresses for $1.25 an hour while attending San Diego Community College. When Sol Price sold Fed-Mart, Sinegal left with Price to help him start the San Diego Price Club store; within a few years, Sol Price's Price Club emerged as the unchallenged leader in member warehouse retailing, with stores operating primarily on the West Coast.

Although he originally conceived Price Club as a place where small local businesses could obtain needed merchandise at economical prices, Sol Price soon concluded that his fledgling operation could achieve far greater sales volumes and gain buying clout with suppliers by also granting membership to individuals—a conclusion that launched the deep-discount warehouse club industry on a steep growth curve.

When Sinegal was 26, Sol Price made him the manager of the original San Diego store, which had become unprofitable. Price saw that Sinegal had a special knack for discount retailing and for spotting what a store was doing wrong (usually either not being in the right merchandise categories or not selling items at the right price points)—the very things that Sol Price was good at and that were at the root of the Price Club's growing success in the marketplace. Sinegal soon got the San Diego store back into the black. Over the next several years, Sinegal continued to build his prowess and talents for discount merchandising. He mirrored Sol Price's attention to detail and absorbed all the nuances and subtleties of his mentor's style of operating—constantly improving store operations, keeping operating costs and overhead low, stocking items that moved quickly, and charging ultra-low prices that kept customers coming back to shop. Realizing that he had mastered the tricks of running a successful membership warehouse business from Sol Price, Sinegal decided to leave Price Club and form his own warehouse club operation.

Costco was founded by Jim Sinegal and Seattle entrepreneur Jeff Brotman (now chairman of the board of directors). The first Costco store began operations in Seattle in 1983, the same year that Wal-Mart launched its warehouse membership format, Sam's Club. By the end of 1984, there were nine Costco stores in five states serving over 200,000 members. In December 1985, Costco became a public company, selling shares to the public and raising additional capital for expansion. Costco became the first ever U.S. company to reach $1 billion in sales in less than six years. In October 1993, Costco merged with Price Club. Jim Sinegal became CEO of the merged company, presiding over 206 PriceCostco locations, which in total generated $16 billion in annual sales. Jeff Brotman, who had functioned as Costco's chairman since the company's founding, became vice chairman of PriceCostco in 1993 and was elevated to chairman in December 1994. Brotman kept abreast of company operations but stayed in the background and concentrated on managing the company's $9 billion investment in real estate operations—in 2006, Costco owned the land and buildings for almost 80 percent of its stores.

In January 1997, after the spin-off of most of its nonwarehouse assets to Price Enterprises Inc., PriceCostco changed its name to Costco Companies Inc. When the company reincorporated from Delaware to Washington in August 1999, the name was changed to Costco Wholesale Corporation. The company's headquarters was in Issaquah, Washington, not far from Seattle.

Exhibit 1 contains a financial and operating summary for Costco for fiscal years 2000–2006.

COSTCO'S MISSION, BUSINESS MODEL, AND STRATEGY

Costco's mission in the membership warehouse business read: "To continually provide our members with quality goods and services at the lowest possible prices." The company's business model was to generate high sales volumes and rapid inventory turnover by offering members low prices on a limited selection of nationally branded and selected private-label products in a wide range of merchandise categories. Management believed that rapid inventory

Exhibit 1   **Financial and Operating Summary, Costco Wholesale Corporation, Fiscal Years 2000–2006 ($ in millions, except for per share data)**

	Fiscal Years Ending on Sunday Closest to August 31				
	2006	2005	2004	2002	2000
Income Statement Data					
Net sales	$58,963	$51,862	$47,146	$37,993	$31,621
Membership fees	1,188	1,073	961	769	544
Total revenue	60,151	52,935	48,107	38,762	32,164
Operating expenses					
Merchandise costs	52,745	46,347	42,092	33,983	28,322
Selling, general, and administrative	5,732	5,044	4,598	3,576	2,755
Preopening expenses	43	53	30	51	42
Provision for impaired assets and store closing costs	5	16	1	21	7
Operating income	1,626	1,474	1,386	1,132	1,037
Other income (expense)					
Interest expense	(13)	(34)	(37)	(29)	(39)
Interest income and other	138	109	52	36	54
Income before income taxes	1,751	1,549	1,401	1,138	1,052
Provision for income taxes	648	486	518	438	421
Net income	$ 1,103	$ 1,063	$ 882	$ 700	$ 631
Diluted net income per share	$ 2.30	$ 2.18	$ 1.85	$ 1.48	$ 1.35
Dividends per share	$ 0.49	$ 0.43	$ 0.20	$ 0.00	$ 0.00
Millions of shares used in per share calculations	480.3	492.0	482.5	479.3	475.7
Balance Sheet Data					
Cash and cash equivalents	$ 1,511	$ 2,063	$ 2,823	$ 806	$ 525
Merchandise inventories	4,569	4,015	3,644	3,127	2,490
Current assets	8,232	8,238	7,269	4,631	3,470
Current liabilities	7,819	6,761	6,170	4,450	3,404
Working capital	413	1,477	1,099	181	66
Net property and equipment	8,564	7,790	7,219	6,523	4,834
Total assets	17,495	16,514	15,093	11,620	8,634
Short-term borrowings	41	54	22	104	10
Long-term debt	215	711	994	1,211	790
Stockholders' equity	9,143	8,881	7,625	5,694	4,240
Cash Flow Data					
Net cash provided by operating activities	$ 1,827	$ 1,776	$ 2,096	$ 1,018	$ 1,070
Warehouses in Operation					
Beginning of year	433	417	397	345	292
Opened	28	21	20	35	25
Closed	(3)	(5)	—	(6)	(4)
End of year	458	433	417	374	313
Primary members at year-end					
Businesses (000s)	5,214	5,050	4,810	4,476	4,358
Gold Star members (000s)	17,338	16,233	15,018	14,597	12,737

Sources: Company 10-K reports 2006, 2005, 2002, and 2000.

turnover—when combined with the operating efficiencies achieved by volume purchasing, efficient distribution, and reduced handling of merchandise in no-frills, self-service warehouse facilities—enabled Costco to operate profitably at significantly lower gross margins than traditional wholesalers, mass merchandisers, supermarkets, and supercenters.

Examples of Costco's incredible annual sales volumes included 96,000 carats of diamonds (2006), 1.5 million televisions, $300 million worth of digital cameras, 28 million rotisserie chickens (over 500,000 weekly), 40 percent of the Tuscan olive oil bought in the United States, $16 million worth of pumpkin pies during the fall holiday season, $3 billion worth of gasoline, 21 million prescriptions, and 52 million $1.50 hot dog/soda pop combinations. Costco was also the world's largest seller of fine wines ($385 million out of total 2006 fine wine sales of $805 million).[4] At one of Costco's largest volume stores, which had annual sales of $285 million and 232,000 members, annual sales volume ran 283,000 rotisserie chickens, 375,000 gallons of milk, and 8.4 million rolls of toilet paper—this store had an average customer bill per trip of $150.[5]

Furthermore, Costco's high sales volume and rapid inventory turnover generally allowed it to sell and receive cash for inventory before it had to pay many of its merchandise vendors, even when vendor payments were made in time to take advantage of early payment discounts. Thus, Costco was able to finance a big percentage of its merchandise inventory through the payment terms provided by vendors rather than by having to maintain sizable working capital (defined as current assets minus current liabilities) to facilitate timely payment of suppliers.

Costco's Strategy

The cornerstones of Costco's strategy were low prices, limited selection, and a treasure-hunt shopping environment.

Pricing. Costco was known for selling top-quality national and regional brands at prices consistently below traditional wholesale or retail outlets. The company stocked only those items that could be priced at bargain levels and thus provide members with significant cost savings; this was true even if an item was often requested by customers. A key element of Costco's pricing strategy was to cap its markup on brand-name merchandise at 14 percent (compared to 20 to 50 percent markups at other discounters and many supermarkets). Markups on Costco's 400 private-label (Kirkland Signature) items could be no higher than 15 percent, but the sometimes fractionally higher markups still resulted in Kirkland Signature items being priced about 20 percent below comparable name-brand items. Kirkland Signature products—which included juice, cookies, coffee, tires, housewares, luggage, appliances, clothing, and detergent—were designed to be of equal or better quality than national brands.

Costco's philosophy was to keep customers coming in to shop by wowing them with low prices. Jim Sinegal explained the company's approach to pricing as follows:

> We always look to see how much of a gulf we can create between ourselves and the competition. So that the competitors eventually say, "These guys are crazy. We'll compete somewhere else." Some years ago, we were selling a hot brand of jeans for $29.99. They were $50 in a department store. We got a great deal on them and could have sold them for a higher price but we went down to $29.99. Why? We knew it would create a riot.[6]

At another time he said:

> We're very good merchants, and we offer value. The traditional retailer will say: "I'm selling this for $10. I wonder whether we can get $10.50 or $11." We say: "We selling this for $9. How do we get it down to $8?" We understand that our members don't come and shop with us because of the window displays or the Santa Claus or the piano player. They come and shop with us because we offer great values.[7]

Indeed, Costco's markups and prices were so low that Wall Street analysts had criticized Costco management for going all out to please customers at the expense of increasing profits for shareholders. One retailing analyst said, "They could probably get more money for a lot of the items they sell."[8] Sinegal was unimpressed with Wall Street calls for Costco to abandon its ultra-low pricing strategy, commenting: "Those people are in the business of making money between now and next Tuesday. We're trying to build an organization that's going to be here 50 years from now."[9] He went on to explain why Costco's approach to pricing would remain unaltered during his tenure:

> When I started, Sears, Roebuck was the Costco of the country, but they allowed someone else to come in under them. We don't want to be one of the casualties. We don't want to turn around and say, "We got so fancy we've raised our prices, and all of a sudden a new competitor comes in and beats our prices."[10]

Product Selection.   Whereas typical supermarkets stocked about 40,000 items and a Wal-Mart Supercenter or a SuperTarget might have as many as 150,000 items for shoppers to choose from, Costco's merchandising strategy was to provide members with a selection of only about 4,000 items.

Costco's product range did cover a broad spectrum—rotisserie chicken, prime steaks, caviar, flat-screen televisions, digital cameras, fresh flowers, fine wines, caskets, baby strollers, toys and games, musical instruments, ceiling fans, vacuum cleaners, books, DVDs, chandeliers, stainless-steel cookware, seat-cover kits for autos, prescription drugs, gasoline, and one-hour photo finishing—but the company deliberately limited the selection in each product category to fast-selling models, sizes, and colors. Many consumable products like detergents, canned goods, office supplies, and soft drinks were sold only in big-container, case, carton, or multiple-pack quantities. For example, Costco stocked only a 325-count bottle of Advil—a size many shoppers might find too large for their needs. Sinegal explained the reason for the deliberately limited selection as follows:

> If you had ten customers come in to buy Advil, how many are not going to buy any because you just have one size? Maybe one or two. We refer to that as the intelligent loss of sales. We are prepared to give up that one customer. But if we had four or five sizes of Advil, as most grocery stores do, it would make our business more difficult to manage. Our business can only succeed if we are efficient. You can't go on selling at these margins if you are not.[11]

Costco's selections of appliances, equipment, and tools often included commercial and professional models because so many of its members were small businesses. The approximate percentage of net sales accounted for by each major category of items stocked by Costco is shown in the following table:

To encourage members to shop at Costco more frequently, the company operated ancillary businesses within or next to most Costco warehouses; the number of ancillary businesses at Costco warehouses is shown in the following table:

	2006	2005	2004
Total number of warehouses	458	433	417
Warehouses having stores with			
Food court and hot dog stands	452	427	412
One-hour photo centers	450	423	408
Optical dispensing centers	442	414	397
Pharmacies	401	374	359
Gas stations	250	225	211
Hearing aid centers	196	168	143
Print shops and copy centers	9	10	10

Treasure-Hunt Merchandising.   While Costco's product line consisted of approximately 4,000 items, about one-fourth of its product offerings were constantly changing. Costco's merchandise buyers remained on the lookout to make one-time purchases of items that would appeal to the company's clientele and that would sell out quickly. A sizable number of these items were high-end or name-brand products that carried big price tags—like $2,000–$3,500 big-screen HDTVs or $800 leather sofas. The idea was to entice shoppers to spend more than they might otherwise by offering irresistible deals on luxury items. According to Jim Sinegal, "Of that 4,000, about 3,000 can be found on the floor all the time. The other 1,000 are the treasure-hunt stuff that's always changing. It's the type of item a customer knows they better buy because it will not be there next time, like Waterford crystal. We try to get that sense of urgency in our customers."[12]

	2006	2005	2004	2003
Food (fresh produce, meats and fish, bakery and deli products, and dry and institutionally packaged foods)	30%	30%	31%	30%
Sundries (candy, snack foods, tobacco, alcoholic and nonalcoholic beverages, and cleaning and institutional supplies)	24	25	25	26
Hard lines (major appliances, electronics, health and beauty aids, hardware, office supplies, garden and patio, sporting goods, furniture, cameras and automotive supplies)	20	20	20	20
Soft lines (apparel, domestics, jewelry, housewares, media, home furnishings, and small appliances)	12	12	13	14
Ancillary and other (gasoline, pharmacy, food court, optical, one-hour photo, hearing aids, and travel)	14	13	11	10

In many cases, Costco did not obtain its luxury offerings directly from high-end manufacturers like Calvin Klein or Waterford (who were unlikely to want their merchandise marketed at deep discounts at places like Costco); rather, Costco buyers searched for opportunities to source such items legally on the gray market from other wholesalers or distressed retailers looking to get rid of excess or slow-selling inventory. Examples of treasure-hunt specials included $800 espresso machines, diamond rings and other jewelry items with price tags of anywhere from $5,000 to $250,000, Italian-made Hathaway shirts priced at $29.99, Movado watches, exotic cheeses, Coach bags, cashmere sports coats, $1,500 digital pianos, and Dom Perignon champagne.

Marketing and Advertising.   Costco's low prices and its reputation for treasure-hunt shopping made it unnecessary for the company to engage in extensive advertising or sales campaigns. Marketing and promotional activities were generally limited to direct mail programs promoting selected merchandise to existing members, occasional direct mail marketing to prospective new members, and special campaigns for new warehouse openings. For new warehouse openings, marketing teams personally contacted businesses in the area that were potential wholesale members; these contacts were supplemented with direct mailings during the period immediately prior to opening. Potential Gold Star (individual) members were contacted by direct mail or by promotions at local employee associations and businesses with large numbers of employees. After a membership base was established in an area, most new memberships came from word of mouth (existing members telling friends and acquaintances about their shopping experiences at Costco), follow-up messages distributed through regular payroll or other organizational communications to employee groups, and ongoing direct solicitations to prospective business and Gold Star members. Management believed that its emphasis on direct mail advertising kept its marketing expenses low relative to those at typical retailers, discounter, and supermarkets.

Growth Strategy.   In recent years, Costco had opened an average 20–25 locations annually; most were in the United States, but expansion was under way internationally as well. The company opened 68 new warehouses in the United States in fiscal years 2002–2006; 16 new warehouses opened in the first four months of fiscal 2007 (between September 1 and December 31, 2006), and management planned to open another 20–24 by the end of fiscal 2007. Five new warehouses were opened outside the United States in fiscal 2005, five more were opened in fiscal 2006, and four were opened in the first four months of fiscal 2007. Going into 2007, Costco had a total of 102 wholly-owned warehouses in operation outside the United States, including 70 in Canada, 18 in the United Kingdom, 5 in Korea, 5 in Japan, and 4 in Taiwan. Costco was a 50–50 partner in a venture to operate 30 Costco warehouses in Mexico. Exhibit 2 shows a breakdown of Costco's geographic operations for fiscal years 2003–2006. (The data for the 30 warehouses in Mexico are not included in the exhibit because the 50–50 venture in Mexico was accounted for using the equity method.)

Costco had recently opened two freestanding high-end furniture warehouse businesses called Costco Home. Sales in 2005 at these two locations increased by 132 percent over 2004 levels, and profits were up significantly. So far, however, rather than opening additional Costco Home stores, management had opted to experiment with adding about 45,000 square feet to the size of selected new Costco stores and using the extra space to stock a much bigger selection of furniture—furniture was one of the top three best-selling categories at Costco's Web site.

A third growth initiative was to expand the company's offerings of Kirkland Signature items. Management believed there were opportunities to expand its private-label offerings from the present level of 400 items to as many as 600 items over the next five years.

Web Site Sales.   Costco operated two Web sites— www.costco.com in the United States and www.costco.ca in Canada—both to provide another shopping alternative for members and to provide members with a way to purchase products and services that might not be available at the warehouse where they customarily shopped, especially such services as digital photo processing, prescription fulfillment, and travel and other membership services. At Costco's online photo center, customers could upload images and pick up the prints at their local warehouse in little over an hour; one-hour photo sales were up 10 percent in fiscal 2005, a year in which the industry overall had negative sales growth. Costco's e-commerce sales totaled $534 million in fiscal 2005 and $376 million in fiscal 2004. (Data for fiscal 2006 e-commerce sales were not available.)

Exhibit 2   **Geographic Operating Data, Costco Wholesale Corporation, Fiscal Years 2003–2006 ($ in millions)**

	United States Operations	Canadian Operations	Other International Operations	Total
Year Ended September 3, 2006				
Total revenue (including membership fees)	$48,465	$8,122	$3,564	$60,151
Operating income	1,246	293	87	1,626
Depreciation and amortization	413	61	41	515
Capital expenditures	934	188	90	1,213
Property and equipment	6,676	1,032	855	8,564
Total assets	14,009	1,914	1,572	17,495
Net assets	7,190	1,043	910	9,143
Number of warehouses	358	68	32	458
Year Ended August 28, 2005				
Total revenue (including membership fees)	$43,064	$6,732	$3,155	$52,952
Operating income	1,168	242	65	1,474
Depreciation and amortization	389	51	42	482
Capital expenditures	734	140	122	995
Property and equipment	6,171	834	786	7,790
Total assets	13,203	2,034	1,428	16,665
Net assets	6,769	1,285	827	8,881
Number of warehouses	338	65	30	433
Year Ended August 29, 2004				
Total revenue (including membership fees)	$39,430	$6,043	$2,637	$48,110
Operating income	1,121	215	50	1,386
Depreciation and amortization	364	40	36	441
Capital expenditures	560	90	55	706
Property and equipment	5,853	676	691	7,220
Total assets	12,108	1,718	1,267	15,093
Net assets	5,871	1,012	742	7,625
Number of Warehouses	327	63	27	417
Year Ended August 31, 2003				
Total revenue (including membership fees)	$35,119	$5,237	$2,189	$42,546
Operating income	928	199	30	1,157
Depreciation and amortization	324	34	34	391
Capital expenditures	699	69	44	811
Long lived assets	5,706	613	642	6,960
Total assets	10,522	1,580	1,089	13,192
Net assets	5,141	784	630	6,555
Number of warehouses	309	61	27	397

Source: Company 10-K reports, 2004 and 2006.

Warehouse Operations

In Costco's 2005 annual report, Jim Sinegal summed up the company's approach to operations as follows:

> Costco is able to offer lower prices and better values by eliminating virtually all the frills and costs histori- cally associated with conventional wholesalers and

retailers, including salespeople, fancy buildings, de- livery, billing, and accounts receivable. We run a tight operation with extremely low overhead which ena- bles us to pass on dramatic savings to our members.

Costco warehouses averaged 140,000 square feet and were constructed inexpensively with concrete floors. Because shoppers were attracted principally by Costco's low prices, its warehouses were rarely located on prime commercial real estate sites. Merchandise was generally stored on racks above the sales floor and displayed on pallets containing large quantities of each item, thereby reducing labor required for handling and stocking. In-store signage was done mostly on laser printers, and there were no shopping bags at the checkout counter—merchandise was put directly into the shopping cart or sometimes loaded into empty boxes. Warehouses generally operated on a seven-day, 69-hour week, typically being open between 10:00 a.m. and 8:30 p.m. weekdays, with earlier closing hours on the weekend; the gasoline operations outside many stores generally had extended hours. The shorter hours of operation—as compared to those of traditional retailers, discount retailers, and supermarkets—resulted in lower labor costs relative to the volume of sales.

Costco warehouse managers were delegated considerable authority over store operations. In effect, warehouse managers functioned as entrepreneurs running their own retail operation. They were responsible for coming up with new ideas about what items would sell in their stores, effectively merchandising the ever-changing lineup of treasure-hunt products, and orchestrating in-store product locations and displays to maximize sales and quick turnover. In experimenting with what items to stock and what in-store merchandising techniques to employ, warehouse managers had to know the clientele who patronized their locations—for instance, big-ticket diamonds sold well at some warehouses but not at others. Costco's best managers kept their finger on the pulse of the members who shopped their warehouse location to stay in sync with what would sell well, and they had a flair for creating a certain element of excitement, hum, and buzz in their warehouses. Such managers spurred above-average sales volumes—sales at Costco's top-volume warehouses often exceeded $5 million a week, with sales exceeding $1 million on many days. Successful managers also thrived on the rat race of running a high-traffic store and solving the inevitable crises of the moment.

Costco bought the majority of its merchandise directly from manufacturers, routing it either directly to its warehouse stores or to one of nine cross-docking depots that served as distribution points for nearby stores. Depots received container-based shipments from manufacturers and reallocated these goods for combined shipment to individual warehouses, generally in less than 24 hours. This maximized freight volume and handling efficiencies. When merchandise arrived at a warehouse, it was moved straight to the sales floor; very little was stored in locations off the sales floor, thereby lowering receiving costs by eliminating many of the costs associated with multiple-step distribution channels, which include purchasing from distributors as opposed to manufacturers; using central receiving, storage, and distribution warehouses; and storing merchandise in locations off the sales floor.

Costco had direct buying relationships with many producers of national brand-name merchandise (including Canon, Casio, Coca-Cola, Colgate-Palmolive, Dell, Fuji, Hewlett-Packard, Kimberly-Clark, Kodak, Levi Strauss, Michelin, Nestlé, Panasonic, Procter & Gamble, Samsung, Sony, KitchenAid, and Jones of New York) and with manufacturers that supplied its Kirkland Signature products. No one manufacturer supplied a significant percentage of the merchandise that Costco stocked. Costco had not experienced any difficulty in obtaining sufficient quantities of merchandise, and management believed that if one or more of its current sources of supply became unavailable, the company could switch its purchases to alternative manufacturers without experiencing a substantial disruption of its business.

Costco warehouses accepted cash, checks, most debit cards, American Express, and a private-label Costco credit card. Costco accepted merchandise returns when members were dissatisfied with their purchases. Losses associated with dishonored checks were minimal because any member whose check had been dishonored was prevented from paying by check or cashing a check at the point of sale until restitution was made. The membership format facilitated strictly controlling the entrances and exits of warehouses, resulting in limited inventory losses of less than two-tenths of 1 percent of net sales—well below those of typical discount retail operations.

Costco's Membership Base and Member Demographics

Costco attracted the most affluent customers in discount retailing—the average income of individual members was about $75,000, with over 30 percent of members having annual incomes of $100,000 or more. Many members were affluent urbanites, living in nice neighborhoods not far from Costco warehouses. One loyal Executive member, a criminal defense lawyer, said, "I think I spend over $20,000–$25,000 a year buying all my products here from food to clothing—except my suits. I have to buy them at the Armani stores."[13] Another Costco loyalist said, "This is the best place in the world. It's like going to church on Sunday. You can't get anything better than this. This is a religious experience."[14]

Costco had two primary types of memberships: Business and Gold Star (individual). Gold Star memberships were for individuals who did not qualify for a Business membership. Businesses—including individuals with a business license, retail sales license, or other evidence of business existence—qualified as Business members. Business members generally paid an annual membership fee of $50 for the primary membership card, which also included a spouse membership card, and could purchase up to six additional membership cards for an annual fee of $40 each for partners or associates in the business; they could also purchase a transferable company card. A significant number of business members also shopped at Costco for their personal needs.

Gold Star members generally paid an annual membership fee of $50, which included a spouse card. In addition, members could upgrade to an Executive membership for an annual fee of $100; Executive members were entitled an additional 2 percent savings on qualified purchases at Costco (redeemable at Costco warehouses), up to a maximum rebate of $500 per year. Executive members also were eligible for savings and benefits on various business and consumer services offered by Costco, including merchant credit card processing, small-business loans, auto and home insurance, long-distance telephone service, check printing, and real estate and mortgage services; these services were mostly offered by third-party providers and varied by state. In 2006, Executive members represented 23 percent of Costco's primary membership base and generated approximately 45 percent of consolidated net sales. Effective May 1, 2006, Costco increased annual membership fees by $5 for U.S. and Canadian Gold Star, Business, and Business Add-on members; the $5 increase, the first in nearly six years, impacted approximately 15 million members.

At the end of fiscal 2006, Costco had almost 48 million cardholders:

Gold Star members (including Executive members)	17,338,000
Business members	5,214,000
Total primary cardholders	22,552,000
Add-on cardholders	25,127,000
Total cardholders	47,679,000

Recent trends in membership are shown at bottom of Exhibit 1. Members could shop at any Costco warehouse; member renewal rates were about 86.5 percent.

Compensation and Workforce Practices

In September 2006, Costco had 71,000 full-time employees and 56,000 part-time employees, including approximately 8,000 people employed by Costco Mexico, whose operations were not consolidated in Costco's financial and operating results. Approximately 13,800 hourly employees at locations in California, Maryland, New Jersey, and New York, as well as at one warehouse in Virginia, were represented by the International Brotherhood of Teamsters. All remaining employees were non-union.

Starting wages for new Costco employees were in the $10–$12 range in 2006; on average, Costco employees earned $17–$18 per hour, plus biannual bonuses. Employees enjoyed the full spectrum of benefits. Salaried employees were eligible for benefits on the first of the month after the date of hire. Full-time hourly employees were eligible for benefits of the first of the month after working a probationary 90 days; part-time hourly employees became benefit-eligible on the first of the month after working 180 days. The benefit package included the following:

• Health and dental care plans. Full-time employees could choose from among a freedom-of-choice health care plan, a managed-choice health care plan, and three dental plans. A managed-choice health care and a core dental plan were available for part-time employees. The company paid about 90 percent of an employee's premiums for health care (far above the more normal 50 percent contributions at many other retailers), but employees did have to pick up the premiums for coverage for family members.

- Convenient prescription pickup at Costco's pharmacies, with co-payments as low as $5 for generic drugs. Generally, employees paid no more than 15 percent of the cost for the most expensive branded drugs.
- A vision program that paid $45 for an optical exam (the amount charged at Costco's optical centers) and had generous allowances for the purchase of glasses and contact lenses.
- A 401(k) plan in which Costco matched hourly employee contributions by 50 cents on the dollar for the first $1,000 annually to a maximum company match of $500 per year. Eligible employees qualified for additional company contributions based on the employee's years of service and eligible earnings. The company's union employees on the West Coast qualified for matching contributions of 50 cents on the dollar to a maximum company match of $250 a year; eligible union employees qualified for additional company contributions based on straight-time hours worked. Company contributions for salaried workers ran about 3 percent of salary during the second year of employment and could be as high as 9 percent of salary after 25 years. Company contributions to employee 410(k) plans were $233.6 million in fiscal 2006, $191.6 million in fiscal 2005, and $169.7 million in fiscal 2004.
- A dependent care reimbursement plan in which Costco employees whose families qualified could pay for day care for children under 13 or adult day care with pretax dollars and realize savings of anywhere from $750 to $2,000 per year.
- Confidential professional counseling services.
- Company-paid long-term disability coverage equal to 60 percent of earnings if out for more than 180 days on a non–worker's compensation leave of absence.
- All employees who passed their 90-day probation period and were working at least 10 hours per week were automatically enrolled in a short-term disability plan covering non-work-related injuries or illnesses for up to 26 weeks. Weekly short-term disability payments equaled 60 percent of average weekly wages up to a maximum of $1,000 and were tax free.
- Generous life insurance and accidental death and dismemberment coverage, with benefits based on years or service and whether the employee worked full-time or part-time. Employees could elect to purchase supplemental coverage for themselves, their spouses, or their children.
- An employee stock purchase plan allowing all employees to buy Costco stock via payroll deduction and avoid commissions and fees.
- A health care reimbursement plan in which benefit eligible employees could arrange to have pretax money automatically deducted from their paychecks and deposited in a health care reimbursement account that could be used to pay medical and dental bills.
- A long-term care insurance plan for employees with 10 or more years of service. Eligible employees could purchase a basic or supplemental policy for nursing home care for themselves, their spouses, or their parents (including in-laws) or grandparents (including in-laws).

Although admitting that paying good wages and good benefits was contrary to conventional wisdom in discount retailing, Jim Sinegal was convinced that having a well-compensated workforce was very important to executing Costco's strategy successfully. He said, "Imagine that you have 120,000 loyal ambassadors out there who are constantly saying good things about Costco. It has to be a significant advantage for you. . . . Paying good wages and keeping your people working with you is very good business."[15] When a reporter asked him about why Costco treated its workers so well compared to other retailers (particularly Wal-Mart, which paid lower wages and had a skimpier benefits package), Sinegal replied: "Why shouldn't employees have the right to good wages and good careers. . . . It absolutely makes good business sense. Most people agree that we're the lowest-cost producer. Yet we pay the highest wages. So it must mean we get better productivity. Its axiomatic in our business—you get what you pay for."[16]

About 85 percent of Costco's employees had signed up for health insurance, versus about 50 percent at Wal-Mart and Target. The Teamsters' chief negotiator with Costco said, "They gave us the best agreement of any retailer in the country."[17] Good wages and benefits were said to be why employee turnover at Costco ran under 6 percent after the first year of employment. Some Costco employees had been with the company since its founding in 1983. Many others had started working part-time at Costco while in high school or college and opted to make a career at the company. One Costco employee told an ABC *20/20* reporter, "It's a good place to work; they take good care of us."[18] A Costco vice president and head baker said working for Costco was a family affair: "My whole family works for Costco, my husband does, my daughter does, my new son-in-law does."[19] Another employee, a receiving clerk who made about $40,000 a year, said, "I want to retire here. I love it here."[20] An employee with over two years of service could not be fired without the approval of a senior company officer.

Selecting People for Open Positions. Costco's top management wanted employees to feel that they could have a long career at Costco. It was company policy to fill at least 86 percent of its higher-level openings by promotions from within; in actuality, the percentage ran close to 98 percent, which meant that the majority of Costco's management team members (including warehouse, merchandise, administrative, membership, front end, and receiving managers) were homegrown. Many of the company's vice presidents had started in entry-level jobs; according to Jim Sinegal, "We have guys who started pushing shopping carts out on the parking lot for us who are now vice presidents of our company."[21] Costco made a point of recruiting at local universities; Sinegal explained why: "These people are smarter than the average person, hardworking, and they haven't made a career choice."[22] On another occasion, he said, "If someone came to us and said he just got a master's in business at Harvard, we would say fine, would you like to start pushing carts?"[23] Those employees who demonstrated smarts and strong people management skills moved up through the ranks.

But without an aptitude for the details of discount retailing, even up-and-coming employees stood no chance of being promoted to a position of warehouse manager. Sinegal and other top Costco executives who oversaw warehouse operations insisted that candidates for warehouse managers be top-flight merchandisers with a gift for the details of making items fly off the shelves; Sinegal said, "People who have a feel for it just start to get it. Others, you look at them and it's like staring at a blank canvas. I'm not trying to be unduly harsh, but that's the way it works."[24] Most newly appointed warehouse managers at Costco came from the ranks of assistant warehouse managers who had a track record of being shrewd merchandisers and tuned into what new or different products might sell well given the clientele that patronized their particular warehouse—just having the requisite skills in people management, crisis management, and cost-effective warehouse operations was not enough.

Executive Compensation. Executives at Costco did not earn the outlandish salaries that had become customary over the past decade at most large corporations. In fiscal 2005, both Jeff Brotman and Jim Sinegal were each paid $350,000 and earned a bonus of $100,000 (versus $350,000 salaries and $200,000 bonuses in fiscal 2004). As of early 2006, Brotman owned about 2.2 million shares of Costco stock (worth about $110 million as of December 2006) and had been awarded options to purchase an additional 1.35 million shares; Sinegal owned 2.7 million shares of Costco stock (worth about $140 million as of December 2006) and had also been awarded options for an additional 1.35 million shares. Several senior officers at Costco were paid 2005 salaries in the $475,000–$500,000 range and bonuses of $47,000–$77,000. Sinegal explained why executive compensation at Costco was only a fraction of the millions paid to top-level executives at other corporations with sales of $50 billion or more: "I figured that if I was making something like 12 times more than the typical person working on the floor, that that was a fair salary."[25] To another reporter, he said: "Listen, I'm one of the founders of this business. I've been very well rewarded. I don't require a salary that's 100 times more than the people who work on the sales floor."[26] Sinegal's employment contract was only a page long and provided that he could be terminated for cause.

Costco's Business Philosophy, Values, and Code of Ethics

Jim Sinegal, who was the son of a steelworker, had ingrained five simple and down-to-earth business principles into Costco's corporate culture and the manner in which the company operated. The following are excerpts of these principles and operating approaches:

1. **Obey the law**—The law is irrefutable! Absent a moral imperative to challenge a law, we must conduct our business in total compliance with the laws of every community where we do business. We pledge to:
    *   Comply with all laws and other legal requirements.

- Respect all public officials and their positions.
- Comply with safety and security standards for all products sold.
- Exceed ecological standards required in every community where we do business.
- Comply with all applicable wage and hour laws.
- Comply with all applicable anti-trust laws.
- Conduct business in and with foreign countries in a manner that is legal and proper under United States and foreign laws.
- Not offer, give, ask for, or receive any form of bribe or kickback to or from any person or pay to expedite government action or otherwise act in violation of the Foreign Corrupt Practices Act.
- Promote fair, accurate, timely, and understandable disclosure in reports filed with the Securities and Exchange Commission and in other public communications by the Company.

2. **Take care of our members**—Costco membership is open to business owners, as well as individuals. Our members are our reason for being—the key to our success. If we don't keep our members happy, little else that we do will make a difference. There are plenty of shopping alternatives for our members, and if they fail to show up, we cannot survive. Our members have extended a trust to Costco by virtue of paying a fee to shop with us. We will succeed only if we do not violate the trust they have extended to us, and that trust extends to every area of our business. We pledge to:

- Provide top-quality products at the best prices in the market.
- Provide high-quality, safe, and wholesome food products by requiring that both vendors and employees be in compliance with the highest food safety standards in the industry.
- Provide our members with a 100 percent satisfaction guaranteed warranty on every product and service we sell, including their membership fee.
- Assure our members that every product we sell is authentic in make and in representation of performance.
- Make our shopping environment a pleasant experience by making our members feel welcome as our guests.

- Provide products to our members that will be ecologically sensitive.
- Provide our members with the best customer service in the retail industry.
- Give back to our communities through employee volunteerism and employee and corporate contributions to United Way and Children's Hospitals.

3. **Take care of our employees**—Our employees are our most important asset. We believe we have the very best employees in the warehouse club industry, and we are committed to providing them with rewarding challenges and ample opportunities for personal and career growth. We pledge to provide our employees with:

- Competitive wages.
- Great benefits.
- A safe and healthy work environment.
- Challenging and fun work.
- Career opportunities.
- An atmosphere free from harassment or discrimination.
- An Open Door Policy that allows access to ascending levels of management to resolve issues.
- Opportunities to give back to their communities through volunteerism and fundraising.

4. **Respect our suppliers**—Our suppliers are our partners in business and for us to prosper as a company, they must prosper with us. To that end, we strive to:

- Treat all suppliers and their representatives as you would expect to be treated if visiting their places of business.
- Honor all commitments.
- Protect all suppliers' property assigned to Costco as though it were our own.
- Not accept gratuities of any kind from a supplier.
- Avoid actual or apparent conflicts of interest, including creating a business in competition with the Company or working for or on behalf of another employer in competition with the Company.

If we do these four things throughout our organization, then we will achieve our ultimate goal, which is to:

5. **Reward our shareholders**—As a company with stock that is traded publicly on the NASDAQ stock exchange, our shareholders are our business partners. We can only be successful so long

as we are providing them with a good return on the money they invest in our company. . . . We pledge to operate our company in such a way that our present and future stockholders, as well as our employees, will be rewarded for our efforts.

COMPETITION

In the discount warehouse retail segment, there were three main competitors—Costco Wholesale, Sam's Club (671 warehouses in six countries—the United States, Canada, Brazil, Mexico, China, and Puerto Rico), and BJ's Wholesale Club (165 locations in 16 states). At the end of 2006, there were just over 1,200 warehouse locations across the United States and Canada; most every major metropolitan area had one, if not several, warehouse clubs. Costco had close to a 55 percent share of warehouse club sales across the United States and Canada, with Sam's Club (a division of Wal-Mart) having roughly a 36 percent share and BJ's Wholesale Club and several small warehouse club competitors about a 9 percent share. The wholesale club and warehouse segment of retailing was estimated to be a $110 billion business, and it was growing about 20 percent faster than retailing as a whole.

Competition among the warehouse clubs was based on such factors as price, merchandise quality and selection, location, and member service. However, warehouse clubs also competed with a wide range of other types of retailers, including retail discounters like Wal-Mart and Dollar General, supermarkets, general merchandise chains, specialty chains, gasoline stations, and Internet retailers. Not only did Wal-Mart, the world's largest retailer, compete directly with Costco via its Sam's Club subsidiary but its Wal-Mart Supercenters sold many of the same types of merchandise at attractively low prices as well. Target and Kohl's had emerged as significant retail competitors in certain merchandise categories. Low-cost operators selling a single category or narrow range of merchandise—such as Lowe's, Home Depot, Office Depot, Staples, Best Buy, Circuit City, PetSmart, and Barnes & Noble—had significant market share in their respective product categories.

Brief profiles of Costco's two primary competitors in North America are presented in the following sections; Exhibit 3 shows selected financial and operating data for these two competitors.

Sam's Club

In 2007, Sam's Club had 693 warehouse locations and more than 49 million members. Wal-Mart Stores opened the first Sam's Club in 1984, and management had pursued rapid expansion of the membership club format over the next 23 years, creating a chain of 579 U.S. locations in 48 states and 114 international locations in Brazil, Canada, China, Mexico, and Puerto Rico as of February 2007. Many Sam's Club locations were adjacent to Wal-Mart Supercenters. The concept of the Sam's Club format was to sell merchandise at very low profit margins, resulting in low prices to members.

Sam's Clubs ranged between 70,000 and 190,000 square feet, with the average being about 132,000 square feet. All Sam's Club warehouses had concrete floors; sparse decor; and goods displayed on pallets, simple wooden shelves, or racks in the case of apparel. Sam's Club stocked brand-name merchandise, including hard goods, some soft goods, institutional-size grocery items, and selected private-label items sold under the Member's Mark, Bakers & Chefs, and Sam's Club brands. Generally, each Sam's Club also carried software, electronics, jewelry, sporting goods, toys, tires and batteries, stationery and books, and most clubs had fresh-foods departments that included bakery, meat, produce, floral products, and a Sam's Café. A significant number of clubs had a one-hour photo processing department, a pharmacy that filled prescriptions, an optical department, and self-service gasoline pumps. Members could shop for a broad assortment of merchandise and services online at www.samsclub.com.

Like Costco, Sam's Club stocked about 4,000 items, a big fraction of which were standard and a small fraction of which represented special buys and one-time offerings. The treasure-hunt items at Sam's Club tended to be less upscale and carry lower price tags than those at Costco. The percentage composition of sales was as follows:

	2006	2005	2004
Food	32%	30%	31%
Sundries	29	31	31
Hard goods	23	23	23
Soft goods	5	5	6
Service businesses	11	11	9

Exhibit 3   **Selected Financial and Operating Data for Sam's Club and BJ's Wholesale Club, 2000–2006**

	2006	2005	2004	2002	2000
Sam's Club[a]					
Sales in United States[c] ($ in millions)	$41,582	$39,798	$37,119	$31,702	$26,798
Operating income ($ in millions)	$1,512	$1,385	$1,280	$1,028	$942
Assets ($ in millions)	$6,345	$5,686	$5,685	$4,404	$3,843
Number of locations at year-end	693	670	642	596	564
United States	579	567	551	525	500
International	114	103	91	71	64
Average sales per U.S. location ($ in millions)	$71.8	$66.7	$67.4	$60.4	$3.6
Average warehouse size (square feet)	132,000	129,400	128,300	125,200	122,100
BJ's Wholesale[b]					
Net sales	$8,303	$7,784	$7,220	$5,729	$4,767
Membership fees and other	$177	$166	$155	$131	$102
Total revenues	$8,480	$7,950	$7,375	$5,860	$4,869
Selling, general, and administrative expenses	$698	$611	$556	$416	$335
Operating income	$144	$204	$179	$220	$209
Net income	$72	$129	$114	$131	$132
Total assets	$1,993	$1,990	$1,892	$1,481	$1,234
Number of clubs at year-end	172	165	157	140	118
Number of members (000s)	Not avail.	8,619	8,329	8,190	6,596
Average sales per location ($ in millions)	$48.3	$47.2	$6.0	$40.9	$40.4

[a]Fiscal years end in January 31; data for 2006 are for year ending January 31, 2007; data for 2005 are for year ending January 31, 2006; and so on.

[b]Fiscal years ending on last Saturday of January; data for 2006 are for year ending January 27, 2007; data for 2005 are for year ending January 28, 2006; and so on.

[c]For financial reporting purposes, Wal-Mart consolidates the operations of all foreign-based stores into a single "international" segment figure; thus, financial information for foreign-based Sam's Club locations is not separately available.

In 2006, Sam's Club launched a series of initiatives to grow its sales and market share:

- *Adding new lines of merchandise, with more emphasis on products for the home as opposed to small businesses.* In particular, Sam's had put more emphasis on furniture, flat-screen TVs and other electronics products, jewelry, and select other big-ticket items.

- *Instituting new payment methods.* Starting November 10, 2006, Sam's began accepting payment via MasterCard credit cards; prior to then, payment was limited to cash, check, Discover Card, and debit cards. Early results with MasterCard were favorable; company officials reported that in the week following the MasterCard acceptance, the average ticket checkout at Sam's increased by 35 percent.

- *Running ads on national TV.* Sam's spent about $50 million annually on advertising and direct mail promotions. During the 2006 holiday season, Sam's ran national TV ads on high-profile TV programs like *Deal or No Deal,* NBC's coverage of the Macy's Thanksgiving Day Parade, and the Thanksgiving Day NFL matchup between the Detroit Lions and Miami Dolphins on CBS. The TV ads and companion print ads featured Sam's Club shoppers showing off their purchases with a background sound track playing "God Only Knows" by the Beach Boys— scenes included a young man watching shark shows on a flat-screen TV from his bathtub, a well-dressed woman buying a hot dog roaster, and a Florida couple buying a supersize inflatable snow globe.

The annual fee for Sam's Club business members was $35 for the primary membership card, with a spouse card available at no additional cost. Business members could add up to eight business associates for $35 each. The annual membership fee for an individual Advantage member was $40, which included a spouse card. A Sam's Club Plus premium membership cost $100 and included health care insurance, merchant credit card processing, Web site operation, personal and financial services, and an auto, boat, and recreational vehicle program. Regular hours of operations were Monday through Friday 10:00 a.m. to 8:30 p.m., Saturday 9:30 a.m. to 8:30 p.m., and Sunday 10:00 a.m. to 6:00 p.m.

Approximately two-thirds of the merchandise at Sam's Club was shipped from the division's own distribution facilities and, in the case of perishable items, from some of Wal-Mart's grocery distribution centers; the balance was shipped by suppliers direct to Sam's Club locations. Like Costco, Sam's Club distribution centers employed cross-docking techniques whereby incoming shipments were transferred immediately to outgoing trailers destined for Sam's Club locations; shipments typically spent less than 24 hours at a cross-docking facility and in some instances were there only an hour. The Sam's Club distribution center network consisted of 7 company-owned-and-operated distribution facilities, 13 third-party-owned-and-operated facilities, and 2 third-party-owned-and-operated import distribution centers. A combination of company-owned trucks and independent trucking companies were used to transport merchandise from distribution centers to club locations.

BJ's Wholesale Club

BJ's Wholesale Club introduced the member warehouse concept to the northeastern United States in the mid-1980s. Since then it had expanded to 163 stores operating in 16 states in the Northeast and the Mid-Atlantic; it also had two ProFoods Restaurant Supply clubs and three cross-dock distribution centers. BJ's had 144 big-box warehouses (averaging 112,000 square feet) and 19 smaller-format warehouses (averaging 71,000 square feet); the two ProFoods clubs averaged 62,000 square feet. Clubs were located in both freestanding and shopping center locations. Construction and site development costs for a full-sized BJ's Club were in the $5 to $8 million range; land acquisition costs could run $5

to $10 million (significantly higher in some locations). Each warehouse generally had an investment of $3 to $4 million for fixtures and equipment. Preopening expenses at a new club were close to $1 million. Full-sized clubs had approximately $2 million in inventory. Merchandise was generally displayed on pallets containing large quantities of each item, thereby reducing labor required for handling, stocking, and restocking. Backup merchandise was generally stored in steel racks above the sales floor. Most merchandise was premarked by the manufacturer so that it did not require ticketing at the club.

Like Costco and Sam's, BJ's Wholesale sold high-quality, brand-name merchandise at prices that were significantly lower than the prices found at supermarkets, discount retail chains, department stores, drugstores, and specialty retail stores like Best Buy. Its merchandise lineup of about 7,500 items included consumer electronics, prerecorded media, small appliances, tires, jewelry, health and beauty aids, household products, computer software, books, greeting cards, apparel, furniture, toys, seasonal items, frozen foods, fresh meat and dairy products, beverages, dry grocery items, fresh produce, flowers, canned goods, and household products; about 70 percent of BJ's product line could be found in supermarkets. Food categories and household items accounted for approximately 59 percent of BJ's total food and general merchandise sales in 2005; about 12 percent of sales consisted of BJ's private-label products, which were primarily premium quality and typically priced well below name-brand products. In some product assortments, BJ's had three price categories for members to choose from—good, deluxe, and luxury.

There were 125 BJ's locations with home improvement service kiosks, 130 clubs with Verizon Wireless kiosks, 44 with pharmacies, and 87 with self-service gas stations. Other specialty products and services, provided mostly by outside operators that leased warehouse space from BJ's, included photo developing, full-service optical centers, brand-name fast-food service, garden and storage sheds, patios and sunrooms, vacation packages, propane tank filling services, discounted home heating oil, an automobile buying service, installation of home security services, printing of business forms and checks, and muffler and brake services.

BJ's Wholesale Club had about 8.6 million members in 2006 (see Exhibit 3). It charged $45 per year for a primary Inner Circle membership that included one free supplemental membership; members in the same household could purchase additional supplemental memberships for $20. A business membership also cost $45 per year, which included one free supplemental membership and the ability to purchase additional supplemental memberships for $20. BJ's launched a membership rewards program in 2003 that offered members a 2 percent rebate, capped at $500 per year, on most all in-club purchases; members who paid the $80 annual fee to enroll in the rewards program accounted for 5 percent of all members and 10 percent of total merchandise and food sales in 2005. Purchases with a co-branded BJ's MasterCard earned a 1.5 percent rebate. BJ's was the only warehouse club that accepted MasterCard, Visa, Discover, and American Express cards at all locations; members could also pay for purchases by cash, check, and debit cards. BJ's accepted returns of most merchandise within 30 days after purchase.

BJ's increased customer awareness of its clubs primarily through direct mail, public relations efforts, marketing programs for newly-opened clubs, and a publication called *BJ's Journal,* which was mailed to members throughout the year; during the holiday season, BJ's engaged in radio and TV advertising, a portion of which was funded by vendors.

Merchandise purchased from manufacturers was shipped either to a BJ's cross-docking facility or directly to clubs. Personnel at the cross-docking facilities broke down truckload quantity shipments from manufacturers and reallocated goods for shipment to individual clubs, generally within 24 hours.

Strategy Features that Differentiated BJ's. Top management believed that several factors set BJ's Wholesale operations apart from those of Costco and Sam's Club:

- Offering a wide range of choice—7,500 items versus 4,000 items at Costco and Sam's Club.
- Focusing on the individual consumer via merchandising strategies that emphasized a customer-friendly shopping experience.
- Clustering club locations to achieve the benefit of name recognition and maximize the efficiencies of management support, distribution, and marketing activities.
- Trying to establish and maintain the first or second industry leading position in each major market where it operated.
- Creating an exciting shopping experience for members with a constantly changing mix of food and general merchandise items and carrying a broader product assortment than competitors.
- Supplementing the warehouse format with aisle markers, express checkout lanes, self-checkout lanes and low-cost video-based sales aids to make shopping more efficient for members.
- Being open longer hours than competitors.
- Offering smaller package sizes of many items.
- Accepting manufacturers' coupons.
- Accepting more credit card payment options.

Endnotes

[1] As quoted in Alan B. Goldberg and Bill Ritter, "Costco CEO Finds Pro-Worker Means Profitability," an ABC News original report on *20/20*, August 2, 2006, http://abcnews.go.com/2020/Business/story?id=1362779 (accessed November 15, 2006).

[2] Ibid.

[3] As described in Nina Shapiro, "Company for the People," *Seattle Weekly*, December 15, 2004, www.seattleweekly.com (accessed November 14, 2006).

[4] 2005 and 2006 annual reports.

[5] Matthew Boyle, "Why Costco Is So Damn Addictive," *Fortune*, October 30, 2006, p. 130.

[6] As quoted in ibid., pp. 128–29.

[7] Steven Greenhouse, "How Costco Became the Anti-Wal-Mart," *New York Times*, July 17, 2005, www.wakeupwalmart.com/news (accessed November 28, 2006).

[8] As quoted in Greenhouse, "How Costco Became the Anti-Wal-Mart."

[9] As quoted in Shapiro, "Company for the People."

[10] As quoted in Greenhouse, "How Costco Became the Anti-Wal-Mart."

[11] Boyle, "Why Costco Is So Damn Addictive," p. 132.

[12] Ibid., p. 130.

[13] As quoted in Goldberg and Ritter, "Costco CEO Finds Pro-Worker Means Profitability."

[14] Ibid.

[15] Ibid.

[16] Shapiro, "Company for the People."

[17] Greenhouse, "How Costco Became the Anti-Wal-Mart."

[18] As quoted in Goldberg and Ritter, "Costco CEO Finds Pro-Worker Means Profitability."

[19] Ibid.

[20] As quoted in Greenhouse, "How Costco Became the Anti-Wal-Mart."

[21] As quoted in Goldberg and Ritter, "Costco CEO Finds Pro-Worker Means Profitability."

[22] Boyle, "Why Costco Is So Damn Addictive," p. 132.

[23] As quoted in Shapiro, "Company for the People."

[24] Ibid.

[25] As quoted in Goldberg and Ritter, "Costco CEO Finds Pro-Worker Means Profitability."

[26] As quoted in Shapiro, "Company for the People."

2

Shearwater Adventures Ltd.

Michelle Reeser

The University of Alabama

Allen Roberts, sitting in his office in the Shearwater Adventures warehouse in Victoria Falls, Zimbabwe, was contemplating his company's future in light of the serious problems it was encountering in conducting its outdoor adventures. Tourism in Zimbabwe was down 75 percent over 1998 highs, and inflation was 1,200 percent, causing prices to double every 22 days. However, over the last two years, Shearwater's sales had risen by 22 percent and 39 percent, respectively. Shearwater was by far the market leader in the Victoria Falls area, with an 80 percent share.

Despite its dominance in the Victoria Falls area and its position as market leader for the entire African continent, Shearwater Adventures had many competitors in the outdoor adventures business. At issue was how to continue to dominate the market while maintaining its reputation as a successful outdoor adventures operator.

As Allen Roberts was preparing to develop his strategy and business plan for the coming year, he was beginning to wonder if there was any future in the adventure industry in Victoria Falls. Roberts and his management team had already cut Shearwater's expenses to the bone and had even given up their company cars for motorbikes.

ALLEN ROBERTS

Allen Roberts was educated in the United Kingdom at Nottingham University, where he majored in quantity surveying. This special course required classes in architecture and detailed cost estimation. However, like a lot of students in their 20s, he was not really interested in going to work, so he followed his passion

of kayaking. He became a competitive kayaker, entering numerous tournaments all over the world. In 1991, Roberts realized he could not make a career of kayaking and acted on a friend's suggestion to go to Victoria Falls and try his luck at rafting the Zambezi River.

As soon as Roberts made his first trip, he was hooked on the Zambezi, and thus a new passion was born. The Zambezi was generally regarded as offering the best white-water rafting in the world. As Roberts said, "The rapids are huge, the water is warm, the weather is great, and the scenery stunning."

After working in Africa for a while, Roberts traveled to the United States and tried his luck at canoeing and white-water rafting in West Virginia and then in Pennsylvania. During his time in the States, Roberts also gained valuable experience making videos of rafting trips and selling the copies to participants. Soon, however, he decided to return to Africa and Victoria Falls for good.

A friend of Roberts's named Mike Davis had, in the previous rafting season, started making videos of Zambezi River rafting trips and had secured the rights to do so for the next season. Knowing that Roberts had been making videos in the States, Davis approached Roberts about working together, and their business soon expanded to produce both videos and photos. The profit was so tremendous on the videos and pictures that Davis and Roberts were making more money than the owners of the rafts. This did not go unnoticed by the raft operators.

Roberts and Davis were having the time of their lives. As single young men, they were making good money with few expenses. Roberts says that his only necessities were food, beer, and the occasional date. The long term was not in his thoughts because he was having too much fun.

In 1995, the manager of Shearwater Adventures approached Mike Davis and asked if he would like to form a partnership. Davis agreed immediately. The

Shearwater owners soon realized that Roberts and Davis were first-rate entrepreneurs, and the two were put in charge of all Shearwater operations. Davis was in charge of running the rafting adventures, and Roberts became a partner in the video and photo section, which at the time was the most profitable area. Roberts was 25 years old.

Business was good for Shearwater at that time. Tourist arrivals to Victoria Falls were growing rapidly. However, in 2000, Davis decided to leave the group to pursue new ventures. Roberts not only stayed on at Shearwater but also assumed the role of CEO, taking a personal 25 percent stake in the company. It was under Roberts's leadership that Shearwater not only grew to dominate the Victoria Falls outdoor adventure market but also became the most well-known adventure tour operator in all of Africa.

THE INDUSTRY

One expert estimated that the extreme and adventure sporting industry was in the $100 million range. However, it was believed that, due to the fragmented nature of the industry, this estimate of the industry's size was too low and that a more accurate estimate would place it in the $400 to $500 million range with over 40 areas of activity and 250,000 operators worldwide. Some players in the industry were experiencing growth rates as high as 12 percent annually. Extreme and adventure sports were growing as working people looked to find more exciting ways to enjoy time away from their jobs.

Thus, the extreme and adventure sports industry not only was fragmented but also had the characteristics of an emerging business. Most companies defined extreme and adventure sports as those activities requiring special equipment and one or more trained guides. The difference between an extreme sport and an adventure sport was simply a matter of word choice: a company's advertising could use either term according to how the company wanted to portray the activities it offered to customers. The wide range of activities included bungee jumping, skiing, hiking, biking, climbing, horseback riding, and going on safaris. The most popular attraction, however, was white-water rafting. Many companies offered individual trips or package deals categorized by the number of days they took.

Like other industries in the 21st century, the extreme and adventure sporting industry had a global presence. Adventure seekers were offered not only a wide range of activities but also a wide range of locations. While one person could seek adventure on a safari in Africa, another could choose to race down the rapids in North America's Rocky Mountains. However, as competitors looked to grow their market share and increase their customer base, they tended to concentrate on competition at the local level while considering attracting customers on the global level to be more of an obstacle. With the average female customer at 46 years old and the average male customer at 50 years old, successful players in this market had to find a way to cater to an aging customer base while continuing to attract college-age and young adult customers.

It was no surprise that the target age in the extreme and adventure sports industry ranged from the mid 40s to early 50s. Those were the years when everyday life became more and more hectic and disposable income increased. With a societal push to stay young at heart and the realization that money can't always buy happiness, adults were looking for ways to break free from the sometimes mundane life of office work and the acquisition of possessions. As one industry expert stated, "How many homes and SUVs can one person own?" In addition to a new mind-set, adults were also influenced by many other factors. An increased focus on healthy lifestyles was prompting consumers to choose vacations that also provided a means of exercise.

Entertainment media were also helping the cause of extreme and adventure sports. ESPN's X Games were gaining popularity, and reality TV shows such as *Survivor* and *Fear Factor* were sparking the interest of millions to take part in their very own adventure. It was also much easier than ever before for people to travel long distances for vacation, making seemingly remote locations such as the Zambezi River not so remote after all. Outdoor adventure companies' knowledge base and the quality of their equipment were also continuing to improve, allowing even the most conservative adventurer to feel safe.

Within this industry, white-water rafting in particular had many positive qualities, but what did it take for a rafting company to be competitive? Players in the field consisted of two types: young college grads looking for adventurous jobs, and experienced tour operators with an average of 15 years in the industry. Mature companies were faced with aging equipment and owners who were getting older and out of shape.

The cost of entering the industry could be as low as $20,000 for a small operation that simply ran rafting trips or as high as $200,000 for a full-service operation offering a combined transport, rafting, shopping, and lodging experience. While it was difficult to start an operation in the United States, due to the cost of permits, opening an adventure operation in some countries such as South Africa could be as easy as just having a white-water raft. However, to achieve long-term sustainability, the leader of the company had to be shrewd and had to know the financial status of the company down to the last penny. Industry leaders were also partnering through acquisitions, organized associations, and reseller networks in order to increase repeat bookings from satisfied customers.

The value chain was critically important for international extreme adventure companies because only 30 percent of customers booked an adventure in advance. If an operator could link up with a travel company such as Thompson Tours (see, e.g., www. thompsonsafrica.com/ZimbabweVictoriaFallsDay ToursAndAdventureExcursion937.aspx), then it could ensure that visitors had prepaid for the adventure and could thus better predict the current demand. Other key success factors included repeat bookings and cross-selling—companies that could offer a variety of activities had a much higher probability of gaining repeat business.

Advertising was key to attract tourists who had not yet chosen an adventure activity upon arrival in the local market. Because competition was concentrated at the local level, marketing techniques had to focus on maximizing operations through local avenues. Adventure sports companies in Victoria Falls,

for example, had to target tourists as soon as they entered the area. They formed partnerships with shuttle drivers from airports and set up offices in key hotels. Credibility was added when locals supported the operation. Another successful means of boosting sales was to expand operations into tourist transportation. Instead of merely investing in partnerships with drivers, an adventure sports company could invest in one or more modes of transportation to directly target customers at the start of their vacation. Placing ads in travel guides, magazines, and high-traffic Internet sources was another way to reach a wider range of customers from different geographical locations and different age brackets.

In the case of Shearwater Adventures, word of mouth played an important role in new sales. After covering advertising on a local level, Shearwater also partnered with leading tour operators such as Jenman African Safaris (www.jenmansafaris.com) to boost its reputation and reach a wider audience.

SHEARWATER ADVENTURES

As Allen Roberts looked to strengthen his 80 percent market share in the Victoria Falls area, one strategy he considered was to acquire other companies. Having a knack for attracting the right person for the right job, he also continued to build a solid management team. Shearwater's financials are shown in Exhibit 1.

Exhibit 1   **Shearwater Adventures' Financials, 2004–2006 (in U.S.$)**

	2004	2005	2006
INCOME STATEMENT DATA			
Revenue	$2,246,680.64	$3,386,586.27	$3,926,063.10
Cost of sales	(673,059.05)	(1,066,122.08)	(1,127,835.02)
Gross profit	$1,573,621.59	$2,320,464.19	$2,798,228.09
Other income (rents, helicopter charters, disposal of old equipment)	158,967.96	820,139.74	352,561.20
Total gross profit	$1,732,589.55	$3,140,603.93	$3,150,789.29
Variable costs	(248,938.18)	(688,884.06)	(741,124.77)
Contribution	$1,483,651.37	$2,451,719.87	$2,409,664.06
Staff overheads	(871,918.83)	(1,737,485.86)	$(927,162.87)
Corporate overheads	(971,329.69)	(1,146,931.73)	(1,167,647.94)
Net profit (loss)	$(359,597.15)	$(432,697.71)	$314,853.25
OTHER DATA			
Customers	26,351	36,056	41,868
Average revenue per customer	$85.26	$93.93	$93.77

Roberts had differentiated Shearwater Adventures by offering far more adventures than any of his competitors—see Exhibit 2.

Roberts knew that Shearwater's competitors had only three options to offer at most—white-water rafting, boating, and riding elephants—but that they could add more in the future. Two concerns were that

(1) it was not expensive for a company to add an adventure to its lineup, and (2) there was talent in the area that could either devise a new adventure or that could simply copy Shearwater's offerings.

One of the bright spots for Shearwater Adventures was its addition of bundled activities—packages allowed customers to choose from a selection activities

Exhibit 2   **Representative of Shearwater Adventures' Offerings**

Jetboat *Adventure*

Zambezi River Jet Boating Trips

Prepare for an action-packed, adreralin-filled 30-minute jetboating experience in one of the most spectacular settings in the world. After donning your lifejacket and helmet and listening to a detailed safety briefing, your driver will take you on a quick warm-up. Nothing quite prepares you for the thrill, when your driver suddenly goes full throttle and you go shooting up the first rapid, heading for the base of the magnificent Falls. In between spurts of wind-swept madness, you will be given a brief talk on the geological formation of the gorçe and Falls and the history of the famous Victoria Falls Bridge.

River Trip includes:
• Courtesy transfers from major hotals / lodges in Vic Falls
• Transfers to and from the gorge
• Minerals and beers after the trip

Remember :
• There is a steep climb into and out of the gorge
• The age-limit for the Shearwater Jet is 8
• The trip takes approximately two and a half hours from pick up to drop off
• All trips are subject to water levels and are governed by weather conditions

Rates

Action Jet Adventure - USD 75

➢ ENQUIRE NOW!

Helicopter *Adventure*

Victoria Falls - Flight Options

"The legendary Flight of Angels"

Coined by David Livingstone when he first documented discovering the Falls; "A sight so wonderful that ange s must have gazed down on it in flight", the "Flight of Angels" is the most popular of the flight options.

Departing from the helipad, located just 3 kilometres from the Victoria Falls town centre, the "Flight of Angels" is a scenic flight over Victoria Falls with an airtime of 12-13 minutes.

Flying lower than a conventional, fixed-wing aircraft, you will fly a complete circuit over the Falls in both directions, giving you the best views of the Falls. A quick trip up river and back over the Zambezi National park completes your flight.

"The Game Flight"

This option is the same as the "Flight of Angels", but with a longer flying time, with the express purpose of spotting game.

30-minutes of airtime takes you firstly over the Falls and then up river and over the Zambezi National Park. The best times for the game flight are early morning and late afternoon. Whilst we cannot guarantee that you will spot game, elephant, buffalo, hippo. crocodile. rhino and giraffe can all be found in the Zambezi National Park and can be seen from the air.

Please Note:

• Each helicopter has a middle seat so there is no guarantee of a window seat. Window seats may not be booked – they are on a first come first served basis.

• Our helicopters provide service to the Medical Air Rescue Service for all its search and rescue operations. Should an emergency arise, your flight may have to be cancelled and rescheduled.

• Flights may also have to be cancelled due to bad weather. Should you not be able to reschedule your flight, a full refund will be given.

Trip includes:

• Transfers from all major hotels in the Victoria Falls town

Rates

Flight of Angels - USD 90.00
Game Flight & Flight of Angels- USD 170.00

➢ ENQUIRE NOW!

GAME DRIVES

DUSK AND DAWN WILDLIFE EXPERIENCES

Join us for a morning or evening game drive. Capture the essence of the African bush at its best in the age old tradition of game driving. Open, well kitted four-wheel drive vehicles will take you on a meander along the shores of a scenic lake, through basalt plains to Teak forests and Kalahari sands within the Nakavango Private Game Reserve.

Let your professional guides impart their immense knowledge of the many species of mammals, birds and other wilderness elements that you will encounter. The reserve is only 20 kilometers out of Victoria Falls yet one feels miles away from the hustle and bustle of daily life. Only two game drive vehicles are permitted in the reserve at any one time, giving you the feeling of absolute exclusivity. The Nakavango Game Reserve is a privately owned estate which is home to an abundant variety of wildlife.

What are the highlights?

• Highly trained professional guides with extensive knowledge in various fields are there to enhance your wildlife knowledge and give you further insight to your game drive experience.

• Only two game drive vehicles are permitted in the reserve at any one time using different routes, thereby ensuring you a peaceful, undisturbed game viewing experience.

• Relax after your night drive, enjoying your bush dinner under the grandeur of the starlit African sky. Listening to the night sounds of the bush as animals draw close to drink by the waterhole.

RATES:

Game Drive (am or pm) - **USD 60.00**
Night Drive - **USD 75.00**

➢ ENQUIRE NOW!

GAME WALKS

NAKAVANGO WILDLIFE TRAILS

Experience wildlife trails in the footprints of your ancestors on the private Nakavango Game Reserve, which is home to abundant wildlife. Let our professional guides show off this magnificent African wildlife paradise.

What are the highlights?

• Experience the laws of nature as you amble through the bush, seeking out in more detail the wonders of the natural world around you.

• Our guides are extremely well versed in all elements of the bush and can pay attention to detail of even the smallest aspects.

• Learn important lessons about the natural elements of being part of this wildlife wonder where we are the visitors. Use these skills to encounter the game more closely.

• Let your natural senses and instincts come to life as you retune your sensory perceptions to the sounds and smells of the wild.

RATES:

Game Walks (am or pm) - **USD 75.00**

➢ ENQUIRE NOW!

LION ENCOUNTER

WALK WITH THE PRIDE

Taking approximately one hour this amazing experience is a great addition to Vic Falls, Africa's adventure capital. No leashes or collars the pride runs freely with you through the bush. You may even be lucky enough to experience a stalk on some of the wildlife species, which abound in the Nakavango game reserve.

What are the highlights?

• Enjoy the spine tingly thrill of your first encounter as the lions brush past you, zigzagging between your legs as they move to take the lead.

• Feel the freedom that these amazing cats enjoy in the wild.

• You will have the opportunity to walk, interact and observe the pride in their natural environment.

• Learn many interesting facts about the lions from your professional guide who has been around these royal African cats for most of his life.

• Watch the cubs in awe as they climb the trees to a surprising height and share in the humour at their indecisiveness as they contemplate their trip back down again.

• You may be lucky enough to feel the intensity of the lions as they attempt a stalk on the various antelope species that abound the game reserve.

• Remember you are not taking the lions for a walk they are allowing you to be part of their pride for a while; this will be your greatest adventure in Africa.

RATES:

Half Day Trip - am or pm - **USD 100.00**

ᐅ ENQUIRE NOW!

SHEARWATER CANOEING

Escape from the mad rush of everyday life with Shearwater upper Zambezi canoeing. Gently paddle your way down the upper Zambezi River, enjoying the playground of the hippo, the shimmering green home of the crocodile and the watering holes of the buffalo and elephant as you canoe against the majestic backdrop of the Zambezi River.

What are the highlights?

• Our guides' expertise and knowledge.

• The peace and tranquility of the upper Zambezi

• Only in a canoe do you have the chance to get up close and "personal" with the African elephant.

• Wonderful bird life

• A true wilderness experience

• Drift past pods of Hippo.

• Ilala Palms standing tall on the islands and banks.

• The canoe trip is an educational trip highly recommended for bird lovers.

RATES:

Half Day - am or pm - **USD 75.00**
Full Day - **USD 95.00**
Two Day and Overnight Camping - **USD 240.00**
Zambezi Wine Route - **USD 60.00**

ᐅ ENQUIRE NOW!

SHEARWATER RIVER SAFARIS

Cruise peacefully exploring the islands and channels, which are home to such southern African mammals as the elephant and hippo and many rare species of birdlife such as the African Finfoot, Open-billed Storks, Yellow-billed Storks and Sacred Ibis. Our guide will describe the flora and fauna, birdlife and game as you sit back and relax in the comfort of our safari boat, venturing into waters un-chartered by the larger cruise boats, enjoying the excitement of a water-borne safari experience.

What are the highlights?

• Watch the spray of the falls, 'the smoke that thunders' as you sit back and enjoy a glass of chilled wine.

• Personalised guided safari of the upper Zambezi River

• Maximum of 10 people per trip

• Our safari operates in the river area just above the Victoria Falls, where larger cruise boats are unable to go.

• A peaceful and secluded safari.

• Encounter game and bird life up close and personal.

• Explore the nesting area of some of Africa's exquisite birds such as the white-faced bee-eater.

• Watch the Sacred Ibis, Cattle Egrets and Spoonbills flocking home to roost.

• Home to many of the southern Zimbabwe specials.

• Enjoy the African sunset and the silhouetted Ilala palms.

RATES:

River Safari - **USD 45.00**

 ENQUIRE NOW!

VICTORIA FALLS BRIDGE TOURS

'Why walk over it when you can walk under it?'

Let us take you on a hundred year journey under the Victoria Falls Bridge. Discover Cecil John Rhodes plans for his Cape to Cairo Railway. Discover how the bridge was constructed and how a full locomotive was transported across the gorge before the actual completion of the bridge and why. Our highly trained and experienced guides will ensure a safe and informative 2½ hours on and around the bridge.

What are the highlights?

• The trouble-free transfer to and from the bridge.

• Seeing and experiencing a hundred years of Victorian Engineering.

• Informative talks on the history of the bridge.

• Magnificent views of the Victoria Falls and Batoka Gorge.

• Seeing a bungi jump up close and personal.

• The camaraderie involved in checking your buddy's safety systems.

RATES:

Historical Bridge Tour - **USD 45.00**

ENQUIRE NOW!

SHEARWATER ULTRALIGHTS

Set your imagination free and get in touch with all your senses as you embark on the flight of a lifetime in our open cockpit ultralights. Taking off from the awesome Zambezi River in our floatplane or from our bush strip in the Zambezi National Park; then flying over the magnificent Victoria Falls for unparalleled viewing and photographic opportunities. Nothing beats the freedom of your ultralight flight.

What are the highlights?

• Being the sole passenger, you receive the one-on-one personal attention of the pilot.

• Ultralight flying offers you the most exhilarating unobstructed, breathtaking view of the magnificent Victoria Falls and surrounding areas——sit back, relax and enjoy it.

• Take your own camera equipment/video equipment and take back a memory of your unique flight exactly as you perceived it.

• Being the only floatplane available in Victoria Falls we offer you a unique opportunity not available through any other operator, as you gently take off and land from the mighty Zambezi, sharing the river with many pods of resident hippos.

• The ultralight aircraft is the quietest aircraft operating in the Falls and allows you to cruise over the game in the Zambezi National Park without disturbing them.

• Cruise above the Zambezi River perhaps spotting elephants crossing from island to island, or pods of Hippo's playing in the water beneath.

• The float plane jetty site is just 3 km's from town situated on the banks of the Zambezi.

• The bush airstrip is situated just 5 km's from the centre of Victoria Falls in the national park.

RATES:

Bush Ultralight Flight of Angels - **USD 100.00**
Ultralight Game Flight & Falls Flight - **USD 170.00**

> **ENQUIRE NOW!**

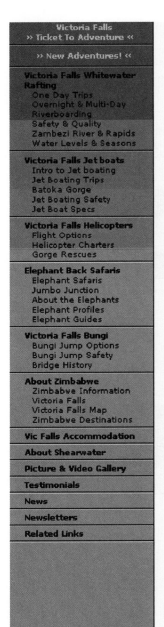

S   A   F   A   R   I   S

PRESS STATEMENT - Elephants, 5th January 2006
This press release is issued in response to a number of reports that have recently appeared in the press concerning Shearwater and the elephants that are in our care.
Download the Press Release

Elephant Back Safaris

Upon arrival, your guide will give a quick introductory talk and safety briefing. You will then be introduced to your induna (elephant carer) and the elephants themselves. On mounting the elephants, the safari begins — view game whilst riding game, savouring the experience of crashing through the African bush atop a gigantic pachyderm. Your safari ends with a short training session and interaction with the elephants followed by breakfast, lunch or snacks (depending on the safari).

Sunrise Safari
Operating all year round, this Safari begins from 06:30 and finishes at 12:00 with a continental breakfast in summer and a full English breakfast during winter.

Sundown Safari
This option also operates all year round, with pick-up from 15:00 and drop-off at 19:00. Snacks and refreshments will be provided after the interaction with the elephants.

Jumbo Junction
Operating all year round, your interaction with these majestic African creatures begins 11:00 and ends after lunch at 14:00. Transfers, lunch and refreshments will be provided.

Please note that the Jumbo Junction does not include a ride on the elephants, merely the chance for you to interact with the elephants.

Elephant Back Safaris includes:

- Educational presentation
- Refreshments and either breakfast, lunch or snacks depending on the Safari
- Bottled water on the ride
- Transfers from all major hotels
- Medical Air Rescue Service

What to bring:

- Neutral coloured clothes: avoid white and bright coloured clothes
- Long trousers, long sleeved shirt and closed comfortable shoes
- Wide brimmed hat
- A sweater is recommended for the months of May to August
- Sun block
- Binoculars
- Glasses and/or sunglasses
- Camera
- Personal medication Insect repellant

Please bear in mind that guests will be responsible for their personal effects whilst they are on the elephant ride. It is therefore advisable that belongings are kept to a reasonable limit.

Rates

Half Day Safari am or pm - USD 100

Source: Company Web site, accessed April 17, 2007.

for one price. Shearwater used the phrase "Ticket to Adventure" to describe its bundled activities—see Exhibit 3.

While Shearwater Adventures faced serious threats, there was a defense or a solution for each one. As Zimbabwe tackled its economic and politi-cal instability, Shearwater could look to neighboring countries for hope. Victoria Falls, however, was a precious commodity, and Shearwater would have to consider that in any plans for relocation. It was crucial for Allen Roberts to increase prebookings of Shearwater adventure tours as a defense against

Exhibit 3   **Shearwater Adventures' Package Offerings**

Shearwater / ticket to adventure

Victoria Falls - Ticket To Adventure

A new and exciting way to buy your adventure activities. You make huge savings and get to choose what to do and when to do it. Choose from any of our special Tick-it to adventure packages shown below.

OPTION ONE

You get a Sunset Cruise (valued at USD 35.00) plus your choice of any **TWO** activities from the list below.

PRICE: USD 170.00
Save up to USD 75.00 off normal prices.
Plus any additional Shearwater product for only USD 70.00.
Cruise to Safari Jet Upgrade USD 20.00

ENQUIRE NOW!

OPTION TWO

Your choice of any **THREE** activities from the list below.

PRICE: USD 205.00
Save up to USD 110.00 off normal prices.
Plus any additional Shearwater product for only USD 70.00

ENQUIRE NOW!

OPTION THREE

Your choice of any **FIVE** activities from the list below.

PRICE : USD 290.00
Save up to USD 230.00 off normal prices.

> **ENQUIRE NOW!**

SHEARWATER ACTIVITIES

Choose from any of the Shearwater activities below:
- Shearwater Rafting
- Zambezi Helicoter Company
- Elephant Company
- Victoria Falls Bungi
- Shearwater Jet
- Shearwater Safaris (Game-drive, Night drive, Game walk)
- River Safari
- Walk with the Pride
- Ultralight flight
- Bridge Tour
- Upper Zambezi canoeing

Source: Company Web site, accessed April 17, 2007.

competition and to use its existing capacity to accommodate more customer bookings for its adventure tours to its advantage. If Shearwater Adventures was to remain the number one adventure tour operator in the Victoria Falls area, what were the next steps in the game plan?

Case 3

The Battle in Radio Broadcasting: XM vs. Sirius vs. Local Radio vs. Internet Radio

Arthur A. Thompson
The University of Alabama

In early 2007, about 220 million people in the United States and Canada listened to radio each week. It was estimated that the average adult listened to radio about three hours daily, with the amount of listening fairly evenly distributed across gender and age groups. But the radio industry in North America was in a state of flux. New technology and changing listening habits were reshaping the competitive structure of the radio marketplace in particular and audio broadcasting in general, precipitating a battle for both listening audiences and advertising dollars. Most motor vehicle manufacturers had begun offering factory-installed or dealer-installed satellite radios in their new vehicles—of the 16 million vehicles expected to be sold in the United States in 2007 at least 5 million were expected to be equipped with satellite radio receivers. Already, almost 15 million U.S. vehicles (about 6 percent of the nation's 230 million registered vehicles) could receive satellite radio broadcasts, and increasing numbers of consumers had begun purchasing satellite radio receivers for their homes. Going into 2007, the two leading satellite radio competitors, XM Radio and Sirius Satellite Radio, had attracted over 14 million U.S. and Canadian subscribers and were expected to add another 3–5 million subscribers in 2007.

In addition, many radio stations were investing in new equipment to begin broadcasting high-definition (HD) digital radio programs. Seven of the top U.S. radio companies had formed a strategic

alliance to accelerate the rollout of HD digital radio broadcasts, and more than 15 manufacturers—including Alpine, Delphi, Panasonic, Polk and Yamaha—were producing digital radio receivers. Clear Channel Communications, Inc., the largest owner of radio stations in the United States, had announced that it expected to install HD digital radio broadcasting capability at 1,000 of its 1,150 stations by the end of 2008. As of early 2007, more than 1,000 radio stations were broadcasting primary signals with HD radio technology, making HD-quality programming available to 80 percent of the U.S. population; another 2,000 U.S. radio stations had announced plans to initiate HD radio broadcasts within several years. HD digital radio eliminated the static, hiss, pop, and fades associated with analog radio signals so that AM-band broadcasts took on the quality of FM broadcasts; furthermore, FM-band broadcasts of HD digital signals produced CD- and DVD-quality sound. HD radio also permitted radio broadcasters to segment a single, existing radio frequency so that it could carry multiple, simultaneous, higher-quality AM and FM broadcast streams as well as wireless data. A number of local radio stations had also taken steps to have their signals relayed over the Internet; in 2007, there were thousands of free online radio stations and a half-dozen or more Internet sites that specialized in helping people locate online radio broadcasts of their liking. Many Internet radio stations are completely independent from traditional ("terrestrial") radio stations and broadcast only on the Internet. Radio listeners with broadband Internet connections had thousands of choices, including Internet-enabled radio stations anywhere in the world—it was very easy to listen to a European radio station from North America or New Zealand. Internet radio was popular with people whose interests were not being met by their local radio stations. Some people were drawn to Internet radio because of the enormously wide genre of programs that were available, because they were traveling or temporarily living in a foreign country, and/or because they were looking to expand their cross-cultural awareness.

An even newer phenomenon was podcasting—an on-the-go, on-demand technology that enabled people to listen to audio files that could be downloaded from the Internet (using some version of podcasting software) to a personal computer, an iPod, a cell phone, or other type of digital media player. Podcast-enabled devices made it simple for the user to download and listen to any of tens of thousands of podcasts whose content ranged from Spanish lessons to headline news to ESPN sports to health information to any type of music imaginable. *BusinessWeek* had emerged as the leading supplier of business-related podcasts. In 2006, podcast enthusiasts downloaded millions of files at Google, Yahoo! Podcasts, MSN, AOL, and Apple's iTunes Music Store. Websites like Podcast.net and Podcast.com had sprung up that allowed podcast producers to post their creations and podcast listeners to sample, find, subscribe, and listen to most any of the tens of thousands of podcasts available worldwide.

Several local radio stations and some of their more entrepreneurial disc jockeys had begun assembling their own customized podcasts of music or other topics and posting the podcasts on Web sites for interested listeners to download. Brian Ibbott, an enterprising disc josckey in a Denver suburb, produced a series of 35-minute music podcasts called Coverville that focused on a new rendition of a previously recorded cover song of an album.[1] Ibbott's podcasts, which were produced in his home and delivered in an informal, relaxed style, usually featured about six selections and included information about the performing artist and source album. Coverville downloads became so popular that Ibbott turned his podcasts into a sideline business, creating his own Web site, Coverville.com, at which he sold advertising and marketed subscriptions to Coverville via Yahoo! and iTunes.

Another increasingly important competitive element in the radio broadcasting market was the exploding use of portable MP3 players; these devices, which sold for approximately $80–$350 and could store up to 20,000 songs, could also be plugged into car outlets and used as a music source while driving. Using MP3 players to listen to music instead of tuning into radio stations was commonplace in 2007 since song files could be readily obtained via numerous file-sharing software programs and on the Web sites of online music retailers, artists, and record labels. At Apple's iTunes Web site, iPod owners could download and purchase over 4 million songs, 100,000 podcasts, 20,000 audio books, 5,000 music videos, 250 feature films, and 350 television shows, as well as convert music on compact disc to digital files. Apple had sold close to 89 million iPods as of January 2007.

Still another, but lesser, competitive element was the recent entry of cable TV companies into the music broadcasting marketplace. Cable TV companies customarily included 40 or so continuous music channels as part of the digital programming package offered to consumers having digital and high-definition TVs.

In 2000, market research indicated that about 75 percent of the population 12 years and older listed to the radio daily and about 95 percent listened at least once weekly.[2] However, in 2006–2007, these percentages were believed to have fallen, particularly among younger age groups due to the enormous popularity of iPods and other brands of portable MP3 players as a primary music source for teen and young adults.

THE RADIO BROADCASTING INDUSTRY

In 2006, there were close to 11,000 commercial radio stations in the United States licensed by the Federal Communications Commission, of which 43.2 percent were AM stations and 66.8 percent were FM stations; there were an additional 2,760 FM educational stations. The number of licensed commercial radio stations had hovered in the range of 10,200 to 11,000 since the mid-1990s. However, the number of radio station owners had been in a long-term decline as more and more stations came under the ownership of a single operator. While there were about 9,300 radio stations in 2006, according to market researcher C. Barnes & Co., the radio broadcasting industry had become increasingly dominated by such large multistation operators as Clear Channel Communications (about 1,150 stations), Cumulus Media (307 stations), Citadel Communications (223 stations), Infinity Broadcasting (178 stations), Entercom Communications (119 stations), and Cox Radio (80 stations). About 30 other operators had 20 or more stations each. In addition to the trend toward greater industry consolidation, a number of multistation operators were restructuring their radio station portfolios. Several larger operators were selling off stations in smaller audience markets in order to better concentrate their attention and resources on midsized and larger markets. Clear Channel, for example, in late 2006 announced plans to sell 448 of its stations that were outside the Top 100 Arbitron Metro areas (it also planned to divest its entire group of 42 television stations, all of which were located in small and midsized geographic areas throughout the United States).

Traditional AM and FM radio stations had a well-established market for their product offering and used an advertising-based business model that provided free broadcast reception paid for by commercial advertising. Stations chose one of several basic programming formats (music, talk, sports, religious, news, educational, ethnic), put their own differentiating spin on the selected programming format, and then tried to make money by selling a sufficient number of advertising spots at rates commensurate with their audience ratings to produce a profitable revenue stream. Radio stations competed for listeners and advertising revenues with other radio stations in their geographic listening area according to such factors as program content, on-air talent, transmitter power, and audience demographics; these factors, along with audience size and the number and characteristics of other radio stations in the area affected the rates they were able to charge for advertising. A growing number of AM and FM radio stations had begun reducing the number of commercials per hour, expanding the range of music played on the air, improving ad copy, and experimenting with new formats in order to provide more entertaining listening and better compete with satellite radio.

Revenues for the licensed commercial stations in the United States in 2006 were about $21.2 billion, of which $20.5 billion or 96.9 percent came from ad sales. According to market research data compiled by C Barnes & Co., radio industry revenues had grown briskly over the past three years, and the brisk growth was expected to continue through 2008:[3]

2004	$15.7 billion
2005	18.4
2006	21.2
2007	24.1
2008	27.1

Each of the 100 largest metro area markets in the United States generated annual radio advertising revenues of $40 million or more. The largest radio market, New York City and the surrounding area, generated ad revenues of just over $1 billion; between 40 and 45 U.S. metro areas generated radio advertising revenues of $100 million or more. However, there were about 650 geographic markets that generated less than 10 million in radio advertising annually.

XM SATELLITE RADIO INC.

XM Satellite Radio was incorporated in 1992 for the purpose of exploiting satellite radio transmission technology and creating a national radio network to compete alongside traditional AM and FM radio stations. XM became a public company in 1999 with an issue of 10.2 million shares of common stock that yielded net proceeds of $114 million. Follow-on offerings of common stock, along with preferred stock issues and secured notes, were undertaken in late 1999 and early 2000 to raise an additional $750 million in capital to help finance the launch of two high-powered Boeing satellites, arrange for the manufacture of satellite radio receivers and other equipment, install terrestrial signal repeaters and other necessary networking equipment, develop programming, conduct market research, and attract subscribers. Program broadcasts began in November 2001, and by December 2002 the company had attracted almost 350,000 subscribers at fees of $9.95 per month. Market research done in 2000–2001 indicated that as many as 49 million people might subscribe to satellite radio service by 2012, assuming a monthly fee of $9.95 and radio receiver prices of $150–$399, depending on the car or home model chosen. A 2002 market research study conducted for XM concluded that there would be about 15 million satellite radio subscribers by the end of 2006. The forecast proved fairly accurate given that both XM and Sirius had recently raised their subscription rates to $12.95 monthly; at year-end 2006, there were 13.6 million satellite radio subscribers in the United States. (XM Radio had 7.63 million subscribers and Sirius had 6.0 million subscribers.) During 2006, XM added 1.7 million net new subscribers, but this was fewer than the 3 million that senior management forecast at the start of 2006.

However, XM had yet to earn a profit from its satellite service; the company had lost money every year of its existence. As shown in Exhibit 1, XM reported losses of $584.5 million in 2003, $642.4 million in 2004, $666.7 million in 2005, and $718.9 million in 2006. Exhibits 2 and 3 show XM Radio's balance sheets and cash flow performance for 2003–2006. In the fourth quarter of 2006, XM Radio reported a positive cash flow from operations despite the sizable losses.

XM Satellite Radio's Business Model and Strategy

In stark contrast to the advertising-based business model of traditional local radio, XM Radio employed a subscription-based business model. The company endeavored to offer a sufficiently broad and appealing selection of digital-quality radio programs that would attract listeners willing to pay $12.95 per month for mostly commercial-free programming. XM had a family plan that allowed subscribers to get a discounted rate of $6.99 per month for additional radios. So far, XM had been restrained in trying to cover some of its costs via ad sales, although a few XM channels did run occasional advertising spots.

Program Offerings   XM's lineup of over 170 channels in early 2007 had broad listener appeal and included 69 commercial-free music channels, 5 commercial music channels, 37 news/talk/commentary channels, 38 sports channels, and 21 instant traffic and weather channels—see Exhibit 4. XM subscribers could listen to original music and talk channels created by XM's programming staff, programs and channels of leading national brand-name content providers like Fox News and ESPN, and live coverage of over 5,000 sporting events annually (including play-by-play broadcasts of Major League Baseball, college football, college men's and women's basketball, and the National Hockey League, plus coverage of PGA Tour, FIFA World Cup soccer, and NASCAR racing events. From time to time, XM added new channels and altered its programs on existing channels to enhance listener appeal and keep its offerings fresh and in step with lifestyle trends for all age groups. The company had broadcast studios in New York City; Washington, D.C.; and the Country Music Hall of Fame in Nashville, Tennessee.

XM's target market included the drivers of the 255+ million registered automobiles and trucks and the 125+ million households with home radios in both the United States and Canada. Management believed that XM Radio had broad market appeal because of its "innovative and diverse programming, nationwide coverage, many commercial-free music channels, and digital sound quality."[4]

Programming could be received via portable receivers suitable for personal and home use and receivers installed in vehicles. Subscribers had online access to more than 85 XM channels over the Internet. In November 2005, XM management partnered with DIRECTV to make 72 channels of XM's music, children's, and talk programming available to the over 16 million customers of DIRECTV. XM also offered an online service through an arrangement with AOL and had partnered with Napster to provide online music purchase and playlist management capability.

XM's Marketing Strategy and Marketing Partnerships

XM's marketing strategy was aimed at building awareness and demand among potential subscribers and in the advertising community. The company made a point of advertising that its satellite radio service had appealing features compared to traditional radio. Advertising and promotional activities were conducted via television, radio, print and the Internet; sample programming and marketing materials were distributed at retail outlets, concert venues, motor sports events, and on the Internet to generate consumer interest. General Motors and Honda sponsored national and local print and television

Exhibit 1   **Consolidation Statement of Operations, XM Radio, 2003–2006
($ in thousands, except per share amounts)**

	2006	2005	2004	2003
Revenue:				
Subscriptions	$825,626	$502,612	$220,468	$78,239
Activation	16,192	10,066	4,814	1,868
Merchandise	21,720	18,182	7,261	6,692
Net ad sales	35,330	20,103	8,485	4,065
Other revenue	34,549	...7,303	3,415	917
Total revenue	933,417	558,266	244,443	91,781
Operating expenses:				
Cost of revenue (excludes depreciation & amortization):				
Revenue share & royalties	149,010	93,874	50,676	26,440
Customer care & billing operations	104,871	76,222	40,887	25,945
Cost of merchandise	48,949	40,707	11,557	9,797
Ad sales	15,961	10,058	6,165	3,257
Satellite & terrestrial	49,019	42,355	35,922	39,692
Broadcast & operations:				
Broadcast	23,049	16,609	10,832	7,689
Operations	34,683	24,460	13,192	12,023
Total broadcast & operations	57,732	41,069	24,024	19,712
Programming & content	165,196	101,008	32,704	23,109
Total cost of revenue	590,738	405,293	201,935	147,952
Research & development (excludes depreciation & amortization)	37,428	31,218	23,513	12,285
General & administrative (excludes depreciation & amortization)	88,626	43,864	28,555	27,418
Marketing (excludes depreciation & amortization):				
Retention & support	31,842	22,275	13,286	7,873
Subsidies & distribution	241,601	264,719	165,704	92,521
Advertising & marketing	147,640	163,312	88,076	64,309
Amortization of GM liability	29,760	37,250	37,250	35,564
Total marketing	450,843	487,556	304,316	200,267
Depreciation & amortization	168,880	145,870	147,165	158,317
Total operating expenses	1,336,515	1,113,801	705,484	546,239
Operating loss	(403,098)	(555,535)	(461,041)	(454,458)
Other income (expense):				
Interest income	21,664	23,586	6,239	3,066
Interest expense	(121,304)	(107,791)	(85,757)	(110,349)
Loss from de-leveraging transactions	(122,189)	(27,552)	(76,621)	(24,749)
Loss from impairment of investments	(76,572)	—	—	—
Equity in net loss of affiliate	(23,229)	(482)		
Other income	5,842	3,389	2,129	1,955
Net loss before income taxes	(718,886)	(664,385)	(615,051)	(584,535)
Provision for deferred income taxes	14	(2,330)	(27,317)	—
Net loss	$(718,872)	$(666,715)	$(642,368)	$(584,535)
Preferred stock dividend requirements	(12,820)	(8,597)	(8,802)	(17,569)
Net loss on Series B and C preferred stock retirement		----		(2,776)
Net loss attributable to common stockholders	$(731,692)	$(675,312)	$(651,170)	$(604,880)
Net loss per share of common stock: basic and diluted	$(2.70)	$(3.07)	$(3.30)	$(4.83)
Weighted average shares used in computing loss per share	270,586,682	219,620,468	197,317,607	125,176,320

Sources: 2005 and 2006 10-K reports and company press release, February 26, 2007.

Exhibit 2   **Consolidated Balance Sheet, XM Radio, 2004–2006 ($ in thousands)**

	2006	2005	2004
ASSETS			
Current assets:			
Cash and cash equivalents	$218,216	$710,991	$717,867
Accounts receivable, net of allowance for doubtful accounts	62,293	47,247	20,182
Due from related parties	13,991	8,629	5,367
Related party prepaid expenses	66,946	54,752	31,160
Prepaid programming content	28,172	65,738	11,390
Prepaid and other current assets	43,040	55,811	18,197
Total current assets	$432,658	943,168	804,163
Restricted investments	2,098	5,438	4,492
System under construction	126,049	216,527	329,355
Net property and equipment	849,662	673,672	461,333
Digital Audio Radio Service (DARS) license from FCC	141,387	141,276	141,227
Intangibles, net of accumulated amortization	4,640	5,902	7,164
Deferred financing fees, net of accumulated amortization	38,601	36,735	44,466
Related party prepaid expenses, net of current portion	160,712	9,809	25,901
Equity investments	80,592	187,403	—
Prepaid and other assets, net of current portion	4,219	3,731	3,534
Total assets	$1,840,618	$2,223,661	$1,821,635
LIABILITIES AND STOCKHOLDERS' EQUITY			
Current liabilities:			
Accounts payable	$51,844	$145,691	$59,986
Accrued expenses	147,591	154,125	88,107
Accrued satellite liability	64,875	104,300	100,100
Accrued interest	18,482	5,603	14,146
Current portion of long-term debt	14,445	7,608	6,556
Due to related parties	46,459	60,750	27,610
Subscriber deferred revenue	340,711	275,944	114,951
Deferred income	9,915	10,137	—
Total current liabilities	694,322	764,158	411,456
Satellite liability, net of current portion	—	23,285	15,000
Long-term debt, net of current portion	1,286,179	1,035,584	948,741
Due to related parties, net of current portion	—	53,901	38,911
Subscriber deferred revenue, net of current portion	86,482	84,694	37,396
Deferred income, net of current portion	140,695	141,073	—
Other non-current liabilities	40,735	40,018	33,968
Total liabilities	2,238,498	2,142,713	1,485,472
Stockholders' equity			
Series A, B, C, and D preferred stock, par value $0.01	54	60	60
Class A common stock, par value $0.01; 600,000,000 shares authorized, 305,781,515 shares, 240,701,988 shares, and 208,249,188 shares issued and outstanding at December 31, 2006,	3,058	2,407	2,082
Accumulated other comprehensive income	3,590	5,985	—
Unearned restricted stock compensation	—	(18,101)	—
Additional paid-in capital	3,093,894	2,870,201	2,446,910
Accumulated deficit	(3,498,476)	(2,779,604)	(2,112,889)
Total stockholders' equity (deficit)	(397,880)	80,948	336,163
Total liabilities and stockholders' equity	$1,840,618	$2,223,661	$1,821,635

Sources: 2005 and 2006 10-K reports; company press release on February 26, 2007.

Exhibit 3   **Selected Cash Flow Data, XM Radio, 2003–2006 ($ in thousands)**

	2006	2005	2004	2003
Cash flows from operating activities:				
Net loss	$(718,872)	$(666,715)	$(642,368)	$(584,535)
Net cash used in operating activities	(462,091)	(168,449)	(85,552)	(245,123)
Cash flows from investing activities:				
Purchase of property and equipment	$(54,895)	$(61,210)	$(25,934)	$(15,685)
Additions to system under construction	(220,124)	(118,583)	(143,978)	(4,108)
Proceeds from sale of assets	7,182	—	—	—
Purchase of equity investments	—	(25,334)	—	—
Net maturity (purchase) of restricted investments	3,390	(996)	(341)	22,750
Insurance proceeds from satellite recoveries	—	—	133,924	—
Other investing activities	—	—	—	11,664
Net cash (used in) provided by investing activities	$(264,447)	$(206,123)	$(36,329)	$14,621
Cash flows from financing activities:				
Proceeds from sale of common stock, net and exercise of stock options	$6,420	$319,637	$236,835	$253,102
Proceeds from issuance of 9.75% senior notes due 2014	600,000			
Proceeds from issuance of senior floating rate notes due 2013	200,000			
Proceeds from issuance of 10% senior secured convertible notes	—	—	—	210,000
Proceeds from issuance of 12% senior secured notes	—	—	—	185,000
Proceeds from issuance of 1.75% convertible senior notes	—	100,000	300,000	—
Proceeds from issuance of floating rate notes	—	—	200,000	—
Proceeds from refinancing of mortgage on corporate facility	—	—	33,300	—
Payments of premiums on de-leveraging transactions	(27,398)	(3,398)	(10,347)	
Repayment of 12% senior secured notes	(100,000)	(15,000)	(70,000)	—
Repayment of 7.75% convertible subordinated notes	—	—	—	(6,723)
Repayment of 14% senior secured notes	(186,545)	(22,824)	(13,028)	—
Repayment of related party long-term debt	—	—	(81,194)	—
Repayment of senior secured floating rate notes due 2009	(200,000)			
Payments on mortgages on corporate facilities	(578)	(381)	(28,247)	(420)
Payments on related party credit facility	—	—	(103,034)	—
Repurchase of Series B preferred stock	(23,960)	—	—	(10,162)
Payments on other borrowings	(12,725)	(9,651)	(40,174)	(2,722)
Deferred financing costs	(21,451)	(2,419)	(13,017)	(12,084)
Net cash provided by financing activities	$233,763	$365,964	$411,094	$615,991
Net increase (decrease) in cash and cash equivalents	$(492,775)	$(6,876)	$299,560	$385,489
Cash and cash equivalents at beginning of period	710,991	717,867	418,307	32,818
Cash and cash equivalents at end of period	$218,216	$710,991	$717,867	$418,307

Sources: 2005 and 2006 10-K reports.

advertising that featured the XM logo and message. The company's 2005 holiday season "Listen Large" marketing campaign featured TV spots with Ellen DeGeneres, Snoop Dogg, Derek Jeter, David Bowie, and Martina McBride. To leverage its extensive sports broadcasting offerings and exclusive relationships with Major League Baseball, XM promoted its "every team, all season long" play-by-play broadcasts of more than 2,500 Major League Baseball spring training, regular season, and playoff games. A free Delphi XM Roady XT satellite radio was offered to every fan at Game One of the 2005 World Series in Chicago. XM promoted its exclusive relationship with the PGA Tour by offering handheld radios for rental and purchase at PGA events. And it had a multiyear agreement with Andretti Green

Exhibit 4   **Comparative Programming and Channel Offerings, XM Radio and Sirius Satellite Radio, February 2007**

	XM Radio	Sirius Satellite Radio
Monthly subscription cost	$12.95	$12.95
Number of channels	Over 170	Over 130
Music		
Music by decades	50s, 60s, 70s, 80s, 90s	50s, 60s, 70s, 80s, 90s
Pop and Hits	11 channels	15 channels
Country	9 channels	7 channels
Rock	14 channels	13 channels
Hip-Hop/Urban/R&B	7 channels	7 channels
Christian/Gospel	3 channels	3 channels
Jazz/Blues	5 channels	5 channels
Classical	3 channels	3 channels
Latin/International	7 channels	7 channels
Dance/Electronic/Standards/Other	9 channels	7 channels
News	Fox News, CNN, CNN Headline, ABC News & Talk, MSNBC, 5 others	Fox News, CNN, CNN Headline, ABC News & Talk, CNBC, 7 others
Talk, Variety & Entertainment	Fox News Talk, C-Span, Open Road (truckers channel), The Power (African American talk), Talk Five (a women's interest channel), Oprah & Family, E!, 6 other channels	NPR Talk, NPR Now, Fox News Talk, Political Talk, C-Span, Howard Stern, Martha Stewart Living, Court TV Radio, Playboy Radio, E!, 3 others
Sports News and Talk	ESPN Radio, ESPN News, Fox Sports Radio, NASCAR Radio, The Sporting News, PGA Tour Network, Home Ice (24/7 hockey talk and play-by-play), MLB Home Plate (24/7 MLB news & talk), 2 others	ESPN Radio, ESPN News, ESPN Deportes, NBA Radio, NFL Radio (non-stop NFL talk), Sports Byline USA, 2 others
Family/Kids	Radio Disney, XM Kids, Radio Classics, Family Talk	LIME, Radio Disney, Kids Stuff, Radio Classics, Discovery Channel Radio
Traffic & Weather	The Weather Channel, Instant Traffic & Weather in 21 urban areas, XM 24/7 Emergency Alert	Local weather & traffic in 11 areas, Canada weather, Sirius weather and emergency
Financial News	CNBC, Bloomberg Radio	CNBC, Bloomberg
Comedy	5 channels	3 channels
Religion	—	3 channels
Special Programming	Opie and Anthony programs, Major League Baseball (play-by-play of games on 14 channels, plus a Spanish language channel), College Sports (ACC, PAC-10, Big Ten, Big East), National Hockey league (play-by-play), Broadcasts of 16 college football bowl games, 6 holiday channels	Dave Ramsey Show Richard Simmons Adam Curry (podcasts) NFL play-by-play of games, NBA play-by-play of 1000 games, NHL play-by-play (up to 40 games per week during the season), Wimbledon tennis championships,

Sources: Company Web sites, accessed December 15, 2006, and March 5, 2007.

Racing (AGR) to be a major associate sponsor of the race car driven by IndyCar Series superstar Danica Patrick. XM Radio service was available on certain AirTran, JetBlue, and United airplanes, and the company had an exclusive multi-year strategic marketing alliance with Starbucks, which included the Starbucks Hear Music channel on XM and a multi-artist music compilation CD series.

Other subscriber acquisition promotional activities included:

- In-store promotional campaigns, including displays located in electronics, music and other retail stores, rental car agencies and automobile dealerships.
- Incentive programs for retailers.
- Jointly funded local advertising campaigns with retailers.

A central element of XM's marketing strategy to grow its business and obtain new subscribers was to have XM receivers installed in new motor vehicles—purchasers of new vehicles equipped with a factory-installed XM receiver typically got a free three-month or six-month trial subscription. Via partnerships with General Motors (an investor in XM Radio), Honda/Acura (also an investor in XM Radio), Toyota/Lexus/Scion, Hyundai, Nissan/Infiniti, Porsche, Volkswagen/Audi, and others (see Exhibit 5), XM Radio was available as a factory-installed or dealer-installed option in more than 140 different vehicle models for model years 2006 and 2007; in a number of these models, XM service was available to new car prospects during vehicle test drives. General Motors offered factory-installed XM receivers as an option on over 55 models; GM had installed over 4 million XM radios as of fall 2006 and expected to install as many as 1.8 million XM receivers in its 2007 models. American Honda planned to equip more than 650,000 vehicles with factory XM radios in 2007. In 2005, Hyundai Motor America became the first automaker to launch XM as standard, factory-installed equipment in every vehicle across its entire model lineup. Harley-Davidson became the first manufacturer of motorcycles to offer XM Radio as an option on all six 2006 model bikes in its touring lineup; XM was standard equipment on Harley-Davidson's Screamin' Eagle Ultra Classic Electra Glide model.

XM's marketing and promotional costs to obtain new subscribers and retain existing subscribers totaled $450.8 million in 2006, $487.6 million in 2005, $304.3 million in 2004, and $200.3 million in 2003 (Exhibit 1). The amounts spent on marketing and promotion to secure new subscribers were exceptionally burdensome, as shown in Exhibit 6.

XM Radio Equipment XM radios ranging in price from $200 to $400 were available at such

Exhibit 5 **Motor Vehicle and Rental Car Brands That Install XM Radio and Sirius Satellite Receivers, December 2006**

Motor Vehicle Partners	
XM Radio	**Sirius Satellite Radio**
Acura	Aston Martin
Alamo Car Rental	Audi
Avis Car Rental	BMW
General Motors (Buick, Cadillac, Chevrolet, Hummer, GMC, Pontiac, Saab, Saturn)	Daimler Chrysler (Chrysler, Dodge, Jeep, Mercedes)
Harley-Davidson	Fleetwood Enterprises (motorhomes)
Honda	Ford/Lincoln/Mercury
Hyundai	Hertz Car Rental
Infiniti	Infiniti
Isuzu	Jaguar
National Car Rental	Kia Motors
Nissan	Land Rover
Porsche	Lexus
Subaru	Mitsubishi
Suzuki	Rolls Royce
Toyota/Lexus/Scion	Volvo
Volkswagen/Audi	

Source: Company Web sites, as of December 2006.

Exhibit 6   **Comparative Measures of XM Radio's Performance per Average Subscriber and as a Percentage of Total Revenue, 2003–2006**

Annual Amounts per Average Subscriber[1]					Amounts as a Percentage of Total Revenue			
2006	2005	2004	2003		2006	2005	2004	2003
$138	$122	$107	$108	Total revenue	100%	100%	100%	100%
122	110	96	92	Subscription revenue	88	90	90	85
5	4	4	5	Net ad sales	4	4	3	4
(87)	(88)	(88)	(177)	Total cost of revenue	63	73	84	164
(22)	(20)	(22)	(31)	Revenue share & royalties	16	17	21	29
(15)	(17)	(18)	(30)	Customer care & billing operations	11	14	17	28
n.a.	(9)	(5)	(11)	Cost of merchandise	n.a.	7	5	11
(7)	(9)	(16)	(46)	Satellite & terrestrial	5	8	15	43
(9)	(9)	(10)	(26)	Broadcast & operations	6	7	10	21
(24)	(22)	(14)	(27)	Programming & content	18	18	13	25
(6)	(7)	(10)	n.a.	Research & development	4	6	10	n.a.
(13)	(10)	(12)	(33)	General & administrative	9	8	12	30
(66)	(106)	(133)	(235)	Total marketing	48	87	124	218
(5)	(5)	(6)	n.a.	Retention & support	3	4	5	n.a.
(36)	(58)	(72)	(108)	Subsidies & distribution	26	47	68	101
(22)	(36)	(38)	(75)	Advertising & marketing	16	29	36	70
(25)	(88)	(136)	(386)	Adjusted EBITDA loss[2]	18	72	128	359

[1] Average subscribers are calculated as the averages of the beginning and ending subscriber balances for each year.

[2] EBITDA — Earnings before interest, taxes, depreciation and amortization.

Sources: Data for 2004–2006 are from the company's 2006 10-K report, p. 40; data for 2003 are from the company's 2005 10-K report, p. 36.

national consumer electronics retailers as Best Buy, Circuit City, and Wal-Mart under the Delphi, Pioneer, Alpine, Audiovox, Tao, Sony, Polk and etón/Grundig brand names. In 2006, numerous mass-market retailers sold support XM's car stereo, home stereo, plug-and-play and portable handheld products. The company had expanded its product line in 2006 to include several new models of XM2go portable receivers and had added both XM Connect-and-Play technology and the capability to download and play MP3 files to several of its radio models. Some models featured customizable sports and stock tickers as well as TuneSelect, which notified the listener when a favorite artist or song was playing on any XM channel. In 2005, the first generation XM2go receivers had won numerous awards for innovation and for consumer technology design and engineering. Five XM products were recognized as honorees for the Innovations 2006 Awards sponsored by the Consumer Electronics Association. XM management planned

to continue to add new receiver features and expand its model lineup in 2007.

XM radios incorporated a proprietary chip set, designed by the company's technology and innovation team in conjunction with others, to decode the signal from XM's satellites and repeaters. Ongoing improvements in the chip-set design had spawned a broad array of XM Radio products, including units significantly smaller and much less expensive than the first-generation models. The latest generation of XM radios included handheld units with memory features and models with customizable sports and stock tickers as well as TuneSelect, which notified the listener when a favorite artist or song was playing on XM.

XM had partnered with Sirius Satellite Radio, its principal competitor, to develop a common receiver platform for satellite radios that would enable buyers to purchase one radio receiver capable of receiving both XM and Sirius signals. The technology was being jointly developed and funded by the two companies, with each company having an ownership interest in the technology. The joint effort to develop a common receiver platform was spurred by FCC rules that required both licensed satellite radio systems to move toward the use of technology that enabled consumers to receive XM and Sirius signals via the same receiver.

Signal Transmission Operations   From 2001 to 2005, XM Radio broadcast its signals throughout the continental U.S. from the two satellites (known as *Rock* and *Roll*) that were launched in 2001. A third satellite (known as *Rhythm*) was launched in February 2005. In the second half of 2006, the company launched a fourth satellite (known as *Blues*) to replace signal transmission by the *Rock* and *Roll* satellites; the company expected to use *Rock* and *Roll* as in-orbit spares for the near term (the licenses for these two satellites expire in 2009). The combination of the new *Rhythm* and *Blues* satellites gave XM the capability to deliver a full complement of digital broadcasts for at least 15 more years (the length of a satellite's useful life). The license for the Rhythm satellite expires in 2013, and the license for Blues satellite expires in 2014, but licenses could be renewed by the Federal Communications Commission absent significant misconduct on XM's part. XM also had a network of approximately 800 terrestrial repeaters, which received and retransmitted the satellite signals in 60 markets to augment the satellite signal coverage that was impaired by buildings, tunnels, or terrain.

Canadian Operations   In November 2005, Canadian Satellite Radio, operating under the name XM Canada, XM's exclusive Canadian licensee, launched its satellite radio service in Canada for a monthly subscription fee of CDN$12.99. XM Canada's 100+ channel lineup included XM's digital-quality commercial-free music, exclusive Canadian channels highlighting Canadian artists, National Hockey League play-by-play coverage of more than 40 games per week, and news/talk. XM Canada had 147,000 subscribers as of November 30, 2006, and had a goal of 1 million subscribers by 2010. XM Canada had an 80 percent share of all factory-installed satellite radios in current 2007 vehicles being marketed in Canada and was available as a factory-installed or dealer-installed option on 115 different models in 2007. XM Satellite Radio owned a 23 percent interest in XM Canada, had two representatives on the board of directors, and received 15 percent of XM Canada's monthly subscription revenues.

Copyright Agreements   Like all radio broadcasters, XM maintained music programming royalty arrangements with and paid license fees to such organizations as Broadcast Music Inc. (BMI) and the American Society of Composers, Authors and Publishers (ASCAP), which negotiated with copyright users, collected royalties, and distributed them to songwriters and music publishers. Under the Digital Performance Right in Sound Recordings Act of 1995 and the Digital Millennium Copyright Act of 1998, broadcasters had to negotiate royalty arrangements with the copyright owners of the sound recordings or, if negotiation is unsuccessful, have the royalty rate established by a copyright royalty board. In July 2006, XM negotiated a new five-year music licensing agreement with ASCAP; however, its other licensing and royalty agreements expired in 2006. XM Radio was participating in a Copyright Royalty Board proceeding in order to set the royalty rate for the six-year period starting in January 2007.

SIRIUS SATELLITE RADIO INC.

Sirius Satellite launched national service in July 2002. Like XM, Sirius employed a subscription-based business model and sought to attract customers with an attractive lineup of channels. By year-end 2003, it had 261,000 subscribers; three years later it had 6 million subscribers (see Exhibit 10 on page C-46). In early 2007, Sirius was broadcasting on 133 channels that included 69 channels of 100 percent commercial-free music and 64 channels of sports, news, talk, entertainment, traffic, weather, and data content for a monthly subscription fee of $12.95. Exhibit 4 shows how Sirius Satellite Radio's programming lineup compared with that of XM Radio.

But despite the company's rapidly expanding subscriber base, Sirius (just like XM) had been gushing red ink, with reported losses of $314 million in 2003, $712 million in 2004, $863 million in 2005, and $1.1 billion in 2006. However, management expected the company to generate positive free cash flow (after capital expenditures) in 2007; Sirius achieved its first ever quarter of positive free cash flow in the fourth quarter of 2006. In the 2005 annual report, Sirius

CEO Mel Karmazin predicted revenues of $3 billion and positive cash flows of approximately $1 billion in 2010. Karmazin said the company was focused on achieving positive cash flow, accelerating along the path to profitability, and providing the best content in all of radio. The company's financial statements are shown in Exhibits 7, 8, and 9.

Sirius Satellite Radio's Marketing Strategy

As was the case with XM Radio, two key components of Sirius Satellite Radio's strategy to grow its subscriber base and market the concept of satellite radio, in addition to appealing programming, were to partner with motor vehicle manufacturers to install satellite radio receivers in new vehicles and to promote the sales of receivers in retail channels. Sirius had partnerships with DaimlerChrysler, Ford, Mitsubishi, BMW, Rolls-Royce, Nissan, Infiniti, Toyota, Lexus, Scion, Volkswagen, Audi, and Subaru to offer Sirius receivers as factory-installed or dealer-installed equipment (see Exhibit 5 for partnership comparisons with XM Radio). As of December 31, 2006, Sirius radios were available as a factory-installed option in 89 vehicle models and as a dealer-installed option in 19 vehicle models; Sirius service was offered to renters of Hertz vehicles at 55 airport locations nationwide. As was the case at XM Radio, Sirius had agreements with some vehicle makers to only offer Sirius brand satellite radios as a factory-installed option. By year-end 2007, Sirius management expected that Sirius Satellite Radio receivers would be available in 150 vehicle models. Executives believed that an increasing proportion of the company's subscribers would be generated through its relationships with automakers. For instance, Sirius had projected that that about 40 percent of the 2007 Chrysler, Dodge, and Jeep vehicles would come with factory-equipped Sirius radios, up from 30 percent in the 2006 model year. Mercedes was installing Sirius radios in about 70 percent of its 2007 vehicles, well ahead of its 50 percent target. Ford Motor was offering Sirius radios as an option on 21 Ford, Mercury, and Lincoln models, up from four models at the beginning of 2006 and 16 models at the end of third-quarter 2006.

As of 2006, consumers could purchase Sirius receivers at some 25,000 consumer electronics retailers and mobile audio dealers, including Best Buy, Circuit City, Crutchfield, Costco, Target, Wal-Mart, Sam's Club, RadioShack, heavy truck dealers, and many truck stops nationwide. Receivers were also available for purchase at Sirius's Web site. The receiver product line included portable and transportable Plug & Play radios with various features and functionality, radios for cars and trucks, and high-end receivers complete with motorized touch-control display screens. The company's strategy was to continue to introduce lighter, thinner, and more feature-rich models. Sirius radios were distributed by Alpine, Audiovox, Brix Group, Clarion, Delphi, Directed Electronics, Eclipse, Eton, Jensen, JVC, Kenwood, Magnadyne, Monster Cable, Pioneer, Russound, Tivoli, Thomson, and XACT Communications. To further broaden its audience and revenue base, Sirius had made its music channels available to DISH satellite television subscribers; certain music channels were offered to Sprint subscribers over multimedia handsets.

In December 2005, Sirius Canada launched service in Canada with 100 channels of commercial-free music and news, sports, talk, and entertainment programming, including 10 channels of Canadian content; as of February 2007, Sirius Canada had 300,000 subscribers and was broadcasting on 110 channels. Sirius Canada enjoyed a 75 percent market share in the Canadian market for satellite radio. Sirius receivers were available in over 3,500 retail outlets in Canada.

Sirius management was concentrating future marketing efforts on (1) enhancing and refining its programming, (2) introducing Sirius radios with new features and functions; and (3) expanding the distribution of Sirius radios through arrangements with automakers and through additional retail points of sale. Sirius was reinforcing its "The Best Radio on Radio" promotional theme with a variety of new initiatives, including the following:

- Launching Sirius Internet Radio (SIR), a CD-quality, online version of the Sirius satellite radio service. SIR delivered more than 75 channels of Sirius programming, without the use of a radio, for a $12.95 monthly subscription fee. To mark the launch of SIR, Sirius allowed free listening for two days.

- Introducing the industry's first portable satellite radio with WiFi capabilities. The model allowed users to listen for the first time to live and recorded Sirius content almost anywhere. This

Exhibit 7   **Consolidated Income Statement, Sirius Satellite Radio, 2003–2006 (in 000s of $, except per share amounts)**

	2006	2005	2004	2003
	—	—	—	—
Revenue:				
Subscriber revenue, including effects of mail-in rebates	$575,404	$223,615	$62,881	$12,615
Advertising revenue, net of agency fees	31,044	6,131	906	116
Equipment revenue	26,798	12,271	2,898	61
Other revenue	3,989	228	169	80
Total revenue	637,235	242,245	66,854	12,872
Operating expenses:				
Satellite and transmission	39,229	27,856	31,157	32,604
Programming and content	230,215	98,607	63,353	29,820
Customer service and billing	68,137	46,653	22,341	23,657
Cost of equipment	35,233	11,827	3,467	115
Sales and marketing	222,492	170,592	154,495	121,165
Subscriber acquisition costs	419,716	349,641	173,702	74,860
General and administrative	87,538	59,831	44,028	36,211
Engineering, design and development	58,732	44,745	30,520	24,534
Depreciation	105,749	98,555	95,370	95,353
Equity granted to third parties and employees/stock-based compensation	437,918	163,078	126,725	12,083
Total operating expenses	1,704,959	1,071,385	745,158	450,402
Loss from operations	(1,067,724)	(829,140)	(678,304)	(437,530)
Other income (expense):				
Debt restructuring	—	—	—	256,538
Interest and investment income	33,320	26,878	9,713	5,287
Interest expense	(64,032)	(45,361)	(41,386)	(50,510)
Loss from redemption of debt	—	(6,214)	—	—
Income (expense) from affiliate	(4,445)	(6,938)	—	—
Other income	79	89	2,016	—
Total other income (expense)	(35,078)	(31,546)	(29,657)	211,315
Loss before income taxes	(1,102,802)	(860,686)	(707,961)	(226,215)
Income tax expense	(2,065)	(2,311)	(4,201)	—
Net loss	$(1,104,867)	(862,997)	(712,162)	(226,215)
Preferred stock dividends	—	—	—	(8,574)
Preferred stock deemed dividends	—	—	—	(79,634)
Net loss applicable to common stockholders	$(1,104,867)	$(862,997)	$(712,162)	$(314,423)
Net loss per share applicable to common stockholders (basic and diluted)	$(0.79)	$(0.65)	$(0.57)	$(0.38)
Weighted average common shares outstanding (basic and diluted)	1,402,619	1,325,739	1,238,585	827,186
	—	—	—	—

Source: 2005 and 2006 10-K reports and company press release, February 28, 2007.

Exhibit 8   **Consolidated Balance Sheets, Sirius Satellite Radio, 2004–2006 ($ in thousands)**

	For the years ending December 31		
	2006	2005	2004
	—	—	—
ASSETS			
Current assets:			
Cash and cash equivalents	$393,421	$762,007	$753,891
Marketable securities	15,500	117,250	5,277
Accounts receivable, net of allowance for doubtful			
accounts of $3,183, $1,550 and $532, respectively	24,189	31,688	7,559
Inventory	34,502	14,256	7,927
Prepaid expenses	52,588	18,248	12,956
Restricted investments	25,000	25,165	4,706
Other current assets	72,066	42,834	18,724
Total current assets	617,266	1,011,448	811,040
Property and equipment, net	810,389	828,357	881,280
FCC satellite radio license	83,654	83,654	83,654
Restricted investments, net of current portion	52,850	82,450	92,615
Deferred financing fees	13,166	16,303	13,140
Other long-term assets	81,203	63,150	75,884
Total assets	$1,658,528	$2,085,362	$1,957,613
LIABILITIES AND STOCKHOLDERS' EQUITY			
Current liabilities:			
Accounts payable and accrued expenses	$437,913	$331,953	$182,447
Accrued interest	24,782	23,546	5,758
Deferred revenue	412,370	251,468	81,309
Total current liabilities	875,065	606,967	269,514
Long-term debt	1,068,249	1,084,437	656,274
Deferred revenue, net of current portion	76,580	56,479	15,691
Other long-term liabilities	27,705	12,511	15,501
Total liabilities	2,047,599	1,760,394	956,980
Commitments and contingencies			
Stockholders' equity:			
Common stock, $0.001 par value: 2,500,000,000 shares authorized, 1,434,635,501 shares, 1,346,226,851 shares, and 1,276,922,634 shares issued and outstanding at December 31, 2005 and 2004, respectively	1,435	1,346	1,277
Additional paid-in capital	3,443,214	3,079,169	2,916,199
Deferred compensation	---	(26,694)	(50,963)
Accumulated other comprehensive loss			(24)
Accumulated deficit	(3,833,720)	(2,728,853)	(1,865,856)
Total stockholders' equity (deficit)	(389,071)	324,968	1,000,633
Total liabilities and stockholders equity	$1,658,528	$2,085,362	$1,957,613

Sources: 2005 and 2006 10-K reports.

Exhibit 9   **Selected Cash Flow Data, Sirius Satellite Radio, 2003–2006 ($ in thousands)**

	For the years ended December 31			
	2006	**2005**	**2004**	**2003**
Cash flows from operating activities:				
Net loss	$(1,104,867)	$(862,997)	$(712,162)	$(226,215)
Net cash used in operating activities	(414,549)	(273,740)	(334,463)	(284,487)
Cash flows from investing activities:				
Additions to property and equipment	(99,827)	(49,888)	(28,589)	(20,118)
Sale of property and equipment	127	72	443	—
Purchases of restricted investments	(12,339)	(21,291)	(89,706)	—
Release of restricted investments	26,000	10,997	—	—
Purchases of available-for-sale securities	(123,500)	(148,900)	—	(24,826)
Sales of available-for-sale securities	229,715	31,850	—	—
Maturities of available-for-sale securities		5,085	25,000	150,000
Net cash (used in) provided by investing activities	20,176	(172,075)	(92,852)	105,056
Cash flows from financing activities:				
Proceeds from issuance of long-term debt, net	—	493,005	518,413	194,224
Proceeds from issuance of common stock, net	—	—	96,025	492,659
Redemption of debt	—	(57,609)		
Costs associated with debt restructuring	—	—	—	(4,737)
Proceeds from exercise of stock options	25,787	18,543	26,051	—
Proceeds from exercise of warrants	—	—	19,850	—
Other	—	(8)	(112)	(111)
Net cash provided by financing activities	25,787	453,931	660,227	682,035
Net increase (decrease) in cash and cash equivalents	(368,586)	8,116	232,912	502,604
Cash and cash equivalents at the beginning of period	762,007	753,891	520,979	18,375
Cash and cash equivalents at the end of period	$393,421	$762,007	$753,891	$520,979

Source: 2005 and 2006 10-K reports and company press release, February 28, 2007.

receiver stored up to 100 hours of live programming (two gigabytes) and could be used to access the company's Internet radio services over an accessible WiFi network and to purchase favorite songs through Yahoo! Music Engine, Yahoo! Music Jukebox, or other compatible download service.

• Devoting an entire channel to such music superstars as the Who, the Rolling Stones, and Elvis Presley (channel 13). In past years, Sirius had dedicated channels to the music of Bruce Springsteen, the E Street Band, country music star George Strait, and David Gilmour of Pink Floyd.

• Entering into a multiyear agreement with the Metropolitan Opera to establish a dedicated channel for opera lovers using Metropolitan Opera content.

• Signing an agreement with the Chelsea Football Club, the two-time defending champions of the Barclays English Premier League, to make Sirius the exclusive satellite radio provider of Chelsea soccer matches.

Sirius billed itself as the leading provider of sports radio programming, broadcasting play-by-play action for every NFL game, over 1,000 NBA games per season, 40 NHL games per week, the Wimbledon tennis championships, several top

Thoroughbred horse races, and football and basketball games of 125 college teams.

Recent Performance and Accomplishments. In 2005–2006, Sirius achieved several important financial and operational milestones in its drive for industry leadership and long-term profitability:

- Parity with XM in distributing satellite radios through retail channels (based on a retail market share of 54 percent for 2005 and 60 percent for the fourth quarter of 2005).[5]
- Rapid acceleration of subscribers coming from motor vehicle partners.
- Extended long-term exclusive agreements with DaimlerChrysler, Ford, and BMW.
- Lower subscriber acquisition costs.
- New programming agreements with Martha Stewart, Richard Simmons, the NBA, Adam Curry's Podcast Show, and NASCAR.
- Introduction of the Sirius S50 receiver, the satellite radio industry's first wearable device with MP3/WMA capabilities.
- The launch of Sirius music on the Sprint wireless network.
- An arrangement for NASCAR to move from XM to Sirius in 2007.

On January 9, 2006, Howard Stern moved his radio show to Sirius Satellite Radio from terrestrial radio as part of two channels programmed by Howard Stern and Sirius. To attract Howard Stern, Sirius agreed to provide a budget of $100 million annually to cover total production and operating costs for the Stern show, including compensation of the show cast and staff, overhead, construction costs for a dedicated studio, and the development of additional programming and marketing concepts. Sirius management estimated that Stern's broadcast presence on Sirius would need to generate approximately 1 million new subscribers in order for Sirius to show a profit on the five-year deal. Stern's interest in moving to Sirius was said, in part, to be a response to avoid "censorship" efforts by the Federal Communications Commission (FCC)—the FCC does not regulate the content of satellite programs. Stern's terrestrial radio shows, known for their raunchy content, had an estimated audience of over 10 million in 2004 when the deal with Sirius was struck. In January 2007, Sirius paid Howard Stern a bonus in stock worth nearly $83 million for exceeding subscriber goals set back in 2004 when the five-year agreement was struck.

Subscription Plans. Most customers subscribed on an annual or monthly basis. Discounts were offered for pre-paid, long-term, and multiple subscriptions. In a number of instances, automakers included a six-month or one-year subscription to Sirius service in the sale or lease price of vehicles equipped with Sirius receivers; frequently, Sirius received subscription payments from automakers in advance of the activation of our service (Sirius reimbursed automakers for a portion of the costs associated with installing Sirius receivers in their vehicles). Sirius received an average of approximately nine months of prepaid revenue per subscriber when service was activated. Other revenue sources included activation fees, the sale of advertising on nonmusic channels, and direct sale of Sirius radios and accessories.

Operations. Sirius transmitted its satellite broadcasts through a proprietary satellite radio system that consisted of three orbital satellites, 140 terrestrial repeaters that received and retransmitted Sirius signals, a satellite uplink facility, and studios in New York City, Los Angeles, Memphis, Nashville, New Orleans, Houston, and Daytona.

As shown in Exhibit 7, Sirius spent $222.5 million for sales and marketing in 2006, $170.6 million in 2005, $154.5 million in 2004, and $121.2 million in 2003. As was the case with XM Radio, Sirius had experienced very high new subscriber acquisition costs—$419.7 million in 2006, $349.6 million in 2005, and $173.7 million in 2004. While the acquisition costs *per subscriber* were trending downward, the company did not realize a positive revenue contribution above marketing costs until a customer's second year of service—see Exhibit 10 for comparisons with XM Radio.

THE PROFITABILITY FORECAST FOR XM AND SIRIUS: SUNNY OR CLOUDY?

While the satellite radio business was an emerging force in radio broadcasting and growing public awareness of both XM and Sirius was helping boost

Exhibit 10   **Comparative Subscriber Statistics, XM Radio versus Sirius Satellite Radio, 2003–2006**

	2006	2005	2004	2003
Number of subscribers at year-end				
XM Radio	7,625,000	5,932,957	3,229,124	1,360,228
Sirius	6,024,555	3,316,560	1,143,258	261,061
Gross subscriber additions				
XM Radio	3,866,481	4,130,437	2,580,515	n.a.
Sirius	3,758,163	2,519,301	986,556	255,798
Net subscriber additions				
XM Radio	1,695,595	2,703,833	1,868,896	1,013,069
Sirius	2,707,995	2,173,302	882,197	231,114
Average monthly subscription revenue per subscriber, after rebates and special promotions				
XM Radio	$10.09	$9.51	$8.68	$8.97
Sirius	10.45	10.06	10.02	9.39
Average monthly net advertising revenue per subscriber				
XM Radio	$0.43	$0.39	$0.33	$0.47
Sirius	0.56	0.28	0.14	0.09
Average revenue per subscriber from both subscriptions and advertising				
XM Radio (includes activation, equipment, and other revenue per subscriber)	$11.41	$10.57	$9.59	$10.52
Sirius	11.01	10.34	10.16	9.48
Subscriber acquisition costs				
XM Radio	$108	$109	$100	$137
Sirius	114	139	177	293
Customer care and billing costs per average subscriber				
XM Radio	n.r.	$1.39	$1.48	$2.53
Sirius	$1.24	2.10	3.56	6.84

n.r. = Not reported.

Sources: XM Satellite Radio 2005 and 2006 10-K reports; XM Satellite Radio press release on February 26, 2007; Sirius 2004, 2005, and 2006 10-K reports; and Sirius press release on February 28, 2007.

subscriber totals, the future of both companies was uncertain. Investors were skeptical about the abilities of the two companies to produce attractive profits and return on invested capital. The stock prices of both XM and Sirius had taken a huge beating on Wall Street during 2006, falling about 50 percent since year-end 2005. XM's stock price had traded as high as $37 in January 2005 but had been trending steadily downward since October 2005 to the $14–$15 range in January 2007. Sirius's stock price hit an all-time high of close to $8 in January 2005 and

traded in the $6.00–$7.50 range for most of 2005; but nervous investors had bid the stock price down to the $3.75–$4.00 range in January 2007.

Most alarming to investors was that both XM and Sirius had recently scaled back their estimates of subscriber growth. At the beginning of 2006, XM management announced a bullish forecast of 9 million subscribers by year-end, but it was forced to issue a series of lower estimates as subscriber growth slowed. XM ended 2006 with just 7.6 million subscribers. XM's president and chief operating officer,

Nate Davis, said that the slower-than-expected growth rate was not due to market indifference but rather to failure to "stimulate the market with new products."[6] Sirius management began 2006 by estimating that the number of Sirius subscribers would grow to 6 million by year-end; estimates were then raised to 6.3 million. But Sirius management had cut its estimates back to 6.1 million by November 2006, and the company ended the year with barely over 6 million subscribers. Sirius management, however, was pleased with the company's performance in 2006 and the gains it was making in challenging XM for leadership in the fledgling satellite radio industry.

XM and Sirius Propose a Merger   On February 19, 2007, executives at Sirius and XM announced a plan to merge the two satellite broadcasters and bring an end to the expensive bidding war for talent and programming that had impaired the profitability of both companies. The merger deal called for Sirius to acquire XM via an exchange of shares of stock, with XM shareholders receiving 4.6 shares of Sirius for each share owned of XM stock. The merger would create a company with about $1.5 billion in revenues and 14 million subscribers. The proposed merger called for the CEO of Sirius, Mel Karmazin, to be CEO of the merged company and for Gary Parsons, the chairman and CEO of XM, to be chairman of the new company (whose name had not been announced). Hugh Panero, the CEO of XM, was scheduled to continue in his current role until the merger closed.

However, the merger proposal was expected to face tough scrutiny from antitrust regulators at the U.S. Department of Justice because it would create a satellite radio broadcasting monopoly. Also, the terms under which the Federal Communications Commission had originally granted the satellite licenses to XM and Sirius expressly prohibited one company from owning both satellite radio licenses—in January 2007, when rumors of a possible XM/Sirius merger surfaced, FCC chairman Kevin Martin said the FCC's rules would not permit a merger between XM and Sirius. Traditional radio stations were expected to oppose the merger as well.

The ramifications of the proposed merger were expected to entail months of regulatory hearings, and many analysts were highly skeptical that merger approval would be granted both by the FCC and the Department of Justice. Nonetheless, executives at Sirius and XM expressed belief that there was greater than a 50–50 chance of winning approval for the merger. XM's chairman Gary Parsons said regulators could be convinced that the merger was in the public interest, due to the existence of competition from the iPod, Internet radio, audio services provided by cable- and satellite-television providers, and other venues. The companies also planned to argue that (1) they could provide greater programming and content choices to consumers as a single entity and (2) the merged companies would be better able to develop and introduce a wider range of lower cost, easy-to-use, and multifunctional receivers through efficiencies in chip-set and radio design and procurement, thus helping keep satellite radio competitive in the consumer electronics–driven world of audio entertainment. Top executives at XM and Sirius were expected to counter the argument that a merger would create a satellite radio monopoly with arguments that satellite radio was in direct competition with free over-the-air AM and FM radio as well as iPods and other brands of MP3 players, mobile phone streaming, HD radio, Internet radio, the digital music channels offered by cable TV companies, and next-generation wireless technologies.[7] At February 2007 hearings before congressional committees overseeing antitrust issues, Mel Karmazin hinted that approval of the proposed XM/Sirius merger might lead to lower monthly subscription rates.

Endnotes

[1] Described in Heather Green, Tom Lowry, and Catherine Yang, "The New Radio Revolution," *BusinessWeek Online*, March 3, 2005, www.businessweek.com (accessed December 5, 2006).
[2] Radio Advertising Bureau, *Radio Marketing Guide and Factbook for Advertisers*, Fall 1999 and Spring 2000, as cited in XM Satellite Radio's 2000 10-K report, p. 2.
[3] C. Barnes & Co, *Barnes Reports: Radio Industry Broadcasting* (NAICS 51311), 2007 Edition, p. 7.

[4] Company 2006 10-K report, p.1.
[5] Based on data made available to the company by market researcher NPD Group.
[6] Eric A. Taub, "Thanks to Stern, Sirius May Be Set for a Merger," *Tuscaloosa News*, January 1, 2007, p. 5B.
[7] Sirius press release, February 19, 2007.

Case 4

Competition in the Bottled Water Industry in 2006

John E. Gamble
University of South Alabama

With global revenues exceeding $62 billion in 2005, bottled water was among the world's most attractive beverage categories. Industry revenues were forecast to grow by an additional 30 percent between 2005 and 2010, to reach approximately $82 billion. Bottled water had long been a widely consumed product in Western Europe and Mexico, where annual per capita consumption approached or exceeded 40 gallons in 2005, but until the mid-1990s bottled water had been somewhat of a novelty or prestige product in the United States. In 1990, approximately 2.2 billion gallons of bottled water were consumed in the United States and per capita consumption approximated 9 gallons. U.S. per capita consumption had grown to more than 25 gallons by 2005. The rising popularity of bottled water in the United States during the late 1990s and early 2000s had allowed the United States to become the world's largest market for bottled water, with annual volume sales of nearly 7.5 billion gallons in 2005. In 2006, emerging-country markets in Asia and South America seemed to be replicating the impressive growth of bottled water in the United States, with annual growth rates exceeding 20 percent. Exhibit 1 presents bottled water statistics for the 10 largest country markets for bottled water in 2004.

The growing popularity of bottled water in the United States was attributable to concerns over the safety of municipal drinking water, an increased focus on fitness and health, and the hectic on-the-go lifestyles of American consumers. Bottled water's convenience, purity, and portability made it the natural solution to consumers' dissatisfaction with tap water and carbonated beverages. The U.S. bottled water market, like most markets outside the United States, was characterized by fierce competitive rivalry as the world's bottled water sellers jockeyed for market share and volume gains. Both the global and U.S. bottled water markets had become dominated by a few international food and beverage producers—such as Coca-Cola, PepsiCo, and Nestlé—but they also included many small regional sellers who were required to either develop low-cost production and distribution capabilities or use differentiation strategies keyed to some unique product attributes. In 2006, competitive rivalry continued to ratchet upward as sellers launched innovative product variations, lowered prices in developed markets, used strategic agreements to strengthen positions in established markets, and acquired smaller sellers to gain footholds in rapidly growing emerging markets. Industry analysts and observers believed the recent moves undertaken by the world's largest sellers of bottled water would alter the competitive dynamics of the bottled water industry and would mandate that certain players modify their current strategic approaches to competition in the industry.

INDUSTRY CONDITIONS IN 2006

Even though it was the world's largest market for bottled water, the United States remained among the faster-growing markets for bottled water since per capita consumption rates of bottled water fell substantially below those in Western Europe, the Middle

Exhibit 1   **Leading Country Markets for Bottled Water, 1999, 2004 (in millions of gallons)**

2004 Rank	Country	Bottled Water Sales		CAGR* (1999–2004)
		1999	2004	
1	United States	4,579.9	6,806.7	8.2%
2	Mexico	3,056.9	4,668.3	8.8
3	China	1,217.0	3,140.1	20.9
4	Brazil	1,493.8	3,062.0	15.4
5	Italy	2,356.1	2,814.4	3.6
6	Germany	2,194.6	2,722.6	4.4
7	France	1,834.1	2,257.3	4.2
8	Indonesia	907.1	1,943.5	16.5
9	Spain	1,076.4	1,453.5	6.2
10	India	444.0	1,353.3	25.0
All others		6,833.5	10,535.0	9.0
Worldwide total		25,993.4	40,756.7	(Avg. CARG) 9.4

* CAGR=Compound annual growth rate

Source: Beverage Marketing Corporation as reported by the International Bottled Water Association, 2006.

East, and Mexico. Bottled water consumption in the United States also lagged per capita consumption of soft drinks by more than a 2:1 margin, but in 2003 bottled water surpassed coffee, tea, milk, and beer to become the second largest beverage category in the United States. In 2005, more than 15.3 million gallons of carbonated soft drinks were consumed in the United States, but concerns about sugar consumption and other nutrition and fitness issues had encouraged many consumers to transition from soft drinks to bottled water. Whereas the bottled water market in the United States grew by 10.7 percent between 2004 and 2005 to reach 7.5 billion gallons, the U.S. carbonated soft drink market declined by 0.6 percent. Industry analysts expected the carbonated soft drink industry to decline by 1.5 percent annually for the foreseeable future as bottled water, energy drinks, and sports drinks gained a larger "share of the stomach." Exhibits 2, 3, and 4 illustrate the growing popularity of bottled water among U.S. consumers during the 1990s and through 2004.

Almost one-half of bottled water consumed in the United States in 1990 was delivered to homes and offices in returnable five-gallon containers and dispensed through coolers. At that time, only 186 million gallons of water was sold in one-liter or smaller single-serving polyethylene terephthalate (PET) bottles. Beginning in the late 1990s, consumers began to appreciate the convenience and portability of water bottled in single-serving PET containers that could be purchased chilled from a convenience store and drunk immediately. By 2005, bottled water sold in two-liter or smaller PET containers accounted for 60.8 percent of industry volume. The unit sales of bottled water packaged in PET containers grew by 22.5 percent between 2004 and 2005. Water sold in five-gallon containers used in the home and office delivery (HOD) market accounted for only 17.8 percent of industry volume in 2005 and grew by only 0.2 percent between 2004 and 2005. Similarly, water sold in 1- or 2.5-gallon high-density polyethylene (HDPE) containers accounted for just 16.5 percent of industry volume in 2005 and grew by only 1.0 percent between 2004 and 2005.

Convenience and portability were two of a variety of reasons U.S. consumers were increasingly attracted to bottled water. A heightened emphasis on healthy lifestyles and improved consumer awareness of the need for proper hydration led many consumers to shift traditional beverage preferences toward bottled water. Bottled water consumers frequently claimed that drinking more water improved the appearance of their skin and gave them more energy. Bottled water analysts also believed that many health-conscious consumers drank bottled water because it was a symbol to others that they were interested in their health.

A certain amount of industry growth was attributable to increased concerns over the quality of tap water provided by municipal water sources.

Exhibit 2 **Per Capita Consumption of Bottled Water by Country Market, 1999, 2004**

2004 Rank	Country	Per Capita Consumption (in gallons)		CAGR* (1999–2004)
		1999	2004	
1	Italy	40.9	48.5	3.5%
2	Mexico	30.9	44.5	7.6
3	United Arab Emirates	29	43.2	8.3
4	Belgium-Luxembourg	32.2	39.1	4.0
5	France	31	37.4	3.8
6	Spain	26.9	36.1	6.1
7	Germany	26.6	33	4.4
8	Lebanon	17.9	26.8	8.4
9	Switzerland	23.8	26.3	2.0
10	Cyprus	17.8	24.3	6.4
11	United States	16.8	23.9	7.3
12	Saudi Arabia	19.9	23.2	3.1
13	Czech Republic	16.4	23	7.0
14	Austria	19.7	21.7	2.0
15	Portugal	18.6	21.2	2.7
	Global Average	4.3	6.4	8.3

* CAGR = compound annual growth rate
Source: Beverage Marketing Corporation as reported by the International Bottled Water Association, 2006.

Exhibit 3 **Global Bottled Water Market Wholesale Value and Volume, 2001–2005, Forecasts for 2006–2010**

Year	Volume Sales (in billions of liters)	Annual Change	Industry Revenues ($ in billions)	Annual Change
2001	92.8	—	$47.3	—
2002	99.5	7.2%	51.3	8.5%
2003	107.9	8.4	56.1	9.4
2004	113.3	5.0	59.1	5.3
2005(e)	119.7	5.6	62.9	6.4
2006(f)	125.9	5.2	66.4	5.6
2007(f)	132.9	5.6	70.4	6.0
2008(f)	139.5	5.0	74.5	5.8
2009(f)	146.4	4.9	78.5	5.4
2010(f)	153.4	4.8	81.9	4.3

(e) = estimated
(f) = forecast

Source: Global Bottled Water Industry Profile, December 2005, Datamonitor.

Consumers in parts of the world with inadequate water treatment facilities relied on bottled water to provide daily hydration needs, but tap water in the United States was very pure by global standards. (Municipal water systems were regulated by the U.S. Environmental Protection Agency and were required

Exhibit 4   **U.S. Per Capita Consumption of Bottled Water, 1991–2005**

Year	Per Capita Consumption (in gallons)	Annual Change
1991	9.3	—
1992	9.8	5.4%
1993	10.5	7.1
1994	11.5	9.5
1995	12.2	6.1
1996	13.1	7.4
1997	14.1	7.6
1998	15.3	8.5
1999	16.8	9.8
2000	17.8	6.0
2001	19.3	8.4
2002	21.2	9.8
2003	22.6	6.6
2004	24	6.2
2005(p)	25.7	7.1

(p) = preliminary

Source: Beverage Marketing Corporation as reported by the International Bottled Water Association, 2006.

to comply with the provisions of the Safe Drinking Water Act Amendments of 2001.) Consumer concerns over the quality of drinking water in the United States emerged in 1993 when 400,000 residents of Milwaukee, Wisconsin, became ill with flu-like symptoms and almost 100 immune-impaired residents died from waterborne bacterial infections. Throughout the 1990s and into the early 2000s, the media sporadically reported cases of municipal water contamination, such as in 2000 when residents of Washington, D.C., became ill after the city's water filtration process caused elevated levels of suspended materials in the water.

Even though some consumers were concerned about the purity of municipal water, most consumers' complaints with tap water centered on the chemical taste of tap water that resulted from treatment processes that included the use of chlorine and other chemicals such as fluoride. In a tap-water tasting in Atlanta hosted by *Southpoint Magazine,* judges rated municipal water on taste and found some cities' waters very palatable. Water obtained from the municipal source in Memphis was said to have "a

refreshing texture." However, other municipal systems did not fare as well with the judges—some of whom suggested Houston's water tasted "like a chemistry lab," while others said Atlanta's municipal water was akin to "a gulp of swimming pool water."[1] However, there were positive attributes to the chemicals added to tap water, as chlorine was necessary to kill any bacteria in the water and fluoride had contributed greatly to improved dental health in the United States. In addition, tap water had been shown to be no less healthy than bottled water in a number of independent studies, including a study publicized in Europe that was commissioned by the World Wide Fund for Nature and conducted by researchers at the University of Geneva.

Bottled water producers in the United States were required to meet the standards of both the Environmental Protection Agency (EPA) and the U.S. Food and Drug Administration (FDA). Like all other food and beverage products sold in the United States, bottled water was subject to such food safety and labeling requirements as nutritional labeling provisions and general good manufacturing practices (GMPs). Bottled water GMPs were mandated under the 1962 Kefauver-Harris Drug Amendments to the Federal Food, Drug and Cosmetic Act of 1938 and established specifications for plant construction and design, sanitation, equipment design and construction, production and process controls, and record keeping. The FDA required bottled water producers to test at least weekly for the presence of bacteria and to test annually for inorganic contaminants, trace metals, minerals, pesticides, herbicides, and organic compounds. Bottled water was also regulated by state agencies that conducted inspections of bottling facilities and certification of testing facilities to ensure that bottled water was bottled under federal GMPs and was safe to drink.

Bottled water producers were also required to comply with the FDA's Standard of Identity, which required bottlers to include source water information on their products' labels. Water labeled as "spring water" must have been captured from a borehole or natural orifice of a spring that naturally flows to the surface. "Artesian water" could be extracted from a confined aquifer (a water-bearing underground layer of rock or sand) where the water level stood above the top of the aquifer. "Sparkling water" was required to have natural carbonation as it emerged from the source, although carbonation could be added to return the carbon dioxide level to what was evident as the water emerged from the source. Even though sparkling water was very popular throughout most of Europe, where it accounted for approximately 54 percent of industry sales, it made up only 8 percent of the bottled water market in the United States.

The FDA's definition of "mineral water" stated that such water must have at least 250 parts per million of total dissolved solids, and its standards required water labeled as "purified" to have undergone distillation, deionization, or reverse osmosis to remove chemicals such as chlorine and fluoride. "Drinking water" required no additional processing beyond what was required for tap water but could not include flavoring or other additives that account for more than 1 percent of the product's total weight. Both "drinking water" and "purified water" had to clearly state that the water originated "from a community water system" or "from a municipal source."

Bottled water producers could also voluntarily become members of the International Bottled Water Association (IBWA) and agree to comply with its Model Code, which went beyond the standards of the EPA, FDA, or state agencies. The Model Code allowed fewer parts per million of certain organic and inorganic chemicals and microbiological contaminants than FDA, EPA, or state regulations and imposed a chlorine limitation on bottled water. Neither the FDA nor the EPA limited chlorine content. IBWA members were monitored for compliance through annual, unannounced inspections administered by an independent third-party organization.

Distribution and Sale of Bottled Water

Consumers could purchase bottled water in nearly any location in the United States where food was also sold. The distribution of bottled water varied depending on the producer and the distribution channel. Typically, bottled water was distributed to large grocers and wholesale clubs directly by the bottled water producer, whereas most producers used third parties like beer and wine distributors or food distributors to make sales and deliveries to convenience stores, restaurants, and delis.

Because of the difficulty for food service distributors to restock vending machines and provide bottled water to special events, Coca-Cola and PepsiCo were able to dominate such channels since they could make deliveries of bottled water along with their deliveries of other beverages. Coca-Cola's and PepsiCo's vast beverage distribution systems made it easy for the two companies to make Dasani and Aquafina available anywhere Coke or Pepsi could be purchased. In addition, the two cola giants almost always negotiated contracts with sports stadiums, universities, and school systems that made one of them the exclusive supplier of all types of nonalcoholic beverages sold in the venue for a specified period. Under such circumstances, it was nearly impossible for other brands of bottled water to gain access to the account.

PepsiCo and Coca-Cola's soft drink businesses had allowed vending machine sales to account for 8 percent of industry sales volume in 2005 and had also aided the two companies in making Aquafina and Dasani available in supermarkets, supercenters, wholesale clubs, and convenience stores. Soft drink sales were important to all types of food stores since soft drinks made up a sizable percentage of the store's sales and since food retailers frequently relied on soft drink promotions to generate store traffic. Coca-Cola and PepsiCo were able to encourage their customers to purchase items across their product lines to ensure prompt and complete shipment of key soft drink products. As a diversified food products company, PepsiCo had exploited the popularity of its soft drinks, Gatorade sports drinks, Frito-Lay snack foods, and Tropicana orange juice in persuading grocery accounts to purchase not only Aquafina but also other non–soft drink brands such as FruitWorks, SoBe, Lipton's Iced Tea, and Starbucks Frappuccino.

Since most supermarkets, supercenters, and food stores usually carried fewer than seven branded bottled waters plus a private-label brand, bottled water producers other than Coke and Pepsi were required to compete aggressively on price to gain access to shelf space. Supermarkets and discount stores accounted for 43.5 percent of U.S. industry sales in 2005 and were able to require bottled water suppliers to pay slotting fees in addition to offering low prices to gain shelf space. Natural foods stores could also require annual contracts and slotting fees but were much more willing than traditional supermarkets to pay higher wholesale prices for products that could contribute to the store's overall level of differentiation. In fact, most natural foods stores would not carry brands found in traditional supermarkets.

Convenience stores were also aggressive in pressing bottled water producers and food distributors for low prices and slotting fees. Most convenience stores carried only two to four brands of bottled water beyond what was distributed by Coca-Cola and Pepsi and required bottlers to pay annual slotting fees of $300 to $400 per store in return for providing 5 to 10 bottle facings on a cooler shelf. Some bottlers offered to provide retailers with rebates of approximately 25 cents per case to help secure distributors for their brand of bottled water. Food and beverage distributors usually allowed bottled water producers to negotiate slotting fees and rebates directly with convenience store buyers.

There was not as much competition among bottled water producers to gain shelf space in delis and restaurants since that channel accounted for only 6.5 percent of U.S. industry sales in 2005. PepsiCo and Coca-Cola were among the better-suited bottled water producers to economically distribute water to restaurants since they likely provided fountain drinks to such establishments.

Suppliers to the Industry

The suppliers to the bottled water industry included municipal water systems; spring operators; bottling equipment manufacturers; deionization, reverse osmosis, and filtration equipment manufacturers; manufacturers of PET and HDPE bottles and plastic caps; label printers; and secondary packaging suppliers. Most packaging supplies needed for the production of bottled water were readily available from a large number of suppliers. Large bottlers able to commit to annual purchases of more than 5 million PET bottles could purchase bottles for as little as 5 cents per bottle, whereas regional bottlers purchasing smaller quantities of bottles or making only one-time purchases of bottles could expect to pay a much as 15 cents per bottle. Suppliers of secondary packaging like cardboard boxes, shrink-wrap, and six-pack rings and suppliers of printed film or paper labels were numerous and aggressively competed for the business of large bottled water producers.

Bottling equipment used for water purification and filling bottles was manufactured and marketed by about 50 different companies in the United States. A basic bottle-filling line could be purchased for about $125,000, whereas a large state-of-the-art bottling facility could require a capital investment of more than $100 million. Bottlers choosing to sell spring water could expect to invest about $300,000 for source certification, road grading, and installation of pumping equipment, fencing, holding tanks, and disinfecting equipment. Bottlers that did not own springs were also required to enter into lease agreements with spring owners that typically ranged from $20,000 to $30,000 per year. Companies selling purified water merely purchased tap water from municipal water systems at industrial rates prior to purifying and bottling the water for sale to consumers. Sellers of purified water were able not only to pay less for water they bottled, but also to avoid spring water's inbound shipping costs of 5 to 15 cents per gallon since water arrived at the bottling facility by pipe rather than by truck.

Key Competitive Capabilities in the Bottled Water Industry

Bottled water did not enjoy the brand loyalty of soft drinks, beer, or many other food and beverage products but was experiencing some increased brand loyalty, with 10 to 25 percent of consumers looking for a specific brand and an additional two-thirds considering only a few brands acceptable. Because of the growing importance of brand recognition, successful sellers of bottled water were required to possess well-developed brand-building skills. Most of the industry's major sellers were global food companies that had built respected brands in soft drinks, dairy products, chocolates, and breakfast cereals prior to entering the bottled water industry.

Bottled water sellers also needed to have efficient distribution systems to supermarket, wholesale club, and convenience store channels to be successful in the industry. It was imperative for bottled water distributors (whether direct store delivery by bottlers or delivery by third parties) to maximize the number of deliveries per driver since distribution included high fixed costs for warehouses, trucks, handheld inventory tracking devices, and labor. It was also critical for distributors and bottlers to provide on-time deliveries and offer responsive customer service to large customers in the highly price-competitive market. Price competition also mandated high utilization of large-scale plants to achieve low production costs. Volume and market share were also key factors in keeping marketing expenses at an acceptable per-unit level.

Recent Trends in the Bottled Water Industry

As the annual growth rate of bottled water sales in the United States slowed from double-digit rates, signs had begun to appear that price competition in the bottled water industry might mirror that of the carbonated soft drink industry. Fierce price competition could be expected to bring volume gains but result in flat or declining revenues for the bottled water industry. Coca-Cola, Nestlé, and PepsiCo had avoided strong price competition through 2004, but during the first six months of 2005 all three of the industry's largest sellers began to offer considerable discounts on 12- and 24-bottle multipacks to boost unit volume. Exhibit 5 presents average U.S. retail prices for 24-bottle multipacks marketed by Nestlé Waters, Coca-Cola, and PepsiCo between 2003 and the first six months of 2005.

The world's largest sellers of bottled water appeared to be positioning for industry maturity by purchasing smaller regional brands. Nestlé had acquired bottled water producers and entered into joint ventures in Poland, Hungary, Russia, Greece, France, Turkey, Algeria, South Korea, Indonesia, and Saudi Arabia between 2000 and 2006. Danone Waters also made a number of acquisitions and entered into strategic alliances and joint ventures during the early 2000s to increase penetration of selected emerging and developed markets.

Danone and Nestlé had long competed against each other in most country markets, but PepsiCo and Coca-Cola were also becoming global sellers of bottled water. Coca-Cola had used a joint venture with Danone Waters to increase its bottled water product line in the United States beyond Dasani and acquired established brands in Europe and Australia to build strength in markets outside the United States. PepsiCo expanded into international markets for bottled water by allowing foreign bottling franchisees to license the Aquafina brand. The strategic maneuvering had created a more globally competitive environment in which the top sellers met each other in almost all of the world's markets and made it difficult for regional sellers to survive. California-based Palomar Mountain Spring Water was one of many casualties of intensifying competitive rivalry. Like many other independent bottled water companies launched in the 1990s, Palomar was forced into bankruptcy in 2003 after losing key supermarket and discount store contracts. After Palomar lost much of its distribution in California supermarkets and discount stores to Nestlé, its 2003 revenues fell to $7 million from $30 million just two years earlier. Exhibit 6 illustrates the extent to which the U.S. bottled water market had consolidated by 2003 and 2004.

The introduction of enhanced waters or functional waters was the most important product innovation since bottled water gained widespread acceptance in the United States, with most sellers in 2006 having introduced variations of their products that included flavoring, vitamins, carbohydrates, electrolytes, and other supplements. The innovation seemed to be a hit with U.S. consumers, as the market for enhanced bottled waters expanded from $20 million

Exhibit 5 **Average Retail Prices of Multipack Bottled Water Marketed by Nestlé Waters, Coca-Cola, and PepsiCo, 2003–2005**

Brands	2003 Average 24-Pack Price	2004 Average 24-Pack Price	2005 Average 24-Pack Price*
Poland Spring (Nestlé Waters)	$5.89	$5.17	$5.10
Dasani (Coca-Cola)	$5.36	$5.88	$5.80
Dannon (Coca-Cola)	$4.70	$4.70	$4.35
Aquafina (PepsiCo)	$5.24	$5.40	$5.01

* January 2005–June 2005.

Source: Morgan Stanley, as reported by the *Atlanta Journal-Constitution*, June 21, 2005.

Exhibit 6   **Top Four U.S. Bottled Water Marketers, 2003–2004**

Rank	Company	Leading Brands	2004 Market Share	2003 Market Share
1	Nestlé Waters	Poland Spring, Deer Park, Arrowhead, Zephyrhills, Ozarka, Ice Mountain	42.1%	39.1%
2	Coca-Cola	Dasani, Evian and Dannon	21.9	24.1
3	PepsiCo	Aquafina	13.6	14.5
4	CG Roxanne	Crystal Geyser	7.4	7.0
	Others/Private-Label		15.0	15.3
	TOTAL		100.0%	100.0%

Source: Morgan Stanley, as reported by the *Atlanta Journal-Constitution*, June 21, 2005.

in 2000 to approximately $1 billion in 2006. Most sellers of bottled water had yet to make functional waters widely available outside the United States. Energy Brands helped create the enhanced water segment in the United States with its 2000 launch of Glacéau Vitamin Water, which contained a variety of vitamins promoting mental stimulation, physical rejuvenation, and overall improved health. Glacéau was the best-selling brand of enhanced water in 2000 and 2001, but it fell to the number two position in the segment upon PepsiCo's launch of Propel Fitness Water. Propel Fitness Water remained the market leader in the U.S. enhanced water segment in 2006. Energy Brands had achieved a compounded annual growth rate of more than 200 percent between 2000 and 2005, to record estimated sales of $350 million and maintain its number two position in the U.S. functional water category.

Coca-Cola, Nestlé, and Danone Waters had begun testing vitamin-enhanced waters in as early as 2002, but all three had changed their approaches to functional waters by 2006. Coke had given up on vitamin-enhanced waters in favor of flavored water, while Nestlé Waters and Danone Waters retained only a fluoride-enhanced water. Like those at Coca-Cola, managers at Nestlé and Danone believed that flavored waters offered substantial growth opportunities in most country markets. The Tata Group, an Indian beverage producer, showed greater confidence in the vitamin-enhanced bottled water market with its purchase of a 30 percent stake in Energy Brands in 2006 for $677 million. The Tata Group's chairman believed that Energy Brands had the potential to become a $3 billion company within 10 years.

PROFILES OF THE LEADING BOTTLED WATER PRODUCERS

Nestlé Waters

Nestlé was the world's leading seller of bottled water, with a worldwide market share of 18.3 percent in 2006. It was also the world's largest food company, with 2005 sales of 91 billion Swiss francs (approximately $71 billion). The company was broadly diversified into 10 food and beverage categories that were sold in almost every country in the world under such recognizable brand names as Nescafé, Taster's Choice, Perrier, Vittel, Carnation, PowerBar, Friskies, Alpo, Nestea, Libby's, Stouffer's, and of course, Nestlé. The company produced bottled water as early as 1843, but its 1992 acquisition of Perrier created the foundation of what has made Nestlé Waters the world's largest seller of bottled water, with 75 brands in 130 countries. In 2005, Nestlé recorded bottled water sales of 8.8 billion Swiss francs (approximately $6.9 billion) and was the global leader in the bottled water industry, with an 18.3 percent worldwide market share in 2005. Nestlé Waters was the number one seller of bottled water in the United States with a 42.1 percent market share in 2004 and the number one seller in Europe with a 20 percent market share. Nestlé was also the number one seller in Africa and the Middle East and was aggressive in its attempts to build market-leading positions in emerging markets Asia and Latin America through the introduction of global Nestlé products and the acquisition of established local brands. The company acquired nearly 20 bottled water producers between 2001 and 2003. In 2006, Nestlé Waters was the number one brand of bottled water in Pakistan, Vietnam, and Cuba; the number two brand in Indonesia and Argentina; and the number three brand in Thailand.

The company's bottled water portfolio in 2006 included two global brands (Nestlé Pure Life and Nestlé Aquarel), five international premium brands (Perrier, Vittel, Contrex, Acqua Panna, and S. Pellegrino), and 68 local brands. Nestlé Pure Life was a purified water product developed in 1998 for emerging markets and other markets in which spring water was not an important differentiating feature of bottled water. Nestlé Aquarel was developed in 2000 for the European market and markets that preferred still spring water over purified water or sparkling spring water. Nestlé's other waters marketed in Europe were either spring water with a higher mineral content or sparkling waters such as Perrier and S. Pellegrino. Almost all brands marketed outside of Europe were either spring water or mineral water with no carbonation. Its brands in the United States included Pure Life, Arrowhead, Ice Mountain, Calistoga, Deer Park, Zephyrhills, Ozarka, and Poland Spring.

During the early 2000s, Nestlé Waters management believed that its broad portfolio of local water brands was among the company's key resource strengths. However, the notable success of Nestlé's two global brands had caused management to reorganize the division in 2006. Pure Life and Aquarel had grown from just 2.5 percent of the division's sales in 2002 to 12.0 percent of the division's 2005 sales. Consumers in the United States seemed to accept the Pure Life brand as well as long-established local brands, with sales of Nestlé Pure Life in the United States increasing by 50 percent between 2004 and 2005. Flavored varieties of Pure Life had also achieved notable success in Canada by capturing a 70 percent share of the flavored water market within the first six months on the market. Nestlé's 68 local brands had accounted for as much as 75.7 percent of division sales in 2002, but local brands had declined to 64.8 percent of sales in 2005. The company's five premium international brands accounted for an additional 23.2 percent of 2005 sales.

Nestlé had test-marketed functional waters fortified with vitamins and plant extracts between 2003 and 2004, but offered only fruit-flavored enhanced waters in 2006. Contrex Lemon Meringue and Strawberry Melba were two innovative calorie-free flavors introduced in 2006. The company had also used packaging innovations to differentiate its bottled water brands, including a spill-proof cap for child-sized bottles of Poland Spring, Deer Park, and Arrowhead. Nestlé Waters also developed a bubble-shaped bottle that was designed to appeal to children. Perrier's new PET container was part of a strategy to revitalize the prestigious brand, which had experienced annual sales declines since the mid-1990s. The new plastic bottle was intended to better match the on-the-go lifestyles of young consumers than Perrier's heavy one-liter glass containers. Nestlé would still package Perrier in glass bottles for consumers who preferred the brand's traditional packaging for dinner parties and other formal settings.

Home and office delivery (HOD) was also an important component of Nestlé's strategy—especially in North America, Europe, and the Middle East. HOD made up nearly 30 percent of Nestlé Waters' sales volume in the United States and was recording double-digit growth in most other country markets in 2005. In 2005, Nestlé competed in the HOD market for bottled water in 30 countries. Between 2000 and 2004, the company had made 8 acquisitions in the European HOD segment to grow from no presence to the leading position, with 32 percent market share. Nestlé had also made acquisitions and entered into joint ventures to develop market leading positions in countries located in the Middle East, Northern Africa, and the Far East. Nestlé's market leading positions in Europe and the United States in HOD and PET channels allowed it to earn the status of low-cost leader in the United States. Exhibit 7 illustrates Nestlé Waters' cost and wholesale pricing advantages relative to Coca-Cola and PepsiCo in U.S. markets. Nestlé Waters' management stated in mid-2002 that it expected to double the division's revenues by 2010.

Groupe Danone

Groupe Danone was established through the 1966 merger of two of France's leading glass makers, who foresaw the oncoming acceptability of plastic as a substitute to glass containers. The management of the newly merged company believed that, rather

Exhibit 7   **Value Chain Comparison for the Bottled Water Operations of Nestlé, PepsiCo, and Coca-Cola**

	Nestlé Waters	PepsiCo	Coca-Cola
Retailer price per case	$8.44	$8.52	$8.65
Retailer margin	35.0%	17.5%	17.6%
Wholesale price per case	$5.49	$7.03	$7.13
Wholesale sales	$5.49	$7.03	$7.13
Support revenue	0.00	0.41	0.52
Total bottler revenue	$5.49	$7.44	$7.65
Expenses			
Water*	$0.01	$1.67	$1.70
PET bottles	1.03	1.16	1.16
Secondary packaging	0.61	0.68	0.68
Closures	0.21	0.23	0.23
Labor/manufacturing	0.70	0.70	0.77
Depreciation	0.07	0.08	0.08
Total cost of goods sold	2.63	4.52	4.62
Gross profit	$2.86	$2.92	$3.03
Selling, general, & administrative	2.29	2.25	2.53
EBITA	$0.57	$0.67	$0.50
EBITA margin	10.4%	9.0%	6.5%

* Includes licensing fees and royalties paid by Coca-Cola and PepsiCo bottlers to Coca-Cola and PepsiCo.

Source: Goldman Sachs Global Equity Research as reported by *Beverage World*, April 2002.

than shifting its focus to the manufacture of plastic containers, the company should enter markets for products typically sold in glass containers. Groupe Danone's diversification outside of glass containers began in 1969 when the company acquired Evian—France's leading brand of bottled water. Throughout the 1970s and 1980s, Groupe Danone acquired additional food and beverage companies that produced beer, pasta, baby food, cereals, sauces, confectionery, dairy products, and baked goods. In 1997, the company slimmed its portfolio of businesses to dairy products, bottled water, and a baked goods division producing cereal, cookies, and snacks. In 2005, Groupe Danone was a leading global food company, with annual sales of €13 billion and was the world's largest producer of dairy products, the number two producer of cereal, cookies, and baked snacks, and the second largest seller of bottled water. The company had been the largest seller of bottled water by

volume in 2005 but was displaced by Nestlé in both terms of volume and dollar sales during 2006.

Danone recorded worldwide bottled water sales of €3.4 billion in 2005. Among Groupe Danone's most important beverage brands were Evian, the world's leading brand of spring water, and Wahaha, the leading brand of bottled water in China. Each brand accounted for more than €1 billion in sales during 2005. During that year, 40 percent of Danone's bottled water sales originated in Europe, 47 percent were in China, and 13 percent were in emerging markets outside of Asia. Danone's local and regional brands held number one shares in many country markets such as Denmark, Germany, Spain, the United Kingdom, Poland, Indonesia, Mexico, and Morocco.

Like Nestlé, Danone had made a number of acquisitions of regional bottled water producers during the late 1990s and early 2000s. During 2002,

Danone acquired a controlling interest in Poland's leading brand of bottled water for an undisclosed amount and purchased Canada's Sparkling Spring brand of waters for an estimated $300–$400 million. The company also entered into a joint venture with Kirin Beverage Company to strengthen its distribution network in Japan and embarked on a partnership with the Rachid Group, an Egyptian firm, to accelerate its development of market opportunities in North Africa and the Near and Middle East. During 2003 and 2004, Groupe Danone acquired three HOD bottled water sellers in Mexico. Danone acquired the leading brand of bottled water in Serbia and an HOD seller in Spain in 2004. In 2006, the company acquired a 49 percent stake in Denmark's leading seller of bottled water.

Danone Waters' revenues had declined by nearly 20 percent between 2000 and 2005 as its U.S. distribution agreement with Coca-Cola began to suffer. Prior to Coca-Cola's launch of Dasani, its bottlers distributed Evian and other non-Coke bottled water brands. Before the introduction of Dasani, about 60 percent of Evian's U.S. distribution was handled by Coca-Cola bottlers. With Coca-Cola bottler's attention directed toward the sale of Dasani, Evian lost shelf space in many convenience stores, supermarkets, delis, restaurants, and wholesale clubs.

Danone Waters and Coca-Cola entered into a joint venture in 2002 that allowed Evian and Dannon water brands to be distributed along with Dasani to convenience stores, supermarkets, and other retail locations serviced by Coca-Cola's bottling operations. In addition, the agreement made Coke responsible for the production, marketing and distribution of Dannon in the United States. Coca-Cola provided Danone an up-front cash payment in return for 51 percent ownership of the joint venture. Danone contributed its five plants and other bottled water assets located in the United States to the joint venture. However, Evian and Dannon continued to suffer under the new distribution arrangement as Coca-Cola continued to put most of its marketing muscle behind Dasani. Danone sold its 49 percent interest in the North American bottled water joint venture to Coca-Cola in 2005.

Danone's home and office delivery businesses were not included in the agreement with Coca-Cola and were combined with Suntory Water Group's assets to form DS Waters in 2003. The combination of Danone Waters' and Suntory Waters assets made

the joint venture the largest HOD distributor in the United States, with sales of approximately $800 million. Brands marketed by DS Waters included Alhambra, Crystal Springs, Sierra Springs, Hinckley Springs, Kentwood Springs, Belmont Springs, and Sparkletts. Groupe Danone and Suntory sold 100 percent of DS Waters to a private investment fund in 2005 for an undisclosed sum. The sale resulted in a €315 million loss for Groupe Danone and completed Groupe Danone's exit from the North American bottled water market. Danone's HOD business remained the worldwide leader in the category with number one rankings in Asia, Argentina, and Canada. Groupe Danone was the second largest HOD provider in Europe in 2005 through a joint venture with Swiss-based Eden Springs.

Groupe Danone had made functional and flavored waters a strategic priority for its beverage business. The company introduced flavored and vitamin-rich versions of Volvic in Europe during 2003 and 2004, and by 2005 it was selling flavored and functional waters in most of its markets. The company held a number one ranking in functional beverage categories in New Zealand and Argentina. Functional and flavored waters accounted for 25 percent of the group's beverage sales in 2005.

The Coca-Cola Company

With 300 brands worldwide, the Coca-Cola Company was the world's leading manufacturer, marketer, and distributor of nonalcoholic beverage concentrates. The company produced soft drinks, juice and juice drinks, sports drinks, water, and coffee and was best known for Coca-Cola, which has been called the world's most valuable brand. In 2005, the company sold more than 20.6 billion cases of beverages worldwide to record revenues of $23.1 billion. Coca-Cola's net income for 2005 was nearly $4.9 billion. Seventy-three percent of Coke's gallon sales were generated outside of North America, with four international markets (Mexico, Brazil, China, and Japan) accounting for 27 percent of Coca-Cola's sales by volume. Sales in the United States also accounted for 27 percent of the company's total volume.

Along with the universal appeal of the Coca-Cola brand, Coca-Cola's vast global distribution system that included independent bottlers, bottlers partially owned by Coca-Cola, and company-owned bottlers made Coke an almost unstoppable international powerhouse. Coca-Cola held market-leading positions in most countries in the cola segment of the soft drink industry, and the strength of the Coca-Cola brand aided the company in gaining market share in most other soft drink segments such as the lemon-lime and diet segments. The company had also been able to leverage Coke's appeal with consumers to gain access to retail distribution channels for new beverages included in its portfolio such as Minute Maid orange juice products, Powerade isotonic beverages, and Dasani purified water.

The Coca-Cola Company did not market and distribute its own brand of bottled water until 1999, when it introduced Dasani. The company created a purified water that included a combination of magnesium sulfate, potassium chloride, and salt to recreate what Coke researchers believed were the best attributes of leading spring waters from around the world. The Dasani formula was a closely guarded secret and was sold to bottlers, just as the company sold its Coke concentrate to bottlers. The Dasani name was developed by linguists who suggested the dual "a"s gave a soothing sound to the name, the "s" conveyed crispness and freshness, and the "i" ending added a foreign ring. Dasani was supported with an estimated $15 million advertising budget during its first year on the market and was distributed through all retail channels where Coke was available. Coca-Cola's U.S. advertising budget for Dasani was $20 million in 2005. Coca-Cola's marketing expertise and vast U.S. distribution system allowed Dasani to become the second largest brand of water sold in the United States by 2001—a position it continued to hold in 2006.

Coca-Cola's 2002 joint venture with Danone Waters allowed Coca-Cola to jump to the rank of second largest bottled water producer in the United States and third largest bottled water producer in the world. The joint venture provided Coke with bottled water products at all price points, with Dasani positioned as an upper-midpriced product, Evian as a premium-priced bottled water, and Dannon as a discount-priced water. Coke management believed the addition of Dannon would allow the company to protect Dasani's near-premium pricing, while gaining spring water brands that could be marketed nationally to challenge Nestlé's regional brands in the spring water segment.

Even though the joint venture allowed Coca-Cola's sales of bottled water to increase from $765 million in 2002 to $1.3 billion in 2003, the three-tier strategy seemed to be failing in some regards since Coke's three water brands had collectively lost 2.2 market share points between 2003 and 2004. Coca-Cola's loss of market share seemed to be attributable, to some to degree, to Nestlé's growth during 2004 and the increasing popularity of private-label brands, which had grown by more than 60 percent during 2004. However, some lost market share for the three brands combined might have been a result of weak support for Evian and Dannon brands. Coca-Cola had committed to increasing advertising and promotion for Evian by 20 percent between 2005 and 2010, but beverage industry analysts believed it was unlikely that Evian would ever return to its previous top-five ranking in the United States.

Coca-Cola tested a vitamin- and flavor-enhanced Dasani NutriWater sub-brand during 2002 and 2003, but it abandoned the concept after poor test-market performance. In 2005, the company did go forward with Splenda-sweetened lemon- and raspberry-flavored varieties of Dasani. The company later added strawberry and grape flavors to the Dasani line. Fruit-flavored Dasani had proved to be successful in the market by 2006, with most retailers stocking at least two flavors of Dasani in addition to unflavored Dasani water. Coca-Cola extended the Dasani line in 2006 with the introduction of Dasani Sensations—a flavored water with light carbonation. Like other varieties of Dasani, Dasani Sensations contained no calories. Powerade Option was another functional water developed by Coca-Cola that was introduced in 2005. Powerade Option was a competing product to Gatorade Propel Fitness Water and was available in grape and strawberry flavors in 2006. As of 2006, Powerade Option had been largely unsuccessful in capturing share from Propel Fitness Water and was unavailable in many retail locations.

Coca-Cola had long produced and marketed, bottled water in foreign countries under local brand names, such as its Bon Aqua brand in the German market and NaturAqua in Hungary, but began efforts to make Dasani an international brand in 2004 with expansion into in Africa, Brazil, and the United Kingdom. Coca-Cola management chose the United Kingdom as its entry point to Western Europe with launches planned for 20 additional European countries by mid-2004. Coca-Cola supported the March 2004 launch of Dasani in the United Kingdom with a $3.2 million advertising budget and a

4-million-bottle sampling campaign but voluntarily recalled all Dasani bottles from retailers' shelves just two weeks after the launch.

The recall was predicated on test results performed by the company that indicated the bottles were tainted with bromate—a cancer-causing agent. Bromate became introduced to the product when calcium, a mandatory ingredient for bottled waters sold in the United Kingdom, was added to Coca-Cola's proprietary formula of minerals used to distinguish Dasani from other bottled waters. The bromate levels present in Dasani exceeded regulatory limits in the United Kingdom but met standards for purity on the European continent. Nevertheless, Coke management believed it best to recall the product and discontinue immediate plans to distribute Dasani not only in the United Kingdom but also in all other European markets. The Dasani launch was viewed by many in the business press as one of the all-time great marketing disasters and resulted in Coke's abandoning the Dasani brand in Europe. Coca-Cola management announced during a June 2006 Deutsche Bank conference for consumer goods that it would expand its line of noncarbonated beverages in Europe through acquisitions. Within two weeks of the announcement, Coca-Cola had acquired the Italian mineral water company Fonti del Vulture and the Apollinaris mineral water brand sold in Germany by Orangina. Coca-Cola also acquired two HOD bottled water producers in Australia during 2006.

PepsiCo Inc.

In 2006, PepsiCo was the world's fourth largest food and beverage company, with sales of approximately $32 billion. The company's brands were sold in more than 200 countries and included such well-known names as Lay's, Tostitos, Mountain Dew, Pepsi, Doritos, Lipton Iced Tea, Gatorade, Quaker, and Cracker Jack. Six of PepsiCo's products were among the top-15 largest selling products sold in U.S. supermarkets. PepsiCo also produced and marketed Aquafina—the best-selling brand of bottled water in the United States between 2002 and 2006.

PepsiCo had made attempts to enter the bottled water market in as early as 1987, when it purchased a spring water company, but its attempts were unsuccessful until its 1997 introduction of Aquafina. After experimenting with spring water and sparkling water for several years, Pepsi management believed

it would be easier to produce a national brand of bottled water that could utilize the same water purification facilities in Pepsi bottling plants that were used to produce the company's brands of soft drinks. Pepsi management also believed that the company could distinguish its brand of purified bottled water from competing brands by stripping all chlorine and other particles out of tap water that might impart an unpleasant taste or smell. PepsiCo began testing a filtration process for Aquafina in 1994 when it installed $3 million worth of reverse osmosis filtration equipment in its Wichita, Kansas, bottling plant to further purify municipal water used to make soft drinks. The system pushed water through a fiberglass membrane at very high pressure to remove chemicals and minerals before further purifying the water using carbon filters. The water produced by Pepsi's process was so free of chemicals that the company was required to add ozone gas to the water to prevent bacteria growth.

Since the company's introduction of Aquafina, PepsiCo had expanded its water brands in the United States to include Gatorade Propel Fitness Water, SoBe Life Water, and functional versions of Aquafina. The product lines for its water business were developed around customer type and lifestyle. Propel was a flavor- and vitamin-enriched water marketed to physically active consumers, while Life Water was a vitamin-enhanced water similar to Glacéau Vitamin Water in formulation and packaging that was marketed to image-driven consumers. The company targeted mainstream water consumers with unflavored Aquafina, Aquafina FlavorSplash (offered in four flavors), and Aquafina Sparkling (a zero-calorie, lightly carbonated citrus or berry-flavored water). Aquafina Alive, planned for a 2007 launch, included vitamins and natural fruit juices. The company's strategy involved offering a continuum of healthy beverages from unflavored Aquafina to nutrient-rich Gatorade. In 2006, Gatorade, Propel, and Aquafina were all number one in their categories, with market shares of 80 percent, 34 percent, and approximately 14 percent, respectively.

PepsiCo was slowly moving into international bottled water markets, with its most notable effort occurring in Mexico. In 2002, PepsiCo's bottling operations acquired Mexico's largest Pepsi bottler, Pepsi-Gemex SA de CV, for $1.26 billion. Gemex not only bottled and distributed Pepsi soft drinks in Mexico but also was Mexico's number one producer of purified water. After its acquisition of Gemex, PepsiCo shifted its international expansion efforts to bringing Aquafina to selected emerging markets in Eastern Europe, the Middle East, and Asia. In 2006, Aquafina was the number one brand of bottled water in Russia and Vietnam and the number two brand in Kuwait.

Other Sellers

In addition to the industry's leading sellers of bottled water, there were hundreds of regional and specialty brands of bottled water in the United States. Most of these companies were privately held bottlers with distribution limited to small geographic regions that competed aggressively on price to make it onto convenience store and supermarket shelves as third-tier brands. Many of these bottlers also sought out private-label contracts with discounters and large supermarket chains to better ensure full capacity utilization and to achieve sufficient volume to purchase bottles and other packaging at lower prices. CG Roxanne was the most successful privately owned bottled water company in the United States. The company's Crystal Geyser brand made it the fourth largest seller of bottled water in the United States in 2004, with a 7.4 percent market share. Crystal Geyser competed at the lower price points in U.S. supermarkets and convenience stores and was bottled from springs in California, Tennessee, South Carolina, and New Hampshire. The company did not disclose its financial performance.

Another group of small bottlers such as Fiji, Voss, Penta and Trinity Springs used differentiating features to avoid the fierce price competition at the low end of the market and sold in the superpremium segment, where bottled water retailed from $1.50 to $2.25 per 16-ounce PET container. Superpremium brands were most often sold in natural foods stores, with Trinity Springs being among the leaders in the channel in 2005. Trinity's differentiation was based on its water source, which was a 2.2-mile-deep artesian well located in the Trinity Mountains of Idaho. Trinity Springs' distribution halted in March 2006

when a court invalidated the 2004 sale of the company to Amcon Distributing. Amcon, which had lost $2 million in fiscal 2005 and another $1.8 million during the first six months of fiscal 2006, shut down its Trinity Springs water division after the ruling and was negotiating a settlement with Trinity Springs shareholders in late 2006.

Penta's differentiation was based on a proprietary purification system that the company claimed removed 100 percent of impurities from tap water. The company had also built brand recognition through product placements in motion pictures, music videos, and more than 25 television series. Penta also sponsored a large number of triathlons across the United States and was endorsed by a wide variety of entertainers and professional athletes. In 2006, Penta was distributed in more than 5,000 health food stores in the United States. Penta was also available in Australia, Japan, the United Kingdom, and Canada. Fiji was also among the best-selling brands of superpremium water sold in natural foods stores in 2006 but was also sold in many supermarkets, convenience stores, and drugstores across the United States. Like Penta, Fiji received considerable exposure from its placement in network television series and motion pictures.

Voss achieved differentiation not only from the purity of its source in Norway but also through its distinctive glass bottle and limited channels of distribution. The brand was available only in the most exclusive hotels, spas, and resorts. Another superpremium brand, Eon, achieved its differentiation through its anti-aging claims. The company's anti-aging properties were said to result from the basic atomic structure of Eon water, which was altered through a proprietary reverse osmosis technology. The structure of Eon was similar to that naturally occurring in snowflakes and glacier ice and was suggested to improve cellular hydration and cell detoxification properties better than unstructured water. Many other superpremium brands of bottled water were sold in the United States during 2006, with each attempting to support its premium pricing with some unique characteristic.

Endnote

As quoted in "The Taste of Water," Bottled Water Web, www.bottledwaterweb.com/watertaste.htm.

Case 5

Blue Nile Inc.: World's Largest Online Diamond Retailer

Arthur A. Thompson
The University of Alabama

A 2006 issue of *Kiplinger's Personal Finance* cited the experience of a couple in Hawaii who were shopping for an engagement ring.[1] The bride-to-be knew what she wanted, so she took a lead role in conducting the search. Several retail jewelry stores in Honolulu quoted her a price of about $7,900 for a nearly flawless diamond ring just under a carat. But the bride-to-be, a policewoman who took pride in thorough investigations, decided to continue her search online. She found a similar ring at BlueNile.com for $4,263 and her fiancé agreed to buy it. As soon as the order was placed, Blue Nile acquired the diamond, which had been selected from the New York diamond cutter whose diamond inventory was displayed on BlueNile.com, and the cutter shipped the diamond overnight to Blue Nile's 13,000-square-foot warehouse in Seattle. A Blue Nile bench jeweler, using a magnifying visor and assorted tools of the trade, mounted the diamond in the setting that the bride-to-be had selected. The ring was cleaned in a tiny hot tub, blasted with steam, placed in a blue-and-silver box that was packed inside a cardboard shipping box, and shipped via FedEx for overnight delivery to the bride in Honolulu. The whole process took just three days. According to the bride-to-be, "It looks absolutely brilliant. It blinds you."[2]

Founded in 1999, Blue Nile had grown to become the world's largest online retailer of certified diamonds and fine jewelry, with sales of $251.6 million in 2006 (up from $169.2 million in 2004). According to *Internet Retailer* magazine, in 2006 Blue Nile was larger than the next three largest online jewelers combined; the magazine had ranked Blue Nile number 48 in its "Top 400 Guide to Retail Web Sites"; in its December 2006 issue, the magazine went a step further and named Blue Nile an Internet Retailer Best of the Web 2007 company (one of five companies cited).[3] *Forbes* magazine had selected Blue Nile as a Forbes Favorite every year during 2000–2005. The company had been awarded the BizRate.com Circle of Excellence Platinum Award, which recognized the best in online customer service as ranked by actual consumers; Blue Nile was the only jeweler to have ever received this award, and had been the recipient of this award every year since 2002. *Kiplinger's Personal Finance* named Blue Nile as the best online jeweler in November 2006.[4] Blue Nile had also received notice in *Time* and *Money* magazines.

In 2006, jewelry in the United States was an estimated $55–$60 billion industry.[5] Annual sales of diamond jewelry were in the $30–$35 billion range, with diamond engagement rings accounting for sales of $4–$5 billion. About 72 percent of Blue Nile's 2005 revenues involved sales of engagement rings; Blue Nile's average engagement ring sale in 2005 was $5,600. Blue Nile management believed that the company's market share of online sales of engagement rings exceeded 50 percent and that its 2005 share of the overall engagement ring market in the United States was approximately 3.2 percent.[6] Sales of diamond jewelry other than engagement rings accounted for 18 percent of Blue Nile's 2005 sales; management considered this segment to present significant growth opportunities because satisfied buyers of Blue Nile engagement rings would likely consider Blue Nile in their future purchases of diamond jewelry. Blue Nile provided engagement rings for over 80,000 couples from 2000 to mid-2006. Sales of jewelry not containing diamonds accounted for 10 percent of Blue Nile's 2005 revenues; sales of these typically lesser-priced items were considered important because they helped develop both trial and repeat purchase opportunities.

BLUE NILE'S BUSINESS MODEL AND STRATEGY

In an industry famous for big markups, frequent closeout sales, and myriad judgments of value that often mystified consumers, the marketing challenge for online jewelers was to convince understandably skittish shoppers to purchase fine jewelry online. It was one thing to shop for a diamond in a reputable jewelry store where one could put on a ring or other jewelry item to see how it looked, perhaps inspect a stone with a magnifying glass or microscope, and have a qualified jeweler describe the features of various stone(s) and cuts, compare the character and merit of various settings, and explain why some items carried higher price tags than others. It was quite another thing to commit to buying expensive jewelry based on pictures and information provided on an Internet Web site.

Blue Nile's strategy to attract customers had two core elements. The first was offering high-quality diamonds and fine jewelry at competitively attractive prices. The second entailed providing jewelry shoppers with a host of useful information and trusted guidance throughout their purchasing process. Top management believed its strategy of providing educational information, in-depth product information, and grading reports—coupled with its wide product selection and attractive prices—was the key driver of the company's success and, ideally, would lead to customers looking upon Blue Nile as their jeweler for life:

> We have established and are continuing to develop a brand based on trust, guidance and value, and we believe our customers view Blue Nile as a trusted authority on diamonds and fine jewelry. Our goal is for consumers to seek out the Blue Nile brand whenever they purchase high quality diamonds and fine jewelry.[7]

Competitive Pricing, Lean Costs, and Supply Chain Efficiency

Blue Nile's domestic and international Web sites showcased as many as 60,000 independently certified diamonds and hundreds of styles of fine jewelry. The product offerings ranged from simple classic designs suitable for wearing every day to an impressive signature collection of some of the finest diamonds in the world. Diamonds were the most significant component of Blue Nile's merchandise offerings, but the selection was limited chiefly to high-quality stones in terms of shape, cut, color, clarity, and carat weight. Complementing the large selection of individual diamonds and gems was a broad range of diamond, platinum, gold, pearl, and sterling silver jewelry that included settings, rings, wedding bands, earrings, necklaces, pendants, bracelets, and watches.

Blue Nile offered a Build Your Own feature that allowed customers to customize diamond rings, pendants, and earrings. Customers could select a diamond and then choose from a variety of ring, earring, and pendant settings that were designed to match the characteristics of each individual diamond.

Blue Nile's economical supply chain and comparatively low operating costs allowed it to sell comparable-quality diamonds, gemstones, and fine jewelry pieces at substantially lower prices than those of reputable local jewelers. The supply chain bypassed the markups of traditional layers of diamond wholesalers and brokers, thus generally allowing Blue Nile to obtain most of its product offerings more cost-efficiently than traditional brick-and-mortar jewelers. The distinctive feature of Blue Nile's supply chain was its set of arrangements that allowed it to display leading diamond and gem suppliers' products on its Web site; some of these arrangements entailed multi-year agreements whereby designated diamonds were offered only at Blue Nile. Blue Nile's suppliers represented more than half of the total supply of high-quality diamonds in the United States.[8] Blue Nile did not actually purchase a diamond or gem from these suppliers until a customer placed an order for it; this enabled Blue Nile to minimize the costs associated with carrying large inventories and limited its risk of potential markdowns. However, Blue Nile did selectively purchase finished pieces (usually bracelets, necklaces, earrings, pendants, wedding bands, and watches), stocking them in its own inventory until customers purchased them. Even so, Blue Nile had inventories of only $11.7 million at year-end 2005 (versus sales of $203.2 million). In contrast, traditional jewelers had far bigger inventories relative to annual sales. For example, Zale Corporation—which not only sold online but also was the parent of Zales Jewelers (780 stores in the United States and Puerto Rico), Zales Outlet, Gordon's Jewelers, Bailey Banks & Biddle (a luxury retail jeweler with 70 locations in 31 states and Puerto Rico), Peoples Jewelers (the largest Canadian jeweler), Mappins Jewelers (another Canadian jewelry chain), and Piercing Pagoda—reported year-end inventories of $853.6 million on 2005 sales of $2.4 billion. Luxury jewelry retailer Tiffany & Co. reported year-end inventories of $1.06 billion on 2005 sales of $2.4 billion.

Blue Nile's supply chain savings gave it a significant pricing advantage. For every dollar that Blue Nile paid suppliers for stones, settings, and other purchased items, it sold its finished jewelry for a markup of about 33 percent over cost (equal to a gross profit margin of 22 percent). In contrast, Zale sold at an average markup of 100 percent over cost of goods sold and Tiffany sold an average markup over cost of goods sold of 127 percent in 2005 (equal to a gross profit margin of 56 percent).

Another cost-saving element of Blue Nile's strategy was lean operating costs. The company had only 146 employees as of early 2006, of whom 133 were full-time; independent contractors and temporary personnel were hired on a seasonal basis. Blue Nile conducted its operations via a combination of proprietary and licensed technologies. It licensed third-party information technology systems for financial reporting, inventory management, order fulfillment, and merchandising. Also, it used redundant Internet carriers to minimize service interruptions and downtime. Management continuously monitored various operating systems using third-party software, and an on-call team responded to any emergencies or technology issues. Management also continuously explored avenues to improve operating efficiency, refine the company's supply chain, and leverage its investment in fixed-cost technology. Blue Nile's selling, general, and administrative (SG&A) expenses were only 13.3 percent of 2005 annual sales, down from 14.1 percent in 2003 and 19.6 percent in 2002; in contrast, SG&A expenses were 41.2 percent of

2005 sales at Zale Corporation and 40.1 percent of 2005 sales at Tiffany & Co.

Blue Nile's agreements with suppliers and low operating costs enabled it to earn respectable profits while selling at prices that ranged from 20 to 40 percent below those of local retail jewelry stores. Blue Nile had a net profit margin of 6.5 percent in 2005, compared to 2005 net profit margins of 4.5 percent at Zale and 10.6 percent at Tiffany.

Blue Nile cut the retail prices of its diamonds in the second quarter of 2006 in an effort to drive sales gains; the price cuts helped produce a 30 percent sales gain in the quarter, the largest increase of the past six quarters. Sales in the second quarter of 2006 included seven customer sales above $100,000 and one sale above $200,000. In the third quarter, the company's biggest sale was a premium-quality seven-carat engagement ring purchased for $324,000. CEO Mark Vadon, in an interview with The Motley Fool, talked about Blue Nile's sales of diamonds at six-figure prices:

> Back in Q2, I believe we announced we had seven transactions in the quarter above $100,000, and over time, as the business has established more of a brand name out there, that part of the market for us is very, very active. We have always had products in that type of price range, and it used to be unusual for us to see a six-figure purchase. Now those are becoming pretty common around here.

What we typically do as our price points rise, we drop our percentage gross margin. So if you look at a purchase at, say, $100,000 price point, we are only making 8% or 9% gross margin on something like that. We are being as aggressive as possible to make the sale, so we will make more selling $100,000 of small rings as opposed to a single $100,000 ring, but we are really excited to have those types of sales.

We are obviously looking at the dollars of profit we are making on the transaction, and we just love that people walk around with a Blue Nile ring that is that extraordinary and [tell] people where they bought it.[9]

Educational Information and Certification

Blue Nile went to considerable lengths to put to rest any concerns shoppers might have about buying fine jewelry online. It employed an informative sales process, striving to demystify and simplify the process of choosing a diamond or some other gemstone. Blue Nile's Web site provided a wealth of easy-to-understand information about the five C's of purchasing diamonds and gems (carat, cut, color, clarity, and cut grade—see Exhibit 1), allowing shoppers to educate themselves about what characteristics determined the quality and value of various stones. In addition to providing substantial educational information, Blue Nile's Web site and its extensively trained customer service representatives provided detailed product information that enabled customers to objectively compare diamonds and fine jewelry products and to make informed decisions in choosing a stone of suitable size/weight, cut, clarity, look, and price.

Exhibit 1   Determining a Diamond's Value: The Five C's

Carat

Refers to a diamond's weight, not its size. One carat equals one-fifth of a gram. While lighter diamonds often carry a lower price per carat, a 1.0 carat diamond might sparkle more than 1.25 carat diamond if it is cut differently or has better color and clarity.

Clarity

The degree to which a diamond is free of flaws or inclusions—blemishes, internal imperfections, scratches, trace minerals, or other tiny characteristics that can detract from a diamond's beauty. Diamonds that are absolutely clear are the most sought after and therefore the most expensive. The lower the clarity (and the greater the flaws and inclusions), the lower the value of the diamond. The naked eye can see flaws in diamonds with very poor clarity, but even using a magnifying glass an untrained person would have trouble seeing flaws in a high-clarity diamond. The 11 grades of clarity—ranging from flawless to included—are based on the number, location, size, and type of inclusions present in a diamond. Inclusions and flaws are more visible to the naked eye in lower-grade emerald cuts than in lower-grade round diamonds.

Color

Concerns a diamond's transparency. Acting as a prism, a diamond can divide light into a spectrum of colors and reflect this light as colorful flashes called fire. Like colored glass, color in a diamond will act as a filter and will diminish the spectrum of color emitted. The less color in a diamond, the more colorful the fire and the better the color grade. A little color in a white diamond could diminish its brilliance. White diamonds with very little color were the most highly valued and are priced accordingly. Color grades range from D (absolutely colorless and extremely rare) to Z. White diamonds with grade of D, E, or F are considered "colorless" grade and very high quality; diamonds with grades of G or H are near colorless and offer excellent value: diamonds with grades of I or J have slightly detectable color but still represent good value; the color in diamonds graded K–Z detracts from the beauty of the stone and is especially noticeable in platinum or white gold settings. (Blue Nile only sold diamonds with color grades of J or higher.) Yellow diamonds (some of which are fancy and highly valued) are graded on a different scale than white diamonds.

Cut

A diamond's shape (round, square, oval, pear, heart, marquise, and so on) and style (width, depth, symmetry, polish, and number/position of flat surfaces). Most diamonds are cut with 58 facets, or separate flat surfaces; it is the diamond cutter's job, using precise mathematical formulas, to align the facets at precise angles in relation to each other to maximize the reflection and refraction of light. Cut style affects how light travels within a diamond, thus determining its brightness, fire, and face-up appearance. The cutter's goal is to transform a diamond in the rough into a sparkling, polished stone of the largest possible size and greatest optical beauty; a poor or less desirable cut can dull the look and brilliance of diamonds with excellent color and clarity. There is no single measurement of a diamond that defines its cut, but rather a collection of measurements and observations that determine the relationship between a diamond's light performance, dimensions, and finish.

Cut Grade

This newest of the 5 C's is perhaps the overall best measure or indicator of a diamond's brilliance, sparkle, and "wow effect." Fewer than 5% of diamonds on the market qualified for the highest cut grade rating. Cut grade was a summary rating that took into account such measures as the diamond's table size (the flat surface at the top of the diamond) as a percentage of the diamond's girth (the widest part of the diamond), the crown of the diamond (the portion above the girth) and the crown angle, the pavilion (the portion of the diamond below the girth)—the height of the pavilion contributed to its brilliance, the pavilion angle, the depth of the diamond (from the top facet to the culet), culet size, the diamond's polish and symmetry, and several other factors affecting sparkle, radiance, and brilliance.

(continued)

Exhibit 1   (continued)

The following table shows price variations in diamonds with varying clarity but the same carat weight and color grade.

Price Comparison: 1 carat, H-color, ideal cut diamond

Clarity Grade	Description	Price
FL	**Flawless** No internal or external finish flaws.	$7,500
IF	**Internally flawless** No internal flaws.	$7,200
VVS1 VVS2	**Very very slightly included** Very difficult to see inclusions under 10× magnification.	$6,900 $6,600
VS1 VS2	**Very slightly included** Difficult to see inclusions under 10× magnification, typically unable to see inclusions with unaided eye.	$6,100 $5,600
SI1 SI2	**Slightly included** Easy to see inclusions under 10× magnification, may not be able to see inclusions with unaided eye.	$5,000 $4,300

The following table compares the prices of diamonds with varying color grades but the same clarity grade (VS1) and carat weight:

Price comparison: 1–1.09 carat VS1 round diamond

	Colorless			Near-Colorless			
	D	E	F	G	H	I	J
Ideal	$8,000	$7,600	$7,200	$6,800	$6,000	$5,200	$4,300
Very Good	$7,500	$7,200	$6,900	$6,200	$5,600	$4,700	$4,200
Good	$7,200	$6,800	$6,700	$6,000	$5,200	$4,600	$4,000
Fair	$7,000	$6,700	$6,600	$5,200	$4,700	$4,200	$3,700

Source: Compiled from a variety of sources, including the educational information posted at www.bluenile.com and www.diamonds.com (accessed August 23, 2006). The two price tables are from www.bluenile.com accessed August 23, 2006.

Blue Nile's management believed that having reputable industry professionals certify and grade each gemstone offered for sale had many advantages. The grading reports provided valuable guidance to consumers in choosing a stone that was right for them and their pocketbook—the carat weight, color, cut, and clarity of a diamond were critical in providing the buyer with the desired sparkle, brilliance, and dazzling or sophisticated look. In addition, a jewelry shopper's ability to immediately review professionally prepared grading reports for a gemstone of particular interest instilled confidence in shopping for fine jewelry at Blue Nile, typically quelling any fears that the stone might not live up to expectations. Furthermore, the grading reports that Blue Nile provided facilitated comparison shopping, allowing jewelry shoppers not only to compare alternative Blue Nile gems but also to see how Blue Nile's products stacked up against the products they might be considering at competing jewelers.

Customers interested in a particular diamond displayed at Blue Nile's Web site could view or print out an accompanying diamond grading or certification report, prepared by an independent team of professional gemologists, that documented the specific characteristics of the diamond—see Exhibit 2. A diamond grading report (also called a diamond certificate or diamond quality document) was, a report created by a team of gemologists who evaluated, measured, and scrutinized the diamond using trained eyes, a jeweler's loupe, a microscope,

Exhibit 2   **Diamond Characteristics Documented in a GIA Diamond Grading Report**

Shape and Cutting Style: The diamond shape and cutting style.

Measurement: The diamond's dimensions in millimeters.

Carat Weight: The weight of diamond listed to the nearest hundredth of a carat.

Color Grade: A grading that assesses the absence of color in a diamond.

Clarity Grade: Clarity grade determined under 10× magnification.

Cut Grade: A grade of cut as determined by a diamond's face-up appearance, design, and craftsmanship. A GIA cut grade was available on round diamonds graded after January 1, 2006. The addition of cut grade to grading reports was particularly important because cut grade was the best indicator of a diamond's sparkle, brilliance, and "wow effect." (A diamond's cut concerned its shape and number of facets but was not a reliable indicator of the sparkle and brilliance across the stone when looking at it face up.) The GIA's cut grades used a five-point scale from Poor to Excellent; in 2006, GIA cut grades were available only for select round diamonds, the most popular cut for engagement rings. GIA was said to be considering expanding its cut grade ratings to stones in other shapes (square, pear, and marquise). (According to one source, fewer than 5 percent of diamonds qualified for the highest cut grade.)

Finish: Grades that represent a diamond's surface and facet placement.

Polish: Rating the overall smoothness of the diamond's surface.

Symmetry: Measuring the shape, alignment and placement of the diamond's facets in relation to one another as well as the evenness of the outline.

Fluorescence: Color and strength of color when diamond is viewed under ultraviolet light.

Comments: A description of additional diamond characteristics not already mentioned in the report.

Clarity Plot: A map of the approximate size, type, and position of inclusions as viewed under a microscope.

Proportion Diagram: A map of the diamond's actual proportions that typically includes information about the following:

- **Culet:** Appearance, or lack thereof, of the culet facet. The culet (pronounced "que-let" or the French-sounding "que-lay") was a tiny flat surface formed by polishing off the tip at the bottom of a diamond. The presence of a culet protected the fragile tip of the diamond from chipping during the cutting, handling, and setting of the diamond. However, Asians often preferred diamonds without a culet, so the practice of downgrading diamonds without culets had been discontinued.
- **Table:** Located at the top of the diamond, the table was the largest facet (or flat surface) of a diamond.
- **Depth:** The height of a gemstone measured from the culet to the table.
- **Girdle:** Range of girdle thickness.

and other industry tools. A completed certificate included an analysis of the diamond's dimensions, clarity, color, polish, symmetry, and other characteristics. Many round diamonds had a cut grade on the report. Every loose diamond sold by Blue Nile was analyzed and graded by either the Gemological Institute of America (GIA) or the American Gem Society Laboratories (AGSL):

- The GIA was regarded as the world's foremost authority in gemology; its mission was to promote public trust in gems and jewelry. In the 1950s, the GIA had created an International Diamond Grading System and established standards that revolutionized the diamond industry. Most recently, the GIA had introduced a new Diamond Cut Grading System, which used computer modeling to assess and predict the cut quality in round brilliant cut diamonds.

The GIA's research revealed that there was no single set of proportions that defined a well-cut round brilliant diamond; according to the GIA, many different proportions could produce attractive diamonds. The GIA had also developed software that provided a method of estimating a cut grade—and a database that was embedded into a number of leading diamond measuring devices so that cut grade estimation could be automated. As a result, manufacturers could plan and, in effect, predict cut grades; buyers could compare cut qualities; and retailers could communicate the effects of cut on round brilliant diamonds. On January 1, 2006, the GIA laboratory introduced new versions of the GIA Diamond Grading Report and Diamond Dossier that provided a single, comprehensive cut grade for all standard round brilliant diamonds falling in the GIA D-to-Z color scale and

Flawless-to-I3 clarity scale. Diamonds received one of five cut grades, from Excellent to Poor.

- Founded in 1996, the AGSL was the only diamond grading laboratory to offer a unique 0 to 10 grading system that provided easy-to-read, clear, and accurate information about each diamond it graded. A cut grade of 10 was the lowest quality, and a grade of 000 was the absolute finest or ideal quality, but so far AGSL had only awarded cut grades to select round and square-cut diamonds. (It was, however, considering expanding the grading system to other cuts.) AGSL grading reports were based on the gemological industry's highest standards of evaluating the four C's of cut, color, clarity, and carat weight. AGSL grades allowed a shopper to compare the quality of the diamond against the price.

These two laboratories, among the most respected laboratories in the diamond industry, were known for their consistency and unbiased diamond grading systems. Diamonds that were accompanied by GIA and AGSL grading reports were the most highly valued in the industry.

In addition to being graded by the GIA or AGSL, all diamonds in Blue Nile's signature collection were also certified by the Gem Certification and Appraisal Lab (GCAL). This provided a second authoritative analysis of the diamond. GCAL verified that a diamond met all the specific quality requirements of the Blue Nile Signature Collection—see Exhibit 3.

Marketing

Blue Nile's marketing strategy was designed to increase Blue Nile brand recognition, generate consumer traffic, acquire customers, build a loyal customer base, and promote repeat purchases. Top executives at Blue Nile believed that jewelry shoppers preferred to seek out high-quality diamonds and fine jewelry from a trusted source in a non-intimidating environment, where information, guidance, reputation, convenience, and value were important characteristics. Hence, a major portion of Blue Nile's marketing effort was focused on making sure that site visitors had a positive, informative experience shopping at Blue Nile, one that inspired their confidence to buy diamonds and fine jewelry from the company. One key initiative to provide a good customer experience was the development of a user-friendly interactive search tool that allowed shoppers to customize their search and quickly identify diamonds with the characteristics they were looking for. An advanced version of Blue Nile's diamond search tool launched in March 2006 allowed site visitors to search Blue Nile's diamond collection according to any of 12 criteria, including price, carat weight, cut,

Exhibit 3   **Contents of a Certificate of Authenticity Issued by the Gem Certification and Appraisal Lab (GCAL)**

Actual Size Photo—A photo of the diamond at its true size.

Laser Inscription Photo—A close-up shot of the laser inscription on the diamond taken at 50× magnification.

Proportion Diagram—A diagram noting the diamond's actual scale, and noting its specific measurements. These measurements were used to determine the cut grade.

Enlarged Photomicrograph—A photo of the diamond from top and bottom.

An Optical Brilliance Analysis—Images of the diamond were captured using a controlled lighting environment and carefully calibrated amounts of light at specific viewing angles. These tests showed the amount of light return or brilliance as it exited the diamond's crown.

Optical Symmetry Analysis—A test analyzing the light exiting the diamond and showing the discrepancies in the balance of the diamond. An even and symmetrical pattern showed that the light was well balanced and indicated exceptional diamond quality.

Certification Statement—A statement signed by the GCAL laboratory director verifying the quality of the graded diamond.

Diamond Grading Analysis—This analysis noted the diamond's shape, measurements, carat weight, and cut grade based on its proportions, polish, symmetry, color, and clarity grades. It also contained any comments regarding the diamond.

Source: www.bluenile.com (accessed August 8, 2006).

color, clarity, polish, symmetry, fluorescence, culet, diamond grading report, depth percentage, and table percentage. The Blue Nile customer experience was designed to empower customers with knowledge and confidence as they evaluated, selected, and purchased diamonds and fine jewelry.

The company's efforts to draw more shoppers to its site and boost awareness of Blue Nile included both online and offline marketing and advertising efforts. Most of Blue Nile's advertising dollars went for ads at Web portals (Yahoo!, America Online, and MSN), search engine sites (Google), and select other sites. The company also did some direct online marketing. Advertising expenses were $4.5 million in 2003, $6.5 million in 2004, $7.6 million in 2005, and $9.7 million in 2006.

Blue Nile pulled back on advertising during December 2005 because the cost to buy keywords on Internet search engines rose dramatically. Search keyword bidding pushed up Blue Nile's cost per click on Google to more than 50 percent above December 2004 levels; moreover, the price of Google's top five keywords rose by over 80 percent. According to Blue Nile's CEO, Mark Vadon, the aggressive competition in the crowded search market converted fewer searchers into Blue Nile buyers.

Customer Service and Support

Blue Nile strove to provide a high level of customer service and was continuously engaged in refining the customer service aspects in every step of the purchase process. Complementing the extensive information resources on its Web site was a call center staffed with knowledgeable, highly trained support personnel. Blue Nile diamond and jewelry consultants were trained to provide guidance on all steps in the process of buying diamonds and fine jewelry, including the process for selecting an appropriate item, the purchase of that item, financing and payment alternatives, and shipping services. Customers with questions could call a prominently displayed toll-free number or send an e-mail to service@ bluenile.com; most calls to the Blue Nile call center were answered within 10 seconds.[10] There were personnel assigned to creating and enhancing the features and functionality of the company's Web site and order processing and fulfillment systems. Policies relating to privacy, security, product avail-

ability, pricing, shipping, refunds, exchanges, and special orders were readily accessed at the company's Web site.

Order Fulfillment Operations

Order fulfillment at Blue Nile was designed to enhance customer value and confidence by filling customer orders accurately and delivering them quickly and securely. When an order for a customized diamond jewelry piece was received, the supplier holding the diamond in inventory generally shipped it to Blue Nile (or an independent third-party jeweler with whom Blue Nile maintained an ongoing relationship for assembly) within one business day. Upon receipt at Blue Nile, the diamond was sent to assembly for setting and sizing, tasks performed by either Blue Nile bench jewelers or independent third-party bench jewelers. Each diamond was inspected upon arrival from suppliers; additionally, each finished setting or sizing was inspected prior to shipment to a customer. Prompt and secure delivery was a high priority, and Blue Nile shipped nearly all diamond and fine jewelry products via FedEx. The company had an on-time order delivery rate of 99.96 percent, which it was striving to push to 100 percent.[11]

Order fulfillment costs, which were included as part of SG&A expenses, totaled $1.5 million in 2003, $1.6 million in 2004, $1.8 million in 2005, and $2.4 million in 2006. These costs included all expenses associated with operating and staffing the Seattle warehouse and order fulfillment center, including costs attributable to receiving, inspecting, and warehousing inventories and picking, preparing, and packaging customers' orders for shipment.

Product Line Expansion

Blue Nile was selectively expanding its product offerings in terms of both price points and product mix. New product offerings included both customized and noncustomized jewelry items. Management believed that the online nature of Blue Nile's business, coupled with its supply arrangements where diamonds and other gemstones were purchased form suppliers only when an order was placed, allowed it to readily test shopper response to new diamond and gemstone offerings and to efficiently add promising new merchandise to its overall assortment of fine jewelry.

Expansion into International Markets

Blue Nile was selectively pursuing opportunities in those international markets where management believed the company could leverage its existing infrastructure and deliver compelling customer value. The decision to enter a new country market was based on the volume of consumer spending on jewelry, the extent to which consumers in a country were adopting online purchasing, the competitive landscape, and other factors. In August 2004, Blue Nile launched a Web site in the United Kingdom (www.bluenile.co.uk), offering a limited number of products; in September 2005, Blue Nile began providing customers at its U.K. Web site with the ability to customize their diamond jewelry purchases and to buy wedding bands. A Web site in Canada (www.bluenile.ca) was launched in January 2005. In 2006, both the U.K. and Canadian Web sites had more limited merchandise selections than the U.S. Web site and less developed search and educational features; the two international sites had combined sales of only $3.3 million in 2005.

Other Strategy Elements

Blue Nile's strategy had three other key elements:
- Blue Nile had a 30-day return policy that gave customers plenty of time to consider their purchase and make sure they had made a good decision. If customers were not satisfied for any reason, they could return any item without custom engraving in its original condition within 30 days of the date of shipment for a refund or an exchange. Requests for a refund or a different item were processed within a few days.
- Blue Nile offered free shipping with every order delivered to a U.S. address; orders were shipped via FedEx Express, FedEx Ground, or U.S. Postal Service, depending on order value and destination. All orders under $250 were shipped via FedEx Ground if within the 48 contiguous states or by U.S. Postal Service for destinations in Hawaii and Alaska. Orders between $250 and $1,000 were shipped via FedEx two-day delivery. All orders over $1,000 and all loose diamond orders were shipped via FedEx Priority Overnight. Customers had the option to upgrade the delivery of items under $1,000 to FedEx Priority Overnight for a $15 charge.

- Blue Nile automatically provided an appraisal stating the approximate retail replacement value of the item to customers who bought (1) a preset engagement ring priced under $2,500; (2) a diamond jewelry item priced $1,000 and over (except preset solitaire engagement rings, preset earrings, or preset solitaire pendants priced $2,500 or over which come with International Gemological Institute appraisals); or (3) any custom diamond ring, earring, or pendant. The appraisal value was based on current market data, typical retail prices, the weight of precious metal included in the item, craftsmanship, and the cut, color, clarity, and carat weight of the gemstone(s). Included with the appraisal was a brief description of the item being appraised, a photograph of the item, and the cut, color, clarity, and either carat weight for any diamonds, or millimeter dimensions for any gemstones. An appraisal represented value-added to customers because a customer had to have one to obtain insurance coverage and determine what constituted equal replacement in case of loss, theft, or damage.

BLUE NILE'S FINANCIAL AND STRATEGIC PERFORMANCE

During the 2001–2006 period, Blue Nile's sales jumped from $48.7 million to $251.6 million, a compound average growth rate of almost 39 percent. Gross profits (sales minus cost of goods sold) rose from $11.1 million in 2001 to $50.9 million in 2006, equal to a compound average growth rate of 35.6 percent. And the company's bottom-line performance was vastly improved, going from a net loss of $7.4 million in 2001 to a net profit of $13.1 million in 2006 (although net profit was flat from 2005 to 2006). The company generated $40.5 million in cash from operations in 2006 and had a largely debt-free balance sheet going into both 2006 and 2007. Exhibit 4 presents highlights of Blue Nile's financial results from fiscal years 2001 through 2006. In fiscal year 2007, Blue Nile's management expected that net sales would be between $290 million and $300 million, with net income in the range of $0.80 to $0.85 per diluted share.

Exhibit 4   **Selected Financial Data, Blue Nile Inc., 2001–2006
($ in thousands, except per share data)**

	Year Ended Jan. 3, 2007	Year Ended Jan. 2, 2006	Year Ended Jan. 1, 2005	Years Ended December 31		
				2003	2002	2001
Income Statement Data						
Net sales	$251,587	$203,169	$169,242	$128,894	$72,120	$48,674
Cost of sales*	200,734	158,025	131,590	99,476	53,967	37,551
Gross profit	50,853	45,144	37,652	29,418	18,153	11,123
Selling, general and administrative expenses	34,296	27,095	22,295	18,207	14,126	15,421
Restructuring charges	—	—	—	(87)	400	1,017
Operating income (loss)	16,557	18,049	14,857	11,298	3,627	(5,315)
Other income (expense)	3,423	2,504	772	(12)	(2,000)	(2,045)
Income (loss) before income taxes	19,980	20,553	15,629	11,286	1,627	(7,360)
Income tax expense (benefit)	6,916	7,400	5,642	(15,700)	—	—
Net income (loss)	$ 13,064	$ 13,153	$ 9,987	$ 26,986	$ 1,627	$(7,360)
Basic net income (loss) per share	$0.79	$0.75	$0.80	$6.98	$0.49	$(2.44)
Diluted net income (loss) per share	$0.76	$0.71	$0.51	$1.65	$0.11	$(2.44)
Weighted average shares outstanding:						
Basic	16,563	17,550	12,450	3,868	3,336	3,015
Diluted	17,278	18,597	17,885	16,363	14,160	3,015
Balance Sheet Data						
Cash and cash equivalents	$ 78,540	$ 71,921	$ 59,499	$ 30,383	$22,597	$16,298
Marketable securities	19,767	42,748	41,868	—	—	—
Accounts receivable	1,640	1,877	1.028	916	481	92
Inventories	14,616	11,764	9,914	10,204	5,181	6,619
Total current assets	116,018	132,496	121,529	47,595	n.a.	n.a.
Accounts payable	66,625	50,157	37,775	26,288	15,791	5,253
Total current liabilities	74,137	55,627	43,691	30,932	n.a.	n.a.
Working capital	41,881	76,869	77,838	16,663	1,795	9,021
Total assets	122,106	138,005	128,382	62,305	30,914	26,545
Total long-term obligations	666	863	1,071	1,126	1,091	10,789
Total stockholders' equity (deficit)	47,303	81,515	83,620	(27,238)	(54,560)	(56,199)
Cash Flow Data						
Net cash provided by operating activities	$ 40,518	$ 31,272	$ 29,751	$ 19,816	$16,730	$ 4,460
Net cash used in investing activities	21,065	(2,053)	(43,296)	(3,503)	(1,041)	n.a.
Net cash provided by (used in) financing activities	(54,964)	(16,797)	42,661	(8,527)	(9,390)	n.a.

*Cost of sales included purchases from suppliers, inbound and outbound shipping costs, insurance on shipments, and jewelry assembly costs.

n.a. = not available.

Source: Company 10-K reports, 2004, 2005, and 2006 and company press release, February 12, 2007.

Exhibit 5   **The Cash-Generating Capability of Blue Nile's Business Model**

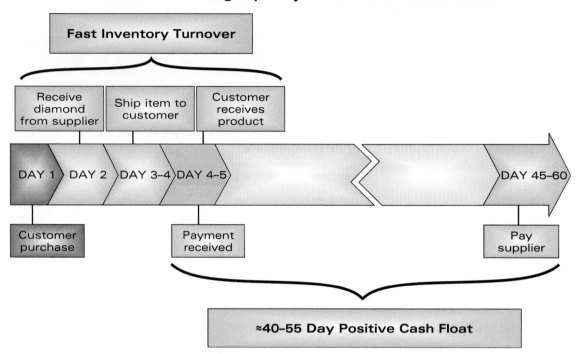

Source: Blue Nile Management Presentation, Goldman Sachs Seventh Annual Internet Conference, May 24, 2006.

One of the big appeals of Blue Nile's business model was the ability to generate cash 40 to 55 days ahead of the need to pay suppliers; in a very real sense, Blue Nile's business model was self-funding because suppliers financed Blue Nile's sales growth—see Exhibit 5. Moreover, the company's business model was readily scalable to substantially higher sales volumes with minimal additional capital investment. Blue Nile's capital expenditures for facilities and equipment were a meager $3.5 million in 2003, $1.4 million in 2004, $1.1 million in 2005, and $1.9 million in 2006. Capital expenditures for fiscal 2007 were budgeted at $4.0 million.

Blue Nile executives believed the company's market position was highly defensible. The company had negotiated exclusive and highly favorable arrangements with a number of diamond and gemstone suppliers that allowed it to offer a broad range and selection of fine jewelry products with minimal inventory, it had a very lean cost structure, and it had created a premium brand name and brand awareness that competitors would have difficulty replicating. While Blue Nile's competitiveness was dependent on maintaining favorable arrangements with its suppliers,

the company was somewhat protected by having negotiated agreements with a variety of suppliers, thus limiting its dependence on particular suppliers—in 2004 and 2005, the top three suppliers accounted for only 25 percent of the company's purchases. Moreover, the supply arrangements were favorable to suppliers, providing them with real-time market intelligence about what items were selling, the potential of high sales volume through a single account, and a way to achieve more inventory turns and otherwise manage their own inventories more efficiently.

Stock Issues and Repurchases

Blue Nile became a public company in 2004, selling some 2.3 million shares of common stock at $20.50 per share and realizing proceeds of $42.5 million after expenses. Trading of the company's stock began on May 20, 2004, on the NASDAQ exchange under the symbol NILE. Since trading began, the stock had traded as low as $22.50 (August 2004) and as high as $43 (December 2005); the stock price hovered in the $30 to $35 range during the January–August 2006 period.

Blue Nile had several stock-based compensation plans, under which stock options could be issued to officers, employees, non-employee directors, and consultants. Going into 2006, stock options for just over 2 million shares were outstanding, about 1.1 million of which were exercisable in 2006. Blue Nile also had an employee stock purchase plan, but no shares had been issued as of January 1, 2006.

Blue Nile repurchased about 3.3 percent of its outstanding shares of common stock in 2005 at a cost of $17.4 million; the company spent $57.4 million to repurchase about 1.8 million shares in 2006.

INDUSTRY GROWTH AND COMPETITION

According to U.S. Department of Commerce data, total U.S. jewelry sales, including watches and fashion jewelry, were $59 billion in 2005, up from $57 billion in 2004. The U.S. jewelry market had grown at a compound annual growth rate of 5.7 percent over the last 25 years. Jewelry sales in the United States grew by 4.6 percent in 2004, 2.9 percent in 2003, 8.0 percent in 2004, and 2.7 percent in 2005; they were forecast to grow 6.0 percent in 2006.[12] Sales were somewhat seasonal, with relatively higher sales in February (Valentine's Day), May (Mother's Day), and the October–December holiday shopping season. Sales of diamond jewelry in the United States were an estimated $32.5 billion in 2005 and were believed to represent about 50 percent of the global diamond jewelry market.[13]

The diamond and fine jewelry retail market was intensely competitive, with sales highly fragmented among locally owned jewelry stores (34 percent); retail jewelry store chains with 100+ stores (13 percent); numerous chain department stores

Exhibit 6   **Major U.S. Retailers of Jewelry, 2005**

	General Retailers of Jewelry			Specialty Retailers of Jewelry	
Rank	Retailer	2005 Sales (in billions)	Retailer		2005 Sales (in billions)
1	Wal-Mart	$2.7	Zale Corp. (2,300+ locations in the United States, Canada, and Puerto Rico)*		$2.4
2	QVC	1.4	Sterling (Kay Jewelers, Jared, and assorted regional retailers)*		2.3
3	JCPenney	1.2	Tiffany (150 stores in U.S. and international locations)		1.2
4	Sears	1.1	Helzberg Diamonds (270 locations)		0.5
5	Finlay	1.0	Fred Meyer (430 stores in 34 states under the brands Fred Meyer Jewelers, Littman Jewelers, and Barclay Jewelers)		0.5
6	Costco	0.4	Whitehall (386 stores in 38 states under the brands Whitehall, Lundstrom, and Marks Bros.)		0.3
7	Home Shopping Network	0.4	Friedman's (420+ locations in 20 states)		0.3
8	Target	0.4	Ross-Simon (14 stores in 9 states, plus catalog sales)		0.3
9	Jewelry Television	0.4	Tourneau (30 locations in 13 states)***		0.3
10	Neiman-Marcus	0.4	Ben Bridge Jeweler (70+ stores in 12 mostly western states)**		0.2
	Share of Overall Market	**15.9%**	**Share of Overall Market**		**13.7%**

*Sterling was a wholly owned subsidiary of Britain-based Signet Group, PLC; Sterling operated 781 Kay's Jewelry stores in 50 states, 110 Jared Galleria of Jewelry showrooms in 26 states, and 330 other regional stores under a variety of brand names in 31 states.

**Became a subsidiary of Warren Buffet's Berkshire Hathaway in 2000.

***Tourneau's sales were heavily concentrated in fine watches.

Source: Company Web sites, plus information posted at www.signetgroupplc.com (accessed August 25, 2006).

(12 percent); online retailers that sold fine jewelry and online auction sites (4 percent); television shopping retailers (4 percent); mass merchants, such as discount superstores and wholesale clubs whose merchandise offerings included fine jewelry (10 percent); and all other retailers, such as general merchandise and clothing stores and catalog retailers (23 percent). The Jewelry Board of Trade estimated that there were some 24,500 specialty jewelry firms in the United States in 2005, down from 26,750 specialty jewelry retailer in 1999. However, the number of stores operated by specialty jewelry retailers increased by about 700 stores over the same period, reflecting a continuing industry trend toward consolidation; the five largest specialty jewelry retailers in the United States had increased their collective share from about 18 percent to about 24 percent of specialty jewelry sales since 1999. Nonetheless, independent jewelers, including those with fewer than 100 stores, accounted for about 70 percent of the sales made by specialty jewelry retailers.

Blue Nile's primary competition came from both online and offline retailers that offered products within the higher value segment of the jewelry market. Many brick-and-mortar jewelry retailers (including market leaders Zale, Sterling, Tiffany, and Helzberg, among many others) had recently begun selling jewelry online at their Web sites. The principal competitive factors in the fine jewelry market were product selection and quality, price, customer service and support, brand recognition, reputation, reliability and trust, and, in the case of online retailers, Web site features and functionality, convenience, and speed of delivery.

The Online Jewelry Industry

Jewelry e-tailers sold approximately $340 million worth of engagement rings in 2005; online sales of other types of rings and jewelry items were another $2 billion in 2005.[14] A majority of those sales were said to be to men, chiefly because they were more amenable than women to shopping for jewelry online. The primary appeal of buying diamonds and jewelry online was lower prices. Most online jewelry retailers employed a business model similar to Blue Nile's, keeping their inventories lean, purchasing stones from suppliers only when an order for a specific stone was received, and delivering the merchandise a few days after the order was placed.

Blue Nile's Online Competitors

There were dozens of online retailers of diamonds in 2006. Some were more reputable than others, and the sites varied considerably in terms of diamond selection, prices, customization options, educational information, product information, and access to professional grading reports, responsive customer service, and return policies. Popular sites, in addition to market leader Blue Nile, included Diamonds.com, Whiteflash.com. Ice.com, JamesAllen.com, Overstock.com, and Amazon.com.

Diamonds.com. Diamonds.com was founded in 2000 and headquartered in Las Vegas; the principal owners had over 25 years experience in all areas of the diamond industry. The company's product offering included over 40,000 loose diamonds sourced from New York City's famed 47th Street diamond district, along with a selection of settings, rings, bracelets, necklaces, and earrings. There was extensive educational information on the Diamonds.com Web site; the discussion of the four C's of purchasing a diamond was lucid and informative. There was a search function that allowed site visitors to search the loose diamond inventory based on shape, carat size, cut, color, clarity, and price. Shoppers had the ability to customize their purchase by choosing a stone and a setting. Diamond grading reports issued by either the Gemological Institute of America or the American Gemological Society Laboratory could be viewed online for all loose diamonds, shipping was free, and orders came with an identifying grading reports and warranty document. Customers could return noncustomized orders for a full refund (excluding shipping, handling, and insurance) for up to 30 days after delivery; returns were not accepted on custom work or special orders unless an error had been made. The staff at Diamonds.com included expert gemologists trained at the world's leading gemological laboratories; shoppers could call a toll-free number for assistance or to place a phone order.

Whiteflash.com. About half of Whiteflash's sales involved orders for customized jewelry. Whiteflash had a small inventory (about 1,000 stones) and was said to charge higher prices than Blue Nile and many other e-tailers.[15] One distinctive strategy element was its trade-up program, whereby a customer could trade in a jewelry item purchased from Whitehall for a higher-priced item and only pay the difference between the new item and the previously purchased item. Whiteflash had a policy of not accepting returns on customized jewelry products unless an error had been made in doing the custom work; for loose stones and standard settings, Whiteflash offered a full refund 10 days from receipt for any reason. The education materials at the Whiteflash Web site included video tutorials.

Ice.com.   Over 300,000 customers had made purchases at Ice.com since it began online operations in 2001. Ice's product line included rings, necklaces, earrings, bracelets, pendants, and watches. Its product offerings were all finished products; no customization options were available. The average purchase was about $210 (versus over $1,600 at Blue Nile). The company had a monthly payment option, provided free shipping on orders over $150, and had an unconditional 30-day money-back guarantee. Bridal and engagement rings came with an appraisal certificate. There was no educational information on the company's Web site, and the information provided about the quality of its diamond jewelry was limited. Customers could make inquiries via a toll-free number or e-mail.

JamesAllen.com.   Founded in 1998 by James Allen Schultz and his wife Michele Sigler, JamesAllen.com had grown to be one of the largest online diamond retailers. The firm's strategy centered around offering "the world's most beautiful engagement rings coupled with the finest laboratory graded diamonds, all at an extraordinary value." It had been featured in such trade magazines as *National Jeweler* and profiled by the *Washington Post, U.S. News & World Report*, NBC News, and National Public Radio. While an estimated 3 percent of the round diamonds sold in the United States qualified as "Ideal" under AGSL grading standards, over 90 percent of the customers shopping at JamesAllen.com chose diamonds from the retailer's Signature Ideal, Ideal, or Premium categories. All stones came with grading reports from either the Gemological Institute of America or the American Gemological Society Laboratory.

Management claimed that no other company offered a finer collection of top-quality cut diamonds. The product offerings at JamesAllen.com product offerings included 55,000 loose diamonds, preset engagement rings, preset wedding and anniversary rings, diamond studs, diamond jewelry, and designer jewelry by Amy Levine, Danhov, and Leo Popov. Shoppers could customize their own diamond rings, studs, and pendants. The JamesAllen.com Web site had a comprehensive Education section that featured an interactive demonstration of the importance of diamond cut, 3D viewing, and tips and search tools. An expert staff answered questions via phone or e-mail. Payment options included credit card, wire transfer, personal check, certified check, or money order. JamesAllen.com provided free overnight shipping via FedEx or UPS on all orders within the United States. Orders outside the United States had to be prepaid via wire transfer and carried a shipping fee of $100. The company had a full 30-day return policy, but loose diamond returns that did not include the original laboratory grading report were subject to a charge of $150.

Endnotes

[1] Sean O'Neill, "Clicks and Stones," *Kiplinger's Personal Finance*, February 2006, www.kiplinger.com/personalfinance/magazine/archives/2006/02/diamonds.html (accessed August 7, 2006).

[2] Ibid.

[3] According to information posted at www.bluenile.com (accessed August 8, 2006).

[4] Sean O'Neill, "Get a Diamond Deal Online," *Kiplinger's Personal Finance*, November 14, 2006, www.kiplinger.com/features/archives/2006/11/diamonds.html (accessed February 1, 2007).

[5] Blue Nile management presentation, Goldman Sachs Seventh Annual Internet Conference, May 24, 2006, available at www.bluenile.com (accessed August 8, 2006).

[6] Ibid.

[7] Blue Nile's 2005 10-K report, p. 4.

[8] Citigroup securities analyst Mark Mahaney, "The Long Case for Online Jewelry Retailer Blue Nile," March 31, 2006, available at

http://internet.seekingalpha.com/article/8418 (accessed August 25, 2006).

[9] Shruti Basavaraj, "The $324,000 Question," The Motley Fool, November 28, 2006, www.fool.com (accessed February 1, 2007).

[10] Sean O'Neill, "Clicks and Stones" *Kiplinger's Personal Finance*, February 2006, www.kiplinger.com/personalfinance/magazine/archives/2006/02/diamonds.html (accessed August 7, 2006).

[11] As cited in "Internet Retailer Best of the Web 2007," *Internet Retailer*, December 2006, www.internetretailer.com (accessed February 1, 2007).

[12] IDEX Online Research, "U.S. Jewelry Sales Strong in June," August 15, 2006, www.idexonline.com (accessed August 25, 2006).

[13] Information posted at www.signetgroupplc.com (accessed August 25, 2006).

[14] O'Neill, "Clicks and Stones."

[15] Ibid.

Eat2Eat.com

Kenneth G. Hardy
University of Western Ontario

EAT2EAT.COM

Eat2Eat.com was the most highly rated Internet-based restaurant reservation service covering major cities in the Asia Pacific region. It was the principal business of Singapore-based Eat2Eat Pte Ltd (Eat2Eat). Eat2Eat.com had firmly established its technology, business model and industry relationships. However, after five years of operation, the Web site's registered user base remained at approximately 12,000 customers. In January 2006, founder and Chief Executive Officer Vikram Aggarwal was considering new ways to promote the company and the Web site. Eat2Eat had limited resources, so Aggarwal knew his methods would have to be innovative, efficient and effective.

Nigel Goodwin prepared this case under the supervision of Professor Kenneth G. Hardy solely to provide material for class discussion. The authors do not intend to illustrate either effective or ineffective handling of a managerial situation. The authors may have disguised certain names and other identifying information to protect confidentiality.

Ivey Management Services prohibits any form of reproduction, storage or transmittal without its written permission. This material is not covered under authorization from CanCopy or any reproduction rights organization. To order copies or request permission to reproduce materials, contact Ivey Publishing, Ivey Management Services, c/o Richard Ivey School of Business, The University of Western Ontario, London, Ontario, Canada, N6A 3K7; phone (519) 661-3208; fax (519) 661-3882; e-mail cases@ivey.uwo.ca.
Copyright © 2006, Ivey Management Services Version: (A) 2006-08-10

COMPANY ORIGIN

In the late 1990s, Aggarwal had been an investment banker specializing in the high-technology sector at Chase Manhattan in Tokyo. He had seen many entrepreneurs launch their own companies and was confident he could do the same. When Chase Manhattan merged with JP Morgan in 2000, Aggarwal's group was dissolved. He accepted an exit package, voluntarily left the bank and decided to launch his own Internet company.

Aggarwal saw an opportunity in online restaurant bookings. He noticed that airline bookings, hotel reservations and car rentals were highly automated processes, with customers frequently searching for information and transacting business online. However, there was little or no similar automation for restaurant reservations. The technology discrepancy was particularly noticeable in the case of hotel restaurants: a consumer could reserve a room at a hotel online, but not a table at the hotel's restaurant.[1] Many corporations—particularly large ones—negotiated special room rates for employees at preferred hotels, but did not negotiate discounts at preferred restaurants. Given that business dinners were a common occurrence, Aggarwal wondered why corporations had not extended their purchasing power to restaurants in the same way they exercised it with hotels.

Aggarwal believed there was a value proposition in connecting diners—both corporate and personal—with restaurants. He believed diners could benefit from accessing a wealth of information on restaurant options, conveniently reserving tables online and receiving loyalty points or discounts. Moreover, he believed restaurants could benefit by having a presence on the Internet, an increasingly popular medium.

ESTABLISHMENT AND BUSINESS MODEL

In 2000, Aggarwal relocated to Singapore, registered Eat2Eat Pte Ltd and began running the company out of his home. He hired a chief technology officer and a programmer, both based in India, to develop the Web site and the supporting technology. Aggarwal himself signed up the first participating restaurants. The English version of the Web site was launched in July 2001. Aggarwal wanted to retain full ownership and control, and subsequently financed the company himself. He invested US$1 million from his personal savings and his exit package from Chase Manhattan. Aggarwal eventually hired two other people to help with the workload, one in Singapore and one in Sydney.

Eat2Eat.com was an Internet-based restaurant portal promoting fine dining in the Asia Pacific region. The Web site was a guide to the region's best restaurants with an online reservation service. Features included restaurant reviews, recipes, interviews with leading chefs and lists of top establishments in various categories. By January 2006, Eat2Eat.com covered more than 800 restaurants in Bangkok, Hong Kong, Kuala Lumpur, Shanghai, Singapore, Seoul, Sydney, Taipei and Tokyo. The company was also launching in Kyoto, Melbourne and Phuket. The original Web site appeared in English, but equivalent sites had also been launched in Japanese and Korean to cover the restaurants in Tokyo and Seoul, respectively.

Core Business: Restaurant Reservations and Advertisements

Eat2Eat.com allowed diners to reserve tables through the Internet, conveniently and with a wealth of supporting information. Aggarwal met with restaurant managers in cities across the Asia Pacific region and encouraged them to participate. (See Exhibit 1 for participating restaurants by city.) He negotiated discounts for corporate customers and commissions for Eat2Eat, and then listed the restaurants on the Web site. A registered customer wishing to make a meal reservation visited the Web site and used a simple booking interface to select a restaurant, date, time and party size.[2] See Exhibit 2 for registered customers by city.

Exhibit 1   **Eat2Eat.com Participating Restaurants by City, 2000–2005**

	Participating Restaurants					
	2000	**2001**	**2002**	**2003**	**2004**	**2005**
Bangkok	–	–	12	32	58	98
Hong Kong	–	18	42	84	97	112
Kuala Lumpur	–	6	30	54	66	72
Shanghai	–	–	6	48	60	62
Singapore	–	24	84	102	120	174
Seoul	–	–	–	4	18	72
Sydney	–	30	66	94	98	137
Taipei	–	–	–	–	–	23
Tokyo	–	–	6	14	44	73
Total	0	78	246	432	561	823

Note: Actual figures have been disguised for the purpose of confidentiality.
Note: Figures do not include Kyoto, Melbourne or Phuket. Eat2Eat was in the process of launching in those cities.
Source: Company files.

Exhibit 2   Eat2Eat.com New Customer Registrations by City, 2000–2005

	Registered Users						
	2000	2001	2002	2003	2004	2005	Total
Bangkok	–	–	30	18	48	100	196
Hong Kong	–	300	324	94	576	804	2,098
Kuala Lumpur	–	60	126	30	324	509	1,049
Shanghai	–	30	65	14	54	70	233
Singapore	–	126	204	42	391	778	1,541
Seoul	–	–	–	84	204	402	690
Sydney	–	48	222	90	120	204	684
Taipei	–	–	–	–	–	300	300
Tokyo	–	152	466	694	1,176	2,580	5,068
Total	0	716	1,437	1,066	2,893	5,747	11,859

Note: Actual figures have been disguised for the purpose of confidentiality.

Note: Figures do not include Kyoto, Melbourne or Phuket. Eat2Eat was in the process of launching in those cities.

Source: Company files.

The restaurants could be searched by various criteria, including location, ambiance, accessibility for disabled diners, smoking preference, cuisine, price range, quality rating and hotel affiliation (if applicable). Customers received loyalty points that could be redeemed during future restaurant visits.

Eat2Eat contacted the restaurant the day after the reservation date, confirmed that the customer had actually eaten there and invoiced the restaurant for the agreed-upon commission.[3] Commissions varied depending on the restaurant in question, but typically were between seven to 10 percent of the customer's bill. In 2005, these reservations contributed 40 percent of Eat2Eat's total revenue of US$478,000. (See Exhibit 3 for annual revenue, profit and loss figures.)

The company also sold Web site banner advertisements to restaurants wanting additional promotion. In 2005, advertisements on Eat2Eat.com contributed an additional 20 percent of the company's total revenue.

Eat2Eat.com had received considerable recognition. A poll taken by the Smart Diners Organization in the United States had rated Eat2Eat.com as the top restaurant information and reservation site in the world. In addition, Google and Yahoo! search engines consistently ranked Eat2Eat.com first in search results for Asian restaurant reviews and reservations.

There were other restaurant portals on the Internet, covering Asia Pacific and other regions, but Eat2Eat.com was different. Most of the other portals derived revenue from advertising alone, and subsequently depended on hits and click-through statistics. Also, the other Asia Pacific portals were city-specific, whereas Eat2Eat.com offered regional coverage.

In 2004 Aggarwal adapted Eat2Eat.com to make its content and booking function accessible through WAP-enabled mobile phones.[4] He believed this added accessibility would significantly extend the company's reach and utilization, considering the high penetration of mobile phones in the region. The service became popular in Tokyo and Seoul, but lagged elsewhere. Aggarwal was disappointed the service had not found greater acceptance in cities such as Hong Kong and Singapore. In the latter cities, virtually every person carried a multi-function mobile phone and people were very savvy about applications such as customized ring tones, photographs and games. Aggarwal suspected people in these cities were uncomfortable in actually making transactions using the new technology.

Complementary Business: Third-Party Sourcing

Aggarwal also engaged in another, complementary business: negotiating preferred arrangements between credit card companies and restaurants for

Exhibit 3   **Eat2Eat Revenue, Profit and Loss by City, 2000–2005**

		Revenue, Profit and Loss (Annual, in US$000's)						
		2000	2001	2002	2003	2004	2005	Total
Bangkok	Revenue	–	–	–	4	6	8	18
	Cost	–	–	18	30	17	30	95
	Profit / (Loss)	–	–	(18)	(26)	(11)	(22)	(77)
Hong Kong	Revenue	–	8	24	6	54	66	158
	Cost	6	28	41	30	24	32	161
	Profit / (Loss)	(6)	(19)	(17)	(24)	30	34	(2)
Kuala Lumpur	Revenue	–	18	31	8	34	56	148
	Cost	4	18	30	30	36	37	155
	Profit / (Loss)	(4)	0	1	(22)	(2)	19	(7)
Shanghai	Revenue	–	–	20	2	24	22	68
	Cost	–	41	66	18	34	44	203
	Profit / (Loss)	–	(41)	(46)	(16)	(10)	(23)	(134)
Singapore	Revenue	–	12	36	18	70	91	227
	Cost	162	180	156	114	144	144	900
	Profit / (Loss)	(162)	(168)	(120)	(96)	(74)	(53)	(673)
Seoul	Revenue	–	–	–	–	12	42	54
	Cost	–	–	–	18	66	36	120
	Profit / (Loss)	–	–	–	(18)	(54)	6	(66)
Sydney	Revenue	–	18	60	48	48	46	220
	Cost	12	96	96	42	36	48	330
	Profit / (Loss)	(12)	(78)	(36)	6	12	(2)	(110)
Taipei	Revenue	–	–	–	–	–	18	18
	Cost	–	–	–	–	–	48	48
	Profit / (Loss)	–	–	–	–	–	(30)	(30)
Tokyo	Revenue	–	–	30	54	90	128	302
	Cost	6	30	70	90	98	114	408
	Profit / (Loss)	(6)	(30)	(40)	(36)	(8)	14	(106)
Total	Revenue	–	56	202	140	337	478	1,213
	Cost	190	392	476	372	455	534	2,419
	Profit / (Loss)	(190)	(336)	(275)	(232)	(118)	(56)	(1,206)

Note: Actual figures have been disguised for the purpose of confidentiality.
Source: Company files.

the benefit of credit card holders. Credit card companies typically offered special deals and perks for cardholders, including discounts at preferred restaurants, spas, sporting venues and retail stores. The card companies' motivations were to attract and retain cardholders by offering superior value, and to encourage cardholders to use the cards, thereby bolstering loyalty and increasing transaction volume.

The credit card companies did not negotiate the arrangements themselves; instead, their marketing teams outsourced the job to third parties. Because Aggarwal already negotiated with restaurants to sign them up for the Web site, he found it was a natural extension to source restaurants for credit card companies as well. In 2005, third-party negotiations contributed the remaining 40 percent of Eat2Eat's revenue.

SEGMENTATION AND APPROACH TO MARKET

Reaching the Restaurants

Aggarwal dealt exclusively with what he described as first-tier restaurants. First-tier restaurants were typically those that accepted reservations, were moderately expensive, or were very popular and busy. Second-tier restaurants did not accept reservations and therefore were of no concern to Aggarwal.

Aggarwal approached the restaurants himself to sign them up as suppliers. This task typically involved traveling to the 12 cities covered by Eat2Eat.com and personally meeting with restaurant managers. In some cities, the restaurants were predominantly chain organizations, while in other cities they were predominantly independently owned. A single chain might have many restaurants, so at first glance a chain-focused approach seemed more efficient. However, it usually took much more time and effort to sign up a chain than a single independent restaurant.

The restaurant reviews posted on Eat2Eat.com were written by Aggarwal and his two employees. He had considered adding reviews by professional restaurant critics, but had decided against it since critics and their publications typically demanded payment for reprinting their reviews. Also, many restaurant reviews in Asia were actually written as promotional pieces on the restaurants' behalf, and Aggarwal felt such reviews were neither independent nor objective. He did consider adding user reviews, as Asia-Hotels.com did for hotels, but had not yet taken any action in that direction.

Market Characteristics

As he traveled, Aggarwal gathered information on the different markets. He was particularly interested in population density, dining habits, the presence of first-tier restaurants, broadband Internet penetration and receptivity to new marketing and distribution tactics. The information helped him select new restaurants to pursue as suppliers. See Exhibit 4 for some of Aggarwal's market observations.

Promotional Strategies

In the beginning, Aggarwal focused his promotional efforts on corporate customers. People who planned business dinners invariably made reservations; by contrast, timing and restaurant choice for personal dining were often spontaneous. Also, Aggarwal thought personal diners were too numerous and, consequently, too difficult and expensive to reach. He thought the corporate approach would bring more value for his efforts and would be the best way to reach customers.

Aggarwal approached large corporations and asked them to encourage their employees to sign up for the service. Because corporations reimbursed their employees for business lunches and dinners, the discounts available for meals reserved through Eat2Eat.com essentially offered the corporations a cost reduction. The service was easy for clients to find, preview and reserve at good restaurants, and users received loyalty points that could be redeemed for free meals in the future.

Aggarwal was pleased with the adoption rates from the targeted corporations. Roughly 80 percent of the companies he approached endorsed the program. At those companies, typically 15 percent of employees would register as Eat2Eat.com users with 10 percent becoming active users. Most of the active users were secretaries and personal assistants to executives because they were the people typically tasked with arranging business functions. They spent most of the workday at their desks with broadband Internet connections, so it was easy for them to access Eat2Eat.com. Also, Eat2Eat.com simplified the task of finding and reserving at an appropriate restaurant.

This approach worked well in most of the cities in question, but Aggarwal found a different strategy worked better in Tokyo. In his opinion, Japanese corporations were reluctant to try new ideas. Also, many first-tier restaurants in Japan had their own Web sites. Those Web sites provided information to customers, but did not support online reservations because the required technology was too complex. Eat2Eat.com enabled the reservations for the restaurants' Web sites, so when a customer viewed a restaurant Web site and wanted to reserve a table,

Exhibit 4 **Market Observations**

City	Description
Bangkok	<ul><li>Fragmented restaurant industry with broad range of dining options</li><li>Opportunities primarily in the mature hotel industry, particularly with established chains that E2E has worked with elsewhere</li><li>Low Internet penetration</li><li>Language issues</li><li>Difficult to gain customer acceptance</li></ul>
Hong Kong	<ul><li>High Internet penetration but low transaction volume</li><li>High population density with easy movement around the island</li><li>Many corporate head offices</li><li>Many restaurants, but choice normally based on proximity to office</li><li>Free local phone calls made it easy to reserve by phone</li><li>Language issues</li></ul>
Kuala Lumpur	<ul><li>Broad restaurant base and large dining population</li><li>Tendency to choose restaurants by the type of food</li><li>High restaurant turnover, which encouraged marketing innovations</li><li>Customers willing to try new technology</li><li>Growing market of visitors from the Middle East</li><li>Spontaneity in dining leading to no-shows and multiple bookings</li><li>Low Internet penetration</li></ul>
Shanghai	<ul><li>Rapidly growing local market</li><li>Strong business from overseas, with visitors to Shanghai willing to book tables in advance</li><li>Unscrupulous restaurant managers posing difficulties for E2E</li><li>Busy restaurants not requiring any promotional support</li><li>Language issues</li><li>Low Internet penetration</li></ul>
Singapore	<ul><li>Vibrant dining scene, with hotel restaurants and many new eateries opening outside hotels as well</li><li>Tendency for restaurants to cluster in common areas</li><li>Willingness to try any restaurant at least once</li><li>Government initiatives to support Internet business</li><li>High Internet penetration but reluctance to transact business online</li><li>Restaurateurs' resistance to new promotion/distribution channels</li></ul>
Seoul	<ul><li>High WAP acceptance</li><li>Busy city with many dining options, so restaurant managers valued the promotional assistance</li><li>Many international visitors willing to book tables</li><li>Language issues</li></ul>
Sydney	<ul><li>Dining well-established as a pastime</li><li>Many new restaurants</li><li>Many visitors from overseas</li><li>Higher margins for Eat2Eat.com</li><li>Reluctance to provide personal information over the Internet</li></ul>
Taipei	<ul><li>Busy city with established dining scene</li><li>High Internet penetration</li><li>Web-based reservations new and considered trendy</li><li>Relatively low number of first-tier restaurants</li></ul>

(*Continued*)

Exhibit 4   **Continued**

City	Description
Tokyo	• High Internet penetration • Widespread WAP use, and marketing on mobile phones widely practiced and accepted • Huge city with established dining culture and countless restaurants • Widespread acceptance among local population • Major foreign presence in the city as well • Difficulty in growing fast enough and keeping up with the ever-changing environment

Note: Information unavailable for Kyoto, Melbourne, and Phuket.
Source: Company files.

that customer was redirected to Eat2Eat.com's own booking engine. This model proved to be popular among Tokyo's personal diners.

The adaptation of Eat2Eat.com for mobile phones also bolstered the Web site's success in Tokyo. As with Korean customers in Seoul, Japanese customers in Tokyo were comfortable finding information and transacting business through that medium.

By the end of 2005, Eat2Eat.com had almost 12,000 registered users. Approximately 43 percent of those users lived in Tokyo, and most of them were personal customers making reservations for their own dining. The remaining 57 percent of registered users lived in other markets, and most of them were secretaries or personal assistants reserving tables for corporate dining.

Expanding in the Personal Market

Although Aggarwal had built a solid user base through the corporate market, he knew he would have to tap the personal market (beyond Tokyo) if Eat2Eat were to reach its potential. However, the company did not have the employees or financial resources needed to pursue such a vast market. Aggarwal believed Eat2Eat would have to partner with other companies that already had large, established user bases and "piggyback" with them.

There were many possible options, including airlines, hotel chains, and local and regional newspapers. "There is no end of possible partners we could work with," he commented, "if we only had the time to approach them, convince them and develop the partnerships."

In May and June of 2004, Eat2Eat partnered with leading regional newspaper, *The Asian Wall Street Journal,* for the first Eat! promotion. The promotion tied in with a regular feature of the paper's Friday section in which food critics sought and reviewed the most authentic and exciting eateries in Asia's culinary capitals. This promotion was one of the paper's most popular features, with readers regularly contacting the paper to request more information or suggest additional eateries.

The three-week promotion featured 70 participating restaurants in Hong Kong, Kuala Lumpur and Singapore, with cuisine ranging from Mediterranean to Asian to fusion. The restaurants offered special set menus for lunch and dinner, featuring more variety and value than their regular offerings. Some restaurants also offered complementary glasses of wine or champagne. Diners could view restaurant details and menus and could make reservations online at www.eat2eat.com/awsj. The promotion was held for a second time in September 2005, when, in addition to the original cities, it was expanded to include Seoul and Taipei for a total of 101 participating restaurants.

The Eat! promotion had little immediate impact on Eat2Eat.com reservations and revenue, but it did give the Web site a great deal of publicity that would likely attract more users and reservations in the longer term. Also, it allowed Aggarwal to expand his restaurant base in current cities and establish his business in new cities, such as Taipei.

Aggarwal thought credit card companies would be another natural avenue for reaching personal customers. He had already negotiated restaurant deals on the companies' behalf so he had the necessary contacts and credibility. He thought it would be logical to extend the arrangements to cover online bookings.

When credit card companies sent monthly statements to cardholders, they often included brochures of benefits for cardholders, including discounts at restaurants, spas, hotels and entertainment venues. The credit card companies also maintained Web sites with the same information, but they were basic information Web sites and were rarely visited by cardholders. Aggarwal wanted to enhance the Web sites by tying them to Eat2Eat.com and providing booking functionality.

Credit card companies would benefit from such arrangements by driving more cardholders to their Web sites. Such interaction would build customer loyalty and also increase transactions on the credit cards, which would be the reason for offering such deals in the first place. Restaurants would likewise benefit by attracting more customers. Finally, Eat2Eat would benefit by leveraging the credit card companies' large user bases. A partnership with a single credit card company might expose Eat2Eat. com to millions of new customers.

The idea made sense to Aggarwal, but he admitted it was hard to convince the credit card companies to buy into it. It required a shift in their thinking, which he was finding difficult to achieve. The marketing teams at credit card companies turned over quickly. Just when Aggarwal made headway with them, the representatives changed and he had to start over with new people. Aggarwal had been trying to negotiate such arrangements for five years and still had not closed any deals, although he felt he was close with at least one company.

RAISING ADDITIONAL CAPITAL

Eat2Eat had established a strong presence with Aggarwal's initial investment, but additional funding would be required to reach the next level. Aggarwal and his two employees spent practically all their time managing the company's day-to-day operations and had little time for additional strategic developments or promotional activities. Aggarwal thought this lack of strategic focus inhibited Eat2Eat's growth

and put the company at a competitive disadvantage. As he commented:

> I feel like I'm in a Formula One race with a private entry car. I compete with professional teams with major funding, and I'm always one or two laps behind, just trying to keep up.

Aggarwal hoped to raise US$2 million in additional capital. Roughly 50 percent of those funds would be allocated to establishing three or four new sales representatives throughout the region. The sales representatives would add more restaurants to the company's inventory. Each representative would be paid US$5,000 to US$6,000 per month and would incur related costs, including computers and travel expenses. It was difficult to estimate the return for investing in new sales representatives, but Aggarwal hoped the additional revenue would outweigh the additional costs by a factor of two to one.

Roughly 40 percent of the new capital would be spent on public relations and marketing activities to reach the personal dining market segment. Aggarwal planned to hire a well-known public relations firm with regional influence and expertise in the hospitality sector. A public relations campaign would begin in a single market, as a test of its effectiveness, before being rolled out to the rest of the region.

The remaining 10 percent of the new capital would be spent on a technology upgrade. The Eat2Eat.com Web site and the supporting software were currently hosted by a third party; Aggarwal wanted to set up his own server and support the Web site in-house. He also wanted to enhance the company's mobile phone functionality to enable more reservations. While the technology upgrade would not have a direct impact on Eat2Eat.com's revenue, it would support the company as a whole and improve operational efficiency.

Potential Sources for Additional Capital

Aggarwal considered debt financing but quickly dismissed the idea. He believed it would be difficult to obtain bank loans because Eat2Eat had not yet established a profitable track record. In fact, he believed it would be difficult for practically any early-stage Internet company to obtain bank loans for this reason. "If I were a banker," he mused, "I wouldn't loan money to this company."

He also contemplated a public stock offering, but likewise dismissed the idea. Eat2Eat simply did not have a big enough profile to make a public offering feasible or worthwhile.

Aggarwal thought he might find another Internet company willing to purchase a stake in Eat2Eat. He pointed to the recent example of Yahoo! purchasing a major stake in Alibaba.com, the Chinese online business-to-business marketplace.[5] The deal had received a great deal of publicity, and Aggarwal hoped it would galvanize the Asian Internet investment scene and inspire more deals in the sector. However, no other Internet companies had yet expressed an interest in buying into Eat2Eat.

Venture capital was a more likely option, although not necessarily a more favorable one. Aggarwal had been approached by several venture capital firms in recent months, but he had low expectations. He believed venture capitalists and entrepreneurs had inherently opposing objectives. The former wanted to buy into companies cheaply while the latter wanted to maximize investment value, so the two parties would naturally dispute the true value of a company's equity. Furthermore, a venture capitalist typically wanted to crystallize a profit from an investment within five years and wanted a return on investment in the 30 percent range. The venture capitalist would also impose a set of conditions (covenants) regarding the company's management and financial performance, and Aggarwal believed that in most cases those conditions might be difficult to meet.

Aggarwal had received telephone calls from other Asian restaurant Web site entrepreneurs trying to sell their businesses to him. Their companies were specific to certain cities, whereas Eat2Eat.com covered the entire region. Aggarwal considered buying or merging with another company to increase his restaurant inventory and user base, but only if such an amalgamation could be accomplished at a reasonable price. However, each of the companies concerned expected several million U.S. dollars for their equity, and Aggarwal was confident he could build or expand his business in any given city organically with a lower investment.

Aggarwal thought he would have to make a decision about new funding in the first half of 2006. He also thought it would be difficult to raise the money. Not only would it be hard to find the right investor, but the task would require more of his time, and his time was already in short supply.

AGGARWAL'S CHALLENGE

Aggarwal was proud of what Eat2Eat had achieved in its first five years, including its technology, industry recognition and value to both diners and restaurants. However, he knew the company would have to significantly expand its user base in 2006 and beyond. Such growth would be a difficult challenge, considering his limited time and financial capital. Aggarwal reviewed his current promotional strategies and tactics and wondered what he should do in the year ahead.

Endnotes

[1] While the example of hotel restaurants gave birth to the concept in Aggarwal's mind, he believed there were also innumerable restaurants not affiliated with hotels that could also benefit from online reservations.

[2] First-time users of the service were required to register as customers and provide some personal details. Registration was free.

[3] Coordination with the restaurants could be automated and conducted online. For restaurants that were not connected to the Internet, the process was conducted using facsimile (fax) machines. Thus, restaurants did not require Internet access to participate, although Internet access made the process more efficient for both the restaurants and for Eat2Eat.com.

[4] WAP, or wireless application protocol, was an open international standard for applications on wireless communication devices. A common example was Internet access on mobile phones.

[5] Alibaba.com operated the world's largest online marketplace for international and domestic China trade, as well as China's most widely used online payment system, AliPay. It had a community of more than 15 million businesses and consumers in more than 200 countries and territories. In 2004, Alibaba.com facilitated more than US$4 billion in trade. In August 2005, Yahoo! Inc. and Alibaba.com announced a long-term strategic partnership in China. The arrangement would promote the Yahoo! brand in China. Also, Yahoo! purchased US$1 billion of Alibaba.com shares, giving Yahoo! approximately 40 percent economic interest in the company.

Case 7

Panera Bread Company

Arthur A. Thompson
The University of Alabama

As Panera Bread Company headed into 2007, it was continuing to expand its market presence swiftly. The company's strategic intent was to make great bread broadly available to consumers across the United States. It had opened 155 new company-owned and franchised bakery-cafés in 2006, bringing its total to 1,027 units in 36 states. Plans were in place to open another 170 to 180 café locations in 2007 and to have nearly 2,000 Panera Bread bakery-cafés open by the end of 2010. Management was confident that Panera Bread's attractive menu and the dining ambience of its bakery-cafés provided significant growth opportunity, despite the fiercely competitive nature of the restaurant industry.

Already Panera Bread was widely recognized as the nationwide leader in the specialty bread segment. In 2003, Panera Bread scored the highest level of customer loyalty among quick-casual restaurants, according to a study conducted by TNS Intersearch.[1] J. D. Power and Associates' 2004 restaurant satisfaction study of 55,000 customers ranked Panera Bread highest among quick-service restaurants in the Midwest and Northeast regions of the United States in all categories, which included environment, meal, service, and cost. In 2005, for the fourth consecutive year, Panera Bread was rated among the best of 121 competitors in the Sandleman & Associates national customer satisfaction survey of more than 62,000 consumers. Panera Bread had also won "best of" awards in nearly every market across 36 states.

COMPANY BACKGROUND

In 1981, Louis Kane and Ron Shaich founded a bakery-café enterprise named Au Bon Pain Company Inc. Units were opened in malls, shopping centers, and airports along the East Coast of the United States and internationally throughout the 1980s and 1990s; the company prospered and became the dominant operator within the bakery-café category. In 1993, Au Bon Pain Company purchased Saint Louis Bread Company, a chain of 20 bakery-cafés located in the St. Louis, Missouri, area. Ron Shaich and a team of Au Bon Pain managers then spent considerable time in 1994 and 1995 traveling the country and studying the market for fast-food and quick-service meals. They concluded that many patrons of fast-food chains like McDonald's, Wendy's, Burger King, Subway, Taco Bell, Pizza Hut, and KFC could be attracted to a higher-quality, quick-dining experience. Top management at Au Bon Pain then instituted a comprehensive overhaul of the newly-acquired Saint Louis Bread locations, altering the menu and the dining atmosphere. The vision was to create a specialty café anchored by an authentic, fresh-dough artisan bakery and upscale quick-service menu selections. Between 1993 and 1997, average unit volumes at the revamped Saint Louis Bread units increased by 75 percent, and over 100 additional Saint Louis Bread units were opened. In 1997, the Saint Louis Bread bakery-cafés were renamed Panera Bread in all markets outside St. Louis.

By 1998, it was clear that the reconceived Panera Bread units had connected with consumers. Au Bon Pain management concluded the Panera Bread format had broad market appeal and could be rolled out nationwide. Ron Shaich believed that Panera Bread had the potential to become one of the leading fast-casual restaurant chains in the nation. Shaich also believed that growing Panera Bread into a national chain required significantly more management attention and financial resources than the company could marshal if it continued to pursue expansion of both the Au Bon Pain and Panera Bread chains. He convinced Au Bon Pain's board of directors that the best course of action was for the company to go exclusively with the Panera Bread concept and divest the Au Bon Pain cafés. In August 1998, the company announced the sale of its Au Bon Pain bakery-café division for $73 million in cash to ABP Corporation; the transaction was completed in May 1999. With the sale of the Au Bon Pain division, the company changed its name to Panera Bread Company. The restructured company had 180 Saint Louis Bread and Panera Bread bakery-cafés and a debt-free balance sheet.

Between January 1999 and December 2006, close to 850 additional Panera Bread bakery-cafés were opened, some company-owned and some franchised. Panera Bread reported sales of $829.0 million and net income of $58.8 million in 2006. Sales at franchise-operated Panera Bread bakery-cafés totaled $1.2 billion in 2006. A summary of Panera Bread's recent financial performance is shown in Exhibit 1.

Exhibit 1   Selected Consolidated Financial Data for Panera Bread, 2002–2006 ($ in millions, except for per share amounts)

	2006	2005	2004	2003	2002
Income Statement Data					
Revenues:					
Bakery-café sales	$666,141	$499,422	$362,121	$265,933	$212,645
Franchise royalties and fees	61,531	54,309	44,449	36,245	27,892
Fresh dough sales to franchisees	101,299	86,544	72,569	61,524	41,688
Total revenues	828,971	640,275	479,139	363,702	282,225
Bakery café expenses:					
Food and paper products	197,182	142,675	101,832	73,885	63,370
Labor	204,956	151,524	110,790	81,152	63,172
Occupancy	48,602	37,389	26,730	18,981	15,408
Other operating expenses	92,176	70,003	51,044	36,804	27,971
Total bakery café expenses	542,916	401,591	290,396	210,822	169,921
Fresh dough costs of sales to franchisees	85,618	75,036	65,627	54,967	38,432
Depreciation and amortization	44,166	33,011	25,298	18,304	13,794
General and administrative expenses	59,306	46,301	33,338	28,140	24,986
Pre-opening expenses	6,173	3,241	2,642	1,531	1,051
Total costs and expenses	738,179	559,180	417,301	313,764	248,184
Operating profit	90,792	81,095	61,838	49,938	34,041
Interest expense	92	50	18	48	32
Other (income) expense, net	(1,976)	(1,133)	1,065	1,592	467
Provision for income taxes	33,827	29,995	22,175	17,629	12,242
Net income	$ 58,849	$ 52,183	$ 38,430*	$ 30,669	$ 21,300
Earnings per share					
Basic	$1.88	$1.69	$1.28	$1.02	$0.74
Diluted	1.84	1.65	1.25	1.00	0.71

(*Continued*)

Exhibit 1   **Continued**

	2006	2005	2004	2003	2002
Weighted average shares outstanding					
Basic	31,313	30,871	30,154	29,733	28,923
Diluted	32,044	31,651	30,768	30,423	29,891
Balance Sheet Data					
Cash and cash equivalents	$ 52,097	$ 24,451	$ 29,639	$ 42,402	$ 29,924
Investments in government securities	20,025	46,308	28,415	9,019	9,149
Current assets	127,618	102,774	58,220	70,871	59,262
Total assets	542,609	437,667	324,672	256,835	195,431
Current liabilities	109,610	86,865	55,705	44,792	32,325
Total liabilities	144,943	120,689	83,309	46,235	32,587
Stockholders' equity	397,666	316,978	241,363	193,805	151,503
Cash Flow Data					
Net cash provided by operating activities	$104,895	$ 110,628	$ 84,284	$ 73,102	$ 46,323
Net cash used in investing activities	(90,917)	(129,640)	(102,291)	(66,856)	(40,115)
Net cash provided by financing activities	13,668	13,824	5,244	6,232	5,664
Net (decrease) increase in cash and cash equivalents	27,646	(5,188)	(12,763)	12,478	11,872

* After adjustment of $239,000 for cumulative effect of accounting change.

Sources: 2006 10-K report, pp. 36–38, 2005 10-K report, pp. 16–17; 2003 10-K report, pp. 29–31; and company press release, February 8, 2007.

THE PANERA BREAD CONCEPT AND STRATEGY

The driving concept behind Panera Bread was to provide a premium specialty bakery and café experience to urban workers and suburban dwellers. Its artisan sourdough breads made with a craftsman's attention to quality and detail and its award-winning bakery expertise formed the core of the menu offerings. Panera Bread specialized in fresh baked goods, made-to-order sandwiches on freshly baked breads, soups, salads, custom roasted coffees, and other café beverages. Panera's target market was urban workers and suburban dwellers looking for a quick-service meal and a more aesthetically pleasing dining experience than that offered by traditional fast food restaurants.

In his letter to shareholders in the company's 2005 annual report, Panera chairman and CEO Ron Shaich said:

> We think our continued commitment to providing crave-able food that people trust, served in a warm, community gathering place by associates who make our guests feel comfortable, really matters. When this is rooted in our commitment to the traditions of handcrafted, artisan bread, something special is created. As we say here at Panera, it's our Product, Environment, and Great Service (PEGS) that we count on to deliver our success—year in and year out.

Panera Bread's distinctive menu, signature café design, inviting ambience, operating systems, and unit location strategy allowed it to compete successfully in five submarkets of the food-away-from-home industry: breakfast, lunch, daytime "chill out" (the time between breakfast and lunch and between lunch and dinner when customers

Exhibit 2   **Selected Operating Statistics, Panera Bread Company, 2000–2006**

	2006	2005	2004	2003	2002	2001	2000
Revenues at company-operated stores (in millions)	$ 666.1	$ 499.4	$ 362.1	$ 265.9	$ 212.6	$ 157.7	$ 125.5
Revenues at franchised stores (in millions)	$1,245.5	$1,097.2	$ 879.1	$ 711.0	$ 542.6	$ 371.7	$ 199.4
Systemwide store revenues (in millions)	$1,911.6	$1,596.6	$1,241.2	$ 976.9	$ 755.2	$ 529.4	$ 324.9
Average annualized revenues per company-operated bakery-café (in millions)	$ 1.967	$ 1.942	$ 1.852	$ 1.830	$ 1.764	$ 1.636	$ 1.473
Average annualized revenues per franchised bakery-café (in millions)	$ 2.074	$ 2.016	$ 1.881	$ 1.860	$ 1.872	$ 1.800	$ 1.707
Average weekly sales, company-owned cafés	$ 37,833	$ 37,348	$ 35,620	$35,198	$33,924	$31,460	$28,325
Average weekly sales, franchised cafés	$ 39,894	$ 38,777	$ 36,171	$35,777	$35,997	$34,607	$32,832
Comparable bakery-café sales percentage increases*							
Company-owned	3.9%	7.4%	2.9%	1.7%	4.1%	5.8%	8.1%
Franchised	4.1%	8.0%	2.6%	(0.4)%	6.1%	5.8%	10.3%
Systemwide	4.1%	7.8%	2.7%	0.2%	5.5%	5.8%	9.1%
Company-owned bakery-cafés open at year-end	391	311	226	173	132	110	90
Franchised bakery-cafés open at year-end	636	566	515	429	346	259	172
Total bakery-cafés open	1,027	877	741	602	478	369	262

* The percentages for comparable store sales are based on annual changes at stores open at least 18 months.

Sources: Company 10-K reports 2000, 2001, 2003, 2005, and 2006; company press releases, January 4, 2007, and February 8, 2007.

visited its bakery-cafés to take a break from their daily activities), light evening fare for eat-in or take-out, and take-home bread. In 2006, Panera began enhancing its menu in ways that would attract more diners during the evening meal hours. Management's long-term objective and strategic intent was to make Panera Bread a nationally recognized brand name and to be the dominant restaurant operator in the specialty bakery-café segment. According to Scott Davis, Panera's senior vice president and chief concept officer, the company was trying to succeed by "being better than the guys across the street" and making the experience of dining at Panera so attractive that customers would be willing to pass by the outlets of other

fast-casual restaurant competitors to dine at a nearby Panera Bread bakery-café.[2] Davis maintained that the question about Panera Bread's future was not *if* it would be successful but *by how much*.

Management believed that its concept afforded growth potential in suburban markets sufficient to expand the number of Panera bread locations by 17 percent annually through 2010 (see Exhibits 3 and 4) and to achieve earnings per share growth of 25 percent annually. Panera Bread's growth strategy was to capitalize on Panera's market potential by opening both company-owned and franchised Panera Bread locations as fast as was prudent. So far, franchising had been a key component of the company's efforts to broaden its market penetration. Panera Bread

Exhibit 3   **Areas of High and Low Market Penetration of Panera Bread Bakery-Cafés, 2006**

High Penetration Markets			Low Penetration Markets		
Area	Number of Panera Bread Units	Population per Bakery-Café	Area	Number of Panera Bread Units	Population per Bakery-Café
St. Louis	40	67,000	Los Angeles	17	1,183,000
Columbus, OH	19	83,000	Miami	2	1,126,000
Jacksonville	12	98,000	Northern California	10	1,110,000
Omaha	12	101,000	Seattle	5	860,000
Cincinnati	26	108,000	Dallas/Fort Worth	10	590,000
Pittsburgh	25	142,000	Houston	12	335,000
Washington D.C./Northern Virginia	26	152,000	Philadelphia	25	278,000

Untapped Markets		
New York City	Phoenix	Austin
Salt Lake City	Tucson	San Antonio
Memphis	District of Columbia	Green Bay/Appleton
New Orleans	Spokane	Shreveport
Atlantic City	Baton Rouge	Toronto
Albuquerque	Little Rock	Vancouver

Source: Panera Bread management presentation to securities analysts, May 5, 2006

had organized its business around company-owned bakery-café operations, the franchise operations, and fresh dough operations; the fresh bread unit supplied dough to all Panera Bread stores, both company-owned and franchised.

Exhibit 4   **Comparative U.S. Market Penetration of Selected Restaurant Chains, 2006**

Restaurant Chain	Number of Locations	Population per Location
Subway	19,965	15,000
McDonald's	13,727	22,000
Starbucks Coffee	7,700	39,000
Applebee's	1,800	166,000
Panera Bread	910	330,000

Note: Management believed that a 17 percent annual rate of expansion of Panera Bread locations through 2010 would result in 1 café per 160,000 people.

Source: Panera Bread management presentation to securities analysts, May 5, 2006.

PANERA BREAD'S PRODUCT OFFERINGS AND MENU

Panera Bread's signature product was artisan bread made from four ingredients—water, natural yeast, flour, and salt; no preservatives or chemicals were used. Carefully trained bakers shaped every step of the process, from mixing the ingredients, to kneading the dough, to placing the loaves on hot stone slabs to bake in a traditional European-style stone deck bakery oven. Exhibit 5 shows Panera's lineup of breads.

The Panera Bread menu was designed to provide target customers with products built on the company's bakery expertise, particularly its 20-plus varieties of bread baked fresh throughout the day at each café location. The key menu groups were fresh baked goods, made-to-order sandwiches and salads, soups, light entrées, and café beverages. Exhibit 6 shows a sampling of the items on a typical Panera Bread menu.

Exhibit 5   **Panera's Lineup of Bread Varieties, 2006**

Sourdough
Panera's signature sourdough bread that featured a golden, crackled crust and firm, moderately structured crumb with a satisfying, tangy flavor. *Available in Baguette, Loaf, XL Loaf, Roll and Bread Bowl.*

Asiago Cheese
Chunks of Asiago cheese were added to the standard sourdough recipe and baked right in, with more Asiago cheese sprinkled on top. *Available in Demi and Loaf.*

Focaccia
A traditional Italian flatbread made with Panera's artisan starter dough, olive oil, and chunks of Asiago cheese. *Available in three varieties—Asiago Cheese, Rosemary & Onion and Basil Pesto.*

Nine Grain
Made with cracked whole wheat, rye, corn meal, oats, rice flour, soy grits, barley flakes, millet and flaxseed plus molasses for a semisweet taste. *Available in Loaf.*

Tomato Basil
A sourdough-based bread made with tomatoes and basil, topped with sweet walnut streusel. *Available in XL Loaf.*

Cinnamon Raisin
A light raisin bread with a swirl of cinnamon, sugar and molasses. *Available in Loaf.*

Artisan Sesame Semolina
Made with enriched durum and semolina flours to create a golden yellow crumb, topped with sesame seeds. *Available in Loaf and Miche.*

Artisan Multigrain
Nine grains and sesame, poppy and fennel seeds blended with molasses, topped with rolled oats. *Available in Loaf.*

Artisan French
Made with Panera's artisan starter to create a nutty flavor with a wine-like aroma. *Available in Baguette and Miche.*

Whole Grain
A moist, hearty mixture of whole spelt flour, millet, flaxseed and other wheat flours and grains, sweetened with honey and topped with rolled oats. *Available in loaf, miche and baguette.*

White Whole Grain
A new bread created especially for Panera Kids sandwiches; a sweeter alternative to the Whole Grain bread with a thin, caramelized crust sweetened with honey and molasses. *Available in Loaf.*

French
A classic French bread characterized by a thin, crackly crust, slightly sweet taste and a lighter crumb than our sourdough. *Available in Baguette, Loaf, XL Loaf and Roll.*

Ciabatta
A flat, oval-shaped loaf with a delicate flavor and soft texture; made with Panera's artisan starter and a touch of olive oil. *Available in Loaf.*

Honey Wheat
A mild wheat bread with tastes of honey and molasses; the soft crust and crumb made it great for sandwiches. *Available in Loaf.*

Rye
Special natural leavening, unbleached flour and chopped rye kernels were used to create a delicate rye flavor. *Available in Loaf.*

Sunflower
Made with honey, lemon peel and raw sunflower seeds and topped with sesame and honey-roasted sunflower seeds. *Available in Loaf.*

Artisan Three Seed
The addition of sesame, poppy and fennel seeds created a sweet, nutty, anise-flavored bread. *Available in Demi.*

Artisan Three Cheese
Made with Parmesan, Romano, and Asiago cheeses and durum and semolina flours. *Available in Demi, Loaf and Miche.*

Artisan Stone-Milled Rye
Made with Panera's artisan starter, chopped rye kernels and caraway seeds, topped with more caraway seeds. *Available in Loaf and Miche.*

Artisan Country
Made from artisan starter with a crisp crust and nutty flavor. *Available in loaf, miche and demi.*

Lower-Carb Pumpkin Seed
Made from Panera's artisan starter dough, pumpkin seeds and flax meal to create a subtle, nutty flavor. *Available in Loaf.*

Lower-Carb Italian Herb
Made from Panera's artisan starter dough, roasted garlic, dried herbs and sesame seed topping. *Available in Loaf.*

Source: www.panerabread.com (accessed July 28, 2006).

Exhibit 6   **Sample Menu Selections, Panera Bread Company, 2006**

Bakery
Loaves of Bread (22 varieties)
Bagels (11 varieties)
Cookies (5 varieties)
Scones (5 varieties)
Cinnamon Rolls Pecan Rolls
Croissants
Coffee Cakes
Muffins (5 varieties)
Artisan and Specialty Pastries (8 varieties)
Brownies (3 varieties)
Mini-Bundt Cakes (3 varieties)

Signature Sandwiches
Pepperblue Steak
Garden Veggie
Tuscan Chicken
Asiago Roast Beef
Italian Combo
Bacon Turkey Bravo
Sierra Turkey
Turkey Romesco
Mediterranean Veggie

Café Sandwiches
Smoked Turkey Breast
Chicken Salad
Tuna Salad
Smoked Ham and Cheese

Hot Panini Sandwiches
Turkey Artichoke
Frontega Chicken
Smokehouse Turkey
Portobello and Mozzarella

Baked Egg Souffles
Four Cheese
Spinach and Artichoke
Spinach and Bacon

Soups
Broccoli Cheddar
French Onion
Baked Potato
Low Fat Chicken Noodle
Cream of Chicken and Wild Rice
Boston Clam Chowder
Low Fat Vegetarian Garden Vegetable
Low Fat Vegetarian Black Bean
Vegetarian Roasted Red Pepper and Lentil
Tuscan Chicken and Ditalini
Tuscan Vegetable Ditalini

Hand Tossed Salads
Asian Sesame Chicken
Fandango
Greek
Caesar
Grilled Chicken Caesar
Bistro Steak
Classic Café
California Mission Chicken
Fuji Apple Chicken
Strawberry Poppyseed and Chicken
Grilled Salmon Salad

Side Choices
Portion of French Baguette
Portion of Whole Grain Baguette
Kettle-cooked or Baked Chips
Apple

Panera Kids
Grilled Cheese
Peanut Butter and Jelly
Kids Deli

Beverages
Coffee
Hot and Iced Teas
Sodas
Bottled Water
Juice
Organic Milk
Organic Chocolate Milk
Hot Chocolate
Orange Juice
Organic Apple Juice
Espresso
Cappuccino
Lattes
Mango Raspberry Smoothie

Source: Sample menu posted at www.panerabread.com (accessed July 29, 2006).

The menu offerings were regularly reviewed and revised to sustain the interest of regular customers, satisfy changing consumer preferences, and be responsive to various seasons of the year. The soup lineup, for example, changed seasonally. Product development was focused on providing food that customers would crave and trust to be tasty. New menu items were developed in test kitchens and then introduced in a limited number of the bakery-cafés to determine customer response and verify that preparation and operating procedures resulted in product consistency and high quality standards. If successful, they were then rolled out systemwide. New product rollouts were integrated into periodic or seasonal menu rotations, which Panera referred to as "Celebrations."

Panera recognized in late 2004 that significantly more customers were conscious about eating "good" carbohydrates, prompting the introduction of whole grain breads. In 2005, several important menu changes were made. Panera introduced a new line of artisan sweet goods made with gourmet European butter, fresh fruit toppings, and appealing fillings; these new artisan pastries represented a significantly higher level of taste and upgraded quality. To expand its breakfast offerings and help boost morning-hour sales, Panera introduced egg soufflés baked in a flaked pastry shell. And, in another health-related move, Panera switched to the use of natural, antibiotic-free chicken in all of its chicken-related sandwiches and salads. During 2006, the chief menu changes involved the addition of light entrées to jump-start dinner appeal; one such menu addition was crispani (a pizzalike topping on a thin crust). In 2006, evening-hour sales represented 20 percent of Panera's business.

PANERA FRESH CATERING

In 2004–2005, Panera Bread introduced a catering program to extend its market reach into the workplace, schools, parties, and gatherings held in homes. Panera saw catering as an opportunity to grow lunch and dinner sales with making capital investments in additional physical facilities. By the end of 2005, catering was generating an additional $80 million in sales

for Panera Bread. Management foresaw considerable opportunity for future growth of Panera's catering operation.

MARKETING

Panera's marketing strategy was to compete on the basis of providing an entire dining experience rather than by attracting customers on the basis of price only. The objective was for customers to view dining at Panera as being a good value—meaning high-quality food at reasonable prices—so as to encourage frequent visits. Panera Bread performed extensive market research, including the use of focus groups, to determine customer food and drink preferences and price points. The company tried to grow sales at existing Panera locations through menu development, product merchandising, promotions at everyday prices, and sponsorship of local community charitable events.

Historically, marketing had played only a small role in Panera's success. Brand awareness had been built on customers' satisfaction with their dining experience at Panera and their tendency to share their positive experiences with friends and neighbors. About 85 percent of consumers who were aware that there was a Panera Bread bakery-café in their community or neighborhood had dined at Panera on at least one occasion.[3] The company's marketing research indicated that 57 percent of consumers who had "ever tried" dining at Panera Bread had been customers in the past 30 days. This high proportion of trial customers to repeat customers had convinced management that getting more first-time diners into Panera Bread cafés was a potent way to boost store traffic and average weekly sales per store.

Panera's research also showed that people who dined at Panera Bread very frequently or moderately frequently typically did so for only one part of the day. Yet 81 percent indicated "considerable willingness" to try dining at Panera Bread at other parts of the day.[4]

Franchise-operated bakery-cafés were required to contribute 0.7 percent of their sales to a national advertising fund and 0.4 percent of their sales as a marketing administration fee and were also required to spend 2.0 percent of their sales in their local markets on advertising. Panera contributed similar amounts from company-owned bakery-cafés toward the national advertising fund and marketing administration. The national advertising fund contribution of 0.7 percent had been increased from 0.4 percent starting in 2006. Beginning in fiscal 2006, national advertising fund contributions were raised to 0.7 percent of sales, and Panera could opt to raise the national advertising fund contributions as high as 2.6 percent of sales.

In 2006, Panera Bread's marketing strategy had several elements. One element aimed at raising the quality of awareness about Panera by continuing to feature the caliber and appeal of its breads and baked goods, by hammering the theme "food you crave, food you can trust," and by enhancing the appeal of its bakery-cafés as a neighborhood gathering place. A second marketing initiative was to raise awareness and boost trial of dining at Panera Bread at multiple meal times (breakfast, lunch, "chill out" times, and dinner). Panera avoided hard-sell or in-your-face marketing approaches, preferring instead to employ a range of ways to softly drop the Panera Bread name into the midst of consumers as they moved through their lives and let them "gently collide" with the brand; the idea was to let consumers "discover" Panera Bread and then convert them into loyal customers by providing a very satisfying dining experience. The third marketing initiative was to increase perception of Panera Bread as a viable evening meal option and to drive early trials of Panera for dinner (particularly among existing Panera lunch customers).

Franchise Operations

Opening additional franchised bakery-cafés was a core element of Panera Bread's strategy and management's initiatives to achieve the company's growth targets. Panera Bread did not grant single-unit franchises, so a prospective franchisee could not open just one bakery-café. Rather, Panera Bread's franchising strategy was to enter into franchise agreements that required the franchise developer to open a number of units, typically 15 bakery-cafés in six years. Franchisee candidates had to be well capitalized, have a proven track record as excellent multi-unit restaurant operators, and agree to meet an aggressive development schedule. Applicants had to

meet eight stringent criteria to gain consideration for a Panera Bread franchise:

- Experience as a multi-unit restaurant operator.
- Recognition as a top restaurant operator.
- Net worth of $7.5 million.
- Liquid assets of $3 million.
- Infrastructure and resources to meet Panera's development schedule for the market area the franchisee was applying to develop.
- Real estate experience in the market to be developed.
- Total commitment to the development of the Panera Bread brand.
- Cultural fit and a passion for fresh bread.

The franchise agreement typically required the payment of a franchise fee of $35,000 per bakery-café (broken down into $5,000 at the signing of the area development agreement and $30,000 at or before a bakery-café opened) and continuing royalties of 4–5 percent on sales from each bakery-café. Franchise-operated bakery-cafés followed the same standards for in store operating standards, product quality, menu, site selection, and bakery-café construction as did company-owned bakery-cafés. Franchisees were required to purchase all of their dough products from sources approved by Panera Bread. Panera's fresh dough facility system supplied fresh dough products to substantially all franchise-operated bakery-cafés. Panera did not finance franchisee construction or area development agreement payments or hold an equity interest in any of the franchise-operated bakery-cafés. All area development agreements executed after March 2003 included a clause allowing Panera Bread the right to purchase all bakery-cafés opened by the franchisee at a defined purchase price, at any time five years after the execution of the franchise agreement.

Exhibit 7 shows estimated costs of opening a new franchised Panera Bread bakery-café. As of 2006, the typical franchise-operated bakery-café averaged somewhat higher average weekly and annual sales volumes than company-operated cafés (see Exhibit 2), was equal to or slightly more profitable, and produced a slightly higher return on equity investment than company-operated cafés (partly because many franchisees made greater use of debt in financing their operations than did Panera, which

Exhibit 7   **Estimated Initial Investment for a Panera Bread Bakery-Café, 2007**

Investment Category	Actual or Estimated Amount	To Whom Paid
Franchise fee	$35,000	Panera
Real property	Varies according to site and local real estate market conditions	
Leasehold improvements	$350,000 to $1,250,000	Contractors
Equipment	$250,000 to $300,000	Equipment vendors, Panera
Fixtures	$60,000 to $90,000	Vendors
Furniture	$50,000 to $70,000	Vendors
Consultant fees and municipal impact fees (if any)	$20,000 to $120,000	Architect, engineer, expeditor, others
Supplies and inventory	$19,000 to $24,175	Panera, other suppliers
Smallwares	$24,000 to $29,000	Suppliers
Signage	$20,000 to $72,000	Suppliers
Additional funds (for working capital and general operating expenses for 3 months)	$175,000 to $245,000	Vendors, suppliers, employees, utilities, landlord, others
Total	$1,003,000 to $2,235,175, plus real estate and related costs	

Source: www.panerabread.com (accessed February 9, 2007).

had no long-term debt at all).[5] During the 2003–2006 period, in four unrelated transactions, Panera purchased 38 bakery-cafés from franchisees.

Panera provided its franchisees with market analysis and site selection assistance, lease review, design services and new store opening assistance, a comprehensive 10-week initial training program, a training program for hourly employees, manager and baker certification, bakery-café certification, continuing education classes, benchmarking data regarding costs and profit margins, access to company developed marketing and advertising programs, neighborhood marketing assistance, and calendar planning assistance. Panera's surveys of its franchisees indicated high satisfaction with the Panera Bread concept, the overall support received from Panera Bread, and the company's leadership. The biggest franchisee issue was the desire for more territory. In turn, Panera management expressed satisfaction with the quality of franchisee operations, the pace and quality of new bakery-café openings, and franchisees' adoption of Panera Bread initiatives.[6]

As of April 2006, Panera had entered into area development agreements with 42 franchisee groups covering 54 markets in 34 states; these franchisees had commitments to open 423 additional franchise-operated bakery-cafés. If a franchisee failed to develop bakery-cafés on schedule, Panera had the right to terminate the franchise agreement and develop its own company-operated locations or develop locations through new area developers in that market. As of mid-2006, Panera Bread did not have any international franchise development agreements but was considering entering into franchise agreements for several Canadian locations (Toronto and Vancouver).

SITE SELECTION AND CAFÉ ENVIRONMENT

Bakery-cafés were typically located in suburban, strip mall, and regional mall locations. In evaluating a potential location, Panera studied the surrounding trade area, demographic information within that area, and information on competitors. Based on analysis of this information, including the use of predictive modeling using proprietary software, Panera developed projections of sales and return on investment for candidate sites. Cafés had proved successful as freestanding units, as both in-line and end-cap locations in strip malls, and in large regional malls.

The average Panera bakery-café was approximately 4,600 square feet. The great majority of the locations were leased. Lease terms were typically for 10 years with one, two, or three 5-year renewal option periods thereafter. Leases typically entailed charges for minimum base occupancy, a proportionate share of building and common-area operating expenses and real estate taxes, and a contingent percentage rent based on sales above a stipulated sales level. The average construction, equipment, furniture and fixture, and signage cost for the 66 company-owned bakery-cafés opened in 2005 was $920,000 per bakery-café after landlord allowances.

Each bakery-café sought to provide a distinctive and engaging environment (what management referred to as "Panera Warmth"), in many cases using fixtures and materials complementary to the neighborhood location of the bakery-café. In 2005–2006, the company had introduced a new G2 café design aimed at further refining and enhancing the appeal of Panera bakery-cafés as a warm and appealing neighborhood gathering place (a strategy that Starbucks had used with great success). The G2 design incorporated higher-quality furniture, cozier seating areas and groupings, and a brighter, more open display case. Many locations had fireplaces to further create an alluring and hospitable atmosphere that patrons would flock to on a regular basis, sometimes for a meal, sometimes to meet friends and acquaintances for a meal, sometimes to take a break for a light snack or beverage, and sometimes to just hang out with friends and acquaintances. Many of Panera's bakery-cafés had outdoor seating, and virtually all cafés featured free wireless high-speed (Wi-Fi) Internet access—Panera considered free Wi-Fi part of its commitment to making its bakery-cafés open community gathering places where people could catch up on some work, hang out with friends, read the paper, or just relax. All Panera cafés used real china and stainless silverware instead of paper plates and plastic utensils.

BAKERY-CAFÉ SUPPLY CHAIN

Panera had invested about $52 million in a network of 17 regional fresh dough facilities (16 company-owned and one franchise-operated) to supply fresh dough daily to both company-owned and franchised bakery-cafés. These facilities, totaling some 313,000 square feet, employed about 830 people who were largely engaged in preparing the fresh doughs, a process that took about 48 hours. The dough-making process began with the preparation and mixing of Panera's all-natural starter dough, which then was given time to rise; other all-natural ingredients were then added to create the different bread and bagel varieties (no chemicals or preservatives were used). Another period of rising then took place. Next the dough was cut into pieces, shaped into loaves or bagels, and readied for shipment in fresh dough form. There was no freezing of the dough, and no partial baking was done at the fresh dough facilities. Each bakery-café did all of the baking itself, using the fresh doughs delivered daily. The fresh dough facilities manufactured about 50 different products, with 11 more rotated throughout the year.

Distribution of the fresh bread and bagel doughs was accomplished through a leased fleet of about 140 temperature-controlled trucks operated by Panera personnel. Trucks on average delivered dough to six bakery-cafés, with trips averaging about 300 miles (but in some cases extending to as much as 500 miles—management believed the optimal trip length was about 300 miles). The fresh dough was sold to both company-owned and franchised bakery-cafés at a delivered cost not to exceed 27 percent of the retail value of the product. Exhibit 8 provides financial data relating to each of Panera's three business segments: company-operated bakery-cafés, franchise operations, and fresh dough facilities. The sales and operating profits associated with the fresh doughs supplied to company-operated bakery cafés are included in the revenues and operating profits of the company-owned bakery-café segment. The sales and operating profits of the fresh dough facilities segment shown in Exhibit 8 all represent transactions with franchised bakery-cafés.

Management claimed that the company's fresh-dough-making capability provided a competitive advantage by ensuring consistent quality and dough-making efficiency. It was more economical to concentrate the dough-making operations in a few facilities dedicated to that function than it was to have each bakery-café equipped and staffed to do all of its baking from scratch.

Panera obtained ingredients for its doughs and other products manufactured at the fresh dough facilities from a variety of suppliers. While some ingredients used at the fresh dough facilities were sourced from a single supplier, there were numerous suppliers of each ingredient and Panera could obtain

Exhibit 8   **Business Segment Information, Panera Bread Company, 2003–2006
(\$ in thousands)**

	2006	2005	2004	2003
Segment revenues:				
Company bakery-café operations	$666,141	$499,422	$362,121	$265,933
Franchise operations	61,531	54,309	44,449	36,245
Fresh dough operations	159,050	128,422	103,786	93,874
Intercompany sales eliminations	(57,751)	(41,878)	(31,217)	(32,350)
Total revenues	$828,971	$640,275	$479,139	$363,702
Segment operating profit:				
Company bakery-café operations	$123,225	$ 97,831	$ 71,725	$ 55,111
Franchise operations	54,160	47,652	39,149	32,132
Fresh dough operations	15,681	11,508	6,942	6,557
Total segment operating profit	$193,066	$156,991	$117,816	$ 93,800
Depreciation and amortization:				
Company bakery-café operations	$ 32,741	$ 23,345	$ 17,786	$ 12,256
Fresh dough operations	7,097	6,016	4,356	3,298
Corporate administration	4,328	3,650	3,156	2,750
Total	$ 44,166	$ 33,011	$ 25,298	$ 18,304
Capital expenditures				
Company bakery-café operations	$ 86,743	$ 67,554	$ 67,374	$ 33,670
Fresh dough operations	15,120	9,082	9,445	8,370
Corporate administration	7,433	5,420	3,610	3,721
Total capital expenditures	$109,296	$ 82,056	$ 80,429	$ 45,761
Segment assets				
Company bakery-café operations	$374,795	$301,517	$204,295	$147,920
Franchise operations	3,740	2,969	1,778	1,117
Fresh dough operations	59,919	37,567	39,968	33,442
Other assets	104,155	95,614	78,631	74,356
Total assets	$542,609	$437,667	$324,672	$256,835

Sources: Company 10-K reports, 2004, 2005, and 2006.

ingredients from another supplier when necessary. Panera contracted externally for the supply of sweet goods to its bakery-cafés. In November 2002, it entered into a cost-plus agreement with Dawn Food Products Inc. to provide sweet goods for the period 2003–2007. Sweet goods were completed at each bakery-café by professionally trained bakers—completion entailed finishing with fresh toppings and other ingredients and baking to established artisan standards.

Panera had arrangements with independent distributors to handle the delivery of sweet goods and other materials to bakery-cafés. Virtually all other food products and supplies for retail operations, including paper goods, coffee, and smallwares, were contracted for by Panera and delivered by the vendors to the designated distributors for delivery to the bakery-cafés. Individual bakery-cafés placed orders for the needed supplies directly from a distributor two to three times per week. Franchise-operated bakery-cafés operate under individual contracts with one of Panera's three primary independent distributors or other regional distributors.

COMPETITION

According to the National Restaurant Association, sales at the 925,000 food service locations in the United States were forecast to be about $511 billion in 2006 (up from $308 billion in 1996), and account for 47.5 percent of consumers' food dollars (up from 25 percent in 1955). Commercial eating places accounted for about $345 billion of the projected

$511 billion in total food service sales, with the remainder divided among drinking places, lodging establishments with restaurants, managed food service locations, and other types of retail, vending, recreational, and mobile operations with food service capability. The U.S. restaurant industry had about 12.5 million employees in 2006, served about 70 billion meals and snack occasions, and was growing about 5 percent annually.[7] Just over 7 out of 10 eating and drinking places in the United States were independent single-unit establishments with fewer than 20 employees.

Even though the average U.S. consumer ate 76 percent of meals at home, on a typical day, about 130 million U.S. consumers were food service patrons at an eating establishment—sales at commercial eating places averaged close to $1 billion daily. Average household expenditures for food away from home in 2004 were $2,434, or $974 per person. In 2003, unit sales averaged $755,000 at full-service restaurants and $606,000 at limited-service restaurants; however, very popular restaurant locations achieved annual sales volumes in the $2.5 million to $5 million range. The profitability of a restaurant location ranged from exceptional to good to average to marginal to money-losing.

The restaurant business was labor-intensive, extremely competitive, and risky. Industry members pursued differentiation strategies of one variety of another, seeking to set themselves apart from rivals via pricing, food quality, menu theme, signature menu selections, dining ambience and atmosphere, service, convenience, and location. To further enhance their appeal, some restaurants tried to promote greater customer traffic via happy hours, lunch and dinner specials, children's menus, innovative or trendy dishes, diet-conscious menu selections, and beverage/appetizer specials during televised sporting events (important at restaurants/bars with big-screen TVs). Most restaurants were quick to adapt their menu offerings to changing consumer tastes and eating preferences, frequently featuring heart-healthy, vegetarian, organic, low-calorie, and/or low-carb items on their menus. It was the norm at many restaurants to rotate some menu selections seasonally and to periodically introduce creative dishes in an effort to keep regular patrons coming back, attract more patrons, and remain competitive.

Consumers (especially those who ate out often) were prone to give newly-opened eating establishments a trial, and if they were pleased with their experience to return, sometimes frequently—loyalty to existing restaurants was low when consumers perceived there were better dining alternatives. It was also common for a once-hot restaurant to lose favor and confront the stark realities of a dwindling clientele, forcing it to either reconceive its menu and dining environment or go out of business. Many

---

Exhibit 9   **Representative Fast-Casual Restaurants Chains and Selected Full-Service Restaurant Chains in the United States, 2006**

Company	Number of Locations, 2005–2006	Select 2005 Financial Data	Key Menu Categories
Atlanta Bread Company	160 bakery-cafés in 27 states	Not available (privately-held company)	Fresh-baked breads, waffles, salads, sandwiches, soups, wood-fired pizza and pasta (select locations only), baked goods, desserts
Applebee's Neighborhood Grill and Bar*	1,730+ locations in 49 states, plus some 70 locations in 16 other countries	2005 revenues of $1.2 billion; average annual sales of $2.5 million per location; alcoholic beverages accounted for about 12 percent of sales	Beef, chicken, pork, seafood, and pasta entrées plus appetizers, salads, sandwiches, a selection of Weight Watchers branded menu alternatives, desserts, and alcoholic beverages
Au Bon Pain	190 company-owned and franchised bakery-cafés in 23 states; 222 locations internationally	Systemwide sales of about $245 million in 2005	Baked goods (with a focus on croissants and bagels), soups, salads, sandwiches and wraps, and coffee drinks

(Continued)

Exhibit 9   **Continued**

Company	Number of Locations, 2005–2006	Select 2005 Financial Data	Key Menu Categories
Baja Fresh	300+ locations across the United States	A subsidiary of Wendy's International	Tacos, burritos, quesadilla, fajitas, salads, soups, sides, and catering services
Bruegger's	260 bakery-cafés in 17 states	2005 revenues of $155.2 million; 3,500 full-time employees	Several varieties of bagels and muffins, sandwiches, salads, and soups
California Pizza Kitchen*	190+ locations in 27 states and 5 other countries	2005 revenues of $480 million; average annual sales of $3.2 million per location	Signature California-style hearth-baked pizzas; creative salads, pastas, soups and sandwiches; appetizers; desserts, beer, wine, coffees, teas, and assorted beverages
Chili's Grill and Bar* (a subsidiary of Brinker International**)	1,074 locations in 49 states and 23 countries	Average revenue per meal of ≈$12.00; average capital investment of $2.4 million per location	Chicken, beef, and seafood entrées, steaks, appetizers, salads, sandwiches, desserts, and alcoholic beverages (13.6 percent of sales)
Chipotle Mexican Grill	500+ locations (all company-owned)	2005 sales of $628 million; 13,000 employees	A selection of gourmet burritos and tacos
Corner Bakery Café (a subsidiary of Brinker International**)	90 locations in 8 states and District of Columbia	Average revenue per meal of ≈$7.44; average capital investment of $1.7 million per location	Breakfast selections (egg scramblers, pastries, mixed berry parfaits); lunch/diner selections (hot and cold sandwiches, salads, soups, and desserts); catering (≈21 percent of sales)
Cracker Barrel	527 combination retail stores and restaurants in 42 states	Restaurant sales of $2.1 billion in 2005; average restaurant sales of $3.3 million	Two menus (breakfast and lunch/dinner); named "Best Family Dining Chain" for 15 consecutive years
Culver's	330 locations in 16 states	Not available (a privately, held company)	Signature hamburgers served on buttered buns, fried battered cheese curds, value dinners (chicken, shrimp, cod with potato and slaw), salads, frozen custard, milkshakes, sundaes, and fountain drinks
Fazoli's	380 locations in 32 states	Not available (a privately-held company)	Spaghetti and meatballs, fettuccine Alfredo, lasagna, ravioli, submarinos and panini sandwiches, salads, and breadsticks
Fuddruckers	200+ locations in the United States and 6 Middle Eastern countries	Not available (a privately-held company)	Exotic hamburgers (the feature menu item), chicken and fish sandwiches, French fries and other sides, soups, salads, desserts
Jason's Deli	150 locations in 20 states	Not available (a privately-held company)	Sandwiches, extensive salad bar, soups, loaded potatoes, desserts; catering services, party trays, and box lunches
McAlister's Deli	200+ locations in 18 states	Not available (a privately-held company)	Deli sandwiches, loaded baked potatoes, soups, salads, and desserts, plus sandwich trays and lunch boxes

(*Continued*)

Company	Number of Locations, 2005–2006	Select 2005 Financial Data	Key Menu Categories
Moe's Southwest Grill	200+ locations in 35 states	Not available (a privately-held company)	Tex-Mex foods prepared fresh—tacos, burritos, fajitas, quesadillas, nachos, salads, chips and salsa
Noodles & Company	120+ urban and suburban locations in 16 states	Not available (a privately-held company)	Asian, Mediterranean and American noodle/pasta entrées, soups and salads
Nothing But Noodles	39 locations in 20 states	Not available (a privately-held company)	Starters, a wide selection of American and Italian pastas, Asian dishes with noodles, pasta-less entrées, soups, salads, and desserts
Qdoba Mexican Grill	280+ locations in 40 states	A subsidiary of Jack in the Box, Inc.; Jack in the Box had 2005 revenues of $2.5 billion, 2,300+ Jack in the Box and Qdoba locations, and 44,600 employees	Signature burritos, a "Naked Burrito" (a burrito served in a bowl without the tortilla), nontraditional taco salads, three-cheese nachos, five signature salsas, and a Q-to-Go Hot Taco Bar catering alternative
Rubio's Fresh Mexican Grill	150 locations in 5 western states	2005 revenues of $141 million; average sales of $960,000 per location	Signature fish tacos; chicken beef, and pork tacos; burritos and quesadillas; salads; proprietary salsas; sides; and domestic and imported beers
Starbucks	7,500+ company-operated and licensed locations in the United States, plus ≈3,000 international locations	2005 revenues of $6.4 billion; estimated retail sales of $1.1 million per company-operated location	Italian-style espresso beverages, teas, sodas, juices, assorted pastries and confections; some locations offer sandwiches and salads

* Denotes a full-service restaurant.

** Brinker International was a multi-concept restaurant operator with over 1,500 restaurants including Chili's Grill & Bar, Chili's Too, Corner Bakery Café, Romano's Macaroni Grill, On the Border Mexican Grill & Cantina, and Maggiano's Little Italy. Brinker had 2005 sales of $3.9 billion.

Sources: Company Web sites and en.wikipedia.org/wiki/Fast_casual_restaurant (accessed August 2, 2006).

restaurants had fairly short lives; there were multiple causes for a restaurant's failure—a lack of enthusiasm for the menu or dining experience, inconsistent food quality, poor service, a bad location, meal prices that patrons deemed too high, and superior competition by rivals with comparable menu offerings.

While Panera Bread competed with specialty food, casual dining, and quick-service restaurant retailers—including national, regional, and locally owned restaurants—its closest competitors were restaurants in the so-called fast-casual restaurant category. Fast-casual restaurants filled the gap between fast-food and casual, full-table-service dining. A fast-casual restaurant provided quick-service dining (much like fast-food enterprises) but were distinguished by enticing menus, higher food quality, and more inviting dining environments; typical meal costs per guest were in the $7–$12 range. Some fast-casual restaurants had limited table service and some were self-service (like fast-food establishments). Exhibit 9 provides information on prominent national and regional chains that were competitors of Panera Bread.

Endnotes

[1] According to information in Panera Bread's press kit; the results of the study were reported in a 2003 *Wall Street Journal* article.

[2] As stated in a presentation to securities analysts, May 5, 2006.

[3] As cited in Panera Bread's presentation to securities analysts on May 5, 2006.

[4] Ibid.

[5] Ibid.

[6] Ibid.

[7] Information posted at www.restaurant.org (accessed August 1, 2006).

Coach Inc.: Is Its Advantage in Luxury Handbags Sustainable?

John E. Gamble
University of South Alabama

In the six years following its October 2000 initial public offering (IPO), Coach Inc.'s net sales had grown at a compounded annual rate of 26 percent and its stock price had increased by 1,400 percent as a result of a strategy keyed to a concept called accessible luxury. Coach created the accessible luxury category in women's handbags and leather accessories by matching key luxury rivals on quality and styling, while beating them on price by 50 percent or more. Not only did Coach's $200–$500 handbags appeal to middle-income consumers wanting a taste of luxury, but affluent consumers with the means to spend $2,000 or more on a handbag regularly snapped up its products as well. By 2006, Coach had become the best-selling brand of women's luxury handbags and leather accessories in the United States, with a 25 percent market share, and was the second best-selling brand of such products in Japan, with an 8 percent market share. Beyond its winning combination of styling, quality, and pricing, the attractiveness of Coach retail stores and high levels of customer service contributed to its competitive advantage.

Much of the company's growth in net sales was attributable to its rapid growth in company-owned stores in the United States and Japan. Coach stores ranged from prominent flagship stores on Rodeo Drive and Madison Avenue to factory outlet stores. In fact, Coach's factory stores had achieved higher comparable store growth during 2005 and 2006 than its full-price stores. At year-end 2006, comparable store sales in Coach factory stores had increased by 31.9 percent since year-end 2005, while comparable

store sales for Coach full-price stores experienced a 12.3 percent year-over-year increase. In 2006, Coach products were sold in 218 full-price company-owned stores, 86 factory stores, 900 U.S. department stores, 118 locations in Japan, and 108 international locations outside Japan.

Going into 2007, the company's executives expected to sustain its impressive growth through monthly introductions of fresh new handbag designs and the addition of retail locations in the United States, Japan, and rapidly growing luxury goods markets in Asia. The company planned to add three to five factory stores per year to eventually reach 105 stores in the United States, add 30 full-price stores per year in the United States to reach 300, and add at least 10 stores per year in Japan to reach as many as 180 stores. The company also expected its licensed international distributors to open new locations in Hong Kong and mainland China. Other growth initiatives included strategic alliances to bring the Coach brand to such additional luxury categories as women's knitwear and fragrances. Only time would tell if Coach's growth could be sustained and its advantage would hold in the face of new accessible luxury lines recently launched by such industry elites as Giorgio Armani, Dolce & Gabbana, and Gianni Versace.

COMPANY HISTORY

Coach was founded in 1941 when Miles Cahn, a New York City leather artisan, began producing women's handbags. The handbags crafted by Cahn and his family in their SoHo loft were simple in style and extremely resilient to wear and tear. Coach's classic styling and sturdy construction proved popular with discriminating consumers, and the company's initial line of 12 unlined leather bags soon developed a loyal following. Over the next 40 years, Coach was able to grow at a steady rate by setting prices about 50 percent lower than those of more luxurious brands, adding new models, and establishing accounts with retailers such as Bloomingdale's and Saks Fifth Avenue. The Cahn family also opened company-owned stores that sold Coach handbags and leather accessories. After 44 years of family management, Coach was sold to diversified food and consumer goods producer Sara Lee.

Sara Lee's 1985 acquisition of Coach left the handbag manufacturer's strategy and approach to operations more or less intact. The company continued to build a strong reputation for long-lasting classic handbags. However, by the mid-1990s, the company's performance began to decline as consumers developed a stronger preference for stylish French and Italian designer brands such as Gucci, Prada, Louis Vuitton, Dolce & Gabbana, and Ferragamo. By 1995, annual sales growth in Coach's best-performing stores fell from 40 percent to 5 percent as the company's traditional leather bags fell out of favor with consumers.

In 1996, Sara Lee made 18-year Coach veteran Lew Frankfort head of its listless handbag division. Frankfort's first move was to hire Reed Krakoff, a top Tommy Hilfiger designer, as Coach's new creative director. Krakoff believed that new products should be based on market research rather than on designers' instincts about what would sell. Under Krakoff, Coach conducted extensive consumer surveys and held focus groups to ask customers about styling, comfort, and functionality preferences. The company's research found that consumers were looking for edgier styling, softer leathers, and leather-trimmed fabric handbags. Once prototypes had been developed by a team of designers, merchandisers, and sourcing specialists, hundreds of previous customers were asked to rate prototype designs against existing handbags. The prototypes that made it to production were then tested in selected Coach stores for six months before a launch was announced. The design process developed by Krakoff also allowed Coach to launch new collections every month. Prior to his arrival, Coach had introduced only two collections per year.

Frankfort's turnaround plan also included a redesign of the company's flagship stores to complement Coach's contemporary new designs. Frankfort abandoned the stores' previous dark wood-paneled interiors in favor of minimalist architectural features that provided a bright and airy ambience. The company also improved the appearance of its factory stores, which carried test models, discontinued models, and special lines that sold at discounts ranging from 15 to 50 percent. Such discounts were made possible by the company's policy of outsourcing production to 40 suppliers in 15 countries. The outsourcing agreements allowed Coach to maintain a sizable pricing advantage relative to other luxury handbag brands in its full-price stores as well. Handbags sold in Coach full-price stores ranged from $200 to $500, which was well below the $700–$800 entry-level price charged by other luxury brands.

Coach's attractive pricing enabled it to appeal to consumers who would not normally consider luxury brands, while the quality and styling of its products were sufficient to satisfy traditional luxury consumers. In fact, a *Women's Wear Daily* survey found that Coach's quality, styling, and value mix was so powerful that affluent women in the United States ranked Coach ahead of much more expensive luxury brands such as Hermès, Ralph Lauren, Prada, and Fendi.[1] By 2000, the changes to Coach's strategy and operations allowed the brand to build a sizable lead in the accessible luxury segment of the leather handbags and accessories industry and made it a solid performer in Sara Lee's business lineup. With the turnaround successfully executed, Sara Lee management elected to spin off Coach through an IPO in October 2000 as part of a restructuring initiative designed to focus the corporation on food and beverages.

Coach Inc.'s performance proved to be stellar as an independent public company. The company's annual sales had increased from $500 million in 1999 to more than $2.1 billion in 2006. Its earnings over the same time frame improved from approximately $16.7 million to $494 million. By late 2006, Coach Inc.'s share price had increased by nearly 15 times from the 2000 IPO price. Exhibit 1 presents income statements for Coach Inc. for fiscal 1999 through fiscal 2006. Its balance sheets for fiscal 2005 and fiscal 2006 are presented in Exhibit 2. Coach's market performance between its October 2000 IPO date and December 2006 is presented in Exhibit 3.

Exhibit 1   **Coach Inc.'s Consolidated Statements of Income, 1999–2006 ($ in thousands, except share amounts)**

	2006	2005	2004	2003	2002	2001	2000	1999
Net sales	$2,111,501	$1,710,423	$1,321,106	$953,226	$719,403	$600,491	$537,694	$500,944
Cost of sales	472,622	399,652	331,024	275,797	236,041	218,507	220,085	226,190
Gross profit	1,638,879	1,310,771	990,082	677,429	483,362	381,984	317,609	274,754
Selling, general and administrative expenses	874,275	738,208	584,778	458,980	362,211	275,727	261,592	248,171
Reorganization costs	—	—	—	—	3,373	4569	—	7108
Operating income	764,604	572,563	405,304	218,449	117,778	101,688	56,017	19,475
Interest income (expense), net	32,623	15,760	3,192	1,059	(299)	(2,258)	(387)	(414)
Income before provision for income taxes and minority interest	797,227	588,323	408,496	219,508	117,479	99,430	55,630	19,061
Provision for income taxes	302,950	216,070	152,504	81,219	41,695	35,400	17,027	2,346
Minority interest, net of tax	—	13,641	18,043	7,608	184	—	—	—
Net income	$ 494,277	$ 358,612	$ 237,949	$130,681	$ 75,600	$ 64,030	$ 38,603	$ 16,715
Net income per share*								
Basic	$1.30	$0.95	$0.64	$0.36	$0.21	$0.20	$0.14	$0.06
Diluted	$1.27	$0.92	$0.62	$0.35	$0.21	$0.19	$0.14	$0.06
Shares used in computing net income per share:								
Basic	379,635	378,670	372,120	359,116	352,192	327,440	280,208	280,208
Diluted	388,495	390,191	385,558	371,684	363,808	337,000	280,208	280,208

* The two-for-one stock splits in April 2005, October 2003 and July 2002 have been retroactively applied to all prior periods.
Source: Coach Inc. 10-K reports.

Exhibit 2   **Coach Inc.'s Balance Sheets, Fiscal 2005–Fiscal 2006 (in thousands)**

	July 1, 2006	July 2, 2005
ASSETS		
Cash and cash equivalents	$ 143,388	$ 154,566
Short-term investments	394,177	228,485
Trade accounts receivable, less allowances	84,361	65,399
of $6,000 and $4,124, respectively		
Inventories	233,494	184,419
Deferred income taxes	78,019	50,820
Prepaid expenses and other current assets	41,043	25,671
Total current assets	974,482	709,360
Long-term investments		122,065
Property and equipment, net	298,531	203,862
Goodwill	227,811	238,711
Indefinite life intangibles	12,007	12,088
Deferred income taxes	84,077	54,545
Other noncurrent assets	29,612	29,526
Total assets	$1,626,520	$1,370,157
LIABILITIES AND STOCKHOLDERS' EQUITY		
Accounts payable	$ 79,819	$ 64,985
Accrued liabilities	261,835	188,234
Revolving credit facility		12,292
Current portion of long-term debt	170	150
Total current liabilities	341,824	265,661
Deferred income taxes	31,655	4,512
Long-term debt	3,100	3,270
Other liabilities	61,207	40,794
Total liabilities	$ 437,786	$ 314,237
Stockholders' equity		
Preferred stock: (authorized 25,000,000 shares; $0.01 par value) none issued		
Common stock: (authorized 1,000,000,000 shares; $0.01 par value) issued and	$ 3,698	$ 3,784
outstanding 369,830,906 and 378,429,710 shares, respectively		
Additional paid-in-capital	775,209	566,262
Retained earnings	417,087	484,971
Accumulated other comprehensive (loss) income	(7,260)	903
Total stockholders' equity	1,188,734	1,055,920
Total liabilities and stockholders' equity	$1,626,520	$1,370,157

Source: Coach Inc. 2006 10-K report.

OVERVIEW OF THE GLOBAL LUXURY GOODS INDUSTRY IN 2006

The world's most well-to-do consumers spent more than $105 billion on luxury goods such as designer apparel, fine watches, and writing instruments, jewelry, and select quality leather goods in 2005. The global luxury goods industry was expected to grow by 7 percent during 2006, to reach $112 billion. Italian luxury goods companies accounted for a 27 percent share of industry sales in 2005, while French luxury goods companies held a 22 percent share, Swiss companies owned a 19 percent share, and U.S. companies accounted for a 14 percent share.

Growth in the luxury goods industry had been attributed to increasing incomes and wealth in developing countries in Eastern Europe and Asia

Exhibit 3   **Performance of Coach Inc.'s Stock Price, 2000–2006**

(a) Trend in Coach's Common Stock Price

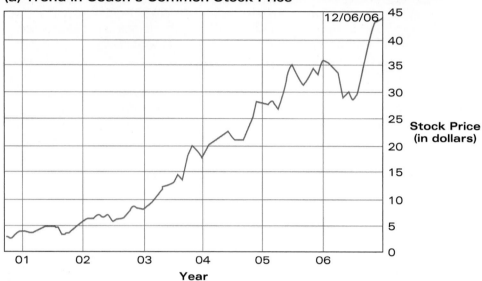

Year

(b) Performance of Coach's Stock Price versus the S&P 500 Index

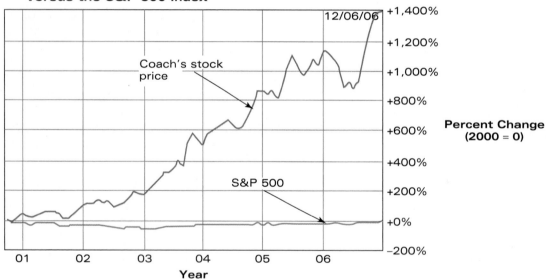

Year

and changing buying habits in the United States. Although traditional luxury consumers in the United States ranked in the top 1 percent of wage earners, with household incomes of $300,000 or better, a growing percentage of luxury goods consumers earned substantially less but still aspired to own products with higher levels of quality and styling. The growing desire for luxury goods by middle-income consumers was thought to be a result of a wide range of factors, including effective advertising and television programming that glorified conspicuous consumption. The demanding day-to-day rigor of a two-income household was another factor suggested to urge middle-income consumers to reward themselves with luxuries.

An additional factor contributing to rising sales of luxury goods was the growth of big-box discounters such as Wal-Mart and Target. Discounters' low prices on everyday items had facilitated a "trade up, trade down"[2] shopping strategy, whereby consumers could buy necessities at very low prices and then splurge on indulgences ranging from premium vodka to $4,000 Viking stoves. The combined effect of such factors had allowed spending on luxury goods to grow at four times the rate of overall spending in the United States.

Both retailers and luxury goods manufacturers had altered their strategies in response to the changing buying preferences of middle-income consumers in the United States. Much of Target's success was linked to its merchandising strategy, which focused on relationships with designers such as Philippe Starck, Todd Oldham, Michael Graves, and Isaac Mizrahi. Target's growth had not gone unnoticed by Wal-Mart, which in 2004 began to closely watch haute couture fashion trends for inspiration for new apparel lines. Wal-Mart hosted fashion shows in Manhattan and Miami's South Beach to launch its Metro 7 collection of women's apparel in fall 2005. Exsto was a designer-inspired menswear line that Wal-Mart introduced in summer 2006.

Wal-Mart also had begun to evaluate new store concepts that might appeal to upscale consumers. In 2006, the company was testing a stylish new Supercenter store in Plano, Texas, that stocked gourmet cheeses, organic produce, and 1,200 different wines. The new store also included a Wi-Fi coffee shop and a sushi bar. A Wal-Mart spokesperson explained the company's experimentation by commenting, "We've always been a top choice for the budget-minded customers. What we're trying to do now is expand our product line, and sell products more relevant to folks who are more discerning in their shopping."[3] Like Wal-Mart, other middle-market retailers had altered their merchandising strategies to accommodate consumers' desires for luxury. During the 2006 Christmas shopping season, J. Crew offered $1,400 cashmere overcoats and Home Depot stocked $2,800 HDTVs for consumers looking for extraordinary gifts.

Manufacturers of the finest luxury goods sought to exploit middle-income consumers' desire for such products by launching "diffusion lines" that offered affordable or accessible luxury.[4] In 2006, most leading designer brands had developed sub-brands that retained the styling and quality of the marquee brand, but sold at considerably more modest price points. For example, while Dolce & Gabbana dresses might

sell at price points between $1,000 and $1,500, very similar-appearing dresses under Dolce & Gabbana's affordable luxury brand—D&G—were priced at $400 to $600. Giorgio Armani's Emporio Armani line and Gianni Versace's Versus lines typically sold at price points about 50 percent less than similar-looking items carrying the marquee labels. Profit margins on marquee brands approximated 40–50 percent, while most diffusion brands carried profit margins of about 20 percent. Luxury goods manufacturers believed that diffusion brands' lower profit margins were offset by the growing size of the accessible luxury market and protected margins on such products by sourcing production to low-wage countries.

Growing Demand for Luxury Goods in Emerging Markets

In 2004, the worldwide total number of households with assets of at least $1 million increased by 7 percent, to reach 8.3 million. The number of millionaires was expected to increase by another 23 percent by 2009, to reach 10.2 million. With much of the increase in new wealth occurring in Asia and the Eastern Europe, demand for luxury goods in emerging markets was projected to grow at annual rates approaching 10 percent. Rising incomes and new wealth had allowed Chinese consumers to account for 11 percent of all luxury goods purchases in 2004. The Chinese market for luxury goods was predicted to increase to 24 percent of global revenues by 2014, which would make it the world's largest market for luxury goods. In 2006, a number of prestigious Western retailers such as Saks Fifth Avenue had opened retail stores in China to build a first-mover advantage in the growing market. Similarly, most luxury goods companies had opened stores in China's largest cities, with Louis Vuitton operating 12 stores in 10 cities in 2006.

Luxury goods producers were also opening retail stores in India, which was another rapidly growing market for luxury goods. In 2005, approximately 50,000 households earned more than 10 million rupees (approximately $250,000) and were the backbone of India's $500 million luxury goods market. The number of households in India with annual incomes of over 10 million rupees was expected to double by 2010. As of 2006, Versace, Louis Vuitton, Dior, Chanel, Hugo Boss, and Tommy Hilfiger had opened retail locations in India. Gucci and Giorgio Armani had announced plans to open flagship stores in India by 2008. LVMH, which was the parent company of Louis Vuitton, Givenchy, Fendi, and others, planned to expand its network of 50 stores in 18 Indian cities to 100 luxury stores in 23 cities by 2008.

Counterfeiting

In 2006, more than $500 billion worth of counterfeit goods were sold in countries throughout the world. European and American companies that produced highly sought-after branded products were most vulnerable to counterfeiting, with fakes plaguing almost every industry. Fake Rolex watches and Ralph Lauren Polo shirts had long been a problem, but by the mid-2000s, counterfeiters were even making knockoffs of branded auto parts and prescription drugs. Counterfeiting had become so prevalent that the Global Congress on Combating Counterfeiting estimated that 9 percent of all goods sold worldwide were not genuine. The European Union's trade commission categorized the problem as "nothing short of an economic crisis."[5] Interpol believed in 2005 that terrorist organizations such as al Qaeda commonly used counterfeiting to fund their activities since fake brands were as profitable as drugs and because there was very little risk of being prosecuted if caught. About two-thirds of all counterfeit goods were produced by manufacturers in China.

One problem in combating counterfeiting was the demand for knockoffs. In the United States, China, and Europe, vendors and consumers who traded in outdoor street markets knowingly bought and sold fakes and had few reservations about doing so. Using Great Britain as an illustration of the problem, experts there believed that 100 million fake luxury goods were sold in Britain in 2005 and that one in eight adult Britons had purchased a fake in the past year. The European Union and the Chinese government took a step toward combating piracy in 2005 with the signing of an agreement that would fine owners of outdoor bazaars in China if vendors were caught selling counterfeit goods. In addition, the agreement called for landlords to terminate the lease of any vendor caught selling counterfeit goods a second time. The Chinese government convicted more than 5,500 individuals of intellectual property rights crimes in 2005. However, many piracy and counterfeiting experts believed the problem would not subside until the Chinese government adopted a zero tolerance policy against fakes.

COACH'S STRATEGY AND INDUSTRY POSITIONING

In 2006, Coach Inc. designed and marketed women's handbags; leather accessories such as key fobs, belts, electronics accessories, and cosmetics cases; and outerwear such as gloves, hats, and scarves. Coach also designed and marketed leather business cases and luggage. The company entered into a licensing agreement with the Movado Group in 1998 to make Coach-branded watches available in Coach retail stores. Coach entered into a similar agreement with the Jimlar Corporation in 1999 that gave Jimlar the right to manufacture and market Coach-branded women's footwear. In 2006, Coach footwear was available in 500 locations in the United States, including department stores and Coach retail stores. Marchon Eyewear became a licensee for Coach-branded eyewear and sunglasses in 2003. Coach sunglasses were sold in Coach retail stores, department stores, and specialty eyewear stores. Coach frames for prescription glasses were sold through Marchon's network of optical retailers.

Handbags accounted for 67 percent of Coach's 2006 sales, while women's accessories accounted for 23 percent of the company's sales, men's accessories accounted for 2 percent of sales, and outerwear made up 2 percent of 2006 net sales. Business cases and luggage each accounted for 1 percent of company 2006 revenues. Royalties from Coach's licensing agreements with Movado, Jimlar, and Marchon accounted for 1 percent, 2 percent, and 1 percent of the company's 2006 net sales, respectively.

Coach held a 25 percent share of the U.S. luxury handbag market and was the second best-selling brand of luxury handbags in Japan, with an 8 percent market share. Through 2006, Coach had focused on Japan and the United States since those two countries ranked numbers one and two, respectively, in global luxury goods spending. Coach's sales in Japan had increased from $144 million in 2002 to more than $420 million in 2006, while the company's market share in the United States had more than doubled from the 12 percent it held in 2002.

Approach to Differentiation

The market research design process developed by Coach's executive creative director, Reed Krakoff, provided the basis of the company's differentiated product line, but the company's procurement process (which selected only the highest-quality leathers) and its sourcing agreements with quality offshore manufacturers were additional contributors to the company's reputation for high quality. Monthly product launches enhanced the company's voguish image and gave consumers reason to make purchases on a regular basis. The company's market research found that its best customers visited a Coach store once every two months and made a purchase once every seven months. In 2006, the average Coach customer purchased four handbags per year, a figure that had doubled since 2002. Lew Frankfort said the increase was attributable to monthly product launches that "increase the frequency of consumer visits" and women's changing style preference of "using bags to complement their wardrobes in the same way they used to use shoes."[6] A retail analyst agreed with Frankfort's assessment of the importance of frequent product introductions, calling it "a huge driver of traffic and sales and has enabled them to capture the . . . customer who wants the newest items and fashions."[7] Seventy percent of Coach's 2006 sales came from products introduced within the fiscal year.

The aesthetic attractiveness of Coach's full-price stores, which were designed by an in-house architectural group under the direction of Krakoff, further enhanced the company's luxury image. A 2006 survey of 2,000 wealthy shoppers by the Luxury Group ranked Coach store environments 10th among luxury brands. The surveyed shoppers found few differences among the 10 highest-rated store atmospheres, with number one Louis Vuitton scoring 88.1 out of 100; number two Hermès scoring 87.9; Armani and Gucci scoring 86; Versace, Ferragamo and Prada all scoring 85; and Burberry and Coach tying at 84.

Coach sought to make customer service experiences an additional differentiating aspect of the brand. Coach had agreed since its founding to refurbish or replace damaged handbags, regardless of the age of the bag. In 2006, the company provided store employees with regular customer service training programs and scheduled additional personnel during peak shopping periods to ensure that all customers were attended to satisfactorily. Through the company's Special Request service, customers were allowed to order merchandise for home delivery if the particular handbag or color wasn't available during a visit to a Coach store.

Retail Distribution

Coach's channels of distribution included direct-to-consumer channels and indirect channels. Direct-to-consumer channels included full-price and factory stores in the United States, Internet sales, catalog sales, and stores in Japan. Wholesale accounts with department stores in the United States and in international markets outside Japan represented the company's indirect sales. Exhibit 4 provides selected financial data for Coach Inc. by channel of distribution.

In the United States, Coach products could be found in approximately 900 department stores, 218 Coach full-price stores, and 86 Coach factory outlet stores. U.S. consumers could also order Coach products through either the company's Web site or its printed catalog. The company mailed about 4.1 million catalogs to strategically selected households in the United States during 2006 and placed another 3.5 million catalogs in Coach retail stores for customers to pick up during a store visit. Sales from catalogs were incidental since the catalogs were primarily used to build brand awareness, promote store traffic, and help shoppers evaluate styles before visiting a Coach retail store. Coach's Web site accomplished the same goals as its catalogs but had become a significant contributor to overall sales. In 2006, the Web site had 40 million unique visitors and generated $54 million in net sales. The company also sent promotional e-mails to 55 million selected customers in 2006.

Full-Price Stores.   Coach's full-price U.S. retail stores accounted for 54 percent of Coach's 2006 net sales. Beginning in 2003, full-price stores were divided into three categories—core locations, fashion locations, and flagship stores. Under Coach's tiered merchandising strategy, the company's flagship stores carried the most sophisticated and highest-priced items, while core stores carried widely demanded lines. The company's fashion locations tended to stock a blend of Coach's best-selling lines

Exhibit 4   **Selected Financial Data for Coach Inc. by Channel of Distribution, Fiscal 2004–Fiscal 2006 ($ in thousands)**

	Direct-to-Consumer	Indirect	Corporate Unallocated*	Total
Fiscal 2006				
Net sales	$1,610,691	$500,810		$2,111,501
Operating income (loss)	717,326	313,689	(266,411)	764,604
Income (loss) before provision				
for income taxes and minority interest	717,326	313,689	(233,788)	797,227
Depreciation and amortization expense	43,177	5,506	16,432	65,115
Total assets	$ 743,034	$ 91,247	792,239	$1,626,520
Additions to long-lived assets	$ 70,440	$ 6,036	57,400	$ 133,876
Fiscal 2005				
Net sales	$1,307,425	$402,998		$1,710,423
Operating income (loss)	548,520	243,276	(219,233)	572,563
Income (loss) before provision				
for income taxes and minority interest	548,520	243,276	(203,473)	588,323
Depreciation and amortization expense	37,275	4,362	8,763	50,400
Total assets	$ 646,788	$ 69,569	$653,800	$1,370,157
Additions to long-lived assets	$ 70,801	$ 4,778	$ 19,013	$ 94,592
Fiscal 2004				
Net sales	$1,002,737	$318,369		$1,321,106
Operating income (loss)	403,884	178,390	(176,970)	405,304
Income (loss) before provision				
for income taxes and minority interest	403,884	178,390	(173,778)	408,496
Depreciation and amortization expense	30,054	3,509	6,537	40,100
Total assets	$ 328,530	$ 64,770	$666,979	$1,060,279
Additions to long-lived assets	$ 57,589	$ 3,884	$ 12,186	$ 73,659

* Breakdown of Coach Inc.'s unallocated corporate expenses, 2004–2006 ($ in thousands):

	Fiscal Year Ended		
	July 1, 2006	July 2, 2005	July 3, 2004
Production variances	$ 14,659	$ 11,028	$ 12,581
Advertising, marketing and design	(91,443)	(70,234)	(56,714)
Administration and information systems	(148,846)	(125,217)	(102,682)
Distribution and customer service	(40,781)	(34,810)	(30,155)
Total corporate unallocated	($266,411)	($219,233)	($176,970)

Source: Coach Inc. 2006 10-K report.

and chic specialty bags. By 2006, the company had successfully graduated many core locations to fashion locations. Management believed that Coach had remaining opportunities in the United States to move core stores to fashion stores and fashion stores to flagship stores.

Coach's site-selection process placed its core and fashion stores in upscale shopping centers and downtown shopping areas, while flagship stores were restricted to high-profile fashion districts in cities such as New York, Chicago, Beverly Hills, and San Francisco. Even though flagship stores were "a beacon for the brand,"[8] as Frankfort described them, the company had been very prudent in the number of flagship stores it operated since such stores, by definition, were required to be located on the world's most expensive parcels of real estate.

Factory Stores. Coach's factory stores in the United States were generally located 50 or more miles from its full-price stores and made up about 19 percent of the company's 2006 net sales. About 75 percent of factory store inventory was produced specifically for Coach's factory stores, while the remaining 25 percent was made up of overstocked items and discontinued models. Coach's 10–50 percent discounts offered in factory stores allowed the company to maintain a year-round full-price policy in full-price stores. Coach's CEO, Lew Frankfort, believed that discounted prices were critical to success in retailing since 80 percent of women's apparel sold in the United States was bought on sale or in a discount store. "Women in the U.S. have been trained to expect to be able to find a bargain if they either go through the hunt . . . or are willing to buy something after the season," said Frankfort.[9]

Coach had found that there was very little overlap between shoppers in full-price stores and factory stores. The company's market research found the typical full-price store shopper was a 35-year-old, college-educated, single or newly married working woman. The typical factory store shopper was a 45-year-old, college-educated, married, professional woman with children. The average annual spending in a Coach store by full-price shoppers was $1,100. Factory store shoppers spent about $770 annually on Coach products, with 80 percent spent in factory stores and 20 percent spent in a full-price store. The 80:20 ratio of spending also applied to full-price store customers. A retail analyst characterized the difference between the two types of Coach customers as "one wants fashion first and the other is a discount shopper. . . . There is no question it is a very different mindset."[10] Coach had found its full-price customers and factory store customers were equally brand loyal.

Coach's factory stores had outperformed full-price stores in terms of comparable store sales growth during 2005 and 2006, with comparable factory store sales increasing by 31.9 percent during 2006 and comparable full-price store sales increasing by 12.3 percent during the year. The company's impressive overall growth in comparable store sales was attributable, to some degree, to its policy of charting sales for every store and every type of merchandise on a

daily basis. During holiday shopping periods, management received sales updates two or three times per day. The frequent updates allowed management to shift production to the hottest-selling items to avoid stockouts.

The company's top-performing factory store during 2005 was its Woodbury Common outlet store, located about 50 miles outside New York City. The store's 2005 sales of $20 million and estimated 2006 sales of $25 million made it as productive as the company's Madison Avenue flagship store. Some degree of Coach's success with its outlet stores resulted from its strategy that valued factory stores as much as full-price stores. The company was committed to providing factory store customers with service and quality equal to that provided to full-price customers. A May 2006 *Consumer Reports* review of outlet stores rated Coach number one in terms of merchandise quality and customer service.

At year-end 2006, Lew Frankfort stated the company would add 3 to 5 factory stores per year until it reached 105, and 30 full-price stores per year to reach 300. Frankfort believed that North America could support 400 full-price Coach stores long term. He did not want factory outlet stores to grow too rapidly, noting, "Our destiny lies in our ability to grow full-price stores."[11] Some analysts were worried that Coach's highly successful factory stores might someday dilute its image. A Luxury Institute analyst described the dilemma faced by Coach and luxury diffusion brands by commenting, "To be unique and exclusive you cannot be ubiquitous."[12] Exhibit 5 shows Coach's growth in retail stores by type and geographic region between 2001 and 2006.

U.S. Wholesale. Wholesale sales of Coach products to U.S. department stores increased by 23 percent during 2006, to reach $232 million. Department stores were becoming less relevant in U.S. retailing, with the average consumer spending less time in malls and shopping in fewer stores during visits to malls. The share of the U.S. retail market held by department stores declined from about 30 percent in 1990 to approximately 20 percent in 2000. However, handbags and accessories remained a better-performing product category for such retailers. Coach had eliminated 500 department store accounts between 2002 and 2006. Macy's, Bloomingdale's, Lord & Taylor,

Exhibit 5   **Coach Inc.'s Retail Stores by Geographic Region, Fiscal 2001–Fiscal 2006**

	2006	2005	2004	2003	2002	2001
North America						
Full price company-owned stores	218	193	174	156	138	121
Net increase vs. prior year	25	19	18	18	17	15
Percentage increase vs. prior year	11.5%	9.8%	10.3%	11.5%	12.3%	12.4%
Retail square footage	562,553	490,925	431,617	363,310	301,501	251,136
Net increase vs. prior year	71,628	59,308	68,307	61,809	50,365	42,077
Percentage increase vs. prior year	12.7%	12.1%	15.8%	17.0%	16.7%	16.8%
Average square footage	2,581	2,544	2,481	2,329	2,185	2,076
Factory stores	86	82	76	76	74	68
Net increase vs. prior year	4	6	0	2	6	5
Percentage increase vs. prior year	4.7%	7.3%	0.0%	2.6%	8.1%	7.4%
Factory square footage	281,787	252,279	231,355	232,898	219,507	198,924
Net increase vs. prior year	29,508	20,924	(1,543)	13,391	20,583	16,414
Percentage increase vs. prior year	10.5%	8.3%	(0)	5.7%	9.4%	8.3%
Average square footage	3,277	3,077	3,044	3,064	2,966	2,925
Coach Japan						
Total locations	118	103	100	93	83	76
Net increase vs. prior year	15	3	7	10	7	6
Percentage increase vs. prior year	12.7%	2.9%	7.0%	10.8%	8.4%	7.9%
Total square footage	194,375	161,632	119,291	102,242	76,975	63,371
Net increase vs. prior year	32,743	42,341	17,049	25,267	13,604	7,229
Percentage increase vs. prior year	16.8%	26.2%	14.3%	24.7%	17.7%	11.4%
Average square footage	1,647	1,569	1,193	1,099	927	834
Other International						
International freestanding stores	21	14	18	n.a.	n.a.	n.a.
International department store locations	63	58	70	n.a.	n.a.	n.a.
Other international locations	24	22	27	n.a.	n.a.	n.a.
Total international wholesale locations	108	94	115	n.a.	n.a.	n.a.

n.a. = Not available

Source: Coach Inc. 10-K reports.

Dillard's, Nordstrom, Saks Fifth Avenue, and Parisian were the highest volume department store sellers of Coach merchandise in 2006.

International Markets

International Wholesale. Coach's wholesale distribution in international markets involved department stores, freestanding retail locations, shop-in-shop locations, and specialty retailers in 18 countries. The company's largest international wholesale accounts were the DFS Group, Lotte Group, Shila Group, Tasa Meng Corporation, and Imaginex. The largest portion of sales by these companies was to traveling Japanese consumers. Coach's largest wholesale country markets were Korea, Hong Kong, Taiwan, Singapore, Japan, Saudi Arabia, Australia, Mexico, Thailand, Malaysia, the Caribbean, China, New Zealand, and France. In 2006, international wholesale accounts amounted to $147 million.

Coach Japan. Coach products in Japan were sold in shop-in-shop department store locations, full-price Coach stores, and Coach factory stores. The company had 118 retail locations in Japan in 2006, although company managers believed Japan could support as many as 180 retail outlets. Coach's expansion plan for Japan called for at least 10 new stores annually, which would more than double its number

Exhibit 6   **Coach Inc.'s Net Sales and Assets by Geographic Region,
Fiscal 2004–Fiscal 2006 ($ in thousands)**

	United States	Japan	Other International	Total
Fiscal 2006				
Net sales	$1,574,285	$420,509	$116,707	$2,111,501
Long-lived assets	266,190	298,087	3,684	567,961
Fiscal 2005				
Net sales	$1,253,170	$372,326	$ 84,927	$1,710,423
Long-lived assets	314,919	288,338	2,995	606,252
Fiscal 2004				
Net sales	$ 982,668	$278,011	$ 60,427	$1,321,106
Long-lived assets	280,938	55,487	2,384	338,809

Source: Coach Inc. 2006 10-K report.

of flagship stores to 15. Coach management believed the increase in stores would allow the company to increase its market share in Japan to 15 percent. The number of Coach retail locations in Japan and other international markets for 2001 through 2006 is presented in Exhibit 5. Coach Inc.'s sales and assets by geographic region are provided in Exhibit 6.

COACH'S STRATEGIC OPTIONS IN 2007

Going into 2007, Lew Frankfort's key growth initiatives involved store expansion in the United States, Japan, Hong Kong, and mainland China; increasing sales to existing customers to drive comparable store growth; and creating alliances to exploit the Coach brand in additional luxury categories. The company's managers believed that there was an opportunity to double the number of full-price retail stores in North America and increase the number of North American factory stores by a third. They also believed that Japan could support approximately 70 additional Coach stores. Licensed distributors in Hong Kong operated 13 locations there and planned to open at least 10 locations on mainland China by 2007.

The company's second growth initiative was to increase same-store sales through continued development of new styles, the development of new usage collections, and the exploitation of gift-giving opportunities. The company had recently begun to prewrap items during holiday shopping periods and had created a new section of its Web site for gift-givers. Coach.com's gift guide recommended items that might appeal to women based on their needs. For example, the Web site recommended handbags preferred by professional women, handbags for formal events, items for fashion-oriented teens, and essential handbags.

During late 2006, Coach launched a women's knitwear collection through a strategic alliance with Lutz & Patmos. The leather- and fur-trimmed cashmere and wool knits ranged from $300 to $1,500. The company also entered into an agreement with a division of the Estée Lauder Company for the development of a fragrance that would be sold in Coach stores beginning in spring 2007.

For the first quarter of fiscal 2007, Coach's comparable store sales for full-price stores increased by 16 percent relative to the same period in 2006. Coach factory stores achieved year-over-year comparable store sales growth of 27.1 percent. The company's indirect sales improved by 11 percent between the first quarter of 2006 and the first quarter of fiscal 2007. Operating income during the first quarter of 2007 increased by 36 percent, while operating margins improved by 340 basis points to reach 35.7 percent. Lew Frankfort attributed the company's continuing sales and profit growth to 19 new store openings in the United States; new handbag collections such as Coach Signature Stripe, Chelsea, Hamptons silhouettes, and Legacy lifestyle; and the increased assortment of gifts under $100 geared to price-sensitive holiday shoppers. The company's stock provided nearly a 35 percent return to shareholders during the 2006 calendar year. The challenge for Lew Frankfort and other key Coach executives was to defend against competitive attacks from French and Italian luxury goods makers and sustain the impressive growth rate the company had achieved since its 2000 IPO.

Endnotes

[1] "How Coach Got Hot," *Fortune* 146, no. 8 (October 28, 2002).

[2] As quoted in "Stores Dancing Chic to Chic," *Houston Chronicle*, May 6, 2006.

[3] Ibid.

[4] "Some Fashion Houses Bolster Lower Priced Lines," *Wall Street Journal*, September 25, 2006.

[5] As quoted in "Gumshoe's Intuition: Spotting Counterfeits at Port of Antwerp," *Wall Street Journal*, December 14, 2006, p. A1.

[6] As quoted in "Fashions Keep Retailer Busy," *Investor's Business Daily*, February 10, 2005, p. A4.

[7] Ibid.

[8] As quoted in "Coach's Split Personality," *BusinessWeek*, November 7, 2005.

[9] As quoted in "Coach Sales Strategy Is in the Bag," *Financial Times*, April 18, 2006, p. 22.

[10] Ibid.

[11] As quoted in "Coach's Split Personality."

[12] As quoted in "Expansion into U.S.: Extending the Reach of the Exclusive Lifestyle Brands," *Financial Times,* July 8, 2006, p. 17.

Case 9

Nucor Corporation: Competing against Low-Cost Steel Imports

Arthur A. Thompson
The University of Alabama

In the 1950s and early 1960s, Nuclear Corporation of America was involved in the nuclear instrument and electronics business. After suffering through several money-losing years and facing bankruptcy in 1964, the company's board of directors opted for new leadership and appointed F. Kenneth Iverson as president and CEO. Shortly thereafter, Iverson concluded that the best way to put the company on sound footing was to exit the nuclear instrument and electronics business and rebuild the company around its profitable South Carolina–based Vulcraft subsidiary, which was in the steel joist business— Iverson had been the head of Vulcraft prior to being named president. Iverson moved the company's headquarters from Phoenix, Arizona, to Charlotte, North Carolina, in 1966 and proceeded to expand the joist business with new operations in Texas and Alabama. Then, in 1968, management decided to integrate backward into steelmaking, partly because of the benefits of supplying its own steel requirements and partly because Iverson saw opportunities to capitalize on newly emerging technologies to produce steel more cheaply. The company adopted the name Nucor Corporation in 1972, and Iverson initiated a long-term strategy to grow Nucor into a major player in the U.S. steel industry.

By 1985, Nucor had become the seventh largest steel company in America, with revenues of $758 million, six joist plants, and four state-of-the-art steel mills that used electric arc furnaces to produce new steel products from recycled scrap steel. Nucor was regarded as an excellently managed company, an accomplished low-cost producer, and one of the most competitively successful manufacturing companies in the country.[1] A series of articles in the *New Yorker* related how Nucor, a relatively small American steel company, had built an enterprise that led the whole world into a new era of making steel with recycled scrap steel. NBC did a business documentary that used Nucor to make the point that American manufacturers could be successful in competing against low-cost foreign manufacturers.

At the turn of the century, Nucor was the second largest steel producer in the United States and charging to overtake longtime leader U.S. Steel. Nucor's sales in 2000 exceeded 11 million tons, and revenues were nearly $4.8 billion. Several years thereafter, Nucor surpassed U.S. Steel as the largest steelmaker in North America, but Nucor fell back into second place in 2006 when a global steel company in Europe made a series of acquisitions in the United States to create a U.S.-based subsidiary (Mittal Steel USA) with greater production capacity than Nucor. (However, Nucor shipped more tons of steel to customers in 2005 than did Mittal Steel.) At the end of 2006, Nucor was solidly entrenched as the second largest steel producer in North America based on total production capacity, with 18 plants having the capacity to produce 25 million tons of steel annually, 2006 revenues of $14.8 billion, and net profits of $1.8 billion. It was the most profitable steel producer in North America in both 2005 and 2006. The company was regarded as the low-cost steel producer in the United States and one of the most efficient and technologically innovative steel producers in the world. Nucor had earned a profit in every quarter and every year since 1966—a truly remarkable accomplishment in a mature and cyclical industry where it was

Exhibit 1   **Nucor's Growth in the Steel Business, 1970–2006**

Year	Tons Sold to Outside Customers	Average Price per Ton	Net Sales (in millions)	Earnings before Taxes (in millions)	Pretax Earnings per Ton	Net Earnings (in millions)
1970	207,000	$245	$ 50.8	$ 2.2	$ 10	$ 1.1
1975	387,000	314	121.5	11.7	30	7.6
1980	1,159,000	416	482.4	76.1	66	45.1
1985	1,902,000	399	758.5	106.2	56	58.5
1990	3,648,000	406	1,481.6	111.2	35	75.1
1995	7,943,000	436	3,462.0	432.3	62	274.5
2000	11,189,000	425	4,756.5	478.3	48	310.9
2001	12,237,000	354	4,333.7	179.4	16	113.0
2002	13,442,000	357	4,801.7	230.1	19	162.1
2003	17,473,000	359	6,265.8	66.9	4	62.8
2004	19,109,000	595	11,376.8	1,731.3	96	1,121.5
2005	20,465,000	621	12,701.0	2,016.4	104	1,310.3
2006	22,118,000	667	14,751.3	2,693.8	129	1,757.7

Source: Company records posted at www.nucor.com (accessed October 3, 2006, and January 31, 2007).

common for companies to post losses when demand for steel sagged. Going into 2007, Nucor had paid a dividend for 135 consecutive quarters. Exhibit 1 provides highlights of Nucor's growth since 1970.

NUCOR IN 2007

Ken Iverson, the architect of Nucor's climb from obscurity to prominence in the steel industry, was regarded by many as a "model company president." Under Iverson, who served as CEO until late 1998, Nucor was known for its aggressive pursuit of innovation and technical excellence, rigorous quality systems, strong emphasis on employee relations and workforce productivity, cost-conscious corporate culture, and ability to achieve low costs per ton produced. The company had a streamlined organizational structure, incentive-based compensation systems, and steel mills that were among the most modern and efficient in the United States. Iverson proved himself as a master in crafting and executing a low-cost leadership strategy, and he made a point of making sure that he practiced what he preached when it came to holding down costs. The offices of executives and division general managers were simply furnished. There were no company planes and no company cars, and executives were not provided with company-paid country club memberships,

reserved parking spaces, executive dining facilities, or other perks. To save money on his own business expenses and set an example for other Nucor managers, Iverson flew coach class and took the subway when he was in New York City.

When Iverson left the company in 1998 following disagreements with the board of directors, he was succeeded briefly by John Correnti and then Dave Aycock, both of whom had worked in various roles under Iverson for a number of years. In 2000, Daniel R. DiMicco, who had joined Nucor in 1982 and risen up through the ranks to executive vice president, was named president and CEO. Under DiMicco, Nucor continued to pursue a rapid-growth strategy, expanding capacity via both acquisition and new plant construction and boosting tons sold from 11.2 million in 2000 to 22.1 million in 2006. Exhibit 2 provides a summary of Nucor's financial and operating performance for 2000–2006.

Product Line

Over the years, Nucor had expanded progressively into the manufacture of a wider and wider range of steel products, enabling it in 2006 to offer steel users one of the broadest product lineups in the industry. Steel products were considered commodities. While some steelmakers had plants where production quality was sometimes inconsistent or on occasions

Exhibit 2 **Seven-Year Financial and Operating Summary, Nucor Corporation, 2000–2006 ($ in millions, except per share data and sales per employee)**

	2006	2005	2004	2003	2002	2001	2000
FOR THE YEAR							
Net sales	$14,751.3	$12,701.0	$11,376.9	$6,265.8	$4,801.8	$4,333.7	$4,756.5
Costs, expenses and other:							
Cost of products sold	11,283.1	10,085.4	9,128.9	5,996.5	4,332.3	3,914.3	3,929.2
Marketing, administrative and other expenses	592.5	493.6	415.0	165.4	175.6	150.7	183.2
Interest expense (income), net	(37.4)	4.2	22.4	24.6	14.3	6.5	(.8)
Minority interests	219.2	110.7	80.9	24.0	79.5	103.1	151.5
Other income	—	(9,200)	(1,596)	(11.6)	(29.9)	(20.2)	—
Total	12,057.5	10,684.6	9,645.6	6,199.0	4,571.7	4,154.3	4,263.0
Earnings before income taxes	2,693.8	2,016.4	1,731.3	66.9	230.1	179.4	493.5
Provision for income taxes	936.1	706.1	609.8	4.1	68.0	66.4	182.6
Net earnings	$ 1,757.7	$ 1,310.3	$ 1,121.5	$ 62.8	$ 162.1	$ 113.0	$ 310.9
Net earnings per share:							
Basic	$5.73	$4.17	$3.54	$0.20	$0.52	$0.37	$0.95
Diluted	5.68	4.13	3.51	0.20	0.52	0.37	0.95
Dividends declared per share	$0.90	$0.925	$0.235	$0.20	$0.19	$0.17	$0.15
Percentage of net earnings to net sales	11.9%	10.3%	9.9%	1.0%	3.4%	2.6%	6.5%
Return on average equity	38.6%	33.9%	38.7%	2.7%	7.2%	5.2%	14.2%
Capital expenditures	$338.4	$331.5	$285.9	$215.4	$243.6	$261.1	$415.4
Depreciation	363.9	375.1	383.3	364.1	307.1	289.1	259.4
Sales per employee (000s)	1,273	1,159	1,107	637	528	531	619
AT YEAR END							
Current assets	$4,675.0	$4,071.6	$3,174.9	$1,620.7	$1,415.4	$1,373.7	$1,379.5
Current liabilities	1,450.0	1,255.7	1,065.8	629.6	591.5	484.2	558.1
Working capital	3,225.0	2,815.9	2,109.2	991.0	823.8	889.5	821.5
Cash provided by operating activities	2,251.2	2,136.6	1,024.8	493.8	497.2	495.1	820.8
Current ratio	3.2	3.2	3.0	2.6	2.4	2.8	2.5
Property, plant and equipment	$2,856.4	$2,855.7	$2,818.3	$2,817.1	$2,932.1	$2,365.7	$2,329.4
Total assets	7,885.0	7,138.8	6,133.2	4,492.4	4,381.1	3,759.3	3,710.9
Long-term debt	922.3	923.6	923.6	903.6	894.6	460.5	460.5
Stockholders' equity	4,826.0	4,279.8	3,456.0	2,342.1	2,323.0	2,201.5	2,131.0
Shares outstanding (000s)	301.2	310.2	319.0	314.4	312.8	311.2	310.4
Employees	11,900	11,300	10,600	9,900	9,800	8,400	7,900

Source: 2005 and 2006 10-K reports and company press release, January 25, 2007.

failed to meet customer-specified metallurgical characteristics, most steel plants turned out products of comparable metallurgical quality—one producer's reinforcing bar was essentially the same as another producer's reinforcing bar, a particular grade of sheet steel made at one plant was essentially identical to the same grade of sheet steel made at another plant.

The commodity nature of steel products forced steel producers to be price-competitive, with the market price of each particular steel product being driven by demand–supply conditions for that product.

Steel Products.   Nucor's first venture into steel in the late 1960s, via its Vulcraft division, was principally one of fabricating steel joists and joist girders from steel that was purchased from various steelmakers; the joists and girders were sold mainly to construction contractors. Vulcraft expanded into the fabrication of steel decking in 1977, most of which was also sold to construction-related customers. Vulcraft's joist, girder, and decking products were used mainly for roof and floor support systems in retail stores, shopping centers, warehouses, manufacturing facilities, schools, churches, hospitals, and, to a lesser extent, multistory buildings and apartments.

In 1979, Nucor began fabricating cold finished steel products. These consisted mainly of cold drawn and turned, ground, and polished steel bars or rods of various shapes—rounds, hexagons, flats, channels, and squares—and were made of carbon, alloy, and leaded steels as per customer specifications or end-use requirements. Cold finished steel of one type or another was used in tens of thousands of products, including anchor bolts, farm machinery, ceiling fan motors, garage door openers, air conditioner compressors, and lawn mowers. Nucor sold cold finished steel directly to large customers in the automotive, farm machinery, hydraulic, appliance, and electric motor industries and to independent steel distributors (usually referred to as steel service centers) that supplied manufacturers buying steel products in relatively small quantities. The total market for cold finished products in the United States was an estimated 2 million tons annually. In 2006, Nucor Cold Finish was the largest producer of cold finished bars in the United States, with a market share of about 17 percent; its 4 cold finish facilities (in Nebraska, South Carolina, Utah, and Wisconsin) had annual capacity of 490,000 tons. Nucor Cold Finish obtained virtually all of the steel needed to produce cold finished bars from Nucor's bar mills.

Nucor's line of steel products also included metal building systems, light-gauge steel framing, and steel fasteners (bolts, nuts, washers, screws, and bolt assemblies). These were produced by the company's building system and fasteners divisions. Nucor Building Systems began operations in 1987 and had four manufacturing facilities (Indiana, South Carolina, Texas, and Utah) in 2007; its wall and roof systems were mainly used for industrial and commercial buildings, including distribution centers, automobile dealerships, retail centers, aircraft hangars, churches, office buildings, warehouses, and manufacturing facilities. Complete metal building packages could be customized and combined with other materials such as glass, wood, and masonry to produce a cost-effective, aesthetically sound building of up to 1 million square feet. The buildings were sold through a builder distribution network. Nucor Building Systems obtained a significant portion of its steel requirements from the Nucor's bar and sheet mills.

The fastener division, located in Indiana, began operations in 1986 with the construction of a $25 million plant. At the time, imported steel fasteners accounted for 90 percent of the U.S. market because U.S. manufacturers were not competitive on cost and price. Iverson said, "We're going to bring that business back; we can make bolts as cheaply as foreign producers." Nucor built a second fastener plant in 1995, giving it the capacity to supply about 20 percent of the U.S. market for steel fasteners.

Steelmaking. In 1968 Nucor got into basic steelmaking, building a mill in Darlington, South Carolina, to manufacture steel bars. The Darlington mill was one of the first plants of major size in the United States to use electric arc furnace technology to melt scrap steel and cast molten metal into various shapes. Electric arc furnace technology was particularly appealing because the labor and capital requirements to melt steel scrap and produce crude steel were far lower than those at conventional integrated steel mills, where raw steel was produced using coke ovens, basic oxygen blast furnaces, ingot casters, and multiple types of finishing facilities to make crude steel from iron ore, coke, limestone, oxygen, scrap steel, and other ingredients. By 1981, Nucor had four bar mills making carbon and alloy steels in bars, angles, and light structural shapes; in 2006, Nucor had 10 such plants with a total annual capacity of approximately 7.7 million tons. The products of bar mills were widely used in metal buildings, farm equipment, automotive products, furniture, and recreational equipment; many types of construction required the use of steel reinforcing rods, or rebar.

In the late 1980s, Nucor entered into the production of sheet steel at a newly constructed plant in Crawfordsville, Indiana. Flat-rolled sheet steel was used in the production of motor vehicles, appliances, steel pipes and tubes, and other durable goods. The Crawfordsville plant was the first in the world to employ a revolutionary thin-slab casting process that substantially reduced the capital investment and costs to produce flat-rolled sheet steel. Thin-slab casting machines had a funnel-shaped mold to squeeze molten steel down to a thickness of 1.5–2.0 inches, compared to the typical 8- to 10-inch-thick slabs produced by conventional casters. It was much cheaper to then build and operate facilities to roll thin-gauge sheet steel from 1.5- to 2-inch-thick slabs than from 8- to 10-inch-thick slabs. The Crawfordsville plant's costs were said to be $50 to $75 per ton below the costs of traditional sheet steel plants, a highly significant cost advantage in a commodity market where the going price at the time was $400 per ton. *Forbes* magazine described Nucor's pioneering use of thin-slab casting as the most substantial technological/industrial innovation in the past 50 years.[2] By 1996, two additional sheet steel mills that employed thin-slab casting technology were constructed and a fourth mill was acquired in 2002, giving Nucor the capacity to produce 10.8 million tons of sheet steel products annually as of 2006.

Also in the late 1980s, Nucor added wide-flange steel beams, pilings, and heavy structural steel products to its lineup of product offerings. Structural steel products were used in buildings, bridges, overpasses, and similar such projects where strong weight-bearing support was needed. Customers included construction companies, steel fabricators, manufacturers, and steel service centers. To gain entry to the structural steel segment, in 1988 Nucor entered into a joint venture with Yamato-Kogyo, one of Japan's major producers of wide-flange beams, to build a new structural steel mill in Arkansas; a second mill was built on the same site in the 1990s that made the Nucor-Yamato venture in Arkansas the largest structural beam facility in the Western Hemisphere. In 1999, Nucor began production at a third structural steel mill in South Carolina. All three mills used a special continuous casting method that was quite cost-effective. As of 2006, Nucor had the capacity to make 3.7 million tons of structural steel products annually.

Starting in 2000, Nucor began producing steel plate of various thicknesses and lengths that was sold to manufacturers of heavy equipment, ships, barges, rail cars, refinery tanks, pressure vessels, pipes and tubes, and similar products. Steel plate was made at mills in Alabama and North Carolina that had combined capacity of about 2.8 million tons.

Exhibit 3 shows Nucor's sales by product category for 1990–2006. The breadth of its product line made Nucor the most diversified steel producer in North America. The company had market leadership in several product categories—it was the largest U.S. producer of steel bars, structural steel, steel joist, steel deck, and cold-rolled bars. Nucor had an overall market share of shipments to U.S.-based steel customers (including imports) of about 17 percent in both 2005 and 2006.

Strategy

Starting in 2000, Nucor embarked on a four-part growth strategy that involved new acquisitions, new plant construction, continued plant upgrades and cost reduction efforts, and joint ventures.

Strategic Acquisitions.   The first element of the four-part strategy was to make acquisitions that would strengthen Nucor's customer base, geographic coverage, and lineup of product offerings. Beginning in the late 1990s, Nucor management concluded that growth-minded companies like Nucor might well be better off purchasing existing plant capacity rather than building new capacity, provided the acquired plants could be bought at bargain prices, economically retrofitted with new equipment if need be, and then operated at costs comparable to (or even below) those of newly constructed state-of-the-art plants. At the time, the steel industry worldwide had far more production capacity than was needed to meet market demand, forcing many companies to operate in the red. Nucor had not made any acquisitions since about 1990, and a team of five people was assembled in 1998 to explore acquisition possibilities.

For almost three years, no acquisitions were made. But then the economic recession that hit Asia and Europe in the late 1990s reached the United States in full force in 2000–2001. The September 11, 2001, terrorist attacks further weakened steel purchases by such major steel-consuming industries as construction, automobiles, and farm equipment. Many steel companies in the United States and other parts of the world were operating in the red. Market conditions in the United States were particularly grim. Between October 2000 and October 2001, 29 steel companies in the United States, including Bethlehem Steel Corporation and LTV Corporation, the nation's third and fourth largest steel producers, respectively, filed for bankruptcy protection. Bankrupt steel companies accounted for about 25 percent of U.S. capacity.

Exhibit 3   **Nucor's Sales of Steel Products, by Product Category, 1990–2006**

| | Tons Sold to Outside Customers (in thousands) | | | | | | | | | |
| | Steel | | | | | | | | | |
Year	Sheet (2006 capacity of ≈10.8 million tons)	Bars (2006 capacity of ≈7.7 million tons)	Structural (2006 capacity of ≈3.7million tons)	Plate (2006 capacity of ≈2.8million tons)	Total (2006 capacity of ≈25 million tons)	Steel Joists (2006 capacity of ≈715,000 tons)	Steel Deck (2006 capacity of ≈435,000 tons)	Cold Finished Steel (2006 capacity of ≈490,000 tons)	Other Steel Products*	Total Tons
2006	8,495	6,513	3,209	2,432	20,649	570	398	327	174	22,118
2005	8,026	5,983	2,866	2,145	19,020	554	380	342	169	20,465
2004	8,078	5,244	2,760	1,705	17,787	522	364	271	165	19,109
2003	6,954	5,530	2,780	999	16,263	503	353	237	117	17,473
2002	5,806	2,947	2,689	872	12,314	462	330	226	110	13,442
2001	5,074	2,687	2,749	522	11,032	532	344	203	126	12,237
2000	4,456	2,209	3,094	20	9,779	613	353	250	194	11,189
1995	2,994	1,799	1,952	—	6,745	552	234	234	178	7,943
1990	420	1,382	1,002	—	2,804	443	134	163	104	3,648

*Includes steel fasteners (steel screws, nuts, bolts, washers, and bolt assemblies), metal building systems, and light-gauge steel framing.

Source: Company records posted at www.nucor.com (accessed October 3, 2006, and January 31, 2007).

The *Economist* noted that of the 14 steel companies tracked by Standard & Poor's, only Nucor was indisputably healthy. Some experts believed that close to half of the U.S. steel industry's production capacity might be forced to close before conditions improved; about 47,000 jobs in the U.S. steel industry had vanished since 1997.

One of the principal reasons for the distressed market conditions in the United States was a surge in imports of low-priced steel from foreign countries. Outside the United States, weak demand and a glut of capacity had driven commodity steel prices to 20-year lows in 1998. Globally, the industry had about 1 billion tons of annual capacity, but puny demand had kept production levels in the 750 to 800 million tons per year range during 1998–2000. A number of foreign steel producers, anxious to keep their mills running and finding few good market opportunities elsewhere, had begun selling steel in the U.S. market at cut-rate prices in 1997–1999. Nucor and other U.S. companies reduced prices to better compete and several filed unfair trade complaints against foreign steelmakers. The U.S. Department of Commerce concluded in March 1999 that steel companies in six countries (Canada, South Korea, Taiwan, Italy, Belgium, and South Africa) had illegally dumped stainless steel in the United States, and the governments of Belgium, Italy, and South Africa further facilitated the dumping by giving their steel producers unfair subsidies that at least partially made up for the revenues lost by selling at below-market prices. Congress and the Clinton administration opted to not impose tariffs or quotas on imported steel, which helped precipitate the number of bankruptcy filings. However, the Bush administration was more receptive to protecting the U.S. steel industry from the dumping practices of foreign steel companies. In October 2001, the U.S. International Trade Commission (ITC) ruled that increased steel imports of semifinished steel, plate, hot-rolled sheet, strip and coils, cold-rolled sheet and strip, and corrosion-resistant and coated sheet and strip were a substantial cause of serious injury, or threat of serious injury, to the U.S. industry. In March 2002, the Bush administration imposed tariffs of up to 30 percent on imports of selected steel products to help provide relief from Asian and European companies dumping steel in the United States at ultra-low prices.

Even though market conditions were tough for Nucor in 2001–2003, management concluded that oversupplied steel industry conditions and the number of beleaguered U.S. companies made it attractive to expand Nucor's production capacity via acquisition. The company proceeded to make a series of acquisitions:

- In 2001, Nucor paid $115 million to acquire substantially all of the assets of Auburn Steel Company's 400,000-ton steel bar facility in Auburn, New York. This acquisition gave Nucor expanded market presence in the Northeast and was seen as a good source of supply for a new Vulcraft joist plant being constructed in Chemung, New York.

- In November 2001, Nucor announced the acquisition of ITEC Steel Inc. for a purchase price of $9 million. ITEC Steel had annual revenues of $10 million and produced load-bearing light-gauge steel framing for the residential and commercial market at facilities in Texas and Georgia. Nucor was impressed with ITEC's dedication to continuous improvement and intended to grow ITEC's business via geographic and product line expansion. ITEC Steel's name was changed to Nucon Steel Commercial Corporation in 2002.

- In July 2002, Nucor paid $120 million to purchase Trico Steel Company, which had a 2.2-million-ton sheet steel mill in Decatur, Alabama. Trico Steel was a joint venture of LTV (which owned a 50 percent interest), and two leading international steel companies—Sumitomo Metal Industries and British Steel. The joint venture partners had built the mill in 1997 at a cost of $465 million, but Trico was in Chapter 11 bankruptcy proceedings at the time of the acquisition and the mill was shut down. The Trico mill's capability to make thin sheet steel with a superior surface quality added competitive strength to Nucor's strategy to gain sales and market share in the flat-rolled sheet segment. By October 2002, two months ahead of schedule, Nucor had restarted operations at the Decatur mill and was shipping products to customers.

- In December 2002, Nucor paid $615 million to purchase substantially all of the assets of Birmingham Steel Corporation, which included four bar mills in Alabama, Illinois, Washington, and Mississippi. The four plants had capacity of approximately 2 million tons annually. The purchase price also included approximately $120 million in inventory and receivables, the assets of Port Everglade Steel Corporation, the assets of Klean Steel, Birmingham Steel's ownership interest in Richmond Steel Recycling, and a mill in Memphis, Tennessee, that was not currently in operation. Top executives believed that the Birmingham Steel acquisition would broaden Nucor's customer base and build profitable market share in bar steel products.

- In August 2004, Nucor acquired a cold-rolling mill in Decatur, Alabama, from Worthington Industries for $80 million. This 1-million-ton mill, which opened in 1998, was located adjacent to the previously acquired Trico mill and gave Nucor added ability to service the needs of sheet steel buyers located in the southeastern United States.

- In June 2004, Nucor paid a cash price of $80 million to acquire a plate mill owned by Britain-based Corus Steel that was located in Tuscaloosa, Alabama. The Tuscaloosa mill, which currently had capacity of 700,000 tons that Nucor management believed was expandable to 1 million tons, was the first U.S. mill to employ a special technology that enabled high-quality wide steel plate to be produced from coiled steel plate. The mill produced coiled steel plate and plate products that were cut to customer-specified lengths. Nucor intended to offer these niche products to its commodity plate and coiled sheet customers.

- In February 2005, Nucor completed the purchase of Fort Howard Steel's operations in Oak Creek, Wisconsin; the Oak Creek facility produced cold finished bars in size ranges up to six-inch rounds and had approximately 140,000 tons of annual capacity.

- In June 2005, Nucor purchased Marion Steel Company located in Marion, Ohio, for a cash price of $110 million. Marion operated a bar mill with annual capacity of about 400,000 tons; the Marion location was in proximity to 60 percent of the steel consumption in the United States.

- In May 2006, Nucor acquired Connecticut Steel Corporation for $43 million in cash. Connecticut Steel's bar products mill in Wallingford had annual capacity to make 300,000 tons of wire rod and rebar and approximately 85,000 tons of

wire mesh fabrication and structural mesh fabrication, products that complemented Nucor's present lineup of steel bar products provided to construction customers.

- In late 2006, Nucor purchased Verco Manufacturing Company for approximately $180 million; Verco produced steel floor and roof decking at one location in Arizona and two locations in California. The Verco acquisition further solidified Vulcraft's market leading position in steel decking, giving it total annual capacity of 530,000 tons.

- In January 2007, Nucor announced plans to acquire all of the shares of Canada-based Harris Steel for a total cash purchase price of about $1.07 billion. Harris Steel had 2005 sales of Cdn$1.0 billion and earnings of Cdn$64 million. The company's operations consisted of (1) Harris Rebar, which was involved in the fabrication and placing of concrete reinforcing steel and the design and installation of concrete post-tensioning systems; (2) Laurel Steel, which manufactured and distributed wire and wire products, welded wire mesh, and cold finished bar; and (3) Fisher & Ludlow, which manufactured and distributed heavy industrial steel grating, aluminum grating, and expanded metal. In Canada, Harris Steel had 24 reinforcing steel fabricating plants, two steel grating distribution centers, and one cold finished bar and wire processing plant; in the United States, it had 10 reinforcing steel fabricating plants, two steel grating manufacturing plants, and three steel grating manufacturing plants. Harris had customers throughout Canada and the United States and employed about 3,000 people. For the past three years, Harris had purchased a big percentage of its steel requirements from Nucor. Nucor planned to operate Harris Steel as an independent subsidiary.

By 2005–2006, steel industry conditions worldwide had improved markedly. Prices in the United States were about 50 percent higher than in 2000 and Nucor's sales and earnings were at all-time highs (see Exhibits 1 and 3). But dumping of foreign-made steel into the U.S. market at below-market prices was still a problem. In April 2005, the U.S. International Trade Commission extended the antidumping and countervailing duty orders and suspension agreement covering imports of hot-rolled steel from Brazil, Japan, and the Russian Federation for an additional five years.

The Commercialization of New Technologies and New Plant Construction.

The second element of Nucor's growth strategy was to continue to be a technology leader and to be aggressive in constructing new plant capacity, particularly when such construction offered the opportunity to be first-to-market with new steelmaking technologies. Nucor management made a conscious effort to focus on the introduction of disruptive technologies (those that would give Nucor a commanding market advantage and thus be disruptive to the efforts of competitors in matching Nucor's cost competitiveness and/or product quality) and leapfrog technologies (those that would allow Nucor to overtake competitors in terms of product quality, cost per ton, or market share).

One of Nucor's biggest and most recent successes in pioneering new technology had been at its Crawfordsville facilities, where Nucor had the world's first installation of direct strip casting of carbon sheet steel—a process called Castrip. After several years of testing and process refinement at Crawfordsville, Nucor announced in 2005 that the Castrip process was ready for commercialization; Nucor had exclusive rights to Castrip technology in the United States and Brazil. The process, which had proved to be quite difficult to bring to commercial reality, was a major technological breakthrough for producing flat-rolled, carbon, and stainless steels in very thin gauges; it involved far fewer process steps to cast metal at or very near customer-desired thicknesses and shapes. The Castrip process drastically reduced capital outlays for equipment and produced savings on operating expenses as well—major expense savings included ability to use lower quality scrap steel and requiring 90 percent less energy to process liquid metal into hot-rolled steel sheets. A big environmental benefit of the Castrip process was cutting greenhouse gas emissions by up to 80 percent. Nucor's Castrip facility at Crawfordsville had the capacity to produce 500,000 tons annually and employed 55 people. In 2006, Nucor was building its second Castrip facility on the site of the Nucor-Yamato beam mill in Arkansas.

Nucor's growth strategy also included investing in the construction of new plant capacity whenever management spotted opportunities to strengthen its market presence:

- In 2006, Nucor announced that it would construct a new facility to produce metal buildings systems in Brigham City, Utah. The new plant, Nucor's fourth building systems plant, was to have capacity of 45,000 tons, employ over 200 people, and cost about $27 million; operations were expect to begin in the first quarter of 2008. The new plant gave Nucor national market reach in building systems products and total annual capacity of more than 190,000 tons.

- In 2006, Nucor announced plans to construct a state-of-the-art steel mill in Memphis, Tennessee, to produce special quality steel bars; the mill was expected to cost $230 million, employ more than 200 people, and have annual capacity of 850,000 tons. Management believed the mill would not only give Nucor one of the industry's most diverse lineups of special quality steel bar products but also provide a significantly better cost structure compared to both foreign and domestic competitors in the special quality steel bar segment. Nucor already had special quality bar mills in Nebraska and South Carolina.

The Drive for Plant Efficiency and Low-Cost Production.

A key part of Nucor's strategy was to continue making capital investments to improve plant efficiency and keep production costs low. From its earliest days in the steel business, Nucor had built state-of-the-art facilities in the most economical fashion possible and then made it standard company practice to invest aggressively in plant modernization and efficiency improvements as technology advanced and new cost-saving opportunities emerged. Nucor management made a point of staying on top of the latest advances in steelmaking around the world, diligently searching for emerging cost-effective technologies it could adopt or adapt in its facilities. Executives at Nucor had a long-standing commitment to provide the company's workforce with the best technology available to get the job done right in a safe working environment.

Nucor management also stressed continual improvement in product quality and cost at each one of its production facilities. Many Nucor locations were ISO 9000 and ISO 14001 certified. The company had a program called BESTmarking aimed at being the industrywide best performer on a variety of production and efficiency measures. Managers at all Nucor plants were accountable for demonstrating that their operations were competitive on both product quality and cost vis-à-vis the plants of rival companies. One trait of Nucor's corporate culture was the expectation that plant-level managers would be aggressive in implementing methods to improve product quality and keep costs per ton low relative to rival plants.

The company's latest initiative involved investments to upgrade and fully modernize the operations of its production facilities. Examples included a three-year bar mill modernization program and the addition of vacuum degassers to its four sheet steel mills. Adding the vacuum degassers not only improved Nucor's ability to produce some of the highest-quality sheet steel available but also resulted in expanded capacity at low incremental cost. Nucor's capital expenditures for new technology, plant improvements, and equipment upgrades totaled $415 million in 2000, $261 million in 2001, $244 million in 2002, $215 million in 2003, $286 million in 2004, $331 million in 2005, and $338 million in 2006. Capital expenditures for 2007 were projected to be $930 million; the big increase over 2006 capital spending was intended to ensure that Nucor plants were kept in state-of-the-art condition and globally competitive on cost. Top executives expected that all of Nucor's plants would have ISO 14001 certified Environmental Management Systems in place by the end of 2007.

Global Growth via Joint Ventures. The fourth component of Nucor's strategy was to grow globally with joint ventures and the licensing of new technologies. Nucor had recently entered into a joint venture with Companhia Vale do Rio Doce (CVRD) to construct and operate an environmentally friendly pig iron project in northern Brazil. Production began in the fourth quarter of 2005. The joint venture at the Brazilian plant involved using fast-growing eucalyptus trees as fuel.[3] Eucalyptus trees reached a mature height of 70 feet in seven years and immediately began to grow back when harvested the first two times, after which they had to be replanted. The project appealed to Nucor because it counteracted global warming. As eucalyptus trees grow, they take in carbon dioxide from the atmosphere and sequester it in their biomass; some goes back into the soil as leaves and twigs fall to the ground, with the remainder being stored in the wood of the tree. While burning the eucalyptus wood to create the charcoal fuel on which this project depended resulted in the release of some of the stored carbon dioxide to the atmosphere and still more was released when the charcoal was combined with iron ore in a mini blast furnace to create pig iron, some of the carbon dioxide was locked up in the pig iron. But the net effect on any global warming due to the release of carbon dioxide was overwhelmingly positive, given that about 500,000 tons of pig iron were being produced and that over 200,000 acres, or about 312 square miles, of eucalyptus forest were being restored or protected. In the overall scheme, the production of pig iron at the Brazilian plant removed about 2,400 pounds of carbon dioxide from the atmosphere for every ton of pig iron produced; this compared quite favorably with the conventional method of producing pig iron, which increased the carbon dioxide in the atmosphere by 4,180 pounds for every ton of pig iron produced.

Nucor had recently partnered with the Rio Tinto Group, Mitsubishi Corporation, and Chinese steelmaker Shougang Corporation to pioneer Rio Tinto's HIsmelt technology at a new plant located in Kwinana, Western Australia. The HIsmelt plant converted iron ore to liquid metal or pig iron and was both a replacement for traditional blast furnace technology and a hot metal source for electric arc furnaces. Rio Tinto had been developing the HIsmelt technology for 10 years and believed that it had the potential to revolutionize iron making and provide low-cost, high-quality iron for making steel. Nucor had a 25 percent ownership in the venture and had a joint global marketing agreement with Rio Tinto to license the technology to other interested steel companies. The Australian plant represented the world's first commercial application of the HIsmelt technology. Production started in January 2006; the plant had a capacity of over 800,000 metric tons and was expandable to 1.5 million metric tons at an attractive capital cost per incremental ton. Nucor viewed the Australian plant as a future royalty stream and raw material source. The technology had also been licensed to a Chinese steelmaker that planned to construct an 800,000-ton steel plant in China using the HIsmelt process for its iron source.

Nucor's third principal international project involved a raw materials strategy initiative to develop a low-cost substitute for scrap steel. Nucor was already the largest purchaser of scrap steel in North America, and the company's rapid growth strategy made it vulnerable to rising prices for scrap steel. In an effort to curtail its dependence on scrap steel as a raw material input, Nucor acquired an idled direct reduced iron plant in Louisiana in September 2004, relocated its operation to Trinidad (an island off the coast of South America near Venezuela), and expanded the project to a capacity of 1.8 million metric tons. Nucor was currently purchasing 6 to 7 million tons of iron annually to use in making higher-quality grades of sheet steel; integrating backward into supplying 25 to 30 percent of its own iron requirements held promise of raw material savings and less reliance on outside iron suppliers. The Trinidad site was chosen because it had a long-term and very cost-attractive supply of natural gas, along with favorable logistics for receiving iron ore and shipping direct reduced iron to Nucor's sheet steel mills in the United States. Production began in January 2007.

Nucor was looking for other opportunities globally. But so far, Nucor's strategy to participate in foreign steel markets was via joint ventures involving pioneering use of new steelmaking technologies. The company did not currently have any plans to build and operate its own steel mills outside the United States—its only company-operated foreign facility was the one in Trinidad.

Operations

Nucor had 49 facilities in 17 states and was the largest recycler of scrap steel in North America. The company recycled over 23 million tons of scrap in 2005 and over 21 million tons in 2006. At Nucor's steel mills, scrap steel and other metals were melted in electric arc furnaces and poured into continuous casting systems. Sophisticated rolling mills converted the billets, blooms, and slabs produced by various casting equipment into rebar, angles, rounds, channels, flats, sheet, beams, plate, and other finished steel products. Nucor's steel mill operations were highly automated, typically requiring fewer operating employees per ton produced than the mills of rival companies. High worker productivity at all Nucor steel mills resulted in labor costs equal to about 8 percent of revenues in

2005–2006—a considerably lower percentage than the labor costs at the integrated mills of companies using union labor and conventional blast furnace technology. Nucor's value chain (anchored in using electric arc furnace technology to recycle scrap steel) involved far fewer production steps, far less capital investment, and considerably less labor than the value chains of companies with integrated steel mills that made crude steel from iron ore.

Nucor's two big cost components at its steel plants were scrap steel and energy. Scrap steel prices were driven by market demand–supply conditions and could fluctuate significantly—see Exhibit 4. Nucor implemented a raw material surcharge in 2004 to cope with sharply increasing scrap steel prices in 2004 and help protect operating profit margins. Total energy costs increased by approximately $7 per ton from 2004 to 2005 as natural gas prices increased by approximately 31 percent and electricity prices increased by approximately 19 percent; energy costs rose another $1 per ton in 2006. Due to the efficiency of Nucor's steel mills, however, energy costs

Exhibit 4   Nucor's Costs for Scrap Steel and Scrap Substitute, 2005–2006

Period	Average Scrap and Scrap Substitute Cost per Ton Used
2000	$120
2001	101
2002	110
2003	137
2004	238
2005	
Quarter 1	272
Quarter 2	246
Quarter 3	217
Quarter 4	240
2006	
Quarter 1	237
Quarter 2	247
Quarter 3	257
Quarter 4	243

Source: Nucor's 10-K reports and information posted at www.nucor.com (accessed October 25, 2006, and January 31, 2007).

remained less than 10 percent of revenues in 2004, 2005, and 2006. In 2006, Nucor hedged a portion of its exposure to natural gas prices out into 2007 and also entered into contracts with natural gas suppliers to purchase natural gas in amounts needed to operate its direct reduced iron facility in Trinidad from 2006 through 2028.

Nucor plants were linked electronically to each other's production schedules, and each plant strived to operate in a just-in-time inventory mode. Virtually all tons produced were shipped out very quickly to customers; consequently, finished goods inventories at Nucor plants were relatively small.

Organization and Management Philosophy

Nucor had a simple, streamlined organization structure to allow employees to innovate and make quick decisions. The company was highly decentralized, with most day-to-day operating decisions made by division or plant-level general managers and their staff. The three building systems plants and the four cold-rolled products plants were headed by a group manager, but otherwise each plant operated independently as a profit center and was headed by a general manager, who in most cases also had the title of vice president. The group manager or plant general manager had control of the day-to-day decisions that affected the group or plant's profitability.

The organizational structure at a typical plant had three management layers:

- General Manager
- Department Manager
- Supervisor/Professional
- Hourly Employee

Group managers and plant managers reported to one of four executive vice presidents at corporate headquarters. Nucor's corporate staff was exceptionally small, consisting of only 66 people in 2006, the philosophy being that corporate headquarters should consist of a small cadre of executives who would guide a decentralized operation where liberal authority was delegated to managers in the field. Each plant had a sales manager who was responsible for selling the products made at that particular plant; such staff functions as engineering, accounting, and personnel management were performed at the group/plant

level. There was a minimum of paperwork and bureaucratic systems. Each group/plant was expected to earn about a 25 percent return on total assets before corporate expenses, taxes, interest, or profit sharing. As long as plant managers met their profit targets, they were allowed to operate with minimal restrictions and interference from corporate headquarters. There was a very friendly spirit of competition from one plant to the next to see which facility could be the best performer, but since all of the vice presidents and general managers shared the same bonus systems, they functioned pretty much as a team despite operating their facilities individually. Top executives did not hesitate to replace group or plant managers who consistently struggled to achieve profitability and operating targets.

Workforce Compensation Practices

Nucor was a nonunion "pay for performance" company with an incentive compensation system that rewarded goal-oriented individuals and did not put a maximum on what they could earn. All employees were covered under one of four basic compensation plans, each featuring incentives related to meeting specific goals and targets:

1. *Production Incentive Plan*—Production line jobs were rated on degree of responsibility required and assigned a base wage comparable to the wages paid by other manufacturing plants in the area where a Nucor plant was located. But in addition to their base wage, operating and maintenance employees were paid weekly bonuses based on the number of tons by which the output of their production team or work group exceeded the standard number of tons. All operating and maintenance employees were members of a production team that included the team's production supervisor, and the tonnage produced by each work team was measured for each work shift and then totaled for all shifts during a given week. If a production team's weekly output beat the weekly standard, team members (including the team's production supervisor) earned a specified percentage bonus for each ton produced above the standard—production bonuses were paid weekly (rather than quarterly or annually) so that workers and supervisors

would be rewarded immediately for their efforts. The standard rate was calculated based on the capabilities of the equipment employed (typically at the time plant operations began), and no bonus was paid if the equipment was not operating (which gave maintenance workers a big incentive to keep a plant's equipment in good working condition)—Nucor's philosophy was that everybody suffered when equipment was not operating and the bonus for downtime ought to be zero. Production standards at Nucor plants were seldom raised unless a plant underwent significant modernization or important new pieces of equipment were installed that greatly boosted labor productivity. It was common for production incentive bonuses to run from 50 to 150 percent of an employee's base pay, thereby pushing their compensation levels up well above those at other nearby manufacturing plants. Worker efforts to exceed the standard and get a bonus involved not so much working harder as practicing good teamwork and close collaboration in resolving problems and figuring out how best to exceed the production standards.

2. *Department Manager Incentive Plan*—Department managers earned annual incentive bonuses based primarily on the percentage of net income to dollars of assets employed for their division. These bonuses could be as much as 80 percent of a department manager's base pay.

3. *Professional and Clerical Bonus Plan*—A bonus based on a division's net income return on assets was paid to employees that were not on the production worker or department manager plan.

4. *Senior Officers Incentive Plan*—Nucor's senior officers did not have employment contracts and did not participate in any pension or retirement plans. Their base salaries were set at approximately 90 percent of the median base salary for comparable positions in other manufacturing companies with comparable assets, sales, and capital. The remainder of their compensation was based on Nucor's annual overall percentage of net income to stockholder's equity (i.e., return on equity, or ROE) and was paid out in cash and stock. Once Nucor's ROE reached a threshold of not less than 3 percent or more than 7 percent (as determined annually by the compensation committee of the board of directors),

senior officers earned a bonus equal to 20 percent of the their base salary. If Nucor's annual ROE exceeded 20 percent, senior officers earned a bonus equal to the 225 percent of their base salary. Officers could earn an additional bonus of up to 75 percent of their base salary based on a comparison of Nucor's net sales growth with the net sales growth of members of a steel industry peer group. There was also a long-term incentive plan that provided for stock awards and stock options; this incentive covered a three-year performance period and was linked to Nucor's return on average invested capital relative to that of other steel industry competitors. The structure of these officer incentives was such that Nucor officers could find their bonus compensation swinging widely—from close to zero (in years like 2003 when industry conditions were bad and Nucor's performance was subpar) to 400 percent (or more) of their base salaries (when Nucor's performance was excellent, as had been the case in 2004–2006).

Nucor management had designed the company's incentive plans for employees so that bonus calculations involved no discretion on the part of a plant/division manager or top executives. This was done to eliminate any concerns on the part of workers that managers or executives might show favoritism or otherwise be unfair in calculating or awarding bonuses. Based on labor costs equal to about 8 percent of revenues, a typical Nucor employee earned close to $91,300 in 2005 in base pay and bonuses. (The average in 2000–2002, when the steel market was in the doldrums, was about $60,000 per employee.)[4] Total worker compensation at Nucor could run double the average earned by workers at other manufacturing companies in the states where Nucor's plants were located. At Nucor's new $450 million plant in Hertford County, North Carolina, where jobs were scarce and poverty was common, Nucor employees earned three times the local average manufacturing wage. Nucor management philosophy was that workers ought to be excellently compensated because the production jobs were strenuous and the work environment in a steel mill was relatively dangerous.

Employee turnover in Nucor mills was extremely low; absenteeism and tardiness were minimal. Each employee was allowed four days of absences and could also miss work for jury duty, military leave, or the death of close relatives. After this, a day's absence cost a worker the entire performance bonus pay for that week, and being more than a half-hour late to work on a given day resulted in no bonus payment for the day. When job vacancies did occur, Nucor was flooded with applications; plant personnel screened job candidates very carefully, seeking people with initiative and a strong work ethic.

Employee Relations and Human Resources

Employee relations at Nucor were based on four clear-cut principles:

1. Management is obligated to manage Nucor in such a way that employees will have the opportunity to earn according to their productivity.
2. Employees should be able to feel confident that if they do their jobs properly, they will have a job tomorrow.
3. Employees have the right to be treated fairly and must believe that they will be.
4. Employees must have an avenue of appeal when they believe they are being treated unfairly.

The hallmarks of Nucor's human resources strategy were its incentive pay plan for production exceeding the standard and the job security provided to production workers—despite being in an industry with strong down cycles, Nucor had made it a practice not to lay off workers.

Nucor took an egalitarian approach to providing fringe benefits to its employees; employees had the same insurance programs, vacation schedules, and holidays as upper level management. However, certain benefits were not available to Nucor's officers. The fringe benefit package at Nucor included:

- *Profit sharing*—Each year, Nucor allocated 10 percent of its operating profits to profit-sharing bonuses for all employees (except senior officers). Depending on company performance, the bonuses could run anywhere from 1 percent to over 20 percent of pay. Twenty percent of the bonus amount was paid to employees in the following March as a cash bonus, and the remaining 80 percent was put into a trust for each employee, with each employee's share being proportional to his or her earnings as a percent of total

earnings by all workers covered by the plan. An employee's share of the profits became vested after one full year of employment. Employees received a quarterly statement of their balance in profit sharing.

- *401(k) plan*—Both officers and employees participated in a 401(k) plan, in which the company matched from 5 percent to 25 percent of each employee's first 7 percent of contributions; the amount of the match was based on how well the company was doing.
- *Medical and dental plan*—The company had a flexible and comprehensive health benefit program for officers and employees that included wellness and health care spending accounts.
- *Tuition reimbursement*—Nucor reimbursed up to $2,750 of an employee's approved educational expenses each year and up to $1,250 of a spouse's educational expenses.
- *Employee stock purchase plan*—Nucor had a monthly stock investment plan for employees whereby Nucor added 10 percent to the amount an employee contributed toward the purchase of Nucor shares; Nucor paid the commission on all share purchases.
- *Service awards*—After each five years of service with the company, Nucor employees received a service award consisting of five shares of Nucor stock.
- *Scholarships*—Nucor provided the children of employees (except senior officers) up to $2,750 worth of scholarship funding each year to be used at accredited academic institutions.
- *Other benefits*—Long-term disability, life insurance, vacation. In 2004, 2005, and 2006 Nucor paid each employee (excluding officers) a special year-end bonus of $2,000; this was in addition to record profit-sharing bonuses and 401(k) matching contributions of $272.6 million in 2006, $206.0 million in 2005, and $172.3 million in 2004 (versus only $8.9 million in 2003). The extra $2,000 bonuses resulted in additional profit-sharing costs of approximately $23.8 million in 2006, $22.6 million in 2005, and $21.0 million in 2004.

Most of the changes Nucor made in work procedures and in equipment came from employees. The prevailing view at Nucor was that the employees knew the problems of their jobs better than anyone else and were thus in the best position to identify ways to improve how things were done. Most plant-level managers spent considerable time in the plant, talking and meeting with frontline employees and listening carefully to suggestions. Promising ideas and suggestions were typically acted on quickly and implemented—management was willing to take risks to try worker suggestions for doing things better and to accept the occasional failure when the results were disappointing. Teamwork, a vibrant team spirit, and a close worker–management partnership were much in evidence at Nucor plants.

Nucor plants did not use job descriptions. Management believed job descriptions caused more problems than they solved, given the teamwork atmosphere and the close collaboration among work group members. The company saw formal performance appraisal systems as added paperwork and a waste of time. If a Nucor employee was not performing well, the problem was dealt with directly by supervisory personnel and the peer pressure of work group members (whose bonuses were adversely affected).

Employees were kept informed about company and division performance. Charts showing the division's results in return on assets and bonus payoff were posted in prominent places in the plant. Most all employees were quite aware of the level of profits in their plant or division. Nucor had a formal grievance procedure, but grievances were few and far between. The corporate office sent all news releases to each division, where they were posted on bulletin boards. Each employee received a copy of Nucor's annual report; it was company practice for the cover of the annual report to consist of the names of all Nucor employees.

All of these practices had created an egalitarian culture and a highly motivated workforce that grew out of former CEO Ken Iverson's radical insight: that employees, even hourly clock punchers, would put forth extraordinary effort and be exceptionally productive if they were richly rewarded, treated with respect, and given real power to do their jobs as best they saw fit.[5] There were countless stories of occasions when managers and workers had gone beyond the call of duty to expedite equipment repairs (in many instances even blowing their weekends to go help personnel at other Nucor plants solve a crisis); the company's workforce was known for displaying unusual passion and company loyalty even when no personal financial stake was involved. As one Nucor worker put it, "At Nucor, we're not 'you guys' and 'us guys.' It's all of us guys. Wherever the bottleneck is, we go there, and everyone works on it."[6]

It was standard procedure for a team of Nucor veterans, including people who worked on the plant floor, to visit with their counterparts as part of the process of screening candidates for acquisition.[7] One of the purposes of such visits was to explain the Nucor compensation system and culture face-to-face, gauge reactions, and judge whether the plant would fit into "the Nucor way of doing things" if it was acquired. Shortly after making an acquisition, Nucor management moved swiftly to institute its pay-for-performance incentive system and to begin instilling the egalitarian Nucor culture and idea sharing. Top priority was given to looking for ways to boost plant production using fewer people and without making substantial capital investments; the take-home pay of workers at newly-acquired plants typically went up dramatically. At the Auburn Steel plant, acquired in 2001, it took Nucor about six months to convince workers that they would be better off under Nucor's pay system; during that time, Nucor paid people under the old Auburn Steel system but posted what they would have earned under Nucor's system. Pretty soon, workers were convinced to make the changeover—one worker saw his pay climb from $53,000 in the year prior to the acquisition to $67,000 in 2001 and to $92,000 in 2005.[8]

New Employees. Each plant/division had a "consul" responsible for providing new employees with general advice about becoming a Nucor teammate and serving as a resource for inquiries about how things were done at Nucor, how to navigate the division and company, and how to resolve issues that might come up. Nucor provided new employees with a personalized plan that set forth who would give them feedback about how well they were doing and when and how this feedback would be given; from time to time, new employees met with the plant manager for feedback and coaching. In addition, there was a new employee orientation session that provided a hands-on look at the plant/division operations; new employees also participated in product group meetings to provide exposure to broader business and technical issues. Each year, Nucor brought all recent college hires to the Charlotte headquarters for a forum intended to give the new hires a chance to network and provide senior management with guidance on how best to leverage their talent.

Pricing and Marketing

The commodity nature of steel products meant that the prices a company could command were driven by market demand–supply conditions that changed more or less continually. As a consequence, Nucor's average sales prices per ton varied considerably from quarter to quarter—see Exhibit 5. Nucor's pricing strategy was to quote the same price and sales terms to all customers, with the customer paying all shipping charges. Its prices were customarily the lowest or close to the lowest in the U.S. market for steel. Nucor's status as a low-cost producer with reliably low prices had resulted in numerous customers entering into noncancelable 6- to 12-month contracts to purchase steel mill products from Nucor. These contracts contained a pricing formula tied to raw material costs (with the cost of scrap steel being the primary driver of price adjustments during the contact period). In 2005–2006, about 45 percent of Nucor's steel mill production was committed to contract customers. All of Nucor's steel mills planned to pursue profitable contract business in the future.

Nucor had recently begun developing its plant sites with the expectation of having several customer companies co-locate nearby to save shipping costs on their steel purchases. In order to gain the advantage of low shipping costs, two tube manufacturers, two steel service centers, and a cold-rolling facility had located adjacent to Nucor's Arkansas plant. Four companies had announced plans to locate close to a new Nucor plant in North Carolina.

Approximately 92 percent of the production of Nucor's steel mills was sold to outside customers in 2005–2006; the balance was used internally by Nucor's Vulcraft, Cold Finish, Building Systems, and Fasteners divisions. Steel joists and joist girder sales were obtained by competitive bidding. Vulcraft supplied price quotes to contractors on a significant percentage of the domestic buildings that had steel joists and joist girders as part of their support systems. Nucor's pricing for steel joists, girders, and decking included delivery to the job site. Vulcraft maintained a fleet of trucks to ensure and control on-time delivery; freight costs for deliveries were less than 10 percent of revenues in 2005–2006. In 2005, Vulcraft had a 40 percent share of the U.S. market for of steel joists. Steel deck was specified in the majority of buildings using steel joists and joist girders. In 2005 and 2006, Vulcraft supplied more than 30 percent of total domestic sales of steel deck; the 2006 Verco acquisition gave Nucor the capability to substantially increase its sales and market share of steel deck in 2007.

Exhibit 5   **Nucor's Average Sales Prices (per ton) for Steel Products, By Product Category, 2005–2006**

Period	Sheet	Bars	Structural	Plate	Steel Joists	Steel Deck	Cold Finished Steel	Overall Price per Ton
2005								
Qtr 1	$675	$514	$605	$763	$1,102	$1,020	$1,012	$663
Qtr 2	609	499	574	708	1,084	972	1,067	621
Qtr 3	523	496	561	625	1,056	935	1,003	571
Qtr 4	583	542	634	684	1,077	931	1,069	630
2006								
Qtr 1	594	543	649	698	1,104	938	1,010	631
Qtr 2	625	567	667	712	1,092	930	1,033	654
Qtr 3	673	601	703	746	1,122	946	1,067	702
Qtr 4	624	576	727	732	1,175	1,031	998	683

Source: Company records posted at www.nucor.com (accessed October 23, 2006, and January 31, 2007).

COMPETITION IN THE STEEL INDUSTRY

The global marketplace for steel was considered to be relatively mature and highly cyclical as a result of ongoing ups and downs in the world economy or the economies of particular countries. In general, competition within the steel industry, both in the United States and globally, was intense and expected to remain so. Numerous steel companies had declared bankruptcy during the past 10 years, either ceasing production altogether or more usually continuing to operate after being acquired and undergoing restructuring to become more cost-competitive.

Worldwide demand had grown by about 6 percent annually since 2000 (well above the 1.1 percent growth rate from 1975 to 2000), but there had been periods of both strong and weak demand during 2000–2006 (see Exhibit 6). Prices for steel products were near record levels throughout most of 2004–2006, driven by strong global demand for steel products (see Exhibit 7). Worldwide sales of steel products were in the $770 to $790 billion range

Exhibit 6   **Estimated Worldwide Production of Crude Steel, with Compound Average Growth Rates, 1975–2005**

Year	Estimated Value of World Steel Production (in billions of $)	World Crude Steel Production (millions of tons)	Compound Average Growth Rates in Steel Production	
			Period	Percentage Rate
1975	n.a.	710	1975–1980	2.2%
1980	n.a.	790	1980–1985	0.1
1985	$250	792	1985–1990	1.4
1990	415	849	1990–1995	−0.5
1995	470	828	1995–2000	2.4
2000	385	934	2000–2005	6.0
2001	270	937		
2002	330	996		
2003	465	1,068		
2004	790	1,176		
2005	770	1,247		

n.a. = not available

Source: International Iron and Steel Institute, *World Steel in Figures, 2006*, www.worldsteel.org (accessed November 6, 2006).

Exhibit 7   **Estimated Consumption of Steel Products, by Geographic Region, 2000–2005 (in millions of tons)**

Region	2000	2001	2002	2003	2004	2005
European Union (25 countries)	177.6	174.6	173.2	176.0	185.2	176.8
Other European countries, Russia, and Ukraine	60.8	64.1	63.0	71.8	75.6	80.1
North America	161.6	145.6	145.9	143.5	164.2	149.7
Central and South America	31.0	31.8	30.4	30.4	36.0	35.8
Africa	17.0	18.4	20.3	21.0	22.6	24.7
Middle East	21.7	25.5	27.9	33.3	33.7	38.2
Asia	353.0	382.7	432.8	496.2	546.7	602.8
Australia, New Zealand	7.4	6.9	7.9	8.3	8.8	8.7
World total	830.2	849.6	901.5	980.6	1,072.9	1,116.8

Source: International iron and Steel Institute, *World Steel in Figures, 2006*, www.worldsteel.org (accessed November 6, 2006).

in 2004–2005; prior to 2004, global sales had never exceeded $500 billion in any one year, according to data compiled by the International Iron and Steel Institute.

Nonetheless, steelmaking capacity worldwide still exceeded global demand in 2005–2006. Many foreign steelmakers, looking to operate their plants as close to capacity as possible or seeking to take advantage of favorable foreign currency fluctuations, had begun exporting steel products to the U.S. market, where strong demand and tight domestic supplies had pushed steel prices to highly profitable levels. According to U.S. Department of Commerce data, steel imports into the United States rose by over 70 percent between November 2005 and September 2006 and were expected to reach a record level of over 45 million tons in 2006 (see Exhibit 8); companies in China, Russia, Korea, Turkey, Taiwan, Japan, India, Australia, and Brazil were particularly aggressive in exporting their production to the U.S. market.[9] Steel imports from China, for example, jumped from 139,300 tons in November 2005 to a monthly average of over 575,000 tons in July, August, and September 2006. Steel imports from Taiwan rose from 48,400 tons in November 2005 to nearly 265,000 tons in September 2006. Steel imports from Russia were 121,300 tons in November 2005 and 517,000 tons in August 2006. Steel imports from Korea were about 115,700 tons in November 2005

and over 260,000 tons in September 2006; imports from Australia were 60,000 tons in November 2005 and 162,000 tons in September 2006. In 2005, foreign steelmakers captured a 22.8 percent share of the U.S. market for steel products (based on tons); foreign steelmakers were expected to achieve close to a 30 percent share of the U.S. market in 2006. Many non-U.S. steel producers were owned and/or subsidized by their governments, a condition that often meant their production and sales decisions were driven by political and economic policy considerations rather than by prevailing market conditions. Steel supplies in the United States (and other countries) were also subject to shifting foreign exchange rates, with more imports pouring in when the local currency was strong and more exports flowing out when the local currency was weak.

In February 2007, Nucor CEO Dan DiMicco applauded the announcement that the U.S. government had requested World Trade Organization (WTO) dispute settlement consultations with China regarding claims that China was violating WTO rules by providing subsidies to Chinese steel exporters.[10] Under the WTO dispute settlement procedures, a request for consultations was the first step in resolving the U.S. claim that the Chinese government was violating WTO rules. If a WTO panel found that China was indeed breaking WTO rules, it could order China to provide compensation to the United States

Exhibit 8   **The U.S. Market for Steel Products, 1995–2005 (in millions of tons)**

Year	U.S. Shipments of Steel Products	U.S. Exports of Steel Mill Products	U.S. Imports of Steel Mill Products	Apparent U.S. Consumption of Steel Mill Products*
1995	97.5	7.1	24.4	114.8
1996	100.9	5.0	29.2	125.0
1997	105.9	6.0	31.2	131.0
1998	102.4	5.5	41.5	138.4
1999	106.2	5.4	35.7	136.5
2000	109.1	6.5	38.0	140.5
2001	98.9	6.1	30.1	122.9
2002	100.0	6.0	32.7	126.7
2003	106.0	8.2	23.1	120.9
2004	111.4	7.9	35.8	139.3
2005	105.0	9.4	32.1	127.7

*Apparent U.S. consumption equals total shipments minus exports plus imports.

Source: American Iron and Steel Institute, as reported in Standard & Poor's Industry Surveys.

by allowing the United States to impose higher tariffs on Chinese goods or take similar measures. Under U.S. countervailing duty law, if a U.S. Department of Commerce investigation confirmed that foreign plants exporting steel to the United States were being subsidized by their government and if the U.S. International Trade Commission determined that the subsidized imports had injured the domestic steel industry, then the United States could apply countervailing duties to offset the subsidies. While the U.S. government had not previously applied countervailing duties when authorized to do so, the Commerce Department was currently considering whether to change this practice. DiMicco saw the U.S. government's request for WTO settlement consultations as only a first step toward leveling the playing field for U.S. steel producers; he said:

> This request does not cover the vast majority of the massive domestic subsidies China provides to its steel industry and other manufacturers. Nor does it address China's gross manipulation of its currency, which provides Chinese exports with a huge advantage in international trade. Free trade is possible only if everyone follows the rules—and China hasn't.[11]

Exhibit 8 shows steel production, steel exports, and steel imports for the U.S. market for 1995–2005. Exhibit 9 shows the value of steel mill shipments by U.S.-based steelmakers for 2004–2005, broken down by product category. Exhibit 10 shows data for the top 20 countries worldwide as concerns total steel production, steel exports, and steel imports;

Exhibit 11 shows the 20 largest steel companies worldwide as of 2005.

STEEL PRODUCTION

Steel was produced by either integrated steel facilities or minimills that employed electric arc furnaces. Integrated mills used blast furnaces to produce hot metal typically from iron ore pellets, limestone, scrap steel, oxygen, assorted other metals, and coke. (Coke was produced by firing coal in large coke ovens and was the major fuel used in blast furnaces to produce hot metal.) Hot metal from the blast furnace process was then run through the basic oxygen process to produce liquid steel. To make flat-rolled steel products, liquid steel was either fed into a continuous caster machine and cast into slabs or else cooled in slab form for later processing. Slabs were further shaped or rolled at a plate mill or hot strip mill. In making certain sheet steel products, the hot strip mill process was followed by various finishing processes, including pickling, cold-rolling, annealing, tempering, or galvanizing. These various processes for converting raw steel into finished steel products were often distinct steps undertaken at different times and in different on-site or off-site facilities rather than being done in a continuous process in a single plant facility—an integrated mill was thus one that had multiple facilities at a single plant site and could therefore not only produce crude (or raw) steel but also run the crude steel through various facilities and finishing

Exhibit 9   **Dollar Value of Shipments of Steel Mill Products by U.S.-Based Steelmakers, by Product Category, 2004–2005 ($ in billions)**

Product Category	2004	2005
Steel ingot and semifinished shapes	$ 4.9	$ 5.7
Hot-rolled sheet and strip, including tin mill products	25.2	24.8
Hot-rolled bars and shapes, plates, structural shapes, and pilings	14.9	17.1
Steel pipe and tube	9.5	10.9
Cold-rolled sheet steel and strip	12.2	13.5
Cold finished steel bars and steel shapes	2.0	2.1
Steel wire	2.3	2.3
All other steel mill products	1.3	1.3
Total	$72.7	$78.3

Source: U.S. Department of Commerce, "Current Industrial Reports, Steel Mill Products, 2005," www.census.gov/mcd (accessed November 2, 2006).

Exhibit 10   **Top 20 Countries: Total Steel Production, Steel Exports, and Steel Imports, 2004–2005 (in millions of tons)**

Rank	Total Steel Production, 2005		Steel Exports, 2004		Steel Imports, 2004	
1	China	385.0	Japan	38.3	China	36.6
2	Japan	124.0	Russia	33.5	United States	36.4
3	United States	104.6	Ukraine	31.1	Germany	21.9
4	Russia	72.8	Germany	30.1	Italy	21.4
5	South Korea	52.7	Belgium	25.9	South Korea	19.5
6	Germany	49.0	China	22.2	France	18.2
7	Ukraine	42.5	France	20.6	Belgium	16.4
8	India	42.0	South Korea	16.5	Taiwan, China	15.1
9	Brazil	34.8	Italy	14.7	Spain	13.0
10	Italy	32.3	Turkey	14.5	Thailand	12.2
11	Turkey	23.1	Brazil	13.2	Canada	10.2
12	France	21.5	Taiwan, China	10.4	United Kingdom	9.6
13	Taiwan, China	20.5	Netherlands	9.9	Turkey	9.0
14	Spain	19.6	United kingdom	8.6	Iran	8.7
15	Mexico	17.9	United States	8.0	Malaysia	8.3
16	Canada	16.9	Spain	7.1	Netherlands	7.2
17	United Kingdom	14.5	Austria	6.4	Hong Kong	6.9
18	Belgium	11.0	Mexico	6.1	Mexico	6.4
19	South Africa	10.5	India	6.1	Vietnam	6.0
20	Iran	10.4	Canada	6.0	United Arab Emirates	5.1

Source: International Iron and Steel Institute, *World Steel in Figures, 2006*, www.worldsteel.org (accessed November 6, 2006).

processes to make hot-rolled and cold-rolled sheet steel products, steel bars and beams, stainless steel, steel wire and nails, steel pipes and tubes, and other finished steel products. The steel produced by integrated mills tended to be purer than steel produced by electric arc furnaces since less scrap was used in the production process. (Scrap steel often contained nonferrous elements that could adversely affect metallurgical properties.) Some steel customers required purer steel products for their applications.

Minimills used an electric arc furnace to melt steel scrap or scrap substitutes into molten metal which was then cast into crude steel slabs, billets or blooms in a continuous casting process; as was the case at integrated mills, the crude steel was then run through various facilities and finishing processes to make hot-rolled and cold-rolled sheet steel products, steel bars and beams, stainless steel, steel wire and nails, steel pipes and tubes, and other finished steel products. Minimills could accommodate short production runs and had relatively fast product change-over time. Minimills typically were able to produce a narrower range of steel products than integrated producers, and their products tended to be more commodity-like. The electric arc technology employed by minimills offered two primary competitive advantages: capital investment requirements that were 75 percent lower than those of integrated mills, and a smaller workforce (which translated into lower labor costs per ton shipped).

GLOBAL STEEL INDUSTRY TRENDS

Over the past five decades, changes in steelmaking technology had revolutionized the world's steel industry. Up until the 1960, steel was produced in large-scale plants using capital-intensive basic oxygen blast furnace technology and open hearth furnace technology where steel was made from scratch using iron ore, coke, scrap steel, limestone, and other raw materials—such companies were referred to as integrated producers because the value chains at such plants involved a number of production steps and processes to convert the raw materials into finished

Exhibit 11   **Top 20 Steel Companies Worldwide, Based on Crude Steel Production, 2005**

		Crude Steel Production (in millions of tons)	
2005 Rank	**Company (Headquarters)**	**2005**	**2004**
1	Mittal Steel* (Netherlands)	69.4	47.2
2	Arcelor* (Luxembourg)	51.5	51.7
3	Nippon Steel (Japan)	35.3	35.7
4	POSCO (South Korea)	33.6	33.3
5	JFE (Japan)	32.9	34.8
6	Baosteel (China)	25.0	23.6
7	US Steel (USA)	21.3	22.9
8	Nucor (USA)	20.3	19.7
9	Corus Group** (Great Britain)	20.1	20.9
10	Riva (Italy)	19.3	18.4
11	ThyssenKrupp (Germany)	18.2	19.4
12	Tangshan (China)	17.7	7.8
13	Evraz (Russia)	15.3	15.1
14	Gerdau (Brazil)	15.1	16.1
15	Severstal (Russia)	15.0	14.1
16	Sumitomo (Japan)	14.9	14.3
17	SAIL (India)	14.8	13.3
18	Wuhan (China)	14.3	10.2
19	Anshan (China)	13.1	12.5
20	Magnitogorsk (Russia)	12.6	12.5

*Mittal Steel and Arcelor merged in 2006.

**Corus Group was acquired by Tata Steel (India) in 2006; Tata Steel was the world's 56th largest producer of steel in 2005.

Source: International iron and Steel Institute, *World Steel in Figures, 2006*, www.worldsteel.org (accessed November 6, 2006).

steel products. But starting in the 1960s, the advent of electric arc furnace technology spurred new start-up companies to enter the steelmaking business. These new companies, called minimills because their plants produced steel on a much smaller scale than did the integrated mills, used low-cost electric arc furnaces to melt scrap steel and cast the molten metal directly into a variety of steel products at costs substantially below those of integrated steel producers.

Initially, minimills were able to only make low-end steel products (such as reinforcing rods and steel bars) using electric arc furnace technology. But when thin-slab casting technology came on the scene in the 1980s, minimills were able to compete in the market for flat-rolled carbon sheet and strip products; these products sold at substantially higher prices per ton and thus were attractive market segments for minimill companies. Carbon sheet and strip steel products accounted for about 50–60 percent of total steel production and represented the last big market category

controlled by the producers employing basic oxygen furnace and blast furnace technologies. Thin-slab casting technology, which had been developed by SMS Schloemann-Siemag AG of Germany, was pioneered in the United States by Nucor at its plants in Indiana and elsewhere. Other minimill companies in the United States and other countries were quick to adopt thin-slab casting technology because the low capital costs of thin-slab casting facilities, often coupled with the lower labor costs per ton, gave minimill companies a cost and pricing advantage over integrated steel producers, enabling them to grab a growing share of the global market for flat-rolled sheet steel and other carbon steel products. Many integrated producers also switched to thin-slab casting as a defensive measure to protect their profit margins and market shares.

By 2005, electric arc furnace technology was being used to produce about 33 percent of the world's steel; basic oxygen furnace technology was used to produce about 65 percent of the all steel products.

Limited supplies of scrap steel and upward-trending prices for scrap steel were said to be the main factors constraining greater use of electric arc technology across the world. Open hearth technology had largely been abandoned as of 2005 and was used only at plants in Russia, the Ukraine, India, and a few other Eastern European countries. In 2003–2006, about 90 percent of the world's production of steel involved the use of continuous-casting technology.

Industry Consolidation.   In both the United States and across the world, the last two industry downturns had resulted in numerous mergers and acquisitions. Some of the mergers/acquisitions were the result of a financially and managerially strong company seeking to acquire a high-cost or struggling steel company at a bargain price and then pursue cost reduction initiatives to make newly-acquired steel mill operations more cost competitive. Other mergers/acquisitions reflected the strategies of growth-minded steel companies looking to expand both their production capacity and their geographic market presence.

In 2006, the world's two largest steel producers, Mittal Steel and Arcelor, both headquartered in Europe but with operations in various parts of the world, merged to form a giant company with total steel production of over 116 million tons (equal to about a 10 percent market share worldwide). Prior to its merger with Arcelor, Mittal Steel in 2005 had acquired International Steel Group, the second largest steel producer in the United States, with 13 major plants in eight states, and Inland Steel, another struggling U.S. steel producer. In 2006, Arcelor Mittal had total production capacity of nearly 125 million tons, annual revenues of $77 billion, earnings of $13.3 billion, plants in 27 countries on five continents (North America, South America, Europe, Asia, and Africa), and 330,000 employees.

Also in 2006, Tata Steel in India acquired Corus Steel (Great Britain), the world's eighth largest steel company; the new company produced over 27 million tons in 2005. Tata Steel was one of the lowest-cost steel producers in the world, with access to low-cost iron ore deposits, and was adding new production capacity at three sites in India, a plant in Iran, and a plant in Bangladesh; Corus was regarded as a relatively high-cost producer but had been profitable in 2004–2005 after posting huge losses in 2000–2003. Corus had a 50 percent share of the steel market in Great Britain and substantial sales in parts of Europe; it was

formed in 1999 as the result of a merger between troubled British Steel and Koninklijke Hoogovens, a well-regarded steel company based in the Netherlands.

Jinan Iron and Steel and Laiwu Steel, the 6th and 7th largest steel producers in China and the 23rd and 24th largest producers in the world, merged in October 2006 to form a company with total sales of almost 23 million tons in 2005; the merged company was named Shandong Iron and Steel. Industry observers believed the Jinan-Laiwu merger was an attempt by Chinese steelmakers to better compete with Arcelor Mittal and other foreign rivals.

In the United States, United States Steel, headquartered in Pittsburgh, had acquired National Steel in 2003, giving it steelmaking capability of 26.8 million tons annually as of 2006. In 2006, U.S. Steel had 12 steelmaking facilities in the United States, one in Slovakia, and two in Serbia. U.S. Steel had a labor-cost disadvantage versus Nucor and Mittal Steel USA (the U.S.-based operations of Arcelor Mittal), partly due to the lower productivity of its unionized workforce and partly due to its pension costs. While Mittal Steel USA also had a union workforce, it had recently downsized the labor force at some of its plants by close to 75 percent and now operated many of its U.S. plants with a very lean workforce in a manner akin to Nucor. Arcelor Mittal's recent acquisitions of Inland Steel and International Steel Group in the United States had transformed Mittal Steel USA into North America's largest steel producer, with operations in 12 states and annual raw steel production capability of about 31 million tons. Mittal Steel USA's principal products included a broad range of hot-rolled, cold-rolled, and coated sheets; tin mill products; carbon and alloy plates; wire rod; rail products; bars and semifinished shapes to serve the automotive, construction, pipe and tube, appliance, container, and machinery markets. All of these products are available in standard carbon grades as well as high-strength, low-alloy grades for more demanding applications.

NUCOR'S CHIEF DOMESTIC COMPETITORS

Consolidation of the industry into a smaller number of larger and more efficient steel producers had heightened competitive pressures for Nucor and most other steelmakers. Nucor had three major rivals headquartered in the United States—Mittal Steel USA, U.S. Steel, and AK Steel. Mittal Steel USA competed only in carbon steel product categories; it had seven integrated mills, three plants that used electric arc furnaces, and four rolling and finishing facilities. About 17,200 of its approximately 20,500 employees were represented by unions. U.S. Steel had mostly integrated steel mills, a unionized workforce, worldwide annual raw steel production

capacity of 26.8 million tons, and worldwide raw steel production of 21.2 million tons in 2005. AK Steel had seven steel mills and finishing plants in four states; about 6,300 of its approximately 8,000 employees were represented by unions. It sold much of its output to automotive companies—its two biggest customers were General Motors and Ford. Exhibit 12 presents selected financial and operating data for these three competitors.

In addition to the three major domestic rivals, there were a number of lesser-sized U.S.-based steelmakers

Exhibit 12   Selected Financial and Operating Data for Nucor's Three Largest U.S.-based Competitors

Company	2005	2004	2003
Mittal Steel USA			
Net sales	$12,237	$12,174	
Cost of goods sold	10,617	10,315	
Selling, general, and administrative expenses	371	301	
Net income	$ 491	$ 1,286	
Net income as a percent of net sales	4.0%	10.6%	
Shipments of finished steel products (millions of tons)	18.8	21.1	
Raw steel production (millions of tons)	20.0	23.9	
U.S. Steel			
Net sales	$14,039	$13,975	$9,328
Cost of sales	11,601	11,368	8,458
Selling, general, and administrative expenses	698	739	673
Income (loss) from operations	1,439	1,625	(719)
Net income	$ 892	$ 1,117	$ (436)
Net income as a % of net sales	10.3%	8.0%	(4.7)%
Shipments of steel products (millions of tons)	19.7	21.8	19.2
Raw steel production (millions of tons)	21.2	23.0	19.8
Domestic	15.3	17.3	14.9
Foreign	5.9	5.7	4.9
Production as a % of total capability			
Domestic	79.1%	89.0%	90.1%
Foreign	79.5	76.8	87.9
AK Steel Group			
Net sales	$5,647.4	$5,217.3	$4,041.7
Cost of products sold	4,996.8	4,553.6	3,886.9
Selling and administrative expenses	208.4	206.4	243.6
Operating profit (loss)	113.1	(79.7)	(651.8)
Net income (loss)	$ (2.3)	$ 38.4	$ (560.4)
Operating profit as a % of net sales	2.0%	(1.5)%	6.0%
Net income as a % of net sales	(0.04)%	4.6%	(13.9)%
Shipments of finished steel products (millions of tons)	6.4	6.3	5.8

Source: Company 10-K reports.

with plants that competed directly against Nucor plants. However, Nucor's most formidable competitive threat in the U.S. market consisted of Mittal Steel USA and foreign steelmakers that were intent on exporting some of their production to the United States; there were many foreign steel producers that had costs on a par with or even below those of Nucor, although their competitiveness in the U.S. market varied significantly according to the prevailing strength of their local currencies versus the U.S. dollar.

Endnotes

[1]Tom Peters and Nancy Austin, *A Passion for Excellence: The Leadership Difference* (New York: Random House, 1985), and "Other Low-Cost Champions," *Fortune*, June 24, 1985.

[2]According to information posted at www.nucor.com (accessed October 11, 2006).

[3]This discussion is based on information posted at www.nucor.com (accessed October 17, 2006).

[4]Nanette Byrnes, "The Art of Motivation," *BusinessWeek*, May 1, 2006, p. 59.

[5]Ibid., p. 57.

[6]Ibid., p. 60.

[7]Ibid.

[8]Ibid.

[9]Based on information in the STAT-USA data base, U.S. Department of Commerce, http://ia.ita.doc.gov/steel/license/SMP/Census/GDESC52/MMT_ALL_ALL_12M.htm (accessed October 27, 2006).

[10]Company press release, February 2, 2007.

[11]Ibid.

The YMCA of London, Ontario

W. Glenn Rowe
University of Western Ontario

As Shaun Elliott, chief executive officer, prepared for the last senior management planning session in 2005, he reflected on what the YMCA of London (the London Y or the association) had achieved in the last four years. Since joining in 2001, Elliott had led the organization from a deficit of $230,000[1] to a projected surplus of almost $1 million by the end of this fiscal year. This turnaround had been accomplished through a careful balance of internal cost cutting and growth through partnering and program expansion. Innovative partnerships with other organizations had allowed the London Y to expand its programs and facilities with minimal capital investment. In addition to its now solid financial performance, the London Y was on track to exceed its targeted participation level of 46,500 individuals by the end of 2005. It was now time for Elliott to turn his attention to achieving the next level of growth: participation levels of 102,000 individuals by 2010. He knew that to achieve an increase of this magnitude, senior management would need to increase their focus and its capacity and that he would need to spend more time on longer term strategic

initiatives and community relations. He wondered if this was possible given the current situation.

THE YMCA

The Young Men's Christian Association (YMCA) was an international federation of autonomous not-for-profit community service organizations dedicated to meeting the health and human service needs of men, women and children in their communities. The YMCA was founded in London, England, in 1844, in response to the unhealthy social conditions resulting from the industrial revolution. Its founder, George Williams, hoped to substitute Bible study and prayer for life on the streets for the many rural young men who had moved to the cities for jobs. By 1851, there were 24 YMCAs in Great Britain and the first YMCA in North America had opened in Montreal. Three years later, in 1854, there were 397 separate YMCAs in seven nations, with a total of 30,400 members.[2]

From its start, the YMCA was unusual in that it crossed the rigid lines that separated the different churches and social classes in England at the time. This openness was a trait that would lead eventually to YMCAs including all men, women and children regardless of race, religion or nationality. In 2005, the YMCA was in more than 120 countries around the world and each association was independent and reflected its own unique social, political, economic and cultural situation. YMCAs worldwide shared a commitment to growth in spirit, mind and body, as well as a focus on community service, social change, leadership development and a passion for youth.[3]

IVEY

Richard Ivey School of Business
The University of Western Ontario

Pat MacDonald prepared this case under the supervision of W. Glenn Rowe solely to provide material for class discussion. The authors do not intend to illustrate either effective or ineffective handling of a managerial situation. The authors may have disguised certain names and other identifying information to protect confidentiality.

Ivey Management Services prohibits any form of reproduction, storage or transmittal without its written permission. This material is not covered under authorization from CanCopy or any reproduction rights organization. To order copies or request permission to reproduce materials, contact Ivey Publishing, Ivey Management Services, c/o Richard Ivey School of Business, The University of Western Ontario, London, Ontario, Canada, N6A 3K7; phone (519) 661-3208; fax (519) 661-3882; e-mail cases@ivey.uwo.ca.

Copyright © 2006, Ivey Management Services Version: (A)2006-04-11

A similar, although separate organization, the Young Women's Christian Association (YWCA) was founded in 1855 in England.[4] It remained a separate organization; however, some YMCA and YWCAs chose to affiliate in order to best serve the needs in their communities.

THE YMCA IN CANADA

The London Y was a member of YMCA Canada, the national body of the 61 Canadian member associations. YMCA Canada's role was to foster and stimulate the development of strong member associations and advocate on their behalf regionally, nationally and internationally. YMCA Canada was a federation governed by a national voluntary board of directors which oversaw national plans and priorities. Volunteer board members were nominated by the member associations. YMCA Canada's President and CEO was accountable to the board for national operations. The national office had only 20 employees in 2005, reflecting the relative autonomy of the member associations.

As in the rest of the world, YMCAs in Canada served people of all ages, backgrounds and abilities and through all stages of life. They were dedicated to helping people attain a healthy lifestyle and encouraging them to get involved in making their community a better place. As charities, the YMCA member associations relied on the support of their communities, the private sector, governments and other agencies. YMCA fundraising campaigns helped to provide better programs and facilities, as well as greater accessibility and financial assistance to include as many people as possible.[5]

Earlier in 2005, YMCA Canada, in conjunction with its member associations, had developed a strong association profile, which comprised a wide range of performance measures similar to a balanced scorecard. Implementation of this measurement tool was voluntary, although YMCA Canada encouraged individual associations to use it to assess their performance and to compare their performance with other associations. According to the YMCA Canada strong association profile, a strong YMCA position profile is as follows:

- Demonstrates that it is having an impact on individuals' spirits, minds and bodies, while building strong kids, strong families and strong communities;
- Assists people to participate in the YMCA who otherwise could not afford to be involved;
- Is seen as a valued contributor to the community;
- Has the capacity to influence the community relative to its strategic priorities;
- Has quality programs that help members meet their personal goals;
- Demonstrates growth in participation over time;
- Offers a variety of programs that are accessible to the community;
- Has a culture of involving their members continually by encouraging them to give their time, talent and treasure to the YMCA;
- Has identified key audiences and has a communications plan that addresses each audience.

The London Y had piloted an earlier version of the strong association profile and had already set annual targets for 2005 through to 2010 (see Exhibit 1). The London Y planned to implement these targets and measures as part of its 2005 strategic planning cycle.

THE YMCA OF LONDON

Founded in 1856, the YMCA of London was a multi-service charity that described its mission as providing "opportunities for personal growth in spirit, mind and body for people of all backgrounds, beliefs and abilities."[6] Its articulated values and the principles by which it operates were:

- **Honesty:** to tell the truth, to act in such a way that you are worthy of trust, to have integrity, making sure your actions match your words.
- **Caring:** to accept others, to be sensitive to the well-being of others, to help others.
- **Respect:** to treat others as you would have them treat you, to value the worth of every person, including yourself.
- **Responsibility:** to do what is right, what you ought to do, to be accountable for your behavior and obligations.

The association served almost 28,000 children annually through child care and camping at 16 child

Exhibit 1   **The YMCA of London Participation Targets**

	2005	2006	2007	2008	2009	2010	5 yr Increase	Average Increase
Childcare								
Infant	70	70	70	70	70	70	0%	0%
Toddler	140	140	140	140	140	140	0%	0%
Preschool	608	672	736	832	928	1,024	68%	14%
School Age	316	316	316	316	316	316	0%	0%
Childcare Total	**1,134**	**1,198**	**1,262**	**1,358**	**1,454**	**1,550**	**37%**	**7%**
Camping and Educational Services								
CQE	1,815	2,215	2,215	2,439	2,471	2,471	36%	7%
Day Camp	5,350	5,457	5,566	5,677	5,791	5,907	10%	2%
Outdoor Education	5,800	6,960	9,048	9,953	10,948	12,043	108%	22%
Children's Safety Village	12,000	13,500	14,000	14,000	14,000	14,000	17%	3%
Community School Programs	1,630	1,880	2,130	2,380	2,630	2,880	77%	15%
Camping Total	**26,595**	**30,012**	**32,959**	**34,449**	**35,840**	**37,301**	**40%**	**8%**
Health Fitness and Recreation								
CBY full fee	5,450	5,580	5,750	5,825	6,000	6,200	14%	3%
CBY asisted	2,210	2,330	2,450	2,500	2,525	2,650	20%	4%
CBY programs	4,200	4,580	4,975	5,750	6,875	8,050	92%	18%
BHY full fee	1,500	1,525	1,900	2,100	2,400	2,700	80%	16%
BHY assisted	300	305	380	420	480	540	80%	16%
BHY programs	1,600	7,565	9,100	10,195	11,480	13,125	720%	144%
ELY full fee		1,025	1,050	1,050	1,075	1,200		
ELY assisted		205	210	210	215	240		
ELY programs		4,085	5,010	5,280	5,755	6,225		
SCY full fee	481	865	1,155	1,155	1,155	1,155	140%	28%
SCY assisted	26	74	100	110	110	110	323%	65%
SCY programs	773	826	865	905	925	945	22%	4%
WDY full fee	1,822	1,844	1,879	1,913	2,400	3,040	67%	13%
WDY assisted	373	405	426	449	600	760	104%	21%
WDY programs	4,900	5,680	6,480	6,935	8,140	9,375	91%	18%
New location full fee	n/a	n/a	n/a	5,000	7,000	7,000		
New location assisted	n/a	n/a	n/a	1,250	1,750	1,750		
HFR Total	**18,735**	**31,214**	**35,250**	**49,797**	**57,135**	**63,315**	**238%**	**48%**
Grand Total of Participants	**46,464**	**62,424**	**69,471**	**85,604**	**94,429**	**102,166**	**120%**	**24%**
Volunteers								
Childcare								
Camping								
CBY								
BHY		55	60	65	70	75		
ELY		15	20	25	30	35		
SCY	20	23	27	30	35	40	100%	20%
WDY	35	38	42	45	60	80		
Total	**55**	**131**	**149**	**165**	**195**	**230**		

(continued)

Exhibit 1 **Continued**

	2005	2006	2007	2008	2009	2010	5 yr Increase	Average Increase
Member Retention Rate								
CBY		76%	76%	76%	76%	76%		
BHY		55%	64%	68%	69%	70%		
ELY		55%	64%	68%	69%	70%		
SCY		55%	65%	68%	72%	75%		
WDY		80%	80%	82%	82%	82%		
New Location								

Source: YMCA of London, 2005 Strategic Planning Documents.

care locations, two residential camps, one outdoor education center and numerous summer day camps and after school program locations. In 2004, the London Y had provided 13,025 health, fitness and recreation (HFR) memberships for children and adults at five branches: three in London, one in Strathroy and one in Woodstock. In addition, the St. Thomas YMCA was operated by London Y senior management under contract. To ensure that no one was turned away because of an inability to pay, in 2004, the association provided 2,994 assisted HFR memberships, 1,100 assisted "camperships" and assistance to 310 children in child care. The association had a very positive brand position in the community and its internal research had shown that referrals were the number one source of new members and participants.

The last four years had been a time of renewal and change for the London Y (see Exhibit 2). Revenue had increased by 50 percent and the association had transformed an operating deficit of $230,000 in 2001 to an expected $1 million operating surplus by the end of 2005 (see Exhibit 3). In 2004, child care contributed 38 percent of total revenue, HFR contributed 27 percent and 16 percent of revenue came from camping (see Exhibit 4 for The YMCA of London—Revenue). The remaining revenue sources included government programs and contracts, community programs, donations and the United Way. Almost 90 percent of the London Y's revenue was self-generated through program and participation fees.

The responsibility for all development and fundraising activity was in the process of being moved

Exhibit 2 **The YMCA of London Growth 2001 to 2005**

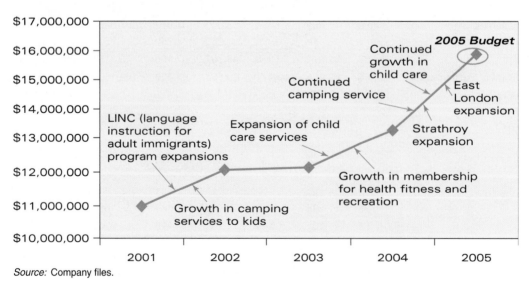

Source: Company files.

Exhibit 3   **The YMCA of London Schedule of Operations, 2001–2005**

	2005 Projected	Year ended Dec. 31, 2004	Year ended Dec. 31, 2003	Year ended Dec. 31, 2002	Year ended Dec. 31, 2001
REVENUE					
Memberships	$3,647,014	$3,560,527	$3,364,190	$3,139,980	$3,183,699
Child Care	6,811,401	4,958,138	4,037,612	4,516,214	4,576,632
Camp Fees	2,192,237	2,121,787	2,023,885	2,020,531	1,978,414
Community Programs	260,676	442,927	532,606	863,573	414,659
Program Service Fees	328,495	228,500	342,727	302,069	299,177
United Way	205,999	185,250	169,989	164,619	178,818
Ancillary Revenue	544,748	519,225	458,768	633,102	252,935
Donations & Fundraising	341,701	297,917	371,996	416,779	128,190
Employment Initiatives	989,141	891,815	792,983		
International Contributions & Grants				41,239	46,023
Total Revenue	$15,321,412	$13,206,086	$12,094,756	$12,098,106	11,058,547
EXPENSES					
Salaries & benefits	$9,550,594	$8,525,862	$7,663,975	$7,718,093	$7,288,194
Program costs	973,935	1,357,277	1,237,143	946,329	1,013,640
Facilities	2,060,400	1,830,450	1,746,122	1,918,676	1,878,400
Promotion	165,180	178,053	140,143	183,441	164,600
Association dues	163,543	157,570	137,985	136,795	132,777
Travel & development	214,130	222,013	238,060		
Office expenses	285,302	276,835	284,382		
Professional & other fees	247,592	247,430	302,695		
Miscellaneous	149,741	168,117	128,503		
Administration				840,048	763,095
International Development				41,239	46,023
Total expenses	$14,399,676	$12,963,607	$11,879,008	$11,784,621	$11,286,729
EXCESS (DEFICIENCY) OF REVENUE OVER EXPENSES	$ 921,736	$ 242,279	$ 215,748	$ 313,485	$ (228,182)

Source: The London YMCA Annual Reports 2004, 2003, 2002, 2001.

into the YMCA of London Foundation, an affiliated but separate organization which had a strong record of investing and securing grants. In its newly expanded role, the foundation was expected to support capital campaigns, conduct annual campaigns and enhance planned giving.

The London Y's structure included the CEO who was accountable to a volunteer board of directors (the board). Seven general managers and one manager reported to the CEO along with three senior directors and one director. The general managers and manager were responsible for service areas or locations including camping and outdoor education, child care, community services, London HFR, the Woodstock District YMCA, the St. Thomas Elgin Family YMCA, the Strathroy-Caradoc Family YMCA, overall facilities, and employment initiatives. The senior directors and director were responsible for finance, development, human resources and communications, respectively (see Exhibit 5). The number of senior managers had not increased in the last four years.

With the introduction of the strong association profile framework for performance measurement, all senior managers would have performance agreements and work-plans that they had planned together. Measures of participation, program quality and financial performance would be tracked and accountability would be to the group. Once the measures and targets were well established, it was

Exhibit 4   **The YMCA London Percent Composition of Revenue, 2004**

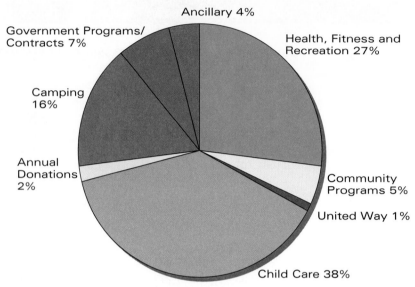

Source: The YMCA of London Annual Report 2004.

expected that compensation decisions would be based on each senior manager's performance against their plans.

In 2005, the association had over 500 permanent staff with an additional 200 seasonal staff. Full-time employees made up 35 to 40 percent of the total and the remaining 60 to 65 percent were part-time employees. Annual staff satisfaction surveys consistently showed high levels of both satisfaction and commitment to the association. However, wages were a persistent issue with staff in the child care centers and finding suitable HFR staff had been particularly challenging.

During the last four years, the board and senior management of the London Y had identified partnering as a key strategy to achieve the association's long-term strategic objectives in its three core service areas: HFR, child care, and camping and outdoor education. Senior management moved quickly to seize opportunities for a number of new partnerships.[7] A new HFR facility in East London was developed in partnership with the London Public Library. Partnerships were established with Kellogg Canada Inc. and John Labatt Ltd. for the London Y to operate their on-site HFR facilities. Child care services had grown more than 50 percent, primarily

as a result of a partnership with the University of Western Ontario.

Some partnerships were opportunistic or tactical but were nonetheless guided by their fit with the long term goals and values of the London Y. For example, a partnership with the Children's Safety Village made resources available to pursue a new full service HFR location in an underserved area of the city, thus expanding service and programs. In the absence of a significant capital infusion, senior management believed that new partnerships were critical to the London Y achieving its participation target of 102,000 individuals by 2010.

CORE SERVICE AREAS

Health, Fitness and Recreation

One of the longest standing services that the London Y provided was HFR. These services were offered through five branches each led by a general manager. These included: the London Centre YMCA (CBY), the Bob Hayward (BHY) and East London (ELY) all located in London; The Strathroy-Caradoc Family YMCA (SCY) located 40 kilometers west of

Exhibit 5   **The YMCA of London Organization Chart, September 2005**

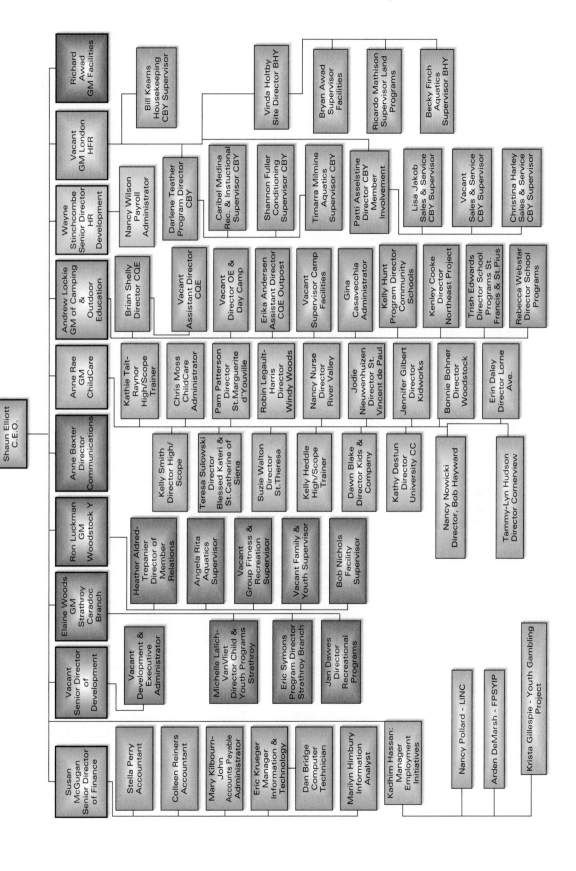

London; and The YMCA of Woodstock and District (WDY) located 50 kilometers east of London. By 2005, the London Y had served more than 18,700 individuals through its HFR programs and by 2010 the association had a target of serving more than 63,000 in six locations, an increase of 238 percent. The St. Thomas Y was located 35 kilometers south of London.

The branches were membership-based and offered health and fitness programs for children, families and adults. Twenty-five percent of the London Y's members received an assisted membership and paid one-third of the cost on average. Programs for children and youth were estimated to cost more than four times the association's programs for adults, yet generated lower fees. Children's programs and services often ran at a loss. The London Y depended on full fee paying adult HFR members to cross-subsidize assisted memberships and children's programs.

The largest challenge to the London Y attracting full fee adult members was the proliferation of fitness facilities for adults. Market-research commissioned by the London Y in 2002, indicated that approximately 30 percent of the 193,845 adults in London would join a fitness facility and that 25.5 percent of adults were already members of a fitness club. The potential for market growth was assessed as limited. The research also showed significant penetration of the market by private sector providers with the primary competition in London coming from the Good Life Clubs with 37 percent market share and The Athletic Club with 22 percent of the market. The London Y was third in the London market with a share of 12 percent. The competition had increased recently with the entrance of the Premier/Mademoiselle chain of fitness clubs into the City of London.

The private clubs operated under a very different economic model than the London Y, typically leasing equipment and facilities. They targeted the adult market only and they did not offer pools or as wide a range of programming as the London Y. In contrast to the private operators, the London Y owned relatively large facilities with pools. Only the two newest branches in London and Strathroy (ELY and SCY) did not have pools, although interest in adding a pool to the SCY had already been raised in the community.

A number of the London Y facilities were aging and required significant capital reinvestment or replacement. The CBY was 25 years old and required ongoing maintenance and refurbishment. The BHY in East London and the WDY were each 50 years old and were not wheelchair accessible. Both buildings required significant capital investment to meet and maintain modern standards. Unfortunately, the BHY was not ideally located so the potential for new members would be limited. More positively, the City of Woodstock had expressed an interest in partnering with the association to develop a new community facility as part of the city's master recreational plan. Replacing the WDY building was considered to be an imperative and partnering with the city was the association's preferred strategy.

Senior management of the London Y believed that to remain relevant in the HFR market as well as meet its targets, the association must develop new facilities in London's north and west ends. The City of London's master recreational plan supported partnership in the delivery of recreational programs and the association had begun discussions with the city regarding development of a new HFR facility in the north end. The city's plan also identified the southwest of the city as a priority site for a HFR facility.

Retention was a key part of membership growth as research showed that two-thirds of new members leave within the first year. Currently, the London Y had relatively high retention rates for members that lasted beyond one year at CBY (76 percent), WDY (80 percent) and BHY (75 percent). ELY and SCY had been in operation less than two years, and retention rates while high were expected to decrease. The association had targeted overall HFR retention rates of 55 percent at BHY, ELY and SCY next year increasing to more than 70 percent by 2010. While the association planned to continue its focus on families and to differentiate itself as a values-based organization, it also planned to offer specialized programs targeted at specific groups such as cardiac rehabilitation, weight loss, osteoporosis treatment, etc. to enhance both member retention and new member attraction. This would require increased staff with increased qualifications, resulting in increased costs. To offset these expected cost increases HFR management would need to determine ways to increase revenues or fees.

Although the CEO managed most of the HFR facilities, each facility was run as a separate unit by its general manager. Each branch did its own hiring, staff training, uniform purchasing, program development, and sales and promotion materials. This had resulted in inconsistencies in program quality, program delivery, member service, staff management, facility maintenance and house-keeping between branches. There were significant economic and operational inefficiencies as well. Senior management believed that increased consist-ency would contribute to increased efficiency, allow-ing the association to serve more members and to retain more of the existing members. However, there were no coordinating mechanisms for HFR other than the CEO. With financial stability and revenue growth as his priorities, he had not had sufficient time to work with each of the HFR general manag-ers. Also, the CEO was not himself an experienced HFR manager, having spent his career in financial services prior to joining the association.

HFR staff tended to be young and at the begin-ning of their careers. Finding and retaining appropri-ate HFR staff had been challenging for the London Y. Work had begun on developing relationships with the local Community College and University to establish a placement/apprentice program to iden-tify strong candidates. Also a skill/aptitude profile of HFR staff was in development based on YMCA Canada's standards and training for HFR staff.

The senior management team had developed a number of strategic initiatives for HFR for the com-ing year. In summary they were:

- Develop a new facility in London in partnership with the city of London.
- Develop a new facility in Woodstock.
- Manage and promote the Bob Hayward and East London facilities as one branch.
- Initiate discussions with the town of Strathroy for the development of a pool.
- Focus on program development and quality, and develop a new revenue structure to support increased quality of service.

Child Care Services

Child care services were the London Y's larg-est source of revenue. These services were offered through 16 child care centers located in London (12 locations), Strathroy (two locations), St. Thomas and Woodstock (one location each). The centers were mostly located in leased premises with only the Woodstock center operating in a facility owned by the association. In 2004, the London Y had served 1,139 children in three categories: infant, toddler and preschooler. By 2010, the association planned to serve an additional 415 preschoolers, for a total of 1,554 children. The London Y child care centers were similar to other providers in offering full-time, part-time and flexible care options and its fees were set between the midpoint and the high end of fees charged in London. Infants are considerably more expensive to serve due to the higher staff-to-child ratios required.

Child care is highly regulated through Ontario's Day Nursery Act (DNA). The DNA prescribes staff-to-children ratios by age, as well as physical space design, procedures, food preparation and all other aspects of operations. Wage enhancement subsidies were established by the provincial government 10 years ago, as private centers were made public and regulations were established. The subsidies were considered to be necessary for the financial fea-sibility of centers; however, they had remained at the same levels since their introduction in the early 1990s. Many levels of government were involved with the regulation and funding of child care, includ-ing the Province of Ontario, the Ministry of Com-munity and Social Services, the Ministry of Health, cities and counties, and in some instances, boards of education. It was expected that the landscape of child care would undergo significant change in 2006 and beyond based on provincial initiatives and pro-grams resulting from proposed increases in federal funding.

Subsidies for child care fees are available to low income families through the cities and counties. These subsidies did not typically cover all of the fees and the London Y absorbed the shortfall as part of its support to the community.

There were two other large child care providers in London: London Children's Connection with 13 centers and London Bridge with 11 centers. Unlike these service providers, the London Y offered unique programming through its use of the High Scope cur-riculum and its values-based programming. In fact, the London Y's curriculum and values focus were key reasons that The University of Western Ontario decided to partner with the association. In addition to the High Scope curriculum, the London Y also offered HFR memberships to each full-time child, discounts for HFR family memberships, summer day camp discounts for customers, swimming as part of their programs and family input through parent advisory committees.

The number of children aged zero to four was expected to decline until the year 2012 in the communities the association currently served. However, senior management believed that opportunities for expansion existed in some of the rural communities and counties that were near existing locations. To continue to maintain full enrollment, the association would need to closely monitor local demographics, competitors' expansion and new subdivision development.

The London Y employed a large number of early childhood educators. Wage scales in the industry were lower than in many other industries. While the London Y had made every effort to provide reasonable compensation and reward good performance, staff satisfaction surveys consistently identified wages as an issue. It was now suspected that the London Y was paying slightly below the average child care wages in the city of London. Management realized that they must carefully balance wage increases and additional managers against their goal of maintaining a surplus.

Communication and consistency among the centers seemed to require constant attention. Some operational processes had been centralized, such as subsidies and collections, while most processes remained with each center, including the purchasing of supplies and food preparation. Procedures had been standardized with a common operation manual, although there were still many opportunities for greater consistency and standardization.

With more than 50 percent growth in child care since 2001, the general manager's scope of authority had become very large. By 2005, she had 18 people reporting directly to her, including all 16 center directors. This created significant barriers to relationship-building, both internally with staff and externally with parents, potential partners, funding organizations and regulators. It was also a challenge during budget review when the general manager of child care had to review 16 center budgets and the overall child care budget in the same time frame as, for example, a general manager in HFR whose one budget might be smaller than one of the larger child care centers.

While the nature and the extent of the changes in programs and program funding were unclear,

senior management believed that the complex regulatory environment gave a distinct advantage to an experienced and competent child care provider. The London Y was confident that it had good working relationships with the cities of London, Woodstock, Strathroy and St. Thomas, the counties in which it operated, and with both the Public and the Roman Catholic School Boards.

Partially in response to the changes expected in the child care environment, the London Y had begun to explore partnership or merger opportunities with other service providers. In addition to operating advantages, management believed a partnership might also enhance their ability to influence government funding.

The senior management team had developed a number of strategic initiatives for child care services in the coming year. In summary they were:

- Explore partnerships or mergers with other providers.
- Identify and initiate opportunities in rural areas.
- Enhance wage structure in balance with budget limitations.
- Monitor changes in government policy, acquire the best and earliest information and develop appropriate contingency plans.

Camping and Outdoor Education

The London Y expected to serve more than 26,500 participants through camping and education programs in 2005. Residential camping programs were delivered in July and August to almost 2,000 children aged 6 to 17 at two sites in Northern Ontario, Camp Queen Elizabeth and Camp Queen Elizabeth (CQE) Outpost. Summer day camps served more than 5,000 children aged 3 to 15 with a variety of programs running from traditional day camps to sports camps and other specialty camps. During the school year more than 1,500 children were served through community school programs delivered in cooperation with school boards. Another 12,000 children were served annually through programs given by police and firefighters at the Children's Safety Village located in the Upper Thames Conservation Authority area near the city of London. Finally, almost 6,000 children and adults participated in outdoor education programs including leadership and team building programs offered at various locations.

Camp Queen Elizabeth had been in operation for 50 years and had an excellent reputation. Each year the camp was booked to capacity and each year those bookings occurred earlier. Similar to other residential camps, much of the activity was outdoors and programming included water sports, crafts and climbing. Fees were among the highest in YMCA camping and the return rate of campers was the highest of all YMCA camps in Ontario. Campers tended to be more homogeneous and from higher income families; however, assisted spots were made available for those unable to afford the fees.

Camp Queen Elizabeth was located on land leased from Parks Canada, a federal department. The current lease was due to expire in 2007 and the London Y had postponed capital investment in the facilities pending renewal of the lease. The association had now received assurance from Parks Canada that the lease would be renewed so a long-overdue refurbishment of the camp's infrastructure could be planned.

The CQE Outpost property had been purchased as a hedge against renewal of the Camp Queen Elizabeth lease as well as for additional capacity to serve older youth with adventure and canoe trips. Service to older youth had not increased as planned and there appeared to be little demand for this type of service. Management was now exploring the possibility of selling the property and using the proceeds towards the renovation of Camp Queen Elizabeth.

The London Y offered a wide variety of day camp and outdoor education programs during all weeks of the summer and, to a limited extent, in the shoulder seasons of spring and fall. During the summer, the association ran a bussing network throughout the city of London to collect and return participants to designated drop-off points. Programming was value-based and emphasized character development more than skill development. Other summer day camp providers included the local university, the city of London, a variety of private businesses and not-for-profit organizations, and churches. The London Y day camps offered the same size groups and staff ratios as other day camp providers and in some cases the offerings were quite undifferentiated. The service needs and selection processes for families and children were not clearly understood by the London Y, although it appeared to management that there were a number of different segments such as skills-based camps, traditional camps and camps that were more like a child care service.

The association had recently invested some capital dollars in its outdoor education program and developed two new sites in partnership with Spencer Hall, run by the Richard Ivey School of Business and Spencer Lodge, run by the Boy Scouts of Canada. With these new partners and facilities the association hoped to increase the number of its outdoor education program participants by more than 100 percent by 2010.

The community school program, funded by the United Way and the London Y, was an after school program aimed at improving the academic performance and the social skills of children in higher risk neighborhoods. The focus was on literacy, social skills and recreation, and the programs were delivered in a number of designated schools. London Y staff worked closely with teachers to identify children who would benefit from participation in the program. This program continued to expand as much as funding and staffing would allow.

Each school year the Children's Safety Village targeted students in grades one to four with its programs on broad safety topics including pedestrian safety, bike safety, fire safety, electrical safety and other household hazards.[8] As a result of their partnership agreement, the London Y's Camping and Outdoor Education operations moved from their dilapidated offices at the association's outdoor education center to the Children's Safety Village site and the London Y took over management of the site. While the London Y was responsible for the physical operation, the Children's Safety Village Board continued to govern the organization, resulting in some overlapping responsibilities.

Camping and outdoor education offered a wide variety of programs in a large number of locations under a number of different names. Each program produced its own sales and promotion materials and parent communications. A number of programs and facilities were not clearly identified as part of the YMCA, such as Camp Queen Elizabeth or the Children's Safety Village. Management believed that there were a number of opportunities to send a more consistent message to the community and to strengthen the London Y's brand.

The senior management team had developed a number of strategic initiatives for camping and outdoor education in the coming year. In summary they were:

- Identify day camp market segments and deliver programs to meet identified needs.
- Sell the CQE Outpost site and use the proceeds to improve Camp Queen Elizabeth, ensuring that current and expected demand can be accommodated.
- Negotiate a new governance model and transfer governance of the YMCA Children's Safety Village to the YMCA of London.
- Ensure that all facilities and programs are clearly identified as part of the London YMCA.
- Leverage opportunities to serve more individuals in outdoor education programs.

ELLIOTT'S CONSIDERATION OF THE SITUATION

Elliott realized that each of the association's three main service areas had very different business models and dynamics and that this created challenges for organizational focus and expertise, resource allocation and communication. He also knew that while the challenges coming from this multi-service approach were abundant and the synergies limited, neither the board of the London Y nor the senior management wished to reduce the range of services that the association provided to the community. Elliott's challenge was how to best manage the association as a whole while appropriately nurturing each of the core service areas. He had a number of concerns.

The recent growth had put significant strain on both the capacity and capabilities of the senior managers. Elliott was concerned that there were simply not enough managers to deliver the targeted growth and, particularly, the new partnership relationships that would need to be established. Over the last few years Elliott felt that he was the "chief business development officer," searching out partnering opportunities with external organizations and developing both the opportunity and the relationship through to the final agreement. The service area leaders had

been focusing on operations and did not have the time, or perhaps the inclination, to think about innovative ways for their areas to serve more people. He believed that it was now time for the service area leaders to take on the development role and to identify and create their own growth opportunities.

In addition to greater capacity, Elliott believed that the senior management team needed to increase its focus on higher level strategic issues affecting the whole association. With 12 people at the table, senior management team meetings were not as effective as they might have been and in fact some members only contributed when the discussion was about their specific location. Also, the meetings tended to over-emphasize day-to-day HFR operations simply because there were so many HFR general managers at the table. This meant that they were perhaps under-emphasizing the association's other key service areas of child care and camping.

Along with decreasing senior management's focus on HFR, Elliott knew that he too needed to spend less time on day-to-day HFR operations and more time on strategic initiatives and community relations. However, with four HFR General Managers reporting to him and with HFR representing the biggest operational challenges and the largest growth target, he knew that HFR needed the undivided attention of a capable senior manager. Also, he did not know how the HFR General Managers would respond to any changes that might be perceived as a loss of status or position.

Elliott had real fears about creating a potentially unnecessary layer of management or, even worse, an elite group that would become out of touch with the staff and the various locations. He worried about becoming out of touch with the operations himself. One of the first things that Elliott had done when he joined the association in 2001 was to eliminate most of the so-called "head office" positions, including the chief operating officer, the head of HFR and the head of development. He did not think that the association could afford those roles at that time and he still believed in carefully balancing expenses and overhead with the need for resources to support expansion. Elliott also had concerns about how the community would perceive a charitable organization that significantly increased its senior management personnel. Finally, he worried about moving too quickly.

CONCLUSION

Elliott recognized that in trying to determine what was best for the London Y, he must consider the business model and strategy of each of the core service areas while taking into account the overall mission and values of the association. He needed to be confident that any changes would increase the management capacity and focus within each area as well as free him up to focus on longer term strategic initiatives. Elliott was concerned about introducing more overhead expense just when the association's financial performance was stable. He did not have much time left to ponder as he wanted the senior management team to consider any potential organizational changes in the last planning session which was scheduled for next week.

Endnotes

[1] All funds in Canadian dollars unless specified otherwise.

[2] http://www.ymca.net/about_the_ymca/history_of_the_ymca.html. Accessed February 23, 2006.

[3] http://www.ymca.ca/eng_worldys.htm. Accessed Feb. 23, 2006.

[4] http://www.ywca.org/site/pp.asp?c=djISI6PIKpG&b=281379. Accessed February 23, 2006.

[5] http://www.ymca.ca/eng_abouty.htm. Accessed February 23, 2006.

[6] http://www.londony.ca/. Accessed February 24, 2006.

[7] All of the London Y's partnering relationships have approximately the same legal structure which involves a facilities lease and an operating or service provision agreement. There are no fees paid to the partners as all services are provided on a fee for service basis and the London Y covers the operating costs of the facility.

[8] http://www.safetyvillage.ca/about.htm. Accessed February 28, 2006.

Case 11

Wild Oats Markets, Inc.

John R. Wells
Harvard Business School

Travis Haglock
Harvard Business School

In 2006, Wild Oats Markets, Inc. (Wild Oats), was the number two natural foods retailer in the fast growing organic and natural foods market. With 111 stores in 25 states at the end of 2005 and sales of $1.1 billion, Wild Oats was struggling to return to the fast growth it had once enjoyed in its early years. Between 1995 and 2000, the company grew from $98.5 million in sales to $838 million, for a compound annual growth rate of 53 percent, and at one point, Wild Oats surpassed the industry leader, Whole Foods Market, Inc. (Whole Foods), in number of stores. However, since 2000, Wild Oats' growth was less stellar, averaging 6 percent annually, and the firm reported cumulative losses as a result of restructuring charges. Meanwhile, Whole Foods grew at 21 percent compound annual rate over the same period and delivered healthy profits. Organic food sales in the United States grew from $6.1 billion in 2000 to $13.8 billion in 2005, a compound rate of about 16 percent per year compared to conventional food sales which grew at a 2–4 percent compound rate.[1]

Early in August 2006, Wild Oats reported that sales at existing stores had grown at a slow 1.3 percent annual rate, and attributed the slow growth to greater competition from conventional supermarkets. Indeed, heavy purchases of organic produce by Wal-Mart and Safeway were causing supply shortages. Meanwhile, Whole Foods had just reported comparable store sales growth of 10 percent. Perry Odak, Wild Oats' chief executive since 2001,

had been struggling for five years to help the company recover from problems created by a string of acquisitions, but some analysts were beginning to doubt whether he was the man to do it. To add to Odak's challenges, the company was being stalked by billionaire grocery store investor Ronald Burkel.[2] The outlook was, at best, uncertain.

EARLY HISTORY

In 1984, 25-year-old husband and wife team Michael Gilliland[3] and Libby Cook raised a mortgage on Gilliland's mother's home and used cash advances on 17 credit cards to acquire a small convenience store across from the University of Colorado.[4] Gilliland, who had once tried opening a crepe stand in New Orleans, Louisiana, and running a parasailing business, recalled, "I was looking for a business I could run on my own. I had a feel for customer service and I knew what the market liked. I fell into retail." Gilliland, an English major, called the store Stella's after the character in *A Streetcar Named Desire*. Gilliland and Cook's first attempt at retailing proved very successful, and sales grew from $100 on the first day to $4,000 a day within six months. Indeed, the store was so popular that the pair had to hire a bouncer. "It became a very cool place for college students to hang out. The fact that we let our employees drink beer on the job added to the party atmosphere."

In 1985, Gilliland and Cook partnered with Randy Clapp to acquire a second convenience store in Boulder, Lolita's, which also proved success.[5] A third store, added in 1986, was more of a challenge. "My wife worked as a lawyer during the day to keep us

9-707-438

afloat," said Gilliland. "Thinking we were infallible, we opened a gourmet/natural foods/convenience store called The French Market in the Basemar Center in Boulder. The store lacked any focus, was terribly mismanaged (by me) and was a disaster for two years. Fortunately, Stella's and Lolita's were profitable enough to keep us afloat."[6] In 1987, Gilliland, Cook, and Clapp acquired the Crystal Market, a vegetarian natural foods store that also sold used bicycles, Guatemalan clothing, and quartz crystals.[7] "It was our first exposure to natural foods. Unlike most people in this industry, we didn't start out as vegetarians. We were converted by the business." Gilliland, Cook, and Clapp changed the name of the Crystal Market to Wild Oats Vegetarian Market and converted one of their convenience stores to a natural foods store. "With Wild Oats, we committed ourselves to good, wholesome foods produced in an earth-friendly, responsible manner. It was a lot more fun than the convenience store–type markets we were running. And it also had more of a future." Two more stores were added, bringing the total by the end of 1990 to six. In 1990, Wild Oats instituted its 5 percent Day Charitable Giving Program. One day, each quarter, each store donated 5 percent of sales to a local charity chosen by store management.

RAPID GROWTH, 1991–1999

In January 1991, Gilliland, Cook, and Clapp, opened a store in Santa Fe, New Mexico, their first store outside of Colorado and their first natural foods supermarket. "It was a slam dunk from opening day on. From there on, we just had great momentum."[8] In May of the following year, the company opened two more stores in New Mexico (Santa Fe and Albuquerque), and another store in Colorado, bringing the total for the company to nine at the end of 1992.[9]

As the chain expanded, the founders felt they were beginning to lose touch, and introduced a staff survey to obtain information that they once obtained informally. "In our business we need to keep our staff happy because they're the first line of defense when customers come into the store," said Cook. In response to the survey results, in 1992, Wild Oats created the Wellness Benefit, which allowed employees to claim up to $2,000 per year for anything they thought would benefit their health, including roller blades, a massage, a snowboard, or a visit to the chiropractor. Over 90 percent of Wild Oats employees participated. Many bought a bike, one a vasectomy. A $200 Baby Benefit covering things related to the care of a baby was also introduced.[10] In 1992, Wild Oats generated sales of $36.6 million and operating income in excess of $1 million.

In 1993, Wild Oats opened another store in Colorado, and acquired a store in Kansas City, Missouri. The employee surveys were increased to twice per year in 1993, and became compulsory; participation increased from under 50 percent of store staff to approximately 90 percent. Wild Oats computerized, compiled, and sorted the results by store, yielding a Happiness Index. Gilliland, Cook, and Clapp then read the results, screening out negative comments they considered nonproductive. "It can bum managers out. If there are 30 great comments and 5 negative ones, they'll fixate on the negative," said Gilliland, who personally delivered and discussed results with store managers. "Every round of surveys brings a surprise," said Gilliland. For example, in one survey, the staff at the store with the best working conditions and most benefits yielded the worst complaints. "We'd assumed it would be the happiest store, but it wasn't," said Cook. In response to feedback, the company introduced a host of changes, including profit sharing, additional training, and other benefits. "Each round brings in about 20 ideas and keeps the corporation in touch with the front lines. For example, I would never have thought of the Wellness Benefit. My idea of what's important is different from an hourly worker's," said Gilliland. Gilliland thought the surveys therapeutic, citing a decline in store staff turnover since their inception.[11]

The company launched a frank, award-winning handbook for new employees in 1993. It began with "A Long, Strange Trip," a history of Wild Oats by Gilliland with the tone of a letter to a friend, and highlighting both the company's early successes and its failings. "Even though we are getting larger, Wild Oats is still pretty much a mom-and-pop store. We wanted people to know it is still owned by the first three people who bought it."[12] In 1993, Gilliland and Cook were named Entrepreneurs of the Year by *The Denver Business Journal*.[13]

In 1994, two stores were acquired in Las Vegas, Nevada, and another was opened in Colorado.[14] In response to its employee survey, Wild Oats introduced a profit sharing plan in which store employees, referred to as "wild things,"[15] received 15 percent of profits exceeding a predetermined monthly net profitability target.[16] "To the average cashier, it might amount to $1 in profit sharing every month. As you progress to higher positions at Wild Oats, the incentives increase," said Mary Beth Lewis, chief financial officer. Wild Oats hoped the plan would increase morale and productivity, boost recruitment, and decrease turnover. Each store posted its profit and loss statement to help employees track performance.[17] Revenues for 1994 reached $65.2 million and operating profits $2.6 million. Funding for the expansion was provided by Chase Venture Capital Associates.[18]

The pace of expansion quickened in 1995 with the opening of five stores (Colorado (two), Kansas, California, and New Mexico) and the acquisition of a further two in northern California. The acquisitions were converted to the Wild Oats Community Markets banner. The activity put a significant strain on the company and, although sales jumped to $98.5 million, operating profits fell to $0.8 million and debt mushroomed. However, the expansion continued. In 1996, the company acquired Alfalfa's Markets, Inc., an 11-store chain generating annual sales of $86 million for $39.1 million in cash and stock. Alfalfa's was Wild Oats' biggest competitor in Colorado, with six stores, and operated two more stores trading as Alfalfa's, in Santa Fe, New Mexico, and Seattle, Washington, and three stores under the name Capers in Vancouver, British Columbia.[19] Wild Oats also acquired a three-store chain in Utah in 1996, and opened a further seven stores. Two underperforming stores were closed the same year. Wild Oats retained the Alfalfa's and Capers names but converted the Utah acquisition to the Wild Oats banner. Alfalfa's and Wild Oats' headquarters in Boulder were consolidated into one. The acquisition of Alfalfa's, begun in 1995, made Wild Oats the number two in the industry behind Whole Foods, displacing Fresh Fields, which had been founded in 1991 and rapidly grown to the number two spot.

To fund Wild Oats' growth, in October 1996 the company made an initial public offering of 1.4 million shares at $25 per share, raising $31.4 million. The stock opened at $25.75 per share and fell immediately. Gilliland commented, "My net worth dropped significantly. It was a shock because it was such a hot deal, supposedly, up until the last minute. The funny thing is they didn't even give us a chance

to screw up. We've exceeded all projections as far as comps and profits and everything else."[20] After the offering, Gilliland, Cook and Clapp owned 50.4 percent of the company.[21] The total store count reached 40 by the end of 1996, sales jumped to $192 million, and operating profits before exceptional items to $11.6 million. After the acquisition, Wild Oats overtook Fresh Fields Inc. to become the second largest natural foods chain behind Whole Foods, and operated in eight U.S. states plus Canada. In June 1996, Whole Foods agreed to acquire Fresh Fields.[22]

Wild Oats stores and Alfalfa's stores were similar in terms of merchandising but not identical. Wild Oats stores were considered better in terms of natural living (e.g., vitamins and supplements, toiletries) and Alfalfa's stores had the edge in perishables (e.g., produce, prepared foods). Wild Oats tried to capitalize on these differences, encouraging the stores to share best practices.[23] To this end, Wild Oats retained Hass Hassan, the founder, CEO, and president of Alfalfa's to be president of Wild Oats. Born in Pakistan, raised in London, and a life-long vegetarian, Hassan founded Alfalfa's in Boulder in 1979. Hassan reportedly clashed with Gilliland, resigning after less than a year. The management style of Wild Oats was more "ready, fire, aim" and the management style of Alfalfa's was more "process-oriented and maybe a little less dictatorial," according to Gilliland. "Both ways [had] their advantages and disadvantages, and I think everyone [tried] to come up with a happy medium."[24]

Wild Oats' expansion did not go unnoticed by the industry leader, Whole Foods. In the company's annual general meeting in March 1996, Whole Foods' chairman, John Mackay, reiterated his commitment to growth at the expense of short-term profitability to prevent competition from getting established. Mackey commented, "It's important to establish dominance. If we do, its unlikely competitors like Fresh Fields and Wild Oats can succeed. We don't mind competition as long as we have overwhelming firepower."[25] In June 1996, Whole Foods announced that it was to acquire Fresh Fields. At the end of 1996, Wild Oats competed with Whole Foods in California and in Florida.

In January 1997, Whole Foods announced that it would open a store in Boulder, Colorado, and intended to open in other markets where Wild Oats competed. Whole Foods' president, Peter Roy, explained, "We're expanding into Boulder because it is an excellent market and it only has one major player. Obviously, our margins in Boulder will not be the highest in the company but that's OK. Whoever does the best job, has the best service and operates in the best location will win the battle. We believe that we're cheaper. Our entry into the market will help consumers. It will bring prices down in many of the stores in Boulder." [26] Wild Oats' stock dropped 26 percent, to $13 a share.

Wild Oats' Mary Beth Lewis commented, "There's plenty of growing room in this business for both of us. The competition between us isn't rational. Why should we beat each other up?" Mackay's view was clear: "It was Wild Oats that first entered our markets in San Francisco, Los Angeles and Chicago. I'm damned if I always want to be the hunted. I've gone into Boulder because I think I can make money there. I also think I can blow up the bomb factory. Boulder is a stronghold of Wild Oats, one of their key markets where they used to be able to extract high profits. Now, no longer. One of my aims is to weaken their company and lessen the competition I face. We're a much bigger and stronger company and can sustain a war of attrition far longer. If we have to fight a war—and they fired the opening shots—I'll fight to win." [27]

Mary Beth Lewis expressed the view that the move would not harm Wild Oats: "Additional stores tend not to take customers away so much as attract new customers. We don't feel particularly threatened by them coming to town despite the tone they've taken with us. Our stores are concentrated in the Western U.S. We are the largest customer from the distributors we buy from. They are locating a single store a thousand miles away from their next nearest store. I don't believe that they can offer lower prices than us." Whole Foods planned to open in a 39,000-square-foot location. Typically, Whole Foods stores generated sales of $10 million in their first year. Wild Oats operated three stores of 25,000 square feet, 13,000 square feet, and 6,500 square feet in Boulder, with combined sales of between $20 million and $25 million, almost 10 percent of total company sales. [28] In response to the announcement, Wild Oats immediately remodeled its two nearest Boulder stores. [29]

Despite the threat, analysts remained bullish on Wild Oats' prospects. Gary Giblin and Mary Cartwrite of Smith Barney identified that Wild Oats' contribution at store level was higher than Whole Foods', but that it had higher central overhead. They wrote: "The good news for [Wild Oats] is that its efficient store model is structural and enduring whereas its lack of corporate expense leverage is temporary. [Wild Oats] has about as good a mouse-trap as [Whole Foods]. We find [Wild Oats'] share valuation compelling. On the key multiples, it is cheaper than [Whole Foods]. Furthermore, it is cheaper than the broader comparable universe of category killer retailers and trades at a deep P/E discount to its growth rate." [30]

In 1997, Wild Oats opened seven new stores and made four small acquisitions, adding two stores in Eugene, Oregon (Oasis Fine Foods); two in Florida; two in Memphis, Tennessee; and three in Arizona. The company retained two of the retail brands acquired (Oasis Fine Foods and Sunshine Grocery) and converted the remaining stores. The company also announced plans to open in Chicago in the first head-to-head competition with Whole Foods. [31] Wild Oats typically paid between two and four times recast store contribution for acquisitions. [32] Margins at acquired stores decreased initially and increased after approximately six months. [33] After acquiring a store, Wild Oats performed a minor remodeling costing approximately $200,000, [34] including décor. The store remained open during the 8- to 16-week remodel period. [35] If the store name was to be changed, the new name was not applied until the remodeling was complete.

Analysts were generally supportive of Wild Oats' acquisition strategy. Mark Hanratty and Adam Cherry of Paine Webber thought that Wild Oats had "the management and systems in place to integrate its recent acquisitions." [36] Gary Giblin and Lisa Cartwright of Smith Barney thought that Wild Oats had integrated gently, "in keeping with its enlightened human resource management and focus on maintaining store level morale and productivity among the truly value-added employees integral to successful natural foods retailing." [37] And one analyst thought that Wild Oats would be shielded from the negative surprises acquisitions "sometimes reveal" because it had made many small acquisitions, creating "a diversified portfolio effect." [38]

Wild Oats looked for store locations offering 15,000 to 35,000 square feet for its supermarket stores and aimed to be an anchor tenant in a neighborhood mall or a high-visibility stand-alone store. For its urban stores, the company looked for 5,000–15,000 square feet in dense residential or commercial areas with high foot traffic. Within these broad parameters, the company was flexible with respect to store format, enabling it to customize its stores to specific sites and local markets. The company believed that this approach allowed it to reach a broader customer base.[39]

The company was also flexible in its merchandising approach, with some stores having a gourmet emphasis, some more mainstream, and one store at least being strictly vegetarian.[40] "I'm a great believer in figuring out where customers are and walking with them. It doesn't do you any good to put a hardcore vegetarian market in the middle of Pasadena, [California,] because you're going to go out of business. In Santa Monica, [California,] for instance, we have a more affluent customer base. We took the bulk bins out. Those customers weren't going to stand around and scoop out flour. But we can sell a $50 bottle of olive oil," said Gilliland.[41] To this end, Wild Oats offered both organic items and non-organic items, aiming to be 80 percent organic. Wild Oats set specific standards for its food products (i.e., preservative-free, organically grown, cruelty-free, not bioengineered, non-radiated, free of artificial coloring and flavoring, free of chemical additives) and natural living products (i.e., preservative-free, cruelty-free, formaldehyde-free, no aluminum packaging, free of artificial coloring and flavoring, full ingredient disclosure, limited animal ingredients).[42] Wild Oats also emphasized locally-grown produce.[43]

The company operated a central purchasing function, which set product standards and negotiated with vendors for volume discounts. Store department managers then decided what to order, allowing each store to customize its offering to its local market. The company had over 3,000 suppliers in 1997, but 20–25 percent of purchases were from one national distributor,[44] United Natural Foods Inc. (UNFI). Most goods were delivered direct to store by local distributors, but the company operated a small distribution center in Denver, and six commissary kitchens to produce deli food, baked goods, and take-out food for delivery to stores over a 100-mile radius. Wild Oats was often one of the highest-volume customers of a regional wholesaler or regional distributor even if it had only a few stores in a region.[45]

In 1997, Wild Oats had between 100 and 150 private-label items in approximately 15 categories, and planned to double this. Private-label lines included chocolate bars, gourmet breads, salsa, salad dressings, chips, pretzels, tortillas, pasta, pasta sauces, oils, canned fruit, and vitamins. Private-label items offered 5 to 10 percent higher margins than branded goods. Private label was approximately 3 percent of sales in 1997, and plans called for this to expand to 10 percent. The strategy was praised by analysts who suggested that natural foods customers were less loyal to brands than conventional foods customers.[46]

Wild Oats' average customer was female, 32 years old, with 15 years of education, a household income of $34,000, and a house worth $140,000;[47] 85 percent of Wild Oats' customer base was female.[48] Wild Oats didn't invest much in advertising except when opening a new store. The emphasis was more on store-level promotions, and in-store experience. Wild Oats aimed to make shopping "theater" in a fun and educational environment, with cooking classes, live music, children's events, harvest fairs, barbecues, and dog washes. Some stores had in-store nutritionists and massage therapists; all offered educational information on food. Stores were festooned with product brochures and recipe cards, and tasting stations allowed consumers to try new products. Most stores also had seating areas and offered juices, while some offered full café service.[49] Wild Oats produced monthly advertising flyers promoting between 30 and 50 items, and distributed them in stores, through newspapers, and sometimes through direct mail.[50] It even tried a major buy-one-get-one-free promotion in 1997.[51]

Wild Oats, like many other natural foods retailers, had relatively unsophisticated information systems compared to most conventional food retailers. In 1997, Wild Oats was installing a point-of-sale system and new inventory control software. It had not established electronic data interchange with its vendors.[52] In 1997, Wild Oats began Fresh-at-Five, a scheduling program to increase store labor hours at peak shopping times. This had been common practice for years for conventional food retailers.[53] Twenty percent of Wild Oats' employees were part-time in 1997, compared to 50 percent for conventional food retailers.[54]

In 1997, Wild Oats launched a $50 Fix-It Fund, available to any store employee to address a customer complaint,[55] and a $30 Birthday Dinner Benefit was introduced. The company instituted its Charity Work Benefit, paying employees for 1 hour of charity work per every 40 hours of Wild Oats work, up to 52 hours per year.[56] It also established Wild Oats University, a training program involving, among other things, a natural products test that employees had to pass before working on the store floor and a refresher course in order to improve retention of important information.[57]

In 1997, Cook began reducing her time commitment as vice president and general counsel in order to pursue other entrepreneurial activities.[58] Gilliland said of their business partnership, "From the start, she has been the voice of reason. I come up with all these ideas, some of which aren't too great, and she acts as a grounding influence. It's a good balance." In December 1997, Wild Oats completed a common stock offering, raising $46.5 million net, and Gilliland and Cook's ownership decreased from 22 to 15 percent each.[59]

In February 1998, Whole Foods opened a new store in Boulder, cutting prices by up to 20 percent and introducing a line of private-label items. Wild Oats' sales decreased by 15 percent in Boulder.[60] Rumors abounded that Whole Foods might attempt a takeover of Wild Oats. In May 1998, Wild Oats adopted certain "poison pill" provisions that required potential acquirers of Wild Oats to negotiate with the board of directors and discouraged coercive takeover attempts.[61] Wild Oats also began offering discounted stock options (15 percent) that vested after five years as part of the profit-sharing plan. Wild Oats' employees with one year of service were eligible.[62]

Wild Oats' pattern of small acquisitions and geographic expansion continued in 1998. In six separate transactions, seven stores were acquired in seven states, four of which were new to Wild Oats. A total of eight new stores were also opened, including Wild Oats' first store in Texas, home state of Whole Foods. Wild Oats entered a total of six new states in 1998. By the end of 1998, the company stores operated under seven banners: Wild Oats Community Market; Alfalfa's Market; Beans, Grains & Things; Ideal Market; Oasis Fine Foods; Sunshine Grocery; and Uptown Whole Foods.

In 1998, the founders of Wild Oats launched a $3 million foundation. The first project to be funded was the creation of a wellness center adjacent to a Wild Oats store, offering alterative healing remedies and more, available to employees for free and to members of the community for a nominal fee.[63] By 1998, Wild Oats had launched the Wild at Heart Foundation, a foundation supporting humanitarian and environmental groups. In 1998, Wild Oats gave at least 7.5 percent of earnings to nonprofit humanitarian and environmental groups.[64] By 1999, Wild Oats had created a second wellness center.[65]

On the merchandising front, in 1998, Wild Oats launched its Dinner-A-Go-Go program, a home meal replacement offering with foods prepared in stores, in commissaries, and by third parties.[66] The company also launched the Wild Card Shopper customer loyalty card program. Half of its customers signed up for a card, but Wild Oats discontinued it after a survey found that customers thought the program was too much like the programs offered by conventional supermarkets.[67] Gilliland, on the Wild Oats Web site, invited customers to return their Wild Cards to stores, where they would be disposed of in an environmentally safe manner, quoting W. C. Fields, "If at first you don't succeed . . . quit before you ruin what you've got."[68]

In 1998, Wild Oats had 10 regional directors responsible for the stores in their area. Store managers reported to the regional director and typically had 10 department managers reporting to them in their stores. Because of the wide size range of stores, Wild Oats had between 25 and 200 employees per store.[69]

By the end of 1998, Wild Oats operated 63 stores under seven banners in 18 states plus Canada. It generated sales of $398.9 million, more than double 1996 levels, and operating income of $18.7 million, more than four times 1996 levels. Gilliland and Cook were named Retail Entrepreneurs of the Year by *Chain Store Age,* a monthly newsmagazine for corporate executives in retail.

In 1999, Wild Oats went on a major acquisition spree, buying 7 Nature's Fresh Northwest stores in Portland, Oregon; 4 Wild Harvest outlets in Boston, Massachusetts; 11 Henry's Marketplace stores in San Diego, California; and 9 Sun Harvest Farms stores in Texas, as well as 3 operating stores in Tucson, Arizona. At the end of 1999, after acquiring a total of 41 stores and opening a further 8, Wild Oats had more stores than Whole Foods. Wild Oats retained the banners of acquired stores, and operated under a total of 12 banners in 1999.[70] Gilliland envisioned a "federation" of regional retailers rather than a national chain of cookie-cutter stores operating under one banner: "Our customers have an anti-chain mentality. They have more of an emotional attachment to the store than to the local Safeway. Maintaining that community connection is very important to us. We try to customize each store to the individual market and take advantage of our size in systems operations buying."[71] In 1999, Wild Oats, converted some of its smaller stores in less expensive locations to People's Markets stores with fewer stock-keeping units (SKUs), lower operating expenses, lower prices, narrower profit margins, the feel of a 1960s co-op, and a name evoking Maoist China.[72]

In 1999, Wild Oats had approximately 400 private-label items, and planned to double this within a year. Private label represented approximately 8 percent of sales, and plans called for this to increase to 20 percent. By 1999, Wild Oats had arranged its Natural Living section to be more accessible, arranging products by function such as cardiovascular health, respiratory health, digestive health and cleansing, and immune system health.[73] In 1999, Wild Oats stopped selling North Atlantic swordfish, marlin, orange roughy, and Chilean sea bass because of conservation concerns.[74] It began offering turtle-safe, certified shrimp—shrimp caught in turtle excluder devices. Wild Oats had been introduced to these devices at its annual Wildstock conference. "It's our version of Woodstock. Every store manager and perishable department manager is invited, and about 120 vendors set up and display their wares."[75]

Wild Oats had a significant number of stock-outs in 1999, for which it considered United Natural Foods Inc. responsible.[76] Sales of $721 million and operating profits of $34.9 million were double 1998 levels. However, the balance sheet was burdened with $80 million of debt, and cash was tight.

CONSOLIDATION 2000–2006

In 2000, the strategic focus shifted to increasing sales per store and 17 underperforming stores were closed. Wild Oats began repositioning itself to attract more mainstream shoppers, increasing the size of its stores and the number of gourmet items, prepared foods, housewares and gift items it offered. One analyst asked, "You seem to be adding a lot more Gucci to the mix. Does this mean that Whole Foods has had it right all along?" "Wild Oats has learned from its competitors and witnessed a convergence of the natural foods and conventional foods markets," said Jim Lee, chief operation officer.[77] In 2000, the company took a charge of $42 million for restructuring, and also wrote off a $2.1 million investment in an e-commerce nutritional company.[78] Operating profits for the year were down to $29.4 million on sales of $838 million, and, because of restructuring charges, the company reported a net loss after taxes of $15.0 million. On December 30, 2001, the company found itself in breach of its financial covenants.[79]

In March 2001, Perry Odak, former chief executive officer of Ben & Jerry's Homemade Inc. was hired as CEO and president. He was faced with a wide variety of stores, 65 percent of which had been acquired, ranging in size between 2,700 square feet and 45,000 square feet; multiple retail brands; weak information technology (IT) infrastructure with a proliferation of systems; a huge number of SKUs, many slow moving; a large number of vendors; pricing inconsistencies across stores; a lack of operational controls; and high out-of-stocks.[80] In the last quarter of 2001, Odak took another $50.4 million restructuring charge.[81] In the next 18 months he replaced the majority of the company's management team; started an SKU rationalization program; switched distributors; centralized buying, merchandising and pricing; introduced operational controls; began installing a data warehouse; and initiated a store relocation program.[82]

The first major change after Odak took over was the Fresh Look program. This involved increased marketing,[83] weekly eight-page flyers instead of monthly, price cuts of between 5 and 25 percent on 2,500 items,[84] and increased staffing to improve service and attract a broader range of customers. The program was rolled out to 44 stores by November 2001. The company reported a larger than expected loss in quarter 2 of 2001, and the chief financial officer resigned, to be replaced by Ed Dunlap, who had experience at Gap Inc. Steve Kaczynski was appointed senior vice president of merchandising, coming from Giant Foods Stores, a large traditional grocer.[85] A banner consolidation program was initiated,[86] and a data warehouse program started. In November 2001, Gilliland and Cook resigned from the board. Wild Oats reported an operating loss before exceptional items of $4.5 million for 2001 on sales of $893 million.

In the first quarter of 2002, Wild Oats returned to profitability. In April 2002, the company unveiled a new supermarket format in a store opened in

California. It included expanded fresh produce and deli areas, lower shelving, reading areas, and new décor.[87] It used a new computerized planogram system for merchandising that was to be applied in all stores. Andrew Wolf, an analyst with BB&T Capital Markets, questioned the wisdom of this mass-market approach, citing Whole Foods' success. He remarked, "Whole Foods is a different economic model from a mass merchant, and is much more assortment driven."[88] Wild Oats initiated an SKU rationalization program to eliminate slow-moving items and replaced them with higher-margin value-added products such as marinated and stuffed meats.[89] The company also commenced IT programs for EDI, automated reordering of merchandise,[90] direct-store delivery receiving, and labor scheduling.[91] In September 2002, the company raised $48.3 million in equity.[92] Operating profits were $18.8 million in 2002 on sales of $919 million. Wild Oats' primary competitor in 2002 was Whole Foods, with which it competed in 70 percent of markets served. Wild Oats claimed that it had higher product standards and more competitive prices than Whole Foods.[93]

On June 14, 2002, Wild Oats announced that it was to switch its primary distribution agreement from United Natural Foods Inc. (UNFI) to Tree of Life Inc. (TOL), effective September 2002. TOL was expected to supply 30 percent of Wild Oats' merchandise.[94] The switch proved problematic, and the company suffered logistics problems and out-of-stocks in 2003. Remodeling stores and the SKU reduction program also proved disruptive, and operating profits fell in 2003 to $9.2 million from $18.8 million the year before. In 2002, Wild Oats and Whole Foods overlapped in 75 percent of markets served.[95]

In January 2004, Wild Oats switched the distribution agreement back to UNFI. A month later it opened its first distribution center, in Riverside, California, to supply fresh produce, private-label groceries, and some other items to the majority of stores west of the Mississippi.[96] In June 2004, the company raised $115 million in convertible bonds, $25 million of which was used to repurchase company stock.[97] In August, the company announced that it was to open health food sections in five Stop & Shop supermarkets.[98] The company made an operating loss of $6.3 million in 2004, which it attributed to disruptions in its logistics pipeline and competitive pressures.[99] Sales passed the billion-dollar mark, at $1.05 billion. Wild Oats also changed its accounting for deferred taxes in 2004, reporting a net loss after taxes of $40.0 million for the year.

On March 31, 2005, the company organized a revolving credit facility of $100 million secured on some of its assets with Bank of America.[100] In June 2005, Wild Oats received a disappointing CCC+ rating from Standard & Poor's on its convertible bonds.[101] However, in the second quarter the company returned to profitability. The company began a merchandising program to broaden the appeal of its product line to attract more mainstream shoppers. It was to offer lower-priced natural products and more gourmet lines, and ethnic offerings.[102] Some analysts questioned this approach, recalling that Wild Oats had tried this before and been unsuccessful. Many of the logistics challenges seemed to have been solved in 2005, and UNFI accounted for 37 percent of the company's purchases.[103] The company reported an operating income of $14.8 million for the year on sales of $1.12 billion.

THE WAY AHEAD: 2006–?

In April, 2006, Wild Oats opened its newest 37,000-square-foot prototype store, and planned to open a 40,000-square-foot store in 2007.[104] The cost to open a new leased store ranged from $2 to $6 million in 2006,[105] while a major refurbishment cost $1 million. Early in August 2006, Wild Oats reported comparable store sales annual growth of 1.3 percent, compared to 5.4 percent a year earlier. By comparison, Whole Foods reported comparable sales up by 10 percent.[106] Wild Oats attributed the slowdown to competition from conventional supermarkets. Perry Odak, chief executive officer since 2001, had long argued that the entry of conventional supermarkets into the organic category was good for specialists, but in 2006, the benefits were far from clear.[107] During the summer, there was a shortage of organic items, such as apples and milk, which was attributed to heavy buying by Wal-Mart and Safeway. Washington State, which produced two-thirds of U.S. certified organic apples, reported growth in demand of 53 percent between the 2003–2004 and 2004–2005 seasons,[108] and prices on some lines of organic produce were reported to be double that of conventionally produced products.

To add to Odak's challenges, in August 2006, Wild Oats was under threat from billionaire grocery store investor Ronald Burkel, ranked 335th in

Forbes' ranking of the world's richest people, who was buying Wild Oats stock. Wild Oats had poison pill provisions in place, preventing anyone from acquiring more than 15 percent of its stock, but Burkel had accidentally exceeded this and reached 17.3 percent. The company had agreed with him that he would limit his purchases to 20 percent.[109] At the time, Burkel was also rumored to be buying a significant stake in Supervalu, another large supermarket chain in the United States.[110]

With cash tight, Odak had limited space for maneuver. He planned to add 10 more stores in 2006, and refurbish six at a cost of $1 million each.[111] He was also driving up the number of private-label Wild Oats–branded items sold through the chain and looking to expand the company's footprint by selling these lines through other retail channels. The company was targeting 1,700 private-label SKUs by calendar year-end 2006,[112] comparable in number to Whole Foods,[113] and up from about 1,000 SKUs in 2000. Wild Oats lines were already selling through Peapod.com, Amazon.com, and in some Stop & Shop supermarkets in the Northeast in August 2006, and Odak was negotiating with more channels to expand this initiative.[114] Whether this would be enough to restore the retailer to its former glory was not clear.

Endnotes

[1]Josee Rose, "Demand for Organic Food Creates Supply Shortages," *Dow Jones News Service,* August 23, 2006.

[2]David Milsead, "Investor Ups Wild Oats Stake," *Rocky Mountain News,* August 15, 2006.

[3]Anonymous, "Retail Entrepreneurs of the Year: Elizabeth Cook; Michael C. Gilliland," *Chain Store Age,* December 1998, p. 66.

[4]Tom Ehrenfeld, "The (Handbook) Handbook," *Inc.,* November 1993, p. 57.

[5]Tom Ehrenfeld, "The (Handbook) Handbook," *Inc.,* November 1993, p. 57.

[6]Tom Ehrenfeld, "The (Handbook) Handbook," *Inc.,* November 1993, p. 57.

[7]Anonymous, "Retail Entrepreneurs of the Year: Elizabeth Cook; Michael C. Gilliland," *Chain Store Age,* December 1998, p. 66.

[8]Anonymous, "Retail Entrepreneurs of the Year: Elizabeth Cook; Michael C. Gilliland," *Chain Store Age,* December 1998, p. 66; and Bill Simpson and Matt Nesland, "1993 Entrepreneur of the Year Awards: Libby Cook and Mike Gilliland," *Denver Business Journal,* June 18, 1993, p. 4B.

[9]Wild Oats Stores Inc., 1996 10-K, p. 20.

[10]Ann Harrison, "'Wellness' Benefits Buy Bikes, Massages," *Boulder County Business Report,* January 1993, p. 13.

[11]"The Motivational Employee-Satisfaction Questionnaire," *Inc.,* February 1994, www.inc.com/magazine/archives (accessed November 2004).

[12]Tom Ehrenfeld, "The (Handbook) Handbook," *Inc.,* November 1993, p. 57.

[13]Bill Simpson and Matt Nesland, "1993 Entrepreneur of the Year Awards: Libby Cook and Mike Gilliland," *Denver Business Journal,* June 18, 1993, p. 4B.

[14]Wild Oats Stores Inc., 1996 10-K, p. 20.

[15]Michelle Conklin, "Growing His Oats," *Rocky Mountain News,* July 7, 1996.

[16]Jonathan H. Ziegler, Salomon Smith Barney, "Wild Oats," May 26, 1998, p. 11.

[17]Michelle Conklin, "Growing His Oats," *Rocky Mountain News,* July 7, 1996.

[18]Wild Oats Markets Inc., Prospectus, October 22, 1996, p. 98.

[19]Wild Oats Markets Inc., Prospectus, October 22, 1996.

[20]Adrienne Brown, "Real Deals," *Colorado Business Magazine,* March 1997, p. 20.

[21]Wild Oats Markets Inc., Prospectus, October 22, 1996, p. 98.

[22]David Orgel, "Whole Foods Market to Acquire Fresh Fields," *Supermarket News,* June 24, 1996.

[23]Adrienne Brown, "Real Deals," *Colorado Business Magazine,* March 1997, p. 20.

[24]Adrienne Brown, "Real Deals," *Colorado Business Magazine,* March 1997, p. 20.

[25]R. Michelle Breyer, "Whole Foods Details Plans for Growth, More Funds," *Supermarket News,* March 18, 1996.

[26]Dan Whipple, "Wheat-Germ Warfare," *Boulder County Business Report,* June 1, 1997, p. 3.

[27]Jay Palmer, "Robust Prospects: Inside the Big-Time Health-Food Supermarket Chains," *Barron's,* January 26, 1998.

[28]Mark Hanratty and Adam Cherry, Paine Webber, "Wild Oats: Abundant and Healthy Growth," July 31, 1997, p. 4.

[29]Diane H. Daggatt and Bobbi K. Hoff, CFA, Dain Bosworth, "Wild Oats Markets, Inc.," October 16, 1997, p. 7.

[30]Gary M. Giblen and Lisa Cartwright, Smith Barney, "Wild Oats Community Market," August 19, 1997, pp. 6–7.

[31]Mary Ellen Podmolik, "Wild Oats Sows Seed of Whole Foods Fight," *Chicago Sun-Times,* April 25, 1997.

[32]Mark Hanratty and Adam Cherry, Paine Webber, "Wild Oats: Abundant and Healthy Growth," July 31, 1997, p. 10.

[33]Mark Hanratty and Adam Cherry, Paine Webber, "Wild Oats: Abundant and Healthy Growth," July 31, 1997, pp. 9–10.

[34]Carole Buyers, Hanifen Imhoff Inc., "Wild Oats Markets, Inc.," December 12, 1997, p. 10.

[35]Jonathan H. Ziegler, Salomon Smith Barney, "Wild Oats," May 26, 1998, p. 11.

[36]Mark Hanratty and Adam Cherry, Paine Webber, "Wild Oats: Abundant and Healthy Growth," July 31, 1997, p. 12.

[37]Gary M. Giblen and Lisa Cartwright, Smith Barney, "Wild Oats Community Market," August 19, 1997, p. 8.

[38]Jonathan H. Ziegler, Salomon Smith Barney, "Wild Oats," May 26, 1998, p. 4.

[39]Wild Oats Markets Inc., 1997 10-K pp. 9, 10.

[40]Molly Clowes, "Wild Oats Growing Via Acquisitions, New Stores," *Frozen Food Age,* May 1997, p. 64.

[41]Molly Clowes, "Wild Oats Growing Via Acquisitions, New Stores," *Frozen Food Age,* May 1997, p. 64.

[42]Allan F. Hickok and Yudi Bahl, Piper Jaffray, "Wild Oats Markets, Inc.," December 1998, p. 8.

[43]David A. Geraty, Dain Rauscher Wessels, "Wild Oats Markets, Inc." July 15, 1999, p. 7.

[44]Wild Oats Markets Inc., 1997 10-K, p. 14.

[45]Mark Hanratty and Adam Cherry, Paine Webber, "Wild Oats: Abundant and Healthy Growth," July 31, 1997, p. 6.

[46]Mark Hanratty and Adam Cherry, Paine Webber, "Wild Oats: Abundant and Healthy Growth," July 31, 1997, p. 9; and Diane H. Daggatt and Bobbi K. Hoff, CFA, Dain Bosworth, "Wild Oats Markets, Inc.," October 16, 1997, p. 10.

[47]Anonymous, "'Healthy' Supermarket Demos: A Snapshot," *Frozen Food Age,* December 1995, p. SS15.

[48]Jonathan H. Ziegler, Salomon Smith Barney, "Wild Oats," May 26, 1998, p. 9.

[49]Diane H. Daggatt and Bobbi K. Hoff, CFA, Dain Bosworth, "Wild Oats Markets, Inc.," October 16, 1997, p. 9.

[50]Diane H. Daggatt and Bobbi K. Hoff, CFA, Dain Bosworth, "Wild Oats Markets, Inc.," October 16, 1997, p. 9.

[51]Gary M. Giblen and Lisa Cartwright, Smith Barney, "Wild Oats Community Market," August 19, 1997, p. 10.

[52]Jonathan H. Ziegler, Salomon Smith Barney, "Wild Oats," May 26, 1998, p. 15.

[53]Gary M. Giblen and Lisa Cartwright, Smith Barney, "Wild Oats Community Market," August 19, 1997, p. 10.

[54]Gary M. Giblen and Lisa Cartwright, Smith Barney, "Wild Oats Community Market," August 19, 1997, p. 12.

[55]Gary M. Giblen and Lisa Cartwright, Smith Barney, "Wild Oats Community Market," August 19, 1997, p. 10.

[56]Susan Greco, "Volunteering: The New Employee Perk," *Inc.*, September 1997, p. 116; and Anonymous, "Retail Entrepreneurs of the Year: Elizabeth Cook; Michael C. Gilliland," *Chain Store Age,* December 1998, p. 66.

[57]Allan F. Hickok and Yudi Bahl, Piper Jaffray, "Wild Oats Markets, Inc.," December 1998, p. 8.

[58]Diane H. Daggatt and Bobbi K. Hoff, CFA, Dain Bosworth, "Wild Oats Markets, Inc.," October 16, 1997, p. 3.

[59]Carole Buyers, Hanifen Imhoff Inc., "Wild Oats Markets, Inc.," December 12, 1997, p. 11.

[60]Bonnie Tonneson, Hambrecht and Quist, "Wild Oats Markets, Inc.," April 21, 1999, p. 7.

[61]Diane Freeman, "Whole Foods Goes Head-to-Head with Competitor Wild Oats Market," *Boulder County Business Report*, June 1, 1998, p. 3A.

[62]Jonathan H. Ziegler, Salomon Smith Barney, "Wild Oats," May 26, 1998, p. 13; and Deutsche Bank, "Wild Oats Markets, Inc.," May 25, 2000, p. 10.

[63]Anonymous, "Retail Entrepreneurs of the Year: Elizabeth Cook; Michael C. Gilliland," *Chain Store Age,* December 1998, p. 66.

[64]Anonymous, "Retail Entrepreneurs of the Year: Elizabeth Cook; Michael C. Gilliland," *Chain Store Age,* December 1998, p. 66.

[65]Bonnie Tonneson, Hambrecht and Quist, "Wild Oats Markets, Inc.," April 21, 1999, p. 7.

[66]Dan Harrison, "Wild Oats Sets '99 Frozen Push," *Frozen Food Age*, January 1999, p. 1.

[67]Elaine Lipson, "Wild Card Loses in Customer Satisfaction Game," May 1999, www.newhope.com/nfm-online/nfm_backs/May_99/wildcard.cfm (accessed November 2004).

[68]Elaine Lipson, "Wild Card Loses in Customer Satisfaction Game," May 1999, www.newhope.com/nfm-online/nfm_backs/May_99/wildcard.cfm (accessed November 2004).

[69]Jonathan H. Ziegler, Salomon Smith Barney, "Wild Oats," May 26, 1998, p. 11.

[70]Wild Oats Community Market; Alfalfa's Market; Bean, Grains & Things; Ideal Market; Oasis Fine Foods; Sunshine Grocery; Uptown Whole Foods; People's Market; Nature's Fresh Northwest; Nature's Northwest; Henry's Marketplace; and Capers Whole Foods.

[71]Anonymous, "Retail Entrepreneurs of the Year: Elizabeth Cook; Michael C. Gilliland," *Chain Store Age,* December 1998, p. 66.

[72]Tara Croft, "Bad Seed," *The Deal.com*, October 13, 2003, p. 1.

[73]David A. Geraty, Dain Rauscher Wessels, "Wild Oats Markets, Inc.," July 15, 1999, p. 14.

[74]Anonymous, "Grocery Chain Agrees to Halt Some Fish Sales," *Journal of Commerce*, August 12, 1999, p. 5.

[75]Anonymous, "Turtle Time at Wild Oats," *ColoradoBiz*, March 1999, p. 21.

[76]Deutsche Bank, "Wild Oats Markets, Inc.," May 25, 2000, p. 10.

[77]Robert Goldfield, "New Owner to Adopt Some of Nature's Ways," *Business Journal*, May 19, 2000, p. 3.

[78]Wild Oats Stores Inc., 2000 10-K, p. 18.

[79]Wild Oats Stores Inc., 2000 10-K, p. 6.

[80]Wild Oats Markets Inc., 2002 10-K, pp. 20, 21.

[81]Wild Oats Markets Inc., 2001 10-K, p. 29.

[82]Wild Oats Markets Inc., 2002 10-K, pp. 20, 21.

[83]Wild Oats Markets Inc., 2002 10-K, p. 13.

[84]"Wild Oats Growing Fresh Look Promotional Campaign," *Supermarket News,* November 5, 2001.

[85]Kelly Pate, "Wild Oats Envisions Return to Profitability," *Denver Post*, March 1, 2002.

[86]Wild Oats Stores Inc., 2001 10-K, p. 3.

[87]Wild Oats Markets Inc., 2003 10-K, p. 6.

[88]Christina Veiders, "Wild Oats' IT Projects Designed to Reignite Business," *Supermarket News*, March 11, 2002.

[89]Wild Oats Markets Inc., 2002 10-K, pp. 9, 10.

[90]Wild Oats Markets Inc., 2002 10-K, p. 14.

[91]Christina Veiders, "Wild Oats' IT Projects Designed to Reignite Business," *Supermarket News*, March 11, 2002.

[92]Wild Oats Markets Inc., 2002 10-K, p. 20.

[93]Wild Oats Markets Inc., 2002 10-K, p. 14.

[94]Wild Oats Markets Inc., 2002 10-K, pp. 12, 28.

[95]Wild Oats Markets Inc., 2003 10-K, p. 11.

[96]Wild Oats Markets Inc., 2005 10-K, p. 16.

[97]Wild Oats Markets Inc., 2005 10-K, pp. 51–52.

[98]Steve Adams, "Wild Oats Looks to Pairing to Keep Pace," *Patriot Ledger*, August 25, 2004.

[99]Wild Oats Markets Inc., 2003 10-K, p. 23.

[100]Wild Oats Markets Inc., 2005 10-K, pp. 51–52.

[101]"Wild Oats Gets CCC+ Rating from Standard & Poor's," *Progressive Grocer*, June 6, 2005.

[102]Heather Draper, "Wild Oats' Move to More Conventional Pdts Could Be Risky," *Dow Jones News Service*, February 22, 2005.

[103]Wild Oats Markets Inc., 2005 10-K, p. 44.

[104]Mike Troy, "Wild Oats Plants Seeds of Success with New Format," *Drug Store News*, May 1, 2006.

[105]Wild Oats Markets Inc., 2005 10-K, p. 24.

[106]David Merrefield, "Whole Foods, Competitors Step Up Convergence," *Supermarket News,* August 7, 2006.

[107]Jon Springer, "Sluggish Sales Challenge Wild Oats," *Supermarket News*, August 14, 2006.

[108]Josee Rose, "Demand for Organic Food Creates Supply Shortages," *Dow Jones News Service*, August 23, 2006.

[109]David Milsead, "Investor Ups Wild Oats Stake," *Rocky Mountain News*, August 15, 2006.

[110]Sandra Guy, "Burkle Looking at Supervalu Stock," *Chicago Sun-Times*, August 11, 2006.

[111]Wild Oats Markets Inc., 2005 10-K, p. 17.

[112]"Q2 2006 Wild Oats Markets Earnings Conference Call," *Voxant Fair Disclosure Wire*, August 3, 2006.

[113]"Event Brief of Q3 2006 Whole Foods Market Earnings Conference Call," *Voxant Fair Disclosure Wire*, July 31, 2006.

[114]Jon Springer, "Wild Oats Expands Private Label," *Supermarket News*, August 7, 2006.

Appendix:

Whole Foods and Wild Oats
Financial Analysis

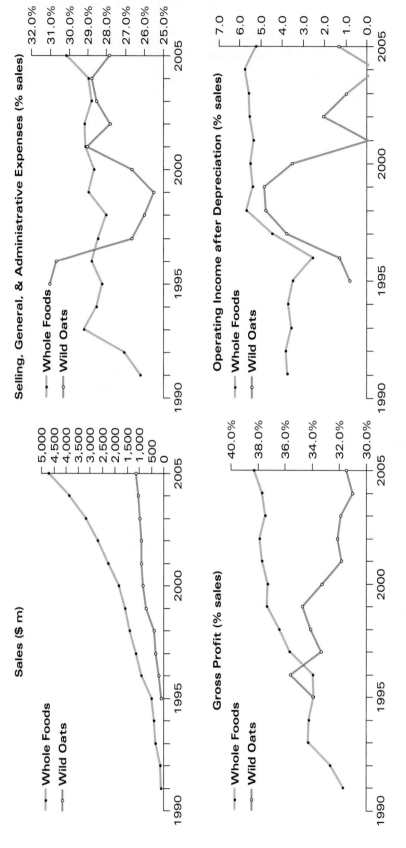

Source: Compiled by casewriter from company reports, analyst reports, the Wharton Research Data Service, and casewriter analysis.

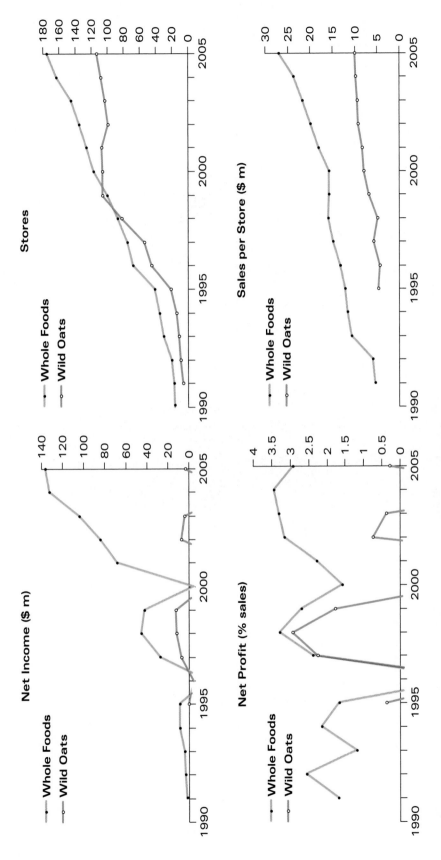

Net Income ($ m)

—— Whole Foods
—— Wild Oats

Net Profit (% sales)

—— Whole Foods
—— Wild Oats

Stores

—— Whole Foods
—— Wild Oats

Sales per Store ($ m)

—— Whole Foods
—— Wild Oats

Source: Compiled by casewriter from company reports, analyst reports, the Wharton Research Data Service, and casewriter analysis.

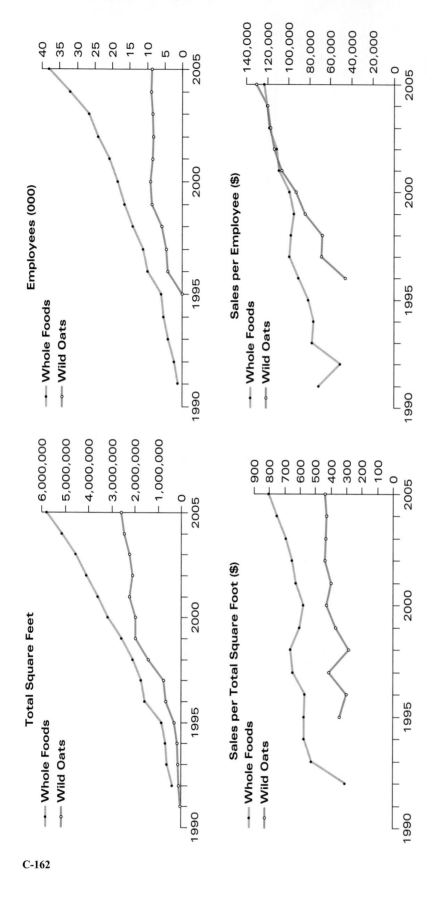

Employees (000)

Whole Foods
Wild Oats

Total Square Feet

Whole Foods
Wild Oats

Sales per Employee ($)

Whole Foods
Wild Oats

Sales per Total Square Foot ($)

Whole Foods
Wild Oats

Source: Compiled by casewriter from company reports, analyst reports, the Wharton Research Data Service, and casewriter analysis.

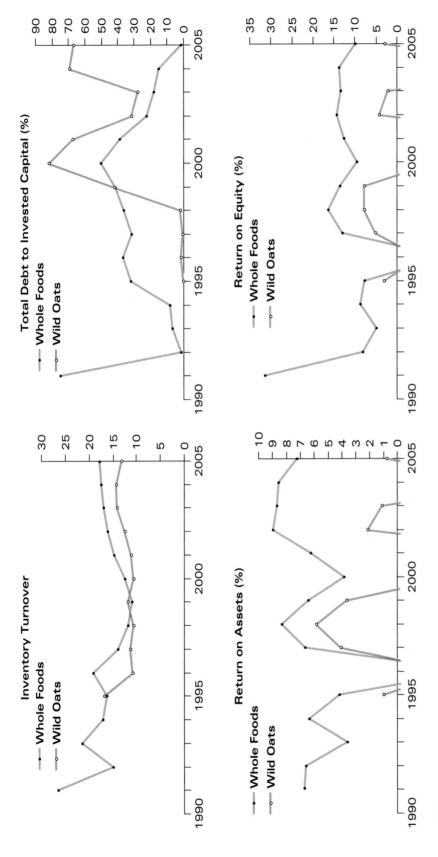

Source: Compiled by casewriter from company reports, analyst reports, the Wharton Research Data Service, and casewriter analysis.

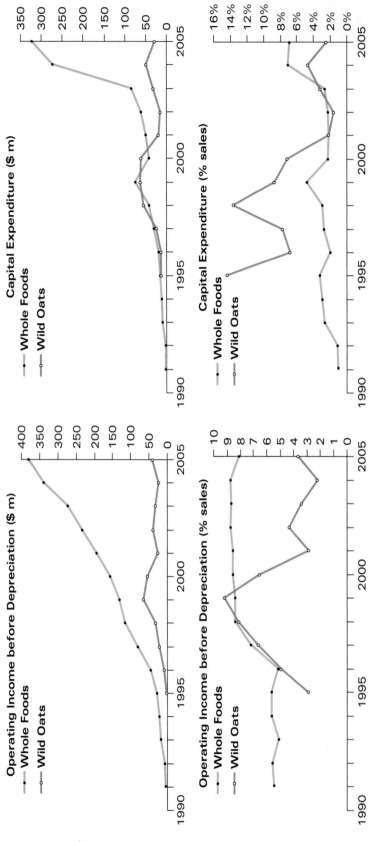

Source: Compiled by casewriter from company reports, analyst reports, the Wharton Research Data Service, and casewriter analysis.

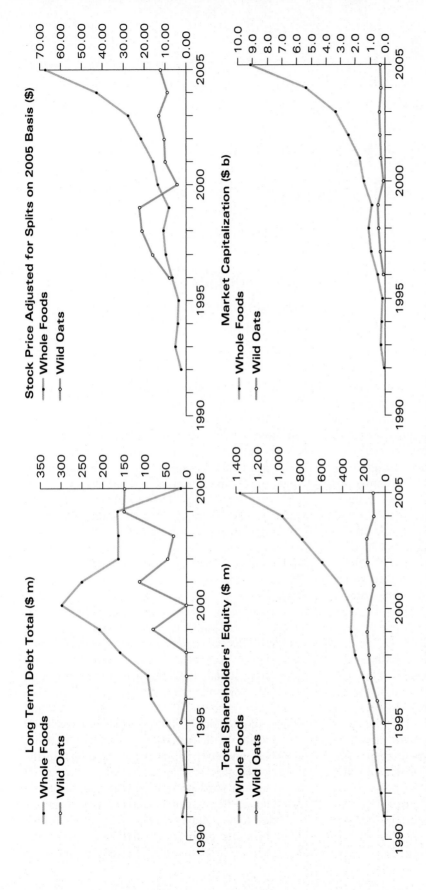

Source: Compiled by casewriter from company reports, analyst reports, the Wharton Research Data Service, and casewriter analysis.

Zune: Microsoft's Entry into the Digital Music Player Market

Louis D. Marino
The University of Alabama

John Hattaway
The University of Alabama

Katy Beth Jackson
The University of Alabama

In the last weeks of July 2006, Chris Stephenson, Microsoft's general manager of marketing for MSN Entertainment, officially confirmed that Microsoft would launch Zune, an umbrella brand for the company's family of hardware and software products that would target a variety of digital entertainment services.[1] Consistent with rumors that had been circulating in the digital music industry for over a year, Microsoft confirmed that the first product launched under the brand would be the Zune itself: a hard-drive-based digital music/video player that had a built-in FM tuner and offered Wi-Fi connectivity. The Zune was coupled with a digital music service, including a media store, in an effort to provide a vertically integrated end-to-end solution, not unlike iPod/iTunes. The ultimate goal of the Zune brand was to make the Zune the center of an entertainment ecosystem built around Microsoft products. Consistent with this goal, Microsoft's original marketing campaign for the Zune included viral marketing and was based on the tagline "Welcome to the Social." This campaign leveraged the Zune's Wi-Fi capabilities, which allowed owners to discover, with appropriate permissions, what was on nearby users' Zunes and then wirelessly beam—or "squirt," as the process was nicknamed—songs or photos to them. The receiving players could then play the acquired song up to three times in three days and view the photos an unlimited number of times.

With the company's announcement and Microsoft's vast resources, a number of music industry analysts believed that the Zune could be the player that would finally break Apple's 70+ percent hold on the digital music player market and become the much-anticipated "iPod killer." They noted the Zune's large, bright screen; innovative use of wireless technology; and relatively intuitive interface. Other analysts, however, were not so sure; they were quick to point out the player's shortcomings and felt that the Zune did not go far enough. Ted Schadler of Forrester Research stated, "I'm very skeptical about its ability to take hold in a market that already has a dominant player. It doesn't feel disruptive enough to gain a foothold."[2] Specific complaints included the fact that the Zune used a proprietary digital encoding system for its content and would not play content based on Microsoft's own PlaysForSure standard, which was used by the company's partners such as Napster and Vongo. Additionally, the player, which was developed in partnership with Toshiba, was criticized as being larger than and not as attractive as the iPod. Finally, critics noted that limitations placed on "squirted" music content were too restrictive and applied to all digital music files, not simply to copyrighted ones.

Prior to the Zune's release on November 14, 2006, the merits of the player and the music service were the center of considerable debate and press coverage. Proponents were convinced that Microsoft had an iPod killer, while critics contended that the Zune would be just another also-ran competitor in a crowded market. The first week it was released, sales were promising: The Zune captured 9 percent of the portable digital media player market, reaching the number two position, but still lagged far behind Apple's 63 percent. However, the Zune's market share fell quickly as SanDisk and other competitors responded with aggressive price cuts. By December, the Zune had fallen to fifth place, with a 2 percent share of the overall market, although Microsoft executives were quick to point out that the Zune owned 10.2 percent of the market for 30-gigabyte devices.

Microsoft's critics were quick to point to the player's weak market share as evidence of the company's inability to prevail in direct competition in the consumer electronics marketplace. Many analysts, however, were reserving their judgment; they noted that Microsoft knew it was not going to win a quick victory against a well-established rival. Scott Erickson, the senior director of product management for the Zune, said, "We entered this market absolutely conscious that this is not a sprint, it's a marathon. We are fully, fully aware it will take some time to have sales numbers that iPod has."[3]

Microsoft's ability and determination to engage in prolonged battles were evidenced by the company's tactics in the smart phone market with Windows Mobile and in the video game market with the Xbox. Some analysts were willing to withhold judgment on Microsoft's ability to catch Apple until as late as 2011, when the company would have had five years to implement its long-term strategy. While the company's critics did not doubt Microsoft's resolve, or its financial resources to wage such a battle, many questioned whether the Zune would eventually be a viable competitor in the Windows-based media player market, let alone the overall market, given Microsoft's largely unproven success in the consumer electronics market.

HISTORY OF THE MP3 PLAYER INDUSTRY

The earliest portable music players were transistor radios introduced by Regency in 1954. While these radios allowed their owners to listen to broadcasts on the go, they generally suffered from relatively weak signal reception, poor sound quality, and the ability to receive AM stations only. It was not until the mid-1970s that consumers had access to portable stereos; the smallest were slightly larger than a shoebox and allowed users not only to listen to both AM and FM radio but also to bring their personal music collections, recorded on cassette tapes, with them wherever they went. However, it was not until 1979 that consumers could purchase the first truly portable personal stereo cassette player, the Sony Walkman, which only played cassettes and did not offer radio reception. By 1984, the cassette tape was beginning to be supplanted by the compact disc (CD), and Sony led the way again with the development of the portable CD player: the CD Walkman or the Discman.

The portable CD player and its more advanced cousin, the minidisc player, were the mechanical precursors to modern digital music players. Mechanical players could hold a relatively limited amount of music and were subject to skipping if bumped or jostled. To overcome these weaknesses, and to capitalize on the growing popularity of digitally encoded music, in 1997 SaeHan information systems developed the MPMan, the world's first nonmechanical digital audio player.[4]

The MPMan player was introduced to the U.S. market in the summer of 1998 as the Eiger Labs MPMan F10. It was a 32-megabyte digital audio player (DAP) and could be expanded, but only by returning it to the manufacturer. The second DAP (also known as an MP3 player) introduced in the U.S. market was the Rio PMP300, which was brought to market by Diamond Multimedia in September 1998. The Rio was so successful in the 1998 Christmas season that it led to significant investment in the MP3 player industry and to a lawsuit by the Recording Industry Association of America for enabling the illegal copying of music. This suit was resolved in Diamond's favor, and digital music players were ruled legal. By the end of 1999, Remote Solutions had introduced the first hard-drive-based player, the Personal Jukebox, which had a 4.8-gigabyte (GB) internal hard drive and could hold about 1,200 songs. Consumers could now choose from flash memory, hard drive, and in-dash digital audio players from a variety of manufacturers.[5]

Growth in the MP3 player market continued fairly slowly until Apple released its legendary iPod in the latter half of 2001. This original hard drive

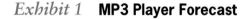

Exhibit 1   **MP3 Player Forecast**

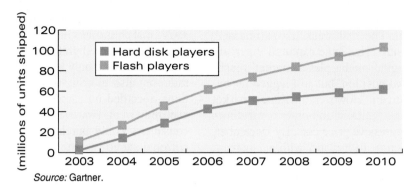

Source: Gartner.

player virtually revolutionized the MP3 market single-handedly, spurring the development of many look-alike models from competing manufacturers. In 2006, over 13.6 million digital music players were sold in U.S. retail outlets, accounting for over $2.5 billion in sales, up 20 percent from the previous year. However, sales of flash-based players were growing much more rapidly than those of hard drive players, which were experiencing a steadily declining growth rate. With only 20 percent of the U.S. population owning an MP3 player in 2006, and much lower penetration rates worldwide, normally conservative analysts were using descriptors such as *boom* and *explosive* to describe growth in MP3 player industry (see Exhibit 1).[6]

TRENDS IN THE MP3 PLAYER INDUSTRY

One important factor that had remained fairly constant in the MP3 industry was the pace of technological innovation. MP3 player manufacturers were continuously working to decrease players' size while increasing their storage capacity and battery life and simplifying their user interface. In developing their offerings, MP3 player manufacturers typically purchased component pieces from various computer hardware vendors and assembled them into the end product. There was not a significant differentiation between the types of batteries used, and many firms developed their user interfaces in-house. However,

the key element that influenced the unit's size and weight was the memory. Firms such as Toshiba, Samsung, and Hatachi that supplied the hard drives and flash memory to the MP3 player manufacturers were constantly trying to cut down the size of their hardware components. Likewise, memory card manufacturers were continuously investigating ways to make their flash cards smaller while maintaining a fairly high level of capacity. While there were numerous manufacturers of hard drives and flash memory, the leading MP3 player manufacturers preferred to partner with the leading memory manufacturers so that they could use the newest and most innovative memory in their players.

Another important trend in the industry was increasing convergence among consumer electronics devices. In response to consumers' increasingly busy lives, and their increasing frustration at having to carry multiple devices, manufacturers of electronic devices, including MP3 players, had recently begun to combine as many features as possible into a single, portable unit. Combinations of cameras, MP3s, PDAs, and even cell phones were becoming abundantly popular. Consumers who were constantly on the go—in the car, exercising, or waiting in line to accomplish some other task—were expressing a desire to carry their music with them so they could essentially "listen while they lived." By 2007, MP3 players had evolved into another piece of technology that many busy consumers could hardly live without; that box the size of a deck of cards could hold their entire music collection and allow them to listen to it anytime, anywhere. The impact of convergence was most apparent in the cell phone industry, with manufacturers offering devices such as the LG Chocolate, the LG enV, the Motorola Rokr, the Nokia N90, the Samsung Blackjack, the Samsung MM-A900, and the Samsung Upstage, all of which advertised the ability to play digital music in addition to the common camera and PDA functions.

In response to consumers' demands for convergence, MP3 player manufacturers were seeking ways to increase their players' multifunctional usage capabilities. Many of the competing models available in 2005 could be used not only as music storage and playback devices but also as calendar/appointment books, data storage devices, and alarm clocks. Consumers could use a hard-drive-based iPod as an external hard drive, a photo album, an alarm clock, a calendar, an appointment book, a game player, and a voice recorder (with the purchase of an accessory). Other possible attributes included a built-in radio tuner and sound manipulating hardware. Some MP3 players could also store videos as well as photographs. As a direct response to the challenge of MP3-enabled cell phones, Apple announced in December 2006 that it would begin selling the iPhone in 2007, and there were rumors of a Microsoft Zune phone as well.

The growth of the Internet, along with customers' access to and comfort with it, was also fueling the MP3 player boom. Not every electronics company had access to retail outlets, but the Internet allowed consumers to shop for just about any MP3 player on the market at the lowest price, no matter where the unit was physically located. After purchasing the player itself online, users could then shop online for brand-new songs to load onto the unit.

Hordes of legitimate subscription and pay-as-you-go online music stores had begun appearing on the Internet. Between January and July 2005, over 184 million tracks were sold online, more than twice the sales in the corresponding period in 2004. Growth of the online digital music market facilitated, and was in turn facilitated by, the increasing popularity of MP3 players. Some MP3 manufacturers operated their own online music stores. This was especially important for Apple, which used a proprietary audio format in programming its MP3 players. Numerous other online music stores were owned by various industry players, including RealNetworks and Wal-Mart.

As MP3 players increasingly became a part of everyday life, they were also becoming fashion statements and status symbols. MP3 players were being seen as the new toy for the young and old alike to sport in their daily lives, and generally, the smaller, lighter, and "prettier" models were the most popular. Apple's product design and color schemes were nearly famous for their elegance and simplicity; the original iPod (about the size of a box of cigarettes) had distinctive white headphones, and the Mini's colorful pastel models (about the size of a credit card) were equally unique and popular. Said one article, "iPod has become so popular it is now a fashion statement."[7] The popularity of those players was partly due to Apple's excellent marketing scheme and partly to the many famous celebrities who were photographed or seen with an Apple player, or happened to mention their iPod during interviews.[8] Additionally, other players were literally being incorporated as fashion. For example, Oakley had introduced a line of sunglasses called Oakley Thump, which had tiny built-in MP3 players and were priced between $395 and $495.[9] Virgin made a player so small that it could be worn as a necklace. The fact that people actually wore MP3 players on the body made their appearance important, and they were extremely popular with younger consumers, a group that often demanded that the products they bought looked just as good as they functioned.

Finally, with the increasing competition in the MP3 player industry, some major players were deciding to exit the market. Specifically, Rio, the company that brought the second MP3 player to the U.S. market, closed its doors in September 2005, and Dell, a giant in the computer industry that had entered the MP3 player market in late 2003 discontinued selling digital music players in late 2006. Rio was owned by Digital Networks North America (a subsidiary of D&M Holdings U.S.). In the fiscal year ended in March 2005, D&M reported an increase in revenues of almost 5 percent over the previous year and an increase in net income of 123 percent over the same year (it reported a large net loss in 2004). However, in July 2005, D&M sold the technology underlying its Rio MP3 players in an effort to recoup some of the losses the Rio subsidiary had generated, but the parent corporation had not yet decided whether to completely terminate the Rio division.[10] The company was still manufacturing its current-generation

Exhibit 2   **PC Magazine Reader Survey of Customer Satisfaction with MP3 Players**

All MP3 Players	Overall Rating out of 10	Quality 1 GB or Less	Quality 1 GB to 10 GB	Quality 10 GB or More	Overall Rating out of 10	Sound Quality out of 10	Ease of Use out of 10	Overall Reliability out of 10	Technical Support out of 10	Percent Needing Repair
Apple (6,292 responses)	8.4	7.8	8.3	8.5	8.4	8.7	8.6	8.3	6.5	8%
Cowon (109)	8.3	–	–	–	8.3	9.0	8.0	8.7	–	6%
Archos (200)	7.8	–	–	7.9	7.8	8.4	7.6	7.9	–	8%
Creative (1814)	7.7	7.4	7.8	8.1	7.7	8.4	7.7	8.1	6.3	5%
iRiver (609)	7.6	7.4	7.7	7.9	7.6	8.4	7.2	8.0	–	4%
mobiBLU (55)	7.5	–	–	–	7.5	8.4	7.1	7.8	–	4%
Dell (400)	7.4	6.8	7.3	7.7	7.4	8.0	7.6	7.6	–	9%
SanDisk (897)	7.4	7.2	8.0		7.4	7.9	7.4	7.8	–	4%
Samsung (307)	7.3	7.5	7.1	–	7.3	8.2	7.4	7.8	–	5%
Sony (682)	7.3	7.0	7.9	8.2	7.3	7.9	7.5	7.7	–	2%
Toshiba (61)	7.0	–	–	–	7.0	7.9	7.2	7.4	–	7%
Rio (662)	6.9	6.5	7.7	8.0	6.9	7.6	7.3	7.3	–	5%
Panasonic (153)	6.8	6.7	–	–	6.8	7.4	7.1	7.3	–	1%
Phillips (163)	6.8	6.3	–	–	6.8	7.7	7.4	7.3	–	4%
MPIO (55)	6.7	–	–	–	6.7	7.7	6.4	7.1	–	4%
RCA (328)	6.6	6.5	–	–	6.6	7.5	7.0	7.2	–	3%
Average	**7.3**	**7.0**	**7.7**	**8.1**	**7.3**	**8.1**	**7.4**	**7.7**	**6.4**	**5%**

Source: *PC Magazine* customer survey, September 20, 2006, www.pcmag.com.

players and shipping them out while making final decisions about Rio's future in the MP3 industry. Early in September 2005, D&M decided to discontinue all Rio products by the end of the month. The company's reason for exiting the MP3 industry was that management felt any investment would be eroded by the high level of competition facing the market.[11]

COMPETITION IN THE MP3 PLAYER INDUSTRY

Although well over 100 companies manufactured MP3 players by the end of 2006, only six could legitimately claim real importance in this market:

Apple, Creative, iRiver, Microsoft, SanDisk, and Sony. Apple clearly dominated, with estimates of the company's market share ranging from 65 to 80 percent, and the other manufacturers having less than 6 percent of the market, although some estimates placed Microsoft's share at as much as 10 percent of the 30-gigabyte hard drive player market. However, for the critical five-week holiday shopping season from November 19 to December 23, 2006, the NPD Group, a leading market research firm, estimated that Apple controlled 57.3 percent of all players sold (flash players, micro drive players, and hard drive players), followed by SanDisk with 19.2 percent (down from 22.1 percent the previous year), Creative with 3.4 percent, and Zune with 2.8 percent.

The leading companies in the industry realized that their continued success depended in large part on how well they could satisfy their current customers as well as on their ability to attract new ones. Research showed that most buyers shopped for players based on song capacity (some users required significantly more capacity than the average user), availability of and compatibility with online music stores, unit battery life, physical size and weight specifications, and ease of use. While price was factor in some consumer purchases, Apple's success had proved that many consumers were willing to pay a premium for some perceived benefit, whether higher quality, more technological sophistication, or greater ease of use. However, industry experts predicted that as competition and rivalry became tougher, price would likely play a more central role in the buyer's decision. Exhibit 2 provides information on the MP3 players offered by the major players in the industry and consumer satisfaction with the players.

Apple

For much of the company's history, Apple had been very good at being the first company to introduce a concept or a new product but then struggling to maintain control of its market share in that product line. Although Apple didn't introduce the first portable MP3 player, it did introduce the first one that gained widespread attention and widespread popularity—the iPod. Upon the iPod's launch in October 2001, many critics did not give the device much of a chance for success, as its introduction came about one month after 9/11 and the product carried a fairly hefty price tag of $399. However, the success of the iPod had reached phenomenal proportions, such that "it is now a fashion statement, and any other digital music player is considered 'Brand X' for many consumers."[12] What Sony did for portable cassette devices with the Walkman in the 1980s, Apple was doing for the digital music industry with the iPod line.

In fiscal year 2005 (ended in September 2006), Apple reported net income of 1.99 billion (up over 49 percent over the previous year) on net sales of $19.3 billion (up over 38 percent from the previous year). During this period, sales of iPods rose by 248 percent to $7.68 billion (39.9 percent of total net

sales) and unit sales rose by 409 percent to $22.5 million. Apple's strategy with regard to its iPods centered largely on quick product innovation and marketing. By January 2007, Apple's iPod digital music player product portfolio included the following:

- The iPod Shuffle, a screenless flash memory player about the size of a matchbook, was offered in a 1GB model that came in five colors and could hold 240 songs ($79).

iPod Shuffle

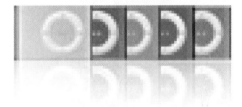

Source: www.apple.com.

- The iPod Nano, a flash-based player about the size of a credit card, but thicker, had a color screen and was offered in a 2GB model that held 500 songs ($149), a 4GB model that was offered in five colors and held 1,000 songs ($199), and an 8GB model that held 2,000 songs ($249). The Nano also had games, a calendar with an appointment scheduler, a contact manager, a world clock, a stopwatch, and password protection. It allowed the user to create custom playlists without a computer, could hold up to 25,000 photos, and boasted a battery life of up to 24 hours.

iPod Nano

Source: www.apple.com.

- The iPod was a hard drive player offered in a 30GB model—which could hold 7,500 songs, 25,000 photos, or 75 hours of video ($249)—and an 80GB model—which held 20,000 songs, over 25,000 photos, or over 150 hours of video. Like the Nano, the iPod had a color screen games, a calendar with an appointment scheduler, a contact manager, and a world clock. However, the iPod also allowed users to watch movies, television shows, and videos.

iPod

Source: www.apple.com.

Aside from the iPod's ease of use, one of the primary factors that contributed to the popularity of the iPod was Apple's iPod/iTunes combination. In fact, some analysts believed that, despite the acclaim that had been heaped on the iPod, without iTunes, the iPod would not have achieved its dominant position. The iTunes site allowed iPod users to manage the content on their iPods, subscribe to free podcasts, and purchase and download music, episodes of television shows, movies, and games. By April 2007, iTunes had reported sales of more than 2.5 billion songs and over 50 million TV shows.

Apple used unique and creative advertising through television and magazine ads as well as several brand alliances—with BMW, HP, Motorola, and U2—in an effort to make the iPod and iTunes *the* choice for buyers in this industry. After the company's success skyrocketed, the MP3 player industry exploded and competition became widespread and intense. Both computer industry regulars and newcomers solely devoted to the MP3 player moved into the industry, quickly making competition intense. As the technology continued to evolve, even traditional cellular phone manufacturers had become potential rivals in this fast-paced market.

Some analysts felt that Apple was merely "making a careful gamble" with regard to the company's tentative entry into the MP3 player/cell phone market by teaming with Motorola to offer a phone that could hold 100 songs.[13] That judgment was based on the fact that other cell phone companies like Nokia and Samsung had introduced phones that could hold up to 3,000 songs and were meant to replace the user's regular MP3 player. The last thing Apple wanted was Motorola users, or anyone else for that matter, to use their cell phones as a replacement for the iPod. However, the possibilities offered by the huge and booming cell phone market were too big to be ignored by any MP3 company. While Apple's partnership with Motorola in the cell phone arena did not produce the results the company hoped, Apple recognized the increasing threat and responded in December 2006 by announcing the launch of the iPhone. The company intended to introduce the phone in the second quarter of 2007 and many iPod fans and cell phone users were eagerly awaiting the device, despite its steep (almost $500) price tag.

Creative Labs

Creative Labs first became known for its Sound Blaster sound cards, which set the standard in PC audio in 1989. Creative had built on this success to become an industry leader in PC audio technology and had earned a strong brand name and a large, loyal user base in this arena. Creative leveraged this brand recognition to originally offer a broad and diverse product line of MP3 players. The company quickly gained recognition in this market, winning the Consumer Electronics Show's prestigious Best of CES Award three years in a row with its Zen Portable Media Center in 2004, the Zen Microphoto in 2005 and the Zen Vision:M in 2006. The Zen Vision:M (30GB $249; 60GB $299), which also was named the best overall product at CES in 2006, was about the same size as an iPod 30GB, although twice as thick, and would play back music, video, and photos. It also included a personal organizer that would sync with Microsoft Outlook to transfer the user's calendar, contacts, and task list. This player was viewed as the first real competition to the iPod, because it would hold about as much content as the iPod but had a superior screen, a battery that lasted twice as long as an iPod's, an FM tuner, and a voice recorder.

Creative's product line in 2007 also included the following:

- Based on the Zen Vision:M multimedia player, the Zen Vision W ($299 30GB, $399 60GB) was a wide-screen multimedia player that used

Windows Media Center Edition software; it won the Best of Digital Life Award in 2005 and a 2006 red dot design award. The Zen Vision W allowed users to listen to, record, and play back WMAs and MP3s (up to 15,000 songs), movies, and television shows (up to 240 hours of video); to view photos (over 20,000); and to listen to and record FM radio.

Zen Vision W

Source: www.creative.com.

- The Zen 8GB Zen Microphoto ($199) featured a 15-hour rechargeable battery; offered a color screen; came in 10 different colors; held up to 4,000 songs; and included an FM radio and recorder, a personal organizer that synced with Microsoft Outlook, and a sleep timer.

Zen Microphoto

Source: www.creative.com.

- The Zen V Plus was a tiny flash-based player in 1GB (84.99), 2GB ($99.99), 4GB ($149.99), and 8GB ($199.99) sizes that would fit in the coin pocket of the user's jeans. This player offered line-in encoding, a built-in microphone to allow users to record music directly from their chosen source, an FM radio, a personal organizer (including a calendar, an alarm clock, and a task manager that synced with Microsoft Outlook), and a screen that could be rotated to suit the user's orientation. The player also featured a scratch-resistant color screen and could

hold short video clips, hundreds of photos, and up to 4,000 songs in the 8GB version.

Zen V plus

Source: www.creative.com.

- MuVo flash players included a 256MB ($19.99) version that featured a monochrome screen, an FM radio, and voice recording. The MuVo players were designed to meet the needs of niche markets and offered a variety of features. The MuVo S200, for example, allowed users to view song lyrics on its LCD, the MuVo TX FM offered voice recording, and the MuVo Slim had a rechargeable battery.

Creative MuVo 200

Source: www.creative.com.

In Creative's fiscal year ending June 30, 2006, the company reported revenues of $1.1 billion (down from $1.2 billion in 2005) and a net loss of $118 million (down from net income of $588 million in 2005). Creative's chairman and CEO, Sim Wong Hoo, attributed this poor performance to unfavorable market conditions that included aggressive price practices, intense competition, and price instability in key supplies such as flash memory. One of the bright points for 2006, Hoo noted, was the U.S. patent Creative had received for the user interface it employed in its portable media players. As a result of this patent, Creative won a $100 million settlement from Apple for using its technology in its iPods. Apple agreed to license the patent from Creative. Despite the patent, Hoo stated that the company planned to focus on higher-margin models only, reduce expenses, and leverage the patent to develop high-margin accessories such as docking stations, portable speaker systems, and earphones and headphones for iPods and other digital music players.

iRiver

iRiver Inc. was owned by the South Korea–based Reigncom Ltd. The company entered the digital music player market relatively early and previously offered a wide variety of music players, including the world's thinnest MP3-compatible portable CD player. While iRiver products were sold worldwide, the brand was especially strong in Korea, controlling over 50 percent of the Korean MP3 player market at one time. Further, in a 2005 survey of Asian consumers designed to gauge the popularity of various MP3 players, iRiver won in Korea, with over 46 percent of people preferring the brand above all others.[14]

In discussing the company's strategy in 2006, iRiver America CEO Jonathan Sasse stated, "We're going to continue to innovate and put out the best products on the market. We feel very confident in our position in this space."[15] When asked about Apple, Sasse stated, "Designing a better product than the iPod is not the real trick. Getting the mindshare of the consumer and getting people aware that there are other places to get good content than iTunes is really our biggest challenge. It won't take a great device to overthrow [Apple]."[16] Sasse noted that, to overcome Apple's dominance in the market, iRiver planned to invest significant resources to form a post-transaction bond with the consumer by offering product updates and fresh content on the company's Web site.

Despite iRiver's bravado—in 2005, for example, the company featured an ad with a person listening to music on an iRiver player while eating an Apple—the company had experienced a series of strategic missteps that diminished its position in the U.S. marketplace. The company significantly underestimated the impact that the Apple Shuffle would have on flash memory prices and seriously underbudgeted, resulting in lower-than-expected profitability. Further, the company seemed to be having a difficulty developing new products and its market share fell significantly. However, by early 2007, the company appeared to be regaining some lost momentum after it narrowed its product line and refocused on product innovation. Leading the company's lineup was the popular and critically acclaimed iRiver Clix, which won multiple awards such as an Editor's Choice Award and a World Class Award from *PC World*; it was featured as one of *PC World*'s Top 100 Products of the Year for 2006. The Clix was also the top-rated flash player on the *Consumer Reports* Web site as of April 1, 2007, beating out players from Apple, SanDisk, and other manufacturers.

In 2007, iRiver offered only two products in the U.S. market:

*   The iRiver Clix was a flash-based player available in 2GB ($169.99) and 4GB ($199.99) sizes. The Clix played music and video files, allowed photo viewing, and offered downloadable games. The player featured a 25-hour battery life, a 2.2-inch color display with customizable digital wallpaper, an integrated voice recorder, and an alarm clock.
*   The iRiver T-10 was a flash-based, ultra-portable digital music player that, depending on its size, held up to 64 hours of music. The player was offered in 2GB ($149.99), 1GB ($119.99), and 512MB ($99.99) sizes and featured an FM tuner and recorder, a color display, and up to 45 hours of battery life. While the player did not support video or photos, it did support subscription music services and audio content from Audible.com.

iRiver Clix 4GB

iRiver T10 4GB

Source: www.iriver.com.

In conjunction with its digital music players, iRiver offered a variety of accessories and provided access to the Online Music Guide, which allowed users of iRiver products to download free games as well as music and videos from new artists. The company also was a partner with Urge, an online service of MTV and Microsoft that offered new iRiver users free trials of services such as Napster, Yahoo! Music, and eMusic.

Heading into 2007, iRiver intended to build on the success of its Clix player to regain lost momentum in the U.S. market. To capitalize on the Clix's success, the company developed a second version of the product, the Clix 2. The widely anticipated product was introduced at the annual Computer Electronics Show (CES), a showcase for the industry's leading companies and products. The product was very well received; a reviewer for Engadget. com, one of the leading technophile Web sites, stated, "It's everything we were hoping for in the Clix followup."[17] While the Clix 2 was not going to be released in the United States until late 2007, analysts believed that this product, along with other iRiver products featured at the CES, clearly indicated that iRiver was back on track to be a serious contender in the digital music player market.

SanDisk

SanDisk, founded in 1988, was one of the world's leading suppliers of flash memory data storage products such as USB storage drives, flash storage cards, and memory sticks for use in digital cameras and digital music players. SanDisk designed, developed, and manufactured its products, which it sold to consumers and to manufacturers of electronic products. SanDisk also licensed its technology to other memory manufacturers. In January 6, 2005, SanDisk announced that it would leverage its experience in manufacturing flash-based memory and memory products to vertically integrate into the flash memory segment of the MP3 player market. SanDisk designed its MP3 players to be small and light, and to be expandable through Secure Digital cards (SD), a form of flash-based memory manufactured by SanDisk and other flash memory manufacturers.

To provide software for its products, SanDisk partnered with Rhapsody, AudioFeast, and Audible. Rhapsody provided SanDisk MP3 player users with a digital jukebox that allowed them to manage their music on their MP3 players and purchase music from Rhapsody's library of over 850,000 songs. AudioFeat was a commercial-free digital radio service that allowed users to update music, news, sports, and entertainment programs and news on their MP3 players and to listen to the content on the go. Finally, Audible was a provider of digital audiobooks, radio programs, and newspapers that users could download to their MP3 players for listening on the go. Analysts applauded SanDisk's expansion into the MP3 player market as a natural extension for the company. The first SanDisk MP3 players were shipped in May 2005, and by June 2005 the company had captured 8.9 percent of the flash memory digital music player market.

SanDisk's original offerings included the 512MB Sansa e130 (240 songs in WMA format), and the 1GB Sansa e140 (up to 480 songs in WMA format). SanDisk's players featured an SD slot for additional storage and a digital FM radio receiver; the company claimed its players could last up to 17 hours on a single AAA battery. SanDisk's players also offered a multiline backlit LCD that provided the title, artists, and album of the song currently being played. In September 2005, SanDisk began offering a car transmitter that would allow the user to play MP3 music through a car radio, and a portable speaker dock for Sansa MP3 players. In 2006, SanDisk planned to aggressively expand its product line and captured a 19.2 percent market share of unit sales for digital music players in the holiday season of that year; the company had revenues of over $300 million in the flash player market in 2006. By April 2007, the company's digital music player portfolio consisted of 10 players:

- The SanDisk Sansa Connect MP3 Player was a 4GB ($249.99) flash-based player that won two CNET Best of CES Awards in 2007 and was introduced to the U.S. market in March 2007. The player held 1,000 songs and featured photo viewing and Internet radio. The lead highlight of the Connect was that it was a Wi-Fi-enabled MP3 player that allowed users to connect to their content through any open wireless hot spot. According to Eric Bone, product marketing director for SanDisk's audio and video line, "The Sansa Connect is a new music experience focused on convenience, instant gratification and social connections."[18] The Connect also included community-building features that allowed users to recommend music and photos to others. The Connect was developed in partnership with a mobile entertainment technology and services company named ZING.

SanDisk Sansa Connect

Source: www.creative.com.

- The SanDisk Sansa Express MP3 Player was a flash-based player introduced in January 2007. The Express was offered in a 1GB ($59.99) version. The player held up to 250 songs in MP3 format or 500 in WMA format. The Express was billed as the first cableless player; it connected directly to a user's PC and included a microSD expansion slot as well as an FM tuner with an FM recorder and a microphone for voice recording.

SanDisk Sansa Express

Source: www.SanDisk.com.

- The SanDisk Sansa View pocket video player was introduced in January 2007 and was an 8GB audio/video player ($299.99) that had a rechargeable, removable battery and held up to 2,000 songs, thousands of photos, or 33 hours of video. The player fit neatly into a pocket and featured an integrated speaker, a 4-inch screen and an SD/SDHC expansion slot.

SanDisk Sansa View

Source: www.SanDisk.com.

- The SanDisk Sansa e200 Series MP3 players were offered in 2GB ($119.99), 4GB ($149.99), 6GB ($169.99), and 8GB ($199.99) capacities. The 2GB player held 32 hours of MP3-encoded music or 500 songs, while the 8GB player held 128 hours of MP4-encoded music or 2,000 songs. The e200 series featured a metal case, a color screen, a removable rechargeable battery that lasted up to 20 hours, a microSD memory expansion slot, and a digital FM tuner and recorder as well as a voice recorder.

SanDisk Sansa e200

Source: www.SanDisk.com.

- The SanDisk Sansa e200R Rhapsody series players were similar to the e200 series players but were optimized for the Best Buy Digital Music store experience powered by Rhapsody. The Rhapsody players were offered in 2GB ($139.99), 4GB ($179.99), 6GB ($219.99), and 8GB ($249.99) capacities. The integration with Rhapsody included unlimited access to millions of songs included in the Rhapsody music service as well as Rhapsody music channels and allowed users to personalize their Rhapsody experience based on their personal preferences.

SanDisk Sansa e200R

Source: www.SanDisk.com.

- The SanDisk Sansa c200 series of MP3 players was introduced in September 2006. Like other SanDisk players, the Sansa c200 players included a digital FM tuner and recorder as well as a voice recorder, supported subscription music services, and an expansion slot. However, they also featured a rechargeable battery, and a color screen that allowed users to view photos and album art. The c200 series included the c240 (1GB, $79.99) and the c250 (2GB $99.99).

SanDisk Sansa c200

Source: www.SanDisk.com.

- The SanDisk Sansa c100 series MP3 players were similar to the c200 series but used an AAA battery instead of a rechargeable battery. The c100 series included the 1GB c140 ($79.99) as well as the 2GB c150 ($109.99).

SanDisk Sansa c100

Source: www.SanDisk.com.

- The SanDisk Sansa m200 series MP3 players were available in January 2006 and were offered in m230 512MB ($49.99), m240 1GB ($69.99), m250 2GB ($99.99), and m260 4GB ($199.99) capacities. The m200 series featured 19 hours of play from a single AAA battery, an FM tuner and recorder, a voice recorder with a built-in microphone and a backlit LCD display.

SanDisk Sansa m260

Source: www.SanDisk.com.

- The SanDisk Sansa e100 series MP3 players were offered in 512MB ($59.99) and 1GB ($89.99) capacities. The e100 players featured a backlit multiline LCD display, a digital FM tuner, and up to 17 hours of playback from a single AAA battery.

SanDisk Sansa e130

Source: www.SanDisk.com.

- SanDisk digital audio players were available in January 2006 in 256MB, 512MB, and 1GB capacities. The digital audio players featured 15 hours of playback from a single AAA battery, a digital FM tuner, a voice recorder with a built-in microphone, and a backlit multiline display.

SanDisk Digital Audio Player 256MB

Source: www.SanDisk.com.

SanDisk was considered by many analysts as the second strongest player in the MP3 player industry and the strongest in the Windows-based segment. SanDisk had made significant strides in the market by offering more features at a lower price than rivals did. For example, the Connect was positioned to compete directly with the iPod Nano, given the Connect's Wi-Fi capabilities, larger screen, expansion slot, and lower price point. The company also attributed its success to aggressive marketing campaigns and retailers who were looking to improve on the razor-thin profit margins Apple allowed its retailers. However, the company was significantly impacted by the fierce competition in the MP3 player industry and the volatile flash memory market. In response to falling profits, the company took measures to reduce production costs and operating expenses. Even with this temporary setback, many analysts viewed SanDisk as the leading challenger to Apple and the main rival for Microsoft to overtake in the fiercely competitive Windows-based MP3 player market.

Sony

Sony was one of world's the best known names in consumer electronics. In fiscal year 2006 (ended in March 2006), the Sony Corporation brought in $63.89 billion in revenue (up 4.4 percent from 2005) and $1.1 billion in net income (down 24.5 percent from 2005). Prior to 2006, net revenues specifically from the electronics segment had fallen in every year from 2002 through 2005. In 2006, revenues in the electronics segment (which accounted for approximately 64 percent of Sony's total revenues) grew by 1.7 percent, but this growth level was still well below the gaming (12 percent of total revenue

and 31.4 percent growth) and financial services (9.3 percent of total revenue and 32.6 percent growth) segments.

In the 1980s, Sony revolutionized mobile the music technology when it introduced the Walkman, a portable cassette tape player that spawned dozens of imitations and look-alikes. Unfortunately, Sony was relatively late to enter the digital music/MP3 player revolution and was forced to be one of the look-alikes in that market. The Sony Network Walkman was released in August 2004—nearly three years after the iPod, which was not even the first MP3 player out on the market. Further, the Network Walkman was criticized for having a confusing interface, being difficult to use, and only playing songs encoded with Sony's proprietary ATRAC3 format rather than MP3. The ATRAC3 format was especially problematic; it took some time for users to copy MP3s to the Network Walkman, because they had to first use Sony software to encode them as ATRAC3s. Sony claimed to use this unusual format because it improved sound quality and helped extend battery life.

However, in the face of declining sales, Sony relented in early 2005 and released its first hard-drive-based MP3 compatible player, the 20GB Sony Network Walkman; it also released an MP3-compatible flash player by year's end. Additionally, Sony allowed users of some earlier hard-drive-based players to upgrade to MP3 compatibility for a fee of $20. However, by this time roles were reversed and Sony was viewed as one of the imitators in the digital music industry. After several additional product rollouts, by late 2005 Sony was finally viewed as competing on a more level playing field with Apple in terms of the price of the models and their capacities, although critics generally viewed the Network Walkman, Sony's core brand in the area, as somewhat inferior to other MP3 players. A 2007 *Consumer Reports* ranking of MP3 players scored Sony's 2GB player in the bottom third of all flash players.

By April 2007, Sony was offering four MP3 players, an MP3 voice recorder, three MP3/ATRAC-enabled portable CD players, a minidisc player, and the MP3-enabled mylo personal communicator, all of which were ATRAC/ATRAC3 and MP3 compatible as well as compatible with the Sony Select online music service. In partnership with cell phone manufacturer Ericsson, Sony also offered eight popular

MP3-enabled music phones. Sony's MP3 players included the following:

- The 2GB ($89.95) Flash MP3 Walkman was Sony's most basic player. This model was offered in six colors and featured a built-in FM tuner, a rechargeable battery that would last up to 28 hours, and a one-line display screen that displayed song information and the current time and date. This model was compatible with both the MP3 and ATRAC formats and could store up to 1,350 songs.

Flash MP3 Walkman

Source: www.sonystyle.com.

- The S2 Sports Walkman MP3 player was offered in both 1GB ($99.95) and 2GB ($119.95) models and was designed to help users get the most out of their workouts. The water-resistant S2 offered many of the same features as the MP3 Walkman but also included a pedometer, a stopwatch that shut off the music after a specified workout time had been reached, a calorie counter, and a five-band equalizer. The S2 allowed users to have a playlist for running or walking that the device would play automatically depending on the user's activity.

S2 Sports Walkman

Source: www.sonystyle.com.

- The Noise Canceling Walkman MP3 player was offered in 1GB ($169.95) and 2GB ($199.95)

models. As the name implied, the key differentiating factor of this model was that it was bundled with premium noise-canceling headphones. Other than features common to Sony's other Walkman MP3 players, this model also included a three-line color rotating display and a JOG shuttle to allow users to easily select a new song or playlist. The Noise Canceling Walkman supported a wide range of encoded and unencoded music formats.

Noise Canceling Walkman

Source: www.sonystyle.com.

- The 8GB Hard Disk Drive Walkman ($199.99) held up to 5,300 songs, supported a wide range of audio formats, and featured an intelligent shuffle function, a 20-hour rechargeable battery, a 1.5-inch color display, and a six-band equalizer.

8GB Hard Disk Drive Walkman

Source: www.sonystyle.com.

- Sony's MP3 voice recorders ranged in size from 256 MB ($99.95) to 1GB ($129.95), were powered by a single AAA battery, and allowed users to listen to MP3 files or use the built-in microphone to record files. In LP mode, users could record up to 125 hours of content on the 256 MB model and up to 502 hours of content on the 1GB player.

Voice Plus All-In-One Digital Voice Recorder

Source: www.sonystyle.com.

Despite Sony's historically dominant position in the electronics market, the manufacturer had failed to gain significant traction in the MP3 player industry. Additionally, analysts noted that the company had committed a series of strategic missteps in the launch of its third-generation gaming console, the PS3. Due to a delayed release of the unit and production difficulties, coupled with unexpectedly stiff competition from the Nintendo Wii, demand for the PS3 had been much lower than expected. Further Blu-ray, Sony's new high-definition DVD standard, was not catching on as quickly as the company had predicted, putting Sony in danger of suffering another setback. Taken in total, the company's series of strategic failings had left a number of analysts wondering how the company that was once the poster child for innovation could regain its leadership of the electronics industry.

Microsoft Zune

Microsoft Corporation, one of the world's best known companies, operated in more than 100 countries, employed over 75,000 people, and had projected annual revenues for the fiscal year ending June 30, 2007, of over $50 billion with operating income in the $19 billion range. In 2007, Microsoft was grouped into three core divisions:

1. The Microsoft Business Solutions Groups accounted for 55.8 percent of Microsoft's revenues in 2006 and included products such as Windows (Microsoft's flagship operating system) and Microsoft Visual Studio.
2. The Microsoft Business Division accounted for 32.72 percent of the company's revenues in 2006 and included Microsoft Office (Word, Access, Excel, Outlook, and PowerPoint).

3. The Microsoft Entertainment and Devices Division accounted for 10.5 percent of Microsoft's revenues in 2006 and included the Windows Mobile operating system, which was used on smart phones and other handheld devices, WebTV, computer games, the Xbox 360, and the Zune.

Microsoft was a late entrant into the MP3 player market, in that it did not release its Zune brand until November 2006. The Zune was offered in a 30GB model that was available in black, brown, or white. It retailed for $249.99 at its release, but the price had fallen to $199.99 by April 2007. The Zune included an FM radio and held 7,500 songs, 25,000 pictures, or 100 hours of video. The player also featured a three-inch color display that could be viewed vertically or horizontally; had up to a 14-hour battery life; was compatible with a wide variety media, including MP3, AAC, and WMA; and played music, videos, photos, and games. The primary distinguishing characteristic of the Zune at the time of its release was its wireless connectivity, which allowed users to share music and photos with other users within 30 feet. A user who received "squirted" songs could listen to the song three times before the Zune's built-in digital rights management (DRM) software prohibited access to the song. Photos had no such limitation. To highlight the song-sharing capability of the Zune, Microsoft marketed the product with the tagline "Welcome to the Social."

Zune

Source: www.zune.net.

Microsoft viewed the Zune's networking feature as a critical element of its strategy for the Zune brand. According to J. Allard, who was charged with overseeing the development of the Zune, Microsoft intended to place this player, and future Zune products, at the center of an "ecosystem" that "helps bring artists closer to their audience and helps people find new music an develop social connections."[19] To further support this ecosystem, Microsoft enlisted over 100 partners to aid in product development, to offer accessories for the Zune, and to provide content on the Zune Marketplace, an online store that was Microsoft's answer to the iTunes store. Users could access the Zune marketplace through the software included with the Zune. At the marketplace, they could purchase accessories for their Zune or select from over 2 million songs, which they could buy outright or could access through an "all-you–can-eat" subscription service known as Zune Pass. For $14.95 a month, the Zune Pass allowed users to download as many songs as they wanted from the Zune Marketplace; once the subscription expired, users could no longer access the downloaded songs.

The Zune's initial launch was met with lukewarm reviews. Critics noted that the market for non-iPod digital music players was already crowded and that the Zune wireless feature was of interest to only a very limited segment of the population—as little as 11 percent, according to Michael Gartner, vice president of JupiterResearch[20]—since it did not allow users to wirelessly download music from the Internet. Further, the Zune was not compatible with Microsoft's own PlaysForSure digital rights management software, so Zune users could purchase music only from the Zune store and not other services such as Napster, which had partnered with Microsoft in the PlaysForSure standard. As evidence of the Zune's shortcomings, the player was ranked only 15th out of the 17 hard drives rated by *Consumer Reports* in 2007, with its main shortcoming in the "Ease of Use" ranking.[21] Finally, critics pointed out that while the Zune had achieved a 10 percent share of the 30GB hard drive player market, its share of this narrow market segment had fallen to less than 9 percent by April 2007. The Zune's share of the overall MP3 player market was less than 2 percent.

Despite the relatively low market share, in early 2007 Microsoft reiterated that it was on pace to sell 1 million Zune players by July 2007. Analysts generally agreed that Microsoft was under no illusion that it would win a quick victory in the MP3 player market and that the company was prepared for an extended battle. Consistent with this belief, the Zune was placed under Allard's charge in the Xbox division rather than in one of Microsoft's more established operations. The intention was that Allard could do for the Zune what he did for the Xbox by making

it a legitimate contender against a deeply entrenched, successful rival over a period of five years. Further, the placement of the Zune in the Entertainment and Devices Division of Microsoft suggested that while Microsoft realized it may not be able to overtake the iPod in the current handheld media market, the company could capture synergies that would enable it to get an early lead in the next generation of handheld media players, such as mobile phones.

THE FUTURE

As Microsoft neared the six-month anniversary of the launch of the Zune, it appeared that it would, indeed, reach its goal of selling 1 million players by June 2007. While this still paled in comparison to Apple's April 9, 2007, announcement that it had sold 100 million iPods since the player's introduction, Microsoft's sales were establishing a toehold in the market that would allow the company to continue to develop and improve the Zune brand of players. A surprising 58 percent of iPod owners who planned to purchase an MP3 player said they would consider purchasing a Zune.[22] There were also credible rumors that Microsoft planned to introduce a Zune phone in response to Apple iPhone. Similarly, it was rumored that Apple planned to launch a subscription-based subscription service similar to the Zune Pass by the end of 2007.

Industry experts such as Van Baker, an analyst for Gartner, believe that Microsoft would first move to consolidate the Windows-based MP3 player market and would then move to more direct competition with the iPod.[23] However, Microsoft's Windows-based rivals were not ready to give up the market without a fight, and companies such as iRiver were working to diligently to keep Microsoft from the market by incorporating wireless technology into their players. There was no doubt that Microsoft had the financial resources and determination to wage a prolonged battle with Apple in the digital music player industry. However, it was apparent that the current iteration of the Zune, while a good start, would not be sufficient to unseat Apple. This left customers and industry experts alike wondering what Microsoft would have to do to meet its stated objective of becoming the leader of the digital music player industry.

Endnotes

[1]Anthony Bruno, "Zune Gets in the Ring," *Billboard* 188, no. 30 (July 29, 2006), p. 6.

[2]Grace Wong, "Zune vs. iPod, Round 1: Holiday Shoppers," www.money.cnn.com/2006/11/07/technology/zune/index.htm (accessed March 16, 2007).

[3]Andy Patrizio, "The Long Journey of the Zune," http://old-www.internet-news.com/storage/article.php/3650651 (accessed March 16, 2007).

[4]http://en.wikipedia.org/wiki/MP3_player (accessed December 23, 2005).

[5]Ibid.

[6]Russ Arensman, "MP3 Leaders Face Off," *Electronic Business*, June 1 2005, www.reed-electronics.com/eb-mag/article/CA603499.html?industryid=43314 (accessed December 16, 2005).

[7]Steve Smith, "iPod's Lessons," *Twice* 19, no. 15 (July 26, 2004), p. 12.

[8]Steven Levy, "iPod Nation" *Newsweek* 144, no. 4 (July 26, 2004), pp. 42–50.

[9]Paul Hansell, "Battle of Form (and Function) in MP3 Players," *New York Times*, October 4, 2004.

[10]Joseph Palenchar, "Rio Foresees Delay for Next Generation Devices," *Twice*, August 8, 2005, p. 6.

[11]Anthony Bruno, "No More Rio," *Billboard*, September 10, 2005, p. 6.

[12]Smith, "iPod's Lessons."

[13]Peter Burrows and Roger O. Crockett, "Apple's Phone Isn't Ringing Any Chimes," *BusinessWeek*, September 19, 2005, p. 58.

[14]Aki Tsukioka, "Info Plant Announces Results of Survey of Youth in East Asia on MP3 Players," *JCN Newswire,* October 3, 2005, p. 1.

[15]J im Welte, "Can iRiver Run through It?," MP3.com, April 7, 2006, www.mp3.com/news/stories/4030.html (accessed April 8, 2007).

[16]Ibid.

[17]Ryan Block, "iRiver Clix 2 Hands-On," Engadget.com, www.engadget.com/2007/01/08/iriver-clix-2-hands-on/ (accessed April 8, 2007).

[18]Company press release, www.sandisk.com/Corporate/PressRoom/PressReleases/PressRelease.aspx?ID=3669 (accessed March 28, 2007).

[19]Steven Levy, "Trying Apple's Tune," *Newsweek* online, September 17, 2006 www.msnbc.msn.com/id/14866932/site/newsweek/ (accessed April 10, 2007).

[20]Stanley Miller, "Zune, Zune, Zune: Microsoft Works to Be Heard," *Knight Ridder Tribune Business News*, November 12, 2006.

[21]"Ratings—MP3 Players," *Consumer Reports*, www.consumerreports.org (accessed April 1, 2007).

[22]Grace Wong, "Zune vs iPod, Round 1: Holiday Shoppers," CNNMoney.com, November 28, 2006, http://money.cnn.com/2006/11/07/technology/zune/index.htm (accessed April 1, 2007).

[23]Andy Patrizio, "The Long Journey of Zune," Internetnews.com, http://old-www.internetnews.com/storage/article.php/3650651 (accessed April 1, 2007).

SkyWest Inc. and the Regional Airline Industry

Annette Lohman

California State University, Long Beach

As 2007 began, SkyWest Inc., the parent holding company of SkyWest Airlines and Atlantic Southeast Airlines (ASA), was the largest independently owned regional airline company in the regional airline subgroup of the airline industry. Its two wholly owned regional airlines' combined operations offered service through over 2,432 departures to 237 U.S. domestic destinations. Prior to its acquisition of Atlantic Southeast Airlines from Delta Airlines in 2005, SkyWest Airlines was the sole airline operation of SkyWest Inc. Previously, SkyWest Inc. had owned SkyWest Airlines, Scenic Airlines, and an Avis car rental company. However, these last two entities had been divested. Prior to the Atlantic Southeast Airlines acquisition from Delta Airlines, SkyWest Airlines and SkyWest Inc., were operated as one company. Exhibit 1 is a map of the destinations served by the combined company.

THE AIRLINE INDUSTRY

The global airline industry was comprised of firms primarily offering domestic air transportation of passengers and/or cargo over regular routes on regular schedules. Airlines operated flights even if they were only partially loaded. Companies whose main business was in providing air transportation of mail on a contract basis were included in this industry.[1] In December 2006, the International Air Transport Association (IATA) predicted that worldwide passenger revenues would rise by 5 percent, to $475 billion, and cargo revenues would rise by 6 percent, to $380 billion in 2007.[2] The IATA also predicted that the industry would post collective profits of about $2.5 billion for the first time since the terrorist attacks in the United States in 2001.[3]

The U.S. Airline Industry

There were three types of domestic airline carriers: (1) network, (2) low-cost, and (3) regional carriers. They operated under three different business models. Network carriers, often referred to as the majors or legacy carriers, operated a significant portion of their flights using what was known as a hub-and-spoke system. At the beginning of 2007, United, Northwest, American, Continental, and Delta airlines were the largest of this group. In 2005, their combined revenues made up about 82 percent of the $25.3 billion generated by the 10 largest U.S. airlines. (See Exhibit 2.) Low-cost carriers were those that the industry generally recognized as operating under a low-cost business model, most often using point-to-point flights. The largest carriers in this segment were Southwest and JetBlue airlines. Several major carriers, in an effort to respond to the loss of revenues from low-cost competitors, had started up their own low-cost airlines. Two examples of this were United's Ted Airlines and Delta's Song Airlines. Regional carriers provided service from small cities, using primarily regional jets, to support the network carriers' hub-and-spoke systems.

The U.S. airline industry was affected by seasonal fluctuations that included increased travel during summer months and inclement weather, primarily

The case author gratefully acknowledges the research assistance that was provided by MBA students Nathan Russell, John Trietsch, and Dave Wippel. Copyright © 2007 by Annette Lohman. All rights reserved.

Exhibit 1   **SkyWest Inc.'s Current Combined Route System**

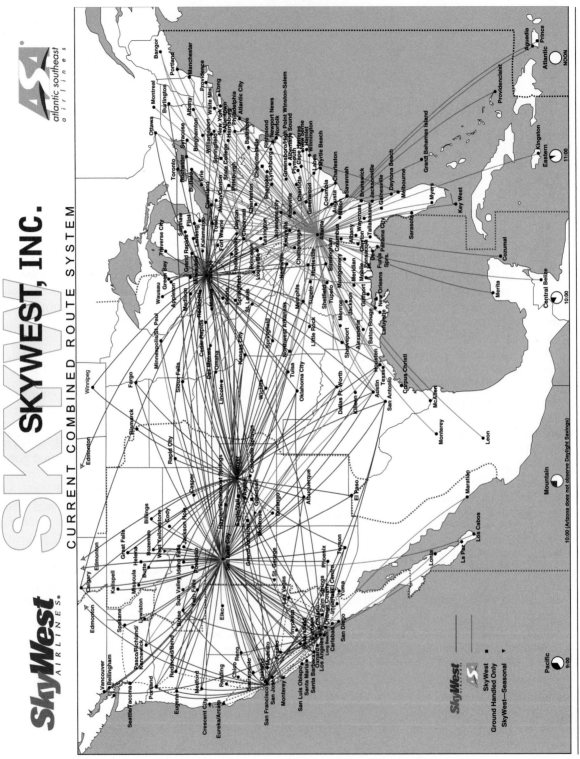

EFFECTIVE DECEMBER: 2006

Source: SkyWest Web site.

Exhibit 2   **Industry Net Profits, 2004–2005, With Forecasts for 2006 and 2007 ($ in billions)**

	Operating Profits				Net Profits			
	2004	2005	2006	2007	2004	2005	2006	2007
Global	3.3	4.3	10.2	10.2	−5.6	−3.2	−0.5	2.5
Regions								
North America	−1.9	−0.3	5.6	6.2	−10.0	−6.7	−3.7	0.2
Europe	2.8	3.0	3.5	3.1	1.1	1.6	1.8	1.5
Asia–Pacific	2.2	1.5	1.4	1.2	3.4	2.1	1.7	1.2
Middle East	0.3	0.4	0.2	0.2	0.2	0.2	0.1	0.1
Latin America	0.2	0.1	0.1	0.1	0.1	−0.1	0.1	0.1
Africa	−0.3	−0.4	−0.5	−0.5	−0.3	−0.4	−0.5	−0.5
Markets								
Domestic (U.S. only)	−3.3	−2.3	3.0	4.0	−9.4	−7.4	−4.9	0.1
International (IATA members only)	4.4	5.1	5.5	4.0	2.5	3.1	3.9	2.3
Other	2.2	1.5	1.7	2.2	1.3	1.1	0.5	0.1

Source: International Civil Aviation Organization (ICAO) data to 2005. IATA forecasts 2006–2007. U.S. net losses includes $6.1 billion restructuring costs in 2006. International Air Transport Association, "New Financial Forecast," December 2006, www.iata.org (accessed January 3, 2007).

Exhibit 3.   **U.S. Major Airlines Financial Results, Quarter Ended September 30, 2004 and 2005 ($ in millions)**

	Operating Revenues		Operating Profit		Net Income	
	2005	2004	2005	2004	2005	2004
AirTran Holdings	$ 374.6	$ 245.6	$1.2	$ (12.0)	$ (0.2)	$ (9.8)
Alaska Air Group	845.7	768.2	90.2	56.8	90.2	74.0
AMR Corp.	5,485.0	4,762.0	39.0	(27.0)	(153.0)	(214.0)
Continental	3,001.0	2,602.0	109.0	22.0	61.0	(18.0)
Delta	4,216.0	3,871.0	(240.0)	(423.0)	(1,134.0)	(651.0)
JetBlue	452.9	323.1	13.8	22.4	2.7	8.1
Northwest	3,378.0	3,052.0	(167.0)	79.0	(475.0)	(46.0)
Southwest	1,989.0	1,674.0	273.0	191.0	227.0	119.0
UAL Corp.	4,655.0	4,305.0	165.0	(80.0)	(1,722.0)	(274.0)
US Airways Group	926.0	679.0	(71.0)	(10.0)	(87.0)	(29.0)
Total	$25,323.2	$22,281.9	$213.2	$(180.8)	$(3,240.3)	$(1,040.7)

Source: Airline reports

during the winter, leading to flight cancellations and delays.[4] For example, SkyWest Inc. reported that one December 2006 storm, during which Denver International Airport was closed for two days, led to the cancellation of 2,850 of its flights, resulting in a decrease to pretax income of approximately $5.2 million.[5] The industry was also highly sensitive to fluctuations in the economy, because a significant portion of travel by leisure and business travelers was discretionary. The recession in the early 2000s

lowered the overall demand for airline services in the United States. This factor—coupled with the major airlines' overexpansion, bloated flight schedules, increasing fuel costs, increased competitive pressures from low-cost carriers, and the post-9/11 fear of flying—translated into huge losses for the major carriers.

Most major airlines started 2006 in serious financial trouble, if not bankruptcy. (See Exhibit 3.) United Airlines and US Airways had filed for bankruptcy in 2002 (with United emerging to post profits in 2006),[6] followed by ATA in 2004, and Northwest and Delta in September 2005. Some analysts believed that the U.S. airline industry, as it existed, was not sustainable and that the time was ripe for serious consolidations to begin. The 2005 US Airways–America West merger, finalized in the fall of 2005, was the most recent example of such consolidation. The newly consolidated airline continued its aggressive push on November 15, 2006, by proposing a takeover of Delta Airlines—a move that was rejected by Delta one month later. There had also been rumors of a potential merger between United and Continental airlines.[7] Analysts viewed mergers from two perspectives. First, they had the potential to take out some of the excess capacity in the industry, leading to more stable profits and less devastating price competition. This was viewed as a positive. On the other hand, they were likely to be accompanied by higher debt and higher costs associated with merging the operations of two airlines. As many airlines were already struggling under heavy debt loads,[8] increased merger activity leading to higher debt could further destabilize the industry.

Airline Passengers

There were two main types of passengers in the airline industry—business travelers and leisure travelers. Business travelers tended to be more profitable for airlines because they flew more often and tended to purchase premier services. Also, a lot of business travel was unplanned, or planned in a short time frame, forcing business travelers to purchase tickets at the last minute at a premium. Leisure travelers flew less and were more price-sensitive than business travelers. For the most part, they did not purchase premier services.[9] The regional airlines, primarily through their contracts with the major carriers, serviced both market segments; however, their passenger base had historically been made up of more business travelers than leisure travelers. Business travelers used regional airlines to commute to and from locations that were considered too far to drive.

Traditionally, the major airlines, through their partnerships with regional airlines, serviced almost the entire business market. However, an increasing number of business travelers had begun to travel on low-cost carriers. The major airlines' share of the business market had dropped to 60 percent, while the low-cost carriers had picked up 20 percent. The

major airlines were responding to these competitive pressures by offering their own low-cost carrier lines, such as United's Ted or Delta's Song. These moves could be expected to potentially lower overall demand for routes traditionally served by the regional carriers.

Safety

The 9/11 terrorist attacks were a major contributor to the decreased demand in the airline industry in the early 2000s. People were afraid to fly and, in an uncertain economy, this translated into less revenue for the major airlines. This factor did not directly affect regional airlines because of the assumption that a smaller, regional aircraft wouldn't be a target for terrorism. However, since regionals derived most, if not all, of their revenues from contracts with the majors, they were affected as well. Regional airlines also suffered from the general view that smaller airplanes were less safe than larger airplanes. In reality, regional airlines had a slightly lower accident rate than the major airlines and had increased safety standards in recent years.

Regulation

The airline industry was heavily regulated given the perceived potential danger found in the service being provided. The Federal Aviation Administration (FAA) oversaw and regulated the safety of the aviation industry. The Department of Transportation (DOT) also oversaw the airline industry and, in conjunction with the Transportation Security Administration (TSA), was responsible meeting the threat of terrorists. Post-9/11 fears of terrorist attacks had lead to stepped-up government intervention in the industry through increased security regulations, leading to additional costs for the airlines.

New regulations posed additional costs for airlines. For example, the Department of Transportation had, in the past, considered implementing a regulation (amending the Air Carrier Access Act of 1986) to require airlines to provide oxygen for passengers needing it. This and other potential rulings could increase the regional airlines' costs through being required to purchase and maintain the equipment and train personnel on its use as well as deal with liability issues. The cost for this regulation was estimated to be between $262 and $577 million to the airline industry over 10 years.[10]

Fuel Cost Increases

The increasing price of jet fuel was a contributing factor to the financial troubles of the major airlines. For most airlines, the costs of fuel made up 10–20 percent of overall costs, with 14–16 percent being the average.[11] Most analysts didn't expect much relief in fuel costs in the foreseeable future. In fact, the recovery of the industry and increased willingness of passengers to fly was expected to increase demand by around 975,000 barrels per day in the five years between 2005 and 2010, compared to growth of 420,000 barrels per day between 2000 and 2005. Rising fuel costs were also a threat for the regional carriers. While their revenue streams tended to be steadier than those of the major airlines and their profitability didn't rely on ticket sales, they still had to keep costs below revenues received to be profitable. This was becoming increasingly difficult as fuel prices rose and the major airline partners were pressuring them for lower fees. The pressures created by increased fuel costs served to increase the importance of efficiency in the operations of airlines.[12]

Labor Unions

The airline business had always been highly labor intensive. It was estimated that 40 percent of an airline's expenses were used to pay airline professionals such as pilots, flight attendants, baggage carriers, and customer service representatives.[13] Most airline employees were represented by one of many labor unions, including the Airline Pilots Association and the Allied Pilots Association, the Professional Flight Attendants' Union, the Transportation Workers Union, the International Association of Machinists, and the Airline Professional Flight Attendants Association. Labor unions and airlines had a history of acrimonious relationships leading to strikes and huge losses for the airlines affected. Some analysts who followed the industry anticipated that labor unions would see the return to profits for the industry as an opportunity for labor to lobby to get its piece of the pie.[14]

THE REGIONAL AIRLINE INDUSTRY

The regional airline industry was made up of air carriers that specialized in short-haul flights that serviced small communities that had neither the facilities nor the frequency of passenger travel to support a larger airport and the accompanying aircraft. Initially, regional airlines operated small, slow planes in one general geographic area. As the industry grew and regional companies partnered with the major airlines, they began to grow their profits and their reach. The introduction of faster, more efficient commuter jets had also helped the regional airlines to expand their service areas.

Regional airlines primarily operated to serve as feeder airlines bringing passengers to and from the small communities they served to a larger hub airport, where passenger air transportation needs were served by larger airlines with larger aircraft and greater geographic reach. About 95 percent of flying by regional airlines was conducted for this purpose.[15] Other regional airlines were formed to serve particular low-use routes and were often most important to small and isolated communities for whom the airline was the only reasonable link to a larger town.

Regional airlines operated mostly through partnerships with the major airlines. Some regional airline companies, such as SkyWest Inc., were independent entities; often, however, they were wholly owned subsidiaries of major airlines where the separate corporate structure allowed the subsidiary to operate under different (and lower) pay schedules. Examples of these were American Eagle, Canada Air Jazz, and Continental Express. In these partnerships, the major carriers paid the regional airlines a contracted fee per departure. The major carriers relied on the regional airlines to make their hubs work efficiently, and the regional airlines gained access to an established customer base and a steady revenue stream. Under these conditions, the revenues of regional airlines were not directly related to ticket sales. A passenger wanting to travel along a route served by a regional airline would book his or her flight with a major carrier that had a partnership with the regional. The identity of the regional carrier was not normally of concern or interest to the passenger.[16]

Regional airlines were subject to a number of operating constraints and problems that their major carrier partners did not face. In the third quarter of 2006, four of the worst on-time records were held by regional carriers. In addition, the six worst carriers in baggage handling were all regionals, and six of the seven worst carriers for canceling flights were regionals. Not all of these problems were directly the fault of the regional airlines. Many of them were caused by their partners, who controlled their scheduling, not allowing enough time to load and unload passengers and luggage. In addition, regional carriers, which were usually limited geographically to one region, were more affected by bad weather, which often threw a monkey wrench into their entire operations. At some hub airports, regional carriers' flights were routinely canceled to make room on runways for major carrier airplanes.[17]

The financial troubles of the major airlines created both opportunities and threats for their regional partners. Many were forced to roll back operations and to outsource more of their routes to the regional airlines. This created opportunities for the regional carriers to expand their service areas and often put them into direct competition with the low-cost carriers, such as Southwest and Jet Blue. Increased pressure on the major carriers to cut costs also forced them to put pressure on their regional partners to accept lower fees, and bankruptcy filings for the majors put extra pressure on the regionals to expand their base of partnership contracts. When Northwest Airlines filed for bankruptcy protection on September 14, 2005, its major regional partner, Mesaba Airlines, followed suit on October 13, 2005, citing the $30 million due it in the Northwest Chapter 11 case.[18]

It was expected that the potential mergers of several of the major airlines could also create tougher times for their regional partners. Consolidations would mean more limited growth opportunities for the regionals that moved the majors' passengers to their hubs from smaller cities. Consolidations would allow carriers to shut down some of their hubs around the country—especially some of the smaller ones that depended more on regional airline flights.[19]

Aircraft

There were two major choices between the types of aircraft used by regional carriers: the turboprop and the regional jet. The uses for these two aircraft differed yet complemented each other. The turboprop was used for short- to medium-haul flights and was able to land on shorter runways. Many travelers were hesitant to ride on turboprops, given the perception that they were loud and uncomfortable. Some of the major turboprops included the Embraer Brasilia, a twin-engine 30-passenger aircraft manufactured by Brazil's Empresa Brasileira de Aeronautica SA, the Jetstream 41, Saab 340, Dornier 328, the de Havilland

Dash 8-100 and 8-200, and the Bombardier Q Series turboprop, which was equipped with noise and vibration reduction devices that reduced the noise and vibration levels to that of a regional jet.

Regional jets, on the other hand, had increasingly been used to service longer-haul flights to destinations up to 1,200 miles away. The Canadair Regional Jet was the main regional jet used in the industry. Its introduction allowed the regional carriers to operate new longer routes and run its current routes more efficiently. Canadair was acquired by Bombardier in 1986 and subsequent regional jets carried the Bombardier name.

Competition

Like competition among the majors and low-cost carriers, competition among the regional airlines for contracts with majors had become increasingly fierce as the regional airlines competed with each other for partnerships with only a few major airlines. Rivalry was expected to continue to increase as the regional airlines compete for new routes being offered and bid out by the major airlines. To be able to successfully acquire contracts with the majors, a regional airline had to be able to:

- *Develop and maintain high levels of customer service.* Airlines had become notorious for providing poor customer service; good customer service could keep customers for life.

- *Develop and maintain a strong safety image.* Passengers would not fly with an airline that had an unsafe image.

- *Maximize on-time arrivals.* To ensure that passengers would continue to fly with a regional airline, the airline had to deliver the passengers to their destination on time so passengers did not miss their connecting flight.

- *Acquire new aircraft.* Regional airlines had to have capital and financing available to them to grow their regional jet fleets to service the longer routes being outsourced by the major airlines. They also had to be able to do this without compromising their scope contracts with labor.

SkyWest Inc. viewed its main rivals in the regional airline industry to be Air Wisconsin Airlines Corporation; American Eagle Airlines Inc., owned by American; Comair Inc., owned by Delta; ExpressJet

Exhibit 4 **Selected Regional Airline Comparisons**

	SKYWEST	MESA Air	Republic Airways	Regional Airline Average
Market Capitalization:	$ 1.69B	$281.50M	$744.25M	$ 1.08B
Employees:	8,095	5,200	3,060	3,450
Quarterly Revenue Growth (year over year):	59.20%	17.30%	33.00%	25.90%
Revenue (trailing twelve months):	$ 3.07B	$ 1.34B	$	$ 1.66B
Gross Margin (trailing twelve months):	21.74%	14.29%	34.52%	36.18%
EBITDA (trailing twelve months):	$530.83M	$126.32M	$290.85M	$162.17M
Operating Margins (trailing twelve months):	11.27%	6.63%	18.43%	8.15%
Net Income (trailing twelve months):	$153.24M	$ 33.97M	$ 77.55M	$ 33.97M
EPS (trailing twelve months):	$ 2.46	$ 0.84	$ 1.80	$ 0.69
Price/Earnings Ratio (trailing twelve months) :	10.71	9.85	9.73	16.74

Source: Yahoo! Finance, SkyWest Competitors, January 5, 2007.

Holdings Inc.; Horizon Air Industries Inc., owned by Alaska Air Group Inc.; Mesa Air Group Inc.; MAIR Holdings Inc.; Pinnacle Airlines Corporation; Republic Airways Holdings Inc.; and Trans State Airlines Inc.[20] See Exhibit 3 for comparative data on the major regional competitors.

MAIR Holdings. MAIR Holdings owned Mesaba Airlines and Big Sky Transportation. Mesaba operated as a commuter for Northwest Airlines out of its hubs in Detroit, Minneapolis/St. Paul, and Memphis. Big Sky Transportation operated flights in Washington, Idaho, Montana, and North Dakota. Forty-one percent of MAIR's 3,779 (as of March 2006) employees were covered by union contracts.[21]

- **Mesaba Airlines.** Mesaba Airlines, in 2006, was the 12th largest regional airline in the United States, offering services through its code-sharing agreement with Northwest Airlines. The company, based in Eagan, Minnesota, provided service to over 100 cities and 31 states and Canada through Northwest Airlines' major hubs in Minneapolis/St. Paul, Detroit, and Memphis. In 2005, Mesaba carried over 5.7 million passengers. The company operated a fleet of 77 regional jets and propjet aircraft primarily under lease agreements with Northwest Airlines. In August 2005, the airline was awarded the Operational Excellence Award by AIG Aviation, the leading underwriter of Aviation Insurance in recognition of its quality safety and loss-prevention

programs.[22] As mentioned above, Northwest Airlines' financial troubles, including its filing for bankruptcy protection on September 14, 2005, left Mesaba in dire straits, and the airline was forced to announce that it had filed for bankruptcy protection. Cited in the announcement were a claim of over $30 million due Mesaba in the Northwest Chapter 11 case and Northwest's decision to reduce the number of aircraft it made available to the airline—effectively reducing its fleet (and flying capabilities) by 28 percent. Mesaba's relationships with its unions had generally been good but had become somewhat strained by the bankruptcy proceedings.[23]

- **Big Sky Transportation.** Based in Billings, Montana, Big Sky Airlines began operations in 1978 with passenger service from Billings to Helena and Kalispell, Montana. In 2006, the airline served 19 cities in six states. Big Sky served markets that it characterized as having unmet demand for affordable access to airline hubs and for air travel between communities. Major states served were Colorado, Idaho, Montana, Oregon, Washington, and Wyoming. The company operated through partnerships with Northwest Airlines, America West Airlines, Alaska Airlines, and Horizon Air.[24]

Mesa Air Group. Mesa Air Group, a publicly held company, operated 188 aircraft with over 1,100 daily system departures to 173 cities, 46 states, the District of Columbia, Canada, and Mexico. On December 22, 2006, the Mesa Air Group signed an agreement with Shenzhen Airlines to create a new regional airline through a joint venture. The new airline was expected to begin operations within 12 months and have twenty 50-seat regional jets flying prior to the Beijing Olympic Games in 2008. The company also operated partnerships with United Airlines, US Airways, Midwest Airlines, and Delta Airlines. Wholly owned subsidiaries included:

- Air Midwest, doing business as Mesa Airlines, primarily served federally subsidized markets across the country through a fleet of twenty 19-passenger, Raytheon 1900D aircraft.
- Freedom Airlines Inc., which operated Delta Connection services primarily in the southeast.
- Go! Hawaii Airlines, a low-cost interisland airline operated by Mesa Airlines that flew 20- to 50-seat planes between the islands of Hawaii.[25]

Republic Airways Holdings. Based in Indianapolis, Indiana, Republic Airways Holdings was an airline holding company that owned Chautauqua Airlines, Republic Airlines, and Shuttle America. The airlines offered scheduled passenger service on approximately 1,000 flights daily to 90 cities in 35 states, Canada, Mexico, and the U.S. Virgin Islands through airline services agreements with four major U.S. airlines. All of the airlines' flights were operated under their major airline partner's brand, such as American Connection, Delta Connection, United Express, and US Airways Express. In 2006, the combined airlines employed over 3,600 people and operated 171 regional jets.[26]

ExpressJet Holdings. ExpressJet Holdings was a publicly held company with operations in the air transportation sector, including ExpressJet Airlines Inc. (operating under the name Continental Express), and ExpressJet Services LLC, which provided third-party maintenance services. The company also invested in other entities that permitted it to leverage the management experience, efficiencies, and economies of scale present in its subsidiaries. ExpressJet Airlines operated as Continental Express, serving 152 destinations in the United States, Canada, Mexico, Central America, and the Caribbean. It operated hubs in New York/Newark,

Cleveland, and Houston. ExpressJet Airlines employed about 6,800 people.[27]

Pinnacle Airlines Corporation. Headquartered in Memphis, Tennessee, Pinnacle Airlines Corporation was the parent of Pinnacle Airlines, which until November of 2003 had been a wholly owned subsidiary of Northwest Airlines. The company conducted its operations under the name of Northwest Airlink, providing flights from Northwest hubs in Detroit, Memphis, Minneapolis/St. Paul, and Indianapolis. The airline employed about 3,900 people and maintained a fleet of 124 all-jet Canadair regional jets. The airline announced in December 2006 that it had reached agreement on an amended service agreement with Northwest Airlines that would provide for Pinnacle to partner with Northwest Airlines through 2017. The companies also reached agreement, subject to approval by the bankruptcy court overseeing Northwest's Chapter 11 proceedings, that Pinnacle would receive an allowed unsecured claim of $377.5 million in settlement of all claims that Pinnacle had against Northwest.[28]

SKYWEST INC.

For the year ending 2006, SkyWest Inc.'s consolidated revenues were $3,114 million, up from $1,964 million the year before. This increase represented the year's internal growth as well growth realized through the acquisition of Atlantic Southeast Airlines, which was complete on September 7, 2005. The company's quarterly financial results for 2006 can be found in Exhibit 5. Exhibit 6 tracks the company's five-year financial history.[29]

Through the end of 2006, SkyWest Inc. operated primarily through partnership contracts with United and Delta. The two legacy carriers had both been in bankruptcy protection, with United emerging from the proceedings early in the year. The company relied almost completely on these carriers for its customers and revenue. Both United and Delta operated with very similar business models and were exposed to the same types of economic and environmental risks. However, United and Delta were expected to outsource more of their flights as they scaled back and restructured their operations. SkyWest was set to take over 20 additional routes from United out of

Exhibit 5   **Skywest, Inc. Condensed Consolidated Statements of Income, by Quarter, 2006 (Dollars and Share in thousands, Except per Share Amounts)**

	Three Months Ended			
	Dec. 31, 2006	Sept. 30, 2006	June 30, 2006	March 31, 2006
Operating Revenue				
Passenger	$783,858	$784,597	$784,332	$734,426
Ground handling and other	5,699	7,244	6,072	8,429
Total	$789,557	$791,841	$790,404	$742,855
Operating Expenses				
Flying operations	$432,996	$447,702	$442,731	$398,466
Customer service	106,988	99,767	99,390	99,676
Maintenance	81,779	78,057	73,779	78,311
Depreciation and amortization	49,714	47,420	47,262	45,489
General and administrative	39,173	31,124	37,621	38,050
	710,650	704,070	700,783	659,992
Operating Income	78,907	87,771	89,621	82,863
Other income (expense):				
Interest income	7,441	5,378	4,225	2,907
Interest expense	(31,952)	(28,987)	(28,519)	(28,543)
Loss on sale of property and equipment	0	0	13	(1,097)
Total other (expense), net	24,511	(23,609)	(24,281)	(26,733)
Income before income taxes	54,396	64,162	65,340	56,130
Provision for income taxes	23,148	23,477	26,054	21,542
Net income	$31,248	$40,685	$39,286	$34,588
Basic earnings per share	$0.49	$0.64	$0.62	$0.59
Diluted earnings per share	$0.48	$0.63	$0.62	$0.57
Weighted average common shares:				
Basic	63,940	63,870	62,970	59,118
Diluted	64,868	64,482	63,501	60,417

Source: Company news releases on 5/3/06, 8/3/2006, 10/30/06, and 2/7/07.

Denver, Chicago, Los Angeles, and San Francisco under the United Express brand. In addition, a bankruptcy court approved a 15-year agreement between Delta and SkyWest in which Delta was expected to begin outsourcing more routes in the United States and Canada to the company as it scaled back its own service.

SkyWest's revenue had become less predictable and more risky because of its reliance on these two companies. However, in December of 2006, SkyWest Inc. announced that SkyWest Airlines had been selected by Midwest Airlines to enter into an airline services agreement, a move that promised to expand and diversify operations and thereby reduce the company's risk.

SkyWest Airlines

SkyWest Airlines was founded in 1972 in St. George, Utah, to facilitate "the connections of passengers to flights of major partners" by partnering with the major airlines to service smaller airports and shorter routes. In June 2007, SkyWest Airlines was scheduled to celebrate its 35th anniversary.[30] The airline's mission/vision as stated in its 2004 annual report was:

Exhibit 6   **SkyWest Inc., Selected Consolidated Financial Data, 2002–2006 ($ in thousands, except per share data)**

	Year Ended December 31				
	2006[3]	2005[2]	2004	2003	2002
Operating revenues	$ 3,114,656	$ 1,964,048	$ 1,156,044	$ 888,026	$ 774,447
Operating income	339,160	220,408	144,776	108,480	119,555
Income before cumulative effect of change in accounting principle	NA	112,267	81,952	66,787	78,277
Net income per common share:					
Basic	$2.33	$1.94	$1.42	$1.16	$1.52
Diluted	$2.30	$1.90	$1.40	$1.15	$1.51
Total Assets	NA	$ 3,320,646	$ 1,662,287	$ 1,529,210	$ 999,384
Current Assets	NA	$ 693,632	$ 712,337	$ 670,368	$ 513,233
Current Liabilities	NA	$ 615,917	$ 170,467	$ 151,959	$ 121,388
Stockholders' equity	NA	$ 913,198	$ 779,055	$ 709,063	$ 638,686
Return on average equity[1]	NA	13.2%	11.0%	9.9%	14.7%

[1] Calculated by dividing net income by the average of beginning and ending stockholders' equity for the year.

[2] Operating results include the consolidated results of SkyWest and ASA. On September 7, 2005, SkyWest, Inc. completed the acquisition of ASA from Delta for $421.3 million in cash. The company paid $5.3 million of transaction fees and ASA assumed approximately $1.25 billion in long-term debt and related assets. 2005 consolidated operating revenues contain 114 days of additional revenue generated by the ASA acquisition.

[3] During the quarter ending December 2006, SkyWest airlines incurred additional maintenance charges for aircraft that were transitioned between Atlantic Southeast Airlines and SkyWest Airlines resulting in a decrease to pretax income of approximately $3.5 million. Additionally, in preparation to fly additional routes for Midwest Airlines and Delta Air Lines, Sky West Airlines incurred training charges which will be reimbursed by Midwest and Delta as the aircraft are brought into service. The impact of the accelerated training resulted in a decrease to pretax income of approximately $1.5 million. The company's net income for the quarter was further reduced by $2.4 million due to the timing of tax deductions for incentive stock options and expenses related to stock option grants.

Source: SkyWest Inc. 2005 annual report and news release of February 7, 2007, announcing fourth-quarter and 2006 annual results.

We understand the value and priceless commodity of time. We respect every individual's quality of life and are committed to promoting dignity and trust in all we do. We strive to be: the airline of choice, the employer of choice and the investment of choice. Our Guiding Principles: health and safety first, excellence in service and quality, personal and operational reliability, fairness and consistency, respect and teamwork, personal and corporate integrity, superior profitability and efficient use of all resources.

At the beginning of January 2007, SkyWest Airlines operations served 135 cities in 38 states, with connecting cities and Canadian provinces for United of 116 and Delta of 81, with 63 shared. Its hubs were in Chicago O'Hare, Los Angeles, San Francisco, Portland, Seattle/Tacoma, Denver, and Salt Lake City; maintenance bases were in Chicago, Colorado Springs, Denver, Fresno, Los Angeles, Palm Springs, Salt Lake City, San Diego, San Francisco,

and Tucson. The airline employed 9,939 people (8,783 full-time equivalents) who are not represented by union contracts.

The company had a good reputation for on-time arrivals. In the Airline Quality Rating study released in April 2005, SkyWest Airlines was on time the most out of the 16 largest U.S. airlines in 2004, and in August 2005, SkyWest Airlines reported 84.5 percent of its flights arrived on time, an on-time arrival rate that was the fourth best of reporting airlines. Meanwhile, SkyWest's cancellation rates, at 1 percent, were half of those of the industry as a whole.

While SkyWest had built a good reputation for on-time service, other factors such as lost baggage (9.53 reports per 1,000—double the industry average) and customer complaints had plagued the company. The Airline Quality Rating study rated SkyWest near the bottom of the list of 16 airlines for overall customer service.[31]

Atlantic Southeast Airlines

Atlantic Southeast Airlines (ASA) was founded in 1979 in Atlanta, Georgia. Until its acquisition by SkyWest Inc., the company was owned and managed by Delta Airlines. At the end of 2006, it served 145 airports with 155 aircraft in 40 U.S. states, Washington, D.C., Canada, Mexico, Belize, the Bahamas, Jamaica, Puerto Rico, and the Turks and Caicos islands. The carrier had hubs in Atlanta, Salt Lake City, Los Angeles, and Cincinnati; its maintenance stations were in Atlanta and Macon, Georgia; Salt Lake City, Utah; Baton Rouge and Shreveport, Louisiana; Columbia, South Carolina; Fort Walt Beach, Florida; and Montgomery, Alabama. The airline employed 5,696 full-time employees, who were represented by the Air Line Pilots Association International, the Association of Flight Attendants–CNA, and the Professional Airline Flight Control Association. In January 2007, the airline had reached an impasse in its negotiations with its unions and mediators and had been unable to resolve the differences between the offers of the company and the demands of its unions.[32]

Prior to the merger, ASA had one of the worst customer service records in the industry. In August 2005, ASA flights were on time only 59.6 percent of the time, which was the worst out of all reporting airlines. ASA also canceled 8 percent of its flights, and its rate of luggage mishandling was 19.95 reports out of 1,000. Both rates were the worst in the industry.

Atlantic Southeast Airlines expressed its vision and values as follows:

ASA aspires to be the most trusted and respected regional airline in the eyes of our customers, team members, shareholders and competitors by:

- Showing every customer our passion for safety and personalized service;
- Attracting and developing team members who contribute to the success of the ASA family;
- Creating a fun and rewarding culture that recognizes the value of individuals and teamwork;
- Being flexible and efficient in everything we do.[33]

Partnerships

Partnership contracts with the two airlines were fairly complex and provided for a number of fixed fees and incentives as well as provisions for early cancellation. SkyWest Inc. operated Delta Connection contracts through both of its airline operations. The combined Delta Connection contracts represented approximately 59.9 percent of the company's capacity and approximately 40.1 percent of capacity was dedicated to its United Express contracts.

Delta Connection. As of December 31, 2005, SkyWest Airlines was operating approximately 400 Delta Connection flights per day between Salt Lake City and designated outlying destinations. Delta was entitled to all passenger, cargo, and other revenues associated with each flight. In exchange for providing the designated number of flights and performing SkyWest Airlines' other obligations under the SkyWest Airlines/Delta Connection Agreement, SkyWest Airlines received from Delta on a weekly basis (1) reimbursement for 100 percent of its direct costs related to the Delta Connection flights, and (2) a fixed dollar payment per completed flight block hour, subject to annual escalation at an agreed rate. Costs directly reimbursed by Delta under the SkyWest Airlines/Delta Connection Agreement included costs related to fuel, ground handling, and aircraft maintenance and ownership.[34]

Under the Atlantic Southeast Airline/Delta Connection Agreement, the company operated more than 850 Delta Connection flights per day between Atlanta, Cincinnati, Salt Lake City, and designated outlying destinations. Under the agreement, Delta was entitled to all passenger, cargo, and other revenues associated with each flight. Commencing in 2008, ASA was guaranteed to maintain its percentage of total Delta Connection flights that it had in 2007, so long as ASA's bid for additional regional flying was competitive with other regional carriers. In exchange for providing the designated number of flights and performing ASA's other obligations under the ASA/Delta Connection Agreement, ASA received from Delta on a weekly basis (1) reimbursement for 100 percent of its direct costs related to Delta Connection flights, and (2) if ASA completed a certain minimum percentage of its Delta Connection flights, an amount equal to a certain percentage of the direct costs related to the Delta Connection flights (not including fuel costs). Costs directly reimbursed by Delta under the ASA/Delta Connection Agreement included costs related to fuel, ground handling and aircraft maintenance and ownership.[35] The ASA/Delta Connection Agreement was scheduled to terminate on September 8, 2020, unless Delta elected to exercise its option to extend.[36]

United Express. In exchange for providing the designated number of flights and performing Sky-West Airlines' obligations under the United Express Agreement, SkyWest Airlines received, from United, compensation (subject to an annual adjustment) of a fixed fee per completed block hour, a fixed fee per completed departure, a fixed fee per passenger, a fixed fee for overhead and aircraft costs, and one-time start-up costs for each aircraft delivered. The United Express Agreement provided for incentives based on SkyWest Airlines' performance, including on-time arrival performance and completion percentage rates. Additionally, certain of SkyWest Airlines' operating costs were reimbursed by United, including costs related to fuel and aircraft ownership and maintenance. Expiration of these contracts, unless options for renewals were exercised, was expected to occur incrementally in 2011, 2013, and 2015.[37]

In competing for these contracts, SkyWest Inc. relied on its ability to achieve and maintain its high safety standard and on-time arrival record and by offering the highest quality service possible through such actions as fleet and safety equipment upgrades. The airlines were also the lowest-cost providers of regional air service for Delta and United—a competitive capability that was becoming increasingly important as the major airlines continued to pressure the regional airlines to accept lower fees.

Midwest Airlines. Under the terms of its new agreement, SkyWest Airlines operations extended to serving markets from Midwest's hubs in Milwaukee and Kansas City. According to December 21, 2006, press release, the agreement provided for an initial term of five years with automatic two-year extensions thereafter. Commenting on the new agreement, Bradford R. Rich, executive vice president, CFO, and treasurer for SkyWest Inc., said, "SkyWest and Midwest have similar corporate cultures and great reputations for quality customer service and we believe that our partnership will be beneficial for customers, employees, and shareholders. . . . This transaction also furthers certain of our strategic diversification objectives."[38]

Safety

SkyWest Inc.'s safety department voluntarily participated in the Aviation Safety Action Program, which was a reporting program for pilots that was designed to determine potential safety hazards. Additionally, the department served as a compliance liaison between SkyWest and the Department of Transportation and Federal Aviation Administration. SkyWest had also implemented Stetson Quality Suite, which was mobile data collection and reporting software used to ensure that SkyWest Inc. was meeting or exceeding its safety and quality standards.

Human Resource Policies

Prior to the acquisition of Atlantic Southeast Airlines, the company's workforce was non-union and its competitive salaries and bonuses, rapid promotion of pilots, retirement plan, and employee stock purchase plan created a level of employee satisfaction that discouraged the unionization of its workforce. The non-union workforce gave SkyWest Airlines more flexibility in making decisions when compared to its competitors. For example, SkyWest's pilots agreed to operate 70- and 90-seat aircraft at the same rate as a 50-seat aircraft. The 2005 acquisition of Atlantic Southeast Airlines changed SkyWest Inc.'s relationship with its workforce as ASA's employees were represented by the Air Line Pilots Association International, the Association of Flight Attendants–CNA, and the Professional Airline Flight Control Association. The airline acknowledged in its 2005 annual report that there existed significant risk to the company should the labor unions associated with the ASA operations seek a "single carrier determination" from the National Mediation Board and attempt to unionize SkyWest's employees.

With the company's growth had also come increases in hiring. SkyWest Airlines had hired 4,000 new employees in 2006 and expected to hire a similar number in 2007. To achieve its hiring goals, the airline planned to hold job fairs throughout the United States.[39] Career opportunities were also regularly posted on the carriers' Web sites.

Employees of both SkyWest Airlines and Atlantic Southeast Airlines were eligible to participate

Exhibit 7   **SkyWest Inc., Selected Operating Highlights, by Quarter, 2006**

Operating Metric	Dec. 31, 2006	Sept. 30, 2006	June 30, 2006	March 31, 2006
Passengers carried	7,740,004	8,171,812	8,144,992	7,408,714
Revenue passenger miles (000)	3,961,246	4,156,637	4,054,909	3,646,400
Available seat miles (000)	5,155,816	5,281,794	5,070,300	4,701,978
Passenger load factor	76.8%	78.7%	80.0%	77.6%
Passenger breakeven load factor	72.2%	72.9%	73.8%	71.9%
Revenue per available seat mile	$0.153	$0.150	$0.156	$0.158
Cost per available seat mile	$0.144	$0.139	$0.144	$0.146
Fuel cost per available seat mile	$0.049	$0.051	$0.052	$0.048
Average passenger trip length (in miles)	512	509	498	492

Source: Unaudited Operating Highlights, company news releases May 3, 2006, August 3, 2006, October 30, 2006, and February 7, 2007.

in company retirement plans in which the company matched, up to a certain point, participant contributions. Employees who had completed 90 days or more of service were also eligible to participate in the company stock purchase plan.[40] In addition to these programs, the company offered a full array of generous benefits, including a credit union; a wellness program; medical, dental, and vision benefits; income protection; travel discounts; an educational savings plan; and a complete package of life and disability insurance programs.[41]

Operations

SkyWest Inc. had been able to achieve a good reputation for safety and on-time arrivals, due in part to having new aircraft in its fleet and through continual fleet upgrades. However, as noted above, ASA operations had suffered from significant problems, not all of the company's own making. Being worst in the industry for on-time arrivals left a lot of room for improvement.

At the beginning of 2007, SkyWest Inc. was operating its SkyWest and ASA operations as separate companies, although it was seeking to reduce costs in some parts of its operations through combining activities in finance, treasury, information technology, and administrative services to realize economies. The company explained that it maintained separate operations to identify best practices that could be applied to both airlines.

The company performed all routine airframe and engine maintenance and periodic inspection of equipment at its airlines' respective maintenance facilities. The airlines also provided the vast majority of training to both company pilots and maintenance personnel at their training facilities. Nonroutine maintenance was handled through contracts with third parties.[42]

Each of the companies had a reputation for low-cost operations. In 2005, SkyWest Inc. was able to reduce its cost per seat mile (a key measure of airline efficiency) from $0.103 to $0.095—a reduction of 7.8 percent, excluding fuel expenses. See Exhibit 7 for selected operating highlights for 2006.

SkyWest Inc.'s Fleet

At the beginning of January 2007, the airline fielded a fleet of 410 aircraft: a mix of 62 Embraer 120 aircraft, 336 regional jets, and 12 ATR72 aircraft. To facilitate the company's expansion plans and improve efficiencies, SkyWest Airlines and Atlantic Southeast Airlines had combined firm orders to acquire additional aircraft. The new regional aircraft were expected to be more cost-efficient to operate than older models, which was important given the increasing costs of operating aircraft. Exhibit 8 outlines the number of Bombardier regional jets that SkyWest and ASA were scheduled to receive during each of the periods set forth below and the expected size and composition of the company's combined fleet following the receipt of these aircraft.[43]

Exhibit 8   **Scheduled Acquisitions of New Aircraft for SkyWest and Atlantic Southeast Airlines Combined, 2007–2009**

	During the Fiscal Year Ended December 31		
	2007	2008	2009
Additional CRJ200s	0	0	0
Additional CRJ700s	8	0	0
Total Bombardier Regional Jets	344	344	344
Total Brasilia Turboprops	60	59	57
Total ATR-72 Turboprops	0	0	0

Source: SkyWest Inc., 2005 annual report.

Bombardier Regional Jets. The Bombardier regional jets were among the quietest commercial jets available and offered many of the amenities of larger commercial jet aircraft, including flight attendant service, a stand-up cabin, overhead and underseat storage, lavatories, and in-flight snack and beverage service. The speed of Bombardier regional jets was comparable to larger aircraft operated by the major airlines, and the jets had a range of approximately 1,600 miles. However, because of their smaller size and efficient design, the per-flight cost of operating a Bombardier regional jet was generally less than that of a 120-seat or larger jet aircraft.

Brasilia Turboprops. The Brasilia turboprops were pressurized 30-seat airplanes designed to operate more economically over short-haul routes than larger jet aircraft. These factors made it economically feasible for SkyWest to provide high-frequency service in markets with relatively low volumes of passenger traffic. Passenger comfort features of the Brasilia turboprops included stand-up headroom, a lavatory, overhead baggage compartments, and flight attendant service. The company expected that Delta and United would want them to continue to operate Brasilia turboprops in markets where passenger load and other factors made the operation of a Bombardier regional jet impractical. As of December 31, 2005, SkyWest operated 62 Brasilia turboprops out of Los Angeles, San Francisco, Salt Lake City, Seattle/Tacoma, and Portland. SkyWest's Brasilia turboprops were generally used in its California markets, which were characterized by high-frequency service on shorter stage lengths.[44]

Growth

SkyWest Inc. had sought growth through the expansion of its current partnerships, geographic growth, through the acquisition of Atlantic Southeast Airlines in 2005, and through the pursuit of new partnerships such as that with Midwest Airlines. These activities had greatly expanded its scope of operations by adding regional jets to its fleet and an anticipated $1 billion to operations. Previously, SkyWest Inc. was mostly based in the western U.S. and had little presence on the East Coast. The acquisition of ASA gave SkyWest Inc. access to the East Coast markets and comprehensive national coverage. It put the company in a better position to serve more routes as they became available from the major airlines. SkyWest Inc. had operated a few routes for Continental in the past, and had expressed an interest in capturing more contracts with the airline in the future. The company had also made some overtures into establishing partnerships with low-cost carriers such as Southwest and Jet Blue, but as yet it had not been successful in attracting business from these two carriers.

The Chapter 11 filings of United and Delta created growth opportunities for SkyWest Inc. as the majors began to outsource more of their routes during the restructuring of their operations. However, the bankruptcies also created risk because of the company's dependence on the airlines.[45] The new contract with Midwest airlines was considered to be a strategic step toward diversifying the company's operations and risk. The company was expected to attempt to build on this newest contract to find ways to grow and diversify its operations.

Endnotes

[1]IBIS World, report on industry risk for scheduled domestic air transportation in the United States, December 30, 2006.

[2]Energy Intelligence Group, "Market Forces: Airlines' Fortunes Look Up," LexisNexis (accessed January 1, 2007).

[3]International Air Transport Association (IATA), "New Financial Forecast," December 2006, www.iata.org/economics (accessed January 5, 2006).

[4]Investopedia.com, "The Industry Handbook—the Airline Industry," www.investopedia.com/features/industryhandbook/airline.asp (accessed January 5, 2007); and SkyWest Inc., 2005 annual report.

[5]SkyWest Inc., news releases dated January 15, 2007, and February 7, 2007.

[6]United Web site, press releases dated February 1, 2006, and July 31, 2006.

[7]James Bernstein, "Industry Analyst Sees More Airline Consolidations on the Radar as Carriers Try to Stay Competitive; Flight Pattern Is Merger," *Newsday*, December 14, 2006.

[8]Susan Carey, "Earnings Digest—Airlines: Return to Profit Has Wings after Massive Losses; Spoilers Could Emerge amid Fragile Recovery; the Merger 'Wild Card,'" *Wall Street Journal*, January 2, 2007, p. C5.

[9]Investopedia.com, "The Industry Handbook."

[10]"Airlines Troubled by DOT's Proposed Oxygen Rules," *Regional Aviation News*, September 25, 2005, p.1.

[11]Investopedia.com, "The Industry Handbook."

[12]Energy Intelligence Group, "Market Forces."

[13]Investopedia.com, "The Industry Handbook."

[14]NPR Radio, "Airline Outlook Improves, While Uncertainties Remain," *Morning Edition*, November 16, 2006.

[15]Roger Cohen, president of Regional Airline Association, letter to the editor, *Wall Street Journal*, January 2, 2007, posted on the RAA Web site (accessed January 3, 2007).

[16]"Regional Airline," Wikipedia.com, http://en.wikipedia.org/wiki/Regional_airline (accessed January 3, 2007).

[17]Scott McCarthy, "The Middle Seat: Flying Gets Rough on Regional Airlines," *Wall Street Journal*, January 2, 2007, p. D.1; and Roger Cohen, letter to the editor.

[18]Mesaba Airlines Web site (accessed January 2, 2007).

[19]Stan Choe, "Regional Airlines May Suffer in Mergers," Forbes.com, December 15, 2006, www.forbes.com/feeds/ap/2006/12/15/ap3259544.html (accessed January 5, 2007).

[20]SkyWest Inc., 2005 annual report, p. 6.

[21]MAIR Holdings Inc., 2006 annual report.

[22]Mesaba Airlines Web site (accessed January 2, 2007).

[23]Ibid.

[24]"Big Sky Airlines," Wikipedia.com, http://en.wikipedia.org/wiki/Big_Sky_Airlines (accessed January 2, 2007).

[25]Mesa Air Group Inc. Web site (accessed January 1, 2007).

[26]"Republic Airlines Extends Deal with U.S. Airways," *Inside Indiana Business with Gerry Dick*, radio show broadcast July 24, 2006, www.insideindianabusiness.com (accessed January 5, 2007).

[27]ExpressJet Holdings Web site (accessed January 4, 2007).

[28]Pinnacle Corporation Web site, press release, December 21, 2006.

[29]SkyWest Inc. Web site (accessed January 1, 2007).

[30]"SkyWest Airlines Continues Coast to Coast Expansion," Yahoo! Finance, December 27, 2006, http://biz.yahoo.com/prnews/061227/law038.html?.v=88 (accessed January 5, 2007).

[31]SkyWest Inc., 2005 annual report.

[32]Atlantic Southeast Airlines Web site (accessed January 2, 2007).

[33]Ibid.

[34]SkyWest Inc., 2005 annual report, pp. 8–9.

[35]Ibid., p. 9.

[36]Ibid.

[37]Ibid., pp. 9–10.

[38]Sky West Inc., news release, December 21, 2006, retrieved from company Web site (accessed January 3, 2007).

[39]"SkyWest Airlines Plans 4,000 More Hires in 2007," *Longview (Washington) Daily News*, December 29, 2007, www.tdn.com/articles/2006/12/29/biz/news04.txt (accessed January 5, 2007).

[40]SkyWest Inc., 2005 annual report, p. 61.

[41]SkyWest Inc. Web site (accessed January 2, 2007).

[42]SkyWest Inc., 2005 annual report, p. 11.

[43]Ibid., p. 23.

[44]Ibid.

[45]Ibid., p. 15.

Competition in Video Game Consoles: Sony, Microsoft, and Nintendo Battle for Supremacy

John E. Gamble
University of South Alabama

About 250 to 300 million people worldwide played video games in 2007. Historically, games were typically played by preteens, teens, and young adults, but by 2005 the average game player age had increased to 33, and 25 percent of gamers were over age 50. In 2000, only 13 percent of gamers were over age 50. In addition to video games appealing to a broader demographic base, gamers were spending more time playing video games. In 2003, the average American was said to spend 75 hours annually playing video games, which was more than double the amount of time spent playing video games in 1997.

More than $35 billion was spent on video game consoles, game software, handheld game devices, mobile games, and online games in 2005. Next-generation consoles launched by Microsoft in November 2005 and by Nintendo and Sony in November 2006 were expected to drive video game–related sales to more than $51 billion by 2010—see Exhibit 1. Sony's PlayStation 3, Microsoft's Xbox 360, and Nintendo's Wii were all equipped with powerful microprocessors, hard drives, Internet connectivity, and high-definition (HD) resolution graphics, giving them new capabilities and visual effects that were expected to spur sufficient interest in video games by traditional gamers and current nongamers to drive sales of video game consoles from $3.9 billion in 2005 to $5.8 billion in 2010.

In 2007, Nintendo, Sony, and Microsoft were locked into a fierce battle for control of the projected $5.8 billion pie. Each company used differing business models to generate revenues and profits and varying strategies to try to build competitive advantage in the marketplace. With the next-generation battle video game hardware in full swing in 2007, the early results made it unclear who the eventual winner might be. Microsoft's one-year head start with next-generation technology gave it an installed base of more than 10 million Xbox 360 units by January 2007, while Sony's installed base of PlayStation 3 units stood at just over 2 million units. Nintendo had been able to sell more than 3 million Wii video game consoles between November 2006 and January 2007. Some analysts believed that Microsoft could sustain its first-mover advantage and achieve a market-leading position by 2011. Others were convinced that Sony's 100-million-plus dedicated PlayStation 2 owners would eventually migrate to the PlayStation 3—giving it another 100-million-unit-selling console by 2012. It was unclear how appealing Nintendo's Wii would prove among video game players, but the Wii was the winner of the 2006 holiday season sales battle. In fact, the combined sales of the Wii and Nintendo's handheld DS and Game Boy Advance systems allowed Nintendo to account for 55 percent of all video game sales during the 2006 holiday gift-buying season. There was some thought that the Wii's innovative wireless wand controller would prove to be a fad and the battle would ultimately be between Microsoft and Sony. With the next-generation battle already fierce, but only into its first months, there was ample opportunity for additional maneuvering by all three rivals.

Exhibit 1   **Size of the Global Video Games Market, by Sector, 2000, 2003, and 2005, with Projections for 2010 ($ in millions)**

	2000	2003	2005	2010
Console hardware	$ 4,791	$ 6,047	$ 3,894	$ 5,771
Console software (both sales and rentals)	9,451	16,449	13,055	17,164
Handheld hardware	1,945	1,501	3,855	1,715
Handheld software (both sales and rentals)	2,872	2,238	4,829	3,113
PC software (both sales and rentals)	5,077	3,806	4,313	2,955
Broadband	70	497	1,944	6,352
Interactive TV	81	249	786	3,037
Mobile	65	587	2,572	11,186
Total	$24,352	$31,370	$35,248	$51,292

Source: Informa Telecoms & Media, "Games Market to Score Big in 2007," press release, October 24, 2005, and "Game Industry Boom Continues," press release, July 24, 2003, both at www.informamedia.com (accessed September 8, 2006).

HISTORY OF VIDEO GAME SYSTEMS

The development of video games began as early as 1947 when engineers working on television projects began to tinker with programs to play simple games using cathode ray tubes. Two noteworthy developments were the creation of Tennis for Two by Brookhaven National Laboratory researcher William A. Higinbotham in 1958 and the invention of Spacewar in 1962 by a trio of Massachusetts Institute of Technology graduate students. Ralph Baer, an engineer at Loral, filed the first patent for a video game in 1968, which led to the development of the Magnavox Odyssey. The Odyssey video game system, introduced to U.S. consumers in 1972, allowed users to play such games as table tennis, hockey, shooting gallery, and football on their black-and-white televisions. The graphics were limited to white lines, dots, and dashes projected on the picture tube, so Magnavox provided users with color transparencies to place on their TV screens to provide the appropriate background for each game. The Odyssey system sold approximately 350,000 units by 1975.

The introduction of Pong, an arcade game produced by Atari, was another key video game launch that occurred in 1972. Atari developed a Pong system for televisions in 1975, but its 1977 launch of the Atari 2600 was the first home game system to achieve success in the marketplace. The Atari 2600 offered full-color output, sound, and cartridge-based games such as Space Invaders. Atari eventually sold more than 30 million 2600 game systems.

By 1983, consumers had tired of simple arcade-type games and, for all practical purposes, the industry was dying. Nintendo rescued the video game industry in 1985 with its introduction of its Nintendo Entertainment System (NES), which was bundled with the soon-to-be ubiquitous Super Mario Brothers video game. Nintendo sold 61.9 million NES systems before its 1991 introduction of the Super NES. Nintendo built on the success of the NES with the launch of the Game Boy handheld model, which allowed users to take their games outside the home. Nearly 120 million Game Boy units had been sold by 2001. Nintendo's ability to resurrect the industry with innovative game systems created a competitive, technology-driven industry environment that remained prevalent into 2007. Exhibit 2 presents a brief description of key video game systems along with their launch prices and number of units sold.

OVERVIEW OF THE GLOBAL MARKET FOR VIDEO GAME CONSOLES

The dramatic increase in the amount of time consumers spent playing video games during the late 1990s and early 2000s was primarily attributable to the improved capabilities of game consoles launched at the turn of the 21st century. The processing capabilities of the Sony PlayStation 2, in particular, allowed game developers to create complex games that were presented at a high screen resolution. Sports games such as NCAA Football, racing games such as Need for

Exhibit 2   **Selected Information for the Best-Selling Video Game Hardware Systems, 1972–2006**

Launch Date	Manufacturer	System Name	Launch Price	Key Features	Units Sold
1972	Magnavox	Odyssey	$100	Black-and-white display, color overlays	350,000
November 1977	Atari	Atari 2600	$200	Color output, sound, cartridge-based games	30 million
October 1985	Nintendo	NES	$199	8-bit processor	61.9 million
August 1989	Sega Enterprises	Sega Genesis	$200	16-bit processor	13 million
August 1989	Nintendo	Game Boy	$109	Handheld system	118.7 million
August 1991	Nintendo	Super NES	$199	16-bit processor	49.1 million
April 1995	Sega Enterprises	Sega Saturn	$399	32-bit processor	1.4 million
September 1995	Sony Computer Entertainment	PlayStation	$299	32-bit processor	102.5 million
September 1996	Nintendo	Nintendo 64	$199	64-bit processor	32.9 million
September 1999	Sega Enterprises	Sega Dreamcast	$199	200 MHz processor, 3D graphics	8.2 million
October 2000	Sony Computer Entertainment	PlayStation 2	$299	294 MHz processor, DVD, backward compatibility with PS One	106.2 million as of December 2006
June 2001	Nintendo	Game Boy Advance	$100	Handheld system, 32-bit processor, 32,000 color video resolution	75.8 million as of December 2006
November 2001	Microsoft	Xbox	$299	733 MHz processor, hard drive, Ethernet port	24 million
November 2001	Nintendo	GameCube	$199	485 MHz processor	20.9 million as of December 2006
November 2004	Nintendo	Nintendo DS/DS Lite	$199	Hand-held system, Wi-Fi connection, touchpad	21.3 million as of December 2006
March 2005	Sony	PlayStation Portable	$249	Hand-held system, 333-MHz processor, 3D graphics, music and movie playback	20 million as of December 2006
November 2005	Microsoft	Xbox 360	$299–$399	3.2 GHz processor, 500 MHz graphics card, Wi-Fi, 1080p HD resolution, 12x DVD, wireless controllers ($399 version only), 20 GB hard drive ($399 version only)	10.4 million as of December 2006
November 2006	Sony	PlayStation 3	$499–$599	3.2 GHz processor, 550 MHz graphics card, Wi-Fi ($599 version only), 1080p HD resolution, Blu-ray optical drive, wireless controllers, 20 or 60 GB hard drive	1.8 million as of December 2006
November 2006	Nintendo	Wii	$249	729 MHz processor, 243 MHz graphics card, Wi-Fi, 512 MB embedded flash memory, motion sensitive wireless controllers	3.2 million as of December 2006

Source: www.businessweek.com (accessed March 1, 2007).

Speed, and shooter games like Call of Duty provided game players with high levels of interaction and backgrounds that were surprisingly realistic looking compared to early video game systems.

The sale of game systems and software tended to decline as the installed base grew and consumers had purchased most "must-have" titles. Industry sales slowed considerably between 2003 and 2005 as gamers postponed purchases until the eagerly awaited Xbox 360, PlayStation 3, and Wii became available. With sales of game software, hardware accessories, and online games expected to exceed $50 billion in 2010, spending on video game hardware and software was projected to account for a larger share of U.S. consumers' entertainment dollars than the motion picture industry. In 2005, U.S. sales of video game hardware exceeded $10 billion, while Americans spent approximately $9 billion at movie theater box offices.

COMPETITION AMONG THE MAKERS OF VIDEO GAME CONSOLES

Technological leadership in computing power and graphics rendering were critical competitive capabilities needed in the console segment of the video game industry. However, such capabilities did not guarantee success in the industry. Sega consistently beat Nintendo and Sony to the market with next-generation computing capabilities but was unable to achieve success and eventually withdrew from the console market in 2001. Sonic the Hedgehog had been Sega's only legitimate "hit" game title, which was not enough incentive for gamers to abandon their Nintendo or Sony systems. With Sega's installed base failing to grow, game software developers focused their efforts on Nintendo and Sony. The small number of new game titles becoming available for Sega's systems further compounded its problems in the marketplace. A survey of 16,670 players of video games conducted by the NPD Group found that, for 87 percent of survey respondents, "appealing game titles" was the single most important feature in choosing a game system.[1]

With the availability of intriguing games so important to gaining sales and increasing the installed base of consoles, Nintendo and, to a lesser extent, Microsoft had established internal game development capabilities. In fact, Nintendo's most popular game titles, including Mario Brothers, Pokémon, and Donkey Kong, had been developed by the company's own software development teams. Software operating profit margins that ranged from 35 to 40 percent had been a consistent contributor to Nintendo's profitability. Independent game publishers such as Electronic Arts, Activision, Take Two Interactive, THQ, Square Enix, Capcom, Atari, and Sega paid console makers royalties on each software copy sold. Independent game publishers tended to spend the lion's share, if not all, of game development budgets on new games for video game consoles with a large installed base and continuing sales growth; consequently, there were far fewer games developed for slow-selling video game systems than was the case for the best-selling consoles.

In addition to cooperative relationships with independent game publishers, makers of video game consoles were also required to collaborate with microprocessor and graphics accelerator producers to develop next-generation game systems. None of the established console manufacturers had the capability to produce all components needed for the assembly of game consoles—especially technologically advanced core components. In developing the PlayStation 3, Xbox 360, and Wii consoles that were launched in 2005 and 2006, Microsoft, Nintendo, and Sony each allied with IBM in the development of the console microprocessor. In all three cases, IBM and the console maker began with standard PowerPC microprocessor technology but customized the microprocessor to perform the complex calculations needed to run game software. The processing tasks needed to run video game software were much different from the processing tasks executed when running productivity software. All three companies maintained similar relationships with makers of graphics processing units (GPUs) to develop the technological capabilities to display HD-quality graphics and 3D effects. Companies such as Nvidia frequently co-developed graphics chips for more than one of the three console makers.

PC manufacturers also collaborated with microprocessor and GPU manufacturers to build computers capable of running 3D and HD video games. AMD's four core, or "brain," microprocessors were developed to perform tasks similar to what the nine-brain PowerPC chip used in the PlayStation 3 could do. Intel released its Core 2 Extreme microprocessor in 2006, which allowed gamers to play processing-intense games on personal computers (PCs). In 2007,

AMD was developing an eight-core microprocessor that would allow extreme gamers to simultaneously play the most graphically intense video game, burn a DVD, download an HD movie, and make a Voice over Internet Protocol (VoIP) telephone call. The Mach V PC marketed by boutique computer maker Falcon Northeast used two gigabytes of memory, an Intel Core 2 Extreme CPU, and a $600 Nvidia 3D GPU to perform such multiple tasks. The Mach V sold for $16,000 and included a 30-inch LCD display and a wireless keyboard and mouse. Dell Inc., the world's leading manufacturer of desktop and laptop computers in 2006, was broadening its product line to include PC models with advanced graphics, wide-screen displays, and multiple processors that greatly enhanced the online gaming experience. Michael Dell believed that Microsoft's new Vista operating system was a great platform for gamers, and Dell Inc. had an advanced technology group working with game developers to explore how to make the PC the best platform for gaming.

Competition in the industry also mandated that game console manufacturers to establish relationships with such value chain allies as discounters, electronics retailers, and toy stores. Big-box retailers such as Wal-Mart, Target, Best Buy, Circuit City, Toys "R" Us, and specialty retailers like Gamestop dedicated ample square footage to video game systems, accessories, and software. There was little price competition among retailers in the sale of video game consoles and software. More price competition at the retailer level was found with video game accessories—especially accessories manufactured and marketed by third parties. Sony, Nintendo, or Microsoft accessories tended to sell at comparable price points across retailers.

Changes in the Competitive Landscape

Console Technology.   Future generations of game systems would undoubtedly include even more impressive technological capabilities than the next-generation consoles launched in 2005 and 2006. Jen-Hsun Huang, CEO of graphic accelerator maker Nvidia, believed there was ample opportunity for higher levels of photorealism in video games since no console was yet able to deliver the industry's aspirational "Toy Story standard."[2] Huang believed the industry was still "a good solid 10 years away from photorealism" and summarized the industry's innovation focus by commenting:

In the next several years, we will still just be learning to do the basics of film, like motion, blur, depth of field—all of that stuff alone chews up a lot of graphics processing. We're pretty excited about moving to high-dynamic range where the color system has the fidelity of what we see in real life. The images don't seem realistic yet. Articulating a human form and human animation, the subtleties of humans and nature, are still quite a ways away for us.[3]

Online Gaming.   The manner in which video game software would be delivered to gamers was also set for change. The addition of Ethernet ports and Wi-Fi cards to video game consoles, coupled with the increased percentage of homes with broadband access, had given rise to online games. As shown in Exhibit 1, online game-playing via broadband connections was expected to constitute a $6.4 billion market worldwide by 2010, up from $1.9 billion in 2005. However, most online game revenue was expected to come from PC gamers, with only about 25 percent of online game subscription revenues in 2010 coming games played on consoles. Even though online games were expected to grow dramatically, DFC Intelligence expected that by 2011 less than 25 percent those owning consoles capable of playing online games would actually subscribe to an online game service.[4]

Mobile Gaming.   Historically, Nintendo's handheld devices had been the dominant leaders in the mobile video game player market segment. The company sold nearly 120 million Game Boy systems between 1989 and 2001. Nintendo introduced the Game Boy Advance in 2001, which was succeeded by the Nintendo DS. Going into 2007, Nintendo had sold more than 75 million Game Boy Advance players, 330 million Game Boy Advance game cartridges, 21 million Nintendo DS devices, and over 60 million games for Nintendo DS models. Sony entered the handheld/mobile gaming segment in 2005 with its PlayStation Portable (PSP), quickly becoming an important market contender, with worldwide sales approaching 20 million units by year-end 2006. Despite the historical popularity of traditional handheld devices (Game Boy, Nintendo DS, and PSP) for game playing, the market for games software for such devices was expected to be stagnant, with projected sales of only $3.1 billion for gaming software on handheld sets in 2010 versus $4.8 billion in 2005.

However, mobile gaming on cellular phones and other wireless devices was expected to explode from a $2.6 billion market in 2005 to a $11.2 billion market in 2010 (see Exhibit 1). In the fall of 2006, Apple announced that it was launching video games for its fifth-generation iPod models, with the games being downloadable directly from Apple's iTunes store. (Buyers of these iPod models could also download over 75 movies and 220 TV shows from iTunes.)

Mobile gaming was a fast-developing market segment because advancing technology made it possible to incorporate high-resolution color displays, greater processing power, and improved audio capabilities on cellular handsets, iPods and other brands of MP3 players, and other sophisticated handheld devices (including those designed just for playing video games). There were over 1.5 billion cell phones in active operation across the world (about 35 percent of which were game enabled), and new models with enhanced game-playing capability were selling briskly—most cell phone users, intrigued by the new features of next-generation models, upgraded their phones every few years. While playing video games on handheld devices had historically been a favorite pastime of preteens and teenagers, the popularity of game-capable cell phones, iPods, and other sophisticated handheld devices was expected to spur increases in mobile gaming among the young adult population worldwide in the years ahead.

THE THREE MAIN CONTENDERS IN VIDEO GAME CONSOLES: MICROSOFT, SONY, AND NINTENDO

In 2007, there were only six leading video game consoles that had enough global market visibility and appeal to generate large-volume sales of new units: Microsoft's Xbox 360; Sony's PlayStation 3 and handheld PSP; and Nintendo's Wii, Game Boy Advance, and DS/DS Lite. The makers of all the other game consoles were niche players for the most part. And, significantly, Microsoft, Sony, and Nintendo each had a differing history in the video game industry and differing competitive approaches.

Microsoft

In the 30 years since its founding in 1976, Microsoft had become the most important software company in the world through the development and sale of

such omnipresent software packages as Windows, Word, Excel, PowerPoint, and Internet Explorer. In 2006, Microsoft's software business, software consulting services business, online MSN service, and entertainment and devices division contributed to total revenues of $44.3 billion and net earnings of $12.6 billion. Microsoft spent almost 15 percent of its revenues on research and development activities in 2006 to ensure its future products offered levels of innovation and functionality necessary to sustain its advantage in the technology sector.

Microsoft's Home and Entertainment Division. Microsoft entered the video console industry in November 2001 with the introduction of the Xbox system, which was the industry's most technologically advanced game console until the November 2005 launch of the Xbox 360. The original Xbox sold 24 million units by 2006. The company's home and entertainment division included the Xbox 360 business and other such products and services as Xbox Live, video game software, Encarta learning products, PC keyboards and mice, and Internet Protocol Television (IPTV). Microsoft's IPTV venture sought to change the delivery of television programming such that viewers could use broadband access and their home computers (or an Xbox 360) to watch TV broadcasts, on-demand programming, or archived episodes of classic TV series.

Revenues and operating losses for the division between 2004 and 2006 are shown in the following table:

	2006	2005	2004
Revenue (in millions)	$ 4,256	$3,140	$ 2,737
Operating Loss (in millions)	$(1,262)	$ (485)	$(1,337)

Source: Microsoft 2006 annual report.

Revenue increases in 2006 were a result of the sale of 5 million Xbox 360 consoles during fiscal 2006, the popularity of Microsoft PC game titles such as Age of Empires III, and an increase in revenues from IPTV. The division's operating loss in 2006 was largely the result of a $1.64 billion increase in cost related to Xbox 360 production and the development of Halo 2. The division's relatively small operating loss in 2005 resulted from declining Xbox production costs and an increase in the sale of high-margin video games for the Xbox. Microsoft discontinued the sale of Xbox units once the Xbox 360 was in production and Xbox inventory was cleared. The company expected the division's operating loss in future years to decline as Xbox 360 production costs became lower and as the volume of video game software for the Xbox 360 increased.

The Xbox 360. Microsoft contracted its manufacturing activities for its game consoles and video game disks to third parties in Asia. The company had multiple sources for the commodity-like components used in the production of the Xbox 360, but it used single sources for core components. The company purchased all microprocessors from IBM, all GPUs from Taiwan Semiconductor Manufacturing Company, and all memory chips from NEC Corporation. Microsoft expected the life cycle for the Xbox 360 to reach five to seven years.

Upon its release, video game industry analysts were quite satisfied with the Xbox 360's capabilities. The Xbox 360's HD graphics impressed many, as did its ease of use. Reviewers were also very pleased with game titles that accompanied the Xbox 360 launch and Microsoft's Xbox Live Arcade games, which could be played over the Internet. Analysts were particularly struck by Xbox 360 games that had been co-developed by Microsoft Game Studios and proven Hollywood screenwriters, directors, and producers. A full list of Xbox 360 features is presented in Exhibit 3.

The November 2005 Xbox 360 launch came one year earlier than the release of next-generation consoles by Sony and Nintendo. The one-year lead in technology gave Microsoft a temporary advantage in building Xbox's installed base and variety of video games. By year-end 2006, more than 160 game titles were available for the Xbox 360. With more than 5 million Xbox 360s installed prior to the launch of the PlayStation 3 or Wii, third-party game developers had little choice but to develop games for the Xbox 360. Gamers were unlikely to buy new software for current-generation consoles once they began to anticipate the launch of a new-generation system. With the exception of annually updated games like Tiger Woods 2007, there was little point in developing new games for the PlayStation 2 or GameCube in 2005 and 2006.

Xbox Live. Microsoft's one-year head start in making its next-generation console available also helped it build traffic to its Xbox Live Web site. Xbox Live provided Xbox users having broadband access the capability to play online games, chat, watch game trailers, demo new game titles, maintain a profile, participate in forums, download television programming and movies, and access massively multiplayer online games (MMOGs). Xbox Live generated revenue from advertising, subscription fees to its premium-level Xbox Live Gold, movie and television program download fees, and download fees charged to Xbox Silver members. Counting the complimentary Xbox Silver memberships, Xbox Live had approximately 6 million registered users by March 2007. The company found that approximately 25 percent of Xbox Silver members purchased the full version of free demo versions of new games.

In late 2006, Microsoft was testing a cross-platform version of Xbox Live called Xbox Live Anywhere that would allow users to play Xbox games from Xbox consoles, cell phones, handheld systems, or PCs. Some industry analysts believed that revenue gains from a cross-platform online gaming site would be limited since surveys had shown that only 18 percent of all gamers play games on consoles, cell phones, handheld systems, and PCs. Of that 18 percent, only 31 percent were interested in cross-platform play. However, 40 percent of gamers who regularly played games on both PCs and console systems were highly interested in cross-platform play.[5] As of March 2007, Microsoft had not made a formal announcement about its plans for Xbox Live Anywhere. Even if Microsoft did not go forward with a launch of Xbox Live Anywhere, PC users using Microsoft's Vista operating system would be able to connect to Xbox Live to play video games.

The addition of downloadable television programs and motion pictures to Xbox Live had the potential to change how Xbox 360 consoles were used. Xbox 360 owners could download TV shows and movies onto their hard drives from Xbox Live's 1,000-hour library of programming for on-demand viewing at a later time. Xbox Live offered movie downloads from Paramount, Lionsgate, and Warner Bros., as well as selected television programming from all major networks and cable channels. Programming pricing was based on usage of points purchased online at Xbox Live or through Xbox 360 retailers. In March 2007, a 1,000-point card sold for $12.50, while a 1,600-point card sold for $19.50. The price of a standard-definition television program download was 160 points. HD programs sold for 240 points. Microsoft charged Xbox Live users 320 points for standard-definition movie downloads and 360 points for downloads of HD movies.

Exhibit 3 **Comparative Features of Microsoft Xbox 360, Sony PlayStation 3, and Nintendo Wii**

	Xbox 360	PlayStation 3	Wii
U.S. launch date	May 12, 2005	November 17, 2006	November 19, 2006
Price	$299—core system $399—premium system	$499—20 GB version $599—60 GB version	$249
Microprocessor	3.2 GHz IBM PowerPC	3.2 GHz IBM PowerPC	729 MHz IBM PowerPC
Graphics processor	ATI 500 MHz	RSX 550 MHz	ATI 243 MHz
Video resolution	720 p, 1080i, 1080p	480i, 480p, 720p, 1080i, 1080p	480p
System memory	512 MB (shared with video)	256 MB dedicated	64 MB (shared with video)
Video memory	512 MB (shared with system)	256 MB dedicated	64 MB (shared with system)
Optical drive	12x DVD; optional HD-DVD priced at $199	Blu-ray HD	DVD available on models produced after late 2007
Storage/hard drive	64 MB memory card with core system; 20 GB hard drive with premium system	20 GB or 60 GB hard drive	512 MB embedded flash memory
Ethernet port	Yes	Yes	Optional Ethernet adapter priced at $29
Wireless networking	Wi-Fi	Wi-Fi available on 60 GB version only	Wi-Fi
Controllers	Wired controller with core system; wireless with premium system	Bluetooth wireless controller w/limited motion-sensing capabilities	Bluetooth wireless full motion-sensing controller
Online services	Free Xbox Live Silver service including online gaming and voice chat and text messaging; Premium Xbox Live service at $49/year; downloadable full-length movies and television programming starting at $2 per download	Web browser; Free PlayStation online gaming Network service providing game demos and game add-ons; online Sony store	Wii Network includes online shopping, weather, news, Web browsing, and e-mail, instant messaging
Game prices	$40–$60	$50–$60	$30–$50
Compatibility with previous generations	Compatible with approximately 300 Xbox titles	Compatible with most PlayStation 2 and PlayStation titles	Compatible with all GameCube titles; online access to titles originally released for Nintendo 64, SNES, NES, Sega Genesis, and TurboGrafx consoles

Sources: Product information published at www.gamestop.com, www.circuitcity.com, www.amazon.com, www.maxconsole.com, www.zdnet.com, and www.biz.gamedaily.com.

The Xbox 360's 20-gigabyte hard drive could store 16 hours of standard definition programs or about 4½ hours of HD programming. Users who deleted programs to free hard drive space were allowed to download previously purchased programs at no charge. Standard-definition programming could be downloaded in minutes, while an HD movie might take hours to download. Even though HD downloads were lengthy, Xbox Live was the only HD programming download service available for televisions in March 2007. Movies downloaded to PCs could be watched only on a PC monitor. Peter Moore, a Microsoft vice president, explained to *The Wall Street Journal* that gaming was the primary selling point for the Xbox 360, but "we look at the console as an entertainment amplifier for the living room."[6]

Marketing. Microsoft used a variety of approaches to market the Xbox 360 and Xbox Live to consumers. The company supported the Xbox 360 with a $150 million ad campaign in fiscal 2007 and regularly entered into promotions to increase awareness of the Xbox 360. In 2006, Microsoft and Burger King agreed to a promotion to made Xbox 360 games available for purchase in Burger King restaurants. Microsoft also established a promotion with the Kellogg Company that placed Xbox-branded green fruit roll-ups on store shelves. In addition, Microsoft provided co-op advertising with its retail partners. During late 2006, Sears ran TV ads that showed a young boy dreaming about playing Xbox 360 games.

Microsoft had also developed highly innovative viral marketing campaigns for the Xbox 360 and its game titles. Viral marketing had proved to be important with gamers since many young consumers did not respond to, and even resented, traditional advertising. One such campaign involved Perfect Dark Zero, an Xbox Live game that relied on users sending links to friends asking them to join in to expand its subscriber base. The viral marketing campaign for Viva Piñata was highly sophisticated. Viva Piñata was Microsoft's attempt at developing a game that might have the same level of appeal with young children that was achieved by Nintendo's Super Mario Brothers and Donkey Kong. The campaign included a new Saturday-morning cartoon based on Viva Piñata characters that aired on Fox Television and a line of electronic action figures produced by Playmates Toys. The Viva Piñata toy could interact with Xbox Live by allowing users to download and upload "special powers" that added to the experience of playing with the toy or playing the video game.

Xbox 360's Early Lead. Some analysts believed that Microsoft had developed a first-mover advantage by beating Nintendo and Sony to market with next-generation technology by a year. In an interview with *BusinessWeek* prior to the launch of the PlayStation 3 and Wii, Kevin Bachus, the former Microsoft executive who originally proposed the Xbox idea to Bill Gates, stated:

> *[The] 360 still has a chance of winning the next-gen battle, but it's far from a certainty. If our industry's brief history has taught us anything it's that there are no set "laws" regarding console adoption—despite what the manufactures might claim. This generation will be decided not on production capabilities or technology, but on brand, price, and content. If Sony can leverage its brand, aggressively cut prices on both hardware and software, and deliver just a few platform-driving franchises as they've done in the past with Final Fantasy, Grand Theft Auto, and others, they can quickly reverse Microsoft's early lead.[7]*

By year-end 2006, Microsoft had sold more than 10.4 million Xbox 360 units, with more than 1.1 million units selling in December alone. By comparison, Sony sold 491,000 PlayStation 3 units in December 2006, while Nintendo sold 604,000 Wii systems. Microsoft expected to sell an additional 2 million units during the first six months of 2007. Microsoft was using its early sales lead to reduce production costs and increase accessories sales to speed profitability. In fact, by November 2006, it was estimated that Microsoft's production costs for the Xbox 360 had fallen to $306 per unit. Microsoft executives expected for the company's entertainment and devices division to become profitable by fiscal 2008. An NPD Group analyst believed that "Xbox is now poised to really take advantage of its lead in this generation's race, provided they (and third-party supporters) keep bringing the games to market that keep consumers wanting to play on that system."[8]

Sony

The Sony Corporation was the world's leading manufacturer and marketer of audio, video, communications, and information technology products, with fiscal 2006 revenues of $64 billion. Sony's video game business contributed $7.8 billion to the company's 2006 total revenues and had generated as much as two-thirds of Sony's total operating profits in past years. However, Sony was confronted with a number of challenges in 2006 and 2007. The company had been unable to capitalize on the exploding growth in digital audio players, was losing market share in the liquid crystal display (LCD) flat-panel TV market, and expected its profits to fall by about 40 percent during fiscal 2007 because of an extensive laptop battery recall and excessive PlayStation 3 development costs and production problems.

Sony's PlayStation and PlayStation 2. Introduced in 1995, the Sony PlayStation was an instant success, selling more than 100,000 units in North America during its first weekend on store shelves. By the PlayStation's six-month anniversary, more than 1 million units had been sold in North America and the company hit the 4 million mark in North America in just over two years. The PlayStation's cutting-edge graphics, CD optical drive, 32-bit processor, and variety of game titles made it much more appealing to adolescents and young adults than Nintendo's Super NES system. Over 100 million PlayStation consoles were eventually sold, which was more than twice the number of Nintendo SNES units sold. By 2001, one in three U.S. households had purchased a PlayStation game console.

Nintendo launched its 64-bit Nintendo 64 console a year after the PlayStation was introduced, but it failed to take a considerable number of sales away from the PlayStation because of Nintendo's limited game categories. While Sony's third-party game developers were creating games that would be appealing to preteens, teenagers, and young adults, Nintendo's game development focus was on smaller children. Because Sony targeted older gamers, it was able to add features to the PlayStation 2 (PS2) that might be difficult for young children to operate. The PS2 was able to play DVDs and could be connected to the Internet with an Ethernet adaptor. The $299 PS2 was powered by a 294-megahertz microprocessor, which was the most powerful game processor until the introduction of the Xbox.

As with the PlayStation, Sony's third-party game developers took advantage of the massive installed base and directed their resources toward developing blockbuster game titles for Sony consoles. Third-party-developed games like Gran Turismo, Final Fantasy, Grand Theft Auto, Madden NFL, Medal of Honor, and Need for Speed were games likely to be found in most game collections. The Sony PS2 was also backward compatible with the game titles that had made the PlayStation a marketplace success. The combination of technological superiority and large number of hit game titles allowed Sony to sell more than 100 million PS2 consoles and achieve a 70 percent worldwide market share in game consoles. Even though Sony introduced the PlayStation

3 in November 2006, it planned to continue producing the PS2. Sony lowered the retail price of the PS2 to $129 in the United States once it began shipping PlayStation 3 consoles.

The Sony PSP. In 2005, Sony challenged Nintendo's dominance in handheld systems with the introduction of the $249 PlayStation Portable (PSP). The PSP used a 333-megahertz microprocessor and a 4.3-inch LCD screen to allow gamers to play 3D games, watch television programs recorded with TiVo, connect to wireless Internet networks, review pictures from digital cameras, listen to MP3s, and watch full-length movies that were available on Universal Media Disc (UMD) minidisks. In addition, up to 16 PSP players in close proximity could connect wirelessly to play multiplayer games. The PSP achieved the status of top-selling handheld game in the United States shortly after its release, but users complained that PSP games were "just rehashes of what you would play on the console."[9] Sony had sold more than 20 million PSP handheld systems by December 2006.

Sony PlayStation 3. Sony hoped to replicate the success of the PlayStation 2 by following a similar strategy with the PlayStation 3. The PlayStation 3 (PS3) was packed with technological features that would allow game developers to create 3D and HD game titles that could exploit the processing power of its 3.2-gigahertz nine-brain processor and Nvidia GPU. (A full list of PlayStation 3 features is presented in Exhibit 3.) The PS3 also had the opportunity to become the central component of a home entertainment system since it included a state-of-the-art Blu-ray HD optical drive and Internet connectivity. Blu-ray was a next-generation DVD drive developed by Sony that could show movies in HD resolution. At the time of the PS3 launch, Sony was in a battle with Toshiba, which had developed a competing HD-DVD player, to become the video disk platform of the future. Clearly, the industry could support only one type of HD disk player. Sony's expectation was that its massive installed base would migrate to the PS3—making it the dominant design in video game consoles and making its Blu-ray drive the industry standard for HD disks.

One of the few flaws evident in Sony's strategy in the first months after the November 2006 launch of the PS3 was the pricing of the console. The PS3 sold at either $499 or $599, depending on hard drive size. Sony's production cost for the PS3 was estimated at $805 for the 20-gigabyte version and $840 for the 60-gigabyte version. The company justified its PS3 pricing by noting the retail price of a Blu-ray player was $1,000. Sony hoped consumers would make the determination that purchasing a PS3 was at least $400 less expensive than purchasing a Blu-ray player and that they would get all of the video game capabilities of the PS3 as an added bonus. Analysts believed that Sony might lose as much as $2 billion on the PS3 in fiscal 2007, but could begin to achieve breakeven on its production costs once about 20 million PS3 units had been sold.

In some ways, the November 2006 launch of the PS3 was a deviation from Sony's intended strategy. Sony had not planned to launch the PS3 when it did, but it was forced into an early launch date because of the November 2005 launch of the Xbox 360 by Microsoft. The PS3 was designed to be backward compatible with more than 16,000 PlayStation and PS2 game titles, but the launch of the system was accompanied by only 24 PS3 game titles. The PS3 had tremendous graphics and processing capabilities, but all of this was not needed to play PS2 games. A PlayStation or PS2 video game was not going to look any better played on a PS3. In addition, the 24 HD games that accompanied the launch did not fully utilize the capabilities of the PS3 since third-party software developers had been forced to shorten their planned development times. Whether or not a consumer owned an HDTV was another consideration that would have to be made before upgrading to a PS3.

Sony was barely able to get the PS3 to market in time for 2006 holiday shopping because of a variety of production problems. Some of its production problems centered on the use of the Blu-ray optical drive. An initial holdup involved the development of copy-protection technology for the Blu-ray drive, which was followed by a problem producing the laser component needed in the assembly of Blu-ray drives. Production problems also affected the PS3's backward compatibility capacity, with many PS2 game titles not working on the PS3 when it was first launched. The cumulative effect of Sony's supply chain and production problems allowed it to ship only an estimated 125,000 to 175,000 units for its North American launch. The company had planned to support the launch with 400,000 units. Sony was

eventually able to ship nearly 500,000 units before the 2006 holiday season ended. However, the production problems continued into 2007, with Sony delaying its European launch of the PS3 until March 2007. Sony expected that 30 PS3 game titles would be available by its European launch.

Another factor that might hinder the sales of PS3 units for some time was the tremendous video game development costs necessary to produce games that could fully utilize the console's capabilities. Even with the PS2, game development costs typically ran $2 to $7 million. Game developers were willing to make such an investment to develop games for the PS2 since a hit could easily sell 5 to 10 million units at $50 per unit. Analysts had projected that game development costs for the PS3 would average $20 million, with some titles requiring much higher investments. Game developers willing to make such an investment based on the PS3's modest installed base of just over 2 million units in early 2007 were taking a huge risk. The president and CEO of game developer THQ commented in November 2006: "Using a crack development team to only sell a few hundred thousand units is not a good use of resources."[10]

With new game titles arriving to the market slowly, Sony could not rely on its PlayStation Network to satisfy the gaming expectations of consumers. Most video game industry analysts found the site's online games to be very limited and no match for Xbox Live. However, the PlayStation Network did offer users free access to a limited number of multiplayer online games and text, voice, and video chat. The combination of the PS3's high price, limited game titles, limited production, and uninspiring online experience made the PS2 its strongest competing game console during late 2006 and early 2007. During the 2006 holiday season, 1.4 million PS2s were sold in the United States, compared to 1.1 million Xbox 360s, 604,000 Nintendo Wii consoles, and 491,000 PS3 systems. Analysts expected that Sony would sell 11 million PS2s in 2007 and the PS2 would continue to outsell the PS3 through 2008. Even given its problems, the Sony PS3 hit the 2 million sales mark in fewer months than the PlayStation or the PlayStation 2.

Nintendo

The playing card manufacturer founded in 1889 in Kyoto, Japan, eventually became known as the Nintendo Company Ltd. in 1963 when it expanded outside playing cards to other types of games. The company had produced electronic toys as early as 1970, but its 1981 introduction of a coin-operated video game called Donkey Kong transformed the company into a household name in North America, Asia, and Europe. By 2007, Nintendo had sold more than 387 million game consoles and 2.2 billion video games worldwide. In the United States, one in four households had a Nintendo game system of one generation or another.

In fiscal 2006, Nintendo recorded revenues of $4.3 billion and earned profits of $840 million through the sale of Nintendo game systems and video game software. The company projected fiscal 2007 revenues and earnings of $7.6 billion and $1.0 billion, respectively.

Nintendo's Strategy.   With the company's business limited to the sale of game consoles, handheld game systems, and game software, the company pursued a different strategic approach than that used by Sony and Microsoft. The company focused on earning profits from the sale of game consoles as well as from game software sales. A company senior vice president commented, "We don't have other sister divisions that can underwrite big losses in our area. So we have to be able to get to breakeven, or profitability pretty quickly on the hardware and then the software-tie ratio becomes the icing on that."[11]

Based on that business model, Nintendo had never held a technological advantage in the industry and didn't attempt to battle Sony and Microsoft for the allegiance of hard-core gamers. It had succeeded by developing game systems that were intuitive and easy to operate. Its video games were fun to play but didn't offer a cinematic experience. Nintendo's strategy was well matched to the interests of children and casual gamers. Nintendo's president, Satoru Iwata, explained in the company's annual report, "Nintendo has implemented a strategy which encourages people around the world to play video games regardless of their age, gender or cultural background. Our goal is to expand the gaming population."[12]

The Nintendo GameCube.   At the time of the November 2001 launch of the GameCube system, its processing capabilities were nearly twice as great as that of the PS2 but far less than what the Xbox was capable of performing. The middle-path strategy did not give consumers much of a reason to get excited about the GameCube, since those wanting

cutting-edge graphics might find the Xbox appealing and those enamored with PlayStation's action games were still quite pleased with their PS2s. With no clear point of differentiation, the GameCube was Nintendo's least successful game console in its history—selling just over 20 million units by year-end 2006. Even though the GameCube's successor, the Wii, was introduced in November 2006, the company retained the GameCube in its product line for especially price-sensitive buyers. The GameCube's retail price in early 2007 was $99.99.

Game Boy Advance and DS/DS Lite.   Few in the video game industry anticipated the runaway success of Nintendo's Game Boy handheld system when it was introduced in 1989. Nintendo paired the Game Boy with its new Pokémon video game in 1996, which was accompanied by an animated series and a line of trading cards. With the help of Pokémon, the low-screen-resolution Game Boy player sold nearly 120 million units. Even though the Game Boy had a life cycle of more than a decade, Nintendo kept its appearance fresh by making the handheld game in different colors and eventually adding a color display. Such cosmetic changes to handheld games were critical to sustaining sales since many children thought of the Game Boy as a fashion accessory.

Nintendo's next-generation successor to the Game Boy was the Game Boy Advance. The Game Boy Advance allowed users to play Pokémon and other games on a larger, higher-resolution screen. Nintendo had sold more than 75 million Game Boy Advance units between its June 2001 launch and December 2006. Even though Nintendo launched the DS (a newer-generation handheld system) in November 2004, it continued to offer the Game Boy Advance through 2007 as a low-priced ($79.99) alternative to the Nintendo DS.

The Nintendo DS was developed to appeal to Nintendo's core youth market as well as to such historically nongamers as women and those over age 35. The system included dual screens, a stylus-operated touchpad, voice recognition, and Wi-Fi capabilities to make operation of the system intuitive rather than an exercise in dexterity. The company developed innovative new games for the DS that would appeal to those who were uninterested in first-person shooters or other genres preferred by the PlayStation aficionados. Nintendo DS games such as Nintendogs, which allowed gamers to play with a virtual pet, and

Brain Training for Adults, which asked gamers to solve arithmetic puzzles, weren't very popular with 18- to 30-year-old males, but they were a huge hit with people who had never before shown an interest in video games. Nintendo planned to introduce 20 new game titles during the first quarter of 2007 to appeal to the interests of new gamers and children.

The retail price of the DS was also an aspect of Nintendo's handheld systems attractive to casual gamers. In March 2007, the retail price of the Nintendo DS Lite was $129.99, compared to a retail price of $199.99 for the Sony PSP. The DS Lite was a slightly smaller and more brightly lit successor to the DS. The Nintendo DS Lite had been the top-selling video game system during the 2006 holiday shopping period, with more than 1 million units sold in November alone. In addition, more than 641,000 Game Boy Advance systems were sold in November 2006, which made it the number three best-selling system during the month. The PS2 was the best-selling console and second best-selling system overall, with 664,000 units sold during November 2006.

The Wii. Nintendo followed its game plan used with the Nintendo DS in developing the Wii. As with the DS, Nintendo attempted to develop a game system that would appeal to nongamers—especially moms. Shigeru Miyamoto, a key Wii developer, explained this key consideration to *BusinessWeek* writers in 2006:

> Our goal was to come up with a machine that moms would want—easy to use, quick to start up, not a huge energy drain, and quiet while it was running. Rather than just picking new technology, we thought seriously about what a game console should be. [CEO Satoru] Iwata wanted a console that would play every Nintendo game ever made. Moms would hate it if they had to have several consoles lying around.[13]

His colleague on the development team, Ken'ichiro Ashida, added, "We didn't want wires all over the place, which might anger moms because of the mess."[14]

The development team considered a variety of controller types that could be wireless and intuitive. Nintendo rejected such design inspirations as cell phones, car navigation remotes, and touch panels for a wireless wand. The wand took over one year to develop and was able to respond to hand motions that were used in throwing a ball, casting a fishing line, swinging a baseball bat, or pointing a gun. A separate "nunchuk" device allowed the user to create motion necessary to play games needing two hands. A

Wedbush Morgan Securities analyst commented on the brilliance of the design by pointing out, "With the Wii remote, the learning curve for most games is 15 minutes or less. I think that will eliminate the intimidation factor and will attract a broader audience."[15]

Although Nintendo executives knew early during the development of the Wii that it would be unable to compete with the next-generation consoles soon to be launched by Microsoft and Sony, they believed the wireless wand controller would have appeal with the masses. Reggie Fils-Aime, the president of Nintendo of America explained:

> What makes the Wii so special is obviously the Wii Remote: the ability to play tennis with a flick of the wrist, to play baseball like you do it on the ball field. That allows the consumer to get more in the game by having a totally different type of interface, plus it allows game developers to create all new different types of games. We have everything from a game like "Trauma Center" from Atlas, where you're the doctor, and you're using the precision of the Wii remote to stitch up a patient and take shards of glass out of their arm—things of that nature. The new way to play "Madden Football," a brand new Madden where you act like the quarterback, where you hike the ball, pass. All of that allows for totally unique game play.[16]

Another consideration was creating a game console that would easily fit within the family budget. Miyamoto explained, "Originally, I wanted a machine that would cost $100. My idea was to spend nothing on the console technology so all the money could be spent on improving the interface and software."[17] As a result, Nintendo wound up using a microprocessor, that although was twice as fast as that used in the GameCube, was less powerful that what Microsoft had used in the original Xbox. Also, the Wii contained only a 512 MB flash memory card to store data instead of a hard drive and could not play DVDs. The Wii could connect to the Internet through a wireless home network, but not with an Ethernet cable. A full list of Wii features is presented in Exhibit 3. Analysts believed that, at launch, Nintendo to earn a profit on every Wii console sold because of its modest components costs.

One additional benefit of Nintendo's low-tech approach to a next-generation console was the low relative development costs needed for Wii video games. Analysts expected that on average the development cost for a Wii video game would be less than half of that necessary to develop games for the Xbox 360 or PS3. As a result, game developers were very interested in creating new games for the Wii. Electronic Arts announced six Nintendo Wii titles during a July 2006 industry trade show, while it said little of its plans for new PS3 games. A video game analyst believed developers saw more opportunity for immediate profits from Wii games than those for PS3 and were "holding off on creating games for Sony" until its installed base grew.[18] In addition to new games, Wii users could also access all older games on Nintendo's Wii Connect24 online gaming site. Wii Connect24 also offered a weather channel, news channel, shopping channel, and Web browser. The Wii console also allowed users to view digital pictures stored on an SD memory card and create personalized Mii interfaces for each member of the family.

THE WINNER OF THE BATTLE FOR SUPREMACY: SONY OR MICROSOFT OR NINTENDO?

In early 2007, there were varying opinions about which company would end up as the market leader in video game consoles in 2010—Sony or Microsoft or Nintendo. During the 2006 holiday season, Nintendo had done surprisingly well, capturing a 55 percent market share based on the combined unit sales of the Wii, DS, DS Lite, and Game Boy Advance. In addition, Nintendo sold more than 1.5 million extra controllers for the Wii during the holidays. Buyers of Wii consoles during November–December 2006 purchased, on average, three video game titles for the Wii. Even so, some observers contended that Microsoft had been the winner of the 2006 holiday season since sales of the Xbox 360 exceeded sales of either the PlayStation 3 or the Wii (although only limited supplies of the PS3 and Wii were available during that period since their production was still in the startup phase). By year-end 2006, Microsoft had sold over 10 million units of the Xbox 360, giving it a sizable lead over the PS3 and the Wii in terms of total users.

But whether Microsoft's first-to-market strategy would translate into a sustainable first-mover advantage was debatable. Microsoft had more than 160 game titles available for the Xbox 360, compared to fewer than 30 for the PS3—but a wave of new games for both the PS3 and the Wii were coming to market in 2007. The Wii was no match for the Xbox 360's HD video resolution, but there were indications that its innovative controller had big appeal to a number of ardent game players. There were also analysts who believed that once Sony opted to lower the price of the PS3 (if indeed Sony management did decide to be more price-competitive), it would replicate the success it had achieved with the PlayStation and PS2. Market research firm Strategy Analytics had forecast that Sony would sell more than 100 million PS3 units by 2012, while Microsoft would sell approximately 60 million Xbox 360s and Nintendo would sell a meager 20–25 million Wii consoles. Merrill Lynch analysts foresaw a much closer contest, forecasting that the Microsoft would achieve a 39 percent market share of the video console market by 2011, with Sony at a 34 percent share and Nintendo at 27 percent. According to one analyst, "There will always be a short-term winner, but there's definitely room in the long run for all three."[19]

Endnotes

[1]"Report from The NPD Group Provides Insight into Consumer Purchase Intent of Next Generation Video Game Consoles," *Business Wire*, November 13, 2006.

[2]As quoted in "Nvidia CEO Talks Console War," *BusinessWeek* (online), July 26, 2006.

[3]Ibid.

[4]"Console Makers Online and on Top," *BusinessWeek* (online), April 5, 2006.

[5]As described in "Microsoft Plays It Cool on Games," *BusinessWeek* (online), September 28, 2006.

[6]As quoted in "Coming to Xbox 360: Films and TV," *The Wall Street Journal* (online), November 7, 2006, p. B3.

[7]As quoted in "Kevin Bachus on Next-Gen Console Wars," *BusinessWeek* (online), April 17, 2006.

[8]As quoted in "Report: Sony Sold 490,700 PS3s in U.S.," *AFX International Focus*, January 13, 2007.

[9]As quoted in "In the Game Wars, Nintendo's All Charged Up," *BusinessWeek* (online), July 28, 2006.

[10]As quoted in "Mysteries of the PS3 and Wii Launch Solved!," *CNNMoney* (online), November 9, 2007.

[11]As quoted in "Nintendo Wii Enters Video Game Fray," *Investor's Business Daily*, November 20, 2006, p. A4.

[12]As quoted in Nintendo's 2006 annual report.

[13]As quoted in "The Big Ideas behind Nintendo's Wii," *BusinessWeek* (online), November 16, 2006.

[14]Ibid.

[15]As quoted in "Nintendo Brings the Games to the People," *BusinessWeek* (online), October 31, 2006.

[16]As quoted in "Nintendo's U.S. head: We're Doing Things Right with the New Console," Associated Press State & Local Wire, November 17, 2006.

[17]As quoted in "The Big Ideas behind Nintendo's Wii."

[18]As quoted in "Will Sony's Pricey PS3 Pay Off?," *BusinessWeek* (online), July 20, 2006.

[19]As quoted in "PS3, Wii Get All the Buzz, but Xbox Could Have the Happiest Holidays," *Advertising Age*, October 30, 2006, p. 3.

15

Electronic Arts in 2007: Can It Retain Its Global Lead in Video Game Software?

Arthur A. Thompson
The University of Alabama

With fiscal 2007 sales of $3.1 billion, Electronic Arts (EA) was the world's leading independent developer, publisher, and marketer of video games. It developed games for play on all the leading home video game consoles (Sony's PlayStation 2 and PlayStation 3, Microsoft's Xbox 360, and Nintendo's Wii); wireless phones and handheld devices such as Nintendo's Game Boy Advance and Sony's PlayStation Portable (PSP); personal computers; and Web sites. EA had more ability than any other game publisher to distribute, market, and sell its game titles to consumers all over the world. It had 31 game titles that sold over 1 million units each in fiscal year 2005 and 27 titles that exceeded sales of 1 million units each in fiscal 2006. EA released sequels of its popular sports titles annually—Madden NFL (professional football), NBA Live (professional basketball), FIFA (professional soccer), NCAA Football, and Tiger Woods PGA Tour. When Madden NFL 07 was introduced in August 2006, it sold a record 2 million copies at retail prices of $59.99 a copy in its first week; the new release of NCAA Football 06 sold over 1 million copies in the first week.

In 2003, Lawrence Probst, EA's chairman and CEO, had confidently predicted the company was on course to become the "biggest and best entertainment company in the world" with revenues eventually rivaling those of Disney (2002 revenues of $25.3 billion) and Time Warner (2002 revenues of $42 billion). But EA's revenues had apparently topped out,

having hovered in the $2.8–$3.1 billion range since 2004. Moreover, EA's net profits had suffered for three years running, partly because of changes in the way that consumers purchased and played video games, partly because of a slower-than-expected transition to next-generation video game platforms, and partly because of significantly higher costs to develop new video games. The company's best year on the bottom line had been in its fiscal year ending March 31, 2004, when it reported earnings of $577 million; since then, net profits had fallen to $504 million in fiscal 2005, $236 million in fiscal 2006, and $76 million in the 2007 fiscal year ending March 31, 2007. Nonetheless, Lawrence Probst believed the company's outlook was quite promising despite the rather profound changes under way in the industry; Probst said:

> Transition is never easy and the combination of new technology, new platforms and new markets makes this one particularly complex. Today, EA is investing ahead of revenue in what we believe will be another period of strong and sustained growth for the interactive entertainment industry. No other company is investing in as many strategic areas; no other company has as much opportunity. Our commitment of financial and creative resources is significant, but so is the potential for long-term growth.[1]

Probst and other EA executives believed that high-speed broadband Internet connections and the newly introduced generation of powerful game-playing consoles gave EA the opening it needed to take video games to heights far beyond what consumers could experience with movies and TV entertainment.

THE VIDEO GAME INDUSTRY

In 2005, the video game industry represented a $35 billion global market. The market was expected to mushroom to a record-setting $58 billion in 2007 as (1) video game enthusiasts rushed to purchase Sony's PlayStation 3 (PS3) or Microsoft's Xbox 360 or Nintendo's Wii (pronounced "we") and video games that exploited the powerful capabilities of these new consoles, and (2) as mobile gaming on cell phones and online gaming via broadband took off—see Exhibit 1. The industry consisted of makers of devices that played video games (consoles, handheld players, and arcade machines), game developers who developed games for play on all the various types of game-playing devices, retailers of video game players and video games, and companies that had Web sites for online game play.

Sony, Microsoft, and Nintendo had incorporated faster processing speeds, digital and high-definition graphics capability, online connectivity, and assorted other innovative features that took the playing of video games on their latest generation of consoles to dramatic new heights. Sony's PS3, for instance,

included Blu-ray technology that exploited the full power of high-definition graphics. Nintendo's Wii had a unique controller. Game developers had responded by creating increasingly sophisticated and exotic games that allowed players to compete in a host of sports and racing events, pilot supersonic fighter jets and spacecraft to defend against all manner of enemies, and enter mystical worlds to untangle ancient webs of treachery and deceit. In 2007, there were games covering all genres, games for players of all ages, and games targeted to both hard-core and casual game players.

Retail sales of video game software soared to record levels in the 1990s, with sales that climbed steadily toward $15 billion annually by 2000. From 1985 to 1994, Nintendo and Sega dominated the market for video game consoles, with combined market shares of around 90 percent. The two rivals sparred back and forth in an escalating battle for market leadership in making the platforms or consoles on which most video games were played. Then, in 1995, competitive rivalry in video games took on a new dimension when Sony entered the market with its new PlayStation. Nintendo and Sega, the longtime industry leaders, found themselves in a fierce battle with Sony, and other small-share console makers scrambled to generate enough sales to survive. There was a huge industry shakeout. By 1998, Sony emerged as the undisputed leader worldwide. In the United States, Sony's PlayStation

Exhibit 1   **Size of the Global Video Games Market, by Sector, 2000, 2003, and 2005, with Projections for 2010 ($ in millions)**

	2000	2003	2005	2010
Console hardware	$ 4,791	$ 6,047	$ 3,894	$ 5,771
Console software (both sales and rentals)	9,451	16,449	13,055	17,164
Handheld hardware	1,945	1,501	3,855	1,715
Handheld software (both sales and rentals)	2,872	2,238	4,829	3,113
PC software (both sales and rentals)	5,077	3,806	4,313	2,955
Broadband	70	497	1,944	6,352
Interactive TV	81	249	786	3,037
Mobile	65	587	2,572	11,186
Total	$24,352	$31,370	$35,248	$51,292*

* Note: Industry analysts expected that industrywide sales would reach a peak of $58 million in 2007 (as games players rushed to buy the new PS3, Wii, and Xbox 360) and then taper off to $51.3 million in 2010 as sales of the newly introduced game-playing consoles tapered off.

Source: Informa Telecoms & Media, "Games Market to Score Big in 2007," press release, October 24, 2005, and "Game Industry Boom Continues," press release, July 24, 2003, both at www.informamedia.com (accessed September 8, 2006).

captured a 70 percent market share, with Nintendo at 26 percent and Sega at only 4 percent. All other video console makers faded into oblivion, and Sega, unable to make any headway in regaining lost market share, exited the market for video consoles in 2001 and turned its full attention to developing video games. The entry of Microsoft's Xbox in 2002 made the video console business a fierce three-way contest.

In 2006, Sony was the undisputed global leader in video game hardware, having shipped more than 100 million PlayStation 2 (PS2) units since its launch in 2000; Sony and independent game developers had introduced more than 7,000 titles for the PS2, and more than 1 billion units had been sold as of 2006. During 2001–2005, the PS2 had about a 70 percent share of the console market. Such market acceptance made PS3 the odds-on favorite for Sony to remain the market leader in video game hardware. But despite PS2's market dominance and huge base of installed users, Microsoft's Xbox 360 and Nintendo's Wii were expected to gain market share against the new PS3. For the first time, the three major console platforms were strongly differentiated from one another, as well as from prior-generation platforms. The Xbox 360 was said to have the best online capabilities, the PS3 the best high-definition graphics, and Nintendo's Wii, while lacking the raw graphics power of the PS3 and Xbox 360, had a novel motion-sensitive controller that allowed users to play games by wielding the controller like a tennis racket, sword, gun, or fishing pole.

In 2007, Sony, Microsoft, and Nintendo were waging an intense global battle for market share in video game consoles. Microsoft's Xbox 360 had a solid first-mover advantage, having been introduced in late 2005 (barely in time for the 2005 holiday sales season). Sony's PS3 had been delayed due to various design and production problems and did not hit the market in Japan and the United States until November 2006—and then only in limited numbers (about 1.5 million units); moreover, it retailed at a hefty $599 per console ($410 in Japan), a far higher price than the $250–$300 introduction prices of prior-generation consoles. The PS3 did not launch in Europe until March 2007, so it would be well into 2008 before a big fraction of the 100 million PS2 users would be able to upgrade to PS3 in the event they chose to do so.

Nintendo's strategy with the Wii was to gain market share by pricing the Wii below both the Xbox 360 and the PS3—at around $250 retail in the United States and $213 in Japan; the Wii, introduced in November 2006, was also late to market because of delays in working out bugs and glitches. Microsoft's Xbox 360 retailed for $399.99 in North America, €299 in Europe, and £209.99 in Great Britain; Microsoft was selling a low-end version of the Xbox 360 at about $255 in Japan (along with two free games) to boost flagging sales. Microsoft expected that its shipments of the Xbox 360 would reach 10 million units worldwide by the end of 2006 and 13–15 million units by June 2007; there were some 160 game titles available for the Xbox 360 in August 2006. Nintendo expected to sell 4 million Wiis by year-end 2006, which would give both Nintendo's Wii and Microsoft's Xbox 360 a nice sales lead over Sony's PS3 heading into 2007. Sony's announced pricing for the PS3 had met strong resistance in some quarters, raising questions about whether the high price would hurt the PS3's chances of attracting a wide audience or whether Sony would be forced into making price cuts early on.

Because the three console makers also developed and marketed games for their respective platforms, independent game publishers were said not to want any single console to dominate the market for this latest generation of game players. A more balanced market share distribution among Sony, Microsoft, and Nintendo would weaken the long-standing leverage that platform manufacturers had in demanding sizable royalty payments from game publishers who wanted to create games played on their platforms. Square Enix, an influential Japan-based games developer that heretofore had made only games for PlayStation (including the showcase Final Fantasy series, with worldwide sales of over 68 million units, and the Dragon Quest series, with worldwide sales of over 40 million units), had announced that it would make games for all three of the new consoles. According to a Square Enix executive, "We don't want the PlayStation 3 to be the overwhelming loser, so we want to support them. But we don't want them to be the overwhelming winner either, so we can't support them too much."[2]

Exhibit 2   **Size of the U.S. Market for Video Games, 1996–2005**

Year	Unit Sales*	Dollar Sales
1996	74.1 million	$2.6 billion
1997	108.4	3.7
1998	153.0	4.8
1999	185.2	5.5
2000	197.1	5.6
2001	211.0	6.1
2002	226.4	7.0
2003	241.4	7.1
2004	250.0	7.4
2005	228.5	7.0

* Includes video games played on PCs as well as games played on video game consoles and handheld devices.

Source: U.S. data are from the NPD Group, point-of-sale information, as reported in "Essential Facts about the Computer and Video Game Industry," Entertainment Software Association, www.theesa.com (accessed September 7, 2006).

The Demographics of Video Game Players

About 250 to 300 million people worldwide were very active or frequent players of video games; game enthusiasts usually owned consoles, handheld players, PCs, or game-capable cell phones and spent six or more hours weekly playing video games. The average American was said to spend 75 hours annually playing video games, more than double the amount spent gaming in 1997 and more than was spent watching rented movies on DVDs or videocassettes.[3] The average gamer in the United States spent over 350 hours annually playing video games; hard-core gamers often spent 700 or more hours annually. Perhaps another 100 million people were infrequent or casual players, using arcade machines in malls and other retail locations, their own personal computers (PCs) during idle moments or as a diversion, the consoles and handheld players of friends and acquaintances, or cell phones.

The majority of video game players were preteens, teenagers, and young adults (those between the ages of 20 and 40). The average age of game players was rising, as people who became game players as preteens or teenagers continued to play in their adult years—in 2005, the average game player age in the United States was 33 and 25 percent were over 50.[4] To broaden the appeal of video games for adults, game developers were creating a growing number of games with mature content. Hard-core gamers purchased 10–15 new games annually and were also among those most attracted to playing games online. Exhibit 3 provides game-player demographics and other video game–related statistics. A substantial number of consumers were not attracted to playing video games, partly because of a lack of interest, partly because they lacked the patience to learn complex controls, and partly because they were unwilling to spend the 20 to 30 hours it took to navigate a game successfully.

The development of video games was considered by some observers to be a niche business, with each game targeted to appeal to a particular subculture. In 2006, increasing numbers of games were being targeted to narrowed-in genres and consumers with specific game-playing preferences. Thinking of the gamers as consisting of just two primary segments—power or hard-core gamers and casual gamers—was overly simplistic. The size of the target niche for a game and the following a game could attract were thus crucial. Unless a game could attract a sizable audience and produce unit sales sufficient to cover development costs, production and packaging costs, and marketing costs, then it ended up a moneyloser. According to one renowned game designer, "Only the top 20 percent is going to make money at any given moment. Most of what we make is destined for the garbage heap of history."[5] Moreover, unless the content of a game could be adapted to other media, the revenue-generating capability of a video game quickly eroded after a few months on the market (and certainly after next-generation consoles were introduced). For instance, even a top-selling title like Madden NFL, usually introduced in August just before the start of football season, generated few sales after December.

Industry Growth

A number of factors had contributed to growth of the video game industry during the 1990–2006 period:[6]

- *Broader game content.* The number and variety of video games had expanded over the years to

Exhibit 3   **Video Game–Playing Statistics, U.S. Households, 2005**

- The average player spent about 6.8 hours per week playing games.
- 31% of all game players in the United States were under age 18, 44% were in the 1–49 age group, and 25% were over age 50 (up from 13% in 2000).
- The average game player in the United States in 2003 was 33 years old.
- 62% of gamers were male.
- The average age of the most frequent game purchaser was 40; 89% of the time parents were present when games were purchased or rented.
- The top four reasons parents played video games with their children:
  - Because they were asked to—79%
  - It's fun for the entire family—75%
  - It's a good opportunity to socialize with the child—71%
  - It's a good time to monitor game content—62%
- 44% of most frequent game players played games online, up from 19% in 2000.
- Best-selling video games by type of genre, 2002 and 2005:

| | 2002 | | 2005 | |
Game Categories	PC Games	PC Games	PC Games	Console Games
Sports	6.3%	19.5%	3.7%	17.3%
Action	—	25.1	4.7	30.1
Strategy/role-playing	35.4	7.4	43.2	—
Racing	4.4	16.6	—	11.1
Fighting	0.1	6.4	—	4.7
Shooting	11.5	5.5	14.4	8.7
Family/child	25.6		19.8	9.3
Adventure	—	5.1	5.8	—
Edutainment	—	7.6	—	—

Note: The categories were "redefined" between 2002 and 2005.

- Computer and video game sales by rating, 2001 and 2005

	2001	2005
Everyone	62.3%	49.0%
Teen	24.6	32.0
Mature	9.9	15.0
Everyone 10+	2.1	4.0

- 16 of the top 20 best-selling console games and 16 of the top 20 best-selling PC games were rated Everyone or Teen.

Source: Interactive Digital Software Association, "Essential Facts about the Computer and Video Game Industry," 2002, www.idsa.com (accessed November 12, 2003), and Entertainment Software Association, "Essential Facts about the Computer and Video Game Industry," 2006, www.theESA.com (accessed September 7, 2006).

the point where there were games for all tastes and all ages.

- *Quantum leaps in the quality of both graphics and play.* The latest generation of consoles introduced in 2005–2007 offered a huge leap in the game-playing experience and had entertainment functions well beyond that of just playing video games. The PS3, Xbox 360, and Wii consoles had high-definition graphics that rendered real-life images, wireless connectivity for surfing the

Internet or playing games online, parental controls, hard drives for saving downloaded games, and multichannel surround sound; they could accommodate wired or wireless controllers and were formatted with a 16:9 widescreen format for high-definition televisions. (However, games would play on standard TVs as well.)

- *The evolution of video game consoles into multifaceted entertainment devices*—The latest generation of consoles had the ability to record TV shows, play music, rip CDs onto the hard drive, and stream video and digital pictures stored on a PC, thus expanding the entertainment value for families.

- *Growing interest in video games by adults.* Demographic research indicated that growing numbers of young adults were continuing to play video games past their teenage and college years. Sports games involving professional and college sports and NASCAR racing were appealing to adults, as were games with mature content.

- *Collaboration between Hollywood movie studios and video game developers to translate popular action movies into video games.* Game developers and Hollywood movie studios had seen the merits of working hand in hand on projects that had both the action component and widespread interest (especially among teenagers) to make a good game. Releasing a game in conjunction with a hit movie—such as a Harry Potter or James Bond movie or *Spider-Man* or *Lord of the Rings*—could increase sales three or four times. Sometimes, film stars recorded dialogue for video games and special scenes were filmed specifically for use in the video game. Game designers would take a movie script and add to the storyline, making it more mission-rich and multifaceted than what appeared onscreen.

- *The growing capability to play games online, often in head-to-head competition with other online players.* Online gaming had allowed game designers to extend their storylines by providing new chapters, adding new missions, and introducing new characters, thus hooking enthusiasts into playing through a never-ending story. Sequels of sports games with the latest player rosters and team schedules spurred continuing interest on the part of online players.

Competitive Structure of the Video Game Software Business

The video game software business was part of the broader entertainment business. Video games competed for the leisure time and discretionary spending of consumers against such other forms of entertainment as motion pictures, television, and music. Industry participants varied in size—from small companies with limited resources to large, diversified companies with considerable financial and marketing clout. Sony, Nintendo, and to a lesser extent Microsoft had in-house personnel assigned to developing game titles exclusively for their respective platforms and were actively marketing their own games against the games of independent game publishers like Electronic Arts, Activision, Take Two Interactive, THQ, Square Enix, Capcom, Atari, Sega, Lucas Arts Entertainment, NCsoft, and numerous others. Well-known media giants such as Disney, Fox, Viacom, and Time Warner, attracted by the growth opportunities in video games and the emergence of related entertainment technologies, were expanding their software game publishing efforts.

Competition among the publishers of video game software was vigorous, revolving around engaging content and game play, number and variety of product offerings, the incorporation of cutting-edge technologies and innovative game features that captured the attention and interest of game players, continuous introduction of new titles, building a brand name that inspired buyer trust and confidence in game quality, gaining access to retail shelf space and visibility in other distribution channels, effective marketing and sales promotion, pricing, and ability to complete game development and time new product releases to match peak sales periods. Success in the marketplace depended heavily on a company's prowess in developing a stream of new titles with mass appeal, marketing them effectively, and having at least several hit titles, outcomes that required ever-increasing budgets for creative game development, advertising, and sales promotion. As a consequence, only companies that could marshal the financial resources needed to support a sizable and talented game development staff and fund a potent sales and marketing effort were likely to prosper or even survive.

Emerging Video Game Distribution Channels and Market Segments

Aside from the transition to next-generation consoles that began in 2005–2006, several other factors were driving market change in video games.

Digital Distribution. Retail sales where consumers bought packaged video games were the industry's most important distribution channel in 2006. Thousands of retail outlets across the world stocked video games—not surprisingly, Wal-Mart was the world's biggest video game retailer, with a market share of about 18 percent. Other key retailers in North America were Target, Best Buy, Circuit City, Blockbuster, Toys "R" Us, and GameStop. In many instances, retailers demanded hefty slotting fees to stock lesser-known or slower-selling games. While some industry observers believed that retailers would remain the primary point of purchase for the foreseeable future, others were less sure. One of the biggest market trends in 2006 was the growing propensity of mainstream consumers to use the Internet to purchase and play video games. Digital distribution via Internet downloads was gaining rapid acceptance because more and more households had broadband or high-speed Internet connections. A broadband connection enabled a consumer to purchase a video game online and download it to a hard drive (on either a PC or a console equipped with a hard drive). In 2006, most PC-based video games were being offered for sale digitally in addition to being available at retail. Moreover, it was becoming quite common for online retailers to promote game sales by offering free downloadable demos. Digital distribution was expected to grow significantly as the installed base of new consoles grew—all three of the leading consoles had hard drives and wireless Internet connections that facilitated downloading of online game purchases. The weaknesses of digital distribution were that downloaded files were not portable (could not be taken to a friend's house or sold at garage sales) and their large file sizes took up considerable hard drive space.

A second driver of digital distribution was the "unlimited shelf space" of Web-based game retailers that enabled them to offer a far wider selection of games than most retailers. With more than 500 titles for PlayStation, 200 titles for Xbox, and 150 titles for GameCube during much of 2003–2006, the big majority of brick-and-mortar retailers tended to award shelf space to only the most popular titles (perhaps 25 to 75, depending on store size and the amount of space devoted to video games) and select new releases. Wal-Mart, for example, generally stocked only about 80–90 games. The shelf life of the average newly released video game was about five weeks, even with expensive in-store merchandising campaigns. Popular video games seldom remained on retail shelves longer than 120 days. Internet retailers, however, could offer a very wide selection of game titles at low incremental cost—indeed, it made sense for Amazon.com or other Internet retailers specializing in video games to stock a big selection of both new releases and older games for all types of platforms and target audiences. Digital distribution had considerable economical appeal to game developers, allowing them to bypass the costs of such game-publishing activities as physical production, packaging, shipping, inventory management, and return processing. In addition, the lower-cost economics of digital distribution created room for game e-tailers to employ price-cutting tactics to spur sales toward the end of a game's life cycle or to induce bargain hunters to purchase a disappointingly slow-selling game.

Rising Popularity of Massively Multiplayer Online Games. High-speed Internet connections greatly enhanced the online game-playing experience, enabling players to compete directly with other online players in what were called massively multiplayer online games (MMOGs). In 2006, with millions of households across the world already having broadband connections and millions more households getting them annually, participation in MMOGs was booming; many enthusiastic online gamers had joined online communities dedicated to the playing of a particular game. Online game-playing via broadband connections was expected to constitute a $6.4 billion market worldwide by 2010, up from $1.9 billion in 2005 (see Exhibit 1). Forecasters expected the growth would be driven not only by PC-based subscriptions but also by the rapidly growing number of video game console systems with online capability—about 75 percent of the online game subscription revenue in 2010 was expected to come from games played on PCs, and 25 percent was expected to come from games played on consoles. By 2008, the installed base of MMOG-capable consoles and PCs was projected to exceed 100 million worldwide. In 2005, over 50 percent of the subscription revenue from online game play came from Asian countries outside Japan, most notably South Korea, China, and Taiwan. In the future online game playing was expected to be more evenly distributed across Asia, North America, and Europe.

The boom in MMOGs had spawned the formation of online communities. A key to success for MMOGs was easy interaction among the players—making it simple to chat with other players, heckle opponents, talk trash, or cooperate with other players to complete certain tasks and missions. MMOG players enjoyed being part of an online gaming community in which they could hang out, chat, engage in head-to-head duels, and check statistics showing their skills versus those of other players. Game play in MMOGs was thus not a solitary interaction between an individual and a technology. Rather, MMOG communities functioned as "third places" (gathering places outside the home and workplace that people used for informal social interaction) where players could hold multiple real-time conversations with fellow players through text or voice, build relationships with other players in different cities and countries, and become exposed to a diversity of worldviews.[7]

The most popular MMOG worldwide in 2006 was said to be World of Warcraft, which had attracted a global following and was available in six languages (English, Korean, German, French, and both simplified and traditional Chinese)—a Spanish version was in development. Online play of World of Warcraft (created by Blizzard Entertainment, a subsidiary of Vivendi International) generated more than $100 million in subscription revenues in each of several countries in its first year alone. MMOG play in major markets like South Korea, China, Japan, and the United States was big enough in 2007 that a highly popular MMOG could generate $100 million in annual revenues per country.

However, MMOGs were more tedious and expensive to build than traditional games (World of Warcraft took nine years to develop), and there were ongoing costs for game masters, servers, technology support, and new content development. Revenues to cover the costs of online game sites came from annual or monthly subscription fees, pay-to-play fees, onsite advertising, and selling digital downloads of games.

The business model for profiting from MMOGs was heavily dependent on subscription revenues, whereas the business model of casual game sites (which typically had higher traffic) entailed a more diverse revenue stream that included site advertising, selling digital downloads, and, to a lesser but increasing extent, subscriptions. In 2006, the business of operating an online game-playing site was considered very risky. A host of online game sites seeking to capitalize on the anticipated market growth in online gaming had sprung up in the 2002–2006 period; many had since gone out of business, and a big majority of the remaining ones were struggling to generate sufficient revenues to be profitable.

Some of the more prominent online gaming sites in North America in 2006 were Microsoft's Xbox Live (which had 2 million subscribers), Sony Online Entertainment's PlayStation site (where games installed on a PlayStation Portable, PlayStation 2, or PlayStation 3 could be played online for monthly fees of $21.99), Electronic Arts' www.ea.com, and CNET Networks Entertainment's www.gamespot.com. Vivendi's Blizzard Entertainment had set up a special Web site, www.worldofwarcraft.com, to handle online play of World of Warcraft. In Asia, there were about 10 companies with significant subscription revenues from online game play, led by South Korean company Ncsoft, which had $300 million in online game revenue in 2005.[8] So far, relatively few companies had generated sizable subscription revenues from online play of MMOGs and casual games—video game developers were finding that earning a profit from online game play with a subscription-based business model was more elusive than relying on the proven business model of selling packaged games through retail channels.

The Emergence of Mobile Gaming.   Historically, Nintendo's Game Boy, Game Boy Color, and Game Boy Advance handheld devices had been the dominant leaders in the mobile video game play market segment. To solidify its market leading position in 2004–2006, Nintendo introduced the Nintendo DS and Nintendo DS Lite portable game players to complement its Game Boy Advance model. Going into 2006, Nintendo had sold over 75 million Game Boy Advance players, 330 million Game Boy Advance game cartridges, 17 million Nintendo DS devices, and over 60 million games for Nintendo DS models. Sony entered the handheld/mobile gaming segment in 2005 with its PlayStation Portable (PSP), quickly becoming an important market contender with worldwide sales approaching 20 million units by year-end 2006. Despite the historical popularity of traditional handheld devices for game playing (Game Boy, Nintendo DS, and PSP), the market for gaming software for such devices was expected to be stagnant, with projected sales of only $3.1 billion for gaming software on handheld sets in 2010 versus $4.8 billion in 2005.

However, mobile gaming on cellular phones and other wireless devices was expected to explode from a $2.6 billion market in 2005 to an $11.2 billion market in 2010 (Exhibit 1). In the fall of 2006, Apple announced that it was launching video games for its fifth-generation iPod models, with the games being downloadable directly from Apple's iTunes store. (Buyers of these iPod models could also download over 75 movies and 220 TV shows from iTunes.)

Mobile gaming was a fast-developing market segment because advancing technology made it possible to incorporate high-resolution color displays, greater processing power, and improved audio capabilities on cellular handsets, iPods and other brands of digital music players, and other sophisticated handheld devices (including those designed just for playing video games). There were over 1.5 billion cell phones in active operation across the world (about 35 percent of which were game enabled), and new models with enhanced game-playing capability were selling briskly—most cell phone users, intrigued by the new features of next-generation models, upgraded their phones every few years. While playing video games on handheld devices had historically been a favorite pastime of preteens and teenagers, the popularity of game-capable cell phones, iPods, and other sophisticated handheld devices was expected to spur increases in mobile gaming among the young adult population worldwide in the years ahead.

To capitalize on the growth opportunities in mobile gaming via cellular handsets and MP3 players, independent game developers had come up with games that customers could download on their cell phones or MP3 players. Cell phone users usually purchased video games through a wireless carrier's branded e-commerce service that was directly accessible from the handset. Purchasers were charged a one-time or monthly subscription fee on their cellular handset invoice for the game; the wireless carrier generally retained a portion of the fee and paid the rest to the game developer. Such wireless distribution also eliminated such traditional game publishing activities as physical production, packaging, shipping, inventory management, and return processing.

PC Games: A Segment in Decline or Poised for Growth?

A number of observers believed the market for PC-based games was in irreversible decline; one forecasting group had predicted that sales and rentals of PC gaming software would represent a worldwide market of only $3.0 billion in 2010, down from $4.3 billion in 2005 (Exhibit 1). Those who saw the market for PC games as fading contended that PCs were not as well suited to playing the most popular video games as were consoles and that the new generation of consoles widened this gap even further. Michael Dell, cofounder and chairman of Dell Inc. and an occasional player of World of Warcraft, believed that multimedia-equipped PCs had a bright future as a gaming platform.[9] Dell Inc. was broadening its product lineup to include models with advanced graphics, wide-screen displays, and multiple processors that greatly enhanced the online gaming experience, particularly MMOGs; further advances in the video performance of PCs were coming to market soon. Michael Dell believed that Microsoft's new Vista operating system was a great platform for gamers and Dell, Inc. had an advanced technology group working with game developers to explore how to make the PC the best platform for gaming. At the Austin Game Conference in September 2006, Michael Dell had a private meeting at his house for 12 game developers.[10] Dell Inc. was the world's leading manufacturer of desktop and laptop computers.

Also in 2006, Microsoft launched a strategic initiative to reenergize the PC gaming market segment by introducing a Games for Windows branding for games that were optimized for play on Windows XP and Vista. Game publishers whose PC-based games met a set of technical guidelines that provided users with easy game installation, high reliability, widescreen viewing, ability to launch from the Windows Media Center, support for the Xbox 360 Controller for Windows, and support for key Windows Vista features (such as the Game Explorer function and parental controls) were authorized to display a Games for Windows logo on the CD or DVD cases of their PC titles. Microsoft's strategic intent in promoting global Games for Windows branding was to help convince PC users that the Windows Vista operating system was a first-class vehicle for gaming.

Sharply Rising Development Costs.   In the early 1980s, a game for an eight-bit Nintendo game player could be developed for less than $100,000. In the early 1990s, game publishers customarily spent around $300,000 to develop a game for Nintendo's Super NES, Sega's Genesis, or PCs. In 1996, a typical PlayStation game cost just under $1 million to develop and retailed for $49. In 2003, development costs for a PlayStation 2 or Xbox game usually ran from $2 to $7 million per title, with retail prices running at $49.99 for hit titles. By 2005, development costs for frontline titles ranged from $5 to $20 million. The costs to develop high-profile hit games for the PS3, Xbox 360, and Wii were predicted to *average* as high as $20 million. Development costs for video console games were climbing for several reasons:

- It took ever bigger and more talented development teams to brainstorm the content of a new game, capitalize on the computing speed and graphics capabilities of each new generation of consoles, and wow game enthusiasts. The gifted and artistic skills it took to conceptualize and flesh out an innovative game were in short supply. As a consequence, talented game developers were becoming a more and more valuable resource, commanding ever higher salaries and bonuses. As game-playing transitioned to PS3, Xbox 360, and Wii, most industry observers believed a large and capable staff of game developers would prove an even more important key success factor.

- Games to fully exploit the capabilities of the latest console generation and capture the rapt attention of game enthusiasts for long periods required far more complicated and detailed animation, graphics, and coding than older 64-bit consoles, making them increasingly time-intensive to prepare and debug. Game development cycles for the PS2, Xbox, GameCube, PCs and the PSP were typically 12 to 24 months, but developing games for the PS3, Xbox 360, and Wii could take from 12 to 36 months, depending on game complexity and scope. Game development times were typically 6 to 9 months for the Game Boy, 9 to 12 months for the Nintendo DS (Dual Screen), and 6 to 9 months for wireless phones.[11] After initial development

of an all-new game for a particular platform, it could take 9 to 12 months to develop a title for other platforms.[12]

- Costs went up when a game had to be reworked or when developers decided to push the technology envelope a bit further and add new or more elaborate features. Game developers often did not know how long it would take or what it would cost to program some games because aspects of many new games had never been done before and it took several rounds of programming to create the desired effects.

- Payments for licensed content or the use of intellectual property owned by others (for rights to use certain characters or celebrities in games or to tie in with hit movies), coupled with the need for special film crews and backdrops to stage certain scenes, could cost game publishers an additional $1 to $10 per game unit.

According to one knowledgeable source, since 1993–1994 the inflation-adjusted budget for creating a game had gone up by 22 times and the amount of data included in a game had grown by 40 to 150 times, yet the industry had only gotten 6 times better at making the content.[13]

Video Game Prices

Retail prices for video games in packaged form varied, depending on popularity, length of time of the market, and the age and popularity of the console for which they were developed. For example, Madden NFL 07 retailed for $59.99 on the Xbox 360; $49.99 on PlayStation 2 and Xbox; $39.99 on GameCube, PSP, and PCs; and $29.99 on Game Boy Advance and Nintendo DS. Hit titles for the newest console generation commanded a premium price as high as $59.99 in 2006, with less popular sellers retailing for $49.99 and $39.99. The prices of titles with lagging sales were frequently discounted after being on the market for several weeks; price discounting was a sales tactic used by many Internet retailers and by big-box retailers like Wal-Mart.

On average, game prices tended to decline once a generation of consoles had been on the market for a significant period (see Exhibit 4), chiefly because there were so many game titles competing for the attention of game players and because the shelf space of game retailers was limited. There were about 50

Exhibit 4   **Average Retail Prices of Video Games, 1995–2002**

Type of Console	1995	1996	1997	1998	1999	2000	2001	2002
16-bit (1989 debut)								
Sega Genesis	$41	$29	$21	$14	$13	$10	$10	$ 7
Super Nintendo	$43	$41	$29	$22	$17	$11	$10	$ 9
32-bit (1995 debut)								
PlayStation	$53	$49	$39	$35	$31	$28	$23	$18
Sega Saturn	$55	$47	$35	$20	$11	$ 5	$14	$ 6
64-bit (1996 debut)								
Nintendo 64		$65	$61	$51	$46	$42	$38	$28
128-bit (2000 debut)								
GameCube							$50	$46
Xbox							$50	$45
PlayStation 2						$49	$48	$41

Source: The NPD Group/NPD FunWorld and www.msnbc.com/news accessed September 8, 2006.

high-profile games scheduled for release during the September–November 2006 period.[14] About 750 new games (or sequels of existing games) were expected to hit the market during 2007–2008; most all game developers were developing new games in expectation that booming sales of PS3, Xbox 360, and Wii would spur big gains in video game purchases. If past sales statistics held true, the top 100 games would account for 50 percent of total sales and half of those might be able to command a premium price.

Royalties Paid to Console Manufacturers

Sony, Nintendo, and Microsoft, aside from creating their own games with in-house staff, licensed independent game developers to create software for use with their respective game-playing systems. The license agreements gave the platform manufacturer the right to set the fee structure that developers had to pay in order to publish games for their platforms. The customary royalty was in the $8 to $10 range on newly released games, but the royalty payment typically decreased as game prices fell. Because royalties did not have to be paid to console manufacturers on PC-based games, the retail prices of PC-based games published by independent game developers were often about $10 cheaper.

The license agreement also gave manufacturers an assortment of controls in other areas. Typically, the game developer was required to submit a prototype for evaluation and approval that included all artwork to be used in connection with packaging and marketing of the product. The console manufacturer had final approval over all games for its consoles (sometimes limiting the number of games approved in a given time frame) and could specify the dates on which new games could be released. Sony and Nintendo were the exclusive producers of the DVDs or game cartridges for their platforms, requiring royalties to be paid based on the number of units manufactured. Microsoft did not engage in production activities but required that titles for Xbox be manufactured by preapproved manufacturers. The manufacture of game titles required that the game publisher place a purchase order with Sony, Nintendo, or a Microsoft-preapproved manufacturer for the desired number of units drawn on its line of credit with the manufacturer for 100 percent of the order cost; the publisher then submitted software code, related artwork, user instructions, warranty information, and brochure and packaging designs for approval. Orders were generally shipped within two weeks of receipt of the purchase order.

All these royalty requirements and the need to maintain good collaborative relationships with console manufacturers tended to increase developer lead times and costs for getting a new game to market. This was especially true when platform manufacturers opted to bring out next-generation platforms with capabilities that entailed more demanding specifications. Moreover, when next-generation platforms were introduced, platform manufacturers required a new license of developers, giving them an opportunity to alter the fee structure and impose new terms and conditions on licensees. Next-generation platforms posed two other risks to game developers. If manufacturers were delayed in introducing next-generation platforms, then the introduction of their new games was delayed as well. And if a manufacturer's new platform met with a poor reception in the marketplace, then the accompanying games of developers had shorter-than-expected life cycles and often ended up as money-losers.

In addition, as online capabilities emerged for video game platforms, platform manufacturers had control over the financial terms on which online game play would be offered to players using their consoles. In each case, compatibility code and the consent of the platform manufacturer were required before a game developer could include online capabilities in their games for a manufacturer's consoles and handheld devices. (This, of course, was not the case for PC-based games.) The forward integration of Microsoft, Sony, and Nintendo into online game sites thus put their strategies and business models in head-on competition with the strategies and business models of independent game developers, like Electronic Arts, that had their own online game-playing businesses.

Marketing and Distribution Costs

Competition for shelf space and efforts to make games into top sellers had prompted game publishers to boost their advertising and promotion efforts.

By and large, the video game software business was hit-title driven and required significant expenditures for marketing and advertising. Game publishers usually promoted their games in several ways:

- Television, print, radio, outdoor, and Internet ads.
- Company Web sites.
- In-store promotions, displays, and retailer-assisted cooperative advertising.
- Trade shows.
- Product sampling through demonstration software.
- Consumer contests and promotions.

Television advertising was often required to create mass-market demand for an altogether new game; a minimal TV advertising campaign for a game cost about $2 million.

About 50 percent of annual video game sales occurred in the fourth quarter of the calendar year; many holiday shoppers considered video game hardware and software as ideal gifts.

Exhibit 5 shows a representative value chain for video games.

ELECTRONIC ARTS

Electronic Arts began operations in 1982 in California and was headquartered in Redwood City, just outside San Francisco. The company developed, published, distributed, and marketed video games

Exhibit 5   **Representative Value Chain for Video Games, 2006**

	PC Game Downloaded from Internet	Packaged DVD for Console
Retail price	$39.99	$59.99
Retailer margin	$ 8.00	$12.00
Wholesale price received by publisher	$31.99	$47.99
Publisher costs		
Manufacturing/packaging	$ 0.00	$ 3.00
Hardware royalty fee (paid to console maker)	$ 0.00	$ 8.00
Licensed content royalties	$0.00–$10.00	$0.00–$10.00
Margin for game development and programming, marketing, other costs, and profit	$21.99–$31.99	$26.99–$36.99

Source: Developed by the case author from information available from Wedbush Morgan Securities and www.msnbc.com/news/924871.asp, accessed September 8, 2006.

for in-home video game consoles (such as Sony's PlayStation 2 and 3, Microsoft's Xbox and Xbox 360, and Nintendo's Game Cube and Wii), personal computers, handheld video game players (such as the PlayStation Portable or PSP, Nintendo DS, and Game Boy Advance), cellular phones, and online play. Like other entertainment companies, EA focused on the creation, acquisition, exploitation, and protection of intellectual property; its intellectual property was primarily lodged in software code, patented technology, and the trade secrets used to develop games and make them run properly on a variety of gaming platforms. In 2006, it had about 7,200 employees, of whom 4,000 were outside the United States.

EA's revenues had more than doubled since 2000 (see Exhibit 6). The company's profits had suffered because of huge operating losses in its online business; as shown in Exhibit 7, the EA.com business segment reported operating losses of $154 million in fiscal 2001, $151 million in fiscal 2002, and $157 million in fiscal 2003. Starting in fiscal 2004, EA eliminated separate reporting for its online operations at EA.com, a move that concealed the financial performance of EA's online operations from public view.

EA's Creative Process

EA's game design staff of 4,100 people consisted of digital animators, programmers, and creative individuals who in many instances had backgrounds in television, the music industry, and the movie industry and were attracted by the creative opportunities in video games and EA's attractive compensation packages of high pay and stock options. Game design personnel were located in five principal design studios in Los Angeles, Redwood Shores (outside San Francisco) Orlando, Vancouver (Canada), and Guildford (England) and smaller design studios in Chicago, Montreal, Shanghai, Chertsey (England), and Tokyo. The dispersion of design studios helped EA to design games that were specific to different cultures—for example, the London studio took the lead in designing the popular FIFA Soccer game to suit European tastes and to replicate the stadiums, signage, and team rosters. No other game software company had EA's ability to localize games or to launch games on multiple platforms in multiple

countries in multiple languages. EA's Harry Potter and the Chamber of Secrets was released simultaneously in 75 countries, in 31 languages, and on seven platforms.[15]

Developing a game from scratch took about 18 months. To create a new game, small teams of EA game developers put together quick prototypes to demonstrate one small scene that represented the "creative center" of a potential game, usually focusing on the activity that would make the game fun to play.[16] If the game was green-lighted, the team fleshed out the idea and created storyboards of every scene, much like moviemakers would illustrate a script. State-of-the-art tools were used to allow for more cost-effective product development and to efficiently convert games designed on one game platform to other platforms. Every 90 days, a large group of EA managers and executives listened to game developers update their works in progress. If the presentation of a game did not come across as promising, EA pulled the plug on further work. Only a few new original games made it through to production and distribution each year.

In the course of creating a number of its games, EA acquired intellectual property and other licensed content from sports leagues, player associations, performing artists, movie studios, music studios, and book authors. Many of its games included the likenesses or voices of various artists, sports personalities, and cartoon characters, along with the musical compositions and performances of film stars and musicians. J. K. Rowling, the author of the Harry Potter books, had written portions of the script for EA's Harry Potter games.

EA's policy was to design only those games that it could be proud of. While some of EA's rivals developed and marketed games with profanity, sex, crime, and violence (e.g., Take-Two Interactive's best-selling Grand Theft Auto game involved doing drug deals, blowing up cars, consorting with a prostitute, and then hacking her to death), EA did not create games that would likely be given a "Mature" rating even though such games could generate millions of dollars in revenues. The chief guardian of this policy was EA's CEO, Lawrence Probst, who had declared, "EA will not publish games with gratuitous sex and violence."[17] In years past, when EA had acquired smaller game developers whose game portfolio

Exhibit 6   **Summary of Electronic Arts' Financial Performance, Fiscal Years 2000–2007 ($ in millions, except for per share data)**

	Fiscal Year Ending March 31						
	2007	2006	2005	2004	2003	2002	2000
Statement of Operations Data							
Net revenues	$3,091	$2,951	$3,129	$2,957	$2,482	$1,725	$1,420
Cost of goods sold	1,212	1,181	1,197	1,103	1,073	815	711
Gross profit	1,879	1,770	1,932	1,854	1,409	910	709
Operating expenses:							
Marketing and sales	466	431	391	370	332	241	189
General and administrative	288	215	221	185	131	107	92
Research and development	1,041	758	633	511	401	381	256
Amortization of intangibles	27	7	3	3	7	25	12
Charge for acquired in-process technology	3	8	13	—	—	—	7
Restructuring charges	15	26	2	9	15	7	—
Asset impairment charges	—	—	—	—	66	13	—
Total operating expenses	1,840	1,445	1,263	1,078	953	774	555
Operating income (loss)	39	325	669	776	456	135	154
Interest and other income, net	99	64	56	21	5	13	16
Income (loss) before provision for income taxes and minority interest	138	389	725	797	461	148	170
Provision for income taxes	66	147	221	220	143	46	53
Income (loss) before minority interest	72	242	504	577	318	102	117
Minority interest in consolidated joint ventures	4	(6)	—	—	(1)	—	—
Net income (loss)	$ 76	$ 236	$ 504	$ 577	$ 317	$ 102	$ 117
Net income per share—diluted	$0.25	$0.75	$1.59	$1.87	$1.08	$0.35	$0.44
Balance Sheet Data at Fiscal Year End							
Cash, cash equivalents, and short-term investments	$2,635	$2,272	$2,958	$2,414	$1,588	$ 797	$ 340
Marketable securities	341	160	140	1	1	7	—
Working capital	2,571	2,143	2,899	2,185	1,334	700	440
Total assets	5,146	4,386	4,370	3,464	2,429	1,699	1,192
Long-term liabilities	88	97	54	42	54	—	—
Total liabilities	1,114	966	861	786	640	453	265
Minority interest	—	12	11	—	4	3	4
Total stockholders' equity	4,032	3,408	3,498	2,678	1,785	1,243	923
Cash Flow Data							
Net cash provided by operating activities	$ 397	$ 596	$ 634	$ 669	$ 714	$ 288	$ 78
Net cash provided by (used in) investing activities	(487)	(108)	(1,726)	288	(464)	(240)	(180)
Net cash provided by (used in) financing activities	190	(503)	200	225	133	84	106

Source: Company 10-K reports, 2001, 2003, and 2006; company press release, May 8, 2007.

Exhibit 7 **EA's Financial Performance by Business Segment, Fiscal Years 2001–2003 ($ in thousands)**

	Fiscal Years		
	2003	2002	2001
Operations of EA Core (or non-online) business segment			
Net revenues	$2,400,669	$1,647,502	$1,280,172
Cost of goods sold	1,056,385	797,894	650,330
Gross profit	1,344,284	849,608	629,842
Total operating expenses	730,747	563,146	506,427
Operating income (loss)	613,537	286,462	123,415
Identifiable assets	$2,287,743	$1,529,422	$1,167,846
Capital expenditures	58,328	38,406	51,460
Operations of EA.com business segment			
Net revenues	$ 81,575	$ 77,173	$ 42,101
Cost of goods sold	16,417	16,889	14,661
Gross profit	65,158	60,284	27,440
Total operating expenses	222,468	211,307	181,171
Operating income (loss)	(157,310)	(151,023)	(153,731)
Identifiable assets	$ 71,790	$ 169,952	$ 211,072
Capital expenditures	780	13,112	68,887

Note: During 2001–2003, EA defined its two business segments as EA Core (which included all non-online operations worldwide) and EA.com (which consisted of all online activities worldwide). Beginning in April 2003 (the start of EA's 2004 fiscal year), EA consolidated the operations of EA.com into its core business operations and eliminated the distinction between the two segments.

Source: 2003 10-K report, pp. 110–12.

included games with Mature ratings, EA had ceased further production and sale of those games. But while forbidding gore and raunchy graphics, EA did include trash talk in its sport games. During the past 25 years, EA had won over 700 awards for outstanding software in the United States and Europe.

Brands and Product Lines

Electronic Arts marketed its video games under four brand names:

- EA SPORTS—Games for this brand included EA's series of realistic sports simulation games for professional and college football, professional and college basketball, World Cup soccer, professional golf, NASCAR racing, rugby, boxing, and fantasy football.
- EA—This brand covered a variety of games (mostly nonsports) and included such titles as Need for Speed, Most Wanted, The Sims 2,

Harry Potter and the Goblet of Fire, and Burnout Revenge.

- EA SPORTS BIG—This brand, used for arcade-style extreme sports games and modified traditional sports games, included such titles as SSX On Tour (skiing and snowboarding) and FIFA Street 2 (soccer).
- Pogo—The Pogo brand was used for EA's online and downloadable casual games (card games, puzzle games, and word games) made available at www.pogo.com; there were three sub-brands of casual games: (1) Pogo (a free online games service), (2) Club Pogo (a premium subscription-based online games service), and (3) Pogo-To-Go (downloadable games).

EA had been highly successful in boosting unit sales volumes and revenues through the development of product families or "franchise" games. For example, most of new versions of most of EA SPORTS titles were released annually, so as to include the latest team rosters, event schedules, venue locations, and so on. Likewise, EA had been successful in creating and marketing sequels for many of its best-selling EA and EA SPORTS BIG products. The company also released "expansion packs" for certain PC titles that provided additional content (characters, storylines, settings, missions) for previously published games—for example, The Sims 2 Open for Business expanded the characters, settings, and game play of the original The Sims 2 game. Annual release games, sequels, and games that spawned expansion packs were considered "franchise" titles.

Co-Publishing and Distribution Products. Electronic Arts partnered with other game development companies to assist them in developing their own interactive games, which EA then published, marketed, and distributed on the partner's behalf—an arrangement the company referred to as co-publishing. Another product category, termed distribution products, involved distributing and marketing video games that were developed and published by other companies.

Distribution Channels

Electronic Arts distributed its games through four channels: retailers, online sellers, cellular handsets, and other manufacturers that bundled EA games with their own products. The console, PC, and handheld games that EA published were usually made available to consumers on a disk that was packaged and typically sold in retail stores and through various online stores (including EA's own online store at www.ea.com). EA referred to these as packaged goods products. EA's games were available in approximately 80,000 retail locations worldwide. In North America, EA's largest market, packaged goods products were sold primarily to mass-market retailers (such as Wal-Mart, Target, and Kmart), electronics specialty stores (such as Best Buy and Circuit City), and specialty retailers (such as Toys "R" Us, Blockbuster, and game software retailer GameStop); about 94 percent of EA's North American revenues were derived from packaged goods sales to retailers. In Europe, sales to about 10 retailers accounted for about 40 percent of sales. In Japan, the biggest fraction of EA's sales were made through a distribution relationship with Sony. Sales to Wal-Mart constituted 13–15 percent of EA's total revenues worldwide.

Online distribution consisted of (1) online-only casual games that EA made available to consumers at www.pogo.com and on certain online services provided by America Online, (2) MMOGs sold to consumers in the form of a CD, DVD, or download file containing the necessary software to play the game online (EA's two MMOGs were Ultima Online and The Sims Online); (3) including capability features in certain packaged PC, PlayStation, PSP, and Xbox games that enabled consumers to participate in online communities and play against one another via the Internet at either EA's site (in the case of PC games) or the sites of the console/handheld makers. Online downloads for certain games were available at the EA.com site, third-party sites such as Gametap and GameStop, and Microsoft's Xbox Live service.

Consumers with cellular phones could purchase and download EA games from wireless carrier services operated by Verizon, Cingular, Sprint, and Vodafone, among others. In an effort to better capitalize on the growth opportunities in this distribution channel, Electronic Arts in 2006 had acquired JAMDAT Mobile, a global publisher of wireless games and other wireless entertainment applications, and merged it with EA's existing cellular handset software game development operations to form EA Mobile. EA executives believed the added resources and expertise provided by the JAMDAT acquisition would enable EA Mobile to rapidly grow the $19 million in cellular game revenues the company received in fiscal 2006.

The fourth and smallest distribution channel involved supplying games to manufacturers in related industries (primarily the makers of PCs and computer software). It was common for PC and other software manufacturers to pay fees to EA for the licensing and distribution rights to include EA games as part of the manufacturer's package sold to consumers. EA called such sales OEM bundles.

Pricing and Marketing

The retail selling prices in North America of EA's games, excluding older titles marketed as classics, typically ranged from $39.99 to $59.99. Classics titles had retail prices from $10 to $30. Outside North America, prices varied widely according to local market conditions.

EA's business was highly seasonal. Retail sales were highest in the calendar year-end holiday season (about 40–50 percent of the annual total) and lowest in the April–May–June period.

EA's expenditures for sales and marketing were climbing (see Exhibit 6). A big part of EA's marketing effort was devoted to promoting the EA SPORTS brand. Management saw sports as a particularly attractive genre. Sports games were appealing to males between the ages of 16 and 40 because they had nearly photo-realistic graphics and gave game-playing sports fans the chance to carry on rivalries that were the trademark of professional and collegiate teams. Sports games were regularly endorsed by the biggest stars in professional sports, which helped spur sales (as well as providing big-name sports stars with lucrative endorsement contracts).

EA had sales offices in 36 countries and was actively pursuing sales in most all parts of the world. The company used a field sales organization and a group of telephone sales representatives to market its games directly to retailers. In markets where direct sales were uneconomical, EA used specialized and regional distributors and rack jobbers to get its products on retailer shelves. Orders from retailers were typically shipped upon receipt, resulting in little or no order backlog. However, sales of digital downloads at EA.com and other online sites were becoming a bigger factor.

Foreign sales were expected to account for a significant and growing portion of EA's revenues. Exhibit 8 shows the geographic distribution of EA's sales for fiscal years 2001–2007.

EA's Suppliers

Electronic Arts used two types of suppliers:

- Sony, Nintendo, and Microsoft's preapproved manufacturers that produced the packaged games for EA titles played on their platforms.
- Third-party vendors that handled the production of EA's PC-based game titles—pressing of CDs or DVDs, printing of user manuals and other packaging-related materials, the packaging of the disk in jewel cases, and shipping.

EA was able to negotiate volume discounts in many cases, and it was the company's practice to have multiple sources of supply for all the functions that were outsourced to third-party suppliers. It was usually able to receive shipment of orders from these suppliers within two weeks. The costs to press a disk, print game instruction booklets, and package a DVD were typically less than $2 per unit.

EA kept only a small inventory of its games on hand because (1) it could obtain additional supplies and fill retailer orders from replenished inventories within two or three weeks, and (2) historically, most sales of a particular game occurred 60–90 days after initial release.

EA's Strategy

EA's near-term strategic objective was to maintain and grow its leadership position in games for the Xbox 360, PS3, and Wii. Toward this end, EA had spent heavily on R&D to develop altogether new games and sequels of existing games (with expanded missions, more elaborate graphics, and other fresh options and features); R&D spending, the lion's share of which was for games development, totaled $1.04 billion in fiscal 2007, $758 million in fiscal 2006, and $633 million in fiscal 2005, amounts about triple the R&D spending in 2000 (see Exhibit 6). The early results on EA's new games for the Xbox 360 were encouraging; in fiscal 2006, 3 of the top 10 games for the Xbox 360 in North America and Europe were EA games. EA had introduced a total of 360 games for the Xbox 360 platform (many of which were upgraded and/or more elaborate versions of games for the original Xbox).

To further capitalize on the opportunities that management saw in the global market for video games, EA management had established a number of strategic objectives and was pursuing initiatives to achieve them:

- *Exploit the opportunity for digital downloading*—To respond to the growing affinity of consumers for buying and downloading games from the Internet, in 2006 EA began offering digital downloads of most of its PC games. Further, starting with the launch of its new Xbox 360 titles, EA had begun promoting several of its newly introduced games by offering free demos at EA.com. As of early 2006, EA's demo for Fight Night Round 3 had been downloaded more than 400,000 times and was the most popular demo on Xbox Live. Although PC game sales via digital downloads had initially been small, EA management believed that growing

Exhibit 8 **EA's Net Revenues by Geographic Area, Fiscal Years 2001–2007 ($ in millions)**

	2007	2006	2005	2004	2003	2002	2001
North America	$1,666	$1,584	$1,665	$1,610	$1,436	$1,093	$ 832
Europe	1,261	1,174	1,284	1,180	879	519	387
Asia-Pacific	164	193	180	167	167	112	104
Total	$3,091	$2,951	$3,129	$2,957	$2,482	$1,724	$1,323

Sources: 2003 10-K report, p.113; 2005 10-K report, p. 96; 2006 10-K report, p. 40; and company press release, May 8, 2007

consumer use of digital downloads would help EA generate incremental revenue and improve operating margins.

- *Grow revenues via "microtransactions"*—This strategy element involved offering buyers of EA games the ability to purchase additional content and game-enhancing features (characters, story-lines, settings, missions, and strategy guides) for games they already owned. Players of EA sports games could pay a modest fee to download new uniforms for their athletes, customized parts for their racing cars, and strategy guides to improve their skills. In fiscal year 2006, EA began offering premium content at price points between $9.99 and $29.99 for its Ultima Online, Club Pogo, Battlefield 2, and The Sims 2 games played on PCs and quickly sold more than 200,000 downloads. Premium content for EA games played on new generation consoles started being sold online via microtransactions in late 2006 and in 2007. EA saw these microtransactions as creating an entirely new revenue stream for many of its most popular games.

- *Make greater use of in-game dynamic advertising technology*—In recent years, EA had begun programming into certain of its games a small number of static ads (quick product messages embedded in the game) that would not intrude on the player's entertainment experience. However, new technology had become available that would allow it to stream ever-changing advertising messages into games played online. For instance, a roadside billboard in Need for Speed could display a soft drink message on one day, a fast-food ad the next day, and an ad to shop at Wal-Mart the third day. While this technology was at an early stage, EA game designers were building additional dynamic ads into

online games to enable EA to grow advertising revenues. According to Nielsen Entertainment, in-game advertising was expected to be a $75 million market in 2006 and grow to $1 billion by 2010.[18]

- *Grow revenue from subscriptions for online game play*—In early 2007, more than 1.5 million players were paying fees of $5 monthly or $30 annually to games and participate in EA's Club Pogo community. More than half of the subscribers at www.pogo.com were women over the age of 35. EA was planning to launch Pogo in China and Europe. As of mid-2006, subscription revenues for playing MMOGs at EA.com had been disappointingly small. Total subscription service revenues were $61 million in fiscal 2006 and $79 million in fiscal 2007, amounts that were less than the revenues from just one of EA's best-selling game titles.

- *Grow revenues from games played on cellular handsets*—To position itself to capitalize on the expected growth in mobile gaming, EA had entered into agreements with 90 wireless carriers in 40 countries to distribute EA's games and applications for wireless phones. These agreements set forth how the amount of the one-time and/or monthly subscription fee would be divided between EA and the carrier. In the years to come, EA expected to enter into agreement with additional wireless carriers. The JAMDAT Mobile acquisition was made specifically to bolster EA's competitiveness in mobile gaming. EA had what management believed was an aggressive plan to migrate many of EA's popular game franchises to the mobile platform, grow its mobile games business in North America where it was already the market leader, and expand its presence in Europe and Asia.

- *Pursue sales in countries and market segments where EA's presence is low and increase the company's global market share*—EA was unrivaled in its ability to market, sell, and distribute its game titles to consumers all over the world. Creating new online games and cultivating new customers was an important part of the company's growth strategy. By early 2007, EA expected to have more than 300 people dedicated to production, marketing, and sales in emerging markets like China, India, and Eastern Europe.

- *Capitalize on the expected mushrooming game player interest in MMOGs*—This strategy element had two related components: develop more PC games (since consumers who played games on their PCs were strong candidates for online game play), and strengthen EA's capabilities in designing games well suited for multiplayers. By some order of magnitude, EA was the world's number one publisher of games for the PC. In fiscal 2006, EA had 4 of the top 10 best-selling PC game titles in North America and 5 of the top 10 in Europe. Flagship franchises like The Sims, Battlefield, and Command & Conquer had millions of loyal players, and new versions were being prepared to extend that success. Several new PC games were in development. In 2006, EA acquired Mythic Entertainment, a critically acclaimed developer of MMOGs with a product line consisting of 15 MMOGs, the best known of which was Dark Age of Camelot. Mythic was based in Virginia and had a staff of more than 170 people. EA management believed that Mythic's proprietary technology, innovative game design, and record of exemplary customer service would enhance EA's resource capabilities and competitiveness in the MMOG segment.

- *Decrease reliance on game content licensed from others and increase the number of games based on ideas from EA's own game development staff*—Because of escalating licensing costs involving the use of content owned by the NFL, the NBA, FIFA, and movie studios (for movie titles like *Harry Potter* and *the Sorcerer's Stone* and *The Godfather*) was putting heavy pressure on operating margins, EA management had set a goal of increasing the percentage of its revenues from games with wholly owned content from 40 percent to 50 percent in the next

cycle of game releases. Management believed that by tapping more heavily into the ideas and creativity of its own game design staff, it would be able to improve both game quality and profit margins. During 2006, EA's game designers were responding to the challenge to create more in-house games—two supposedly innovative games, SPORE and Army of Two, were scheduled for release in 2007, and creative sequels to six other popular EA franchise titles were in the works.

While top executives at Electronic Arts saw online gaming as a critical component of their overall strategy to grow sales of the company's existing and future products, they recognized that there were many questions surrounding the global market for online gaming. At what pace would households continue to switch from dial-up to broadband Internet connections? What fraction of video game enthusiasts would become enamored with playing games online? How fast would online gaming grow, and how big would the global market for online gaming get? Would interest in online gaming prove to be permanent or a passing fad? Would other innovative online entertainment experiences emerge to erode the interest in online gaming? To what extent would gamers be willing to pay for online game content (game-enhancing microtransactions and/or monthly subscriptions)? Should EA concentrate on developing online games with global market appeal or games targeted at the preferences of consumers in just a few countries?

Exhibit 9 shows the number of new title releases by console for fiscal years 2005–2007. Roughly 70 percent of EA revenues came from new releases of existing games. Exhibit 10 presents a breakdown of EA's revenues by game platform and product category for fiscal years 2001–2007. Management expected that revenues from prior-generation platforms would continue to erode while those from current and future generation platforms would rise.

EA'S COMPETITORS

Electronic Arts faced several different groups of competitors. In the console and handheld segment, EA's main rivals included Sony, Microsoft, and Nintendo (all of which made games for their own

Exhibit 9   New EA Game Titles for Selected Platforms, Fiscal Years 2005–2007

Platform	Number of New Game Title Releases		
	Fiscal 2007	Fiscal 2006	Fiscal 2005
PlayStation 2		28	27
PlayStation 3	8–12	—	—
PlayStation Portable	n.a.	16	3
Xbox		28	26
Xbox 360	15–20	7	—
Nintendo Wii	4+	—	—
GameCube		14	20

n.a. = Not available.

Source: Company annual reports and press releases.

platform brands), along with perhaps 20 other independent game developers, including Activision, Atari, Sega, Square Enix (a big game developer in Japan), Take Two Interactive, and THQ. Diversified media companies like Disney, Fox, Viacom, and Fox were expanding their efforts in publishing and marketing video games. In the casual games portion of the online market segment, EA's chief rivals included Yahoo!, Popcap, MSN, and Real Networks. In MMOGs, EA competed against NCsoft, Sony, Atari, Blizzard Entertainment, and an assortment of lesser-known Asian companies. In the cell phone segment, EA's principal competitors included Disney, Gameloft, Sony, Yahoo!, THQ Wireless, Infospace, Mforma, Sorrent, and Verisign.

Small game developers were struggling to absorb the rising costs of developing games in preparation for wide-scale market adoption of the new generation of consoles. They were more capital constrained, had less predictable revenues and cash flow, lacked product diversity, and were forced to spread fixed costs over a smaller revenue base—factors that were prompting the industry to consolidate to a smaller number of larger developers. Since 2000, a number of game developers across the world had

Exhibit 10   EA's Revenues by Product Line, Fiscal Years 2001–2007 ($ in millions)

Revenue Source	2007	2006	2005	2004	2003	2002	2001
Games for Consoles							
Sony PlayStation 3	$ 93	—	—	—	—	—	—
Sony PlayStation 2	885	$1,127	$1,330	$1,315	$ 911	$ 483	$ 259
Sony PlayStation	—	1	10	30	100	190	310
Microsoft Xbox 360	481	140	—	—	—	—	—
Microsoft Xbox	157	400	516	384	219	78	—
Nintendo Wii	65						
Nintendo GameCube	61	135	212	200	177	52	—
All consoles	1,742	1,803	2,068	1,929	1,407	803	569
Games for PCs	498	418	531	470	500	456	405
Games for Mobile Devices							
Nintendo Game Boy Advance and Game Boy Color	39	55	77	78	105	82	
PlayStation Portable (PSP)	248	252	18	—	—	—	—
Nintendo DS	104	67	23	—	—	—	—
Cellular handsets	139	19	—	—	—	—	—
All mobile devices	530	393	118	78	105	82	
Co-publishing and distribution	175	213	283	398	376	269	222
Internet subscription services	79	61	55	49	38	31	29
Licensing, advertising, and other	57	63	74	33	57	84	97
Total	$3,091	$2,951	$3,129	$2,957	$2,482	$1,725	$1,322

Source: EA's 2003, 2006, and 2007 10-K reports; company press release, May 8, 2007.

merged or been acquired. Several had gone bankrupt (including 3DO and Acclaim Entertainment) and several more (including Atari and Midway Games) were in financial distress as of 2006. Many struggling developers were having trouble convincing potential buyers that the value of their game titles and development teams outweighed the risks of taking on their entire enterprise, given that they were either losing money or barely breaking even.

Brief profiles of selected rivals are presented in the following paragraphs. Exhibit 11 provides summary information on these and other rivals.

Activision.   Activision was founded in 1979 and headquartered in Santa Monica, California; its mission was to be one of the largest, most profitable, and most highly respected interactive entertainment companies in the world. In 2006, Activision was the second largest independent U.S. publisher of video game software (behind Electronic Arts). It released 17 major titles in fiscal 2006, versus 14 in fiscal 2005. The company posted net revenues of $1.47 billion for the fiscal year ended March 31, 2003, almost double the $786 million reported for fiscal 2002. It reported 2006 net income of $41.9 million, versus a net of $138.3 million in 2005 and $77.7 million in 2004, and ended its 2006 fiscal year with $1 billion in cash. Geographically, Activision's 2006 revenues were divided almost equally between the United States and Europe; only $40 million in revenues came from other parts of the world market.

Activision management believed that the revenue opportunities created by the new-generation platforms would produce the greatest growth period in the industry's history. It expected that online gaming, wireless gaming, and in-game advertising would play significant roles in both the company's and the industry's long-term performance.

Activision's strategy was grounded around four elements:

- Developing and marketing games for a wide range of product categories and target audiences.
- Focusing on games that were, or had the potential to become, "franchise properties" with sustainable consumer appeal and brand recognition.
- Strengthening the company's international presence—the company had recently begun selling its games in Norway, Austria, and Denmark.
- Exerting stronger control over game development costs and variable marketing expenses so as to improve profit margins—the company was working to improve the efficiency of the game development process and have its various development studios share tools and technologies.

Activision's biggest competitive strength was in games based on superheroes such as Spider-Man and James Bond, animated characters such as Shrek, and skateboard legend Tony Hawk—the company's series of Tony Hawk games had generated combined revenues exceeding $1 billion. It was also strong in action sports games other than skateboarding, having signed long-term agreements with athletes in biking, surfing, snowboarding, and wakeboarding. Activision released four new game titles concurrent with the launch of the Xbox 360 and, as of early 2006, had the top-selling game on the Xbox 360, Call of Duty 2. It released three new titles to correspond with the introduction of the PS3, and three new titles concurrent with the introduction of Wii.

In June 2006, in the latest of a series of acquisitions over the past nine years, Activision purchased video game publisher RedOctane, the developer of the popular Guitar Hero franchise; this acquisition gave Activision early leadership in music-based gaming, which management believed would be one of the fastest-growing genres in the coming years.

Take Two Interactive Software Inc.   Take Two's games were concentrated in the action, racing, strategy, sports, and simulation genres and were marketed under four brands: Rockstar Games, 2K Games, 2K Sports, and Global Star Software. In 2005, Take Two released 14 new internally developed titles and 28 new titles developed by third parties; in 2005, the company released 15 new internally developed titles and 18 titles developed by third parties. Of the total of 29 internally developed titles developed in 2005 and 2006, six sold more than 1 million units across all platforms and four sold more than 500,000 units; five of the 46 externally developed titles sold more than 500,000 units. Many of Take Two Interactive's titles were rated M (age 17 and over) or AO (age 18 and over)—Take Two was the leading publisher of games for mature audiences. The company's top franchise was its M-rated Grand Theft Auto series, which had sales of over 7 million copies in 2005 and accounted for 38.1 percent of Take Two's 2005 revenues. Management saw the Grand Theft Auto series as a "uniquely original popular culture phenomenon." Take Two expected to release at least 25 new titles during 2007.

Exhibit 11   **Financial Performance of Selected Game Developers, 2004–2006 ($ in millions)**

	Fiscal Years		
	2006	**2005**	**2004**
Activision*			
Net revenues	$1,468.0	$1,405.9	$947.7
Cost of sales—product costs	734.9	658.9	475.5
Cost of sales—intellectual property licenses and royalties	205.5	186.0	91.6
Net income	41.9	138.3	77.7
Net cash provided by operating activities	86.0	215.3	67.4
Cash and cash equivalents	923.9	915.4	675.8
THQ*			
Net sales	$806.6	$756.7	$640.8
Cost of sales	287.9	255.2	234.6
License amortization and royalties	80.5	85.9	71.1
Software development amortization	116.4	93.6	105.6
Product development	84.2	73.0	36.9
Selling and marketing	123.6	110.5	87.1
Net income	34.3	63.0	35.8
Net cash provided by operating activities	42.8	60.5	71.2
Cash and cash equivalents	371.6	331.2	253.0
Take Two Interactive**			
Net revenues	$1,037.8	$1,202.6	$1,127.7
Product costs	538.8	593.4	619.7
Royalties	206.8	164.3	114.1
Software development costs	79.9	28.4	15.9
Selling and marketing	139.3	157.7	117.6
Research and development	64.3	73.2	43.3
Net income	(184.9)	37.5	65.4
Net cash provided by operations	43.4	40.0	20.5
Cash and cash equivalents	132.5	107.2	155.1
Midway Games**			
Net revenues	$165.6	$150.1	$161.6
Product costs and distribution	67.3	56.2	62.7
Royalties and product development	68.9	75.8	41.3
Research and development expense	37.0	39.7	25.6
Selling and marketing expense	43.2	57.2	41.2
Net loss	(77.8)	(112.5)	(24.7)
Net cash used in operations	(92.9)	(100.4)	(46.1)
Cash and cash equivalents	73.4	98.4	118.3

* Fiscal years ending March 31.
** Fiscal years ending December 31.
Source: Company 10-K reports and press releases.

The company had 12 game development studios in the United States, Canada, and England and a game development staff of 1,140 employees as of October 2005. Its game development personnel had the technical capabilities to develop and localize software titles for all major hardware platforms and the PC. Its localization capabilities included both translating game content into foreign languages and making changes in game content to enhance local appeal. Management closed 3 of the company's 12 game development studios in 2006 in response to declining sales and mounting losses.

Take Two had sales offices in 13 countries and a marketing and sales staff of about 256 people. During 2003–2005, the company spent progressively larger amounts for advertising—$56 million in 2003, $72 million in 2004, and $101 million in 2005, but trimmed its advertising and promotional activities in 2006 as an economizing measure due to a downturn in sales revenues. In 2006, the company derived 69 percent of its revenues from sales in North America, 28 percent from sales in Europe, and 3 percent from sales in other parts of the world. Sales to Take Two's largest five customers accounted for almost 41 percent of 2005 revenues and over 49 percent of 2006 revenues; Wal-Mart was Take Two's largest customer, accounting for 15.4 percent of 2006 revenues. Financial data on Take Two Interactive are shown in Exhibit 11.

THQ Inc.   THQ was one of the world's fastest-growing video game publishers with a diverse portfolio of game titles catering to every segment of the gaming audience. With fiscal 2006 revenues of $807 million, it was the fourth largest independent U.S. developer and publisher of video games. Headquartered in Los Angeles, THQ employed 1,700 people; its game development resources included some 1,300 people in 15 studio locations in North America, the United Kingdom, and Australia. THQ developed games for all console and handheld game systems, PCs, and cell phones; it was the leading independent publisher of games for handheld systems (the Game Boy, Nintendo DS, and PSP). THQ games were on retail shelves in more than 75 countries and it distributed wireless content in every major worldwide market. In fiscal 2005, 39 percent of THQ's sales were outside North America, up from 29 percent in 2004. The company's revenues had grown for 11 consecutive years.

At the end of fiscal 2006, THQ had shipped more than 25 million units of games based on its series of World Wrestling Entertainment games, 17 million units of its SpongeBob SquarePants games, more than 8.5 million units of games based on *Finding Nemo*, and more than 7.5 million units of games based on *The Incredibles*. It had a number of other "franchise" titles and several all-new games

scheduled for release in 2006–2007. THQ's financial and strategic priorities were to grow revenues at above-market rates, increase operating margins, and boost sales outside North America. The company's strategy to grow revenues in 2007–2008 were to expand its share of games sold to core gamers, emphasize more casual game content suitable for cellular phones, continue to acquire small developers and thereby expand its internal game development capabilities, acquire additional licensed intellectual content, expand its digital downloading and micro-transaction offerings, and incorporate additional in-game advertising.

Selected financial performance data for THQ are shown in Exhibit 11. Management had forecast that sales for fiscal 2007 would rise by 12–18 percent, resulting in sales of $900 to $950 million.

Midway Games Inc.   In 2006, Midway was struggling, having lost over $330 million in 2003–2006. (Recent financial data are shown in Exhibit 11.) To help stem the tide of losses, the company reduced the size of its workforce by about 10 percent during 2006. About 88 percent of the company's stock was owned by Sumner Redstone, CEO and chairman of Viacom.

Historically, Midway had been strong in games for mature audiences—versions of its best-known title, Mortal Kombat, had sold over 20 million copies. The company also developed over-the-top sports games characterized by extreme game play and the exaggerated abilities of characters; its best-seller in this genre was NBA Ballers. Over 86 percent of the company's 2005 revenues came from games played on the PlayStation 2 and Xbox; about 19 percent of the company's revenues came from sales of Mortal Kombat.

Midway had six game design studios and an internal product development staff of 650 employees, up from 330 in 2003. Four new studios had been added since 2004, and one in Australia was closed. The company released 12 new titles in 2004, 18 new titles in 2005, and 28 titles in 2006. Midway spent $27.7 for advertising in 2006, $41.2 million in 2005, and $28.3 million in 2004. To conserve on game development costs in 2006, Midway was standardizing its preproduction and planning process, sharing technology across all studios, and instituting peer review and intrastudio resource sharing. Midway's costs to develop games for the PlayStation 2 and Xbox had ranged from $4 million to $16 million; management expected that development costs for PS3 and Xbox 360 games would run between $10 and $25 million per game and take 24 to 36 months.

To try to capitalize on the expected surge in spending for games for newly introduced platforms, Midway had bolstered its distribution capabilities in Europe, opened a new sales office in the United Kingdom to orchestrate sales of Midway titles in Europe and Australia, increased its product development efforts in games for children and for PCs (neither of which had been a significant part of the company's business in recent years), and increased its development efforts in multiaction games that allowed players to have multiple experiences (such as shooting, driving, and fighting) within a single game. In September 2006, Midway released The Grim Adventures of Billy and Mandy, a humorous animated fighting/adventure game for children based on licensed content from a popular TV show on Cartoon Network. Management expected these initiatives along with its portfolio of new titles for 2007 (which included *The Lord of the Rings Online*) to produce full-year 2007 revenues of $225 million and reduced losses of $40 million.

Endnotes

[1]Letter to the stockholders, 2006 proxy statement, and annual report, p. 3.

[2]As quoted in Yukari Kane and Nick Wingfield, "Problems for PlayStation 3 Could Bring Other Sony Setbacks," *Wall Street Journal*, September 25, 2006, p. B6.

[3]Peter Lewis, "The Biggest Game in Town," *Fortune*, September 15, 2003, p. 135.

[4]Entertainment Software Association, "Essential Facts about the Computer and Video Game Industry," 2006, www.theesa.com (accessed September 7, 2006).

[5]Raph Koster, "The Age of Dinosaurs," speech to Austin Game Conference on September 7, 2006; as reported by Mark Wallace in "AGC: Koster Says Game Industry Dinosaur 'Doomed,'" www.gamasutra.com (accessed September 13, 2006).

[6]Paul A. Paterson, "Synergy and Expanding Technology Drive Booming Video Industry," *TD Monthly* 2, no. 8 (August 2003), www.toydirectory.com/monthly/Aug2003 (accessed November 15, 2003).

[7]Constance Steinkuehler and Dmitri Williams, "Where Everybody Knows Your (Screen) Name: Online Games as 'Third Places,'" *Journal of Computer-Mediated Communication* 11, no. 4 (July 2006), Article 1, http://jcmc.indiana.edu (accessed September 12, 2006).

[8]DFC Intelligence, "Who Will Benefit from the Growth of Online Game Subscription Revenue?," press release, March 7, 2006.

[9]Mark Wallace, "Michael Dell on the Future of PC Gaming," a transcript of a public Q&A session with Michael Dell at the Austin Game Conference in September 2006, September 11, 2006, www.gamsutra.com (accessed September 13, 2006).

[10]Lilly Rockwell, "Dell Forges Closer Ties to Gamers," *Austin American-Statesman*, September 9, 2006, www.statesman.com (accessed September 14, 2006).

[11]As cited in THQ Inc.'s 2006 10-K report, pp. 6–7.

[12]According to information in Take Two Interactive Software's 2005 10-K report, p. 6.

[13]Statistics attributed to MMOG designer Raph Koster and reported in Carolyn Koh, "AGC Talk: Raph Koster's 'The Age of Dinosaurs,'" *Game News*, September 13, 2006, http://home.nestor.minsk.by/game/news/2006/09/1303.html (accessed September 13, 2006).

[14]Lou Kesten, "Video-Game News in Brief: Fall Releases; a 'Madden' Record; Ads in Games," September 7, 2006, www.deseretnews.com (accessed September 11, 2006).

[15]Associated Press, "Electronic Arts: A Powerhouse Well-attuned to Public Tastes," news release, August 18, 2003.

[16]Dean Takahashi, "Electronic Arts Grows to $2.5 Billion in Annual Sales," *San Jose Mercury News*, May 5, 2003.

[17]As quoted in Ashby Jones, "The Rules of the Game," *Corporate Counsel* 3, no. 7 (July 1, 2003), pp. 72ff., www.law.com/jsp/cc/pubarticleCC.jsp?id=1055463668855 (accessed December 4, 2003).

[18]As cited in Activision's 2006 annual report, p. 12.

Sun Microsystems

Scott Jacobs
Morgan Stanley

Prescott C. Ensign
University of Ottawa

The fourth quarter ended June 30, 2005. The 2005 fiscal year was over. On July 26, 2005, Sun Microsystems (Sun) unveiled fiscal year (FY) 2005 results: Q4 revenues were US$2.98 billion (2004 Q4 revenues were US$3.11 billion, but had included income of US$1.6 billion from a legal settlement with Microsoft); for the full fiscal year 2005, Sun Microsystems reported revenues of US$11.07 billion (FY2004 revenues were US$11.19 billion).

Sun Microsystems Chief Financial Officer (CFO), Steve McGowan, commented, "We achieved impressive operational improvements in fiscal 2005 . . . our 16th consecutive year of generating positive cash flow from operations." Sun Microsystems employees, investors and analysts recognized that Bill Gates had helped out last year. But what explained this year? Perhaps Sun was righting itself?

"Putting our cash to work, we've expanded our product portfolio and announced plans to acquire companies that deepen and broaden our systems strategy. We've maintained our R&D commitment and delivered crown jewels like Solaris 10 to the market," said Scott McNealy, chairman and chief executive officer (CEO) of Sun Microsystems. "Big-time progress in FY05. The company is now in a position to take advantage of the investments we have made over the past few years and we believe there is more to come in FY06."

McNealy continued, "Our demand indicators for Q4 were positive. We have great partners, lots of cash, and a strong team across the board. FY05 was a year of stabilized revenue and earnings. Our opportunity for FY06 is sustained growth and profitability."

"Profitability?" was the incredulous reaction of many who had followed Sun's struggle.

A STRATEGIC CRISIS

At the beginning of 2004, Sun Microsystems found itself at a serious inflection point (see Exhibits 2, 3 and 4 beginning on page C-242). It had lost money in eight of the last 10 quarters and allowed its market share to slip again, this time from 12.1 percent in 2002 to 10.3 percent in 2003, Sun announced its largest product offering update in company history. The products were intended to stop the bleeding that had caused the company's share price to plummet to only one-tenth of its high value in 2000, a decline that in 2003 raised speculation of a takeover. The chief executive officer and chairman of the board of directors was Scott McNealy, cofounder of the company originally named Stanford Unified Networks when it began in 1982.

Since developing the vision that had endured throughout the company's history, "The Network is the Computer," McNealy had come under great scrutiny as many industry analysts relentlessly questioned Sun's business-level strategy. Specifically, many doubted the effectiveness and competitiveness of the products that the company offered during its recent decline in profitability.

On December 8, 2004, Scott McNealy delivered a keynote address at an industry show in San Francisco, California. He relayed some statistics about Sun's Java platform: 579 million Java-enabled phones by the end of the year, almost one billion java smart cards and nearly 900 companies were now contributing to Java. He spoke of how the world had envisioned the computer 50 years prior and remarked, "It's hard to imagine where we'll be 50 years from now." Some in the audience were scratching their heads wondering where Sun was headed in the very near future.

Fiscal year 2005 had just closed and it was now July. With catchy newspaper headlines, "The Sun Always Rises"; "Dawn of a New Era for Sun"; and "Will Sun Shine Again?", it was evident that Sun Microsystems was at a crossroads, and it was time for serious reflection on the part of Scott McNealy. The company, based in Santa Clara, California, had been through a lot in the last 10 years. It had learned from some experiences and was still learning from others.

BOOM TO BUST

In 1997, Thailand could no longer prop up its currency, the baht. High levels of debt and years of trade deficits had resulted in a spectacular crash in the value of the baht. The ensuing economic crisis engulfed most of Asia and spread throughout the entire world, slowing down economies from east to west. Most importantly for Sun, the crisis adversely impacted Japan, its largest single source of foreign revenue, at nine percent.

The global economic collapse continued in January of 1999 when Brazil devalued its currency, the real. The devaluation dashed any immediate growth plans and delayed future growth there indefinitely. Brazil had been one of the countries on which Sun had been counting to lead information technology (IT) spending in South America.

The Brazilian and Asian financial crises provided compelling evidence that, while Sun's diverse portfolio appeared to protect it from individual blips in economic stability, its product sales were highly sensitive to macroeconomic conditions. In 1998, the company reported that more than 45 percent of its revenues was generated outside of the United States. By 2003, Sun's reliance on foreign revenue had increased to more than 50 percent, and the economic crises had unfolded into a worldwide economic slowdown—with some analysts using the label "recession."

However, economic conditions alone did not lead to Sun's fall from profitability. Rather, the economic macro-environment was a catalyst for change towards affordable enterprise computing. In addition, technological advancements led to performance improvements in the x86 platform.[1] Making use of these advancements along with utilizing various sources of leverage to lower cost structures, many firms were able to offer products similar to Sun's but at a fraction of the price.

Sun's expensive high-margin products lagged in demand while the company attempted in vain to continue presenting its same value proposition. To compound the adverse effect of developments in the x86 hardware space, competitive pressure was also being applied to Sun by an inexpensive, competitive and very contrary x86-based software product, named Linux. This singular platform would change Sun's competitive environment drastically. Open source software on inexpensive standard hardware began to unravel Sun's offering: a product where software, hardware and service were bundled.

BILLION-DOLLAR BETS

In 2000, shares of Sun Microsystems hovered near US$60 per share. Around that same time, Scott McNealy, CEO, put Masood Jabbar in charge of managing Sun's worldwide sales. McNealy was counting on Jabbar to formulate the right plan and strategy to capitalize on Sun's momentum and reputation for innovation. McNealy needed Jabbar to grow the business and build shareholder wealth.

In response, Jabbar developed a strategy that focused on five countries that were each potential billion-dollar-a-year markets for Sun's server business. They were Brazil, Spain, China, India and Italy. Shareholders were optimistic about Sun's potential for growth.

Although shareholders responded positively to Sun's future, managers of the U.S. business at Sun's

Palo Alto, California, headquarters were getting tense. It seemed as though a meeting could not take place without attention being diverted from the U.S. business toward conversations about foreign interest rates, political regimes and foreign legal language. U.S. business managers simply could not have discussions on policy and strategy without some "foreign distractions." Many of the U.S. managers involved began to feel that those managers representing Mexico, South America and Canada were muddying the waters with talk about fluctuating currency exchange rates and political instability. In fact, those territories accounted for less than a few percent of Sun's business at the time. The United States had nearly always accounted for roughly half of Sun's multibillion-dollar annual sales.

However, Jabbar's "billion-dollar bets" required that these emerging areas get attention in order to shift the distribution of sales. And yet, international managers felt they were getting little cooperation and support to expand business in their emerging markets. Jabbar also knew that under the current structure, U.S. managers could not focus on their own strategy and planning, which meant that a considerable portion of Sun's revenue could be threatened. The current organizational structure was just not working. Something at Sun had to change.

Jabbar approached Bob MacRitchie, who at that time was already managing the South American, Mexican and Canadian lines of business under the umbrella of the U.S. organizational division. The infrastructure was already in place. What remained was an official transition that emphasized Sun's commitment to pursuing its billion-dollar bets. "I just got on the phone with Bob and told him what we were doing," Jabbar later said, "It took only a minute."

However, the transition itself was not so easy. The same U.S. business managers that previously decried the waste of precious resources on those underperforming emerging markets felt a sense of loss they had not anticipated—a loss of power. "Egos were involved here," Jabbar explained, "It was hard to get those guys to give up the control."

Apart from being a functional decision, the decision was symbolic of the attention and commitment Sun would give to these emerging areas. Sun's strategy was to develop these "billion-dollar bets." The economy was booming and the demand for enterprise computing products was growing quickly.

Sun did not have to chase customers. The sales, it seemed, were coming to them. However, neither Sun nor any other company could contend with the competitive pressure created by the volatile nature of the new global economy.

ATTACK OF THE GIANT PENGUIN—LINUX

"We're saying that Linux will eat Unix,"[2] was the prediction for 2003, issued by John Gantz, International Data Corporation's (IDC's) chief research officer. The irony was subtle—the Linux mascot was an innocuous penguin. Linux, an operating system named after its creator Linus Torvalds, took the enterprise computing industry by storm. Its open source, community approach to application creation was not only revolutionary in theory, but in practice as well.

Linux is open source, inexpensive and scalable. Adoption of Linux products spread rapidly, especially internationally. In fact, countries outside the United States found Linux to be a viable alternative to Microsoft's Windows operating system, which many critics felt was unsecure and not readily scalable. In 2003, Brazil's government urged its federal agencies to adopt Linux in an effort to cut costs. Brazil represented no small piece of the pie; it imported more than US$1 billion more in software than it exported in 2001. In moving to Linux, Brazil was not alone. It joined China, Japan and South Korea in using Linux to get IT spending under control.

Sun had resisted Linux for a long time since Sun designed its own operating system, Solaris. In addition, Sun's past success was due in large part to its strategy of integrating proprietary software (Solaris), hardware and its own "SPARC" Unix microprocessor.[3] By developing not only its own microprocessors, but also its own operating system, the company could have complete control of the integration of the system hardware and software. This strategy ensured optimization and control over the entire design process. In effect, Sun created a lot of value for its customers through this integration. However, Sun's strategic focus on its operating system, Solaris, and its SPARC microprocessors prevented it from seeing the threat that Linux presented. Eventually, an x86 or

Unix server running Linux offered customers a close substitute to Sun's products.

In February of 2002, after years of denial, Sun Microsystems could no longer fend off the waves of criticism—it gave in to Linux. To demonstrate its commitment to Linux, Scott McNealy gave his keynote speech (in a penguin suit) at a Sun trade show to announce the company's new Linux products. Typically, Sun attacked other platforms by suggesting that they were not as reliable or did not offer the features of its own Unix servers. However, with the advent of Linux, users found a new, reliable, inexpensive choice to expensive Sun products.

The problem was serious. If Sun refused to offer Linux products, it would be cutting itself out of a considerable portion of the server market. Linux was dominating the inexpensive x86 server space. Yet, if Sun were to produce its own x86 products, it would have to purchase microprocessors from a third party for a new line of x86 hardware. Since there was essentially one company that was developing highly respected enterprise-level x86 microprocessors, Sun had few choices. Entering the x86 market would mean teaming up with a tried and true competitor—Intel.

For Sun, doing business with Intel would not only mean accepting the rise of Linux, but also the commoditization of enterprise computing, at least at the low end. Moreover, Sun's value proposition became increasingly diminished as the company lost control of the integration process. By using Intel chips, Sun would no longer offer value to customers through engineering and innovation as it had previously, but rather via an assembly of outsourced components. Although very similar to some of its competitors, that value proposition was a substantial departure from Sun's original model. To counteract this change, Sun developed its own middleware, the Java Enterprise System, that would operate in Unix or Linux and offered a unique pricing model that made scalable enterprise computing more affordable.

In 2003, the People's Republic of China and Sun announced a deal. The arrangement was for 500,000 to one million copies per year of Sun's Java Enterprise System. Most industry observers believed the blockbuster result of this deal would not be the revenue, but rather the market share. Indeed the revenue would likely not be significant and would even take quite a while to capture, given the extended

time frame of the agreement. With Java Enterprise System, Sun was trying to inject value into its offerings through research and development, one of Sun's competitive advantages.

Continuing to partner with Intel, however, remained a strategic disadvantage. After years of competition, joining forces and integrating development initiatives with Intel seemed unrealistic. Sun's future in the x86 space continued to look uncertain until November of 2003, when Sun announced a newly formed strategic alliance with an emerging x86 microprocessor developer—AMD.

A NEW ENTRANT, OLD COMPETITORS AND BIG THREATS

In 2003, Advanced Micro Devices, also known as AMD, agreed to collaborate with Sun in a new strategic venture. By providing its x86-based Opteron chips for use in Sun's low-end servers, AMD stood to combat years of dominance by rival, Intel. AMD's new Opteron technology took its x86 technology to 64 bits,[4] a feat Intel had yet to master. In doing so, it became an industry leader. Along with that status came new friends. Sun was not the only firm to form an alliance with AMD—HP and IBM both struck similar deals, although seemingly less integrated than Sun's alliance.

Intel leveraged its technology, manufacturing capabilities and market share in the PC space to produce chips able to compete in the enterprise computing domain, at least in the low-end segment. And, it certainly did not suffer from diminishing relations with Sun. Dell capitalized in the low-end space by selling a large volume of servers running Linux on Intel. Finding operating efficiencies allowed Dell, the fourth largest server maker behind Sun, to turn the low-end server market into a battlefield by steadily dropping prices.[5]

Sun attempted to compete on the basis of price, but found it difficult to out-price companies like Dell and even IBM that reduced costs through sources of leverage, such as unit volume and consulting services, respectively. As a result, Sun was losing the low-end battle against Dell, IBM and HP, and there continued to be little demand in the high-end for its expensive

Unix servers. As if this were not bad enough, another competitor was posing a significant threat to Sun.

Japan's Fujitsu, which ranked as the fifth largest server maker, licensed Sun's proprietary Ultra-SPARC chip designs to power its own SPARC64 chips found in its line of Unix servers. Fujitsu had great success in taking Sun's SPARC chips and turning them into more powerful SPARC64 Fujitsu chips—and winning Sun customers in the process. Fujitsu was much quicker to market than Sun, which was reliant on Texas Instruments to churn out its chips. The situation presented a very difficult decision for Sun. Should it discontinue its relationship with Fujitsu or get in even tighter with the Japanese giant?

Sun Microsystems desperately needed the revenue from the licensing agreement, so it was extremely reluctant to cease the licensing contracts. To complicate matters further, Fujitsu was not only licensing Sun's chipset designs, it was also a leading reseller of Sun product. Fujitsu was more than a manufacturer; it served also as a reseller or channel partner. In fact, Fujitsu's role was significant. Sales to Fujitsu accounted for a large portion of Sun sales in Japan, Sun's leading foreign market in revenue terms.

Rumors surfaced in 2003 about a possible alliance or even merger with the Japanese firm. However, for Sun, forming a tighter alliance with Fujitsu might cause more problems than it would address. For instance, if Sun were to begin using the SPARC64 chips, it might mean spurning its longstanding chip-producing partner, Texas Instruments. Given a very large installed base, such bridges were not to be burned hastily. Moreover, despite the fact that Sun and Fujitsu used the same instruction set for the microprocessors, Sun and Fujitsu products could not be used together without some reprogramming. Adopting the SPARC64 chips would mean massive reconstruction of its current products and the products it had in the pipeline, which suggested that Fujitsu would remain a competitor in the future.

EXECUTIVE EXODUS

A month-long executive exodus culminated with the Chief Operating Officer (COO) and President Ed Zander resigning. He and four other high-level officers—all with at least 15 years each at Sun—departed effective July 1, 2002. The naysayers on Wall Street were having a field day—"the Captain goes down with the ship." McNealy was going to do it alone—he named no successor for the president and COO's position. There were also now vacancies for the vice-president, two executive VPs and the CFO. On July 18, 2002, it was announced that Masood Jabbar would retire from Sun after 16 years of service. The stock was at a 52-week low, hovering around US$7 per share.

And things did get worse—at least according to the stock market. The share price slowly but steadily, in the coming years, fell to a mark below US$3. It would be almost two years before a president and COO was named—the 38-year-old, pony-tailed Jonathan Schwartz received the nod from McNealy in April 2004. Schwartz had come to Sun in 1996 when it acquired Lighthouse Design, Ltd.—the firm Schwartz was then CEO of.

ALL BETS ARE OFF

Growth in the server industry was not flat by any means. IDC expected tech spending would increase in 2005 and beyond, regaining some of its lost momentum from the bubble burst of 2000.

Scott McNealy's vision of everything and everyone connected to the network was probably not that far from the eventual truth (see Exhibit 1). Yet, Sun's ability to determine the long-term direction of computing was more refined than its value-added strategy.

Most of Sun's billion-dollar bets that were developed by Masood Jabbar failed to materialize. In fact, Sun Microsystems was now desperate, fighting for revenue each quarter. In retrospect, Sun might have put the cart before the horse. Instead of focusing on the evolution of its competitive environment, it was distracted by the economic euphoria that reigned in the late 1990s. McNealy admitted to as much, "Looking back, we probably hired too many people and signed too many leases, but we had a very natural and understandable desire to fill all the orders we could."

The network was still the computer—even increasingly so—but recent product offerings and industry conferences suggested Sun Microsystems

Exhibit 1   **Sun Microsystems' Strategic Direction**

> A singular vision—"The Network Is The Computer"—guides Sun in the development of technologies that power the world's most important markets. Sun's philosophy of sharing innovation and building communities is at the forefront of the next wave of computing: the Participation Age.
>
> **VISION: Everyone and everything connected to the network.**
>
> Eventually every man, woman, and child on the planet will be connected to the network. So will virtually everything with a digital or electrical heartbeat—from mobile phones to automobiles, thermostats to razor blades with RFID tags on them. The resulting network traffic will require highly scalable, reliable systems, from Sun.
>
> **MISSION: Solve complex network computing problems for governments, enterprises, and service providers.**
>
> At Sun, we're tackling complexity through system design. Through virtualization and automation. Through open standards and platform-independent Java technologies. In fact, we're taking a holistic approach to network computing in which new systems, software, and services are all released on a regular, quarterly basis. All of it integrated and pretested to create what we call the Network Computer.

Source: http://www.sun.com (accessed February 11, 2006).

and especially McNealy had succumbed to some inevitable truths about the competitive environment of the industry. One was that the x86 platform was not going away as McNealy had once envisioned. It became clear that Sun's future strategy would include x86- and Linux-based products, as well as more compelling and competitive high-end Unix servers.

To sell Sun product, McNealy was banking on a healthy return on research and development. He asserted, "Sun is doing things that Intel isn't doing or AMD isn't doing." Innovation, however, was costly. Sun's R&D budget had been around US$2 billion annually for the last few years, dwarfing its competitors. Innovation was a key component of Sun's current strategy, but the results were not yet readily quantifiable. Still, McNealy claimed, "[Over the decade,] we're going to spend $20 billion to $30 billion minimum on R&D." Clearly, Sun was intent on continuing to add value through innovation rather than being relegated to a game of economies of scale and efficiencies.

Charles Cooper, editor of CNETNEWS.com, remarked, "[Sun's] strategy—if you can call it that—has been to throw a lot of stuff against the wall and wait to see what sticks." It was still hard to tell what the firm and specifically Scott McNealy were learning from the devolution of Sun's business. The well-known CEO admitted to strategic missteps but quipped "I try to make a mistake only once." "If your strategy isn't controversial, you have zero chance of making money." "You have to have a wildly different strategy and you have to be right. It's that second part that gets tricky." McNealy recognized, "There's lots more to do." Now was the time to do it.

Exhibits 2, 3, and 4 (on pages C-242 through C-244) present financial statement data for Sun Microsystems for fiscal years 1996–2005.

Endnotes

[1]x86 hardware stands for x86 central processing units (CPUs) developed by Intel. This CPU forms the base of PCs. History of the chip: 286, 386, 486, 586 (dubbed "Pentium"), Pentium Pro, Pentium II, Celeron, Pentium III, Pentium IV, etc. Other manufacturers, such as Advanced Micro Devices (AMD) and Cyrix, have used the same CPU machine code with their own architecture to create equivalent chips, but with a lower price-to-performance ratio.

[2]Unix software is an abbreviation for UNiplexed Information and Computing System, originally spelled "Unics." It is an interactive time-sharing operating system developed at Bell Labs in 1969. In the 1990s, Unix was the most widely used multi-use general-purpose operating system in the world. Unix is presently offered by many manufacturers and is the subject of international standardization efforts.

[3]SPARC is an abbreviation for Scalable Processor ARChitecture, designed by Sun Microsystems in 1985. SPARC is not a chip per se, but a specification. The first standard product based on SPARC was produced by Sun and Fujitsu in 1986. In 1989, Sun transferred ownership of the SPARC specifications to an independent, non-profit organization, SPARC International.

[4]64 bit is a computer architecture term, which refers to the bandwidth of the arithmetic logic unit, registers (high-speed memory locations in the CPU) and data bus (connections between and within the CPU, memory and peripherals).

[5]HP was the server market leader, followed by IBM.

Exhibit 2   **Sun Microsystems' Income Statement, 1996–2005 (US$ millions)**

	1996	1997	1998	1999	2000	2001	2002	2003	2004	2005
Revenue	$7,094.8	$8,598.4	$9,790.8	$11,726.3	$15,721.0	$18,250.0	$12,496.0	$11,434.0	$11,185.0	$11,070.0
Cost of Goods Sold	3,972.0	4,320.5	4,693.3	5,648.4	7,549.0	10,041.0	7,580.0	6,492.0	6,669.0	6,481.0
Gross Profit	**3,122.7**	**4,277.9**	**5,097.5**	**6,077.9**	**8,172.0**	**8,209.0**	**4,916.0**	**4,942.0**	**4,516.0**	**4,589.0**
Operating Expenses										
Selling, General and Administrative	1,732.7	2,402.4	2,777.3	3,173.0	4,137.0	4,544.0	3,812.0	3,329.0	3,317.0	2,919.0
Research and Development	657.1	826.0	1,190.2	1,383.2	1,642.0	2,093.0	1,835.0	1,841.0	1,996.0	1,785.0
Other	57.9	23.0	—	—	–	261.0	517.0	2,496.0	393.0	262.0
Operating Income	**675.0**	**1,026.5**	**1,130.1**	**1,521.8**	**2,393.0**	**1,311.0**	**(1,248.0)**	**(2,724.0)**	**(1,190.0)**	**(377.0)**
Other Income and Expenses										
Net Interest Income and Other	33.9	94.7	46.1	83.9	378.0	273.0	200.0	71.0	1,627.0	193.0
Earnings Before Taxes	**708.9**	**1,121.2**	**1,176.2**	**1,605.7**	**2,771.0**	**1,584.0**	**(1,048.0)**	**(2,653.0)**	**437.0**	**(184.0)**
Income Taxes	232.5	358.8	413.3	574.4	917.0	603.0	(461.0)	776.0	825.0	(77.0)
Earnings After Taxes	**476.4**	**762.4**	**762.9**	**1,031.3**	**1,854.0**	**981.0**	**(587.0)**	**(3,429.0)**	**(388.0)**	**(107.0)**
Accounting Changes						(54.0)				
Net Income	**$ 476.4**	**$ 762.4**	**$ 762.9**	**$ 1,031.3**	**$ 1,854.0**	**$ 927.0**	**($587.0)**	**($3,429.0)**	**($388.0)**	**($107.0)**
Diluted EPS Continuing Operations	$0.15	$0.25	$0.24	$0.32	$0.55	$0.29	($0.18)	($1.07)	($0.12)	($0.03)
Diluted EPS	$0.15	$0.25	$0.24	$0.32	$0.55	$0.27	($0.18)	($1.07)	($0.12)	($0.03)
Shares of Common Stock (in millions)	3,147.0	3,111.0	3,154.0	3,256.0	3,378.0	3,417.0	3,242.0	3,190.0	3,277.0	3,368.0

Source: company files.

Exhibit 3   **Cash Flow Data for Sun Microsystems, 1996—2005 (US$ millions)**

	1996	1997	1998	1999	2000	2001	2002	2003	2004	2005
Cash from Operating Activities										
Net Income	$476.4	$ 762.4	$ 762.9	$ 1,031.3	$ 1,854.0	$ 927.0	($587.0)	($3,429.0)	($388.0)	($107.0)
Depreciation/Amortization	284.1	341.7	439.9	627.0	776.0	1,229.0	1,092.0	918.0	730.0	671.0
Deferred Taxes	–	–	–	–	–	–	(673.0)	706.0	620.0	(315.0)
Other	(72.2)	0.9	323.7	858.6	1,124.0	(67.0)	1,048.0	2,842.0	1,264.0	120.0
Cash from Operations	**688.3**	**1,105.1**	**1,526.5**	**2,516.9**	**3,754.0**	**2,089.0**	**880.0**	**1,037.0**	**2,226.0**	**369.0**
Cash from Investing Activities										
Cap Expenditures	(295.6)	(554.0)	(830.1)	(738.7)	(982.0)	(1,292.0)	(559.0)	(373.0)	(249.0)	(257.0)
Purchase of Business	–	(23.0)	(244.0)	(130.3)	(89.0)	(18.0)	(49.0)	(30.0)	(201.0)	(95.0)
Other	170.9	33.3	(94.8)	(1,227.1)	(3,154.0)	(244.0)	647.0	(125.0)	(1,861.0)	(73.0)
Cash from Investing	**(124.7)**	**(543.7)**	**(1,169.0)**	**(2,096.1)**	**(4,225.0)**	**(1,554.0)**	**39.0**	**(528.0)**	**(2,311.0)**	**(425.0)**
Cash from Financing Activities										
Net Issuance of Stock	(467.5)	(374.8)	(190.8)	(242.7)	(285.0)	(899.0)	(354.0)	(317.0)	239.0	218.0
Net Issuance of Debt	–	–	–	–	1,500.0	–	(13.0)	(201.0)	(28.0)	(252.0)
Dividends	–	–	–	–	–	–	–	–	–	–
Other	18.9	(55.3)	(4.6)	88.7	4.0	(13.0)	–	–	–	–
Cash from Financing	**(448.6)**	**(430.1)**	**(195.5)**	**(154.0)**	**1,219.0**	**(912.0)**	**(367.0)**	**(518.0)**	**211.0**	**(34.0)**
Currency Adjustments	–	–	–	–	–	–	–	–	–	–
Change in Cash	115.0	131.3	162.1	266.7	748.0	(377.0)	552.0	(9.0)	126.0	(90.0)
Free Cash Flow										
Cash from Operations	688.3	1,105.1	1,526.5	2,516.9	3,754.0	2,089.0	880.0	1,037.0	2,226.0	369.0
Capital Expenditures	(295.6)	(554.0)	(830.1)	(738.7)	(982.0)	(1,292.0)	(559.0)	(373.0)	(249.0)	(257.0)
Free Cash Flow	**$392.7**	**$ 551.1**	**$ 696.4**	**$ 1,778.2**	**$ 2,772.0**	**$ 797.0**	**$ 321.0**	**$ 664.0**	**$1,977.0**	**$ 112.0**

Source: company files.

Exhibit 4   **Balance Sheet Data for Sun Microsystems, 1996–2005 (US$ millions)**

	1996	1997	1998	1999	2000	2001	2002	2003	2004	2005
Assets										
Cash and Equivalent	$ 528.9	$ 660.2	$ 822.3	$1,089.0	$ 1,849.0	$ 1,472.0	$ 2,024.0	$ 2,015.0	$ 2,141.0	$ 2,051.0
Short-term Investments	460.7	452.6	476.2	1,576.1	626.0	387.0	861.0	1,047.0	1,460.0	1,345.0
Account Receivable	1,206.6	1,666.5	1,845.8	2,286.9	2,690.0	2,955.0	2,745.0	2,381.0	2,339.0	2,231.0
Inventory	460.9	438.0	346.5	307.9	557.0	1,049.0	591.0	416.0	464.0	431.0
Other Current Assets	376.6	511.2	656.8	856.5	1,155.0	2,071.0	1,556.0	920.0	899.0	1,133.0
Total Current Assets	**3,033.7**	**3,728.5**	**4,147.5**	**6,116.4**	**6,877.0**	**7,934.0**	**7,777.0**	**6,779.0**	**7,303.0**	**7,191.0**
Net Property, Plant, and Equipment	533.9	799.9	1,300.6	1,608.9	2,095.0	2,697.0	2,453.0	2,267.0	1,996.0	1,769.0
Intangibles						2,041.0	2,286.0	417.0	533.0	554.0
Other Long-term Assets	233.3	168.9	262.9	695.1	5,180.0	5,509.0	4,006.0	3,522.0	4,671.0	4,676.0
Total Assets	**$3,800.9**	**$4,697.3**	**$5,711.1**	**$8,420.4**	**$14,152.0**	**$18,181.0**	**$16,522.0**	**$12,985.0**	**$14,503.0**	**$14,190.0**
Liabilities and Stockholders' Equity										
Accounts Payable	$ 325.1	$ 468.9	$495.6	$ 753.8	$ 924.0	$ 1,050.0	$ 1,044.0	$ 903.0	$ 1,057.0	$ 1,167.0
Short-term Debt	87.6	100.9	47.2	1.7	7.0	3.0	205.0	–	257.0	–
Taxes Payable	134.9	118.6	188.6	402.8	422.0	90.0				
Accrued Liabilities	801.6	963.0	1,126.5	1,646.6	2,117.0	1,862.0	1,739.0	1,506.0	1,930.0	1,727.0
Other Short-term Liabilities	140.2	197.6	265.0	422.1	1,289.0	2,141.0	2,069.0	1,720.0	1,869.0	1,872.0
Total Current Liabilities	**1,489.3**	**1,849.0**	**2,122.9**	**3,227.0**	**4,759.0**	**5,146.0**	**5,057.0**	**4,129.0**	**5,113.0**	**4,766.0**
Long-term Debt	60.2	106.3			1,720.0	1,705.0	1,449.0	1,531.0	1,175.0	1,123.0
Other Long-term Liabilities			74.6	381.6	364.0	744.0	215.0	834.0	1,777.0	1,627.0
Total Liabilities	**1,549.4**	**1,955.3**	**2,197.4**	**3,608.6**	**6,843.0**	**7,595.0**	**6,721.0**	**6,494.0**	**8,065.0**	**7,516.0**
Total Equity	**2,251.5**	**2,741.9**	**3,513.6**	**4,811.8**	**7,309.0**	**10,586.0**	**9,801.0**	**6,491.0**	**6,438.0**	**6,674.0**
Total Liabilities and Equity	**$3,800.9**	**$4,697.3**	**$5,711.1**	**$8,420.4**	**$14,152.0**	**$18,181.0**	**$16,522.0**	**$12,985.0**	**$14,503.0**	**$14,190.0**

Source: company files.

Toyota's Strategy and Initiatives in Europe: the Launch of the Aygo

Kazuo Ichijo
International Institute of Management Development

George Rädler
International Institute of Management Development

Since 2000 the output of the global [auto] industry has risen by about 3 million vehicles to some 60 million: of that increase, [more than] half came from Toyota alone. While most attention over the past four years has focused on a spectacular turnaround at Nissan, Toyota has undergone a dramatic growth spurt all round the world.

—*The Economist,* January 29, 2005, p. 61

For Toyota Motor Europe (TME), locally designed cars and the availability of diesel engines led to impressive results: 2005 was the ninth consecutive year of record sales for Toyota in Europe. Sales grew by almost 50 percent from 2000 to 2005. The new strategy paid off financially, too. According to *BusinessWeek*, the operating profit increased ninefold to $654 million in 2003.

After plant openings in France, Turkey, Poland, and the Czech Republic, local production was expected to reach 60 percent in 2006. This lowered exposure to exchange rates and import tariffs. Within Toyota, sales increases from Europe were needed to meet ambitious global sales targets.

But for the European marketing team of Toyota's Aygo minicar, the challenge continued. In a fiercely competitive market they had to find 100,000 buyers annually for the 3.41-meter Aygo. This segment was seen as a difficult market: low prices meant low margins. Mercedes-Benz's "MCC smart" recorded losses of €4 billion between 2000 and 2005.[1] Other competitors also had difficulties making money in this segment.

With the launch of the Aygo, Toyota challenged many of its traditional views: the car was specifically designed for the European market and exclusively sold there. The factory was a 50/50 joint venture with the Peugeot/Citroën Group (PSA) in the Czech Republic. But for the marketing managers of the Aygo, the challenge was how to sell the 100,000 units annually they guaranteed to buy from the factory in the Czech Republic.

TOYOTA GLOBAL: BECOMING NUMBER 1[2]

Toyota Motor Corporation (Toyota) had posted record growth. Sales reached 7.97 million units in 2005, an increase of about 2.5 million since 2000 (Exhibit 1).

For Toyota, North America remained the most important international market and its market share was increasing rapidly. In 2005 sales hit the 2 million unit level for the first time and Toyota held 13.7 percent of the important U.S. market (up from 9.3

Exhibit 1   **Vehicle Sales of Toyota Motor Corporation**

	1999	2000	2001	2002	2003	2004	2005
Global sales (million units)	5,182	5,526	5,543	6,113	6,719	7,400	7,970

Note: Toyota publishes its numbers for the financial year ending March 31.
Source: Various annual reports, press reports.

percent in 2000). Sixty percent of the American demand was satisfied by 12 plants in the NAFTA region.

For 2006 Toyota was expected to reach 9 million units in production—with luxury brand Lexus reaching the 500,000 units mark for the first time (up from 400,000 units in 2004). Between 1990 and 2005, the number of Toyota plants increased from 20 factories in 14 countries to 47 factories in 26 countries. Within Toyota, there was concern that such rapid expansion could hurt the company. Toyota president Katsuaki Watanabe explained:

> Everyone should be dissatisfied with the present situation and should constantly try to improve or change things. It's important to realize that there is always something more we need to aim at. That's what needs to be recognized by every individual. When you are growing you are satisfied with the status quo, and that's no good.[3]

A European supplier, listening to a presentation by former chairman Fujio Cho in 2004, later remembered:

> Listening to them [the top management], you get the impression that Toyota is facing its biggest crisis in history.[4]

The company was one of nine members of the "$10 billion club," indicating a net income in excess of $10 billion (2005: net income of $12.35 billion on revenues of $189 billion; revenue grew by 14 percent). Toyota was one of two manufacturing companies on that list, the other seven companies were in either oil/gas or financial services. In order to avoid complacency, Toyota set the ambitious goal of reaching 15 percent global share by 2010 (up from 11 percent in 2005). On the financial markets, Toyota had the reputation of delivering on its ambitious goals. As of March 2006, Toyota accounted for 35 percent of the total market capitalization in the global automotive industry (refer to Exhibit 2).

It was expected that as early as 2006, Toyota could overtake General Motors (GM) as the world's

Exhibit 2   **Shares of Global Sales and Market Capitalization (2006)**

	Share of Global Vehicle Sales	Share of Global Market Capitalization
Toyota	11.0%	35.0%
Honda	5.2	11.0
Nissan	5.4	8.5
DaimlerChrysler	7.7	7.5
Ford	11.0	2.9
General Motors	13.0	2.2

Note: According to this study, Asian manufacturers accounted for no more than 43 percent of all passenger cars sold in the world but for 73 percent of the worth of all car makers. GM's sales data are likely to include volume from foreign manufacturers, in which GM holds a minority stake.
Source: Wall Street Journal Europe, March 23, 2006, p. 4.

largest car manufacturer. But Jim Farley, Toyota's VP of marketing in the U.S. was cautious: "And if we do become No. 1, we'll still act like we're No. 3 or 4, because that's the Toyota Way."[5] A spokesperson explained: "Our goals are not directly positioned against competitors. Our goals are around customers." However, in order to reach the 15 percent share by 2010, continued growth in Europe was essential.

TOYOTA IN EUROPE: "WE ARE GROWING STEP-BY-STEP"[6]

With the launch of the Yaris model in 1999, Toyota's sales took off. The initial goal of reaching a European sales volume of 800,000 units was reached two years ahead of time—in 2003 instead of 2005 (refer to Exhibit 3).

Besides attractive models from the design center in Nice (France), Toyota benefited from the much better availability of diesel engines (starting

Exhibit 3   **Unit Sales and Market Share for Toyota in Western and Eastern Europe**

	2000	2001	2002	2003	2004	2005
Sales (thousand units)	656	666	756	835	916	964
Market share	3.56%	3.58%	4.4%	4.7%	4.9%	5.1%

Source: Toyota in Europe (2005): 15; Toyota Web site www.toyota-europe.com.

in 2002), which reached penetration rates of almost 40 percent in 2005. Moreover, Toyota's position in the market was different: for the first time the company was able to exploit a more emotional positioning around "green issues." The Prius hybrid model won the coveted "2005 [European] Car of the Year Award." In 2005 Toyota sold around 18,000 units of Prius in Europe (global sales: 180,000 units) and by 2010 was expecting to sell 1,000,000 units worldwide. Hybrid technology gave Toyota a good opportunity to position itself as a technology leader since the competition had only just started to sell hybrid models. The technology was also launched in the Lexus RX 400h in 2005. The hybrid version fetched a price premium of €6,200* over the gasoline-powered RX 300. In Europe, Toyota was also one of the first to offer its D-Cat diesel engines with a diesel particulate filter. Toyota's environmental initiatives were widely recognized. In a 2006 survey on "who builds the most environment-friendly car," Toyota came first in the five biggest European markets plus Poland.[7]

* Exchange rate: €1 = $1.27 (May 7, 2006)

Toyota drivers were on average around 53 years of age.[8] Customers were very loyal and Toyota usually topped customer satisfaction indexes such as J. D. Power. Lexus continued to secure top ratings in J. D. Power surveys, but its sales continued to be below expectations, with the volume fluctuating around 25,000 units—compared to over 250,000 units in the U.S. In Europe, Lexus models were sold with extended warranties, including a six-year warranty, three years of free services, maintenance, and roadside assistance (compared with two years at most luxury car manufacturers).

Apart from Lexus, Toyota was in the passing lane in Europe. It had considerably increased its sales volumes in Europe, unlike some of the other Japanese manufacturers (refer to Exhibit 4 for annual sales in Western Europe).

In 2005 Toyota's largest markets were: UK (138,500 units), Italy (130,507 units), Germany (130,275 units), France (92,024 units), and Spain (65,498 units). However, Toyota executives believed there was still a huge potential for the brand. Despite record sales in Europe, Toyota made it to the top-10

Exhibit 4   **Annual Sales of Asian Brands of Motor Vehicles in Western Europe, 2000 vs. 2005**

		2000		2005	
Brand	Country of Origin	Units Sold	Market Share	Units Sold	Market Share
Honda	Japan	181,600	1.2%	238,368	1.6%
Mazda	Japan	181,710	1.2	226,427	1.6
Mitsubishi	Japan	160,281	1.1	127,351	0.9
Nissan	Japan	393,736	2.7	343,023	2.4
Suzuki	Japan	131,587	0.9	182,415	1.3
Toyota	Japan	542,771	3.7	762,736	5.3
Daewoo	South Korea	202,058	1.4	12,972	0.1
Hyundai	South Korea	227,210	1.5	298,389	2.1
Kia	South Korea	68,300	0.5	232,309	1.6

Note: The Kia numbers are for 2001 (not 2000).
Source: ACEA.

Exhibit 5   **Top-10 Car Registrations in Four Largest European Countries, 2005**

France		Germany		Italy		United Kingdom	
Models	**Units**	**Models**	**Units**	**Models**	**Units**	**Models**	**Units**
Renault Megane	188,373	VW Golf	237,990	Fiat Punto	173,502	Ford Focus	145,010
Renault Clio	132,982	Opel Astra	122,841	Fiat Panda	130,972	Opel Astra	108,461
Peugeot 206	119,907	Audi A4	100,910	Ford Fiesta	69,946	Opel Corsa	89,463
Peugeot 307	113,484	VW Passat	98,136	**Toyota Yaris**	**66,271**	Renault Megane	87,093
Citroën C3	79,259	BMW 3-series	96,311	Lancia Ypsilon	64,436	Ford Fiesta	83,803
Peugeot 407	68,130	MB A-Class	85,691	Ford Focus	63,050	VW Golf	67,749
Citroën C4	63,798	Ford Focus	78,899	VW Golf	60,004	Peugeot 206	67,450
Renault Modus	61,877	MB C-Class	77,845	Renault Megane	58,896	Ford Mondeo	57,589
Ford Focus	48,930	VW Touran	76,077	Citroën C3	58,152	Renault Clio	56,538
Renault Twingo	45,594	VW Polo	71,061	Opel Astra	54,972	BMW 3-series	44,844

Source: Auto Motor Sport, March 2006, p. 12.

best-selling list only for Italy (refer to Exhibit 5 for the top registrations in the largest four markets in Europe).

But Toyota wanted more: It stated its sales goal of 1.2 million units annually in Europe by 2010. However, the press was already speculating on whether the goal could be reached two years earlier.[9]

LOCALIZING PRODUCTION IN EUROPE

After the 1992 opening of Toyota's first car and engine plant in the UK, the speed of plant openings accelerated in the new millennium. A car plant in France started production in 2001; in the same year Toyota produced over 200,000 cars in Europe for the first time. Only three years later, the company was producing 583,000 cars per year in Europe (see Exhibit 6).

Exhibit 6   **Toyota's Production in Europe, 2004**

UK	245,000 units	Avensis: 180,000 units, Corolla Hatchback
France	204,000 units	All Yaris
Turkey	134,000 units	Corolla Sedan/ Wagon/ Verso
Total	583,000 units	

By 2005 Toyota had produced 638,000 vehicles in Europe and this was expected to increase to over 800,000 units in 2006. Exhibit 7 gives an overview of the factory openings in Europe.

By 2005, Toyota had a total of eight plants in six countries (total investment: about €6 billion since 1990). A spokesperson for the company explained the dilemma they were facing, "We really don't want to be perceived as a Japanese invader."[10] But the question was, how to get round it?

TOYOTA AND PSA JOIN FORCES

The automotive industry was surprised when Toyota and PSA (holding company for the Peugeot and Citroën brands) announced a 50/50 joint venture in late 2001. The factory, to be located in Kolin, Czech Republic (about 60 km to the east of Prague), was planned for an annual capacity of 300,000 units. The joint venture was limited to manufacturing, with cars being sold separately through the Toyota/Peugeot/Citroën distribution channels. Manufacturing, purchasing and R&D accounted for around 70 percent of value-added in car manufacturing (refer to Exhibit 8 for the business system).

The objective was to produce a minicar with 93 percent common parts between the Toyota, Peugeot, and Citroën cars. For Toyota, this was a completely new segment. Peugeot's aim was to produce the replacement model for the Peugeot 106. This model

Exhibit 7   **Timeline for Toyota's Factory Openings in Europe**

Start of production	2001	2002	2002	2002	2005	2005
Type of factory	Car	Petrol engines	Transmissions, later also engines	Car	Diesel engines	Car (JV with PSA)
Location	Valenciennes, France	Valenciennes, France	Walbrzych, Poland	Adapazari, Turkey	Jelcz-Laskowice, Poland	Kolin, Czech Republic
Capacity	240,000 units		250,000 engines; 550,000 transmissions	134,000 units	180,000 engines	300,000 units, of which Toyota will take 100,000
Total investment	€ 790 m	See 2001	€ 400 m	€ 730 m	€ 200 m	€1.3 billion (Toyota: 50%)

Source: Various Toyota documents.

Exhibit 8   **Value Chain System in the Automotive Industry**

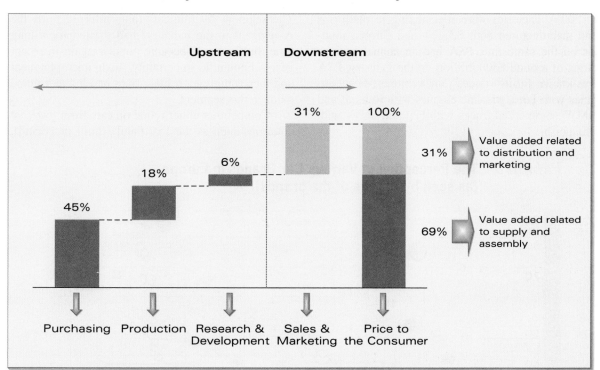

Source: McKinsey, ATKearney

was on sale between 1991 and 2004 and sold a total of 2.8 million units over that period. It was also sold under the Citroën Saxo brand between 1997 and 2003. Until the Kolin factory opened in mid-2005, PSA did not have a replacement for the Peugeot 106 and the Citroën Saxo.

PSA Company Background

Paris-based PSA had been the big success story of the European automobile sector. Although the PSA name was almost unknown to the majority of end customers, the company's two brands (Peugeot and

Citroën) were very popular. Sales increased from 2.8 million units in 2000 to 3.39 million units in 2005 (5.5 percent share globally). Non-European sales surpassed 1 million units in 2005 for the first time ever. The non-European growth averaged 17 percent up to 2005 (mostly from Asia and South America).

In the five years up to 2003, PSA increased its European share from 12 percent to 15.5 percent, but it fell to 14 percent in 2005. Nevertheless, it remained Europe's second biggest manufacturer (after the VW Group). The company was praised for its good vehicle designs, diesel engines, clever advertising and excellent cost position in manufacturing, but it was disappointed by the results of quality surveys (refer to Exhibit 9 for an overview of quality ratings).

PSA strongly pushed its platform strategy. By 2008, the three main platforms were expected to account for 3 million units (up from 1.5 million in 2005). Factories were specializing in platforms and manufactured both Peugeot and Citroën models on the same line. PSA had an annual savings target of around €600 million. In the industry, PSA was known for its various joint ventures: diesel engines with Ford, gasoline engines with Renault and BMW, commercial trucks with Fiat and SUVs with Mitsubishi.

At the same time, PSA was actively involved in Eastern Europe. In addition, the company also opened a new factory in Slovakia (annual capacity: 300,000 units). It was estimated that PSA would source 15 percent of its total European production from Eastern Europe by 2008, up from 0 percent in 2004.[11] Industry sources were expecting the factory in Slovakia to grow to 500,000 units. This would make it the fifth largest car plant in Europe.

INTRICACIES OF THE MINICAR SEGMENT

The Challenge: Operating Profitably

The segment for minicars (also referred to as the A-segment in the industry) had existed for a long time, but had only became popular again in recent years. Economic uncertainty, high unemployment and increasingly high fuel prices had led to volume gains in this segment.

Competitors either relied on cars from low-cost countries such as the Fiat Panda (built in Poland),

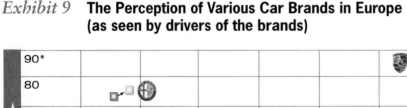

Exhibit 9   **The Perception of Various Car Brands in Europe (as seen by drivers of the brands)**

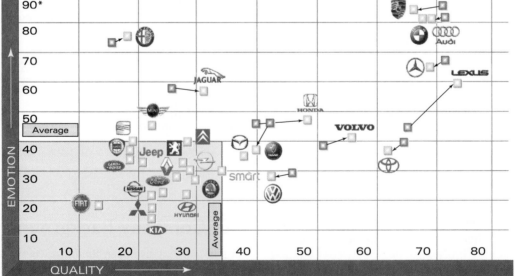

*in Percent   ■ 2005   □ 2006

Source: Auto Motor und Sport, "Best Cars 06," 6/2006: 139

VW Fox (Brazil), Hyundai Getz (South Korea). Some other competitors opted for very long product life cycles: Renault's Twingo had sold for over a decade without major changes, as had the former model of the Nissan Micra (both models were built in Western Europe). The base price for this category was normally below €10,000, but it could increase with the addition of features.

In the case of MCC smart, the company went furthest in differentiating their offering. The car was positioned as a fashion item. Customers could have the color of the plastic exterior body panels completely changed within 90 minutes at a cost of between €825 and €1,225. However, only 0.8 percent of customers made use of this option—mostly after accidents or other damage. Most other innovative features around the car such as the mobility concept, for example special rates at parking garages, were either stopped or drastically reduced. Cumulated losses reached in excess of €4 billion between 2000 and 2005 and the future of the car remained uncertain.

Volkswagen Group tried entering this segment by offering the technological advanced aluminum frame for its Audi A2 model and offering a 3-liter version of its VW Lupo minicar with a fuel consumption of less than 3 liters/100 km. However, the Audi model became too expensive and the 3-liter Lupo initially lacked convenience features, such as power windows and power steering in order to keep the fuel consumption low. Neither of the models reached sales targets and both were discontinued in 2004. Soon afterwards, Volkswagen started to import the Fox model as a replacement for the Lupo. BMW's MINI model was relaunched in 2001 and stressed its rich heritage. At average transaction prices in excess of €22,000, it sold around 200,000 units in 2005 (refer to Exhibit 10 for the actual sales data).

Minicars Please Regulators

Regardless of the economics around minicars, they were helping car makers to make big improvements with regard to their voluntary target for reducing carbon dioxide by 2008. Under a 1999 agreement with the European Union, the European car industry pledged to reduce the per-car carbon dioxide (CO_2) emissions to 140 grams per kilometer by the year 2008, compared to 175 grams per kilometer in 1999. Japanese and Korean manufacturers also accepted this challenge, but they were given an

Exhibit 10   **New Vehicle Registrations in Europe in the Minicar Segment, 2001–2005**

Brand, Model Name	2001	2002	2003	2004	2005
Toyota Aygo	0	0	0	0	21,224
Peugeot 107	0	0	0	0	19,552
Citroën C1	0	0	0	0	17,730
BMW Mini	24,980	144,119	176,465	184,357	200,428
Chevrolet Matiz	0	0	0	22,066	53,247
Daewoo Matiz	91,476	72,232	59,176	36,528	1,879
Citroën Saxo	243,962	164,477	71,478	1,737	19
Fiat Panda	101,924	117,959	131,677	224,055	228,106
Hyundai Atos	60,606	40,130	19,679	37,186	37,450
Kia Picanto	0	0	0	58,135	83,076
MCC smart	115,000	120,000	123,000	152,000	125,000
Mercedes A-Class	165,915	151,646	132,911	125,950	172,539
Opel/ Vauxhall Agila	86,236	79,218	74,518	55,237	37,143
Peugeot 106	109,244	67,764	38,656	1,919	11
Renault Twingo	168,358	143,441	116,472	85,580	76,853
VW Fox	0	0	0	0	50,862

Note: The data cover 19 European countries.
Chevrolet took over Daewoo and is fading out the Daewoo brand.
The numbers for BMW Mini and MCC smart are world-wide sales data.
Source: Toyota, various annual reports, press releases.

additional year to implement it. Car makers took this seriously, as such a voluntary agreement could easily find its way into regulations. The best way to reduce CO_2 was to reduce fuel consumption. Minicars usually had small engines and hence low fuel consumption. While the popularity of diesel engines greatly helped (they consumed less fuel), the increasing consumer demand for air conditioning, more horsepower, big SUVs, as well as new regulations including better protection for pedestrians, often added additional weight to the car and new sources for electricity consumption (hence higher fuel consumption). So fuel-efficient engines became crucial for meeting the needs of this voluntary target. PSA developed a new 1.6-liter engine which consumed 10 percent less fuel, but this development came at a cost of €610 million.[12] PSA decided to share this cost with BMW.

TOYOTA PEUGEOT CITROËN AUTOMOBILE (TPCA) IN THE CZECH REPUBLIC*

Setup: Simple, Slim, Lean

The TPCA factory was the biggest foreign direct investment ever made in the Czech Republic at a cost of €1.3 billion. Located in Kolin, it was about 60 km from Mlada Boleslav, the home town of Skoda Auto (member of the VW Group) and many suppliers.

The factory was set up by Masatake Enomoto from Toyota. A lawyer by training, he led the negotiations that resulted in the establishment of the Kolin plant. The negotiations ended with a clear arrangement on the financial side. Jean-Martin Folz, CEO of PSA, later explained, "We shared the development cost and we paid for only two-thirds of the new factory in Kolin."[13] The pillars of the agreement included: PSA would absorb 200,000 units annually and Toyota half of that. Toyota would be responsible for running the factory (according to the Toyota Production System [TPS]) and would

be responsible for the development of the three vehicles to be produced at the factory (including the Peugeot 107 and Citroën C1). This helped greatly to build in the 93 percent parts commonality between the different brands. In return, PSA would handle all purchasing and supplier relations including their selection. Toyota was hoping to benefit from PSA's experience with European suppliers. Each partner would also bring one engine to the venture with the right [size] specification. Toyota would produce a 3-cylinder gasoline engine (also to be used in the bigger Toyota Yaris model) and PSA would bring a 4-cylinder diesel engine (also used in the Peugeot 206, Citroën C2 and C3). Engines were among the most expensive components of a car, averaging at around 32 percent of total vehicle cost.[14]

Enomoto oversaw the construction and start-up. This could explain why the factory looked very much like a Toyota factory. *Automotive News*, an industry newspaper, reported:

> In many ways, the Kolin plant is a typical Toyota factory. The principles of efficient production that Toyota has established over the years are practiced in full at TPCA, including kaizen (continuous improvement), jidoka (fixing problems right away, where they occur), and just-in-time delivery.[15]

Much of this can be attributed to Satoshi Takae. Takae was a Toyota veteran who started in Kolin as factory manager and was promoted to president of TPCA in 2005. His goal for the factory was very clear: "To be the number one plant in Europe."

In order to realize this, he had to work together with not only his 30 expatriate colleagues from Toyota, but also with nine permanent members of staff from PSA. For Takae, this meant exposing the Toyota Way, the "mysterious" Toyota DNA to outsiders (refer to Exhibit 11 for the key concepts of the Toyota Way). At the same time, this working arrangement implied transferring control of suppliers to PSA.

Role of PSA

With an increasing trend toward outsourcing, PSA's task to manage all purchasing functions was hugely important to the outcome. Developing the local supply infrastructure, which accounted for 80 percent of all parts purchased (by value and volume), was seen as a major task. TPCA was directly dealing with

---

* Readers of this case are strongly encouraged to have a look at the official Web site of TPCA for a virtual factory tour. http://www.tpca-cz.com/en/about_factory_how.php#

Exhibit 11   **The Toyota Way**

Section 1: Long-Term Philosophy

Principle 1: Base your management decisions on a long-term philosophy, even at the expense of short-term financial goals.

Section 2: The Right Process Will Produce the Right Results

Principle 2: Create continuous process flow to bring problems to the surface.

Principle 3: Use "pull" systems to avoid "overproduction."

Principle 4 : Level out the workload (Heijunka).

Principle 5: Build a culture of stopping to fix problems, to get quality right the first time.

Principle 6: Standardized tasks are the foundation for continuous improvement and employee empowerment.

Principle 7: Use visual control so no problems are hidden.

Principle 8: Use only reliable, thoroughly tested technology that serves your people and processes.

Section 3: Add Value to the Organization by Developing Your People and Partners

Principle 9: Grow leaders who thoroughly understand the work, live the philosophy, and teach it to others.

Principle 10: Develop exceptional people and teams who follow your company's philosophy.

Principle 11: Respect your extended network of partners and suppliers by challenging them and helping them to improve.

Section 4: Continuously Solving Root Problem Drives Organizational Learning

Principle 12: Go and see for yourself to thoroughly understand the situation (Genchi Genbutsu).

Principle 13: Make decisions slowly by consensus, thoroughly considering all options; implement decisions rapidly (Nemawashi).

Principle 14: Become a learning organization through relentless reflection (hansei) and continuous improvement (Kaizen).

Source: Jeffrey K. Liker, *The Toyota Way* (New York: McGraw-Hill, 2004).

around 150 Tier-1 suppliers. These were the big suppliers at the top of the hierarchy and many of them were the Czech or Slovak subsidiaries of the big international suppliers.

Within the automotive industry, PSA was known for its cost focus and its various JVs. Nicolas Guibert, TPCA's executive VP and highest ranking PSA official in Kolin and previously a plant manager in one of Peugeot's French factories, explained:

> PSA is one of the most joint-ventured companies [in the industry]. But this JV is different from other JVs. Usually, the responsibilities are clearly shared and each company works with high autonomy for what it is in charge. PSA has two JVs with Fiat—one in Italy and one in France. In Italy, Fiat does the design, process engineering and production operation and PSA pays for each car. In France, it is the contrary. Our engine JV with Ford is structured in a similar way: PSA is in charge of some engines from design to manufacturing and Ford of others. In our engine JV with BMW, they do the design and we do the industrialization. But here it is slightly different. We also share the tasks within the production operation. In TPCA we are not only spectators but also actors.

The level of difference could be seen in Guibert's role. He was reporting to Takae. Guibert was also responsible for accounting and finance functions of the factory.

Supplier Selection

European suppliers were very eager to supply TPCA since this was seen as the entry point for supplying Toyota. European suppliers were struggling, as many of their traditional customers had cut their production volumes considerably in recent years. Therefore, by supplying TPCA they hoped to grow with Toyota in Europe. TPCA was quite clear on what it would not do. The company did not outsource external surfaces and key structural parts for quality reasons.

While supplying Toyota was an excellent reference in the industry, dealing with the company was not seen to be easy. Toyota's search for simplicity and economic efficiency was still a big question mark for many suppliers. Takae explained:

> We are relationship-oriented with regards to the suppliers. We were surprised to see this transaction orientation with some of the suppliers here.

Suppliers to TPCA could also qualify for PSA's factory in neighboring Slovakia, about 250 km from Kolin. PSA had big plans at this factory, too.

RUNNING TPCA

Toyota's Production System (TPS) was running all over the world, but in each market, it needed some minor adjustments. In the case of TPCA, the rapid ramp-up worked well (reaching full production capacity in less than 12 months). The factory produced four body types (both Toyota and PSA had a 3-door and 5-door version of their respective models) on the same line. TPCA had around 3,000 employees. Extensive training took place at various European factories and in Japan for the senior positions. The training sessions lasted for a anywhere between one month and six months.

The normal shift system saw employees working for four days (10 hours each) and then they were off for three days. Newspapers reported:

> Few line workers have cars. Many live far from Kolin, often staying locally during the workweek and returning home only on days off.[16]

Management at TPCA soon started to wonder about high absenteeism among employees. A detailed analysis showed that in some cases, employees were asked to work six days in a row. And often, they did not show up on the sixth day. TPCA's management soon changed the allocation of shifts and it lowered absenteeism. But turnover remained an issue.

Regarding talent management, the question was, what would happen once competitor Hyundai Motor started hiring for its new Czech factory? Would employees switch to the new factory or would they stay with TPCA?

Overall, the management made every effort to embed the TPS at TPCA. It was willing to make some of the displays (ANDON) showing the status of the plant operation using pictures only, with no text, unlike in Japan and the US. With regard to running TPCA, Takae explained:

> Of course, we had to overcome cultural and language barriers. We are dealing here with three national cultures—Japanese, French and Czech—and two company cultures with very different histories and production systems. But we found an overriding

principle—cost reduction. Everything would depend on cost. In order to overcome the language barriers, we visualized everything; we never had to do this before [to this extent].

At the same time, TPCA actively tried to work around local regulations. *Automotive News Europe* reported:

> To keep a promise it would not bring weekend heavy-truck traffic through town to the plant, TPCA must stockpile extra parts before the weekend starts. . . . It's built a parking lot. . . . The new parking lot can hold up to 180 trailers full of parts and raw materials. Then as the assembly lines move on Saturday and Sunday, logistics workers can move the parts via forklifts and cranes into the plant. It is an indication of how flexible the joint venture between PSA and Toyota is being to accommodate public feeling in its new Czech home. Because of local political pressures, the automaker gave up its promised exemption to Czech laws that limit weekend truck traffic. These laws ban trucks of 7.5 tons and larger between midnight and 10 pm on Sundays and during the summer months from 7 am to 8 pm on Saturdays.[17]

It seems that this also created a lot of goodwill within the company.

Meeting Structure

Managers at TPCA had to represent the interests of both TPCA and their employers. In order to minimize miscommunication, TPCA had a systematic meeting structure:

- Daily production meeting: This meeting took place every morning at 8:30. At this meeting, most managers were present in order to discuss quality, absenteeism and announce major decisions.

- Project Leaders Meeting: Managers from both companies originally met on a monthly basis and then only once a quarter. These meetings were attended by 10 to 20 managers from PSA and around 30 to 40 from Toyota.

- Steering Committee—TPCA's highest decision-making committee: Critical decisions were discussed here. There were five members from each side including Takae and Guibert. The meetings took place either at Toyota's HQ in Tokyo or PSA's HQ in Paris. This committee met twice a year.

Kolin, the New Travel Destination

Kolin became the new travel destination for plant managers and other executives from both Toyota and PSA. The factory was of interest, as it was a place for both companies to try new things. Generally speaking, with only 100,000 square meters, this factory was seen as having very little space. Guibert commented:

> In this project we see interesting new methodologies compared to PSA's production system. But first, the TPS is a lot more than what we see and secondly, we cannot modify deeply our system because it is coherent and it has also its strong points. While both systems have their qualities, they are above all different.

Nevertheless, within TPCA there were a few things that were off-limits to managers from the parent companies, as they were protected by patents or seen as proprietary.

UNDERSTANDING THE MARKET SPACE

As the construction of the factory was progressing, marketing managers at Toyota were getting ready for the positioning of the Aygo. The marketing challenge for selling the Aygo was considerable:

- How could a car with 93 percent standardized parts be differentiated in the marketplace from its two siblings? Colors were one differentiator, but only to a limited extent. There were six shared colors among the three brands and two colors were specific to each brand.
- Toyota also launched the new Yaris in 2005. The car was a bit bigger than the Aygo, but 3,000 more expensive. Sales representatives were likely to push the more expensive Yaris, as commissions were normally based on transaction prices.
- The plant setup with fixed volumes of 200,000 units for PSA and 100,000 for Toyota was unusual. In comparable joint ventures, there was normally a transfer pricing agreement, so the production volumes could be determined according to the market situation.

- The average age of Toyota's customers was relatively high (50+ years in Europe). The dealerships were not really accustomed to serving younger clients.
- Toyota had neither a recent history of selling cars in the A-segment nor a loyal customer base in that segment.
- The agreement with PSA prohibited the use of car pictures until the launch of the car.

For marketing managers working on the launch of the Aygo, this was a tough list to work on. For Andrea Formica, marketing manager at Toyota's European HQ in Brussels, these constraints were seen as a challenge:

> We will take the car out of the traditional showroom and bring it to the customer through special events, experience centers and concept cafes.[18]

But would younger customers select the Toyota?

Knowing Younger Customers: What Makes Generation Y Different?

Roughly speaking, Generation Y were those customers born after 1976 and was expected to be bigger than Generation X (1965–1976). Market research revealed major differences for Generation Y:

1. Consumers were more individualistic. Cars were not just transportation, they were another form of fashion apparel—it's about "making it mine."
2. Young consumers were Internet-savvy—generally they had done their homework online before physically inspecting the car.
3. This group was immune to traditional advertising. Members of Generation Y were not likely to sit in front of the TV. A study by McKinsey found that American teenagers spent 2.4 hours per day online, about six times the average of the overall population.[19] By contrast, teenagers spent less than half the time watching TV compared with the overall population.

Generation Y was definitely attractive size-wise, but reaching them would require many changes to the existing ways of doing things.

LAUNCHING THE AYGO

Given the challenge of entering a new segment, there were different approaches for launching the Aygo in Europe. As one manager put it, "It is difficult to co-ordinate between the different countries. And what is good for one country may not necessarily be good for another." To capture the European spirit, Toyota asked 10 artists from different European countries to redo the outside of an Aygo. These cars could be seen at many European car shows. Although the European HQ provided some background marketing material, the approaches for launching were different.

In Sweden, initially it was not even possible to buy the Aygo. Until May 2006, customers could only lease it as part of a mobility package, for €190 per month, including insurance, service and repairs. This was seen as a way to make the cost of owning the car more transparent.

An Example from the German Market

Markus Schrick, managing director of Toyota in Germany, outlined the initial situation:

> With Aygo we had a historic opportunity: Targeting young people who were new to Toyota with a completely new and appealing product in a [for Toyota] new segment of the market.
>
> The launch was phased in several steps, of which the first ones were the most important and maybe also the most impressive ones: (1) Identifying trendsetters amongst young people, (2) getting in touch with them personally to "promote" Aygo via (3) so-called "players." These players followed the trends discovered and created by the trendsetters and brought them to a broad young mainstream audience.
>
> This is what "viral marketing" is all about—but we needed to remain credible with our brand and product in order not to fail or to be misunderstood.
>
> "Go to where the people are" was one of our central ideas—and all together it worked well. And of course the fact that we discussed our strategies prior to our actions with these respective people helped a lot in understanding their lifestyle, attitudes and dreams.

Soon, it became apparent that the 18–30 age group was going to be the target market. Michael Potthast, Toyota's product manager for the Aygo in Germany, remembered the beginning:

> In hindsight, this was the most exciting launch I have done in my career.
>
> We wanted to sell into a market that Toyota did not know but, as always, understanding the customers was important. We had to make the car attractive to young, first-time buyers. We wanted to position ourselves as young, but we had to be credible in what we do.
>
> [Generation Y] was definitely a good target group, but they were difficult to get in touch with. Our dealers were not used to them as customers, except when the parents were buying a car for their children. We had a similar reaction in focus groups. One of our main findings, which became a motto for the Aygo retail experience was the Generation Y attribute: "Don't sell to me, make me buy."

For Aygo's product managers in Europe, reaching the customers would require new approaches (refer to Exhibit 12 for pictures of the car). At the same time, they could not change everything. For example, Toyota did not want—under any circumstances—to alter its reputation of having sufficient safety equipment on board. Starting with the first Aygo models sold, the standard equipment included six airbags, ABS and power steering at price points below €9,000.

Early Promotional Activities   For the executives around Potthast and the agencies involved, it became clear that Generation Y could not be reached through "traditional marketing" practices. They would rely on very little traditional advertising, opting instead for direct contact with potential customers at the places they frequented:

- ***Phase 1*** *(about nine months prior to the launch)*: Toyota started communication with potential customers very early on. They created an interactive "Aygo online community" without the Toyota name. Visitors to the Web site wondered: Who/what is Aygo? At that point, there were no answers to that question. The goal was to get into dialogue with this market. The Web site included, among other things, videogames.

- ***Phase 2*** (*a few months before the launch in July 2005*): Aygo trendscouts arrived at discotheques and pointed visitors to the Aygo booths inside the venue. There, booths for playing videogames were set up. The highest scorers of the evening would get attractive prizes, including leather cowboy hats, which were very popular at the time. Visitors could also continue their

Exhibit 12   **The Aygo (3-door and 5-door)**

Source: Toyota.

game from home via the Aygo Web site. Inside another booth, pictures and video messages of visitors were taken. The pictures were posted on the Web site; the video messages could be sent to any e-mail address. The cowboy hats and other prizes were marked, "Aygo by Toyota," with "by Toyota" in a much smaller font size. Other prizes included mints in the shape of "ecstasy" drug pills and were also marked, "Aygo by Toyota."

Toyota also became involved in sponsoring rap concerts, among others a popular rap band—Fantastischen Vier. While the rappers did not actively promote the car during the concert, an Aygo poster was hanging on the stage. By sending text messages from their mobiles, visitors could win tickets to an after-hour VIP party with the band, which was sponsored by Toyota. The band also produced four video clips and a music contest. Here the public could send in their music files and the best one would then be recorded professionally. This partnership attracted a lot of attention by the media, and eventually led to an open-air concert, which was also sponsored by MTV, a popular TV station among teenagers.

Getting Closer to the Launch   Besides the Web site, Toyota put great emphasis on other ways of communicating with potential customers. The goal was to launch Aygo as a lifestyle vehicle. Besides a thorough dealer training, there were several innovative ways to reach customers:

- *Dealer Training:* As dealers did not have much experience with young customers, they were sent to an extensive dealer training. The location, an unused subway station in the center of Berlin, provided an unusual location. The subway station was remodeled into a living room. The goal was to get the dealers in the minds of the core customers in the 18–30 age group. This covered everything from how do these people live to what kind of technologies were important to them, for example MP3 players. The subway station was also used for the press launch.

- *Aygo Nights:* The launch was on a Friday night in early July 2005 and it was intended to be something special. The logic was to take the car to where the customers were. The dealers either picked their showroom or, if they felt that their location was unsuitable for the target group, various other locations where young people would go. Some organized beach parties/volleyball tournaments, disco nights and concerts.

- *Aygo Lifestyle Magazine:* On the one hand, this was a car brochure dealing with the Aygo, but on the other hand, it was a real lifestyle magazine covering typical topics such as fashion, travel, food and sports. The lifestyle side also included commercials from Calvin Klein, Samsonite, and Fossil watches. It was also used for communicating product news, such as the arrival of new colors. The magazine was initially published every quarter and subsequently twice a year. It was produced on a European basis, with some variation according to countries.

- *Aygo City Tour:* to the biggest universities. This was a way for university students to test-drive the Aygo. But it was far from a normal test-drive. The Tour consisted of several renovated caravans from the 1970s. One caravan was for booking test-drives. Another caravan was converted into a lounge, another one was set up for sending video messages via the Internet.

- *Mobile Services:* Potential customers could have car specifications sent to their mobile phones and register for brochures via SMS, a technology heavily used by members of Generation Y.

Features of the Aygo   The Aygo had emission rates that were among the lowest—only 109 grams per kilometer. This was an important argument for the target market. The car came with a full warranty for three years or 100,000 km. But here the commonalities with other car manufacturers stopped. The interest rates for the cars were calculated according to the age of the driver. An 18-year-old customer would pay 1.8 percent interest, a 30-year-old customer had to pay 3.0 percent. The positioning of the Aygo was quite different from its siblings (refer to Exhibit 13 for pictures and different positioning of the vehicles).Customers could also opt for a package including insurance and service contracts; they could get better rates on the insurance if they joined a one-day driving training.

Accessories   It was possible to select from a wide range of accessories including window covers in "crazy" colors, costing €179. Covers for the side were available at €215.

In early 2006 Aygo was doing extremely well on the forecasted resale values of the major leasing companies. This limited the risk Toyota had to take when financing the cars. The launch was widely seen as successful and Toyota won the coveted "best media strategy award" in Germany. This was the trophy everyone wanted to have, but for managers at Toyota in Europe in 2006, the question was, how to keep up the momentum?

Exhibit 13   **Different Positioning**

Model	Toyota Aygo	Peugeot 107	Citroën C1
Sales goal	100,000 units	100,000 units	100,000 units
Predecessor	—	Peugeot 106	Citroën Saxo
Base price	€8,950	€8,890	€8,390
Target market	First-time buyers (18–30)	Women (18–35)	Lifestyle oriented people
Ways of reaching the targets	Non-traditional ways, such as through the Internet, SMS, etc.	Mostly in women's magazines,TV magazines	

Source: Pia Krix, "Von Schweinen, Frauen und Lifestyle," *Automobilwoche*, June 11, 2005.

Endnotes

[1]Hillebrand, Walter. "Zetsche's Schlachtplan." *Capital* 9/2006: 44.

[2]Parts of the global overview of Toyota were taken from IMD-case "Toyota: Repositioning the Brand in Europe (D): Growing Step-by-step" (Case IMD-5-0701), by George Rädler and Dominique Turpin, 2006.

[3]"10 Questions for Katsuaki Watanabe." Interview in *Time* magazine, August 22, 2005: 10.

[4]"Formel Toyota." *Manager Magazin*, December 2004. 72 ff.

[5]"Toyota searches for love." *Wall Street Journal Europe*, January 11, 2006. 28.

[6]Toyota press release January 12, 2006. Quote taken from Mr. Shinichi Sasaki, President & CEO of Toyota Motor Europe (TME).

[7]See *Auto Motor Sport* 6/2006.

[8]Krix, Pia. "Von Schweinen, Frauen und Lifestyle." *Automobilwoche Online*, June 11, 2005

[9]*Automotive News*, July 11, 2005.

[10]Kanter, James. "Toyota leads Asia drive in Europe." *International Herald Tribune*, July 23, 2005.

[11]Jonas, Adam and David Cramer. "PSA Peugeot Citroën—The Toyota of Europe." *Morgan Stanley Company Update*, November 18, 2005: 7.

[12]*Automotive News Europe*, July 25, 2005: 19.

[13]Eschment, Wolfgang. "PSA plant keine weiteren Kooperationen." *Automobilwoche Online*, March 12, 2005.

[14]Radtke, Philipp and Eberhard Abele/ Andreas E. Zielke. "Die smarte Revolution in der Automobilindustrie." *Ueberreuter* (Redline Wirtschaft), 2004: 133.

[15]Kochan, Anna. "Toyota transfers high standards to Czech factory." *Automotive News Europe*, July 11, 2005: 26.

[16]Frink, Lyle. "Day One at Kolin: Czech plant starts regular output of PSA." *Automotive News Europe,* March 7, 2005.

[17]Frink, Lyle. "Add a shift? Build a Parking Lot." *Automotive News Europe*, September 19, 2005: 4.

[18]Weernink, Wim Oude. "Toyota taps US Scion brand for Aygo Marketing." *Automotive News*, March 7, 2005: 18.

[19]Court, David C., Jonathan W. Gordon and Jesko Perry. "Boosting returns on marketing investment." *McKinsey Quarterly* 2005, Number 2: 37–47.

Econet Wireless International's Expansion across Africa

Bruce Mtigwe
National University of Science and Technology

In its elegant Sandton offices near Johannesburg, South Africa, under the watchful eye of the legendary champion of mobile communications for Africa's poor, Strive Masiyiwa, founder and CEO of Econet Wireless International (EWI), the EWI top executive team was putting together its game plan for entering the next country market in Africa. The EWI footprint stretched across several African countries; however, the company did not have a network license to operate in South Africa, Africa's largest mobile phone market and headquarters of EWI's international operation. The company used a variety of ownership structures and had acquired a sizable number of network licenses. Its rapid expansion on the African continent had put it on a collision course with the Big Five mobile phone operators: South African giants MTN and Vodacom, Orascom Telecom of Egypt, Kuwait's MTC, and Luxembourg-based Millicom.

Navigating the precarious African business environment had not been easy for the international upstart; EWI had spent a significant amount of its attention and resources on legal battles with governments, partners, and competitors. It was expanding faster than it could marshal the financial and technical resources to fully develop the markets in which it had won the licenses to operate. The company had resisted all merger and takeover attempts, preferring to maintain its African identity and continue its

global expansion crusade. Although EWI had operations in 10 countries on three continents, its brand remained obscured by MTN, Vodacom, Orascom, MTC, and Millicom.

There were four strategic challenges facing the Masiyiwa-led management team. First was whether to continue to provide a complete package of telecommunications solutions (mobile networks, fixed networks, and Internet and data-streaming services) or to focus only on operating mobile networks, where EWI had a successful track record. A second issue was whether to focus on the African continent or to internationalize without regard to where licenses might be acquired. Third was the issue of whether to continue bidding for more new licenses or to zero in on building a critical mass of subscribers in the markets where it already operated, thereby avoiding spreading resources too thin and being relegated to second-tier status in all the regional markets where it operated. Fourth was the major challenge of how best to finance further growth and international expansion.

BACKGROUND

Econet Wireless was launched in Zimbabwe in 1993 by a consortium headed by Strive Masiyiwa, a young and aggressive entrepreneur who had formerly worked as a telecom engineer at the state-owned Posts and Telecommunications Corporation (PTC) before founding a successful electrical firm called Retrofit. With the advent of mobile communications on the African continent in the mid-1990s, and the deregulation of the sector globally, the stage was set for the transformation of the communications landscape. In 1993, Masiyiwa proposed a joint venture to establish Zimbabwe's first mobile network with his former employer PTC, which held a monopoly over all telecommunications at the time. PTC turned down the proposal, arguing that there was no need for the service in Zimbabwe. Masiyiwa went to court seeking to overturn PTC's monopoly over telecommunications so that he could start his own mobile telephone company. In 1995, the Supreme Court of Zimbabwe agreed with the plaintiff that the state's monopoly over telecommunications through PTC was unconstitutional and thus granted Masiyiwa the right to operate a mobile phone network. Econet, in partnership with Ericsson of Sweden, began setting up base stations around Harare, the capital of Zimbabwe.

In February 1996, however, a presidential decree barred the establishment of any private mobile networks—offenders were subject to a two-year jail term. Again Masiyiwa went to court, this time challenging the constitutionality of the presidential decree. In the meantime, the government, through PTC, began a frantic effort to establish its own mobile network (NetOne) and avoid the inconvenience of competition. At the same time, the government sought to block the entry of the Masiyiwa-led group into the market by announcing that there would be two Global System for Mobile Communications (GSM) network licenses, one of which was to be awarded to NetOne and the other to the Telecel consortium (a member of the Orascom Telecom group). Yet again Masiyiwa went to court, arguing that the Telecel consortium did not meet the tender specifications and therefore should be disqualified.

By the end of 1997, Masiyiwa had won both court cases and for the final time was granted a license to operate. This time he was also supported by the then vice president, Joshua Nkomo, to whom he had appealed to end the embarrassing travesty of justice. In a face-saving move, the government issued a third GSM network license in order to accommodate the Telecel Consortium that was led locally by some prominent members of the ruling party. In 1997, while awaiting the final determination of the

cases pending in the courts, Econet formed a consortium involving Portugal Telecom to bid for a 15-year GSM network license in Botswana, which it won in 1998. Econet launched its mobile phone service in July 1998 and then went on to list itself on the Zimbabwe Stock Exchange in September 1998, raising capital to retire debts, finance network expansion, and pursue new international opportunities. In the meantime, NetOne had been operating for two years and had entrenched itself as the market leader.

Since its launch, Econet had become popular with the general public as a symbol of resistance; moreover, its innovative product range and low prices made it the network of choice for many. Consequently, the demand for Econet lines far outstripped the company's ability to supply them; this led to the birth of a black market for Econet lines, in which a line could cost as much as 20 times its official retail price. Within one year Econet had overtaken NetOne as the market leader, and by 2006 it had a 60 percent market share, with NetOne and Telecel sharing the balance. By the end of 2005, Econet had become one of the four largest firms on the Zimbabwe Stock Exchange, with a market capitalization of over US$300 million.

Not wishing to be restricted in its international ambitions by the economic and political meltdown occurring in Zimbabwe at the time, Econet decided to relocate its headquarters to Johannesburg in 2000. Since then, it had entered a number of foreign markets, including Nigeria, Kenya, Burundi, Lesotho, Morocco, Malawi, the United Kingdom, and New Zealand. By 2006, Econet had become a recognized player in the African mobile phone market. For some time, the company had been considering a London Stock Exchange listing to facilitate raising up to US$500 million in capital to develop its global business and become a larger player in the telecom marketplace.

MOBILE TELEPHONY IN AFRICA

Like elsewhere in the world, the telecommunications sector in Africa had historically been dominated by state monopolies. Due to the undercapitalization of these state monopolies and guaranteed government subsidies, there was no pressure for innovative management practices; consequently, service delivery and telephone penetration rates across Africa were low. The average density in 2000 was one telephone line for every 70 people, although the density rates differed markedly by country. In Chad, for example, the penetration rate was one land-based line per 700 people. However, between 2000 and 2005, the use of mobile phones in Africa grew at the highest rates in the world: The number of mobile phone subscribers skyrocketed from 15.6 million to 135 million subscribers (an average compound rate of 54 percent versus a global average of 24 percent). Within the space of 12 years (1994–2006) the Africa and Middle East market (combined population of 1.2 billion) grew from almost zero to US$25 billion and counting. Still, since Africa's population was approximately 1 billion, the mobile phone penetration rate stood at less than 15 percent against a global average of 33 percent (2 billion mobile phone users worldwide from a world population of 6 billion). Mobile phone users accounted for 83 percent of Africa's telephone users, indicating the poor state of the fixed telephone infrastructure. But in spite of that, network coverage was still very low at an average of 15 percent. Consequently, it was not uncommon for subscribers to subscribe to two networks depending on where they were located or where they traveled.

Mobile phone capital investments in Africa had exploded to approximately US$14 billion in the last five years, while the average revenue per user (ARPU) had declined to between US$5 and US$10 a month from rates as high as US$40 (e.g., in Nigeria) in the early days of mobile communications. With a few exceptions, most countries in Africa had at least two mobile phone operators, and in some cases governments wishing to cash in on mobile operator license fees had overlicensed the sector, meaning that operators were not able to fully benefit from their investments. A case in point was Burundi, with a population of 7 million but four licensed mobile phone operators.

The number of traditional land-based telephone lines in Africa rose from 25.1 million in 2003 to 27.3 million in 2006, a sluggish 2.8 percent compound annual growth rate. Historically, growth in the number of land-based lines had averaged less than 7 percent annually. For the most part, the state-owned and operated telecommunications enterprises in Africa were capital-poor and had not invested very aggressively

in modern telecommunications technologies. As a consequence, interconnectivity between calls made on mobile phones and land-based telephones had suffered; this, in turn, had restricted the range of services that mobile operators could provide, since some of these depended on good interconnections with land-based telephone networks and their customers. For example, the use of telephone systems for high-speed data transfer and Internet services had been slow to take off because of the poor fixed-line infrastructural backbone, relatively high user costs, and low literacy levels in the population. Mobile communications systems were thus used chiefly for voice communications. Ironically, mobile phone subscribers in Africa had benefited from the poor state of land-based telephone networks because they gained speedier access to fast-advancing mobile technologies at competitive prices from mobile phone operators, most of which were subsidiaries of large international network operators. These new technologies included broadband and even third-generation (3G) technology that supported color phone handsets, digital photography, television, Internet services, and other high-technology facilities that older first- and second-generation (1G and 2G) phones, available at the beginning of telecommunications revolution, could not support. All this rapid access to leading-edge technology on such a large scale on the African continent might not have been possible had there been a high subscription rate to traditional landline telephone networks.

The cash-rich Middle Eastern operators and the cash-rich South African operators had been jockeying for acquisitions in a strategic effort to build a strong competitive position in the African mobile phone marketplace, where the potential for sustained long-term growth seemed so promising. The five largest competitors had led the drive to acquire smaller competitors and consolidate the supply side of the market. Recent major acquisitions included MTN's US$5.5 billion acquisition in 2006 of Investcom, a player in the African and the Middle Eastern markets, and MTC's US$3.4 billion acquisition in 2005 of Celtel, a major player in 14 African countries. However, there were a few remaining attractive acquisition candidates, including Portugal Telecom's African interests, France Telecom's interests, and even Econet Wireless. The prospect of South Africa's MTN, one of the Big Five, being itself a takeover target either by one or a consortium of Gulf-based telecom companies, had also been

Exhibit 1   **Market Capitalization and Subscriber Base of Big Five Mobile Telecom Operators in Africa**

Company	Headquarters	Market Capitalization US$ Billion (2006)	Revenues US$ Billion (2006)	Subscriber Base Africa (Worldwide)	Countries
Millicom	Luxembourg	5.8	$1.4	3.2 (13.0)	16
MTC	Kuwait	14.5	3.0	14.2 (22.9)	20
MTN	South Africa	20.5	3.0	28.6 (31.5)	21
Orascom	Egypt	12.8	2.1	19.4 (46.0)	9
Vodacom	South Africa	Not available	3.0	20.2 (28.2)	5

Source: Economist, Company financial statements.

mentioned in some press reports. Some observers believed the Big Five in Africa were destined to become the Big Three.

Exhibit 1 presents comparative data for the five biggest mobile telecom operators in Africa.

GSM technology was the standard for mobile phone operators in Africa. However, there were five fairly important mobile operators in Africa that employed Code Division Multiple Access (CDMA) technology: Movicel in Angola, Telecel in the Democratic Republic of the Congo (DRC), Kasapa Telecom in Ghana, Telecel in Zambia, and five in Nigeria that accounted for 2 percent of Nigeria's nearly 30 million mobile phone subscribers. One difficulty that subscribers encountered in areas where some competing operators used CDMA technology and other operators used GSM technology was that subscribers with CDMA handsets could not switch to an operator using GSM technology without buying a new handset—and vice versa. CDMA handsets were more expensive that GSM handsets.

Moreover, over 90 percent of Africa's mobile phone business was conducted on a prepaid basis, and many GSM mobile phone users had purchased prepaid cards from two or more GSM mobile phone operators in order to be able to make calls in areas where their GSM subscriber did not have good coverage. For example, a mobile phone subscriber of a particular GSM network, say MTN, might also have a prepaid card to make calls on Celtel (also a GSM network) in order to (1) be able to make calls in areas where Celtel had coverage and MTN did not, or (2) take advantage of lower charges that Celtel might offer on specific occasions. The propensity of subscribers to have prepaid cards for different network operators had the further effect of limiting a subscriber's loyalty to a particular network and provided subscribers to a GSM network the flexibility to switch between GSM mobile service providers at low cost.

PROFILES OF THE STRATEGIES AND POSITIONS OF AFRICA'S BIG FIVE MOBILE OPERATORS

Millicom

Luxembourg-based Millicom was formed in 1990. Millicom executives had anticipated the worldwide mobile telecom revolution early, and the company had been a first-mover in acquiring operating licenses in the developing world when they were relatively cheap. The population under license in Africa, Asia, and South America was approximately 433 million in 2006. Millicom's subscriber base was 13 million worldwide (3.2 million in Africa)—see Exhibit 2. Millicom had sales revenues of US$1.4 billion in 2006, with its African operations contributing over US$200 million in revenues. Millicom had market leader status in three relatively fragmented markets within South America (El Salvador, Honduras, and Paraguay) and one market in South East Asia (Cambodia); the combined population of these four areas was 34 million. In Africa, where Millicom had operations in seven countries, the company had market challenger status in four markets and market share laggard status in the remaining three. The biggest market in Africa by population where Millicom had operations was the Democratic Republic of Congo (population 60 million), where it had a 100 percent ownership of local mobile operator, Oasis.

From a strategic point of view, Millicom had followed a mass-market strategy anchored around the appeal of low pricing. Millicom employed a multi-branding strategy, using the Millicom brand in only 3 (Chad, Sierra Leone, and Laos) of its 16 markets. Given its investment strategy of going for relatively low population markets with a sprinkling of relatively high population markets, and a less aggressive business approach, Millicom was the weakest competitor of the Big Five. It had been the target of a takeover by China Mobile; the deal eventually failed to go through because Millicom considered the price offered by China Mobile unsatisfactory. However, several other operators were said to be interested in acquiring Millicom.

MTC

MTC, established in 1983, was the first mobile operator in the Middle East and Africa. It had revenues of US$3 billion during the first nine months of 2006, employed 12,000 people, and had operations in 6 Middle Eastern countries and 14 African countries. MTC's market capitalization at the end of 2006 was approximately US$15 billion. In 2005, it paid US$3.36 billion to acquire Celtel International BV, a company that had mobile network operations in 14 African countries (and market-leader status in 10 of them). This acquisition was followed by increasing its ownership from 39 percent to 100 percent of Mobitel of Sudan and to 65 percent in Vee-Mobile of Nigeria (formerly Econet Wireless Nigeria), at costs of US$1.3 billion and US$1 billion, respectively. These transactions catapulted MTC into major-player status in both Africa and the Middle East and gave it a total subscriber base of 23 million (see Exhibit 2). However, there was potential for substantially greater subscriber growth, in that there were 400 million people in the countries where MTC had mobile phone licenses.

MTC's strategic approach was to fully segment the market, building a formidable competitive web in each segment that was difficult for competitors to penetrate. The company aimed to capture more than a 50 percent share in markets where it had market-leader status and at least a 30 percent share in countries where it had enough competitive strength to be an up-and-coming market challenger. Its investment strategy was to concentrate resources on large population markets with relatively low mobile phone penetration rates, fast mobile phone adoption rates, and relatively high rates of economic growth. MTC was an aggressive player, striving to dominate the African and Middle Eastern mobile phone markets in which it operated. In Africa, MTC had continued to operate under the Celtel brand in all the markets where Celtel had operated prior to its acquisition by MTC. Similarly, it operated as Mobitel in Sudan after the acquisition. The MTC brand was employed in Middle Eastern countries, except in Jordan, where MTC operated under the Fastlink brand.

MTN

MTN, with a current workforce of 8,360 people, began operations in 1994 after winning the second of three mobile phone operator licenses awarded by the South African government. In South Africa, a market with a population of 47 million and a mobile phone penetration rate of 72 percent, it had 10 million subscribers (versus 20 million for major competitor Vodacom). MTN had begun entering other countries in Africa in 1997 when it acquired a license in Uganda. This was followed by the acquisition of operating licenses in Rwanda, Swaziland, and Cameroon in 1998–2000. In 2001, MTN acquired a license to operate in Nigeria, Africa's most populous country, with approximately 151 million people. The mobile phone penetration rate in Nigeria was 19 percent; MTN had a 41 percent market share (12 million subscribers) in 2006, making it the market leader ahead of Globacom (29 percent), Celtel, (24 percent), M-Tel (4 percent), and CDMA Networks (2 percent).

MTN was focused on expanding northward into the Middle Eastern market, currently awash with petrodollars owing to high oil prices. The mobile phone market in the Middle East was growing rapidly, but competition among regional and European market contenders was quite strong. In 2006, MTN acquired Investcom for US$5.5 billion, giving it a foothold in 10 new country markets (Benin, Ghana, Guinea Bissau, Guinea Republic, Liberia, Sudan,

Syria, Yemen, Cyprus, and Afghanistan). MTN had a regional office in Iran, where it had an ownership interest in IranCell. MTN expected its investments in Investcom and IranCell would be the platforms for building its business in the Middle Eastern market. In 2006 MTN's mobile phone operations extended to 21 countries in Africa and Middle East with a total subscriber base of 32 million, making it the biggest and arguably the most successful mobile phone company in Africa, ahead of its arch-rival Vodacom. MTN had mobile phone licenses in countries with a total population close to 500 million.

MTN's international strategy had two main elements: leveraging existing businesses and growing new markets. Consequently, the group had pursued license acquisition opportunities in emerging markets that consolidated their regional positions and economies of scale. This made it possible for the group to acquire small, otherwise uneconomic licenses in some markets where the group had as much as 100 percent of the market (for example, Swaziland and Rwanda). MTN's strategy also balanced the use of existing infrastructure with its own research and development to develop new applications for market opportunity exploitation. The company remained exclusively focused on mobile phone operations, providing a wide product range, including 3G technology-based services and a strong retailing and franchising system. It operated under a single corporate brand name in all its markets.

Orascom

Orascom was an Egypt-based conglomerate with telecom revenues of US$2.1 billion; it had 15,000 employees. Orascom had both mobile, fixed-line, and Internet operations in nine markets: Egypt, Tunisia, Algeria, Iraq, Malta, Pakistan, Bangladesh, Zimbabwe, and the British Virgin Islands. Rather than expand further in Africa, the company had been disposing of its shareholdings in several African mobile operators in Africa and was currently targeting high-population, high-growth markets in Europe, the Middle East, and Asia that had relatively low mobile phone penetration rates. Orascom had attracted a critical mass of 7 million mobile phone subscribers in the Egyptian market, equal to a 51 percent market share; Egypt had a population of 62 million people. In terms of subscriber numbers, Orascom was the biggest mobile phone operator in

Africa, with over 46 million subscribers in its operating regions (Africa, the Middle East, and South Asia). There were about 460 million people in the countries where Orascom had licenses to operate a mobile phone network. Orascom also owned 19.3 percent of Hutchison Telecom, which had operations in eight Asian countries. Orascom operated under several brand names—Mobinil in Egypt and Pakistan, Bangalink in Bangladesh, IraQna in Iraq, Tunisiana in Tunisia, and Telecel in Zimbabwe.

Vodacom

Vodacom was a US$3 billion South Africa–based company that employed 5,300 people. Vodacom was the product of a 50–50 joint venture between Vodafone Group PLC and Telkom SA. Vodafone Group was the world's largest mobile phone operator based on revenues (China Mobile was the biggest based on the number of subscribers), and Telkom in 1994 had won the first of three mobile phone licenses awarded in South Africa. The Vodacom Group used a business model paralleling that of Vodafone Group—it operated mobile networks, was an important retailer of mobile phones and accessories, and had a business franchising service. Vodacom was the least internationalized of the Big Five, operating in only five African countries; its largest subscriber base was in South Africa, where it had a 59 percent market share against MTN's 35 percent and Cell-C's 6 percent. Prior to November 2006, Vodacom was limited to operating south of the Equator due to an agreement with Vodafone Group, but that agreement had expired. Vodacom had adequate resources for expansion and was actively searching for investment opportunities chiefly in Africa. But it was also focusing on cementing its position as the number one operator in South Africa, the most prosperous mobile phone market in all of Africa. Vodacom, like its rival MTN, had invested heavily in 3G technology, even though the evidence from Europe and elsewhere so far had been that 3G systems had not delivered the expected big profits for the operators that had deployed 3G technology. To date, Vodacom's expansion in Africa had been in countries that were neighbors of South Africa: Lesotho, Mozambique, Tanzania, and the Democratic Republic of Congo (DRC). DRC, with a population of 60 million, was Vodacom's second largest country market in Africa, followed by Tanzania (population of 37 million).

Exhibit 2   **Comparative Number of Subscribers of Selected Mobile Telecom Operators, June 2006 (in millions)**

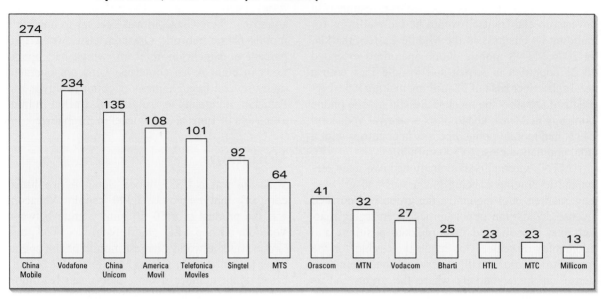

Source: Orascom 2006 Financial statement.

Vodacom had belatedly tried to enter Nigeria via a management contract with Econet Wireless Nigeria (EWN) in 2004, attracted by the spectacular good fortune that the Nigerian market had brought to MTN. But Vodacom's agreement with EWN lasted only two months, allowing MTN to reign supreme in Nigeria. However, observers believed that Nigeria was too important a market for Vodacom to ignore for long, leading to speculation that Vodacom might return to the Nigerian market via an acquisition of one of the GSM operators, possibly Globacom.

See Exhibit 2 for comparative numbers of subscribers of selected mobile telecom operators.

THE ECONET WIRELESS GROUP IN AFRICA

The Econet Wireless Group had a subscriber base of 5 million in four networks and a workforce of 1,400. Its most successful majority-owned network was in Zimbabwe, where it was the leading network, with a subscriber base of about 800,000 in a market with a population of 14 million. Econet Wireless Holdings owned 51 percent of Econet Wireless International. Econet's efforts to expand into other African countries had been weakened by its strong dependence on its Zimbabwean operations. However, Econet's ability to tap its substantial cash flows from its Zimbabwe operations were largely blocked due to Zimbabwe's lack of foreign currency and stringent government controls on hard currency remittances. The blocked funds had been partly used to acquire sizable equity investments in selected blue-chip companies in Zimbabwe and to buy back the company's shares on the Zimbabwe Stock Exchange. (Econet's stock had a market capitalization of Z$1.5 trillion, or US$375 million, at January 2007—the exchange rate was US$1 = Z$4000.)

Until 2006, mobile phone licenses in Africa were cheap by international standards. Consequently, Econet had been able, with the help of various consortium partnerships in which Econet had a minority position, to acquire mobile licenses in such important markets in Africa as Nigeria and Kenya. In each of these markets, the licenses were for second, third, or fourth network operator licenses.

Econet's internationalization sequence had been to enter Botswana in 1998 through a 20 percent stake in Mascom; Morocco in 2000 through a 35 percent stake in Gulfsat Maghreb SA; New Zealand in 2001 through a 65 percent stake in Econet New Zealand; Nigeria in 2001 through a 5 percent stake in Econet Wireless Nigeria; Lesotho in 2002 through a 21 percent stake in Mountain Kingdom Communications; Kenya in 2004 through a 10 percent stake in the Econet Consortium; Malawi in 2006 through a 60 percent stake in Telecom Networks Malawi; and Burundi in 2006 through a 65 percent stake in ST Cellular, formerly Spacetel Burundi. The Econet brand was used in all the markets where the company had a controlling stake or where it was able negotiate use of its brand name (Nigeria and Lesotho).

Econet's original business model and strategy was to be exclusively a mobile phone company that offered an up-to-date and comprehensive product range at competitive prices. Over time, Econet Wireless International's business model and strategy had evolved into becoming a full-service communications company offering mobile telephony, traditional landline telephony, Internet services, data streaming services, transactions systems, and contract services for other operators.

Early on, Econet had partnered with Ericsson (its supplier of base stations, network equipment, and cheap handsets), which had helped propel Econet's exponential growth in the mobile phone market in Zimbabwe. More recently, a new technical partnership had been developed with China's Huawei Technologies for the supply of base stations and other network equipment in some markets, particularly in New Zealand.

From a human resources point of view, Econet combined an ethnocentric approach with a polycentric approach. Experts from the parent company were sent to operating subsidiaries for periods of up to six months and on two-year contracts. Host country nationals were generally put in charge of each country's operations, with finance functions usually under the direction of an expatriate manager from Econet Wireless International.

The size of the total population in countries where Econet Wireless International had licenses to operate and had established mobile networks in competition with rivals was approximately 188 million

(Exhibit 3). This figure excluded Kenya (population: 33 million), Malta (population: 383,000), Morocco (population: 31 million), and New Zealand (population: 3.8 million), where Econet had licenses to operate but had not yet begun network operations and the process of signing up subscribers.

Econet in Nigeria

Mobile phone operators considered Nigeria to be the most attractive long-term country market in Africa because it had the largest population on the continent (151 million people) and because of the expected rapid growth in mobile phone use in Nigeria—predictions called for the number of Nigerian subscribers to surpass the number of subscribers in South Africa by 2010 and reach as many as 90 million subscribers in the post-2010 period. Nigeria had nine mobile phone network competitors, four of which used GSM technology and five of which had CDMA systems. Econet and its consortium partners had entered Nigeria in 2001, even before MTN, and had grown to be the second largest mobile operator in Nigeria. Econet was a 5 percent shareholder in the consortium of 21 partners but had the option of increasing its ownership stake to 33 percent. Econet had not exercised this option early on due to lack of funds; more recently, Econet's consortium partners had resisted a higher stake for Econet, believing Econet lacked the financial means and resources to invest in strengthening the partnership's competitive position in Nigeria.

On the first day of operation in Nigeria, the Econet consortium signed up 30,000 subscribers. But its growth in Nigeria was held back by having to wait for more than a year for Nitel, the government-controlled telecom operator, to provide transmission links to some of Nigeria's states. These delays worked to MTN's advantage because MTN had its own network transmission backbone and was not dependent on Nitel for essential customer connection services. In 2002, Econet opted to suspend the sale of its prepaid Buddie cards for six months due to quality problems; use of prepaid cards was highly popular among Nigerian mobile phone users. Econet's decision proved somewhat catastrophic because it triggered a mass exodus of subscribers over to MTN. Indeed, MTN's network was temporarily overwhelmed by the unanticipated burst in call

Exhibit 3   **Econet Wireless International Mobile Networks in Africa, 2006**

Country	Population (Millions)	Networks	Equity Holding % (1 Jan 2007)	Econet Market Position*	Market Share	Mobile Penetration %
Botswana	1.7	Mascom* Orange	20%	1st	70%	43%
Burundi	7.6	Safaris Telecel EWBurundi*	65%	3rd	13%	2.2%
Kenya	33.0	Safaricom EWKenya* Celtel	51%	0	0	12%
Lesotho	2.5	Econet* Vodacom	21%	2nd	20%	15%
Malawi	11.2	Celtel Callpoint*	60%	2nd	35%	4%
Nigeria	150.6	MTN Globacom Celtel* Mtel MTS Multi-links Intercellular Starcomms Reltel	5%	3rd	24%	19%
Zimbabwe	14.3	Econet* Telecel NetOne	64%	1st	60%	10%

*Econet's market position (or market ranking as 1st, 2nd, 3rd) is based on size of the subscriber base and amount of generated revenues.

volume brought on by the new subscribers switching from Econet, but the sudden surge of growth stimulated MTN to aggressively expand the call volume that its network could handle reliably. When Econet later reintroduced its Buddie card, it priced the cards so cheaply that the number of new subscribers quickly soared. Unfortunately, the resulting growth in call volume strained the Econet network's call-carrying capacity and led to network quality problems. However, unlike MTN, which had experienced a call-volume problem earlier, Econet did not have the money to upgrade its network and came under government threat of having its license revoked for failing to provide an acceptable mobile phone service. To resolve its difficulties, Econet managed to secure a $75 million loan from the U.S.-based Export-Import Bank to finance network expansion and save its fledgling Nigerian business. While

Econet's network expansion was in process, Econet management decided to limit the number of days that subscribers could access the network, a highly unpopular move that worked to MTN's advantage and solidified its status as the market leader in Nigeria (a position MTN had held since it launched operations in Nigeria in August 2001).

In April 2004, Econet Wireless Nigeria (EWN) entered into an agreement that would lead to Vodacom becoming a 51 percent ownership partner in the EWN consortium within 18 months. The intent of the arrangement to bring Vodacom in as a consortium partner was to give EWN access to the resources to increase EWN's network capacity and put EWN in a stronger position to rapidly grow its subscriber base and serve the fast-growing Nigerian market. EWN management and other consortium partners in Econet Wireless Nigeria believed that allying with a new strategic partner having stronger financial resources and network operating experience was vital to the long-term interests of their business. Econet Wireless International, with only a 5 percent ownership in the Econet Wireless Nigeria consortium, bitterly opposed the arrangement between EWN and Vodacom, believing that Vodacom control of the business would permanently limit Econet Wireless International's role and future in the Nigerian business that it helped establish. Econet Wireless International argued that it had preemptive rights to increase its ownership to 33 percent before Vodacom or any other entity could be offered shares. EWI executives accused Econet Wireless Nigeria management of acting in bad faith and even in rebellion, claiming that EWI had not been given an opportunity to exercise its rights before Vodacom was offered the 51 percent ownership stake. Econet Wireless International also accused Vodacom of corruptly inducing Econet Wireless Nigeria management to enter into the agreement with Vodacom at the expense of Econet Wireless International's preemptive rights. EWI opted to file a lawsuit against Vodacom seeking $1.8 billion in damages. For its part, EWN management argued that Econet Wireless International had demonstrated difficulty and even inability to raise the capital required to compete effectively. EWN management claimed that a joint venture with Vodacom was essential for EWN to compete on a more equal footing with MTN and eventually overtake MTN as the market leader in Nigeria.

Vodacom's interest in assuming a 51 percent ownership of the EWN venture was to use EWN's market position as a platform not only for competing with MTN in Nigeria but also for better competing with MTN across Africa—MTN's success in Nigeria had catapulted MTN into the number one mobile phone operator in Africa. The attraction of using EWN as its entry vehicle into the Nigerian market had galvanized Vodacom management to vigorously defend against Econet Wireless International's legal challenge. Prior to signing the agreement to be a 51 percent partner in the EWN venture, Vodacom had conducted a nine-month due diligence exercise that concluded that all was well at Econet Wireless Nigeria.

The Vodacom-EWN relationship began with a management agreement to provide technical and managerial expertise and to finance expansion of the EWN network. In return, Vodacom was to receive a 51 percent controlling stake in Econet Wireless Nigeria that was valued at $150 million. Econet Wireless Nigeria was to be rebranded Vodacom Nigeria (Vee-Mobile). Two months after the agreement came into force, it emerged that Econet Wireless Nigeria had paid nearly $3 million to three parties as commission/brokerage payments for its investment in the company. This was determined to be lawful in Nigeria, but Vodacom's principal shareholders—Telkom SA, Vodafone Group PLC, and U.S. telecom company SBC, all of whom were listed on the New York Stock Exchange (NYSE)—took a different view. They concluded that it was corruption and demanded that Vodacom pull out of Nigeria immediately, fearing possible U.S. prosecution under laws that forbade U.S. firms from engaging in corrupt practices abroad. Such prosecution could lead to jail terms for offenders or fines that could run into hundreds of millions of U.S. dollars for offending companies.

These unexpected developments broke the two-month-old Vodacom-EWN marriage apart, leaving EWN with an identity crisis since a switch had already been made to the Vodacom Nigeria (Vee-Mobile) brand. It also left EWN without the resources to compete on a more level playing field against market leader MTN. Vodacom agreed to let EWN use its brand name for three months and to keep Vodacom's technical and managerial staff at EWN for six months to smooth the transition. In return for this gesture, EWN agreed not to sue Vodacom for breach of contract. In spite of Vodacom's exit in Nigeria, EWI did not drop its lawsuit against Vodacom. EWN management moved quickly to consider new strategic partners to fill the void left by Vodacom; three operators became the focus of attention: Orascom, MSI-Celtel of the Netherlands, and Orange, a company based in the United Kingdom. In the interim, Econet Wireless International managed to raise $1 billion and made an offer to purchase 65 percent of Vee-Mobile; the other consortium partners in EWN spurned Econet Wireless International's offer. In May 2006, Celtel announced that it had acquired a 65 percent controlling stake in Vee-Mobile (formerly EWN) and proceeded to rebrand the operation as Celtel Nigeria.

In spite of Econet Wireless International's legal and other efforts, the Econet brand disappeared from the Nigerian mobile phone landscape, as did any hope of amicable business relationships with its former EWN partners. At the beginning of 2007, Celtel Nigeria (formerly Econet Wireless Nigeria and Vee-Mobile) had approximately 7 million subscribers in Nigeria versus MTN's 12 million.

Econet in Kenya

In 2004 the Econet Wireless Consortium—whose owners consisted of Econet Wireless International (10 percent), Kenya National Federation of Co-operatives (82 percent), Rapsel Limited (4 percent), and Corporate Africa Limited (4 percent)—bid $27 million and won Kenya's third GSM mobile phone license. Econet Wireless Kenya was privately registered without the knowledge and agreement of the original partners in order to gain sole control of the Kenyan operation. The Kenya Telecommunications Investment Group (KTIG), an interested party in the GSM mobile license, argued to the Communication Commission of Kenya that Econet Wireless Kenya was a different entity from the one that had won the license. Econet Wireless Kenya was accused of abusing the goodwill of its Kenyan partners, drafting them into a partnership for the specific purpose of winning the license only to drop them from the partnership after qualification. Consequently, KTIG's argument was that the Communication Commission of Kenya erred in giving a license to a company that was different in name and ownership from the consortium that had won the tender and that therefore Econet Wireless Kenya should not be allowed to operate and the whole license award process should be started afresh.

Two months after the license award, the license was canceled by the Kenyan authorities, citing irregularities in the award process and the failure by the consortium to fully honor the license fee obligations within the stipulated period. In relation to the license fee, the Kenyan government maintained that Econet Wireless International's partners in Kenya had failed to come up with their part of the license fee even though EWI had paid its part of the fee and had guaranteed the payment of the amounts owed by its partners. A series of lawsuits followed, involving EWI as both plaintiff and defendant. One of these lawsuits involved Econet Wireless International suing the Kenyan Minister of Information, Raphael Tuju, for $989 million for damaging the Econet trademark and for loss of business owing to the minister's remarks that Econet Wireless Kenya lacked the financial capability to roll out a network in Kenya and that it had won the license under questionable circumstances.

Whether Econet would gain a license to operate in Kenya was still up in the air in early 2007.

Econet and Altech

In a move to strengthen its capabilities to establish mobile phone operations in more parts of Africa, in 2004 Econet Wireless International entered into a 50–50 joint venture with Altech, a communication and technology firm listed on the Johannesburg Stock Exchange, to establish Newco; each partner contributed $70 million to the venture. Newco was expected to eventually take control of all of Econet Wireless International's interests except those in Zimbabwe (because of foreign exchange restrictions and the political and economic climate) and in Kenya and Nigeria (because of the ongoing legal wrangles in those two countries).

Both parties believed there was a good strategic fit and operational synergies to be gained from the venture. The directors of Econet Wireless International felt that EWI could benefit from Altech's technology products, finance, and administrative structures. For Altech, the benefit lay in diversifying into the mobile phone business, the growth prospects of Econet's existing mobile telecommunications networks, the appeal of jointly expanding in other mobile operations across Africa and elsewhere, and improving Altech's Black Economic Empowerment credentials (which put Altech in better position to take advantage of South African government contracts where there was a stipulation of significant black share participation in a company before it could be awarded any government business. Barely a year after the announcement of the partnership, it was dissolved amid allegations of breach of contract and racism against Econet's black leadership. In 2005, Econet paid $87.5 million to walk away from the contract.

ECONET IN NEW ZEALAND AND EUROPE

In New Zealand, which had a population of 3.8 million people and 3.3 million mobile phone users, Econet had a license to operate a mobile network in partnership with the Maori investment group, Hautaki. The partnership bought an open (not limited to GSM or CDMA) network license in 2001 at a cost of NZ$13.2 million. The mobile phone market in New Zealand was a duopoly, with a GSM network operated by Vodafone (which had a 66 percent share) and a CMDA network owned by Telecom (which had a 34 percent share). The lack of competition between the two networks had resulted in New Zealand having the highest mobile phone calling rates of all 30 countries that belonged to the Organization for Economic Cooperation and Development (OECD). Even before the network rollout, Econet complained to the New Zealand Telecom's regulator that the playing field was tilted in favor of the two incumbent mobile phone operators who acted aggressively and even unfairly to block any chance of a third operator could enter the New Zealand market and be competitively successful. This had prompted Econet to join forces with groups in other OECD countries in lobbying for amendments to the Telecommunications Act of 2001 that would promote greater ease of entry and competition among more mobile phone operators.

As of early 2007, Econet New Zealand did not have a network in New Zealand, some six years after the license award. It had not been able to raise the hundreds of millions of U.S. dollars needed to establish a network and fund a startup operation. The company was spending a small fortune monthly to maintain the New Zealand office with revenue from other operations. A decision had recently been made to reduce the staffing in the Econet New Zealand office to the barest minimum consistent with maintaining efforts to find the necessary funding to enter into competition against Vodafone and Telecom.

In Europe and the Middle East, Econet Wireless International did not operate any mobile phone network as of 2007 and had not announced any plans to begin any such operations despite having some operating licenses. However, Econet Wireless International did have fragmented interests in that region through operating subsidiaries and equity investments in such telecom-based service ventures as Econet Satellite Services, a London-based satellite and broadband service; Ecoweb Malta, an Internet service provider that was a joint venture with Comtel of Malta; and Gulfsat Maghreb, a VSAT technology–based company in Morocco in which Econet had a 35 percent ownership.

Bibliography

"Africa and the Mobile Phone: It's Not All Good News." 2006. www.scidev.net/features/index.cfm?fuseaction=readFeatures &itemid=564&language=1.

"Altech and the Econet Wireless Group in R1 Billion Venture." 2004. www.altrongroup.com/content/news-corporate.asp?list_231581646.

"Cell-Phone Firms Wary as Foreign Players Jockey for Slice of Africa." *Financial Gazette,* November 16–22, 2006.

Dagli, P. "CellPhone Use in Africa." 2005. fellows.rdvp.org/parasdagli/blog/cellphoneuseinafrica?PHPSESSID=c30481fc812ab.

De Wet, P. "Vodacom to Pull Out of Nigeria Over Scandal." *ThisDay,* May 31, 2004, p. 2.

"Econet Acquires 65 Percent Stake in Burundi GSM Operator." 2006. www.telegeography.com/cu/article.php?article_id=12725&email=html.

"Econet Offered $ 1 BN Ticket into Nigerian Market." 2006. www.econetwirless.com/press_office/articles/2006/ewi-069.htm?B1.x=17&B1.y=4.

"Econet Sues Minister for Defamation." 2006. www.telegeography.com/cu/article.php?article_id=7388&email=html.

"Econet Wins Race for Kenya Mobile Phone License." 2003. www.fingaz.co.zw/fingaz/2003/September/September25/1343.shtml.

Gray, V. "The Un-wired Continent: Africa's Mobile Success Story." 2006. www.itu.int/ITU-D/ict/statistics/at_glance/Africa_EE2006_e.pdf.

"GSM Today." 2003. www.mail-archive.com/gsmtoday@freelists.org/msg00068.html.

"Huawei Teams with Econet on Kiwi Wireless." 2005. www.physorg.com/news8728.html.

Keown, J. "Econet Still Whistling in the Dark for Funds." 2006. www.nzherald.co.nz/section/story.cfm?c_id=5&ObjectID=10406370.

Khabuchi, L. "Firm Wants Econet Mobile License Revoked on Technicality." 2006. www.timesnews.co.ke/03dec06/business/buns1.html

Millicom International Cellular 2006 financial report.

Mobile Africa. "Nigeria Will Be Africa's Largest Mobile Phone Market." www.mobileafrica.net/n1783.htm

MTN Group 2006 financial report.

Ndlela, D. "Econet Board Pleads for Investor Backing." 2003. www.fingaz.co.zw/fingaz/2003/September/September25/1302.shtml.

"The New Zealand Cellular Mobile Phone Environment." www.ewnz.co.nz/html/nz-mob-environ.htm.

Ngunjiri, P. "Kenya: Govt Dares Econet to Sue Over GSM License." 2006. http://allafrica.com/stories/200611140145.html.

Orascom Telecom Holdings 2006 financial report.

"Out of Africa." www.economist.com/business/display-story.cfm?story_id=8381911.

Population World Web site. www.populationworld.com.

Sutherland, E. "Multi-national Operators in African Mobile Markets." 2006. www.3wan.net.

"Telecom's Statement Illustrative of Monopoly." 2006. www.scoop.co.nz/stories/BU0608/S00118.htm.

"Vodacom and Econet Wireless Nigeria Sign Management Agreement." 2004. www.vodafone.com/article_with_thumbnail/0,3038,OPCO%253D40002%2526CA.

Vodacom Group 2006 financial report.

White, D. "Telecommunications: A Dynamic Revolution." 2006. www.ft.com/cms/s/1868125e-6e5f-11db-b5c4-0000779e2340,dwp_uuid=1f2588a0-76.

PepsiCo in 2007: Strategies to Increase Shareholder Value

John E. Gamble
University of South Alabama

PepsiCo was the world's largest snack and beverage company, with 2006 net revenues of approximately $35 billion. The company's portfolio of businesses in 2007 included Frito-Lay salty snacks, Quaker Chewy granola bars, Pepsi soft drink products, Tropicana orange juice, Lipton Brisk tea, Gatorade, Propel, SoBe, Quaker Oatmeal, Cap'n Crunch, Aquafina, Rice-A-Roni, Aunt Jemima pancake mix, and many other regularly consumed products. Gatorade, Propel, Rice-A-Roni, Aunt Jemima, and Quaker Oats products were added to PepsiCo's arsenal of brands through the $13.9 billion acquisition of Quaker Oats in 2001. The Quaker Oats acquisition was the final strategic move in a major portfolio restructuring initiative that began in 1997. Since the restructuring, the company had consistently increased the value delivered to PepsiCo shareholders through share price appreciation and a rising dividend. A summary of PepsiCo's financial performance is shown in Exhibit 1. Exhibit 2 tracks the performance of PepsiCo's stock price between 1997 and March 2007.

In 2007, the company's top managers were focused on sustaining the impressive performance that had been achieved since its restructuring through strategies keyed to product innovation, close relationships with distribution allies, international expansion, and strategic acquisitions. Newly introduced products generated an additional $1 billion in sales during 2006 and had accounted for 15–20 percent of all new growth in recent years. New product innovations that addressed consumer health and

wellness concerns were the greatest contributors to the company's growth, with PepsiCo's better-for-you and good-for-you products accounting for 15 percent of its 2006 snack sales in North America, 70 percent of net beverage revenues in North America during 2006, and 55 percent of its 2006 sales of Quaker Oats products in North America. The company also planned to increase the percentage of healthy snacks in markets outside North America, since consumers in most developed countries wished to reduce their consumption of saturated fats, cholesterol, transfats, and simple carbohydrates.

The company's Power of One retailer alliance strategy had been in effect for nearly 10 years and was continuing to help boost PepsiCo's volume and identify new product formulations desired by consumers. Under the Power of One strategy, PepsiCo marketers and retailers collaborated in stores and during offsite summits to devise tactics to increase consumers' tendency to purchase more than one product offered by PepsiCo during a store visit. In addition, some of PepsiCo's most successful new products had been recommended by retailers.

PepsiCo's international sales had grown by 14 percent during 2006 and by 15 percent between 2004 and 2005, but the company had many additional opportunities to increase sales in markets outside North America. The company held large market shares in many international markets for beverages and salty snacks, but it had been relatively unsuccessful in making Quaker branded products available outside the United States. In 2006, 75 percent of Quaker Oats' international sales of $500 million was accounted for by just six countries.

Exhibit 1   **Financial Summary for PepsiCo Inc., 1997–2006
($ in millions, except per share amounts)**

	2006	2005	2004	2003	2002	2001	2000	1999	1998	1997
Net revenue	$35,137	$32,562	$29,261	$26,971	$25,112	$23,512	$20,438	$20,367	$22,348	$20,917
Net income	5,642	4,078	4,212	3,568	3,000	2,400	2,183	2,050	1,993	1,491
Income per common share—basic, continuing operations	$3.42	$2.43	$2.45	$2.07	$1.69	$1.35	$1.51	$1.40	$1.35	$0.98
Cash dividends declared per common share	$1.16	$1.01	$0.85	$0.63	$0.60	$0.58	$0.56	$0.54	$0.52	$0.49
Total assets	$29,930	$31,727	$27,987	$25,327	$23,474	$21,695	$18,339	$17,551	$22,660	$20,101
Long-term debt	2,550	2,313	2,397	1,702	2,187	2,651	2,346	2,812	4,028	4,946

Source: PepsiCo 10-K reports, various years.

For the most part, PepsiCo's strategies seemed to be firing on all cylinders in early 2007. If the company's current growth rates were sustained, projected free cash flows of approximately $15 billion would be generated between 2007 and 2009. PepsiCo had made only $1.2 billion in acquisitions between 2003 and 2005, which had allowed it to pay $4 billion in dividends and complete an $8 billion share buyback plan during that time. Going forward, PepsiCo management would need to consider what strategy changes were still needed and how to best use its operating cash flows to further build shareholder value.

COMPANY HISTORY

PepsiCo Inc. was established in 1965 when Pepsi-Cola and Frito-Lay shareholders agreed to a merger between the salty snack icon and soft drink giant. The new company was founded with annual revenues of $510 million and such well-known brands as Pepsi-Cola, Mountain Dew, Fritos, Lay's, Cheetos, Ruffles, and Rold Gold. PepsiCo's roots can be traced to 1898 when New Bern, North Carolina, pharmacist Caleb Bradham created the formula for a carbonated beverage he named Pepsi-Cola. The company's salty snacks business began in 1932 when Elmer Doolin of San Antonio, Texas, began manufacturing and marketing Fritos corn chips and Herman Lay started a potato chip distribution business in Nashville, Tennessee. In 1961, Doolin and Lay agreed to a merger between their businesses to establish the Frito-Lay Company.

During PepsiCo's first five years as a snack and beverage company, it introduced new products such as Doritos and Funyuns, entered markets in Japan and Eastern Europe, and opened, on average, one new snack food plant per year. By 1971, PepsiCo had more than doubled its revenues to reach $1 billion. The company began to pursue growth through acquisitions outside snacks and beverages as early as 1968, but its 1977 acquisition of Pizza Hut significantly shaped the strategic direction of PepsiCo for the next 20 years. The acquisitions of Taco Bell in 1978 and Kentucky Fried Chicken in 1986 created a business portfolio described by Wayne Calloway (PepsiCo's CEO between 1986 and 1996) as a balanced three-legged stool. Calloway believed the combination of snack foods, soft drinks, and fast food offered considerable cost sharing and skills transfer opportunities and he routinely shifted managers between the company's three divisions as part of the company's management development efforts.

PepsiCo also strengthened its portfolio of snack foods and beverages during the 1980s and 1990s with acquisitions of Mug root beer, 7-Up International, Smartfood ready-to-eat popcorn, Walker's Crisps (UK), Smith's Crisps (UK), Mexican cookie company Gamesa, and SunChips. Calloway also added quick-service restaurants Hot-n-Now in 1990; California Pizza Kitchens in 1992; and East Side Mario's, D'Angelo Sandwich Shops, and Chevy's Mexican Restaurants in 1993. The company expanded beyond carbonated beverages via a 1992 agreement with Ocean Spray to distribute single-serving

Exhibit 2 **Monthly Performance of PepsiCo Inc.'s Stock Price, 1997 to March 2007**

(a) Trend in PepsiCo Inc.'s Common Stock Price

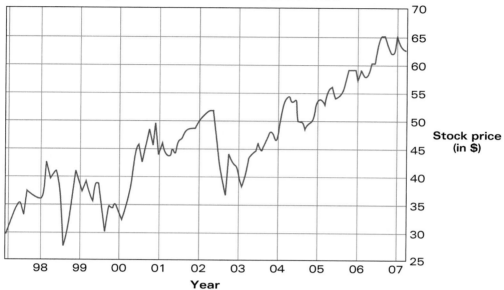

(b) Performance of PepsiCo Inc.'s Stock Price versus the S&P 500 Index

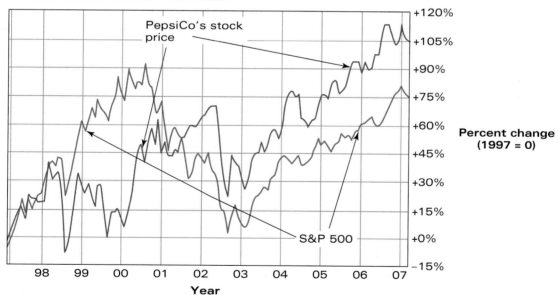

juices, the introduction of Lipton ready-to-drink (RTD) teas in 1993, and the introduction of Aquafina bottled water and Frappucino ready-to-drink coffees in 1994.

By 1996, it had become clear to PepsiCo management that the potential strategic fit benefits existing between restaurants and PepsiCo's core beverage and snack businesses were difficult to capture. In addition, any synergistic benefits achieved were more than offset by the fast-food industry's fierce price competition and low profit margins. In 1997, CEO

Roger Enrico spun off the company's restaurants as an independent, publicly traded company to focus PepsiCo on food and beverages. Soon after the spin-off of PepsiCo's fast-food restaurants was completed, Enrico acquired Cracker Jack, Tropicana, Smith's Snackfood Company in Australia, SoBe teas and alternative beverages, Tasali Snack Foods (the leader in the Saudi Arabian salty snack market), and the Quaker Oats Company.

The Quaker Oats Acquisition

At $13.9 billion, Quaker Oats was PepsiCo's largest acquisition and gave it the number-one brand of oatmeal in the United States, with a 60+ percent category share; the leading brand of rice cakes and granola snack bars; and other well-known grocery brands such as Cap'n Crunch, Rice-A-Roni, and Aunt Jemima. However, Quaker's most valuable asset in its arsenal of brands was Gatorade.

Gatorade was developed by University of Florida researchers in 1965 but was not marketed commercially until the formula was sold to Stokley–Van Camp in 1967. When Quaker Oats acquired the brand from Stokely–Van Camp in 1983, Gatorade gradually made a transformation from a regionally distributed product with annual sales of $90 million to a $2 billion powerhouse. Gatorade was able to increase sales by more than 10 percent annually during the 1990s, with no new entrant to the isotonic beverage category posing a serious threat to the brand's dominance. PepsiCo, Coca-Cola, France's Danone Group, and Swiss food giant Nestlé all were attracted to Gatorade because of its commanding market share and because of the expected growth in the isotonic sports beverage category. PepsiCo became the successful bidder for Quaker Oats and Gatorade with an agreement struck in December 2000, but would not receive U.S. Federal Trade Commission (FTC) approval until August 2001. The FTC's primary concern over the merger was that Gatorade's inclusion in PepsiCo's portfolio of snacks and beverages might give the company too much leverage in negotiations with convenience stores and ultimately force smaller snack food and beverage companies out of convenience store channels. In its approval of the merger, the FTC stipulated that Gatorade with PepsiCo's soft drinks could not be jointly distributed for 10 years.

Acquisitions after 2001

After the completion of the Quaker Oats acquisition in August 2001, the company focused on integration of Quaker Oats' food, snack, and beverage brands into the PepsiCo portfolio. The company made a number of small, "tuck-in" acquisitions such as Stacey's bagel and pita chips, Izze carbonated beverages, Netherlands-based Duyvis nuts, and Star Foods (Poland) in 2006. Tuck-in acquisitions made during the first quarter of 2007 included Naked Juice fruit beverages and New Zealand's Bluebird snacks. Acquisitions in 2006 totaled $522 million, about half the $1.1 billion it spent on acquisitions in 2005. PepsiCo's largest acquisition in 2005 was the $750 million acquisition of Generals Mills' minority interest in Snack Ventures Europe. The company's management sought to identify additional small, fast-growing food and beverage companies in the United States and internationally that could broaden its portfolio of brands. The combination of acquisitions with PepsiCo's core snacks and beverages business had allowed the company's revenues to increase from approximately $20 billion in 2000 to more than $35 billion in 2006. Exhibit 3 presents PepsiCo's consolidated statements of income for 2004–2006. The company's balance sheets for 2005–2006 are shown in Exhibit 4; operating cash flows for 2004–2006 are shown in Exhibit 5.

BUILDING SHAREHOLDER VALUE IN 2007

Three people had held the position of CEO since PepsiCo began its portfolio restructuring in 1997. Even though Roger Enrico was the chief architect of PepsiCo's diversified business lineup as it stood in 2007, his successor, Steve Reinemund, and the company's CEO in 2007, Indra Nooyi, were both critically involved in the restructuring. Nooyi had emigrated to the United States in 1978 to attend Yale's Graduate School of Business and had worked with Boston Consulting Group, Motorola, and Asea Brown Boveri before arriving at PepsiCo in 1994. She developed a reputation as a tough negotiator who engineered the 1997 spin-off of Pepsi's restaurants, spearheaded the 1998 acquisition of Tropicana, and played a critical role in the 1999 IPO of Pepsi's

Exhibit 3   **PepsiCo Inc.'s Consolidated Statements of Income, 2004–2006 ($ in millions, except per share amounts)**

	2006	2005	2004
Net revenue	$35,137	$32,562	$29,261
Cost of sales	15,762	14,176	12,674
Selling, general and administrative expenses	12,774	12,314	11,031
Amortization of intangible assets	162	150	147
Restructuring and impairment charges	—	—	150
Operating profit	6,439	5,922	5,259
Bottling equity income	616	557	380
Interest expense	(239)	(256)	(167)
Interest income	173	159	74
Income from continuing operations before income taxes	6,989	6,382	5,546
Provision for income taxes	1,347	2,304	1,372
Income from continuing operations	5,642	4,078	4,174
Tax benefit from discontinued operations	—	—	38
Net income	$ 5,642	$ 4,078	$ 4,212
Net income per common share—basic			
Continuing operations	$3.42	$2.43	$2.45
Discontinued operations	—	—	0.02
Total	$3.42	$2.43	$2.47
Net income per common share—diluted			
Continuing operations	$3.34	$2.39	$2.41
Discontinued operations	—	—	0.02
Total	$3.34	$2.39	$2.44

Source: PepsiCo Inc., 2006 10-K report.

bottling operations. After being promoted to chief financial officer, Nooyi was also highly involved in the 2001 acquisition of Quaker Oats. She was selected as the company's CEO upon Reinemund's retirement in October 2006.

In 2007, PepsiCo's corporate strategy had diversified the company into salty and sweet snacks, soft drinks, orange juice, bottled water, ready-to-drink (RTD) teas and coffees, purified and functional waters, isotonic beverages, hot and ready-to-eat breakfast cereals, grain-based products, and breakfast condiments. Many PepsiCo brands had achieved number one or number two positions in their respective food and beverage categories through strategies keyed to product innovation, close relationships with distribution allies, international expansion, and strategic acquisitions. A relatively new element of PepsiCo's corporate strategy was product reformulations to make snack foods and beverages less unhealthy. The company believed its efforts to develop good-for-you (GFY) or better-for-you

(BFY) products would create growth opportunities from the intersection of business and public interests.

The company was organized into four business divisions, which all followed the corporation's general strategic approach. Frito-Lay North America manufactured, marketed, and distributed such snack foods as Lay's potato chips, Doritos tortilla chips, Cheetos cheese snacks, Fritos corn chips, Quaker Chewy granola bars, Grandma's cookies, and Smartfood popcorn. PepsiCo's North American beverage business manufactured, marketed and sold beverage concentrates, fountain syrups, and finished goods under such brands as Pepsi, Gatorade, Tropicana, Lipton, Dole, and SoBe. PepsiCo International manufactured, marketed and sold snacks and beverages in approximately 200 countries outside the United States. Quaker Foods North America manufactured and marketed cereals, rice and pasta dishes, and other food items that were sold in supermarkets. A full listing of Frito-Lay

Exhibit 4 **PepsiCo, Inc.'s Consolidated Balance Sheets, 2005–2006**
($ in millions, except per share amounts)

	December 30, 2006	December 31, 2005
ASSETS		
Current assets		
Cash and cash equivalents	$ 1,651	$ 1,716
Short-term investments	1,171	3,166
Accounts and notes receivable, net	3,725	3,261
Inventories	1,926	1,693
Prepaid expenses and other current assets	657	618
Total current assets	$ 9,130	$10,454
Property, plant and equipment, net	9,687	8,681
Amortizable intangible assets, net	637	530
Goodwill	4,594	4,088
Other non-amortizable intangible assets	1,212	1,086
Non-amortizable intangible assets	5,806	5,174
Investments in noncontrolled affiliates	3,690	3,485
Other assets	980	3,403
Total assets	$29,930	$31,727
LIABILITIES AND SHAREHOLDERS' EQUITY		
Current liabilities		
Short-term obligations	$274	$ 2,889
Accounts payable and other current liabilities	6,496	5,971
Income taxes payable	90	546
Total current liabilities	6,860	9,406
Long-term debt obligations	2,550	2,313
Other liabilities	4,624	4,323
Deferred income taxes	528	1,434
Total liabilities	$14,562	$17,476
Commitments and contingencies		
Preferred stock, no par value	41	41
Repurchased preferred stock	(120)	(110)
Common shareholders' equity		
Common stock, par value 1²/₃¢ per share (issued 1,782 shares)	30	30
Capital in excess of par value	584	614
Retained earnings	24,837	21,116
Accumulated other comprehensive loss	(2,246)	(1,053)
	23,205	20,707
Less: repurchased common stock, at cost	(7,758)	(6,387)
(144 and 126 shares, respectively)		
Total common shareholders' equity	$15,447	$14,320
Total liabilities and shareholders' equity	$29,930	$31,727

Source: PepsiCo Inc., 2006 10-K report.

snacks, PepsiCo beverages, and Quaker Oats products is presented in Exhibit 6. Selected financial information for PepsiCo's four divisions is presented in Exhibit 7.

Frito-Lay North America

In 2006, Frito-Lay brands accounted for 31 percent of PepsiCo's total revenues and 51 percent of

Exhibit 5 **PepsiCo's Cash Flows from Operations, 2004–2006 (in millions of $)**

	2006	2005	2004
Net cash provided by operating activities	$6,084	$5,852	$5,054
Capital spending	(2,068)	(1,736)	(1,387)
Sales of property, plant and equipment	49	88	38
Net cash flows from operations	$4,065	$4,204	$3,705

Source: PepsiCo Inc., 2006 10-K report.

Exhibit 6 **PepsiCo Inc.'s Snack, Beverage, and Quaker Oats Brands, 2007**

Frito-Lay Brands	PepsiCo Beverage Brands	Quaker Oats Brands
• Lay's potato chips • Maui Style potato chips • Ruffles potato chips • Doritos tortilla chips • Tostitos tortilla chips • Santitas tortilla chips • Fritos corn chips • Cheetos cheese flavored snacks • Rold Gold pretzels & snack mix • Funyuns onion flavored rings • Go Snacks • SunChips multigrain snacks • Sabritones puffed wheat snacks • Cracker Jack candy coated popcorn • Chester's popcorn • Grandma's cookies • Munchos potato crisps • Smartfood popcorn • Baken-ets fried pork skins • Oberto meat snacks • Rustler's meat snacks • Churrumais fried corn strips • Frito-Lay nuts • Frito-Lay, Ruffles, Fritos and Tostitos dips & salsas • Frito-Lay, Doritos and Cheetos snack crackers • Fritos, Tostitos, Ruffles and Doritos snack kits	• Pepsi-Cola • Mountain Dew • Mountain Dew AMP energy drink • Mug • Sierra Mist • Slice • Lipton Brisk (Partnership) • Lipton Iced Tea (Partnership) • Dole juices and juice drinks (License) • FruitWorks juice drinks • Aquafina purified drinking water • Frappuccino ready-to-drink coffee (Partnership) • Starbucks DoubleShot (Partnership) • SoBe juice drinks, dairy, and teas • SoBe energy drinks (No Fear and Adrenaline Rush) • Gatorade • Propel • Tropicana • Tropicana Twister • Tropicana Smoothie • Izze • Naked Juice **Outside North America** • Mirinda • 7UP • Pepsi • Kas • Teem	• Quaker Oatmeal • Cap'n Crunch cereal • Life cereal • Quaker 100% Natural cereal • Quaker Squares cereal • Quisp cereal • King Vitaman cereal • Quaker Oh's! Cereal • Mother's cereal • Quaker grits • Quaker Oatmeal-to-Go • Aunt Jemima mixes & syrups • Quaker rice cakes • Quaker rice snacks (Quakes) • Quaker Chewy granola bars • Quaker Dipps granola bars • Rice-A-Roni side dishes • Pasta Roni side dishes • Near East side dishes • Puffed Wheat • Harvest Crunch cereal • Quaker Baking Mixes • Spudz snacks • Crisp'ums baked crisps • Quaker Fruit & Oatmeal bars • Quaker Fruit & Oatmeal Bites • Quaker Fruit and Oatmeal Toastables • Quaker Soy Crisps • Quaker Bakeries

(Continued)

Exhibit 6   **Continued**

Frito-Lay Brands	PepsiCo Beverage Brands	Quaker Oats Brands
• Hickory Sticks	• Manzanita Sol	**Outside North America**
• Hostess Potato	• Paso de los Toros	• FrescAvena beverage powder
• Lay's Stax potato crisps	• Fruko	• Toddy chocolate powder
• Miss Vickie's potato chips	• Evervess	• Toddynho chocolate drink
• Munchies snack mix	• Yedigun	• Coqueiro canned fish
• Stacy's Pita Chips	• Shani	• Sugar Puffs cereal
• Flat Earth Fruit and Vegetable Chips	• Fiesta	• Puffed Wheat
	• D&G (License)	• Cruesli cereal
Outside North America	• Mandarin (License)	• Hot Oat Crunch cereal
• Bocabits wheat snacks	• Radical Fruit	• Quaker Oatso Simple hot cereal
• Crujitos corn snacks	• Tropicana Touche de Lait	• Scott's Porage Oats
• Fandangos corn snacks	• Alvalle gazpacho fruit juices and vegetable juices	• Scott's So Easy Oats
• Hamka's snacks	• Tropicana Season's Best juices and juice drinks	• Quaker Bagged cereals
• Niknaks cheese snacks	• Looza juices and nectars	• Quaker Mais Sabor
• Quavers potato snacks	• Copella juices	• Quaker Oats
• Sabritas potato chips	• Frui'Vita juices	• Quaker oat flour
• Smiths potato chips		• Quaker Meu Mingau
• Walkers potato crisps		• Quaker cereal bars
• Gamesa cookies		• Quaker Oatbran
• Doritos Dippas		• Corn goods
• Sonric's sweet snacks		• Magico chocolate powder
• Wotsits corn snacks		• Quaker Vitaly Cookies
• Red Rock Deli		• 3 Minutos Mixed Cereal
• Kurkure		• Quaker Mágica
• Smiths Sensations		• Quaker Mágica con Soja
• Cheetos Shots		• Quaker Pastas
• Quavers Snacks		• Quaker Frut
• Bluebird Snacks		

Source: Information posted at www.pepsico.com, accessed February 27, 2007.

Exhibit 7   **Selected Financial Data for PepsiCo Inc.'s Business Segments, 2004–2006 ($ in millions)**

	2006	2005	2004
Net Revenues			
Frito-Lay North America	$10,844	$10,322	$9,560
Pepsi Bottling North America	9,565	9,146	8,313
Pepsi International	12,959	11,376	9,862
Quaker Foods North America	1,769	1,718	1,526
Total division	35,137	32,562	29,261
Corporate	—	—	—
Total	$35,137	$32,562	$29,261

(Continued)

	2006	2005	2004
Operating Profit			
Frito-Lay North America	$ 2,615	$ 2,529	$ 2,389
Pepsi Bottling North America	2,055	2,037	1,911
Pepsi International	1,948	1,607	1,323
Quaker Foods North America	554	537	475
Total division	7,172	6,710	6,098
Corporate	(733)	(788)	(689)
	6,439	5,922	5,409
Restructuring and impairment charges	—	—	(150)
Total	$ 6,439	$ 5,922	$ 5,259
Capital Expenditures			
Frito-Lay North America	$ 499	$ 512	$ 469
Pepsi Bottling North America	492	320	265
Pepsi International	835	667	537
Quaker Foods North America	31	31	33
Total division	1,857	1,530	1,304
Corporate	211	206	83
Total	$ 2,068	$ 1,736	$ 1,387
Total Assets			
Frito-Lay North America	$ 5,969	$ 5,948	$ 5,476
Pepsi Bottling North America	6,567	6,316	6,048
Pepsi International	11,274	9,983	8,921
Quaker Foods North America	1,003	989	978
Total division	24,813	23,236	21,423
Corporate	1,739	5,331	3,569
Investments in bottling affiliates	3,378	3,160	2,995
Total	$29,930	$31,727	$27,987
Depreciation and Other Amortization			
Frito-Lay North America	$ 432	$ 419	$ 420
Pepsi Bottling North America	282	264	258
Pepsi International	478	420	382
Quaker Foods North America	33	34	36
Total division	1,225	1,137	1,096
Corporate	19	21	21
Total	$ 1,244	$ 1,158	$ 1,117
Amortization of Other Intangible Assets			
Frito-Lay North America	$ 9	$ 3	$ 3
Pepsi Bottling North America	77	76	75
Pepsi International	76	71	68
Quaker Foods North America	—	—	1
Total division	162	150	147
Corporate	—	—	—
Total	$ 162	$ 150	$ 147

Source: PepsiCo Inc., 2006 10-K report.

the company's profits. Frito-Lay also accounted for nearly 50 percent of the snack food industry's total sales in the United States, which had grown by 3 percent annually since 2000 to reach $24.6 billion in 2005. Three key trends that were shaping the industry were convenience, a growing awareness of nutritional content of snack foods, and indulgent snacking. A product manager for a regional snack producer explained, "Many consumers want to reward themselves with great-tasting, gourmet flavors and styles. . . . The indulgent theme carries into seasonings as well. Overall, upscale, restaurant-influenced flavor trends are emerging to fill consumers' desires to escape from the norm and taste snacks from a wider, often global, palate."[1] Most manufacturers had developed new flavors of salty snacks such as jalapeno and cheddar tortilla chips and pepper jack potato chips to attract the interest of indulgent snackers. Manufacturers had also begun using healthier oils when processing chips and had expanded lines of baked and natural salty snacks to satisfy the demands of health-conscious consumers. Snacks packaged in smaller bags also addressed over-eating concerns and were additionally convenient to take along on an outing. In 2007, Frito-Lay owned the top-selling chip brand in each U.S. salty snack category and held nearly a two-to-one lead over the next largest snack food maker in the United States. The following table presents shares of the U.S. convenience food market for leading manufacturers in 2006. Convenience foods include chips, pretzels, ready-to-eat popcorn, crackers, dips, snack nuts and seeds, candy bars, cookies, and other sweet snacks.

Manufacturer	Market Share
PepsiCo	21%
Kraft Foods	12
Hershey	9
Kellogg	6
Master Foods	5
General Mills	2
Procter & Gamble	1
Private Label	7
Others	37
Total	100%

Note: The share information shown above excludes data from certain retailers such as Wal-Mart that do not report data to Information Resources Inc. and A. C. Nielsen Corporation.
Source: PepsiCo Inc., 2006 10-K report.

Frito-Lay North America's (FLNA) revenues increased by 5 percent during 2006 as a result of double-digit growth in sales of SunChips, Quaker Rice Cakes, and multipacks of other products. FLNA's better-for-you (BFY) and good-for-you (GFY) snacks also grew at double-digit rates during 2006 and represented 15 percent of the division's total revenue. Sales of Lay's and Doritos branded products declined slightly between 2005 and 2006. In 2007, improving the performance of the division's core salty brands and further developing health and wellness products were key strategic initiatives. The company had eliminated trans fats from all Lay's, Fritos, Ruffles, Cheetos, Tostitos, and Doritos varieties and was looking for further innovations to make its salty snacks more healthy. The company had introduced Lay's Classic Potato Chips cooked in sunflower oil that retained Lay's traditional flavor, but contained 50 percent less saturated fat. The company had also developed new multigrain and flour tortilla Tostitos varieties that appealed to indulgent snackers and were healthier than traditional Tostitos. Other new indulgent Doritos flavors included Fiery Habañero and Blazin' Buffalo & Ranch. FLNA had also expanded the number of flavors of SunChips to sustain the brand's double-digit growth. New SunChips flavors included Garden Salsa and Cinnamon Crunch. SunChips were also introduced in 100-calorie minipacks and 20-bag multipacks.

PepsiCo's 2006 acquisition of Flat Earth fruit and vegetable snacks offered an opportunity for the company to exploit consumers' desires for healthier snacks and address a deficiency in most diets. Americans, on average, consumed only about 50 percent of the U.S. Department of Agriculture's recommended daily diet of fruits and vegetables. Flat Earth Cheddar, Tangy Tomato Ranch, Garlic Herb Garden Veggie Crisps and Peach Mango, Apple Cinnamon, Wild Berry Fruit Crisps were all launched in February 2007. Other GFY snacks included Stacy's Pita Chips, which was also acquired in 2006, and Quaker Chewy Granola Bars. In 2007, Stacy's Pita Chips came in Multigrain, Cinnamon Sugar, Whole Wheat, and Simply Cheese flavors. Quaker Chewy Granola Bars had achieved a number two rank in the segment with a 25 percent market share in 2006. Some of the success of Quaker Chewy Granola products was related to product innovations such as reduced calorie oatmeal and raisin bars. PBNA also distributed Quaker Rice Cakes, which had added chocolate drizzled and multigrain varieties in 2006.

PepsiCo Beverages North America

PepsiCo was the largest seller of liquid refreshments in the United States, with a 26 percent share of the market in 2006. Coca-Cola was the second largest non-alcoholic beverage producer with a 23 percent market share. Cadbury Schweppes and Nestlé were the third and fourth largest beverage sellers in 2006 with market shares of 10 percent and 8 percent, respectively. Like Frito-Lay, PepsiCo's beverage business contributed greatly to the corporation's overall profitability and free cash flows. In 2006, PepsiCo Beverages North America (PBNA) accounted for 27 percent of the corporation's total revenues and 39 percent of its profits. Revenues for PBNA had increased by 7.5 percent annually between 2004 and 2006 as the company broadened its line of noncarbonated beverages like Gatorade, Tropicana fruit juices, Lipton ready-to-drink tea, Propel, Aquafina, Dole fruit drinks, Starbucks cold coffee drinks, and SoBe. Carbonated soft drinks (CSDs) were the most consumed type of beverage in the United States in 2006, with a 50.9 percent of share of the stomach, but carbonated soft drink volume declined by 1.1 percent between 2005 and 2006 as consumers searched for healthier beverage choices. In contrast, noncarbonated beverages grew by 7 percent and bottled water grew by 8 percent between 2005 and 2006. The following table presents U.S. liquid refreshment beverage volume and volume share by beverage category in 2006.

Beverage Category	Millions of Gallons		Volume Share	
	2005	2006	2005	2006
Carbonated soft drinks	15,271.6	15,103.6	52.9%	50.9%
Bottled water	7,537.1	8,253.1	26.1%	27.8%
Fruit beverages	4,119.0	4,020.1	14.3%	13.5%
Isotonic sports drinks	1,207.5	1,348.8	4.2%	4.5%
Ready-to-drink tea	555.9	701.5	1.9%	2.4%
Energy drinks	152.5	227.4	0.5%	0.8%
Ready-to-drink coffee	38.9	43.0	0.1%	0.1%
Total	28,882.5	29,697.5	100.0%	100.0%

Source: Beverage Marketing Corporation.

PepsiCo's Carbonated Soft Drinks Business. During the mid-1990s, it looked as if Coca-Cola would dominate the soft drink industry, with every Pepsi-Cola brand except Mountain Dew losing market share to Coca-Cola's brands. Coca-Cola's CEO at the time, Roberto Goizueta, had stated that the company's strategic intent was to control 50 percent of the U.S. cola market by 2000; he seemed convinced PepsiCo could do little to stop the industry leader. Goizueta summed up his worries about Pepsi as a key rival in an October 28, 1996, *Fortune* article entitled "How Coke Is Kicking Pepsi's Can" by saying, "As they've become less relevant, I don't need to look at them very much anymore."

Pepsi-Cola management engineered a dramatic comeback in the late 1990s and early 2000s by launching new brands like Sierra Mist and new flavors of existing brands such as Mountain Dew Code Red and by focusing on strategies to improve local distribution. Among Pepsi's most successful strategies to build volume and share in soft drinks was its Power of One strategy, which attempted to achieve the synergistic benefits of a combined Pepsi-Cola and Frito-Lay envisioned by shareholders of the two companies in 1965. PepsiCo had found that even though Frito-Lay and Pepsi-Cola products were consumed together 58 percent of the time, they were purchased together only 22 percent of the time. The Power of One strategy called for supermarkets to place Pepsi and Frito-Lay products side-by-side on shelves. Roger Enrico visited the CEOs of the 25 largest supermarket chains to encourage their companies to participate in the plan, citing research finding that supermarket profit margins on PepsiCo's products were typically 9 percent, compared with an average profit margin of 2 percent on other items sold by supermarkets. In addition, Enrico stressed that PepsiCo products accounted for only 3 percent of supermarket sales, but 20 percent of retailers' cash flows. By 2001, Power of One and other PepsiCo strategies allowed Pepsi-Cola to draw within two percentage points of market leader Coca-Cola. In 2006, PepsiCo added to its Power of One program "Innovation Summits," whereby retailers could share their views on consumer shopping and eating habits. PepsiCo used the information gleaned from the summits in developing new products like SoBe Life Water and Lay's Potato Chips cooked in sunflower oil.

In 2007, PBNA was attempting to reinvent carbonated diet soft drinks as energy boosting drinks to better appeal to health-conscious consumers, since market research had found that 43 percent of consumers wanted drinks that would invigorate them. Diet Mountain Dew's energy-boosting properties had helped its volume increase by 8.5 percent during 2006 and PBNA added Diet Pepsi Max energy drink to its product line in 2007. The company also expanded the Mountain Dew line in 2006 to include Mountain Dew Amp energy drinks. SoBe Essential Energy beverages were also launched in 2006.

The company was attempting to develop new types of sweeteners for its soft drinks that would lower their calorie content of nondiet drinks. PepsiCo also planned a packaging redesign for Diet Pepsi in 2007 and planned to launch as many as 35 new designs for Pepsi cans, bottles, cartons, vending machines, and fountain cups during the year. The company also hoped its 2006 acquisition of Izze lightly carbonated sparkling fruit drinks would prove popular with consumers. Tava was an additional sparking beverage PBNA scheduled for a U.S. launch in 2007.

PepsiCo's Noncarbonated Beverage Brands.
Although carbonated beverages made up the largest percentage of PBNA's total beverage volume, much of the division's growth was attributable to the success of its noncarbonated beverages. In 2006, total case volume for the division increased by 4 percent, which was driven by a 14 percent increase in noncarbonated beverages. Carbonated soft drink volume declined by 2 percent during 2006.

Aquafina, the number one brand of bottled water in the United States, grew by 21.9 percent between 2005 and 2006. Bottled water was a particularly attractive segment for PepsiCo since U.S. bottled water consumption had from increased 4.6 billion gallons in 1999 to 6.8 billion gallons in 2004. PepsiCo's Frappucino RTD coffee and Lipton RTD teas made it the leader in the RTD tea and RTD coffee categories as well. The RTD tea category grew by 26.2 percent between 2005 and 2006, while RTD coffees grew by 10.4 percent during 2006. New flavors like Doubleshot Light and Italian Roast Iced Coffee were expected to contribute further growth for Starbucks RTD coffees. PBNA also introduced Starbucks RTD coffee vending machines in 2006.

In 2007, PBNA's Propel Fitness Water was the leading brand of functional water. In 2006, the company had also introduced SoBe Life Water and functional versions of Aquafina. The product lines for its water business were developed around customer type and lifestyle. Propel was a flavor- and vitamin-enriched water marketed to physically active consumers, while Life Water was a vitamin-enhanced water marketed to image-driven consumers. The company targeted mainstream water consumers with unflavored Aquafina, Aquafina FlavorSplash (offered in four flavors), and Aquafina Sparkling (a zero-calorie, lightly carbonated citrus- or berry-flavored water). Aquafina Alive, launched in 2007, included vitamins and natural fruit juices. The company's strategy involved offering a continuum of healthy beverages from unflavored Aquafina to nutrient-rich Gatorade. In 2006, Gatorade, Propel, and Aquafina were all number one in their categories, with market shares of 80 percent, 34 percent, and approximately 14 percent, respectively.

Gatorade's volume had grown by 21 percent in 2005 and by 12 percent in 2006 to reach sales of over $3 billion. Gatorade's impressive growth had come about through the introduction of new flavors, new container sizes and designs, new multipacks, world-class advertising, and added points of distribution. Analysts believed that Gatorade could achieve even stronger performance once the FTC's 10-year prohibition on bundled beverage contracts with retailers and joint Gatorade–soft drink distribution came to an end. Gatorade's broker-distribution system also allowed Tropicana and Lipton RTD teas to double sales volume between the 2001 acquisition of Quaker Oats and year-end 2006. Volume gains for Tropicana and Lipton were also aided by the addition of new flavors and packaging.

Tropicana was not only the number one brand in the $3 billion orange juice industry but also among the fastest-growing beverage brands, with 10.3 percent growth in 2006. Tropicana achieved double-digit volume growth during 2006 even though the fruit beverage category declined by 2.4 percent that year. Tropicana had achieved volume and revenue growth through the introduction of such new products as Tropicana Pure superpremium blended juice drinks, Tropicana Essentials Omega-3 fortified orange juice, and Tropicana Organic orange juice. The combined sales of PBNA's BFY and GFY beverages made up 70 percent of the division's net revenue in 2006.

PepsiCo International

All PepsiCo snacks, beverages, and food items sold outside North America were included in the company's PepsiCo International division. International snack volume grew by 9 percent in 2006, with double-digit growth in emerging markets such as Russia, Turkey, Egypt, and India. Beverage volume in international markets increased by 9 percent as well during 2006, with the fastest growth occurring in the Middle East, China, Argentina, Russia, and Venezuela. The company made three small acquisitions of snack brands in the Netherlands, Poland, and New Zealand in 2006.

PepsiCo's Sale of Beverages in International Markets.   PepsiCo also found that it could grow international sales through its Power of One strategy. A Pepsi-Cola executive explained how the company's soft drink business could gain shelf space through the strength of Frito-Lay's brands. "You go to Chile, where Frito-Lay has over 90 percent of the market, but Pepsi is in lousy shape. Frito-Lay can help Pepsi change that."[2] PepsiCo's market share in carbonated soft drinks in its strongest international markets during 2006 is presented in the following table.

Country/Region	PepsiCo's Carbonated Soft Drink Market Share
Middle East	75%+
India	49
Thailand	49
Egypt	47
Venezuela	42
Nigeria	38
China	36
Russia	24

Source: PepsiCo Investor Presentation by Mike White, CEO PepsiCo International, 2006.

PepsiCo International management believed that further opportunities in other international markets existed. In 2006, the average consumption of carbonated soft drinks in the United States was 32 servings per month, while the average consumption of CSDs in other developed countries was 17 servings per month and in developing countries was 5 servings per month. The company also saw a vast opportunity for sales growth in the $70 billion market for noncarbonated beverages in international markets. In 2006, PepsiCo International recorded less than $1 billion in noncarbonated beverage sales outside North America. The company was rapidly rolling out Tropicana to international markets and had acquired two international juice brands to capture a larger share of the $37 billion international markets for juice drinks. Also, PepsiCo was making Gatorade available in more international markets to capture a share of the $5 billion isotonic sports drink market outside the United States. Sales of Gatorade in Latin America more than doubled between 2001 and 2006 to give the sports drink a 72 percent market share in the entire Latin American region in 2006. PepsiCo International was also moving into new markets with Lipton RTD tea to gain a share of the $15 billion international RTD tea market. In 2007, Gatorade was available in 42 international markets, Tropicana was in 27 country markets outside North America, and Lipton was sold in 27 international markets. Tropicana was the number one juice brand in Europe and had achieved a 100 percent increase in sales in the region between 2001 and 2006. By 2012, PepsiCo planned to launch Gatorade in 15 additional country markets, Tropicana in 20 new markets, and Lipton in 5 new international markets.

PepsiCo had moved somewhat slowly into international bottled water markets, with its most notable effort occurring in Mexico. In 2002, PepsiCo's bottling operations acquired Mexico's largest Pepsi bottler, Pepsi-Gemex SA de CV for $1.26 billion. Gemex not only bottled and distributed Pepsi soft drinks in Mexico but was also Mexico's number one producer of purified water. After its acquisition of Gemex, PepsiCo shifted its international expansion efforts to bringing Aquafina to selected emerging markets in Eastern Europe, the Middle East, and Asia. In 2006, Aquafina was the number one brand of bottled water in Russia and Vietnam and the number two brand in Kuwait.

PepsiCo's Sales of Snack Foods in International Markets.   Frito-Lay was the largest snack chip company in the world, with sales of approximately $7 billion outside the United States and a 40 percent+ share of the international salty snack industry in 2006. Frito-Lay held commanding shares of the market for salty snacks in many country markets. The following table presents PepsiCo's salty snack market share in selected countries in 2006.

Country	PepsiCo's Salty Snack Market Share
Mexico	75%
Holland	59
South Africa	57
Australia	55
Brazil	46
India	46
United Kingdom	44
Russia	43
Spain	41
China	16

Source: PepsiCo Investor Presentation by Mike White, CEO PepsiCo International, 2006.

PepsiCo management believed international markets offered the company's greatest opportunity for growth since per capita consumption of snacks in the United States averaged 13.9 servings per month, while per capita consumption in other developed countries averaged 8.8 servings per month, and per capita consumption averaged 1.9 servings per month in developing countries. PepsiCo executives expected that, by 2010, China and Brazil would be the two largest international markets for snacks. The United Kingdom was projected to be the third largest international market for snacks, while developing markets Mexico and Russia would be the fourth and fifth largest international markets, respectively.

Developing an understanding of consumer taste preferences was a key to expanding into international markets. Taste preferences for salty snacks were more similar from country to country than many other food items, which allowed PepsiCo to make only modest modifications to its snacks in most countries. For example, classic varieties of Lay's, Doritos, and Cheetos snacks were sold in Latin America. However, the company supplemented its global brands with varieties spiced to local preferences such as Lay's Artesanas chips sold in Latin America and Lay's White Mushroom potato chips sold in Russia. In addition, consumer characteristics in the United States that had forced snack food makers to adopt better-for-you or good-for-you snacks applied in most other developed countries as well. In 2007, PepsiCo was eliminating trans fats from its snacks and expanding the nutritional credentials of its snacks sold in Europe since demand for health and wellness products in Europe was growing by 10–13

percent per year. The annual revenue growth for core salty snacks in Europe was growing at a modest 4–6 percent per year. Among PepsiCo's fastest-growing snacks in the United Kingdom was Walker's Low Fat Ready Salted potato chips. which had 70 percent less saturated fat and 25 percent less salt than regular Walker's chips. The company's Potato Heads natural chip line, which also boasted less fat and reduced salt, became the number one food launch in the United Kingdom during 2005. In addition, Walker's Baked Potato Chips had outperformed forecast sales in 2006 by 100 percent.

International Sales of Quaker Oats Products. PepsiCo International also manufactured and distributed Quaker Oats oatmeal and cereal in international markets. In 2006, 75 percent of Quaker Oats' international sales of $500 million was accounted for by just six countries. The United Kingdom was Quaker's largest market outside the U.S., where it held more than a 50 percent market share in oatmeal. The company had launched new oatmeal products in the United Kingdom, including Organic Oats, OatSo Simple microwaveable oatmeal and oatmeal bars, and Oat Granola and Oat Muesli cereals. PepsiCo also added new varieties of Quaker Oatmeal products in Latin America to double the brand's sales in the region from the time of its acquisition by PepsiCo to year-end 2006. Exhibit 8 presents a breakdown of PepsiCo's net revenues and long-lived assets by geographic region.

Quaker Foods North America   Quaker Oats produced, marketed, and distributed hot and ready-to-eat cereals, pancake mixes and syrups, and rice and pasta side dishes in the United States and Canada. The division recorded sales of nearly $1.8 billion in 2006. Net revenues during 2006 increased by 3 percent during the year with Quaker Oatmeal, Life cereal, and Cap'n Crunch cereal volumes increasing at single-digit rates. Sales of Aunt Jemima syrup and pancake mix and Rice-A-Roni rice and pasta kits declined slightly during 2006. Quaker Oats was the star product of the division, with a 58 percent market share in North America in 2006. Rice-A-Roni held a 33 percent market share in the rice and pasta side dish segment of the consumer food industry. Although Quaker Foods was just the third largest ready-to-eat cereal maker, with a 14 percent market share in 2005, it was the only cereal producer to increase volume during the year. Quaker sales increased by 3.1

Exhibit 8   **PepsiCo Inc.'s U.S. and International Sales and Long-Lived Assets, 2004–2006 ($ in millions)**

	2006	2005	2004
Net Revenues			
United States	$20,788	$19,937	$18,329
Mexico	3,228	3,095	2,724
United Kingdom	1,839	1,821	1,692
Canada	1,702	1,509	1,309
All other countries	7,580	6,200	5,207
Total	$35,137	$32,562	$29,261
Long-Lived Assets			
United States	$11,515	$10,723	$10,212
Mexico	996	902	878
United Kingdom	1,995	1,715	1,896
Canada	589	582	548
All other countries	4,725	3,948	3,339
Total	$19,820	$17,870	$16,873

Source: PepsiCo Inc., 2006 10-K report.

percent during 2005, while Kellogg's sales declined by 0.8 percent and General Mills' sales declined by 6.1 percent during the year. Some of Quaker's gains were a result of new cereal varieties such as Take Heart cereal that included heart-healthy Omega-3s, Oatmeal Crunch, Oatmeal Squares, Natural Granola, and Oat Bran cereals. In 2005, Kellogg's held a 30 percent share of the $6 billion ready-to-eat cereal market and General Mills held a 26 percent market share. Quaker grits and Aunt Jemima pancake mix and syrup competed in mature categories and all enjoyed market leading positions. Fifty-five percent of Quaker Foods' 2006 revenues was generated by BFY and GFY products.

Value Chain Alignment between PepsiCo Brands and Products

PepsiCo's management team was dedicated to capturing strategic fit benefits within the business line-up throughout the value chain. The company shared marketed research information to better enable each division to develop new products likely to be hits with consumers, consolidated its purchasing to reduce costs, and manufactured similar products in common facilities whenever possible. The company

had also consolidated sales and marketing functions of similar products to eliminate duplication of effort and to present one face to customers.

The efforts to achieve synergies undertaken upon the acquisition of Quaker Oats had delivered an estimated $160 million in cost savings by 2005 through the combined corporate-wide procurement of product ingredients and packaging materials. Also, the combination of Gatorade and Tropicana hot fill operations had saved an estimated $120 million annually by 2005. The joint distribution of Quaker snacks and Frito-Lay products had reduced distribution expenses by an estimated $40 million by 2005.

PEPSICO'S INVESTMENT PRIORITIES IN 2007

PepsiCo's financial managers expected the company's lineup of snack, beverage, and grocery items to generate cumulative management operating cash flows of $15 billion between 2007 and 2009. The company's priorities for free cash flow were to reinvest in its core businesses, provide cash dividends to shareholders, and identify strategic growth opportunities that would provide attractive returns. From the close of the Quaker Oats acquisition in 2001 through early 2007, the company had chosen to make only small "tuck-in" acquisitions. The company's executives expected to continue to make additional tuck-in acquisitions totaling approximately $500 million per year. Future capital expenditures for existing businesses were expected to range from 5 to 7 percent of net revenues. Dividends to shareholders had grown at a compounded annual rate of 15 percent between 2001 and 2006 to reach $1.16 per share. Between 2003 and 2005, PepsiCo had completed $1.2 billion in acquisitions, made $4.5 billion in capital expenditures, paid $4 billion in dividends, and completed an $8 billion share repurchase program. In May 2006, the company's board announced a new $8.5 billion share repurchase program that would expire on June 30, 2009. The company repurchased shares totaling $1.1 billion in 2006, which left $7.4 billion remaining on the share repurchase program.

Endnotes

[1] As quoted in "Snack Attack," *Private Label Buyer*, August 2006, p. 26.
[2] "PepsiCo's New Formula," *BusinessWeek Online*, April 10, 2000.

Spectrum Brands' Diversification Strategy: A Success or a Failure?

Arthur A. Thompson
The University of Alabama

John E. Gamble
University of South Alabama

In 2003, top executives at Rayovac Corporation, concerned about fierce competition and limited growth opportunities in its global consumer battery business, decided to embark on a long-term program to diversify the company's revenue stream away from such heavy dependence on selling alkaline and rechargeable AA and AAA batteries, coin batteries for watches and calculators, hearing aid batteries (where it was the worldwide leader), and flashlight products. Three years later, via a series of acquisitions, Rayovac had transformed itself into a global branded consumer products company with positions in seven major product categories: consumer batteries, portable lighting, pet supplies, lawn and garden, electric shaving and grooming, electric personal care products, and household insect control. The resulting change in the company's revenue mix was dramatic:

Product Category	Percentage of Company Net Sales, Fiscal Year Ending September 30			
	2003	2004	2005	2006
Consumer batteries	90%	67%	42%	34%
Portable lighting	10	6	4	3
Pet supplies	—	—	12	21
Lawn and garden	—	—	18	20
Electric shaving and grooming	—	19	12	10
Electric personal care products	—	8	6	6
Household insect control	—	—	6	6
	100%	100%	100%	100%

In recognition of the strategic shift in its business composition, Rayovac changed its name to Spectrum Brands in May 2005.

Exhibit 1   **Consolidated Statement of Operations for Spectrum Brands, Fiscal Years 2002–2006 ($ in millions, except per share data)**

	Fiscal Years Ending September 30				
	2006	2005	2004	2003	2002
Net sales	$2,551.8	$2,307.2	$1,417.2	$922.1	$572.7
Cost of goods sold	1,576.1	1,427.1	1,417.2	922.1	334.1
Restructuring and related charges, cost of goods sold	22.5	10.5	(0.8)	21.1	1.2
Gross profit	953.2	869.5	606.1	351.5	237.4
Operating expenses					
Selling	557.3	475.6	293.1	185.2	104.4
General and administrative	182.0	142.6	121.3	80.9	56.9
Research and development	30.6	29.3	23.2	14.4	13.1
Restructuring and related charges	33.6	15.8	12.2	11.5	—
Goodwill and intangibles impairment	433.0	—	—	—	—
Total operating expenses	1,236.5	673.5	449.9	291.9	174.4
Operating income (loss)	(283.2)	196.1	156.2	59.6	63.0
Interest expense	177.0	134.1	65.7	37.2	16.0
Other income, net	(4.1)	0.9	0.0	0.6	(1.3)
Income (loss) from continuing operations before income taxes	(456.1)	62.9	90.5	23.0	45.7
Income tax expense (benefit)	(27.6)	21.5	34.4	7.6	16.4
Income (loss) from continuing operations	(428.5)	41.3	56.2	15.5	29.2
Income (loss) from discontinued operations, net of tax benefits	(5.5)	5.5	(0.4)	—	—
Net income (loss)	$ (434.0)	$ 46.8	$ 55.8	$ 15.5	$ 29.2
Net income (loss) per common share					
Basic	$ (8.77)	$ 1.07	$ 1.67	$ 0.49	$ 0.92
Diluted	(8.77)	1.03	1.61	0.48	0.90
Weighted average shares of common stock outstanding					
Basic	49.5	43.7	33.4	31.8	31.8
Diluted	49.5	45.6	34.6	32.6	32.4

Source: Company 10-K reports, 2006 and 2003.

But while the company's revenues had jumped from $573 million in fiscal 2002 to $2.55 billion at the end of fiscal 2006, its financial performance and financial condition were less than inspiring. Net income had dropped from $55.8 million in fiscal 2004 to $46.8 million in fiscal 2005 to a loss of $434 million in fiscal 2006. Despite the company's much bigger size and revenue stream, net cash flows from operations in 2006 were below the level in 2002. The company had long-term debt of more than $2.2 billion and interest expenses of $177 million in 2006 versus long-term debt of $188 million and interest expenses of $16 million in 2002. Moreover, investors were a bit uneasy about Spectrum Brands' future prospects. Spectrum's stock price, which had traded as high as $46 in February 2005, traded in the $6 to $12 range between July 2006 and February 2007. Exhibits 1 and 2 present recent financial performance data for Spectrum Brands.

Exhibit 2   **Selected Consolidated Balance Sheet and Cash Flow Data for Spectrum Brands, Fiscal Years 2002–2006 ($ in millions)**

	Fiscal Years Ending September 30				
	2006*	2005*	2004*	2003**	2002**
Balance Sheet Data					
Cash and cash equivalents	$ 28.4	$ 29.9	$ 14.0	$ 107.8	$ 9.9
Inventories	460.7	451.6	264.7	219.3	84.3
Current assets	959.8	1,048.0	648.7	675.3	259.3
Property, plant, and equipment, net	311.8	304.3	182.4	150.4	102.6
Goodwill	1,130.2	1,429.0	320.6	398.4	30.6
Intangible assets, net	1,016.1	1,154.4	422.1	253.1	88.9
Total assets	3,549.3	4,022.1	1,634.2	1,576.5	533.2
Current liabilities	562.6	557.4	396.8	405.5	118.8
Long-term debt, net of current maturities	2,234.5	2,268.0	806.0	870.5	188.5
Total shareholders' equity	452.2	842.7	316.0	202.0	174.8
Cash Flow and Related Data					
Net cash provided by operating activities	$ 44.5	$ 216.6	$ 96.1	$ 76.2	$ 66.8
Capital expenditures	60.4	62.8	26.9	26.1	15.6
Depreciation and amortization	87.5	68.6	40.6	35.0	20.3
Working capital	397.2	490.6	251.9	269.8	140.5

* Figures for 2004–2006 are as reported in the company's 10-K reports for 2005 and 2006.

** Figures for 2002 and 2003 are as reported in the company's 10-K report for 2003.

Sources: Company 10-K Reports, 2006, 2005, and 2003.

COMPANY BACKGROUND

In 1906, a company founded as the French Battery Company began operations in a plant in Madison, Wisconsin; French Battery was renamed Ray-O-Vac in 1930. Over the next several decades, Ray-O-Vac gained a reputation for innovation in batteries and flashlights:

In 1946, company sales surpassed 100 million batteries for the first time; Ray-O-Vac produced its one billionth leakproof cell battery in 1950.[1] In 1981, Ray-O-Vac debuted a new logo and a new corporate name minus the hyphens, Rayovac. During the 1970s and 1980s, Rayovac established firmly itself as the leading marketer of value-priced batteries in

1933	Patented the first wearable hearing aid tube
1939	Introduced the first leak-proof "sealed in steel" dry cell battery
1949	Introduced the crown cell alkaline for hearing aids and launched its soon-to-be-famous steel Sportsman flashlight
1970	Patented a silver oxide button cell battery
1972	Introduced the first heavy-duty, all-zinc chloride battery with double the life of general purpose batteries
1984	Introduced the Workhorse premium flashlight with lifetime warranty
1988	Introduced a battery to power the real-time clocks of personal computers
1993	Introduced a line of long-life rechargeable batteries
2001	Introduced breakthrough chargers for high-capacity Nickel Metal Hydride (NiMH) batteries; developed a new zinc air battery that combined long life and unprecedented power for hearing aids used by the severely hearing impaired
2002	Introduced 15-minute battery recharging technology

North America—the company's core competitive strategy was to sell a battery comparable in quality to those of competing brands but at prices averaging about 10–15 percent less.

During the early 1990s, Rayovac suffered an erosion of market share to its two primary competitors, Duracell and Energizer, becoming a distant third in market share. In 1996, a private-equity company, Thomas H. Lee Partners, purchased Rayovac and instituted a number of restructuring initiatives and organizational changes. David A. Jones was made chairman and CEO in September 1996. In 1997, Thomas H. Lee Partners took the company public with an initial offering of common stock; trading of shares began on the New York Stock Exchange in November 1997. However, Thomas H. Lee Partners retained a sizable ownership share in the company; it was the company's largest shareholder as of early 2007, controlling about 23 percent of the company's outstanding shares. Rayovac had sales of $427 million and profits of $6 million in 1997, the year it went public.

Shortly after Rayovac became a public company, CEO David Jones put it on a long-term course to rejuvenate its battery business and spur sales growth. The strategy to reshape Rayovac and grow market share was comprehensive, involving efforts to (1) build the Rayovac brand via increased advertising and promotion, (2) broaden the battery lineup via technological innovation, (3) improve merchandising and attractiveness of packaging, (4) expand distribution to include more retailers of Rayovac in more countries, (5) revamp battery manufacturing operations to slash production costs and increase plant capacity, (6) refine the supply chain and consolidate purchasing, (7) offer very attentive customer service, and (8) create a results-oriented, entrepreneurial culture.

Starting in 1999, Jones embarked on a strategy to globalize Rayovac's battery and flashlight business via a series of acquisitions in key foreign markets:[2]

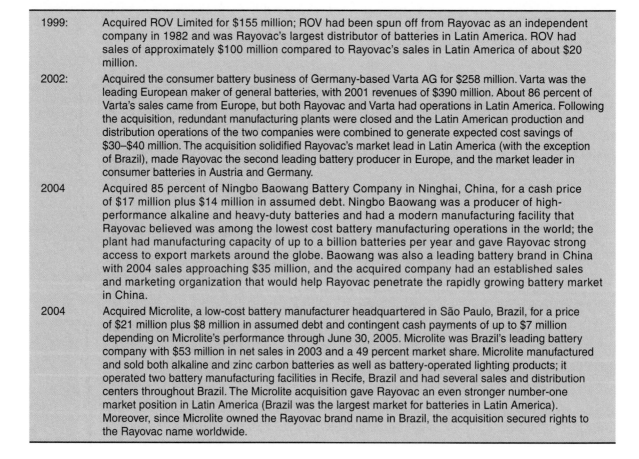

1999:	Acquired ROV Limited for $155 million; ROV had been spun off from Rayovac as an independent company in 1982 and was Rayovac's largest distributor of batteries in Latin America. ROV had sales of approximately $100 million compared to Rayovac's sales in Latin America of about $20 million.
2002:	Acquired the consumer battery business of Germany-based Varta AG for $258 million. Varta was the leading European maker of general batteries, with 2001 revenues of $390 million. About 86 percent of Varta's sales came from Europe, but both Rayovac and Varta had operations in Latin America. Following the acquisition, redundant manufacturing plants were closed and the Latin American production and distribution operations of the two companies were combined to generate expected cost savings of $30–$40 million. The acquisition solidified Rayovac's market lead in Latin America (with the exception of Brazil), made Rayovac the second leading battery producer in Europe, and the market leader in consumer batteries in Austria and Germany.
2004	Acquired 85 percent of Ningbo Baowang Battery Company in Ninghai, China, for a cash price of $17 million plus $14 million in assumed debt. Ningbo Baowang was a producer of high-performance alkaline and heavy-duty batteries and had a modern manufacturing facility that Rayovac believed was among the lowest cost battery manufacturing operations in the world; the plant had manufacturing capacity of up to a billion batteries per year and gave Rayovac strong access to export markets around the globe. Baowang was also a leading battery brand in China with 2004 sales approaching $35 million, and the acquired company had an established sales and marketing organization that would help Rayovac penetrate the rapidly growing battery market in China.
2004	Acquired Microlite, a low-cost battery manufacturer headquartered in São Paulo, Brazil, for a price of $21 million plus $8 million in assumed debt and contingent cash payments of up to $7 million depending on Microlite's performance through June 30, 2005. Microlite was Brazil's leading battery company with $53 million in net sales in 2003 and a 49 percent market share. Microlite manufactured and sold both alkaline and zinc carbon batteries as well as battery-operated lighting products; it operated two battery manufacturing facilities in Recife, Brazil and had several sales and distribution centers throughout Brazil. The Microlite acquisition gave Rayovac an even stronger number-one market position in Latin America (Brazil was the largest market for batteries in Latin America). Moreover, since Microlite owned the Rayovac brand name in Brazil, the acquisition secured rights to the Rayovac name worldwide.

Following these moves, Rayovac established itself as the leading value brand of alkaline batteries in North America and Latin America, the top supplier of rechargeable batteries in the United States and Europe, and the world's largest manufacturer and marketer of hearing aid batteries (with a market share approximating 60 percent). Since 1997, the company's sales of battery and lighting products sales had grown from $427 million to just over $1 billion at the end of fiscal 2004. Going into fiscal 2005, Rayovac's battery and lighting products were sold by 19 of the world's 20 largest retailers and were available in 1 million store locations in 120 countries.[3] It had a full lineup of battery products and was continuing to introduce new products. Rayovac had more hearing aid battery patents than all of its competitors combined.

SPECTRUM BRANDS' DIVERSIFICATION STRATEGY

Starting in 2003, David Jones and other top executives at Rayovac determined that the company needed to expand beyond its battery and lighting products business, partly due to stiff competition in batteries and partly due to a maturing global market demand for batteries that diminished the company's prospects for achieving 8–10 percent annual growth in revenues and profits. Just as the strategy for becoming a global battery company had been predicated largely on acquisition, so also was the strategy to diversify into new businesses and product categories. During the 2003–2005 period, the company made four important diversification-related acquisitions:[4]

2003:	Acquired Remington Products Company, a leading designer and distributor of battery-powered electric shavers, beard and mustache trimmers, grooming products, and personal care appliances. The purchase price was $222 million, including the assumption of Remington's debt; in the 12 months prior to the acquisition, Remington had sales of $360 million and net income of $20 million.
	Headquartered in Bridgeport, Connecticut, Remington was the number one selling brand in the United States in the combined dry shaving and personal grooming products categories based on units sold. Remington had acquired Clairol's worldwide personal care appliance business (consisting of hair dryers, stylers, hot rollers, and lighted mirrors) in 1993.
	Remington products were sold in more than 20,000 retail outlets in the United States; more than 70 percent of Remington's sales were in North America. Remington's core North American shaving and grooming products business had grown an average of 18 percent per year from 1998 through 2002. Internationally, Remington products were sold through a network of subsidiaries and distributors in more than 85 countries.
	Following the acquisition, Rayovac closed Remington's headquarters, transferred all of Remington's headquarters operations to Rayovac's headquarters, moved all of Remington's manufacturing operations to a Rayovac plant in Wisconsin, merged Remington and Rayovac R&D functions into a single department, and closed Remington's distribution operations and 65 U.S. service centers and relocated their functions to Rayovac's North American and European facilities. In North America, Rayovac and Remington sales management, field sales operations, and marketing were merged into a single North American sales and marketing organization.
2005	Acquired privately owned United Industries Corporation, for a total value of approximately $1.2 billion including the assumption of approximately $880 million of United Industries debt and a cash tax benefit of $140 million. United Industries, based in St. Louis, was a leading manufacturer and marketer of consumer products for lawn and garden care and household insect control; United also manufactured and marketed premium-branded specialty pet supplies. In lawn and garden products and household insect control, United operated as Spectrum Brands in the United States and NuGro in Canada. In pet supplies, it operated as United Pet Group. United's brands included Spectracide, Vigoro, Sta-Green, Schultz, and C.I.L in the lawn and garden market; Hot Shot, Cutter and Repel in the household insect control market; and Marineland, Perfecto, and Eight in One in pet supply products. United had sales of approximately $950 million in 2004; major customers included Home Depot, Lowe's, Wal-Mart, PETCO, and PETsMART.

(Continued)

(Continued)

2005	Acquired Tetra Holding, a privately held supplier of fish and aquatics supplies headquartered in Melle, Germany. The purchase price was approximately €415 million. Tetra was the leading global brand in foods, equipment, and care products for fish and reptiles, along with accessories for home aquariums and ponds. Tetra currently operated in over 90 countries worldwide and held leading market positions in Germany, the United States, Japan and the United Kingdom. It had approximately 700 employees and annual sales of about €200 million. The Tetra acquisition strengthened Rayovac's newly created strategic position in pet supplies. According to CEO David Jones, "Tetra's superior brand equity and demonstrated record of product innovation make it a premiere property in this industry. The combination of Tetra with our United Pet Group business means Rayovac becomes the world's largest manufacturer of pet supplies, a position with which we can leverage our company's worldwide operations, supply chain and information systems infrastructure to better meet the needs of our global retailer customers." United Pet Group President John Heil stated, "The Tetra brand is arguably the most recognized global brand name in the pet supplies industry. The acquisition of Tetra is a linchpin to our goal of becoming the most important pet supplies provider in the world."
2005	Acquired Jungle Labs for $29 million, with the potential for additional payments contingent on Jungle Labs' meeting defined future growth objectives. Based in San Antonio, Texas, Jungle Labs had sales of approximately $14 million and was a leading manufacturer and marketer of premium water and fish care products, including water conditioners, plant and fish foods, fish medications, and other products designed to maintain an optimal environment in aquariums or ponds. Jungle was known for such innovative high-end products as Tank Buddies fizz tablets for easy fish and water care, and Quick Dip test strips for fast, accurate water testing. Spectrum Brands' CEO David Jones believed that Jungle Labs' product line and its strong track record of innovative product development and marketing in water and fish care complemented the previously acquired Tetra, Marineland, ASI, and Perfecto aquatics brands and strengthened Spectrum's position in aquatic supplies.

These acquisitions drove Rayovac's decision to change its name to Spectrum Brands and prompted management to begin touting Spectrum Brands as "a brand new 100-year-old company."[5] Exhibit 3 shows the performance of Spectrum Brands' stock price as it became a more broadly diversified company.

AN OVERVIEW OF SPECTRUM BRANDS' BUSINESSES AND PRODUCT CATEGORIES

Beginning with fiscal year 2006, Spectrum Brands began managing its business in four reportable segments:

1. North America, which consisted of the sales and operations of its consumer battery, shaving and grooming, personal care, lawn and garden, household insect control, and portable lighting product categories in the United States and Canada.

2. Latin America, which consisted of the sales and operations of its consumer battery, shaving and grooming, personal care, lawn and garden, household insect control, and portable lighting product categories in Mexico, Central America, South America, and the Caribbean ("Latin America").

3. Europe/Rest of the World, which consisted of the sales and operations of its consumer battery, shaving and grooming, personal care, lawn and garden, household insect control, and portable lighting product categories in the United Kingdom, continental Europe, China, Australia, and all other countries not included in the first two segments.

4. Global Pet, which consists of the acquired operations of United Pet Group, Tetra Holdings, and Jungle Labs.

Exhibit 4 shows the company's operating performance and selected financial data for these four segments for the period 2003–2006.

The Global Battery Business

Going into 2007, most consumer batteries around the world were manufactured and marketed by one of four companies: Procter & Gamble (manufacturer/distributor of the Duracell brand), Energizer

Exhibit 3   **Performance of Spectrum Brands' Stock Price, November 1997–December 2006**

(a) Performance of Spectrum Brands' Stock Price and Key Acquisition Dates

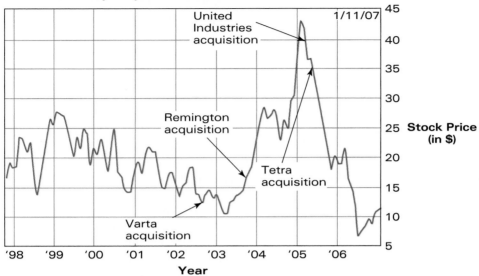

(b) Performance of Spectrum Brands' Stock Price versus the S&P 500

Holdings (the maker/distributor of the Energizer brand of batteries), Spectrum Brands (the maker/distributor of VARTA batteries in Europe and Rayovac batteries in the rest of the world), and Matsushita (manufacturer/distributor of the Panasonic brand).[6] Some major retailers, especially in Europe, marketed private-label brands of batteries. Duracell was the market leader worldwide, followed in order by Energizer, Rayovac/VARTA, and Panasonic.

Batteries were used chiefly to power toys and games; remote-control devices for a variety of electronics products (TVs, DVD players); handheld video game players; MP3 players like the Apple iPod; digital cameras; clocks and watches; hearing aids;

and flashlights. Growth in consumer battery sales was in the low single digits in the United States and much of Europe, owing to already widespread battery use and a mature marketplace. In Latin America and Southeast Asia (particularly China), consumer use of batteries was much lower and there was good long-term potential for sales growth in the high single digits as consumers purchased more devices powered by batteries. In North America and Europe, most consumers purchased alkaline batteries; less expensive zinc carbon batteries were most popular in Latin America, but the Latin American market was slowly converting to alkaline batteries as disposable incomes increased.

In 2001, the global market for batteries was about a $21 billion industry and had grown at a historical rate of about 6–7 percent. About one-third of total sales occurred in the United States. Since 2001, global growth had slowed to an average of 4–5 percent, resulting in global sales close to $25 billion in 2006. However, battery sales were affected by ups and downs in the economy and by the strength of sales of battery-using products.

Spectrum Brands manufactured and distributed alkaline and zinc carbon batteries, hearing aid batteries, rechargeable batteries and battery chargers, photo batteries, lithium batteries, silver oxide batteries, keyless entry batteries, and coin cells for use in watches, cameras, calculators, communications equipment, and medical instrumentation. A full line of alkaline batteries (AA, AAA, C, D, and nine-volt sizes) was sold to both retail and industrial customers, primarily under the VARTA brand in Europe and under the Rayovac brand in the rest of the world. Alkaline batteries were also manufactured for sellers of private-label batteries. Zinc carbon batteries (used primarily for low- and medium-drain battery-powered devices), Nickel Metal Hydride (NiMH) rechargeable batteries, and a variety of battery chargers were marketed primarily under the Rayovac and VARTA brands.

In the U.S. alkaline battery marketplace, the Rayovac brand was positioned as a value brand offering comparable performance to the Duracell and Energizer brands at a lower price. In Europe, the VARTA brand was competitively priced with other premium brands. In Latin America, where zinc carbon batteries outsold alkaline batteries, the Rayovac brand was also competitively priced against other

leading brands. In 2005–2006, Rayovac was the third-ranked brand in North America, with an estimated 19 percent market share (based on dollar sales).[7] VARTA was the second-ranked brand in Europe, with an estimated market share of 25 percent; in Latin America, Rayovac was the leading brand.

The retailers of private-label batteries typically sold their batteries at prices below the leading name brands; however, private-label brands were normally not supported by advertising or promotional activities. On the whole, competition in the global battery marketplace was relatively strong, but competitive pressures varied by geographic location. Competitive factors included distribution capability (as measured by the ability to win the battle for limited space on retailer's shelves), brand-name recognition (affected by advertising and promotion strategies), perceived product quality, price, product performance, and product packaging and design innovation. The main barriers to entry for new competitors were investment in technology research, the cost of building manufacturing capacity, and the expense of building retail distribution channels and brand awareness.

Industry leader Duracell had a 45 percent U.S. market share in 2005 and extended its lead in 2006. Some of Duracell's growth in the United States came at Rayovac's expense as Spectrum Brands' U.S. battery sales declined by $18 million between 2005 and 2006. Spectrum Brands' battery sales declined by $89 million outside the United States as consumers showed a growing preference for private-label alkaline batteries and since the company had elected not to bid on certain private-label contracts. Declining sales of VARTA batteries in Europe took the company partly by surprise because sales of private-label batteries grew unexpectedly fast in Germany, France, Italy, and several other countries.

Spectrum Brands' battery business also suffered from declining gross margins in 2006 as increases in raw materials prices reduced gross profit by $18 million. However, market leaders Duracell and Engergizer were able to avoid margin declines by increasing prices in the United States. Spectrum Brands management addressed the cost disadvantage in batteries in 2005 and 2006 by relocating production from Europe to its recently acquired manufacturing facilities in China. The company also restructured operations in its German packaging center to reduce its total workforce in Europe by 350.

Pet Supplies

The United Industries, Tetra, and Jungle Labs acquisitions resulted in a global pet supplies group with broad representation in products for fish, dogs, cats, birds, and other small domestic animals.[8] The aquatics lineup included such consumer and commercial aquatics products as integrated aquarium kits, stand-alone tanks and stands, filtration systems, heaters, pumps, sea salt, aquarium hoods and lights, and other aquarium supplies and accessories. The largest aquatics brands were Tetra (aquarium and pond supplies, world's leading brand of fish flakes); Marineland (aquarium heaters, filters, and décor); Perfecto (aquariums and fish tanks; aquarium stands, hoods, lights, and filters); Jungle (aquariums, pond kits, fountain maintenance, fizz and water conditioner products for ponds); and Instant Ocean (aquarium salt). The lineup of products for birds and animals include animal treats, stain and odor removal products, grooming aids, bedding products, premium food, medications; and vitamin supplements. The largest specialty pet brands were 8in1 (dog shampoos and conditioners, bird food and health care products, cat litter and health care products, stain and odor products); Nature's Miracle (stain and odor products); Dingo (dog chews and bones); Wild Harvest (bird food); and Firstrax (pet bedding, crates, and toys).

John Heil, the president of the United Pet Group at Spectrum Brands, was bullish on the group's growth prospects in 2007 and beyond due to several key trends:[9]

- Projected continued growth in the number of households owning pets (pet ownership was growing fastest in the 55–64 age group).

- Increases in the number of pets per household (47 percent of households had more than one pet).

- Pets were increasingly viewed as family members.

- Spending by pet owners on pet supplies was relatively insensitive to ups and downs in the economy.

- The number of major retailers of pet supplies was consolidating—in the United States, for example, Wal-Mart, Target, PETsMart, PETCO, and large supermarket chains were accounting for a bigger percent of total pet supply sales.

Spectrum Brands had also begun accelerating plans to source its pet supply production from Chinese contract manufacturers.

The global pet supply industry was highly fragmented, consisting primarily of small companies with limited product lines; in the United States alone, there were over 500 manufacturers. Global sales of pet supplies of all types were an estimated $60 billion in 2006. Global growth in specialty pet supplies was in the 4–6 percent range. Spectrum Brands' management estimated that the retail value of the U.S. pet supplies industry in just those product categories where it competed was about $8 billion in 2004, with another $4 billion in Europe. The industry had grown at a 6–8 percent rate annually in the United States since the mid-1990s and was expected to grow in the 4–7 percent range in the near future.

Spectrum Brands' global pet supplies group had an estimated 8 percent market share worldwide in the product categories where it competed, with broad distribution in North America, Europe, and Japan.[10] Its largest competitors in North America were Hartz Mountain and Central Garden & Pet Company. Hartz Mountain, acquired by Sumitomo Corporation in 2004, marketed over 1,500 products for dogs, cats, birds, hamsters, reptiles, and other animals; Hartz's acquisition by Sumitomo had provided the resources to pursue the development of new markets and distribution channels in Asia and Europe. Central Garden and Pet's product line consisted of six brands of aquatics products, seven brands of dog and cat products, three brands of bird and small animal products, and five brands of animal health and insect control products. Sales of pet products at Central Garden and Supply were $569 million in fiscal 2004, $639 million in fiscal 2005, and $819 million in fiscal 2006; operating income from sales of pet products before deduction of corporate-level expenses totaled $61 million in 2004, $84 million in 2005, and $105 million in 2006.[11] Central marketed its pet products only in the United States, where its sales of $819 million in 2006 made it far and away the sales leader—Spectrum Brands and Hartz were tied at second, with U.S. sales of approximately $350 million in 2006. (However, Spectrum's international sales were greater than Hartz Mountain's, making it number two in terms of worldwide sales.) Central management estimated that total U.S. sales of pet products in 2006 amounted to about $39 billion, that the product categories in which it competed had total U.S. sales of $13 billion, and that its brands typically ranked first or second in market share in their respective segments.

Doskocil, the fourth largest seller of pet supplies in the United States, with 2006 sales of $160 million, was the only other U.S. manufacturer of pet supplies that competed in a broad number of product categories. Most other manufacturers had limited product lines that included only such specialized products as sea salt, aquariums, pet treats, or bird seed.

Lawn and Garden

Spectrum Brands' lawn and garden business consisted of several leading lawn and garden care products, including lawn fertilizers, professional fertilizers, lawn control products, herbicides, garden and indoor plant foods, plant care products, potting soils and other growing-media products and grass seed. During fiscal 2006, three new lawn and garden products were introduced—Mulch with Weed Stop (the first premium landscape mulch with weed preventer), the Smart Seeder (the first ready-to-use combination grass seed container and spreader), and the only termite killing stakes product for the do-it-yourself market. Brands with the largest sales were Spectracide, Schultz, Real-Kill, Garden Safe, and Vigoro. The company distributed its branded products primarily through Wal-Mart, Lowe's, and Home Depot and also produced private-label fertilizers for all three retailers. Sta-Green fertilizer was produced exclusively for Lowe's, Vigoro was produced exclusively for Home Depot, and Expert Gardener fertilizers were made exclusively for Wal-Mart. In Canada, lawn and garden products were sold under the Wilson, Nu-Gro, and So-Green brands.

In lawn and garden products, as in batteries, Spectrum Brands targeted value-conscious consumers who preferred products that sold at lower prices than premium-priced brands but that were still very comparable in quality and packaging. Management believed that its lawn and garden business had a strong second-place market share of 23 percent in the North American lawn and garden segments where it had product offerings, with its brands primarily positioned as value-priced alternatives.[12]

Primary competitors in the lawn and garden market were:[13]

- The Scotts Miracle-Gro Company, which marketed lawn and garden products under the Scotts, Ortho, Roundup, Osmocote, and Miracle-Gro brand names. Scotts Miracle-Gro products were number one in every major category in which the company competed—management believed the company had an overall market share of 52 percent in the segments where it had product offerings. Scotts also owned Smith & Hawken, a leading retailer of garden-inspired products that included pottery, watering equipment, gardening tools, outdoor furniture, and live plants. Scotts had sales of $2.1 billion in 2004, $2.4 billion in 2005, and $2.7 billion in 2006; over 80 percent of sales were in the United States, with the remainder in Europe. Net income was $101 million in 2004, $101 million in 2005, and $133 million in 2006. Scotts' recorded market share and revenue gains in all categories during 2006, with sales of Scotts fertilizer increasing by 14 percent, sales of Miracle-Gro garden soils increasing by 17 percent, and sales of Ortho insect control products increasing by 7 percent.

- Central Garden & Pet Company, which had a product line consisting of wild bird feed, grass seed, lawn and garden chemicals and fertilizers, and indoor and outdoor pottery products. Products were marketed under 20 brands, including AMDRO (fire ant bait), Sevin (insecticides), and Pennington (the leader in both grass seed and wild bird feed). Sales of lawn and garden products at Central Garden and Supply were $698 million in fiscal 2004, $741 million in fiscal 2005, and $802 million in fiscal 2006; operating income from sales of lawn and garden products before deduction of corporate level expenses totaled $43 million in 2004, $47 million in 2005, and $57 million in 2006. Management estimated that the lawn and garden categories in which it participated had total U.S. sales of approximately $27 billion in 2006.

- Bayer AG, which marketed lawn and garden products under the Bayer Advanced brand name in North America, Europe, and Latin America and was the fourth leading seller behind Scotts,

Central Garden, and Spectrum. Bayer's product line consisted of weed and insect control products, fire ant killer granules, lawn disease control products, potting mixes, and fertilizers for flowers, shrubs, and trees. Bayer, headquartered in Germany and best known for its aspirin and other health care products, had 2006 sales of about €28 billion worldwide, of which about €6 billion involved crop protection and seed treatment products, fungicides, insecticides, herbicides, fertilizers, and other crop, lawn, and garden products. Bayer's 2006 sales in the United States were said to be about $125 million.

Favorable demographic trends were expected to continue to spur sales of lawn and garden products, leading to mid-single-digit growth. Gardening was the number one leisure activity in the United States, with approximately 80 percent of homeowners working in their lawns on a regular basis. The industry, with $5 billion in 2006 retail sales, was expected to grow at 3–5 percent as the number of retirees grew and spent more time at home. Due to the rapid expansion of mass merchants with lawn and garden departments (Home Depot, Lowe's, and others) and full-line lawn and garden centers in the past 15 years, the buying power of retailers selling lawn and garden supplies had increased considerably.

Electric Shaving and Grooming

This product/business group consisted of Remington-branded men's rotary and foil shavers, women's shavers, beard and mustache trimmers, nose and ear trimmers, haircut kits, and related accessories. During fiscal 2006, several new products designed to improve the comfort and closeness of the shaving experience were introduced. These products were distributed broadly in North America and the United Kingdom and had been recently introduced in continental Europe and Latin America.

The worldwide retail sales of men's and women's electric shavers totaled $3.3 billion in 2006. The industry grew by 3 percent in 2006 and was expected to grow at a comparable rate during the next five years. Remington's two primary competitors in the electric shaving and grooming market were Norelco, a division of Koninklijke Philips Electronics NV (Philips), which sold and marketed rotary shavers, and Braun, a division of the Procter & Gamble Company, which

sold and marketed foil shavers (Remington sold both foil and rotary shavers). Philips Norelco had long held the number one position in every geographic region of the world and increased its market share in North America from 46 percent in 2005 to 53 percent in 2006. Similarly, Norelco's share of the Western European market for men's and women's electric shavers increased from 56 percent in 2005 to 59 percent in 2006. The keys to Philips Norelco's growth were design and performance innovations. Test-marketing results indicated that the company's new Williams F1 electric shaver, which resembled a handheld industrial power tool and could be washed and cleaned in seconds, would prove to be very popular in 2007. Procter & Gamble's Braun was the world's best-selling brand of foil shavers and the second largest seller of men's and women's electric shavers overall, with 28 percent of the worldwide market in 2006.

Remington-branded shaving products had an overall market share of approximately 30 percent in North America. In North America, Spectrum management estimated that the Remington brand was number two in men's rotary shavers; number one in men's foil shavers; number one in women's shavers; and number one in men's beard and mustache trimmers, nose and ear trimmers, haircut kits, and related accessories.[14] Worldwide, Remington shavers were estimated to be the third best-selling brand. Both Braun and Remington experienced sales declines in North America and Europe due to Norelco's gains in market share in 2006. Braun's sales in other parts of the world increased during 2006.

Household Insect Control

The company's household insect control business was comprised of several leading products that enabled consumers to maintain a pest-free household and repel insects. These included spider, roach, and ant killer; flying insect killer; insect foggers; wasp and hornet killer; flea and tick control products; and roach and ant baits. It also manufactured and marketed a line of insect repellents. The largest brands were Hot Shot, Cutter, and Repel. The company enjoyed broad distribution of its insect control products across North America and a second-ranking market share of about 23 percent.[15] The North American market for insect control products was growing at around 4–6 percent.

Chief competitors in the household insect control market were (1) S. C. Johnson & Son, Inc., which marketed the Raid and OFF! brands of insecticide and repellent products; (2) the Scotts Miracle-Gro Company, the marketer of Ortho household insect control products; and (3) Henkel KGaA, which marketed Combat brand products.

Spectrum Brands estimated the size of the U.S. household insect control industry at approximately $1 billion in 2003. The company's management expected the industry to slightly exceed its historical 4 percent annual growth rate over the next several years because of an increasing awareness of the West Nile virus and eastern equine encephalitis. Spectrum Brands' Hot Shot, Cutter, and Repel were distant seconds to the Raid and OFF! brands marketed by S. C. Johnson. S. C. Johnson was a privately held business that also produced such well-known household products as Windex glass cleaner, Ziploc bags, Glade air freshener, and Pledge furniture polish.

Electric Personal Care Products

Electric personal care products were marketed under the Remington brand name and included hair dryers, straightening irons, curling irons, and hair setters. Remington personal care products had an estimated 21 percent share in the United Kingdom, and Remington was the number two brand in Western Europe.[16]

The global market for such electric personal care products as hair dryers, curling irons, hair straighteners, and lighted mirrors grew by 1.2 percent in 2006, to approximately $2.6 billion. Conair had been the worldwide best-selling brand of such products for decades. In addition to electrical hair care products, Conair also manufactured and marketed Cuisinart and Waring kitchen appliances, Weight Watchers bathroom scales, and Pollenex shower heads. Conair management believed that its success in the industry was related to its low-cost production capabilities and its ability to quickly bring products popularized in salons to consumers.

Vidal Sassoon, Remington, and Revlon were other brands of personal care products frequently carried by U.S. retailers. In 2005, about 59 percent of electric personal care products were sold by discounters like Wal-Mart or Target, 7 percent were sold by department stores, 23 percent were sold by drugstores and supermarkets, 7 percent were sold by specialty stores, and 4 percent were sold by other types of retailers.

Portable Lighting

Spectrum Brands sold a broad line of flashlights, lanterns, and other portable battery-powered devices for both retail and industrial markets. These were marketed under both the Rayovac and VARTA brand names, under several other brand names, and under licensing arrangements with third parties. The three major competitors were Energizer Holdings, Mag Instrument, and Eveready. Sales of Rayovac and VARTA lighting products had been flat for the past four years (see Exhibit 3).

Global retail sales of flashlights and lanterns had remained flat at about $1.5 billion during 2003–2006; no significant market growth was expected in the future. However, flashlights equipped with light emitting diodes (LEDs) were growing in popularity because of their small size, bright light, and low power usage. The industry was fragmented geographically and included few global brands. Maglite, Rayovac, and Eveready were the best-selling brands of portable lights in the United States. Mag Instruments' flashlights were considered the highest quality in the industry since the 1979 introduction of the Maglite. The all-aluminum flashlights were first marketed to police departments because of their exceptionally bright light, durability, and reliability, but consumers quickly became the biggest purchasers of the superior Mag flashlights. Maglite flashlights had been recognized for design excellence by the Japan Institute of Design and by the Museum for Applied Art in Cologne, Germany, and were named by *Fortune* as one of the 100 products "America makes best."[17] Eveready and Rayovac produced much less expensive plastic flashlights and lanterns.

SPECTRUM BRANDS' ORGANIZATION AND OPERATING PRACTICES

Sales and Distribution

Spectrum Brands used a variety of distribution channels, including retailers, wholesalers and distributors, hearing aid professionals, industrial products distributors, and original equipment manufacturers (OEMs). Sales to Wal-Mart stores accounted for about 18 percent of consolidated net sales in fiscal 2005 and for about 19 percent in fiscal 2006; no other customer accounted for more than 10 percent of total sales in fiscal 2005 or 2006. Sales and distribution practices in each of the four reporting segments were as follows:[18]

- *North America:* Spectrum Brands' sales force in North America was organized by distribution channel, with separate sales groups for (1) retail sales and distribution channels, (2) hearing aid professionals, and (3) industrial distributors and original equipment manufacturers (OEMs). In some cases, independent brokers were used to service customers in selected North American distribution channels.

- *Latin America:* The sales force in Latin America was organized both by distribution channel and geographic territory. The Latin American sales force sold directly to large retailers, wholesalers, distributors, food and drug chains and retail outlets in both urban and rural areas. In Latin American countries having no company sales representatives, the company used independent distributors who marketed Spectrum products through all channels in that country.

- *Europe/ROW:* A sales force group, supplemented by an international network of distributors, promoted the sale of Spectrum products in Europe and the rest of the world (ROW). Sales operations throughout Europe/ROW were organized by geographic territory and three different sales channels: (1) food/retail, which includes mass merchandisers, discounters, drugstores, and food stores; (2) specialty trade, which includes wholesale clubs, consumer electronics stores, department stores, photography stores, and wholesalers/distributors; and (3) industrial, government, hearing aid professionals, and OEMs.

- *Global Pet:* The sales force for pet supplies was aligned by type of customer—mass merchandisers, grocery and drug chains, pet superstores, independent pet stores, and other retailers.

Manufacturing, Raw Materials, and Suppliers

Spectrum operated two major alkaline battery plants (one in Wisconsin and one in Germany), a combination zinc carbon/alkaline battery plant in China, three zinc carbon manufacturing plants and a zinc carbon battery component plant in Latin America, and two plants that made zinc air button cell plants, one of which also produced lithium cell batteries and foil shaver components for its Remington shavers.[19] Substantially all of the company's rechargeable batteries and chargers, portable lighting products, hair care and other personal care products and electric shaving and grooming products were manufactured by third-party suppliers primarily located in the Asia/Pacific region. The lawn and garden group had four combination production-distribution facilities; eight blend, pack, and warehouse facilities, and three distribution facilities that with shared with other Spectrum product groups. The pet supplies group had five production facilities (four in the United States and one in Germany), a specialty pet facility, and three distribution centers, one of which was shared with lawn and garden products. A number of manufacturing facilities had been closed during the past five years. Management believed that existing facilities were adequate for the company's present and foreseeable needs.

The principal raw materials used in manufacturing battery products—zinc powder, granular urea, electrolytic manganese dioxide powder, and steel—were sourced on either a global or a regional basis. The prices of these raw materials were susceptible to price fluctuations due to supply/demand trends, energy costs, transportation costs, government regulations and tariffs, changes in currency exchange rates, price controls, economic conditions, and other unforeseen circumstances. As a consequence, Spectrum regularly engaged in forward purchase and hedging derivative transactions to manage raw material costs in the upcoming 12 to 24 months.

Research and development activities were centralized at a single facility in Madison, Wisconsin. The company's R&D strategy was focused on new product development and performance enhancements of existing products.[20] Management saw efforts to introduce innovative products and improve the designs and functionality existing products as keys to organic sales growth and enhanced value to consumers. However, while R&D expenditures had increased from $13.1 million in fiscal 2002 to $30.6 million in fiscal 2006, R&D expenditures as a percentage of net sales had declined from 2.3 percent in fiscal 2002 to 1.2 percent in fiscal 2006 (see Exhibit 1).

Exhibit 4   **Selected Data for Spectrum Brands, by Business Segment and/or Geographic Area, Fiscal Years 2002–2006 ($ in millions)**

	Fiscal Years Ending September 30				
	2006	**2005**	**2004**	**2003**	**2002**
Net sales to external customers					
North America	$1,212.4	$1,155.8	$ 654.0	$ 375.6	$435.6
Europe/ROW	559.9	657.7	618.0	421.5	52.5
Latin America	236.2	208.1	145.3	125.0	84.7
Global Pet	543.2	285.6	—	—	—
Segment total	$2,551.7	$2,307.2	$1,417.2	$ 922.1	$572.7
Segment profit					
North America	$ 146.4	$ 164.8	$ 130.7	$ 64.8	$ 85.5
Europe/ROW	55.2	94.5	96.2	53.8	5.1
Latin America	23.4	19.0	11.7	17.7	5.3
Global Pet	83.6	28.7	—	—	—
Segment total	$ 308.6	$ 307.0	$ 238.7	$ 136.3	$ 95.9
Product line net sales					
Batteries	$ 861.0	$ 968.3	$ 939.1	$ 832.3	$506.9
Lighting products	88.0	93.8	90.1	89.8	65.8
Electric shaving and grooming	252.0	273.0	271.7	—	—
Personal care	150.0	141.0	116.3	—	—
Lawn and garden	507.0	402.0	—	—	—
Household insect control	151.0	143.0	—	—	—
Pet products	543.0	285.6	—	—	—
Segment total	$2,552.0	$2,307.0	$1,417.2	$ 922.1	$572.7
Segment total assets					
North America	$1,503.6	$2,246.4	$ 684.8	$ 625.5	$256.4
Europe/ROW	551.3	556.5	619.5	537.4	31.4
Latin America	239.6	368.5	322.2	203.9	191.0
Global Pet	1,170.8	790.9	—	—	—
Segment total	3,465.4	3,962.3	1,626.5	1,366.8	478.8
Corporate	83.9	59.8	7.7	209.7	54.4
Company total	$3,549.3	$4,022.1	$1,634.2	$1,576.5	$533.2
Depreciation and amortization					
North America	$ 50.8	$ 36.3	$ 20.5	$ 15.5	$ 15.4
Europe/ROW	10.6	15.7	16.2	13.5	0.7
Latin America	4.5	5.0	3.9	2.6	2.9
Global Pet	21.7	11.6	—	—	—
Segment total	$ 87.5	$ 68.6	$ 40.6	$ 31.6	$ 19.0
Capital expenditures					
North America	$ 23.5	$ 22.8	$ 14.6	$ 14.6	$ 13.2
Europe/ROW	18.6	23.2	9.1	9.5	1.0
Latin America	5.1	8.5	3.1	2.0	1.5
Global Pet	13.2	8.2	—	—	—
Segment total	$ 60.4	$ 62.8	$ 26.9	$ 26.1	$ 15.7

Note: Totals may not add due to rounding; segment accounting treatments and allocation methodology may not be entirely consistent for 2002 and 2003 data versus 2004–2006 data.

Sources: Company 10-K reports, 2006, 2005, and 2003.

RECENT EVENTS AT SPECTRUM BRANDS

In January 2006, Spectrum Brands sold its fertilizer technology and Canadian professional fertilizer products businesses of Nu-Gro (Nu-Gro Pro and Tech) to Agrium Inc. for net proceeds of approximately $83 million. Monies from the sale were used to reduce outstanding debt. Spectrum management was using earnings and cash flows from operations to reinvest in its businesses and to pay down debt—since going public in 1997, the company had never paid a dividend to shareholders and did not expect to pay a dividend in the near future.

Exhibit 5 shows the composition of the company's long-term debt and the repayment schedule as of year-end fiscal 2006.

Late in fiscal 2006, Spectrum management began to contemplate the divestiture of portions of its business portfolio in order to better sharpen the company's focus on strategic growth businesses, reduce outstanding indebtedness, and increase the company's lackluster stock price. Wall Street advisers were engaged to assist with any divestitures; the plan was to complete any asset sales by mid-2007. Proceeds from any asset sales were expected to be used for debt repayment.

Spectrum Brands failed to capture all of the expected $100 million in cross-business strategic fits

Exhibit 5   **Spectrum Brands' Debt Obligations, Fiscal Years 2005 and 2006**

| | September 30, | | | |
| | 2006 | | 2005 | |
	Amount	Rate[A]	Amount	Rate[A]
Senior Subordinated Notes, due February 1, 2015	$ 700,000	7.4%	$ 700,000	7.4%
Senior Subordinated Notes, due October 1, 2013	350,000	8.5%	350,000	8.5%
Term Loan, US Dollar, expiring February 6, 2012	604,827	8.6%	651,725	5.8%
Term Loan, Canadian Dollar, expiring February 6, 2012	72,488	7.4%	74,081	4.9%
Term Loan, Euro, expiring February 6, 2012	134,721	6.3%	137,142	4.7%
Term Loan, Euro Tranche B, expiring February 6, 2012	332,315	6.2%	338,288	4.4%
Term C Loan, expiring September 30, 2009	—	—	—	—
Euro Term C Loan, expiring September 30, 2009	—	—	—	—
Revolving Credit Facility, expiring February 6, 2011	26,200	10.3%	—	—
Revolving Credit Facility, expiring September 30, 2008	—	—	—	—
Euro Revolving Credit Facility, expiring February 6, 2011	—	—	—	—
Other notes and obligations	42,698	5.7%	38,701	—
Capitalized lease obligations	13,922	5.0%	17,396	—
Total long-term debt	2,277,171		$2,307,333	
Less current maturities payable in upcoming fiscal year	42,713		39,308	
Long-term debt outstanding	$2,234,458		$2,268,025	

Aggregate scheduled maturities of debt as of September 30, 2006:

2007	$ 42,713
2008	9,575
2009	8,939
2010	8,711
2011	242,172
Thereafter	$1,965,061
	$2,277,171

Source: Company 10-K report, 2006, pp.105–6.

by year-end 2006, but management believed the company would be more successful in 2007. Kent Hussey pinpointed the difficulties in April 2006:

> When you make acquisitions in categories that are outside your core competency, there's a certain amount of learning that takes place, developing your own business model and dealing with new competitors in new marketplaces. So far, we think we've been very successful, but we're still in the early stages of the acquisitions in lawn and garden and pet supplies.[21]

Top executives at Spectrum Brands announced a new organizational structure in January 2007 that was expected to aid efforts to capture the expected cost-savings from cross-business strategic fits. Starting in 2007, management decided to abandon the four operating segment structure in favor of a three business-segment structure—Global Batteries & Personal Care, Home & Garden, and Global Pet Supplies. According to CEO David Jones, the new structure would enable "Spectrum to operate more efficiently and profitably by eliminating duplicative staff functions and overhead in each of our business units, and downsizing our corporate infrastructure."[22] In addition, Jones said:

> By streamlining the business into three product-oriented operating units, we will significantly enhance our competitive focus and improve our cost structure. These changes will allow us to go to market faster with new, innovative products, as well as improve our ability to efficiently allocate resources on a worldwide basis. This business unit realignment will also facilitate the orderly execution of the asset sale process we announced in July.[23]

In February 2007, Spectrum announced net sales of $564.6 million and a net loss of $0.38 per share for the first quarter of fiscal 2007 that ended December 31, 2006. Global battery sales declined 6 percent as compared to the first quarter of fiscal 2006, as strong results from Latin America were offset by sales declines in North America and Europe/ROW. Sales of Remington branded products increased by 7 percent on a worldwide basis. Global Pet reported sales growth of 4 percent. Favorable foreign exchange rates had a $16.2 million positive impact on net sales during the quarter, mostly driven by the strong euro. The company generated operating income of $37.5 million versus $67.6 million in fiscal 2006's first quarter. The primary reasons for the decline in operating income were increased advertising and marketing expense of approximately $14 million and higher commodity costs, including an increase of $7 million in zinc costs.

Endnotes

[1] Information posted at www.spectrumbrands.com (accessed January 28, 2007).
[2] Various company press releases; 2004 10-K report, p. 15.
[3] 2004 annual report, p. 2.
[4] Various company press releases; company 10-K reports for 2003 and 2005.
[5] 2005 annual report.
[6] 2006 10-K report, p. 6.
[7] Company annual report, 2005, p. 8.
[8] 2006 10-K report.
[9] Investor presentation by John Heil, March 24, 2006; posted at www.spectrumbrands.com (accessed January 29, 2007).
[10] 2005 annual report, p. 9.
[11] Central Garden and Pet Company, 2006 10-K report, p. 66.
[12] Company annual report, 2005, p. 9.
[13] Company Web sites, SEC filings, and annual reports.
[14] 2005 annual report, p. 8.
[15] Ibid., p. 9.
[16] Ibid., p. 8.
[17] Mag Instruments Company History (www.maglite.com/history.asp).
[18] 2006 10-K report, pp. 3–4.
[19] 2006 10-K report, p. 5.
[20] Ibid.
[21] As quoted in an interview with The Wall Street Transcript, April 2006.
[22] Company press release, January 10, 2007.
[23] Ibid.

Sara Lee Corporation: Retrenching to a Narrower Range of Businesses

Arthur A. Thompson
The University of Alabama

John E. Gamble
University of South Alabama

In February 2005, Brenda Barnes, Sara Lee's newly appointed president and CEO, announced a bold and ambitious multiyear strategic plan to transform Sara Lee into a more tightly focused food, beverage, and household products company. The centerpiece of Barnes's transformation plan was the divestiture of weak-performing business units and product categories accounting for $8.2 billion in sales (40 percent of Sara Lee's annual revenues). While the divestitures would cut Sara Lee's revenues from $19.6 billion to about $11.4 billion, Barnes believed that Sara Lee would be better off concentrating its financial and managerial resources on a smaller number of business segments where market prospects were promising and Sara Lee's brands were well positioned.[1] Once the retrenchment initiatives were completed, the plan was to drive the company's growth via initiatives to boost the sales, market shares, and profitability of the key remaining brands: Sara Lee breads and bakery products, Ball Park meats, Douwe Egberts coffees, Hillshire Farm meats, Jimmy Dean sausage, Kiwi shoe care products, Sanex personal care products, Ambi Pur air fresheners, and Senseo single-serve coffee products.

By focusing on strong brands with good growth potential, company executives estimated that Sara Lee's sales revenues would grow to $14 billion in fiscal 2010 and that the company's operating profit margin would increase to at least 12 percent (versus an 8.1 percent operating profit margin in fiscal 2004).[2] The improved operating margin was

expected to result from a combination of an increase in the mix of more profitable and innovative value-added products plus expected annual cost savings of between $575 and $800 million. However, some of the annual cost savings would be partially offset by spending an incremental $250 million annually on media advertising and promotion and on research and development. In addition, Sara Lee executives believed that the retrenchment strategy would generate sufficient cash flows to pay the company's total debt down to between $1.5 and $2 billion by fiscal 2010 (versus total debt of $4.8 billion in fiscal 2004), pay substantial dividends to shareholders, and repurchase shares of common stock.

COMPANY BACKGROUND

Sara Lee Corporation originated in 1939 when Nathan Cummins acquired C. D. Kenny Company, a small wholesale distributor of sugar, coffee, and tea that had net sales of $24 million. The purchase of Sprague, Warner & Company in 1942 prompted a name change to Sprague Warner–Kenny Corporation and a shift in the headquarters location from Baltimore to Chicago; the company's shares began trading on the New York Stock Exchange in 1946. In 1954, the company's name was changed to Consolidated Foods Corporation to emphasize its diversified role in food processing, packaging, and distribution. In 1956, Consolidated Foods acquired Kitchens of Sara Lee and also entered the retail food business by acquiring 34 Piggly Wiggly supermarkets (later divested in 1966). The next 40 years were marked by a series of related and unrelated acquisitions:

1962	Jonker Fris, a Dutch producer of canned goods
1966	Oxford Chemical Corporation
	E. Kahn's Sons Company, a producer of meats
1968	Bryan Foods, a meat products producer
	Electrolux, a direct seller of vacuum cleaners
	Gant, an apparel producer
	Country Set, an apparel producer
	Canadelle, a producer of women's intimate apparel
1969	Aris Gloves (later renamed Aris Isotoner)
1971	Hillshire Farm, a meat producer
	Rudy's Farm, a meat producer
1972	Erdal, a Dutch company that produced and marketed personal care products (later renamed Intradal)
1978	Chef Pierre, a manufacturer/distributor of frozen prepared desserts Douwe Egberts, a Dutch coffee and grocery company
1980	Productos Cruz Verde, a Spanish household products company
1982	Standard Meat Company, a processor of meat products
1984	Jimmy Dean Meats, a manufacturer of various meat, food, and leather products
	Nicholas Kiwi Limited, an Australian-based manufacturer and marketer of personal, household, shoe, and car care products and home medicines
1987	Bil Mar Foods, a producer of turkey-based products
	Dim SA, the leading hosiery brand in France
1988	Adams-Millis Corporation, a manufacturer of hosiery products (provided an entry into the men's basic sock business)
1989	Champion Products, manufacturer of professional-quality knit athletic wear
	Van Nelle, a Dutch company active in coffee and tea
	Hygrade Food Products, a manufacturer of hot dogs, luncheon meats, bacon, and ham (which included the Ball Park and Hygrade hot dog brands)
1990	Henson-Kickernick Inc., a manufacturer of high-quality foundations and daywear
1991	Playtex Apparel Inc., an international manufacturer and marketer of intimate apparel products
	Rinbros, a manufacturer/marketer of men's and boys' underwear in Mexico
1992	BP Nutrition's Consumer Foods Group
	Giltex Hosiery
	Bessin Corporation
	The furniture care businesses of SC Johnson Wax
	A majority interest in Maglificio Bellia, SpA
	Select assets of Mark Cross Inc.
1993	SmithKline Beecham's European bath and body care brands
1997	Aoste, a French meats company
	Lovable Italiana SpA, an Italian intimate apparel manufacturer
	Brossard France SA, a French manufacturer of bakery products
1998	NutriMetics
	Café do Ponto
1999	Wechsler Coffee
	Chock full o'Nuts
	Continental Coffee
2000	Hills Bros., MJB, and Chase & Sanborn coffee brands (acquired from Nestlé USA)
	Courtaulds Textiles, UK-based producer of intimate apparel brands Gossard and Berlei.
	Café Pilão, the number one coffee company in Brazil, Sol y Oro, the leading company in women's underwear in Argentina
2001	The Earthgrains Company, the number two player in the U.S. bakery market
	A major European bakery company

John H. Bryan, former head of Bryan Meats (which the company acquired in 1968), became president and CEO in 1975 and served as CEO until 2000; Bryan was appointed chairman in 1976, a position he held until 2001. Bryan was the chief architect of the company's acquisition strategy during 1975–2000, guiding both its diversification efforts and its emergence as a global corporation. By 1980, sales had reached $5 billion. In 1985, Consolidated Foods changed its name to Sara Lee Corporation. Sales reached $10 billion in 1988, $15 billion in 1994, and $20 billion in 1998. But revenues peaked at the $20 billion level in 1998–1999, as management struggled to manage the company's broadly diversified and geographically scattered operations.

In 2000, C. Steven McMillan succeeded John Bryan as CEO and president of Sara Lee; Bryan remained chairman until he retired a year later, at which time McMillan assumed the additional title. McMillan launched strategic initiatives to narrow Sara Lee's focus on a smaller number of global branded consumer packaged goods segments— Food and Beverage, Intimates and Underwear, and Household Products. McMillan orchestrated several divestitures to begin the process of sharpening Sara Lee's business focus:

1966	Piggly Wiggly supermarket chains
2000	PYA/Monarch (sold to Royal Ahold's U.S. Foodservice for nearly $1.6 billion)
	Champion Europe
	Coach
	The International Fabrics division of Courtaulds
	The international bakery businesses in France, India, China, and the United Kingdom
2004	Filodoro, an Italian intimate apparel business

Brenda C. Barnes, a former president of PepsiCo North America from 1996 to 1998, joined Sara Lee as president and chief operating officer in July 2004. At the time of her appointment, Barnes, age 50, was a board of directors member at Avon Products, the New York Times Company, Sears Roebuck, and Staples. During her 22-year career at PepsiCo, Barnes held a number of senior executive positions in operations, general management, manufacturing, sales, and marketing. From November 1999 to March 2000, she served as interim president and chief operating officer

of Starwood Hotels & Resorts. Brenda Barnes's appointment as president and CEO of Sara Lee was announced on February 10, 2005, the same day as the announcement of the plan to transform Sara Lee into an even more tightly focused company. McMillan, in announcing Barnes's elevation to CEO, said:

> Our decision to fundamentally transform Sara Lee presents an ideal time for Brenda Barnes to transition to her new role as chief executive officer. We recruited Brenda last year to be my successor, and her contributions and leadership have exceeded all expectations. Brenda has played a key leadership role in designing our transformation plan and, for continuity and focus, it is appropriate that she lead its execution from the outset. Also, to ensure a smooth transition, I will remain chairman through the annual shareholders meeting in October. During these nine months, I will focus on the divestitures included in our plan.[3]

SARA LEE'S RETRENCHMENT INITIATIVES

The first phase of Brenda Barnes's transformation plan for Sara Lee was to exit seven businesses that had been targeted as nonstrategic:

- **Direct Selling**—A $450 million business that sold cosmetics, skin care products, fragrances, toiletries, household products, apparel, and other products to consumers through a network of independent salespeople in 18 countries around the world, most notably in Mexico, Australia, the Philippines, and Japan. In August 2005, Sara Lee announced a definitive agreement to sell its direct selling business to Tupperware Corporation for $557 million in cash.[4] The sale included products being sold under such brands as Avroy Shlain, House of Fuller, House of Sara Lee, NaturCare, Nutrimetics, Nuvó Cosméticos, and Swissgarde.

- **U.S. Retail Coffee**—A $213 million business that marketed well-known Chock full o'Nuts, Hills Bros., MJB, and Chase & Sanborn coffees plus several private-label coffees. Not included in the divestiture plan was the sale of Sara Lee's fast-growing global coffee brand, Senseo, which had sales of approximately $85 million. The U.S. retail coffee business was sold to Italy-based Segafredo Zanetti Group for $82.5 million in late 2005.[5]

- **European Apparel**—A Sara Lee business unit that marketed such well-known brands as Dim, Playtex, Wonderbra, Abanderado, Nur Die, and Unno in France, Germany, Italy, Spain, the United Kingdom, and much of Eastern Europe; it also included Sara Lee Courtaulds, a UK-based maker of private-label clothing for retailers. The branded European apparel business had nearly $1.2 billion in sales in fiscal year 2005, ending July 2, 2005; the Sara Lee Courtaulds business had fiscal 2005 sales of about $560 million. In November 2005, Sara Lee sold the branded apparel portion of the European apparel business unit to an affiliate of Sun Capital Partners, a U.S. private equity company, based in Boca Raton, Florida, for about $115 million plus possible contingent payments based on future performance.[6] In May 2006, a big fraction of Sara Lee Courtaulds was sold to PD Enterprise Ltd., a global garment producer with nine facilities that produced more than 120 million garments annually, including bras, underwear, nightwear, swim- and beachwear, formal wear, casual wear, jackets and coats, baby clothes, and socks; the deal with PD Enterprise did not include three Sara Lee Courtaulds facilities in Sri Lanka. (Sara Lee was continuing its efforts to find a buyer for the Sri Lanka operations.) Sara Lee received no material consideration as a result of the sale and remained liable for certain obligations of Sara Lee Courtaulds after the disposition, the most significant of which was the defined benefit pension plans that were underfunded by $483 million at the end of 2005.

- **European Nuts and Snacks**—A business with approximately €88 million in annual sales in fiscal 2005 that marketed products under the Duyvis brand in the Netherlands and Belgium as well as the Bénénuts brand in France. Sara Lee sold its European nuts and snacks business in the Netherlands, Belgium, and France to PepsiCo for approximately $150 million in November 2005.[7]

- **U.S. Meat Snacks**—A small unit with annual sales of $33 million in fiscal 2005 and $25 million in fiscal 2006. This business was sold in June 2006 for $9 million.[8]

- **European Meats**—A $1.1 billion packaged-meats business in Europe that had respectable market positions in France, the Benelux region, and Portugal and included such brands such as Aoste, Justin Bridou, Cochonou, Nobre, and Imperial. Headquartered in Hoofddorp, the Netherlands, Sara Lee's European meats operation generated $1.1 billion in sales in fiscal 2005, and employed approximately 4,500 people. In June 2006, Sara Lee completed the sale of this unit to Smithfield Foods for $575 million in cash; based in Smithfield, Virginia, Smithfield Foods was the world's largest grower of hogs and producer of pork products and had subsidiaries in France, Poland, Romania, and the United Kingdom that marketed meats under various brands, including Krakus and Stefano's.[9]

- **Sara Lee Branded Apparel**—Sara Lee's strategy for exiting branded apparel (2004 sales of $4.5 billion) was to spin the entire business off as an independent company named Hanesbrands Inc. The operations of Sara Lee Branded Apparel consisted of producing and marketing 10 brands of apparel: Hanes, L'eggs, Champion, Bali, Barely There, Playtex, Wonderbra, Just My Size, Duofold (outdoor apparel), and Outer Banks (golf, corporate, and stylish sportswear); sales of these brands were chiefly in North America, Latin America, and Asia. Two top executives of Sara Lee Branded Apparel were named to head the new company. The spin-off was completed in September 2006 when Sara Lee distributed 100 percent of the common stock of Hanesbrands to Sara Lee shareholders; shares were traded on the New York Stock Exchange under the symbol HBI.

Sara Lee management expected the retrenchment initiatives would generate combined net after-tax proceeds in excess of $3 billion. Exhibit 1 provides financial data relating to the divested businesses. The next section provides additional details about the Hanesbrands spin-off.

The Spin-Off of Hanesbrands

Sara Lee management's decision to exit the branded apparel business was driven principally by eroding sales and weak returns on its equity investment in branded apparel (Exhibit 2). But rather than sell the business, management determined that shareholders would be better served by spinning off the branded apparel business as a stand-alone company. Sara Lee shareholders received one share of Hanesbrands stock for every eight shares owned. Hanesbrands began independent operations in September 2006 and organized its business around four product/geographic segments, as shown in Exhibit 3.

However, the spin-off of Hanesbrands had some unique financial features. The terms of the spin-off called for Hanesbrands to make a one-time "dividend" payment of $2.4 billion to Sara Lee immediately following the commencement of independent operations. But in order to make the $2.4 billion

Exhibit 1   Financial Data for Sara Lee's Divested Businesses, Fiscal Years 2004–2006

(a) Sales and Income of Divested Businesses, Fiscal Years 2004–2006 ($ in millions)

	Fiscal Years		
	2006	2005	2004
Net sales of divested businesses			
Direct selling	$ 202	$ 473	$ 447
U.S. retail coffee	122	213	206
European branded apparel	641	1,184	1,276
European nuts and snacks	54	64	66
Sara Lee Courtaulds	437	558	536
U.S. meat snacks	25	30	33
European meats	1,114	1,176	1,111
Total net sales	$2,595	$3,698	$3,675
Pretax income (loss) of divested businesses			
Direct selling	$ 14	$ 55	$ 55
U.S. retail coffee	(46)	(39)	(2)
European branded apparel	(186)	(302)	67
European nuts and snacks	8	7	12
Sara Lee Courtaulds	(69)	—	14
U.S. meat snacks	(14)	(1)	(1)
European meats	(57)	90	101
Total pretax income (loss)	$ (350)	$ (190)	$ 246
After-tax income (loss) of divested businesses			
Direct selling	$ 54	$ (12)	$ 34
U.S. retail coffee	(39)	(33)	—
European branded apparel	(153)	(296)	68
European nuts and snacks	3	3	7
Sara Lee Courtaulds	(71)	(1)	26
U.S. meat snacks	(9)	(1)	—
European meats	(41)	(22)	86
Total after-tax income (loss)	$ (256)	$ (362)	$ 221

(b) Proceeds Realized from the Sales of the Divested Businesses ($ in millions)

	Sale Price	Pretax Gain on Sale	Tax Benefit (Charge)	After-Tax Gain
Direct selling	$ 557.0	$327	$(107)	$220
U.S. retail coffee	82.5	5	(2)	3
European branded apparel	≈115.0	45	41	86
European nuts and snacks	≈150.0	66	4	70

(Continued)

Exhibit 1   Continued

	Sale Price	Pretax Gain on Sale	Tax Benefit (Charge)	After-Tax Gain
Sara Lee Courtaulds	No material consideration**	22	—	22
U.S. meat snacks	9.0	1	(1)	—
European meats*	575.0	42	(2)	40
Totals	$1,488.5***	$508	$ (67)	$441

* This unit was divested in early fiscal 2007; data regarding the gains from the sale is from company press release on November 7, 2006 reporting results for first quarter of fiscal 2007.

** Sara Lee retained liability for unfunded pension benefits of $483 million at Sara Lee Courtaulds and made payments of approximately $93 million to remedy its liability during 2006.

*** The actual amount realized from the sales of these businesses was closer to $1.3 billion after taking into account the payments made to remedy unfunded pension liabilities at Sara Lee Courtaulds and other costs incurred in discontinuing the operations of all these businesses.

Sources: Company 2006 10-K report, p. 56, and various company press releases announcing the sale and disposition of the businesses.

Exhibit 2   Performance of Hanesbrands Prior to Spin-Off by Sara Lee, Fiscal Years 2002–2006 ($ in thousands)

	Fiscal Years Ending				
	June 29, 2002	June 28, 2003	July 3, 2004	July 2, 2005	July 1, 2006
Statements of Income Data					
Net sales	$4,920,840	$4,669,665	$4,632,741	$ 4,683,683	$4,472,832
Cost of sales	3,278,506	3,010,383	3,092,026	3,223,571	2,987,500
Gross profit	1,642,334	1,659,282	1,540,715	1,460,112	1,485,332
Selling, general and administrative expenses	1,146,549	1,126,065	1,087,964	1,053,654	1,051,833
Charges for (income from) exit activities	27,580	(14,397)	27,466	46,978	(101)
Income from operations	468,205	547,614	425,285	359,480	433,600
Interest expense	2,509	44,245	37,411	35,244	26,075
Interest income	(13,753)	(46,631)	(12,998)	(21,280)	(8,795)
Income before income taxes	479,449	550,000	400,872	345,516	416,320
Income tax expense (benefit)	139,488	121,560	(48,680)	127,007	93,827
Net income	$ 339,961	$ 428,440	$ 449,552	$ 218,509	$ 322,493
Balance Sheet Data					
Cash and cash equivalents	$ 106,250	$ 289,816	$ 674,154	$ 1,080,799	$ 298,252
Total assets	$4,064,730	$ 3,915,573	$4,402,758	$4,237,154	$4,891,075
Noncurrent liabilities:					
Noncurrent capital lease obligations	12,171	10,054	7,200	6,188	2,786
Noncurrent deferred tax liabilities	10,140	6,599	—	7,171	5,014
Other noncurrent liabilities	37,660	32,598	28,734	40,200	42,187
Total noncurrent liabilities	59,971	49,251	35,934	53,559	49,987
Total Sara Lee equity investment	$1,762,824	$2,237,448	$2,797,370	$2,602,362	$3,229,134

Source: Hanesbrands fiscal 2006 10-K report.

Exhibit 3   **Hanesbrands' Lineup of Products and Brands, 2006**

Product/Geographic Segments	Primary Products	Primary Brands
Innerwear	Intimate apparel, such as bras, panties and bodywear	Hanes, Playtex, Bali, Barely There, Just My Size, Wonderbra
	Men's underwear and kids' underwear	Hanes, Champion, Polo Ralph Lauren**
	Socks	Hanes, Champion
Outerwear	Activewear, such as performance T-shirts and shorts	Hanes, Champion, Just My Size
	Casual wear, such as T-shirts,	Hanes, Just My Size, Outerbanks,
Hosiery	Hosiery	L'eggs, Hanes, Just My Size
International	Activewear, men's underwear, kids' underwear, intimate apparel, socks, hosiery and casual wear	Hanes, Wonderbra,* Playtex,* Champion, Rinbros, Bali

* Terms of the February 2006 sale of Sara Lee's European branded apparel business prevented Hanesbrands from selling Wonderbra and Playtex branded products in the European Union, several other European countries, and South Africa.

** Hanesbrands had a license agreement to sell men's underwear and kids' underwear under the Polo Ralph Lauren label.

Source: Company 10-K report for fiscal 2006.

payment to Sara Lee and to fund its own operations, Hanesbrands borrowed $2.6 billion, thus saddling itself with a huge debt that prompted Standard & Poor's to assign the company a B+ credit rating (which put Hanesbrands in the bottom half of apparel companies from a credit rating standpoint). The company's debt-to-equity ratio was extraordinarily high, raising some questions about whether the interest expenses associated with the high debt would still leave Hanesbrands with sufficient funds and financial flexibility to invest in revitalizing its brands and growing its business. Exhibit 4 shows the impact of the $2.4 billion payment to Sara Lee on Hanesbrands' balance sheet.

A *BusinessWeek* reporter speculated that the reason for the unusually outsized dividend payment to Sara Lee was that the proceeds Sara Lee realized from the sales of the divested units (Exhibit 1) fell far short of the hoped-for $3 billion that was an integral part of the retrenchment strategy and restructuring announced by CEO Brenda Barnes in February 2005.[10] To make up for the shortfall, Sara Lee supposedly opted to get more cash out of the Hanesbrands spin-off.

In February 2007, Hanesbrands reported that sales for the first six months of fiscal 2007 were $2.25 billion, down 3 percent from the comparable period in fiscal 2006. Net income for the six-month period was $74.1 million, down 60.7 percent from $188.6 million in the first two quarters of fiscal 2006. The decrease in net income reflected increased interest expense, reduced operating profit, and a higher income tax rate. However, strong cash flows from operations allowed the company to pay down long-term debt by more than $106 million and make a voluntary $48 million contribution to reduce the underfunded liability for qualified pension plans to $173 million. In its first six months, Hanesbrands announced the closure of four plants and three distribution centers as part of a plan to create a lower-cost global supply chain; it also notified retirees and employees that the company would phase out premium subsidies for early retiree medical coverage, move to an access-only plan for early retirees by the end of 2007, and eliminate the medical plan for retirees aged 65 and older as a result of recently expanded Medicare coverage.

Hanesbrands' stock price, which began trading at around $22 per share in early September 2006, had trended upward to the $25–$27 range as of February 2007. Exhibit 5 compares Sara Lee's financial situation at the end of fiscal 2004 (just prior to the transformation plan) with that at the end of fiscal 2006 (when the divestitures and the Hanesbrands spin-off were completed).

Exhibit 4   Balance Sheet for Hanesbrands, Just Prior to and Immediately Following the 2006 Spin-Off ($ in thousands)

	September 30, 2006 (just after the spin-off)	July 1, 2006 (prior to the spin-off)*
Assets		
Cash and cash equivalents	$ 209,080	$ 298,252
Accounts receivable, less allowances of $44,380 at September 30, 2006 and $41,628 at July 1, 2006	516,778	523,430
Inventories	1,262,961	1,236,586
Deferred tax assets and other current assets	168,810	151,263
Due from related entities	—	273,428
Notes receivable from parent companies	—	1,111,167
Funding receivable with parent companies	—	161,686
Total current assets	$2,157,629	$3,755,812
Property, net	609,048	617,021
Trademarks and other identifiable intangibles, net	138,395	136,364
Goodwill	278,725	278,655
Deferred tax assets and other noncurrent assets	417,406	103,223
Total assets	$3,601,203	$4,891,075
Liabilities and Owners' Equity		
Accounts payable and bank overdrafts	$ 203,972	$ 483,033
Accrued liabilities and other	403,905	368,561
Notes payable to banks	4,751	3,471
Current portion of long-term debt	26,500	—
Due to Sara Lee Corporation	26,306	—
Due to related entities	—	43,115
Notes payable to parent companies	—	246,830
Notes payable to related entities	—	466,944
Total current liabilities	665,434	1,611,954
Long-term debt	2,573,500	—
Other noncurrent liabilities	346,034	49,987
Total liabilities	$3,584,968	$1,661,941
Stockholders' or parent companies' equity:		
Common stock (500,000,000 authorized shares; $.01 par value)		
Issued and outstanding—96,306,232 as of September 30, 2006	963	—
Additional paid-in capital	73,074	—
Retained earnings (for the period subsequent to September 5, 2006)	9,230	—
Accumulated other comprehensive loss	(67,032)	(8,384)
Sara Lee's equity investment	—	3,237,518
Total owners' equity	16,235	3,229,134**
Total liabilities and owners' equity	$3,601,203	$4,891,075

* Equity investment of Hanesbrands shareholders.

** Equity investment of Sara Lee Corporation in its branded apparel business unit.

Source: Hanesbrands 10-Q Report for the quarter ending September 30, 2006.

Exhibit 5   **Sara Lee's Financial Performance in the Fiscal Years Before and After the Divestitures and the Spin-off of Hanesbrands ($ in millions)**

	Fiscal Years ending	
	July 1, 2006	July 3, 2004
Results of continuing operations		
Net sales	$11,471	$19,566
Cost of sales	7,035	12,017
Gross profit	4,436	7,549
Gross profit margin	38.7%	38.6%
Selling, general, and administrative expenses	3,791	5,897
SG&A expenses as a % of net sales	33.0%	30.1%
Operating income	477	1,485
Operating profit margin	4.2%	8.1%
Interest expense	288	271
Interest income	(71)	(90)
Income from continuing operations before taxes	267	1,542
Income taxes	179	270
Net income	$ 233	$ 1,272
Net profit margin	2.0%	8.0%
Other financial and operating information		
Cash and cash equivalents	$ 1,933	$ 638
Inventories	916	2,779
Total assets	9,631	14,883
Net cash flow from operating activities	721	2,042
Number of employees	60,000	150,400

Note: Data for fiscal 2004 are from Sara Lee's 2004 10-K report. Data for fiscal 2006 reflect case author adjustments to the figures in Sara Lee's 2006 10-K report, made in order to account for the spin-off of Hanesbrands business and consequent exit from the branded apparel business; Sara Lee's financial results for fiscal included branded apparel because the spin-off was not effective until a few weeks after fiscal 2006 ended.

Sources: Sara Lee's 10-K reports for fiscal 2004 and fiscal 2006; Hanesbrands 10-K report for fiscal 2006.

SARA LEE'S POSTRETRENCHMENT STRATEGY: INITIATIVES TO REVITALIZE SALES AND BOOST PROFITABILITY

Upon the completion of Sara Lee Corporation's disposition of "nonstrategic" businesses in September 2006, Sara Lee management turned its full attention to growing the sales, market shares, and profitability of its remaining businesses. The two chief goals were to boost top line sales by 2–4 percent

annually to reach $14 billion by 2010 and to achieve a 12 percent operating profit margin by 2010. Sara Lee planned to achieve its objectives by developing three competitive capabilities in all of its remaining businesses. The company believed all of its business units must develop a strong focus on consumer and customer needs and on operating excellence. The company's management believed that competitive pricing, innovative new products, and brand-building capabilities were essential to its efforts to please consumers. Category management and leverage through size were thought to be necessary for the company to win new accounts with supermarket and discount store customers. Operating excellence was the third key element of its corporate strategy, which was critical to competitive pricing. Major operations initiatives under way at Sara Lee included lean manufacturing, centralized purchasing to achieve economies of scope, and the implementation of a common corporate-wide information systems platform.

The organizational structure developed by Brenda Barnes and other key Sara Lee managers that would best enable its businesses to contribute to corporate goals was a three-division structure built around customer types. The Sara Lee Food & Beverage division included the company's North American meats brands, North American bakery products, and Senseo single-serving coffee products sold in North American supermarkets and discount stores. Sara Lee Foodservice included the sales of meat products, bakery products, and coffee and tea products sold to food-service accounts in North America. The Sara Lee International division included sales of coffee and tea products, bakery goods, and household and body care brands sold outside North America.

Sara Lee Food & Beverage

Sara Lee's Food & Beverage division (SLFB) included Ball Park franks, Jimmy Dean sausage, Hillshire Farm deli meats, Sara Lee deli meats, Sara Lee bakery products, Sara Lee frozen desserts, and Senseo single serving coffeemakers and coffee pods. Sara Lee's sales of Hillshire Farm, Jimmy Dean, Ball Park, State Fair, and Sara Lee meat products made it the second-largest seller of such products in the $9.6 billion North American packaged-meat industry. The combined sales of Sara Lee's meat products gave it a 19.6 percent share of the North American retail meat industry in 2006. Kraft was the largest seller of packaged meats in North America, with a 21 percent market share during 2006. Smithfield Foods, ConAgra, and Hormel were the next largest meat producers in North America in 2006, with respective market shares of 9 percent, 8 percent, and 5 percent.

North American Retail Meat. Sales of meats in North America improved by 5 percent and operating income increased by 36 percent relative to 2005 through new product innovations like Jimmy Dean Breakfast Bowls, Hillshire Farms Chicken Caesar Entrée Salads, and Sara Lee Thin Sliced Virginia Brand Baked Ham. In 2007, SLFB had four times as many products under development than were under development in 2005. Promotions tied

to key holidays and sports events helped Sara Lee increase the sales of its meat products during 2006. The company's Power Events used a combination of in-store displays, newspaper ads, and discounts to boost sales volume of deli meats by 22 percent, on average, during event dates. The company also used Power Events for other division products, including Jimmy Dean frozen breakfast items, Sara Lee fresh bread, and Sara Lee frozen desserts. The combination of product innovations and effective promotions was expected to allow the Jimmy Dean brand to increase sales from approximately $400 million in 2005 to more than $500 million in 2007, even though sales of Jimmy Dean sausage and bacon were expected to remain level.

North American Retail Bakery. The company's chief managers also expected significant growth from its fresh bakery business. Sara Lee's fresh bakery sales had improved from $91 million in 2003 to $697 million in 2006. SLFB's ability to negotiate with supermarket buyers to increase shelf space allocated for its bakery products accounted for much of the growth in bakery sales during 2006. In several cases, SLFB was able to increase space on the bread aisle from 18 inches to four feet. Average weekly sales tripled in stores where Sara Lee gained shelf space. Sara Lee's sales growth in the fresh bakery sales had made it the number one national brand of bread, with a 7.2 percent market share. Number two Pepperidge Farm recorded sales of $509 million in 2006 and held 5.3 percent of the market. Innovations that contributed to Sara Lee's boost in sales of fresh bread included wide-pan loaf breads and Hearty & Delicious thick-sliced sandwich loaves.

In addition to producing the number one brand of fresh loaf bread, Sara Lee was also the number one brand of hot dog buns, hamburger buns, and bagels and other breakfast breads in North America in 2006. Sara Lee's 2006 breakfast bread sales total of $21.2 million was more than seven times greater than the second best-selling brand's 2006 sales of $3 million. Similarly, the sales of Sara Lee's thick-sliced Hearty & Delicious fresh bread of $22.2 million was five times greater than the second best-selling brand of thick-sliced bread in 2006. The company's whole-grain white bread 2006 sales total of $90 million was more than twice that of its closest rival. Sara Lee's combined sales of fresh bread, breakfast breads, buns and rolls, bagels, and specialty breads gave it a

14 percent share of the $101 billion North American retail bread industry in 2006. Wesson was the largest baked-goods maker in North America, with a 22 percent market share in 2006, while IBC was the third largest national bakery, with a 13 percent market share. Flowers Bread was the fourth largest bakery in North America, with a 10 percent market share in 2006. Exhibit 6 presents sales and operating profits for Sara Lee's three divisions and major business segments for 2005 and 2006.

Sara Lee did not anticipate significant growth for its frozen desserts like cheesecake, pound cake, pies, coffeecakes, or croissants, with projected 2007 sales approximating $75 million. Consumer eating patterns did not favor growth in home desserts, and sales of Sara Lee frozen desserts had experienced no meaningful growth in five years. The division's Senseo single-serving coffeemakers and coffee pods had also experienced little growth in 2006. Only 5 percent of coffeemakers sold during 2006 were single-serving coffeemakers, according to an NPD Group survey. The survey also found that one-half of those who purchased single-serving coffeemakers rated them as "fair" or "poor." Only about one-third of survey respondents said coffee pods were convenient to find.[11]

Sara Lee Foodservice

Sara Lee's food-service division marketed and sold products available to consumers in North American supermarkets to food service distributors such as U.S. Foodservice and Sodexho. Sara Lee Foodservice (SLF) also sold meat, bakery, and coffee products to national restaurant chains like Sonic, Dunkin' Donuts, Waffle House, Quiznos Sub, and Burger King. Most of the division's sales were standard Sara Lee, Jimmy Dean, Hillshire Farm, Ball Park, and State Farm branded products, although the division did customize meat and bakery products for its largest customers. Coffee brands sold to North American food-service accounts included Douwe Egberts and Superior Coffee. SLF also provided commercial-grade coffee machines and espresso makers to food-service customers.

The food-service industry offered Sara Lee a considerable growth opportunity since industry sales were projected to grow from $476 billion in 2006

Exhibit 6   **Sales and Operating Profits for Sara Lee Corporation's Three Business Units after the Restructuring and Retrenchment, 2005–2006**

	2006		2005	
	Sales	**Operating Profit**	**Sales**	**Operating Profit**
Sara Lee Food & Beverage				
North America Retail Meats	$ 2.5 billion	$ 197 million	$ 2.4 billion	$144 million
North America Retail Bakery	$ 1.8 billion	$ 9 million	$ 1.8 billion	($10) million
Subtotal	$ 4.3 billion	$ 206 million	$ 4.2 billion	$134 million
Significant items	$ 38 million	($254) million	$ 36 million	$ 41 million
Total	$ 4.4 billion	($48) million	$ 4.3 billion	$175 million
Sara Lee Foodservice	$ 2.2 billion	$ 141 million	$ 2.1 billion	$179 million
Significant items	—	($20) million	—	$ 3 million
Total	$ 2.2 billion	$ 121 million	$ 2.1 billion	$182 million
Sara Lee International				
International Beverage	$ 2.4 billion	$ 400 million	$ 2.2 billion	$417 million
H&BC	$ 1.8 billion	$ 244 million	$ 1.8 billion	$300 million
International Bakery	$742 million	$ 64 million	$739 million	$ 72 million
Subtotal	$ 4.9 billion	$ 708 million	$ 4.8 billion	$789 million
Significant items	—	($88) million	$174 million	($4) million
Total	$ 4.9 billion	$ 620 million	$ 5.0 billion	$785 million

Source: Presentations by Sara Lee Management Team Members at the 2006 "Meet the Management" Analyst Day, www.saralee.com (accessed March 23, 2007).

to $522 billion in 2010 as Americans continued to eat a higher percentage of meals away from home. In 2006, industrywide sales of meats to the food-service industry exceeded $7 billion, while sales of frozen bakery products amounted to $2 billion and fresh bakery item sales approximated $5 billion. The sales of coffee and tea to the food-service industry also approximated $5 billion in 2006. In 2006, the coffee and tea and meat segments grew by nearly 5 percent, while the bakery segment of the food-service industry grew by about 2 percent. SLF was positioned to capture a significant portion of industry growth, since in 2006 it held a 9 percent market share in deli meats sold to food-service customers, an 11 percent market share in relevant baked goods, and an 18 percent share of coffee and tea products sold to food-service customers. Beverages made up $836 million of the division's 2006 sales of $2.2 billion. Baked goods sales and meat product sales amounted to $748 million and $616 million, respectively, in 2006.

Sara Lee Foodservice had benefited from the innovations developed by Sara Lee Food & Beverage since the food-service trends mirrored those in the grocery industry. For example, presliced deli meats that were intended to satisfy consumers' desires for convenience also made sense for food-service accounts. Food-service customers had found that it was more cost effective and more sanitary to purchase presliced meat than to purchase bulk meat for restaurant employees to slice. SLF had also provided complete sandwich solutions to customers such as Quiznos that dramatically lowered restaurants' labor costs and customer wait times. Sara Lee Signature Sandwiches were made with premium Sara Lee presliced meats and Sara Lee sandwich loaves. Sara Lee's dessert and bakery brands like Sara Lee, Bistro Collection, and ChefPierre also benefited from innovations developed for consumers. Lower calorie pies developed by SLFB helped SLF capture 50 percent of the market for pies in the food-service industry. The company held 5–15 percent market shares in upscale desserts and cheesecakes, pastries, cake, bread, and muffins sold to the food-service industry.

Sara Lee International

Sara Lee's international brands included Douwe Egberts and Maison du Café coffee, Pickwick teas, Bimbo bread, Kiwi shoe care products, Sanex body care products, Ridsect, Vapona, and GoodKnight insecticides, and Ambi Pur air fresheners. Seventy-three percent of the division's 2006 sales of $4.9 billion were made in Western Europe. Twelve percent of the division's sales were made in Asia/Australia, while 7 percent of division sales originated in Eastern Europe, 6 percent originated in South America, and 2 percent of sales were made in Africa.

During 2006, management in the division had focused on improving marketing and sales, sharing administrative services, establishing a culture of continuous improvement, and accelerating the product development process. In addition, Sara Lee International (SLI) had undergone restructuring during 2006 that eliminated 1,300 jobs. SLI management had implemented continuous improvement programs in five European factories in 2005 and 2006 and expected to bring continuous improvement programs to all 30 factories outside the United States by May 2008.

International Beverage.   Sara Lee was the world's second largest seller of coffee in retail channels, with a global market share of about 9 percent. The total value of coffee sales in retail channels was approximately $24.5 billion in 2006. SLI recorded sales of $1.7 in retail channels in Europe during 2006, with Douwe Egberts generating 2006 sales of $379 million. Senseo's single-serving coffee pods were its second best-selling coffee product in Europe with 2006 sales of $336 million. SLI had sold more than 11 million Senseo coffeemakers and 11 billion coffee pods in Europe since 2001. The company expected sales of Senseo coffeemakers and coffee pods to continue to grow in Europe, as it launched new Senseo coffee products in 2007 that included cappuccino, espresso, and mug-size pods. The company also planned to launch ready-to-drink hot and cold coffee drinks in European retail channels in 2007. About $700 million of SLI's beverage sales of $2.4 billion were to restaurants and other out-of-home channels. SLI's European sales of tea in retail channels totaled $136 million in 2006.

International Bakery.   Bimbo was the number one brand of packaged bread in Spain with a 54 percent market share. Bimbo's strongest rival in packaged bread in 2006 was private-label brands, which accounted for 25 percent of the market. Private-label brands were expected to grow faster than branded bread sales between 2007 and 2010. SLI's limited ability to increase sales in other European countries was a result of consumer preference for fresh-baked bread. In 2005, packaged bread made up only 12 percent of the €4 billion total bread market in Europe. Packaged bread was expected to grow by 7–8 percent annually to account for 25 percent of industry sales by 2015.

Household & Body Care.   The SLI's Household & Body Care unit's Kiwi brand was the number one shoe care brand worldwide, with distribution in 200 countries and a global market share of 63 percent in 2006. Kiwi accounted for $280 million of the business unit's 2006 sales of $1.8 billion. Sanex was the number one brand of bath and shower products in Europe with a 14.7 percent share of the $1.7 billion market. Bath and shower care products grew by 0.9 percent during 2006. Sanex was also the fourth largest deodorant brand in Europe in 2006. Sanex's 2006 sales reached $800 million, with significant sales in Spain, France, the Netherlands, the United Kingdom, Germany, Italy, South Africa, the Philippines, and Indonesia.

The company's insecticide brands held a collective market share of 28.1 percent in Europe during 2006 and contributed $205 million to the unit's revenues during 2006. SLI's largest country markets for its insecticides were India, Malaysia, Spain, and France. SLI had focused growth initiatives for its insecticides and other household and body care products on emerging markets in Asia. Its fastest-growing markets in Asia were Malaysia, India, Indonesia, and the Philippines. SLI's European strategy was keyed to maintenance of market share and product innovations such as exfoliator bath products and dermo-active deodorants.

Ambi Pur was the third largest brand of air freshener in the $2.3 billion European air care market, with 2006 sales of $335 million. The European air care market declined by 1.4 percent between 2005 and 2006. Ambi Pur was strongest in Spain, the United Kingdom, the Netherlands, Italy, and France, where its market share was as high as 25 percent. There was reason to believe that Ambi Pur could dramatically increase its market share in Europe based on the dramatic results achieved by the Ambi Pur 3volution air freshener launched in the United Kingdom in March 2006. The 3volution air freshener cycled through three different fragrances every 45 minutes since research had indicated that individuals quit detecting a scent once they have been continuously exposed to it for 30 minutes to an hour. Ambi Pur's market share in the United Kingdom increased from 16 percent at the time of the 3volution launch to nearly 26 percent at year-end 2006.

THE FUTURE

Top executives at Sara Lee believed that fiscal 2007 would be an inflection point for the company's performance, resulting in positive top- and bottom-line growth trends across all businesses. New product introductions, new marketing programs, increased in-store promotions, and improved product placement were expected to drive sales increases. Brenda Barnes said that the company expected to grow sales by 2 to 4 percent annually and achieve steady expansion in profit margins in the coming years.[12]

As a result of raising more than $3.7 billion from the disposition of businesses, management said the company had ample cash to invest in the business and return to shareholders. The company's chief financial officer expected cash from operations to be between $400 and $500 million, although the cash costs to repatriate money from outside the United States cut into the company's ability to deploy all of these funds for corporate purposes.[13] Management expected to return significant value to shareholders in fiscal 2007 by delivering a healthy $370 million dividend payout, repurchasing $500 million of shares, and reducing net debt by $1 to $2 billion. Executives indicated that the previously stated long-term targets, while aggressive, were attainable.

Endnotes

[1]Company press release, February 10, 2005.
[2]Company press releases on February 10, 2005, and February 25, 2005.
[3]Company press release, February 10, 2005.
[4]Company press release, August 10, 2005.
[5]Company press release, October 26, 2005.
[6]Company press release, November 14, 2005.
[7]Company press release November 22, 2005.

[8]Company 10-K report for fiscal 2006.
[9]Company press release, June 27, 2006.
[10]Jane Sasseen, "How Sara Lee Left Hanes in Its Skivvies," *Business-Week*, September 18, 2006, p. 40.
[11]As discussed in "Kraft Foods' Beverage Machine Is Slow to Sell," *The Morning Call*, February 11, 2007.
[12]Letter to Shareholders, 2006 annual report, p.13.
[13]Company press release, September 16, 2006.

Robin Hood

Joseph Lampel
New York University

It was in the spring of the second year of his insurrection against the High Sheriff of Nottingham that Robin Hood took a walk in Sherwood Forest. As he walked he pondered the progress of the campaign, the disposition of his forces, the Sheriff's recent moves, and the options that confronted him.

The revolt against the Sheriff had begun as a personal crusade. It erupted out of Robin's conflict with the Sheriff and his administration. However, alone Robin Hood could do little. He therefore sought allies, men with grievances and a deep sense of justice. Later he welcomed all who came, asking few questions and demanding only a willingness to serve. Strength, he believed, lay in numbers.

He spent the first year forging the group into a disciplined band, united in enmity against the Sheriff and willing to live outside the law. The band's organization was simple. Robin ruled supreme, making all important decisions. He delegated specific tasks to his lieutenants. Will Scarlett was in charge of intelligence and scouting. His main job was to shadow the Sheriff and his men, always alert to their next move. He also collected information on the travel plans of rich merchants and tax collectors. Little John kept discipline among the men and saw to it that their archery was at the high peak that their profession demanded. Scarlock took care of the finances, converting loot to cash, paying shares of the take, and finding suitable hiding places for the surplus. Finally, Much the Miller's son had the difficult task of provisioning the ever-increasing band of Merrymen.

The increasing size of the band was a source of satisfaction for Robin, but also a source of concern.

The fame of his Merrymen was spreading, and new recruits were pouring in from every corner of England. As the band grew larger, their small bivouac became a major encampment. Between raids the men milled about, talking and playing games. Vigilance was in decline, and discipline was becoming harder to enforce. "Why," Robin reflected, "I don't know half the men I run into these days."

The growing band was also beginning to exceed the food capacity of the forest. Game was becoming scarce, and supplies had to be obtained from outlying villages. The cost of buying food was beginning to drain the band's financial reserves at the very moment when revenues were in decline. Travelers, especially those with the most to lose, were now giving the forest a wide berth. This was costly and inconvenient to them, but it was preferable to having all their goods confiscated.

Robin believed that the time had come for the Merrymen to change their policy of outright confiscation of goods to one of a fixed transit tax. His lieutenants strongly resisted this idea. They were proud of the Merrymen's famous motto: "Rob the rich and give to the poor." "The farmers and the townspeople," they argued, "are our most important allies. How can we tax them, and still hope for their help in our fight against the Sheriff?"

Robin wondered how long the Merrymen could keep to the ways and methods of their early days. The Sheriff was growing stronger and becoming better organized. He now had the money and the men and was beginning to harass the band, probing for its weaknesses. The tide of events was beginning to turn against the Merrymen. Robin felt that the campaign must be decisively concluded before the Sheriff had a chance to deliver a mortal blow. "But how," he wondered, "could this be done?"

Robin had often entertained the possibility of killing the Sheriff, but the chances for this seemed increasingly remote. Besides, killing the Sheriff might satisfy his personal thirst for revenge, but it would not improve the situation. Robin had hoped that the perpetual state of unrest, and the Sheriff's failure to collect taxes, would lead to his removal from office. Instead, the Sheriff used his political connections to obtain reinforcement. He had powerful friends at court and was well regarded by the regent, Prince John.

Prince John was vicious and volatile. He was consumed by his unpopularity among the people, who wanted the imprisoned King Richard back. He also lived in constant fear of the barons, who had first given him the regency but were now beginning to dispute his claim to the throne. Several of these barons had set out to collect the ransom that would release King Richard the Lionheart from his jail in Austria. Robin was invited to join the conspiracy in return for future amnesty. It was a dangerous proposition. Provincial banditry was one thing, court intrigue another. Prince John had spies everywhere, and he was known for his vindictiveness. If the conspirators' plan failed, the pursuit would be relentless, and retributions swift.

The sound of the supper horn startled Robin from his thoughts. There was the smell of roasting venison in the air. Nothing was resolved or settled. Robin headed for camp promising himself that he would give these problems his utmost attention after tomorrow's raid.

Dilemma at Devil's Den

Allen Cohen
Babson College

Kim Johnson
Babson College

My name is Susan, and I'm a business student at Mt. Eagle College. Let me tell you about one of my worst experiences. I had a part-time job in the campus snack bar, The Devil's Den. At the time, I was 21 years old and a junior with a concentration in finance. I originally started working at the Den in order to earn some extra spending money. I had been working there for one semester and became upset with some of the happenings. The Den was managed by contract with an external company, College Food Services (CFS). What bothered me was that many employees were allowing their friends to take free food, and the employees themselves were also taking food in large quantities when leaving their shifts. The policy was that employees could eat whatever they liked free of charge while they were working, but it had become common for employees to leave with food and not to be charged for their snacks while off duty as well.

I felt these problems were occurring for several reasons. For example, employee wages were low, there was easy access to the unlocked storage room door, and inventory was poorly controlled. Also, there was weak supervision by the student managers and no written rules or strict guidelines. It seemed that most of the employees were enjoying freebies, and it had been going on for so long that it was taken for granted. The problem got so far out of hand that customers who had seen others do it felt free to do it whether they knew the workers or not. The employees who witnessed this never challenged anyone because, in my opinion, they did not care and they feared the loss of friendship or being frowned upon by others. Apparently, speaking up was more costly to the employees than the loss of money to CFS for the unpaid food items. It seemed obvious to me that the employees felt too secure in their jobs and did not feel that their jobs were in jeopardy.

The employees involved were those who worked the night shifts and on the weekends. They were students at the college and were under the supervision of another student, who held the position of manager. There were approximately 30 student employees and 6 student managers on the staff. During the day there were no student managers; instead, a full-time manager was employed by CFS to supervise the Den. The employees and student managers were mostly freshmen and sophomores, probably because of the low wages, inconvenient hours (late weeknights and weekends), and the duties of the job itself. Employees were hard to come by; the high rate of employee turnover indicated that the job qualifications and the selection process were minimal.

The student managers were previous employees chosen by other student managers and the full-time CFS day manager on the basis of their ability to work and on their length of employment. They received no further formal training or written rules beyond what they had already learned by working there. The student managers were briefed on how to close the snack bar at night but still did not get the job done properly. They received authority and responsibility over events occurring during their shifts as manager, although they were never actually taught how and

when to enforce it! Their increase in pay was small, from a starting pay of just over minimum wage to an additional 15 percent for student managers. Regular employees received an additional nickel for each semester of employment.

Although I only worked seven hours per week, I was in the Den often as a customer and saw the problem frequently. I felt the problem was on a large enough scale that action should have been taken, not only to correct any financial loss that the Den might have experienced but also to help give the student employees a true sense of their responsibilities, the limits of their freedom, respect for rules, and pride in their jobs. The issues at hand bothered my conscience, although I was not directly involved. I felt that the employees and customers were taking advantage of the situation whereby they could "steal" food almost whenever they wanted. I believed that I had been brought up correctly and knew right from wrong, and I felt that the happenings in the Den were wrong. It wasn't fair that CFS paid for others' greediness or urges to show what they could get away with in front of their friends.

I was also bothered by the lack of responsibility of the managers to get the employees to do their work. I had seen the morning employees work very hard trying to do their jobs, in addition to the jobs the closing shift should have done. I assumed the night managers did not care or think about who worked the next day. It bothered me to think that the morning employees were suffering because of careless employees and student managers from the night before.

I had never heard of CFS mentioning any problems or taking any corrective action; therefore, I wasn't sure whether they knew what was going on, or if they were ignoring it. I was speaking to a close friend, Mack, a student manager at the Den, and I mentioned the fact that the frequently unlocked door to the storage room was an easy exit through which I had seen different quantities of unpaid goods taken out. I told him about some specific instances and said that I believed that it happened rather frequently. Nothing was ever said to other employees about this, and the only corrective action was that the door was locked more often, yet the key to the lock was still available upon request to all employees during their shifts.

Another lack of strong corrective action I remembered was when an employee was caught pocketing cash from the register. The student was neither suspended nor threatened with losing his job (nor was the event even mentioned). Instead, he was just told to stay away from the register. I felt that this weak punishment happened not because he was a good worker but because he worked so many hours and it would be difficult to find someone who would work all those hours and remain working for more than a few months. Although a customer reported the incident, I still felt that management should have taken more corrective action.

The attitudes of the student managers seemed to vary. I had noticed that one in particular, Bill, always got the job done. He made a list of each small duty that needed to be done, such as restocking, and he made sure the jobs were divided among the employees and finished before his shift was over. Bill also stared down employees who allowed thefts by their friends or who took freebies themselves; yet I had never heard of an employee being challenged verbally, nor had anyone ever been fired for these actions. My friend Mack was concerned about theft, or so I assumed, because he had taken some action about locking the doors, but he didn't really get after employees to work if they were slacking off.

I didn't think the rest of the student managers were good motivators. I noticed that they did little work themselves and did not show much control over the employees. The student managers allowed their friends to take food for free, thereby setting bad examples for the other workers, and allowed the employees to take what they wanted even when they were not working. I thought their attitudes were shared by most of the other employees: not caring about their jobs or working hard, as long as they got paid and their jobs were not threatened.

I had let the "thefts" continue without mention because I felt that no one else really cared and may even have frowned upon me for trying to take action. Management thus far had not reported significant losses to the employees so as to encourage them to watch for theft and prevent it. Management did not threaten employees with job loss, nor did they provide employees with supervision. I felt it was not my place to report the theft to management, because I was just an employee and I would be overstepping the student managers. Also, I was unsure whether management would do anything about it anyway—maybe they did not care. I felt that talking to the student managers or other employees would be useless, because they were either abusing the rules themselves or were clearly aware of what was going on and just ignored it. I felt that others may have frowned upon me and made it uncomfortable for me to continue working there. This would be very difficult for me, because I wanted to become a student manager the next semester and did not want to create any waves that might have prevented me from doing so. I recognized the student manager position as a chance to gain some managerial and leadership skills, while at the same time adding a great plus to my résumé when I graduated. Besides, as a student manager, I would be in a better position to do something about all the problems at the Den that bothered me so much.

What could I do in the meantime to clear my conscience of the freebies, favors to friends, and employee snacks? What could I do without ruining my chances of becoming a student manager myself someday? I hated just keeping quiet, but I didn't want to make a fool of myself. I was really stuck.

Case 24

Enterprise Rent-a-Car

Lou Marino
The University of Alabama

Kimberly Swan
The University of Alabama

R. Glenn Richey
The University of Alabama

When Jack Taylor founded the Executive Leasing Company in St. Louis in 1957, he based his business model on a very simple concept: "Take care of your customers and employees *first,* and growth and profits will follow."[1] This simple philosophy was imprinted across the company and became the foundation for the company's strategic operations. Over the next 50 years, the company, renamed Enterprise Rent-a-Car, grew to become the largest and most prosperous auto rental company in America, achieving approximately $9 billion from its multinational operations. In 2007, Enterprise was the leading auto rental company in North America, with more than 6,900 local market and on-airport rental locations and more than 878,000 rental and fleet service vehicles. The company operated through an extensive network of local neighborhood offices, each powered by small, highly entrepreneurial teams that had a high level of autonomy. Enterprise's network consisted of offices in the United States, Canada, the United Kingdom, Ireland, and Germany, where they handled tens of millions of transactions annually. Eventually the company had achieved a domestic saturation rate in the United States that put an Enterprise location within 15 miles of 90 percent of the U.S. population.

In its drive to the top of the auto rental industry, Enterprise remained true to Taylor's founding principles. The company received numerous awards for customer satisfaction and for being one of the best employers. As a tribute to the company's customer service, in November 2006 J. D. Power named Enterprise the auto rental company with the highest customer satisfaction, a distinction the company had achieved for seven of the previous eight years. In February 2007, Media Metrix ranked Enterprise as the leading auto rental company in its 2006 Hospitality Awards, a distinction it had achieved 17 out of a total 18 times. The company was similarly recognized for the way it treated its employees— being recognized in 2006 by *BusinessWeek* as the fifth best company in which to start a career, and in 2003, 2004, and 2006 as one of the 50 best employers in Canada. The Princeton Review additionally rated Enterprise as one of the best entry-level employers for college graduates and as the largest college recruiter in the United States.

Despite the company's outstanding performance and top rankings, Enterprise's chairman and chief executive officer, Andrew Taylor, remained "constructively paranoid" about his rivals. He was committed to continued growth to remain on top of the auto rental industry.[2] In early 2007, several developments in the auto rental industry indicated that Taylor's concerns for the activities of his rivals were justified. These developments included a possible merger between Dollar Thrifty Automotive Group (owner of Dollar and Thrifty auto rental companies) and Vanguard Car Rental (owner of National and

Alamo), as well as direct attacks on Enterprise's off-airport rental markets and insurance company clients by Hertz, the number two auto rental company in the industry.

U.S. AUTOMOBILE RENTAL INDUSTRY

The inception of the auto rental industry was widely attributed to two individuals. The first was Joe Saunders, who in 1916 in Omaha, Nebraska, began renting a secondhand Model-T for 10 cents a mile. His first customer was purported to have been a traveling salesman who had a date with a local girl and was in need of transportation. By 1925, Saunders had purchased over $1 million worth of automobiles from Chrysler and had operations in 21 states. Unfortunately, Saunders went bankrupt during the Great Depression in the early 1930s.[3] A second pioneer in the industry was Walter L. Jacobs, who in 1918 started a small company in Chicago that bought, repaired, and rented Model T automobiles. Within five years, the company was generating annual revenues of approximately $1 million; it was purchased by John Hertz, then president of Yellow Cab and Yellow Truck and Coach Manufacturing Company. Hertz renamed the company Hertz Drive-Ur-Self System and sold it to General Motors in 1926.

In 2006, total industry revenues were approximately $20 billion (Exhibit 1), with the top six companies having combined market shares of over 90 percent.

In 1932, the first airport auto rental facility was opened at Chicago's Midway Airport by Hertz, which also established the first fly/drive program later that year.[4] World War II led to significant restrictions on the automotive rental industry and caused the market to stagnate, but following the war the industry grew rapidly due to expansion in the airline industry. Auto rental companies responded to this opportunity by building locations in airports.[5] While most auto rental companies also maintained off-airport locations, it would not be until the late 1990s that off-airport locations became a significant force in the industry due to the efforts of Enterprise Rent-a-Car. In 1994, the off-airport segment represented only $2.5 billion of the $10.7 billion industry; however, by February 2006, off-airport revenue accounted for a greater proportion of the industry's total $20.08 billion revenue than did airport locations. The market shares of the leading companies in the on-airport and off-airport segments in 2005 are shown in Exhibits 2 and 3.

In addition to the growth in the off-airport segment, the industry was also seeing significant international growth as large U.S. auto rental companies sought to build global brands. In 2005, the total global market was estimated to be close to $30 billion. The United States represented 50.20 percent of the total global market, followed by Europe (31.30 percent) and Asia-Pacific (8.30 percent). Analysts predicted that from 2005 to 2010, growth in the U.S. market would slow from 7.2 percent in 2005 to 5.6 percent in 2010, with a total compound annual growth rate over this time of 6.3 percent. However, the market outside the United States was expected to

Exhibit 1   **U.S. Automobile Rental Revenues by Company, 2000–2006 ($ in billions)**

	2006	2005	2004	2003	2002	2001	2000
Avis	$ 2.75	$ 2.45	$ 2.28	$ 2.14	$ 2.25	$ 2.38	$ 2.40
Budget	1.43	1.22	1.13	0.94	1.00	1.70	1.80
Dollar*	1.53	1.39	1.01	0.92	0.91	0.89	0.94
Enterprise	7.00	6.40	5.83	5.49	5.25	5.10	4.50
Hertz	3.90	3.87	3.50	3.11	3.05	2.90	3.98
Vanguard	2.14	1.93	1.84	1.80	2.00	NA	NA
Other	1.33	1.65	2.05	2.05	1.97	5.23	5.78
Total	$20.08	$18.91	$17.64	$16.45	$16.43	$18.20	$19.40

* Data for 2005 and 2006 represent the combined operations of Dollar and Thrifty, which was acquired by Dollar.

Source: "United States Car Rental Industry Revenues for 2005." *Auto Rental News,* February 28, 2005, www.fleet central. com/arn/t_inside.cfm?action=statistics.

Exhibit 2   **United States On-Airport Segment Market Share as of October 31, 2006**

	2006*	2005	2004	2003	2002
Hertz	28.4%	29.2%	29.6%	29.0%	29.2%
ABG Brands					
Avis	19.9	20.2%	20.2%	21.2%	22.3%
Budget	10.4	10.5	10.2	10.4	10.8
Vanguard (National/Alamo brands)	19.7	19.4	19.8	20.8	21.8
DTG Brands					
Dollar	7.2	7.1	7.7	7.4	7.2
Thrifty	4.4	4.3	4.5	4.4	3.2
Enterprise	7.6	7.0	6.0	5.0	3.9
Other	2.4	2.3	2.0	1.8	1.6

* Estimated based on the first ten months of 2006

Source: Hertz annual report 2006, https://images.hertz.com/pdfs/HTZ_2006_annual_report.pdf (accessed April 28, 2007).

grow faster over this time frame and through 2020, with especially rapid growth forecast in Asia.

In the early 1970s, the fuel crisis and growing government regulations forced a number of auto rental companies to change the mix of cars they offered on their lots to include more fuel-efficient models. These trends, coupled with a decrease in the fleet discounts offered by automakers and rising

Exhibit 3   **Estimated On-Airport and Off-Airport Market Shares, 2005**

(a) On-Airport Market Segment

Alamo	5%
Avis	21
Budget	11
Dollar	7
Enterprise	7
Hertz	28
National	15
Thrifty	4
Other	2

(b) Off-Airport Market Segment

Avis/Budget	7%
Enterprise	65
Hertz	9
Others	19

Source: Avis Budget Group Presentation to Investors, November 2006, http://library.corporate-ir.net/library/11/119/119532/items/221139/Investorupdate1106.pdf.

auto prices, forced auto rental companies to shift their business models and to begin selling their used cars directly to the public. By 1980, Hertz was one of the largest used auto dealers in the United States. The success of Hertz in this business led companies such as Avis to move away from leasing cars from automobile manufacturers to purchasing the vehicles outright so that they could be sold to the public as used cars. In 2007, the sale of used vehicles represented a significant portion of most automotive rental company revenues.

Selling used cars directly to the public was viewed as a more profitable way of managing fleet sizes, adding flexibility to operations. Some of the auto rental companies had extensive networks of sales outlets; Enterprise had 170 locations throughout the United States, allowing for significant market penetration in the sale of its auto rentals to the public. Over the last two decades, to further diversify their revenue streams, auto rental companies had also sought to expand their brand portfolios. An example of this was Budget Rental Group, which owned Budget, Ryder, and a variety of other transportation-related companies. Broader brand portfolios allowed the rental companies to share fleets, integrate systems, and smooth out their business cycles. The trend toward broader portfolios had led to further industry consolidation, as evidenced by the February 2007 announcement that the Dollar Thrifty Automotive group—which was formed by a 2002 consolidation of the Dollar and Thrifty Car rental brands, both owned by Thrifty Inc.—was in merger talks with Vanguard.

From the earliest days of the auto rental industry, auto rental company purchases had been an important revenue stream for automakers. In some years, fleet purchases from auto rental companies accounted for as much as 10 percent of the total auto sales of the Big Three U.S. automakers. The relationship between auto rental companies and automakers had always been close, but in 1987 Ford Motor Company took the relationship to the next level when it partnered with the management of Hertz to form a company that purchased Hertz from United Airlines. Similarly, in 1988, Ford purchased a 45 percent share of National Rent-a-Car and in 1989 purchased a 25 percent share of Avis. Automobile companies justified these investments because auto rental companies were their largest customers. They also viewed auto rental companies as an important marketing tool, because they allowed automakers to expose potential customers to new models and to get feedback on auto design and quality. In return for these benefits, auto companies gave rental firms favorable fleet pricing similar to volume discounts despite very thin profit margins for the automakers. Additionally, the automakers would sometimes guarantee to repurchase the cars from the rental firms. While the auto companies benefited from this ownership, it was not as clear that the rental companies were benefiting since the auto companies would often put their strategic needs—such as smoothing out the auto sales cycle—ahead of the operational needs of the auto rental firms.

In the early 2000s, many of the auto rental companies were divested by the automakers, allowing the auto rental companies to focus on profitability and enhancing internal operations and profitability. This split had allowed auto rental companies to expand their rental fleets to include autos from a variety of domestic and foreign manufacturers. However, the fleet discounts offered by automakers were still an important element of the business models of many major rental companies. In late 2006 and early 2007, the domestic automakers announced that they would be scaling back the low-margin fleet sales to rental auto companies in an effort to improve their profit margins.

Auto rental companies traditionally had not focused on technological innovations. An innovative change started in 1966 when National Car Rental brought computers into its daily reservation operations by introducing its Telemax computer system into its regional offices. However, it was not until the late 1980s that auto rental companies began to increasingly leverage technology. In the mid-1990s, technology and the Internet were becoming increasingly important in the auto rental industry, as they were in most other industries as well. By 2007, successful auto rental companies were leveraging technology throughout their operations to help reduce costs and promote operational efficiency through programs such as automated auto return programs and sophisticated inventory management, as well as to enhance the rental experience, through rental offerings such as GPS and an auto wireless Internet access, and to promote customer loyalty. Recognizing the need to further improve customer service, many auto rental firms were also investing in customer relationship management (CRM) software, which allowed companies to gather and analyze data about customers' rental habits and experiences. However, some industry experts believed that these systems were not yet sufficiently developed and would benefit from additional attention by many of the auto rental firms.

Technology was also important in the reservation process, with the most successful automobile rental companies having Web sites that were ranked highly in terms of customer support, competitive prices, and easy-to-use rental search/reservation processes. In a 2006 Keynote survey of 2,000 online customers, Travelocity was ranked as the best overall auto rental Web site, but the Budget, Enterprise, and Avis sites were rated highest in terms of satisfaction with the reservation process. In response to the popularity of travel consolidation Web sites such as Travelocity and customer demands for increased Web access to auto rental information, auto rental companies were forming preferred partnerships with some of the travel aggregator Web sites. The alliance between Hertz and Expedia.com, for example, allowed Hertz preferential placement on Expedia's Web site in return for making the company's lowest rental rates available only to Expedia clients.

As technology became an increasingly important factor in customers' automobile rental decisions—with sites such as Orbitz, for example, allowing customers to easily see competing quotes—auto rental companies had increasingly invested in customer service to attract and retain their best customers. One tool was the frequent-renter (customer continuity) program. In 1987, National Car Rental introduced its Emerald Club as the first comprehensive frequent-renter program. By 2007, every major auto rental company had a frequent-renter program that offered perks such as free upgrades, free rental days, express pickup and return, and choice of car. These frequent renter programs were especially important to business customers who placed a premium on their time and who rented more often than leisure renters. The goal of these programs was to increase customer usage through penetration of the existing market.

ENTERPRISE RENT-A-CAR

Back in 1957, Jack Taylor did not aspire to build the largest automobile rental company in the United States. His original goals for the company were much more humble: "I never thought," he said, "it would be more than a small to medium-sized business. I knew I wanted to live reasonably comfortably and to get a couple of new autos every two or three years and I thought that if I was really successful, I would have maybe a condominium in Florida and a reasonably nice house in St. Louis."[6] This vision was reflected in Taylor's early strategic decisions for his company. For example, the original location for his auto leasing company was the basement of a Cadillac dealership. While this decision was made for practical reasons at the time, it ended up having a significant impact on the company's long-term strategy.

In expanding the leasing business, Enterprise stayed with its core strategy and located offices in downtown locations, a pattern that facilitated the company's focus on off-airport rentals and simplified the overall business model. In 1962, Enterprise entered the daily rental market in response to inquiries from its leasing customers who asked about renting autos when their leased autos were in the shop. Seeing an opportunity, Enterprise expanded into the daily rental market and also began selling used autos. This strategic position served as the company's fundamental business model and is still reflected in its current operations.

The company's management philosophy of encouraging an entrepreneurial spirit among its employees had also been in place since its early operations. When Enterprise decided to expand its rental business in downtown St. Louis, the company's president, Don Ross, was visiting office buildings to identify clients who might need to rent autos. By chance, a secretary in one of the buildings mentioned that there was going to be a meeting of insurance adjustors the next day. Ross stood outside the meeting and handed out coffee, Danish, and business cards. This proactive approach secured Enterprise's first insurer as a customer, and insurance companies have been the company's single largest customer segment throughout the company's history.

Enterprise did not simply encourage an entrepreneurial attitude among its employees; it also supported corporate innovation as it constantly sought to identify the best practices originating anywhere in the company and then to transfer this knowledge throughout the organization. For example, Enterprise's famous slogan "We'll pick you up" originated with an Orlando branch manager who was looking for a way to differentiate his operations. The idea, consistent with Enterprise's focus on customer service, was so successful that the company made it a cornerstone of its operations.

Although Enterprise continued to concentrate on customer service and maintained a focus on its off-airport rental operations, the company's business model had not stagnated, as shown in Exhibit 4. In 1993, Enterprise expanded internationally by opening its first office in Canada; by 1995, it had made its move into the on-airport segment. By 2007, Enterprise had 6,000 offices in the United States and more than 900 in Canada, the United Kingdom, Germany, and Ireland with over 225 airport locations. These airport locations accounted for more than 7 percent of the total on-airport market.

Additionally, Enterprise Fleet Management, one of the nation's leading fleet management companies, operated one of the nation's largest service departments. Located in St. Louis, the service department consisted of more than 40 Automotive Service Excellence (ASE) certified technicians. Enterprise Fleet Management had the largest share of the mid-sized market—business fleets of 15–125 vehicles—in 2007. Annually, the firm carefully evaluated new vehicle models coming out of Detroit, Tokyo, and Stuttgart and then provided guidance and additional products for businesses to manage their fleets for the highest productivity level at the lowest cost. Enterprise also offered financial consulting to help customers improve cash flow, lower costs, and expand credit lines. As such, Enterprise handled licensing and taxes following acquisition and delivery. It

Exhibit 4 **Enterprise Rent-a-Car Milestones**

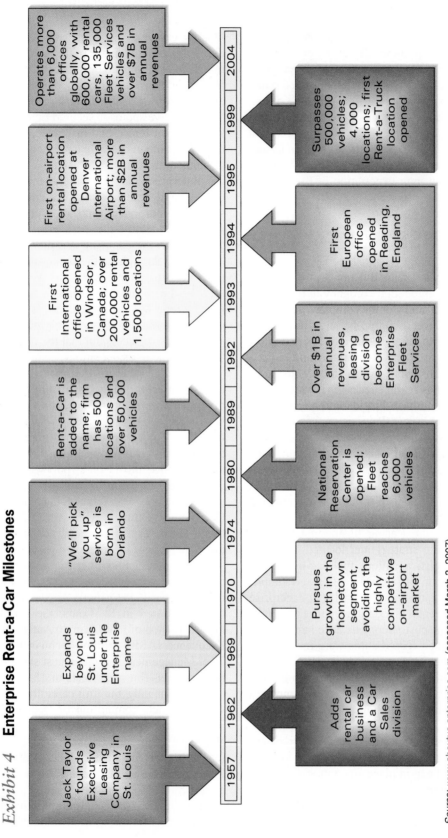

Year	Milestone
1957	Jack Taylor founds Executive Leasing Company in St. Louis
1962	Adds rental car business and a Car Sales division
1969	Expands beyond St. Louis under the Enterprise name
1970	Pursues growth in the hometown segment, avoiding the highly competitive on-airport market
1974	"We'll pick you up" service is born in Orlando
1980	National Reservation Center is opened; Fleet reaches 6,000 vehicles
1989	Rent-a-Car is added to the name; firm has 500 locations and over 50,000 vehicles
1992	Over $1B in annual revenues, leasing division becomes Enterprise Fleet Services
1993	First International office opened in Windsor, Canada; over 200,000 rental vehicles and 1,500 locations
1994	First European office opened in Reading, England
1995	First on-airport rental location opened at Denver International Airport; more than $2B in annual revenues
1999	Surpasses 500,000 vehicles; 4,000 locations; first Rent-a-Truck location opened
2004	Operates more than 6,000 offices globally, with 600,000 rental cars, 135,000 Fleet Services vehicles and over $7B in annual revenues

Source: www.aboutus.enterprise.com (accessed March 3, 2007).

could tailor risk management and maintenance-management products, assist in vehicle disposal, and provide fuel-card programs and 24-hour roadside assistance to its fleet clients.[7]

Enterprise's Businesses Segments

Enterprise was organized into six primary market segments: the off-airport market, the on-airport market, after-market used auto sales, California Vanpool Services, Rent-a-Truck, and International Operations. Enterprise generated most of its revenues from its non-airport operations and received most of its business from downtown and suburban locations. Over the last two decades, the company consistently achieved revenue growth across all business segments, with double-digit growth in the on-airport market over the last six years. Industry analysts largely attributed this success to Enterprise's service-focused business practices, including picking customers up and focusing marketing efforts on repair shops, insurance companies, and policyholders whose cars have been damaged or stolen.[8] While the company catered to a large variety of clients, its most vital customers were auto insurance companies whose policies included coverage to defray the cost of an auto rental if an accident put a policyholder's vehicle in a repair shop.[9]

Off-Airport Market   Renting at neighborhood locations was a trend pioneered by Enterprise, which started out renting replacement vehicles to families when their automobiles were in the repair shop. In early 2007, more than half of all vehicle rentals in almost any given state or community were made by local residents who needed temporary replacement cars or vehicles for special occasions. In 2005, Enterprise controlled nearly 55 percent of the off-airport auto rental leisure market, operating more than four times as many local branches in the United States as its largest competitor and more than all of its national competitors combined. Ninety-five percent of Enterprise's business took place in the home city, primarily serving leisure travelers and value-minded business travelers who wanted exceptional customer service coupled with a great price. The strategic choice to focus on this segment was based on Enterprise's desire to avoid the concession fees and extended staffing requirements of airport locations and to develop

lean operations that would enable the company to offer competitive prices in all of its markets, although it was not always the low-price leader. In 2004, for the first time more revenue was generated in the auto rental industry by neighborhood-based locations than by airport locations, with home-city rentals accounting for $9.5 billion (roughly 54 percent of the total auto rental market).[10] The growth in the home-city business was partly driven by Enterprise's strategy to develop this market.

On-Airport Market   Enterprise's original strategy was to operate solely in the off-airport market. However, in 1995 the company entered the airport market at the urging of customers who demanded easier access to the Enterprise brand and customer service away from home. The first location opened at Denver International Airport, and the firm now had 230 on-site airport locations throughout the United States, plus locations in Canada, the United Kingdom, Germany, and Ireland. Despite intense competition and flat industry growth in the overall airport auto rental segment, Enterprise had evolved into the fastest-growing auto rental company in this segment, with a 20 percent annual growth rate since 1999. Enterprise's market share in the on-airport market had almost quadrupled over the past five years, making the company the fifth largest of eight major players in this segment, which was led by rival Hertz. In building this market, Enterprise had continued to focus on service and to offer prices at airports that tended to be 20 percent below the industry average.

In focusing on the on-airport market, one challenge Enterprise faced was that the on-airport customers, many of whom were businesspeople, often viewed customer service differently from off-airport customers. One complaint among on-airport business travelers was that while Enterprise's friendly customer service was nice, they would rather focus on the transaction and get out the door faster than spend time with pleasantries.

After-Market   In a move away from auto rental industry tradition, Enterprise decided to sell its cars itself rather than use reverse logistics to move them back to the auto manufacturer.[11] Enterprise Used Car Sales began in 1962, when Jack Taylor established a haggle-free buying policy—customers got a fair price that was clearly posted on every vehicle without having to negotiate. All vehicles sold were below the Kelley Blue Book suggested retail value. Enterprise developed a second policy—worry-free ownership. Each Enterprise vehicle passed a 109-point inspection conducted by an ASE-certified technician and came with a seven-day repurchase agreement. During this time, customers could return the vehicle for any reason, no questions asked. Enterprise also offered buyers a 12-month/12,000-mile limited power train warranty and one year of roadside assistance.

Enterprise's climb had made it the largest buyer of cars in the world (in fiscal year 2006, the company purchased more than 800,000 vehicles), giving the company strong buying power over suppliers. Enterprise Used Car Sales was one of the largest sellers of certified used vehicles in the United States. During fiscal 2005, Enterprise sold around 775,000 cars through its referral auto sales division, which operated more than 175 auto sales locations across the United States. Enterprise offered customers one of the industry's most diverse, continually revolving inventories and had been awarded a 97 percent customer satisfaction rating two years in a row. The division created value-added partnerships with national and local financial institutions, such as credit unions, that provided members with easy access to high-quality used vehicles.

California Vanpool Services   Founded in 1994, Enterprise Rideshare was headquartered in Orange County, California, and specialized in providing vanpool and carpool commuter services to individuals and companies throughout Northern and Southern California. In 2007, Enterprise operated over 700 vehicles and transported more than 7,000 commuters daily. Enterprise's pricing varied according to the size of the van, the round-trip distance, and the type of equipment in the van. The average cost per rider was $75–$125/month. Enterprise's California Vanpool Services competed with Midway Ride Share, which operated in several metropolitan areas including Houston, San Francisco, Los Angeles, Chicago,

Seattle, Las Vegas, New York City, Orlando, Atlanta, and Washington, D.C.

Rent-a-Truck   Enterprise Rent-a-Truck was Enterprise's newest division. Opened in 1999, the division served businesses with replacement or supplemental transportation needs. As of 2006, Enterprise Rent-a-Truck had 105 locations throughout 23 states. Trucks were available for daily, weekly, or monthly rentals and included three-quarter- to one-ton pickups, cargo vans, box trucks, and stake bed trucks, all specifically equipped for commercial use. Similar to the consumer auto rental business, customer service was top priority and the company offered consolidated and customized billing, special delivery, and 24-hour roadside assistance.

International Operations   The first Enterprise office outside the United States opened in Windsor, Canada, in 1993, as seen in Exhibit 5. In 2007, Enterprise had more than 900 international branches with more than 7,000 employees. In 2006, Enterprise generated a record $819 million in revenue outside the United States, representing a 13 percent increase in its international business. Each international office operated with the same commitment to the community as the U.S. locations. The offices hired locally, bought cars locally, and provided comprehensive service to the neighborhood markets they served. Enterprise's international focus was also primarily on the off-airport market, providing temporary replacement cars, corporate travel vehicles, and fleet management to firms with temporary transportation needs and serving local dealerships and service shops for loaner purposes.[12]

Mission and Values

When Jack Taylor founded Enterprise, he clearly articulated his business philosophy:

Exhibit 5   Enterprise Rent-a-Car International Operations

Canada (opened in 1993)	More than 380 branch offices including several airport locations
United Kingdom (opened in 1997)	More than 300 branch offices including locations at Heathrow and Gatwick airports
Germany (opened in 1997)	More than 150 branch offices
Ireland (opened in 1998)	More than 20 branch offices

Source: Company Web site http://aboutus.enterprise.com/what_we_do/intl_operations.html (accessed February 20, 2007).

- "Take care of your customers and your employees, and profit will take care of itself."
- "Treat customers the way you would want to be treated as a customer."
- "Repeat customers are the quickest way to build a solid base of business."
- "Never promise what you can't deliver; deliver more than you promise."
- "After dealing with us, we want customers to say, 'This is the best place I've ever done business.'"[13]

Enterprise had remained true to these basic principles. They were reflected in the company's mission statement, shown in Exhibit 6.

Taylor's philosophy was also reflected in a tool called the Enterprise Cultural Compass, shown in Exhibit 7. The company developed the compass to guide its service-oriented employees in conducting business and in interactions with each customer, each other, and their local communities. The compass was also intended to aid employees in focusing on key areas throughout the organization. To help promote the values depicted in the compass, Enterprise developed an award named the Jack Taylor Founding Values Award, which provided winners with a grant from the Enterprise Rent-a-Car Foundation that could be used for qualified nonprofit causes in the winners' local communities. Employees were expected to adhere to these principles in all of their business dealings. A failure to do so could result in disciplinary action or dismissal.

Enterprises' ability to live up to this ambitious philosophy and mission were demonstrated by the multiple awards the company had won in the areas of customer service, job satisfaction, and hiring practices. For example, between August 2006 and February 2007, *BusinessWeek* recognized Enterprise as both one of the best places to start a career and as a Customer Service Champ.

In 2007, Jack Taylor's founding principles were also sustained by his son Andrew (Andy) Taylor, who served as the company's CEO. The Taylor family was still the principal owner of Enterprise and the company was one of the 20 largest private companies in the United States. Andy Taylor became president of Enterprise in 1980 and had been CEO since 1994. At age 16, Andy jockeyed cars at Enterprise and later received an undergraduate degree in business at the University of Denver. Andy was known throughout the organization for his strong belief in Enterprise's founding principles and his relentless work ethic. Andy flew up to 300 hours annually on business and would come into his St. Louis office on Saturdays when home. An inspirational leader, Andy Taylor stated that his father had worked on weekends and that if Enterprise employees were expected to work on Saturday, then so should he. His willingness to work alongside branch managers was a powerful motivational tool for his employees and had won him their respect and dedication.

Focus on Customer Service

Customer service was at the core of Enterprise's business philosophy. However, until 1989 Enterprise did not systematically measure customer service. After launching a national advertising campaign,

Exhibit 6   **Enterprise Rent-a-Car Mission Statement, 2007**

Our mission is to fulfill the automotive and commercial truck rental, leasing, car sales and related needs of our customers and, in doing so, exceed their expectations for service, quality and value.

We will strive to earn our customers' long-term loyalty by working to deliver more than promised, being honest and fair and "going the extra mile" to provide exceptional personalized service that creates a pleasing business experience.

We must motivate our employees to provide exceptional service to our customers by supporting their development, providing opportunities for personal growth and fairly compensating them for their successes and achievements.

We believe it is critical to our success to promote managers from within who will serve as examples of success for others to follow.

Although it is our goal to be the best and not necessarily the biggest or the most profitable, our success at satisfying customers and motivating employees will bring growth and long-term profitability.

Source: Company Web site http://aboutus.enterprise.com/who_we_are/mission.html (accessed February 20, 2007).

Exhibit 7   **Enterprise Rent-a-Car's Cultural Compass**

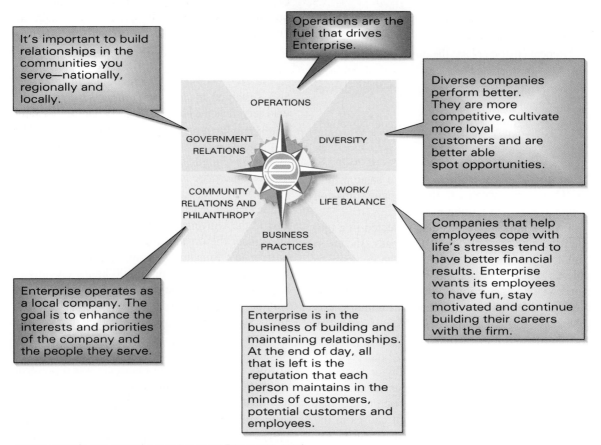

It's important to build relationships in the communities you serve—nationally, regionally and locally.

Operations are the fuel that drives Enterprise.

Diverse companies perform better. They are more competitive, cultivate more loyal customers and are better able spot opportunities.

OPERATIONS

GOVERNMENT RELATIONS

DIVERSITY

COMMUNITY RELATIONS AND PHILANTHROPY

WORK/ LIFE BALANCE

BUSINESS PRACTICES

Enterprise operates as a local company. The goal is to enhance the interests and priorities of the company and the people they serve.

Enterprise is in the business of building and maintaining relationships. At the end of day, all that is left is the reputation that each person maintains in the minds of customers, potential customers and employees.

Companies that help employees cope with life's stresses tend to have better financial results. Enterprise wants its employees to have fun, stay motivated and continue building their careers with the firm.

Source: www.aboutus.enterprise.com (accessed February 20, 2007).

the company decided to measure the effectiveness of the new ad program. In the survey of 250 people that was used to measure advertising effectiveness, the company asked customers how satisfied they were, overall, with their enterprise experience. From the initial survey in 1989 the overall satisfaction index was 90 out of 100, but only 66 percent of the respondents answered that they were completely satisfied. Another 26 percent were moderately satisfied, 3 percent were slightly satisfied, 2 percent were slightly dissatisfied, 1 percent was moderately dissatisfied, and 2 percent were completely dissatisfied. Enterprise calculated a "top box" score of 61 by subtracting all of the customers who noted they were dissatisfied (5 percent) from those who were completely satisfied. From 1990 to 1993 the satisfaction index ranged from 86 to 89, and the top box score ranged from 53 to 71.[14]

In 1994, the company's top box score fell to 50 with an overall satisfaction index of 86. In 1996, Jack Taylor approached his son Andy, who was then CEO at senior management retreat, and said, "Andrew, we have a *big* problem . . ."[15] Jack was concerned that the company's rapid growth of the previous decade had caused Enterprise to lose its focus on customer service. While Andy had been getting anecdotal information that this might be true, additional investigation by Andy revealed that other top managers were getting indications that customer service failures were occurring in the organization. In response to this troubling information, the company undertook an extensive process over more than a year to develop and execute a systematic customer service survey. The company received approximately 400 responses from the first survey; the initial results seemed promising in that less than 10 percent of the respondents indicated that they were somewhat dissatisfied or completely dissatisfied. However, only 67 percent of respondents indicated that they were completely satisfied. While this number was discouraging, the truly problematic statistic was the range of scores between the geographic regions. While some regions were in the mid-80s, others, such as Enterprise's largest and most profitable market in Southern California, scored in the mid-50s.[16]

Not surprisingly, the first step in solving this problem was to convince the managers of the regions with the low scores that they actually had a problem. The managers in these regions attacked the validity of the survey and criticized the way it was administered. However, when further research showed that 70 percent of the customers who said they were completely satisfied would rent from Enterprise again (as opposed to only 22 percent of those who were somewhat satisfied), managerial attention turned to how the company could strengthen the survey and address the problems it raised. Additional research also showed that the three main factors customers cared about were the attitude and helpfulness of Enterprise employees, transaction speed, and the cleanliness of the cars. Of these, the attitude and helpfulness of the staff was by far the most important factor.

By the time the process was complete, Enterprise had invested over $10 million in developing the Enterprise Service Quality Index (ESQi) to ensure that it was a reliable, accurate, and useful management tool. Despite the significant investment in the ESQi, Enterprise did not see any significant changes in its business processes or customer service rankings until it tied individual compensation and career advancement to it. Operating reports were redesigned to highlight the ESQi score, and each region's score was communicated widely across the entire organization. Customer satisfaction was put on the agenda of every meeting at Enterprise and managers were held publicly responsible for their scores. A few managers who tried to game the system (by asking customers for high scores on the survey, or by devising schemes to ensure that dissatisfied customers were not contacted) were terminated from the company when their activities were discovered. Even with these efforts, it was not until 1999 that the company felt it had turned the corner.

The company had continued to improve customer service as well as the ESQi. By 2007, the survey process had been redesigned so that 1 out of every 15 customers was contacted for a quick phone survey. These customers are asked: (1) On a scale ranging from "completely satisfied" to "completely dissatisfied," how would you rate your last Enterprise rental experience? and (2) Would you rent from Enterprise again? Answers from the first question were compiled into an index for each branch. Approximately 98 percent of the customers who were contacted participated in the survey, and in early 2007 the company average ESQi score had reached 80 (meaning that 80 percent of all survey respondents answered "completely satisfied") and the company had been ranked top in customer service in the auto rental business for three consecutive years.

Hiring and Store Operations

Unlike many other auto rental companies, or large organizations in general, Enterprise encouraged its employees to be entrepreneurial and gave its branch managers significant autonomy in running their local operations. The typical Enterprise branch had a team of five to seven employees and a fleet of 125 cars. Branches much larger than this were divided, and assistant managers at these growing branches could be promoted to branch managers at the new locations. The basic philosophy used to staff Enterprise branches was to hire well-educated, competitive, social individuals with a strong work ethic and then give them a sense of ownership and nurture their entrepreneurial spirit through training and a strong inventive program.

In achieving this culture, Enterprise employed a highly decentralized structure that relied on independent field managers, who resembled franchisees. These new employers were taught how to run their own businesses through an award-winning training program, known as a "virtual MBA," that provided new hires with a broad set of skills. These diverse skills were essential, because each field manager was responsible for managing a range of branch operations, including determining the need for cars, opening branches, selling used cars, and setting local rental prices, within corporate limits. While students seeking specialized employment might not pursue employment at Enterprise, many students sought the challenge of a diverse work environment. In fact, the company had been recognized multiple times as being one of the best places to start a new career and was the largest employer of new college graduates. In 2007, the company was slated to hire over 8,000 new graduates and had a new-hire retention rate ranging from 50 to 70 percent.

While Enterprise encouraged an entrepreneurial spirit among its employees, the company still enforced some corporate control over branch operations to ensure consistency and to implement corporate goals. For example, staff members were required to be in business dress and Enterprise closely monitored pricing to ensure that the firm's most valuable customers, insurers, did not complain that their rivals were getting better rental prices. Additionally, the sense of ownership Enterprise sought to instill in its employees could lead them to become very vocal when overhead costs imposed by headquarters started to cut into branch profits or when strategic change mandated from corporate cut personal earnings.

In the 1980s, when Jack Taylor thought the firm needed to advertise on national television, the field argued that the expense was unnecessary. Taylor still decided to go ahead with the program and hired a New York–based agency that came up with the Enterprise auto wrapped in brown paper. While the campaign was successful, some branch managers complained that it only served to make firms such as Hertz aware that Enterprise was a serious competitor.

Compensation and Incentives

Enterprise's compensation and incentive structure were keys in promoting an entrepreneurial spirit throughout the company. All new hires started out washing cars and earning anywhere from $30,000 to $38,000. After being with the company a year and a half, employees were eligible to be promoted to assistant branch manager, where their total compensation included a salary plus a percentage of the branch's profits at the end of each month. However, an employee could not be promoted if his or her branch's ESQi score was not at or above the corporate average.

In Enterprise's compensation system, each branch was treated as a profit center and the total compensation of each branch manager and assistant manager was largely contingent on the branch's profitability. The company believed that this strongly aligned the interests of the employees with those of the company. From this level all the way to the top of the company, individuals' salaries were tied to the performance of operations for which they were responsible. In effect, the company's operations formed a series of pyramids, with managers at any given level earning a percentage of all that was made below them.

The compensation system often resulted in employees being willing to work more than the company's 49½-hour maximum workweek. Some workers had sued, claiming that they deserved overtime pay. However, for those employees who made it into the managerial ranks, the compensation could be significant. The vast majority of Enterprise's top managers had started their careers working in a branch, and at the upper echelons of the company managers could earn millions of dollars a year through the company's hierarchical compensation system.

Information Technology

Enterprise used the Automated Rental Management System (ARMS), a proprietary system that linked all of the company's locations using simple desktop technology to automatically update and send vehicle status reports directly to insurance companies via the Internet. Enterprise had grown by focusing on insurers and their close collaborators, auto repair shops, and currently received one-third of its total revenue, around $3 (billion) from U.S. insurers. Enterprise was the "preferred provider" for dozens of the biggest insurance companies and even had employees implanted full-time in many of the insurers' offices. The firm had gotten so big that insurers wanted alternative providers, which gave competitors such as Hertz an opportunity to move in. Nevertheless, for the past decade the insurance industry had used the ARMS, which worked by facilitating and streamlining three-way communication between Enterprise, insurers, and auto repair shops. The ARMS initiated auto rental reservations, monitored repairs, and authorized payment through electronic funds transfer, speeding up the entire process and increasing customer satisfaction. Over 60,000 adjusters and more than 500 worldwide insurance companies currently use the ARMS.

In February 2006, Enterprise announced a strategic partnership with FIX AUTO Network, one of the biggest providers of business solution technology to the collision industry to expand the reach of the company's ARMS. Through this agreement, Enterprise planned to integrate its ARMS with FIX AUTO's technology system to create a more efficient way to streamline collision repair and rental status reports for monitoring by insurance companies.

Exhibit 8   **Enterprise's Revenues, 2000–2006**

Fiscal Year	Worldwide Revenue
2000	$5.6 billion
2001	$6.3 billion
2002	$6.5 billion
2003	$6.9 billion
2004	$7.4 billion
2005	$8.2 billion
2006	$9.0 billion

Source: www.enterprise.com (accessed February 20, 2007).

Financial Performance

Enterprise was privately held, so standard financial performance information was not publicly available. However, management had indicated the company had achieved a compound annual revenue growth rate of 20 percent for the past 25 years; 2006 revenues were in the $9 billion range (see Exhibit 8). According to Standard & Poor's Ratings Services, Enterprise's credit ratios were by far the strongest in the auto rental industry. Its strong balance sheet had resulted in an A rating on unsecured debt and interest rates around 6.2 percent. *Fortune* estimated that Enterprise's profits for fiscal year 2006, on its $9 billion in revenues, would be upward of $700 million.[17] In addition, Enterprise's true equity market value was estimated to be around $17 billion. The company ranked number 16 on the most recent *Forbes* magazine "America's Largest Private Companies" list, and its $9.04 billion in revenues would have placed it

number 259 in the most recent Fortune 500 ranking of publicly held U.S. companies. In just over a decade, the firm had moved up the equivalent of nearly 200 places in the annual Fortune 500 rankings.

Enterprise produced superior financial results relative to its competitors for several reasons: Its business was not particularly cyclical (mostly because of the little exposure to the volatilities of air travel), its balance sheet was not highly leveraged, it generated strong cash flows from operations, and it had proven ability to curtail capital spending, allowing it to continue funding vehicle purchases and servicing debt.

COMPETITORS

Hertz

Headquartered in Park Ridge, New Jersey, Hertz was a global leader in the auto rental market and also offered rental of industrial and construction equipment. The Hertz family of companies is shown in Exhibit 9. For the fiscal year ending December 2005, Hertz generated revenues of $7,314.7 million, an increase of 11.9 percent over the previous year. The company reported a net income of $398.8 million for fiscal 2005, an increase of 3.3 percent over fiscal 2004.

The company was founded in Chicago, Illinois, in 1918 and in 1932, introduced the first fly/drive auto rental program. In 1984, Hertz developed and introduced computerized driving directions (CDD) and then became the first auto rental company to offer this service. Directions were available in six languages at customer rental locations through self-serve

Exhibit 9   **Hertz Family of Companies**

Hertz Local Edition	Opened for over 80 years; the second largest auto rental company in the world, on- and off-airport locations
Hertz Equipment Rental	Rental and sale of heavy equipment and tools for construction and industrial needs
Hertz Car Sales	Sale of one-year-old vehicles from the rental fleet with low fixed prices
Hertz Claim Management	Claim management services for liability exposures; specializing in auto and general liability claims
Hertz Truck & Van Rental	Truck and van rentals for all moving needs
Hertz Lease	Offers a wide range of operational leasing and fleet management services through a franchise network around Europe, the Middle East, and Africa

Source: www.hertz.com (accessed February 20, 2007).

touch screen kiosks. In 1995, Hertz introduced its NeverLost navigation system to the United States. In 1998, it collaborated with Magellan in an exclusive joint venture so that Magellan could oversee the expansion and operation of the NeverLost system. In 2001, Hertz launched its premium auto rental service, the Hertz Prestige Collection, which included rentals from Jaguar, Land Rover, Lincoln, and Volvo. In 2004, they introduced wireless, high-speed Internet access to more than 50 major airport locations across the United States. In December 2005, an indirect, wholly-owned subsidiary of Hertz Holdings acquired all of Hertz's common stock from Ford Holdings. In January 2006, Hertz introduced the Hertz Fun Collection, with vehicles tailor-made for travelers seeking exciting driving experiences featuring a selection of convertibles, coupes/roadsters, and SUVs. In addition, all Fun Collection vehicles feature SIRIUS Satellite Radio and customers can reserve the cars by brand and model. Also in 2006, Hertz introduced its Green Collection of fuel-efficient, environmentally friendly cars, which customers could reserve by make and model.

Hertz had been a perennial runner-up to Enterprise in terms of total market share in the auto rental business, but its core competency lay in the on-airport business, where it had around 28 percent of the market. Hertz operated approximately 3,100 auto rental locations in the United States and approximately 4,600 international locations, representing more than 150 foreign countries, including France, Germany, Italy, the United Kingdom, Australia, Canada, Spain, the Netherlands, and Switzerland. Hertz operated in two major segments: auto rental and equipment rental. It also generated revenues from customer airport concession fee reimbursements and vehicle licensing costs, fueling charges, and charges for supplemental products and services that included child seats, ski racks, loss or collision damage waiver, liability insurance, Hertz NeverLost navigation system, and satellite radios. Hertz maintained auto repair centers at some airports, as well as in urban and suburban areas. Many of these repair shops were eligible to perform and receive reimbursement for warranty work from auto manufacturers and insurers.

Hertz's primary focus was the on-airport market, but it increased the number off-airport locations by 44 percent (to 1,200) between 2005 and 2007 with the intent to expand further. With a goal of increasing its share of the rapidly growing leisure business,

the company had also taken direct aim at Enterprise's auto insurer business. Although Enterprise had a solid lock on this market, some insurers did not want to be overly reliant on Enterprise and were willing to explore options with other auto rental companies. Enterprise and Hertz were also engaged in a struggle over Enterprise's ARMS software. Hertz had been accused of software infringement on Enterprise's ARMS; if found guilty, Hertz would have to pay damages but, more significantly, might suffer a disadvantage in growing its off-airport business. Despite its clashes with Enterprise, Hertz had steadily grown its revenue since 2000 (see Exhibit 10) and had made significant improvements in net income since 2002.

Avis Budget Group

In 2007 Avis Budget Group had about a 32 percent share of the on-airport auto rental market via its Avis and Budget brands, and its Budget Truck Rental operation was the second largest consumer truck rental business in the United States. The Avis, Budget, and Budget Truck brands accounted for approximately 61 percent, 31 percent, and 8 percent of 2006 revenues, respectively. Management believed that the company gained significant economies from operating two distinct brands targeting different market segments while sharing the same fleet, maintenance facilities, technology, and administrative infrastructure. Exhibit 11 shows the company's income statement for 2004–2006.

Avis Budget Group operated about 6,700 auto and truck rental locations in North America, Australia, New Zealand, Latin America, the Caribbean, and portions of the Pacific region. The rental fleet averaged around 410,000 vehicles, with the company completing more than 28 million auto rental transactions worldwide in 2006. In 2006, the company's domestic car rental business, which included almost 330,000 vehicles, generated approximately 89 million rental days and realized average revenue per day of $40.01. The international car rental business had a rental fleet of approximately 53,310 vehicles, generated approximately 14 million rental days, and realized average revenue per day of $39.61 per vehicle. The truck rental fleet (about 30,500 vehicles) generated approximately 4.6 million rental days and realized average revenue per day of $86.28 per vehicle.

The Avis brand was positioned as a leading supplier to the premium commercial and leisure

Exhibit 10   **Hertz Income Statement, 2001–2005 ($ in millions)**

	2005	2004	2003	2002	2001
Revenues					
Auto rental	$5,949.9	$5,430.8	$4,819.3	$4,537.6	$4,366.6
Equipment rental	1,414.9	1,162.0	1,037.8	1,018.7	1,128.7
Other	104.4	83.2	76.6	82.1	101.6
Total revenues	7,469.2	6,676.0	5,933.7	5,638.4	5,596.9
Expenses					
Direct operating expenses	4,189.3	3,734.4	3,316.1	3,093.0	3,248.0
Depreciation of revenue earning equipment	1,599.7	1,463.3	1,523.4	1,499.5	1,462.3
Selling, general, & administrative	638.5	591.3	501.7	463.1	479.2
Interest, net of interest income	500.0	384.4	355.0	366.4	404.7
Total expenses	6,927.5	6,173.4	5,696.2	5,422.0	5,594.2
Income (loss) before income taxes and minority interest	541.7	502.6	237.5	216.4	2.7
(Provision) benefit of taxes on income	(151.6)	(133.9)	(78.9)	(72.4)	20.6
Minority interest	(12.6)	(3.2)			
Income (loss) before cumulative effect of change in accounting principle	377.5	365.5	158.6	144.0	23.3
Cumulative effect of change in accounting principle	—	—	—	(294.0)	—
Net income (loss)	$ 377.5	$ 365.5	$ 158.6	$ (150.0)	$ 23.3

Source: Company 10-K report for 2005, p. 46.

segments of the travel industry. Avis rented vehicles at approximately 2,000 locations in the United States, Canada, Puerto Rico, the U.S. Virgin Islands, Argentina, Australia, and New Zealand. Budget was a well-recognized value brand aimed at serving the price-conscious rental auto segment; Budget rented vehicles at about 1,800 locations in the United States, Canada, Puerto Rico, Australia, and New Zealand. Like Hertz, Avis was focused on expanding its off-airport locations. In 2006, Avis Budget's truck rental business consisted of a fleet of 30,500 vehicles that were rented through a network of 2,400 dealer-operated locations, 210 company operations, and about 100 franchise-operated locations across the continental United States.

Avis Budget Group's financial and strategic objectives included expanding revenue sources, maximizing profits, and pursuing growth in the off-airport market. The company intended to increase sales of its optional insurance products and push at-the-counter upgrades (called "up sells"), as well as boost sales of ancillary rental products such as Where2 global positioning navigation. Management expected to open

200 new rental locations in both 2006 and 2007, and add Budget auto rentals to the product offerings at its truck dealerships. New locations were expected to reach break-even in six to nine months.

National Car Rental and Alamo Car Rental

Vanguard Car Rental USA Inc., the parent company of National Car Rental and Alamo Rent a Car, operated more than 3,000 locations in the United States and Canada, the United Kingdom, Germany, Sweden, Latin America, the Caribbean, Japan, Australia, New Zealand, and Singapore. Its fleet consisted of about 275,000 vehicles that were rented to about 15 million travelers. Exhibit 12 shows selected financial and operating data for 2004–2006.

Vanguard Car Rental Group operated National and Alamo as two separate brands under common ownership. National was positioned to target commercial and corporate accounts, frequent business travelers, and premium leisure renters. Commercial

Exhibit 11   **Avis Budget Group's Income Statement, 2004–2006 (in millions of $)**

	2006	2005	2004
Revenues			
Vehicle rental	$4,519	$4,302	$3,860
Other	1,170	1,098	960
Total	5,689	5,400	4,820
Expenses			
Operating	2,887	2,729	2,413
Vehicle depreciation and lease charges, net	1,416	1,238	988
Selling, general and administrative	818	857	784
Vehicle interest, net	320	309	244
Non-vehicle related depreciation and amortization	105	116	115
Interest expense related to corporate debt, net:			
Interest expense	236	172	251
Early extinguishment of debt	313	—	18
Separation costs	261	15	—
Restructuring charges	10	26	—
Total expenses	6,366	5,462	4,813
Income (loss) before income taxes	(677)	(62)	7
Benefit from income taxes	(226)	(51)	(64)
Income (loss) from continuing operations	(451)	(11)	71
Income from discontinued operations, net of tax	478	1,088	1,822
Gain (loss) on disposal of discontinued operations, net of tax	(1,957)	549	198
Income (loss) before cumulative effect of accounting changes	(1,930)	1,626	2,091
Cumulative effect of accounting changes, net of tax	(64)	(8)	—
Net income (loss)	$(1,994)	$1,618	$2,091

Source: 2006 10-K report.

and corporate accounts represented National's largest source of revenue, with National serving more than one-third of the Fortune 500 companies. The Alamo brand was primarily focused as a value brand intended to serve the needs of less-frequent leisure travelers and tour operators.

National had a history of innovation in the industry and had developed several industry features to improve the rental experience for its customers. In 1954, National became the first auto rental company to offer one-way rentals for customers wishing to rent cars in one town and return them in another. In 1966, National equipped its regional reservation offices with the Telemax computer system, officially becoming the first auto rental company to bring computers into daily reservation operations. After the deregulation of the airline industry in 1976, National opened its doors to the new segment of

leisure travelers when it became the first company to offer flat rates to auto renters.

As one of the first auto rental companies to initiate corporate account business in the late 1970s, National made a commitment to the corporate travelers early on. In 1987, National introduced the industry's first comprehensive frequent-renter program, the Emerald Club, and the Paperless Express Rental Agreement, which used information stored in the company's customer database system to speed auto rental transactions and heighten its appeal to time-sensitive business travelers. Other National innovations included (1) the Emerald Aisle, that permitted customers to select their own cars, complete a rental transaction without filling out any paperwork, and bypass the rental counter completely; (2) the Choice Rental Process, which gave customers the ability to select their own vehicle; and (3) the QuickRent

Exhibit 12   **Selected Financial Statement and Operating Data, Vanguard Car Rental, 2004–2006 ($ in millions)**

	First Six Months, 2006	2005	2004
Rental revenues	$1,456.8	$2,815.5	$2,632.0
Total revenues	1,496.6	2,891.1	2,701.6
Costs and expenses			
Direct vehicle and operating costs	690.8	1,279.1	1,215.2
Selling, general, and administrative expenses	239.9	469.4	487.8
Vehicle depreciation and lease charges	381.5	688.9	595.0
Vehicle interest expense, net	119.9	231.9	162.1
Non-vehicle interest expense, net	17.8	39.6	41.2
Net (gain) loss from derivatives	(10.6)	(0.8)	2.0
Other (income) expense, net	2.8	(1.8)	(3.4)
Income before provision for income taxes	54.5	184.8	201.7
Provision for income taxes	15.9	79.5	30.0
Net Income	$38.6	$105.3	$171.7
Selected balance sheet data			
Cash and cash equivalents	$288.3	$253.9	$172.6
Total assets	7,101.7	6,547.9	5661.7
Total debt	5,709.2	5,107.7	4,487.2
Stockholders' equity	291.2	279.0	182.2
Selected operating data			
Rental revenue per day	$42.33	$41.08	$41.36
Rental revenue per vehicle per month	$1,007.93	$990.83	$993.32
Average paid fleet	240,885	236,760	220,804
Rental days	34,416,332	68,521,486	63,642,013

Source: Vanguard Car Rental Group Inc., Form S-1/A filed September 20, 2006.

service, which offered customers not enrolled in the Emerald Club the ability to bypass the counter by completing their rental transactions online.

In an effort to fund future growth and offset increasing fleet costs and pressure from automobile manufacturers, Vanguard registered for an initial public offering (IPO) of $300 million in August 2006. Despite the planned IPO, rumors of a potential merger between Vanguard and the Dollar Thrifty Group began to circulate in late 2006. In March 2007 no definitive plans for a merger had been announced and Vanguard was still scheduled for an IPO.

Dollar/Thrifty

The Dollar/Thrift Group (DTG) operated the Dollar and Thrifty rental car companies as separate value

brands with company-owned stores in the top 75 airport markets and key leisure markets in the United States and the top 8 airport markets in Canada under DTG Canada. While the two brands were operated separately, they shared vehicles, a single corporate management structure, and, where available, back-office employees and facilities.

The Thrifty brand was originally focused on franchising and franchise support services. In 2003, Thrifty's strategy changed and began to focus on acquiring franchises and operating company-owned stores. By 2007, Thrifty was operating approximately 478 locations in the United States and Canada with 271 franchise locations and 207 company-owned stores. Of these 478 locations, 109 were located at in-terminal locations in the United States. In 2006, Thrifty's total revenue was $616 million for the entire year, with 80 percent of the revenue coming from the airport market and the remaining 20 percent derived from the local market.

The Dollar brand had the majority of its locations at or near airports and was primarily focused on serving business and leisure travelers in the airport vehicle market. In 2007, the company had 358 locations (200 company-owned stores and 159 franchise locations) with 107 in-terminal airport locations. In fiscal year 2006, Dollar's total revenue at company-owned stores was $923 million.

In the United Sates there was some duplication of coverage between the Dollar and Thrifty brands. For example, while Dollar operated in 58 of the top 75 U.S. airport locations and Thrifty operated in 53, both brands operated in direct competition in 47 of these markets. Internationally, both the Thrifty and Dollar brands offered master franchises, generally on a countrywide basis. As of December 31, 2006, Thrifty had franchised locations in 66 countries and Dollar had franchised locations in 51 countries. The master franchisee in a given country could either operate all of the locations in a given country or award subfranchises. Total revenues from franchise locations outside the United States and Canada in 2006 totaled $8.2 million. The income statement for the Dollar Thrifty Group is presented in Exhibit 13.

Heading into 2007, three of the primary concerns of the DTG included overreliance on revenues from airport locations; high concentration in key leisure destinations (over 60 percent of total

Exhibit 13   **Selected Income Statement Data, Dollar Thrifty Group, 2004–2006 ($ in millions)**

	2006	2005	2004
Revenues			
Vehicle rentals	$1,539	$1,380	$1,256
Vehicle leasing	57	63	80
Fees and services	47	50	54
Other	18	15	13
Total revenues	1,661	1,508	1,403
Costs and Expenses			
Direct vehicle and operating	827	788	693
Vehicle depreciation and lease charges, net	380	295	316
Selling, general and administrative	260	236	223
Interest expense, net of interest income of $29,387, $18,388 and $6,929	96	88	91
Total costs and expenses	1,563	1,407	1,323
(Increase) decrease in fair value of derivatives	9	−30	−24
Income before income taxes	89	131	104
Income tax expense	37	54	42
Income before cumulative effect of a change in accounting principle	52	77	62
Cumulative effect of a change in accounting principle	—	—	4
Net income	$ 52	$ 77	$ 66
Basic Earnings Per Share			
Income before cumulative effect of a change in accounting principle	$ 2.14	$ 3.04	$ 2.51
Cumulative effect of a change in accounting principle	—	—	0.15
Net income	$ 2.14	$ 3.04	$ 2.66
Diluted Earnings Per Share			
Income before cumulative effect of a change in accounting principle	2.04	2.89	2.39
Cumulative effect of a change in accounting principle	—	—	0.14
Net income	$ 2.04	$ 2.89	$ 2.53

revenue was derived from Florida, Hawaii, California, and Nevada); and increased pressure from vehicle manufacturers. In response to these pressures, the DTG was exploring a merger with Vanguard. DTG management perceived that the two companies had complementary operations and that administration could be easily rationalized since both companies were headquartered in Tulsa, Oklahoma.

THE FUTURE AT ENTERPRISE RENT-A-CAR

In early 2007, there were several challenges emerging on the horizon that caused Enterprise concern. The first was that the potential DTG/Vanguard merger could change the face of the industry. Separately, neither of these companies represented a significant threat to Enterprise. Through consolidation, however, they would be the third largest auto rental company in the United States. A second challenge was that in response to Enterprise's significant growth in the on-airport market, Hertz had made concerted efforts to expand into Enterprise's lucrative off-airport market. While Enterprise had a big market-share edge in the off-airport market segment and was the leader in this segment by a long margin, Hertz grew its off-airport revenue by 46 percent between 2004 and 2005. Additionally, Avis and Budget planned to increase their off-airport locations by 20 percent annually. Finally, Hertz was actively working to break Enterprise's hold on renting vehicles to people whose car insurance paid for car rental charges while their vehicles were being repaired due to an accident; it had been making some progress with major insurance carriers, including State Farm. In response to these challenges, CEO Andy Taylor stated: "We own the high ground in this business, and we aren't going to give it up."[18]

Endnotes

[1] http://aboutus.enterprise.com/what_we_believe/social_responsibility.html.

[2] Carol J. Loomis, "The Big Surprise Is Enterprise," *Fortune,* July 24, 2006, p. 142.

[3] www.answers.com/topic/passenger-car-rental (accessed February 20, 2007).

[4] www.hertz.com/rentacar/abouthertz/index.jsp (accessed February 21, 2007).

[5] www.answers.com/topic/passenger-car-rental (accessed February 20, 2007).

[6] Loomis, "The Big Surprise Is Enterprise," p. 142.

[7] Enterprise Rent-a-Car Company Web site, www.enterprise.com (accessed February 20, 2007).

[8] Enterprise Rent-a-Car Career Web site. www.erac.com/recruit/where_going.asp?navID=where_going (accessed February 20, 2007).

[9] Loomis, "The Big Surprise Is Enterprise."

[10] Company press release, January 2, 2006.

[11] Chad W. Autry, Patricia J. Daugherty, and R. Glenn Richey, "The Challenge of Reverse Logistics: Electronics Catalog Retailing" *International Journal of Physical Distribution and Logistics Management* 31, no. 1 (2001), pp. 26–37.

[12] www.aboutus.enterprise.com (accessed February 27, 2007).

[13] Andy Taylor, "Top Box: Rediscovering Customer Satisfaction," *Business Horizons* 46, no. 5 (September/October 2003), p. 3.

[14] Ibid.

[15] Ibid.

[16] Ibid.

[17] Loomis, "The Big Surprise Is Enterprise," p. 142.

[18] Ibid.

Case 25

Manpower Australia: Using Strategy Maps and the Balanced Scorecard Effectively

Suresh Cuganesan
Macquarie Graduate School of Management

Guy Ford
Macquarie Graduate School of Management

Haider Khan
Macquarie Graduate School of Management

The 2004 financial performance was very encouraging for Varina Nissen, who was then in the second year of her role as managing director for Manpower Australia. Revenue had increased by 10 percent, while costs were well below target. The overall measure of performance, return on sales, had been improved. Scott McLachlan, the CFO and director of corporate services, announced confidently, "We have achieved the budget targets. It's never happened before in the history of Manpower Australia." The corporate strategy developed by Nissen and her team, and executed through the balanced scorecard (BSC), had achieved the short-term financial objectives for the company and a turnaround in a relative short time. However, future challenges awaited Nissen and McLachlan, not least of which was how to use the BSC to secure further performance improvements.

The recruitment industry in Australia heading into 2005 continued to become more challenging. Since the industry had reached relative maturity, profit margins were being eroded. Manpower's major competitors had also focused on improving productivity and were often able to offer clients better prices. This had affected the company's core business of temporary placements, which had been flat for the last couple of years. There were also candidate shortages in certain segments of the market, while customers were demanding total solutions for their human resource management needs, ranging from the existing recruiting services to learning/development and performance management/succession planning activities. An opportunity existed for growth through innovation—developing and marketing new products and services to target customers.

Under Nissen's leadership, a new strategic vision had been developed and communicated: Manpower was to become a "leader in innovative people solutions." The emphasis was on innovation and growth of higher-margin business, such as human resource services, while maintaining high service-delivery speed at lower costs in Manpower's core business of recruitment. To help communicate and implement her strategy, Nissen had developed and implemented a Strategy Map and BSC for the organization in 2004. According to Manpower's senior management, the BSC at Manpower had been important in communicating the key behaviors required for improved productivity and demonstrating the financial impacts of doing so, with the improved financial performance in 2004 being seen as proof that it worked.

However, given the changing business environment, Nissen wanted to know whether the value

Exhibit 1   **Sizes of Market Sectors in Employment Services Industry in Australia, 1999–2003 (A$ in millions)**

	1999	2003
Executive search	A$ 579.5	A$1,191.2
General permanent jobs	2,429.1	2,883.9
General temporary jobs	2,273.2	4,727.1
Outplacement consultancy	497.5	877.7
Specialist agencies	2,038.7	2,858.9

Source: Euromonitor International.

propositions were being delivered to targeted customers and, if so, whether they were leading to improved customer and financial outcomes. Was the company progressing fast enough in performing activities and services that were valued by targeted customers? In addition, the CFO of Manpower's global operations was still concerned over the slow pace of productivity gains in Manpower Australia as compared to Manpower's global standards. Beating the productivity targets agreed on with the parent company represented another challenge for Manpower Australia, where return on revenue had to be increased by 2 percent and the expense to gross profit ratio decreased by 10 percent.

Nissen and McLachlan both felt that the BSC could help the business implement its strategy more effectively and attain a higher level of performance than that already achieved. However, they were also aware that the BSC was not being used as extensively as they had envisaged in some parts of the business and, in some cases, was being totally ignored in managerial decision making. Also, there was a lack of consistent communication to teams on effective progress on performance. Overall, they thought that the BSC needed to be improved if it was to focus the entire organization on the critical leading indicators of success for the business.

THE AUSTRALIAN RECRUITMENT EMPLOYMENT SERVICES INDUSTRY

Market Size

The Australian market for employment services was estimated at A$12.5 billion (US$8.1 billion) in 2003, and had grown by 13.0 percent from 2002. During

the last five years, the market had grown by over 60 percent. One of the major drivers for this growth was that companies were focusing more on investing and strengthening their core competencies, and turning to strategic alliances with employment service providers to manage and operate noncore activities such as staff recruitment and related human resource management activities.

General temporary jobs, growing by 107.9 percent during 1999–2003 (see Exhibit 1), constituted the largest sector in employment services industry, with 37.7 percent (A$4.7 billion) of the total revenue mix. Temporary employment provided flexibility for organizations in times of economic uncertainty as well as flexibility on the side of employees. Although executive employment market remained flat during 2003, there was consistent growth in this sector due to increased pressure to improve corporate performance and the growth of global firms. In Australia, the demand for talent and experience had increased at most levels in organizations, particularly in information technology (IT) and financial services–related jobs.

Competitor Dynamics

Industry statistics revealed that there were approximately 2,750 organizations in the employment services (recruiting) industry in 2002/2003. The employment services industry in Australia was highly fragmented, with low barriers to entry and the nondominance of global players. Adecco Group SA had been the market leader for the last six years, with a market share of 11.6 percent. Manpower Services (Australia) Pty. Ltd. had the second largest market share (6.0 percent), while Skilled Engineering, a strong performer in temporary placement, was third with a market share of 5.8 percent (see Exhibit 2). There were also a number of niche service providers

Exhibit 2   **Market Shares of Leading Employment Services Providers in Australia, 2003**

Adecco Group SA	11.6%
Manpower Services (Australia) Pty. Ltd.	6.0
Skilled Engineering Ltd.	5.8
Hudson Global Resources	4.6
Chandler Macleod Group Pty. Ltd.	3.1
Hays Personnel Services (Australia) Pty. Ltd.	3.0
Kelly Services Australia	2.5
Spherion Group	1.7
Julia Ross	1.6
Candle Australia Ltd.	1.6
Drake	1.5
Integrated Group	1.5
Michael Page	0.7

Source: Euromonitor International.

that focused on higher-margin areas such as executive search specifically.

Market Growth Forecasts

The recruiting (employment services) market was forecast to grow 61.7 percent from 2003 to 2008, to reach a value of A$20.3 billion (US$13.2 billion). The major drivers for growth were the positive economic outlook, existing low unemployment levels (which, at 5.6 percent, were the lowest in 14 years), and high confidence levels positively affecting investments in human resources. While general temporary jobs were projected to continue to be the largest sector in the Australian employment services market, with a value of A$7.6 billion and 37.5 percent of total industry revenues, the other forecasted growth sector was executive search, with a forecast of 61 percent growth.

In addition, companies were looking to outsource more of the human resource management function. Alongside the provision of core recruiting and staff services, opportunities existed for participants in the employment services industry to provide core human resource management functions such as employee records maintenance, payroll services, and health/wealth benefits services, together with learning/development and performance/succession planning advice. Overall, opportunities existed for recruitment firms to become more proactive in offering solutions to their clients across the entirety of the human resource management spectrum.

MANPOWER GLOBAL

Manpower Inc., established in 1948 in Milwaukee, Wisconsin, was a world leader in the employment services industry, offering customers a continuum of services to meet their needs throughout the employment and business cycle. A Fortune 500 company, it specialized in permanent, temporary, and contract recruitment; employee assessment; training; career transition; and organizational consulting services. Manpower's global network of 4,300 offices in 74 countries and territories enabled the company to meet the needs of its 440,000 customers per year. These ranged from small and medium-sized enterprises across all industry sectors to some of the world's largest multinational corporations. During 2003, the company's 21,400 staff employees and 1.6 million temporary workers worldwide supplied 780 millions of hours of work. Manpower Inc. claimed to be able to help any company—no matter where it was in its business evolution—to raise productivity through improved strategy, quality, efficiency, and cost reduction, thereby enabling clients to concentrate more on their core business activities.

Manpower had shown impressive financial performance worldwide during financial year 2004. Revenues from services increased by 22.5 percent, to US$14.9 billion; gross profit increased by 30.5 percent, to US$ 2.8 billion; and net earnings per share, diluted, increased by 53.3 percent, to US$ 2.59. The company's global vision, strategies, and values (see Exhibit 3) represented a framework for direction and

Exhibit 3   **Manpower Global: Vision, Strategies, and Values**

Vision

To be the best worldwide provider of higher-value staffing services and center for quality employment opportunities.

Strategies

- **Revenue**—Rigorously focus on industries, geographies and customers that have the strongest long-term growth opportunities for staffing services and solutions.
- **Efficiency**—Continuously improve profit margins and returns through disciplined internal processes and increased productivity.
- **Acquisitions**—Identify and pursue opportunities for strategic acquisitions that have the best potential to catalyze and enrich the core temporary staffing business.
- **Technology**—Aggressively explore and implement the transformational opportunities of information technology and e-commerce to continuously develop defensible competitive advantage in all aspects of the company's activities.
- **Organization and culture**—Capitalize on our entrepreneurial corporate culture to make the most of our internal talent and develop meaningful career paths for employees, striving toward "best practices" in everything we do throughout the global organization.

Values

Manpower global core values are based on three principles pertaining to people, knowledge and innovation.

People—*We care about people and the role of work in their lives.*

- We respect all our people as individuals, enabling and trusting them to meet the needs of colleagues, customers and the community.
- We are committed to developing professional service according to our high quality and ethical standards.
- We recognize everyone's contribution to our success.
- We help people develop their careers through planning, work experience, coaching and training.

Knowledge—*We learn and grow by sharing knowledge and resources.*

- We actively listen to our people and customers and act upon this information to improve our relationships and services.
- We pursue the adoption of the best practices worldwide.
- We share one global identity and act as one company while recognizing the diversity of national cultures and working environments.
- We reward team behavior.

Innovation—*We dare to innovate and be pioneers.*

- We thrive on our entrepreneurial spirit and speed of response.
- We take risks, knowing that we will not always succeed.
- We are willing to challenge each other and not accept the status quo.
- We lead by example.

priorities in making decisions, developing opportunities, and building relationships for Manpower's people and customers around the world.

MANPOWER AUSTRALIA

Manpower had been operating in Australia and New Zealand as a human resources solution provider for over three decades. It was first established as a franchised operation in 1965 but was later purchased by Manpower Inc. in 1996. There were 72 offices in Australia/New Zealand, with 34,000 temporary workers. During 2003, over 85,000 permanent and temporary jobs were filled in Australia/New Zealand by Manpower. In Australia, Manpower operated under the brand names of Manpower, Right Management Consultants, Manpower Executive, Elan, and Manpower City. The company's current organization structure is shown in Exhibit 4.

The company had four divisions: Recruitment & Staffing Solutions (R&SS), Major Client Services (MCS), Corporate Services, and Strategic Services. R&SS, the retail arm of the company, operated

Exhibit 4   **Manpower Organizational Chart**

through a network of 58 branches and was generally organized by regions, whereas MCS was generally structured into teams that serviced the needs of high-volume clients such as major information technology companies. The core business of R&SS and MCS was the fulfilment of both temporary jobs (temps) and permanent jobs (perms). Across both business units, the Manpower consultant was responsible for servicing client needs through the sourcing of the right candidate.

In general, the MCS business was considered to be at the lower-margin end of the spectrum of Manpower's offerings, while executive permanent recruitment and human resources (HR) services tended to be of higher margin. In recognition of this, a significant effort had been made to augment the existing portfolio of clients with volume business with HR services as well as compete in retail and, in particular, expand its executive placement business.

The Strategy

Varina Nissen joined Manpower Australia and New Zealand as managing director in 2003. According to Nissen and McLachlan, when Nissen joined Manpower, the company was facing a number of significant challenges:

- Manpower Australia had experienced flat growth for the past two years against the Manpower global standard of year-on-year growth.
- There had been little successful new product development.
- The company had been underperforming against the Manpower global standard for the measure of gross profit/total salary cost.

- The company was challenged by competitor discounting.
- Culture and processes did not support innovation or have the capability of the company's rapid commercialization.

All key areas of the business were thus challenged to create value and improve the company's financial performance; however, there was no explicit strategy in place to give managers direction and focus. In the absence of a specific Australian strategy, the newly appointed managing director decided to develop a corporate strategy based on the corporate vision: "To be recognised as the Australasian Leader in delivering innovative people solutions." Three strategic themes were identified:

1. A focus on clients and candidates.
2. The expansion of service offerings to provide people solutions throughout the HR value chain.
3. Supply capability to grow communities and sectors/industries.

To make these strategic themes operational, Manpower required significant marketplace repositioning, cultural change, operational redirection, and an overall improvement in all major aspects of the business. Five strategic initiatives were proposed to address these challenges:

- Grow market share in growth industries and sectors.
- Contribute to the employment growth in communities.
- Meet industry benchmarks.
- Reposition the Manpower brand as "the authority on work."
- Proactively manage risk.

In Australia, the market conditions for the recruiting industry were volatile. According to Scott McLachlan, the CFO of Manpower:

> The recruiting industry in Australia is highly competitive and extremely fragmented. The market leader has only 10–11 percent of total market share and there are around 3,000 agencies in the country. There are all types of competitors across the board and also competitors in key categories and niche providers. The market has shifted from being volume and price driven to being profitable growth driven. It is a low return, low cost of entry market and therefore the purchasing power is starting to shift. The successful company is one that is both a low-cost provider and delivers products that are better than the competitors. Also, 70 percent of cost is related to people; therefore, the best gross profit return per consultant is important to achieve.

Initially, the focus was mainly on developing and clarifying Manpower Australia's vision and strategy. However, Nissen was also concerned about the organization's agility in aligning itself with the rapidly changing business environment and the strategy that had been developed. She knew that the mind-set and behaviors of the Manpower consultant, being the customer- and candidate-facing resource, were the keys to achieving this agility. In one meeting, she raised her concerns with other members of her team:

> Recruiting is a commoditized industry with competitive margins at retail and margin squeeze in volume accounts. Therefore, in order to perform, our front-line staff, whether consultant or support staff must be able to understand and implement the company's strategy. This could also be where we have our single-most potential point of failure—in the field. Our people need to understand, from the company's strategy, what they can deliver to our customers and candidates, and how to price it, with effective operations and sales tools.

To help communicate and drive strategic priorities, Nissen developed a strategy map and a balanced scorecard (BSC) at Manpower.

The Strategy Map and Balanced Scorecard

After developing and finalizing strategic initiatives, the next challenge was to implement the strategy and measure the impact on business performance. Nissen and her team chose the BSC as the strategy implementation tool. According to both Nissen and McLachlan, the BSC was selected by Manpower because:

- Manpower's vision and strategy needed to be translated into actions, with a common language, particularly a common, fact-based approach to measurement.
- Key changes were required in the measurement systems that would impact customer relationships, core competencies, and organizational capabilities.
- There was a need for a measurement and management framework that could link long-term financial success to current customers, internal processes, employees, and systems performance.
- BSC used measurements to inform employees about the drivers of current and future success.
- With BSC it was easier to channel collective energy, enthusiasm, knowledge, and abilities in the pursuit and achievement of long-term common goals.

According to Nissen, "The balanced scorecard is an easy to adopt methodology and is value focused. It clarifies the cause and effect linkages between employee, customers and financials. It's a modern tool that helps analyse business effectively." McLachlan was likewise happy with the selection of the BSC as the company's strategic measurement system; he said, "The scorecard will monitor how we are going in our journey." The CFO added, "Previously, the management was more focused on short term gains. With balanced scorecard, the management team started looking across at least a year's horizon and the operational team started focusing on quarterly horizons."

The management team decided to implement the BSC first in the R&SS division. It was envisaged that once successes were created, the program could then be rolled out efficiently and effectively to the entire organization. R&SS was selected because the company wanted to leverage its branch network to focus on growth sectors and occupations through the implementation of various strategic initiatives, and it was felt that the BSC framework could help this process.

To achieve clarity around Manpower's strategy, a strategy map (see Exhibit 5) was first developed during various strategy sessions with the executive management. The strategy map was used to describe the corporate strategy and elaborate how the value would be created through the execution of strategy.

Exhibit 5   **Manpower Australia's Strategy Map, 2003–2004**

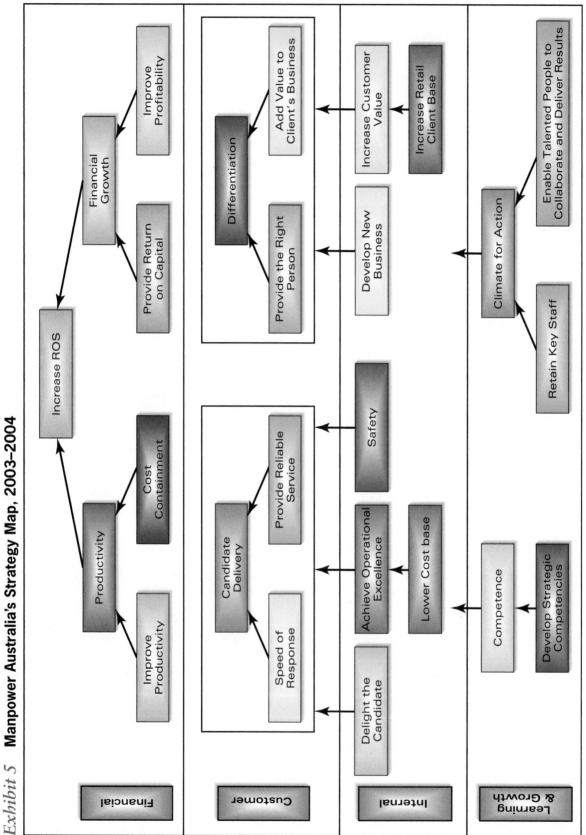

Exhibit 6 **Manpower Australia's Recruiting & Staffing Solution (R&SS) Scorecard, 2004**

Themes	Objectives	Measures
Financial Perspective		
Growth	• Provide return on capital • Improve profitability	• YTD Return on sales • Sales revenue • Gross profit • Operating unit profit • YTD gross profit margin • Gross profit growth YoY
Productivity	• Improve productivity • Cost containment	• Debtors over 29 days • DSO days • SG&A Growth YoY • SG&A as % of gross profit • YTD Gross profit/Total personnel cost
Customer Perspective		
Candidate delivery	• Speed of response	• Job fill rate contract • Job fill rate perm • Job fill rate temp • Job vacancy days contract • Job vacancy days permanent • Job vacancy days temporary
Internal Business Perspective		
Increase customer value	• Increase the retail client base as a % of gross profit	• Client retention—lapsed
Achieve operational excellence	• Lower the cost base of the business	• Pay Bill error rate
Safety	• Safety	• Lost time injury frequency rate (LTIFR) rolling average
Learning and Growth Perspective		
Climate for action	• Retain key staff	• Staff retention

One of the Manpower's directors highlighted how Varina Nissen supported the strategy mapping process: "The major reason for adopting the strategy map was its cause and effect linkage and it was Varina who focused the team towards the cause and effect relationship. She repeatedly conveyed during various strategy meetings how the employee engagement and customer measures drove financial results." The first version of the strategy map was developed by Nissen prior to discussion with senior management, most of whom agreed to its cause-and-effect linkages. A key feature of the strategy map was the integration and alignment of all levels of her management team and the overall organization. Nissen said, "The strategy map was developed to unite the leadership team by linking the divisions and business units through higher corporate goals like ROS, Expenses as a percent of gross profit, etc."

Having developed the strategy map, the R&SS scorecard (see Exhibit 6) was developed and implemented in 2004. The scorecard was built from the top down using four steps:

1. Financial outcomes were set.
2. Key customer outcomes that created related financial outcomes were identified.
3. Internal processes relating to customers and productivity outcomes were identified.
4. The infrastructure needed to achieve all of the above was identified.

Initially, effort was not directed toward developing new measures for processes, as shown in the strategy map, but rather focus was on leveraging the existing information. Nissen emphasized, "Initially the focus was on capturing what was already available."

Exhibit 7   **Financial Perspective**

Themes	Objectives	Measures
Growth	• Provide return on capital • Improve profitability	• YTD Return on sales • Sales revenue growth • Gross profit • Operating unit profit • YTD gross profit margin • Gross profit growth YoY
Productivity	• Improve productivity • Cost containment	• Debtors over 29 days • DSO days • SG&A growth • SG&A as % of gross profit • Gross profit/Total personnel cost

The R&SS scorecard consisted of four perspectives, seven strategic themes, nine objectives, and 21 measures. The four perspectives of the BSC were:

1. Financial
2. Customer
3. Internal Processes
4. Learning & Growth

Financial Perspective   Financial measures indicated whether a company's strategy, implementation, and execution were contributing to bottom-line improvement. Manpower was in the "sustain" stage of its life cycle, as the recruiting industry had reached maturity. Most companies in the sustain stage used measures related to accounting income, such as operating profit and gross margins. Manpower had chosen both growth and productivity themes for maximizing income (see Exhibit 7).

The financial perspective of the R&SS scorecard had two strategic themes, four objectives, and 11 measures. Return on sales (ROS) as the overall financial objective was driving the business toward operational efficiency. Thus, debtor measures were incorporated to improve asset utilization through improvement in the cash cycle, and the measures on the selling, general, and administration expenses focused on cost reduction. The productivity focus highlighted the company's strategy to deal with the highly competitive market conditions with squeezing margins, while the various growth metrics were aimed at capturing the performance of Manpower in expanding its scale of business, share of revenue, and profit.

Customer Perspective   The customer perspective articulated the customer-and market-based strategy that would deliver superior future financial returns. This perspective usually included identification of the customer and market segments, with common metrics comprising outcome measures and attributes of the specific value proposition offered that would drive the outcomes sought by the business. Common outcome measures usually included customer satisfaction, customer retention, customer acquisition, customer profitability, and market and account share in targeted segments. Measures of the value proposition typically focused on product/service attributes, the customer relationship, and/or brand image and reputation.

The customer perspective of the R&SS scorecard had one strategic theme, one objective, and six measures (see Exhibit 8). The focus on speed in candidate delivery clearly indicated the company's emphasis on productivity, which was considered one of the major requirements for efficient branch operations.

Internal Business Process Perspective   In the internal business perspective, critical processes were identified at which the organization must excel to achieve its financial and customer objectives. Internal processes accomplished two vital components of an organization's strategy: (1) they produced and delivered the value proposition for customers, and (2) they directly impacted the productivity theme in the financial perspective. The organization's internal processes could be grouped into four clusters: operations management processes, innovation processes,

Exhibit 8   **Customer Perspective**

Theme	Objective	Measures
Candidate delivery	• Speed of response	• Job fill rate contract • Job fill rate permanent • Job fill rate temporary • Job vacancy days contract • Job vacancy days permanent • Job vacancy days temporary

Exhibit 9   **Internal Business Process Perspective**

Themes	Objectives	Measures
Increase customer value	• Increase the retail client base as a % of gross profit	• Client retention—lapsed
Achieve operational excellence	• Lower the cost base of the business	• Pay bill error rate
Safety	• Safety	• Lost time injury frequency rate (LTIFR) rolling average

customer management processes, and regulatory and social processes.

Manpower had focused mainly on three clusters of internal processes. Manpower's corporate scorecard had three strategic themes, three objectives, and three measures under the internal business process perspective (see Exhibit 9). The customer and candidate management processes were focused on client retention and ensuring the longevity of the customer base. The operational excellence theme was geared to reducing the cost structure by reducing invoicing and other errors/disputes that impacted prompt client payments. Safety was given priority under the regulatory and social processes of the company, with the Lost Time Injury Frequency Rate (LTFIR) metric focused on candidates' occupational health and safety issues, risk management, and cost related to injury compensation.

Learning and Growth Perspective   The objectives in the learning and growth perspective provided the infrastructure to enable objectives in the other three perspectives to be achieved. This perspective focused on the longer-term enablers of the business and its readiness to implement the chosen strategy. Enablers were grouped into human capital readiness focused on employee skills and competencies (with common outcome measures comprising employee retention, productivity, and satisfaction), information system capabilities, and overall cultural alignment and values.

The learning and growth perspective in the R&SS scorecard had one theme, one objective, and one measure (see Exhibit 10). The main focus was on retaining key staff. Staff retention was arguably an outcome measure for employees' satisfaction.

The Implementation Process

Having developed the BSC for R&SS, Nissen developed BSCs for the other business units and cascaded down to regions and branches within R&SS. The monthly business review meeting, led by Nissen and

Exhibit 10   **Learning and Growth Perspective**

Theme	Objectives	Measures
Climate for action	• Retain key staff	• Staff retention

Exhibit 11   **Survey Results on Role in BSC Development**

Role Identified	% Response*
Not a part of strategic objective formulation	39%
Only responsible for metrics in my business area	22
I adopted the objectives suggested	11
Involved in initial conversations and workshops	11
Reviewed objectives with my team	6
Senior management developed it along with IT	6
Change scorecard to suit business needs	6
	100%

*Responses rounded to the next whole number.

comprising her senior management team, undertook to assess the development of BSCs, the selection of right measures, and the linking of initiatives with strategy, and to review the progress at each meeting. In addition, the initial implementation and rollout of the BSC at Manpower was made the responsibility of the general manager of human resources, and the BSC and strategic initiatives progress were reported in the monthly intranet communication to all staff.

A BSC evaluation interview-survey conducted at Manpower revealed that the BSC formulation process had been relatively top-down, with most of the respondents indicating that they had not been directly involved in the formulation of BSC objectives (see Exhibit 11). For most of the survey respondents, their journey started after receiving instructions from Nissen or her senior management team to develop the scorecard, with the majority of these adopting the strategic objectives and metrics that were prescribed.

A series of road shows and education workshops was held throughout Manpower and its branches to communicate the rationale for the BSC and how it was to be used, with a number of these led by Nissen. To ensure adoption and take-up of the BSC, periodic BSC reviews were made a part of the management reviews early in the implementation phase. These reviews monitored the progress of the BSC and its impact on the business. In addition, the BSC reporting and analysis was to be facilitated through technology and Manpower's intranet. According to Nissen, "It was important to signal our revitalization of our Manpower company, that everyone should have a modern looking tool—not an Excel spreadsheet but a tool through which they could analyze the data and reach a fact-based conclusion." As many measures were already in the company's management infor-

mation system, personnel responsible for maintaining this were also given responsibility to feed the data manually into the BSC reporting tool. Within R&SS in particular, a scoreboard form (Exhibit 12) was developed to ensure that the BSC was reviewed at the branch level on a timely basis and actions were taken by the branch managers in five areas: sales, staffing, skills, systems, and safety.

The BSC measures were also linked to compensation. Quarterly bonuses were introduced that were linked to the achievement of the financial numbers, with the BSC aimed at enabling learning about which lead indicators drove financial results. Nissen encouraged the team, "It's okay to be away from your numbers. This is an opportunity for understanding and learning. Learn from the deviations and understand what to do in the future to meet the numbers." In addition, the company also developed 27 incentive plans that were linked with the other nonfinancial measures on the BSC. While there was a common perception that these plans needed to be simplified and rationalized, linking incentives with the BSC measures suggested that Manpower's leadership strongly believed in the BSC. One of the directors claimed, "HR incentive plans at Manpower are in place for sustainable performance and they are aligned with the balanced scorecard objectives and measures."

In mid-2004, responsibility for the BSC was handed over to the directors of the individual business units to drive to lower levels of their respective areas. The BSC Evaluation Survey indicated that significant benefits had been achieved through the BSC implementation at Manpower (see Exhibit 13) in addition to the improvement in the company's financial performance. Specifically, 85 percent of responses to an interview survey pointed out that the BSC had

Exhibit 12   **Scoreboard Form**

Financials		Customer		Internal Business		Learning & Growth	
Operating profit margin (ROS as % revenues)		Temporary job fill rate/ cycle time		Pay bill error rate		Retention	
Gross profit/Total salary cost		Temporary job fill rate/ cycle time		Last time injury frequency rate		Fill rate of internal jobs	
Gross profit/branch personnel cost		Temporary job fill rate/ cycle time					

	From this period	To next period	Target period

	From what	To what	Target
Sales	Action points:		

	From what	To what	Target
Staffing	Action points:		

	From what	To what	Target
Skills	Action points:		

	From what	To what	Target
System	Action points:		

	From what	To what	Target
Safety	Action points:		

Team name	
Date agreed	
Next review date	

Exhibit 13   **Survey Results: Benefits of BSC**

Benefits Identified	% Response*
Helped in understanding of business	22%
Gives focus and insight on key issues	19
Helped in developing management team	14
Nothing will happen if BSC taken out	11
Consistency of communication by providing a common language	8
Gives a good snapshot of business	5
Improved decision making	3
Helped improved business results	3
Drives behavior	3
Helps in changing culture	3
Doesn't drive business decision-making	3
Greater visibility	3
Mechanism for rewarding people	3
Drives business	3
	100%

*Responses rounded to the next whole number.

provided a better understanding of business, more focus on key issues, and learning and development of management team. However, the perception of the BSC as a strategic management system was still low among the participants, with 11 percent of responses indicating that Manpower would not be different without the BSC and 3 percent indicating that it did not drive business decision-making.

PROBLEMS AND CHALLENGES

The Balanced Scorecard

Although the initial implementation of the BSC had resulted in productivity gains for Manpower, Nissen and McLachlan didn't want to stop there. They were focused on leveraging this success by refining the BSC so that innovative and growth objectives could be better achieved. However, one problem was that there appeared to be a blockage in the business using the information embedded in the BSC to identify and better manage the critical lead indicators that would lead to success. Information from the BSC evaluation survey found low usage of the BSC (see Exhibit 14), especially by teams working under the senior to middle management. When the leadership team was questioned regarding the extent of their direct reports usage of the BSC, 65 percent of them

reported low or no usage by their direct reports. They attributed this low take-up to the quality of the information presented on the scorecard. The measures were limited to past performance, lagging, not relevant, and at times inaccurate. Only 17 percent of responses claimed that the direct reports used it for business analysis purposes.

Business Challenges

The external business environment was also becoming increasingly challenging for the company. Discussions among Manpower's senior and middle managers revealed issues relating to the external environment of clients, candidates, and competitors, while internal factors related to systems/processes, employees, and culture.

The major issues and challenges related to clients were identified as comprising:

- Pressure for low price.
- Required speedy service.
- Lack of understanding of customer needs.
- High level of service expectations.
- Increasing customer bargaining power.

The customers' focus was on price, speed, and quality. However, there was a need for better understanding at Manpower for the customer needs and requirements. One of the general managers explained, "There are different industrial sectors and each sector

Exhibit 14   **Survey Results: BSC Usage**

Usage Identified	% Response*
Use it extensively for business analysis	17%
BSC don't have any new info to review	17
Only interested in summary level data on monthly basis	14
Weekly financial reports are more relevant and useful	14
BSC information lagging—not useful	7
Drive behavior as it impacts incentives	7
Its part of their job	7
Measures not relevant to business	7
Not interested	3
Don't have access to BSC	3
Accuracy of BSC questionable	3
	100%

*Responses rounded to the next whole number.

is at a different stage of life cycle—therefore their demands and needs are different. There is no one-fits-all solution. We need to be more focused and analyze each of the sectors in detail to successfully execute our strategy."

The major candidate issues were:

- Candidate shortage.
- Decreasing candidate loyalty and stability.
- Poor candidate care.

There was a severe shortage of candidates, especially in certain skill categories. A regional operations manager of Manpower within R&SS raised the candidate-related issues: "Sourcing candidates with the right skill set is a big issue. In addition to this shortage, candidate loyalty is another issue. Whether we are preferred supplier or not, it is a candidate-driven market and the candidate will move even for an extra 50 cents per hour."

In relation to competition, the market had already matured with rivalry intensifying and a number of niche competitors emerging targeting higher margin business. In this scenario, the main issues and challenges that Manpower currently faced from this highly competitive market were:

- Offering low prices.
- Growth of niche agencies.
- Developing brands.

Another R&SS regional operations manager explained the market conditions as follows: "It's a very competitive market. Pricing has become an issue as we choose to be profitable and the competition

chooses to get the business at any cost." Similarly, the general manager of one of the business units was worried about the increasing number of niche agencies, commenting: "As the market entry barriers are low there is a huge growth of consultants, usually a one-person or two-person company. This increasing competition has meant that clients preferred to maintain more suppliers on their preferred list."

Internally, Manpower's systems and processes were identified as an area that needed improvement. Key issues were identified as being:

- Lack of standardization/consistency in branches and between teams.
- Old and slow processes.
- Inefficient candidate handling processes.
- Too many applications and no end-to-end solution.

One of the R&SS regional operations managers identified processes as one of the greatest challenges: "Our processes are very long. They are not fully integrated and therefore we double handle a lot of work." Furthermore, the lack of integration was seen as having competitive impacts, with one of the members of the senior management team explaining: "Our technology needs continuous upgrading. We don't have an end-to-end recruiting system. We've got various brilliant applications but at times we lose speed as they are not totally integrated. We need to focus on our databases and make them more aligned towards customers' and consultants' needs and requirements. They should be made more users friendly and precise. For example, one should be quickly able to search for job specs or other requirements. We have got legacy systems and there is a cost of changing them."

The nature of the industry also posed significant challenges in relation to the management of human capital. While the consultant was important—being the candidate- and client-facing resource—hiring and retaining skilled and effective consultants was difficult. McLachlan, who was also director of corporate services, claimed, "For the company there is a continuous battle in finding the right consultant, the client- and candidate-facing resources. The industry has a large attrition rate that we need to manage. We are continuously bridging the gaps, if any, in the leadership and management skills at business unit level." The current issues with the people side of the business were many, but the most important were:

- Finding the right consultant.
- Low staff retention.
- Slow career growth.

Finally, in implementing the new strategic direction, the whole organization was going through a change management process. Many within the organization considered it important to inculcate the right culture to support these initiatives. Challenges identified related to developing a high performance culture were:

- Changing the bureaucratic corporate culture.
- Shift required from customer service to sales culture.

The issues relating to the cultural readiness of Manpower to pursue the new strategic initiatives were summarized by one member of the senior management team as follows: "We need to focus on staff advocacy and engagement for achieving our targets. There is a service culture. Our people do selling but not as a selling culture. A selling culture is that if you have ten candidates you will place all of them, but in a service culture you will only focus on what is demanded by the customer and not what you can sell. We want to move to that culture of selling."

WHAT NEXT?

Varina Nissen and her team believed their biggest challenge was to use the available information to evaluate the implementation and achievement of current strategic objectives and the initiatives, to help focus the business on the lead indicators of success, and refine the current strategic thinking if required to adapt to the emerging conditions and issues.

Abercrombie & Fitch: An Upscale Sporting Goods Retailer Becomes a Leader in Trendy Apparel

Janet L. Rovenpor
Manhattan College

On November 10, 2005, Abercrombie & Fitch (A&F) celebrated the opening of a new 36,000-square-foot, four-level flagship store on Fifth Avenue and 56th Street in Manhattan. The timing was perfect—right ahead of the busy Christmas shopping season during which the retailer hoped to sell large quantities of cashmere sweaters, Henley long-sleeved fleeces, hand-knit wool sweaters, polo shirts, and jeans. The Fifth Avenue store, considered a prototype for other flagship stores, featured dark interiors, oak columns, bronze fixtures, and a central staircase with frosted glass-block flooring. A mural by the artist Mark Beard of muscular, skin-showing rope climbers in a setting from the 1930s was prominently displayed. "We're really excited to be back on Fifth Avenue. We're really trying to build the character of the brand. We had a little store in Trump Tower that closed in 1986, and we have been looking on Fifth Avenue for a few years. This is a prestige location and great for the positioning of the brand," commented CEO Michael Jeffries.[1]

In an attempt to gauge customer reaction to the opening of the new store, *New York Magazine* surveyed 75 teenagers, asking them what the A&F brand meant to them. Answers were varied: "It's gross." "It's overpriced." "It's stylish and sleek." "It's very logotistical." "It projects the typical image of the perfect American male—good at school and masculine." "It was cool up until we were 16. Then it got this dumb-jock-meathead image."[2] Perhaps

such contradictory statements were just what A&F's senior executives wanted. Consumers either loved or hated the company, its products, and its image. Part of the trendy retailer's competitive strategy, in fact, was to stir up controversy, go against convention, and appeal emotionally to its youthful customers.

A&F's Fifth Avenue store symbolized the values the retailer held: sensuality, a youthful lifestyle, a love for the outdoors, and fun with friends. It was the culmination of the retailer's creative endeavors to design and implement an exciting store format that drew shoppers in and captivated them. The loud music, appealing visuals, and perfumed interiors encouraged teenagers to hang out and browse.

A&F had come a long way from its early beginnings in 1892. Back then, A&F was considered a luxury sporting goods retailer with conservative tastes that appealed to affluent clients, including adventurers, hunters, presidents, and heads of royal families. President Theodore Roosevelt, for example, purchased snake-proof sleeping bags for a 1908 African safari at an Abercrombie store. Admiral Richard Byrd bought equipment for his 1950s expedition to Antarctica.

A&F's competitive strategies seemed to be working. In 2006, the specialty retailer operated 850 stores in 49 states, the District of Columbia, and Canada. It had 6,900 full-time and 69,200 part-time employees. Its 2005 revenues were $2.78 billion, and its net income was $334 million. It planned to open its first European store in London in 2007. *Apparel* magazine ranked A&F number four in terms of profitability (net income as a percentage of sales) among apparel retailers in 2006 (up from number five in 2005).

At the same time, questions existed regarding the retailer's long-term success. Would teenagers, A&F's primary target market, remain loyal to the company and its products? Could A&F bring back some of the shoppers it had alienated because of its treatment of minority employees and its racy slogans on its T-shirts? Would A&F be able to maintain its competitive advantage in a fragmented industry in which new entrants from both the United States as well as from overseas markets were intent on imitating A&F's strategies? Should CEO Jeffries be concerned with the exodus of talented senior executives from his top management team? Who would eventually succeed Jeffries? Would the retailer's new corporate governance and diversity initiatives pay off?

THE U.S. SPECIALTY APPAREL INDUSTRY

A&F was considered a specialty retailer. Retailers in this category sold products in specific merchandise categories (e.g., apparel, footwear, office supplies, home furnishings, books, jewelry, toys). Numerous small to midsized firms existed. They survived by catering to local tastes and preferences. Sometimes, their financial performance was adversely affected when a competitor entered their niche or when the preferences, lifestyles, and demographics of their target markets changed. As young people became interested in electronics and began spending more and more time playing video games, for example, the fortunes of retailers like Best Buy rose at the expense of retailers like Toys "R" Us.[3]

Specialty apparel retailers opened stores in shopping malls and constructed freestanding units along major roadways. The firms enhanced their capabilities to sell products via directing mailings of catalogs and through Web sites equipped with shopping-cart technologies. To compete with mass merchandisers and department stores, they tried to: (1) maintain high prices and high-quality merchandise; (2) cultivate customer loyalty through various membership programs; and (3) promote their own private-label brands. J. Crew, for example, offered high-end, limited-edition items (e.g., crocodile sling backs and silk wedding dresses) that created excitement and enticed

consumers to buy early at full prices. Chico's FAS Inc. offered a customer loyalty program, Passport Club, that gave customers discounts and other benefits when their purchases exceeded $500.

In 2005 and 2006, the price of oil surged above $70 a barrel. This contributed to a corresponding rise in gasoline prices (e.g., the average retail price for a gallon of gasoline reached $3.07 in 2005, up 65.9 percent from 2004).[4] As consumers used more of their income on fuel and drove their vehicles less frequently, they spent less on goods and services. Retailers who catered primarily to low- to moderate-income Americans (e.g., Gap Inc.'s Old Navy division) experienced a decline in same-store sales. Retailers who served more affluent Americans (e.g., Chico's FAS and Nordstrom's) or who served teenagers and children (e.g., A&F, American Eagle Outfitters, and Wet Seal) benefited from an increase in same-store sales. The latter group of retailers was not significantly affected by rising energy costs.[5]

Believing that "trend transcends age," A&F catered to cool, attractive, fashion-conscious consumers offering products to meet their needs through different life stages—from elementary school to postcollege.[6] The retailer managed four brands:

- A&F: Repositioned in 1992, A&F offered apparel that reflected the youthful lifestyle of the East Coast and Ivy League traditions for college students. In 2006, there were 361 A&F brand stores in the United States (close to its capacity of 400 stores).

- Abercrombie: Launched in 1998, Abercrombie targeted customers ages 7–14 with fashions similar to the A&F line. There were 163 stores in 2006.

- Hollister Company: Launched in 2000, Hollister Company targeted high school students with lower-priced casual apparel, personal care products, and accessories. It promoted the laid-back, California surf lifestyle. There were 318 stores in 2006, a number that had the potential to double.

- Ruehl: Launched in 2004, Ruehl sold casual sportswear, trendy apparel, and leather goods to postcollege consumers ages 22 to 35. Its line of clothing was inspired by the lifestyle of New York City's Greenwich Village. The merchandise was more upscale and more expensive than the A&F line. There were eight stores in 2006.

A&F had three main competitors. Two—American Eagle Outfitters Inc. (AEOS) and Gap Inc.—were publicly held firms, and one—J. Crew Group, Inc. (JC)—was a privately held firm. For basic comparative financial data, see Exhibit 1. Data for JC were unavailable because the retailer was privately held.

Based in Warrendale, Pennsylvania, AEOS sold lower-priced casual apparel and accessories to men and women ages 15–25. The Schottenstein family (who held interests in Value City Department and Furniture Stores) owned 14 percent of the retailer. AEOS operated over 850 stores in the United States and Canada, with approximately 40 percent of its stores located west of the Mississippi River. Revenues in 2005 were $2.3 billion (an increase of 22.7 percent from 2004); net income reached $294 million (an increase of 38 percent from 2004). AEOS planned to launch two new store concepts in 2006. Martin + Osa would be a clothing store selling denim and active sportswear targeting men and women ages 24–40. Aerie was an intimate apparel sub-brand that would be operated adjacent to existing AEOS stores and as stand-alone stores.

JC operated 200 retail and outlet stores in the United States. With a joint venture partner, it also had 45 stores in Japan. Millard "Mickey" Drexler, former CEO of Gap Inc., headed the retailer; Texas Pacific Group (a private equity firm) owned 56 percent of JC. While revenues in 2005 were $804 million (up 14 percent from 2004), the company suffered a net loss of $100 million (double the losses in 2004). JC planned to launch Madewell, a casual clothing store for women selling merchandise at prices 20 to 30 percent lower than JC prices. It also was preparing an initial public offering of common stock of $355 million.

Whereas JC was the smallest of A&F's direct competitors, Gap was the largest, with 3,000 stores worldwide. Gap stores sold basic casual clothing and accessories for children, men, and women. Revenues in 2005 were $16 billion (a decrease of 1.5 percent from 2004); net income was $1.1 billion (a decrease of 3 percent from 2004). Gap Inc. also operated Banana Republic (high-quality, fashionable apparel) and Old Navy (low-priced trendy clothing). Its most recent entry was Forth & Towne (stylish apparel for women over 35). Gap's CEO, Paul Pressler, struggled to turn around the retailer's poor performance, which began in 2000 (before he arrived) when the company overexpanded, assumed too much debt, and made a few fashion-related miscalculations.

A&F'S EARLY BEGINNINGS

A&F was founded in 1892 by David T. Abercrombie (see Exhibit 2 for key milestones in A&F's history). Abercrombie was a civil engineer, topographer, and colonel in the Officers Reserve Corps. He was also an avid hunter and fisherman. The first store was located on Water Street in lower Manhattan. Ezra Fitch, a lawyer and one of Abercrombie's best customers, became a partner in 1900. The two men frequently argued. Fitch continued to run the company after Abercrombie resigned in 1907.

A&F's 12-story building on Madison Avenue and 45th Street opened in 1917. It featured a log cabin and casting pool on the roof and a rifle range in the basement. The store's location was excellent. By 1923, Madison Avenue and 45th Street had become the "heart" of the "specialized shop trade."[7] Near A&F's flagship store were Brooks Brothers, Tiffany Studios, Eastman Kodak, and Maillard's. The Roosevelt Hotel was just undergoing construction. Abercrombie died in 1931 at the age of 64; Fitch died of a stroke aboard his yacht in Santa Barbara, California, in 1930 at the age of 65.

A&F's managers promoted it as "The Finest Sporting Goods Store in the World." An early advertisement announcing the opening of a new store on 36th Street appears in Exhibit 3. A&F was known for its expensive and exotic goods as well as for its affluent clientele. It was possible to buy an antique miniature cannon for $300, a custom-made rifle for $6,000, or a Yukon dog sled for $1,188. Presidents William Taft and Warren Harding purchased golf clubs at A&F. President Dwight Eisenhower bought hunting boots for $55 for his walks in the woods at Camp David. Other famous customers were: Amelia Earhart, Greta Garbo, Charles Lindberg, Clark Gable, the Duke of Windsor, Howard Hughes, and Ernest Hemingway.

A&F was not just a place to purchase sporting goods and rugged apparel. It was also a place where individuals could learn new skills and get involved in the community. In 1923, the Adirondack Club held its annual meeting in A&F's log cabin. Its members discussed whether or not an open season should be declared on beavers whose dam-building activities were causing floods that damaged timber and ruined trout streams. In 1966, A&F held a lecture on how

Exhibit 1 **Comparative Financial Information for Abercrombie & Fitch (A&F), American Eagle Outfitters, and Gap**

	A&F				American Eagle Outfitters				Gap			
	2005	2004	2003	2002	2005	2004	2003	2002	2005	2004	2003	2002
Operating revenues (in millions)	$2,785	$2,021	$1,708	$1,596	$2,309	$1,881	$1,520	$1,463	$16,023	$16,267	$15,854	$14,455
Net income (in millions)	$334	$216.4	$204.8	$194.9	$294	$213.3	$60	$88.7	$1,113	$1,150	$1,030	$477.5
Net income as a % of operating revenues	12.0%	10.7%	12.0%	12.2%	12.7%	11.3%	3.9%	6.1%	6.9%	7.1%	6.5%	3.3%
Earnings per share ($)	$3.83	$2.33	$2.12	$1.98	$1.94	$1.55	$0.59	$0.62	$1.26	$1.29	$1.15	$0.55
Return on assets	18.7%	15.8%	17.2%	22.1%	18.3%	16.0%	7.5%	12.6%	12.6%	11.3%	10.2%	5.4%
Return on equity	33.6%	28.3%	25.5%	29.0%	27.8%	26.7%	9.8%	16.4%	20.5%	23.7%	24.4%	14.3%
Current ratio	1.9	1.6	2.4	2.8	2.99	3.3	2.8	3.0	2.7	2.8	2.7	2.1
Debt/capital ratio (%)	0	0	0	0	0	0	2.1%	2.8%	16.5%	27.6%	34.2%	44.2%
Debt as a % of net working capital	0	0	0	0	0	0	4.1%	5.7%	NA	46.4%	59.3%	96.1%
Annual high-low stock price	$74.10–44.17	$47.45–23.07	$33.65–20.65	$33.85–14.97	$34.04–19.45	$23.88–7.91	$11.69–6.60	$15.22–4.88	$22.70–15.90	$25.72–18.12	$23.47–12.01	$17.14–8.35

NM = Not meaningful.

NA = Not available.

Sources: Standard & Poor's Industry Surveys: Retailing Specialty; data for 2005 from company 10-K reports and Hoover's.

Exhibit 2   **Key Milestones in A&F's History**

1892	A&F was founded by David T. Abercrombie, an engineer, topographer, outdoorsman and colonel.
1900	Ezra Fitch, a lawyer from Kingston, New York, became Abercrombie's business partner.
1907	Abercrombie resigned from the company.
1917	A&F's 12-story building on Madison Avenue and 45th Street opened.
1928	Ezra Fitch resigned as president. He was succeeded by James S. Cobb.
1929	A&F acquired an interest in Von Lengerke & Detmold, a gun, camp, and fishing chain based in Chicago.
1935	A&F earned a net profit of $148,123, up from $123,424 in the previous year.
1940	Otis Guernsey was elected president and CEO.
1943	A&F earned a net profit of $286,694.
1958	A store in San Francisco opened.
1961	John H. Ewing became president and CEO, succeeding Guernsey. Earl Angstadt became the president and CEO in the mid-1960s.
1962	A&F opened a store in Colorado Springs.
1963	A&F's opened a store in Short Hills, New Jersey.
1967	A&F acquired the Crow's Nest, a nautical supply store with a national mail order business.
1968	Sales peaked at $28 million and net income rose to $866,000.
1970	Angstadt resigned. He was replaced by William Humphreys. Henry Haskell, a major shareholder, soon replaced Humphreys as CEO. A&F lost money every year until 1977.
1972	A store in a Chicago suburb opened.
1977	A&F declared bankruptcy.
1978	A&F was acquired by Oshman's Sporting Goods Inc.
1988	The Limited acquired A&F from Oshman's.
1989	Sally Frame-Kasaks was named president and chief executive of A&F. She left the company in 1992.
1992	Michael Jeffries became president and chief executive of A&F.
1996	A&F was spun off from The Limited as an independent company.
1999	There were 186 A&F stores and 13 Abercrombie stores.
2001	A&F opened a new 260,000-square-foot corporate office and a 700,000-square-foot distribution center in New Albany, Ohio.

to capture a musk ox bare-handed without harming it. In 1967, A&F ran a fishing clinic in which experts discussed tackle, knot tying, and trout angling techniques. In 1973, A&F served flambé quail, prepared in the log cabin's fireplace, in celebration of a talking cookbook it had produced. The cookbook contained two 40-minute cassettes and a booklet of recipes printed on waterproof and greaseproof plastic.

Throughout its early history, A&F did a good job keeping up with its customers and with changing fashions. During World War II, when activities such as parlor skeet and military board games were popular, A&F sold a wooden box that could be filled with water and used to blow sailboats from side to side. In the 1940s, barbeque picnics in fields outside country homes became the latest fad arriving from the West. A&F sold high-quality BBQ equipment and insulated canvas bags to keep drinks cold. In 1964, A&F made a splash when it developed the capacity to sell

a cashmere sweater with a lifelike reproduction one's pet embroidered on it. It sold resort wear with a fruit motif in the 1940s and Bermuda length culottes in the 1960s. A&F had a clearly defined target market. CEO Anstadt said, "We aren't out for the teenage business. Our customers are on the go and have the time and the money to enjoy travel and sport."[8]

A&F had its share of problems. Some were typical of all retailers throughout the decades, and some were atypical. During the early 1940s, A&F stores were low on inventory. Commerce had been disrupted by the wartime effort. It was difficult to import goods from abroad. Manufacturers were busy making binoculars, field glasses, saddles, and marine clocks for use by the Army and Navy. A&F wrote to its customers, asking them if they would like to sell optical or sporting goods in satisfactory condition back to the retailer so that the items could be refurbished and resold to new customers. One year, the Office

Exhibit 3 **An Early A&F Advertisement in the *New York Times* 1912**

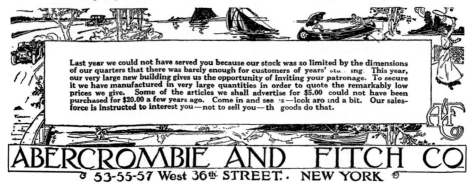

Opening

We Cordially Invite You to Inspect Our New Store

We maintain at this address, the finest Sporting Goods Store in the world. We want you to visit the establishment—we are proud of it, and we are proud of the stock we have to show you. It comprises everything for the Great Out of Doors, each article the BEST for its purpose and most of them exclusive. You can't get them elsewhere.

For a good many years, this concern, The Abercrombie & Fitch Co., occupied a small, exclusive store at 57 Reade Street, in the dingy downtown district where buyers came only because they HAD to—because they could not buy elsewhere the things they bought from us. We have been known the world over not only as the one place where the big Nimrods, Explorers, Hunters, Trappers, Fishermen,—the whole Out-of-Door Brotherhood were outfitted, but as a sort of informal clearing house of information for them. We outfitted Col. Roosevelt for his trip into Africa—Stewart Edward White speaks of our outfits in his textbooks—our peculiar specialty of having the RIGHT thing, the CORRECT thing and finally the EXCLUSIVE thing was recognized by the adept many years ago. Our business grew by word of mouth—by talks over camp fires and at club tables, because when once a man or woman found us, they had found the ONLY one there was and took a pride in passing on the good news. We outgrew our store—we outgrew the building—and now we have our own building on 36th Street. So long as we

had to move, we moved to a place where you could get at us—right in the centre of your shopping district.

We have the finest store of its kind in the world. We have not merely the finest stock of our sort in the world, but we carry the ONLY correct things for the purpose. We have broadened our business and to bring this about, we have manufactured in quantities impossible before because of the restrictions of space in our old quarters. All the economies due to manufacturing and buying on a wholesale plan are reflected in the very low prices of the goods we offer you.

We want you to see our Out-of-Door Clothing for Men and Women and for Boys. We want you to see our complete outfits for camping, for canoeing, for fishermen, for golfers, for every 'one of the sports. We want you to see to what lengths we have gone to provide not only the best, but the exactly RIGHT and the EXCLUSIVE thing for your favorite sport, the thing you have always wanted but couldn't get elsewhere because it didn't EXIST elsewhere.

EZRA H. FITCH, President

Last year we could not have served you because our stock was so limited by the dimensions of our quarters that there was barely enough for customers of years' sta .. ing. This year, our very large new building gives us the opportunity of inviting your patronage. To secure it we have manufactured in very large quantities in order to quote the remarkably low prices we give. Some of the articles we shall advertise for $5.00 could not have been purchased for $20.00 a few years ago. Come in and see s—look aro nd a bit. Our salesforce is instructed to interest you—not to sell you—th goods do that.

ABERCROMBIE AND FITCH CO
53-55-57 West 36th STREET. · NEW YORK

of Price Administration placed limits on civilian consumption of rubber products. This caused a rush on golf balls sold by A&F. A&F joined other retailers in asking customers to do their Christmas shopping early—in November. A lack of manpower had overwhelmed the postal services and caused delays.

At least twice in A&F's history, a customer used one of the guns on display in an A&F shop to commit suicide. The first shooting occurred in 1932, when the son of a famous horse breeder killed himself. The second shooting occurred in 1968 when an immigrant from Czechoslovakia killed himself. Subsequently, extra care was taken to ensure that every gun was fitted with a trigger lock and kept in locked showcases. Customers were no longer handed guns or ammunition over the counter; upon purchase, the firearms were delivered to their homes.

Employee theft and shoplifting occurred. In 1915, for example, Gustave Touchard Jr., a champion tennis player, was charged with stealing 48 dozen golf balls worth $288 from an A&F store on 36th Street. He had worked at the store as a manager of its sporting department. In 1923, a well-dressed woman was caught with 21 yards of Scotch tweed cloth hidden in the ulster (i.e., a bulky overcoat) she was wearing. The theft occurred a few weeks after two sisters who shopped at Macy's while carrying small dogs in their arms were caught with stolen items in their wide sleeves. In 1969, inventory shrinkage (from bookkeeping errors, internal theft, and shoplifting) totaled $1 million (up from between $600,000 and $700,000 the previous year). This contributed to the retailer's pretax loss for the year.[9]

Between 1970 and 1976, A&F continued to incur financial losses. In the fiscal year ending January 31, 1976, A&F incurred a net loss of $1 million on sales of $23.8 million.[10] The loss followed annual deficits ranging from $287,000 to $540,000 every year since 1970.[11] A&F's best year had been in 1968, when it reported pretax earnings of $866,000 on sales of $28 million.[12] Managers began to search for a possible buyer of the firm. No one was seriously interested.

In August 1976, A&F filed for bankruptcy. It held a sale to liquidate its inventory of $8.5 million. A sign in the retailer's Madison Avenue store read: "They say we're stuffy so we're moving the stuff out at tremendous reductions on all floors."[13] After the sale, the stores were closed. A&F's difficulties were attributed to several factors: competition from mass marketers (e.g., Hermann's World of Sporting Goods) that sold discounted merchandise; the lack of professional managers and leadership turnover (the retailer had had three different CEOs in its last six years); high overhead costs; and a dearth of customers who could afford its exotic, high-priced items.

In 1978, Oshman's Sporting Goods Inc. of Houston acquired A&F's name, trademark, and mailing list for $1.5 million. A&F's slogan was changed from "The Finest Sporting Goods Store in the World" to "The Adventure Goes On." The new owners had studied A&F's business model for two years. According to A&F president Jerry Nanna, "We examined the original business, took it apart and retained the good qualities. We also retained some of the legendary old products that Abercrombie had and expanded their variety. But we dropped most of the tailored clothing that proved to be a drain."[14] The owners believed that they could bring A&F styles up-to-date for the 1980s. The chain expanded to 12 stores; sales of $20 million were expected in 1982.

In 1988, The Limited Inc. acquired 25 A&F stores and the A&F catalog business for $47 million from Oshman's. Two additional stores were closed. At the time, The Limited operated a chain of 3,100 stores that sold women's apparel. In 1992, Michael Jeffries became president and chief executive of A&F, a retailing unit of The Limited. A new format was introduced. The chain began to carry casual, classic American clothes for 20-something men and women. A&F became one of The Limited's fastest-growing divisions. The number of stores grew from 40 in 1992 to 113 in 1996. Its sales increased at a compounded annual rate of 40.3 percent during those same years.[15] In 1996, The Limited spun off A&F. Jeffries stayed on as CEO.

SENIOR EXECUTIVES AND CORPORATE GOVERNANCE

Michael Jeffries got his start in retailing at an early age when he helped his father select the toys that were sold in the family's chain of party supply stores. He also enjoyed organizing and designing the window and counter displays. Born in 1944, Jeffries received a BA in economics from Claremont McKenna College and an MBA from Columbia University. He entered the management training program of Abraham & Straus (a New York department store that belonged to Federated) in 1968. From there, he went on to start a women's clothing store, Alcott & Andrews, which later failed. He worked in merchandising at Paul Harris, which also went bankrupt.[16]

In his flip-flops, polo shirt, and torn jeans, Jeffries embodied the casual look of A&F more than anyone else. He made sure that A&F's apparel reflected the lifestyles of college students. Teams of designers, merchandisers, and marketers visited college campuses once a month to talk to students and find out what they liked and how they spent their time. On one of those visits in 1998, Jeffries saw someone wearing nylon wind pants. A&F was quick to make its own version of the pants. Tom Lennox, A&F's director of corporate communications and investor relations once said, "We just believe that it is our job to position Abercrombie and Fitch as the coolest brand, the brand with the greatest quality, the aspirational brand of college students."[17]

A&F's success did not make Jeffries complacent. He was quoted as saying, "Every morning I'm scared. I'm superstitious. I come in every morning being afraid to look a yesterday's figures, and I want everyone else to have that same kind of fear."[18] He worked hard and constantly traveled from store to store. He was always thinking of ways to extend the A&F brand, with a fifth concept in the planning stage. Jeffries had a few eccentric habits. He went through revolving doors twice, parked his black Porsche at an odd angle in the company's parking lot, and wore the same lucky shoes when he reviewed financial reports.[19] It was almost as if he felt that his firm's good fortune could change at any time. Perhaps he realized that his primary target audience—teenagers—was fickle and that trendy apparel quickly became outdated.

Between 2003 and 2006, A&F had three different chief financial officers and two different chief operating officers. The latter position remained unfilled. In July 2003, Wesley McDonald, who had been A&F's chief financial officer (CFO) for four years, left to become CFO of Kohl's Corporation. He was replaced in February 2004 by Susan Riley, who had held CFO positions at Mount Sinai Medical Center, Dial Corporation, and Tambrands Inc. In August 2005, Riley resigned for family reasons and returned to her home in New York City. Michael Kramer became A&F's new CFO. He had been the CFO of the retail unit of Apple Inc. He also had retail experience working for Gateway Inc., The Limited, and Pizza Hut. He had a BA in business administration and accounting from Kansas State University and was a certified public accountant.

Seth Johnson was A&F's chief operating officer (COO) between 2000 and 2004. Before that, he had been its CFO. Johnson was credited with keeping costs down by reducing payroll and travel expenses. He was responsible for installing computer systems to help A&F's distribution system run more efficiently. He had aspired to a CEO position and was offered such an opportunity at Pacific Sunwear of California Inc. Robert Singer, the former CFO of Gucci, became the next president and COO in 2004. After 15 months on the job, Singer resigned to become the CEO of Barilla Holdings SpA. Disagreements about international expansion were cited as the reason for his departure. Singer's duties were divided between John Lough (executive vice president of logistics and store operations) and Michael Kramer (CFO). Search for a replacement began.

Unlike other retailers, A&F did not have division presidents for its brands. Merchants from different businesses reported directly to the CEO. They did not work within a particular brand. Instead, they led categories (e.g., denim or outerwear). They were responsible for these brands across each of the company's divisions. That way, their expertise and knowledge could best be leveraged and exploited.

A&F encountered criticism from shareholders regarding executive compensation and the composition of its board of directors. In February 2005, shareholders charged A&F directors with wasting corporate assets by paying CEO Jeffries $22.9 million in salary, bonus, and stock options. The company settled the lawsuit and Jeffries agreed to reduce his $12 million bonus to $6 million and to forgo new stock options for two years. The bonus was contingent on meeting specific earnings targets. Jeffries would receive the full $6 million bonus if A&F's earnings per share increased by 13.5 percent between February 1, 2005, and January 31, 2009.[20]

Shareholders also expressed concern over the independence of A&F's board of directors. John W. Kessler, chair of the compensation committee, had financial ties to the retailer. As chair of a real estate development firm owned by The Limited's CEO, Les Wexner (Jeffries's former boss), Kessler sold the land on which A&F built its headquarters in 1999. He received a fee for finding the site. Kessler's son-in-law, Thomas D. Lennox, was A&F's director of investor relations and communications. Samuel Shahid, president and creative director of the advertising agency that received $2 million a year from A&F for its services, was a board member until May 2005. He was replaced by Allan A. Tuttle, an attorney for the luxury goods maker Gucci Group. While

Tuttle did not have financial ties to A&F, he was a friend of Robert Singer, who at the time was A&F's president and COO.

A&F denied wrongdoing and settled the lawsuits to "avoid the uncertainty, harm and expense of litigation."[21] As part of its agreement with shareholders, A&F promised to provide more public information about executive compensation and to add independent members to its board and its compensation committee.

A&F underwent a formal investigation by the U.S. Securities and Exchange Commission regarding insider selling of stock. In June and July 2005, when A&F's stock price was high, Jeffries sold 1.6 million shares worth $120 million. In August, share prices declined after the company announced it would miss Wall Street expectations regarding its second-quarter earnings. A&F was also sued for making false and misleading statements of monthly and quarterly sales figures and for failing to disclose that profit margins were declining and inventory rising. The company announced that it was cooperating with the SEC and that the shareholder lawsuit had no merit.

STORE CONCEPT AND MARKETING STRATEGIES

When customers walked into an A&F clothing store in a local mall, they were often greeted by a young, handsome salesperson wearing the latest fashion in casual attire. The store's lights were dimmed and posters of attractive models wearing its trademark cargo pants and polo shirts adorned the walls. In some stores, chandeliers made of fake deer antlers or whitewashed moose antlers hung from the ceilings. Apparel was neatly folded and placed on long wooden tables. The retailer's hip, trendy, all-American look was reinforced by the playing of loud dance music and the spraying of men's cologne. The intent was to provide a sensual experience that appealed to a shopper's senses of sight, smell, and sound. According to marketing expert Pam Danziger, "Shoppers are rejecting the old concept of 'hunting and gathering' shopping in favor of a more involved, interesting, dynamic retail experience."[22] A&F was able to successfully implement an exciting store format.

Every A&F store was designed according to one of several specific models created at company headquarters. The retailer wanted complete control over its brand and to communicate a consistent message in all stores across the nation. Jeffries himself made sure the model stores were "perfect."[23] The prototypes were photographed and sent to the store managers of the individual outlets for replication. Jeffries was known for paying attention to every detail. He visited stores and made sure that the clothes were folded correctly. He approved of the background music to be played in the stores and selected the appropriate volume level for all locations. He even gave suggestions on how mannequins could be made to look more rugged and masculine.

A&F's Web site (www.abercrombie.com/anf/lifestyles/) was created to match the feel and aura of its stores as much as possible. It featured striking black-and-white images of young people in outdoor settings. Through the "A&F Lifestyle" link, Web surfers could download screen savers or send e-postcards to one another. According to *Forbes* magazine, the A&F Web site's best feature was the photo gallery showing images of the models that made A&F famous. Its worst feature was that the models pictured did not have the effect of showcasing the company's line of clothing.[24]

A&F had an enviable target market. It catered to teenagers, whose population in the United States was expanding. In 2003, there were 32 million teens living in the United States This number was expected to rise to 35 million by 2010. Moreover, teens spent approximately $170 billion on goods and services in 2002, with one-third of that amount going toward apparel.[25] Spending in 2005 was lower—$159 billion[26]—but teen retailing was considered to be somewhat recession-proof. Although teens worked for low wages, they had multiple revenue streams—babysitting, paper routes, part-time jobs, and assistance from parents.[27] They usually did not have financial obligations (no mortgages or bills to pay). Also, parents were more likely to spend money on their children than on themselves.

A&F's busy seasons were spring and fall The company hired extra employees during the back-to-school and holiday seasons. A&F was typically able to sell its merchandise at its customary premium prices without resorting to frequent off-price sales and deep discounting. Management feared that greatly reduced sale prices would cheapen the A&F brand. The company economized on advertising and promotional expenditures by relying extensively on word-of-mouth advertising. The retailer claimed that it spent less than 2 percent of net sales on marketing in 2004.[28] It also kept careful watch on administrative expenses and bargained hard for lower prices from its suppliers. Premium prices and economical operating costs were a merchandising formula that worked well for A&F.

A&F tried to introduce two or three new items in its stores every week. It launched a new men's line, Ezra Fitch, which featured high-quality apparel made from cashmere, velvet, and leather. A&F cultivated brand loyalty. Shoppers could join Hollister's Club Cali and receive gift cards based on how much they spent. Instead of marking down items the day after Thanksgiving (the start of the busy Christmas shopping season), the company issued invitations to after-hours parties with new bands., In 2004, preferred customers who spent $1,000 a year or more were invited to a live concert given by Ryan Cabrera. The concert was also shown on big-screen televisions in 50 other Hollister stores around the nation.

A&F generated controversy. Adults often reacted negatively to the company's catalog photographs, revealing clothes, and racy slogans. But teenagers and young adults were thought to respond positively to A&F's provocative advertising, perhaps in a show of rebellion against the traditional values and/or because they closely identified with the life-style images and hip trends portrayed in A&F ads. Teens were reluctant to shop in the same stores as their parents. Some observers believed that A&F purposely created controversy and engaged in risky practices to attract attention, draw in shoppers, and sell more products. As an analyst with Midwest Research in Cleveland remarked, "Abercrombie is not a company that really cares about backing away from controversy. They use controversy as a free advertising gig and are successful in driving traffic into the stores."[29]

The following is a list of some of A&F's controversial moves:

- In July 1998, a story entitled "Drinking 101" appeared in an A&F back-to-school catalog. It featured recipes for alcoholic beverages and a game for helping students decide which drink to mix. After being criticized by Mothers Against Drunk Driving (MADD), A&F deleted the story and sent postcards to students who received the publication by mail reminding them to "be responsible, be 21, and don't ever drink and drive."[30]
- In April 2002, A&F sold a line of T-shirts with Asian cartoon characters and matching ethnic slogans: "Wong Brothers Laundry Service Two Wongs Can Make It White"; "Wok-N-Bowl"; "Buddha Bash: Get Your Buddha on the Floor." The retailer took the T-shirts off store shelves after protests from college students from campuses around the country. A&F's spokesperson Hampton Carney apologized, saying, "It is not, and never has been, our intention to offend anyone. These were designed to add humor and levity to our fashion line. Since some of our customers were offended by these T-shirts, we removed them from all our stores."[31]
- In May 2002, A&F sold thong underwear for girls ages 10 and up with sexual phrases such as "Eye Candy" and "Wink, Wink" printed on the front. Family-advocacy groups and Christian organizations protested. The line was recalled in Washington, D.C., area stores.[32]
- In December 2003, under heavy criticism from parents and consumer groups, A&F decided to stop publishing its provocative catalog, A&F Quarterly. Its holiday issue featured nude models and articles about group sex and masturbation.[33]
- In March 2004, Bob Wise, governor of West Virginia, asked A&F to pull from its shelves T-shirts with the slogan "It's All Relative in West Virginia." Wise explained that the slogan was offensive because it referred to a stereotype that West Virginia was a state that condoned incest.[34]
- In October 2004, officials of USA Gymnastics sought the immediate removal of a T-shirt depicting a male gymnast performing on the still rings alongside the phrase "L is for Loser." They wrote a letter to Jeffries saying its members would be encouraged to withdraw their support of the chain.[35]
- In May 2005, A&F quietly pulled a line of T-shirts from its stores with slogans that read "I Brews Easily," "Candy is Dandy but Liquor is Quicker," and "Don't Bother I'm Not Drunk Yet." The company was criticized for glorifying underage drinking and promoting a lifestyle that was illegal for its target audience. Pressure came from the International Institute for Alcohol Awareness, a public advocacy group that worked to reduce underage drinking. This time, A&F responded to criticism before the issue was reported in national newspapers.[36]

- In November 2005, 24 participants in the Allegheny County Girls as Grantmakers program organized a "girlcott" of A&F stores to protest its "attitude T-shirts," which featured such slogans as "Who needs brains when you have these?"; "Blondes Are Adored, Brunettes Are Ignored"; "All Men Like Tig Old Bitties." Other groups—such as Peace Project, an antidiscrimination student club in Norwalk, Connecticut, and the Women & Girls Foundation of Southwestern Pennsylvania—joined in. A&F pulled two of the more offensive T-shirts, and its executives agreed to meet with several of the protestors. The girls suggested that the retailer print more appropriate slogans, such as "All This and Brains to Match" and "Your Future Boss." They hoped the firm would launch such a line and donate a portion of revenue to groups like theirs.[37]

LOGISTICS AND SUPPLY CHAIN MANAGEMENT

A&F operated solely as a retailer. It assumed responsibility for creating and managing its brands. Unlike other businesses, A&F did not distribute its apparel and accessories through wholesaling, licensing, or franchising. Abercrombie clothing could not be purchased in department stores or in discount stores. It could, however, be purchased online via the A&F Web site. E-commerce transactions generated over $100 million in business a year.[38]

During 2005, A&F purchased merchandise from approximately 246 factories and suppliers located around the globe, primarily in Southeast Asia and Central and South America. It did not source more than 50 percent of its apparel from any single factory or supplier. The design and development process for a garment took anywhere from 6 to 12 weeks.[39] Retailers struggled to reduce this time so as not to get stuck with merchandise that had lost its fashion appeal. A&F made the process more efficient by centralizing its design services at its New Albany, Ohio, headquarters, which reduced overseas travel of executives.

A&F also operated a distribution center in New Albany, Ohio. Merchandise was received, inspected, and then distributed to stores via contract carriers. It was here that concepts for new divisions were created and prototypes for new stores were constructed. The new formats were kept secret until their launch dates.

A&F launched an anticounterfeiting program in an effort to protect its brand and prevent low-cost manufacturers in Asian factories from making imitations of its products. Local authorities seized 300,000 pairs of fake Abercrombie jeans (worth $20 million) in a raid of a Chinese warehouse in 2006. The retailer hired a former FBI agent to head a 10-person department to conduct investigations overseas and to work with foreign authorities.[40]

A&F began experimenting with radio frequency identification (RFID) technology in its Rhuel stores, which sold higher-priced and higher-quality merchandise than its other stores. Tags that could be monitored electronically were sewn into the seams of garments. Employees could thus track garments, enabling them to quickly return items that had been left in dressing rooms or placed in the wrong spots on the sales floor. The technology could also be used to prevent theft and to differentiate between authentic products and counterfeit goods.

A&F'S FINANCIAL PERFORMANCE

In 2005, A&F achieved revenues of $2.785 billion, an increase of 37.8 percent from 2004. Its net income rose to $334 million, an increase of 54.3 percent from 2004 (see Exhibit 4). Earnings per share rose to $3.66 from $2.28. A&F opened 63 new stores and added 20,600 employees to its payroll. It had no long-term debt. It repurchased 1.8 million shares of common stock for $103.3 million and paid dividends of 60 cents a share, for a total of $52.2 million.

A&F'S SOCIALLY RESPONSIBLE PRACTICES

A&F held fund-raising activities that benefited local charities and communities. Every Christmas holiday season, shoppers were invited into its stores to have their picture taken with its models. The fee was $1, which the retailer matched. The proceeds were donated to foundations such as Toys for Tots or the Juvenile Diabetes Research Foundation. It held the "A&F Challenge," an action-packed outdoor event, at its headquarters in New Albany, Ohio.

Exhibit 4   **Summary of A&F's Financial Performance, 2001–2005**

	2005	2004	2003	2002	2001
Operating revenues (in thousands)	$2,784,711	$2,021,253	$1,707,810	$1,595,757	$1,364,853
Gross profit (in thousands)	1,851,416	1,341,224	1,083,170	980,555	817,325
Operating income (in thousands)	542,738	347,635	331,180	312,315	268,004
Net income (in thousands)	$ 333,986	$ 216,376	$ 204,830	$ 194,754	$ 166,600
Earnings per share	$3.66	$2.28	$2.06	$1.94	$1.62
Dividends declared per share	$0.60	$0.50	0	0	0
Total assets (in thousands)	$1,789,718	$1,386,791	$1,401,369	$1,190,615	$929,978
Capital expenditures (in thousands)	$256,422	$185,765	$159,777	$145,662	$171,673
Long-term debt (in thousands)	0	0	0	0	0
Shareholder's equity (in thousands)	$995,227	$669,326	$857,765	$736,307	$582,395
Number of stores	851	788	700	597	491
Gross square feet of store space	6,025,000	5,590,000	5,016,000	4,358,000	3,673,000
Number of employees	69,100	48,500	30,200	22,000	16,700

Source: A&F 10-K report

Participants, who paid an entry fee of $25, went on a 20-mile cycling tour, a 5K inline skating tour, and a 5K run. They heard live music from a band, enjoyed food and drinks, and received a T-shirt. All proceeds went to the Center for Child and Family Advocacy in Columbus, Ohio. The company's largest donation—$10 million—went to a children's hospital in Columbus in June 2006. The hospital's new trauma center would bear the A&F name.

A&F also sometimes got involved in issues at the supplier end of its business. In 2004, it joined a boycott of Australian merino wool in an effort to force ranchers to end a cruel procedure known as mulesing; although intended to protect lambs from flies, the procedure was said to cause pain and suffering. Even though A&F did not purchase much Australian wool, wool producers feared that the retailer would set a precedent and that other retailers would soon join the boycott. They agreed to end the practice of mulesing by 2010 or sooner.[41]

ORGANIZATIONAL CULTURE AND HUMAN RESOURCE MANAGEMENT

A&F's core corporate values were "nature, friendships and having fun."[42] These values were reflected in everything from the decor of the retailer's stores and the casual attire of its employees to the layout of A&F's headquarters in New Albany, Ohio, and to the firm's advertising messages. If there were no customers to serve, employees might throw a football to one another in the store. The retailer's home page on its Web site featured a tree house that could be downloaded as wallpaper.

A&F's headquarters, built in 2001, was situated in the woods along Blacklick Creek in New Albany, Ohio. Its campuslike setting served as a continual reminder to employees that the firm's target audience was college students. It was also designed to encourage teamwork and creativity. Instead of sitting at desks in individual cubicles, employees engaged in collaborative work at long tables in doorless conference rooms. Employees could walk along paths in the woods to relax, think, or seek inspiration for a new idea. There was no executive suite. Jeffries had no desk or office. He also worked in a conference room with a view of the grounds from large windows.

Employees enjoyed healthy meals that included roast chicken, international dishes, salads, fruit juices, and gourmet coffees in the full-service cafeteria. They traveled from building to building on scooters and were allowed to bring their skateboards. A bonfire pit provided the atmosphere of an outdoor summer camp. Employees worked out in the gym. One of the architects said, "A&F wants to give back to the people who work there. That's why they can go to that rusty barn the first thing in the morning, or get sweaty in the gym and then go to work, have a great meal and then go back to work again. It reinforces the idea that this is community."[43]

Store managers visited nearby fraternities and sororities to recruit salespeople, or "brand representatives." They were encouraged to ask attractive shoppers in their stores if they wanted to apply for a sales position. Tom Lennox, A&F's investor relations and communications director, acknowledged that the firm liked to hire job candidates who looked great. "Brand representatives are ambassadors to the brand. We want to hire brand representatives that will represent the Abercrombie & Fitch brand with natural classic American style, look great while exhibiting individuality, project the brand and themselves with energy and enthusiasm, and make the store a warm, inviting place that provides a social experience for the customer," Lennox said.[44] The company ran a manager-in-training program for seniors and graduates. Promotion to store manager could occur one year after completing the training.

Brand representatives were expected to adhere to a dress code outlined in an Abercrombie Associate's Handbook. Hair was to be neatly combed and attractive; makeup was to be worn to enhance natural features and create a fresh, natural appearance; fingernails were not to extend more than a quarter of an inch beyond the tip of the finger, and nail polish was to be a natural color; mustaches, goatees, and beards were unacceptable; jewelry was to be simple and classic—only women were allowed to wear earrings, they could have no more than two earrings in each ear, and each earring could be no larger than a dime and could not dangle.[45]

In 2000, the California Department of Industrial Relations received complaints from several A&F employees who said that they were forced to buy and wear the company's clothes on the job. One woman, in another part of the country, later claimed that she spent more on clothes for work than she earned at the store. Such company policy might have violated a state work uniform law that required employers to supply the clothing when they wanted workers to wear specific apparel. In 2003, A&F settled the lawsuit in California for $2.2 million without admitting wrongdoing. Employees received reimbursements ranging from $180 to $490 depending on their job status and the amount of money spent on clothing.[46] The case spurred similar lawsuits across the state and the rest of the nation against The Limited, Gap, Chico's, and Polo Ralph Lauren. In some states,

lawyers used the federal Fair Labor Standards Act, which required employers to pay minimum wage, to argue that sales associates ended up with less than minimum wage after spending their earnings on store clothing.

A&F's legal problems were only just beginning. In July 2003, two former A&F employees filed a lawsuit accusing the company of failing to pay overtime wages when they were required to work 50–60 hours a week. The plaintiffs claimed that they were sales associates, with no management responsibilities, but were classified as managers so that the retailer could avoid paying overtime. According to the Federal Fair Labor Standards Act and the Ohio Minimum Fair Wage Standards Act, non-exempt employees had to be paid time and a half for work in excess of 40 hours a week.

In June 2003, lawyers for nine plaintiffs filed a lawsuit against the retailer for discriminating against minorities in its hiring practices and job placement. It allegedly cultivated an "overwhelmingly white workforce" and steered minority applicants into less visible jobs.[47] Former A&F employees appeared on CBS's television program *60 Minutes* and said that A&F was interested in hiring employees who fit a certain look. Anthony Ocampo worked at an Abercrombie store during his Christmas break from Stanford University. When he returned to get a summer job, he was told that he could not be rehired because the store already had too many Filipinos working there. Eduardo Gonzalez, another Stanford University student who was Latino, was told that he could only work in the store's stockroom or as part of the overnight crew; at Banana Republic, he was asked if he was applying for a management position. Carla Grubb, an African American student at California State University at Bakersfield, felt she was not treated fairly because she was scheduled to work only during closing times and was asked to wash the front windows, vacuum, and clean the mannequins.

In November 2003, another lawsuit was filed against A&F on behalf of a New Jersey woman who claimed that her application for a sales-associate position was denied because she was African American. A&F denied that it discriminated against minorities. It claimed that minorities represented 13 percent of all its store associates (which exceeded national averages). The U.S. Equal Employment Opportunity Commission also initiated a lawsuit, claiming that

A&F violated parts of the Civil Rights Act of 1964. Store managers reported that they were instructed to discard job applications if the candidates did not possess the right look.

In November 2004, A&F paid $50 million (including legal fees) to settle the discrimination lawsuits. It agreed to hire a vice president of diversity, provide training in diversity and inclusion to its employees and managers, increase the number of minority employees in sales and store management positions, enhance its compliance and oversight processes, and use more minority models in its advertising. The retailer promised that within two years its sales force would consist of 9 percent African Americans, 9 percent Latinos, its current percentage of Asians, and 53 percent women.[48] A&F was told to stop recruiting from predominantly white fraternities and sororities. It agreed to hire 25 full-time diversity recruiters who would seek new hires from historically black colleges, minority job fairs, and minority recruiting events. Michael Jeffries issued a statement: "We have, and always have had, no tolerance for discrimination. We decided to settle this suit because we felt that a long, drawn-out dispute would have been harmful to the company and distracting to management."[49]

Todd Corley became A&F's new vice president of diversity. Due to his efforts, A&F established a $300,000 grant for scholarships for the United Negro College Fund, became a sponsor of the Organization of Chinese Americans' College Leadership Summit, became a sponsor of the National Black MBA Association, and offered internships for minority college juniors seeking retail-management careers through Inroads Inc.

A&F'S FUTURE

A&F was likely to face increased competition. One of its direct rivals, American Eagle Outfitters, was able to outperform A&F in terms of profitability and assume the number three rank (compared to A&F's fourth-place rank) among U.S. publicly traded apparel companies in 2006, as listed by *Apparel* magazine. Newcomers to the specialty apparel industry, as well as large department stores, sought to imitate A&F's product offerings. Metropark, for example, a West Coast chain for 20- to 35-year-old shoppers, opened its 15th store in Atlanta, Georgia. It planned to open an additional 50 stores by 2007. The retailer

sold brand-name casual apparel made by such designers as True Religion and Joe's Jeans. It also tried to create a nightclub-like atmosphere in its stores with flat-screen televisions playing music videos and a lounge offering energy drinks and magazines.

Department stores, too, began to diversify their lines by stocking merchandise from new suppliers and by promoting their own in-house labels. Oved Apparel launched Company 81 in 2005 as "an Abercrombie for department stores."[50] It began to sell distressed denim, chinos, shorts, golf jackets, blazers, and graphic T-shirts at the wholesale level. It provided department stores with in-store signage and imagery from its advertising campaign to complement its merchandise. Federated Department Stores, which operated Macy's and Bloomingdale's, created an in-house label called American Rag. Its merchandise was similar in style to A&F's but priced more moderately.

As if sensing the encroachment of competitors, A&F began an unusual effort to improve its customer service. In the past, brand representatives acted more like models than salespeople. They were known for their snobbish disregard of shoppers. They did not talk to customers until they were within five feet of each other.[51] Some customers felt intimidated. Under COO Singer, store greeters were positioned in the entrance to each store and salespeople were posted in every section. A vice president of training was hired to work with store staff. The number of employees was increased and hours of store operations were extended. The added attention helped reduce merchandise shrinkage.[52] Nonetheless, progress in customer service may have been derailed by the departure of Singer from the company.

A&F also needed to be vigilant regarding the needs and preferences of its target markets. Teenagers were perceived as being fickle. According to experts on the reactions of millennials to pop culture, they were difficult to influence because they thought more independently and changed their minds more frequently than previous generations. They would find the "emphasis on the physicality of models" in A&F advertisements unappealing.[53] The emerging trend toward ethical consumption was also something to be watched. Young people began to purchase food products and clothing with Fair Trade labels. They were committed, for example, to purchasing coffee that was organically grown from suppliers who paid bean pickers higher wages than the going rate.

They bought T-shirts that were not made in overseas sweatshops.

The challenges for A&F executives in 2006 and beyond were to anticipate competitor moves, to improve customer service, and to maintain consumer loyalty. They needed to hire talented top managers who could work well alongside CEO Jeffries. These domestic imperatives came at a critical time for the retailer. It was just about to enter the European market, with its first store on Savile Row in London. Pamela Quintiliano, a WR Hambrecht retail analyst, gave the expansion plan a nod of approval: "Abercrombie is an incredibly strong brand name, and there's a hunger for American brands around the world."[54]

Endnotes

[1]J. E. Palmierie and D. Moin., "A&F Hits Fifth Avenue Fray," *DNR 35* (November 14, 2005), p. 4. Retrieved April 19, 2006, from ABI/Inform (Proquest) database.

[2]D. Penny, "The Abercrombie Report," *New York* 38 (November 21, 2005), p. 6. Retrieved April 19, 2006, from ABI/Inform (Proquest) database.

[3]M. Souers and M. Normand, "Specialty Retailers Demonstrate Resilience in Face of Adversity," *Standard & Poor's Industry Surveys: Retailing: Specialty*, January 12, 2006.

[4]Ibid.

[5]Ibid.

[6]A&F, 10-K report; J. Sheban, "Oh, Canada!," *Knight Ridder Tribune Business News*, February 26, 2006, p. 1. Retrieved April 18, 2006, from ABI/Inform (ProQuest) database.

[7]"Rapid Growth in Specialized Shop Trade Madison Avenue in the Forties The Centre," *New York Times*, February 18, 1923. Retrieved April 21, 2006, from ProQuest Historical Newspapers database.

[8]"New Face for Fashion at Abercrombie & Fitch," *New York Times,* September 11, 1965, p. 14. Retrieved April 21, 2006, from ProQuest Historical Newspapers database.

[9]"Changes Weighed for Abercrombie," *New York Times*, September, 1970, p. 73. Retrieved April 21, 2006, from ProQuest Historical Newspapers database.

[10]"Abercrombie Reports Loss of $1 Million in Fiscal Year," *New York Times*, August 26, 1976, p. 68. Retrieved April 21, 2006, from ProQuest Historical Newspapers database.

[11]R. Hanley, "Abercrombie & Fitch Put Up for Sale," *New York Times*, July 20, 1976. Retrieved April 21, 2006, from ProQuest Historical Newspapers database.

[12]I. Barmash, "Abercrombie & Fitch in Bankruptcy Step," *New York Times*, August 7, 1976, p. 47. Retrieved April 21, 2006, from ProQuest Historical Newspapers database.

[13]C. G. Fraser, "'Stuffy' Abercrombie's Gets Sale Relief," *New York Times*, August 29, 1976, p. 47. Retrieved April 21, 2006, from ProQuest Historical Newspapers database.

[14]I. Barmash, "New Guise for Abercrombie's," *New York Times*, November 9, 1982, p. D1. Retrieved April 21, 2006, from ProQuest Historical Newspapers database.

[15]D. Canedy, "After Unbuttoning Its Image, a Retail Legend Comes to Market," *New York Times*, September 1996, p. F3. Retrieved April 21, 2006, from ProQuest Historical Newspapers database.

[16]R. Berner, "Flip-Flops, Torn Jeans—And Control," *BusinessWeek*, May 30, 2005, p. 68. Retrieved December 12, 2005, from ABI/Inform (ProQuest) database.

[17]M. Cole, "Facing a Brave New World," *Apparel* 45 (July 2004), p. 22. Retrieved April 20, 2006, from ProQuest Historical Newspapers database.

[18]M. Pledger, "Abercrombie & Fitch Focuses on American College Audience," *The Plain Dealer*, June 22, 1999, p. 2S. Retrieved April 19, 2006, from Lexis/Nexis Academic database.

[19]Berner, "Flip-Flops."

[20]"Abercrombie CEO Benefits Settlement OKd." *Los Angeles Times*, June 15, 2005. Retrieved May 18, 2006, from ABI/Inform (Proquest) database.

[21]Ibid.

[22]M. Wilson, "The 'Pop' Factor," *Chain Store Age* 82 (April 2006), p. 78. Retrieved May 18, 2006, from ABI/Inform (Proquest) database.

[23]Denizet-Lewis, "The Man."

[24]"Web Site Reviews: Abercrombie & Fitch," Forbes.com, www.forbes.com/bow/b2c/review. jhtml?id=6833 (accessed May 1, 2006).

[25]J. Ablan, "Trend Setter," *Barron's* 83 (March 31, 2003), p. 21. Retrieved April 20, 2006, from ABI/Inform (Proquest) database.

[26]P. B. Erikson, "Companies Focus on Youthful Influence for Prosperity," *Knight Ridder Tribune Business News*, April 16, 2006, p. 1. Retrieved April 21, 2006, from ABI/Inform (Proquest) database.

[27]Ibid.; Ablan, "Trend Setter."

[28]Presentation at the Merrill Lynch Retailing Leaders & Household Products & Cosmetics Conference, March 25, 2005, www.abercrombie.com (accessed April 22, 2006).

[29]T. Turner, "Retailer Abercrombie & Fitch Angers West Virginia Residents with New T-Shirt," *Knight Ridder Tribune Business News*, March 24, 2004, p. 1. Retrieved November 8, 2004, from ABI/Inform (Proquest) database.

[30]"Abercrombie & Fitch Plans to Delete Drinking Section," *The Wall Street Journal*, July 30, 1998, p. 1. Retrieved November 8, 2004, from ABI/Inform (Proquest) database.

[31]G. Kim, "Racism Doesn't Belong on T-shirts," *Knight Ridder Tribune Business News*, April 28, 2002, p. 1. Retrieved April 21, 2006, from ABI/Inform (Proquest) database.

[32]D. DeMarco, "Abercrombie & Fitch Pulls Children's Thong," *Knight Ridder Tribune Business News*, May 23, 2002, p. 1. Retrieved November 8, 2004, from ABI/Inform (Proquest) database.

[33]J. Caggiano, "Abercrombie & Fitch Drops Racy Publication," *Knight Ridder Tribune Business News,* December 11, 2003, p. 1. Retrieved November 8, 2004, from ABI/Inform (Proquest) database.

[34]T. Turner, "Retailer Abercrombie & Fitch."

[35]"USA Gymnastics Upset with Abercrombie & Fitch," *Washington Post*, October 8, 2004, p. D2. Retrieved November 8, 2004, from ABI/Inform (Proquest) database.

[36]K. S. Shalett, "Shamed off Shelves," *Times-Picayune*, May 20, 2005, p. 1. Retrieved December 12, 2005, from ABI/Inform (Proquest) database.

[37]M. Haynes, "'Girlcott' Organizers Meet with Abercrombie & Fitch Execs over T-shirts," *Knight Ridder Tribune Business News*, December 6, 2005, p. 1. Retrieved December 12, 2005, from ABI/Inform (Proquest) database.

[38]"Abercrombie & Fitch Co. at Banc of America Securities Consumer Conference," *Fair Disclosure Wire*, March 17, 2005. Retrieved May 24, 2006, from ABI/Inform (Proquest) database.

[39]K. Showalter, "A&F Readies $10 Million Expansion," *Business First of Columbus*, March 11, 2005, http://columbus.bizjournals.com/columbus/stories/ 2005/03/14/story5.html (accessed April 29, 2006).

[40]J. Sheban, "Fighting Fakes: Abercrombie Enlists Expert to Help It Combat Counterfeiting," *Knight Ridder Tribune Business News*, February 3, 2006, p. 1. Retrieved April 23, 2006, from ABI/Inform (Proquest) database.

[41]J. Sheban, "Abercrombie & Fitch's Wool Boycott Helps End 'Mulesing' Practice," *Knight Ridder Tribune Business News*, November 12, 2004, p. 1. Retrieved April 19, 2006, from ABI/Inform (Proquest) database.

[42]D. Gebolys, "Inside Abercrombie & Fitch," *Columbus Dispatch*, May 24, 2001, p. 1F. Retrieved April 19, 2006, from LexisNexis Academic database.

[43]K. Showalter, "Abercrombie & Fitch: Campus Reflects the True Nature of New Albany Firm's Culture," *Business First of Columbus*, August 24, 2001, http://columbus. bizjournals.com/ columbus/stories/2001/08/27/focus1.html?page=3 (accessed April 29, 2006).

[44]S. Greenhouse, "Going for the Look, but Risking Discrimination," *New York Times*, July 13, 2003, p. 12. Retrieved November 9, 2004, from ABI/Inform (Proquest) database.

[45] B. Paynter, "Don't Hate Me Because I'm Beautiful," *Kansas City Pitch Weekly*, September 4, 2003. Retrieved February 12, 2005, from LexisNexis Academic database.

[46]"Abercrombie & Fitch Settles Dress Code Case," *Houston Chronicle*, June 25, 2003, p. 2. Retrieved November 4, 2004, from ABI/Inform (Proquest) database.

[47]T. Turner, "Cincinnati Suit Charges Abercrombie & Fitch with Failing to Pay Overtime," *Knight Ridder Tribune Business News*, July 9, 2003, p. 1.

[48]J. Sheban, "Abercrombie & Fitch: The Face of Change," *Columbus Dispatch*, July 31, 2005, p. F1. Retrieved April 19, 2006, from ABI/Inform (Proquest) database.

[49]S. Greenhouse, "Abercrombie & Fitch Bias Case Is Settled," *New York Times*, November 17, 2004, p. A16. Retrieved May 24, 2006, from ABI/Inform (Proquest) database.

[50]L. Bailey, "The New South: Young Men's & Streetwear," *DNR* 35 (August 22, 2005), p. 94. Retrieved June 1, 2006, from ABI/Inform (Proquest) database.

[51]Paynter, "Don't Hate."

[52]S. King, "Style and Substance: Abercrombie & Fitch Tries to Be Less Haughty," *Wall Street Journal*, June 17, 2005, p. B1. Retrieved June 23, 2005, from ABI/Inform (Proquest) database.

[53]V. Seckler, "Brands' Challenge: Bridging Gap with Young People," *Women's Wear Daily* 77 (April 12, 2006). Retrieved June 1, 2006, from ABI/Inform (Proquest) database.

[54]Sheban, "Oh Canada!"

New Balance Athletic Shoe Inc.

H. Kent Bowen
Harvard Business School

Robert S. Huckman
Harvard Business School

Carin-Isabel Knoop
Harvard Business School

On a pleasant August evening in 2005, Jim and Anne Davis enjoyed what was meant to be a relaxing dinner at home. As they finished their meal, however, they could not help but turn their attention to a headline in that morning's *Boston Globe*, a copy of which sat on their kitchen table: "Adidas to buy Reebok." For over 30 years, the Davises had been the sole owners of New Balance Athletic Shoe Inc., one of the top five producers of athletic footwear in the world. Given their experience in the industry, they had suspected for some time that an Adidas–Reebok transaction might be in the works. Nevertheless, the formal announcement caused them to wonder about the implications of this deal for New Balance. By bringing together Adidas and Reebok—the second- and third-largest producers of athletic footwear, respectively—this transaction would create a juggernaut that would rival Nike, the largest competitor in the industry. Although the Davises did not have to answer to Wall Street concerning their competitive plans, they knew that many in the industry—including their own employees—would soon be asking for their response.

Lately, the Davises had focused significant attention on an initiative called New Balance Executional Excellence (NB2E), the goal of which was to increase the quality and efficiency of the company's operational processes through the application of lean manufacturing. Started less than one year earlier,

NB2E already had provided evidence of early improvement, and the Davises did not want to lose the growing enthusiasm for this initiative among New Balance's 2,600 associates. Further, they realized the importance of staying true to the private company's unique operating philosophy, strategy, culture, and history. Nonetheless, they could not help but wonder whether New Balance's priorities needed to be adjusted in light of the shifting competitive landscape.

THE U.S. ATHLETIC SHOE INDUSTRY[1]

The United States was the world's largest market for athletic shoes and apparel, accounting for roughly 50 percent of the $32 billion spent globally each year. Between 2004 and 2009, the number of pairs of athletic footwear sold in the United States was expected to grow at a 6.3 percent annual growth rate (8.4 percent growth among women who accounted for 58 percent of all pairs purchased), reaching 530 million pairs in 2009. Industry trade group Sporting Goods Intelligence projected that the $9 billion branded-shoe market in the United States would grow by 8 percent in 2005. Growth was slowing in part because of a maturation in consumer interest in sports and fitness activities.

In recent years, manufacturers moved to combine fashion and comfort to appeal to a broader range of consumers, namely those who wore athletic shoes for casual purposes. Concurrently, a combination of technological developments and style improvements in athletic footwear helped drive growth.

Exhibit 1   **Comparative Data on Major Athletic Footwear and Apparel Companies, 2004**

	Worldwide Sales ($ million)	Footwear Sales ($ million)	Total Assets ($ million)	Net Income ($ million)	Employees
Nike, Inc.	$13,739.7	$7,299.7	$8,793.6	$1,211.6	26,000
Adidas-Salomon AG	8,057.0	3,384.0	6,015.8	402.3	17,023
Reebok International Ltd.	3,785.3	2,430.3	2,440.6	192.4	9,100
Puma	1,903.3	1,065.8	1,263.1	320.0	3,910
New Balance	1,500.0	NA	NA	NA	2,600
Asics	1,330.0	811.3	1,146.0	43.8	4,160
Fila USA	955.2	NA	NA	(85.0)	2,300
K-Swiss	508.6	508.6	336.2	75.2	480
Vans	330.2	NA	NA	(30.0)	1,890
Saucony	166.7	140.8	96.3	10.4	340

Note: All figures are for 2004, except Vans (2003) and Fila USA (2002).

Source: Standard & Poor's Research Insight, Hoover's, *BrandWeek*, June 20, 2005, p. S53, www.newbalance.com (accessed April 15, 2006).

While leather continued to be the most popular material for athletic footwear uppers, some firms, such as Adidas-Salomon (Adidas), had developed shoes with so-called "smart textiles" and microchips that adjusted fit based on the wearer's activity, height, weight, and running terrain.

Nike maintained a comfortable lead ahead of its competitors with 43 percent of the total global market for athletic shoes and apparel (see Exhibit 1 for sales and financial data for leading firms in the industry). Within the U.S. footwear market, Nike accounted for 36 percent of the market, while Adidas, Reebok and New Balance held on to a variable 8–12 percent each (Exhibit 2). Appendix A provides a brief description of each of the top competitors in the industry.

The acquisition of Reebok by Adidas would create a firm that rivaled Nike in terms of size and would boost Adidas's share to roughly 20 percent of the U.S. footwear market. Though the Adidas-Reebok transaction was notable for its size, it reflected a broader recent trend of consolidation in the athletic footwear industry. In July 2003, Nike acquired Converse, a Massachusetts based manufacturer of court and casual shoes, for $305 million. In June 2005, Stride Rite—the maker of casual footwear brands Keds and Sperry Top Sider—announced its intention to acquire Saucony, a $170 million manufacturer of specialty running shoes and apparel based in Peabody, Massachusetts.

With respect to worldwide marketing, Nike outspent its rivals, spending $213 million in measured media in 2004, compared to Adidas' $89 million and Reebok's $42 million.[2] For the first 10 months

of 2005, for example, New Balance total advertising expenditure was $17.3 million.[3] For all companies, a large portion of worldwide media expenditure was geared toward the marketing of footwear brands in the United States (Exhibit 2).

In addition to spending more on marketing than New Balance, most of its competitors produced their shoes outside of the United States, largely because the manufacturing of athletic footwear was highly labor intensive and required relatively low levels of worker skill. As a result, China had become the largest manufacturer of athletic footwear for the U.S. market, commanding 85 percent of the category.[4] The U.S. trade deficit in shoes was expected to continue to deepen, as more manufacturers shifted production offshore. The deficit had increased about 7 percent per year since 1999, reaching 379 million pairs in 2004. Overall, Americans purchased 2.2 billion pairs of shoes and boots in 2004, enough to give each man, woman and child there 7.7 new footwear options that year.[5]

Distribution Channels

In 2005, the American sneaker market was divided into several discrete retail channels catering to periodically overlapping demographics that defined themselves by distinctive tastes, buying patterns, and price elasticity. Foremost among these were the "big box" chains such as Wal-Mart, Target, and Sears which together sold an estimated $12 billion in athletic apparel and equipment per year.[6] The second-largest group by sales volume included national

Exhibit 2   **U.S. Athletic Footwear Sales and Media Expenditure by Brand, 2004**

Brand	U.S. Athletic Footwear Sales ($ million)	U.S. Athletic Footwear Media Expenditure ($ million)	Brand Familiarity
Nike	$3,225.0	$134.1	88%
Reebok	1,087.0	31.0	82
New Balance	1,022.0	10.9	58
Adidas	790.0	52.0	80
K-Swiss	395.0	29.0	41
Converse	305.0	3.9	66
Vans	240.0	4.6	27
Puma	209.0	6.2	54

Note: Excludes brands with athletic footwear sales less than $200 million. The total U.S. athletic footwear market was estimated at $9 billion in sales in 2004.

Source: BrandWeek, June 20, 2005, p. S53.

sellers such as Foot Locker, The Sports Authority, Finish Line, and The Athlete's Foot. Next were smaller urban chains that maintained strong ties to tastemakers and arbiters of fashion. These chains typically either sold brands at heavy discounts to younger consumers or catered to high-end customers with very specific needs (e.g., high-performance running). The leading sneaker manufacturers, such as Nike and Adidas, also maintained showcase stores that featured new products in lavish displays accompanied by TV screens and music. These branded outlets were less retail stores than museums to the sneakers of tomorrow and the "classics" made legendary by the likes of Pelé, Chuck Taylor, and Michael Jordan.

With 4,000 stores around the world, Foot Locker was widely recognized as the world's leading retailer of athletic shoes and apparel. Foot Locker contributed slightly less than 10 percent to Nike's annual sales, but Nike products represented as much as 50 percent of sales for Foot Locker. The Sports Authority had 400 U.S. stores, but maintained a broader product base, selling workout equipment, basketball gear, sneakers and sports apparel. Finally, with 598 stores in the United States, Finish Line, originally started in the early 1980s as a discounter whose primary business was in "closeout" sales, prided itself in offering prices that were typically $5 less than other retailers.

Although beholden to the vagaries of fashion and manufacturers' ability to design hit products that would drive traffic into their stores, larger retailers held a great deal of sway over the fortunes of the sneaker companies. For example, even though Converse sneakers were sold through many retail and on-line outlets nationwide, Foot Locker accounted for roughly 20 percent of all Converse sales. Any decision by Foot Locker about Converse's product placement thus could have a material impact on the brand's sales. In another case, a 2003 dispute over promotional practices for Nike shoes caused a costly one-year rift between the manufacturer and Foot Locker.

THE MAKING OF NEW BALANCE

New Balance was founded in Boston in 1906 as New Balance Arch[7] by William J. Riley, a 33-year-old British émigré who committed himself to helping people with problem feet by making arch supports and prescription footwear to improve shoe fit. In 1934, Riley went into partnership with his leading salesman, Arthur Hall. In 1954, Arthur Hall sold the business to his daughter and son-in-law, Eleanor and Paul Kidd. Arch supports and prescription footwear remained the cornerstone of the business until 1961, when they manufactured the Trackster, the world's first performance running shoe made with a ripple sole and available in multiple widths.

During the 1960s, New Balance's reputation for manufacturing innovative performance footwear available in multiple widths grew through word of mouth and grassroots promotions. When Jim Davis bought the specialized shoe manufacturer from the Kidds on the day of the Boston Marathon in 1972, he committed himself to uphold the company's founding values of fit, performance, and manufacturing. He recalled:

> I wanted to buy a company, I was young and single. I didn't have anything, so I had nothing to lose. I looked at it a year before I bought it. At the time, I was in electronics. I passed, because I knew nothing about footwear and not much about sporting goods, other than what I knew from doing sports in college. I got a pair of the shoes, started running in them, and people would come up to me and comment that I must be a good runner. Unable to put a deal together in electronics, with the company still available, I went back, and the guy was desperate to sell it. We paid $100,000 for the company; we put $10,000 down, and the rest of the $90,000 was generated from lowering inventory.

At the time New Balance was primarily a mail-order business with only a handful of U.S. retailers. Jim Davis started traveling around the country to expand retail distribution, and sales grew from $100,000 to around $300,000 over a two-year period. Anne, who would marry Jim in 1984, joined New Balance in 1978 and focused on building a distinct culture for New Balance associates and those who would do business with the company around the globe. Indeed, New Balance's first international sales office and first European manufacturing facility both opened in 1978 in Europe. Since then the brand had expanded from Europe and Asia to the Middle East, Latin America, and Africa.

In the early 1980s New Balance set up new manufacturing facilities in New England and signed on international distributors. In 1982, the company reached the $60 million mark and debuted the well-received 990 running shoe, the first athletic shoe priced at $100.[8] In the 1990s, the company unveiled its New Balance Suspension System to telegraph its emphasis on cutting-edge R&D and its dedication to meeting the needs of performance-oriented runners. The company's commitment to multiple sneaker widths remained a selling point that was reflected in the brand's iconic marketing logo of three differently sized feet.[9]

Being Different

Herb Spivak, executive vice president of operations and a 12-year veteran of the company, provided a picture of New Balance's unique features. He observed:

> Our values have been very, very consistent and reinforced continuously by Jim and Anne Davis. We do not endorse athletes, as an example. We aim to make every one of our shoes a performance product as opposed to just a fashion product. We sell every shoe that we make in multiple widths, because we believe that fit is a critical performance characteristic. We maintain a great percentage of our product in inventory for replenishment, so that dealers can continually get fill-ins when they sell and when they need certain sizes and widths. In contrast, competitors pretty much tell retailers, "OK, tell us six months in advance what you're going to want to buy and we'll deliver it. But it's fixed, and we don't plan on having future inventory." These basic factors, combined with the maintaining of our domestic factories all come together to describe what makes us unique.

Because the company had remained private, Jim Davis felt that he and his colleagues could act more nimbly and be more socially responsible than their more well-heeled competitors. "If we were a public company, I am sure the shareholders would say, 'Close your factories and make the product abroad because you will make more dough for me and my quarterly dividend,'" Davis told the *Boston Globe* in 2004.[10] Davis also felt that the company had products capable of providing solid margins needed to generate the cash flow required to finance growth. As such, the company's balance sheet remained very strong with a seven-to-one ratio of assets to liabilities.

Beyond financial flexibility, other aspects of the company's operations and strategy suggested that it was somehow different from competitors. President and Chief Operating Officer Jim Tompkins noted:

> One thing that sets us apart and that is we are manufacturers. But we are mediocre marketers by design. Our marketing spend as a percent of net revenue is much lower than our competitors. The message that we talk about in the marketplace is different from our competitors' message. And that's what makes the company unique—it is that we are manufacturing- and operations-based, not marketing-based.

Jim Davis emphasized this distinction:

> In the early to mid-1980s, Nike and Reebok were both becoming major players, and everybody said, "You ought to really do this because Nike and Reebok are doing it." Well, we tried a couple times with product and programs and whatever, and we failed, drastically. So then I woke up one morning and I said, "We're not

any good at that. We're really good at this." So we concentrated on doing this instead of that, and thus differentiated ourselves.

Culture

Similar to its unique business model, New Balance's corporate culture developed over time. Teamwork was a critical component. "When you're young and starting up," Jim Davis recalled, "you don't really think in terms of a culture. You just sort of do things a certain way. One day we realized that we're very team-oriented, and that we empower people. When we got to a certain size and maturity, we realized that that's basically what we were all about." Further, New Balance developed a long-standing commitment to social responsibility that, according to Anne Davis, "made people feel good about dealing with the company." For example, after the 2004 Asian Tsunami, New Balance declared that it would match whatever its associates donated. Then retailers wanted to participate, so New Balance decided to match their contributions for a total contribution of $1 million. The company also promised to donate another $1 million if 100 percent participation was reached among associates. In the end, every person in the organization contributed something.

The company's culture was also very entrepreneurial, starting with the owners' willingness to take risks and encourage others to do the same. Anne emphasized that this culture of change and challenge extended to the factory, noting that manufacturing employees, mostly organized in cross-functional teams, represented one of the greatest forces for change in the company. This spirit was also reflected across New Balance's senior managers. Chief Financial Officer John Withee observed, "Continuous improvement is a mantra here. Do the best you can, work cross-functionally, and work towards a common goal."

As an example of a major risk taken relatively early on by the company, Jim Davis pointed to the introduction of the 990 series running shoe in the 1980s, the first $100 shoe at a time when athletic shoes were retailing for about $50. "People said we were nuts," Jim mused, "but we couldn't make them fast enough. People learned from that and became more confident in pushing the envelope." As of 2005, the 990 series still represented the top-selling product for New Balance, accounting for roughly 3.5 percent of the company's sales.

Endorsed by No One

In an industry dominated by endorsement deals and large print and TV campaigns featuring celebrity athletes, New Balance put its energies and investment into research, design, and domestic manufacturing, and let the resulting products speak for themselves. New Balance felt it could eschew celebrity endorsements and position itself as a brand for performance-oriented runners less swayed by fashion trends and popular personalities. New Balance extended its product-focused strategy to its branding efforts in 1992 with its "Endorsed by No One" campaign despite holding only 3 percent of the U.S. market for athletic shoes at the time.[11]

New Balance introduced edgier iterations of the campaign that culminated with an anti-endorsement ad message that actually chided professional athletes for losing sight of the game and focusing disproportionately on endorsement deals. With slightly older core customers (between 25 and 49), New Balance concluded it could afford to take this irreverent tone in commercials. The "For Love or Money" campaign was unveiled in February 2005.[12] The slogan felt "natural to us because it was something that only New Balance can stand in front of," said Paul Heffernan, executive vice president of global marketing. "It's all about everyday athletes playing for the love of the game."[13] By contrast, Reebok introduced a new ad campaign of its own that same month featuring basketball icon Yao Ming, Olympic gold medalist Kelly Holmes, actress Lucy Liu, and tennis player Andy Roddick, with the tagline "I Am What I Am."[14]

The New Balance campaign featured a young basketball player admonishing "some of the pros out there," for their swagger and potentially unsportsmanlike conduct on and off the court that had become accepted behavior in some quarters. Most notably, a game-ending brawl during a Detroit Pistons game in Auburn Hills, Michigan, on November 19, 2004, that erupted after Indiana Pacers' forward Ron Artest leapt into the stands to retaliate against a spectator who had lobbed a cup of beer at players from the stands. The New Balance campaign took a direct approach with an unassailable jibe: "Is fighting in sports ever justified?"[15]

In addition to 30-second TV spots, the campaign included print, billboard, and online ads that posed a series of questions about athletes'—and by extension, their fans'—core values: "Can a losing coach still be a good coach?" and "Which teaches a player more, winning or losing?" Yet another New Balance ad from the same series was even more direct and confrontational: "Just in case you forgot, this is what a pass looks like. . . . *This* is what a floor burn looks like." New Balance was reportedly planning to spend $21 million on its 2006 advertising campaign, which was close to its entire promotional budget for the year.[16]

PRODUCT DESIGN

According to Paul Heffernan, New Balance's focus on width sizing and fit had historically dictated the design of many of the company's products. He explained:

> A 15-year-old who wants a pair of Nike Air Jordans might curl his toes or put on six pairs of socks to make that shoe fit. In that case, purchases are made based on how a shoe looks rather whether it really fits well. The market that is interested in width sizing and fit is a little bit older and more mature; those customers demand a product that is a bit more conservative in its presentation and style. They tend to like a product and buy it again and again and again. It's like a white button-down shirt. I own a white button-down, it wears out, I buy another white button-down.

New Balance had approximately 60 people in product design and development who were involved with efforts on two fronts. One was incremental development of existing models. The second involved the incorporation of new technologies such as Absorb EX—a premium, visible-cushioning technology—and Zip, a patented responsive-cushioning technology scheduled to debut in 2006. Both technologies were oriented toward a younger customer base.

Despite New Balance's desire for long-lived products, Heffernan knew that the company had to remain capable of delivering products to the shorter-cycle, fashion-oriented segments of the market. He noted:

> The 991 series—our franchise shoe of 25 years—stays in line three years. With three years to update that shoe, we can afford to take our time and be more thoughtful. But the more fashion-oriented products often need to churn every 60 to 90 days, which creates a completely different model for product design. The fashion segment cares less about widths and more about time to market, so we need to work under tighter timelines for these products.

Jim Davis felt that in the past five or six years, New Balance had "dropped the ball in a few places, and design is one of them." He added:

> Right now, we are emphasizing design more than we have in the past and are raising the level and stature of design within the organization. Design is going to become more important as time goes on, a much larger factor than it has been. We tend to be a little bit more conservative with design than our competition and stay within a certain realm for a relatively long period of time. Then we find that we might have hit a wall, so we have to come back and reinvent ourselves a little bit and move forward. The manufacturing folks do that every day. The rest of the company is sort of playing catch-up there, and we have to re-invent ourselves a little bit more often than we have in the past.

SALES AND DISTRIBUTION

New Balance had focused more on smaller retailers, running specialty shops, and family footwear shops. John Withee explained, "We are heavily focused on supporting the smaller type of service-oriented customer." New Balance sold its products through approximately 3,500 retailers representing over 12,000 sites, commonly referred to as "doors." Its largest retail customer was Foot Locker, a major chain that, on its own, accounted for over 3,000 doors in the United States. New Balance divided its retailers into two groups—key accounts and specialty dealers (see Exhibit 3). Key accounts were further divided into six strategic accounts and 49 other key accounts. Specialty retailers were subdivided into three major channels: elite running stores (i.e., specialty stores for serious runners); independently owned and operated New Balance stores; and other independent dealers, which were primarily family shoe stores.

Fran Allen, executive vice president for sales and service, noted that strong relationships with both small and large retailers were critical for New Balance. "The importance of independent, specialty retailers to the image of our brand far exceeds their 25 percent share of our sales volume. Obviously, large accounts are extremely important in terms of their sales volume. Consequently, we give both groups a lot of attention and work hard to give each what they need to be successful."

In contrast to competitors, New Balance relied on a sales force that was composed of independent agents. Allen noted, "In the sporting goods industry

Exhibit 3   **New Balance Sales Summary**

Category	Number of Accounts	Number of Outlets	Total New Balance Revenues ($000s)
Specialty Retailers			
Elite running stores	250	350	$ 25,000
New Balance stores	70	130	75,000
Other independent stores	3,100	3,500	150,000
Key Retailers			
Strategic accounts	6	6,000	$360,000
Other key accounts	49	3,000	450,000

Source: Company documents.

there is an unwritten rule—or maybe it is just natural selection—that as you get to a certain point in sales volume, you grow out of an independent sales force. You bring the sales organization in house. At New Balance, we do not have any in-house accounts. We prefer using independent, dedicated sales agencies with an entrepreneurial mindset."

Indeed, all the company's sales agents were independent of—but exclusive to—New Balance. These sales agencies were compensated through a sales-based commission. Under this system, new salespeople might earn $40,000 to $50,000 per year (from which they would cover their own expenses) while the most experienced salespeople could make several hundred thousand per year. Large retail accounts were managed by a total of 10 head sales agents, 6 of whom were strategic account managers (SAMs). Specialty accounts were managed by approximately 100 agents, who worked for independent sales agencies, but were managed by five regional managers employed by New Balance (see Exhibit 4). New Balance was investing in a sales force automation system to increase the agents' productivity.

Despite the fact that these agents were not direct employees of New Balance, Allen—who had been with New Balance 15 years as sales manager—noted that the company was not concerned about these relationships that were unique to the industry. "We have a loyal group of salespeople, and their longevity of service provides us with a distinct edge over our competitors," he explained, attributing this loyalty to the strength of New Balance's leadership and culture. He added:

In 1991, my first year at New Balance, the company sold $84 million in footwear in the United States; last year, we did a little over $1 billion. One of the reasons

Jim Davis liked this sales organization was that he had head sales agents who had been with him for 15 or 20 years before I got here and had gone through some difficult times and stuck with the company.

For smaller, privately owned retailers, New Balance had historically paid an independent sales representative to take product orders and either key them into the New Balance order system or fax them to New Balance's corporate sales office at company headquarters in Allston, Massachusetts. To speed the ordering process, the company had recently invested in what Chief Financial Officer John Withee termed a "state-of-the-art" distribution center and was using technology to leverage this resource, support its retailers, and strengthen its retail relationships. In terms of information technology, a new sales force automation system enabled sales representatives to place direct orders remotely, access New Balance's inventory information, and check on delivery status business-to-business (B2B). A B2B application promised to enable retailers—particularly smaller retailers—to do the same without intervention by the sales representative. Withee added, "This application helps manage the flow of product through the supply chain and is about as vital as you can get in determining our performance."

Going forward, Withee explained, the B2B application would help retailers directly manage basic ordering, thereby freeing up the sales representative to engage with the retailer and make recommendations about new items to carry or options for reducing inventory levels. Concerning retailers, Jim Davis explained:

If you've been selling New Balance shoes for the last 10 years, to sell 1,000 pairs you had 400 pairs in inventory. Assuming you are selling all domestic

Exhibit 4 **Organizational Structure of New Balance's Sales Force**

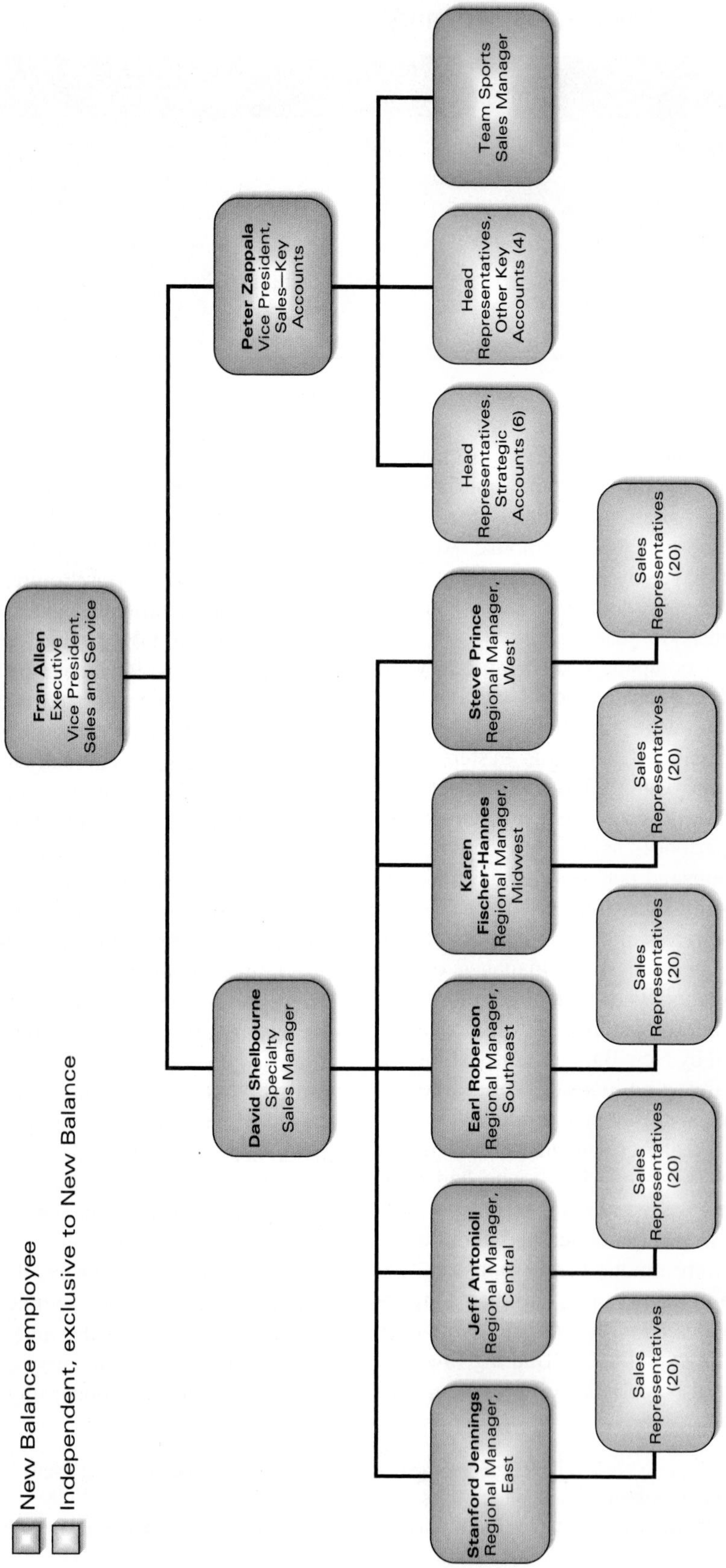

■ New Balance employee

□ Independent, exclusive to New Balance

Source: Company documents.

product, which some of our accounts do, we would say: "We think we can increase your sales next year and lower your inventory at the same time. We will ship to you the day after you order the product, so your inventories can be decreased dramatically. Rather than carrying 400 pairs, you can carry 200 pairs, and sell maybe 1,200 pairs instead of 1,000. And your markdowns are negligible, because your inventory's so low." And we think that's a very compelling argument. We are taking all the risk when we do that.

By shipping quickly and accurately, New Balance offered retailers the ability to build loyal customers of their own. Indeed, according to Jim Davis, New Balance had far the greater consumer loyalty than any of its competitors. "That translates well for the retailer, especially if that retailer's able to satisfy the customer with that 13EEEE, because that customer always wants that 13EEEE. He or she will generally go back to that same retailer to get that product. And retailers know that."

SUPPLY CHAIN AND MANUFACTURING

In contrast to Nike and Reebok, who outsourced nearly all of their production to Asian manufacturers, New Balance used outsourcers for only 75 percent of its U.S. volume. For the remaining 25 percent, final product assembly took place in one of New Balance's five factories in the Northeastern United States. One-third of these domestically assembled shoes were referred to as "cut through assembly" product. For these shoes, New Balance would import finished soles and the raw materials for the upper from Asian suppliers. The uppers would then be fully manufactured and attached to soles in the United States. The remaining two-thirds of New Balance's domestic product was referred to as "sourced upper." For sourced-upper shoes, New Balance would import finished uppers and soles from Asia and would complete the assembly by attaching the appropriately sized uppers and soles at its U.S. factories. The more time-intensive cut-through-assembly product was manufactured at New Balance's factories in Lawrence, Massachusetts; Skowhegan, Maine; and Norridgewock, Maine. Sourced-upper shoes were assembled at these three sites, as well as another factory in Norway, Maine.[17] Exhibit 5 provides an overview of the manufacturing network and supply chain.

Foreign Suppliers

New Balance sourced the soles for most of its shoes from two suppliers in China (suppliers A and B in Exhibit 5). Depending on the shoe, these two firms also supplied either finished uppers or kits containing a significant portion of the materials required to stitch uppers in the United States.[18] Finally, these firms provided a limited amount of fully assembled shoes. These firms shipped to New Balance's three materials warehouses, two in Skowhegan, Maine, and one in Lawrence, Massachusetts.

Historically, it would take approximately one week for New Balance to place a purchase order for components (e.g., soles, uppers, or kits) and have it accepted by the appropriate supplier in China. It would then take roughly six weeks for the supplier to manufacture the required components and an additional five weeks to ship them by boat across the Pacific and transfer them to cross-country transport for delivery to the designated warehouse. Until the early 2000s, New Balance tended to place orders for a particular sole on a monthly basis in batches as large as 20,000 pairs. For a single type of sole, each order would include roughly 20 different SKUs, reflecting different shoes' lengths and widths such as 9D, 10½E, and 12EEE.

John Wilson, vice president for manufacturing, noted that the company had taken several steps in recent years to reduce the lead times from Asian suppliers. First, New Balance had shifted to placing smaller orders of between 2,000 and 10,000 pairs on a weekly basis. In addition, New Balance made arrangements with these suppliers to enable them to "pre-buy" their own raw materials on behalf of the company, thereby reducing the lead time required to produce an order. Based on the above initiatives and other efforts to reduce lead time, the average time from placing a component order with a supplier to having those items available at the New Balance materials warehouses fell from 12 weeks to approximately 9 weeks by 2005.

New Balance also contracted with two other Chinese manufacturers who were responsible for 75 percent of New Balance's foreign final product assembly. These firms shipped finished shoes to several of New Balance's smaller international divisions, but most were bound for the United States and were sent via ship directly to New Balance's product distribution centers in Lawrence, Massachusetts, or Ontario, California. The order-to-delivery lead time

Exhibit 5 **New Balance Supply Chain**

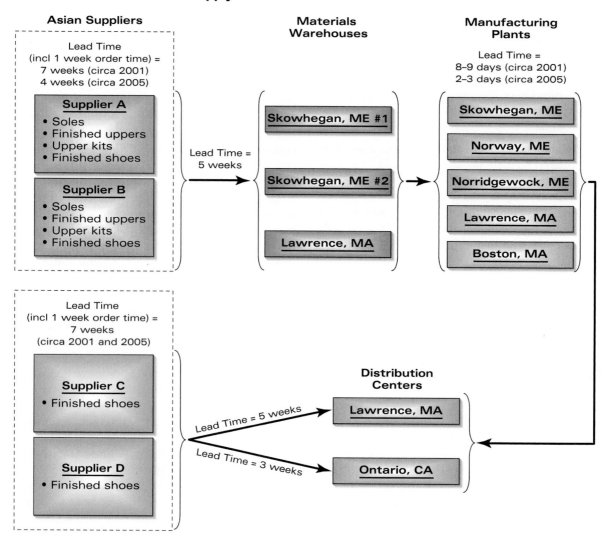

Source: Company documents.

was approximately 12 weeks and 10 weeks for shoes going to Lawrence and Ontario, respectively.

To further shorten lead times, New Balance continued to forge closer partnerships with its Asian suppliers. Jim Davis explained:

> What we learn by doing things domestically, we share with our partners abroad. We are focusing on lead-time optimization, asking them to go downstream two or three levels and work with suppliers to react more quickly to us. In other words, we will share with them how many shoes of a particular type that we are forecasting over the next few months so that they can

go back to their suppliers to let them know what their requirements are going to be.

Materials Warehousing, Manufacturing, and Distribution

As of August 2005, the three warehouses in Skowhegan and Lawrence held approximately $9 million—or 4.5 weeks—worth of raw materials inventory. For shoes that were assembled in the United States,

Exhibit 6   **Standard Process for a "Cut Through Assembly" Conventional Shoe (Flat-Lasted Process)**

- Materials are received and inspected.
- Materials are webbed in the Webbing Dept. This consists of laying several layers of materials, face to face, so when the pieces are cut, they become the left and right parts with one single cut.
- Webbed materials are sent to the Cutting Department, where all the parts for all styles are cut.
- Some shoe parts are sent to the Radio Frequency machine for embossing and bonding of a reinforcing material.
- Other shoe parts are sent to Embroidery, where the emblems are embroidered.
- All shoe parts are kept together in racks with cases of 12 pairs each in the Pre-Fit Department.
- The racks are sent to the Orisol Departments, where many shoe components are stitched together in single pass. This has helped NB to reduce the cost per shoe.
- Some styles require the "N" stitched into each shoe, they are sent to the "N" department.
- All the above operations are done in the flat stage, the sewn parts are two-dimensional (2D). Everything continues to travel in cases of 12 pairs and are sent to the Closing Department.
- In the Closing Department, the shoe components begin to take the form of a shoe as the they are being converted from flat shoe components to their 3D shape.
- From the closing department, the shoes are sent to the Upper-Prep Department. Here uppers, soles and other shoe components are cased together.
- With all of the parts cased together they are sent to the Assembly Department. In this department, the shoes are "Lasted." Tasks in the lasting department consist of:

  — Upper conditioning
  — Slip lasting
  — ToelLasting
  — Side/heel lasting
  — Pounding, which is the act of sanding down any excess material under the shoes
  — Washing or priming as recommended by the Bonding Department
  — Marking the periphery of the sole
  — Cementing to the sole line
  — Cement drying
  — Sole and upper cement activation
  — Sole setting
  — Sole pressing
  — Extracting the last
  — Inserting shoe insert
  — Lacing the shoes
  — Cleaning and/or repairing
  — Inspecting
  — Boxing the shoes in pairs and in cases of 12 pairs

Source: Company documents.

each of the five manufacturing plants placed orders for materials to these warehouses. The required materials arrived at the requesting plant by the next day.

Upon arriving at the factory, the materials were held in inventory briefly before moving to production. Sourced-upper and cut-through-assembly shoes followed different flow paths through the factory. A description of the standard production process for cut-through-assembly shoes appears in Exhibit 6. Industry experts estimated that the labor content for a pair of cut-through-assembly shoes was approximately 25 minutes. In terms of manufacturing cost, labor and overhead each accounted for roughly

25 percent of the total, while materials accounted for the remaining 50 percent. Estimates of the total cost for a cut-through-assembly pair of shoes assembled in the United States was approximately $13 greater than a similar product fully manufactured in Asia. For "sourced upper" pairs, this difference was thought to be about $0.50, due to import duties placed on finished goods entering the United States.

In 2001, the average lead time for a cut-through-assembly batch (typically consisting of 12 pairs of shoes) through a New Balance plant—measured from arrival of the raw materials to loading on the truck as finished product—was roughly 8.5 days. By 2005, the company had reduced this time to 2.5 days through significant attention to process improvement and work-in-process reduction within the plants. Wilson and his colleagues believed that further reductions in manufacturing lead time were attainable.

Following production, domestically assembled pairs were transported via truck either directly to the retailer (in the case of large strategic accounts) or to inventory in the Lawrence or Ontario distribution center. Each of those sites received and filled orders from smaller retailers. Combined, these two distribution centers held roughly 6.4 million pairs of finished shoes.

The New Balance Workforce— A Key to Operations Improvement

The Davises believed that improving the production process at New Balance required widespread initiative and involvement from the company's front line workers. Before joining the New Balance team, these manufacturing employees went through a lengthy selection process. New Balance screened potential employees for their professional or personal experience in team-based environments. For example, the company often looked for employees who had played team sports in high school or college.

New hires were paired up with an experienced employee, known as a "buddy," and were placed in a training team for six to eight weeks until they were comfortable enough to go on a regular production team. "As soon as new employees come in, we train them in the foundations of associate involvement, continuous improvement, and leadership," Anne Davis explained, "but we don't want to put them immediately into an existing team and have them intimidated by the skills that the more experienced members already have."

Another important feature of the company's U.S. workforce was that it was not unionized. Some employees performed two or three jobs on teams—a feature that would not be possible under a strict job classification system. "If one area of the factory is slow and the other one is loaded up," Anne Davis explained, "people willingly go to the next area to make their numbers for the day, and we would not be able to do that if they were unionized."

"It's a flexibility issue. The factories are always changing," Jim Davis explained. "The folks on the factory floor are always pushing us to change things so they can do it better. We wouldn't be able to do that if we were unionized." He added:

> Annie and I are constantly amazed at how flexible these folks are, and how engaged they are in what they're doing. They go home, and they come to work the next day thinking, "How can I do things better? How can I be more productive?" And what we're trying to do is get the whole company to think that way.

Beyond the organization of the workforce, compensation also played a key role in the ability of New Balance's management to leverage employee knowledge and initiative. A few years ago, New Balance briefly moved from individual-based hourly wages to team-based piece rates, but then quickly moved back to the hourly system. Jim Davis explained:

> Teammates put too much pressure on each other under the team-based compensation system. If one person was out of work because she had a sick child at home, there would be too much pressure on the rest of the team to perform, and she came in feeling guilty the next day. So we have also a culture of mutual respect here, and we sat down with our supervisors and we talked about how we might better accommodate these people, and one of the things that we came up with was hourly pay. We did a pilot run for a month or so, and we found that the production when we were compensating them on an hourly

basis was equal to if not better than under the team-based piecework system.

Anne Davis added that the maintenance of hourly compensation helped gain support for continued training of the workforce. "Under the team-based rate, many supervisors saw training as another project, as taking their people away from the job," she said. "With hourly pay they were more willing to send people to training, and by doing training early on, people know right away whether or not they fit in the company."

LEAN MANUFACTURING— NEW BALANCE EXECUTIONAL EXCELLENCE (NB2E)

In 2004, New Balance began New Balance Executional Excellence (NB2E) to apply the principles of the Toyota Production System (TPS) to shoe production. One of the key goals of NB2E was to further reduce the lead time from a retailer's order to its delivery. Tompkins clearly stated his objective for NB2E:

> Our goal is 100 percent delivery of requested product within 24 hours. It may be impossible, but we are going to work toward something very, very close to that—to a position where, for that two or three percent that we can't deliver within 24 hours—we can certainly replenish within, say, four days at the most. And that would be only for the worst-case scenario where we got completely surprised by an order.

According to Tompkins, an essential component of NB2E would be to move the company's manufacturing plants from batch production to single-pair flow. He added:

> Over a period of time I would like to know that when a part of an upper gets cut to what pair of shoes that part is heading. . . . And we might be making several different models in a given factory on a given day, but we would still know that *that* part right there and the one in the other factory over there are going to end up in a shoe that is put on *that* trailer heading to *that* customer. That is where I would like to get to.

Before NB2E, to improve product availability, New Balance was required to resort to what Spivak called "brute force" by greatly increasing finished goods inventory. For the company's flagship shoe, the 991, inventory was doubled to ensure availability for all colors, sizes, and widths. Though there was a significant increase in sales of the 991, the inventory cost was very high.

If NB2E were to be successful—approaching Tompkins' goal of 100 percent availability within 24 hours while reducing inventory levels—manufacturing cycle times would need to be dramatically reduced. These changes required complete realignment of factory operations. Spivak observed:

> Our factory had a classic arrangement with a cutting, an embroidery, a stitching, and an assembly department. Each department did their particular tasks for all styles, and the factory worked on a batch basis. To realign that under NB2E would require a big change. Instead of moving a day's worth of production, we needed to move toward a more continuous flow. Doing this would require us to reduce work in process significantly and get the line associates and supervisors to embrace that change. The real challenge would be to keep making shoes every day while this transformation was ongoing.

THE MARATHON

Glimpsing the brilliant evening sun outside their kitchen window, the Davises could not imagine a more fitting time for reflection. Though New Balance traditionally had competed on the basis of its manufacturing, service to retailers, and its ability to build loyalty among a core set of customers for its high-margin, long-lived shoe models, 2005 had not been a stellar year mostly because of operational issues. "We did a very poor job of executing in the first half of the year," Jim Davis noted. "We had a lot of quality problems, late deliveries, late samples, which inhibited the effectiveness of our salespeople." To Jim Davis, the answer to the company's problems was "basically doing everything we've always done before, only doing it better." Yet as New Balance grew well beyond $1 billion in revenue, the question of scalability came up.

John Withee mirrored Davis' concern:

New Balance is very good culturally at knocking down all walls to get something done. But then it's easy to regret that. That may be why we have so many styles and so many SKUs. Everyone's trying to work harder. You try to do things efficiently and have the right type of metrics, and all of a sudden it's just too many balls to juggle. And there's the balance of the entrepreneurial—which is certainly a cultural thing here—and the fact that you wake up and you haven't got a good handle on your inventory. Your inventory is too high, the wrong color, or on the wrong coast.

The confluence of so many opportunities forced the Davises to consider whether and how the company should react to the Adidas–Reebok announcement. Did New Balance need to consider making its own acquisitions? Did it need to consider reducing its level of domestic manufacturing? Did it need to get better at the promotional tactics used by its competitors? Or should the company remain focused on scaling its current business model and improving operational performance via the NB2E initiative? Which option would provide New Balance with an acceptable level of future growth in light of industry consolidation?

Jim Davis felt that the impact of the Adidas–Reebok transaction would be felt most by retailers, a fact that would play into New Balance's hand. "Before this deal, the industry had one 800-pound gorilla; now there are two. Those big guys tend to dictate a little bit, but they don't move as quickly as a smaller company, and they don't really establish the partnerships that we do. We see this as a major opportunity for us." As an example of the possible opportunities, Jim Davis noted that a major customer recently told New Balance that it planned on doing more business with the company after the Adidas–Reebok merger, in part because they knew New Balance—and its stable roster of salespeople and managers— so well.

Having finished their dinner, the Davises wondered what to have for dessert.

Appendix A: Brief Overview of Main Competitors

NIKE

Headquartered in Beaverton, Oregon, and started with a handshake between two self-described running geeks in 1972, University of Oregon running coach Bill Bowerman and entrepreneur Phil Knight. Nike was the leading supplier of athletic footwear to the U.S. market in 2004 and the largest marketer of athletic apparel in the world. In 2004, Nike's sales exceeded $13.7 billion and it employed approximately 26,000 people in May 2005. U.S. footwear sales (virtually all of which were manufactured overseas) totaled approximately $3.2 billion in 2004. That year, the company's top-selling footwear product categories were running, basketball, children's, cross-training and women's shoes. Although Nike focused mainly on athletic shoes, it also offered dress and casual footwear through its Cole Haan subsidiary.[19] Virtually all of its products were manufactured by independent contractors. Virtually all footwear and apparel products were produced outside the United States, while equipment products were produced both in the United States and abroad.

REEBOK

Founded in 1895 and headquartered in Canton, Massachusetts, Reebok was the second largest supplier of athletic footwear in the United States and produced athletic apparel and accessories in addition to non-athletic, casual clothing and footwear. Reebok's sales reached nearly $3.8 billion in 2004, of which $2.1 billion was in the United States, and the company employed 9,100 people. Product lines marketed under the Reebok brand name included RBK, targeted at young, fashion-oriented consumers; Performance, designed for sport-specific activities and utilizing such features as the Pump inflation technology; and Classic, whose products included long-time consumer footwear favorites.[20] Like Nike, virtually all of its footwear was manufactured by independent manufacturers outside of the United States. According to its 2004 annual report, the company sourced some of its apparel and some of the component parts used in its footwear from independent manufacturers located in the United States.

ADIDAS-SALOMON

Headquartered in Herzogenaurach, Germany, Adidas-Salomon was the third leading supplier of athletic footwear to the U.S. market in 2004 and also produced athletic clothing and equipment. Its products were available in virtually every country in the world. The 80-year-old company described its strategy as "simple: [to] continuously strengthen our brands and products to improve our competitive position and financial performance."[21] Adidas-Salomon's 2004 sales totaled roughly $8 billion, of which North America accounted for $1.8 billion. In an effort to build brand recognition in North America, Adidas had recently opened concept stores in city centers, mirroring Nike's approach of showcasing its products in glossy Niketown outlets. In 2004, the Adidas line of branded products accounted for $6.4 billion of sales and encompassed three divisions: Sport Performance, focused on introducing innovative, technology-based products for sport-specific activities; Sport Heritage, which offered classic style footwear for casual use; and Sport Style, targeted at cosmopolitan consumers.

OTHERS

Niche players such as Puma were making a strong push into lifestyle models. Also headquartered in Herzogenaurach, Germany, Puma's marketing aspired to develop an iconic brand that defined the culture of what they called Sport-lifestyle. In January 2005, the company partnered with Ferrari AG to become the official licensee of replica and fan merchandise as well as supplier of Scuderia Ferrari Marlboro Formula 1 team.[22]

Founded by two Swiss brothers in California, K-Swiss introduced its "Classic" tennis shoe in 1966. In 2005, the company sold athletic, training, and children's shoes; apparel (including shirts and dresses); and accessories. Sales for K-Swiss totaled $508.6 million and the company employed 480 employees in 2004.[23]

Vans sold footwear and apparel for casual wear and for use in activities such as skateboarding, snowboarding, surfing, and bicycle motocross (BMX). The company was acquired by VF Corporation in 2004.[24]

Established in Japan in 1949 as Onitsuka Company Ltd., Asics made footwear, sportswear, uniforms, and accessories. In 2004, the company employed over 4,100 people and totaled $1.3 billion in sales. Founded with the philosophy "bringing up sound youth through sports," the name Asics is an acronym of a Latin phrase meaning, "you should pray to have a sound mind in a sound body."[25]

Endnotes

[1]Drawn from "Industry Overview: Freedonia Focus On Athletic Foot-wear," The Fredonia Group, April 1, 2005, available on http://freedonia.ecnext.com/coms2/summary_0285-284466_ITM (accessed February 10, 2006).

[2]Rich Thomaselli, "Adidas Deal Sets Stage For Full-Scale War With Nike; Pooled Might Makes For Fairer Match Up In Bid For Endorse-ments, Share," Advertising Age, August 8, 2005, available on www.factiva.com (accessed February 21, 2006).

[3]Rich Thomaselli, "Adidas Deal Sets Stage For Full-Scale War With Nike; Pooled Might Makes For Fairer Match Up In Bid For Endorse-ments, Share," Advertising Age, August 8, 2005, available on www.factiva.com (accessed February 21, 2006).

[4]Stephanie Nall, "Putting A Fashionable Foot Forward," Pacific Shipper, September 23, 2005, available on www.factiva.com (accessed April 17, 2006).

[5]Stephanie Nall, "Putting A Fashionable Foot Forward," Pacific Shipper, September 23, 2005, available on www.factiva.com (accessed April 17, 2006).

[6]"Doing The Math: Retail Top 100," Sporting Goods Business, June 1, 2004, available on www.factiva.com (accessed April 17, 2006)

[7]Business Wire, "New Balance Achieves Its Centennial Year; Global Athletic Manufacturer Recognizes Past Milestones and Looks to Innovative Future," January 5, 2006, available on www.factiva.com (accessed March 1, 2006).

[8]Business Wire, "New Balance Achieves Its Centennial Year; Global Athletic Manufacturer Recognizes Past Milestones and Looks to Innovative Future," January 5, 2006, available on www.factiva.com (accessed March 1, 2006).

[9]Business Wire, "New Balance Achieves Its Centennial Year; Global Athletic Manufacturer Recognizes Past Milestones and Looks to Innovative Future," January 5, 2006, available on www.factiva.com (accessed March 1, 2006).

[10]Steve Bailey, "Mom and Pop Billionaires," The Boston Globe, October 6, 2004, available on www.factiva.com (accessed March 1, 2006).

[11]Joe Pereira, "New Balance Sneaker Ads Jab At Pro Athletes' Preten-sions," The Wall Street Journal, March 10, 2005, available on www.factiva.com (accessed March 1, 2006).

[12]Naomi Aoki, "New Balance's Latest Ads Celebrate The Older Ama-teur," The Boston Globe, February 28, 2005, available on www.factiva.com (accessed March 1, 2006).

[13]Naomi Aoki, "New Balance's Latest Ads Celebrate The Older Ama-teur," The Boston Globe, February 28, 2005, available on www.factiva.com (accessed March 1, 2006).

[14]Naomi Aoki, "New Balance's Latest Ads Celebrate The Older Ama-teur," The Boston Globe, February 28, 2005, available on www.factiva.com (accessed March 1, 2006).

[15]Naomi Aoki, "New Balance's Latest Ads Celebrate The Older Ama-teur," The Boston Globe, February 28, 2005, available on www.factiva.com (accessed March 1, 2006).

[16]Joe Pereira, "New Balance Sneaker Ads Jab At Pro Athletes' Preten-sions," The Wall Street Journal, March 10, 2005, available on www.factiva.com (accessed March 1, 2006).

[17]New Balance also had a small factory in Boston, Massachusetts, that manufactured roughly 500,000 pairs of shoes per year for groups that needed particular types of footwear for various occupational uses. This

factory completed all aspects of production, including the manufacturing of soles.

[18]Typically, all materials except leather and certain mesh fabrics were sourced from these Chinese suppliers. For models assembled in the United States, leather and mesh were sourced domestically.

[19]Fredonia report and Nike Web site www.nike.com/nikebiz/nikebiz.jhtml?page=3 (accessed February 10, 2006).

[20]Ibid.

[21]Ibid.

[22]Puma Web site, http://about.puma.com/puma.jsp?type=company&lang=eng (accessed March 3, 2006).

[23]"K-Swiss Company Overview," available from Hoover's, www.hoovers.com (accessed March 3, 2006).

[24]"Vans Company Overview," available from Hoover's, www.hoovers.com (accessed March 3, 2006).

[25]Hoover's report and Asics Web site, www.asics.com/shoeshistory/index_e.html (accessed March 3, 2006).

Ryanair: European Pioneer of Budget Airline Travel

Eleanor R. E. O'Higgins
*University College Dublin and
London School of Economics
and Political Science*

SHOCK AND AWE

"He never fails to surprise, that man—it's incredible." This was the reaction of a prominent Irish bookmaker to the shocking news that Ryanair, Europe's leading budget airline, led by its CEO, Michael O'Leary, had launched a €1.48 billion bid for its Irish rival, Aer Lingus, just a week after Aer Lingus had become a public company.[1] Ryanair revealed that it had already procured 19.2 percent of Aer Lingus shares through its stockbroker and claimed that its all-cash offer of €2.80 a share represented a 27 percent premium over the initial stock issue price of €2.20. Its intentions were to retain the Aer Lingus brand and

> up-grade their dated long-haul product, and reduce their short-haul fares by 2.5 percent per year for a minimum of 4 years. . . . The combination of Aer Lingus and Ryanair into one strong Irish airline group will be rewarding for consumers and will enable both to vigorously compete with the mega carriers in Europe. . . . There are significant opportunities, by combining the purchasing power of Ryanair and Aer Lingus, to substantially reduce operating costs, increase efficiencies, and pass these savings on in the form of lower fares to Aer Lingus' consumers.[2]

Among those surprised by the bid were many Ryanair investors, who were concerned that it could distract the carrier from its heretofore successful ruthless approach to cost-cutting, by taking on an airline with long-haul routes. In the past it had made a

successful acquisition, but it was of a small-budget, short-haul carrier, Buzz, which had only 2 million passengers and was easily absorbed. While perceived as a departure from its organic growth model, that deal had nevertheless been greeted as a coup for Ryanair. Apart from the bargain purchase price, it was a golden opportunity to pick up a ready-made bundle of take-off and landing slots at London Stansted Airport.

It had been quite an achievement by the Irish government to have finally privatized Aer Lingus after many false starts and much agonizing over a number of years. Once they recovered their collective breaths, Aer Lingus and its board firmly rejected the purchase offer from Ryanair. They said that Ryanair had acted in "a hostile, anticompetitive manner designed to eliminate a rival at a derisory price." A combined Ryanair–Aer Lingus operation would account for 80 percent of all flights between Ireland and other European countries. Aer Lingus's chief executive, Dermot Mannion, said his company was fundamentally opposed to a merger with Ryanair, even if it raises its price. "I cannot conceive of the circumstances where the Aer Lingus management and Ryanair would be able to work harmoniously together," Mannion said in an interview. "This is simply a reflection of the fact that these organizations have been competing head to head, without fear or favor, for 20 years. It would be like merging Manchester United and Liverpool football clubs. You just wouldn't do it."[3]

In fact, the bid was opposed by a loose alliance representing almost 47 percent of the Aer Lingus shares. This included the Irish government, which still retained a 25.4 percent holding, two investment funds operated on behalf of Aer Lingus pilots accounting for about 4 percent of shares, and Irish telecom tycoon Denis O'Brien, who bought 2.1 percent of shares explicitly to complicate Ryanair's move. A critical 12.6 percent of the shares was controlled by members of the Aer Lingus employee share ownership trust (ESOT). The ESOT had the right to appoint two directors to the Aer Lingus board and a stake in future profits, under an agreement reached with the airline ahead of the initial public stock offering. Given Ryanair's traditional anti–trade union stance, the trade unions campaigned successfully against acceptance of the bid by ESOT members, dismissing Ryanair's claim that each ESOT member stood to receive an average of €60,000 from the transaction, saying it would actually amount to €32,000 after borrowing costs.

By the time Ryanair announced its excellent first-half 2007 results in early November, it virtually admitted defeat for its bid, given expected opposition from the ESOT. Michael O'Leary declared that "Aer Lingus has no long-term future," and that if the bid did not go through, Ryanair would not increase its price, but would continue to be a minority shareholder and exercise what influence it could to encourage Aer Lingus to reduce costs and offer lower fares.[4] Ryanair's contentment to be a significant minority shareholder was confirmed when it acquired a further 31.8 million shares in Aer Lingus in late November 2006, giving it a 25.2 percent stake. This was seen as a way of blocking any major transactions requiring shareholder approval, such as asset disposals, by Aer Lingus.

OVERVIEW OF RYANAIR

Ryanair was founded in 1985 by the Ryan family, headed by Tony Ryan, to provide scheduled passenger airline services between Ireland and the United Kingdom, as an alternative to the then state monopoly carrier, Aer Lingus. Initially, Ryanair was a full-service conventional airline, with two classes of seating, leasing three different types of aircraft. Despite a growth in passenger volumes, by the end of 1990, the company had flown through a great deal of turbulence, disposing of five chief executives and accumulating losses of IR£20 million. Its fight to survive in the early 1990s, saw the airline restyle

itself to become Europe's first low-fare, no-frills carrier, built on the model of Southwest Airlines, the highly successful Texas-based operator. A new management team was appointed by Tony Ryan, led by Michael O'Leary, then a reluctant recruit. The new formula produced a turnaround in the fortunes of the company. In 2006, Ryanair's common stock, which first began trading on the Dublin Stock Exchange in 1997, was quoted on both the Dublin and London Stock exchanges and on NASDAQ; Ryanair was made a part of the NASDAQ 100 Index in 2002.

RYANAIR IN FULL FLIGHT

The World's Most Profitable Airline

Up to Ryanair's announcement that it was bidding for Aer Lingus, it appeared to be business as usual for the company. It was continuing to outperform all other airlines, not only in its own European battleground but also globally. In August 2006, an *Air Transport World* magazine announced that Ryanair was the most profitable airline in the world, on the basis of its operating and net profit margins, on a per-airplane and per-passenger basis.

In November 2006, the airline announced record half-year profits of €329 million for the first half of fiscal 2007. Traffic grew by 23 percent to 22.1 million passengers, and yields increased by 9 percent as total revenues rose by 33 percent to €1.256 billion. Ancillary revenues grew by 27 percent. Unit costs increased by 7.5 percent as fuel costs rose by 42 percent to €337 million. Despite these significantly higher fuel costs, Ryanair's after tax margin for the half year rose by 1 point to 26 percent.

Ryanair's financial data are presented in Exhibits 1 and 2, while operating data are given in Exhibit 3.

Growth and Expansion

At its 2006 annual general meeting on September 21 in Dublin and its investor briefing day in New York on September 26, Ryanair offered its investors good news. The airline had delivered a 12 percent increase in net profit, despite a 74 percent increase in fuel costs. Traffic had grown by 26 percent, from 27.6 million passengers in 2005 to 34.8 million in

Exhibit 1   Ryanair Profit Statement, 2005–2007 (€ in thousands)

	Years Ending March 31		
	First Six Months, Fiscal 2007	2006	2005
Operating revenues			
Scheduled revenues	€1,092,102	€1,433,377	€1,128,116
Ancillary revenues	164,321	259,153	190,921
Total operating revenues—continuing operations	1,256,423	1,692,530	1,319,037
Operating expenses			
Staff costs	113,844	171,412	141,673
Depreciation	71,622	124,405	110,357
Fuel & oil	337,042	462,466	265,276
Maintenance, materials & repairs	21,313	37,417	26,280
Marketing & distribution costs	11,608	13,912	19,622
Aircraft rentals	25,394	47,376	21,546
Route charges	98,384	164,577	135,672
Airport & handling charges	139,097	216,301	178,384
Other	52,312	79,618	79,489
Total operating expenses	870,616	1,317,484	978,299
Operating profit—continuing operations	385,807	375,046	340,738
Other income (expenses)			
Foreign exchange gains (losses)	(1,229)	(1,234)	(2,302)
Gain on disposal of property, plant and equipment	—	815	47
Finance/interest income	28,923	38,219	28,342
Finance/interest expense	41,311	73,958	57,629
Total other income (expenses)	13,617	36,158	31,542
Profit before taxation	372,190	338,888	309,196
Tax on profit on ordinary activities	43,063	32,176	29,153
Profit for the financial period	€ 329,127	€ 306,712	€ 280,043
Earnings per ordinary share (in € cent)			
Basic	42.67	40.00	36.85
Diluted	42.39	39.74	36.65
Adjusted earnings per ordinary share (in € cent)			
Basic	42.67	39.32	35.28
Diluted	42.39	39.07	35.09
Weighted average number of ordinary shares (in 000's)			
Basic	711,413	766,833	759,911
Diluted	776,456	771,781	764,003

Source: Ryanair 20F September 2006.

Exhibit 2   **Ryanair Balance Sheet, 2005–2007 (€ in thousands)**

	Year Ending March 31		
	First Six Months, Fiscal 2007	2006	2005
Noncurrent assets			
Property, plant, and equipment	€2,550,162	€2,532,988	€2,117,891
Intangible assets	46,841	46,841	46,841
Derivative financial instruments	3,888	763	—
Available for sale financial asset	185,363	—	—
Total non-current assets	2,786,254	2,580,592	2,164,732
Current assets			
Inventories	3,627	3,422	2,460
Other assets	48,842	29,453	24,612
Trade receivables	24,207	29,909	20,644
Derivative financial instruments	502	18,872	
Restricted cash	204,040	204,040	204,040
Financial assets: cash >3 months	824,314	328,927	529,407
Cash and cash equivalents	1,064,692	1,439,004	872,258
Total current assets	2,170,224	2,053,627	1,653,421
Total assets	€4,956,478	€4,634,219	€3,818,153
Current liabilities			
Trade payables	€ 87,903	€ 79,283	€ 92,118
Accrued expenses and other liabilities	519,835	570,614	418,653
Current maturities of long term debt	158,049	153,311	120,997
Derivative financial instruments	69,854	27,417	
Current tax	46,331	15,247	17,534
Total current liabilities	881,972	845,872	649,302
Noncurrent liabilities			
Provisions	22,723	16,722	7,236
Derivative financial instruments	74,864	81,897	
Deferred income tax liability	134,881	127,260	104,180
Other creditors	68,396	46,066	29,072
Long term debt	1,476,874	1,524,417	1,293,860
Total noncurrent liabilities	1,777,738	1,796,362	1,434,348
Shareholders' equity			
Issued share capital	9,807	9,790	9,675
Share premium account	602,664	596,231	565,756
Retained earnings	1,796,750	1,467,623	1,158,584
Other reserves	(112,453)	(81,659)	488
Shareholders' equity	2,296,768	1,991,985	1,734,503
Total liabilities and shareholders' equity	€4,956,478	€4,634,219	€3,818,153

Source: Ryanair 20F September 2006.

2006, giving a 27 percent increase in passenger revenues. Indeed, on the cover of its 2006 annual report, Ryanair designated itself as the "World's Favourite Airline," on the basis that it predicted that it would be carrying 42 million passengers in 2007, surpassing even Lufthansa, which carried over 39 million

Exhibit 3   **Ryanair Operating Statistics, 2005–2006**

	2006	2005	Change %
Total aircraft	103	87	18%
Average aircraft age (years)	2.4	7	−65%
Available seat miles (billions)	24.3	17.8	37%
Average daily aircraft hours	9.6	9.3	3%
Passengers (millions)	34.8	27.6	26%
Revenue passenger miles (billions)	18.8	13.9	35%
Average length of haul (miles)	585	541	8%
Average passenger fare (€)	44.63	43.95	2%
Revenue per revenue passenger mile (€)	0.076	0.081	−6%
Revenue per available seat mile (€)	0.058	0.063	−8%
Operating costs per available seat mile (€)	0.052	0.053	−2%
Break-even load factor (%)	68	65	5%
Load factor (%)	77.6	77.8	−0.2%
Average staff	3063	2604	18%
Average staff per aircraft	29.7	29.9	−0.3%
Passengers per employee	11,351	10,596	7%
Average staff cost (€)	50,582	53,306	−5%
Airport costs per passenger (€)	6.36	6.86	−7%
Marketing costs/scheduled revenue	1.70%	2.00%	−15%
Airports served	111	95	17%

Source: Ryanair 20F September 2006.

passengers on its intra-European routes in 2005. (However, Southwest Airlines, which had carried 77+ million passengers in 2005, was not mentioned as a comparator.) Ryanair reported that it flew out of 18 European airports with a fleet of over 100 new Boeing 737-800 aircraft, and firm orders for a further 138 new aircraft to be delivered over the next six years. These additional aircraft would allow Ryanair to double in size, transporting 80 million passengers per year by 2012.

More immediate growth plans included the delivery of 30 aircraft between September 2006 and April 2007 to dovetail with planned new capacity coming onstream in the winter season. The company was cautious in its outlook for the second half of fiscal 2007, because of the capacity expansion, which would entail slightly lower load factors, and in the face of significantly higher oil prices. However, yield stability was expected in a benign yield environment where some competitors were imposing fuel surcharges. As a result, it was expected that the increase in net profit after tax for fiscal 2007 would be approximately 16 percent, or €350 million.

Ryanair affirmed that it would continue to offer the lowest fares in every market. In particular, Michael O'Leary declared, "[We] guarantee our customers no fuel surcharges not today, not tomorrow, not ever." This was an allusion to those airlines that had added fuel surcharges to their fares when oil prices rose precipitously in 2005 and even further in 2006. Many of the surcharges were levied by carriers with long-haul routes, where the surcharge would not form a significant proportion of the overall fare. Examples were British Airways and Lufthansa.

Ancillary Revenues

Meanwhile, ancillary revenues had climbed by 36 percent in 2006, considerably faster than passenger revenues, generating €7.70 per passenger, with very high margins. Ancillary revenues include nonflight scheduled services (hotels, travel insurance, excess baggage charges, flight change fees, car rental services, in-flight sales, rail and bus ground transport services, commission from Ryanair's credit card with MBNA and personal loans). It was claimed that Ryanair's Web site was the largest travel Web site in Europe and the fifth most recognized brand on Google, offering huge potential for Ryanair to convert this traffic into e-commerce and advertising revenues.[5]

Ancillary revenue initiatives—for example, on-board and online gambling, and an in-flight mobile phone service—continued to be introduced. A poll of readers of the *Financial Times* produced a 72 percent negative response to the question "Should mobile phones be allowed on aircraft?" Among the comments were that passengers do not wish to be disturbed and "Just another reason not to fly Ryanair."[6] However, when introducing the phone service, Michael O'Leary declared, "If you want a quiet flight, use another airline. Ryanair is noisy, full and we are always trying to sell you something."[7] Not all ancillary service initiatives were successful. In 2005, Ryanair pulled an in-flight entertainment system. Passengers had resisted paying €8 to rent a games and entertainment console, probably because they did not consider it a worthwhile investment for short flights.

Investor Perspectives

Prior to its bid for Aer Lingus, Ryanair had come in for some criticism for sitting on a €2 billion cash pile, instead of distributing it to investors, blaming uncertainty of demand in the second half of fiscal 2007 for its cautious approach.[8] However, announcing its excellent first-half 2007 results in November 2006, the airline stated it was looking into a number of options for payouts to shareholders by the end of 2007 calendar year, irrespective of the Aer Lingus bid. The options included an annual dividend policy, share buyback, and a one-off dividend. It also intended to seek shareholder approval for a 2-for-1 stock split intended to improve the marketability and liquidity of the stock.

The shares rose by 3.6 percent, to €9.28, a record high. The stock had gained 12 percent during the year. Yet, despite its superior profit performance, historically, Ryanair was only mid-range or below average in its P/E multiple relative to peers like easyJet, whose shares had risen 46 percent during the year. However, this offered an upside potential for capital gains, and a low risk of derating, according to the company's stockbrokers, Davy.

RYANAIR'S OPERATIONS IN 2006

To quote Michael O'Leary, "Any fool can sell low airfares and lose money. The difficult bit is to sell the lowest airfares and make profits. If you don't make profits, you can't lower your air fares or reward your people or invest in new aircraft or take on the really big airlines like BA and Lufthansa."[9] Certainly, Ryanair had stuck closely to the low-cost/low-fares model. Ever decreasing costs was Ryanair's mantra, as it constantly adapted the model to the European arena and changing circumstances.

The Ryanair Fleet

Ryanair continued its policy of fleet commonality to keep staff training and aircraft maintenance costs as low as possible, using Boeing 737 planes. Over the years, Ryanair replaced its fleet of old aircraft with new, more environmentally friendly aircraft, reducing the average age of its fleet to 2.4 years, the youngest fleet of any major airline in Europe. The larger seat capacity of the new aircraft did not need more crew. The newer aircraft produced 50 percent less emissions, 45 percent less fuel burn, and 45 percent lower noise emissions per seat. Also, a winglet modification program on the fleet was providing better aircraft performance and a 2 percent reduction in fleet fuel consumption, a saving which the company believed could be improved over the next year.

Staff Costs and Productivity

In fiscal 2006, Ryanair's employee count rose by more than 700, to 3,500 people, comprising over 25 different nationalities. The new intake was almost entirely accounted for by flight and cabin crew to service the airline's expansion. Ryanair claimed in its 2006 annual report that its average pay, including commissions to cabin crew for on-board sales, was €49,612, a higher figure than any other major European airline. Nonetheless, by tailoring rosters, the carrier maximized productivity and time off for crew members, complying with European Union regulations, which impose a ceiling on pilot flying hours to prevent dangerous fatigue. The airline adhered to the general rule of a maximum of 900 hours flying time per annum, averaging 18 hours per week.

Passenger Service Costs

In 2006, Ryanair introduced cost-cutting/yield-enhancing measures for passenger check-in and luggage handling. Estimates were that these tactics could save an average of more than €1 per passenger. One such measure was Web-based check-in from March 2006, and priority boarding, with over half of passengers availing of this, thus saving Ryanair costs on check-in staff and airport facilities, as well as time. Another was charging for check-in bags, which encouraged passengers to travel with few check-in bags or, if possible, none, again saving on costs and enhancing speed. Other rivals were also introducing charges for hold luggage, including Aer Lingus and FlyBE. After ruling out a similar move in February 2006, easyJet succumbed in September of the same year, charging passengers for any more than one item of hold luggage.

Airport Charges and Route Policy

Consistent with the budget airline model, Ryanair's routes continued to be point-to-point only. Anxious to increase passenger throughput, Ryanair reduced airport charges by avoiding congested main airports and choosing secondary and regional airports. Most of these airports are significantly farther from the city centers they serve than the main airports are. For example, Ryanair uses Frankfurt Hahn (123 kilometers from Frankfurt), Torp (100 kilometers from Oslo), and Charleroi (60 kilometers from Brussels). In December 2003, the Advertising Standards Authority rebuked Ryanair and upheld a misleading advertising complaint against it for attaching "Lyon" to its advertisements for flights to St. Etienne. A passenger had turned up at Lyon Airport, only to discover that her flight was leaving from St. Etienne, 75 kilometers away. The airline dismissed the ruling on the basis that Lyon was written only in small print underneath St. Etienne, so was not misleading.

In 2006, airport and handling charges increased by 21 percent, a smaller increase than the growth in passenger numbers, reflecting a net reduction in costs from deals at new airports and bases, despite increased costs at certain existing airports, such as Stansted. Route charges also increased by 21 percent because of an increase in the number of sectors flown and an 8 percent increase in average sector length, as Ryanair ventured further afield into the new EU member states, such as Poland, Hungary, and Slovakia, as well as ex-EU destinations, such as Marrakech in Morocco.

Ryanair continued to protest at charges and conditions at some airports, especially Stansted and Dublin, two of its main hubs. It vehemently opposed the British Airport Authority (BAA) airport monopoly plans to build a "£4bn gold-plated Taj Mahal at Stansted which we believe could be built for £1bn." The airline was "deeply concerned by continued understaffing of security at Stansted which has led to repeated passenger and flight delays . . . management of Stansted security is inept, and BAA has again proven that it is incapable of providing adequate or appropriate security services at Stansted. This shambles again highlights that BAA is an inefficient, incompetent airport monopoly."[10]

Further, Ryanair continued:

> The tragedy at Dublin airport continues where the Dublin Airport Authority (DAA) monopoly recently obtained planning approval for a second terminal at a cost of €750 million, 4.5 times more than the €170 million cost it announced just 11 months earlier in Sept. 2005. Only a government owned monopoly would seek a cost increase of over 4 fold—with no increase in passenger capacity . . . DAA has recently proposed an outrageous 60 percent increase in charges at Dublin Airport to recoup the inflated cost of this facility which Ryanair passengers will never use. Ryanair will continue to oppose this waste and has appealed the planning decision.

RISKS AND CHALLENGES

At the same time, Ryanair faced various challenges as it entered the second half of fiscal 2007. The airline itself predicted that its extra capacity building would create uncertainty about the success of new routes and locations and other difficulties. These were extra marketing and discounted fare costs incurred in launching new routes, as well as overcapacity leading to price cutting by rivals.

Fuel Prices

Ryanair was especially vulnerable to rising fuel prices from 2005, but especially in 2006. Its low-fare policy limited its ability to pass on increased fuel costs to passengers through increased fares. Coupled with a guarantee that it would not impose any fuel surcharges on its customers, this placed extra pressure on the carrier to find cost savings in other spheres of its operations. Its fuel costs represented 35 percent of operating costs in 2006, compared to 27 percent the year before. Since jet fuel cost fluctuations are subject to unpredictable and volatile world events, Ryanair could neither predict nor control these costs, and was dependent on hedging, based on educated guessing. Moreover, the fact that jet fuel prices are denominated in U.S. dollars compounds the risk by introducing exchange rate exposure, also requiring hedging. Ryanair had not hedged early, so it was paying $70 per barrel of oil up to October 2006, and $73 to $74 up to March 2007 while better-hedged competitors such as Lufthansa, Air France–KLM, and Iberia had the bulk of their fuel needs hedged at an average of $50 to $60 a barrel until the end of calendar year 2006. Meanwhile, the price of oil stood at about $60 a barrel in late September 2006, with forward prices for January 2007 Brent Crude at $62 a barrel.

Compensation to Passengers

On February 17, 2005, a new EU regulation came into effect, intended to reduce the inconvenience caused to air passengers by delays, cancellations, and denied boarding. The regulation provides for standardized and immediate assistance for air passengers where these events occur. The rights in the regulation apply to all passengers departing from EU airports, as well as to those passengers departing from outside the EU arriving at an EU airport on an EU-licensed carrier. It was expected that the compensation costs would amount to a sectorwide bill of €200 million annually; one large carrier estimated that it would increase its costs by an annual €35 million.

Passengers affected by cancellations had to be offered a refund or rerouting and free care and assistance while waiting for their rerouted flight—specifically, meals, refreshments, and hotel accommodation where an overnight stay was necessary. Financial compensation of up to €600 was also payable for flight cancellation, unless the airline could prove that it was caused by extraordinary circumstances that could not have been avoided even if all reasonable measures had been taken. Examples of circumstances that may fall within this exception are political instability, weather conditions incompatible with the operation of the flight, security and safety risks, and strikes. For Ryanair, the typical compensation cost would likely fall into the €250 category, based on the typical distance of its flights. Passengers subject to long delays would also be entitled to similar assistance, including meals and hotel accommodation. Obviously, for budget carriers, such assistance and compensation costs would be out of all proportion to the fares paid by passengers.

Terrorism and Security

Past terrorist attacks on airliners and in urban and holiday centers had inflicted added risks and costs to the airline industry worldwide. In August 2006, UK authorities imposed severe security measures at all UK airports in the face of an alleged imminent terrorist plot to attack up to 10 aircraft on transatlantic routes. These measures applied to all passengers, including short-haul ones, so they were to be body-searched and banned from carrying liquids and gels in their carry-on luggage. Airports serving London were especially affected. Ryanair had to cancel 279 flights in the days immediately following the incident and refunded €2.7 million in fares to approximately 40,000 passengers. In addition, Ryanair was estimated to have suffered a loss of €1.9 million in reduced bookings. British Airways reported a second-quarter profit fall of 1.8 percent as the impact of stricter security measures at Heathrow and other airports reached £100 million.

While the restrictions were relaxed somewhat in November, they still severely limited the contents of carry-on luggage and made it more likely that passengers would have to bring check-in bags, thus impeding the efficiency of the budget airlines, which relied on quick check-in and aircraft turnarounds, with a minimum of check-in luggage. There was also a threat that passengers would choose other forms of transport, such as trains, rather than face the inconvenience and expense of checking in luggage, as well as the extra time spent in airport security queues.

In the past, Ryanair had recovered quickly from terrorist episodes and alerts, after initial dips in traffic, namely, after the terrorist attacks on airliners in the United States on September 11, 2001, and the aftermath of attacks on London transport on July 7, 2005, and abortive attempts two weeks later on July 21. This had affected flight bookings to London for some weeks. Michael O'Leary's verdict on the new August 2006 security measures was that they were "farcical" and that terrorists "must be rolling around in their caves in Pakistan laughing at us."[11] While various other airline executives protested, too, Ryanair was on its own in launching two legal cases against the British government. One was a claim of €4.6 million to compensate the carrier for lost flights and bookings. In the other case, Ryanair was challenging the legality of the new security measures and sought to return to those in operation prior to August 2006. Another effect of the 9/11 attacks was significantly increased insurance costs for all commercial airlines. Ryanair had passed these costs on in its fares.

Environmental Concerns

Environmental concerns about greenhouse gases continued to climb up the public and political agenda worldwide, and especially in Europe, with an ever greater focus on the impact of aviation. Aviation represented 2.6 percent of CO_2 emissions in the European Union, but an Oxford University study predicted that carbon dioxide from aviation would accelerate, so that adverse climate impacts would far outweigh the positive effects of aviation.[12] Another report warned that failure to curtail greenhouse gases would lead to catastrophic human and economic consequences. Hence, the report said, airlines should pay environmental taxes for the contributions they make to global warming.[13]

Heretofore, aviation fuel was exempt from taxation, since International Civil Aviation Organization rules precluded levying taxes on fuel carried on international services. However, despite the difficulties in finding fair and workable tax arrangements on an international level, there was mounting pressure to tax aviation fuel, and some plan to do so within the EU area seemed probable by 2010. In addition, aviation was likely to become part of some form of emissions trading scheme that could cost up to €9 for a return ticket within Europe.

Ryanair argued that aviation contributed only a small proportion of carbon emissions relative to the benefits of easily accessible cheap air travel. Moreover, taxes have proved ineffective in reducing road vehicle use. Nonetheless, the carrier had pledged to behave responsibly by deploying more efficient aircraft that used less fuel and produced less pollution. Ryanair had urged that any environmental taxation scheme should be to the benefit of more efficient carriers, so airlines with low load factors that generated high fuel consumption and emissions per passenger, and airlines that offered connecting rather than point-to-point flights should be penalized.

Industrial Relations

Ryanair's industrial relations with staff, especially its pilots, were fraught. Ryanair had come under fire from trade unions representing workers in the airline industry for refusing to recognize unions and allegedly providing poor working conditions—for example, staff were banned from charging their own mobile phones at work to reduce the company's electricity bill. Ryanair did not recognize the Irish Airline Pilots' Association (IALPA), the largest pilots' union in Ireland. There was also pressure from the British Airline Pilots Association to recruit Ryanair pilots based in Britain. Ryanair was appealing to the Irish Supreme Court a previous ruling allowing collective bargaining by its pilots. In the absence of unions, Ryanair negotiated with all its employees through internally elected Employee Representation Committees.

In July 2006, an Irish High Court judge found that Ryanair had bullied pilots to force them to agree to new contracts. In 2004, Ryanair had told pilots they would have to pay retraining costs of €15,000 if they left the airline, or if the company were forced to negotiate with unions during the following five years. Moreover, some Ryanair managers had given false evidence in court. Meanwhile, Ryanair was contesting the claims of pilots comprising 3.5 percent of the pilot workforce, for victimization under the new contracts. It was conceded by the company that a ruling in favor of the pilots could incur damages of €100,000 per pilot. In another legal case, Ryanair was ordered to pay well in excess of €1 million in legal costs after a court refused the airline access to the names and addresses of pilots who posted critical comments about the company on a site hosted by the British and Irish pilots' unions. Ryanair, led by Michael O'Leary, had claimed that anonymous pilots were using a Web site to intimidate and harass foreign-based pilots and dissuade them from working for the company. The pilots involved used code names such as "ihateryanair" and "cant-fly-wontfly."

Ryanair declared that its pilots were recognized as the best-paid short-haul pilots in Europe. Remuneration packages included a share option scheme. The company claimed that Ryanair pilots enjoy a stable roster pattern, offering a facility to plan time off, apparently unique in aviation. No planned overnights meant that pilots were home every night. However, in the autumn of 2006, pilots in Ryanair lodged a pay claim with the Irish Labor Relations Commission on the basis that there were significant differences in take-home pay between Ryanair and Aer Lingus pilots. It also claimed that Ryanair training pilots were working for nothing. Nonetheless, in effect, Ryanair appeared to have had no problems recruiting cabin staff, including pilots, to meet its needs. Whether this would continue in the face of rapid expansion remained to be seen.

Sundry Legal Actions

Apart from litigation over industrial relations and airport security measures, Ryanair was in dispute with various airports over landing charges. A ruling in 2004 deemed that the carrier was in illegal receipt of state aid under the terms of its deal with publicly-owned Charleroi Airport, its Brussels base. Ryanair was ordered to repay €4 million, which it placed into an escrow account, pending an appeal in the European Court. The Walloon authorities were claiming back a further €2.3 million in the Irish courts for its reimbursement to Ryanair of start-up costs at Charleroi. Sundry other legal challenges by competitors to Ryanair were also under way in 2006/2007. These were based on allegations of unfair discrimination favoring Ryanair over other airlines at various publicly-owned airports, such as Lübeck and Frankfurt Hahn in Germany, and Shannon in Ireland, constituting illegal state aid. Ryanair was vigorously defending these actions.

Often, Ryanair took the initiative over illegal aid to rivals. For example, it filed a complaint with the European Commission accusing rival Air France–KLM of trying to block competition after the French airline took action to prevent Ryanair from using Marseille airport. The complaint by Ryanair was in response to Air France filing a case, alleging that Marseille was breaching the law by offering discount airlines cut-price fees at its second, no-frills terminal. Ryanair had planned to base two planes at Marseille, serving 13 routes. The latest complaint came a month after Ryanair called on the commission to investigate allegations that Air France had received almost €1 billion in illegal state aid, benefiting unfairly from up to 50 percent discounted landing and passenger charges on flights within France, and should repay the cash.

Adverse rulings on these airport cases could have the effect of curtailing Ryanair's growth, if the company was prevented from striking advantageous deals with publicly-owned airports and confined to the smaller number of privately-owned airports across Europe.

Other legal cases against Ryanair accused it of misleading passengers on its Web site by exaggerating the prices of its competitors in making comparisons. The carrier was also being sued by Sweden's prime minister and a former foreign minister over an advertising campaign that used their pictures alongside the tagline "Time to leave the country?" The company's Scandinavian sales manager quipped, "This must be the first time that a Swedish politician has objected to his image being used in a newspaper."[14]

Safety Issues

Safety was taken very seriously by Ryanair, with extensive safety training and protocols. A Safety Committee reported to the board at each board meeting. The airline was aware of the permanent damage to the company that could follow a serious accident to one of its aircraft. Indeed, any serious accident to a budget airliner could have knock-on effects on all the other budget carriers, and some industry experts had questioned the safety of the low-cost model on the basis of "human factors."

Ryanair's detractors have attempted to disparage its safety record, with reports of various incidents of near-miss accidents, accusing the company of placing crew under such intensive pressurized work schedules that alertness levels were compromised. In February 2006, a British television channel, Channel 4, broadcast a documentary titled "Ryanair Caught Napping." Two undercover reporters obtained jobs as Ryanair cabin crew based at London Stansted

Airport, and secretly recorded Ryanair training program and cabin crew procedures. The documentary
criticized Ryanair's training policies, security procedures, and aircraft hygiene, as well as highlighting
poor staff morale. It filmed Ryanair cabin crew sleeping on the job, using aftershave to cover the smell of
vomit in the aisle rather than cleaning it up, ignoring
warning alerts on the emergency slide, encouraging
staff to falsify references for airport security passes,
and asking staff not to recheck passengers' passports
before they boarded flights.

Ryanair denied the allegations and published its
correspondence with Channel 4 on its Web site. It
claimed to have forwarded all 20 allegations to the
British and Irish aviation authorities, both of which
agreed that there was no substance to them. It also
alleged that the program was misleading and that
promotional materials, in particular a photograph
of a stewardess sleeping, had been faked. Much
of the subsequent coverage of the program in the
media considered that the documentary was over-
blown and failed to make substantive claims against
the airline, with some going so far as to label the
attempted exposé as a vindication for Ryanair.
Following the documentary, Ryanair launched new
services and a free flights offer.

Customer Services and Perceptions

In 2003, Ryanair published a Passenger Charter,
which embraced a number of doctrines, mainly
dealing with low fares, redress, and punctuality.
However, in a poll of 4,000 travelers around the
world by TripAdvisor in October 2006, Ryanair was
voted the world's least favorite airline, with easyJet
coming second worst. Unfriendly staff were cited as
the worst part of the Ryanair experience, followed
by delays and poor legroom. In fact, Ryanair scored
badly in virtually all categories, which also included
"comfortable seats," "safe/secure," "never lose my
luggage," "best amenities (snacks/food; TV/mov-
ies; magazines/newspapers; hot towels; eye shades)."
However, it scored very well on "best fares." Ryanair's
"ultra-frugal approach to flying wins millions of customers but very few fans."[15] Southwest Airlines,
Ryanair's role model emerged as the world's fifth
most favorite airline in the survey.

There had been suggestions that Ryanair's "obsessive focus on the bottom line may have dented its

public image. In one infamous incident, it charged a
man with cerebral palsy £18 (€25) to use a wheelchair."[16] In response to protests over the charge,
Ryanair imposed a 50-cent wheelchair levy on
every passenger ticket. Campaigners for the disabled accused Ryanair of profiteering from its extra
charges, declaring that the levy should be no more
than 3 cents—the company would still have collected €1,000,000. Ryanair defended its position, saying that it costs €37 per person to transport disabled
passengers at Stansted, and the airline carried 1.5
million such passengers every year. Ryanair was the
only major airline in Britain to impose such wheelchair charges.

Further, *The Guardian* newspaper had alleged that the insurance fee that Ryanair charged
each passenger was unreasonably high. The insurance surcharge amounted to more than 10 percent
of Ryanair's average fare, the newspaper estimated.
Rival easyJet claimed: "Ryanair's insurance charges
appear to be far higher than they actually incur. . . .
Either this is poor cost management on Ryanair's behalf or it's a fuel surcharge in disguise."[17]

Critics had accused Ryanair of poor treatment
of customers whose flights had been canceled. The
airline formerly refused to provide accommodation or meal vouchers when flights were canceled
or delayed, until it became illegal to do so in 2005.
Ryanair also refused to refund taxes and fees when
passengers canceled their tickets, but revised this
practice by introducing an "administration fee" of
€20 per ticket for handling refunds, a fee that often
exceeded the amount for which passengers were
eligible. Norwegian consumer authorities had fined
Ryanair €64,000 for this practice. However, it was
not uncommon for airlines to charge an administration fee for changes or refunds.

In response to various complaints, Ryanair had
declared that, in effect, customers voted with their
feet by choosing Ryanair for its low fares. It also
claimed to be number one for punctuality among
European airlines, with the lowest level of complaints, fewest cancellations, and fewest lost bags.
Exhibits 4 and 5 show comparative fare levels and
punctuality statistics for Ryanair versus other airlines. There were no externally verified published
data on customer complaints, lost baggage, and
flight cancellations.

In March 2006, Davy, Ryanair's stockbrokers, reported on a quarterly customer survey conducted by

Exhibit 4 Comparative Fare Levels (same booking dates and approximate departure times)

Route: Dublin—London: Weekend Return (2 Nights)

Airline	From	To	Total Price
Aer Lingus	Dublin	Heathrow	€198.07
Bmi British Midland	Dublin	Heathrow	188.18
British Airways	Dublin	Gatwick	193.03
Ryanair	Dublin	Gatwick	147.03
Ryanair	Dublin	Stansted	104.96
Ryanair	Dublin	Luton	103.91

Route: Dublin—London: Weekday Return (3 Nights)

Airline	From	To	Total Price
Aer Lingus	Dublin	Heathrow	€ 98.07
Bmi British Midland	Dublin	Heathrow	62.18
British Airways	Dublin	Gatwick	163.03
Ryanair	Dublin	Gatwick	52.07
Ryanair	Dublin	Stansted	45.00
Ryanair	Dublin	Luton	43.95

Route: Rome—London: Weekend Return (2 Nights)

Airline	From	To	Total Price
Alitalia	Rome (Fiumicino)	Heathrow	€192.85
British Airways	Rome (Fiumicino)	Gatwick	235.85
British Airways	Rome (Fiumicino)	Heathrow	144.77
easyJet	Rome (Ciampino)	Gatwick	85.46
Ryanair	Rome (Ciampino)	Stansted	61.88
Ryanair	Rome (Ciampino)	Luton	65.83

Route: Rome—London: Weekday Return (3 Nights)

Airline	From	To	Total Price
Alitalia	Rome (Fiumicino)	Heathrow	€192.85
British Airways	Rome (Fiumicino)	Gatwick	179.77
British Airways	Rome (Fiumicino)	Heathrow	154.85
easyJet	Rome (Ciampino)	Gatwick	111.46
Ryanair	Rome (Ciampino)	Stansted	68.9
Ryanair	Rome (Ciampino)	Luton	72.85

Route: Berlin—London: Weekend Return (2 Nights)

Airline	From	To	Total Price
Air Berlin	Berlin (Tegel)	Stansted	€314.00
British Airways	Berlin (Tegel)	Heathrow	254.71
easyJet	Berlin (Schonefeld)	Luton	144.44
Ryanair	Berlin (Schonefeld)	Stansted	113.67

Route: Berlin—London: Weekday Return (3 Nights)

Airline	From	To	Total Price
Air Berlin	Berlin (Tegel)	Stansted	€194.00
British Airways	Berlin (Tegel)	Heathrow	578.71
easyJet	Berlin (Schonefeld)	Luton	142.44
Ryanair	Berlin (Schonefeld)	Stansted	133.67

Exhibit 4 **Continued**

Airports Distance to City Centre (point 0)	
Airports	**Distance**
Stansted	61 Kilometers
Heathrow	25
Luton	55
Gatwick	45
Dublin	12
Rome (Fiumicino)	32
Rome (Ciampino)	15
Berlin (Tegel)	8
Berlin (Schonefeld)	18

Exhibit 5 **Comparative Punctuality Statistics, May 2006**

Airline Name	Origin	Reporting Airport	Average Delay Mins	Early to 15 Mins late %	16 to 30 Mins late %	31 to 60 Mins Late %
Aer Lingus	Dublin	Heathrow	19.40	59.30	20.10	13.32
Bmi British Midland	Dublin	Heathrow	26.43	52.11	19.47	15.79
British Airways	Dublin	Gatwick	15.85	71.43	16.96	8.04
Ryanair	Dublin	Gatwick	24.66	50.65	17.53	21.43
Ryanair	Dublin	Stansted	12.76	70.47	15.44	12.42
Ryanair	Dublin	Luton	15.53	60.40	22.77	14.85
Alitalia	Rome (Fiumicino)	Heathrow	14.15	72.33	10.06	12.58
British Airways	Rome (Fiumicino)	Gatwick	31.16	35.48	32.26	22.58
British Airways	Rome (Fiumicino)	Heathrow	17.54	62.58	14.84	17.42
easyJet	Rome (Ciampino)	Gatwick	16.03	69.35	16.13	8.06
Ryanair	Rome (Ciampino)	Stansted	16.17	71.79	16.67	7.69
Ryanair	Rome (Ciampino)	Luton	16.06	67.74	16.13	3.23
British Airways	Lyon	Heathrow	16.25	73.91	9.78	7.61
easyJet	Lyon	Stansted	22.65	61.29	9.68	12.90
Ryanair	St Etienne	Stansted	13.65	77.42	6.45	9.68
Air Berlin	Berlin (Tegel)	Stansted	14.05	70.37	12.04	12.96
British Airways	Berlin (Tegel)	Heathrow	14.21	70.32	14.19	10.32
easyJet	Berlin (Schonefeld)	Luton	19.56	69.51	8.54	17.07
Ryanair	Berlin (Schonefeld)	Stansted	11.81	74.19	11.29	11.29
easyJet	Almeria	Gatwick	9.10	83.87	6.45	3.23
easyJet	Almeria	Stansted	3.58	90.32	6.45	3.23
easyJet	Murcia San Javier	Gatwick	18.68	70.97	16.13	6.45
Ryanair	Almeria	Stansted	7.00	87.18	5.13	2.56
Ryanair	Murcia San Javier	Stansted	14.44	73.77	14.75	4.92

Ryanair in 2005, with responses from about 20,000 passengers, with "huge" repeat business.[18] The respondents were evenly split between business travelers, leisure travelers, and travelers who were visiting friends and relatives. Unlike external surveys, satisfaction levels with Ryanair were overwhelmingly "excellent" or "good" and certainly above average on check-in at the airport, boarding and departure, cabin cleanliness, and cabin crew service. Seating space was regarded as largely average, as was onboard catering.

Davy concluded that the positive results were actually likely to improve with the new aircraft coming onstream. The only disappointing results pertained to on-board sales, which, although improving, were not much above €1.30 per passenger.

Other comparative customer rating data for airlines are shown in Exhibit 6. The star ratings, compiled by Skytrax, are based on the perception of delivered front-line product and service quality.

RYANAIR'S COMPETITORS IN EUROPE

The potential of the budget airline sector in Europe was underlined by its growth, as low-cost carriers had 18 percent of the market for all European flights in the three months ended September 30, 2006, compared with 15 percent a year earlier. Davy saw the European market as healthy, with huge potential, and only incremental growth, even if many of the competitors were losing money. Some carriers were withdrawing from routes where they clashed with Ryanair (e.g., MyTravelLite from the Dublin-Birmingham route), or avoiding such routes altogether.

The attractiveness of the budget sector in Europe was signified by the large number of entrants and rivals, although as many as 50 had gone bankrupt, been taken over, disappeared, or never got off the ground.[19] Exhibit 6 gives an overview of the main budget carriers in Europe as of 2006.

The following section describes Ryanair's budget airline competitors and some selected other carriers. See Exhibits 7 and 8 for financial and operational comparisons with competitors and benchmark airline operators.

easyJet

easyJet was Ryanair's greatest rival, given that both operated an important hub at Stansted, and encountered each other in the same markets. The two airlines frequently attacked each other as part of their "public relations." When accused by easyJet of introducing stealth charges, Ryanair retaliated by pointing out that, even with taxes included, its average fare was well below easyJet's. Ryanair said that easyJet had charged each passenger £14 (€20) more per ticket than Ryanair, thereby overcharging their passengers by £413 (€600) million in a year.

easyJet, based at London Luton Airport, was founded by Greek Cypriot easyGroup entrepreneur Sir Stelios Haji-Ioannou. Listed on the London Stock Exchange, the company was approximately 49 percent owned by members of the Haji-Ioannou family. In October 2004, the FL Group, owner of airlines Icelandair and Sterling, purchased an 8.4 percent stake in easyJet, and kept increasing its share periodically to 16.9 percent, fueling speculation that it would mount a takeover bid for the British carrier. However, in April 2006, FL sold its stake for €325m, securing a profit of €140m on its investment.

The business model of easyJet was somewhat different from Ryanair's in that it used more centrally located airports, thus incurring higher airport charges, but more actively courting the business traveler. For example, Schiphol in Amsterdam and Orly Airport in Paris were hubs, while the airline also used Charles de Gaulle Airport in Paris. In June 2006, the easyJet Web site was awarded the Best Airline Web site award. Judges commented that although actual contact with the airline could be hard, the Web site was "user-friendly and pleasing to the eye." EasyJet had come under criticism in Germany for months of delay in reimbursing passengers for flight cancellations, when passengers had the right to be reimbursed within one week. Allegedly, easyJet did not return the fare unless massive pressure was exerted.

Compared to Ryanair, easyJet struggled on the profit front, as it strove to bring down its costs. Its first-half results for 2006 showed a pretax loss of £40 (€60) million, "better than expected," although it was forecasting pretax profit growth of 10 to 15 percent for the full year, after an expected bumper summer. Like Ryanair, easyJet had been expanding capacity

Exhibit 6 **Overview of Low Cost Airline Carriers in Europe**

Airline	Millions of Passengers	% of total	Principal bases	Bases	Aircraft in service	Skytrax star rating*	Comment
Ryanair	34.9	29.90%	Stansted, Dublin	16	107	2	Dominant lowest cost producer: gross cash > €1.8bn
easyJet	30.3	25.90%	Stansted, Luton	16	109	3	65% of passenger UK based, but becoming pan-European player
Air Berlin/Niki	13.8	11.80%	Berlin	9	47	4	Founded in 1979 as charter operator, operates Majorca shuttle. Set up City Shuttle in October 2002. Partnership with Niki in Austria
FlyBE	5.5	4.70%	Southampton	6	35	3	Independent regional UK LCC owned by the Walker Trust
Germanwings	5.5	4.70%	Cologne-Bonn, Stuttgart, Hamburg	4	14	3	Majority owned by Lufthansa through its regional associate airline Eurowings; potentially expand fleet to 20 aircraft
Sterling/Maersk	3.8	3.30%	Bilund, Copenhagen	2	29	3	Sterling merged with Maersk Air in 2005 but now owned by FL Group
bmibaby	3.5	3.00%	Cardiff, East Midlands	5	16	2	Part of BMI British Midland Group
dba	3	2.60%	Munich, Berlin	2	16	4	Largely domestic high-frequency German airline
Hapag Lloyd Express	2.7	2.30%	Cologne-Bonn	5	15	3	Part of TUI Group, Europe's largest travel group
Vueling	2.5	2.10%	Barcelona, Valencia	2	9	3	$30m start-up investment from Apax Partners and other investors, including JetBlue top managers
Norwegian Air Shuttle	2.1	1.80%	Largely domestic Norway	1	14	3	Listed on the Oslo Stock Exchange in 2003
Virgin Express	2	1.70%	Brussels	1	10	3	Merged with SN Brussels (formally Sabena)
SkyEurope	1.9	1.60%	Bratislava	4	15	2	Listed on Vienna Exchange in late 2005
Wizz	1.9	1.60%	Katowice, Budapest	3	6	3	Start-up funding of $34m from US private equity fund Indigo Partners. Focused on leased aircraft
Wind Jet	1	0.90%	Sicily	2	8		Sicilian based, largely Italian domestic carrier
Air Baltic	1	0.90%	Riga	1	16	3	Majority owned Latvian state, SAS have 47% stake
Fly Me	0.5	0.40%	Gothenburg	1	4		Gothenburg-based LCC operating intra-Scandinavia
Jet2	0.5	0.40%	Leeds, Manchester	3	9	3	Bases at Leeds, Manchester and Belfast
Monarch Scheduled	0.5	0.40%	Luton, Manchester, Gatwick	3	10		Scheduled part of Monarch Group flying to Spanish/Mediterranean destinations and the Canary Islands
Totals	116.9				489		
Total Ryanair+easyJet		55.80%					

* Skytrax survey scale, 1 star low to 5 star high

Source: Table adapted from Davy, March 2006.

Exhibit 7　**Comparative Airline Financial Statistics, 2005**

	Aer Lingus 2005(€millions)	British Airways 2005(£millions)	easyJet 2005 (£millions)	Lufthansa 2005 (€millions)	Southwest 2005($ millions)
Total Revenue	€1,002.6	£8,515	£1,341.4	€18,065	$7,584
Operating Costs:					
Employee Costs	249.4	2,346	136.2	4,853	2,702
Sales & Marketing	42.4	449	48.4	924	
Airport Charges	178.7	559	230.1		454
Ground Handling	89.9	955	130.5		
Fuel	134.1	1,632	260.2	2,700	1,342
Maintenance	75.3	559	119.2		430
Lease Charges	44.9	112	123.7	594	163
Depreciation	60.8	717	36.5	1,398	469
Operating Profit (Loss)	89.9	705	48.7	719	820
Net Profit (Loss)	€ 88.9	£ 467	£ 42.6	€ 612	$ 548
Net Profit Margin (%)	8.9%	5.5%	3.2%	3.4%	7.2%

Sources: Company annual reports

Exhibit 8   **Comparative Airline Operating Statistics, 2005**

	Aer Lingus 2005(€)	British Airways 2005(£)	easyJet 2005(£)	Lufthansa 2005(€)	Southwest 2005($)	Aer Berlin(€) 1st half 2006	FlyBE 2005
Number of Aircraft in Fleet	27	284	108	339	445	58	38
Average Daily Hours of Flight Time per Aircraft	9.6	10.14	11.7		12.5	10.2	
Capacity (billions)[b]	4.6	147.9	32.1	144.2	85.2	12.4	3.8
Annual Number of Passengers (millions)	3.6	35.6	29.6	51.3	77.7	6.9	4.7
Revenue Passenger Distance Units (billions)[c]	3.4	111.9	27.4	108.2	60.2	9.7	2.6
Average Length of Flight	869 km	627 km	926 km		775 miles	1393 km	
Revenue per Passenger	66.81		42.43		93.68		
Revenue per Revenue Passenger Distance Unit		.061/RPK			.121/RPM	.064/RPK	
Revenue per Capacity Unit		.046/ASK	.042/ASK		.089/ASM	.050/ASK	
Operating Cost per Capacity Unit			.039/ASK		.079/ASM		
Load Factor (%)	76	75.6	85.2	75	70.7	77.6	67.8
Average Staff	3,475	47,012	3,875	37,042	31,729	3,158	1,638
Destinations	54	151	66	163	62	65	34

[a] Short haul except for staff, i.e., total for company.

[b] Available seat kilometers (ASK) except Southwest available seat miles (ASM).

[c] Revenue per kilometer (RPK) except for Southwest revenue per mile (RPM).

Sources: Company annual reports.

rapidly, often in the same geographic locations, and its ancillary revenues were rising faster than its passenger ones.

Air Berlin

Originally a charter airline that started operations from Berlin in 1979, Air Berlin expanded into scheduled services and styled itself as a low-cost airline. However, it did not operate with a pure low-cost carrier model. Most notably, instead of only point-to-point service, Air Berlin offered guaranteed connections via its hubs. The airline also offered free services including in-flight meals and drinks, newspapers, assigned seating, and a frequent flyer program. *Skytrax* named Air Berlin as the best low-cost carrier in Europe in 2006.

In January 2004, Air Berlin announced cooperation with former Formula One racing driver Niki Lauda's newly founded airline, Niki. The two airlines considered their cooperation a "low fares alliance." Air Berlin held 24 percent of Lauda's enterprise, operating a mixed fleet of Boeing 737s and Airbus A320s. The airline's initial stock issue took place in May 2006, with its initial share-price range reduced from €15.0–€17.5 before finally opening at €12, due to rising fuel costs and other market pressures. As a result of the initial public offering, the company claimed to have over €400 million in the bank, to be used to fund further expansion, including aircraft purchases. On August 17, 2006, it was announced that Air Berlin had acquired dba, formerly Deutsch British Airways, a budget airline based at Munich. Dba would continue to operate as an independent company but would be marketed as Air Berlin, "powered by dba." Having incurred losses during 2005 and the first half of 2006, Air Berlin was expecting "a considerable profit for the 2006 financial year."[20]

bmibaby

In March 2003, bmi British Midland began operating its low-fares subsidiary, bmibaby, from its own base at East Midlands Airport. A Birmingham base, launched in January 2005, was at the forefront of bmibaby's effort to become one of the leading low-cost carriers in the Midlands and northern England. In 2005, bmibaby carried almost 3.5 million passengers with a load factor of just under 80 percent.

The airline had expanded into 29 airports in various UK cities, Ireland, Spain, Portugal, France, Italy, and the Czech Republic, with 14 Boeing 737s in service. It appeared to compete with its parent company on some of its routes. The parent company, bmi, was the United Kingdom's second largest scheduled service operator, serving domestic, European, and American routes. It made a modest profit in 2005. It was a competitor on the Dublin–London Heathrow route.

FlyBE

In the summer of 2002, British European Airways, a regional carrier, restyled itself as FlyBE, incorporating aspects of the budget airline model. These included a change in its booking practices away from travel agents to the Internet, passenger payment for on-board services, no ticket refunds (since illegal), a charge for itinerary changes, and credit card booking. The network was also redesigned to focus on more leisure-type destinations. However, it did provide an economy-plus product offering frequent-flyer points, a lounge, priority check-in, and complimentary onboard service, alongside the standard product. In December 2005, the airline announced that passengers would be charged for hold luggage, although fares would be slightly reduced, to encourage passengers with hand baggage only who would pay less overall. FlyBE CEO Jim French acknowledged that the adoption of the low-cost model was a cultural challenge. He also described FlyBE as not in the same low-cost bracket as Ryanair. In terms of fare and service levels, it was just ahead of easyJet but below the mainline carriers.

In 2006, FlyBE served destinations in the United Kingdom, Ireland, France, Spain, Austria, the Netherlands, Switzerland, and the Czech Republic from six bases across the United Kingdom and Channel Islands. It chose primary airports, such as London Heathrow and Paris Charles de Gaulle. In early 2003, the carrier was planning to standardize its fleet to Bombardier Dash-8 Q400 turboprop jets. The average seat costs of the sub-120-seat capacity of these aircraft were higher than those of the larger 737s, but French argued that the airline competed not on seat costs, but on higher frequencies than 737s.

FlyBE, privately owned by one of the family trusts of a steel millionaire, Jack Walker, had plans for a possible stock offering or trade sale in 2007. It achieved a net profit of $11.5 (€9) million in 2005, having made a loss of $5.5 (€4.3) million the year before. This loss was despite a windfall secured through the joint sale with Air France of takeoff and landing slots at Heathrow Airport.

In November 2006, FlyBE reached an agreement to purchase BA Connect, British Airways' regional operation. British Airways would acquire a 15 percent stake in the new business. The acquisition (which did not include BA Connect's London City or Manchester to JFK routes) was expected to significantly increase FlyBE's route network in both the United Kingdom and continental Europe making FlyBE Europe's largest regional airline. The new FlyBE would have 159 routes, including 35 new routes; 10 million passengers; and €900 million in revenues. Also, it would operate from 23 UK and 36 European airports and would have 70 aircraft by the end of 2007.

Aer Lingus

Aer Lingus, operating short- and long-haul services, was the national state-owned airline of Ireland, until it became a publicly-owned company in October 2006. The events of 9/11 were particularly traumatic for Aer Lingus, as the airline teetered on the verge of bankruptcy. It brought an end to plans for an initial public stock offering that had already been postponed several times. In late 2001, the choice was to change, to be taken over, or liquidated. Led by a determined and focused chief executive, Willie Walsh (who was to become the CEO of British Airways in 2005) and his senior management team, the company set about cutting costs. One ingredient of its cost reduction was a severance program costing over €100 million, whereby 2,000 of its 6,000 employees left the group. By the end of 2002, Aer Lingus had turned 2001's €125 million loss into a €33 million profit, and it improved still further with a net profit of €88.9 million in 2005.

In essence, Aer Lingus maintained that it had transformed itself into a low-fare airline, and that it matched Ryanair fares on most routes, or that it was only very slightly higher. The airline's chief operating officer said:

> Aer Lingus no longer offers a gold-plated service to customers, but offers a more practical and appropriate service. . . . It clearly differentiates itself from no-frills carriers. We fly to main airports and not 50 miles away. We assign seats for passengers, we beat low fares competitors on punctuality, even though we fly

to more congested airports, and we always fulfill our commitment to customers—unlike no frills carriers.[21]

In its defense document against the Ryanair takeover bid in October 2006, the airline proclaimed a strong track record of growth, with a return on capital and operating margin second only to Ryanair in the European airline industry, leading the Irish market in terms of technological innovation and value-added service innovations such as self-check-in, advance seat selection, Web check-in and a dynamic and easy-to-use online booking service. Its customer proposition was "Low Fares, Way Better," and it emphasized flying to more convenient airports and posting leading punctuality statistics at Heathrow. A survey conducted by the airline found that customers considered Aer Lingus better value for money than Ryanair, even if they paid slightly higher fares. Aer Lingus achieved more than three times as much short-haul passenger growth as Ryanair from Dublin in 2005, with substantial opportunities to grow ancillary revenues. Staff productivity improved from 6,108 to 3,475 employees per passenger between 2001 and 2005.

LEADING RYANAIR INTO THE FUTURE

In November 2005, Michael O'Leary, age 44, announced that he had set 2008 as his own departure date from Ryanair. At that stage he would have been with the airline for 20 years. He declared that he would sever all links with the airline, refusing to "move upstairs" as chairman. "I think it is one of the worst things you can do; you have to get out, otherwise you will be like Banquo's ghost, hanging around the corridors," he said. "You don't need a doddery old bastard hanging around the place."[22]

O'Leary bred horses at Gigginstown Stud, a farm about 50 miles (80 kilometers) from Dublin. His horse War of Attrition won the Cheltenham Gold Cup, one of the most prestigious races in steeplechasing, in 2006.

In 2006, Michael O'Leary was Ryanair's largest shareholder, with 4.53 percent of the share capital. Although O'Leary consistently praised his management team, Ryanair was inextricably identified with its dynamic chief executive. He was credited with single-handedly transforming European air transport.

The airline won various international awards, such as Best Managed Airline. In 2001, O'Leary was awarded the European Businessman of the Year Award by *Fortune* magazine; in 2004, *The Financial Times* named Michael O'Leary as one of 25 European "business stars," who are expected to make a difference. The newspaper described him as personifying "the brash new Irish business elite" and possessing "a head for numbers, a shrewd marketing brain and a ruthless competitive streak."[23] In 2005, he was ranked eighteenth among the World's Most Respected Business Leaders in a *Financial Times/PricewaterhouseCoopers* poll.

Present and former staff had praised O'Leary's leadership style. "Michael's genius is his ability to motivate and energize people. . . . There is an incredible energy in that place. People work incredibly hard and get a lot out of it. They operate a very lean operation for a company of its size. It is without peer," said Tim Jeans, a former sales and marketing director of Ryanair, currently CEO of a small low-cost rival, MyTravelLite.[24]

O'Leary's publicity-seeking antics had earned him a high profile. These included his declaration of war on easyJet when, wearing an army uniform, he drove up in a tank to easyJet's headquarters in Luton Airport. In similar vein, he flew to Milan Bergamo when Ryanair opened its hub there aboard a jet bearing the slogan "Arrivederci Alitalia." He had also dressed up as St. Patrick and as the Pope to promote ticket offers.

It was O'Leary's outspokenness that had made him a figure of public debate. One article noted, "He is called everything from 'arrogant pig' to 'messiah.'"[25] He had certainly made investors very happy, and even detractors credited Ryanair with opening up the era of inexpensive air travel. At the same time, O'Leary was a reviled figure among trade unionists, and he had antagonized Irish government circles with his continuous attacks on the state airport authority. Michael O'Leary was very personally involved in Ryanair's battles with the European Union, and some pundits believed that his abrasive style had only served to annoy the commissioners. Indeed, the Belgian commissioner, Philippe Busquin, denounced Michael O'Leary as "irritating" and added that he was "not the only Commissioner who is allergic to the mere mention of the name of Ryanair's arrogant chief."[26]

Irish Times columnist John McManus suggested that "maybe it's time for Ryanair to jettison O'Leary."[27] McManus claimed that O'Leary had become a caricature of himself, fulfilling all 15 warning signs of an executive about to fail. These 15 signs had been identified by Professor Sydney Finklestein of the Tuck Business School at Dartmouth College, in the United States; they fell under five main headings: ignoring change, the wrong vision, getting too close, arrogant attitudes, and old formulae. After apparently demonstrating how well O'Leary fit the Finklestein criteria, McManus nonetheless concluded: "So, is it time for Ryanair to dump Mr. O'Leary? Depends whether you prefer the track record of one of the most successful businessmen in modern aviation, or the theories of a US academic from an Ivy League school."

Perhaps the last words should go to Michael O'Leary himself: "We could make a mistake and I could get hung," he said. He reiterated a point he had often made before: "It is okay doing the cheeky chappie, running around Europe, thumbing your nose, but I am not Herb Kelleher [the legendary founder of the original budget airline, Southwest Airlines, in the United States]. He was a genius and I am not."[28]

In what could have been his darkest hour, O'Leary was irrepressible: "This is the most fun you can have without taking your clothes off. It is much more fun when the world is falling apart than when things are boring and going well," he declared on the day he announced a shock profits warning in January 2004.[29]

So, how do these upbeat comments and the Aer Lingus bid fit with Michael O'Leary's declaration to part company with Ryanair? Would he really retire in 2008 and, if so, what would happen to Ryanair and its ambitions? No one really knew the answer to these questions, but it would certainly lie in Michael O'Leary's propensity to surprise his admirers and detractors alike.

Endnotes

[1]Companies UK, "Ryanair Sets Its Cap at Local Rival Aer Lingus," *Financial Times*, October 7, 2006, p. 21.

[2]Statement made at Ryanair's half-yearly results presentation, November 6, 2006.

[3]S. Pogatchnik, "Aer Lingus Rejects Ryanair Takeover Offer," *Business-Week* online, October 5, 2006. Manchester United and Liverpool have a long-standing legendary rivalry in English football (i.e., soccer).

[4]E. Oliver, "Ryanair's Profits Rise 38% as Aer Lingus Bid Falters," *Irish Times*, November 7, 2006, p. 21.

[5]S. Furlong, *Ryanair as a Consumer Growth Company: Inside the 21st Century European Travel Phenomenon* (Dublin: Davy Stockbrokers, March 2006).

[6]*Financial Times*, September 9, 2006, p. 16.

[7]K. Done and T. Braithwaite, "Ryanair to Allow Mobile Phone Calls Next Year," *Financial Times*, August 31, 2006, p. 1.

[8]Lex, "Ryanair," *Financial Times*, August 2, 2006, p. 14.

[9]Ryanair annual report, 2001

[10]Ryanair 2007 half-yearly results.

[11]FT Reporters, "Airlines in Backlash Over Travel Restrictions," *Financial Times*, August 19/20, 2006, p. 1.

[12]S. Cairns and C. Newson, *Predict and Decide: Aviation, Climate Change and UK Policy* (Oxford: ECI Research Report 33, Environmental Change Institute, University of Oxford, 2006).

[13]Sir Nicholas Stern, "Economics of Climate Change," review for UK government, 2006.

[14]P. Munter, "Swedish Premier and Ex-Minister Sue Ryanair Over Adverts with Their Pictures," *Financial Times*, April 7, 2006, p. 9.

[15]D. Milmo, "Ryanair—The World's Least Favourite Airline," *The Guardian*, October 26, 2006.

[16]Ibid.

[17]A. Clark, "Ryanair . . . the Low-Fare Airline with the Sky-High Insurance Levy," *The Guardian*, May 8, 2006.

[18]Furlong, *Ryanair as a Consumer Growth Company*.

[19]Information posted at Low Cost Graveyard Web site, www.etn.nl/lcostgra.htm.

[20]Air Berlin Investor Relations Web site, August 2006.

[21]S. Creaton, "Aer Lingus's New Model Airline Takes Off," *Irish Times*, August 8, 2003.

[22]D. Dalby, "I'm Going for Good, O'Leary Tells Ryanair," *Sunday Times*, November 20, 2005, News Section, p. 3.

[23]B. Groom, "Leaders of the New Europe: Business Stars Chart a Course for the Profits of the Future," *Financial Times*, April 20, 2004.

[24]G. Bowley, "How Low Can You Go?" *Financial Times Magazine*, no.9 (June 21, 2003).

[25]Ibid.

[26]S. Creaton, "Turbulent Times for Ryanair's High-Flier," *Irish Times*, January 31, 2004.

[27]J. McManus, "Maybe It's Time for Ryanair to Jettison O'Leary," *Irish Times*, August 11, 2003.

[28]Bowley, "How Low Can You Go?"

[29]Creaton, "Turbulent Times."

Monitoring Foreign Suppliers: The Challenge of Detecting Unethical Practices

Arthur A. Thompson
The University of Alabama

Importers of goods from China, Indonesia, Cambodia, Vietnam, Malaysia, Korea, Pakistan, Bangladesh, Sri Lanka, India, the Philippines, Peru, Honduras, the Dominican Republic, Tunisia, and other less developed countries had long had to contend with accusations by human rights activists that they sourced goods from sweatshop manufacturers that paid substandard wages, required unusually long work hours, used child labor, operated unsafe workplaces, and habitually engaged in assorted other unsavory practices. Since the 1990s, companies had responded to criticisms about sourcing goods from manufacturers in developing nations where working conditions were often substandard by instituting elaborate codes of conduct for foreign suppliers and by periodically inspecting the manufacturing facilities of these suppliers to try to eliminate abuses and promote improved working conditions. In several industries where companies sourced goods from common foreign suppliers, companies had joined forces to conduct plant monitoring; for example, Hewlett-Packard, Dell, and other electronics companies that relied heavily on Asia-based manufacturers to supply components or assemble digital cameras, handheld devices, and PCs had entered into an alliance to combat worker abuse and poor working conditions in supplier factories.

But a number of unscrupulous foreign manufacturers had recently gotten much better at concealing human rights abuses and substandard working conditions. In November 2006, *BusinessWeek* ran a cover story detailing how shady foreign manufacturers were deceiving inspection teams and escaping detection.[1] According to the *BusinessWeek* special report, Ningbo Beifa Group—a top Chinese supplier of pens, mechanical pens, and highlighters to Wal-Mart, Staples, Woolworth, and some 400 other retailers in 100 countries—was alerted in late 2005 that a Wal-Mart inspection team would soon be visiting the company's factory in the coastal city of Ningbo. Wal-Mart was Beifa's largest customer and on three previous occasions had caught Beija paying its 3,000 workers less than the Chinese minimum wage and violating overtime rules; a fourth offense would end Wal-Mart's purchases from Beifa. But weeks prior to the audit, an administrator at Beifa's factory in Ningbo got a call from representatives of Shanghai Corporate Responsibility Management & Consulting Company offering to help the Beifa factory pass the Wal-Mart inspection.[2] The Beifa administrator agreed to pay the requested fee of $5,000. The consultant advised management at the Beifa factory in Ningbo to create fake but authentic-looking records regarding pay scales and overtime work and make sure to get any workers with grievances out of the plant on the day of the audit. Beifa managers at the factory were also coached on how to answer questions that the auditors would likely ask. Beifa's Ningbo factory reportedly passed the Wal-Mart inspection in early 2006 without altering any of its practices.[3] A lawyer for Beifa confirmed that the company had indeed employed the Shanghai consulting firm but said that factory personnel engaged in no dishonest actions to pass the audit; the lawyer indicated that the factory passed the audit because it had taken steps to correct the problems found in Wal-Mart's prior audits.

GROWING USE OF STRATEGIES TO DELIBERATELY DECEIVE PLANT INSPECTORS

In 2007, substandard wages and abusive working conditions were thought to be prevalent in factories in a host of countries—China, Indonesia, Cambodia, Vietnam, Malaysia, Korea, Pakistan, Bangladesh,

Sri Lanka, India, the Philippines, Peru, Honduras, the Dominican Republic, Tunisia, and several other countries in Latin America, Eastern Europe, the Middle East, and Africa. (See Exhibit 1 for a sample of the problems in eight countries.) Factories in China were particularly in the spotlight because of China's prominence as the world's biggest source of low-priced goods. China was the largest single source of goods imported into both the United States and the 25 countries comprising the European Union. U.S. imports from Chinese manufacturers amounted to about $280 billion in 2006.

Political support in many countries for growing trade ties with offshore manufacturers, especially those in China, often hinged on the ability of companies with global sourcing strategies to convince domestic governmental officials, human rights groups, and concerned citizens that they were doing all they

Exhibit 1   **Comparative Labor and Workplace Conditions in Eight Countries, 2006**

Country	Labor and Workplace Overview
Brazil	Primary problems in the manufacturing workplace are forced labor, inadequate occupational safety (work accidents are common in several industries), and wage discrimination (wages paid to females are 54% to 64% of those paid to males).
China	Factories are most prone to ignore minimum wage requirements, underpay for overtime work, subject workers to unsafe and unhealthy working conditions, and suppress worker attempts to join independent unions.
India	Most common issues concern underpayment of minimum wages, overtime pay violations, use of child labor (according to one estimate some 100 million children ages 5 to 14 work and at least 12.6 million work full-time), the use of forced labor (perhaps as many as 65 million people), and inattention to occupational safety.
Indonesia	The stand-out issues concern weak enforcement of minimum-wage rules and work hours in factories, overtime pay violations in factories, subpar occupational safety (especially in mining and fishing), and use of underage labor (particularly in domestic service, mining, construction, and fishing industries).
Mexico	Problem areas include sweatshop conditions in many assembly plants near the U.S. border and elsewhere, fierce opposition to unions, insistence on pregnancy tests for female job applicants of child-bearing age, and use of child labor in non-export economic sectors.
Peru	Worst workplace conditions relate to lack of enforcement of wage and overtime provisions in factories, mandatory overtime requirements for many workers, and inattention to occupational safety.
South Africa	Most frequent offenses entail failure to observe minimum-wage and overtime pay rules (particularly in garment industry), use of child labor, occupational safety violations (especially in non-export sectors where outside monitoring is nonexistent), and low pay for women.
Sri Lanka	Most frequent violations relate to underpayment of wages, forced overtime requirements, compulsory work on Sundays and holidays, and inattention to worker health and safety (such as excessive noise, blocked exits, and disregard for worker safety—one study found 60% of grain and spice mill workers lost fingers in work-related accidents and/or contracted skin diseases).

Source: Compiled by the author from information in "How China's Labor Conditions Stack Up Against Those of Other Low-Cost Nations," *BusinessWeek Online,* November 27, 2006, www.businessweek.com (accessed January 26, 2007). The information was provided to *BusinessWeek* by Verité, a Massachusetts-based nonprofit social auditing and research organization with expertise in human rights and labor abuses in supplier factories around the world.

could do to police working conditions in the plants of suppliers in low-wage, poverty-stricken countries where sweatshop practices were concentrated. A strong program of auditing the offshore plants of suspect employers was a way for a company to cover itself and negate accusations that it was unfairly exploiting workers in less developed countries.

Workplace Rules in China

Minimum wages in China were specified by local or provincial governments and in 2006 ranged from $45 to $101 per month, which equated to hourly rates of $0.25 to $0.65 based on a 40-hour workweek.[4] According to Chinese government income data compiled by the U.S. Bureau of Labor Statistics and a Beijing consulting firm, the average manufacturing wage in China was $0.64 per hour (again assuming a 40-hour workweek). While the standard workweek in Chinese provinces officially ranged from 40 to 44 hours, there were said to be numerous instances where plant personnel worked 60 to 100 hours per week, sometimes with only one or two days off per month. Such long work hours meant that the actual average manufacturing wage in China was likely well below $0.64 per hour in 2005–2006. According to estimates made by a veteran inspector of Chinese factories, employees at garment, electronics, and other plants making goods for export typically worked more than 80 hours per week and earned an average of $0.42 per hour.[5]

Overtime pay rules in Chinese provinces officially called for time-and-a-half pay for all work over eight hours per day and between double and triple pay for work on Saturdays, Sundays, and holidays. However, it was commonplace for Chinese employers to disregard overtime pay rules, and governmental enforcement of minimum wage and overtime requirements by both Beijing officials and officials in local Chinese provinces was often minimal to nonexistent. At a Hong Kong garment plant where 2,000 employees put in many overtime hours operating sewing and stitching machines, worker pay averaged about $125 per month—an amount that the owner acknowledged did not meet Chinese overtime pay requirements. The owner said that overtime rules were "a fantasy. Maybe in two or three decades we can meet them."[6] Many young Chinese factory workers were tolerant of long hours and less than full overtime pay because they

wanted to earn as much as possible, the idea being to save enough of their income to return to their homes in the countryside after a few years of factory employment.

Chinese export manufacturing was said to be rife with tales of deception to frustrate plant monitoring and escape compliance with local minimum wage and overtime rules and supplier codes of conduct. Indeed, a new breed of consultants had sprung up in China to aid local manufacturers in passing audits conducted both by customer companies and industry alliance groups.[7]

Emerging Strategies to Frustrate Plant Monitoring Efforts

The efforts of unscrupulous manufacturers in China and other parts of the world to game the plant monitoring system and use whatever deceptive practices it took to successfully pass plant audits had four chief elements:

1. *Maintaining two sets of books*—Factories generated a set of bogus payroll records and time sheets to show audit teams that their workers were properly paid and received the appropriate overtime pay; the genuine records were kept secret. For example, at an onsite audit of a Chinese maker of lamps for Home Depot, Sears, and other retailers, plant managers provided inspectors with payroll records and time sheets showing that employees worked a five-day week from 8 a.m. to 5:30 p.m. with a 30-minute lunch break and no overtime hours; during interviews, managers at the plant said the records were accurate. But other records auditors found at the site, along with interviews with workers, indicated that employees worked an extra three to five hours daily with one or two days off per month during peak production periods; inspectors were unable to verify whether workers at the plant received overtime pay.[8] According to a compliance manager at a major multinational company who had overseen many factory audits, the percentage of Chinese employers submitting false payroll records had risen from 46 percent to 75 percent during the past four years; the manager also estimated that only

20 percent of Chinese suppliers complied with local minimum-wage rules and that just 5 percent obeyed hour limitations.[9]

2. *Hiding the use of underage workers and unsafe work practices*—In some instances, factories in China, parts of Africa, and select other countries in Asia, Eastern Europe, and the Middle East employed underage workers. This was disguised either by falsifying the personnel records of underage employees, by adeptly getting underage employees off the premises when audit teams arrived, or by putting underage employees in back rooms concealed from auditors. A memo distributed in one Chinese factory instructed managers to "notify underage trainees, underage full-time workers, and workers without identification to leave the manufacturing workshop through the back door. Order them not to loiter near the dormitory area. Secondly, immediately order the receptionist to gather all relevant documents and papers."[10] At a toy plant in China, a compliance inspector, upon smelling strong fumes in a poorly ventilated building, found young female employees on a production line using spray guns to paint figurines; in a locked back room that a factory official initially refused to open, an apparently underage worker was found hiding behind co-workers.[11]

3. *Meeting requirements by secretly shifting production to subcontractors*—On occasions, suppliers met the standards set by customers by secretly shifting some production to subcontractors who failed to observe pay standards, skirted worker safety procedures, or otherwise engaged in abuses of various kinds.

4. *Coaching managers and employees on answering questions posed by audit team members*—Both managers and workers were tutored on what to tell inspectors should they be interviewed. Scripting responses about wages and overtime pay, hours worked, safety procedures, training, and other aspects related to working conditions was a common tactic for thwarting what inspectors could learn from interviews. However, in instances where plant inspectors were able to speak confidentially with employees away from the worksite, they often got information at variance with what they were told during onsite interviews—plant personnel were more inclined

to be truthful and forthcoming about actual working conditions and pay practices when top-level plant management could not trace the information given to inspectors back to them.

There was a growing awareness among companies attempting to enforce supplier codes of conduct that all factories across the world with substandard working conditions and reasons to hide their practices from outside view played cat-and-mouse games with plant inspectors. In many less-developed countries struggling to build a manufacturing base and provide jobs for their citizens, factory managers considered deceptive practices a necessary evil to survive, principally because improving wages and working conditions to comply with labor codes and customers' codes of conduct for suppliers raised costs and imperiled already thin profit margins. Violations were said to be most prevalent at factories making apparel, but more violations were surfacing in factories making furniture, appliances, toys, and electronics.

However, large global corporations such as General Electric, Motorola, Dell, Nestlé, and Toyota that owned and operated their own offshore manufacturing plants in China and other low-wage countries had not been accused of mistreating their employees or having poor working conditions. The offshore factories of well-known global and multinational companies were seldom subject to monitoring by outsiders because the workplace environments in their foreign plants were relatively good in comparison to those of local manufacturing enterprises who made a business of supplying low-cost components and finished goods to companies and retailers in affluent, industrialized nations.

FOREIGN SUPPLIER COMPLIANCE PROGRAMS AT NIKE AND WAL-MART

Corporate sensitivity to charges of being socially irresponsible in their sourcing of goods from foreign manufacturers had prompted hundreds of companies to establish supplier codes of conduct and to engage in compliance monitoring efforts of one kind or another manner. Most companies with global sourcing strategies and factory compliance programs worked proactively to improve working conditions globally, preferring to help suppliers achieve the expected standards rather than abruptly and permanently cutting off purchases. The most commonly observed problems worldwide related to benefits such as pensions and insurance (medical, accident, unemployment) not being paid. Other frequent issues included workers not being paid for all hours worked, the use of false books, and incomplete or insufficient documentation.

Nike and Wal-Mart were two companies with supplier codes of conduct and rather extensive programs to monitor whether suppliers in low-wage, low-cost manufacturing locations across the world were complying with their codes of conduct. Both companies initiated such efforts in the 1990s because they came under fire from human rights activist groups for allegedly sourcing goods from sweatshop factories in China and elsewhere.

Nike's Supplier Code of Conduct and Compliance Monitoring Program

Nike was the world's leading designer, distributor, and marketer of athletic footwear, sports apparel, and sports equipment and accessories, but it did no manufacturing. All Nike products were sourced from contract manufacturers. In April 2005, Nike reported that there were over 730 factories actively engaged in manufacturing its products; of these, about 135 were in China (including Hong Kong and Macau); 73 in Thailand, 39 in Indonesia, 35 in Korea, 34 in Vietnam, 33 in Malaysia, 25 in Sri Lanka, and 18 in India.[12] Nike's contract factories employed roughly 625,000 workers, the majority of whom were women between the ages of 19 and 25 performing entry-level, low-skill jobs.

Nike drafted a code of conduct for its contract factories in 1991, distributed the code to all of its contract factories in 1992, and directed them to post the code in a visible place and in the appropriate local language. The code had been modified and updated over the years, and in 2007 also included a set of leadership standards that was adopted in 2002. Nike's code of conduct is presented in Exhibit 2. In 1998, in a move to strengthen its opposition to the use of child labor in factories, Nike directed its contract factories to set age standards for employment at 16 for apparel and 18 for footwear; these age standards were more demanding than those set in 1991 and exceeded the International Labor Organization's age minimum of 15 years.

Nike's System for Monitoring Contract Manufacturers.   During 2003–2006, Nike used three approaches to plant monitoring:[13]

- *Basic monitoring or SHAPE inspections:* SHAPE inspections, used since 1997, sought to gauge a factory's overall compliance performance, including environment, safety, and health. They were typically performed by Nike's field-based production staff and could be completed in one day or less. Nike's stated goal was to conduct two SHAPE audits on each active factory each year, but the actual number of such audits had fallen short of that target.

- *In-depth M-Audits:* The M-Audit was designed to provide a deeper measure of the working conditions within contract factories. As a general rule, Nike focused its plant inspection efforts on factories where noncompliance was most likely to occur. Factories located in highly regulated countries where workers were more informed about their rights and workplace laws and regulations were enforced were deemed less likely to be out of compliance. In 2003, Nike focused its M-audits on factories presumed to have the highest risk of noncompliance and the greatest size (as measured by worker population). In 2004 M-audits were focused on factories believed to be of medium risk for noncompliance. Nike's stated goal was to conduct M-audits for approximately 25–33 percent of its active factory base each year. The M-Audit included four major categories of inquiry (hiring practices, worker treatment, worker–management communications, and compensation) and covered more than 80 labor–management issues.

  In 2004 Nike had 46 employees who regularly conducted M-Audits. The typical M-Auditor was under the age of 30, and 74 percent were women. Nike tried to hire auditors who were local nationals and understood the local language and culture. In 2003–2004, over 9,200 factory workers were individually interviewed as part of the M-Audit process. Each interview took approximately 30 minutes. The typical M-Audit took an average of 48 hours to complete, including

Nike, Inc. was founded on a handshake

Implicit in that act was the determination that we would build our business with all of our partners based on trust, teamwork, honesty and mutual respect. We expect all of our business partners to operate on the same principles.

At the core of the NIKE corporate ethic is the belief that we are a company comprised of many different kinds of people, appreciating individual diversity, and dedicated to equal opportunity for each individual.

NIKE designs, manufactures, and markets products for sports and fitness consumers. At every step in that process, we are driven to do not only what is required by law, but what is expected of a leader. We expect our business partners to do the same. NIKE partners with contractors who share our commitment to best practices and continuous improvement in:

1. Management practices that respect the rights of all employees, including the right to free association and collective bargaining
2. Minimizing our impact on the environment
3. Providing a safe and healthy workplace
4. Promoting the health and well-being of all employees

Contractors must recognize the dignity of each employee, and the right to a workplace free of harassment, abuse or corporal punishment. Decisions on hiring, salary, benefits, advancement, termination or retirement must be based solely on the employee's ability to do the job. There shall be no discrimination based on race, creed, gender, marital or maternity status, religious or political beliefs, age or sexual orientation.

Wherever NIKE operates around the globe we are guided by this Code of Conduct and we bind our contractors to these principles. Contractors must post this Code in all major workspaces, translated into the language of the employee, and must train employees on their rights and obligations as defined by this Code and applicable local laws.

While these principles establish the spirit of our partnerships, we also bind our partners to specific standards of conduct. The core standards are set forth below.

Forced Labor

The contractor does not use forced labor in any form—prison, indentured, bonded or otherwise.

Child Labor

The contractor does not employ any person below the age of 18 to produce footwear. The contractor does not employ any person below the age of 16 to produce apparel, accessories or equipment. If at the time Nike production begins, the contractor employs people of the legal working age who are at least 15, that employment may continue, but the contractor will not hire any person going forward who is younger than the Nike or legal age limit, whichever is higher. To further ensure these age standards are complied with, the contractor does not use any form of homework for Nike production.

Compensation

The contractor provides each employee at least the minimum wage, or the prevailing industry wage, whichever is higher; provides each employee a clear, written accounting for every pay period; and does not deduct from employee pay for disciplinary infractions.

Benefits

The contractor provides each employee all legally mandated benefits.

Hours of Work/Overtime

The contractor complies with legally mandated work hours; uses overtime only when each employee is fully compensated according to local law; informs each employee at the time of hiring if mandatory overtime is a condition of employment; and on a regularly scheduled basis provides one day off in seven, and requires no more than 60 hours of work per week on a regularly scheduled basis, or complies with local limits if they are lower.

Environment, Safety and Health (ES&H)

The contractor has written environmental, safety and health policies and standards, and implements a system to minimize negative impacts on the environment, reduce work-related injury and illness, and promote the general health of employees.

Documentation and Inspection

The contractor maintains on file all documentation needed to demonstrate compliance with this Code of Conduct and required laws; agrees to make these documents available for Nike or its designated monitor; and agrees to submit to inspections with or without prior notice.

Source: www.nike.com (accessed January 25, 2007).

travel to and from the factory—travel hours accounted for between 25 and 30 percent of total M-Audit time.

- *Independent external monitoring:* Beginning in 2003, Nike became a member of the Fair Labor Association, an organization that conducted independent audits of factories that provided goods to members. The FLA applied a common set of compliance standards in all of its factory audits. About 40 factories supplying goods to Nike were audited by the FLA in 2003.

In 2004, Nike's compliance team consisted of 90 people based in 24 offices in 21 countries. The typical Nike compliance team in each country spent about one-third of their time on monitoring and auditing activities, about half their time assisting and tracking factory remediation activities, and the remainder of their time on troubleshooting and collaboration/outreach work.[14] In its 2004 Corporate Responsibility Report, Nike said

> With an average of one compliance staff for more than 10 factories—some of which are remote and some of which are large and complex businesses with 10,000 or more employees—tracking and assisting factory remediation is at times an overwhelming and incomplete body of work.[15]

Nike's factory audits were announced rather than unannounced because "much of the information we require in our evaluation of a factory is dependent upon access to relevant records and individuals within factory management."[16] When a factory was found to be out of compliance with the code of conduct, Nike's compliance team worked with factory management and the Nike business unit for which products were being manufactured to develop a Master Action Plan (MAP) that specified the factory's needed remediation efforts. The Nike production manager responsible for the business relationship with the contract factory monitored MAP progress and exchanged information about progress or obstacles with Nike's country compliance team. The Nike general manager for production monitored the progress of all factories within his or her purview, and weighed in when factory remediation progress was too slow.

To further facilitate factory compliance with Nike's Code of Conduct for suppliers, the company conducted or sponsored training and education programs for factory personnel. In 2004, over 16,500 factory managers and workers attended programs relating to labor issues, worker health and safety, and environmental protection.[17]

Nike's Compliance Rating System. Nike's factory ratings for SHAPE and M-Audits resulted in numeric scores ranging from 0 to 100 (a score of 100 indicated full compliance); these numeric scores were then converted to one of four overall grades:[18]

Grade	Criteria
A	No more than 5 minor violations on a factory's Master Action Plan for improving working conditions and achieving higher levels of compliance with Nike's Code of Conduct, and no more than 20 percent of MAP items past due.
B	No more than 5 minor violations, but no serious or critical issues outstanding on the MAP and no more than 30 percent of MAP items past due.
C	One or more C-level compliance issues outstanding on the MAP and no more than 30 percent of MAP items past due—examples of C-level issues included excessive work hours per week (more than 60 but less than 72), not providing 1 day off in 7, verbal or psychological harassment of workers, exceeding legal annual overtime work limit for 10% or more of workforce, conditions likely to lead to moderate injury or illness to workers, and conditions likely to lead to moderate harm to environment or community.
D	One or more D-level issues outstanding on the factory's MAP or past due correction of prior D-level issues; or more than 40 percent of open MAP items past due. Examples of D-level issues included unwillingness to comply with code standards, falsified records, coaching of workers to falsify information, use of underage workers or forced labor, paying below the legal wage, no verifiable timekeeping system, exceeding daily work hour limit or work in excess of more than 72 hours per week for more than 10% of workforce, not providing one day off in 14, and conditions that could lead to serious worker injury or harm to the environment.

Note: A grade of E was assigned to factories for which there was insufficient information.

Exhibit 3   **Summary Results of Nike's Compliance Ratings for Contract Suppliers, Fiscal Years 2003–2004**

	Geographic Region				
	Americas	**Europe, Middle East, Africa**	**Northern Asia**	**Southern Asia**	**Worldwide Total**
Number of SHAPE audits in 2004	178	157	378	303	1,016
Number of M-Audits in 2003 and 2004	148	56	198	167	569
M-Audit Numeric Scores in 2003–2004					
Lowest score	46	49	25	20	20
Average score	78	70	58	58	65
Highest score	94	96	95	95	99
Compliance Ratings for Contact Factories as of June 2004					
Grade of A	32	15	34	25	106 (15%)
Grade of B	64	40	147	76	327 (44%)
Grade of C	18	7	33	65	123 (17%)
Grade of D	5	35	14	8	62 (8%)
Grade of E	18	7	22	70	117 (16%)

Note: Worker population in M-Audited factories was 375,000 in fiscal year 2003 and 213,000 in fiscal year 2004.

Source: Nike's 2004 Corporate Responsibility Report, pp. 20, 34, and 35.

Exhibit 3 presents a summary of Nike's latest available factory ratings.

Cutting Off Orders to Noncomplying or Nonperforming Suppliers. A factory was cut from Nike's supplier base when, over a specified period, Nike management determined that factory management lacked the capacity or the will to correct serious issues of noncompliance. One supplier in China, for example, was cited for repeated violations of overtime standards and falsification of records. The compliance team established action plans, which three different Nike business units worked with the factory to implement. After six months of continuous efforts, and no improvement, the factory was dropped. In November 2006, Nike severed its business relationship with a Pakistani supplier of soccer balls that failed to correct serious code of conduct violations.

More typically, Nike's decisions to end a business relationship with problem suppliers was based on a balanced scorecard of factory performance that took into account labor code compliance along with such measures such as price, quality, and delivery

time. For example, a manufacturing group in South Asia had performed poorly on a range of issues, from overtime and worker–management communication to the quality of product and shipping dates. After a series of performance reviews, Nike management informed the factory group that it would not be placing orders for the next season. Nike did not report on factories dropped solely from noncompliance reasons related to its code of conduct because, management said, "it is often difficult to isolate poor performance on compliance as the sole reason for terminating a business relationship."[19]

To give its contract manufacturers greater incentive to comply with Nike's workplace standards and expectations, during crunch production periods Nike management and plant auditors had given some factories latitude to institute long workweeks (above 72 hours) and not hold them to a strict standard of 1 day off out of every 14 days if the employer gave workers more days off during slack production periods. Nike was also working to streamline its methods of designing shoes and placing orders with key suppliers and helping foreign factories develop more efficient production techniques, so as to help contract factories eliminate the need to institute long workweeks and excessive overtime. According to Nike's vice president for global footwear operations, "If you improve efficiency and innovation, it changes the cost equation" for factories.[20]

Wal-Mart's Supplier Code of Conduct and Compliance Monitoring Program

In 1992, Wal-Mart established a set of standards for its suppliers and put in place an ethical standards program to monitor supplier compliance with these standards.[21] Since then, Wal-Mart's standards for suppliers had been periodically evaluated and modified based on experience and feedback from the ethical sourcing community. The company's standards for suppliers covered compensation, working hours, forced labor, underage labor, discrimination, compliance with applicable national laws and regulation, health and safety practices, environmental abuse, freedom of association and collective bargaining, rights concerning foreign contract workers, and the right of audit by Wal-Mart.

Prior to contracting with any supplier, Wal-Mart required suppliers to review and sign a supplier agreement, which incorporated an expectation that the supplier would comply with Wal-Mart's standards for suppliers. In addition, it was mandatory that all suppliers display Wal-Mart's "Standards for Suppliers" poster in all of the suppliers' factories. Factory management was required to sign that it had read and fully understood the "Standards for Suppliers" poster, and a copy of the poster in the relevant language had to be posted in a public place within the factory. Wal-Mart's "Standards for Suppliers" poster was available in 25 languages.

In February 2002, Wal-Mart created the Global Procurement Services Group (GPSG), which was charged with identifying new suppliers, sourcing new products, building partnerships with existing suppliers, managing Wal-Mart's global supply chain of direct imports, providing workplace standards training to suppliers, and enforcing compliance with Wal-Mart's supplier standards. All Wal-Mart personnel engaged in monitoring supplier compliance became part of the GPSG organization. In 2007, GPSG consisted of about 1,600 people working

from offices in 23 countries, including China, Indonesia, India, Pakistan, Sri Lanka, Bangladesh, Honduras, Nicaragua, Guatemala, Mexico, Brazil, and Turkey (countries where supplier compliance presented big challenges).

In 2005–2006, Wal-Mart purchased goods from about 7,200 factories in over 60 countries; about 2,000 of the 7,200 factories had recently come into Wal-Mart's compliance and factory audit system due to mergers, acquisitions, and new factory construction. About 200 Wal-Mart personnel scattered across GPSG's offices in all 23 countries were engaged in monitoring suppliers for compliance with Wal-Mart's standards for suppliers. Suppliers covered by Wal-Mart's ethical standards program had to disclose the factory (or factories) used to fulfill each order placed by Wal-Mart.

Wal-Mart's Supplier Auditing Program and Compliance Rating System

During 2005, Wal-Mart audited more factories than any other company in the world, performing 14,750 initial and follow-up audits of 7,200 supplier factories; in 2004, Wal-Mart conducted 12,561 factory audits. The company's audit methodology and its factory rating system are described in Exhibit 4. A summary of Wal-Mart's audit findings for 2004 and 2005 is contained in Exhibit 5. Wal-Mart management said that the greater incidence of violations in 2005 compared to 2004 was primarily due to a 100 percent increase in unannounced audits, increased rigor of supplier standards, a reclassification of violations to strengthen and reinforce their severity, the implementation of team audits, and greater auditor familiarity with the factories and their workers.

Rather than banning the placement of orders at supplier factories receiving Yellow (medium-risk violations) and Orange (high-risk violations) ratings, Wal-Mart's policy was to work with supplier factories to reduce violations and achieve steady improvement of workplace conditions, a position widely endorsed by most human rights activists, concerned citizens groups, and nongovernmental agencies striving for better factory conditions for low-wage workers. To help promote higher levels of supplier compliance, Wal-Mart trained more than 8,000 supplier personnel in 2004 and another 11,000

Exhibit 4   **Wal-Mart's Factory Audit Methodology and Factory Ratings System, 2005**

- **Opening Meeting**—The Opening Meeting consisted of (1) confirmation of the factory and its information, (2) an introduction by the Wal-Mart auditors to factory management and supplier representatives, (3) a presentation and signing of the Wal-Mart Gifts & Gratuity Policy (which forbids any offer or receipt of gifts or bribes by the factory or the auditor), and (4) a request by the auditors of factory documentation related to personnel, production, time and pay records.
- **Factory Tour**—The auditors conducted a factory walk-through to examine factory conditions. The walk-through had minimal factory managers present because auditors asked production employees questions about machinery operation and other working conditions. Auditors also followed up with workers interviewed in previous audits about conditions since the last audit. The tour lasted up to three hours, depending on the size of the factory.
- **Worker Interviews**—During factory tours, auditors typically choose workers off the shop floor to interview, although additional workers could be requested to verify factory records during the documentation review process. Factory management had provide a private location for interviews, and under no circumstances were interviews conducted with factory management or supplier representatives present. Workers were interviewed in same-sex groups. The objectives of the interviews were to discover what interviewees had to say relevant to the audit, verify findings and observations made by the auditors, and ensure that workers understood their rights. A minimum of 15 workers were interviewed. The number of workers interviewed depended on the size of the factory.
- **Factory Documentation Review**—Auditors conducted an on-site inspection of appropriate production documents. For Initial and Annual audits, document review required records dating back at least three months and up to one year. Follow-up audits not only included reviewing findings from the previous audit, but also always included review of hours and compensation. Any factory that failed or refused to comply with this requirement was subject to immediate cancellation of any and all outstanding orders.
- **Closing Meeting**—Auditors summarized the audit findings, described any violations found, made recommendations to remedy the violations, and gave factory management a chance to ask any questions about the audit. Factory management and the auditor both signed the on-site audit report. Auditors left a copy of the signed audit findings and recommendations. Factory management was expected to act on all the recommendations in the on-site report and to present a completed action plan to the auditor during the follow-up audit opening meeting so auditors could validate that the actions were taken. Suppliers and factory management were encouraged to contact the regional Wal-Mart Ethical Standards office to discuss any concerns or questions about the on-site report and recommendations.
- **Factory Ratings**—Factories were rated Green, Yellow, Orange, or Red. A Green assessment was assigned for no or minor violations; a Yellow rating signified medium-risk violations; an Orange rating entailed high-risk violations (and was an automatic rating for factories where the use of one or two underage workers was discovered); and a Red rating indicated failure to pass the audit (factories found to use prison or forced labor, have extremely unsafe working conditions, have more than two underage workers, engage in serious worker abuse, or have other serious violations were immediately assigned a Red rating). Red-rated factories were permanently banned from producing merchandise for Wal-Mart. Starting in 2006, Green-rated factories had re-audits every 2 years instead of annually. Yellow- and Orange-rated factories had follow-up audits after 120 days to allow time for corrections and verification that corrective actions had been implemented. Factories rated Orange with underage labor violations for only one or two workers were an exception to the timeline for re-audits; such factories were re-audited within 30 days. If the follow-up audit for these factories indicated that the use of underage labor had been corrected, the factory could continue production for Wal-Mart; a failure on the follow-up 30-day audit resulted in a Red rating and a permanent order ban. A factory receiving an Orange assessment four times in a two-year period was banned from producing for Wal-Mart for up to one year (the ban on orders for such factories was extended from 90 days to one year starting January 1, 2005, in order to strengthen the seriousness of program non-compliance).
- **Use of Outside Auditors**—When Wal-Mart sourced goods for its foreign stores from suppliers in the same country in which the foreign stores were located, it used outside auditors to check supplier compliance. In 2005, the outside auditing firms used were Accordia, Bureau Veritas, Cal Safety Compliance Corporation (CSCC), Global Social Compliance, Intertek Testing Services, and Société Générale de Surveillance.

Source: Wal-Mart's 2005 Report on Ethical Sourcing, posted at www.walmart.com (accessed January 25, 2007).

suppliers and members of factory management in 2005. The training focused on increasing supplier familiarity with Wal-Mart's standards for suppliers and encouraging an exchange of information about factory operating practices. Wal-Mart also actively worked with its foreign suppliers on ways to do better

Exhibit 5   **Comparison of Wal-Mart's 2004 and 2005 Factory Audit Results**

	2004	2005
Number of factory audits	12,561	14,750
Audits resulting in Green ratings	20.7%	9.6%
Audits resulting in Yellow ratings	42.6%	37.0%
Audits resulting in Orange ratings	35.6%	52.3%
Number of factories permanently banned from receiving orders	1,211	164 (141 of these related to the use of underage labor)

Source: Wal-Mart's 2005 Report on Ethical Sourcing, posted at www.walmart.com (accessed January 25, 2007).

production planning, enhance plant efficiency, better educate and train workers, make supply chain improvements, and adopt better factory operating practices. Wal-Mart also consulted with knowledgeable outside experts and organizations on ways to accelerate ethical compliance and the achievement of better working conditions in supplier factories.

Upon learning of the incident in the *Business-Week* report cited in the opening of this case, Wal-Mart began an investigation of the Beifa factory in Ningbo. Wal-Mart acknowledged that some of its suppliers were trying to deceive plant monitors and avoid complying with Wal-Mart's standards for suppliers.

COMPLIANCE EFFORTS OF INDUSTRY GROUPS AND NONGOVERNMENTAL ORGANIZATIONS—THE FAIR LABOR ASSOCIATION

Some companies, rather than conducting their own supplier monitoring and compliance effort, had banded together in industry groups or multi-industry coalitions to establish a common code of supplier conduct and to organize a joint program of factory inspections and compliance efforts. For example, Hewlett-Packard, Dell, and other electronics companies that relied heavily on Asia-based manufacturers to supply components or else assemble digital cameras, handheld devices, and personal computers had entered into an alliance to combat worker abuse and poor working conditions in the factories of their suppliers.

The Fair Labor Association

One of the most prominent and best organized coalitions was the Fair Labor Association (FLA), whose members and affiliates included 194 colleges and universities, a number of concerned nongovernmental organizations, and a group of 35 companies that included Nike, the Adidas Group (the owner of both Reebok and Adidas brands), Puma, Eddie Bauer, Liz Claiborne, Patagonia, Cutter & Buck, Russell Corporation, and Nordstrom. As part of its broad-based campaign to eliminate human rights abuses and improve global workplace conditions, the FLA had established its Workplace Code of Conduct, a document to which all members and affiliates had subscribed. To aid in winning supplier compliance with the Workplace Code of Conduct, the FLA conducted unannounced audits of factories across the world that supplied its members and affiliates.

In 2004, FLA's teams of independent plant monitors conducted inspections at 88 factories in 18 countries, the results of which were published in FLA's 2005 annual public report. The audits, all of which involved factories that were supplying goods to one or more FLA members, revealed 1,603 instances of noncompliance with FLA's Workplace Code of Conduct, an average of 18.2 violations per factory (versus an average of 15.1 per factory in 2003).[22] The violations included excessive work hours, underpayment of wages and overtime, failure to observe legal holidays and grant vacations (27.5 percent); health and safety problems (44 percent);

and worker harassment (5.1 percent). The FLA concluded that the actual violations relating to underpayment of wages, hours of work, and overtime compensation were probably higher than those discovered because "factory personnel have become sophisticated in concealing noncompliance relating to wages. They often hide original documents and show monitors falsified books."[23]

In its 2006 public report, the FLA said that accredited independent monitors conducted unannounced audits of 99 factories in 18 countries in 2005; the audited factories employed some 77,800 workers.[24] The audited factories were but a small sample of the 3,753 factories employing some 2.9 million people from which the FLA's 35 affiliated companies sourced goods in 2005; however, 34 of the 99 audited factories involved facilities providing goods to 2 or more of FLA's 35 affiliated companies. The 99 audits during 2005 revealed 1,587 violations, an average of 15.9 per audit. The greatest incidence of violations was found in Southeast Asia (chiefly factories located in China, Indonesia, Thailand, and India), where the average was about 22 violations per factory audit. As was the case with the audits conducted in 2004, most of the violations related to health and safety (45 percent); wages, benefits, hours of work, and overtime compensation (28 percent); and worker harassment and abuse (7 percent). Once again, the FLA indicated that the violations relating to compensation and benefits were likely higher than those detected in its 2005 audits because "factory personnel have become accustomed to concealing real wage documentation and providing falsified records at the time of compliance audits, making any noncompliances difficult to detect."[25]

The Fair Factories Clearinghouse

The Fair Factories Clearinghouse (FFC)—formed in 2006 by World Monitors Inc. in partnership with L. L. Bean, Timberland, Federated Department Stores, Adidas/Reebok, the Retail Council of Canada, and several others—was a collaborative effort to create a system for managing and sharing factory audit information that would facilitate detecting and eliminating sweatshops and abusive workplace conditions in foreign factories; membership fees were based on a company's annual revenues, with annual fees ranging

from as little as $5,000 to as much as $75,000 (not including one-time initiation fees of $2,500 to $11,500). The idea underlying the FFC was that members would pool their audit information on offshore factories, creating a database on thousands of manufacturing plants. Once a plant was certified by a member company or organization, other members could accept the results without having to do an audit of their own.

Audit sharing had the appeal of making factory audit programs less expensive for member companies; perhaps more important, it helped reduce the audit burden at plants having large number of customers that conducted their own audits. Some large plants with big customer bases were said to undergo audits as often as weekly and occasionally even daily; plus, they were pressured into having to comply with varying provisions and requirements of each auditing company's code of supplier conduct—being subject to varying and conflicting codes of conduct was a factor that induced cheating. Another benefit of audit sharing at FFC was that members sourcing goods from the same factories could band together and apply added pressure on a supplier to improve its working conditions and comply with buyers' codes of supplier conduct.[26]

THE OBSTACLES TO ACHIEVING SUPPLIER COMPLIANCE WITH CODES OF CONDUCT IN LOW-WAGE, LOW-COST COUNTRIES

Factory managers subject to inspections and audits of their plants and work practices complained that strong pressures from their customers to keep prices low gave them a big incentive to cheat on their compliance with labor standards. As the general manager of a factory in China that supplied goods to Nike said, "Any improvement you make costs more money. The price [Nike pays] never increases one penny but compliance with labor codes definitely raises costs."[27]

The pricing pressures from companies sourcing components or finished goods from offshore factories in China, India, and other low-wage, low-cost locations were acute. Since 1996, the prices paid for men's shirts and sweaters sourced in China were said to have dropped by 14 percent, while the prices of clocks and lamps had dropped 40 percent and the prices of toys and games had fallen by 30 percent.[28] Such downward pressure on prices made it financially difficult for foreign manufacturers to improve worker compensation and benefits, make their workplaces safer and more pleasant, introduce more efficient production methods, and overhaul inefficient plant layouts. Many factory managers believed that if they paid workers a higher wage, incurred other compliance costs, and then raised their prices to cover the higher costs that their customers would quickly cut and run to other suppliers charging lower prices. Hence, the penalties and disincentives for compliance significantly outweighed any rewards.

In a 2006 interview with *BusinessWeek*, the CEO of the Fair Labor Association, Auret van Heerden, offered a number of reasons why underpayment of wages and excessive overtime in supplier factories in China were such difficult problems to resolve:

> The brands book and confirm orders really late. And they often change their orders after booking. The brands want to order later and they don't want to hold product. Then you add price pressures into that and it is really tough for the supplier [to not overwork its workers].
>
> But the factory often doesn't order the materials until too late and they are often delivered late [to the factory], too. The factory production layout is often a mess, so the supplier gets behind schedule and over budget even before they know it. Then they have to catch up. And to save money, they extend hours, but don't pay overtime premiums. And the suppliers also lack proper training. The styles [of clothing and footwear] are becoming more complicated and are changing more frequently.
>
> Multiple codes are a big problem. The classic example is the height that a fire extinguisher should be kept off the ground—how high varies according to different codes. Companies like McDonald's, Disney, and Wal-Mart are doing thousands of audits a year that are not harmonized. That's where audit fatigue comes in.
>
> And auditing in itself tells you a little about the problem, but not enough, and not why there is a problem. So you have an overtime problem, but you don't know why. Is it because of electricity shortages, labor shortages, or a shorter order turnaround time? You don't know.[29]

Endnotes

[1] Dexter Roberts and Pete Engardio, "Secrets, Lies, and Sweatshops," *BusinessWeek*, November 27, 2006, pp. 50–58.
[2] Ibid., p. 50.
[3] Ibid.
[4] Ibid., p. 52.
[5] Ibid., p. 54.
[6] Ibid., p. 54.
[7] Ibid., p. 50.
[8] Ibid., p. 55.
[9] Ibid., p. 53.
[10] Ibid., pp. 55–56.
[11] Ibid., p. 53.
[12] Information posted at www.nike.com/nikebiz/nikebiz.jhtml?page=25&cat=activefactories (accessed January 26, 2007).
[13] Information posted at www.nikebiz.com (accessed January 26, 2007); Nike's 2004 Fiscal Year Corporate Responsibility Report, pp. 21–24.
[14] Nike's 2004 Fiscal Year Corporate Responsibility Report, p. 28.
[15] Ibid., p. 29.
[16] Ibid., p. 20.
[17] Ibid., p. 30.
[18] Ibid., p. 25.
[19] Ibid., p. 26.
[20] Pete Engardio and Dexter Roberts, "How to Make Factories Play Fair," *BusinessWeek*, November 27, 2007, p. 58.
[21] The content of this section was developed by the case author from information posted in the supplier section at www.walmartstores.com (accessed January 25, 2007).
[22] These results of the audits were published in the Fair Labor Association's 2005 annual public report, posted at www.fairlabor.org (January 23, 2007).
[23] Fair Labor Association, 2005 annual public report, p. 38; also quoted in Roberts and Engardio, "Secrets, Lies, and Sweatshops," p. 54.
[24] Fair Labor Association, 2006 annual public report, posted at www.fairlabor.org (January 23, 2007).
[25] Ibid., p. 40.
[26] Roberts and Engardio, "Secrets, Lies, and Sweatshops," p. 58.
[27] As quoted in ibid., p. 53.
[28] Ibid., p. 58.
[29] As quoted in Dexter Roberts, "A Lion for Worker Rights," *BusinessWeek Online*, November 27, 2006, www.businessweek.com (accessed January 23, 2007).

Queensland Rainforest Resort

Janine S. Hiller
Virginia Tech

France Belanger
Virginia Tech

Sam A. Hicks
Virginia Tech

Nancy G. McGehee
Virginia Tech

Built in 1987, Queensland Rainforest Resort (QRR) was the first Australian resort to be developed by Adventures Hotels and Resorts Inc., whose headquarters office, along with two additional resorts, was located in California. Adventures Hotels and Resorts (AHR) was a hospitality company committed to showcasing and preserving the extraordinary destinations in which their properties were located. On the homepage of the resort was a statement by QRR's executive director, Abe Grant, which read as follows:

> Explore wild Australia in luxurious comfort in our award-winning resorts. We are committed to sharing Australia's beauty with the world while protecting it. Our properties are managed within strict environmental guidelines; we are committed to sustainable tourism management practices, to energy-efficiency, recycling and waste management programs. From the red heart to the rainforest, from canyons to the Reef, here are landscapes to ravish the senses and refresh the spirit.

QRR was located two hours north of Cairns, Australia, in the Daintree Rainforest, and was the only place in the world where two World Heritage listed environments existed alongside each other, or as the locals said, where "the rainforest meets the reef." QRR was a full-service luxury resort that offered both a lodge with deluxe accommodation rooms and private cabins set farther back in the

rainforest. All rooms and cabins had direct access to the white sand beach.

Every element of QRR was designed to take advantage of the natural setting while staying attuned to ecological and sustainable growth ideals. For example, the minimal amount of timber removed for the development of the resort was used to build the cabins and lodge; a local spring provided all the water for the resort; plumbing and water filtration systems had been developed using state-of-the-art conservation techniques; all the soaps and detergents used at the resort (both in rooms and in the restaurants) were biodegradable; and all indigenous flora and fauna located in or around the 450 million-year-old rainforest surrounding the resort were treated as "honored guests," including tropical birds, tree kangaroos, and monitor lizards.

Amid the natural beauty, however, not all was well. Although the resort attracted visitors from all over the world, in part due to the strength of its presence on the Internet, the global downswing in international travel, fueled by the decrease in visitors from the United States, was a significant problem for QRR. Everyone was tense about the decrease in visitors, and things were very tight. Adventure Hotels and Resorts (AHR), the corporate headquarters located in California, had made it quite clear that unless profitability increased, some real cost-saving measures would have to be instituted. Lost jobs and cutbacks in service were all possibilities in the near future if things did not show improvement. Part of the corporate strategy to save money and increase profitability was to use technology to improve and streamline both internal and external functions. Although the resort's appeal was based on the natural environment, QRR sought to be thoroughly modern and efficient, especially in the area of information technology.

QRR's information technology evolved, as with many resorts, from a few bulky computers at the accountant's desk to tabulate accounting data and print bills to a highly sophisticated technology environment companywide. In addition to standard accounting and payroll systems, QRR had adopted point-of-sale systems for its restaurants, automated credit card processing systems at all areas receiving guest payments, e-mail systems within the resort and across the corporate environment, connections to the Internet, and even Web registration and payment services.

At QRR the information system function reported to the vice president of operations. The day-to-day IT operations were managed by Peter Myers, the information technology director. However, because of limited resources, QRR made a strategic decision four years ago to outsource a large part of the information systems function. This was triggered by the need for an online reservation system. Peter evaluated and discussed the possibility of in-house development with the executive committee; but in the end it was felt they had neither the resources nor the expertise to make it happen. Instead QRR contracted with CibCo, an outside company, to provide online reservation functions.

Jessica Austin was the CibCo account representative for QRR. In her sales presentation to QRR executives, Jessica suggested that many more existing functions could be outsourced at lower costs than in-house development and greater efficiency. QRR agreed. Today, CibCo had a contract to host and maintain the Web site and hosting applications at QRR, including inventory control, payment, and payroll applications. However, a few IT services were managed centrally at AHR, such as the e-mail server functions.

At QRR, the basic systems environment was a series of three Ethernet LANs connected through a router and a bridge. There were three local servers. One was used as a database server accessed by all stations and point-of-sale locations at the resort while another was used as an application server, running applications such as front desk registrations, phone reservations, and the local accounting applications. Finally, the resort had its own Private Branch Exchange (PBX) for handling all of the phone connections for the resort.

THE LETTER

Caitlin Murphy, vice president of customer relations at Queensland Rainforest Resort (QRR) had just read a letter she received from a particularly loyal, but also particularly irate, customer regarding a recent visit to QRR. "Maybe I should not have transferred from the corporate office of AHR," she thought to herself. "Australia seemed such a beautiful place to live for a few years and a good place to distinguish myself for further advancement."

She decided to read the letter again:

Dear Queensland Rainforest Resort Management:

My family recently spent our third vacation at your property, traveling all the way from the United States (California), and I have to tell you that it may be our last. While we always enjoy traveling to the Daintree Rainforest, this last trip was dampened by a number of problems related to our interactions with the Queensland Rainforest Resort. Our problems with the resort all began when we arrived at the resort and found that there was no reservation in our name, even though we registered online a full 6 months ahead of time and had a copy of our confirmation e-mail. Your front desk staff was very nice, and luckily there were rooms available, but there were some pretty tense moments until we found that out for sure. Things then proceeded to go well for a day or so, but we ran into additional trouble when we decided to eat at the Billabong. Each time we visited the restaurant our order was either wrong, or cold, or slow to arrive. The waitress was very apologetic, even "comped" our meal the third time, but she seemed to be frustrated by the system she was using to place our orders.

The rest of the visit went well, but after we returned home, our problems seemed to follow us. Almost as soon as we got home we began to be inundated with brochures, e-mail, and telephone calls from similar types of other high-end resorts; it appeared that Queensland Rainforest Resort had sold our personal information, which we found very disappointing. Next, several of the incidental charges we incurred at the resort (meals, room service, long distance, spa visits, the reef tour) were not charged to our credit card until almost 6 months after we returned from our trip. When we called our credit card agency, they informed us that it had taken that long for Queensland Rainforest Resort to submit the charges. When we e-mailed the accounting department about the problem (numerous times) we never received an answer. Instead we received numerous undeliverable e-mail responses.

All these things were an inconvenience and a bother, but nothing prepared us for the final straw: 8 months after the trip, we were victims of identity theft! Someone spent over $25,000.00 on our credit cards. Luckily they were caught and prosecuted, but the authorities traced the source of the problem to your resort. In addition, a family we met from England with whom we have maintained e-mail correspondence had similar problems to ours, and they have suggested that we all should receive some form of compensation. I have to say I agree with that idea, and have been contemplating calling my lawyer, just to see what our rights are. I find it very distressing that a resort that bills itself as a luxury experience, and charges room rates accordingly, has such problems with its information technology.

Let me just say that we are incredibly disappointed, because we have LOVED our trips to your resort over the years, but we cannot justify returning if our interactions continue to result in so many problems for us. I hope that my complaints will result in some improvements. If you are unable to demonstrate changes to us soon, we will have to begin to search for a new vacation destination for next year, as well as recommending to our friends and colleagues that they refrain from visiting your resort.

Sincerely,

Spencer Benjamin, M.D.
Los Angeles, CA

Obviously, there were numerous issues that needed to be addressed. While Dr. Benjamin was the only customer to complain about all of these issues, many customers had complained at different times about various problems related to the resort's online registration and reservation system, restaurant orders, credit card transactions, and e-mail. As a new employee, Caitlin Murphy herself had been the victim of a slow payroll system when she had to wait almost two months before receiving her first paycheck. While the problems seemed a bit overwhelming, Caitlin knew something had to be done.

DATA COLLECTION

While Caitlin Murphy was beginning her investigation into Dr. Benjamin's complaint, information technology was at the center of attention in another part of the resort as well. Martha Hines, marketing director for QRR, was in her office after just returning from a seminar in Orlando, Florida, entitled

"Make the Most of Your Customers: One-to-One Marketing and Other Profit Enhancing Techniques." She was excited to bring back ideas to incorporate into the new marketing plan. In fact, Martha had been energized by the conference ideas. At the last QRR executive committee meeting, it had been decided to task the marketing department with creating an aggressive plan to increase guest nights in response to the sagging bottom line. According to what the conference speaker said, it would seem that QRR was sitting on a gold mine of information. And, by using the Internet, she could reach millions of people for an extraordinarily small investment. If she could put some of these ideas to work, then QRR could increase its profits even without renting any additional rooms! Martha could taste the promotion that she would receive if she could pull this off.

The list of new marketing techniques included the following possibilities:

- Use e-mail lists from private vendors to send information about QRR all over the world.

- Trade e-mail lists and guest information with others who also market to resort and ecotourists.

- Sell e-mail addresses and other guest information, such as the address of customers, to other related businesses such as outdoor equipment manufacturers and wildlife groups.

- Subscribe to an advertising program to place pop-up ads for the resort on surfers' computer screens.

- Collect information about the Web sites that guests access while staying at the resort. Use this information to create a database of products and services that would be targeted to the guests.

All that was needed now was to pull together a presentation to the executive committee. Martha called together the marketing staff for a work session. To her surprise, not everyone was as excited and enthusiastic as she was about the ideas, and in fact Terry Travis, one of her marketing specialists, was an absolute spoiler. "I don't see how you can even think about this! What you are doing is sending spam. I don't want to become a spammer; I absolutely hate the spam that I receive now. I'd rather quit than work on this. And I don't see how you can violate the confidence of the customers. If it were me, I wouldn't come here if I knew that you would use my information like that."

Samantha Hu also spoke up: "This company stands for high ideals: preserving the environment while still opening it up for visitors. I think these new marketing ideas violate the overall values of our company. Besides, what if it backfires on us? Did anyone else besides me receive that memo about the disgruntled customer from the States? I think his name was Benjamin—who was outraged because his information was somehow leaked from QRR—including his e-mail address? At some point, customers will revolt and take their business elsewhere, and that's really not what we need to see happen right now."

But Lee Woods disagreed, saying, "High ideals are all well and good, but not if you are out of a job. And, while you are on your high horse, someone else is already out there taking advantage of the data and customer information. Face it; we don't have any privacy anymore, and we would not be doing anything that other resorts aren't already doing. Everyone expects you to use the information already."

BACKDOOR POLITICS

Unaware of the brewing controversies in other resort departments, Jody Antopolis had information technology concerns of her own. "Peter, you may want to sit down to hear what I am about to tell you. We have a huge problem, one that could cost a lot of money to fix." Jody Antopolis walked into the office of her boss and IT director, Peter Myers, and proceeded to tell him about her discovery of a hole in QRR's reservation system and Web site.

At first, Jody was sure that it must be a mistake. The company had paid an arm and a leg for the e-commerce Web site and reservation system from CibCo. Jody ran the program again, just to make sure that it was not an aberration. "No, there it was," she thought. "CibCo must have left a backdoor in the program so that they could disable it if payments were not made on time." She remembered the discussion about the backdoor and the jokes around the IT group about electronic warfare between the two companies if a disagreement broke out. Now, anyone with an advanced knowledge of the programming language could easily access QRR's customer information, including addresses, names of children, and e-mail addresses. "Thankfully," she thought, "the credit card numbers are encrypted, so at least they are protected." It was at this point that Jody decided to report the problem at once to Peter.

She took a deep breath and continued her story. "So, I am afraid that we need to shut the system down, Peter. I believe I can get my group to work around the clock to reinstall our old in-house system. It won't allow for reservation updates, and it won't link the information to the database created by the new system, but it is secure, I am sure of that."

"Now hold on, Jody," said Peter. "I am not at all convinced that we should shut the system down. After all, it would take a person with a considerable amount of knowledge to break in. And it hasn't happened yet, has it? I think that we should continue to use the system until such time as we actually know that someone has broken into it. Really, all we have now is a possibility of the information being lost, and if anything happens, it will be CibCo's fault, not ours."

Flabbergasted at Peter's curt response and quick decision, Jody left the office. She now had a decision of her own to make. By simply doing what she was told, she knew she was participating in a breach of trust with QRR's customers. On the other hand, if she were a QRR guest, she would not like to find out that her private information had been compromised in that way. Should she stay the course and follow her boss's instructions?

Jody was suddenly reminded that just yesterday she had been copied on an e-mail memo informing the staff about a particularly troublesome complaint letter. The guest, a doctor from the United States, had experienced an awful series of IT-related problems after a recent stay at QRR. She had only skimmed the letter at the time, but she was sure she remembered that the guest had experienced an influx of spam shortly after his visit. Could someone from CibCo be accessing the QRR Web site and selling the data? Just the thought made Jody sick with worry. This pointed to a second option for her decision about the hole in the system. Jody could send e-mails to all the guests in the database. "After all," she thought, "they have a right to know, and perhaps this would bring pressure on QRR to fix the problem."

EYES ON THE INSIDE

The meeting with Jody was disturbing, but Peter had other issues to attend to, and he needed to particularly focus on the report that he was scheduled to give at the next executive committee meeting. As he turned back to his work, his mind wandered back to the meeting that had started it all.

Exhibit 1   **QRR Computer Acceptable Use Policy**

All employees at QRR granted access to information systems and networks owned or operated by QRR must follow company policies, and local, district, and national laws. Access also imposes certain responsibilities and obligations. Acceptable use always is ethical, reflects honesty, and shows restraint in the consumption of shared resources. It demonstrates respect for intellectual property, ownership of data, system security mechanisms, and individuals' rights to privacy and to freedom from intimidation and harassment.

The company considers any violation of acceptable use principles or guidelines to be a serious offense and reserves the right to copy and examine any files or information resident on its systems allegedly related to unacceptable use, and to protect its network from systems and events that threaten or degrade operations.

General Guidelines:

In making acceptable use of resources you must:

- use resources only for authorized purposes.
- protect your account and computer from unauthorized use. You are responsible for all activities on your account or that originate from your system.
- access only information that is your own, that is publicly available, or to which you have been given authorized access.
- use only legal versions of copyrighted software in compliance with vendor license requirements.
- be considerate in your use of shared resources. Refrain from monopolizing systems, overloading networks with excessive data, degrading services, or wasting computer time, connect time, disk space, printer paper, manuals, or other resources.

In making acceptable use of resources you must NOT:

- use another person's computer, account, password, files, or data without permission.
- use software to decode passwords or access control information.
- attempt to circumvent or subvert system or network security measures.
- engage in any activity that might be purposefully harmful to systems or to any information stored thereon, such as creating or propagating viruses, disrupting services, or damaging files or making unauthorized modifications to university data.
- use corporate systems for commercial or partisan political purposes, such as using electronic mail to circulate advertising for products or for political candidates.
- make or use illegal copies of copyrighted materials or software, store such copies on university systems, or transmit them over university networks.
- use mail or messaging services to harass or intimidate another person, for example, by broadcasting unsolicited messages, by repeatedly sending unwanted mail, or by using someone else's name or account.
- waste computing resources or network resources, for example, by intentionally placing a program in an endless loop, printing excessive amounts of paper, or by sending chain letters or unsolicited mass mailings.
- use the company's systems or networks for personal gain; for example, by selling access to your account or to systems or networks, or by performing work for profit with company resources in a manner not authorized by the company.
- engage in any other activity that does not comply with the General Guidelines presented above.

The purpose of the meeting was to review CibCo's contract concerning the outsourcing of certain IT functions and to discuss projects for the upcoming year. During the discussion, Abe Grant, executive director of QRR, had asked Jessica Austin, CibCo's account representative for QRR, a provocative question: "Is it possible to monitor all of QRR's employees? How about employees' general use of e-mail and the Internet?"

"Of course," Jessica replied. She went on to describe various options for monitoring employees' use of the Internet. Although Peter recommended moving more slowly, Abe agreed to the service and asked for it to be implemented immediately. Peter was assigned the responsibility of summarizing the monitoring reports for Abe, and making a presentation to the executive committee about the status of the new monitoring (see Exhibit 1).

Now, a month later, Peter was reminded of that meeting as he reviewed the first set of reports. Jessica's team had provided him with a log of who sent e-mails to whom and when, with the subject line's content. The content of the e-mails was not included in the report. Peter glanced through the report and saw that a certain Mike Howell in front desk operations sent many "lunch together?" e-mails to a Julia Robertson in food and beverage. "An office romance, no doubt," Peter reflected. Should he report this? What if one of them was married? What other information is in these e-mail logs? As he thought about this, Peter realized he might not be able to delegate the job of summarizing these reports to one of his employees, as he was first tempted to do. What if they used the information in the wrong way?

Still puzzling about what to do, Peter continued looking at the Web access reports. These reports were in a different format. Each user account was listed in alphabetical order, with the user's top five Web sites ranked according to the number of times accessed, and then the top five Web sites ranked by quantity of time spent on those sites. Immediately, Peter knew that this was going to be an ugly job. He browsed through the lists and found three accounts where the top Web site use seemed excessive. He then found to whom the accounts belonged and visited those sites. The following is a summary of his major findings and thoughts:

- Maria Jones, a reservationist, went to an online games site every day for almost one hour.

- Anthony Vega, a food and beverage manager, looked at a stock market Web site very frequently, although he spent much more time overall looking at a food and beverage equipment auction site.

- Jared Michaels, a maintenance manager, went mainly to an adult entertainment Web site where pictures of nude or almost-nude young women were plentiful, and were available for downloading. Peter made a note to see what other suspicious "files" might be saved to Jared's computer.

Smithfield Foods' Vertical Integration Strategy: Is It Environmentally Correct?

LaRue T. Hosmer

The University of Michigan

In 2005, Smithfield Foods was the largest hog producer and pork processor in the world. The company raised 14 million hogs domestically (a 14 percent U.S. share) and processed 27 million hogs annually (a 27 percent U.S. share). Smithfield marketed chops, roasts, ribs, loins, ground pork, bacon, hams, sausages, and sliced deli meats under such brands as Smithfield, Smithfield Lean Generation, John Morrell, Gwaltney, Patrick Cudahy, Stefano's, Farmland, Quick-n-Easy, and Jean Caby (France), plus it had the two best-known meat brands in Poland—Krakus and Morliny. Smithfield specialized in producing exceptionally lean hogs; the company had exclusive U.S. franchise rights to a proprietary breed of SPG sows that accounted for about 55 percent of its herd and provided live hogs for its best-selling Smithfield Lean Generation Pork products. In 2005 Smithfield operated 52 pork processing plants and 7 beef processing plants. A new state-of-the-art ham processing plant opened in 2005.

Since 1981, the company had made some 32 acquisitions to expand geographically, diversify into new product segments, and vertically integrate its pork business. Smithfield's acquisitions of Moyer Packing Company and Packerland Holdings in 2002 made it the fifth largest beef producer in the United States. In 1998, Smithfield began expanding into foreign markets, making acquisitions in Canada, France, Romania, and Poland and establishing joint ventures in Mexico, Spain, and China. Two meat processors in Poland and Romania were acquired in 2004, along with a Romanian hog farming opera-

tion with 15,000 sows producing 200,000 market hogs annually. Management believed its acquisitions and joint ventures gave the company strong market positions, high-quality manufacturing facilities, and excellent growth and exporting potential to serve regions that already had high pork consumption levels and that were emerging as major meat consumers. Executives were particularly excited about the company's opportunities in the European Union.

In pork, Smithfield had pursued a vertical integration strategy, establishing operations in hog farming, feed mills, meat packing plants, and distribution. Smithfield's hog processing group, the chief subsidiary of which was Murphy-Brown LLC, owned and operated hog farms with close to 900,000 sows in North Carolina, South Carolina, Virginia, Utah, Colorado, Texas, Oklahoma, South Dakota, Iowa, Missouri, Illinois, Mexico, Romania, and Poland.

Smithfield Foods was headquartered in Smithfield, Virginia, where it operated two large hog processing plants. But large parts of the company's operations were in North Carolina—Smithfield's biggest pork processing plant was in Bladen County, North Carolina, and the company's Murphy-Brown hog production subsidiary had a very sizable hog farming operation in eastern North Carolina. Smithfield opened a new state-of-the-art ham processing plant in Kinston, North Carolina, in 2005 that employed 206 workers; the Kinston plant was expected to be the most efficient premier-cooked-ham plant in the United States, employing the newest technologies available and meeting the highest food standards in the industry. Smithfield's large southern base provided low wages and relatively

Exhibit 1   **Financial and Operating Summary, Smithfield Foods, 1995–2004 ($ in millions, except per share amounts)**

	2004	2003	2001	1999	1995
Operations					
Sales revenues	$9,267.0	$7,135.4	$5,123.7	$3,550.0	$1,526.5
Gross profit	938.9	602.2	762.3	448.6	126.9
Selling, general, and administrative expenses	570.8	497.9	416.2	280.4	62.4
Depreciation expense	167.5	151.5	114.5	59.3	19.7
Interest expenses	121.3	87.8	81.5	38.4	14.1
Income from continuing operations	162.7	11.9	214.3	89.6	31.9
Net income	$ 227.1	$ 26.3	$ 223.5	$ 94.9	$ 27.8
Earnings per share	$2.03	$0.24	$2.03	$1.16	$0.40
Financial position					
Working capital	$1,056.6	$ 833.0	$ 635.4	$ 215.9	$ 60.9
Total assets	4,813.7	4,410.6	3,250.9	1,771.6	550.2
Total debt	1,801.5	1,642.3	1,188.7	610.3	234.7
Shareholders' equity	1,617.2	1,299.2	1,053.1	542.2	184.0
Current ratio	2.09	2.02	2.01	1.46	1.35
Total debt to total capitalization	52.7%	55.8%	53.0%	53.0%	58.4%
Other statistics					
Capital expenditures	$151.4	$172.0	$113.3	$92.0	$90.6
Number of employees	46,400	44,100	34,000	33,000	9,000

Source: 2004 annual report.

low operating costs across much of its integrated operations, factors that helped pave the way for Smithfield's competitive prices and strong growth.

The company's longtime chairman and CEO, Joseph W. Luter III, continually emphasized the need to drive down costs and push up sales. Top executives at Smithfield Foods wanted to continue the company's rapid and profitable expansion and were constantly on the lookout for opportunities to grow the company's business. Going into 2006, Smithfield had annualized sales of close to $11 billion, up from $1.5 billion in 1995; revenues had grown at a compound average rate of close to 24 percent during the past decade. Exhibit 1 provides historical financial data.

OPPOSITION TO SMITHFIELD'S EXPANSION

Over the last decade, Smithfield Foods had met with mounting opposition to expansion of its business,

particularly in hog farming. The chief pockets of opposition to Smithfield's hog farming activities came from rural residents in eastern North Carolina, where there were some 8,000 hog farms. Neighboring residents complained that commercial hog farming had essentially been imposed on them and that it entailed substantial adverse impacts in the form of low wages and environmental discharges.

Eastern North Carolina and Smithfield's Hog Farming Operations

Eastern North Carolina, essentially the area extending about 150 miles from Raleigh (the state capital) to the Atlantic coast, is a region of flat land, sandy soil, and ample rainfall. At one time it was a relatively prosperous region, with thousands of small family farms, each of which had a tobacco allotment. During the 1930s far more tobacco had been grown than was needed, and the price plummeted. One of the government initiatives of the Depression era was a restriction on the total amount of tobacco that could be grown, and this total amount was divided up among the existing growers by restricting each to a set percentage of the amount of their land that had been devoted to the crop during a given base year. These restrictions on growth first stabilized and later increased the price, and the possession of an allotment almost guaranteed the financial prosperity of the farm.

The typical family farm would have 150 to 200 acres. Perhaps 15 acres would be devoted to tobacco, and the balance would be sown in corn, wheat, rye, or soybeans, or left as pasture for cattle or—more frequently—hogs. The grains grown locally would be trucked to the nearest town within the region to be milled into feed and then returned to the farm for the livestock. The cattle and hogs produced locally would be trucked to the nearest town to be sold at auction, and then slaughtered and processed at a nearby packing plant. These towns were also relatively prosperous, as the farmers and their families purchased clothing and household goods at local stores and automobiles and farm machinery at local dealers.

This prosperity started downhill in the 1970s as the national campaigns against smoking led to continual reductions in the size, and consequently the profitability, of the tobacco allotments, which eventually came almost to an end. Local prosperity continued to decline in the 1980s as very large feed lots in Nebraska, Iowa, and Kansas developed a much less costly means of raising hogs prior to slaughter; the piglets spent only the first 12 to 15 months of their lives on the farms where they were bred before being brought to fenced open-air corrals where they were closely confined but fed continuously to gain weight. Farmers in eastern North Carolina had to compete against this new and far more efficient production process. Prices for the hogs raised in eastern North Carolina declined sharply, and many of the local packing plants went out of business.

Local prosperity stabilized to some extent in the 1990s, though with a greatly changed distribution of income, as Smithfield Foods introduced the concept of the factory farm. Large metal sheds with concrete floors were built, each designed to hold up to 1,000 hogs. Feeding was by means of a mechanized conveyor that carried food alongside both walls. Waste was removed by hosing it off the floors to a central trough that carried it to a storage lagoon. Temperature was controlled by huge fans at each end of each shed. Every effort was made to reduce costs. Feed grains were no longer grown, purchased, and milled locally; instead most grains were grown, purchased, and milled in the Midwest and transported to eastern North Carolina by unit feed trains, which were strings of covered hopper cars that moved as a unit, without switching, from the feed mill in Nebraska or Iowa directly to one of the company's distribution centers in North Carolina. Some feed grains were grown and purchased even more cheaply abroad, primarily in Australia and Argentina, and then carried by ship to a company-leased milling facility and distribution center in Wilmington (a port in southeastern North Carolina, near the South Carolina border).

Limited farm machinery was needed for this new method of raising hogs, given that few feed grains were grown locally, but the little that was needed was purchased by the Smithfield headquarters office directly from the manufacturer. Many farm equipment dealers within the region were forced to close. Even diesel fuel, needed for the trucks that transported the feed grains to the farms and the mature hogs to the packing plants, was purchased from the refinery, transported by railway tank cars to large storage tanks at the distribution centers, and pumped directly into the trucks. Local fuel dealers got little or none of this business. All truck purchases were arranged by bid from national dealers located in Detroit (auto companies had refused to sell outside their dealer chains, but they allegedly gave favored prices to very large dealers near their corporate headquarters) at very low prices, and all subsequent truck repairs were done at company-owned repair shops located at the company-owned distribution centers. Some truck dealers in the region were forced to close.

Executives at Smithfield Foods did not apologize for the business model that they had created. Their attitude could be summed up as follows: "This is the way the world is going and this is what the market demands. All we have done is to create a competitive system that works. Moreover, we have saved farms and brought jobs to the eastern North Carolina region through this system, and we have provided better (leaner) pork products at lower prices to our customers." Smithfield's development of a "competitive system that works" had won Joseph Luter an award as Master Entrepreneur of the Year in 2002;

a Smithfield news release dated December 21, 2002, said:

> Joseph W. Luter III has been named the Ernst & Young 2002 Virginia Master Entrepreneur of the Year. The Ernst & Young program recognizes entrepreneurs who have demonstrated excellence and extraordinary success in such areas as innovation, financial performance and personal commitment to their businesses and communities . . .
>
> Since becoming chairman and chief executive officer of Smithfield Foods, Inc. in 1975, Mr. Luter transformed the company from a small, regional meat packer with sales of $125 million and net worth of $1 million to an international concern with annual sales of $8 billion and a net worth of $1.4 billion.

Smithfield Foods did not own the farms that raised the hogs. Instead, company representatives would select a reasonably large farm, one that had been successful in the past and therefore was financially solvent now, and negotiate a contract with the owning family to raise hogs at a set price per animal. The farm family would frequently use a loan provided through the Smithfield Corporation and a contractor licensed by the Smithfield Corporation to build metal barns with concrete floors, feed conveyors, ventilation fans, and waste systems; connect the waste systems to storage lagoons (five to eight acres in size); construct feed bins and loading ramps; and be ready for business. Smithfield Corporation would then deliver the hogs at piglet stage, provide a constant supply of feed grains mixed with antibiotics (to prevent disease in the crowded conditions of the metal barns), and offer free veterinarian service. The responsibility of the farm family was to raise those hogs to marketable weight as quickly and as efficiently as possible. This was termed *contract farming;* it was described in the following terms in a five-part investigative series that ran February 19–26, 1995, in the *Raleigh News and Observer:*

> Greg Stephens is the 1995 version of the North Carolina hog farmer. He owns no hogs. Stephens carries a mortgage on four new confinement barns that cost him $300,000 to build. The 4,000 hogs inside belong to a company called Prestage Farms, Inc. (one of the larger suppliers of Smithfield Foods). Prestage simply pays Stephens a fee to raise them . . .
>
> This arrangement is called contract farming, and it's hardly risk-free. But for anyone wanting to

break into the swine business these days, it's the only game in town. "Without a contract, there's no way I'd be raising hogs," says Stephens, "and even if I had somehow gotten in, my pockets aren't nearly deep enough to let me stay in."

Welcome to corporate livestock production, the force behind the swine industry's explosive growth in North Carolina. The backbone of the new system is a network of hundreds of contractors like Stephens, the franchise owners in a system that more closely resembles a fast-food chain than traditional agriculture.

Nowhere in the nation has this change been as dramatic, or as officially embraced, as in North Carolina. As a result, the hog population has more than doubled in four years, and nearly all of that growth has occurred on farms controlled by the big companies. Meanwhile, independent farmers have left the business by the thousands.

In 1998, Smithfield Foods reportedly had a two-year waiting list of farmers wishing to obtain hog farming contracts. Industry observers, however, worried about the practice of saddling hundreds of small farmers with thousands of dollars of debt. As one elected state representative said, "Why invest your capital when you can get a farmer to take the risk? Why own the farm when you can own the farmer?"[1]

The problem foreseen by industry observers was the possibility that a company could cancel its contract with only 30 days' notice, leaving the farmer with the debt and no income to repay it, or could threaten to cancel and then renew the contract only with a sharply lower price per animal. Both sudden cancellations and lower prices were said to have happened frequently in the poultry industry:

> The changes that are sweeping the swine industry today were pioneered by chicken and turkey growers in the 1960s and '70s. Total confinement housing, vertical integration, and contract farming are all standard practices in the feather world. As a result, you need only look at chickens to see where pork is headed.
>
> The poultry industry today is fully integrated— meaning a handful of companies control all phases of production—and the labor is performed by an army of contract growers, some of them decidedly unhappy. "It's sharecropping, that's what it is," said Larry Holder, a chicken farmer and president of the Contract Poultry Growers Association.

The *Raleigh News and Observer* interviewed a number of farmers with hog-growing contracts in

North Carolina. One farmer with 10 years of experience growing for Carroll Farms (another large supplier of Smithfield Foods), said, "They've been nothing but good to me."[2] Greg Stephens, the farmer quoted earlier, told the *News and Observer* that in his case the biggest selling point had been his freedom from market risk: "If hog prices go south, as they did two months ago, the contract farmer is barely affected. The company that owns the pigs takes on more risk than you do."[3]

The survival of over 1,000 family farms as contract hog growers was cited as one of the major benefits of the industrialization of agriculture in eastern North Carolina. Another was the creation of new agricultural jobs. Each of the contract farms averaged 7,500 animals. The owning families could not care for all those animals, even though the hogs are closely confined and automatically fed and watered. The typical farm employed five people from the community at wages of $7 to $8 an hour; working conditions were hard and unpleasant. Most of the people filling such jobs were untrained and poorly educated area residents.

Smithfield's three newest slaughterhouses in North Carolina employed about 3,200 people. Many of the jobs at these plants were regarded as hard and unpleasant; some involved killing and disemboweling the hogs. The killing was said to be painless, and much of the early processing (scraping the carcass to remove the hair, and dealing with the internal organs) was automated. One of the more labor-intensive tasks involved preparing cuts of meat for packaged sale at grocery chains. Most grocery chains, to reduce their internal costs, had eliminated the position of store butchers, opting instead to buy their fresh meats cut, wrapped, packaged, and ready for sale. The cutting at meatpacking facilities was done on a high-speed assembly line, using very sharp laser-guided knives; workers were under continual pressure to perform and were exposed to dangers of injury. Workers who became skilled at this cutting and were able to endure the stress earned $10 to $12 an hour; turnover was relatively high because of the strenuous job demands. Many of the workers at the high-volume packing plants in eastern North Carolina were immigrants from Central or South America. The jobs were described in the following terms by an undercover reporter for the *New York Times* who worked at one of the Smithfield packing plants for three weeks on what was termed the picnic line:

One o'clock means it is getting near the end of the workday [for the first shift]. Quota has to be met, and the workload doubles. The conveyor belt always overflows with meat around 1 o'clock. So the workers redouble their pace, hacking pork from shoulder bones with a driven single-mindedness. They stare blankly, like mules in wooden blinders, as the butchered slabs pass by.

It is called the picnic line: 18 workers lined up on both sides of a belt, carving meat from bone. Up to 16 million shoulders a year come down that line here at Smithfield Packing Co., the largest pork production plant in the world. That works out to about 32,000 per shift, 63 a minute, one every 17 seconds for each worker for eight and a half hours a day. The first time you stare down at that belt you know your body is going to give in way before the machine ever will.[4]

Smithfield's vertical integration strategy, which had resulted in very limited purchasing of feed, machinery, and fuel from local sources; the debt-laden nature of the farm contracts, which fueled concerns about the possibility of future contract cancellations or price reductions; and the low-pay/low-quality nature of the jobs that had been created at both the farms and the packing plants had combined to create strong, often vocal, opposition on the part of many local residents to any planned expansion of Smithfield Foods within eastern North Carolina.

A much bigger and far more intense issue, however, was the alleged impact of a concentrated cluster of hog farms on the environment:

Imagine a city as big as New York suddenly grafted onto North Carolina's Coastal Plain. Double it. Now imagine that this city has no sewage treatment plants. All the wastes from 15 million inhabitants are simply flushed into open pits and sprayed onto fields.

Turn those humans into hogs, and you don't have to imagine at all. It's already here. A vast city of swine has risen practically overnight in the counties east of Interstate 95. It's a megalopolis of 7 million animals that live in metal confinement barns and produce two to four times as much waste, per hog, as the average human.

All that manure—about 9.5 million tons a year—was stored in thousands of earthen pits called lagoons.

These pits were open so that sunlight would decompose the wastes and kill the harmful bacteria; the manure was then spread on farm fields as organic fertilizer. The lagoon system was the source of most hog farm odor, but industry officials said it was a proven and effective way to keep harmful chemicals and bacteria out of water supplies. New evidence said otherwise:

- The *News and Observer* has obtained new scientific studies showing that contaminants from hog lagoons are getting into groundwater. One N.C. State University report estimates that as many as half of existing lagoons—perhaps hundreds—are leaking badly enough to contaminate ground water.

- The industry also is running out of places to spread or spray the waste from lagoons. On paper, the state's biggest swine counties already are producing more phosphorous-rich manure than available land can absorb, state Agriculture Department records show.

- Scientists are discovering that hog farms emit large amounts of ammonia gas, which returns to earth in rain. The ammonia is believed to be contributing to an explosion of algae growth that's choking many of the state's rivers and estuaries.[5]

Raising hogs was admitted even by farm families to be a messy and smelly business. Hogs eat more than other farm animals, and they excrete more. And those excretions smell far, far worse. Having 50 to 100 hogs running free in a fenced pasture was one thing. The odor was clearly noticeable, but that sharp and pungent smell was felt to be part of rural living. Having 5,000 to 10,000 hogs closely confined in metal barns, with large ventilation fans moving the air continually from each barn, and the wastes from those hogs collected in huge open-air lagoons was something else. People who lived near one of the large hog farms said that, unless you've experienced it, you just can't know what it is like:

At 11 o'clock sharp on a Sunday morning the choir marched into the sanctuary of New Brown's Chapel Baptist Church. And the stench of 4,800 hogs rolled right in with them.

The odor hung oppressively in the vestibule, clinging to church robes, winter coats and fancy hats. It sent stragglers scurrying indoors from the parking lot, some holding their noses. Sherry Leveston, 4, pulled her fancy white sweater over her face as she ran. "It stinks," she cried.

It was another Sunday morning in Brownsville, a Greene County North Carolina hamlet that's home to 200 people and one hog farm. Like many of its

counterparts throughout the eastern portion of the state, the town hasn't been the same since the hogs moved in a couple of years ago.

To some, each new gust from the south [the direction of the farm] is a reminder of serious wrongs committed for which there has been no redress. "We've basically given up," said the Rev. Charles White, pastor at New Brown's Chapel.

In scores of rural neighborhoods down east [the eastern portion of North Carolina] the talk is the same. There's something new in the air, and people are furious about it.

Hog odor is by far the most emotional issue facing the pork industry—and the most divisive. Growers assert their right to earn a living; neighbors say they have a right to odor-free air. Hog company officials, meanwhile, accuse activists of exaggerating the problem to stir up opposition . . .

For other residents [of Brownsville, close to New Brown's Chapel] hog odor has simply become an inescapable part of their daily routine. It's usually heaviest about 5 a.m., when Lisa Hines leaves the house for her factory job. It seeps into her car and follows her on her commute to work. It clings to her hair and clothes during the day. And it awaits her when she returns home in the afternoon.

"It makes me so mad," she said. "The owner lives miles away from here, and he can go home and smell apples and cinnamon if he wants to. But we have no choice."[6]

Lagoons had been the accepted means for disposing of animal wastes on small family farms for centuries. It was a method fully protected by federal, state, and local laws; a hog farmer—whether a small family or large contract farm—could not be sued for any inconveniences brought about by the hogs, unless those inconveniences were the result of clear negligence in caring for the hogs.

The difference now, of course, came from the huge expansion of scale. Again, the wastes of 50 to 100 animals were easily accommodated. There was a noticeable effect on air quality, but that was felt to be a natural consequence of living in the country, and the smell came from your own farm, or that of your neighbor, or that of a person who had been there for years. There was a probable effect on water quality, but farm wells were always located uphill and a substantial distance from manure piles, and it was thought that neighbors would be protected by natural filtration through the clay subsoils of the region. No one worried very much about possible public health effects of small numbers of farm animals.

The wastes from 5,000 to 10,000 animals could not be so easily accommodated, and people did worry about the possible public health effects of very large numbers of farm animals. Debilitating asthma had become a much more frequent condition among young children who lived near large hog farms, and there was concern that waste was leaking from the lagoons and contaminating the groundwater. The conventional wisdom about the lagoons was that the heavier sludge was supposed to settle on the bottom and form a seal that would prevent the escape of harmful bacteria or destructive chemicals:

> As recently as two years ago, the U.S. Division of Environmental Management told state lawmakers in a briefing that lagoons effectively self-seal within months with "little or no groundwater contamination." Wendell H. Murphy, a former state senator who was also [in partnership with Smithfield Corporation] the nation's largest producer of hogs, said in an interview this month that "lagoons will seal themselves" and that "there is not one shred, not one piece of evidence anywhere in this nation that any groundwater is being contaminated by any hog lagoon."
>
> What Murphy didn't know was that a series of brand-new studies, conducted among Eastern North Carolina hog farms, showed that large numbers of lagoons are leaking, some of them severely.[7]

The *Raleigh News and Observer* had reported that researchers at North Carolina State University had dug test wells near 11 lagoons that were at least seven years old. They found that more than half of the lagoons were leaking moderately to severely; even those lagoons that were described as leaking only moderately still produced groundwater nitrate levels up to three times the allowable limit. The researchers also found that lagoons were not the only source of groundwater contamination. They dug test wells and examined water quality in fields where hog waste had been sprayed as fertilizer, and found evidence of widespread bacterial and chemical contamination. It was felt that fully as much water contamination came from the practice of attempting to dispose of the decomposed waste through spraying on crops as from the earlier storage of decomposing waste in the lagoons. According to the *Raleigh News and Observer* reporter, too much waste was being sprayed on too few fields, even though almost all farmers in the region now accepted this natural fertilizer in lieu of buying commercial products.

The researchers from North Carolina State University, however, did not urge rural residents to rush out to buy bottled water. In most of the cases they concluded that the contaminants appeared to be migrating laterally toward the nearest ditch or stream, and they found no evidence that a private well had been contaminated. But they did find evidence that numerous streams had been contaminated, partially from leakage but primarily from spills and overflows:

> Frequently major spills are cleaned up quickly so that the public never hears about them. That's what happened in May 1995 when a 10-acre lagoon ruptured on Murphy's Farms' 8,000-hog facility in Magnolia, North Carolina. A limestone layer beneath the lagoon collapsed, sending tons of waste cascading into nearby Millers Creek in an accident that was never reported to state water-quality officials.
>
> An employee of the town's water department discovered the problem when he saw corn kernels and hog waste floating by in the creek that runs through the center of town. He alerted the company, and within hours a task force had been assembled to plug the leak.
>
> It took four days to find the source and fix the problem. But neither Magnolia town officials nor Murphy Farms executives ever notified the state about the spill.
>
> "In retrospect, maybe we should have," Wendell Murphy said, "but I would also say that to my knowledge no harm has ever come of it."
>
> Former employees of hog companies, however, told *News and Observer* reporters that spills were a common occurrence. "Hardly a week goes by," said a former manager for one of the largest hog farms in the state, "that there isn't some sort of leak or overflow. Almost any heavy rain will bring an overflow. When that happens, workers do the best they can to clean it up. After that it's just pray no one notices and keep your mouth shut," he explained.[8]

The waste lagoons could not be covered with a roof to prevent overflows associated with heavy rains, or enclosed with a building to prevent the escape of odors; They were simply too large—five to eight acres—and it was necessary to have direct sunlight to create the natural conditions that would break down the toxic chemicals and kill the harmful bacteria in the wastes. Company officials seemed to believe that there was no possible solution to the problem of the extremely bad odors; essentially they said it would just be necessary for people to learn to live with the smell, which extends up to two miles from the open lagoons and the sprayed fields. According to the *Raleigh News and Observer,*

> Wendell Murphy, chairman of Murphy Family Farms [part of the Murphy Brown hog farming subsidiary of Smithfield Foods] said that while the hog industry is extremely sensitive to the odor problem, he thinks the industry's economic importance should be considered in the equation. "Should we expect the odor to never drift off the site to a neighbor's house? If so, then we're out of business. We all have to have some inconvenience once in a while for the benefits that come with it."[9]

As the *Raleigh News and Observer* reported, feelings ran high among eastern North Carolina residents in opposing further expansion of hog farming in the region:

> Three weeks ago, the tiny town of Faison held a referendum of sorts on whether its residents wanted a new industrial plant, with 1,500 new jobs, built in their community. The jobs lost.
>
> Because the industry in question was a hog-processing plant, people packed the local fire station an hour early to blast the idea. They jeered and hissed every time the county's industrial recruiter mentioned pigs or the plant. "I want to know two things," thundered one burly speaker thrusting a finger at that much smaller industrial recruiter, Woody Brinson. "How can we stop this thing, and how can we get you fired?"
>
> The town council's eventual 3–0 vote against the proposed IBP [a subsidiary of Smithfield Foods] hog slaughterhouse may have little effect on whether the plant is built. [Zoning within rural North Carolina is controlled by the county, not the municipality, and agriculturally related zoning has always been very loosely applied, to benefit local farmers.] What was striking about this meeting, and this vote, was that both occurred in the heart of Duplin County, an economic showcase for the hog industry.
>
> With a pigs-per-person ratio of 32-to-1, Duplin has seen big payoffs from eastern North Carolina's hog revolution in the past decade. The county's revenues from sales and property taxes have soared, and Duplin's per capita income has risen from the lowest 25 percent statewide to about the middle.
>
> Pork production also has spawned jobs in support businesses in Duplin and neighboring counties. People in the hog business say farm odor—"the smell of money"—is a small price to pay for a big benefit. "These hog farms are putting money in people's

pockets," says Woody Brinston [the county's director of industrial development]. "Duplin County is booming."

> But even here, some bitterly resent the way the industry has transformed the way the countryside looks and smells. Some say that their property has gone down in value. Others note the contrasts in the economic picture. In Duplin County, just 70 miles east of the booming Research Triangle [an area located between Raleigh, Durham, and Chapel Hill with a large number of advanced electronic and biotechnology firms], the population hasn't grown in 10 years. Farm jobs are dwindling despite the rise in hog production.
>
> Daryl Walker, a newly elected Duplin County commissioner, says he hears these arguments all the time. "If this is prosperity," he says, "many of my constituents would just as soon do without it. They are scared to death that there are just going to be more and more hogs, and more and more of the problems that come with those hogs.[10]

A subsequent letter to the editor of the *Raleigh News and Observer* said:

> Last Sunday, returning from a weekend at Wrightsville Beach, we stopped at an Interstate 40 rest area near Clinton. When we stepped from our car the stench brought tears to our eyes. So add to the ever-mounting environment damage the poor image our state now leaves with tourists heading towards our beautiful coast. We'll never know how many big tourism bucks are now and soon will be going elsewhere.[11]

SMITHFIELD'S EFFORTS TO ADDRESS CONCERNS ABOUT THE ENVIRONMENTAL IMPACT OF ITS VERTICAL INTEGRATION STRATEGY

Smithfield management was endeavoring to combat opposition to its operations in eastern North Carolina and elsewhere and to respond to the environmental challenges that its pork business presented. Exhibit 2 describes examples of Smithfield's environmental improvement projects during 2000–2004. Exhibit 3 presents Smithfield Foods' environmental

Exhibit 2   **Examples of Smithfield Foods' Environmental Projects, 2000–2004**

- In 2000, Smithfield signed an agreement with the Office of the North Carolina Attorney General to contribute $2 million per year for 25 years to a fund used for such environmental enhancement projects as constructing and maintaining wetlands, preserving environmentally sensitive lands, and promoting similar projects. In 2003, the attorney general used Smithfield's contributions for grants to five recipients: the Cape Fear River Assembly, Save Our State, the Green Trust Alliance, the North Carolina Coastal Land Trust, and the North Carolina Foundation for Soil and Water Conservation Districts.

- Smithfield had funded a $15 million research project at North Carolina State University to investigate 18 different technologies to modify or replace current methods of swine waste removal at hog farms. A major goal of the project was to achieve cleaner air by finding ways to reduce methane and ammonia emissions of the swine waste lagoons. Smithfield had agreed to implement the recommended technologies, if they were commercially feasible, at all of its hog farms.

- In 2001, all of Murphy-Brown's company-owned swine production farms in North Carolina, South Carolina, and Virginia implemented "environmental management systems" (EMSs) to identify and manage parts of Smithfield's activities that have, or could have, an impact on the environment—the objective was to monitor environmental performance, pinpoint problem areas, and implement any needed preventive and corrective action. These farms then went an extra step and achieved ISO 14001 certification, making Murphy-Brown the first livestock operation in the world to do so—ISO 14001 certification was considered the gold standard for environmental excellence in implementing methods to monitor and measure the environmental impact of production operations and pinpoint problem areas. Since that time, Murphy-Brown has completed EMS implementation and achieved ISO 14001 certification for all company-owned farms in the United States.

- Smithfield was investing up to $20 million in a majority-owned subsidiary, BEST BioFuels, to build a waste collection system and a central treatment facility in southwestern Utah that used proprietary technology to convert livestock waste (which contained methane, a greenhouse gas) into biomethanol. Biomethanol could be processed with a variety of vegetable- or animal-based oils to create biodiesel, an environmentally friendly alternative to petroleum diesel. The waste-to-biomethanol treatment facility in Utah, which began operations in 2004, was connected by an underground sewage network to 23 area farms and received waste from approximately 257,000 hogs over the course of a year. The Utah plant shipped much of its 2.7 million gallons of biomethanol to a newly constructed BEST Biofuels plant in Texas, where it was processed with used cooking oil, rendered animal fat, or other oil feedstock to create biodiesel, an environmentally friendly alternative to petroleum diesel that emitted nearly 50 percent less carbon monoxide and hazardous particulate matter than regular petroleum diesel. Fuel distributors then blended biodiesel with conventional petroleum diesel in a 20/80 ratio to create a cleaner diesel fuel.

- Cooling towers were installed at four of Smithfield's company processing plants to recirculate water needed in operating the plants; these water conservation measures reduced use of groundwater and relieved stresses on local water tables.

- Smithfield had partnered with its primary corrugated packaging suppliers to pursue cardboard recycling in its operations. Since 2002, close to 50,000 tons of cardboard had been recycled rather than being sent to landfills.

- Several Smithfield plants had modified their facilities to allow biogas—a fuel source derived from plant wastewater—to be used as an energy source. Most all Smithfield plants were pursuing projects to conserve on the use of electric energy.

Source: Information contained in Smithfield's 2003 Stewardship Report and information posted at www.smithfieldfoods.com (accessed December 26, 2002, and November 23, 2004).

policy statement. Exhibit 4 presents senior management's statement regarding the company's "Strategy for Responsible Growth." Exhibit 5 presents excerpts from the company's Code of Business Conduct.

During the spring of 2003, the highest seasonal rainfall in North Carolina's recorded history caused elevated lagoon levels at many eastern North Carolina

hog farms. Farmers reported the levels to the state agency, as was the standard practice, but officials at North Carolina's Department of Environment and Natural Resources nonetheless sent out hundreds of notices of violations (NOVs), 55 of which were to farms operated by Smithfield's Murphy-Brown subsidiary. While elevated lagoon levels did not compromise the structural integrity of the lagoons,

Exhibit 3   Smithfield Foods' Environmental Policy Statement, 2004

It is the corporate policy of Smithfield Foods, Inc., and its subsidiaries to conduct business in a manner consistent with continual improvement in regard to protecting the environment.

- Smithfield Foods, Inc., is committed to protecting the environment through pollution prevention and continual improvement of our environmental practices.
- Smithfield Foods, Inc., seeks to demonstrate its responsible corporate citizenship by complying with relevant environmental legislation and regulations, and with other requirements to which we subscribe. We will create, implement, and periodically review appropriate environmental objectives and targets.
- Protection of the environment is the responsibility of all Smithfield Foods, Inc., employees.

Source: www.smithfieldfoods.com (accessed November 23, 2004).

they did decrease the reserve designated for storage of rainfall accumulated over a 24-hour period from intense storms. Many farmers and legislative leaders protested the number of NOVs issued, prompting the Department of Environment and Natural Resources to reconsider their having issued so many NOVs; a substantial number were subsequently reclassified as notices of deficiency (NODs). Following the severe

Exhibit 4   Statement of Smithfield Foods' Management Regarding the Company's Strategy for Responsible Growth

Over the past few years, our company has set the foundations for continuous improvement in our stewardship responsibilities, which include our environmental, employee safety and animal welfare–related performance. We have firmly established the necessary policies, organizations, management systems, programs, funding, and expertise.

This foundation is now in place within the majority of our U.S. operations. We continue to move forward guided by the principles of accountability, transparency, and sustainability, and by our primary objectives:

- Achieve 100 percent regulatory compliance, 100 percent of the time.
- Move well beyond compliance in stewardship responsibilities.
- Reduce the frequency and severity of injuries to employees.
- Enhance communications and transparency with external stakeholders.
- Continue to expand community involvement.

We also have a more ambitious vision, and that is to be recognized as the industry leader for stewardship. To do this, we will continue to explore approaches to the issues that are unique to our industry. We will continue to find ways to participate productively in key industry and multi-stakeholder groups where we can help facilitate win–win solutions. We will share our experiences and best practices with our peers and other interested parties. We will also work toward policy changes that promote industry innovation and enable our company to better deliver financial, environmental, and social value.

In 2003, Smithfield embarked on a major project, committing to invest $20 million to implement technology beneficial to the environment and that will also play a key role in the solution for our global energy needs. We are using the untapped energy stored in livestock waste to create a fully renewable motor fuel—biodiesel. Our renewable fuel project at Circle Four Farms in Utah will produce in excess of 7,000 gallons of biomethanol per day. Blended with rendered fats, this biomethanol is converted to biodiesel that would meet the daily fuel requirements for about 300 over-the-road trucks, offsetting the need to import crude oil to produce that quantity of traditional diesel fuel. The project is highlighted in more detail in other sections of this report and is expected to be in full operation in late spring 2004.

We are very encouraged by the results we have seen over the past few years. Moving forward, Smithfield's strategy for responsible growth can be summed up as follows: more of the same. And by that we mean more management systems, more measurement and target setting, more innovative thinking and partnering, further support of environmentally superior waste management technologies, more communication, transparency and relationship building, more improvement—and more listening. This is what Smithfield will strive to accomplish.

Source: Smithfield Foods, *2003 Stewardship Report,* pp. 11–12.

Exhibit 5   **Excerpts from Smithfield Foods' Code of Business Conduct, 2004**

Smithfield is committed to compliance with the laws, rules, and regulations applicable to the conduct of our business wherever we operate. Our ultimate goal is 100% compliance, 100% of the time. Employees must avoid activities that could involve or lead to involvement of Smithfield or its personnel in any unlawful practice.

Employee awareness of Smithfield operating practices must include knowledge of the environmental laws and Smithfield policies governing their operations. Employees must immediately control and report all spills and releases as required by applicable regulations and facility rules.

The nature of Smithfield's business requires it to conduct various monitoring, inspecting, and testing to ensure compliance with applicable laws and regulations. Such monitoring, inspecting, and testing must be performed, and accurate records thereof made and retained, in compliance with all applicable legal requirements. Employees who have questions about legal requirements applicable to such areas should consult their supervisor or a member of the Smithfield Law Department.

Smithfield employees are expected to comply with all federal, state, local, and foreign environmental laws and all Smithfield policies related to environmental affairs. We expect 100% compliance 100% of the time. It is each employee's responsibility to know and understand the legal, policy, and operating practice requirements applicable to his or her job and to notify management when the employee believes that a violation of law or Smithfield policies has occurred. Any employee who has concerns regarding compliance in this area should immediately consult with the environmental contact for his or her facility or subsidiary, a senior environmental officer, or the Smithfield Law Department. The Smithfield Foods, Inc. Employee Hotline (1-877-237-5270) is available for reporting employee concerns anonymously.

Compliance with environmental laws and all Smithfield policies is the single highest priority for the company's environmental program. Our employees' job performance is important to us, and is evaluated not only on business results achieved, but also on whether our employees, and particularly our management team, operate within our expectations for environmental performance. We hold all of our employees to a high standard of conduct and accountability for environmental performance.

Compliance with the Smithfield Foods, Inc., Code of Business Conduct and Ethics is a condition of employment. Failure to comply may result in a range of disciplinary actions, including termination. Failure by any Smithfield employee to disclose violations of these standards and practices by other Smithfield employees or contract workers is also grounds for disciplinary action.

Source: Smithfield Foods' Code of Business Conduct, www.smithfieldfoods.com (accessed November 23, 2004).

weather, Smithfield moved swiftly to get its lagoon levels back to compliance levels and no further regulatory actions were taken. All told, Smithfield received 77 notices of violations or noncompliance in 2003, resulting in fines of $124,204. The biggest fine ($77,000) was for a wastewater incident at its Moyer beef processing plant in Pennsylvania, and a $17,875 fine was imposed for an ammonia release at a Georgia plant.

Endnotes

[1] Quoted in the five-part series by Joby Warrick and Pat Stith, "Boss Hog: North Carolina's Pork Revolution—Hog Waste Is Polluting the Ground Water," *Raleigh News and Observer,* February 19, 1995. This series, based on a seven-month investigation and run in the *News and Observer,* February 19–26, 1995, was awarded the Pulitzer Prize for Public Service Journalism in 1996.
[2] Ibid.
[3] Ibid.
[4] Charlie LeDuff, "At a Slaughterhouse, Some Things Never Die," *New York Times,* June 16, 2000, p. A1.
[5] *Raleigh News and Observer,* February 19, 1995.

[6] Joby Warrick and Pat Stith, "Boss Hog: North Carolina's Pork Revolution—Money Talks," *Raleigh News and Observer,* February 24, 1995, p. A9.
[7] Ibid.
[8] Ibid.
[9] Ibid.
[10] Joby Warrick and Pat Stith, "Boss Hog: North Carolina's Pork Revolution—Pork Barrels," *Raleigh News and Observer,* February 26, 1995.
[11] *Raleigh News and Observer,* March 4, 1995, p. A10.

Endnotes

Chapter 1

[1] Costas Markides, "What Is Strategy and How Do You Know If You Have One?" *Business Strategy Review* 15, no. 2 (Summer 2004), pp. 5–6.

[2] For a discussion of the different ways in which companies can position themselves in the marketplace, see Michael E. Porter, "What Is Strategy?" *Harvard Business Review* 74, no. 6 (November–December 1996), pp. 65–67.

[3] For an excellent treatment of the strategic challenges posed by high-velocity changes, see Shona L. Brown and Kathleen M. Eisenhardt, *Competing on the Edge: Strategy as Structured Chaos* (Boston: Harvard Business School Press, 1998), Chapter 1.

[4] See Henry Mintzberg and Joseph Lampel, "Reflecting on the Strategy Process, *Sloan Management Review* 40, no. 3 (Spring 1999), pp. 21–30; Henry Mintzberg and J. A. Waters, "Of Strategies, Deliberate and Emergent," *Strategic Management Journal* 6 (1985), pp. 257–72; Costas Markides, "Strategy as Balance: From 'Either-Or' to 'And,'" *Business Strategy Review* 12, no. 3 (September 2001), pp. 1–10; Henry Mintzberg, Bruce Ahlstrand, and Joseph Lampel, *Strategy Safari: A Guided Tour through the Wilds of Strategic Management* (New York: Free Press, 1998), 7; and C. K. Prahalad and Gary Hamel, "The Core Competence of the Corporation," *Harvard Business Review* 70, no. 3 (May–June 1990), pp. 79–93.

[5] Joseph L. Badaracco, "The Discipline of Building Character," *Harvard Business Review* 76, no. 2 (March–April 1998), pp. 115–24.

[6] Joan Magretta, "Why Business Models Matter," *Harvard Business Review* 80, no. 5 (May 2002), p. 87.

Chapter 2

[1] For a more in-depth discussion of the challenges of developing a well-conceived vision, as well as some good examples, see Hugh Davidson, *The Committed Enterprise: How to Make Vision and Values Work* (Oxford: Butterworth Heinemann, 2002), Chapter 2; W. Chan Kim and Renée Mauborgne, "Charting Your Company's Future," *Harvard Business Review* 80, no. 6 (June 2002), pp. 77–83; James C. Collins and Jerry I. Porras, "Building Your Company's Vision," *Harvard Business Review* 74, no. 5 (September–October 1996), pp. 65–77; James C. Collins and Jerry I. Porras, *Built to Last: Successful Habits of Visionary Companies* (New York: HarperCollins, 1994), Chapter 11; and Michel Robert, *Strategy Pure and Simple II*

(New York: McGraw-Hill, 1998), Chapters 2, 3, and 6.

[2] Davidson, *Committed Enterprise,* pp. 20, 54.

[3] Ibid., pp. 36, 54.

[4] Jeffrey K. Liker, *The Toyota Way* (New York: McGraw-Hill, 2004), and Steve Hamm, "Taking a Page from Toyota's Playbook," *BusinessWeek,* August 22/29, 2005, p. 72.

[5] As quoted in Charles H. House and Raymond L. Price, "The Return Map: Tracking Product Teams," *Harvard Business Review* 60, no. 1 (January–February 1991), p. 93.

[6] Robert S. Kaplan and David P. Norton, *The Strategy-Focused Organization* (Boston: Harvard Business School Press, 2001), p. 3.

[7] Ibid., p. 7. Also, see Kevin B. Hendricks, Larry Menor, and Christine Wiedman, "The Balanced Scorecard: To Adopt or Not to Adopt," *Ivey Business Journal* 69, no. 2 (November–December 2004), pp. 1–7; and Sandy Richardson, "The Key Elements of Balanced Scorecard Success," *Ivey Business Journal* 69, no. 2 (November–December 2004), pp. 7–9.

[8] Information posted on the Web site of the Balanced Scorecard Institute, www. balancedscorecard.org (accessed August 22, 2005).

[9] Darrell Rigby, "Management Tools Survey 2003: Usage Up as Companies Strive to Make Headway in Tough Times," *Strategy & Leadership* 31, no. 5 (May 2003), p. 6.

[10] Information posted on the Web site of Balanced Scorecard Collaborative, www.bscol.com (accessed August 22, 2005). This Web site was created by the co-creators of the balanced scorecard concept, Professors Robert S. Kaplan and David P. Norton, Harvard Business School.

[11] The concept of strategic intent is described in more detail in Gary Hamel and C. K. Prahalad, "Strategic Intent," *Harvard Business Review* 89, no. 3 (May–June 1989), pp. 63–76; this section draws on their pioneering discussion. See also Michael A. Hitt, Beverly B. Tyler, Camilla Hardee, and Daewoo Park, "Understanding Strategic Intent in the Global Marketplace," *Academy of Management Executive* 9, no. 2 (May 1995), pp. 12–19.

[12] For a fuller discussion of strategy as an entrepreneurial process, see Henry Mintzberg, Bruce Ahlstrand, and Joseph Lampel, *Strategy Safari: A Guided Tour through the Wilds of Strategic Management,* (New York: Free Press, 1998), Chapter 5. Also see Bruce Barringer and Allen C. Bluedorn, "The Relationship Between Corporate Entrepreneurship and Strategic Management," *Strategic Management*

Journal 20 (1999), pp. 421–444, and Jeffrey G. Covin and Morgan P. Miles, "Corporate Entrepreneurship and the Pursuit of Competitive Advantage," *Entrepreneurship: Theory and Practice* 23, no. 3 (Spring 1999), pp. 47–63.

[13] The strategy-making, strategy-implementing roles of middle managers are thoroughly discussed and documented in Steven W. Floyd and Bill Wooldridge, *The Strategic Middle Manager* (San Francisco: Jossey-Bass Publishers, 1996), Chapters 2 and 3.

[14] "Strategic Planning," *Business Week,* August 26, 1996, pp. 51–52.

[15] For an excellent discussion of why a strategic plan needs to be more than a list of bullet points and should in fact tell an engaging, insightful, stage-setting story that lays out the industry and competitive situation as well as the vision, objectives, and strategy, see Gordon Shaw, Robert Brown, and Philip Bromiley, "Strategic Stories: How 3M Is Rewriting Business Planning," *Harvard Business Review* 76, no. 3 (May–June 1998), pp. 41–50.

[16] For a discussion of what it takes for the corporate governance system to function properly, see David A. Nadler, "Building Better Boards," *Harvard Business Review* 82, no. 5 (May 2004), pp. 102–5; Cynthia A. Montgomery and Rhonda Kaufman, "The Board's Missing Link," *Harvard Business Review* 81, no. 3 (March 2003), pp. 86–93; and John Carver, "What Continues to Be Wrong with Corporate Governance and How to Fix It," *Ivey Business Journal* 68, no. 1 (September–October 2003), pp. 1–5. See also Gordon Donaldson, "A New Tool for Boards: The Strategic Audit," *Harvard Business Review* 73, no. 4 (July–August 1995), pp. 99–107.

Chapter 3

[1] There are a large number of studies of the size of the cost reductions associated with experience; the median cost reduction associated with a doubling of cumulative production volume is approximately 15 percent, but there is a wide variation from industry to industry. For a good discussion of the economies of experience and learning, see Pankaj Ghemawat, "Building Strategy on the Experience Curve," *Harvard Business Review* 64, no. 2 (March–April 1985), pp. 143–49.

[2] The five-forces model of competition is the creation of Professor Michael Porter of the Harvard Business School. For his original presentation of the model, see Michael E. Porter, "How Competitive Forces Shape Strategy," *Harvard Business Review* 57, no. 2

(March–April 1979), pp. 137–45. A more thorough discussion can be found in Michael E. Porter, *Competitive Strategy: Techniques for Analyzing Industries and Competitors* (New York: Free Press, 1980), Chapter 1.

3. Many of these indicators of whether rivalry produces intense competitive pressures are based on Porter, *Competitive Strategy,* pp. 17–21.

4. The role of entry barriers in shaping the strength of competition in a particular market has long been a standard topic in the literature of microeconomics. For a discussion of how entry barriers affect competitive pressures associated with potential entry, see J. S. Bain, *Barriers to New Competition* (Cambridge: Harvard University Press, 1956); F. M. Scherer, *Industrial Market Structure and Economic Performance* (Chicago: Rand McNally, 1971), pp. 216–20, 226–33; and Porter, *Competitive Strategy,* pp. 7–17.

5. Porter, "How Competitive Forces Shape Strategy," p. 140, and Porter, *Competitive Strategy,* pp. 14–15.

6. For a good discussion of this point, see George S. Yip, "Gateways to Entry," *Harvard Business Review* 60, no. 5 (September–October 1982), pp. 85–93.

7. Porter, "How Competitive Forces Shape Strategy," p. 142, and Porter, *Competitive Strategy,* pp. 23–24.

8. Porter, *Competitive Strategy,* p. 10.

9. Ibid., pp. 27–28.

10. Ibid., pp. 24–27.

11. For a more extended discussion of the problems with the life-cycle hypothesis, see ibid., pp. 157–62.

12. Ibid. p. 162.

13. Most of the candidate driving forces described here are based on the discussion in ibid., pp. 164–83.

14. Ibid., Chapter 7.

15. Ibid., pp. 129–30.

16. For an excellent discussion of how to identify the factors that define strategic groups, see Mary Ellen Gordon and George R. Milne, "Selecting the Dimensions That Define Strategic Groups: A Novel Market-Driven Approach," *Journal of Managerial Issues* 11, no. 2 (Summer 1999), pp. 213–33.

17. Porter, *Competitive Strategy,* pp. 152–54.

18. Strategic groups act as good reference points for predicting the evolution of an industry's competitive structure. See Avi Fiegenbaum and Howard Thomas, "Strategic Groups as Reference Groups: Theory, Modeling and Empirical Examination of Industry and Competitive Strategy," *Strategic Management Journal* 16 (1995), pp. 461–76. For a study of how strategic group analysis helps identify the variables that lead to sustainable competitive advantage, see S. Ade Olusoga, Michael P. Mokwa, and Charles H. Noble,

"Strategic Groups, Mobility Barriers, and Competitive Advantage," *Journal of Business Research* 33 (1995), pp. 153–64.

19. Porter, *Competitive Strategy,* pp. 130, 132–38, and 154–55.

20. For a discussion of legal and ethical ways of gathering competitive intelligence on rival companies, see Larry Kahaner, *Competitive Intelligence* (New York: Simon & Schuster, 1996).

21. Ibid., pp. 84–85.

22. Some experts dispute the strategy-making value of key success factors. Professor Pankaj Ghemawat has claimed that the "whole idea of identifying a success factor and then chasing it seems to have something in common with the ill-considered medieval hunt for the *philosopher's stone,* a substance which would transmute everything it touched into gold." Pankaj Ghemawat, *Commitment: The Dynamic of Strategy* (New York: Free Press, 1991), p. 11.

Chapter 4

1. Many business organizations are coming to view cutting-edge knowledge and intellectual resources of company personnel as a valuable competitive asset and have concluded that explicitly managing these assets is an essential part of their strategy. See Michael H. Zack, "Developing a Knowledge Strategy," *California Management Review* 41, no. 3 (Spring 1999), pp. 125–45, and Shaker A. Zahra, Anders P. Nielsen, and William C. Bogner, "Corporate Entrepreneurship, Knowledge, and Competence Development," *Entrepreneurship Theory and Practice,* Spring 1999, pp. 169–89.

2. In the past decade, there's been considerable research into the role a company's resources and competitive capabilities play in crafting strategy and in determining company profitability. The findings and conclusions have coalesced into what is called the resource-based view of the firm. Among the most insightful articles are Birger Wernerfelt, "A Resource-Based View of the Firm," *Strategic Management Journal,* September–October 1984, pp. 171–80; Jay Barney, "Firm Resources and Sustained Competitive Advantage," *Journal of Management* 17, no. 1 (1991), pp. 99–120; Margaret A. Peteraf, "The Cornerstones of Competitive Advantage: A Resource-Based View," *Strategic Management Journal,* March 1993, pp. 179–91; Birger Wernerfelt, "The Resource-Based View of the Firm: Ten Years After," *Strategic Management Journal* 16 (1995), pp. 171–74; Jay Barney, "Looking Inside for Competitive Advantage," *Academy of Management Executive* 9, no. 4 (November 1995), pp. 49–61; Christopher A. Bartlett and Sumantra Ghoshal, "Building Competitive Advantage through People,"

MIT Sloan Management Review 43, no 2, (Winter 2002), pp. 34–41; and Danny Miller, Russell Eisenstat, and Nathaniel Foote, "Strategy from the Inside Out: Building Capability-Creating Organizations," *California Management Review* 44, no. 3 (Spring 2002), pp. 37–54.

3. George Stalk Jr. and Rob Lachenauer, "Hard Ball: Five Killer Strategies for Trouncing the Competition," *Harvard Business Review* 82, no. 4 (April 2004), p. 65.

4. For a more extensive discussion of how to identify and evaluate the competitive power of a company's capabilities, see David W. Birchall and George Tovstiga, "The Strategic Potential of a Firm's Knowledge Portfolio," *Journal of General Management* 25, no. 1 (Autumn 1999), pp. 1–16, and Nick Bontis, Nicola C. Dragonetti, Kristine Jacobsen, and Goran Roos, "The Knowledge Toolbox: A Review of the Tools Available to Measure and Manage Intangible Resources," *European Management Journal* 17, no. 4 (August 1999), pp. 391–401. Also see David Teece, "Capturing Value from Knowledge Assets: The New Economy, Markets for Know-How, and Intangible Assets," *California Management Review* 40, no. 3 (Spring 1998), pp. 55–79.

5. See Barney, "Firm Resources," pp. 105–9, and David J. Collis and Cynthia A. Montgomery, "Competing on Resources: Strategy in the 1990s," *Harvard Business Review* 73, no. 4 (July–August 1995), pp. 120–23.

6. Donald Sull, "Strategy as Active Waiting," *Harvard Business Review* 83, no. 9 (September 2005), p. 121–122.

7. Ibid., p. 122.

8. Ibid., pp. 124–26.

9. See Jack W. Duncan, Peter Ginter, and Linda E. Swayne, "Competitive Advantage and Internal Organizational Assessment," *Academy of Management Executive* 12, no. 3 (August 1998), pp. 6–16.

10. The value chain concept was developed and articulated by Professor Michael Porter at the Harvard Business School and is described at greater length in Michael E. Porter, *Competitive Advantage* (New York: Free Press, 1985), Chapters 2 and 3.

11. Ibid., p. 36.

12. Ibid., p. 34.

13. The strategic importance of effective supply chain management is discussed in Hau L. Lee, "The Triple-A Supply Chain," *Harvard Business Review* 82, no. 10 (October 2004), pp. 102–112.

14. M. Hegert and D. Morris, "Accounting Data for Value Chain Analysis," *Strategic Management Journal* 10 (1989), p. 180; Robin Cooper and Robert S. Kaplan, "Measure Costs Right: Make the Right Decisions," *Harvard Business Review* 66, no. 5 (September–October, 1988), pp. 96–103; and John K. Shank and Vijay

Govindarajan, *Strategic Cost Management* (New York: Free Press, 1993), especially Chapters 2–6, 10.

[15]For more on how and why the clustering of suppliers and other support organizations matter to a company's costs and competitiveness, see Michael E. Porter, "Clusters and the New Economics of Competition," *Harvard Business Review* 76, no. 6 (November–December 1998), pp. 77–90.

[16]For discussions of the accounting challenges in calculating the costs of value chain activities, see Shank and Govindarajan, *Strategic Cost Management,* especially Chapters 2–6, 10, and 11; Cooper and Kaplan, "Measure Costs Right"; and Joseph A. Ness and Thomas G. Cucuzza, "Tapping the Full Potential of ABC," *Harvard Business Review* 73, no. 4 (July–August 1995), pp. 130–38.

[17]For more details, see Gregory H. Watson, *Strategic Benchmarking: How to Rate Your Company's Performance Against the World's Best* (New York: John Wiley, 1993); Robert C. Camp, *Benchmarking: The Search for Industry Best Practices That Lead to Superior Performance* (Milwaukee: ASQC Quality Press, 1989); Christopher E. Bogan and Michael J. English, *Benchmarking for Best Practices: Winning through Innovative Adaptation* (New York: McGraw-Hill, 1994); and Dawn Iacobucci and Christie Nordhiem, "Creative Benchmarking," *Harvard Business Review* 78 no. 6 (November–December 2000), pp. 24–25.

[18]Jeremy Main, "How to Steal the Best Ideas Around," *Fortune,* October 19, 1992, pp. 102–3.

[19]Shank and Govindarajan, *Strategic Cost Management,* p. 50.

[20]Some of these options are discussed in more detail in Porter, *Competitive Advantage,* Chapter 3.

[21]An example of how Whirlpool Corporation transformed its supply chain from a competitive liability to a competitive asset is discussed in Reuben E. Stone, "Leading a Supply Chain Turnaround," *Harvard Business Review* 82, no. 10 (October 2004), pp. 114–21.

[22]James Brian Quinn, *Intelligent Enterprise* (New York: Free Press, 1993), p. 54.

[23]Ibid., p. 34.

Chapter 5

[1]This classification scheme is an adaptation of a narrower three-strategy classification presented in Michael E. Porter, *Competitive Strategy: Techniques for Analyzing Industries and Competitors* (New York: Free Press, 1980), Chapter 2, especially pp. 35–40 and 44–46. For a discussion of the different ways in which companies can position themselves in the marketplace, see Michael E. Porter, "What Is Strategy?" *Harvard Business Review* 74, no. 6 (November–December 1996), pp. 65–67.

[2]Porter, *Competitive Advantage*, p. 97.

[3]Iowa Beef Packers' value chain revamping was first reported in ibid., p. 109. Since then the company has successfully extended its efforts to reconfigure the meat industry value chain, including an entry into the pork segment. IBP was acquired in 2001 by Tyson Foods after a heated bidding war with Smithfield Foods drove Tyson's acquisition price up to $14 billion. Tyson is now applying many of the same value chain revamping principles in chicken, beef, and pork.

[4]Ibid., pp. 135–38.

[5]For a more detailed discussion, see George Stalk, Philip Evans, and Lawrence E. Schulman, "Competing on Capabilities: The New Rules of Corporate Strategy," *Harvard Business Review* 70, no. 2 (March–April 1992), pp. 57–69.

[6]The relevance of perceived value and signaling is discussed in more detail in Porter, *Competitive Advantage,* pp. 138–42.

[7]Ibid., pp. 160–62.

[8]Gary Hamal, "Strategy as Revolution," *Harvard Business Review* 74, no. 4 (July–August 1996), p. 72.

Chapter 6

[1]Yves L. Doz and Gary Hamel, *Alliance Advantage: The Art of Creating Value through Partnering* (Boston: Harvard Business School Press, 1998), pp. xiii, xiv.

[2]Jason Wakeam, "The Five Factors of a Strategic Alliance," *Ivey Business Journal* 68, no. 3 (May–June 2003), pp. 1–4.

[3]Jeffrey H. Dyer, Prashant Kale, and Harbir Singh, "When to Ally and When to Acquire," *Harvard Business Review* 82, no. 7/8 (July–August 2004), p. 109.

[4]Salvatore Parise and Lisa Sasson, "Leveraging Knowledge Management across Strategic Alliances," *Ivey Business Journal* 66, no. 4 (March–April 2002), p. 42.

[5]David Ernst and James Bamford, "Your Alliances Are Too Stable," *Harvard Business Review* 83, no. 6 (June 2005), p. 133.

[6]An excellent discussion of the portfolio approach to managing multiple alliances and how to restructure a faltering alliance is presented in ibid., pp. 133–41.

[7]Michael E. Porter, *The Competitive Advantage of Nations* (New York: Free Press, 1990), p. 66. For a discussion of how to realize the advantages of strategic partnerships, see Nancy J. Kaplan and Jonathan Hurd, "Realizing the Promise of Partnerships," *Journal of Business Strategy* 23, no. 3 (May–June 2002), pp. 38–42; Parise and Sasson, "Leveraging Knowledge Management," pp. 41–47; and Ernst and Bamford, "Your Alliances Are Too Stable," pp. 133–41.

[8]A. Inkpen, "Learning, Knowledge Acquisition, and Strategic Alliances," *European Management Journal* 16, no. 2 (April 1998), pp. 223–29.

[9]For a discussion of how to raise the chances that a strategic alliance will produce strategically important outcomes, see M. Koza and A. Lewin, "Managing Partnerships and Strategic Alliances: Raising the Odds of Success," *European Management Journal* 18, no. 2 (April 2000), pp. 146–51.

[10]Doz and Hamel, *Alliance Advantage,* Chapters 4–8; Patricia Anslinger and Justin Jenk, "Creating Successful Alliances," *Journal of Business Strategy* 25, no. 2 (2004), pp. 18–23; Rosabeth Moss Kanter, "Collaborative Advantage: The Art of the Alliance," *Harvard Business Review* 72, no. 4 (July–August 1994), pp. 96–108; Joel Bleeke and David Ernst, "The Way to Win in Cross-Border Alliances," *Harvard Business Review* 69, no. 6 (November–December 1991), pp. 127–35 and Gary Hamel, Yves L. Doz, and C. K. Prahalad, "Collaborate with Your Competitors—and Win," *Harvard Business Review* 67, no. 1 (January–February 1989), pp. 133–39.

[11]This same 50 percent success rate for alliances was also cited in Ernst and Bamford, "Your Alliances Are Too Stable," p. 133; both co-authors of this *HBR* article were McKinsey personnel.

[12]Doz and Hamel, *Alliance Advantage,* pp. 16–18.

[13]Dyer, Kale, and Singh, "When to Ally and When to Acquire," p. 109.

[14]For an excellent discussion of the pros and cons of alliances versus acquisitions, see ibid., pp. 109–15.

[15]For an excellent review of the strategic objectives of various types of mergers and acquisitions and the managerial challenges that different kinds of mergers and acquisitions present, see Joseph L. Bower, "Not All M&As Are Alike—and That Matters," *Harvard Business Review* 79, no. 3 (March 2001), pp. 93–101.

[16]For a more expansive discussion, see Dyer, Kale, and Singh, "When to Ally and When to Acquire," pp. 109–10.

[17]See Kathryn R. Harrigan, "Matching Vertical Integration Strategies to Competitive Conditions," *Strategic Management Journal* 7, no. 6 (November–December 1986), pp. 535–56; for a more extensive discussion of the advantages and disadvantages of vertical integration, see John Stuckey and David White, "When and When Not to Vertically Integrate," *Sloan Management Review* (Spring 1993), pp. 71–83.

[18]The resilience of vertical integration strategies despite the disadvantages is discussed in

Thomas Osegowitsch and Anoop Madhok, "Vertical Integration Is Dead or Is It?" *Business Horizons* 46, no. 2 (March–April 2003), pp. 25–35.

[19]This point is explored in greater detail in James Brian Quinn, "Strategic Outsourcing: Leveraging Knowledge Capabilities," *Sloan Management Review* 40, no. 4 (Summer 1999), pp. 9–21.

[20]Dean Foust, "Big Brown's New Bag," *BusinessWeek*, July 19, 2004, pp. 54–55.

[21]"The Internet Age," *BusinessWeek,* October 4, 1999, p. 104.

[22]For a good discussion of the problems that can arise from outsourcing, see Jérôme Barthélemy, "The Seven Deadly Sins of Outsourcing," *Academy of Management Executive* 17, no. 2 (May 2003), pp. 87–100.

[23]For an excellent discussion of aggressive offensive strategies, see George Stalk Jr. and Rob Lachenauer, "Hardball: Five Killer Strategies for Trouncing the Competition," *Harvard Business Review* 82, no. 4 (April 2004), pp. 62–71. A discussion of offensive strategies particularly suitable for industry leaders is presented in Richard D'Aveni, "The Empire Strikes Back: Counterrevolutionary Strategies for Industry Leaders," *Harvard Business Review* 80, no. 11 (November 2002), pp. 66–74.

[24]George Stalk, "Playing Hardball: Why Strategy Still Matters," *Ivey Business Journal* 69, no. 2 (November–December 2004), pp. 1–2.

[25]Ian C. MacMillan, "How Long Can You Sustain a Competitive Advantage?" in *The Strategic Planning Management Reader,* ed. Liam Fahey (Englewood Cliffs, NJ: Prentice Hall, 1989), pp. 23–24.

[26]Ian C. MacMillan, Alexander B. van Putten, and Rita Gunther McGrath, "Global Gamesmanship," *Harvard Business Review* 81, no. 5 (May 2003), pp. 66–67; also, see Askay R. Rao, Mark E. Bergen, and Scott Davis, "How to Fight a Price War," *Harvard Business Review* 78, no. 2 (March–April, 2000), pp. 107–16.

[27]Stalk and Lachenauer, "Hardball," p. 64.

[28]Stalk, "Playing Hardball," p. 4.

[29]Stalk and Lachenauer, "Hardball," p. 67.

[30]For an interesting study of how small firms can successfully employ guerrilla-style tactics, see Ming-Jer Chen and Donald C. Hambrick, "Speed, Stealth, and Selective Attack: How Small Firms Differ from Large Firms in Competitive Behavior," *Academy of Management Journal* 38, no. 2 (April 1995), pp. 453–82. Other discussions of guerrilla offensives can be found in Ian MacMillan, "How Business Strategists Can Use Guerrilla Warfare Tactics," *Journal of Business Strategy* 1, no. 2 (Fall 1980), pp. 63–65; William E. Rothschild, "Surprise

and the Competitive Advantage," *Journal of Business Strategy* 4, no. 3 (Winter 1984), pp. 10–18; Kathryn R. Harrigan, *Strategic Flexibility* (Lexington, MA: Lexington Books, 1985), pp. 30–45; and Liam Fahey, "Guerrilla Strategy: The Hit-and-Run Attack," in *The Strategic Management Planning Reader,* ed. Liam Fahey (Englewood Cliffs, NJ: Prentice Hall, 1989), pp. 194–97.

[31]The use of preemptive strike offensives is treated comprehensively in Ian MacMillan, "Preemptive Strategies," *Journal of Business Strategy* 14, no. 2 (Fall 1983), pp. 16–26.

[32]W. Chan Kim and Renée Mauborgne, "Blue Ocean Strategy," *Harvard Business Review* 82, no. 10 (October 2004), pp. 76–84.

[33]Philip Kotler, *Marketing Management,* 5th Edition (Englewood Cliffs, N.J.: Prentice Hall, 1984), p. 400.

[34]Michael E. Porter, *Competitive Advantage* (New York: Free Press, 1985), p. 518.

[35]For an excellent discussion of how to wage offensives against strong rivals, see David B. Yoffie and Mary Kwak, "Mastering Balance: How to Meet and Beat a Stronger Opponent," *California Management Review* 44, no. 2 (Winter 2002), pp. 8–24.

[36]Stalk, "Playing Hardball," pp. 1–2.

[37]Porter, *Competitive Advantage,* pp. 489–94.

[38]Ibid., pp. 495–97. The list here is selective; Porter offers a greater number of options.

[39]For a more extensive discussion of how the Internet impacts strategy, see Michael E. Porter, "Strategy and the Internet," *Harvard Business Review* 79, no. 3 (March 2001), pp. 63–78.

[40]Porter, *Competitive Advantage,* pp. 232–33.

[41]For research evidence on the effects of pioneering versus following, see Jeffrey G. Covin, Dennis P. Slevin, and Michael B. Heeley, "Pioneers and Followers: Competitive Tactics, Environment, and Growth," *Journal of Business Venturing* 15, no. 2 (March 1999), pp. 175–210 and Christopher A. Bartlett and Sumantra Ghoshal, "Going Global: Lessons from Late-Movers," *Harvard Business Review* 78, no. 2 (March–April 2000), pp. 132–45.

[42]For a more extensive discussion of this point, see Fernando Suarez and Gianvito Lanzolla, "The Half-Truth of First-Mover Advantage," *Harvard Business Review* 83, no. 4 (April 2005), pp. 121–27.

[43]Gary Hamel, "Smart Mover, Dumb Mover," *Fortune,* September 3, 2001, p. 195.

[44]Ibid., p. 192.

[45]Costas Markides and Paul A. Geroski, "Racing to be 2nd: Conquering the Industries of the Future," *Business Strategy Review* 15, no. 4 (Winter 2004), pp. 25–31.

Chapter 7

[1]For an insightful discussion of how much significance these kinds of demographic and market differences have, see C. K. Prahalad and Kenneth Lieberthal, "The End of Corporate Imperialism," *Harvard Business Review* 76, no. 4 (July–August 1998), pp. 68–79.

[2]Joseph Caron, "The Business of Doing Business with China: An Ambassador Reflects," *Ivey Business Journal* 69, no. 5 (May–June 2005), p. 2.

[3]Extrapolated from 2002 statistics reported by the U.S. Department of Labor.

[4]Michael E. Porter, *The Competitive Advantage of Nations* (New York: Free Press, 1990), pp. 53–54.

[5]Ibid., p. 61.

[6]For more details on the merits of and opportunities for cross-border transfer of successful strategy experiments, see C. A. Bartlett and S. Ghoshal, *Managing Across Borders: The Transnational Solution,* 2nd ed. (Boston: Harvard Business School Press, 1998), pp. 79–80 and Chapter 9.

[7]H. Kurt Christensen, "Corporate Strategy: Managing a Set of Businesses," in *The Portable MBA in Strategy,* ed. Liam Fahey and Robert M. Randall (New York: Wiley, 2001), p. 42.

[8]Porter, *Competitive Advantage*, pp. 53–55.

[9]Ibid., pp. 55–58.

[10]C. K. Prahalad and Yves L. Doz, *The Multinational Mission* (New York: Free Press, 1987), p. 60.

[11]Porter, *Competitive Advantage*, p. 57.

[12]Ibid., pp. 58–60.

[13]Several other types of strategic offensives that companies have occasionally employed in select foreign market situations are discussed in Ian C. MacMillan, Alexander B. van Putten, and Rita Gunther McGrath, "Global Gamesmanship," *Harvard Business Review* 81, no. 5 (May 2003), pp. 63–68.

[14]Canadian International Trade Tribunal, findings issued June 16, 2005 and posted at www. citttcce.gc.ca (accessed September 28, 2005).

[15]George Stalk, "Playing Hardball: Why Strategy Still Matters," *Ivey Business Journal* 69, no. 2 (November–December 2004), pp. 1–2.

[16]For two especially insightful studies of company experiences with cross-border alliances, see Joel Bleeke and David Ernst, "The Way to Win in Cross-Border Alliances," *Harvard Business Review* 69, no. 6 (November–December 1991), pp. 127–35, and Gary Hamel, Yves L. Doz, and C. K. Prahalad, "Collaborate with Your Competitors—and Win," *Harvard Business Review* 67, no. 1 (January–February 1989), pp. 133–39.

[17]See Yves L. Doz and Gary Hamel, *Alliance Advantage* (Boston, MA: Harvard Business School Press, 1998), especially Chapters 2–4; Bleeke and Ernst, "The Way to Win," pp. 127–33; Hamel, Doz, and Prahalad, "Collaborate with Your Competitors," pp. 134–35; and Porter, *Competitive Advantage,* p. 66.

[18]Christensen, "Corporate Strategy," p. 43.

[19]For an excellent presentation on the pros and cons of alliances versus acquisitions, see Jeffrey H. Dyer, Prashant Kale, and Harbir Singh, "When to Ally and When to Acquire," *Harvard Business Review* 82, no. 7/8 (July–August 2004), pp. 109–15.

[20]For additional discussion of company experiences with alliances and partnerships, see Doz and Hamel, *Alliance Advantage,* Chapters 2–7, and Rosabeth Moss Kanter, "Collaborative Advantage: The Art of the Alliance," *Harvard Business Review* 72, no. 4 (July–August 1994), pp. 96–108.

[21]Details are reported in Shawn Tully, "The Alliance from Hell," *Fortune,* June 24, 1996, pp. 64–72.

[22]Jeremy Main, "Making Global Alliances Work," *Fortune,* December 19, 1990, p. 125.

[23]Prahalad and Lieberthal, "The End of Corporate Imperialism," p. 77.

[24]Ibid.

[25]This point is discussed at greater length in Prahalad and Lieberthal, "The End of Corporate Imperialism," pp. 68–79; also see David J. Arnold and John A. Quelch, "New Strategies in Emerging Markets," *Sloan Management Review* 40, no. 1 (Fall 1998), pp. 7–20. For a more extensive discussion of strategy in emerging markets, see C. K. Prahalad, *The Fortune at the Bottom of the Pyramid: Eradicating Poverty through Profits* (Upper Saddle River, NJ: Wharton, 2005), especially Chapters 1–3.

[26]Brenda Cherry, "What China Eats (and Drinks and . . .)," *Fortune,* October 4, 2004, pp. 152–53.

[27]Prahalad and Lieberthal, "The End of Corporate Imperialism," pp. 72–73.

[28]Tarun Khanna, Krishna G. Palepu, and Jayant Sinha, "Strategies That Fit Emerging Markets," *Harvard Business Review* 83 no. 6 (June 2005), p. 63.

[29]Prahalad and Lieberthal, "The End of Corporate Imperialism," p. 72.

[30]Khanna, Palepu, and Sinha, "Strategies That Fit Emerging Markets," pp. 73–74.

[31]Ibid., p. 74.

[32]Ibid., p. 76.

[33]Niroj Dawar and Tony Frost, "Competing with Giants: Survival Strategies for Local Companies in Emerging Markets," *Harvard Business Review* 77, no. 1 (January–February 1999), p. 122; see also Guitz Ger, "Localizing in the Global Village: Local Firms Competing in Global Markets," *California Management Review* 41, no. 4 (Summer 1999), pp. 64–84.

[34]Dawar and Frost, "Competing with Giants," p. 124.

[35]Ibid., p. 125.

[36]Steve Hamm, "Tech's Future," *Business Week,* September 27, 2004, p. 88.

[37]Dawar and Frost, "Competing with Giants," p. 126.

[38]Hamm, "Tech's Future," p. 89.

Chapter 8

[1]Michael E. Porter, *Competitive Strategy: Techniques for Analyzing Industries and Competitors* (New York: Free Press, 1980), pp. 216–23.

[2]Phillip Kotler, *Marketing Management,* 5th ed. (Englewood Cliffs, NJ: Prentice Hall, 1984), p. 366, and Porter, *Competitive Strategy,* Chapter 10.

[3]Several of these were pinpointed and discussed in Charles W. Hofer and Dan Schendel, *Strategy Formulation: Analytical Concepts* (St. Paul, MN: West, 1978), pp. 164–65.

[4]Ibid., pp. 164–65.

[5]Porter, *Competitive Strategy,* pp. 238–40.

[6]The following discussion draws on ibid., pp. 241–46.

[7]Kathryn R. Harrigan and Michael E. Porter, "End-Game Strategies for Declining Industries," *Harvard Business Review* 61, no. 4 (July–August 1983), pp. 112–13.

[8]R. G. Hamermesh and S. B. Silk, "How to Compete in Stagnant Industries," *Harvard Business Review* 57, no. 5 (September–October 1979), p. 161, and Kathryn R. Harrigan, *Strategies for Declining Businesses* (Lexington, MA: Heath, 1980).

[9]Hamermesh and Silk, "How to Compete," p. 162; Harrigan and Porter, "End-Game Strategies," p. 118.

[10]Hamermesh and Silk, "How to Compete," p. 165.

[11]Harrigan and Porter, "End-Game Strategies," pp. 111–21; Harrigan, *Strategies for Declining Businesses;* and Phillip Kotler, "Harvesting Strategies for Weak Products," *Business Horizons* 21, no. 5 (August 1978), pp. 17–18.

[12]The strategic issues companies must address in fast-changing market environments are thoroughly explored in Gary Hamel and Liisa Välikangas, "The Quest for Resilence," *Harvard Business Review* 81, no. 9 (September 2003), pp. 52–63; Shona L. Brown and Kathleen M. Eisenhardt, *Competing on the Edge: Strategy as Structured Chaos* (Boston: Harvard Business School Press, 1998); and Richard A. D'Aveni, *Hyper-Competition: Managing the Dynamics of Strategic Maneuvering* (New York: Free Press, 1994). See also Richard A. D'Aveni, "Coping with Hypercompetition: Utilizing the New 7S's Framework," *Academy of Management Executive* 9, no. 3 (August 1995), pp. 45–56, and Bala Chakravarthy, "A New Strategy Framework for Coping with Turbulence," *Sloan Management Review* (Winter 1997), pp. 69–82.

[13]Brown and Eisenhardt, *Competing on the Edge,* pp. 4–5.

[14]Ibid., p. 4.

[15]For deeper insight into building competitive advantage through R&D and technological innovation, see Shaker A. Zahra, Sarah Nash, and Deborah J. Bickford, "Transforming Technological Pioneering into Competitive Advantage," *Academy of Management Executive* 9, no. 1 (February 1995), pp. 32–41.

[16]Brown and Eisenhardt, *Competing on the Edge,* pp. 14–15. See also Kathleen M. Eisenhardt and Shona L. Brown, "Time Pacing: Competing in Markets That Won't Stand Still," *Harvard Business Review* 76, no. 2 (March–April 1998), pp. 59–69.

[17]The circumstances of competing in a fragmented industry are discussed at length in Porter, *Competitive Strategy,* Chapter 9; this section draws on Porter's treatment.

[18]What follows is based on the discussion in Eric D. Beinhocker, "Robust Adaptive Strategies," *Sloan Management Review* 40, no. 3 (Spring 1999), p. 101.

[19]Gary Hamel, "Bringing Silicon Valley Inside," *Harvard Business Review* 77, no. 5 (September–October 1999), p. 73.

[20]Beinhocker, "Robust Adaptive Strategies," p. 101.

[21]Kotler, *Marketing Management,* Chapter 23; Michael E. Porter, *Competitive Advantage* (New York: Free Press, 1985), Chapter 14; and Ian C. MacMillan, "Seizing Competitive Initiative," *Journal of Business Strategy* 2, no. 4 (Spring 1982), pp. 43–57. For a perspective on what industry leaders can do when confronted with revolutionary market changes, see Richard D'Aveni, "The Empire Strikes Back: Counterrevolutionary Strategies for Industry Leaders," *Harvard Business Review* 80, no. 11 (November 2002), pp. 66–74.

[22]The value of being a frequent first-mover and leading change is documented in Walter J. Ferrier, Ken G. Smith, and Curtis M. Grimm, "The Role of Competitive Action in Market Share Erosion and Industry Dethronement: A Study of Industry Leaders and Challengers," *Academy of Management Journal* 42, no. 4 (August 1999), pp. 372–88.

[23]George Stalk Jr. and Rob Lachenauer, "Five Killer Strategies for Trouncing the Competition," *Harvard Business Review* 82, no. 4 (April 2004), pp. 64–65.

[24]Ibid., pp. 67–68.

[25]For more details, see R. G. Hamermesh, M. J. Anderson, and J. E. Harris, "Strategies for Low Market Share Businesses," *Harvard Business Review* 56, no. 3 (May–June 1978), pp. 95–96.

[26]Porter, *Competitive Advantage*, p. 514.

[27]Some of these options are drawn from Kotler, *Marketing Management,* pp. 397–412; Hamermesh, Anderson, and Harris, "Strategies for Low Market Share Businesses," pp. 97–102; and Porter, *Competitive Advantage,* Chapter 15.

[28]William K. Hall, "Survival Strategies in a Hostile Environment," *Harvard Business Review* 58, no. 5 (September–October 1980), pp. 75–85. See also Frederick M. Zimmerman, *The Turnaround Experience: Real-World Lessons in Revitalizing Corporations* (New York: McGraw-Hill, 1991), and Gary J. Castrogiovanni, B. R. Baliga, and Roland E. Kidwell, "Curing Sick Businesses: Changing CEOs in Turnaround Efforts," *Academy of Management Executive* 6, no. 3 (August 1992), pp. 26–41.

[29]A study performed by Crest Advisors, a boutique investment firm and reported in Leigh Gallagher, "Avoiding the Pitfalls of Orphan Stocks," www.forbes.com, April 24, 2003.

[30]Phillip Kotler, "Harvesting Strategies for Weak Products," *Business Horizons* 21, no. 5 (August 1978), pp. 17–18.

Chapter 9

[1]For a further discussion of when diversification makes good strategic sense, see Constantinos C. Markides, "To Diversify or Not to Diversify," *Harvard Business Review* 75, no. 6 (November–December 1997), pp. 93–99.

[2]Michael E. Porter, "From Competitive Advantage to Corporate Strategy," *Harvard Business Review* 45, no. 3 (May–June 1987), pp. 46–49.

[3]Michael E. Porter, *Competitive Strategy: Techniques for Analyzing Industries and Competitors* (New York: Free Press, 1980), pp. 354–55.

[4]Ibid., pp. 344–45.

[5]Yves L. Doz and Gary Hamel, *Alliance Advantage: The Art of Creating Value through Partnering* (Boston: Harvard Business School Press, 1998), Chapters 1 and 2.

[6]Michael E. Porter, *Competitive Advantage* (New York: Free Press, 1985), pp. 318–19 and pp. 337–53, and Porter, "From Competitive Advantage," pp. 53–57. For an empirical study confirming that strategic fits are capable of enhancing performance (provided the resulting resource strengths are competitively valuable and difficult to duplicate by rivals), see Constantinos C. Markides and Peter J. Williamson, "Corporate Diversification and Organization Structure: A Resource-Based View," *Academy of Management Journal* 39, no. 2 (April 1996), pp. 340–67.

[7]For a discussion of the strategic significance of cross-business coordination of value chain activities and insight into how the process works, see Jeanne M. Liedtka, "Collaboration across Lines of Business for Competitive Advantage," *Academy of Management Executive* 10, no. 2 (May 1996), pp. 20–34.

[8]"Beyond Knowledge Management: How Companies Mobilize Experience," *Financial Times,* February 8, 1999, p. 5.

[9]For a discussion of what is involved in actually capturing strategic fit benefits, see Kathleen M. Eisenhardt and D. Charles Galunic, "Coevolving: At Last, a Way to Make Synergies Work," *Harvard Business Review* 78, no. 1 (January–February 2000), pp. 91–101. Adeptness at capturing cross-business strategic fits positively impacts performance; see Constantinos C. Markides and Peter J. Williamson, "Related Diversification, Core Competences and Corporate Performance," *Strategic Management Journal* 15 (Summer 1994), pp. 149–65.

[10]Peter Drucker, *Management: Tasks, Responsibilities, Practices* (New York: Harper & Row, 1974), pp. 692–93.

[11]While arguments that unrelated diversification are a superior way to diversify financial risk have logical appeal, there is research showing that related diversification is less risky from a financial perspective than is unrelated diversification; see Michael Lubatkin and Sayan Chatterjee, "Extending Modern Portfolio Theory into the Domain of Corporate Diversification: Does It Apply?" *Academy of Management Journal* 37, no. 1 (February 1994), pp. 109–36.

[12]For a review of the experiences of companies that have pursued unrelated diversification successfully, see Patricia L. Anslinger and Thomas E. Copeland, "Growth through Acquisitions: A Fresh Look," *Harvard Business Review* 74, no. 1 (January–February 1996), pp. 126–35.

[13]Of course, management may be willing to assume the risk that trouble will not strike before it has had time to learn the business well enough to bail it out of almost any difficulty. But there is research that shows this is very risky from a financial perspective; see, for example, Lubatkin and Chatterjee, "Extending Modern Portfolio Theory," pp. 132–33.

[14]For research evidence of the failure of broad diversification and trend of companies to focus their diversification efforts more narrowly, see Lawrence G. Franko, "The Death of Diversification? The Focusing of the World's Industrial Firms, 1980–2000," *Business Horizons* 47, no. 4 (July–August 2004), pp. 41–50.

[15]For an excellent discussion of what to look for in assessing these fits, see Andrew Campbell, Michael Gould, and Marcus Alexander, "Corporate Strategy: The Quest for Parenting Advantage," *Harvard Business Review* 73, no. 2 (March–April 1995), pp. 120–32.

[16]Ibid., p. 128.

[17]Ibid., p. 123.

[18]A good discussion of the importance of having adequate resources, and also the importance of upgrading corporate resources and capabilities, can be found in David J. Collis and Cynthia A. Montgomery, "Competing on Resources: Strategy in the 90s," *Harvard Business Review* 73, no. 4 (July–August 1995), pp. 118–28.

[19]Ibid., pp. 121–22.

[20]Drucker, *Management,* p. 709.

[21]See, for, example, Constantinos C. Markides, "Diversification, Restructuring, and Economic Performance," *Strategic Management Journal* 16 (February 1995), pp. 101–18.

[22]For a discussion of why divestiture needs to be a standard part of any company's diversification strategy, see Lee Dranikoff, Tim Koller, and Antoon Schneider, "Divestiture: Strategy's Missing Link," *Harvard Business Review* 80, no. 5 (May 2002), pp. 74–83.

[23]Drucker, *Management,* p. 94.

[24]See David J. Collis and Cynthia A. Montgomery, "Creating Corporate Advantage," *Harvard Business Review* 76, no. 3 (May–June 1998), pp. 72–80.

[25]Drucker, *Management,* p. 719.

[26]Evidence that restructuring strategies tend to result in higher levels of performance is contained in Markides, "Diversification, Restructuring," pp. 101–18.

[27]Company press release, October 6, 2005.

[28]Dranikoff, Koller, and Schneider, "Divestiture," p. 76.

[29]C. K. Prahalad and Yves L. Doz, *The Multinational Mission* (New York: Free Press, 1987), p. 2.

[30]Ibid., p. 15.

[31]Ibid., pp. 62–63.

[32]For a fascinating discussion of the chess match in strategy that can unfold when two DMNC's go head-to-head in a global marketplace, see Ian C. MacMillan, Alexander B. van Putten, and Rita Gunther McGrath, "Global Gamesmanship," *Harvard Business Review* 81, no. 5 (May 2003), pp. 62–71.

Chapter 10

[1] James E. Post, Anne T. Lawrence, and James Weber, *Business and Society: Corporate Strategy, Public Policy, Ethics,* 10th ed. (Burr Ridge, IL: McGraw-Hill/Irwin, 2002), p. 103.

[2] For research on what are the universal moral values (six are identified—trustworthiness, respect, responsibility, fairness, caring, and citizenship), see Mark S. Schwartz, "Universal Moral Values for Corporate Codes of Ethics," *Journal of Business Ethics* 59, no. 1 (June 2005), pp. 27–44.

[3] See, for instance, Mark. S. Schwartz, "A Code of Ethics for Corporate Codes of Ethics," *Journal of Business Ethics* 41, nos. 1–2 (November–December 2002), pp. 27–43.

[4] For more discussion of this point, see ibid., pp. 29–30.

[5] T. L. Beauchamp and N. E. Bowie, *Ethical Theory and Business* (Upper Saddle River, NJ: Prentice Hall, 2001), p. 8.

[6] Based on information in U.S. Department of Labor, "The Department of Labor's 2002 Findings on the Worst Forms of Child Labor," www.dol.gov/ILAB/media/reports, 2003.

[7] ILO-IPEC (SIMPOC), *Every Child Counts: New Global Estimates on Child Labour,* www.ilo.org/public/english/standards/ipec/simpoc/others/globalest.pdf, April 2002. The estimate of the number of working children is based on the definition of the "economically active population," which restricts the labor force activity of children to "paid" or "unpaid" employment, military personnel, and the unemployed. The definition does not include children in informal work settings, non-economic activities, "hidden" forms of work, or work that is defined by ILO Convention 182 as the worst forms of child labor.

[8] W. M. Greenfield, "In the Name of Corporate Social Responsibility," *Business Horizons* 47, no. 1 (January–February 2004), p. 22.

[9] For a study of why such factors as low per capita income, lower disparities in income distribution, and various cultural factors are often associated with a higher incidence of bribery, see Rajib Sanyal, "Determinants of Bribery in International Business: The Cultural and Economic Factors," *Journal of Business Ethics* 59, no.1 (June 2005), pp. 139–45.

[10] For a study of bribe-paying frequency by country, see Transparency International, *2003 Global Corruption Report,* p. 267; this report can be accessed at www.globalcorruptionreport.org.

[11] Roger Chen and Chia-Pei Chen, "Chinese Professional Managers and the Issue of Ethical Behavior," *Ivey Business Journal* 69, no, 5 (May/June 2005), p.1.

[12] Thomas Donaldson and Thomas W. Dunfee, "When Ethics Travel: The Promise and Peril of Global Business Ethics," *California Management Review* 41, no. 4 (Summer 1999), p. 53.

[13] John Reed and Erik Portanger, "Bribery, Corruption Are Rampant in Eastern Europe, Survey Finds," *Wall Street Journal,* November 9, 1999, p. A21.

[14] See Transparency International, *Global Corruption Report* for 2003, 2004, and 2005; these reports can be accessed at www.globalcorruptionreport.org.

[15] For a study of "facilitating" payments to obtain a favor (such as expediting an administrative process, obtaining a permit or license, or avoiding an abuse of authority), which are sometimes condoned as unavoidable or are excused on grounds of low wages and lack of professionalism among public officials, see Antonio Argandoña, "Corruption and Companies: The Use of Facilitating Payments," *Journal of Business Ethics* 60, no. 3 (September 2005), pp. 251–64.

[16] Donaldson and Dunfee, "When Ethics Travel," p. 59.

[17] Thomas Donaldson and Thomas W. Dunfee, *Ties That Bind: A Social Contracts Approach to Business Ethics* (Boston: Harvard Business School Press, 1999), pp. 35, 83.

[18] Based on a report in M. J. Satchell, "Deadly Trade in Toxics," *U.S. News and World Report,* March 7, 1994 p. 64, cited in Donaldson and Dunfee, "When Ethics Travel," p. 46.

[19] Chen and Chen, "Chinese Professional Managers," p. 1.

[20] Two of the definitive treatments of integrated social contracts theory as applied to ethics are Thomas Donaldson and Thomas W. Dunfee, "Towards a Unified Conception of Business Ethics: Integrative Social Contracts Theory," *Academy of Management Review* 19, no. 2 (April 1994), pp. 252–84, and Donaldson and Dunfee, *Ties That Bind,* especially Chapters 3, 4, and 6. See also Andrew Spicer, Thomas W. Dunfee, and Wendy J. Bailey, "Does National Context Matter in Ethical Decision Making? An Empirical Test of Integrative Social Contracts Theory," *Academy of Management Journal* 47, no. 4 (August 2004), p. 610.

[21] P. M. Nichols, "Outlawing Transnational Bribery through the World Trade Organization," *Law and Policy in International Business* 28, no. 2 (1997), pp. 321–22.

[22] Donaldson and Dunfee, "When Ethics Travel," pp. 55–56.

[23] Archie B. Carroll, "Models of Management Morality for the New Millennium," *Business Ethics Quarterly* 11, no. 2 (April 2001), pp. 367–69.

[24] Ibid., pp. 369–70.

[25] John R. Wilke and Don Clark, "Samsung to Pay Fine for Price-Fixing," *The Wall Street Journal,* October 14, 2005, p. A3.

[26] For survey data on what managers say about why they sometimes behave unethically, see John F. Veiga, Timothy D. Golden, and Kathleen Dechant, "Why Managers Bend Company Rules," *Academy of Management Executive* 18, no. 2 (May 2004), pp. 84–89.

[27] For more details see Ronald R. Sims and Johannes Brinkmann, "Enron Ethics (Or: Culture Matters More Than Codes)," *Journal of Business Ethics* 45, no. 3 (July 2003), pp. 244–46.

[28] As reported in Gardiner Harris, "At Bristol-Myers, Ex-Executives Tell of Numbers Games," *The Wall Street Journal,* December 12, 2002, pp. A1, A13.

[29] Ibid., p. A13.

[30] Veiga, Golden, and Dechant, "Why Managers Bend the Rules," p. 36.

[31] The following account is based largely on the discussion and analysis in Sims and Brinkmann, "Enron Ethics," pp. 245–52. Perhaps the definitive book-length account of the corrupt Enron culture is Kurt Eichenwald, *Conspiracy of Fools: A True Story* (New York: Broadway Books, 2005).

[32] Chip Cummins and Almar Latour, "How Shell's Move to Revamp Culture Ended in Scandal," *The Wall Street Journal,* November 2, 2004, p. A14.

[33] Gedeon J. Rossouw and Leon J. van Vuuren, "Modes of Managing Morality: A Descriptive Model of Strategies for Managing Ethics," *Journal of Business Ethics,* 46, no. 4 (September 2003), pp. 389–400.

[34] Empirical evidence that an ethical culture approach produces better results than the compliance approach is presented in Terry Thomas, John R. Schermerhorn, and John W. Dienhart, "Strategic Leadership of Ethical Behavior," *Academy of Management Executive* 18, no. 2 (May 2004), p. 64.

[35] Anna Wilde Mathews and Barbara Martinez, "E-Mails Suggest Merck Knew Vioxx's Dangers at Early Stage," *The Wall Street Journal,* November 1, 2004, pp. A1 and A10.

[36] Archie B. Carroll, "The Four Faces of Corporate Citizenship," *Business and Society Review* 100/101 (September 1998), p. 6.

[37] Business Roundtable, "Statement on Corporate Responsibility," New York, October 1981, p. 9.

[38] Sarah Roberts, Justin Keeble, and David Brown, "The Business Case for Corporate Citizenship," a study for the World Economic Forum, www.weforum.org/corporatecitizenship, October 14, 2003, p. 3.

[39] N. Craig Smith, "Corporate Responsibility: Whether and How," *California Management Review* 45, no. 4 (Summer 2003), p. 63.

[40] Jeffrey Hollender, "What Matters Most: Corporate Values and Social Responsibility," *California Management Review* 46, no. 4 (Summer 2004), p. 112. For a study of the

corporate social responsibility reports of leading European companies, see Simon Knox, Stan Maklan, and Paul French, "Corporate Social Responsibility: Exploring Stakeholder Relationships and Program Reporting across Leading FTSE Companies," *Journal of Business Ethics* 61, no. 1 (September 2005), pp. 7–28.

[41]World Business Council for Sustainable Development, "Corporate Social Responsibility: Making Good Business Sense," www.wbscd.ch, January 2000 (accessed October 10, 2003), p. 7. For a discussion of how companies are connecting social initiatives to their core values, see David Hess, Nikolai Rogovsky, and Thomas W. Dunfee, "The Next Wave of Corporate Community Involvement: Corporate Social Initiatives," *California Management Review* 44, no. 2 (Winter 2002), pp. 110–25, and Susan Ariel Aaronson, "Corporate Responsibility in the Global Village: The British Role Model and the American Laggard," *Business and Society Review,* 108, no. 3 (September 2003), p. 323.

[42]www.chick-fil-a.com (accessed November 4, 2005).

[43]Smith, "Corporate Responsibility," p. 63. See also World Economic Forum, "Findings of a Survey on Global Corporate Leadership," www.weforum.org/corporatecitizenship, (accessed October 11, 2003).

[44]Roberts, Keeble, and Brown, "The Business Case," p. 6.

[45]Ibid., p. 3.

[46]Wallace N. Davidson, Abuzar El-Jelly, and Dan L. Worrell, "Influencing Managers to Change Unpopular Corporate Behavior through Boycotts and Divestitures: A Stock Market Test," *Business and Society,* 34, no. 2 (1995), pp. 171–196.

[47]Tom McCawley, "Racing to Improve Its Reputation: Nike Has Fought to Shed Its Image as an Exploiter of Third-World Labor, Yet It Is Still a Target of Activists," *Financial Times,* December 2000, p. 14, and Smith, "Corporate Social Responsibility," p. 61.

[48]Based on data in Amy Aronson, "Corporate Diversity, Integration, and Market Penetration," *BusinessWeek,* October 20, 2003, pp. 138 ff.

[49]Smith, "Corporate Social Responsibility," p. 62.

[50]See Social Investment Forum, *2001 Report on Socially Responsible Investing Trends in the United States* (Washington, DC: Social Investment Forum, 2001).

[51]Smith, "Corporate Social Responsibility," p. 63.

[52]See James C. Collins and Jerry I. Porras, *Built to Last: Successful Habits of Visionary Companies,* 3rd ed. (London: HarperBusiness, 2002); Roberts, Keeble, and Brown, "The Business Case," p. 4; and Smith, "Corporate Social Responsibility," p. 63.

[53]Roberts, Keeble, and Brown, "The Business Case," p. 4.

[54]Smith, "Corporate Social Responsibility," p. 65; Lee E. Preston and Douglas P. O'Bannon, "The Corporate Social-Financial Performance Relationship," *Business and Society* 36, no. 4 (December 1997), pp. 419–29; Ronald M. Roman, Sefa Hayibor, and Bradley R. Agle, "The Relationship between Social and Financial Performance: Repainting a Portrait," *Business and Society* 38, no. 1 (March 1999), pp. 109–25; and Joshua D. Margolis and James P. Walsh, *People and Profits* (Mahwah, NJ: Lawrence Erlbaum, 2001).

[55]Smith, "Corporate Social Responsibility," p. 71.

[56]Business Roundtable, "Statement on Corporate Governance," Washington, DC, September 1997, p. 3.

[57]Henry Mintzberg, Robert Simons, and Kunal Basu, "Beyond Selfishness," *MIT Sloan Management Review* 44, no. 1 (Fall 2002), p. 69.

[58]For a good discussion of the debate between maximizing shareholder value and balancing stakeholder interests, see H. Jeff Smith, "The Shareholders versus Stakeholders Debate," MIT *Sloan Management Review* 44, no. 4 (Summer 2003), pp. 85–91.

[59]Smith, "Corporate Social Responsibility," p. 70.

[60]Based on information in Edna Gundersen, "Rights Issue Rocks the Music World," *USA Today,* September 16, 2002, pp. D1, D2.

[61]This information is based on Charles Gasparino, "Salomon Probe Includes Senior Executives," *The Wall Street Journal,* September 3, 2002, p. C1; Randall Smith, "How a Star Banker Pressed for IPOs," *The Wall Street Journal,* September 4, 2002, pp. C1, C14; Randall Smith and Susan Pulliam, "How a Technology-Banking Star Doled Out Shares of Hot IPOs," *The Wall Street Journal,* September 23; 2002, pp. A1, A10; and Randall Smith, "Goldman Sachs Faces Scrutiny for IPO-Allocation Practices," *The Wall Street Journal,* October 3, 2002, pp. A1, A6.

Chapter 11

[1]As quoted in Steven W. Floyd and Bill Wooldridge, "Managing Strategic Consensus: The Foundation of Effective Implementation," *Academy of Management Executive* 6, no. 4 (November 1992), p. 27.

[2]Jack Welch with Suzy Welch, *Winning* (New York: HarperBusiness, 2005), p. 135.

[3]For an excellent and very pragmatic discussion of this point, see Larry Bossidy and Ram Charan, *Execution: The Discipline of Getting Things Done* (New York: Crown Business, 2002), Chapter 1.

[4]For an insightful discussion of how important staffing an organization with the right people is, see Christopher A. Bartlett and Sumantra Ghoshal, "Building Competitive Advantage through People," *MIT Sloan Management Review* 43, no. 2 (Winter 2002), pp. 34–41.

[5]The importance of assembling an executive team with exceptional ability to see what needs to be done and an instinctive talent for figuring out how to get it done is discussed in Justin Menkes, "Hiring for Smarts," *Harvard Business Review* 83, no. 11 (November 2005), pp. 100–9 and Justin Menkes, *Executive Intelligence* (New York: HarperCollins, 2005), especially Chapters 1–4.

[6]Welch with Welch, *Winning,* p. 139.

[7]See Bossidy and Charan, *Execution: The Discipline of Getting Things Done,* Chapter 1.

[8]Menkes, *Executive Intelligence,* pp. 68, 76.

[9]Bossidy and Charan, *Execution;* Chapter 5.

[10]Welch with Welch, *Winning,* pp. 141–42.

[11]Menkes, *Executive Intelligence,* pp. 65–71.

[12]Jim Collins, *Good to Great* (New York: HarperBusiness, 2001), p. 44.

[13]John Byrne, "The Search for the Young and Gifted," *BusinessWeek,* October 4, 1999, p. 108.

[14]James Brian Quinn, *Intelligent Enterprise* (New York: Free Press, 1992), pp. 52–53, 55, 73–74, 76. Also see Christine Soo, Timothy Devinney, David Midgley, and Anne Deering, "Knowledge Management: Philosophy, Processes, and Pitfalls," *California Management Review* 44, no. 4 (Summer 2002), pp. 129–51, and Julian Birkinshaw, "Why Is Knowledge Management So Difficult?" *Business Strategy Review* 12, no. 1 (March 2001), pp. 11–18.

[15]Robert H. Hayes, Gary P. Pisano, and David M. Upton, *Strategic Operations: Competing through Capabilities* (New York: Free Press, 1996), pp. 503–7. Also see Jonas Ridderstråle, "Cashing in on Corporate Competencies," *Business Strategy Review* 14, no. 1 (Spring 2003), pp. 27–38, and Danny Miller, Russell Eisenstat, and Nathaniel Foote, "Strategy from the Inside Out: Building Capability-Creating Organizations," *California Management Review* 44, no. 3 (Spring 2002), pp. 37–55.

[16]Quinn, *Intelligent Enterprise,* p. 43.

[17]Quinn, *Intelligent Enterprise,* pp. 33, 89; James Brian Quinn and Frederick G. Hilmer, "Strategic Outsourcing," *Sloan Management Review* 35, no. 4 (Summer 1994), pp. 43–55; Jussi Heikkilä and Carlos Cordon, "Outsourcing: A Core or Non-Core Strategic Management Decision," *Strategic Change* 11, no. 3 (June–July 2002), pp. 183–93; and James Brian Quinn, "Strategic Outsourcing: Leveraging Knowledge Capabilities," *Sloan Management Review* 40, no. 4 (Summer 1999), pp. 9–22. A strong case for outsourcing is presented in

C. K. Prahalad, "The Art of Outsourcing," *The Wall Street Journal,* June 8, 2005, p. A13. For a discussion of why outsourcing initiatives fall short of expectations, see Jérôme Barthélemy, "The Seven Deadly Sins of Outsourcing," *Academy of Management Executive* 17, no. 2 (May 2003), pp. 87–98.

[18] Quinn, "Strategic Outsourcing," p. 17.

[19] For a more extensive discussion of the reasons for building cooperative, collaborative alliances and partnerships with other companies, see James F. Moore, *The Death of Competition* (New York: HarperBusiness, 1996), especially Chapter 3; Quinn and Hilmer, "Strategic Outsourcing"; and Quinn, "Strategic Outsourcing."

[20] Quinn, *Intelligent Enterprise,* pp. 39–40; also see Barthélemy, "The Seven Deadly Sins."

[21] The importance of matching organization design and structure to the particular needs of strategy was first brought to the forefront in a landmark study of 70 large corporations conducted by Professor Alfred Chandler of Harvard University. Chandler's research revealed that changes in an organization's strategy bring about new administrative problems that, in turn, require a new or refashioned structure for the new strategy to be successfully implemented. He found that structure tends to follow the growth strategy of the firm—but often not until inefficiency and internal operating problems provoke a structural adjustment. The experiences of these firms followed a consistent sequential pattern: new strategy creation, emergence of new administrative problems, a decline in profitability and performance, a shift to a more appropriate organizational structure, and then recovery to more profitable levels and improved strategy execution. See Alfred Chandler, *Strategy and Structure* (Cambridge, MA: MIT Press, 1962).

[22] The importance of empowering workers in executing strategy and the value of creating a great working environment are discussed in Stanley E. Fawcett, Gary K. Rhoads, and Phillip Burnah, "People as the Bridge to Competitiveness: Benchmarking the 'ABCs' of an Empowered Workforce," *Benchmarking: An International Journal* 11, no. 4 (2004), pp. 346–60.

[23] Iain Somerville and John Edward Mroz, "New Competencies for a New World," in *The Organization of the Future,* ed. Frances Hesselbein, Marshall Goldsmith, and Richard Beckard (San Francisco: Jossey-Bass, 1997), p. 70.

[24] Exercising adequate control over empowered employees is a serious issue. For example, a prominent Wall Street securities firm lost $350 million when a trader allegedly booked fictitious profits; Sears took a $60 million write-off after admitting that employees in its automobile service departments recommended unnecessary repairs to customers. Several makers of memory chips paid fines of over $500 million when over a dozen of their employees conspired to fix prices and operate a global cartel—some of the guilty employees were sentenced to jail. For a discussion of the problems and possible solutions, see Robert Simons, "Control in an Age of Empowerment," *Harvard Business Review* 73 (March–April 1995), pp. 80–88.

[25] For a discussion of the importance of cross-business coordination, see Jeanne M. Liedtka, "Collaboration across Lines of Business for Competitive Advantage," *Academy of Management Executive* 10, no. 2 (May 1996), pp. 20–34.

[26] Michael Hammer and James Champy, *Reengineering the Corporation* (New York: HarperBusiness, 1993), pp. 26–27.

[27] Ibid. Although functional organization incorporates Adam Smith's division-of-labor principle (every person/department involved has specific responsibility for performing a clearly defined task) and allows for tight management control (everyone in the process is accountable to a functional department head for efficiency and adherence to procedures), *no one oversees the whole process and its result.*

[28] Rosabeth Moss Kanter, "Collaborative Advantage: The Art of the Alliance," *Harvard Business Review* 72, no. 4 (July–August 1994), pp. 105–6.

[29] For an excellent review of ways to effectively manage the relationship between alliance partners, see Kanter, "Collaborative Advantage," pp. 96–108.

Chapter 12

[1] For a discussion of the value of benchmarking in implementing strategy, see Christopher E. Bogan and Michael J. English, *Benchmarking for Best Practices: Winning Through Innovative Adaptation* (New York: McGraw-Hill, 1994), Chapters 2 and 6; Mustafa Ungan, "Factors Affecting the Adoption of Manufacturing Best Practices," *Benchmarking: An International Journal* 11, no. 5 (2004), pp, 504–20; and Paul Hyland and Ron Beckett, "Learning to Compete: The Value of Internal Benchmarking," *Benchmarking: An International Journal* 9, no. 3 (2002), pp. 293–304; and Yoshinobu Ohinata, "Benchmarking: The Japanese Experience," *Long-Range Planning* 27, no. 4 (August 1994), pp. 48–53.

[2] Michael Hammer and James Champy, *Reengineering the Corporation* (New York: HarperBusiness, 1993), pp. 26–27.

[3] Gene Hall, Jim Rosenthal, and Judy Wade, "How to Make Reengineering Really Work," *Harvard Business Review* 71, no. 6 (November–December 1993), pp. 119–131.

[4] For more information on business process reengineering and how well it has worked in various companies, see James Brian Quinn, *Intelligent Enterprise* (New York: Free Press, 1992), p. 162; Ann Majchrzak and Qianwei Wang, "Breaking the Functional Mind-Set in Process Organizations," *Harvard Business Review* 74, no. 5 (September–October 1996), pp. 93–99; Stephen L. Walston, Lawton R. Burns, and John R. Kimberly, "Does Reengineering Really Work? An Examination of the Context and Outcomes of Hospital Reengineering Initiatives," *Health Services Research* 34, no. 6 (February 2000), pp. 1363–88; and Allessio Ascari, Melinda Rock, and Soumitra Dutta, "Reengineering and Organizational Change: Lessons from a Comparative Analysis of Company Experiences," *European Management Journal* 13, no. 1 (March 1995), pp. 1–13. For a review of why some company personnel embrace process reengineering and some don't, see Ronald J. Burke, "Process Reengineering: Who Embraces It and Why?" *TQM Magazine* 16, no. 2 (2004), pp. 114–19.

[5] For some of the seminal discussions of what TQM is and how it works written by ardent enthusiasts of the technique, see M. Walton, *The Deming Management Method* (New York: Pedigree, 1986); J. Juran, *Juran on Quality by Design* (New York: Free Press, 1992); Philip Crosby, *Quality Is Free: The Act of Making Quality Certain* (New York: McGraw-Hill, 1979); and S. George, *The Baldrige Quality System* (New York: Wiley, 1992). For a critique of TQM, see Mark J. Zbaracki, "The Rhetoric and Reality of Total Quality Management," *Administrative Science Quarterly* 43, no. 3 (September 1998), pp. 602–36.

[6] For a discussion of the shift in work environment and culture that TQM entails, see Robert T. Amsden, Thomas W. Ferratt, and Davida M. Amsden, "TQM: Core Paradigm Changes," *Business Horizons* 39, no. 6 (November–December 1996), pp. 6–14.

[7] For easy-to-understand overviews of Six Sigma, see Peter S. Pande and Larry Holpp, *What Is Six Sigma?* (New York: McGraw-Hill, 2002); Jiju Antony, "Some Pros and Cons of Six Sigma: An Academic Perspective," *TQM Magazine* 16, no. 4 (2004), pp. 303–6; Peter S. Pande, Robert P. Neuman, and Roland R. Cavanagh, *The Six Sigma Way: How GE, Motorola and Other Top Companies Are Honing Their Performance* (New York: McGraw-Hill, 2000); and Joseph Gordon and M. Joseph Gordon Jr., *Six Sigma Quality for Business and Manufacture* (New York: Elsevier, 2002). For how Six Sigma can be used in smaller companies, see Godecke Wessel and Peter Burcher, "Six Sigma for Small and Medium-sized Enterprises," *TQM Magazine* 16, no. 4 (2004), pp. 264–72.

[8] Based on information posted at www.isixsigma.com, November 4, 2002.

[9]Kennedy Smith, "Six Sigma for the Service Sector," *Quality Digest Magazine,* May 2003, posted at www.qualitydigest.com (accessed September 28, 2003).

[10]Del Jones, "Taking the Six Sigma Approach," *USA Today,* October 31, 2002, p. 5B.

[11]Pande, Neuman, and Cavanagh, *The Six Sigma Way,* pp. 5–6.

[12]Smith, "Six Sigma for the Service Sector."

[13]Jones, "Taking the Six Sigma Approach," p. 5B.

[14]Terry Nels Lee, Stanley E. Fawcett, and Jason Briscoe, "Benchmarking the Challenge to Quality Program Implementation," *Benchmarking: An International Journal* 9, no. 4 (2002), pp. 374–87.

[15]For a recent study documenting the imperatives of establishing a supportive culture, see Milan Ambroz, "Total Quality System as a Product of the Empowered Corporate Culture," *TQM Magazine,* 16, no. 2 (2004), pp. 93–104. Research confirming the factors that are important in making TQM programs successful in both Europe and the United States is presented in Nick A. Dayton, "The Demise of Total Quality Management," *TQM Magazine,* 15, no. 6 (2003), pp. 391–96.

[16]Judy D. Olian and Sara L. Rynes, "Making Total Quality Work: Aligning Organizational Processes, Performance Measures, and Stakeholders," *Human Resource Management* 30, no. 3 (Fall 1991), pp. 310–11, and Paul S. Goodman and Eric D. Darr, "Exchanging Best Practices Information through Computer-Aided Systems," *Academy of Management Executive* 10, no. 2 (May 1996), p. 7.

[17]Thomas C. Powell, "Total Quality Management as Competitive Advantage," *Strategic Management Journal* 16 (1995), pp. 15–37. See also Richard M. Hodgetts, "Quality Lessons from America's Baldrige Winners," *Business Horizons* 37, no. 4 (July–August 1994), pp. 74–79; and Richard Reed, David J. Lemak, and Joseph C. Montgomery, "Beyond Process: TQM Content and Firm Performance," *Academy of Management Review* 21, no. 1 (January 1996), pp. 173–202.

[18]Based on information at www.utc.com and www.otiselevator.com (accessed November 14, 2005).

[19]Fred Vogelstein, "Winning the Amazon Way," *Fortune,* May 26, 2003, pp. 70, 74.

[20]*BusinessWeek,* November 21, 2005, pp. 87–88.

[21]Such systems speed organizational learning by providing fast, efficient communication, creating an organizational memory for collecting and retaining best practice information, and permitting people all across the organization to exchange information and updated solutions. See Goodman and Darr, "Exchanging Best Practices Information," pp. 7–17.

[22]*BusinessWeek,* November 21, 2005, pp. 85–90.

[23]Vogelstein, "Winning the Amazon Way," p. 64.

[24]For a discussion of the need for putting appropriate boundaries on the actions of empowered employees and possible control and monitoring systems that can be used, see Robert Simons, "Control in an Age of Empowerment," *Harvard Business Review* 73 (March–April 1995), pp. 80–88.

[25]Ibid. Also see David C. Band and Gerald Scanlan, "Strategic Control through Core Competencies," *Long Range Planning* 28, no. 2 (April 1995), pp. 102–14.

[26]The importance of motivating and empowering workers so as to create a working environment that is highly conducive to good strategy execution is discussed in Stanley E. Fawcett, Gary K. Rhoads, and Phillip Burnah, "People as the Bridge to Competitiveness: Benchmarking the 'ABCs' of an Empowered Workforce," *Benchmarking: An International Journal* 11, no. 4 (2004), pp. 346–60.

[27]Jeffrey Pfeffer and John F. Veiga, "Putting People First for Organizational Success," *Academy of Management Executive* 13, no. 2 (May 1999), pp. 37–45; Linda K. Stroh and Paula M. Caliguiri, "Increasing Global Competitiveness through Effective People Management," *Journal of World Business* 33, no. 1 (Spring 1998), pp. 1–16; and articles in *Fortune* on the 100 best companies to work for (various issues).

[28]As quoted in John P. Kotter and James L. Heskett, *Corporate Culture and Performance* (New York: Free Press, 1992), p. 91.

[29]For a provocative discussion of why incentives and rewards are actually counterproductive, see Alfie Kohn, "Why Incentive Plans Cannot Work," *Harvard Business Review* 71, no. 6 (September–October 1993), pp. 54–63.

[30]See Steven Kerr, "On the Folly of Rewarding A While Hoping for B," *Academy of Management Executive* 9, no. 1 (February 1995), pp. 7–14; Steven Kerr, "Risky Business: The New Pay Game," *Fortune,* July 22, 1996, pp. 93–96; and Doran Twer, "Linking Pay to Business Objectives," *Journal of Business Strategy* 15, no. 4 (July–August 1994), pp. 15–18.

[31]Kerr, "Risky Business," p. 96.

Chapter 13

[1]Joanne Reid and Victoria Hubbell, "Creating a Performance Culture," *Ivey Business Journal* 69, no.4 (March–April 2005), p. 1.

[2]John P. Kotter and James L. Heskett, *Corporate Culture and Performance* (New York: Free Press, 1992), p. 7. See also Robert Goffee and Gareth Jones, *The Character of a Corporation* (New York: HarperCollins, 1998).

[3]Kotter and Heskett, *Corporate Culture and Performance,* pp. 7–8.

[4]Ibid., p. 5.

[5]John Alexander and Meena S. Wilson, "Leading across Cultures: Five Vital Capabilities," in *The Organization of the Future,* ed. Frances Hesselbein, Marshall Goldsmith, and Richard Beckard (San Francisco: Jossey-Bass, 1997), pp. 291–92.

[6]Terrence E. Deal and Allen A. Kennedy, *Corporate Cultures* (Reading, MA: Addison-Wesley, 1982), p. 22. See also Terrence E. Deal and Allen A. Kennedy, *The New Corporate Cultures: Revitalizing the Workplace after Downsizing, Mergers, and Reengineering* (Cambridge, MA: Perseus, 1999).

[7]Vijay Sathe, *Culture and Related Corporate Realities* (Homewood, IL: Richard D. Irwin, 1985).

[8]Kotter and Heskett, *Corporate Culture and Performance,* Chapter 6.

[9]See Kurt Eichenwald, *Conspiracy of Fools: A True Story* (New York: Broadways, 2005).

[10]Reid and Hubbell, "Creating a Performance Culture," pp. 2, 5.

[11]This section draws heavily on the discussion of Kotter and Heskett, *Corporate Culture and Performance,* Chapter 4.

[12]There's no inherent reason why new strategic initiatives should conflict with core values and business principles. While conflict is always possible, most strategy makers lean toward choosing strategic initiatives that are compatible with the company's character and culture and that don't go against ingrained values and beliefs. After all, the company's culture is usually something that strategy makers have had a hand in building and perpetuating, so they are not often anxious to undermine core values and business principles without serious soul searching and compelling business reasons.

[13]Kotter and Heskett, *Corporate Culture and Performance,* p. 52.

[14]Ibid., p. 5.

[15]Avan R. Jassawalla and Hemant C. Sashittal, "Cultures That Support Product-Innovation Processes," *Academy of Management Executive* 16, no. 3 (August 2002), pp. 42–54.

[16]Kotter and Heskett, *Corporate Culture and Performance,* pp. 15–16. Also see Jennifer A. Chatham and Sandra E. Cha, "Leading by Leveraging Culture," *California Management Review* 45, no. 4 (Summer 2003), pp. 20–34.

[17]Judy D. Olian and Sara L. Rynes, "Making Total Quality Work: Aligning Organizational Processes, Performance Measures, and Stakeholders," *Human Resource Management* 30, no. 3 (Fall 1991), p. 324.

[18]Information posted at www.dardenrestaurants. com (accessed November 25, 2005); for more specifics, see Robert C. Ford, "Darden Restaurants' CEO Joe Lee on the Importance of Core Values: Integrity and Fairness," *Academy of Management Executive* 16, no. 1 (February 2002), pp. 31–36.

[19]For several perspectives on the role and importance of core values and ethical behavior, see Joseph L. Badaracco, *Defining Moments: When Managers Must Choose between Right and Wrong* (Boston: Harvard Business School Press, 1997); Joe Badaracco and Allen P. Webb, "Business Ethics: A View from the Trenches," *California Management Review* 37, no. 2 (Winter 1995), pp. 8–28; Patrick E. Murphy, "Corporate Ethics Statements: Current Status and Future Prospects," *Journal of Business Ethics* 14 (1995), pp. 727–40; and Lynn Sharp Paine, "Managing for Organizational Integrity," *Harvard Business Review* 72, no. 2 (March–April 1994), pp. 106–17.

[20]For a study of the status of formal codes of ethics in large corporations, see Emily F. Carasco and Jang B. Singh, "The Content and Focus of the Codes of Ethics of the World's Largest Transnational Corporations," *Business and Society Review* 108, no. 1 (January 2003), pp. 71–94, and Murphy, "Corporate Ethics Statements." For a discussion of the strategic benefits of formal statements of corporate values, see John Humble, David Jackson, and Alan Thomson, "The Strategic Power of Corporate Values," *Long Range Planning* 27, no. 6 (December 1994), pp. 28–42. An excellent discussion of whether one should assume that company codes of ethics are always ethical is presented in Mark S. Schwartz, "A Code of Ethics for Corporate Codes of Ethics," *Journal of Business Ethics* 41, nos. 1–2 (November–December 2002), pp. 27–43.

[21]See Schwartz, "A Code of Ethics," p. 27.

[22]Ford, "Darden Restaurants' CEO Joe Lee."

[23]For excellent discussions of the problems and pitfalls in leading the transition to a new strategy and to fundamentally new ways of doing business, see Larry Bossidy and Ram Charan, *Confronting Reality: Doing What Matters to Get Things Right* (New York: Crown Business, 2004); Larry Bossidy and Ram Charan, *Execution: The Discipline of Getting Things Done* (New York: Crown Business, 2002), especially Chapters 3 and 5; John P. Kotter, "Leading Change: Why Transformation Efforts Fail," *Harvard Business Review* 73, no. 2 (March–April 1995), pp. 59–67; Thomas M. Hout and John C. Carter, "Getting It Done: New Roles for Senior Executives," *Harvard Business Review* 73, no. 6 (November–December 1995), pp. 133–45; and Sumantra Ghoshal and Christopher A. Bartlett, "Changing the Role of Top Management: Beyond Structure to Processes," *Harvard Business Review* 73, no. 1 (January–February 1995), pp. 86–96.

[24]For a pragmatic, cut-to-the-chase treatment of why some leaders succeed and others fail in executing strategy, especially in a period of rapid market change or organizational crisis, see Bossidy and Charan, *Confronting Reality.*

[25]Fred Vogelstein, "Winning the Amazon Way," *Fortune,* May 26, 2003, p. 64.

[26]For a more in-depth discussion of the leader's role in creating a results-oriented culture that nurtures success, see Benjamin Schneider, Sarah K. Gunnarson, and Kathryn Niles-Jolly, "Creating the Climate and Culture of Success," *Organizational Dynamics,* Summer 1994, pp. 17–29.

[27]Jeffrey Pfeffer, "Producing Sustainable Competitive Advantage through the Effective Management of People," *Academy of Management Executive* 9, no.1 (February 1995), pp. 55–69.

[28]For some cautions in implementing ethics compliance, see Robert J. Rafalko, "A

Caution about Trends in Ethics Compliance Programs," *Business and Society Review* 108, no. 1 (January 2003), pp. 115–26. A good discussion of the failures of ethics compliance programs can be found in Megan Barry, "Why Ethics and Compliance Programs Can Fail," *Journal of Business Strategy* 26, no. 6 (November–December 2002), pp. 37–40.

[29]For documentation of cross-country differences in what is considered ethical, see Robert D. Hirsch, Branko Bucar, and Sevgi Oztark, "A Cross-Cultural Comparison of Business Ethics: Cases of Russia, Slovenia, Turkey, and United States," *Cross Cultural Management* 10, no. 1 (2003), pp. 3–28, and P. Maria Joseph Christie, Ik-Whan G. Kwan, Philipp A. Stoeberl, and Raymond Baumhart, "A Cross-Cultural Comparison of Ethical Attitudes of Business Managers: India, Korea, and the United States," *Journal of Business Ethics* 46, no. 3 (September 2003), pp. 263–87.

[30]James Brian Quinn, *Strategies for Change: Logical Incrementalism* (Homewood, IL: Richard D. Irwin, 1980), pp. 20–22.

[31]Ibid., p. 146.

[32]For a good discussion of the challenges, see Daniel Goleman, "What Makes a Leader," *Harvard Business Review* 76, no. 6 (November–December 1998), pp. 92–102; Ronald A. Heifetz and Donald L. Laurie, "The Work of Leadership," *Harvard Business Review* 75, no. 1 (January–February 1997), pp. 124–34; and Charles M. Farkas and Suzy Wetlaufer, "The Ways Chief Executive Officers Lead," *Harvard Business Review* 74, no. 3 (May–June 1996), pp. 110–22. See also Michael E. Porter, Jay W. Lorsch, and Nitin Nohria, "Seven Surprises for New CEOs," *Harvard Business Review* 82, no. 10 (October 2004), pp. 62–72.

ORGANIZATION

Note: Page numbers preceded by C- indicate material in Cases.

NAME INDEX

Page numbers followed by n indicate notes; page numbers preceded by C- indicate material in Cases; page numbers preceded by EN- indicate endnotes.

SUBJECT INDEX

Page numbers in *italics* indicate material in illustrations; page numbers followed by t indicate material in tables; page numbers preceded by C- indicate material in Cases.